Administrative Law

Administrative Law

Cases and Materials

EIGHTH EDITION

The Late Charles H. Koch Jr.
DUDLEY WARNER WOODBRIDGE PROFESSOR OF LAW
THE COLLEGE OF WILLIAM AND MARY SCHOOL OF LAW

William S. Jordan III
EMERITUS PROFESSOR OF LAW
THE UNIVERSITY OF AKRON SCHOOL OF LAW

Richard W. Murphy
AT&T PROFESSOR OF LAW
TEXAS TECH UNIVERSITY SCHOOL OF LAW

Louis J. Virelli III
PROFESSOR OF LAW
STETSON UNIVERSITY COLLEGE OF LAW

CAROLINA ACADEMIC PRESS
Durham, North Carolina

LCCN: 2019951734
ISBN: 978-1-5310-1681-4
eISBN: 978-1-5310-1682-1

Carolina Academic Press
700 Kent Street
Durham, North Carolina 27701
Telephone (919) 489-7486
Fax (919) 493-5668
www.cap-press.com

Printed in the United States of America

We dedicate this edition to the memory of Charles H. Koch, Jr., the first author of this casebook and the creator of the Wine Trade Commission.

Contents

Table of Cases

Preface

Administrative law is tremendously exciting. The administrative process affects each of us every day, probably in more ways than we can recognize or count. The car we drive, the fuel it uses, the air we breathe, the water we drink, the drugs we take, and so much more reflect the complex interaction among the elected branches of government, agency employees, the judiciary, and a seemingly infinite number of private interest groups. Indeed, the administrative process is the way that more than 300 million people make the collective decisions that shape virtually every aspect of our lives.

The characteristics that make administrative law exciting also make its study a daunting task. Any body of law governing such a complex and dynamic process must itself be complex and dynamic. While the safety of our tires or our children's toys are intensely practical concerns, administrative law is by necessity not only complicated, but highly abstract. Administrative law practitioners must know not only the statutes and regulations of the particular agencies with which they deal, but also the general principles of administrative law that apply across the board.

While we cannot hope to teach the details of the nation's regulatory and administrative programs, we can impart the principles that govern the interpretation and implementation of the various statutes through which Congress has created the programs of the administrative state. Whether dealing with the Clean Air Act, the Federal Trade Commission Act, the Social Security Disability benefits program, or the many state-level programs such as workers compensation, the lawyer must pay close attention to the language of those statutes — both the substantive mandates and the procedural requirements. In addition, the administrative law practitioner must understand how the Constitution applies to administrative agencies and the requirements of the Administrative Procedure Act and other generally applicable statutes, from information disclosure to administrative procedures to judicial review.

This casebook approaches this complexity and abstraction at a highly practical level. It employs a "simulation" involving the creation of a new agency, the Wine Trade Commission. Students will follow two central characters, both newly-minted lawyers (one in the agency, one representing the regulated industry), through the implementation of a new regulatory program. This approach facilitates learning administrative law in various ways. First, it presents the issues from the point of view of those who actually practice administrative law — an intensely practical perspective that is easy for students to grasp. This provides a firm foundation from which to grapple with the many highly theoretical concepts of the field. Second, it reveals how cases and principles governing other agencies apply as well to this new regulatory body. An opinion dealing with the Nuclear Regulatory Commission, for example, must be used by the characters (and the students) in designing rulemaking for the fictitious agency. Third, the practical orientation helps the student understand that the administrative process involves more than a body of highly theoretical propositions or technical legal details. It is a deeply human enterprise in which success derives as much from careful management as from expert legal analysis.

We hope you will enjoy this approach to a fascinating topic. No doubt clever students will take the opportunity to suggest a wine tasting to accompany the academic enterprise. With the passing of Professor Koch in 2012, Professors Jordan, Murphy, and Virelli are honored to continue and build upon his legacy in this pathbreaking approach to teaching administrative law. We raise our glasses to his memory.

Richard W. Murphy, Texas Tech University School of Law, Lubbock, Texas
Louis J. Virelli III, Stetson University College of Law, Gulfport, Florida
William S. Jordan, III, University of Akron School of Law, Akron, Ohio
Fall 2019

Administrative Law

Chapter 1

Administrative Law: An Introduction and Structural Constitutional Issues

A. An Overview of the Casebook

If you are reading this sentence, it is likely that you are taking a course in administrative law, which is the law governing government. You made a wise choice. Every legal practice confronts administrative law, and every practitioner must understand it in order fully to serve her clients. Practice in areas such as employment law and environmental law, among many others, is dominated by administrative processes at all governmental levels. Even some areas not generally considered administrative law practices are consistently involved in administrative processes. A property practitioner, for example, practices before zoning boards or wetland agencies; a criminal lawyer represents clients before parole boards or in prison proceedings. Administrative law is pervasive because it provides the legal principles that determine how governmental agencies must make their decisions and justify their actions. As American administrative law serves an array of changing governmental and societal goals, it has been and will continue to be dynamic and eclectic.

It also has a reputation for being very abstract and hard to learn. One reason for this reputation is that government agencies come in many different forms and serve a bewildering variety of functions. Subject to exceptions that need not detain us at the moment, the Administrative Procedure Act (APA), which serves as a kind of quasi-constitution for the federal administrative state, defines the term "agency" as "each authority of the Government of the United States, whether or not it is within or subject to review by another agency." 5 U.S.C. § 551(1). This vague and capacious term encompasses, among countless other examples, the Environmental Protection Agency, the Department of Defense, the National Park Service, the Securities and Exchange Commission, the Food and Drug Administration, and the Consumer Financial Protection Bureau. You will no doubt be able to add scores more federal agencies to this list—and of course there are countless other examples occupying local, state, international, and even global levels of administration. We will sometimes reference these other systems, but we will concentrate on the federal, confident that once students have figured out one system, they will be able to steer through others with a bit of work. Even when focused on just federal law, however, it can be very easy to lose one's way in an administrative law course. Different cases present different doctrines in the context of actions by a multitude of different agencies.

This casebook responds to this difficulty on two levels. The first strategy, which is common to all administrative law casebooks, is to identify and examine unifying legal principles that apply across the vast variety of agencies. At some level of abstraction, agency actions present a recurring set of generic issues. For example, any system that authorizes agencies to make rules will need to identify procedures for rulemaking. Any system that involves judicial review of agency decisionmaking will need to identify which agency actions are subject to review, as well as who can seek such review and when. The responses to these issues developed by legislatures, courts, and agencies compose the body of administrative law. Primary sources of such law include glosses on constitutional law (especially regarding separation of powers and due process), statutory law (especially agency "enabling acts" and the APA), and a quasi-common law developed by the courts. The casebook marches through these materials in, we hope, a logical and orderly fashion.

The second strategy to help you avoid getting lost among numberless agencies is to build a set of discussion problems around a single, fictitious federal agency, the Wine Trade Commission (WTC). Federal agencies are creatures of statute, enjoying only those powers that Congress has chosen to give them in an "enabling act," such as the EPA's Clean Air Act. (Sometimes we refer to "enabling acts" as "organic statutes.") Our fictitious agency is a creature of the equally fictitious Wine Trade Commission Act (WTCA), which you will find in Appendix 1. Our late colleague, Professor Charles Koch, created the WTCA by piecing together real statutory provisions from the enabling acts of various agencies. Like other enabling acts, the WTCA defines its agency's missions, grants and limits powers, and sets terms for judicial review. Each section of the casebook begins with a "lesson" that raises one or more issues relating to powers, procedures, or actions of the WTC. Discussion of the lesson will require you to apply administrative law principles explored in the case excerpts and note materials that follow them. Applying these administrative law principles to one agency subject to one (fictitious but realistic) enabling act will help you see how the various pieces of administrative law hang together in one (fairly) coherent whole.

To provide more orientation to the task at hand, here is a chapter-by-chapter overview of the core administrative law principles we will address:

Chapter 1—Administrative Law: An Introduction and Structural Constitutional Issues: After an overview of the casebook, this chapter briefly discusses various rationales that are commonly invoked to justify using administrative government to alter outcomes that would otherwise obtain in the world. Suppose, for just a moment, that we were governed solely by common law principles—e.g., contract law, tort law, etc. The world produced by this system of regulation would have some level of pollution, contain some number of parks, pay workers various amounts, allocate wealth in some way, and so on. We ask you to consider both why we might want government to change these outcomes as well as why we might think that administrative government provides a good means for doing so. We offer a thumbnail history of American administrative law along the way.

Most of Chapter 1, however, is devoted to squaring the administrative state with our eighteenth-century Constitution and its commitment to separation of powers. The Constitution vests the federal government's legislative power in Congress and its judicial power in the federal courts. Nonetheless, Congress has over the centuries passed many statutes empowering a vast array of agencies to promulgate "rules," and some of these rules carry the "force of law." In addition, Congress has delegated adjudicative power to many agencies to find facts and apply law to determine legal consequences that are then embedded in agency orders. In short, Congress has empowered agencies to act as "junior varsity" legislatures and courts. Chapter 1 examines some of the leading Supreme Court cases that attempt to reconcile these agency powers with the Constitution's allocations of legislative and judicial power.

Administrative law also implicates another set of separation-of-powers issues bearing on the centuries-old struggle between Congress and presidents to control the administrative bureaucracy. Chapter 1 closes by taking a look at some of the constitutional doctrines that have evolved out of this struggle, paying particular attention to doctrines governing the appointment and removal of agency officials.

Chapter 2—The Basic Procedural Categories of Administrative Law: This chapter introduces you to two fundamental dichotomies in American administrative law—the distinction between rulemaking and adjudication and the distinction between formal and informal agency action.

It is important to distinguish rulemaking from adjudication as the legal effects and procedural controls of the two differ. You might well think that this task should be easy. After all, rulemaking involves making rules that are roughly comparable to statutes, while adjudication involves deciding individual cases. But this distinction proves tricky on the margin. For instance, if an agency adjudication, as a practical matter, bars many private entities from engaging in certain conduct, is it really a "rule"? Or if an agency promulgates a rule that governs only the conduct of one entity, is the rule really an adjudicative "order"?

Legislation is a means for making general policy determinations, but, as anyone with the slightest sophistication about the law knows, judicial precedents, too, can serve a similar policymaking function. Agencies, unlike legislatures or courts, commonly possess both rulemaking and adjudicative powers. They therefore often can choose between using rulemaking or adjudication to make policy decisions. The middle of Chapter 2 explores both the legal principles and policy concerns that bear on this choice.

Chapter 2 closes with a brief survey of the range of procedural forms that rulemaking and adjudication might take. One reason for including these materials is a suspicion that, by now, the judicial model for decisionmaking likely dominates your intuitions regarding how governmental procedures should operate. The judicial model is often (but not always) inapt for administrative business, however, and administrative procedures can take many different forms with varying degrees of formality. Along these lines, administrative law commonly distinguishes between "formal" and "informal" procedures. "Formal" procedures, whether for rulemaking or adjudication, can resemble those of a court. Procedures that do not look especially court-like fall into the catch-all category of "informal."

Chapter 3 — Rulemaking: This chapter examines both the various types of "rules" that agencies can promulgate, as well as the statutory procedural requirements for rulemaking. It begins with a discussion of the legal principles governing the existence and scope of agency authority to issue "legislative" rules, which are those rules that carry the "force of law." (Not all of them do, as it turns out.)

Chapter 3 then turns to the basic procedures for promulgating rules. To determine what procedures an agency must follow to promulgate a rule, the first thing to do is to find and read any relevant portions of the agency's enabling act. Where, however, an enabling act does not contain instructions on rulemaking procedures, the default procedures established by Congress in the APA — the quasi-constitution of administrative law mentioned a few paragraphs ago — may apply. (The APA's basic model for rulemaking has been very influential over the decades, and the rulemaking procedures set forth in agency enabling acts are often variations on that APA model.)

The APA's usual method for promulgating legislative rules is "notice and comment." As the name implies, this process requires an agency to give "notice" to the public regarding proposed rules and to accept "comments" from the public on these proposals. As you will see, thanks to later congressional, judicial, and executive encrustations, notice-and-comment rulemaking has become far more onerous than it was back in 1946 when the APA was enacted. We nonetheless continue to refer to notice-and-comment rulemaking as "informal" in administrative-law speak.

The APA contemplates that notice and comment is unnecessary or counterproductive for certain types of rules. It therefore exempts from notice-and-comment requirements "nonlegislative" rules, (which lack the "force of law"), procedural rules, and a few other special categories. Also, an agency can avoid notice and comment where it has "good cause" to do so. Chapter 3 explores the law, some of it rather confused and confusing, for determining whether a rule falls into one of these exempt categories.

In addition to examining statutory procedural controls on agency rulemaking, Chapter 3 also takes a quick look at centralized White House control of rulemaking. Generally speaking, Congress delegates final rulemaking authority to agency heads — e.g., Congress vested the EPA's rulemaking power in the EPA's Administrator, not the president. Presidents, however, have strong incentives to control agency rulemaking authority and at least a colorable basis to do so given that the Constitution vests the "executive power" in "a President of the United States of America." (Whether the Constitution, properly understood, requires that the president enjoy final control over agency rulemaking discretion has prompted a long-running, ideologically charged debate that will last as long as the Republic.) In any event, for the last forty years or so, presidents of both parties have issued or relied upon executive orders to institute centralized review of agency rules in a White House office called the Office of Information and Regulatory Affairs (sometimes called "the most important agency no one has ever heard of").

Chapter 4—Adjudication: This chapter begins by exploring the APA's two default models for procedural control of agency adjudication. We refer to the more elaborate of these models as "formal" or "on the record" or "trial-type" adjudication. As these names suggest, formal adjudication can resemble a judicial bench trial, except that the adjudicator will generally be an official known as an "Administrative Law Judge" (ALJ).

Where the APA's requirements for formal adjudication are not triggered, the "informal adjudication" model applies instead. The APA imposes very little in the way of procedural requirements on informal agency adjudications. Other bodies of law often do, however. Congress may impose additional procedural requirements in the agency's enabling act, and the agency itself might impose additional procedures on itself by adopting procedural rules. In addition, and most to the present point, where an adjudication threatens deprivation of life, liberty, or property, it implicates procedural due process. The last half of Chapter 4 examines some of the core case law applying procedural due process principles to administrative adjudications.

Chapter 5—Judicial Review of Agency Action: You will recollect from your Civil Procedure course that there are various bodies of law that limit access to appellate review of district court judgments (e.g., the final judgment rule). There are also doctrines that establish standards of review that modulate how closely appellate courts scrutinize various types of issues (e.g., the clearly erroneous standard). You will not be surprised to learn that administrative law similarly imposes limits on access to judicial review of agency actions as well as on the intensity of such review. Chapter 5, which is a big one, explores some of these limits.

Issues bearing on access to the courts include:

- Which "agency actions" are "reviewable"?
- Who has "standing" to contest them in court?
- Does sovereign or official immunity apply to block a suit?
- Is the timing right for a judicial challenge? I.e.,
  - Is the agency action "ripe" for review?
  - Is the agency action "final"?
  - Have administrative remedies been "exhausted"?

The last half of the chapter explores doctrines that govern the scope of judicial review of agency action. There are separate doctrines governing review of fact, policy, and law. We are happy to report that, as you might expect since agencies are supposed to be the experts on their respective domains, the bottom line is that judicial review of agency fact and policy determinations is generally highly deferential. The body of law governing review of agency determinations of law is regrettably complex.

Chapter 6 — Agency Power to Gather Information: This brief chapter examines administrative authority to gather information in connection with law enforcement. It discusses agency power to require private parties to provide information, whether in the form of required filings or reports, or in responses to subpoenas or similar demands. It also examines agency authority to physically inspect property.

Chapter 7 — Open Government: This chapter is in some ways a mirror image of Chapter 6, as it examines statutes that enable those outside the government to obtain information from those inside the government. Chapter 7 focuses in particular on the Freedom of Information Act, a very complex statute that establishes both a broad baseline duty of agencies to provide information as well as a set of exemptions and exclusions from this duty.

Let's Pause to Take a Breath: We wouldn't blame you a bit if you found that quick tour a little overwhelming. But if you look again, you will see that, for the most part, this casebook focuses on a small handful of principles and themes:

- What is the scope and nature of agency rulemaking authority, and what procedures govern it?

- What is the scope and nature of agency adjudicatory authority, and what procedures govern it?

- What principles govern judicial review of agency actions?

Now let's start getting to know our fictitious agency, the Wine Trade Commission.

A Quick Introduction to the WTC

The Wine Trade Commission (WTC or Commission) is a fictional agency, but there is a very real history of government regulation of alcohol. Alcoholic beverages have long been heavily regulated by federal, state, and local authorities both to tax and control consumption. The federal government taxed distilled spirits in 1791 to raise revenue to reduce the national debt. This prompted the Whiskey Rebellion of 1794, which was suppressed by militia led by President Washington. In the early twentieth century, the Eighteenth Amendment to the Constitution, in combination with the Volstead Prohibition Enforcement Act, effectively criminalized alcoholic beverages in America until the Twenty-First Amendment repealed prohibition in 1933. Skipping ahead to near the present, the Homeland Security Act of 2002 reorganized the administration of alcohol laws, creating the Alcohol and Tobacco Tax and Trade Bureau (TTB) within the Treasury Department. TTB's functions include enforcement and administration of federal laws governing taxation, production, non-retail distribution, and use of alcohol and tobacco products. TTB has enforced provisions of the Federal Alcohol Administration Act controlling labeling and advertising of alcoholic beverages and barring deceptive trade practices. (If you have a mind to learn more about TTB's mission and history, the agency has kindly provided a video for you to watch, which you can find at https://www.ttb.gov/about/story.shtml.)

Now for a bit of alternative history. Wine is big business in the United States. The rapid development of the internet allowed people from every walk of life to learn about, purchase, and taste wines from all over the country and the world more easily and cheaply than ever before. When coupled with a similar explosion in popularity of the culinary arts in America, wine has been on the minds and lips of the American public in an unprecedented fashion. Not surprisingly, the American wine industry does not want to miss out on the economic opportunities provided by its newfound popularity. Major players in the wine industry grew unhappy with TTB, contending that it was "unresponsive" to the special needs of the wine industry. Some wine producers contacted their representatives in Congress to inform them of the benefits of a robust wine industry for the national economy in terms of job creation, investment, and exports. They encouraged Congress to help promote the wine industry through government investment and protection against uncontrollable losses such as natural disasters.

Other wine makers and retailers, however, objected to this appeal for government assistance. They contended that the government has no place in promoting any private industry and feared that further meddling by the legislative or executive branches would only restrain businesspeople and consumers from taking advantage of the benefits of the free market. They argued that the satisfaction of the consuming public will promote the industry in the healthiest possible way—by rewarding wineries that meet the needs and expectations of consumers and punishing, through lost profits, those that do not.

The wine industry was not the only entity to take an interest in the recent increase in wine's popularity. Consumers and consumer advocates were concerned that as the industry grows, market forces alone will be unable to maintain quality controls, and it will become easier for unscrupulous wine makers to take advantage of unsuspecting customers. These consumer groups demanded that Congress create greater controls on what manufacturers can put into their wines and on how they describe the nature and quality of those wines. Other factions of society have more basic concerns, for example, about the dangers of alcoholic consumption in general, and they wanted to make sure that Congress considered these fundamental issues before it decided whether to take action regarding the wine industry.

This wide-ranging interest in the wine industry motivated Congress to create a more focused agency to handle federal regulation of wine by enacting the Wine Trade Commission Act (WTCA or Act). A quick run-through of the Act's provisions, which are set forth in full in Appendix 1, suggests that it was a political compromise with something for just about everyone.

- Section 1 establishes the Wine Trade Commission (WTC), which is composed of five members (agency heads), one of whom is chair.

- Section 2 provides definitions of statutory terms.

- Section 3 charges the Commission with promoting the American wine industry.

- Section 4 establishes an Emergency Trust Fund to insure against crop failures and other natural disasters.

- Section 5 bars unfair trade practices in the wine industry.

- Section 6 establishes a licensing scheme for wine merchants as well as a self-regulatory organization, the Wine Merchants Association.

- Section 7 grants the Commission adjudicatory authority to issue orders to enforce the Act or rules promulgated pursuant to it.

- Section 8 grants the Commission rulemaking authority and provides procedures for exercising it.

- Section 9 establishes a right to judicial review of various Commission actions and contains provisions concerning timing, standing, and scope of review.

- Section 10 provides for judicial enforcement of Commission orders.

- Section 11 provides authority to the Commission to impose administrative penalties for violations of the Act and rules promulgated pursuant to it.

- Section 12 establishes a statutory cause of action for any person to initiate a civil suit against persons who violate Commission rules or orders or against the Commission itself for failure to take legally required action.

It may be helpful to divide the preceding provisions into three different conceptual piles:

- One pile, including §§ 3–5, charges the Commission with various substantive tasks—e.g., develop the wine industry; stop fraudulent trade practices, etc.

- Another pile, including §§ 7, 8, and 11, grants the agency rulemaking and adjudicatory authority and provides procedural instructions for deploying them.

- A third pile, including §§ 9, 10, and 12, provides paths for judicial control of agency action.

We will be getting to know various provisions of the WTCA very well as we march through the casebook's chapters. For now, the important thing to see is how, in general terms, the provisions empowering and limiting our fictitious agency implicate the legal doctrines outlined earlier in this introduction—e.g., the WTC is, within its domain, a kind of junior varsity legislature and court subject to various judicial controls.

Even this brief description of the WTC shows that it enjoys considerable powers both to regulate the behavior of private actors and coerce those who do not comply. Before examining these powers in detail, let's step back and consider briefly some very big questions relating to *whether* administrative government should exist and in *what form.* The first of these questions explores justifications for the government using its coercive powers to change outcomes that might otherwise obtain in what we might guardedly call the "market." Answers to this question will depend in part on widely differing moral, political, and economic views on the appropriate role of government controls and their effectiveness. The second question explores why, assuming government does decide to change these outcomes, it might wish to use the forms of administrative government to achieve its ends. More concretely, why should Congress delegate rulemaking and adjudicative powers to agencies rather than write the laws itself and leave it to the courts to enforce them through the litigation process?

B. The Administrative State: Rationales and History

1. What Justifies Government Intervention?

Before we tackle the corpus of administrative law itself, this opening section seeks to prompt discussion of a critical threshold question that precedes the creation of any regulatory scheme: Recognizing that reasonable people will disagree on this point, what circumstances, in your view, justify government intervention to alter the outcomes obtained in the "free market"? (We put "free market" in scare quotes because, for our intents and purposes, all markets are subject to some level of government control—e.g., the law of contract.) Following the lesson, which, in addition to introducing you to some of the WTC's cast of characters, raises questions far too big to answer completely, you will find some notes discussing various prominent rationales for government intervention as well as a thumbnail history of the regulatory state.

Lesson 1B.1: Abby is a very recent law school graduate who is living in Washington, D.C. She has just joined a large Washington law firm that specializes in government practice. Gallery, one of the nation's largest wine makers with a twenty percent market share and responsibility for more than one hundred brands, is one of the firm's biggest clients. Abby has been told she will be working primarily with Rock, a young partner, to help represent Gallery in matters related to the new WTC.

Today is a very big day for Abby, as she has just received notice that she passed the D.C. bar exam. She had been anxiously awaiting the results (keeping her job at the firm depended on them, after all), so after calling her parents to let them, and by extension the rest of her rural Midwestern hometown, know that she passed, she began looking for a way to celebrate. Unfortunately, she didn't really know anyone in D.C. yet. Undaunted, she left her apartment and headed for a nearby bar. At least she could toast herself before she called it a night. As luck would have it, she did not have to celebrate alone.

At the bar she ran into Ben, also a new attorney who, by happy chance, has just joined the General Counsel's office of the newly formed WTC after a clerkship for a judge on the United States Court of Appeals for the District of Columbia Circuit. Ben grew up in a fancy northeastern suburb. Ben's father had a successful solo practice that he started over his parents' grocery store. Ben's mother is an irrepressible public interest advocate. Together they gave him his values and the best education in the world. It was natural then for him to take a job in a consumer protection agency despite offers from the top firms in the country. While protecting wine consumers was not exactly poverty law, it promised to be an entertaining venture in the defense of the public interest. As his judge advised him at the time: "Working for a new or revitalizing agency is the most fun in government."

After noting the irony of their meeting one another over glasses of wine, Abby and Ben got to talking about the WTC and its potential effects on the wine industry. Ben turned out to be a treasure trove of information about the people at the WTC. He told Abby that the chair of the five-member Commission, Carl, was recently defeated in a hotly contested congressional race. The party rewarded his loyalty with a position at the Department of Agriculture and, when the WTC was created, its chair. Although nominally a lawyer, his entire career has been in politics and government. Ben explained that Carl can rely on the support of the two other commissioners from the president's party, who Ben thinks are appropriately named Fred and Barney for their stone-age mentality. Fred is a lawyer from a state bond firm in Sacramento, and Barney is a lawyer turned commercial real-estate developer from Denver. Ben believes that Carl can also rely on the fourth commissioner, Angela, who is not a lawyer but an economist. The oddball, in Ben's view, is Sarah. Even though a commissioner from outside the president's party was required by the WTCA, Sarah's views are even more radical than expected. As the one truly independent member of the Commission, it seemed she would be harmless if sometimes uncomfortably vocal.

As for the major players in his office, Ben informed Abby that the WTC's General Counsel, Chris, began her career as a campaign manager and then staffer to several members of Congress, and was a senior career lawyer in the Department of Health and Human Services when Carl offered her the General Counsel position at the WTC. Ben described Chris as shrewd rather than brilliant, and said he would not make jokes about her partly because he respects her abilities and partly because "she knows everything said or done in this town." Ben also expressed admiration for Ralph, the Assistant General Counsel. Ralph had a reputation as a brilliant criminal trial attorney before coming to the WTC and is the consummate professional advocate; he sees and can argue every side of a controversy. As someone who anticipates working closely with all of them in the very near future, Abby was thrilled to get the inside scoop on some of the most influential people at the WTC before even meeting them.

After this tutorial on the major players at the WTC, Abby turned the conversation toward the agency's mission. It quickly became clear that Abby and Ben have very different attitudes about government regulation. Ben proclaimed himself an unapologetic fan of activist government. He took the view that government interference with private behavior is often needed to help the weak and check the strong. He is skeptical about the ability of the market alone to keep big corporations in line and thinks the WTC's most important contribution will be creating the market controls sought by consumer groups. Abby responded that Ben lacks sufficient respect for personal liberty or for the power of markets to allocate resources where people, rather than governments, want them. Also, she chides him for neglecting the law of unintended consequences, which has so often caused good governmental intentions to lead to bad societal results. She is sympathetic with the portion of the wine industry that would prefer the government leave it alone so that the experts can run their business as they and the market see fit.

With which of our two new lawyers do you find yourself most sympathetic? To be a bit more specific, § 3 of the WTCA commands the Commission to promote the wine industry. Is it a proper role of government to devote resources to such a task? More generally, are there examples of government redistribution of resources that do strike you as justified? As not justified?

Section 5 essentially bars deceptive practices (including materially misleading omissions) in the wine trade, and §§ 7 and 11 give the Commission power to enforce this bar. What justifies this sort of government intervention? Aside from fairness and moral concerns, are there any market "failures" to cure here? More broadly, what are some examples of agency actions or programs that, in your view, properly address market failures?

And, finally, do you generally trust government, and government officials, to act in the "public interest" (whatever that may be)? Why or why not?

The following notes provide grist for thought and discussion by exploring both the evolution of the administrative state and rationales commonly offered to justify its efforts to redistribute resources and regulate "private" conduct.

Notes on Rationales for the Administrative State

1. Nonmarket rationales (to do the right thing). The concept of the "public interest" is problematic given that the hundreds of millions of people who live in the United States have many divergent interests. Still, one should expect supporters of any given government intervention to contend that it supports some reasonable vision of a broader "public interest," and one might expect opponents often to argue that it instead serves some narrow set of special interests. For instance, a coal company that has successfully pressed for a new regulation that relaxes pollution controls might argue that the new regulation saves jobs and enables the sale of cheaper energy to consumers. An environmental group might counter that the new regulation is a corrupt giveaway to the coal company that will cause widespread damage to health and accelerate global climate change. It is, of course, the domain of politics to argue over such competing visions of the public interest.

At an extremely high level of abstraction, one can divide public interest rationales for government intervention into two groups. One set addresses concerns for economic efficiency. We will discuss prominent examples of efficiency rationales, which have a technocratic air some might find comforting, in the next note. The other set, very broadly speaking, concerns non-market values of fairness and morality more generally. Put another way, this set of rationales involves "doing the right thing" for reasons other than efficient wealth maximization. Of course, people disagree about what fairness requires, what role government should play in achieving it, and which programs effectively serve this end.

One obvious driver of governmental interventions is a sense that economic fairness requires redistribution of resources within society. Social safety net programs, such as Social Security retirement and disability programs, Medicare, Medicaid, and welfare reflect this impulse. Minimum wage laws serve the same motivation less directly by regulating private conduct rather than making direct transfer payments.

Some administrative schemes proscribe private conduct chiefly on moral, rather than economic, grounds. For instance, although one can make a good case that racial discrimination is economically inefficient, surely the core rationale for barring such conduct and creating agencies such as the Equal Employment Opportunity Commission is that racial discrimination is morally wrong.

Public health and safety programs also plainly have a strong moral dimension. One motivation for implementing a regulatory ban on harmful pollution is that it is wrong—a problem often worsened by the tendency of such harms to be concentrated in disadvantaged communities. Nor should firms require workers to be exposed to needlessly dangerous working conditions.

Some government interventions reflect a mix of aesthetic and moral concerns. For instance, President Theodore Roosevelt, sometimes called the "conservation president," did not double the number of national parks because someone explained to him that parks are "public goods" that the market will not provide at efficient levels. He expanded the park system for "nonmarket" reasons, such as his love of nature and desire to preserve its more spectacular sites for the public's benefit. Great nations are supposed to have great parks.

Of course, government interventions will commonly serve some complex mix of rationales, and good arguments can often be made that such interventions enhance both fairness and efficiency.

2. Economic efficiency and fixing market "failures." In a common metaphor, redistribution relates to the politically contentious project of carving up the economic pie whereas "economic efficiency" relates to growing the pie—i.e., maximizing welfare and making the world wealthier. In perfect competition, the market, with its many buyers and sellers all with perfect information, is supposed to generate efficient outcomes, allocating resources to those who will value them most. A market that is not generating such outcomes has in some sense "failed," leaving space for intervention to improve its operation to make it more efficient (and generate that bigger pie). Accordingly, much of the economically oriented discussion of rationales for regulation focuses on fixing "market failures." Examples of causes of purported "market failure" include, among others: (a) monopoly power, (b) information asymmetries, (c) externalities, and (d) public goods.

a. Monopoly power. A firm with monopoly power enjoys the ability to profitably raise its prices above those that would hold in a competitive market. Pervasive price regulation of some firms, such as utilities, has often been justified on the ground that they are "natural" monopolies. Natural monopolies exist where one firm can supply an entire market at a lower cost than a greater number could. *See* RICHARD

A. Posner, Economic Analysis of the Law 377–81 (5th ed. 1998) (providing a concise introduction to the economics of natural monopoly). For instance, suppose that there is a bridge across a river, a bridge that is big enough to allow all who wish to cross to do so. Given that this bridge can satisfy the market, building a second bridge near the same spot would waste resources that could be put to more productive ends. The problem, of course, is that a bridge owner who faces no competition can charge supra-competitive prices. A traditional regulatory answer to this problem has been to impose price and output controls on natural monopolies.

b. Information asymmetries. A market cannot function "perfectly" unless participants have sufficient information concerning what they are buying and selling. Sometimes, one side of the "deal" has control over information that the other side does not. For instance, a drug manufacturer will know more about its drug's side effects than a typical consumer. Likewise, a mine owner may know more about the risks of collapse and black lung than a prospective miner. Where such information asymmetries exist, government may step in to correct them. Sometimes, sufficient disclosures may correct the problem. In other instances, absorbing the relevant information may be so costly that it makes better sense to ban the transaction (e.g., bar the sale of drugs even with full disclosure unless they have been approved by the FDA).

c. Externalities (and the Coasean response). The "externalities" theory of market failure is associated with Arthur Pigou, a Cambridge economist of the last century, who observed that the private costs of a firm's activity might not include all of its "social costs." For example, to produce its widget, a factory will have to pay for inputs including labor and materials, but it might not have to bear the cost of the damages its air pollution inflicts on others downwind. The price that the factory charges for its widget will not reflect these pollution costs that it has "externalized" onto others. Consumers will therefore pay less than they should for the widget, resulting in inefficiently high production and consumption. Pigou proposed that government force firms to internalize the costs that they might otherwise impose on others.

In 1960, Ronald Coase, an economist at the University of Chicago, offered a powerful critique of the connection between "externalities" and inefficiency. Ronald Coase, *The Problem of Social Cost*, 3 J. L. Econ. 1 (1960). Coase argued that market participants would, in the absence of transaction costs, negotiate their way to efficient deployment of resources—notwithstanding any initial assignment of legal rights. A well-known example uses the problem of a factory smokestack that emits pollutants that damage the laundry that five nearby residents regularly hang out to dry. Assume that pollution from the smokestack would, if left uncontrolled, cause each of the five residents $75 in damage to their laundry, or $375 in total damages. Assume also that this damage could be avoided if the factory installs a $150 screen or if each of the residents purchases a $50 mechanical dryer. The efficient solution is obviously for the factory to spend $150 on the screen rather than the residents to spend $250 on dryers or incur $375 in damages. Coase's insight was that, in the absence of transaction costs, the interested parties should reach this efficient solution regardless of whether the factory has a right to pollute or the residents have a right to clean air. If residents have a right to clean air, the factory will pay for the $150 screen to avoid paying damages to the residents. If the factory has the right to pollute, the residents will pay for the $150 screen to avoid paying $250 for the dryers. The choice of legal rule thus has important distributional consequences (who gets what part of the pie), but it does not affect efficiency (size of the pie). *See* A. Mitchell Polinsky, An Introduction to Law and Economics 13 (3d ed. 2003).

One might, of course, object that, in real life, transaction costs do exist—it is costly for the neighbors to get together to negotiate with each other and the factory regarding the laundry. A more nuanced approach to the Coase Theorem responds to this fact of life by suggesting that legal rules should be selected to minimize transaction costs. *Id.* at 16.

Consider: What would be a good example of a government regulatory program that curbs externalities? Does the Coase Theorem undermine the case for this program?

d. Public goods. "Public goods" are marked by nonexcludability and nonrivalrous consumption. Nonexcludability means that someone who wants to enjoy the good cannot be excluded from doing so—at least not easily. Nonrivalrous means that enjoyment of the good by one person does not lessen its availability to others. One common example of a public good is national defense, and another is street lighting. Once the system of street lighting is in place, anyone walking down the street will be able to take advantage of its illumination, and one person's use of the light does not decrease its availability to others. A banana, by contrast, is not a public good. If you own a banana, you can stop other people from eating it, and, if you eat it, no one else can.

Public goods implicate market failure due to a free rider problem. The idea here is that, because of the characteristics of public goods, consumers can enjoy their benefits without paying for them. The failure of the free rider to pay for the benefits she obtains from a public good reduces the incentive of a private producer to provide it, leading to inefficient levels of production.

3. A public choice critique of the public interest. Your views on government intervention may depend in part on whether you believe that Congress and the regulators that it empowers consistently act in the "public interest"—whatever that may be. But do they? Public choice theory, which applies the tools of economic analysis to the political realm, submits that it is more illuminating to regard political actors, including agency bureaucrats, as rational maximizers of their own utility. Dispensing with the jargon, they look out for themselves, or at least we should think of them as behaving this way for the purpose of modeling and predicting their behavior.

On this view, just as those in business compete with others to accumulate consumer dollars that will bring them wealth, politicians compete with each other for electoral support that keeps them in office (their "wealth") and bureaucrats deal with the public and the legislature to accumulate power, prestige, tenure, etc. The persons most willing to invest heavily in supporting public officials are those persons who stand to benefit the most from policies they expect those public officials to implement. This premise suggests that we should expect legislation and regulation to favor delivery of concentrated benefits to powerful vested interests rather than delivery of diffuse benefits spread thinly over the public at large. This conclusion naturally breeds suspicion of regulatory schemes that purport to serve the "public interest." One might expect to find, on close examination, that regulation that purports to set industry standards to protect consumers instead favors that industry's major players and blocks entry of new competition. (Does the bar exam spring to mind?)

Certainly it is true that special interest legislation and regulation are familiar features of the governmental landscape. But does the public choice account describe or predict how real legislators, officials, and other people behave? Critics of public choice theory note that it has trouble explaining why, for instance, people vote. Notwithstanding the Florida fiasco of the Bush-Gore presidential election of 2000, the likelihood that any given person's vote will determine the outcome of any election involving a substantial number of voters is vanishingly small. So why do voters bother? Public choice theory also has trouble accounting for the enactment of legislation that, on its face, seems to scatter benefits across a diffuse public while concentrating costs on a relative few. Major environmental statutes, such as the Clean Air Act, may fall into this category. More generally, critics of public choice theory contend that its fundamental premise, that political actors maximize some narrow self-interest, is wrong; that its predictions are often banal, untestable, or wrong; and that, perhaps worst of all, propounding this theory undermines the whole notion that there is a "public interest" that political actors should pursue.

Where does this all leave public choice theory? After surveying the literature exemplifying and criticizing public choice theory, one leading public law scholar concluded:

> [I]t would be nice if we could simply accept the public choice approach to either understanding or designing public institutions or reject it. But that seems not to be our fate. We must instead mine the field for insights and usable knowledge, while avoiding either overly enthusiastic acceptance or derisive dismissal of PCT analyses. If public law is to pursue the public interest, it must do so in part by attempting to learn from those who here sometimes seemed to suggest that the public interest could not possibly exist.

Jerry L. Mashaw, *Public Law and Public Choice: Critique and Rapprochement, in* Daniel A. Farber & Anne Joseph O'Connell, Research Handbook on Law and Public Choice (2009). The debate over the merits of public choice theory is likely to proceed indefinitely. Are you inclined, as a general matter, to think that those in government seek to serve the public interest? Does public choice help explain your own behavior? Can it explain why you vote, for instance?

Notes on the Evolution of the Administrative State

4. Early Republic. It has been fairly typical, at least until recently, to characterize the federal administrative state as a creature of the late nineteenth century that grew exponentially during the twentieth. The federal government has, however, necessarily been in the business of administration since its beginning. The First Congress established Departments of War, Treasury, and Foreign Affairs. The Tariff Act of 1789 created an administrative structure for collection of duties and designated administrative officials for carrying out this task. Jerry Mashaw, Creating the Administrative Constitution 35–38 (2012). The Patent Act of 1790 authorized a patent board consisting of the Secretary of State, Secretary of War, and the Attorney General to issue patents. Congress passed legislation providing for the payment of military pensions "to the invalids who were wounded and disabled during the late war . . . under such regulations as the President of the United States may direct." In 1791, Congress created the first Bank of the United States, and in 1792, it reorganized the Postal Service. More generally, Professor Mashaw recounts that "[f]rom the earliest days of the Republic federal statutes regulated seaman's contracts, trade with Indian tribes, and access to . . . fisheries. The central government licensed commercial vessels, created patent monopolies, regulated bankruptcy, and enforced the substantive provisions of state quarantine and product quality statutes." *Id.* at 187.

During this early era, judicial review of agency action was limited and rare. Where an official's action violated a person's common law rights, that person might bring a common law action for damages against the official, who would plead the defense that his actions were justified by law. (This general method of seeking official accountability has been carried forward in the modern era by § 1983 actions for violations by state officials of civil rights.) In addition, a party might seek judicial review via prerogative writs developed at common law, notably including mandamus and certiorari. (You may recall that Marbury tried to use a writ of mandamus to force Madison to turn over Marbury's commission.) Courts, however, sharply limited use of such writs to review of nondiscretionary action.

5. A watershed moment in the late nineteenth century. Although hardly a new phenomenon, regulation of private economic activity by the federal government did become far more prominent during the late nineteenth century, partially in response to the growing power of "big business," especially the railroads. A primary justification for such regulation was the need to control monopoly power to raise prices and limit output or engage in price discrimination. The national scope of entities such as railroad corporations required a federal response.

This response came in 1887 with the passage of the Interstate Commerce Act, which created the Interstate Commerce Commission (ICC). Congress charged the ICC with the tasks of ensuring "just and reasonable" railroad rates and barring price discrimination. The ICC is generally regarded as the first "modern" regulatory agency and as marking the dawn of the modern administrative state. It was run by a group of five commissioners appointed by the president with the advice and consent of the Senate to serve set terms of years. The ICA provided that the president could remove a commissioner during her term only for "inefficiency, neglect of duty, or malfeasance in office." We refer to agencies protected from presidential control in this way as "independent" agencies. (We will revisit the definition and role of independent agencies near the close of this chapter.)

The ICC served as the model for future independent federal agencies created later during the Progressive Era or the New Deal, such as the Federal Trade Commission, the Federal Communications Commission, the Securities and Exchange Commission, and the National Labor Relations Board.

6. The New Deal and the APA. During the 1930s, Congress and the Roosevelt administration combated the Great Depression with an "alphabet soup" of new, powerful agencies. Many of these new agencies were designed to regulate the conduct of business interests. The most aggressive regulatory statute was the National Industrial Recovery Act of 1933, which granted the president authority to promulgate "codes of fair competition" in consultation with industry trade groups. This delegation of authority proved too much for the Supreme Court, which struck it for violating the Nondelegation Doctrine in *Schechter Poultry Corp. v. United States,* 295 U.S. 495 (1935). (The Nondelegation Doctrine is discussed at Chapter 1C.1.) Other statutes created powerful independent agencies such as the Securities and Exchange Commission to regulate the securities industry, the Federal Communications Commission to regulate interstate communications, and the National Labor Relations Board to regulate collective bargaining and enforce laws against unfair labor practices. A very partial list of other agencies created during the early New Deal includes: the Agricultural Adjustment Administration, the Civilian Conservation Corps, the Civil Works Administration, the Federal Aviation Administration, the Farm Credit Administration, the Federal Deposit Insurance Corporation, the Federal Housing Administration, the Public Works Administration, and the Tennessee Valley Authority.

In addition to expanding regulation of private conduct, the New Deal also greatly expanded federally administered social programs. The Social Security Act provided for old-age insurance (or pensions) for the aged; unemployment insurance for the jobless; and public assistance to dependent children in single-parent families, disabled children, and the blind. In addition, the Act provided federal aid to the states to encourage them to undertake certain social programs. In addition to creating the Social Security Administration to administer these programs, the Act also gave states a role in administration, which led to the growth of massive state human service bureaucracies. These federal, state, and local agencies now constitute the dominant segment of the administrative government.

New Deal critics, led by the American Bar Association, charged that this massive increase in federal administrative authority came at the expense of separation of powers and that the New Deal agencies constituted a headless fourth branch of government. Years of legislative debate ensued over how to control the newly expanded administrative state. This debate culminated in the 1946 passage of the Administrative Procedure Act (APA), which has been described as "the bill of rights for the new regulatory state." George B. Shepherd, *Fierce Compromise: The Administrative Procedure Act Emerges from New Deal Politics*, 90 Nw. U. L. Rev. 1557, 1558 (1996).

You will be studying the APA, which you can find at Appendix 2 of this book, in detail as this course proceeds. For now, suffice it to recall that the APA established default templates for agency rulemaking and adjudication. For instance, the APA establishes the notice-and-comment process for "informal" rulemaking, which an agency can satisfy by: (a) publishing its proposal in the *Federal Register*; (b) allowing interested parties an opportunity to submit comments on the proposal; and (c) incorporating in the final rule a "concise general statement of . . . basis and purpose." 5 U.S.C. § 553. In addition to creating templates for rulemaking and adjudication, the APA also codified judicial authority to review agency action to ensure its legality and rationality. *Id.* at §§ 701–06.

7. A burst of quality-of-life regulation in the 1960s and 1970s. Several decades after the New Deal, another powerful group of agencies was created to address health, safety, and environmental concerns. Members of this group include the Environmental Protection Agency (EPA), Occupational Safety and Health Administration (OSHA), and Consumer Product Safety Commission (CPSC).

The history of the movement that produced these agencies is very interesting from a political perspective. The late 1960s and 1970s saw "a remarkable resurgence of regulatory reform activity." Although difficult to attribute to any one source, these new programs were enacted over strong industry objections about the costs of additional regulation. "[B]ig business was truly on the defensive . . . . The political climate made it virtually impossible to oppose such programs in principle." Robert Rabin, *The Federal Regulation in Historical Perspective*, 38 Stan. L. Rev. 1189, 1293 (1986). Interestingly, unlike civil rights legislation, for example, these reforms did not derive from a strong social movement or interest group pressures, but "as instances of 'entrepreneurial politics'—situations in which astute politicians adopted anticipatory strategies, setting the agenda for regulatory action prior to clearly articulated interest group demands for change." *Id.* at 1293–94. This form of political anticipation by lawmakers was not necessarily new, as the New Deal and President Lyndon Johnson's Great Society were also arguably examples of anticipatory reforms. What was unique about the quality of life regulations of the 1970s, however, was that they were inspired by Congress, rather than the president. Whereas Presidents Roosevelt and Johnson are seen as the driving forces behind the major reforms during their administrations, President Nixon "was an uneasy participant from the outset in the movement for 'quality of life' regulation . . . [his] main constituency was quite clearly the business community." *Id.* at 1294. Prominent figures like Senator Edmund Muskie in the area of environmental protection and well-known consumer protection advocate Ralph Nader served as primary catalysts for regulatory change.

8. A deregulatory backlash. The burst of public-interest regulations of the 1970s pro-voked a deregulatory response. Economists led this charge, arguing that government directives about how businesses must operate led to increased costs and unnecessary inefficiencies. A common criticism of the expanded administrative state focused on the heavy-handed nature of command-and-control regulatory techniques:

> These command-control programs, designed specifically to avoid bureau-cratic discretion and undue industry influence in the administrative pro-cess, created serious problems as uniform federal standards were applied inflexibly in all instances. Not only were extraordinarily high regulatory costs a possible outcome, but ironically strict adherence to highly specific rules tended to stifle technological developments that could achieve desired results more effectively or efficiently.

RICHARD HARRIS & SIDNEY MILKIS, THE POLITICS OF REGULATORY CHANGE: A TALE OF TWO AGENCIES 7–8 (1989).

In response to this critique, some regulatory programs shifted away from the command-and-control model toward the use of markets as a means to achieve reg-ulatory goals. For instance, the 1990 Clean Air Act Amendments used this approach to control sulfur dioxide, one of the major causes of acid rain. Rather than enforce predetermined limits on plant-specific emissions, this program capped aggregate emissions and established a system of tradable emissions allowances. If a plant's sul-fur dioxide emissions exceed its allowances, it can either reduce its emissions or buy more allowances on the market, and will presumably do whichever is less expensive. There will only be allowances available to buy, however, if some plants are able to sell because they have reduced their emissions below their allowances. *See gener-ally* Paul L. Joskow & Richard Schmalensee, *The Political Economy of Market Based Environmental Policy: The U.S. Acid Rain Program*, 41 J.L. & ECON. 37 (1998). More recently, governments around the world, most notably the European Union, have formed trading schemes for controlling greenhouse gas emissions.

Another, deeper criticism of the regulatory state decried excessive regulation for its interference with liberty. Critics argued, "the new social regulation was incon-sistent, even antithetical, to the American notion of liberal democracy." RICHARD HARRIS & SIDNEY MILKIS, THE POLITICS OF REGULATORY CHANGE: A TALE OF TWO AGENCIES 7–8 (1989). Under this view, it was not sufficient for government "simply to work more efficiently; . . . it [needed] to work less." *Id.* This focus on a smaller, rather than a more effective, government is a defining feature of the deregula-tory movement. It was reflected in the Reagan administration's frequent use of the phrase "regulatory relief," over the more traditional "regulatory reform," to describe its policy agenda. *Id.* A decade later, President Bill Clinton suggested the rhetorical success of the deregulatory movement when he said in his 1996 State of the Union Address that "the era of big government is over."

9. The Great Recession and aftermath. In 2008, the United States and the world became mired in the greatest economic crisis since the Great Depression. This crisis undermined the laissez-faire ideology that had tended to dominate the regulatory environment of the preceding several decades. In this vein, Alan Greenspan, the former chair of the Federal Reserve, remarked, "[t]hose of us who have looked to the self-interest of lending institutions to protect shareholders' equity, myself included, are in a state of shocked disbelief." *See* Edmund L. Andrews, *Greenspan Concedes Error on Regulation*, N.Y. TIMES, Oct. 23, 2008.

Judge Richard Posner, a father of the law-and-economics movement, prophesied:

> Capitalism will survive the current depression as it did the Great Depression of the 1930s. It will survive because there is no alternative that hasn't been thoroughly discredited, which wasn't as clear in the 1930s. It is clear now. The Soviet, Maoist, "corporatist" (fascist Italy), Cuban, Venezuelan, etc. alternatives to capitalism are unappealing, to say the least. Yet capitalism may survive only in a compromised form—think of the spur that the Great Depression gave to collectivism. Spawned in the depression the New Deal ushered in a long era of heavy-handed government regulation of the economy; and likewise today there is both advocacy and the actuality of renewed regulation and an impending increase in the size of government.

RICHARD A. POSNER, A FAILURE OF CAPITALISM 234 (2009).

During the brief period of unified Democratic control of the Congress and White House from 2009 to 2010, Congress did indeed pass major legislation expanding regulation. For instance, Congress passed the Dodd-Frank Wall Street Reform and Consumer Protection Act to strengthen and rationalize regulation of the financial services industry. Dodd-Frank created a powerful new agency, the Consumer Financial Protection Bureau, to protect consumers from predatory financial products. Congress also passed the Affordable Care Act, which in addition to expanding access to health care through "Obamacare" markets and by expanding Medicaid, also imposed minimum coverage requirements on insurance plans.

The Great Recession did not, however, convince everyone that greater governmental involvement in regulating the economy is needed. The two major American political parties have sharply divergent ideologies regarding the proper role of government regulation of private economic actors. The rollback of regulations, especially environmental regulations, is a primary goal of the Trump administration.

2. Why Use Agencies to Govern?

Once we determine that government should address some social problem, we must then confront the question of how it should do so. Generally speaking, the branch of the federal government empowered to solve such problems—at least initially—is the Congress. Congress is the "law making" branch of the federal government, and as such is the first actor in any government effort or program.

Congress's tool for solving problems is the enactment of federal statutes, or legislation. Federal legislation can be used to address any issue over which Congress has constitutional authority to legislate. *See* U.S. CONST. art. I, § 8. Where Congress wishes to impose regulatory controls, it confronts a choice between two basic mechanisms that are most relevant to the present discussion. The first is direct control. Direct control is what you likely think of first when you hear about legislation addressing an issue. It occurs when Congress enacts a statute telling individuals or groups what they may or may not do. An easy example of this is the criminal law, where Congress enacts a statute prohibiting, for instance, the possession or use of certain types and quantities of drugs. Law enforcement officials investigate and prosecute violations of these congressional instructions, which are ultimately enforced in the courts. Such direct control may be the most straightforward way in which Congress can use its power to regulate, but it is not the only way.

Another approach, and the one that is most important for our study of administrative law, is the use of legislation to delegate to another governmental entity—an administrative agency—the responsibility to tackle the problem at hand. When Congress chooses this approach, we refer to the statute as an "enabling act." An enabling act defines the scope of an agency's authority both substantively and procedurally: substantively in terms of the types of policy questions the agency is empowered to address (think environmental issues for the EPA and food safety for the FDA), and procedurally in terms of the legal mechanisms it may employ to achieve its substantive goals (such as rulemaking, adjudication, and investigations).

Given that Congress can choose direct control or delegation to an administrative agency, why in a particular context should it choose one over the other?

Lesson 1B.2. You will recall that Abby just got a job as an associate at a D.C. firm for which Gallery, a major wine producer, is a big client. After getting her bar results, Abby, a dutiful child, called her parents to update them on the latest details of her life. Abby's dad is a big fan of all the lawyer shows on television. Strange to say, none of them focus on administrative law, and when Abby tells him that she will be representing Gallery before a new agency, the Wine Trade Commission, her father asks for further explanation. Abby explains that the WTC has the power to make rules that Gallery and other industry players must obey, to hold hearings to determine if they have been violated, and to order penalties against violators. Appalled, Abby's dad responds—"Isn't it Congress's job to make the rules? And the courts' job to decide who broke them? What do we pay them for if they are just going to make somebody else do their work for them?" He is considering writing his member of Congress and sending a stern letter to the editor of his local newspaper to alert them of the WTC's un-American usurpation of power.

How might the following materials help Abby explain why we rely on administrative processes to carry out certain community goals? Do you find the arguments these materials make persuasive?

The Legislative Process

Informed discussion of the choice between direct control and delegation requires a basic grounding in the legislative process itself. How does Congress actually go about enacting legislation, and what does the way legislation is made tell us about the strengths of direct control versus delegation?

The short answer to how a statute comes about is contained in Article I of the Constitution, which states that "[e]very Bill which shall have passed the House of Representatives and the Senate, shall, before it become a law, be presented to the President of the United States." U.S. Const. art. I, § 7, cl. 2. This process of "bicameralism and presentment" reflects what we all learned in our middle school social studies class about how a bill becomes law: it has to be passed by a majority of both houses of Congress, and either the president must sign it or Congress must override his veto. But where does a bill come from, and how does it get to the honored position of even being voted on in Congress?

The answer to where a bill comes from is simultaneously simple and complex. The simple response is that legislation may be drafted by anyone, including members of Congress and their staffs, executive branch officials, public or private interest groups, individual citizens, or any combination thereof, but it may not be formally considered by either the House or Senate until it is introduced by a member of that chamber while the Congress is in session. Steven S. Smith, Jason M. Roberts, & Ryan J. Vander Wielen, The American Congress 233 (8th ed. 2013). Why might a member of Congress choose to formally introduce a bill? Perhaps the member of Congress has become interested in a particular issue, either personally or on behalf of her constituents. Perhaps she has heard from concerned individuals or groups (often described as "special interests") that are frequently experts in the field and ideologically committed to a particular cause, from the president or some other member of the executive branch, or even from public opinion more generally. While some of these influences (like the president, for instance) may have more sway over congressional actors than others, it is impossible to outline a reliable formula for how the political development of a statute occurs. It is safe to say, however, that without some impetus for a member of Congress to act, legislation cannot be passed.

Once one or more members of Congress have determined that a statute is a good idea, the technical aspect of legislating in a bicameral legislature begins. Here the Constitution again provides a short answer to how bills progress in each house of Congress by declaring that "[e]ach House may determine the rules of its proceedings." U.S. Const. art. I, § 5, cl. 2. The internal rules of each house of Congress determine how a bill gets reviewed and advanced by the members of that house. While the House of Representatives and Senate do not have identical processes for considering proposed legislation, there are some common themes.

In both houses, once a bill has been introduced, it is referred to one or more of the standing committees.[1] Committees are usually defined by subject matter and

---

1. A list of House committees can be found at http://www.house.gov/committees/, and of Senate committees at http://www.senate.gov/pagelayout/committees/d_three_sections_with_teasers /committees_home.htm.

are staffed by members of the chamber in which they reside. The Speaker of the House and the Senate Majority Leader (with the assistance of their respective parliamentarians) make the determination as to which committees should consider a bill. Once a bill is assigned to a committee, that committee may choose to pass the bill along to one or more of its subcommittees for initial consideration. Committees and subcommittees may hold hearings or commission studies relevant to the bill. They may offer amendments or even rewrite the bill in its entirety before deciding whether to "report" the bill back to the floor of their chamber. They may also, however, choose to do nothing at all. Failure to act results in the bill dying in the committee. This is by far the most common outcome, making committee consideration a hugely consequential part of the legislative process. The small percentage of bills that are reported out of committee are accompanied by a committee report, which is often drafted by committee staff members and serves as an important piece of legislative history if the bill is ultimately passed into law.

A bill that is reported out of committee next goes to the floor of the chamber for debate and, potentially, a vote. In the House of Representatives, the Rules Committee is critical to this process. The Rules Committee issues a "rule" for each bill establishing how the entire House of Representatives will consider that bill. The rule addresses issues such as scheduling consideration of the bill, the amount of time for general debate, and the appropriateness and number of amendments. The Senate, by contrast, works much less formally. Bringing up a bill in the Senate is simply a matter of a Senator making a motion. The difficulty arises, however, in the scope of debate allowed. Senate rules allow for unlimited debate, which allows opponents of a bill an opportunity to kill it either through endless talking on the Senate floor or, far more commonly, by the procedural device of invoking a motion for "cloture." This tactic of extending debate to prevent a final vote on a bill, commonly referred to as a "filibuster," can be overcome only by a successful cloture motion. A cloture motion must be signed by at least sixteen Senators, and seeks to end the debate on a bill and proceed to a final vote on its merits. Senate Rule XXII. In order for cloture to be achieved, the motion must be approved by at least three-fifths (sixty) of Senators. This supermajority requirement makes cloture difficult to achieve and thus leaves the filibuster as a powerful and often successful tool for blocking legislation in the Senate.

In November 2013, the Senate eliminated cloture requirements for the confirmation of presidential nominees to executive offices and the lower courts. In April 2017, during confirmation proceedings for Justice Gorsuch, the Senate eliminated cloture requirements for Supreme Court justices. These controversial changes were achieved through a parliamentary procedure that allows the Senate to amend its own rules by a simple majority vote, without the prospect of a filibuster. This procedure is referred to as the "nuclear option" because it is a drastic break from the Senate's long-standing custom of requiring a supermajority of votes to overcome a filibuster and, perhaps more importantly, because its use could result in a dramatic power shift within the Senate. The Senate has traditionally been the slower moving, more deliberative of the two houses of Congress. The nuclear option threatens that tradition by stripping the minority party of the blocking power of the filibuster, thus enabling the majority party to pursue its own agenda unopposed. The fact that the nuclear option has been employed recently (and after years of unfulfilled threats) suggests a live possibility that the filibuster may be further narrowed or eliminated.

Assuming that both houses vote to enact a bill, the next step is to assure that both the House of Representatives and Senate versions of the bill are identical before their presentment to the president in accordance with Article I, § 7. This process is called reconciliation and can be done in a number of ways. One house can simply adopt the other's version of the bill, or the two can exchange amendments until they reach a consensus. A third way is called a conference, in which each house appoints members (selected by the Speaker of the House and the Senate Majority Leader) to a conference committee. The conference committee is charged with negotiating a version of the bill that is acceptable to both houses. The conference process is subject to the same internal and external political pressures as the rest of the legislative process, and thus may not result in an acceptable bill. A successful conference results in the houses approving a single version of the bill to be presented to the president, the "enrolled bill," and a conference report explaining the compromises reached at the conference. All that remains at this juncture is the president's signature or, in the alternative, a veto. U.S. Const. art. I, § 7, cl. 2. A signature results in the bill becoming law, whereas a veto prevents the bill from becoming law and returns it to the originating chamber with an explanation of the president's objections to enactment. If a two-thirds majority of each house of Congress votes at this stage to enact the bill, it becomes law over the president's veto.

This very brief exegesis on the legislative process offers some insight into the significant obstacles confronting an even slightly controversial bill. In the initial stages, political pressure and procedural obstacles can be brought to bear to defeat a bill before it even escapes its reviewing committees. For a bill that survives committee review and emerges onto the floor of the House of Representatives or the Senate, a new set of procedural and political challenges arise that again make it extremely difficult to enact a single chamber's preferred version of a bill, let alone one that is also acceptable to the other chamber. Finally, presidential approval is the ultimate gatekeeper, with only a supermajority of legislators standing between a presidential veto and the bill's demise.

Understanding how a statute came about is useful to aspiring lawyers, and in our case aspiring practitioners of administrative law, for at least three reasons. First, it helps lawyers advise their clients how to become more involved in the lawmaking process, either through lobbying or more public participation. As we will see later, interaction between agencies and their constituencies is an important and influential part of administrative law. Due to Congress's power over administrative agencies, that interaction often involves discussions of *legislative*, as well as agency, activity. Second, understanding the details of how a statute is made may enhance our understanding of what that statute *means*. Much of what agencies and administrative lawyers do involves detailed statutory interpretation. Legislative history—information developed throughout the enactment of a statute—is a powerful tool for finding statutory meaning when a particular statutory provision is either vague or not clearly determinative in a given situation. A better understanding of the steps involved in enacting a statute leads to a more thorough understanding of the legislative history accompanying that statute, and in turn of the full range of arguments about its meaning. We discuss administrative law's approach to statutory interpretation in far greater detail in Chapter 5. For now, it is enough to understand that statutes are fundamental to both governmental regulation in general and administrative law.

Third, and most important for the present discussion about how Congress should regulate, knowledge of the legislative process helps explain why Congress often chooses to delegate complicated policy questions to administrative agencies, rather than simply tackling those questions itself. The bottom line is that enacting legislation is a politically difficult and time-consuming process. So difficult, in fact, that it may be impossible for Congress to directly address more than a handful of the numerous important issues facing the nation at any given time. When confronted with the potentially insurmountable task of providing legislative responses to all of our national issues, delegation becomes more attractive. That is not to say that delegation is the only defensible way to regulate. On the contrary, strong arguments can be made for making the process more manageable by asking Congress to simply do less of it. Regardless of whether one subscribes to the argument for smaller government, it is clear that the intricacies of the legislative process are at least relevant to the question of why Congress may choose delegation over direct regulation.

Benefits of Administrative Government

The preceding discussion of the legislative process suggests a kind of negative argument in favor of delegation: Congress needs to delegate power to agencies because the legislative process is so politically and procedurally difficult. We now switch the emphasis to explore some of the positive benefits claimed for administrative government by its proponents.

Agencies come in a mind-boggling array of shapes and sizes, and their powers vary widely. That said, the Federal Trade Commission (FTC) can serve as a good example of an archetypal modern agency for the purpose of this discussion. Congress has granted the FTC very broad jurisdiction—charging it with the tasks of rooting out "unfair methods of competition" and "unfair or deceptive acts or practices" in interstate commerce. Congress has also granted the FTC the power to promulgate "rules." This means the FTC has the power to identify particular behaviors or practices that are "unfair" under the Federal Trade Commission Act. These rules can carry the "force of law"—i.e., they are binding on the public in the same way as congressional statutes. The FTC also has authority to initiate enforcement actions against those it determines may have violated its rules or the statute and to adjudicate these violations (subject to judicial review). The upshot is that the FTC, within its jurisdiction, combines what might be fairly called legislative, executive, and adjudicative powers. Why, as a matter of policy, might Congress prefer to create such agencies rather than use other entities such as the FBI (or similar enforcement agencies) and Article III courts to implement federal laws and programs?

Final Report of the Attorney General's Committee on Administrative Procedure 11–18 (1941)

What are the reasons why Congress thus resorted, continuously and with increasing frequency, to the administrative process as an instrument for the execution of the policies which it has enacted into law? No single or simple explanation can be given. The reasons are both varied and numerous, reflecting the variety and number of the agencies themselves. Discussion frequently requires classification in terms of the differing functions which the agencies perform.

1. *Advantages of administration as compared with executive action.* — One of the principal alternatives to the administrative process is the more extensive use of ordinary executive officers. This alternative appears in a distinctive field of governmental action, comprising those numerous functions which commonly are regarded, for historical or other reasons, as belonging peculiarly to the executive department. An instance is the issuance of passports, the task of the Passport Division in the Department of State. Another is the actual expenditure, as distinguished from the appropriation, of public funds. Congress itself cannot or should not issue passports or make payments of money. Nor have these been thought of as appropriate tasks for the courts. This being so, two alternatives, broadly speaking, are available. Congress can establish an administrative tribunal for the task. Or it can make use of executive officers, charged with acting substantially as officers by the Business Enterprises Act.

The difference between these alternatives is not easy of exact statement, yet it appears readily enough from a comparison of extremes. It can be illustrated by the contrast between the Works Progress Administration and the Veterans' Administration. Both agencies disburse benefits. The former, however, proceeds in fluid executive fashion under a statute so framed that it confers upon individuals no "rights" to relief in stated circumstances. It issues no regulations giving notice of how it will act or limiting its own discretion. The latter, administering law embodied in statute and regulations, adjudicates "rights" by a relatively formal hearing procedure. The former the Committee has not regarded as an "administrative" agency falling within its purview; the latter it has. In this and analogous situations weighty reasons may often lead Congress to frame statutes upon the executive, more broadly discretionary, pattern. But the alternative of administrative adjudication, where practicable, insures greater uniformity and impersonality of action. In this area of Government the administrative process, far from being an encroachment upon the rule of law, is an extension of it.

A substantial number of existing administrative agencies represent an effort to discharge in a fashion analogous to the judicial a function which might have been discharged executively or even legislatively. . . .

2. *Constitutional limitations upon the powers of courts.* — Many of the functions just discussed might, as far as the Constitution is concerned, have been assigned directly to the courts. Congress, for example, might conceivably have empowered the Federal district courts to hear claims for social security benefits under the Social Security Act and, when a claim was approved, to enter a money judgment against the United States. For reasons of expediency or appropriateness Congress did not use this method. In other situations, however, no such choice under the Constitution is open to Congress. Federal courts created under Article III can be authorized only to decide "cases and controversies," to use the constitutional phrase; and from an early day the Supreme Court has regarded this restriction as an important one, to be scrupulously observed. "Cases and controversies," broadly speaking, are matters in which a court can determine with finality the rights of adverse parties by applying the law to the facts as found. Thus the whole field of rule-making (with the exception of rules of judicial procedure) is outside the constitutional competence of the courts, for rules do not determine the rights of specific litigants but, like statutes, are addressed to people generally. Again, the Supreme Court has held that the Federal courts cannot be empowered to fix rates or prices, although they can review rate orders made by administrative agencies. Nor can they be authorized to issue broadcasting licenses, or to perform many other functions involving similarly wide discretion with respect to future conduct or arrangements. This insistence of the courts upon confining themselves to judicial, as distinguished from executive or legislative, functions has made inevitable the conferring of a wide range of powers, if the powers were to be conferred at all, upon some one of the executive departments or upon an independent agency.

3. *The trend toward preventive legislation.* — If administrative agencies did not exist in the Federal Government, Congress would be limited to a technique of legislation primarily designed to correct evils after they have arisen rather than to prevent them from arising. The criminal law, of course, operates in this after-the-event fashion. Congress declares a given act to be a crime. The mere declaration may act as a deterrent. But if it fails to do so the courts can only punish the wrongdoer; they cannot wipe out or make good the wrong. Traditional noncriminal, private law operates for the most part in the same after the event fashion. A statute or the common law gives one individual a right to go into court and sue another. This procedure is likely to be expensive. It is uncertain. At best, in the ordinary action for money damages, it leads only to compensation for the injury, which is seldom as satisfactory as not having been injured at all. To be sure, courts of equity administer a substantial measure of preventive justice by giving injunctions against threatened injuries. But it is necessary to prove the threat, and other limitations confine the scope of this mode of relief. The desire to work out a more effective and more flexible method of preventing unwanted things from happening accounts for the formation of many (although by no means all) Federal administrative agencies.

The rate-making powers of the Interstate Commerce Commission afford an apt illustration. . . . A more recent example is the Securities and Exchange Commission.

Within rather severe limits, the common law recognized a right in a purchaser of securities to recover damages from the seller resulting from false statements made in effecting the sale. The importance of truth in securities led to a demand that honest statements, as well as fuller and more informative statements, be assured so far as possible in advance. If this end were to be accomplished, it could only be done by creating an administrative agency. A similar purpose, effected in a great variety of ways, underlies the formation of many other agencies. Thus, licensing is one of the most significant of all preventive devices. It would be possible to permit anyone to act as the pilot of a ship or a plane, and then to punish those whose incompetence led to accidents or to prohibit them from acting as pilots again. People have preferred, however, to attempt by a licensing method to assure competence in advance; and administrative agencies have had to be created to carry out the licensing system. . . .

4. *Limitations upon effective legislative action.* — Many of the functions of existing Federal administrative agencies obviously could not, in any view, be performed by Congress. Others, however, could. Thus, State legislatures once fixed rates by statute, although Congress seems never to have done so. Congress once disposed of all money claims against the United States by a private bill procedure; much[,] although not all, of this work has now been passed on to other agencies. Apart from instances of this character, the full range of rule-making activity of Federal administrative agencies represents work of a type which Congress could do if it had the time and deemed it wise to do it. Independently of the comparative advantages of administrative action, various inherent limitations upon its own functioning militate in these cases against action by Congress itself. The total time available is the most obvious. Time spent on details must be at the sacrifice of time spent on matters of broad public policy. Lack of specialized information is another; lack of a staff or a procedure adapted to acquiring it is a third. The complexity of the problems which have to be determined, even after basic policy has been settled, is the governing consideration. Even if Congress had the time and facilities to work out details, there would be constant danger of harmful rigidity if the result were crystallized in the form of a statute. Thus comes a steady pressure — which may, of course, be yielded to over readily — to assign such tasks to the controlled discretion of some other agency.

5. *Limitations upon exclusively judicial enforcement.* — If Congress chooses to rely upon the courts instead of assuming the tasks itself, discretion[,] as already pointed out, must not be so broad as to require the exercise of nonjudicial functions. Although this difficulty can be avoided, however, other limitations operate. The 94 Federal district and territorial courts are structurally incapable of the same uniformity in the application of law as a single centralized agency. The problem of uniformity, and other problems as well, arise also with respect to the initiative of enforcement which, of course, the judges themselves cannot assume. Action must be brought either in the name of the Government or by private individuals. If brought by the Government, the 94 district and territorial attorneys will vary in their enforcement policy as will the courts in their decisions. If brought by private

individuals, there is cast upon these individuals a burden which it is one of the prime purposes of administrative agencies to avoid. Certain agencies, it is essential to recognize, represent an effort, whether wise or unwise, to place upon the Government—rather than upon millions of people of often limited resources—a large share of the responsibility for making effective policies which the people through their Government have declared.

6. *The advantages of continuity of attention and clearly allocated responsibility.*— In contrast to the limitations of other agencies, just discussed, are certain advantages which administrative agencies, properly organized, may have. The need of bringing to bear upon difficult social and economic questions the attention of those who have time and facilities to become and remain continuously informed about them was recognized very early. . . .

Each of the agencies . . . specializes in the regulation of a single industry or phase of industry—railroad transportation, or shipping, or investment, or banking. But Congress has also employed the administrative process to perform specialized and continuing regulation not of particular industries but of activities cutting across many industries. . . .

It is thus apparent that varied types of subject matters, from rate control of railroad carriers to collection of employees' wages and disciplining of seamen, have been entrusted by Congress to administrative agencies at least in part for similar reasons: in order to assure continuous attention to and clearly allocated responsibility for the effectuation of legislative policies.

7. *The need for organization to dispose of volume of business and to provide the necessary records.*—The volume of cases arising under certain laws is very great. . . .

These same agencies illustrate another and related reason for employing the administrative process. This is the need of specialized staffs and machinery to keep and make available the records upon which judgment must be based.

Notes

1. How well has the Final Report held up? The Final Report was authored by a blue-ribbon commission created by President Roosevelt in the aftermath of the New Deal. It tells us what those most ardently, and to some extent uncritically, committed to bureaucratic solutions to social problems thought they could accomplish through the administrative process. What, according to the report, are the advantages of administration as opposed to those of regulation? Of adjudication by the courts? Of what the report calls "executive" action?

2. Ask the experts? Confidence in experts has been a major justification for committing many community issues to administrative agencies. There is, however, a long history of the "best and brightest" leading the country into big trouble. Expertise may carry certain cognitive biases that make expert judgment less accurate than might be expected. *E.g.,* Colin Camerer & Eric Johnson, *The Process-Performance Paradox in Expert Judgment: How Can Experts Know So Much and Predict So Badly?,* *in* TOWARDS A GENERAL THEORY OF EXPERTISE: PROSPECTS AND LIMITS 195 (Ericsson & Smith ed. 1991) (surveying studies of expertise). *But see* CASS R. SUNSTEIN, RISK AND REASON 55 (2002) (criticizing the view that "ordinary" people enjoy a "rival" and "richer" rationality than experts; concluding, "[w]hen they disagree, experts are generally right, and ordinary people are generally wrong"). The good news is that experts seem to understand their limitations better than nonexperts. Moreover, experts seem to be better at certain tasks, such as searching for information and pattern recognition. But, let's face it, experts are often wrong. Under what circumstances should non-experts (e.g., politicians, judges, the public) trump the judgments of the people who are supposed to know the most?

3. Unleash the bureaucrats? Complaining about the government is a national sport—thus the old joke, "I'm from the government, and I'm here to help." Responding to this attitude, it is virtually a tradition that each incoming president forms a blue ribbon group that produces a report on how to reform governmental operations. One prominent theme in some of these reports is the need for quality personnel who are given the freedom to carry out their missions. For example, the "Landis" report, commissioned by President Kennedy, urged that the key to improvement lay in independence for government personnel. JAMES M. LANDIS, REPORT ON REGULATORY AGENCIES TO THE PRESIDENT-ELECT 68 (1960). Several decades later, a report issued under the auspices of Vice President Gore emphasized the importance of "deregulating" government personnel and creating "entrepreneurial government." Two of its four "key principles" focus on that issue:

> Effective, entrepreneurial governments . . . reorient their control systems to prevent problems rather than simply punish those who make mistakes. They strip away unnecessary layers of regulation that stifle innovation. And they deregulate organizations that depend upon them for funding, such as lower levels of government. . . .

> Effective, entrepreneurial governments transform their culture by decentralizing authority. They empower those who work on the front lines to make more of their own decisions and solve more of their own problems.

REPORT OF THE NATIONAL PERFORMANCE REVIEW 6–7 (1993). In spite of such calls for more bureaucratic independence or "discretion," it seems fair to say that the bureaucracies that regulate us are themselves highly regulated. Should this be the case? Does the "rule of law" require it?

4. Public participation in administration and administrative shaping of the public. The operations of the modern administrative state raise the specter of unelected bureaucrats wielding unaccountable power. Administrative law lessens this concern to some extent by allowing public participation in administrative procedures, especially rulemaking. Public participation can provide agencies with helpful substantive information about regulatory problems, as well as information concerning the policy preferences of participants. How, though, should agencies make use of information concerning public preferences?

Robert Reich distinguished between two dominant approaches to this problem in administrative law. Under the "interest-groups intermediation" model, "[t]he public administrator's central responsibility came to be understood as ensuring that *all* those who might be affected by agency action were represented in decisionmaking deliberation." Robert Reich, *Public Administration and Public Deliberation: An Interpretive Essay*, 94 YALE L.J. 1617 (1985). On this view, an agency might be said to serve as a forum for an alternative type of participatory democracy. The administrator was to serve as a referee whose job was "to accommodate — to the extent possible — the varying demands placed upon government by competing groups."

The "net-benefit maximization" model, by contrast, contemplates that the administrator serves as an analyst who chooses "the policy option yielding the largest net benefit or greatest 'social utility.'" Preferences of members of the public still play a role in this analysis insofar as efforts to calculate utility look to how much people are willing to pay for various goods — even though some non-market goods, such as clean air, do not have readily determinable market values.

According to Reich, both of these models miss a profoundly important point by assuming that administration is a matter of giving people what they want — where what they want is taken as given. But administration itself, as Reich observes, "can have a profound effect on perceptions and, hence, on individual preferences." For example, Reich notes that, by placing a monetary value on a wilderness area, an administrator makes a "public statement that feelings towards such wilderness areas *can* be expressed in dollars and cents" and "thereby transforms wilderness areas into consumer goods whose worth depends upon how well they satisfy us, rather than entities with their own inherent value."

What do you think the proper relationship of an agency should be to the broader public? In designing rules, should an agency's focus be on ensuring broad participation and accommodation of all those affected? Or should it focus on what Reich refers to as "net-benefit" maximization? Relating to Reich's deeper point, what role should an agency such as the EPA (or the WTC, for that matter) attempt to play in *shaping* the public's preferences?

C. Separation of Powers and the Administrative State

In addition to granting enumerated powers to the United States government, the Constitution also famously restricts these powers through a regime of checks-and-balances and separation of powers. Article I of the Constitution vests the federal government's "legislative" powers in the Congress; Article II vests the "executive" power in the president, and Article III vests the "judicial" power of the United States in the federal courts. This structure inevitably creates tensions among the three branches and raises difficult questions regarding whether one branch has intruded upon another. These questions are particularly acute in administrative law given

Congress's practice of authorizing agencies to issue binding regulations and to resolve case-specific disputes (albeit typically subject to judicial review). These activities give rise to powerful arguments that agencies within the executive branch are improperly exercising legislative and adjudicative power. Moreover, efforts by Congress and the courts to control the vast powers that Congress has delegated to agencies sometimes lead to charges that these branches have usurped the executive power.

The rest of this chapter will address the Supreme Court's leading efforts to reconcile the modern administrative state with the structural requirements of our eighteenth-century Constitution. As you reflect on these efforts, consider: Why did the Constitution insist on some form of separation of powers in the first place? Writing in *The Federalist No. 47*, James Madison claimed that "[t]he accumulation of all powers, legislative, executive, and judiciary, in the same hands, whether of one, a few, or many, and whether hereditary, self-appointed, or elective, may justly be pronounced the very definition of tyranny." He gave a partial explanation for this claim in the same number of *The Federalist* in a brief exegesis on Montesquieu, the eighteenth-century French philosopher who served as an oracle on separation-of-powers doctrine for the Framers:

> The reasons on which Montesquieu grounds his maxim are a further demonstration of his meaning. "When the legislative and executive powers are united in the same person or body," says he, "there can be no liberty, because apprehensions may arise lest *the same* monarch or senate should *enact* tyrannical laws to execute them in a tyrannical manner." Again: "Were the power of judging joined with the legislative, the life and liberty of the subject would be exposed to arbitrary control, for *the judge* would then be *the legislator*. Were it joined to the executive power, *the judge* might behave with all the violence of *an oppressor*."

So, for Madison, the purpose of separation of powers is to protect liberty and block tyranny. Certainly, it seems correct to say that we would not enjoy much "liberty" (whatever that term means) if one governmental entity enjoyed all the powers of Congress, the president, and the federal courts. But does agency rulemaking threaten the demise of liberty and rise of tyranny? Agency adjudication? If so, are there means to reduce these risks to acceptable levels? And, if these risks are reduced to acceptable levels, does that make modern regulatory agencies constitutional?

1. Agencies as "Legislators"

Article I, § 1 provides that "[a]ll legislative Powers herein granted shall be vested in a Congress of the United States which shall consist of a Senate and House of Representatives." According to the nondelegation doctrine, this constitutional provision bars Congress from delegating legislative authority to other actors, including agencies. Nonetheless, agencies commonly enjoy the power to create rules that carry the force of law (i.e., "legislative rules"). The following materials explore how the Court has managed the tension among these propositions.

Lesson 1C.1. To prepare for her work, Abby spends some quality time studying the Wine Trade Commission Act (WTCA). She immediately sees that the WTCA charges the Wine Trade Commission (WTC) with a variety of responsibilities. Section 3 instructs the agency to promote the American wine industry. Section 4 grants it power to supervise states in the administration of a cooperative disaster fund program. Section 5 directs the agency to police the wine industry against fraud and deceit. Section 6 grants it authority to license "wine merchants" and to supervise the Wine Merchant's Association, an industry self-regulatory organization.

Most notably for the immediate purpose, § 8 grants the WTC "the power to make rules and regulations for the purpose of carrying out the provisions of this Act." The WTC thus can promulgate rules designed to aid administration and enforcement of its various statutory duties, such as policing against fraud under § 5 and licensing wine merchants under § 6. Under §§ 7, 10, and 11, violators of these rules may be subject to civil, administrative, or criminal penalties. The agency thus has power, in effect, to create a sort of criminal code governing the wine industry. Abby, whom we regret to report did not take Administrative Law in law school, wonders how it could conceivably be constitutional for the WTC to exercise this type of power. What light do the following materials shed on this problem?

Background of *Whitman v. American Trucking Assoc., Inc.*

The Clean Air Act requires the Environmental Protection Agency to promulgate national ambient air quality standards (NAAQS) for various pollutants. Under § 109(b)(1) of the Act, these standards must be "requisite to protect the public health" with "an adequate margin of safety." Carrying out this incredibly important task requires EPA to make difficult scientific determinations concerning the effects of regulated pollutants and to follow a complex set of procedures. Uncertainty and judgment calls are inevitable, and the whole process can take many years.

The *Whitman* case arose out of EPA's revisions of the NAAQS for ozone and particulate matter. These revised NAAQS provoked intense reactions by environmental groups that thought them too weak and by industrial groups that thought them too tough. Scores of entities, including the U.S. Chamber of Commerce, states such as Ohio and West Virginia, and various utilities and manufacturers, challenged the rules before the D.C. Circuit. Sending shock waves through the worlds of environmental and administrative law, a majority of the panel concluded that EPA's rulemaking authority violated the nondelegation doctrine. In support of this conclusion, the court observed that the agency's approach to its authority left it free to set emissions levels at "any point between zero and a hair below the concentrations yielding London's Killer Fog." *American Trucking Ass'n v. EPA*, 175 F.3d 1027, 1037 (D.C. Cir. 1999). The court declined, however, to throw out a critical provision of the Clean Air Act as unconstitutional decades after its adoption. Instead, the court vacated the revised NAAQS and remanded to the agency with instructions to develop an "intelligible principle" that would narrow its discretion to acceptable levels. The stage was thus set for a major discussion by the Supreme Court of the scope of agency rulemaking authority under the Constitution.

Whitman v. American Trucking Assoc., Inc.

531 U.S. 457 (2001)

JUSTICE SCALIA delivered the opinion of the Court. . . .

Section 109(a) of the CAA [Clean Air Act], as added, 84 Stat. 1679, and amended, 42 U.S.C. § 7409(a), requires the Administrator of the EPA to promulgate NAAQS [national ambient air quality standards] for each air pollutant for which "air quality criteria" have been issued. Once a NAAQS has been promulgated, the Administrator must review the standard (and the criteria on which it is based) "at five-year intervals" and make "such revisions . . . as may be appropriate." These cases arose when, on July 18, 1997, the Administrator revised the NAAQS for particulate matter (PM) and ozone. American Trucking Associations, Inc., and its co-respondents in No. 99-1257 which include, in addition to other private companies, the States of Michigan, Ohio, and West Virginia, challenged the new standards in the Court of Appeals for the District of Columbia Circuit, pursuant to 42 U.S.C. § 7607(b)(1).

The District of Columbia Circuit accepted some of the challenges and rejected others. It agreed with the No. 99-1257 respondents (hereinafter respondents) that § 109(b)(1) delegated legislative power to the Administrator in contravention of the United States Constitution, Art. I, § 1, because it found that the EPA had interpreted the statute to provide no "intelligible principle" to guide the agency's exercise of authority. The court thought, however, that the EPA could perhaps avoid the unconstitutional delegation by adopting a restrictive construction of § 109(b)(1), so instead of declaring the section unconstitutional the court remanded the NAAQS to the agency. (On this delegation point, Judge Tatel dissented, finding the statute constitutional as written.) . . .

Section 109(b)(1) of the CAA instructs the EPA to set "ambient air quality standards the attainment and maintenance of which in the judgment of the Administrator, based on [the] criteria [documents of § 108] and allowing an adequate margin of safety, are requisite to protect the public health." 42 U.S.C. § 7409(b)(1). The Court of Appeals held that this section as interpreted by the Administrator did not provide an "intelligible principle" to guide the EPA's exercise of authority in setting NAAQS. "[The] EPA," it said, "lack[ed] any determinate criteria for drawing lines. It has failed to state intelligibly how much is too much." The court hence found that the EPA's interpretation (but not the statute itself) violated the nondelegation doctrine. We disagree.

In a delegation challenge, the constitutional question is whether the statute has delegated legislative power to the agency. Article I, § 1, of the Constitution vests "[a]ll legislative Powers herein granted . . . in a Congress of the United States." This text permits no delegation of those powers, *Loving v. United States* (1996) (SCALIA, J., concurring in part and concurring in judgment), and so we repeatedly have said that when Congress confers decisionmaking authority upon agencies Congress must "lay down by legislative act an intelligible principle to which the person or body authorized to [act] is directed to conform." *J. W. Hampton, Jr., & Co. v. United States* (1928). We have never suggested that an agency can cure an unlawful delegation of legislative power by adopting in its discretion a limiting construction of the statute. Both *Fahey v. Mallonee* (1947) and *Lichter v. United States* (1948) mention agency regulations in the course of their nondelegation discussions, but *Lichter* did so because a subsequent Congress had incorporated the regulations into a revised version of the statute, and *Fahey* because the customary practices in the area, implicitly incorporated into the statute, were reflected in the regulations. The idea that an agency can cure an unconstitutionally standardless delegation of power by declining to exercise some of that power seems to us internally contradictory. The very choice of which portion of the power to exercise, that is to say, the prescription of the standard that Congress had omitted, would itself be an exercise of the forbidden legislative authority. Whether the statute delegates legislative power is a question for the courts, and an agency's voluntary self-denial has no bearing upon the answer.

We agree with the Solicitor General that the text of § 109(b)(1) of the CAA at a minimum requires that "[f]or a discrete set of pollutants and based on published air quality criteria that reflect the latest scientific knowledge, [the] EPA must establish uniform national standards at a level that is requisite to protect public health from the adverse effects of the pollutant in the ambient air." Requisite, in turn, "mean[s] sufficient, but not more than necessary." These limits on the EPA's discretion are strikingly similar to the ones we approved in *Touby v. United States* (1991), which permitted the Attorney General to designate a drug as a controlled substance for purposes of criminal drug enforcement if doing so was "'necessary to avoid an imminent hazard to the public safety.'" They also resemble the Occupational Safety and Health Act provision requiring the agency to "'set the standard which most adequately assures, to the extent feasible, on the basis of the best available evidence, that no employee will suffer any impairment of health,'" which the Court upheld in *Industrial Union Dept., AFL-CIO v. American Petroleum Institute* (1980), and which even then-JUSTICE REHNQUIST, who alone in that case thought the statute violated the nondelegation doctrine (opinion concurring in judgment), would have upheld if, like the statute here, it did not permit economic costs to be considered. *See American Textile Mfrs. Institute, Inc. v. Donovan* (1981) (REHNQUIST, J., dissenting).

The scope of discretion § 109(b)(1) allows is in fact well within the outer limits of our nondelegation precedents. In the history of the Court we have found the requisite "intelligible principle" lacking in only two statutes, one of which provided literally no guidance for the exercise of discretion, and the other of which conferred authority to regulate the entire economy on the basis of no more precise a standard than stimulating the economy by assuring "fair competition." *See Panama Refining Co. v. Ryan* (1935); *A.L.A. Schechter Poultry Corp. v. United States* (1935). We have, on the other hand, upheld the validity of § 11(b)(2) of the Public Utility Holding Company Act of 1935, which gave the Securities and Exchange Commission authority to modify the structure of holding company systems so as to ensure that they are not "unduly or unnecessarily complicate[d]" and do not "unfairly or inequitably distribute voting power among security holders." *American Power & Light Co. v. SEC* (1946). We have approved the wartime conferral of agency power to fix the prices of commodities at a level that "'will be generally fair and equitable and will effectuate the [in some respects conflicting] purposes of th[e] Act.'" *Yakus v. United States* (1944). And we have found an "intelligible principle" in various statutes authorizing regulation in the "public interest." *See, e.g., National Broadcasting Co. v. United States* (1943) (FCC's power to regulate airwaves); *New York Central Securities Corp. v. United States* (1932) (ICC's power to approve railroad consolidations). In short, we have "almost never felt qualified to second-guess Congress regarding the permissible degree of policy judgment that can be left to those executing or applying the law." *Mistretta v. United States* (1989) (SCALIA, J., dissenting).

It is true enough that the degree of agency discretion that is acceptable varies according to the scope of the power congressionally conferred. While Congress need not provide any direction to the EPA regarding the manner in which it is to define "country elevators," which are to be exempt from new-stationary source regulations governing grain elevators, it must provide substantial guidance on setting air standards that affect the entire national economy. But even in sweeping regulatory schemes we have never demanded, as the Court of Appeals did here, that statutes provide a "determinate criterion" for saying "how much [of the regulated harm] is too much." In *Touby*, for example, we did not require the statute to decree how "imminent" was too imminent, or how "necessary" was necessary enough, or even most relevant here how "hazardous" was too hazardous. Similarly, the statute at issue in *Lichter* authorized agencies to recoup "excess profits" paid under wartime Government contracts, yet we did not insist that Congress specify how much profit was too much. It is therefore not conclusive for delegation purposes that, as respondents argue, ozone and particulate matter are "nonthreshold" pollutants that inflict a continuum of adverse health effects at any airborne concentration greater than zero, and hence require the EPA to make judgments of degree. "[A] certain degree of discretion, and thus of lawmaking, inheres in most executive or judicial action." *Mistretta v. United States* (SCALIA, J., dissenting) (emphasis deleted). Section 109(b)(1) of the CAA, which to repeat we interpret as requiring the EPA to set air quality standards at the level that is "requisite" that is, not lower or higher than is necessary to protect the public health with an adequate margin of safety, fits comfortably within the scope of discretion permitted by our precedent.

We therefore reverse the judgment of the Court of Appeals remanding for reinterpretation that would avoid a supposed delegation of legislative power. It will remain for the Court of Appeals on the remand that we direct for other reasons to dispose of any other preserved challenge to the NAAQS under the judicial review provisions contained in 42 U.S.C. § 7607(d)(9). . . .

To summarize our holdings in these unusually complex cases: . . . [as to the issue of delegation] Section 109(b)(1) does not delegate legislative power to the EPA in contravention of Art. I, § 1, of the Constitution.

JUSTICE THOMAS, concurring.

I agree with the majority that § 109's directive to the agency is no less an "intelligible principle" than a host of other directives that we have approved. I also agree that the Court of Appeals' remand to the agency to make its own corrective interpretation does not accord with our understanding of the delegation issue. I write separately, however, to express my concern that there may nevertheless be a genuine constitutional problem with § 109, a problem which the parties did not address.

The parties to this case who briefed the constitutional issue wrangled over constitutional doctrine with barely a nod to the text of the Constitution. Although this Court since 1928 has treated the "intelligible principle" requirement as the only constitutional limit on congressional grants of power to administrative agencies, *see J.W. Hampton, Jr., & Co. v. United States*, the Constitution does not speak of "intelligible principles." Rather, it speaks in much simpler terms: "*All* legislative Powers herein granted shall be vested in a Congress." U.S. Const., Art. 1, § 1 (emphasis added). I am not convinced that the intelligible principle doctrine serves to prevent all cessions of legislative power. I believe that there are cases in which the principle is intelligible and yet the significance of the delegated decision is simply too great for the decision to be called anything other than "legislative."

As it is, none of the parties to this case has examined the text of the Constitution or asked us to reconsider our precedents on cessions of legislative power. On a future day, however, I would be willing to address the question whether our delegation jurisprudence has strayed too far from our Founders' understanding of separation of powers.

JUSTICE STEVENS, with whom JUSTICE SOUTER joins, concurring in part and concurring in the judgment.

Section 109(b)(1) delegates to the Administrator of the Environmental Protection Agency (EPA) the authority to promulgate national ambient air quality standards (NAAQS). In Part III of its opinion, the Court convincingly explains why the Court of Appeals erred when it concluded that § 109 effected "an unconstitutional delegation of legislative power." I wholeheartedly endorse the Court's result and endorse its explanation of its reasons, albeit with the following caveat.

The Court has two choices. We could choose to articulate our ultimate disposition of this issue by frankly acknowledging that the power delegated to the EPA is "legislative" but nevertheless conclude that the delegation is constitutional because adequately limited by the terms of the authorizing statute. Alternatively, we could pretend, as the Court does, that the authority delegated to the EPA is somehow not "legislative power." Despite the fact that there is language in our opinions that supports the Court's articulation of our holding, I am persuaded that it would be both wiser and more faithful to what we have actually done in delegation cases to admit that agency rulemaking authority is "legislative power."

The proper characterization of governmental power should generally depend on the nature of the power, not on the identity of the person exercising it. If the NAAQS that the EPA promulgated had been prescribed by Congress, everyone would agree that those rules would be the product of an exercise of "legislative power." The same characterization is appropriate when an agency exercises rulemaking authority pursuant to a permissible delegation from Congress.

My view is not only more faithful to normal English usage, but is also fully consistent with the text of the Constitution. In Article I, the Framers vested "All legislative Powers" in the Congress, Art. I., § 1, just as in Article II they vested the "executive Power" in the President, Art. II, § 1. Those provisions do not purport to limit the authority of either recipient of power to delegate authority to others. *See Bowsher v. Synar* (1986) (STEVENS, J., concurring in judgment) ("Despite the statement in Article I of the Constitution that 'All legislative powers herein granted shall be vested in a Congress of the United States,' it is far from novel to acknowledge that independent agencies do indeed exercise legislative powers"); *INS v. Chadha* (1983) (WHITE, J., dissenting) ("[L]egislative power can be exercised by independent agencies and Executive departments. . . ."); 1 Davis [& Pierce, Administrative Law Treatise] § 2.6, p. 66 ("The Court was probably mistaken from the outset in interpreting Article I's grant of power to Congress as an implicit limit on Congress' authority to delegate legislative power"). Surely the authority granted to members of the Cabinet and federal law enforcement agents is properly characterized as "Executive" even though not exercised by the President. *Cf. Morrison v. Olson* (1988) (SCALIA, J., dissenting) (arguing that the independent counsel exercised "executive power" unconstrained by the President).

It seems clear that an executive agency's exercise of rulemaking authority pursuant to a valid delegation from Congress is "legislative." As long as the delegation provides a sufficiently intelligible principle, there is nothing inherently unconstitutional about it. Accordingly, . . . I would hold that when Congress enacted § 109, it effected a constitutional delegation of legislative power to the EPA.

Notes

1. Big changes may be coming: *Gundy v. United States* **(2019).** Since early in the twentieth century, the Supreme Court's touchstone for applying the nondelegation doctrine has been whether Congress has limited agency authority with an "intelligible principle." It has proven terrifically difficult to persuade courts to strike a grant of authority for lacking such an "intelligible principle." As Justice Scalia observed in *Whitman*, the Supreme Court has taken this step just twice in more than two hundred years, striking provisions of the National Industrial Recovery Act in the Depression-era cases of *Panama Refining Co. v. Ryan*, 293 U.S. 388 (1935), and *A.L.A. Schechter Poultry Corp. v. United States*, 295 U.S. 495 (1935). The more important of these two, *Schechter*, challenged an extraordinarily broad grant of authority to the president to create or approve "codes of fair competition" regulating trade and industry. The Court rejected this "virtually unfettered" power to create "whatever laws [the president] thinks may be needed or advisable for the rehabilitation and expansion of trade or industry" as "an unconstitutional delegation of legislative power." *Id.* at 542.

In every other case that has reached the Supreme Court, it has found the "intelligible principle" needed to defuse a nondelegation challenge. Toward the end of his *Whitman* opinion, Justice Scalia documented this point by citing impressively broad grants of discretionary agency authority that the Court has approved in the past. Twelve years earlier, in his dissenting opinion in *Mistretta v. United States*, 488 U.S. 361 (1989), he explained why this toothless approach was, in his view, appropriate:

> But while the doctrine of unconstitutional delegation is unquestionably a fundamental element of our constitutional system, it is not an element readily enforceable by the courts. Once it is conceded, as it must be, that no statute can be entirely precise, and that some judgments, even some judgments involving policy considerations, must be left to the officers executing the law and to the judges applying it, the debate over unconstitutional delegation becomes a debate not over a point of principle but over a question of degree. As Chief Justice Taft expressed the point for the Court in the landmark case of *J. W. Hampton, Jr., & Co. v. United States*, the limits of delegation "must be fixed according to common sense and the inherent necessities of the governmental coordination." Since Congress is no less endowed with common sense than we are, and better equipped to inform itself of the "necessities" of government; and since the factors bearing upon those necessities are both multifarious and (in the nonpartisan sense) highly political — including, for example, whether the Nation is at war, or whether for other reasons "emergency is instinct in the situation" — it is small wonder that we have almost never felt qualified to second-guess Congress regarding the permissible degree of policy judgment that can be left to those executing or applying the law.

Mistretta, 488 U.S. at 415–16 (Scalia, J., dissenting).

Read together, the three opinions issued in *Gundy v. United States*, 139 S. Ct. 2116 (2019), indicate that the Court's well-settled and lax approach to the nondelegation doctrine may soon be changing substantially. This case raised a nondelegation challenge to the Sex Offender Registration and Notification Act (SORNA), which Congress passed to strengthen and rationalize registration of sex offenders. SORNA requires sex offenders to register before completing their sentences of imprisonment. This requirement obviously could not apply to persons who had completed their sentences before SORNA itself was enacted. To deal with such persons, SORNA delegated to the Attorney General the authority to "specify the applicability" of registration requirements and to "prescribe rules for registration." 34 U.S.C. § 20913(d). Gundy, a pre-SORNA offender, was convicted of failing to follow registration requirements adopted by the Attorney General. He challenged this conviction on the ground that the delegation of authority to the Attorney General to "specify the applicability" of SORNA registration requirements to pre-Act offenders violated the nondelegation doctrine. The Supreme Court affirmed the lower courts' rejection of this claim by a 5-3 vote that nonetheless demonstrated that at least four justices are ready for serious reconsideration of the nondelegation doctrine—and Justice Kavanaugh, who did not participate in the case, likely would take this number to five.

Justice Kagan wrote a plurality opinion joined by the other three relatively "liberal" justices. She emphasized that the Court had in an earlier opinion, *Reynolds v. United States*, 565 U.S. 432 (2012), already determined that the Attorney General's statutory authority to specify the applicability of SORNA registration requirements was quite constrained in light of congressional purpose, the Act's definition of sex offender, and the Act's history. Understood in this light, SORNA required the Attorney General to require registration by pre-Act offenders "as soon as feasible." Given this statutory construction, it was an easy matter for Justice Kagan to conclude that the delegation at issue satisfied the "intelligible principle" requirement. She pointedly added that, "if SORNA's delegation is unconstitutional, then most of Government is unconstitutional."

Justice Alito concurred in the judgment. In his short opinion, he characterized the Court's precedents as authorizing "agencies to adopt important rules pursuant to extraordinarily capacious standards." He then declared, "[i]f a majority of this Court were willing to reconsider the approach we have taken for the past 84 years, I would support that effort. But because a majority is not willing to do that, it would be freakish to single out the provision at issue here for special treatment."

Justice Gorsuch wrote a dissenting opinion joined by the Chief Justice and Justice Thomas. He opened with this salvo:

> The Constitution promises that only the people's elected representatives may adopt new federal laws restricting liberty. Yet the statute before us scrambles that design. It purports to endow the nation's chief prosecutor with the power to write his own criminal code governing the lives of a half-million citizens. Yes, those affected are some of the least popular among us. But if a single executive branch official can write laws restricting the liberty of this group of persons, what does that mean for the next?

> Today, a plurality of an eight-member Court endorses this extraconstitutional arrangement but resolves nothing. Working from an understanding of the Constitution at war with its text and history, the plurality reimagines the terms of the statute before us and insists there is nothing wrong with Congress handing off so much power to the Attorney General. But Justice Alito supplies the fifth vote for today's judgment and he does not join either the plurality's constitutional or statutory analysis, indicating instead that he remains willing, in a future case with a full Court, to revisit these matters. Respectfully, I would not wait.

Justice Gorsuch, in stark contrast to Justice Kagan, construed SORNA as granting the Attorney General untrammelled authority to determine the applicability of registration provisions to pre-Act offenders. Having maximized agency discretion on a statutory level, he then turned to discussion of "guiding principles" for applying the nondelegation doctrine.

The first of these principles is that "as Congress makes the policy decisions when regulating private conduct, it may authorize another branch to 'fill up the details.'" For support for this principle, Justice Gorsuch turned to Chief Justice Marshall's opinion in *Wayman v. Southard*, 23 U.S. 1 (1825), in which the Court upheld the constitutionality of a congressional statute that instructed federal courts to use state-court procedural rules but also authorized them to make "alterations and additions." Justice Gorsuch observed that, to justify this authority, the Chief Justice had "distinguished between those 'important subjects, which must be entirely regulated by the legislature itself,' and 'those of less interest, in which a general provision may be made, and power given to those who are to act . . . to fill up the details.'" As another example of Congress permissibly delegating power to fill up details, Justice Gorsuch also cited *United States v. Grimaud*, 220 U.S. 506 (1911), in which the Court upheld a delegation that authorized "the Secretary of Agriculture to adopt rules regulating the 'use and occupancy' of public forests to protect them from 'destruction' and 'depredations.'"

A second principle is that "once Congress prescribes the rule governing private conduct, it may make the application of that rule depend on executive fact-finding." In other words, Congress is free to make its instructions to agencies conditional, telling them to embark on some course of action only if they first find certain triggering facts to be true. For an early example of this practice, Justice Gorsuch cited *Cargo of Brig Aurora v. United States*, 11 U.S. 382 (1813), which had authorized the president during the Napoleonic Wars to impose a trade embargo on Great Britain if the president determined that France had stopped interfering with American trade or a trade embargo on France if the president determined that Great Britain had stopped interfering with American trade.

The third principle implicates the idea that some authorities overlap among the branches. No separation-of-powers problem arises where Congress instructs the executive or judicial branches to take actions that they are constitutionally empowered to take without congressional authorization. Justice Gorsuch noted that "the foreign-affairs-related statute in *Cargo of the Brig Aurora* may be an example of this kind of permissible lawmaking, given that many foreign affairs powers are constitutionally vested in the president under Article II," and that Chief Justice Marshall's holding in *Wayman* "might be explained by the same principle" given judicial power to regulate judicial practice.

Justice Gorsuch characterized the "intelligible principle" doctrine, adopted by the Court in *J.W. Hampton, Jr., & Co. v. United States*, 276 U.S. 394 (1928), as a "misadventure" that "has no basis in the original meaning of the Constitution, in history, or even in the decision from which it was plucked" and that "has been abused to permit delegations of legislative power that on any other conceivable account should be held unconstitutional." He did not identify which delegations of the last century he would reject that the Court has mistakenly upheld.

Going forward, it seems likely that, when Justice Kavanaugh joins the fray, the conservative wing of the Court will rework the nondelegation doctrine along Justice Gorsuch's preferred lines. Applying his framework will raise its own set of difficult line-drawing questions. Where is the line between policy determinations that Congress must make and those details that agencies can permissibly "fill up"? At what point does permissible executive "factfinding" become so value-laden that it veers into impermissible policymaking? Circling back to our lead excerpt, under Justice Gorsuch's approach, did *Whitman* reach the right conclusion in upholding a delegation of authority to the EPA's Administrator to promulgate ambient air quality standards "requisite to protect the public health" with "an adequate margin of safety"? And, circling back to the *Mistretta* quote near the opening of this note, do Justice Gorsuch's principles provide an adequate response to Justice Scalia's concerns about second-guessing Congress on the scope of permissible delegations?

2. What is the nondelegation doctrine for, anyway? This question has been much discussed over the years and cannot be given a short yet exhaustive answer. That said, Justice Rehnquist, concurring in *Industrial Union Dep't, AFL-CIO v. American Petroleum Inst.*, 448 U.S. 607, 685 (1980), offered the following concise discussion:

> As formulated and enforced by this Court, the nondelegation doctrine serves three important functions. First, and most abstractly, it ensures to the extent consistent with orderly governmental administration that important choices of social policy are made by Congress, the branch of our Government most responsive to the popular will. Second, the doctrine guarantees that, to the extent Congress finds it necessary to delegate authority, it provides the recipient of that authority with an "intelligible principle" to guide the exercise of the delegated discretion. Third, and derivative of the second, the doctrine ensures that courts charged with reviewing the exercise of delegated legislative discretion will be able to test that exercise against ascertainable standards.

In this same opinion, Justice Rehnquist insisted, "[i]t is the hard choices, and not the filling in of blanks, which must be made by the elected representatives of the people." *Id.* at 687.

If Congress could not delegate "hard" policy choices to agencies, would there be more or less regulation? How would a court tell whether Congress made or punted on a "hard" choice?

3. Should agencies be able to "cure" nondelegation violations? As the Court reported in *Whitman*, the D.C. Circuit concluded that, as interpreted by the Administrator, the EPA's NAAQS authority was so broad as to violate the nondelegation doctrine. For the lower court, the core of the problem lay in the EPA's criteria for evaluating pollution, which included "the nature and severity of the health effects involved, the size of the sensitive populations(s) at risk, the types of health information available, and the kind and degree of uncertainties that must be addressed." *American Trucking Ass'n, Inc. v. EPA*, 175 F.3d 1027, 1034–35 (D.C. Cir. 1999). The D.C. Circuit concluded that the indeterminate nature of these factors left the agency largely free to decline to regulate the pollutants at issue at all or to go so far as to require deindustrialization. Rather than create a limiting construction of the agency's authority itself, the court instead invoked a variation on the canon of constitutional avoidance to give the EPA a chance to fix the problem:

> Where (as here) statutory language and an existing agency interpretation involve an unconstitutional delegation of power, but an interpretation without the constitutional weakness is or may be available, our response is not to strike down the statute but to give the agency an opportunity to extract a determinate standard of its own. . . . The agency will make the fundamental policy choices. But the remand does ensure that the courts not hold unconstitutional a statute that an agency, with the application of its special expertise, could salvage.

Id. at 1036–37. The D.C. Circuit conceded that this "curative" approach would leave the power to make fundamental policy choices with agencies, but also noted that it would serve two other basic rationales for the nondelegation doctrine by (a) reducing the likelihood of arbitrary agency action; and (b) enhancing the likelihood of meaningful judicial review. *Id*. at 1038. Justice Scalia's majority opinion rejected this approach out of hand. Was he right to do so?

4. The nondelegation doctrine, the canon of constitutional avoidance, and statutory construction. Although the Supreme Court has not used the nondelegation doctrine to strike a grant of authority as unconstitutional since 1935, the Court has invoked the doctrine to justify narrowly construing agency authority as a statutory matter. A well-established principle of statutory construction, the canon of constitutional avoidance, holds that courts should, where reasonably possible, avoid statutory constructions that raise serious constitutional problems. In *Industrial Union Department, AFL-CIO v. American Petroleum Institute*, 448 U.S. 607 (1980), the controlling plurality opinion invoked this canon to adopt a narrow construction of OSHA's statutory authority to fend off a potentially serious nondelegation challenge. Section 3(8) of the OSH Act provides a basic definition of "occupational safety and health standard":

> The term "occupational safety and health standard" means a standard which requires conditions, or the adoption or use of one or more practices, means, methods, operations, or processes, reasonably necessary or appropriate to provide safe or healthful employment and places of employment.

In addition, §6(b)(5) instructs that "[t]he Secretary, in promulgating standards dealing with toxic materials . . . , shall set the standard which most adequately assures, to the extent feasible, on the basis of the best available evidence, that no employee will suffer material impairment of health or functional capacity." For carcinogens, the Secretary had "taken the position that no safe exposure level can be determined and that § 6(b)(5) requires him to set an exposure limit at the lowest technologically feasible level that will not impair the viability of the industries regulated."

As the plurality viewed the matter, given the omnipresence of carcinogens and suspected carcinogens, a broad understanding of the Secretary's statutory authority invited "pervasive regulation limited only by the constraint of feasibility." 448 U.S. at 645. If the Act granted, in essence, the power to regulate the entire industrial economy, then it "would make such a 'sweeping delegation of legislative power' that it might be unconstitutional under the Court's reasoning in *A.L.A. Schechter Poultry Corp. v. United States* and *Panama Refining Co.*" *Id.* at 646. The plurality avoided this problem by focusing on the meaning of the term "safe" as used by § 3(8). It concluded that "safe" does not mean "risk free"; as examples of risky activities commonly regarded to be "safe," it cited "driving a car or breathing city air." *Id.* at 642. Section 3(8) therefore does not authorize the creation of standards to eliminate *all* risks of harm; rather, it authorizes elimination only of "significant risk of harm." *Id.* It followed that, "before he can promulgate *any* permanent health or safety standard, the Secretary is required to make a threshold finding that a place of employment is unsafe—in the sense that significant risks are present and can be eliminated or lessened by a change in practices. . . ." *Id.*

5. Should the nondelegation "fiction" be dropped? Do you agree with Justice Stevens's concurrence in *Whitman* that the Court should drop the fiction that agency legislative rulemaking power is not "legislative" in nature? The consequences of such an admission depend on which justice you ask. For Justice Stevens, this admission would make the law clearer and more candid. It would not force abandonment of the administrative state because the Constitution, properly understood, does not bar delegations of legislative power. Justice Thomas agrees that legislative rulemaking, insofar as it formulates "generally applicable rules of private conduct," involves the exercise of legislative power. *Dep't of Transp. v. Ass'n of American RR*, 135 S. Ct. 1225, 1242 (2015) (Thomas, J., concurring). He, however, concludes that the Constitution does bar delegations of legislative power. Therefore, legislative rulemaking, and by extension much of the modern administrative state that has evolved over the last century, are unconstitutional. For an extended discussion of Justice Thomas's views on this point, see *id.* at 1242–52 ("We should return to the original meaning of the Constitution: The Government may create generally applicable rules of private conduct only through the proper exercise of legislative power."). *See also Kisor v. Wilkie*, 139 S. Ct. 2400, 2438 n.84 (2019) (Gorsuch, concurring; joined by Justices Thomas, Alito, and Kavanaugh) (citing Justice Thomas's concurrence in *Ass'n of American RR* for the striking proposition, "[t]o be sure, our precedent allowing executive agencies to issue legally binding regulations to govern private conduct may raise constitutional questions of its own").

6. Delegations to private entities. Government agencies are not the only entities that adopt standards that control others' conduct. Private entities create such standards all the time. Organizations such as the Underwriters Laboratories create safety standards for various types of products. Professional organizations, such as bar associations, play important roles in "self regulation." Many functions that might be performed by government, such as running prisons, have been outsourced to private contractors, which must create and administer rules to run their operations.

The intertwined roles of public and private entities in governance highlight the problem of determining the degree to which government can "outsource" rule-making authority to private entities. Whatever one might think of their legality or efficiency, government agencies are supposed to serve the public interest and are subject to legal restrictions, such as due process, designed to help ensure that they do. Private entities are not subject to the same restrictions, and the job of a profit-maximizing firm, generally speaking, is to make money rather than serve the public interest as such.

The law's black-letter response to this issue has been that the government cannot delegate regulatory authority to private entities. *Carter v. Carter Coal Co.*, 298 U.S. 238, 311 (1936) (finding unconstitutional a statute that allowed a majority of miners and mine-operators to set binding rules on wages and hours). Private entities may, however, "help a government agency make its regulatory decisions." *Ass'n of American Railroads v. U.S. Dept. of Trans.*, 721 F.3d 666, 671 (D.C. Cir. 2013), *rev'd on other grounds by*, 135 S. Ct. 1225 (2015). The trick, of course, is to tell when permissible "help" slides into impermissible control. The Supreme Court has held that private parties may propose regulations so long as a public agency retains final control over their approval, rejection, or modification. *Sunshine Anthracite Coal Co. v. Adkins*, 310 U.S. 381, 388 (1940).

7. Combining legislative and executive power in parliamentary systems. Is separation of legislative from executive power necessary to protect liberty and the rule of law from an overreaching government? In some parliamentary systems, control of the legislative body determines control of the executive power. In the United Kingdom, for instance, the majority of the House of Commons selects the Prime Minister. If the Prime Minister and her "government" lose the support of the parliamentary majority, then the government falls. Does the modern United Kingdom strike you as especially tyrannical?

2. Agencies as "Courts"

Suppose that Congress charges some regulatory agency with, say, ensuring clean water. This agency has authority to promulgate regulations barring water pollution and to investigate to ensure compliance. As agency officials conduct investigations, they must determine facts on the ground in individual cases (e.g., did firm X dump sludge in the stream?) and apply those facts to pertinent law (e.g., do agency regulations bar dumping sludge into streams?). It may make considerable policy sense to give the agency's determinations on these matters substantial, even dispositive, weight. The agency, after all, is supposed to be the "expert" on water pollution and how to control it. The legislature might therefore authorize the agency to issue cease-and-desist orders commanding regulated entities to halt violations. The legislature might even go so far as to authorize the agency to issue citations penalizing violators.

An obvious potential constitutional roadblock to this type of scheme lies in Article III, § 1 of the Constitution, which provides that the "judicial Power of the United States shall be vested in one supreme Court, and in such inferior Courts as the Congress may from time to time ordain and establish." To ensure decisional independence, this provision adds that "[t]he Judges, both of the supreme and inferior Courts, shall hold their Offices during good Behavior, and shall, at stated Times, receive for their Services, a Compensation, which shall not be diminished during their Continuance in Office." In other words, the Constitution requires that officials wielding the judicial power of the United States must enjoy both life tenure and salary protection. In exercising this power, courts find facts and apply law to arrive at final, binding orders that determine case outcomes. An agency's adjudicative order that carries too much "binding" force threatens to usurp this judicial power.

The Supreme Court's efforts to draw the line between acceptable agency adjudicative authority and unacceptable usurpation of judicial power have resulted in an extremely complex and difficult body of law. As you work through these materials, it may be helpful to consider: Why should this line matter in the first place? Are there reasons to trust judges more than administrators? If so, how should these reasons affect efforts to define Article III's "judicial power"?

Lesson 1C.2. After reluctantly concluding that the WTC's rulemaking authority is constitutional under long established doctrine, Abby examined the agency's adjudicative authority. She saw that § 7 authorizes the agency to conduct a trial like process to determine if a regulated party has violated the WTCA or regulations promulgated pursuant to it. As part of these proceedings, the agency can issue orders designed to "cure" such violations. Section 10 authorizes judicial proceedings in which civil and criminal penalties and injunctive relief may be imposed against violators of the WTCA, WTC rules, or WTC orders. The agency need not go to court to impose a penalty, however, because § 11 authorizes the WTC to impose "administrative penalties" in its own internal proceedings. Compounding all this power, § 9, to Abby's surprise, substantially limits judicial review of agency decisionmaking.

Abby finds it particularly distressing that §§ 7 and 11 of the Act appear to grant the same "judicial power" to the Commission that Article III vests in life tenured federal judges. Can the WTC constitutionally apply these provisions to issue orders against regulated parties?

Next, suppose that the WTC is contemplating adopting a rule that will allow private parties to initiate § 7 proceedings against regulated winemakers for violation of § 5's anti-fraud provisions. Using its authority under § 7 to issue "curative" orders, the WTC will order parties found liable to pay compensatory damages to plaintiffs. Is this scheme consistent with Article III?

Background of *CFTC v. Schor*

Schor was president and majority stockholder of Mortgage Services of America (collectively, Schor). Schor issued mortgage loans and then sold them to third parties. The value of such loans depends on movements in interest rates. To hedge against this risk, Schor purchased financial futures contracts through ContiCommodity Services, Inc. (Conti). Contracts to buy at some future date are characterized as "long." Contracts to sell at some future date are characterized as "short." At the time of the events that led to the litigation, Schor's position was heavily long and his margin account was underfunded by the terms of his agreement with Conti. According to Schor, he contacted Conti to take up short positions, but Conti failed to carry out his instructions. Schor then informed Conti that later margin calls on the account would not be satisfied. Conti liquidated Schor's accounts, which had a negative value.

The Commodity Exchange Act (CEA) empowers the Commodity Futures Trading Commission (CFTC) to order reparations against commodity brokers who violate the Act. The CFTC has adopted a rule claiming power to adjudicate counterclaims for debts that arise out of reparations claims. Schor filed a reparations action before the CFTC, charging, among other things, that Conti had failed to issue margin calls properly, failed to follow his instructions, and improperly liquidated his account. Conti counterclaimed for the debt represented by the deficit in Schor's liquidated account. The administrative law judge rejected Schor's claims and upheld Conti's counterclaim; the CFTC declined to review this result; Schor sought judicial review. The D.C. Circuit raised the issue of whether the agency's assertion of authority to determine the counterclaim violated Article III. The court evaded resolving this issue, however, by concluding that the agency lacked statutory authority over the counterclaim under the CEA. The Supreme Court reversed on this statutory point, and proceeded to address the constitutional question.

Commodity Futures Trading Commission v. Schor
478 U.S. 833 (1986)

JUSTICE O' CONNOR delivered the Opinion of the Court. . . .

Article III, § 1, directs that the "judicial Power of the United States shall be vested in one Supreme Court and in such inferior Courts as the Congress may from time to time ordain and establish," and provides that these federal courts shall be staffed by judges who hold office during good behavior, and whose compensation shall not be diminished during tenure in office. Schor claims that these provisions prohibit Congress from authorizing the initial adjudication of common law counterclaims by the CFTC, an administrative agency whose adjudicatory officers do not enjoy the tenure and salary protections embodied in Article III.

Although our precedents in this area do not admit of easy synthesis, they do establish that the resolution of claims such as Schor's cannot turn on conclusory reference to the language of Article III. Rather, the constitutionality of a given congressional delegation of adjudicative functions to a non-Article III body must be assessed by reference to the purposes underlying the requirements of Article III. This inquiry, in turn, is guided by the principle that "practical attention to substance rather than doctrinaire reliance on formal categories should inform application of Article III."

Article III, § 1, serves both to protect "the role of the independent judiciary within the constitutional scheme of tripartite government," and to safeguard litigants' "right to have claims decided before judges who are free from potential domination by other branches of government." Although our cases have provided us with little occasion to discuss the nature or significance of this latter safeguard, our prior discussions of Article III, § 1's guarantee of an independent and impartial adjudication by the federal judiciary of matters within the judicial power of the United States intimated that this guarantee serves to protect primarily personal, rather than structural, interests.

Our precedents also demonstrate, however, that Article III does not confer on litigants an absolute right to the plenary consideration of every nature of claim by an Article III court. Moreover, as a personal right, Article III's guarantee of an impartial and independent federal adjudication is subject to waiver, just as are other personal constitutional rights that dictate the procedures by which civil and criminal matters must be tried. Indeed, the relevance of concepts of waiver to Article III challenges is demonstrated by our decision in *Northern Pipeline* [1982], in which the absence of consent to an initial adjudication before a non-Article III tribunal was relied on as a significant factor in determining that Article III forbade such adjudication.

In the instant cases, Schor indisputably waived any right he may have possessed to the full trial of Conti's counterclaim before an Article III court. Schor expressly demanded that Conti proceed on its counterclaim in the reparations proceeding rather than before the District Court, and was content to have the entire dispute settled in the forum he had selected until the ALJ [Administrative Law Judge] ruled against him on all counts; it was only after the ALJ rendered a decision to which he objected that Schor raised any challenge to the CFTC's consideration of Conti's counterclaim.

Even were there no evidence of an express waiver here, Schor's election to forgo his right to proceed in state or federal court on his claim and his decision to seek relief instead in a CFTC reparations proceeding constituted an effective waiver. Three years before Schor instituted his reparations action, a private right of action under the CEA was explicitly recognized in the Circuit in which Schor and Conti filed suit in District Court. Moreover, at the time Schor decided to seek relief before the CFTC rather than in the federal courts, the CFTC's regulations made clear that it was empowered to adjudicate all counterclaims "aris[ing] out of the same transaction or occurrence or series of transactions or occurrences set forth in the complaint." Thus, Schor had the option of having the common law counterclaim against him adjudicated in a federal Article III court, but, with full knowledge that the CFTC would exercise jurisdiction over that claim, chose to avail himself of the quicker and less expensive procedure Congress had provided him. In such circumstances, it is clear that Schor effectively agreed to an adjudication by the CFTC of the entire controversy by seeking relief in this alternative forum.

As noted above, our precedents establish that Article III, § 1, not only preserves to litigants their interest in an impartial and independent federal adjudication of claims within the judicial power of the United States, but also serves as "an inseparable element of the constitutional system of checks and balances." Article III, § 1 safeguards the role of the Judicial Branch in our tripartite system by barring congressional attempts "to transfer jurisdiction [to non-Article III tribunals] for the purpose of emasculating" constitutional courts, and thereby preventing "the encroachment or aggrandizement of one branch at the expense of the other." To the extent that this structural principle is implicated in a given case, the parties cannot by consent cure the constitutional difficulty for the same reason that the parties by consent cannot confer on federal courts subject-matter jurisdiction beyond the limitations imposed by Article III, § 2. When these Article III limitations are at issue, notions of consent and waiver cannot be dispositive because the limitations serve institutional interests that the parties cannot be expected to protect.

In determining the extent to which a given congressional decision to authorize the adjudication of Article III business in a non-Article III tribunal impermissibly threatens the institutional integrity of the Judicial Branch, the Court has declined to adopt formalistic and unbending rules. Although such rules might lend a greater degree of coherence to this area of the law, they might also unduly constrict Congress' ability to take needed and innovative action pursuant to its Article I powers. Thus, in reviewing Article III challenges, we have weighed a number of factors, none of which has been deemed determinative, with an eye to the practical effect that the congressional action will have on the constitutionally assigned role of the federal judiciary. Among the factors upon which we have focused are the extent to which the "essential attributes of judicial power" are reserved to Article III courts, and, conversely, the extent to which the non-Article III forum exercises the range of jurisdiction and powers normally vested only in Article III courts, the origins and importance of the right to be adjudicated, and the concerns that drove Congress to depart from the requirements of Article III.

An examination of the relative allocation of powers between the CFTC and Article III courts in light of the considerations given prominence in our precedents demonstrates that the congressional scheme does not impermissibly intrude on the province of the judiciary. The CFTC's adjudicatory powers depart from the traditional agency model in just one respect: the CFTC's jurisdiction over common law counterclaims. While wholesale importation of concepts of pendent or ancillary jurisdiction into the agency context may create greater constitutional difficulties, we decline to endorse an absolute prohibition on such jurisdiction out of fear of where some hypothetical "slippery slope" may deposit us. Indeed, the CFTC's exercise of this type of jurisdiction is not without precedent. Thus, in *Reconstruction*

Finance Corp. v. Bankers Trust Co. (1943), we saw no constitutional difficulty in the initial adjudication of a state law claim by a federal agency, subject to judicial review, when that claim was ancillary to a federal law dispute. Similarly, in *Katchen v. Landy* (1966), this Court upheld a bankruptcy referee's power to hear and decide state law counterclaims against a creditor who filed a claim in bankruptcy when those counterclaims arose out of the same transaction. We reasoned that, as a practical matter, requiring the trustee to commence a plenary action to recover on its counterclaim would be a "meaningless gesture."

In the instant cases, we are likewise persuaded that there is little practical reason to find that this single deviation from the agency model is fatal to the congressional scheme. Aside from its authorization of counterclaim jurisdiction, the CEA leaves far more of the "essential attributes of judicial power" to Article III courts than did that portion of the Bankruptcy Act found unconstitutional in *Northern Pipeline*. The CEA scheme in fact hews closely to the agency model approved by the Court in *Crowell v. Benson* (1932).

The CFTC, like the agency in *Crowell*, deals only with a "particularized area of law," whereas the jurisdiction of the bankruptcy courts found unconstitutional in *Northern Pipeline* extended to broadly "all civil proceedings arising under title 11 or arising in or *related to* cases under title 11." 28 U.S.C. § 1471(b) (quoted in *Northern Pipeline*) (emphasis added). CFTC orders, like those of the agency in *Crowell*, but unlike those of the bankruptcy courts under the 1978 Act, are enforceable only by order of the district court. CFTC orders are also reviewed under the same "weight of the evidence" standard sustained in *Crowell*, rather than the more deferential standard found lacking in *Northern Pipeline*. The legal rulings of the CFTC, like the legal determinations of the agency in *Crowell*, are subject to *de novo* review. Finally, the CFTC, unlike the bankruptcy courts under the 1978 Act, does not exercise "all ordinary powers of district courts," and thus may not, for instance, preside over jury trials or issue writs of habeas corpus.

Of course, the nature of the claim has significance in our Article III analysis quite apart from the method prescribed for its adjudication. The counterclaim asserted in this litigation is a "private" right for which state law provides the rule of decision. It is therefore a claim of the kind assumed to be at the "core" of matters normally reserved to Article III courts. Yet this conclusion does not end our inquiry; just as this Court has rejected any attempt to make determinative for Article III purposes the distinction between public rights and private rights, there is no reason inherent in separation of powers principles to accord the state law character of a claim talismanic power in Article III inquiries.

We have explained that "the public rights doctrine reflects simply a pragmatic understanding that when Congress selects a quasi-judicial method of resolving matters that 'could be conclusively determined by the Executive and Legislative Branches,' the danger of encroaching on the judicial powers" is less than when private rights, which are normally within the purview of the judiciary, are relegated as an initial matter to administrative adjudication. Similarly, the state law character of a claim is significant for purposes of determining the effect that an initial adjudication of those claims by a non-Article III tribunal will have on the separation of powers for the simple reason that private, common law rights were historically the types of matters subject to resolution by Article III courts. The risk that Congress may improperly have encroached on the federal judiciary is obviously magnified when Congress "withdraw[s] from judicial cognizance any matter which, from its nature, is the subject of a suit at the common law, or in equity, or admiralty" and which therefore has traditionally been tried in Article III courts, and allocates the decision of those matters to a non-Article III forum of its own creation. Accordingly, where private, common law rights are at stake, our examination of the congressional attempt to control the manner in which those rights are adjudicated has been searching. In this litigation, however, "[l]ooking beyond form to the substance of what" Congress has done, we are persuaded that the congressional authorization of limited CFTC jurisdiction over a narrow class of common law claims as an incident to the CFTC's primary, and unchallenged, adjudicative function does not create a substantial threat to the separation of powers.

It is clear that Congress has not attempted to "withdraw from judicial cognizance" the determination of Conti's right to the sum represented by the debit balance in Schor's account. Congress gave the CFTC the authority to adjudicate such matters, but the decision to invoke this forum is left entirely to the parties and the power of the federal judiciary to take jurisdiction of these matters is unaffected. In such circumstances, separation of powers concerns are diminished, for it seems self-evident that just as Congress may encourage parties to settle a dispute out of court or resort to arbitration without impermissible incursions on the separation of powers, Congress may make available a quasi judicial mechanism through which willing parties may, at their option, elect to resolve their differences. This is not to say, of course, that if Congress created a phalanx of non-Article III tribunals equipped to handle the entire business of the Article III courts without any Article III supervision or control and without evidence of valid and specific legislative necessities, the fact that the parties had the election to proceed in their forum of choice would necessarily save the scheme from constitutional attack. But this case obviously bears no resemblance to such a scenario, given the degree of judicial control saved to the federal courts, as well as the congressional purpose behind the jurisdictional delegation, the demonstrated need for the delegation, and the limited nature of the delegation.

When Congress authorized the CFTC to adjudicate counterclaims, its primary focus was on making effective a specific and limited federal regulatory scheme, not on allocating jurisdiction among federal tribunals. Congress intended to create an inexpensive and expeditious alternative forum through which customers could enforce the provisions of the CEA against professional brokers. Its decision to endow the CFTC with jurisdiction over such reparations claims is readily understandable given the perception that the CFTC was relatively immune from political pressures, and the obvious expertise that the Commission possesses in applying the CEA and its own regulations. This reparations scheme itself is of unquestioned constitutional validity. It was only to ensure the effectiveness of this scheme that Congress authorized the CFTC to assert jurisdiction over common law counterclaims. Indeed, as was explained above, absent the CFTC's exercise of that authority, the purposes of the reparations procedure would have been confounded.

It also bears emphasis that the CFTC's assertion of counterclaim jurisdiction is limited to that which is necessary to make the reparations procedure workable. The CFTC adjudication of common law counterclaims is incidental to, and completely dependent upon, adjudication of reparations claims created by federal law, and in actual fact is limited to claims arising out of the same transaction or occurrence as the reparations claim.

In such circumstances, the magnitude of any intrusion on the Judicial Branch can only be termed *de minimis*. Conversely, were we to hold that the Legislative Branch may not permit such limited cognizance of common law counterclaims at the election of the parties, it is clear that we would "defeat the obvious purpose of the legislation to furnish a prompt, continuous, expert and inexpensive method for dealing with a class of questions of fact which are peculiarly suited to examination and determination by an administrative agency specially assigned to that task." *Crowell v. Benson.* We do not think Article III compels this degree of prophylaxis.

Nor does our decision in *Bowsher v. Synar* (1986) require a contrary result. Unlike *Bowsher*, this case raises no question of the aggrandizement of congressional power at the expense of a coordinate branch. Instead, the separation of powers question presented in this litigation is whether Congress impermissibly undermined, without appreciable expansion of its own power, the role of the Judicial Branch. In any case, we have, consistent with *Bowsher*, looked to a number of factors in evaluating the extent to which the congressional scheme endangers separation of powers principles under the circumstances presented, but have found no genuine threat to those principles to be present in this litigation.

In so doing, we have also been faithful to our Article III precedents, which counsel that bright-line rules cannot effectively be employed to yield broad principles applicable in all Article III inquiries. Rather, due regard must be given in each case to the unique aspects of the congressional plan at issue and its practical consequences in light of the larger concerns that underlie Article III. We conclude that the limited jurisdiction that the CFTC asserts over state law claims as a necessary incident to the adjudication of federal claims willingly submitted by the parties for initial agency adjudication does not contravene separation of powers principles or Article III.

Justice Brennan, with whom Justice Marshall joins, dissenting. . . .

On its face, Article III, § 1, seems to prohibit the vesting of *any* judicial functions in either the Legislative or the Executive Branch. The Court has, however, recognized three narrow exceptions to the otherwise absolute mandate of Article

III: territorial courts, courts martial, and courts that adjudicate certain disputes concerning public rights. Unlike the Court, I would limit the judicial authority of non-Article III federal tribunals to these few, long-established exceptions and would countenance no further erosion of Article III's mandate. . . .

The Court states that in reviewing Article III challenges, one of several factors we have taken into account is "the concerns that drove Congress to depart from the requirements of Article III." The Court identifies the desire of Congress "to create an inexpensive and expeditious alternative forum through which customers could enforce the provisions of the CEA against professional brokers" as the motivating congressional concern here. The Court further states that "[i]t was only to ensure the effectiveness of this scheme that Congress authorized the CFTC to assert juris-diction over common-law counterclaims[;] . . . absent the CFTC's exercise of that authority, the purposes of the reparations procedure would have been confounded." Were we to hold that the CFTC's authority to decide common-law counterclaims offends Article III, the Court declares, "it is clear that we would 'defeat the obvious purpose of the legislation.'" Article III, the Court concludes, does not "compe[l] this degree of prophylaxis."

I disagree—Article III's prophylactic protections were intended to prevent just this sort of abdication to claims of legislative convenience. The Court requires that the legislative interest in convenience and efficiency be weighed against the com-peting interest in judicial independence. In doing so, the Court pits an interest the benefits of which are immediate, concrete, and easily understood against one, the benefits of which are almost entirely prophylactic, and thus often seem remote and not worth the cost in any single case. Thus, while this balancing creates the illusion of objectivity and ineluctability, in fact the result was foreordained, because the bal-ance is weighted against judicial independence. The danger of the Court's balancing approach is, of course, that as individual cases accumulate in which the Court finds that the short-term benefits of efficiency outweigh the long-term benefits of judicial independence, the protections of Article III will be eviscerated. . . .

According to the Court, the intrusion into the province of the Federal Judiciary caused by the CFTC's authority to adjudicate state-law counterclaims is insignifi-cant, both because the CFTC *shares* in, rather than displaces, federal district court jurisdiction over these claims and because only a very narrow class of state-law issues are involved. The "sharing" justification fails under the reasoning used by the Court to support the CFTC's authority. If the administrative reparations proceed-ing is so much more convenient and efficient than litigation in federal district court that abrogation of Article III's commands is warranted, it seems to me that com-plainants would rarely, if ever, choose to go to district court in the first instance. Thus, any "sharing" of jurisdiction is more illusory than real.

Notes

1. **Justice O'Connor versus Justice Brennan.** What factors did Justice O'Connor identify as important for determining "the extent to which a given congressional

decision to authorize the adjudication of Article III business in a non-Article III tribunal impermissibly threatens the institutional integrity of the Judicial Branch"? How did these factors play out in *Schor*? How might the analysis have changed had Schor not "waived" his personal right to an Article III tribunal by bringing his reparations claims to the CFTC?

In his dissent, Justice Brennan accepted that Article III is subject to "narrow" exceptions for "territorial courts, courts martial, and courts that adjudicate certain disputes concerning public rights." How could it be constitutional for these three to trump what he describes as an "otherwise absolute mandate"? Once one accepts these three, why not accept some more? And what does Justice Brennan have against the values of legislative convenience and efficiency?

Recall from our earlier discussion that, for Madison, the purpose of separation of powers is to protect liberty and block tyranny. Broadly speaking, how does Article III seek to protect liberty? Was Schor's liberty threatened by the CFTC's exercise of jurisdiction over Conti's common-law counterclaim in an action initiated by Schor himself? Did Schor's invocation of this option threaten anyone else's liberty?

2. The judicial power's "arcane distinctions and confusing precedents." Many agencies, like the CFTC (and our fictional WTC, for that matter) can act in ways that look very much like a court, conducting trial-like procedures to find facts, apply law, and issue orders to specific parties. Although it may seem difficult to square this power with Article III, non-Article III tribunals have been determining matters that seem amenable to judicial resolution throughout the history of the Republic. *See, e.g., American Ins. Co. v. 356 Bales of Cotton*, 26 U.S. 511, 546 (1828) (affirming exercise by non-Article III "territorial court" of jurisdiction over admiralty claim). The scope of congressional power to grant adjudicatory authority to non-Article III tribunals has presented one of the thorniest problems in all of constitutional law. *Northern Pipeline Constr. Co. v. Marathon Pipe Line Co.*, 458 U.S. 50, 90 (1982) (Rehnquist, J., concurring) (observing that this doctrine is rife with "frequently arcane distinctions and confusing precedents"). Would it be fair to say that *Schor's* response to the difficulty of determining the permissible scope of non-Article III adjudicative authority was to punt?

3. "Adjuncts" can help the courts. No one doubts that a judge can, consistent with Article III, properly hire a clerk to carry out tasks such as the initial drafting of opinions. This type of assistance does not threaten usurpation of the "judicial power" so long as the judge retains sufficient control over the decisionmaking process and outcome. This idea finds expression in legal doctrine in the "adjunct theory" of administrative adjudication, which is closely associated with *Crowell v. Benson*, 285 U.S. 22 (1932). *Cf.* Richard Fallon, *Of Legislative Courts, Administrative Agencies, and Article III*, 101 HARV. L. REV. 915, 933 (1988) (arguing for an "appellate review" approach to the Article III problem, under which "sufficiently searching review of a legislative court's or administrative agency's decision by a constitutional court will always satisfy the requirements of article III").

Crowell addressed the constitutionality of a federal statutory scheme that required employers to provide compensation on a strict liability basis for work-related injuries that occurred on navigable waters of the United States. The statute gave the task of determining facts to the United States Employees' Compensation Commission. The Commission's findings were subject to deferential judicial review to determine if they were "supported by evidence." Responding to this allocation of factfinding power, the Court observed, "there is no requirement that, in order to maintain the essential attributes of the judicial power all determinations of fact in constitutional courts shall be made by judges." 285 U.S. at 51. Indeed, in common law cases, juries are constitutionally required for this purpose; in equity and admiralty, courts have commonly used masters, commissioners, and assessors to determine certain factual matters, such as amounts of damages. *Id.* Turning to the particulars of the scheme in *Crowell*, the Court concluded that the Commission could, consistent with Article III, determine "nonjurisdictional" facts subject only to deferential review because: (a) the agency's jurisdictional reach was limited in scope, "being confined to the relation of master and servant"; (b) its role in factfinding was similar to "the familiar practice of commissioners and assessors"; (c) the courts maintained "full authority . . . to deal with matters of law"; and (d) factfinding by the Commission was "essential in order to apply [statutory] standards to the thousands of cases involved, thus relieving the courts of a most serious burden while preserving their complete authority to insure the proper application of the law." *Id.* at 54.

The Court reserved special treatment for questions of "jurisdictional" or "constitutional" fact. In *Crowell*, jurisdictional facts included whether an injury occurred on navigable waters of the United States and whether a master-servant relation existed. These conditions had to be satisfied for the Commission to have statutory and constitutional authority to act. The Court held that Article III courts must retain *de novo* control over the determination of such "fundamental" facts. This distinction—between "ordinary" facts on the one hand and "jurisdictional" or "constitutional" or "fundamental" facts on the other—proved very hard to maintain, and administrative law has essentially abandoned it.

Fifty years later, in *Northern Pipeline Const. Co. v. Marathon Pipe Line Co.*, 458 U.S. 50 (1982), the Court refused to apply the adjunct theory to save the newly reorganized bankruptcy courts from an Article III attack. The Bankruptcy Act of 1978 granted bankruptcy courts jurisdiction to issue final judgments "in all civil proceedings arising under title 11 or arising in or related to cases under title 11." Bankruptcy judges, however, do not enjoy the constitutional tenure and salary protections of Article III judges. Justice Brennan's plurality opinion distinguished *Crowell* on grounds including: (a) the bankruptcy judges' subject matter jurisdiction, as just noted, was far broader; (b) whereas the agency in *Crowell* "possessed only limited power to issue compensation orders pursuant to specialized procedures," the bankruptcy judges could "exercise all ordinary powers of district courts," including, inter alia, issuing "any order, process, or judgment appropriate for the enforcement of the provisions of Title 11"; and (c) the agency orders in *Crowell* required judicial enforcement to become effective, whereas bankruptcy judges issued final judgments that became binding absent appeal. *See also Stern v. Marshall*, 131 S. Ct. 2594, 2618–19 (2011) (applying these same factors to conclude that bankruptcy courts could not be considered "adjuncts" of the district courts for the purpose of resolving a common-law tort counterclaim brought by a debtor in bankruptcy against a creditor). (For further discussion of *Stern*, see the next note.)

What role did the "adjunct" theory seem to play in *Schor*?

4. The difficult "public rights" doctrine. Both Justices O'Connor and Brennan referred in *Schor* to the "public rights" doctrine, which defies neat summary, but we will give it a try. This exception to Article III jurisdiction is generally traced back to *Murray's Lessee v. Hoboken Land & Imp. Co.*, 59 U.S. 272 (1856), which challenged the validity of proceedings by which the federal government, acting without judicial authorization, seized and sold the property of a federal customs collector after an audit of his accounts showed he owed the government $1,374,119. In the course of upholding this extra-judicial process, the Court observed:

> [W]e think it proper to state that we do not consider congress can either withdraw from judicial cognizance any matter which, from its nature, is the subject of a suit at the common law, or in equity, or admiralty; nor, on the other hand, can it bring under the judicial power a matter which, from its nature, is not a subject for judicial determination. At the same time there are matters, involving public rights, which may be presented in such form that the judicial power is capable of acting on them, and which are susceptible of judicial determination, but which congress may or may not bring within the cognizance of the courts of the United States, as it may deem proper.

59 U.S. at 284. The sale of the collector's property fell on the "public rights" side of this dichotomy because it could be challenged only if Congress waived the government's sovereign immunity. As Chief Justice Roberts explained many years later, commenting on the "whole point" of *Murray's Lessee*, "Congress may set the terms of adjudicating a suit when the suit could not otherwise proceed at all." *Stern v. Marshall*, 131 S. Ct. 2594, 2612 (2011).

In his plurality opinion in *Northern Pipeline Constr. Co. v. Marathon Pipe Line Co.*, 458 U.S. 50 (1982), Justice Brennan used this notion of "public rights" to justify ruling that the newly reorganized bankruptcy courts could not constitutionally resolve contract claims between private parties. He explained that the public rights doctrine "extends only to matters arising between the Government and persons subject to its authority in connection with the performance of the constitutional functions of the executive or legislative departments, . . . and only to matters that historically could have been determined exclusively by those departments." *Id*. at 67 (citations omitted). By contrast, "the liability of one individual to another under the law as defined, is a matter of private rights." *Id*. at 69 (quotation marks omitted). The contract claim in *Northern Pipeline* was, on this approach, clearly a "private right," and it therefore could not be adjudicated by non-Article III bankruptcy courts.

Justice Brennan's effort to confine non-Article III tribunals with a bright-line approach to "public rights" soon met obstacles. In *Thomas v. Union Carbide Agricultural Prod. Co.*, 473 U.S. 568 (1985), the Court rejected an Article III challenge to provisions of the Federal Insecticide, Fungicide, and Rodenticide Act (FIFRA) designed to streamline registration of pesticides with EPA. Providing the health, safety, and environmental data necessary for registration is expensive. FIFRA authorized EPA to use data provided by earlier registrants to consider the applications of later applicants seeking to register similar products. Firms benefiting from this process were required to compensate the firms that developed the data. In case of disagreement, the statute provided for binding arbitration. If the category of "public rights" encompasses only disputes to which the federal government is a party, then such arbitrations would necessarily involve matters of "private right." Foreshadowing *Schor*, Justice O'Connor's majority opinion in *Union Carbide* adopted a more expansive view of the scope of "public rights." She observed that Justice Brennan's categorical approach in *Northern Pipeline* had not captured a majority and insisted that "practical attention to substance rather than doctrinaire reliance on formal categories should inform application of Article III." *Id.* at 586–87. She rejected the contention that "the right to an Article III forum is absolute unless the Federal Government is a party of record." *Id.* Instead, "Congress, acting for a valid legislative purpose pursuant to its constitutional powers under Article I, may create a seemingly 'private' right that is so closely integrated into a public regulatory scheme as to be a matter appropriate for agency resolution with limited involvement by the Article III judiciary." *Id.* at 593–94.

A year later and consistent with *Union Carbide*, Justice O'Connor authored the majority opinion in *Schor* adopting a multi-factor test for determining the Article III issue. On this approach, as you will recall, the fact that a claim implicates a private right does not, by itself, block resolution of that claim by a non-Article III federal tribunal. Together, *Union Carbide* and *Schor* thus: (a) blurred the outlines of the distinction between "public" and "private" rights; and (b) established that this distinction was not, in any event, dispositive.

For the moment, *Schor* remains good law, but it is unclear how long this will remain the case given changes in Supreme Court personnel. One wing of the Court, which has grown in strength, seems to accept the blurring of the public/private right dichotomy but also, *contra Schor*, favors a categorical rule that bars non-Article III tribunals from adjudicating matters of private right. Chief Justice Roberts's majority opinion in *Stern v. Marshall*, 131 S. Ct. 2594 (2011), which returned to the problem of determining Article III limits on the powers of bankruptcy judges, illustrates this approach. At issue was whether a bankruptcy court could constitutionally determine a compulsory counterclaim for tortious interference with an expected gift brought by Vickie Lynn Marshall (popularly known as "Anna Nicole Smith") against Pierce Marshall, the son of Vickie's deceased husband, octogenarian Texas billionaire J. Howard Marshall II. Vickie claimed that J. Howard, whom she had married about a year before his death, intended to establish a trust for her benefit, but that Pierce tortiously interfered with the gift. By the time the litigation reached the Supreme Court for a second time in 2011, both Vickie and Pierce were dead, but their estates carried on the battle. Writing for a five-justice majority, Chief Justice Roberts concluded that the bankruptcy court could not determine the state-law counterclaim consistent with Article III because: (a) the claim did not implicate public rights; and (b) the bankruptcy court was not acting as an "adjunct" to an Article III court.

Consistent with the Court's post-*Northern Pipeline* cases, the Chief Justice characterized the category of "public rights" very broadly, reaching "cases in which the claim at issue derives from a federal regulatory scheme, or in which resolution of the claim by an expert government agency is deemed essential to a limited regulatory objective within the agency's authority." *Id*. at 2613. "Public rights" must be "integrally related to particular federal government action." *Id*. With the stage thus set, the Chief Justice attempted to reconcile *Schor*'s multi-factor framework with the categorical approach that *Schor* had expressly rejected. He explained that *Schor* had rested on the following observations:

> (1) the claim and the counterclaim concerned a "single dispute" — the same account balance; (2) the CFTC's assertion of authority involved only "a narrow class of common law claims" in a "'particularized area of law'"; (3) the area of law in question was governed by "a specific and limited federal regulatory scheme" as to which the agency had "obvious expertise"; (4) the parties had freely elected to resolve their differences before the CFTC; and (5) CFTC orders were "enforceable only by order of the district court."

Stern, 131 S. Ct. at 2613 (quoting *Schor*). The most important of these factors was that *Schor* and *Conti* were fighting about the same account balance, and it was therefore "necessary" to allow the agency to determine Conti's common-law counterclaim to preserve the functioning of the reparations system that Congress had designed. *Id*. Casting this point in terms of the Chief Justice's definition of "public rights," it was "essential" to allow the CFTC, an "expert agency," to resolve the counterclaim in order to effectuate "a limited regulatory objective within the agency's authority." *Cf. id*. at 2613. *Schor* was, despite all appearances, thus a "public rights" case after all.

Vickie's counterclaim for tortious interference, by contrast, could not be shoehorned into the category of public rights. The counterclaim was a creature of state-law that bore no necessary connection to the outcome of any claim created by federal law. *Id*. at 2614. The Court also found it significant that: (a) Pierce, unlike Schor, had not genuinely consented to non-Article III resolution of the claim; and (b) the bankruptcy courts, unlike the CFTC, were not confined to a "particularized area of the law" and had no special expertise for resolving common-law tort claims. *Id*. at 2615.

Justice Breyer, dissenting for four justices, criticized the majority for disregarding *Schor*'s multi-factor approach that treats the public-private dichotomy as one factor among several bearing on the Article III question. *Id*. at 2625–26. In response, the majority expressly limited the implications of *Stern* for agency authority, observing that the bankruptcy and agency contexts are "markedly distinct" and that "we do not in this opinion express any view on how the [public rights] doctrine might apply in that different context." *Id*. at 2615.

It took four years for the pendulum to swing back from *Stern*'s categorical approach to reaffirming the primacy of *Schor*'s multi-factor approach. In *Wellness Internat'l Network v. Sharif*, 135 S. Ct. 1932 (2015), a bankruptcy court issued a final judgment determining that assets Sharif claimed belonged to a trust were properly part of the bankruptcy estate. Justice Sotomayor, writing for a five-justice majority, characterized *Schor* as the "foundational case in the modern era." *Id*. at 1942. Where a litigant waives her personal right to Article III adjudication, the problem remains of determining whether structural concerns regarding the institutional integrity of the courts should block non-Article III adjudication. Courts should resolve this question not with "formalistic and unbending rules" but by pragmatic application of the *Schor* factors. *Id*. at 1944 (quoting *Schor*). Applying these factors, the Court observed: (a) bankruptcy courts hear matters only on reference from the district courts, which, if they wish, can withdraw these references; (b) bankruptcy courts decide "a narrow class of common law claims as in incident to [their] primary, and unchallenged, adjudicative function" of disposing of bankruptcy estates; and (c) given the Article III courts' extensive control over the bankruptcy courts, "there is no indication that congress gave bankruptcy courts" the power at issue "to aggrandize itself or humble the judiciary." *Id*. at 1944–45. These factors together led to the conclusion that bankruptcy courts can issue final judgments over "claims for which litigants are constitutionally entitled to an Article III adjudication" so long as they have the parties' consent. The majority opinion did not turn on or discuss the public rights doctrine. Its resounding endorsement of *Schor*, however, suggests that this factor is once again, notwithstanding *Stern*, one factor among several rather than a categorical test. Chief Justice Roberts, you will not be surprised to learn, dissented and accused the majority of authoring an "imaginative reconstruction of *Stern*," which, "in constitutional analysis . . . spanning 22 pages, contained exactly one affirmative reference to the lack of consent." *Id*. at 1957 (Roberts, C.J., dissenting).

In *Oil States Energy Services, LLC v. Greene's Energy Group, LLC*, 138 S. Ct. 1365 (2018), the Court deployed the public rights doctrine again, but also signaled the instability of the *Schor* regime. The petitioner, Oil States Energy Services, LLC (Oil States), obtained a patent relating to hydraulic fracturing and sued respondent Greene's Energy Group, LLC (Greene's Energy) for infringement. Greene's Energy challenged the validity of the patent via "inter partes review," an administrative proceeding authorized by the America Invents Act, which went into effect in 2012. *Inter partes* review allows a petitioner to request cancellation of patent claims in adversarial proceedings that are held before the Patent Trial and Appeal Board (PTAB). Greene's Energy persuaded the PTAB to cancel two claims from the Oil States patent. In response, Oil States challenged *inter partes* review as a violation of Article III.

Justice Thomas, a stalwart defender of a categorical approach to separation of powers, authored the majority opinion upholding *inter partes* review. The gist of his opinion was very simple: The government's decision to grant a patent creates a form of public right; it follows that the PTAB could reconsider this type of grant consistent with Article III. Justice Breyer added a short concurrence to emphasize that "the Court's opinion should not be read to say that matters involving private rights may never be adjudicated other than by Article III courts, say, sometimes by agencies." 138 S. Ct. at 1379 (Breyer, J., concurring). Translated: *Schor* is still good law. In a dissent joined by the Chief Justice, the newly installed Justice Gorsuch chided the concurrence in a footnote for suggesting that "depart[ures] from the requirements of Article III" are allowable where the benefits outweigh the costs. 138 S. Ct. at 1381 n.1 (Gorsuch, J., dissenting) (quoting *Commodity Futures Trading Comm'n v. Schor*, 478 U.S. 833, 851 (1986)). Translation: I want to throw out *Schor*'s squishy framework.

Now that you have worked through this long note, consider: Does the public rights doctrine further the policy goals that plainly underlie Article III? The Constitution grants life tenure and salary protections to federal judges to protect their decisional independence. Might the need for such independence be at its greatest when a person is in a dispute with the federal government? For further discussion of the public rights doctrine, see Caleb Nelson, *Adjudication in the Political Branches*, 107 Colum. L. Rev. 559 (2007); James E. Pfander, *Article I Tribunals, Article III Courts, and the Judicial Power of the United States*, 118 Harv. L. Rev. 643 (2004); Richard Fallon, *Of Legislative Courts, Administrative Agencies, and Article III*, 101 Harv. L. Rev. 915, 933 (1988).

5. Formalism vs. functionalism. The opinions in *Schor* usefully illustrate the clash between what are commonly called "formalist" and "functionalist" approaches to separation of powers. Very broadly speaking, "formalism" takes the view that the Court should dispose of separation-of-powers disputes by applying the definitions of the "legislative," "executive," and "judicial" powers. Thus, for Justice Brennan dissenting in *Schor*, the CFTC could not resolve Conti's common-law counterclaim for debt because to do so would require an exercise of "judicial power." Justice Brennan's opinion neatly illustrates that formalism is commonly married to a functionalism of its own—as he saw the matter, adhering to a definitional approach to the limits of the "judicial power" would prevent the Court from sliding down a slippery slope to evisceration of Article III's protections. Justice O'Connor's majority opinion in *Schor*, by contrast, is a classic example of the "functionalist" approach. It expressly rejects the proposition that "formalistic and unbending rules" should be used to determine claims that administrative adjudication infringes on Article III. What grounds does Justice O'Connor give for rejecting a definitional approach? What "functions" does the majority opinion's "functionalism" seek to protect?

More provocatively, is "functionalism" just a fancy name for making up doctrines that ignore constitutional text? Is an uncompromising formalism compelled by the Constitution? Consider this critique of the definitional approach from the 8-justice majority opinion in *Morrison v. Olson:*

The difficulty of defining such categories of "executive" or "quasi-legislative" officials is illustrated by a comparison of our decisions in cases such as *Humphrey's Executor, Buckley v. Valeo*, and *Bowsher*. In *Buckley*, we indicated that the functions of the Federal Election Commission are "administrative," and "more legislative and judicial in nature," and are "of kinds usually performed by independent regulatory agencies or by some department in the Executive Branch under the direction of an Act of Congress." In *Bowsher*, we found that the functions of the Comptroller General were "executive" in nature, in that he was required to "exercise judgment concerning facts that affect the application of the Act," and he must "interpret the provisions of the Act to determine precisely what budgetary calculations are required." Compare this with the description of the FTC's powers in *Humphrey's Executor*, which we stated "occupie[d] no place in the executive department": "The [FTC] is an administrative body created by Congress to carry into effect legislative policies embodied in the statute in accordance with the legislative standard therein prescribed, and to perform other specified duties as a legislative or as a judicial aid." As Justice White noted in his dissent in *Bowsher*, it is hard to dispute that the powers of the FTC at the time of *Humphrey's Executor* would at the present time be considered "executive," at least to some degree.

487 U.S. 654, 689 n.28 (1988). According to Professor Peter Strauss, a leading academic of administrative law, formalism requires a game of pretend that is neither necessary nor worthwhile:

> A shorthand way of putting the argument is that we should stop pretending that all our government (as distinct from its highest levels) can be allocated into three neat parts. . . .

> Thus, while the actual text of the Constitution says little about the structure of the federal government beneath the apex, the structure and history of the Constitution makes clear the framers' decisions concerning the interdependence of the three branches and the place of the agencies as subsidiaries to all three. . . .

> The seeming bright-line simplicity of separation of powers, never in fact fully embraced by those who wrote the Constitution, is neither necessary as a matter of text, context or past interpretation for those parts of government not named in the Constitution itself, nor possibly successful in describing that bulk of government as it is. Courts have been able to reconcile the reality of modern administrative government and the strict separation-of-powers model only by blind feats of definition. . . .

Peter Strauss, *The Place of Agencies in Government: Separation of Powers and the Fourth Branch*, 84 COLUM. L. REV. 573, 579, 604, 625, 640–42 (1984).

Keep the formalism-functionalism clash in mind as you read the excerpt of *Morrison v. Olson* below—especially Justice Scalia's dissent, a tour-de-force for formalism.

3. Political Branch Control of Agency Power

For whom do agencies work, as it were? Congress has the Article I legislative power to create agencies, define their missions, and fund them. Article II, however, vests the executive power in the president and charges that officer to "take Care that the Laws be faithfully executed." It should come as no surprise that this constitutional division has given rise to centuries of competition between the branches for control of agency power. Much of this competition has focused on control of the power to appoint and remove agency officers. Obviously, those who appoint the officers who directly control an agency can have a vast impact on how that agency actually implements its statutory missions. The Constitution provided the legal framework for competition over this power in the Appointments Clause, Art. II, § 2, cl. 2. It is equally obvious that agency officers will tend to listen rather well to the wishes of those with the power to fire them. The Constitution provides for impeachment by Congress, Art. I, § 2, cl. 5; Art. I § 3, cl. 6–7, but does not otherwise expressly govern removal of agency officials. This gap has left room for unending debate regarding whether Congress can legally impose "good cause" requirements on presidential removal of agency officials, thus protecting these officials to some degree from presidential control. Agencies headed by officials enjoying such protections are commonly called "independent" agencies and are distinguished from "executive" agencies, which are run by officials who lack this protection from presidential removal. Regardless of this lingering debate, however, independent agencies have been a fixture of American government for more than a century.

The following materials introduce you to constitutional doctrines that have evolved to control competition between the political branches to control agency power. They focus mostly on appointment and removal, but the closing notes briefly address other avenues of potential control, such as the legislative veto, oversight, appropriations, and centralized review of rulemaking.

Lesson 1C.3. Ben, an attorney at the WTC, is no fan of Commissioners Fred and Barney, whom he regards as political hacks. For a moment he takes solace in the idea that, if and when a new administration comes to town, it will install its own people in place, and they might even have relevant expertise. But then Ben snapped to his senses after recalling § 1 of the WTCA. Why is it that removing Fred and Barney as commissioners is not so simple a matter as Ben had thought? Should it be easier, as a constitutional matter, for a new president, who "runs" the entire executive branch as it were, to remove WTC Commissioners? Turning to appointments, could a sympathetic Congress vest in the president the power to appoint WTC Commissioners without Senate confirmation?

Suppose now for the sake of argument that the WTCA creates the position of General Counsel and grants this officer the sole power to determine whether to initiate administrative enforcement actions against regulated entities under §§ 7 and 11. The Act also specifies that the president shall appoint the General Counsel for a four-year term subject to removal for good cause by the Commission. The Act does not require Senate confirmation. Are these appointment and removal provisions constitutional?

Background of *Morrison v. Olson*

In May 1973, Attorney General Elliot Richardson appointed Archibald Cox to serve as a special prosecutor to investigate the Watergate scandal that eventually led to the fall of President Richard Nixon. After Cox subpoenaed Nixon to obtain copies of taped conversations in the Oval Office, Nixon ordered Richardson to fire Cox. Rather than follow this order, Richardson resigned, as did Deputy Attorney General William Ruckelshaus. This left the task of firing Cox to Solicitor General Robert Bork. This series of events became known as the "Saturday Night Massacre." In the aftermath of the Saturday Night Massacre and Watergate, Congress enacted the Ethics in Government Act of 1978, which included provisions creating the office of independent counsel for the investigation and prosecution of high-level government officials. To create insulation between the executive branch and independent counsels, the Act included provisions for a panel of judges to appoint these officers at the request of the Attorney General; it also provided that independent counsel could be removed by the Attorney General only for cause.

Morrison v. Olson arose out of a dispute over production of documents by EPA to House subcommittees investigating the agency's expenditure of funds for cleanup of hazardous waste sites. Following direction of the Department of Justice, EPA declined to provide some documents on the ground that they were enforcement-sensitive. The subcommittees subpoenaed EPA's Administrator, who refused to comply based on executive privilege. The House cited the Administrator for contempt; the United States and the Administrator responded by suing the House. The Administrator and the House subcommittees subsequently compromised on the document production. A subcommittee of the House Judiciary Committee, however, had begun an investigation of the Department of Justice's conduct in the matter. As part of this investigation, Assistant Attorney General Theodore Olson testified. The House Judiciary Committee later sought appointment of an independent counsel to investigate Olson based on this testimony. Olson, and other department officials, refused to honor subpoenas requiring them to appear before a grand jury. They were held in contempt, which they appealed on the ground that the statutory provisions authorizing independent counsels were unconstitutional.

Morrison v. Olson

487 U.S. 654 (1988)

Chief Justice Rehnquist delivered the opinion of the Court.

This case presents us with a challenge to the independent counsel provisions of the Ethics in Government Act of 1978. We hold today that these provisions of the Act do not violate the Appointments Clause of the Constitution, Art. II, § 2, cl. 2, or the limitations of Article III, nor do they impermissibly interfere with the

President's authority under Article II in violation of the constitutional principle of separation of powers.

I

Briefly stated, Title VI of the Ethics in Government Act allows for the appointment of an "independent counsel" to investigate and, if appropriate, prosecute certain high-ranking Government officials for violations of federal criminal laws. The Act requires the Attorney General, upon receipt of information that he determines is "sufficient to constitute grounds to investigate whether any person [covered by the Act] may have violated any Federal criminal law," to conduct a preliminary investigation of the matter. When the Attorney General has completed this investigation, or 90 days has elapsed, he is required to report to a special court (the Special Division) created by the Act "for the purpose of appointing independent counsels." If the Attorney General determines that "there are no reasonable grounds to believe that further investigation is warranted," then he must notify the Special Division of this result. In such a case, "the division of the court shall have no power to appoint an independent counsel." If, however, the Attorney General has determined that there are "reasonable grounds to believe that further investigation or prosecution is warranted," then he "shall apply to the division of the court for the appointment of an independent counsel." The Attorney General's application to the court "shall contain sufficient information to assist the [court] in selecting an independent counsel and in defining that independent counsel's prosecutorial jurisdiction." Upon receiving this application, the Special Division "shall appoint an appropriate independent counsel and shall define that independent counsel's prosecutorial jurisdiction."

With respect to all matters within the independent counsel's jurisdiction, the Act grants the counsel "full power and independent authority to exercise all investigative and prosecutorial functions and powers of the Department of Justice, the Attorney General, and any other officer or employee of the Department of Justice." The functions of the independent counsel include conducting grand jury proceedings and other investigations, participating in civil and criminal court proceedings and litigation, and appealing any decision in any case in which the counsel participates in an official capacity. . . . [T]he counsel's powers include "initiating and conducting prosecutions in any court of competent jurisdiction, framing and signing indictments, filing informations, and handling all aspects of any case, in the name of the United States." . . . The Act also states that an independent counsel "shall, except where not possible, comply with the written or other established policies of the Department of Justice respecting enforcement of the criminal laws." . . .

Two statutory provisions govern the length of an independent counsel's tenure in office. The first defines the procedure for removing an independent counsel. Section 596(a)(1) provides:

"An independent counsel appointed under this chapter may be removed from office, other than by impeachment and conviction, only by the personal action of the Attorney General and only for good cause, physical disability, mental incapacity, or any other condition that substantially impairs the performance of such independent counsel's duties."

If an independent counsel is removed pursuant to this section, the Attorney General is required to submit a report to both the Special Division and the Judiciary Committees of the Senate and the House "specifying the facts found and the ultimate grounds for such removal." Under the current version of the Act, an independent counsel can obtain judicial review of the Attorney General's action by filing a civil action in the United States District Court for the District of Columbia. Members of the Special Division "may not hear or determine any such civil action or any appeal of a decision in any such civil action." The reviewing court is authorized to grant reinstatement or "other appropriate relief."

The other provision governing the tenure of the independent counsel defines the procedures for "terminating" the counsel's office. Under § 596(b)(1), the office of an independent counsel terminates when he or she notifies the Attorney General that he or she has completed or substantially completed any investigations or prosecutions undertaken pursuant to the Act. . . .

Finally, the Act provides for congressional oversight of the activities of independent counsel. An independent counsel may from time to time send Congress statements or reports on his or her activities. The "appropriate committees of the Congress" are given oversight jurisdiction in regard to the official conduct of an independent counsel, and the counsel is required by the Act to cooperate with Congress in the exercise of this jurisdiction. The counsel is required to inform the House of Representatives of "substantial and credible information which [the counsel] receives . . . that may constitute grounds for an impeachment." In addition, the Act gives certain congressional committee members the power to "request in writing that the Attorney General apply for the appointment of an independent counsel." The Attorney General is required to respond to this request within a specified time but is not required to accede to the request. . . .

III

The Appointments Clause of Article II reads as follows:

"[The President] shall nominate, and by and with the Advice and Consent of the Senate, shall appoint Ambassadors, other public Ministers and Consuls, Judges of the Supreme Court, and all other Officers of the United States, whose Appointments are not herein otherwise provided for, and which shall be established by Law: but the Congress may by Law vest the Appointment of such inferior Officers, as they think proper, in the President alone, in the Courts of Law, or in the Heads of Departments." U.S. Const., Art. II, § 2, cl. 2.

. . . The initial question is, accordingly, whether appellant is an "inferior" or a "principal" officer. If she is the latter, as the Court of Appeals concluded, then the Act is in violation of the Appointments Clause.

The line between "inferior" and "principal" officers is one that is far from clear, and the Framers provided little guidance into where it should be drawn. . . . We need not attempt here to decide exactly where the line falls between the two types of officers, because in our view appellant clearly falls on the "inferior officer" side of that line. Several factors lead to this conclusion.

First, appellant is subject to removal by a higher Executive Branch official. Although appellant may not be "subordinate" to the Attorney General (and the President) insofar as she possesses a degree of independent discretion to exercise the powers delegated to her under the Act, the fact that she can be removed by the Attorney General indicates that she is to some degree "inferior" in rank and authority. Second, appellant is empowered by the Act to perform only certain, limited duties. An independent counsel's role is restricted primarily to investigation and, if appropriate, prosecution for certain federal crimes. Admittedly, the Act delegates to appellant "full power and independent authority to exercise all investigative and prosecutorial functions and powers of the Department of Justice," but this grant of authority does not include any authority to formulate policy for the Government or the Executive Branch, nor does it give appellant any administrative duties outside of those necessary to operate her office. The Act specifically provides that in policy matters appellant is to comply to the extent possible with the policies of the Department.

Third, appellant's office is limited in jurisdiction. Not only is the Act itself restricted in applicability to certain federal officials suspected of certain serious federal crimes, but an independent counsel can only act within the scope of the jurisdiction that has been granted by the Special Division pursuant to a request by the Attorney General. Finally, appellant's office is limited in tenure. There is concededly no time limit on the appointment of a particular counsel. Nonetheless, the office of independent counsel is "temporary" in the sense that an independent counsel is appointed essentially to accomplish a single task, and when that task is over the office is terminated, either by the counsel herself or by action of the Special Division. Unlike other prosecutors, appellant has no ongoing responsibilities that extend beyond the accomplishment of the mission that she was appointed for and authorized by the Special Division to undertake. In our view, these factors relating to the "ideas of tenure, duration . . . and duties" of the independent counsel . . . are sufficient to establish that appellant is an "inferior" officer in the constitutional sense. . . .

V

We now turn to consider whether the Act is invalid under the constitutional principle of separation of powers. Two related issues must be addressed: The first is whether the provision of the Act restricting the Attorney General's power to remove the independent counsel to only those instances in which he can show "good cause," taken by itself, impermissibly interferes with the President's exercise of his constitutionally appointed functions. The second is whether, taken as a whole, the Act violates the separation of powers by reducing the President's ability to control the prosecutorial powers wielded by the independent counsel.

A

Two Terms ago we had occasion to consider whether it was consistent with the separation of powers for Congress to pass a statute that authorized a Government official who is removable only by Congress to participate in what we found to be "executive powers." *Bowsher v. Synar*, 478 U.S. 714, 730 (1986). We held in *Bowsher* that "Congress cannot reserve for itself the power of removal of an officer charged with the execution of the laws except by impeachment." A primary antecedent for this ruling was our 1926 decision in *Myers v. United States*, 272 U.S. 52 (1926). *Myers* had considered the propriety of a federal statute by which certain postmasters of the United States could be removed by the President only "by and with the advice and consent of the Senate." There too, Congress' attempt to involve itself in the removal of an executive official was found to be sufficient grounds to render the statute invalid. As we observed in *Bowsher*, the essence of the decision in *Myers* was the judgment that the Constitution prevents Congress from "draw[ing] to itself . . . the power to remove or the right to participate in the exercise of that power. To do this would be to go beyond the words and implications of the [Appointments Clause] and to infringe the constitutional principle of the separation of governmental powers."

Unlike both *Bowsher* and *Myers*, this case does not involve an attempt by Congress itself to gain a role in the removal of executive officials other than its established powers of impeachment and conviction. The Act instead puts the removal power squarely in the hands of the Executive Branch; an independent counsel may be removed from office, "only by the personal action of the Attorney General, and only for good cause." § 596(a)(1). There is no requirement of congressional approval of the Attorney General's removal decision, though the decision is subject to judicial review. § 596(a)(3). In our view, the removal provisions of the Act make this case more analogous to *Humphrey's Executor v. United States*, 295 U.S. 602 (1935), and *Wiener v. United States*, 357 U.S. 349 (1958), than to *Myers* or *Bowsher*.

In *Humphrey's Executor*, the issue was whether a statute restricting the President's power to remove the Commissioners of the Federal Trade Commission (FTC) only for "inefficiency, neglect of duty, or malfeasance in office" was consistent with the Constitution. We stated that whether Congress can "condition the [President's power of removal] by fixing a definite term and precluding a removal except for cause, will depend upon the character of the office." Contrary to the implication of some dicta in *Myers*, the President's power to remove Government officials simply was not "all-inclusive in respect of civil officers with the exception of the judiciary provided for by the Constitution." At least in regard to "quasi-legislative" and "quasi-judicial" agencies such as the FTC, "[t]he authority of Congress, in creating [such] agencies, to require them to act in discharge of their duties independently of executive control . . . includes, as an appropriate incident, power to fix the period during which they shall continue in office, and to forbid their removal except for cause in the meantime." In *Humphrey's Executor*, we found it "plain" that the Constitution did not give the President "illimitable power of removal" over the officers of independent agencies. Were the President to have the power to remove FTC Commissioners at will, the "coercive influence" of the removal power would "threate[n] the independence of [the] commission." . . .

Appellees contend that *Humphrey's Executor* and *Wiener* are distinguishable from this case because they did not involve officials who performed a "core executive function." They argue that our decision in *Humphrey's Executor* rests on a distinction between "purely executive" officials and officials who exercise "quasi-legislative" and "quasi-judicial" powers. In their view, when a "purely executive" official is involved, the governing precedent is *Myers*, not *Humphrey's Executor*. . . .

We undoubtedly did rely on the terms "quasi-legislative" and "quasi-judicial" to distinguish the officials involved in *Humphrey's Executor* and *Wiener* from those in *Myers*, but our present considered view is that the determination of whether the Constitution allows Congress to impose a "good cause"-type restriction on the President's power to remove an official cannot be made to turn on whether or not that official is classified as "purely executive." The analysis contained in our removal cases is designed not to define rigid categories of those officials who may or may not be removed at will by the President, but to ensure that Congress does not interfere with the President's exercise of the "executive power" and his constitutionally appointed duty to "take care that the laws be faithfully executed" under Article II. *Myers* was undoubtedly correct in its holding, and in its broader suggestion that there are some "purely executive" officials who must be removable by the President at will if he is to be able to accomplish his constitutional role.[2] . . . At the other end of the spectrum from *Myers*, the characterization of the agencies in *Humphrey's Executor* and *Wiener* as "quasi-legislative" or "quasi-judicial" in large part reflected our judgment that it was not essential to the President's proper execution of his Article II powers that these agencies be headed up by individuals who were removable at will. We do not mean to suggest that an analysis of the functions served by the officials at issue is irrelevant. But the real question is whether the removal restrictions are of such a nature that they impede the President's ability to perform his constitutional duty, and the functions of the officials in question must be analyzed in that light.

Considering for the moment the "good cause" removal provision in isolation from the other parts of the Act at issue in this case, we cannot say that the imposition of a "good cause" standard for removal by itself unduly trammels on executive authority. There is no real dispute that the functions performed by the independent counsel are "executive" in the sense that they are law enforcement functions

---

2. The dissent says that the language of Article II vesting the executive power of the United States in the President requires that every officer of the United States exercising any part of that power must serve at the pleasure of the President and be removable by him at will. This rigid demarcation—a demarcation incapable of being altered by law in the slightest degree, and applicable to tens of thousands of holders of offices neither known nor foreseen by the Framers—depends upon an extrapolation from general constitutional language which we think is more than the text will bear. . . .

that typically have been undertaken by officials within the Executive Branch. As we noted above, however, the independent counsel is an inferior officer under the Appointments Clause, with limited jurisdiction and tenure and lacking policymaking or significant administrative authority. Although the counsel exercises no small amount of discretion and judgment in deciding how to carry out his or her duties under the Act, we simply do not see how the President's need to control the exercise of that discretion is so central to the functioning of the Executive Branch as to require as a matter of constitutional law that the counsel be terminable at will by the President.

Nor do we think that the "good cause" removal provision at issue here impermissibly burdens the President's power to control or supervise the independent counsel, as an executive official, in the execution of his or her duties under the Act. This is not a case in which the power to remove an executive official has been completely stripped from the President, thus providing no means for the President to ensure the "faithful execution" of the laws. Rather, because the independent counsel may be terminated for "good cause," the Executive, through the Attorney General, retains ample authority to assure that the counsel is competently performing his or her statutory responsibilities in a manner that comports with the provisions of the Act. Although we need not decide in this case exactly what is encompassed within the term "good cause" under the Act, the legislative history of the removal provision also makes clear that the Attorney General may remove an independent counsel for "misconduct." Here, as with the provision of the Act conferring the appointment authority of the independent counsel on the special court, the congressional determination to limit the removal power of the Attorney General was essential, in the view of Congress, to establish the necessary independence of the office. We do not think that this limitation as it presently stands sufficiently deprives the President of control over the independent counsel to interfere impermissibly with his constitutional obligation to ensure the faithful execution of the laws.

B

The final question to be addressed is whether the Act, taken as a whole, violates the principle of separation of powers by unduly interfering with the role of the Executive Branch. . . .

We observe first that this case does not involve an attempt by Congress to increase its own powers at the expense of the Executive Branch. *Cf. Commodity Futures Trading Comm'n v. Schor.* Unlike some of our previous cases, most recently *Bowsher v. Synar*, this case simply does not pose a "dange[r] of congressional usurpation of Executive Branch functions." [S]ee also INS v. Chadha, 462 U.S. 919, 958 (1983). Indeed, with the exception of the power of impeachment — which applies to all officers of the United States — Congress retained for itself no powers of control or supervision over an independent counsel. The Act does empower certain Members of Congress to request the Attorney General to apply for the appointment of an independent counsel, but the Attorney General has no duty to comply with the request, although he must respond within a certain time limit. Other than that,

Congress' role under the Act is limited to receiving reports or other information and oversight of the independent counsel's activities, functions that we have recognized generally as being incidental to the legislative function of Congress. . . .

Finally, we do not think that the Act "impermissibly undermine[s]" the powers of the Executive Branch, or "disrupts the proper balance between the coordinate branches [by] prevent[ing] the Executive Branch from accomplishing its constitutionally assigned functions." It is undeniable that the Act reduces the amount of control or supervision that the Attorney General and, through him, the President exercises over the investigation and prosecution of a certain class of alleged criminal activity. The Attorney General is not allowed to appoint the individual of his choice; he does not determine the counsel's jurisdiction; and his power to remove a counsel is limited. Nonetheless, the Act does give the Attorney General several means of supervising or controlling the prosecutorial powers that may be wielded by an independent counsel. Most importantly, the Attorney General retains the power to remove the counsel for "good cause," a power that we have already concluded provides the Executive with substantial ability to ensure that the laws are "faithfully executed" by an independent counsel. No independent counsel may be appointed without a specific request by the Attorney General, and the Attorney General's decision not to request appointment if he finds "no reasonable grounds to believe that further investigation is warranted" is committed to his unreviewable discretion. The Act thus gives the Executive a degree of control over the power to initiate an investigation by the independent counsel. In addition, the jurisdiction of the independent counsel is defined with reference to the facts submitted by the Attorney General, and once a counsel is appointed, the Act requires that the counsel abide by Justice Department policy unless it is not "possible" to do so. Notwithstanding the fact that the counsel is to some degree "independent" and free from executive supervision to a greater extent than other federal prosecutors, in our view these features of the Act give the Executive Branch sufficient control over the independent counsel to ensure that the President is able to perform his constitutionally assigned duties.

VI

In sum, we conclude today that it does not violate the Appointments Clause for Congress to vest the appointment of independent counsel in the Special Division; that the powers exercised by the Special Division under the Act do not violate Article III; and that the Act does not violate the separation-of-powers principle by impermissibly interfering with the functions of the Executive Branch. The decision of the Court of Appeals is therefore

Reversed.

Justice Scalia, dissenting. . . .

To repeat, Article II, § 1, cl. 1, of the Constitution provides:

"The executive Power shall be vested in a President of the United States."

. . . [T]his does not mean some of the executive power, but all of the executive power. It seems to me, therefore, that the decision of the Court of Appeals invalidating the present statute must be upheld on fundamental separation-of-powers principles if the following two questions are answered affirmatively: (1) Is the conduct of a criminal prosecution (and of an investigation to decide whether to prosecute) the exercise of purely executive power? (2) Does the statute deprive the President of the United States of exclusive control over the exercise of that power? Surprising to say, the Court appears to concede an affirmative answer to both questions, but seeks to avoid the inevitable conclusion that since the statute vests some purely executive power in a person who is not the President of the United States it is void.

The Court concedes that "[t]here is no real dispute that the functions performed by the independent counsel are 'executive,'" though it qualifies that concession by adding "in the sense that they are law enforcement functions that typically have been undertaken by officials within the Executive Branch." The qualifier adds nothing but atmosphere. In what *other* sense can one identify "the executive Power" that is supposed to be vested in the President (unless it includes everything the Executive Branch is given to do) *except* by reference to what has always and everywhere—if conducted by government at all—been conducted never by the legislature, never by the courts, and always by the executive. There is no possible doubt that the independent counsel's functions fit this description. She is vested with the "full power and independent authority to exercise all *investigative and prosecutorial* functions and powers of the Department of Justice [and] the Attorney General." 28 U.S.C. § 594(a) (emphasis added). Governmental investigation and prosecution of crimes is a quintessentially executive function.

As for the second question, whether the statute before us deprives the President of exclusive control over that quintessentially executive activity: The Court does not, and could not possibly, assert that it does not. That is indeed the whole object of the statute. Instead, the Court points out that the President, through his Attorney General, has at least some control. That concession is alone enough to invalidate the statute, but I cannot refrain from pointing out that the Court greatly exaggerates the extent of that "some" Presidential control. "Most importan[t]" among these controls, the Court asserts, is the Attorney General's "power to remove the counsel for 'good cause.'" This is somewhat like referring to shackles as an effective means of locomotion. As we recognized in *Humphrey's Executor*—indeed, what *Humphrey's Executor* was all about—limiting removal power to "good cause" is an impediment to, not an effective grant of, Presidential control. . . . What we in *Humphrey's Executor* found to be a means of eliminating Presidential control, the Court today considers the "most importan[t]" means of assuring Presidential control. . . .

Moving on to the presumably "less important" controls that the President retains, the Court notes that no independent counsel may be appointed without a specific request from the Attorney General. As I have discussed above, the condition that renders such a request mandatory (inability to find "no reasonable grounds to believe" that further investigation is warranted) is so insubstantial that the Attorney General's discretion is severely confined. And once the referral is made, it is for the

Special Division to determine the scope and duration of the investigation. And in any event, the limited power over referral is irrelevant to the question whether, once appointed, the independent counsel exercises executive power free from the President's control. Finally, the Court points out that the Act directs the independent counsel to abide by general Justice Department policy, except when not "possible." The exception alone shows this to be an empty promise. Even without that, however, one would be hard put to come up with many investigative or prosecutorial "policies" (other than those imposed by the Constitution or by Congress through law) that are absolute. Almost all investigative and prosecutorial decisions including the ultimate decision whether, after a technical violation of the law has been found, prosecution is warranted—involve the balancing of innumerable legal and practical considerations. . . . In sum, the balancing of various legal, practical, and political considerations, none of which is absolute, is the very essence of prosecutorial discretion. To take this away is to remove the core of the prosecutorial function, and not merely "some" Presidential control.

As I have said, however, it is ultimately irrelevant *how much* the statute reduces Presidential control. The case is over when the Court acknowledges, as it must, that "[i]t is undeniable that the Act reduces the amount of control or supervision that the Attorney General and, through him, the President exercises over the investigation and prosecution of a certain class of alleged criminal activity." . . . It is not for us to determine, and we have never presumed to determine, how much of the purely executive powers of government must be within the full control of the President. The Constitution prescribes that they all are. . . .

The Court has . . . replaced the clear constitutional prescription that the executive power belongs to the President with a "balancing test." What are the standards to determine how the balance is to be struck, that is, how much removal of Presidential power is too much? Many countries of the world get along with an executive that is much weaker than ours—in fact, entirely dependent upon the continued support of the legislature. Once we depart from the text of the Constitution, just where short of that do we stop? The most amazing feature of the Court's opinion is that it does not even purport to give an answer. It simply announces, with no analysis, that the ability to control the decision whether to investigate and prosecute the President's closest advisers, and indeed the President himself, is not "so central to the functioning of the Executive Branch" as to be constitutionally required to be within the President's control. Apparently that is so because we say it is so. Having abandoned as the basis for our decision-making the text of Article II that "the executive Power" must be vested in the President, the Court does not even attempt to craft a substitute criterion—a "justiciable standard," however remote from the Constitution—that today governs, and in the future will govern, the decision of such questions. Evidently, the governing standard is to be what might be called the unfettered wisdom of a majority of this Court, revealed to an obedient people on a case-by-case basis. This is not only not the government of laws that the Constitution established; it is not a government of laws at all.

In my view, moreover, even as an ad hoc, standardless judgment the Court's conclusion must be wrong. Before this statute was passed, the President, in taking action disagreeable to the Congress, or an executive officer giving advice to the President or testifying before Congress concerning one of those many matters on which the two branches are from time to time at odds, could be assured that his acts and motives would be adjudged—insofar as the decision whether to conduct a criminal investigation and to prosecute is concerned—in the Executive Branch, that is, in a forum attuned to the interests and the policies of the Presidency. That was one of the natural advantages the Constitution gave to the Presidency, just as it gave Members of Congress (and their staffs) the advantage of not being prosecutable for anything said or done in their legislative capacities. *See* U.S. Const., Art. I, §6, cl. 1. It is the very object of this legislation to eliminate that assurance of a sympathetic forum. Unless it can honestly be said that there are "no reasonable grounds to believe" that further investigation is warranted, further investigation must ensue; and the conduct of the investigation, and determination of whether to prosecute, will be given to a person neither selected by nor subject to the control of the President—who will in turn assemble a staff by finding out, presumably, who is willing to put aside whatever else they are doing, for an indeterminate period of time, in order to investigate and prosecute the President or a particular named individual in his administration. The prospect is frightening . . . even outside the context of a bitter, interbranch political dispute. Perhaps the boldness of the President himself will not be affected—though I am not even sure of that. (How much easier it is for Congress, instead of accepting the political damage attendant to the commencement of impeachment proceedings against the President on trivial grounds—or, for that matter, how easy it is for one of the President's political foes outside of Congress—simply to trigger a debilitating criminal investigation of the Chief Executive under this law.) But as for the President's high-level assistants, who typically have no political base of support, it is as utterly unrealistic to think that they will not be intimidated by this prospect, and that their advice to him and their advocacy of his interests before a hostile Congress will not be affected, as it would be to think that the Members of Congress and their staffs would be unaffected by replacing the Speech or Debate Clause with a similar provision. It deeply wounds the President, by substantially reducing the President's ability to protect himself and his staff. That is the whole object of the law, of course, and I cannot imagine why the Court believes it does not succeed. . . .

III

As I indicated earlier, the basic separation-of-powers principles I have discussed are what give life and content to our jurisprudence concerning the President's power to appoint and remove officers. The same result of unconstitutionality is therefore plainly indicated by our case law in these areas.

Article II, §2, cl. 2, of the Constitution provides as follows:

"[The President] shall nominate, and by and with the Advice and Consent of the Senate, shall appoint Ambassadors, other public Ministers and Consuls, Judges of the supreme Court, and all other Officers of the United

States, whose Appointments are not herein otherwise provided for, and which shall be established by Law: but the Congress may by Law vest the Appointment of such inferior Officers, as they think proper, in the President alone, in the Courts of Law, or in the Heads of Departments."

Because appellant . . . was not appointed by the President with the advice and consent of the Senate, but rather by the Special Division of the United States Court of Appeals, her appointment is constitutional only if (1) she is an "inferior" officer within the meaning of the above Clause, and (2) Congress may vest her appointment in a court of law.

As to the first of these inquiries, the Court does not attempt to "decide exactly" what establishes the line between principal and "inferior" officers, but is confident that, whatever the line may be, appellant "clearly falls on the 'inferior officer' side" of it. The Court gives three reasons: First, she "is subject to removal by a higher Executive Branch official," namely, the Attorney General. Second, she is "empowered by the Act to perform only certain, limited duties." Third, her office is "limited in jurisdiction" and "limited in tenure."

The first of these lends no support to the view that appellant is an inferior officer. Appellant is removable only for "good cause" or physical or mental incapacity. By contrast, most (if not all) *principal* officers in the Executive Branch may be removed by the President at will. I fail to see how the fact that appellant is more difficult to remove than most principal officers helps to establish that she is an inferior officer. And I do not see how it could possibly make any difference to her superior or inferior status that the President's limited power to remove her must be exercised through the Attorney General. If she were removable at will by the Attorney General, then she would be subordinate to him and thus properly designated as inferior, but the Court essentially admits that she is not subordinate. If it were common usage to refer to someone as "inferior" who is subject to removal for cause by another, then one would say that the President is "inferior" to Congress.

The second reason offered by the Court—that appellant performs only certain, limited duties—may be relevant to whether she is an inferior officer, but it mischaracterizes the extent of her powers. As the Court states: "Admittedly, the Act delegates to appellant [the] '*full power and independent authority to exercise all investigative and prosecutorial functions and powers of the Department of Justice.*'" Ante quoting 28 U.S.C. § 594(a) (emphasis added). Moreover, in addition to this general grant of power she is given a broad range of specifically enumerated powers, including a power not even the Attorney General possesses: to "contes[t] in court . . . any claim of privilege or attempt to withhold evidence on grounds of national security." § 594(a)(6). Once all of this is "admitted," it seems to me impossible to maintain that appellant's authority is so "limited" as to render her an inferior officer. . . .

The final set of reasons given by the Court for why the independent counsel clearly is an inferior officer emphasizes the limited nature of her jurisdiction and tenure. Taking the latter first, I find nothing unusually limited about the independent counsel's tenure. To the contrary, unlike most high-ranking Executive Branch officials, she continues to serve until she (or the Special Division) decides that her work is substantially completed. This particular independent prosecutor has already served more than two years, which is at least as long as many Cabinet officials. As to the scope of her jurisdiction, there can be no doubt that is small (though far from unimportant). But within it she exercises more than the full power of the Attorney General. The Ambassador to Luxembourg is not anything less than a principal officer, simply because Luxembourg is small. And the federal judge who sits in a small district is not for that reason "inferior in rank and authority." If the mere fragmentation of executive responsibilities into small compartments suffices to render the heads of each of those compartments inferior officers, then Congress could deprive the President of the right to appoint his chief law enforcement officer by dividing up the Attorney General's responsibilities among a number of "lesser" functionaries. . . .

V

The purpose of the separation and equilibration of powers in general, and of the unitary Executive in particular, was not merely to assure effective government but to preserve individual freedom. Those who hold or have held offices covered by the Ethics in Government Act are entitled to that protection as much as the rest of us, and I conclude my discussion by considering the effect of the Act upon the fairness of the process they receive. . . .

Under our system of government, the primary check against prosecutorial abuse is a political one. The prosecutors who exercise this awesome discretion are selected and can be removed by a President, whom the people have trusted enough to elect. Moreover, when crimes are not investigated and prosecuted fairly, nonselectively, with a reasonable sense of proportion, the President pays the cost in political damage to his administration. If federal prosecutors "pick people that [they] thin[k] [they] should get, rather than cases that need to be prosecuted," if they amass many more resources against a particular prominent individual, or against a particular class of political protesters, or against members of a particular political party, than the gravity of the alleged offenses or the record of successful prosecutions seems to warrant, the unfairness will come home to roost in the Oval Office. I leave it to the reader to recall the examples of this in recent years. . . .

That is the system of justice the rest of us are entitled to, but what of that select class consisting of present or former high-level Executive Branch officials? If an allegation is made against them of any violation of any federal criminal law (except Class B or C misdemeanors or infractions) the Attorney General must give it his attention. That in itself is not objectionable. But if, after a 90-day investigation without the benefit of normal investigatory tools, the Attorney General is unable to say that there are "no reasonable grounds to believe" that further investigation is warranted, a process is set in motion that is not in the full control of persons "dependent on the people," and whose flaws cannot be blamed on the President. An independent counsel is selected, and the scope of his or her authority prescribed, by a panel of judges. What if they are politically partisan, as judges have been known to be, and select a prosecutor antagonistic to the administration, or even to the particular individual who has been selected for this special treatment? There is no remedy for that, not even a political one. Judges, after all, have life tenure, and appointing a surefire enthusiastic prosecutor could hardly be considered an impeachable offense. So if there is anything wrong with the selection, there is effectively no one to blame. The independent counsel thus selected proceeds to assemble a staff. As I observed earlier, in the nature of things this has to be done by finding lawyers who are willing to lay aside their current careers for an indeterminate amount of time, to take on a job that has no prospect of permanence and little prospect for promotion. One thing is certain, however: it involves investigating and perhaps prosecuting a particular individual. Can one imagine a less equitable manner of fulfilling the executive responsibility to investigate and prosecute? . . . It seems to me not conducive to fairness. But even if it were entirely evident that unfairness was in fact the result — the judges hostile to the administration, the independent counsel an old foe of the President, the staff refugees from the recently defeated administration — there would be no one accountable to the public to whom the blame could be assigned. . . .

The notion that every violation of law should be prosecuted, including — indeed, *especially* — every violation by those in high places, is an attractive one, and it would be risky to argue in an election campaign that that is not an absolutely overriding value. *Fiat justitia, ruat coelum.* Let justice be done, though the heavens may fall. The reality is, however, that it is not an absolutely overriding value, and it was with the hope that we would be able to acknowledge and apply such realities that the Constitution spared us, by life tenure, the necessity of election campaigns. I cannot imagine that there are not many thoughtful men and women in Congress who realize that the benefits of this legislation are far outweighed by its harmful effect upon our system of government, and even upon the nature of justice received by those men and women who agree to serve in the Executive Branch. But it is difficult to vote not to enact, and even more difficult to vote to repeal, a statute called, appropriately enough, the Ethics in Government Act. If Congress is controlled by the party other than the one to which the President belongs, it has little incentive to repeal it; if it is controlled by the same party, it dare not. By its shortsighted action today, I fear the Court has permanently encumbered the Republic with an institution that will do it great harm.

Worse than what it has done, however, is the manner in which it has done it. A government of laws means a government of rules. Today's decision on the basic issue of fragmentation of executive power is ungoverned by rule, and hence ungoverned by law. It extends into the very heart of our most significant constitutional function the "totality of the circumstances" mode of analysis that this Court has in recent years become fond of. Taking all things into account, we conclude that the power taken away from the President here is not really *too* much. The next time executive power is assigned to someone other than the President we may conclude, taking all things into account, that it is too much. That opinion, like this one, will not be confined by any rule. We will describe, as we have today (though I hope more accurately) the effects of the provision in question, and will authoritatively announce: "The President's need to control the exercise of the [subject officer's] discretion is so central to the functioning of the Executive Branch as to require complete control." This is not analysis; it is ad hoc judgment. And it fails to explain why it is not true that—as the text of the Constitution seems to require, as the Founders seemed to expect, and as our past cases have uniformly assumed—all purely executive power must be under the control of the President.

The ad hoc approach to constitutional adjudication has real attraction, even apart from its work-saving potential. It is guaranteed to produce a result, in every case, that will make a majority of the Court happy with the law. The law is, by definition, precisely what the majority thinks, taking all things into account, it ought to be. I prefer to rely upon the judgment of the wise men who constructed our system, and of the people who approved it, and of two centuries of history that have shown it to be sound. Like it or not, that judgment says, quite plainly, that "[t]he executive Power shall be vested in a President of the United States."

Notes

1. Round the horn in *Morrison*. Under the Ethics in Government Act, how were independent counsel appointed? Why did Congress choose such a complex system? Who had the better end of the argument regarding whether independent counsel are "inferior" officers—the majority or Justice Scalia? (Note well: As you will see below, Justice Scalia later had the chance to write a majority opinion on how to distinguish "principal" and "inferior" officers.)

What test did the majority devise for determining whether a limitation on removal authority impermissibly infringes on the president's executive power? Are there any executive officials whom Congress could not protect with a "good cause" limitation on removal? Where do *Meyers* and *Humphrey's Executor* fit into the *Morrison* removal analysis? What were Justice Scalia's particular criticisms of the majority's removal analysis?

Putting to one side his more specific criticisms of the Act's appointment and removal provisions, why did Justice Scalia broadly conclude that independent counsels violate separation of powers? What was wrong with what he described as the majority's "balancing test" approach?

More generally, what role did functionalist as opposed to formalist thinking play in the *Morrison* opinions' discussions of separation of powers? Was either approach more persuasive to you?

Notes about Appointment

2. The appointment power—the meaning of "Officers of the United States." In *Buckley v. Valeo*, 424 U.S. 1 (1976), the Supreme Court addressed a challenge to the constitutionality of provisions governing appointment of members of the Federal Election Commission. At the time of this challenge, the Commission had what the Court called "extensive rulemaking and adjudicative powers" as well as "direct and wide ranging" powers to enforce the requirements of the Federal Election Campaign Act. These enforcement powers included, *inter alia*, authority to seek injunctive or other relief from the courts to enforce the Act's provisions and authority to disqualify candidates from running for federal office.

The power to appoint the eight FEC Commissioners was distributed as follows:

> The Secretary of the Senate and the Clerk of the House of Representatives are *ex officio* members of the Commission without the right to vote. Two members are appointed by the President *pro tempore* of the Senate "upon the recommendations of the majority leader of the Senate and the minority leader of the Senate." Two more are to be appointed by the Speaker of the House of Representatives, likewise upon the recommendations of its respective majority and minority leaders. The remaining two members are appointed by the President. Each of the six voting members of the Commission must be confirmed by the majority of both Houses of Congress, and each of the three appointing authorities is forbidden to choose both of their appointees from the same political party.

Id. at 113. A moment's reflection may suggest why Congress might have designed this particular structure for officials with jurisdiction over, among other things, congressional elections.

Whatever the wisdom of Congress's plan, the Court deemed it unconstitutional because of the role it gave Congress in appointing "Officers of the United States." The Court vaguely explained that this phrase, as used by the Appointments Clause, captured "any appointee exercising significant authority pursuant to the laws of the United States." *Id.* at 126. It attempted to give some flesh to this standard by noting precedents that had treated postmasters first class and clerks of district courts as "inferior officers." *Id.*

The Court also distinguished "Officers of the United States" from two other kinds of functionary—"employees" and what might be termed "officers of Congress." "Employees" are "lesser functionaries subordinate to officers of the United States. . . ." *Id.* at 126 n.162. "Officers of Congress" are persons whom Congress may properly appoint to "perform duties only in aid of those functions that Congress may carry out itself or in an area sufficiently removed from the administration and enforcement of the public law as to permit their being performed by persons not 'Officers of the United States.'" *Id.* at 139. For example, Congress may grant its *own* officers powers of "an investigative or informative nature" because they fall into the "same general category as those powers which Congress might delegate to one of its own committees." *Id.* at 137. In short, Congress may appoint persons to help it perform properly legislative functions without complying with Appointments Clause requirements.

Given their "significant" authority, it was plain that FEC Commissioners were not "employees." Also, as the Court explained, they possessed many powers that could not be exercised by an "officer of Congress." In this regard, the Commissioners' powers to seek discretionary judicial relief to enforce the Act were particularly problematic given the executive nature of prosecution. *Id.* at 138. More broadly:

> All aspects of the Act are brought within the Commission's broad administrative powers: rulemaking, advisory opinions, and determinations of eligibility for funds and even for federal elective office itself. These functions, exercised free from day-to-day supervision of either Congress or the Executive Branch, are more legislative and judicial in nature than are the Commission's enforcement powers, and are of kinds usually performed by independent regulatory agencies or by some department in the Executive Branch under the direction of an Act of Congress. Congress viewed these broad powers as essential to effective and impartial administration of the entire substantive framework of the Act. Yet each of these functions also represents the performance of a significant governmental duty exercised pursuant to a public law. While the President may not insist that such functions be delegated to an appointee of his removable at will, none of them operates merely in aid of congressional authority to legislate or is sufficiently removed from the administration and enforcement of public law to allow it to be performed by the present Commission. These administrative functions may therefore be exercised only by persons who are "Officers of the United States."

Id. at 140–41.

It followed that the FEC Commissioners were "Officers of the United States" within the meaning of the Appointments Clause. Given that they were, identify two ways in which their appointments technically violated that clause.

3. The appointment power—ALJs as "officers." You may recall earlier references in the casebook to "administrative law judges" (ALJs). We discuss their functions in Chapter 4 on administrative adjudications. The important thing to know about them for the moment is that the APA authorizes these agency functionaries to act as front-line decisionmakers for "formal" adjudications by agencies. During these formal adjudications, an ALJ functions much like a judge running a bench trial. Unlike an Article III judge, however, their decisions are typically subject to plenary review by their employing agencies—e.g., the FTC can overrule decisions by its ALJs that it does not like. Seventy years after adoption of the APA, a circuit split developed regarding whether ALJs are "officers of the United States" subject to Article II's Appointments Clause. The Supreme Court decided that the SEC's ALJs are such officers in *Lucia v. SEC,* 138 S. Ct. 2044 (2018).

Justice Kagan, writing for the Court, relied on two Supreme Court precedents to articulate a two-part test for whether someone is an "officer" within the meaning of the Appointments Clause. She explained that "an individual must occupy a 'continuing' position established by law to qualify as an officer," *id.* at 2051 (quoting *United States v. Germaine*, 99 U.S. 508, 510, 511 (1879)), and must "exercis[e] significant authority pursuant to the laws of the United States." *Id.* (quoting *Buckley v. Valeo*, 424 U.S. 1, 126 (1976)). Everyone involved in the litigation agreed that SEC ALJs satisfy the first part of this test given that they hold career appointments in posts created by statute. *Id.* at 2053.

Turning to the second part, Justice Kagan declined to elaborate on the meaning of "significant authority." Instead, she resolved the issue on the narrow ground that SEC ALJs should be regarded as "officers" because their powers are virtually indistinguishable from those of Special Trial Judges (STJs) of the United States Tax Court, whom the Court had determined were "officers" in *Freytag v. Commissioner*, 501 U.S. 868, 881–82 (1991). Justice Kagan explained:

> [T]he Commission's ALJs exercise the same "significant discretion" when carrying out the same "important functions" as STJs do. Both sets of officials have all the authority needed to ensure fair and orderly adversarial hearings—indeed, nearly all the tools of federal trial judges. Consider in order the four specific (if overlapping) powers *Freytag* mentioned. First, the Commission's ALJs (like the Tax Court's STJs) "take testimony." More precisely, they "[r]eceiv[e] evidence" and "[e]xamine witnesses" at hearings, and may also take pre-hearing depositions. Second, the ALJs (like STJs) "conduct trials." . . . [T]hey administer oaths, rule on motions, and generally "regulat[e] the course of" a hearing, as well as the conduct of parties and counsel. Third, the ALJs (like STJs) "rule on the admissibility of evidence." . . . And fourth, the ALJs (like STJs) "have the power to enforce compliance with discovery orders." In particular, they may punish all "[c]ontemptuous conduct," including violations of those orders, by means as severe as excluding the offender from the hearing. So point for point—straight from *Freytag*'s list—the Commission's ALJs have equivalent duties and powers as STJs in conducting adversarial inquiries.

Id. at 2053 (citations omitted). Justices Sotomayor and Ginsburg dissented, reasoning that SEC ALJs did not exercise the significant authority required for "officer" status given that their decisions were subject to de novo review by agency heads. *Id.* at 2065–67.

4. The appointment power—the meaning of "inferior." In *Edmond v. United States*, 520 U.S. 651 (1997), the Supreme Court revisited the problem of distinguishing principal and inferior officers within the meaning of the Appointments Clause. The petitioners in this case sought to overturn their court-martial convictions on the ground that the judges of the Coast Guard Court of Criminal Appeals (CGCCA) who had affirmed their convictions had been appointed by the Secretary of Transportation, which was improper because they were, in fact, principal officers who should have been appointed by the president with the advice and consent of the Senate. Justice Scalia—who you will recall lost on the inferior officer issue in *Morrison*—authored an 8-1 opinion rejecting this claim. He explained:

Generally speaking, the term "inferior officer" connotes a relationship with some higher ranking officer or officers below the President: Whether one is an "inferior" officer depends on whether he has a superior. It is not enough that other officers may be identified who formally maintain a higher rank, or possess responsibilities of a greater magnitude. If that were the intention, the Constitution might have used the phrase "lesser officer." Rather, in the context of a Clause designed to preserve political accountability relative to important Government assignments, we think it evident that "inferior officers" are officers whose work is directed and supervised at some level by others who were appointed by Presidential nomination with the advice and consent of the Senate.

520 U.S. at 662–63. On this view, judges of the CGCCA are "inferior" because they are subject to the joint supervision of the Judge Advocate General of the Coast Guard and the Court of Appeals for the Armed Forces (CAAF). The Judge Advocate General may not reverse or otherwise attempt to influence the decisions of the CGCCA, but may "remove a [CGCCA] judge from his judicial assignment without cause." *Id.* at 664. CGCCA decisions are, moreover, subject to review by the CAAF. The scope of review as to fact is quite limited, checking only to ensure that "there is some competent evidence in the record to establish each element of the offense beyond reasonable doubt." *Id.* at 665. Notwithstanding this limited scope of review, the Court concluded that the judges of the CGCCA are not principal officers as they "have no power to render a final decision on behalf of the United States unless permitted to do so by other Executive officers." *Id.* at 665.

5. The appointment power—the Supreme Court applies *Edmond* in *Free Enterprise Fund*. In *Free Enterprise Fund v. Public Co. Accounting Oversight Bd.*, 130 S. Ct. 3138 (2010), the Free Enterprise Fund (FEF) challenged the constitutionality of statutory provisions governing appointment and removal of members of the Public Company Accounting Oversight Board (PCAOB or Board). Congress had created the Board in the aftermath of the Enron and WorldCom scandals to "oversee the audit of public companies that are subject to the securities laws." 15 U.S.C. § 7211(a). Chief Justice Roberts offered the following summary of the PCAOB's structure and powers:

> The Board is charged with enforcing the Sarbanes-Oxley Act, the securities laws, the Commission's rules, its own rules, and professional accounting standards. §§ 7215(b)(1), (c)(4). To this end, the Board may regulate every detail of an accounting firm's practice.... § 7213(a)(2)(B).
>
> ... The willful violation of any Board rule is treated as a willful violation of the Securities Exchange Act of 1934, 48 Stat. 881, 15 U.S.C. § 78a et seq.—a federal crime punishable by up to 20 years' imprisonment or $25 million in fines ($5 million for a natural person). §§ 78ff(a), 7202(b)(1) (2006 ed.). And the Board itself can issue severe sanctions in its disciplinary proceedings, up to and including the permanent revocation of a firm's registration, a permanent ban on a person's associating with any registered

firm, and money penalties of $15 million ($750,000 for a natural person). §7215(c)(4)....

The Act places the Board under the SEC's oversight, particularly with respect to the issuance of rules or the imposition of sanctions (both of which are subject to Commission approval and alteration). §§7217(b)–(c). But the individual members of the Board...are substantially insulated from the Commission's control. The Commission cannot remove Board members at will, but only "for good cause shown," "in accordance with" certain procedures. §7211(e)(6).

130 S. Ct. at 3147–48.

FEF contended that assigning power to the SEC to appoint Board members violated the Constitution because: (a) Board members were not "inferior" officers and therefore needed to be appointed by the president; (b) even if Board members were inferior, the SEC could not appoint them because it is not a "department" within the meaning of the Appointments Clause; and (c) the Commission as a group could not appoint members of the Board because, even if the SEC is a "department," its true head is its Chairman—not all of the Commissioners acting together. *Id.* at 3162–64.

The justices made speedy work of rejecting these arguments. Following *Edmond*, they held that Board members are "inferior" insofar as they are subject to the control of the SEC—the Board's superior, as it were. The SEC is a "department" as it is "a freestanding component of the Executive Branch, not subordinate to or contained within any other such component." *Id.* at 3162. Lastly, the Court quickly disposed of the argument that the Chairman is the sole head of the SEC, noting that its powers "are generally vested in the Commissioners jointly." *Id.* at 3163.

6. Fixing an appointment problem by making principal officers into inferior officers. In *Intercollegiate Broadcasting System, Inc. (IBS) v. Copyright Royalty Board*, the D.C. Circuit faced a constitutional challenge to a ruling by Copyright Royalty Judges (CRJs) on the basis that the CRJs' appointment by the Librarian of Congress violated the Appointments Clause. The court concluded that CRJs are, as defined by statute, principal officers, and, as such, could not be constitutionally appointed by the Librarian. 684 F.3d 1332 (D.C. Cir. 2012). Rather than toss out the entire CRJ scheme as unconstitutional, the court instead transformed them into inferior officers by making them easier to remove. *Id.* at 1340 (relying on *Free Enterprise Fund v. Public Company Accounting Oversight Bd.*, 130 S. Ct. 3138, 3161 (2010)).

CRJs have authority to set "reasonable" copyright royalty rates where negotiations among the interested parties fail. 17 U.S.C. §801(b)(1). As a practical matter, CRJs have considerable discretion in determining what is "reasonable." The Librarian of Congress, an officer appointed by the president with the advice and consent of the Senate, appoints the three CRJs to staggered six-year terms. The Librarian approves the CRJ's procedural regulations, issues ethical rules governing CRJs, and provides CRJs with logistical support. *Id.* at 1338. The Register of the Library of Congress is appointed by the Librarian and subject to his direction. *Id.* The Register has authority to issue interpretations of law that bind the CRJs and to review their decisions for legal error. Subject to this caveat, CRJ decisions are not subject to correction by any other entity within the executive branch. *Id.* at 1340.

The D.C. Circuit applied three factors drawn from *Edmond v. United States*, 520 U.S. 651 (1997), bearing on the principal-inferior divide: (1) the degree of supervision and control exercised by higher executive authorities; (2) removability; and (3) power to render final decisions uncorrectable by other executive authorities. The first factor suggested that CRJs are principal officers given that the real heart of their power lies in their control over discretionary, fact-bound royalty determinations. The Register's authority over legal determinations does little to check this practical power. By statute, the Librarian could remove a CRJ only for cause. Therefore, the second factor, removability, favored principal officer status. (The court conceded, however, that an officer protected by a for-cause restriction on removal could, under some circumstances, be an inferior officer in light of *United States v. Morrison*, 487 U.S. 654 (1988).) As for the third factor, no executive authority could review the CRJs' rate determinations to the degree they rested on facts.

The court concluded that the Librarian could not constitutionally appoint CRJs insofar as they are principal officers. To remedy this problem, the court did not throw out the entire CRJ statutory scheme as unconstitutional. Instead, following the lead of the Supreme Court in *Free Enterprise Fund*, the court severed the statutory provision that imposed a good-cause limitation on removal of CRJs by the Librarian. Subjecting CRJs to plenary removal authority by the Librarian transformed them into inferior officers whom the Librarian could appoint consistent with the Appointments Clause.

Notes about Removal

7. Removal power and "independent" agencies. Thanks in part to the Constitution's lack of a "Removal Clause," the scope of presidential removal authority has been the subject of debate from the dawn of the Republic. The most aggressive congressional effort to limit this power came in the Tenure of Office Act of 1867 as Congress and President Andrew Johnson struggled for power in the aftermath of the Civil War. This Act required Senate approval for removal of Cabinet officers. Johnson defied the Act, firing the Secretary of War. The House subsequently impeached him, and he only narrowly escaped Senate conviction.

The Supreme Court addressed the issue of whether Congress could require Senate consent as a condition of presidential removal of executive officers in *Myers v. United States*, 272 U.S. 52 (1926). Myers was removed from his office as a regional postmaster in Oregon without the Senate approval required by statute. The Court, in an opinion authored by a Chief Justice who happened to be a former President (Taft), held this restriction infringed on the "executive" power vested in the president by Article II, §1. The Court reasoned that, to secure unitary and uniform execution of the laws, the president must have the power to discipline subordinate "executive officers," including the power to remove them from office.

Nine years later, the Court revisited control over removal in *Humphrey's Executor v. United States*, 295 U.S. 602 (1935). Humphrey was a Commissioner of the Federal Trade Commission appointed during the Hoover administration. After he declined to resign, President Roosevelt removed him from office. The statutory removal restriction at issue did not, unlike *Myers*, require affirmative Senate approval. It did, however, limit removal to instances of "inefficiency, neglect of duty, or malfeasance in office." This for-cause limitation on removal followed the model of the Interstate Commerce Commission created in 1887. *Myers* placed the constitutionality of this model in doubt.

The *Humphrey's Executor* Court explained that Congress had intended the FTC to function as a nonpartisan, expert body "free to exercise its judgment" in carrying out legislative policies "without leave or hindrance from any other official or any department of government." Conceding to the president an unlimited power to remove FTC Commissioners would thwart this aim. *Myers* did not compel this result as the regional postmaster in that case performed "purely executive" duties, whereas the FTC

> ... cannot in any proper sense be characterized as an arm or an eye of the executive. Its duties are performed without executive leave and, in the contemplation of the statute, must be free from executive control. In administering the provisions of the statute in respect of "unfair methods of competition"—that is to say in filling in and administering the details embodied by that general standard—the commission acts in part quasi legislatively and in part quasi judicially. ...
>
> We think it plain under the Constitution that illimitable power of removal is not possessed by the President in respect of officers of the character of those just named. The authority of Congress, in creating quasi legislative or quasi judicial agencies, to require them to act in discharge of their duties independently of executive control cannot well be doubted; and that authority includes, as an appropriate incident, power to fix the period during which they shall continue, and to forbid their removal except for cause in the meantime. For it is quite evident that one who holds his office only during the pleasure of another cannot be depended upon to maintain an attitude of independence against the latter's will.

Id. at 628–29.

Agencies like the FTC headed by officers protected by for-cause restrictions on presidential removal are commonly referred to as "independent" agencies. This category includes, among many others, the Securities and Exchange Commission, the Commodity Futures Trading Commission, the Federal Energy Regulatory Commission, and the Equal Employment Opportunity Commission. Agencies headed by persons whom the president can remove at will are called "executive" agencies. The

Departments of State, Defense, and Treasury are familiar examples. In addition to for-cause restrictions on removal, a number of other attributes tend to be associated with "independent" status. For instance, independent agencies are commonly, but not in every case, headed by a multi-member group rather than a single officer. Also, for agencies headed by multi-member groups, a statutory requirement of partisan balance often limits the number of agency heads that can come from one party.

Criticisms of the legal concept of the independent agency come from two very different directions. Proponents of the "unitary executive" theory of presidential power, consistent with Chief Justice Taft's opinion in *Myers*, contend that independent agencies improperly deprive the president of executive power vested in him by Article II of the Constitution. *See, e.g., In re Aiken County*, 645 F.3d 428, 438–48 (D.C. Cir. 2011) (Kavanaugh, J., concurring) (arguing for a unitary executive approach to presidential power; sharply criticizing *Humphrey's Executor*); Steven G. Calabresi & Saikrishna B. Prakash, *The President's Power to Execute the Laws*, 104 Yale L.J. 541, 549 (1994) ("The Executive Power Clause actually does what it says it does, i.e., it vests (or grants) a power over law execution in the President, and it vests that power in him alone.").

Other critics focus their objections not on the legality of removal restrictions as such, but on the terms of the debate. On this view, the notion that agency "independence" turns just on statutory limitations on presidential removal authority is far too facile and ignores an extremely complex set of legal and political realities. Along these lines, Justice Breyer, dissenting in *Free Enterprise Fund v. Public Company Accounting Oversight Bd.*, explained:

> Agency independence is a function of several different factors, of which "for cause" protection is only one. Those factors include, inter alia, an agency's separate (rather than presidentially dependent) budgeting authority, its separate litigating authority, its composition as a multimember bipartisan board, the use of the word "independent" in its authorizing statute, and, above all, a political environment, reflecting tradition and function, that would impose a heavy political cost upon any President who tried to remove a commissioner of the agency without cause.

561 U.S. 477, 546 (2010) (citing Breger & Edles, *Established by Practice: The Theory and Operation of Independent Federal Agencies*, 52 Admin. L. Rev. 1111, 1135–55 (2000)). The "independence" of independent agencies is easy to overstate given that, among other factors, presidents designate chairs of multi-member commissions and, over time, select commissioners. Budgetary control often offers another especially potent avenue for influence. *See* Rachel E. Barkow, *Insulating Agencies: Avoiding Capture Through Institutional Design*, 89 Tex. L. Rev. 15, 42–43 (2010) ("If you want to locate power in Washington (and just about any place else), you must follow the money. This holds true for agency authority as well.").

On the other side of the coin, the "dependence" of executive agencies on presidential will is easy to exaggerate as well. There are severe practical limits to the control that the president, or White House staff purporting to work in her name, can exercise over the vast federal bureaucracy. Peter L. Strauss, *The Place of Agencies in Government: Separation of Powers and the Fourth Branch*, 84 COLUM. L. REV. 573, 586 (1984) ("As Presidents and political scientists are fond of remarking, the White House does not control policymaking in the executive departments."). Cabinet secretaries do not enjoy statutory protection from removal, but presidents do not casually fire them as doing so carries political costs. *Id.* at 590. Moreover, high-ranking, political agency heads exercise only limited control over agency staffers, who enjoy bureaucratic advantages of substantive expertise, time, and Civil Service protections. When the president says, "Jump!" the government does not always respond with a hearty "How high?"

The preceding points largely speak to practical realities of agency independence and presidential control. Turning to constitutional theory, a core premise of many unitary executive theorists is that the vesting of the executive power in the president necessarily gives her constitutional authority to control agency action. A corollary is that the president can instruct an agency head how to exercise discretion that has been statutorily vested in the agency. Thus, even though the Clean Air Act, by its terms, vests rulemaking authority in the EPA Administrator, the president has final legal authority over the exercise of this power. According to Professor Peter Strauss, this premise misapprehends the nature of presidential authority. Where a law vests decisionmaking authority in an agency head for ordinary administrative functions, the president discharges her constitutional duty by "overseeing" the agency's actions to ensure their legality rather than by seizing direct control of them, which would violate rather than implement Congress's statutory allocation of power. Peter L. Strauss, *Overseer or "the Decider"? The President in Administrative Law*, 75 GEO WASH. L. REV. 696, 704 (2007). This point holds regardless of whether the agency at issue falls on the "independent" or "executive" side of the line. On this view, many proponents of the unitary executive wish to see the president exercise a level of control over independent agencies that she should not properly exercise over executive agencies.

8. Removal power and double "for-cause" protections. Take another look at Chief Justice Roberts' description of the Public Company Accounting Oversight Board (PCAOB or Board) back in note 5. As you will recall, the Court unanimously disposed of Appointments Clause challenges to the Board in *Free Enterprise Fund v. Public Co. Accounting Oversight Bd.*, 130 S. Ct. 3138 (2010).

Removal presented a far thornier problem, prompting a 5-4 split. The majority started from the premise that two layers of for-cause protection insulated Board members from presidential control—i.e., the president could remove SEC Commissioners only for cause, and the SEC Commissioners could remove Board members only for cause. According to the majority, this double insulation weakened presidential control of Board members too much:

> A second level of tenure protection changes the nature of the President's review. Now the Commission cannot remove a Board member at will. The

President therefore cannot hold the Commission fully accountable for the Board's conduct, to the same extent that he may hold the Commission accountable for everything else that it does. The Commissioners are not responsible for the Board's actions. They are only responsible for their own determination of whether the Act's rigorous good-cause standard is met. And even if the President disagrees with their determination, he is powerless to intervene—unless that determination is so unreasonable as to constitute "inefficiency, neglect of duty, or malfeasance in office." . . .

This novel structure does not merely add to the Board's independence, but transforms it. Neither the President, nor anyone directly responsible to him, nor even an officer whose conduct he may review only for good cause, has full control over the Board. The President is stripped of the power our precedents have preserved, and his ability to execute the laws—by holding his subordinates accountable for their conduct—is impaired.

That arrangement is contrary to Article II's vesting of the executive power in the President. Without the ability to oversee the Board, or to attribute the Board's failings to those whom he can oversee, the President is no longer the judge of the Board's conduct. He is not the one who decides whether Board members are abusing their offices or neglecting their duties. He can neither ensure that the laws are faithfully executed, nor be held responsible for a Board member's breach of faith. This violates the basic principle that the President "cannot delegate ultimate responsibility or the active obligation to supervise that goes with it," because Article II "makes a single President responsible for the actions of the Executive Branch."

Id. at 3154. To remedy this problem, the Court invalidated the for-cause restriction on removal of Board members by Commissioners, but, to FEF's disappointment, otherwise left the Board intact.

The four-justice dissent, led by Justice Breyer, strongly disagreed on a number of levels. Most striking of all, he observed that SEC Commissioners are not in fact protected by any statutory restriction on their removal! *Id.* at 3182–84. This fact is not so surprising once one realizes that Congress created the SEC between issuance of *Myers* and *Humphrey's Executor*—a time when congressional authority to restrict presidential removal authority was in doubt. The *Free Enterprise* majority evaded this problem by declaring that it proceeded with the "understanding" that SEC Commissioners could be removed only for good cause because all the parties agreed with this position. *Id.* at 3148–49.

In addition, Justice Breyer contended: (a) in the absence of clearly controlling constitutional text, history, or precedent, the Court should have deferred to the shared judgments of the political branches on structuring of the Board; (b) as a practical matter, the for-cause limitation on removal of Board members was unlikely to matter much given that Sarbanes-Oxley "provides the Commission with full authority and virtually comprehensive control over all of the Board's functions,"

Id. at 3172; and (c) the majority's rule was sufficiently murky that it might "sweep[ ] hundreds, perhaps thousands of high level government officials within the scope of the Court's holding, putting their job security and their administrative actions and decisions constitutionally at risk." *Id.* at 3179.

Justice Breyer's dissent also contained broad reflections on the nature of agency independence and the many factors that bear on real levels of presidential control. Agency independence, he opined, is about much more than for-cause restrictions on removal:

> In practical terms no "for cause" provision can, in isolation, define the full measure of executive power. This is because a legislative decision to place ultimate administrative authority in, say, the Secretary of Agriculture rather than the President, the way in which the statute defines the scope of the power the relevant administrator can exercise, the decision as to who controls the agency's budget requests and funding, the relationships between one agency or department and another, as well as more purely political factors (including Congress' ability to assert influence) are more likely to affect the President's power to get something done. That is why President Truman complained . . . "'the powers of the President amount to'" bringing "'people in and try[ing] to persuade them to do what they ought to do without persuasion.'" C. Rossiter, *The American Presidency* 154 (2d rev. ed. 1960).

Id. at 3170. Understood in the context of these underlying realities, Justice Breyer insisted that the for-cause restriction on removal of Board members by Commissioners was constitutionally unobjectionable.

9. Removal power and single-headed "independent" agencies. As a descriptive matter, independent agencies almost always have some common features: they are headed by a multi-member commission or board, and their leaders are protected from removal by statutory provisions that require some variation of good cause. The Consumer Financial Protection Bureau (CFPB), which was created in 2010, departs from the usual model as it is headed by a single Director protected from removal by the president except in instances of "inefficiency, neglect of duty, or malfeasance in office." 12 U.S.C. § 5491(c)(3).

In 2014, the CFPB brought an enforcement action against PHH Corporation ("PHH") for illegal mortgage insurance referrals. Among its other defenses, PHH argued that the CFPB's structure unduly interfered with presidential control over the executive branch because it concentrated power in a single individual who was not fully accountable to the president. Unlike the singular head of an executive agency, the CFPB Director cannot be removed at will, and unlike the members of other independent agencies, the Director is not constrained by other board members or commissioners. A three-judge panel of the D.C. Circuit accepted this structural argument, *PHH Corp. v. CFPB*, 839 F.3d 1 (D.C. Cir. 2016), but the en banc court reversed, 881 F.3d 75 (D.C. Cir. 2018) (en banc).

To justify its reversal, the en banc court focused on two questions. First, "is the means of independence permissible?" *Id.* at 78. The court gave an affirmative answer to this question given the Supreme Court's long tradition of upholding similar for-cause removal provisions. Second, "does 'the nature of the function that Congress vested in' the agency call for that means of independence?" *Id.* (quoting *Wiener v. United States*, 357 U.S. 349, 353 (1958)). The court concluded that the CFPB's independence was proper given that the agency, rather than serve "core executive functions" like, for instance, the Secretary of State, was instead "one of a number of federal financial regulators—including the Federal Trade Commission, the Federal Reserve, the Federal Deposit Insurance Corporation, and others—that have long been permissibly afforded a degree of independence" by Supreme Court precedent. *Id.* at 84.

We bring this new wrinkle in the case law to your attention in part because the author of the reversed panel opinion was none other than Justice Kavanaugh, who will likely someday have the chance to say more on the subject. *See Collins v. Mnuchin*, 896 F.3d 640 (5th Cir. 2018) (holding for-cause limitation on removal of Director of Federal Housing Finance Agency unconstitutionally limited presidential control), *reh'g en banc granted,* 908 F.3d 151 (5th Cir. 2018).

Notes on Other Political Branch Controls of Agencies

10. The demise of the legislative veto. Congress naturally takes a strong interest in monitoring and controlling administrative exercise of delegated powers. Of course, in theory, Congress can override administrative action by passing a statute, but doing so is notoriously hard to do given that it requires enactment by the House and Senate and either a presidential signature or an override of a presidential veto. In response to this problem, Congress included "legislative veto" provisions in hundreds of enactments since 1929 as the modern administrative state took shape and grew in power. Such provisions authorize a portion of Congress (e.g., just the House acting alone) to block administrative action without obtaining bicameral approval or undergoing presentment to the president as the Constitution requires for legislation. Article I, §§ 1, 7, cls. 2, 3. The legislative veto, in short, makes it cheaper for interested elements in Congress to block administrative actions they do not like.

In *INS v. Chadha*, 462 U.S. 919 (1983), the Supreme Court ruled that legislative vetoes are unconstitutional. The facts of the case were not good for fans of this device. Under the statutory scheme at issue, the Attorney General had discretion to suspend the deportation of persons of good moral character who would suffer extreme hardship if deported; one house of Congress could by resolution block such suspension. An immigration judge determined that Mr. Chadha met these requirements and suspended deportation. Subsequently, Representative Eilberg, Chairman of the Judiciary Subcommittee on Immigration, Citizenship, and International Law, introduced a resolution in the house to block suspension of deportation of a half-dozen aliens—one of them Mr. Chadha. The Supreme Court described the subsequent legislative process this way:

> On December 16, 1975, the resolution was discharged from further con-
> sideration by the House Committee on the Judiciary and submitted to the
> House of Representatives for a vote. 121 Cong.Rec. 40800. The resolution
> had not been printed and was not made available to other Members of the
> House prior to or at the time it was voted on. *Ibid.* So far as the record
> before us shows, the House consideration of the resolution was based on
> Representative Eilberg's statement from the floor that "[i]t was the feeling
> of the committee, after reviewing 340 cases, that the aliens contained in the
> resolution . . . did not meet these statutory requirements, particularly as it
> relates to hardship; and it is the opinion of the committee that their depor-
> tation should not be suspended." *Ibid.*

Id. at 926.

Chief Justice Burger's majority opinion striking the legislative veto is often cited as an example of a formalistic approach to separation of powers. Simplifying some-what, he reasoned: (a) when Congress alters legal rights it is passing a law; (b) when Congress passes a law, it needs to satisfy the constitutional requirements of bicam-eralism and presentment, which are designed to promote deliberation and protect liberty; and (c) these requirements hold regardless of whether the legislative veto is, from a functional point of view, a "useful political invention," which is a debatable point in any event.

Justice White's dissent is a classic opinion in the functionalist mold. He stressed in particular that the legislative veto was vital to Congress's ability to balance dele-gation of power and its control:

> Without the legislative veto, Congress is faced with a Hobson's choice:
> either to refrain from delegating the necessary authority, leaving itself with
> a hopeless task of writing laws with the requisite specificity to cover endless
> special circumstances across the entire policy landscape, or in the alter-
> native, to abdicate its law-making function to the executive branch and
> independent agencies. To choose the former leaves major national prob-
> lems unresolved; to opt for the latter risks unaccountable policymaking by
> those not elected to fill that role. Accordingly, over the past five decades, the
> legislative veto has been placed in nearly 200 statutes. The device is known
> in every field of governmental concern: reorganization, budgets, foreign
> affairs, war powers, and regulation of trade, safety, energy, the environment
> and the economy.

Id. at 967–68 (White, J., dissenting). He also observed that it was rather odd for the Court to take such a strict view of the procedural limits on congressional authority given that the Court had, in essence, allowed Congress to delegate to agencies the power to make laws without undergoing bicameralism and presentment.

11. Congress has the money. The Supreme Court's *Chadha* opinion did not alter the fundamental political fact that Congress has the power to make life quite diffi-cult for an agency and its officials. For instance, congressional oversight committees can require agencies to produce information and agency officials to testify—which can be quite time-consuming and unpleasant for the official. But even more to the point, as we all learn in high school, Congress controls the purse strings. The significance of this power for the practical import of *Chadha* was revealed in a telling anecdote recounted by Fisher and Devins about NASA's abortive effort to make use of that decision:

> The agency contested a legislative veto provision in its appropriations act. Congress responded by providing insufficient funds and then requiring the agency to come back for supplemental appropriations. NASA quickly succumbed in this unequal contest. The unconditional surrender was executed by this letter from the NASA administrator to the congressional subcommittee controlling its appropriations:

> As you are aware, the Supreme Court in 1983 held legislative vetoes to be unconstitutional, and the Department of Justice, in applying that decision to [our] appropriation act, has indicated that provisions for Committee approval to exceed ceilings on certain programs specified in the legislation are unconstitutional.

> ... The House Committee on Appropriations has proposed ... deletion of all Committee approval provisions, leaving inflexible, binding funding limitations on several programs. Without some procedure for adjustment, other than a subsequent separate legislative enactment, these ceilings could seriously impact the ability of NASA to meet unforeseen technical changes or problems that are inherent in challenging R&D programs. We believe that the present legislative procedure [providing for committee approval] could be converted by this letter into an informal agreement by NASA not to exceed amounts for Committee designated programs without the prior approval of the Committee on Appropriations. . . .

> We appreciate the support NASA has received from the Committees of both the House and the Senate, and wish to assure the Committees that NASA will comply with any ceilings imposed by the Committees without the need for legislative ceilings which could cause serious damage to NASA's ongoing programs.

L. Fisher & N. Devins, Constitutional Law: Readings in Institutional Dynamics (1991). *See also* L. Fisher, *The Legislative Veto: Invalidated, It Survives*, 56 Law & Contemp. Problems 273 (1993) ("The legislative veto continues to thrive, however, as a practical accommodation between executive agencies and congressional committees.").

12. The Congressional Review Act—the legislative veto (partially) revived. In 1996, Congress created a partial substitute for the legislative veto in the Congressional Review Act (CRA), 5 U.S.C. §§ 801–08. The CRA provides that major rules cannot take effect until sixty days after they are submitted to Congress. It also provides streamlined procedures for Congress to consider and enact a joint resolution of disapproval for rules, which, unlike a legislative veto, must survive the present-ment process to take effect. To prevent an agency from making an end run around the CRA, it provides that an invalidated rule "may not be reissued in substantially the same form, and a new rule that is substantially the same . . . may not be issued, unless the reissued or new rule is specifically authorized by law enacted after the date of the joint resolution disapproving the original rule." 5 U.S.C. §801(b)(2). This is sometimes called the CRA's "salt the earth" provision.

As a CRA resolution must pass both houses and survive presentment, its provisions are likely to be useful only where control of the presidency has recently shifted to a party that also controls both houses of Congress. Prior to 2017, the stars had aligned for invoking the CRA just once. After Republicans took control of both houses of Congress and the White House in the 2000 election, they promptly invalidated a hotly contested OSHA regulation adopted late in the Clinton Administration to address repetitive motion injuries. The CRA then lay dormant for sixteen years, until 2017 when the presidency again switched from Democratic to Republican control while the Republicans controlled both houses of Congress. This time, the CRA carved a much broader swathe of regulatory destruction, eliminating fourteen of the fifteen regulations considered for repeal. The lone survivor was an Interior Department rule to limit methane emissions that was saved by one vote in the Senate, 51-49.

13. Centralized presidential control of rulemaking. Statutory delegations of rule-making authority generally run to agency heads rather than to the president — e.g., Congress delegates to the EPA administrator, not the president, the authority to promulgate national ambient air quality standards. Does the president nonetheless have legal authority to control how agency heads use their rulemaking discretion? The president's position at the apex of the executive branch suggests the existence of such authority. But then, the Constitution instructs the president to "take Care that the Laws be faithfully executed," and Congress generally has, by law, vested rulemaking authority in agency heads. Can Congress constitutionally limit the president's authority to control agency rulemaking? Or, given the level of informal presidential influence over even "independent" agencies, does the "legal" answer to this question matter?

These questions are prompted by presidential efforts over the last several decades to rationalize and centralize agency rulemaking through executive orders that require executive agencies to, among other things, conduct cost-benefit analyses of significant rules. These orders also subject significant agency rules to centralized review by the Office of Information and Regulatory Affairs, an agency within the Office of Management and Budget, which is part of the Executive Office of the President. An executive order issued by the Clinton administration more than twenty-five years ago, E.O. 12,866, 58 Fed. Reg. 51, 735 (Sept. 30, 1993), has largely controlled this process. In 2017, the Trump administration issued E.O. 13771, 82 Fed. Reg. 9339 (Feb. 3, 2017), the most significant order governing centralized review since E.O. 12,866. Among other things, this more recent executive order requires agencies to follow a "regulatory budget" that limits the incremental costs that new regulations can impose and to remove two regulations for every one they promulgate. We will discuss these executive orders in greater detail as part of our treatment of agency rulemaking in Chapter 3.

For very different assessments of centralized review of rulemaking by two leading scholars of administrative law, *compare* Peter L. Strauss, *Presidential Rulemaking*, 72 Chi.-Kent L. Rev. 965, 984 (1997) (contending that presidential control threatens to unduly politicize rulemaking); *with* Elena Kagan, *Presidential Administration*, 114 Harv. L. Rev. 2245, 2252 (2001) (contending that "the new presidentialization of administration renders the bureaucratic sphere more transparent and responsive to the public, while also better promoting important kinds of regulatory competence and dynamism").

14. Special counsels as a regulatory substitute for independent counsels. We will end this chapter by circling back to independent counsels. As you have read, the Supreme Court upheld their constitutionality in *Morrison v. Olson*. They fell victim, however, to the political branches. Critics long complained that independent counsels engaged in heavy-handed, expensive, interminable inquiries. An investigation of the Iran-Contra Affair by Independent Counsel Lawrence Walsh led to prosecutions of a National Security Advisor and a Secretary of Defense. Independent Counsel Kenneth Starr's investigation of President Clinton led to his impeachment. The statutory provisions authorizing independent counsels were subject to sunset provisions requiring periodic reauthorization. In 1999, after high-ranking executive officials of both parties had been sufficiently discomfited by independent counsels, Congress declined to reauthorize their existence.

The DOJ responded to the demise of independent counsels authorized by statute by adopting a set of regulations authorizing special counsels. 28 C.F.R. §§ 600.1–10. These regulations provide for the appointment of a special counsel where the Attorney General determines that the "investigation or prosecution of . . . [a] person or matter by a United States Attorney's Office or litigating division of the Department of Justice would present a conflict of interest for the Department or other extraordinary circumstances." *Id.* at § 600.1(a). Within her jurisdiction, the special counsel "shall exercise . . . the full power and independent authority to exercise all investigative and prosecutorial functions of any United States Attorney." *Id.* at § 600.6. Of special note, "[t]he Attorney General may remove a Special Counsel for misconduct, dereliction of duty, incapacity, conflict of interest, or for other good cause, including violation of Departmental policies." *Id.* at § 600.7(d).

You no doubt recall the most famous Special Counsel investigation of recent years—Special Counsel Robert Mueller's wide ranging investigation of potential conspiracies between the Trump campaign and the Russian government and of obstruction of justice. As of this writing, the consequences of that investigation are still unfolding.

Chapter 2

The Basic Procedural Categories of Administrative Law

Although administrative law encompasses the separation-of-powers issues discussed in Chapter 1, it concentrates on the law controlling government decision-making. Administrative law seeks answers to questions such as: What sorts of decisions can an agency make? What procedures must an agency follow when it makes these decisions? What rights do members of the public—regulated entities, consumers, and the like—have to participate in and influence agency decisions?

Legal control of agency action starts with the Constitution, particularly procedural due process principles derived from the Fifth and Fourteenth Amendments. With that foundation, Congress has enacted two basic types of statutes governing agency authority and procedure. First, the Administrative Procedure Act (APA) and several other statutes (e.g., the Freedom of Information Act) apply across the board to most or all government agencies. Second, specific "enabling acts" create and empower the various agencies (e.g., the Federal Trade Commission Act). Both the agencies and the courts develop administrative decisionmaking principles from these sources.

At both a constitutional and statutory level, administrative law draws a fundamental distinction between two types of administrative processes: adjudication and rulemaking. Broadly speaking, adjudication, as the name suggests, is the process that agencies use to determine facts and apply relevant law to them to determine individual rights or duties. Factual issues tend to revolve around determinations of the "who did what to whom" variety. For instance, in *CFTC v. Schor*, an administrative law judge, crediting Conti's testimony over Schor's, determined that Schor had not placed any market orders. Administrative law refers to facts like these, which are specific to particular individuals or situations, as "adjudicative facts." Adjudication is a retrospective enterprise insofar as it is devoted to determining legal consequences of past actions. Like courts, however, agencies can use adjudications to create precedents that, in effect, make policy.

Rulemaking is a process designed for supporting and making generally applicable policy decisions that seek to promote societal goals or values. For example, in *Whitman v. American Trucking Association, Inc.*, the EPA made a policy decision to set pollution control requirements at a certain level to protect the public health and safety. To make such policy decisions reasonably, an agency must, of course, suitably investigate relevant facts—such as, in *Whitman*, the effects of inhaling particulate

matter on human lungs. Note that, unlike adjudicative facts, the facts supporting rulemaking have a generalized quality. In *Whitman*, for instance, the EPA did
not investigate whether breathing particulate matter is bad for EPA Administrator
Whitman's lungs; rather, the issue focused on the effects of breathing particulate
matter on everyone's lungs. Administrative law refers to these sorts of facts, which
lack the "who did what to whom" focus of adjudicative facts, as "legislative facts."
By and large, rulemaking is a forward-looking, generalized enterprise.

Administrative law also draws an important distinction between "formal" and
"informal" proceedings. "Formal" proceedings, which in theory can be used for
either rulemaking or adjudication, can look much like a judicial bench trial. (We
also refer to "formal" proceedings sometimes as "trial-type" or "on the record.") At
some point, procedures deviate far enough from the trial model that administrative
law refers to them as "informal." There is no single model for what it means to be
"informal"; rather, procedural informality spreads out along a continuum. Mixing
and matching the elements of the rulemaking-adjudication and formal-informal
dichotomies leads to four basic procedural categories: formal adjudication, informal adjudication, formal rulemaking, and informal rulemaking.

The bulk of this brief chapter explores aspects of the rulemaking-adjudication
dichotomy. We will examine:

- How, for the purpose of due process, to tell the two apart—which may prove
  trickier than you might think;
- The legal consequences of rules as opposed to adjudicative precedents;
- The use of rules to shape the issues subject to adjudication; and
- The policy concerns and legal constraints that guide agencies as they choose
  whether to use rulemaking or adjudication to make policy.

The last section of the chapter will turn attention to the formal-informal dichotomy. It will provide examples of the wide range of procedures that agencies use, and
it will briefly consider what might justify these differences.

But, before we begin examining these issues in detail, it may be helpful to provide a relatively concrete example of how rulemaking and adjudication can work
together in one complete administrative process. Congress established the Social
Security Administration (SSA) during the New Deal to administer several benefits
programs, such as retirement and children's welfare. Eventually, Congress added to
the SSA's responsibilities a program to support people who are too disabled to work.
A person is disabled under the Social Security Act if she cannot "engage in any substantial gainful activity by reason of any medically determinable physical or mental
impairment." The Act instructed the SSA that in order to obtain disability benefits
a person must "not only [be] unable to do his previous work but [must be unable],
considering his age, education, and work experience, [to] engage in any other kind
of substantial gainful work which exists in the national economy."

The SSA has established elaborate procedures for adjudication of disability
claims. This process starts with the filing of a claim. The claim is assigned to a

"claims representative" who helps the claimant develop a supporting file, including medical and work records. That file is sent to a central "Disability Determination Service" (DDS) administered by the state. The DDS assigns the claim to a team made up of a staff member and a doctor. Many claims are granted at this initial level. But if a claim is denied, the claimant may ask for "reconsideration," and a second team reviews the claim. If the second team denies the claim, the claimant may "appeal," and a hearing is held before an administrative law judge (ALJ). The ALJ hearing has some of the elements of a trial, e.g., witnesses and a presiding official, but in other ways it tends more to the informal end of our procedural continuum. If the ALJ denies the claim, the claimant may appeal that ruling to the Appeals Council. If the claimant fails at this last administrative level, he or she may seek judicial review, starting with a federal district court, possibly up to the Supreme Court.

The SSA eventually found that determinations as to employability based on age, education, and work experience in these individual adjudications were often inconsistent. Therefore, in 1978 it promulgated a body of "rules" in which it established a matrix or "grid" for weighing these factors. In *Heckler v. Campbell*, discussed in Note 1 following *United States v. Storer Broadcasting* in subchapter 2A.3, the Supreme Court reviewed a determination in which an ALJ had denied benefits based on the grid. The disappointed claimant asserted that she had a right to an individual hearing on all the statutory factors regardless of the SSA's rules. This challenge went from the federal District Court for the Eastern District of New York to the Court of Appeals for the Second Circuit to the Supreme Court. The Supreme Court ruled that an agency may issue a rule to resolve general issues that do not depend upon the facts of a particular individual dispute. Such a rule would determine the outcome of such general issues arising in individual disputes and would preclude individual consideration of those issues in individual hearings.

Here we have an example of the working parts of the administrative process. Congress establishes the agency and gives it a substantive mandate. The agency makes individual determinations through a specially designed adjudicative process and uses rulemaking to establish general principles to be applied in those adjudications. The courts may review either these individual adjudicative decisions or the general rules. Together these parts combine into the administrative process for disability benefits determinations.

A. The Rulemaking-Adjudication Dichotomy

1. The Due Process Distinction between Rulemaking and Adjudication

Our first task is to grasp the distinction between rulemaking and adjudication, the essential processes of administrative law. This distinction exists on two different but intertwining legal levels—constitutional and statutory. Here, we focus on the constitutional distinction, which is critical for determining due process rights. On a statutory level, the APA, as well as many enabling acts, define and provide procedures for rulemaking and adjudication. We will focus on these statutory procedures in Chapter 3 on rulemaking and Chapter 4 on adjudication. For now, consider what the two classic cases excerpted below tell us about the rulemaking-adjudication distinction and its significance for due process.

Lesson 2A.1. To plan the activities of the new agency, Carl, the first Chair of the Commission, asked Ralph, the Assistant General Counsel, to head a special task force. Ralph assigned Ben to serve on the staff of this task force and to learn as much as possible about the history of wine and about current production and marketing practices in the wine industry. Ben has learned that the traditional method of making rosé wine involves leaving the skins of red grapes in the fermenting juice to impart the pink color. He has also discovered that, rather than follow this traditional process, Gallery and other wine producers mix red and white wines together and label the product as "rosé." He notes that WTCA § 5 makes it unlawful to engage in deceptive practices or "to omit to state a material fact" in connection with the purchase or sale of wine. He suggests that the WTC should use that section to prevent producers from labeling a wine as rosé unless it has been produced by the traditional method. Ben would also like to establish a general principle that wine producers must disclose on their labels both the varieties of grapes used as well as any artificial ingredients added during the winemaking process. (Ben had been shocked to learn that, prior to adoption of the WTCA, winemakers were under no general legal obligation to disclose artificial ingredients on labels—e.g., calcium pantothenate, chitosan, beta-glucanase, folic acid, polyvinyl-pyrrolodine, potato protein isolate, etc.)

Ralph and Ben consider whether the task force should recommend that the WTC promulgate a rule under § 8 before taking any enforcement action, or whether instead the WTC should immediately initiate enforcement proceedings against Gallery pursuant to the adjudicative procedures of § 7 for violation of § 5.

In light of the decisions below, could the agency, consistent with due process, use rulemaking to resolve whether the sale of wine labeled "rosé" that was not produced through traditional methods violates § 5? If so, would due process require the agency to give Gallery an opportunity to participate in the rulemaking process? Could the agency use rulemaking to resolve whether Gallery violated § 5 by selling wine labeled as "rosé" that was not produced through traditional methods? Would your answer to any of these questions change if you knew that Gallery was the only producer making "rosé" wine in this new way? More generally, for the purpose of due process analysis, where is the line between rulemaking and adjudication, and why does it matter?

Background of the *Londoner* and *Bi-Metallic* Decisions

The following decisions both arose in Denver, Colorado, and both involved disputes over taxation. Note carefully the differences between the two decisions. In, *Londoner*, owners of land along a certain road disputed taxes imposed to pay for improvements to the road. They sought hearing rights with respect to two distinct issues, (1) the decision to incur costs by improving the road, and (2) the allocation of improvement costs to individual landowners. How did the Court resolve each of those issues?

In *Bi-Metallic*, by contrast, landowners in Denver disputed a city-wide increase in property valuation, which would result in increased property taxes. They, too, sought individual opportunities to be heard with respect to that decision. How did the Court rule in *Bi-Metallic*, and how did that decision compare to *Londoner*, just seven years earlier?

Londoner v. City & County of Denver
210 U.S. 373 (1908)

JUSTICE MOODY delivered the opinion of the Court.

[A state statute empowered the Denver board of public works to improve the city streets and assess the cost to those who owned land abutting the improvement. At the board's request, the city council enacted an ordinance authorizing improvement of the road. The board then paved the street and assessed a tax for the cost. The tax was apportioned according to the extent that each landowner had specially benefited. Usually the apportionment was according to the amount of land fronting on the improvement, but unique situations might be determined by less mechanical methods. The Colorado Supreme Court held that the tax had been assessed in conformity with the Constitution and the laws of the state.]

[First, the owners asserted that the decision to make the improvement was invalid because they had been afforded no notice or opportunity to be heard before that decision was made.]

The proceedings, from the beginning up to and including the passage of the ordinance authorizing the work did not include any assessment or necessitate any assessment, although they laid the foundation for an assessment, which might or might not subsequently be made. Clearly all this might validly be done without hearing to the landowners, provided a hearing upon the assessment itself is afforded. . . .

[In the alternative, the landowners insisted that the individual assessments on their lands had been made without notice and opportunity for hearing. The record showed that notification had been published as the statute required. It showed also that the landowners had filed written objections. Thereafter, without further notice or hearing, the city council, "sitting as a board of equalization," enacted an ordinance of assessment confirming and approving the apportionment of assessment made by the board of public works.]

. . . The first step in the assessment proceedings was by the certificate of the board of public works of the cost of the improvement and a preliminary apportionment of it. The last step was the enactment of the assessment ordinance. From beginning to end of the proceedings the landowners, although allowed to formulate and file complaints and objections, were not afforded an opportunity to be heard upon them. Upon these facts was there a denial by the State of the due process of law guaranteed by the Fourteenth Amendment to the Constitution of the United States?

In the assessment, apportionment and collection of taxes upon property within their jurisdiction the Constitution of the United States imposes few restrictions upon the States. In the enforcement of such restrictions as the Constitution does impose this court has regarded substance and not form. But where the legislature of a State, instead of fixing the tax itself, commits to some subordinate body the duty of determining whether, in what amount, and upon whom it shall be levied, and of making its assessment and apportionment, due process of law requires that at some stage of the proceedings before the tax becomes irrevocably fixed, the taxpayer shall have an opportunity to be heard, of which he must have notice, either personal, by publication, or by a law fixing the time and place of the hearing. It must be remembered that the law of Colorado denies the landowner the right to object in the courts to the assessment, upon the ground that the objections are cognizable only by the board of equalization.

If it is enough that, under such circumstances, an opportunity is given to submit in writing all objections to and complaints of the tax to the board, then there was a hearing afforded in the case at bar. But we think that something more than that, even in proceedings for taxation, is required by the due process of law. Many requirements essential in strictly judicial proceedings may be dispensed with in proceedings of this nature. But even here a hearing in its very essence demands that he who is entitled to it shall have the right to support his allegations by argument however brief, and, if need be, by proof, however informal. It is apparent that such a hearing was denied to the plaintiffs in error. The denial was by the city council, which, while acting as a board of equalization, represents the State. The assessment was therefore void, and the plaintiffs in error were entitled to a decree discharging their lands from a lien on account of it. . . .

The CHIEF JUSTICE and JUSTICE HOLMES dissent.

Bi-Metallic Investment Co. v. State Board of Equalization
239 U.S. 441 (1915)

JUSTICE HOLMES delivered the opinion of the Court.

This is a suit to enjoin the State Board of Equalization and the Colorado Tax Commission from putting in force, and the defendant Pitcher as assessor of Denver from obeying, an order of the boards increasing the valuation of all taxable property in Denver forty per cent. . . . The plaintiff is the owner of real estate in Denver and brings the case here on the ground that it was given no opportunity to be heard and that therefore its property will be taken without due process of law, contrary to the Fourteenth Amendment of the Constitution of the United States. That is the only question with which we have to deal. . . .

For the purposes of decision we assume that the constitutional question is presented in the baldest way—that neither the plaintiff nor the assessor of Denver, who presents a brief on the plaintiff's side, nor any representative of the city and county, was given an opportunity to be heard, other than such as they may have had by reason of the fact that the time of meeting of the boards is fixed by law. On this assumption it is obvious that injustice may be suffered if some property in the county already has been valued at its full worth. But if certain property has been valued at a rate different from that generally prevailing in the county the owner has had his opportunity to protest and appeal as usual in our system of taxation, so that it must be assumed that the property owners in the county all stand alike. The question then is whether all individuals have a constitutional right to be heard before a matter can be decided in which all are equally concerned—here, for instance, before a superior board decides that the local taxing officers have adopted a system of undervaluation throughout a county, as notoriously often has been the case. The answer of this court . . . was that it was hard to believe that the proposition was seriously made.

Where a rule of conduct applies to more than a few people it is impracticable that every one should have a direct voice in its adoption. The Constitution does not require all public acts to be done in town meeting or an assembly of the whole. General statutes within the state power are passed that affect the person or property of individuals, sometimes to the point of ruin, without giving them a chance to be heard. Their rights are protected in the only way that they can be in a complex society, by their power, immediate or remote, over those who make the rule. If the result in this case had been reached as it might have been by the State's doubling the rate of taxation, no one would suggest that the Fourteenth Amendment was violated unless every person affected had been allowed an opportunity to raise his voice against it before the body entrusted by the state constitution with the power. In considering this case in this court we must assume that the proper state machinery has been used, and the question is whether, if the state constitution had declared that Denver had been undervalued as compared with the rest of the State and had decreed that for the current year the valuation should be forty per cent higher, the objection now urged could prevail. It appears to us that to put the question is to answer it. There must be a limit to individual argument in such matters if government is to go on. In *Londoner v. Denver*, a local board had to determine 'whether, in what amount, and upon whom' a tax for paving a street should be levied for special benefits. A relatively small number of persons was concerned, who were exceptionally affected, in each case upon individual grounds, and it was held that they had a right to a hearing. But that decision is far from reaching a general determination dealing only with the principle upon which all the assessments in a county had been laid.

Notes

1. **Distinguishing rulemaking and adjudication (for due process).** What characteristics distinguished the decision in *Londoner* from that in *Bi-Metallic*? In which

of these cases did it make more sense to allow unhappy taxpayers to be "heard" in administrative proceedings?

Together, *Londoner* and *Bi-Metallic* established a lasting working distinction between adjudication and rulemaking for the purpose of due process analysis. Government decisions that threaten deprivation of life, liberty, or property and that fall on the *Londoner* side (adjudication) trigger a due process right to some sort of hearing. Decisions that fall on the *Bi-Metallic* side (rulemaking) do not.

Adjudication determines individual rights or duties. American legal institutions tend to make such decisions through an adversary process, often a trial, and hence lawyers tend to think of adjudication as synonymous with a trial. Adjudication, however, is any process that focuses on individualized considerations specific to a party. On this broad understanding, a father deciding on a toy for his child or the Catholic Church deciding on canonization for a particular candidate saint both involve adjudications. Administrative law refers to individualized facts—often of the "who did what to whom" variety—as "adjudicative" facts. The unique circumstances of the individual properties at issue in *Londoner* involved adjudicative facts.

Rulemaking focuses on policymaking—the promotion of societal goals or values. Rules have general applicability and are usually prospective, although they are sometimes given retroactive effect. The factual support for rulemaking focuses on general or "legislative" facts, rather than individualized or "adjudicative" facts. The factual issue embedded in *Bi-Metallic* of whether property in Denver had been generally undervalued provides an example of a legislative fact.

2. It isn't just a question of numbers. In *Bi-Metallic*, Justice Holmes distinguished *Londoner* on the ground that, in the former case, "[a] relatively small number of persons was concerned, who were exceptionally affected, in each case upon individual grounds." Does it follow that numbers are dispositive? Suppose the WTC adopts a "rule" barring labeling wine as "rosé" if it was not produced via traditional methods, but suppose also that the WTC knows that Gallery is the only winemaker not following this practice. Has the agency improperly used a rulemaking to conduct an adjudication?

Notwithstanding Justice Holmes's reference in *Bi-Metallic* to a "relatively small number of persons" involved in *Londoner,* numbers do not provide a dispositive guide to the adjudication-rulemaking distinction. It is the nature of the decision and the dominant issues involved that are determinative. Adjudications are decisions that directly affect particular rights or duties based upon facts specific to those affected, regardless of the number of individuals directly affected. Rulemaking has more broad-ranging implications and is based upon legislative facts—factual determinations that are not specific to individual circumstances. Consideration of legislative facts can, however, lead to promulgation of a rule that, in practice, directly affects a class of just one. Suppose, for instance, that an agency bans emission of a pollutant based on the legislative fact that it is toxic. As a matter of adjudicative fact, just one firm emits that pollutant. Even though the ban, in one sense, regulates just this one firm, it remains a rule in the *Londoner-Bi-Metallic* sense.

3. An application of the rulemaking-adjudication distinction to land use. In *Horn v. County of Ventura*, 596 P.2d 1134 (Cal. 1979), the Supreme Court of California provided a nice discussion and application of *Londoner/Bi-Metallic* principles in the context of land use decisionmaking. When a landowner sought approval of a subdivision, a neighbor challenged the request and sought a hearing to demonstrate that the particular land was not suitable for residential construction. Echoing *Londoner,* the California court held that the neighbor was entitled to a hearing because the decision was adjudicative in nature:

> Due process principles require reasonable notice and opportunity to be heard before governmental deprivation of a significant property interest.

> It is equally well settled, however that only those governmental decisions which are adjudicative in nature are subject to procedural due process principles. *Legislative* action is not burdened by such requirements. The rationale of the "legislative-adjudicatory" distinction was well expressed many years ago by Justice Holmes in *Bi-Metallic Co. v. Colorado.* . . .

> We adopted similar reasoning recently in which we concluded that the enactment of a general zoning ordinance by a city's voters under the initiative process, being "legislative" in character, required no prior notice and hearing, even though it might well be anticipated that the ordinance would deprive persons of significant property interests. In so holding, we distinguished "adjudicatory" matters in which "the government's action affecting an individual [is] determined by facts peculiar to the individual case" from "legislative" decisions which involve the adoption of a "broad, generally applicable rule of conduct on the basis of general public policy."

> We expressly cautioned . . . that land use planning decisions less extensive than general rezoning could not be insulated from notice and hearing requirements by application of the "legislative act" doctrine. We noted: "We are thus not faced in the instant case with any of the great number of more limited 'administrative' zoning decisions, such as the grant of a variance or the award of a conditional use permit, which are adjudicatory in nature and which thus involve entirely different constitutional considerations."

> Subdivision approvals, like variances and conditional use permits, involve the application of general standards to specific parcels of real property. Such governmental conduct, affecting the relatively few, is "determined by facts peculiar to the individual case" and is "adjudicatory" in nature. . . .

> Resolution of these issues involves the exercise of judgment, and the careful balancing of conflicting interests, the hallmark of the adjudicative process. The expressed opinions of the affected landowners might very well be persuasive to those public officials who make the decisions, and affect the outcome of the subdivision process.

The Supreme Court of California emphasized that the crucial factor is not the number of people affected or the significance of the impact, but whether the outcome depended upon "facts peculiar to the individual case." Since the outcome of this dispute depended upon facts peculiar to the property in question, the court considered the matter to be an adjudication and required a hearing.

4. The statutory distinction between adjudication and rulemaking. In addition to providing a trigger for due process rights, the rulemaking-adjudication distinction is deeply embedded in fundamental statutory law governing agency procedures, including both the federal and state APAs. One year after enactment of the federal APA, an important document, the ATTORNEY GENERAL'S MANUAL ON THE ADMINISTRATIVE PROCEDURE ACT, was distributed to the agencies as a guide to following the new statute's commands. Regarding the rulemaking-adjudication distinction, the ATTORNEY GENERAL'S MANUAL explains:

> [T]he entire Act is based upon the dichotomy between rule making and adjudication. . . . Rule making is agency action which regulates the future conduct of either groups of persons or a single person; it is essentially legislative in nature, not only because it operates in the future but also because it is primarily concerned with policy considerations. The object of the rule making proceeding is the implementation or prescription of law or policy for the future, rather than the evaluation of a respondent's past conduct. Typically, the issues relate not to the evidentiary facts, as to which the veracity and demeanor of witnesses would often be important, but rather to the policy-making conclusions to be drawn from the facts. . . . Conversely, adjudication is concerned with the determination of past and present rights and liabilities. Normally, there is involved a decision as to whether past conduct was unlawful, so that the proceeding is characterized by an accusatory flavor and may result in disciplinary action.

ATTORNEY GENERAL'S MANUAL ON THE ADMINISTRATIVE PROCEDURE ACT 14 (1947).

We will spend a lot of time in Chapters 3 and 4 working through the federal APA's provisions governing rulemaking and adjudication. For the moment, note that the APA's definitional section defines "rule," "rulemaking," "order," and "adjudication." 5 U.S.C. § 551(4)–(7). Later sections, notably including § 553 and § 554, respectively, provide statutory procedures for rulemaking and adjudication. (You might take a glance at these provisions, which you will find in Appendix 2 of the casebook. Don't worry about parsing them closely now, though—we will work on them later.)

2. The Legal Consequences of (Legislative) Rules and Agency Precedents

Once we understand the difference between rulemaking and adjudication, the question becomes how an agency can use these procedural techniques to perform its essential functions of developing agency policy and enforcing its statutes and regulations in individual cases. The answer to this question depends in part on the legal consequences of agency rules and adjudicative orders. Put another way, we must determine: What is the potential "binding" force of agency rules and orders?

Lesson 2A.2. Recall that Gallery makes its rosé wines by mixing red and white wines together rather than through the traditional method of leaving grape skins in the juice to impart color during the fermenting process. Ben and Ralph are both interested in challenging this conduct, but they have different ideas about how to do it. Ben is primarily interested in establishing the principle that § 5 of the WTCA requires the wine industry to disclose grape quality, artificial additives, and any practices (such as mixing red and white wines) inconsistent with traditionally understood production methods. He knows that an enforcement action against Gallery challenging its rosé label might change that particular company's behavior, but he wants to establish a general rule, or at least a precedent, that will govern the entire industry. He is therefore inclined to think that the Commission should use its § 8 rulemaking authority to impose the disclosure rule he favors. Ralph, by contrast, is concerned that the agency does not yet know enough about the many different winemaking practices prevailing in the industry to draft a general rule. He is also concerned that using § 8 rulemaking authority would deprive the agency of flexibility in the future. He therefore suggests that the agency should bring an enforcement action against Gallery under § 7 of the WTCA, claiming that Gallery's labeling practice regarding its "rosé" violates § 5's bar on deceptive trade practices.

Assume that if the WTC brought an enforcement action against Gallery with respect to the company's "rosé" label, the agency would issue an order finding Gallery in violation of § 5 because that provision, properly understood, requires labels to disclose all grape varieties used in production and whether wines were produced using the methods consumers are likely to expect. In light of the following materials, could the WTC rely on the binding force of this precedent in later enforcement actions against other producers? If the WTC later changed its position and determined that the practice of labeling a mix of red and white wines as "rosé" is not deceptive, could the WTC change its position in a later decision?

What if, on the other hand, the WTC used the rulemaking process to establish that the failure to disclose mixed "rosé" violates § 5? Could the WTC later change that position without going through rulemaking? What does your answer suggest about how the agency should draft its rules?

Background of the *Wyman-Gordon* Decision

Under the National Labor Relations Act, employees who want to form a union (usually with the support of an existing union) may, if they meet certain requirements, petition the National Labor Relations Board (NLRB or Board) to order an election among the members of a "bargaining unit" within the company. In addition to ordering the election, the Board supervises the election in various ways to assure compliance with the Act. In *Wyman-Gordon*, the Board had ordered the company to furnish a list of the names and addresses of employees in the bargaining unit, but the company had refused to comply. When the unions involved lost the election, they complained to the Board, and the Board asked the courts to enforce its order to supply the names and addresses of employees.

As you read *Wyman-Gordon*, you will see reference to an earlier decision by the Board, *Excelsior Underwear Inc.*, which also involved a dispute over employee address lists in an election. The Board and many other agencies publish their decisions in much the same way as courts publish their decisions, so it is relatively easy to research and refer to previous agency decisions. Indeed, the Freedom of Information Act, 5 U.S.C. § 552(a)(2)(A), requires each agency to "make available for public inspection and copying—final opinions, including concurring and dissenting opinions, as well as orders, made in the adjudication of cases." Thus, the parties in *Wyman-Gordon* were able to find and cite the Board's previous decision, just as you have found and cited previous judicial decisions.

Many consider *Wyman-Gordon* to be very confusing, but it actually reveals some very basic and relatively simple principles governing agency use of adjudications. Pay close attention to what the Board actually did in *Excelsior Underwear*. How does it differ from what the court did in *Wyman-Gordon*? What justifies the majority's decision to uphold the NLRB in *Wyman-Gordon* despite the plurality's treatment of the Board's *Excelsior Underwear* decision?

NLRB v. Wyman-Gordon Co.

394 U.S. 759 (1969)

Mr. Justice Fortas announced the judgment of the Court and delivered an opinion in which the Chief Justice, Mr. Justice Stewart, and Mr. Justice White join.

On the petition of the International Brotherhood of Boilermakers and pursuant to its powers under § 9 of the National Labor Relations Act, the National Labor Relations Board ordered an election among the production and maintenance employees of the respondent company. At the election, the employees were to select one of two labor unions as their exclusive bargaining representative, or to choose not to be represented by a union at all. In connection with the election, the Board ordered the respondent to furnish a list of the names and addresses of its employees who could vote in the election, so that the unions could use the list for election purposes. The respondent refused to comply with the order, and the election was held without the list. Both unions were defeated in the election.

. . . .

. . . The Court of Appeals thought that the order in this case was invalid because it was based on a rule laid down in an earlier decision by the Board, *Excelsior Underwear Inc.* [NLRB 1966], and the *Excelsior* rule had not been promulgated in accordance with the requirements that the Administrative Procedure Act prescribes for rule making, 5 U.S.C. § 553. We granted certiorari to resolve a conflict among the circuits concerning the validity and effect of the *Excelsior* rule.

The *Excelsior* case involved union objections to the certification of the results of elections that the unions had lost at two companies. The companies had denied the unions a list of the names and addresses of employees eligible to vote. In the course of the proceedings, the Board "invited certain interested parties" to file briefs and to participate in oral argument of the issue whether the Board should require the employer to furnish lists of employees. Various employer groups and trade unions did so, as *amici curiae*. After these proceedings, the Board issued its decision in *Excelsior*. It purported to establish the general rule that such a list must be provided, but it declined to apply its new rule to the companies involved in the *Excelsior* case. Instead, it held that the rule would apply "only in those elections that are directed, or consented to, subsequent to 30 days from the date of [the] Decision."

Specifically, the Board purported to establish "a requirement that will be applied in all election cases. . . . [T]he employer must file with the Regional Director an election eligibility list, containing the names and addresses of all the eligible voters. The Regional Director, in turn, shall make this information available to all parties in the case. Failure to comply with this requirement shall be grounds for setting aside the election whenever proper objections are filed."

Section 6 of the National Labor Relations Act empowers the Board "to make . . . , in the manner prescribed by the Administrative Procedure Act, such rules and regulations as may be necessary to carry out the provisions of this Act." The Administrative Procedure Act contains specific provisions governing agency rule making, which it defines as "an agency statement of general or particular applicability and future effect." The Act requires, among other things, publication in the Federal Register of notice of proposed rule making and of hearing; opportunity to be heard; a statement in the rule of its basis and purposes; and publication in the Federal Register of the rule as adopted. [The Board asks us to hold] that it has discretion to promulgate new rules in adjudicatory proceedings, without complying with the requirements of the Administrative Procedure Act.

The rule-making provisions of the Act, which the Board would avoid, were designed to assure fairness and mature consideration of rules of general application. They may not be avoided by the process of making rules in the course of adjudicatory proceedings. There is no warrant in law for the Board to replace the statutory scheme with a rule-making procedure of its own invention. Apart from the fact that the device fashioned by the Board does not comply with statutory command, it obviously falls short of the substance of the requirements of the Administrative Procedure Act. The "rule" created in *Excelsior* was not published in the Federal Register, which is the statutory and accepted means of giving notice of a rule as adopted; only selected organizations were given notice of the "hearing," whereas notice in the Federal Register would have been general in character; under the Administrative Procedure Act, the terms or substance of the rule would have to be stated in the notice of hearing, and all interested parties would have an opportunity to participate in the rule making.

The Solicitor General does not deny that the Board ignored the rule-making provisions of the Administrative Procedure Act. But he appears to argue that *Excelsior*'s command is a valid substantive regulation, binding upon this respondent as such, because the Board promulgated it in the *Excelsior* proceeding, in which the requirements for valid adjudication had been met. This argument misses the point. There is no question that, in an adjudicatory hearing, the Board could validly decide the issue whether the employer must furnish a list of employees to the union. But that is not what the Board did in *Excelsior*. The Board did not even apply the rule it made to the parties in the adjudicatory proceeding, the only entities that could properly be subject to the order in that case. Instead, the Board purported to make a rule: *i.e.*, to exercise its quasi-legislative power.

Adjudicated cases may and do, of course, serve as vehicles for the formulation of agency policies, which are applied and announced therein. They generally provide a guide to action that the agency may be expected to take in future cases. Subject to the qualified role of *stare decisis* in the administrative process, they may serve as precedents. But this is far from saying, as the Solicitor General suggests, that commands, decisions, or policies announced in adjudication are "rules" in the sense that they must, without more, be obeyed by the affected public.

In the present case, however, the respondent itself was specifically directed by the Board to submit a list of the names and addresses of its employees for use by the unions in connection with the election. This direction, which was part of the order directing that an election be held, is unquestionably valid. Even though the direction to furnish the list was followed by citation to "*Excelsior Underwear Inc.*," it is an order in the present case that the respondent was required to obey. Absent this direction by the Board, the respondent was under no compulsion to furnish the list because no statute and no validly adopted rule required it to do so.

Because the Board in an adjudicatory proceeding directed the respondent itself to furnish the list, the decision of the Court of Appeals for the First Circuit must be reversed.

MR. JUSTICE BLACK, with whom MR. JUSTICE BRENNAN and MR. JUSTICE MARSHALL join, concurring in the result.

I agree with Parts II and III of the prevailing opinion of MR. JUSTICE FORTAS, holding that the *Excelsior* requirement that an employer supply the union with the names and addresses of its employees prior to an election is valid on its merits and can be enforced by a subpoena. But I cannot subscribe to the criticism in that opinion of the procedure followed by the Board in adopting that requirement in the *Excelsior* case. . . .

In the present case . . . I am convinced that the *Excelsior* practice was adopted by the Board as a legitimate incident to the adjudication of a specific case before it, and for that reason I would hold that the Board properly followed the procedures applicable to "adjudication" rather than "rule making." Since my reasons for joining in reversal of the Court of Appeals differ so substantially from those set forth in the prevailing opinion, I will spell them out at some length.

Most administrative agencies, like the Labor Board here, are granted two functions by the legislation creating them: (1) the power under certain conditions to make rules having the effect of laws, that is, generally speaking, quasi-legislative power; and (2) the power to hear and adjudicate particular controversies, that is quasi-judicial power. The line between these two functions is not always a clear one and in fact the two functions merge at many points. For example, in exercising its quasi-judicial function an agency must frequently decide controversies on the basis of new doctrines, not theretofore applied to a specific problem, though drawn to be sure from broader principles reflecting the purposes of the statutes involved and from the rules invoked in dealing with related problems. If the agency decision reached under the adjudicatory power becomes a precedent, it guides future conduct in much the same way as though it were a new rule promulgated under the rule-making power, and both an adjudicatory order and a formal "rule" are alike subject to judicial review. Congress gave the Labor Board both of these separate but almost inseparably related powers. No language in the National Labor Relations Act requires that the grant or the exercise of one power was intended to exclude the Board's use of the other.

Nor does any language in the Administrative Procedure Act require such a conclusion. The Act does specify the procedure by which the rule-making power is to be exercised, requiring publication of notice for the benefit of interested parties and provision of an opportunity for them to be heard, and, after establishment of a rule as provided in the Act, it is then to be published in the Federal Register. Congress had a laudable purpose in prescribing these requirements, and it was evidently contemplated that administrative agencies like the Labor Board would follow them when setting out to announce a new rule of law to govern parties in the future. In this same statute, however, Congress also conferred on the affected administrative agencies the power to proceed by adjudication, and Congress specified a distinct procedure by which this adjudicatory power is to be exercised. The Act defines "adjudication" as "agency process for the formulation of an order," and "order" is defined as "the whole or a part of a final disposition, whether affirmative, negative, injunctive, or declaratory in form, of an agency in a matter other than rule making but including licensing." Thus, although it is true that the adjudicatory approach frees an administrative agency from the procedural requirements specified for rule making, the Act permits this to be done whenever the action involved can satisfy the definition of "adjudication" and then imposes separate procedural requirements that must be met in adjudication. Under these circumstances, so long as the matter involved can be dealt with in a way satisfying the definition of either "rule making" or "adjudication" under the Administrative Procedure Act, that Act, along with the Labor Relations Act, should be read as conferring upon the Board the authority to decide, within its informed discretion, whether to proceed by rule making or adjudication. Our decision in *SEC v. Chenery Corp.* [1947], though it did not involve the Labor Board or the Administrative Procedure Act, is nonetheless equally applicable here. As we explained in that case, "the choice made between proceeding by general rule or by individual, *ad hoc* litigation is one that lies primarily in the informed discretion of the administrative agency."

[Justice Black then argued that the *Excelsior* decision was the product of an "adjudication" under the Administrative Procedure Act despite the fact that the NLRB had not applied the principle to the parties in that case. Thus, Justice Black would have upheld the Board's reliance on the principle it had announced in *Excelsior*.]

[Justices Douglas and Harlan dissented on the ground that the APA requires a new principle with future effect to be adopted through the rulemaking process.]

Notes

1. Distinguishing the force of "legislative rules" and "precedents" on the public. In law school, we learn to identify "rules" produced by judicial opinions. This way of talking about judicial opinions creates a natural inclination to speak of "rules" produced by agency adjudications. As *Wyman-Gordon* illustrates, however, this usage creates complications in administrative law given that the legal force of "rules" produced via rulemaking and "rules" produced by adjudication (i.e., agency precedents) can differ.

Rules that we refer to as "legislative rules" carry, as their name suggests, the force of law. As the plurality opinion in *Wyman-Gordon* put it, these are "'rules' in the sense that they must, without more, be obeyed by the affected public."

To make this distinction more concrete, suppose that Congress enacted the Anti-Speeding Act, which states, "it is illegal to drive at an unsafe speed." The Act also granted the Anti-Speeding Commission rulemaking and adjudicatory authority to enforce the Act. The Commission brings an enforcement action against you for driving 90 miles per hour on the freeway. Under the Act, the material question in the enforcement proceeding is whether you drove at an "unsafe speed." This may leave you with argumentative space to contend that you were driving safely notwithstanding your speed because there was no other traffic and you are an excellent driver. Suppose now, however, that, before the Commission brought its enforcement action against you, it had adopted a legislative rule stating, "it is illegal to drive faster than 75 miles per hour on the freeway." This rule, with its "force of law," changes the underlying question for the enforcement proceeding, which now turns not on whether you drove at an "unsafe speed," but instead on whether you exceeded 75 miles per hour. Your defense that you are a terrific driver has become irrelevant.

There is a reason, however, that we refer to judicial precedents as producing "rules." Thanks to the operation of stare decisis, we expect courts to follow their precedents. Among other benefits, this consistency helps ensure equal treatment of similarly situated litigants and protects reliance interests. A similar logic applies to agency precedents. As Justice Fortas's plurality opinion explained:

> Adjudicated cases may and do, of course, serve as vehicles for the formulation of agency policies, which are applied and announced therein. They generally provide a guide to action that the agency may be expected to take

in future cases. Subject to the qualified role of *stare decisis* in the administrative process, they may serve as precedents.

A wise regulated party should, of course, take heed of such precedents as, all other things being equal, an agency is likely to follow its precedents in later adjudications. These adjudications do not technically, however, enjoy the same "force of law" as a legislative rule. Circling back to our Anti-Speeding Act example, suppose that the Commission has not, after all, adopted a legislative rule imposing a 75-miles-per-hour speed limit on freeway driving. It has, however, issued a series of orders after enforcement proceedings in which it has found drivers liable for driving at an "unsafe speed" because they exceeded 75 miles per hour. An enforcement action has been brought against you for driving 90 miles per hour. It may be a pretty good bet that you will be found liable in light of agency precedents. Technically, however, the underlying legal question remains whether you drove at an "unsafe speed," opening up the possibility for you to explain what a wonderful driver you are.

2. So what was wrong with *Excelsior*? According to the *Wyman-Gordon* plurality, the Board could not properly rely in *Wyman-Gordon* on the *Excelsior* "rule" as it lacked the force of either a legislative rule or a precedent. Why didn't *Excelsior* produce a proper "rule"? Why not a proper "precedent"? → *DIDN'T IMPOSE COMMAND ON COMPANY*

3. *Wyman-Gordon* and purely prospective adjudication. The *Wyman-Gordon* plurality seems to exclude the possibility of purely prospective agency adjudications — i.e., the decision in *Excelsior* was not a proper adjudication because the Board did not apply the new disclosure principle it announced in that case to the facts of that case itself. Cobbling together a majority on this point, Justices Douglas and Harlan agreed. *Wyman-Gordon*, 394 U.S. at 777 (Douglas, J., dissenting) (explaining, "an agency is not adjudicating when it is making a rule to fit future cases"); *id.* at 780 (Harlan, J., dissenting) (contending, "[t]he language of the Administrative Procedure Act does not support the Government's claim that an agency is 'adjudicating' when it announces a rule which it refuses to apply in the dispute before it").

This approach is hard to square with a case you will likely read for the next assignment, *SEC v. Chenery Corp.*, 332 U.S. 194 (1947), which stated that whether an agency adjudication should be applied retroactively is subject to a balancing test that compares the "mischief of producing a result which is contrary to a statutory design or to legal and equitable principles" to the "ill effect of the retroactive application of a new standard." *See also Verizon Telephone Co. v. FCC*, 269 F.3d 1098 (D.C. Cir. 2001) (discussing standards for determining whether retroactivity is acceptable for agency adjudications). In a recent case, Justice Gorsuch, while still a judge of the Tenth Circuit, resolved this tension by reading *Wyman-Gordon* not as a bar on prospective adjudication generally but rather as a bar on agency efforts to use adjudicatory procedures to evade the burden of rulemaking. *De Niz Robles v. Lynch*, 803 F.3d 1165, 1177 (10th Cir. 2015). The *Wyman-Gordon* plurality provided support for this reading by noting that the Board had never used APA rulemaking procedures and had been much criticized for this evasion. *Wyman-Gordon*, 394 U.S. at 765 n.3 (citation omitted).

Note well, however, that the plurality, although it held that the *Excelsior* opinion, in light of its prospectivity, did not produce a proper adjudicative precedent, nonetheless upheld the Board. How did the plurality justify this result?

4. The qualified force of agency precedents on agencies. Justice Fortas's plurality opinion refers to the "qualified role of *stare decisis* in the administrative process." What is this "qualified role"? Suppose our Commission adopts a very narrow interpretation of §5 in its first adjudication (e.g., rejecting the argument that Gallery must disclose how it makes "rosé" wines). Might the Commission adopt a broader interpretation in a later proceeding? Or is it stuck with its original precedent?

Compared to the operation of judicial *stare decisis*, the *stare decisis* effects of an agency precedent are generally modest. In essence, when an agency changes course, it needs to acknowledge that it is doing so and offer a reasonable explanation for its new approach. *FCC v. Fox Television Stations, Inc.*, 556 U.S. 502 (2009). The relatively relaxed nature of precedential force in an administrative context is justified in part by agency expertise — i.e., as agencies learn about their regulatory domains, their policies should evolve accordingly. Politics provides another justification. Unlike the Article III courts, agencies, by design, are supposed to be responsive to the political branches. A relaxed approach to precedential force enhances agency political accountability by enabling agencies to shift policy in response to shifts in control of the political branches. Put another way, elections are supposed to have consequences.

The net effect is that an agency may use the adjudicatory process to establish a precedent regarding some principle or interpretation, but, subject to legal constraints — notably including due process's notice requirement and a duty of reasonable explanation   the agency may change its position in a later action.

5. The binding force of legislative rules on agencies. An agency is bound by its own legislative rules (and certain procedural rules) until it properly changes them. One landmark decision on this point is *Service v. Dulles*, 354 U.S. 363, 388 (1957), in which the Secretary of State had sought to dismiss an employee whose loyalty to the country was in question. Although the Secretary would otherwise have had complete statutory discretion to dismiss the employee, the agency had previously adopted a regulation imposing additional dismissal constraints. The regulation controlled even though it went beyond the statute. *See also United States ex rel. Accardi v. Shaughnessy*, 347 U.S. 260 (1954) (holding the Attorney General bound by valid regulations "as long as the regulations remain operative"); *Am. Fed'n of Gov't Employees, AFL-CIO, Local 3090 v. Fed. Labor Relations Auth.*, 777 F.2d 751 (D.C. Cir.1985) (agency bound by valid legislative rule until amended or repealed).

If it were trivially easy for an agency to adopt a legislative rule, then this principle that an agency is bound by its own legislative rules would have little bite. To change a legislative rule, however, an agency needs to adopt a new legislative rule. As you will see in Chapter 3, the legislative rulemaking process can be time-consuming and difficult.

EFFECT OF AGENCY PRECEDENT

3. Using Rules to Shape Adjudications

As we saw in the last subchapter, although agency adjudicative precedents lack the binding force of legislative rules, they still can function as a means of developing and enforcing agency policymaking. Adjudication thus can serve as a partial substitute for at least some rulemaking. Here, we explore a related, almost obverse issue — can rulemaking displace adjudication? We already know, thanks to *Londoner/Bi-Metallic*, that sometimes the answer to this question is no: Where an issue turns on adjudicative facts, an agency may not use rulemaking procedures to deprive a person of an opportunity to be heard otherwise guaranteed by due process. Often, however, an adjudication, in addition to requiring findings of adjudicative fact, will also turn on more generalized facts or policy concerns. The following cases examine the power of agencies to shape adjudications by resolving such issues via rulemaking.

Lesson 2A.3. Although the WTC could begin the process of implementing its pro-disclosure policy by bringing an enforcement action against Gallery challenging its labeling of its rosé as deceptive within the meaning of § 5, Chris, the agency's general counsel, suggests the agency should first use its § 8 authority to promulgate a rule requiring disclosure of additives, grape varieties, and use of non-traditional production methods. Ralph notes, however, that Gallery will surely have some specific arguments about why its labeling of a mix of red and white wines as "rosé" is not misleading and therefore does not violate § 5. He argues that, even if the agency promulgates the proposed disclosure rule, Gallery has a statutory right under WTCA § 7 to a "full hearing" before the agency on the issue of whether its labeling practice is misleading. Is Ralph right?

Consider the following materials.

United States v. Storer Broadcasting Co.
351 U.S. 192 (1956)

Mr. Justice Reed delivered the opinion of the Court.

The Federal Communications Commission [FCC] . . . rules provide that licenses for broadcasting stations will not be granted if the applicant, directly or indirectly, has an interest in other stations beyond a limited number. The purpose of the limitations is to avoid overconcentration of broadcasting facilities. . . .

Respondent [Storer] alleged it owned or controlled, within the meaning of the Multiple Ownership Rules, seven standard radio, five FM radio and five television broadcast stations. It asserted that the Rules complained of were in conflict with the statutory mandates that applicants should be granted licenses if the public interest would be served and that applicants must have a hearing before denial of an application. . . .

In its petition for review Storer prayed the court to vacate the provisions of the Multiple Ownership Rules insofar as they denied to an applicant already controlling the allowable number of stations a "full and fair hearing" to determine whether additional licenses to the applicant would be in the public interest. . . .

We do not read the hearing requirement, however, as withdrawing from the power of the Commission the rulemaking authority necessary for the orderly conduct of its business. As conceded by Storer, "Section 309(b) does not require the Commission to hold a hearing before denying a license to operate a station in ways contrary to those that the Congress has determined are in the public interest." The challenged Rules contain limitations against licensing not specifically authorized by statute. But that is not the limit of the Commission's rulemaking authority. [The act grants] general rulemaking power not inconsistent with the Act or law. . . .

. . . We read the Act and Regulations as providing a "full hearing" for applicants who have reached the existing limit of stations upon their presentation of applications that set out adequate reasons why the Rules should be waived or amended. The Act, considered as a whole, requires no more. We agree with the contention of the commission that a full hearing, such as is required by § 309(b), would not be necessary on all such applications. As the Commission has promulgated its Rules after extensive administrative hearings, it is necessary for the accompanying papers to set forth reasons, sufficient if true, to justify a change or waiver of the Rules. We do not think Congress intended the Commission to waste time on applications that do not state a valid basis for a hearing. If any applicant is aggrieved by a refusal, the way for review is open.

Notes

1. **Other instances in which rules overcame a statutory right to a hearing.** In *Federal Power Comm'n v. Texaco, Inc.*, 377 U.S. 33 (1964), the Supreme Court clarified that the *Storer* holding applies to all agencies. The FPC rule at issue provided for summary rejection of contracts with price provisions other than those specified in the regulations. The Supreme Court held that "the statutory requirement for a hearing [in the Natural Gas Act] does not preclude the Commission from particularizing statutory standards through the rulemaking process and barring at the threshold those who neither measure up to them nor show reasons why in the public interest the rule should be waived." *Id.* at 39.

The Supreme Court confirmed the continuing vitality of the *Storer* doctrine in *Heckler v. Campbell*, 461 U.S. 458, 467 (1983), which involved a claim for disability benefits under the Social Security Act. Campbell, the claimant, had a statutory right to a *de novo* hearing after the agency initially denied her application. The case involved two factual questions: (1) the extent of the claimant's disability, and (2) "whether jobs exist in the national economy that a person having claimant's qualifications could perform." On the first question, Campbell received an "individualized determination based on evidence adduced at a hearing." As to the second question, however, the agency relied upon "medical-vocational guidelines" that it had recently issued through the rulemaking process. The guidelines consisted of a matrix of the four statutory factors, physical ability, age, education and work experience, and conclusively established the availability (or non-availability) of jobs for claimants with various combinations of the four factors. According to the guidelines, jobs existed for Campbell to perform given her physical condition. Despite her right to a *de novo* hearing, she was not permitted to litigate the second issue by presenting evidence to the contrary. Relying on *Storer Broadcasting* and *FPC v. Texaco*, the Court said that Campbell's statutory hearing right

> does not bar the Secretary from relying on rulemaking to resolve certain classes of issues. The Court has recognized that even where an agency's enabling statute expressly requires it to hold a hearing, the agency may rely on its rulemaking authority to determine issues that do not require case-by-case determination. A contrary holding would require the agency continually to relitigate issues that may be established fairly and efficiently in a single rulemaking proceeding.

The Court noted, however, that disability claimants had "ample opportunity . . . to offer evidence that the guidelines do not apply to them." Thus, if a claimant showed her condition did not fit in the matrix, the rule could not govern her claim. *See also id.* at 467 n.11 (adding that both *Texaco* and *Storer* "were careful to note that the statutory scheme at issue allowed an individual applicant to show that the rule promulgated should not be applied to him").

Similarly, in *American Hosp. Ass'n v. NLRB*, 499 U.S. 606, 611–12 (1991), a challenge to a NLRB rule defining the appropriate bargaining units in acute care hospitals, the Court found:

> [T]he Board's decision is presumably to be guided not simply by the basic policy of the Act but also by the rules that the Board develops to circumscribe and to guide its discretion either in the process of case-by-case adjudication or by the exercise of its rulemaking authority. The requirement that the Board exercise its discretion in every disputed case cannot fairly or logically be read to command the Board to exercise standardless discretion in each case. . . .

> [*Storer, Texaco* and *Campbell*] confirm that, even if a statutory scheme requires individualized determinations, the decisionmaker has the authority to rely on rulemaking to resolve certain issues of general applicability unless Congress clearly expresses an intent to withhold that authority.

Why is the Court so willing to allow agencies to circumvent the individual hearing requirement?

2. What about *Londoner/Bi-Metallic*? In *Storer, Texaco,* and *Campbell*, rules overcame a statutory right to a hearing. What about constitutional rights? Why didn't *Londoner/Bi-Metallic* principles require that the petitioners in these three cases have the chance to be heard on their issues by the agency?

4. Choosing Between Rulemaking and Adjudication for Policymaking

An agency, unlike a legislature or a court, can often choose either rulemaking or adjudication as a vehicle to develop policy. In this section, we consider both: (1) why an agency, as a matter of policy (or meta-policy, if you like) might prefer one method rather than the other; and (2) the legal constraints limiting agency discretion to choose between them.

Lesson 2A.4. It is clear to Chris, the general counsel, that the Commission can use its rulemaking authority under § 8 to require disclosure of grape varieties and additives on labels. She also thinks that simple fairness requires the WTC to promulgate such a rule before proceeding with an individual enforcement action. She sees adjudication as a long and cumbersome process for enforcing and developing the law and believes that it would be more efficient and inclusive for the WTC to make policy through rulemaking rather than adjudication.

But, on the other hand, Chris also believes the agency needs to gain more experience with the industry before it can confidently propose a rule that would address the full range of industry practices. As a result, with some reluctance, she is considering bringing an enforcement action against particular firms for violating § 5 of the WTCA, which bars various deceptive practices. Ben has reported that Gallery, like many other winemakers, does not disclose its use of artificial additives in the winemaking process. Gallery also labels one of its wines as "Gallery Reserve Rosé" even though the firm produces it by blending red and white wines rather than through the traditional method of using red grape skins to impart color. Chris intends to seek an order under § 7 of the WTCA forbidding Gallery from marketing "Gallery Reserve Rosé" without disclosing on its label all artificial additives and that Gallery produces it by blending. She is also contemplating seeking administrative penalties under § 11 of the WTCA to sanction Gallery's past marketing of the wine without proper disclosures.

What do the following materials suggest as to whether Chris should choose rulemaking or adjudication as a matter of policy? Put another way, would it be *better* to use rulemaking or adjudication?

Turning to law, does the WTC have legal authority to bring an enforcement action against Gallery for its disclosure practices before the agency uses rulemaking to clarify Gallery's obligations? What arguments might Gallery make to challenge the WTC's use of adjudication rather than rulemaking? How would the WTC respond? Do these arguments play out differently for a § 7 order enjoining future conduct than for a § 11 order sanctioning past conduct?

Background of *SEC v. Chenery Corp.*

The following is the second of two major *Chenery* decisions involving a company reorganization plan required by the Public Utility Holding Company Act of

1935 (Act). The SEC rejected a reorganization plan proposed by managers of the Federal Water Service Company on the ground that the plan violated judicially recognized fiduciary duties that the managers owed to shareholders. In *Chenery I,* the Supreme Court held that the courts had not actually imposed these particular fiduciary duties on company officers and directors. The SEC contended that the Court should nonetheless affirm because, in its expert judgment, the reorganization plan violated the requirements of the Act itself, which requires that reorganizations be "fair" and "equitable." Announcing the legal proposition for which the case is famous, the Court rejected the SEC's argument in light of the principle that "an administrative order cannot be upheld unless the grounds upon which the agency acted in exercising its powers were those upon which its action can be sustained." The Court added that, if the SEC had "intended to create new standards growing out of its experience in effectuating the legislative policy, it failed to express itself with sufficient clarity and precision to be so understood." The Court therefore set aside the SEC's rejection of the Chenery reorganization plan and remanded to the agency for further proceedings.

After the remand, the SEC again rejected the Chenery reorganization plan. Having gotten the message from its earlier trip to the Supreme Court, this time the agency asserted that the reorganization plan violated principles established by the Act, which required that reorganization plans be "fair and equitable to the persons affected thereby." The Court of Appeals struck down the SEC's action as prohibited by the Court's decision in *Chenery I.*

SEC v. Chenery Corp. [Chenery II]

332 U.S. 194 (1947)

MR. JUSTICE MURPHY delivered the opinion of the Court.

This case is here for the second time. In *S.E.C. v. Chenery Corp [Chenery I]*, 318 U.S. 80 [1943], we held that an order of the Securities and Exchange Commission could not be sustained on the grounds upon which that agency acted. We therefore directed that the case be remanded to the Commission for such further proceedings as might be appropriate. On remand, the Commission reexamined the problem, recast its rationale and reached the same result. The issue now is whether the Commission's action is proper in light of the principles established in our prior decision.

When the case was first here, we emphasized a simple but fundamental rule of administrative law. That rule is to the effect that a reviewing court, in dealing with a determination or judgment which an administrative agency alone is authorized to make, must judge the propriety of such action solely by the grounds invoked by the agency. If those grounds are inadequate or improper, the court is powerless to affirm the administrative action by substituting what it considers to be a more adequate or proper basis. To do so would propel the court into the domain which Congress has set aside exclusively for the administrative agency.

The latest order of the Commission definitely avoids the fatal error of relying on judicial precedents which do not sustain it. This time, after a thorough reexamination of the problem in light of the purposes and standards of the Holding Company Act, the Commission has concluded that the proposed transaction is inconsistent with the standards of §§ 7 and 11 of the Act. It has drawn heavily upon its accumulated experience in dealing with utility reorganizations. And it has expressed its reasons with a clarity and thoroughness that admit of no doubt as to the underlying basis of its order.

The argument is pressed upon us, however, that the Commission was foreclosed from taking such a step following our prior decision. It is said that . . . , the Commission could not determine by an order in this particular case that [the managers' actions were] inconsistent with the statutory standards. . . . Under this view, the Commission would be free only to promulgate a general rule outlawing such profits in future utility reorganizations; but such a rule would have to be prospective in nature and have no retroactive effect upon the instant situation.

We reject this contention, for it grows out of a misapprehension of our prior decision and of the Commission's statutory duties. We held no more and no less than that the Commission's first order was unsupportable for the reasons supplied by that agency. But when the case left this Court, the problem whether Federal's management should be treated equally with other preferred stock-holders still lacked a final and complete answer. It was clear that the Commission could not give a negative answer by resort to prior judicial declarations. And it was also clear that the Commission was not bound by settled judicial precedents in a situation of this nature. Still unsettled, however, was the answer the Commission might give were it to bring to bear on the facts the proper administrative and statutory considerations, a function which belongs exclusively to the Commission in the first instance. The administrative process had taken an erroneous rather than a final turn. Hence we carefully refrained from expressing any views as to the propriety of an order rooted in the proper and relevant considerations.

When the case was directed to be remanded to the Commission for such further proceedings as might be appropriate, it was with the thought that the Commission would give full effect to its duties in harmony with the views we had expressed. This obviously meant something more than the entry of a perfunctory order giving parity treatment to the management holdings of preferred stock. . . . After the remand was made, therefore, the Commission was bound to deal with the problem afresh, performing the function delegated to it by Congress. It was again charged with the duty of measuring the proposed treatment of the management's preferred stock holdings by relevant and proper standards. Only in that way could the legislative policies embodied in the Act be effectuated.

The absence of a general rule or regulation governing management trading during reorganization did not affect the Commission's duties in relation to the particular proposal before it. The Commission was asked to grant or deny effectiveness to a proposed amendment to Federal's reorganization plan whereby the management would be accorded parity treatment on its holdings. It could do that only in the form of an order, entered after a due consideration of the particular facts in light of the relevant and proper standards. That was true regardless of whether those standards previously had been spelled out in a general rule or regulation. Indeed, if the Commission rightly felt that the proposed amendment was inconsistent with those standards, an order giving effect to the amendment merely because there was no general rule or regulation covering the matter would be unjustified.

It is true that our prior decision explicitly recognized the possibility that the Commission might have promulgated a general rule dealing with this problem under its statutory rule-making powers, in which case the issue for our consideration would have been entirely different from that which did confront us. But we did not mean to imply thereby that the failure of the Commission to anticipate this problem and to promulgate a general rule withdrew all power from that agency to perform its statutory duty in this case. To hold that the Commission had no alternative in this proceeding but to approve the proposed transaction, while formulating any general rules it might desire for use in future cases of this nature, would be to stultify the administrative process. That we refuse to do.

Since the Commission, unlike a court, does have the ability to make new law prospectively through the exercise of its rule-making powers, it has less reason to rely upon *ad hoc* adjudication to formulate new standards of conduct within the framework of the Holding Company Act. The function of filling in the interstices of the Act should be performed, as much as possible, through this quasi-legislative promulgation of rules to be applied in the future. But any rigid requirement to that effect would make the administrative process inflexible and incapable of dealing with many of the specialized problems which arise. Not every principle essential to the effective administration of a statute can or should be cast immediately into the mold of a general rule. Some principles must await their own development, while others must be adjusted to meet particular, unforeseeable situations. In performing its important functions in these respects, therefore, an administrative agency must be equipped to act either by general rule or by individual order. To insist upon one form of action to the exclusion of the other is to exalt form over necessity.

In other words, problems may arise in a case which the administrative agency could not reasonably foresee, problems which must be solved despite the absence of a relevant general rule. Or the agency may not have had sufficient experience with a particular problem to warrant rigidifying its tentative judgment into a hard and fast rule. Or the problem may be so specialized and varying in nature as to be impossible of capture within the boundaries of a general rule. In those situations, the agency must retain power to deal with the problems on a case-to-case basis if the administrative process is to be effective. There is thus a very definite place for the case-by-case evolution of statutory standards. And the choice made between proceeding by general rule or by individual, *ad hoc* litigation is one that lies primarily in the informed discretion of the administrative agency.

Hence we refuse to say that the Commission, which had not previously been confronted with the problem of management trading during reorganization, was forbidden from utilizing this particular proceeding for announcing and applying a new standard of conduct. That such action might have a retroactive effect was not necessarily fatal to its validity. Every case of first impression has a retroactive effect, whether the new principle is announced by a court or by an administrative agency. But such retroactivity must be balanced against the mischief of producing a result which is contrary to a statutory design or to legal and equitable principles. If that mischief is greater than the ill effect of the retroactive application of a new standard, it is not the type of retroactivity which is condemned by law.

And so in this case, the fact that the Commission's order might retroactively prevent Federal's management from securing the profits and control which were the objects of the preferred stock purchases may well be outweighed by the dangers inherent in such purchases from the statutory standpoint. If that is true, the argument of retroactivity becomes nothing more than a claim that the Commission lacks power to enforce the standards of the Act in this proceeding. Such a claim deserves rejection.

[The Court then turned to the merits of the SEC's application of the statute, which required all organizations to be "fair and equitable to the persons affected" thereby. The Court noted that "the Commission avoided placing its sole reliance on inapplicable judicial precedents. Rather it has derived its conclusions from the particular facts in the case, its general experience in reorganization matters and its informed view of statutory requirements." The Court upheld the SEC's application of the statute to the facts of the *Chenery* reorganization.]

MR. JUSTICE JACKSON, dissenting.

The Court by this present decision sustains the identical administrative order which only recently it held invalid. As the Court correctly notes, the Commission has only "recast its rationale and reached the same result." There being no change in the order, no additional evidence in the record and no amendment of relevant legislation, it is clear that there has been a shift in attitude between that of the controlling membership of the Court when the case was first here and that of those who have the power of decision on this second review.

I feel constrained to disagree with the reasoning offered to rationalize this shift. It makes judicial review of administrative orders a hopeless formality for the litigant, even where granted to him by Congress. It reduces the judicial process in such cases to a mere feint. While the opinion does not have the adherence of a majority of the full Court, if its pronouncements should become governing principles they would, in practice, put most administrative orders over and above the law. . . .

The reversal of the position of this Court is due to a fundamental change in prevailing philosophy. The basic assumption of the earlier opinion as therein stated was, "*But before transactions otherwise legal can be outlawed or denied their usual business consequences, they must fall under the ban of some standards of conduct prescribed by an agency of government authorized to prescribe such standards.*" The basic assumption of the present opinion is stated thus: "*The absence of a general rule or regulation governing management trading during reorganization did not affect the Commission's duties in relation to the particular proposal before it.*" This puts in juxtaposition the two conflicting philosophies which produce opposite results in the same case and on the same facts. The difference between the first and the latest decision of the Court is thus simply the difference between holding that administrative orders must have a basis in law and a holding that absence of a legal basis is no ground on which courts may annul them.

As there admittedly is no law or regulation to support this order we peruse the Court's opinion diligently to find on what grounds it is now held that the Court of Appeals, on pain of being reversed for error, was required to stamp this order with its approval. We find but one. That is the principle of judicial deference to administrative experience. That argument is five times stressed in as many different contexts, and I quote just enough to identify the instances: "The Commission," it says, "has drawn heavily upon its accumulated experience in dealing with utility reorganizations." "Rather it has derived its conclusions from the particular facts in the case, its general experience in reorganization matters and its informed view of statutory requirements." "Drawing upon its experience, the Commission indicated . . . ," etc., ". . . the Commission has made a thorough examination of the problem, utilizing statutory standards and its own accumulated experience with reorganization matters." And finally, of the order the Court says, "It is the product of administrative experience," etc.

What are we to make of this reiterated deference to "administrative experience" when in another context the Court says, "Hence we refuse to say that the Commission, *which had not previously been confronted with the problem of management trading during reorganization*, was forbidden from utilizing this particular proceeding for announcing and applying a *new standard of conduct.*" (Emphasis supplied.)

The Court's reasoning adds up to this: The Commission must be sustained because of its accumulated experience in solving a problem with which it had never before been confronted! . . .

Background of *NLRB v. Bell Aerospace Co.*

Under the National Labor Relations Act, when a union petitions for an election, the Board must determine the appropriate "bargaining unit," which is the particular group of employees who would participate in the election and, in the case of an affirmative vote, be represented by the union. In the following case, a union had petitioned the NLRB for a representation election to determine whether it could represent Bell Aerospace buyers (the "bargaining unit") in collective bargaining. The dispute relevant here involved the question of whether the Bell Aerospace buyers fell within the definition of "managerial employee." As the Supreme Court held in the first part of the decision below (not excerpted here), "managerial employees" do not have the right to seek union representation under the NLRA. That left the question of whether the Board could determine that some buyers are not "managerial employees." The Court of Appeals held that the Board could hold that some buyers are not "managerial employees," but that a long line of the Board's own decisions to the contrary meant that the Board would have to make this change of position in rulemaking, rather than through adjudication. In the decision below, the Supreme Court disagreed.

NLRB v. Bell Aerospace Co.

416 U.S. 267 (1974)

MR. JUSTICE POWELL delivered the opinion of the Court.

This case presents two questions: first, whether the National Labor Relations Board properly determined that all "managerial employees," except those whose participation in a labor organization would create a conflict of interest with their job responsibilities, are covered by the National Labor Relations Act; and second, whether the Board must proceed by rulemaking rather than by adjudication in determining whether certain buyers are "managerial employees." We answer both questions in the negative.

. . . [T]he present question is whether on remand the Board must invoke its rulemaking procedures if it determines, in light of our opinion, that these buyers are not "managerial employees" under the Act. The Court of Appeals thought that rulemaking was required because *any* Board finding that the company's buyers are not "managerial" would be contrary to its prior decisions and would presumably be in the nature of a general rule designed "to fit all cases at all times."

A similar issue was presented to this Court in its second decision in *SEC v. Chenery Corp.* (*Chenery II*) [1947]. There, the respondent corporation argued that in an adjudicative proceeding the Commission could not apply a general standard that it had formulated for the first time in that proceeding. Rather, the Commission was required to resort instead to its rulemaking procedures if it desired to promulgate a new standard that would govern future conduct. In rejecting this contention, the Court first noted that the Commission had a statutory duty to decide the issue at hand in light of the proper standards and that this duty remained "regardless of whether those standards previously had been spelled out in a general rule or regulations." The Court continued:

> "The function of filling in the interstices of the [Securities] Act should be performed, as much as possible, through this quasi-legislative promulgation of rules to be applied in the future. But any rigid requirement to that effect would make the administrative process inflexible and incapable of dealing with many of the specialized problems which arise. . . ."

The Court concluded that "the choice made between proceeding by general rule or by individual, *ad hoc* litigation is one that lies primarily in the informed discretion of the administrative agency."

And in *NLRB v. Wyman-Gordon Co.* [1969], the Court upheld a Board order enforcing an election list requirement first promulgated in an earlier adjudicative proceeding in *Excelsior Underwear Inc.* The plurality opinion of MR. JUSTICE FORTAS, joined by THE CHIEF JUSTICE, MR. JUSTICE STEWART, and MR. JUSTICE WHITE, recognized that "[a]djudicated cases may and do . . . serve as vehicles for the formulation of agency policies, which are applied and announced therein," and that such cases "generally provide a guide to action that the agency may be expected to take in future cases." The concurring opinion of MR. JUSTICE BLACK, joined by MR. JUSTICE BRENNAN and MR. JUSTICE MARSHALL, also noted that the Board had both adjudicative and rulemaking powers and that the choice between the two was "within its informed discretion."

The views expressed in *Chenery II* and *Wyman-Gordon* make plain that the Board is not precluded from announcing new principles in an adjudicative proceeding and that the choice between rulemaking and adjudication lies in the first instance within the Board's discretion. Although there may be situations where the Board's reliance on adjudication would amount to an abuse of discretion or a violation of the Act, nothing in the present case would justify such a conclusion. Indeed, there is ample indication that adjudication is especially appropriate in the instant context. As the Court of Appeals noted, "[t]here must be tens of thousands of manufacturing, wholesale and retail units which employ buyers, and hundreds of thousands of the latter." Moreover, duties of buyers vary widely depending on the company or industry. It is doubtful whether any generalized standard could be framed which would have more than marginal utility. The Board thus has reason to proceed with caution, developing its standards in a case-by-case manner with attention to the specific character of the buyers' authority and duties in each company. The Board's judgment that adjudication best serves this purpose is entitled to great weight.

The possible reliance of industry on the Board's past decisions with respect to buyers does not require a different result. It has not been shown that the adverse consequences ensuing from such reliance are so substantial that the Board should be precluded from reconsidering the issue in an adjudicative proceeding. Furthermore, this is not a case in which some new liability is sought to be imposed on individuals for past actions which were taken in good-faith reliance on Board pronouncements. Nor are fines or damages involved here. In any event, concern about such consequences is largely speculative, for the Board has not yet finally determined whether these buyers are 'managerial.'

It is true, of course, that rulemaking would provide the Board with a forum for soliciting the informed views of those affected in industry and labor before embarking on a new course. But surely the Board has discretion to decide that the adjudicative procedures in this case may also produce the relevant information necessary to mature and fair consideration of the issues. Those most immediately affected, the buyers and the company in the particular case, are accorded a full opportunity to be heard before the Board makes its determination.

Background of *Ford Motor Company v. FTC*

By contrast to the two previous decisions, the Ninth Circuit in *Ford Motor Company* held that the FTC could not adopt a new policy in the particular adjudication. Here, the agency had initiated enforcement adjudications against all of the major actors in the automobile industry, settling with all except the Francis Ford dealership. The agency had also initiated but had not yet concluded a rulemaking proceeding that would address essentially the same issues. Why should the outcome here differ from either *Chenery II* or *Bell Aerospace*?

Ford Motor Company v. FTC

673 F.2d 1008 (9th Cir. 1981)

GOODWIN, CIRCUIT JUDGE.

Francis Ford, Inc. petitions this court to review an F.T.C. order finding it in violation of § 5 of the F.T.C. Act, (unfair trade practices). We have reviewed the petition, and set aside the order.

Francis Ford, Inc. is an Oregon automobile dealership. Its practice in repossessing cars has been to credit the debtor for the wholesale value of the car, charge him for indirect expenses (*i.e.*, overhead and lost profits) as well as direct expenses (*i.e.*, refurbishing) associated with repossession and resale, and sell the repossessed vehicle at retail keeping the "surplus." In doing so, Francis Ford claims it is doing what is commonly done throughout its industry.

The F.T.C. does not approve of the described practice. Nor does it approve of a number of other credit practices now commonly in use in a wide variety of industries. See its investigations of the credit business, and its recent attempted rulemaking. In re Proposed Trade Regulation Rule: Credit Practices, 40 Fed.Reg. 16,347 (1975).

In order to attack Francis Ford's practice, the F.T.C. began in 1976 an adjudicatory action against Ford Motor Co., Ford Credit Co., and Francis Ford, Inc. The commission alleged that the respondents had violated § 5 of the F.T.C. Act by failing to give defaulting customers more than wholesale value for their repossessed cars, and by improperly charging them with indirect expenses such as overhead and lost profits. Parallel proceedings were commenced against Chrysler Corp. and General Motors, their finance subsidiaries, and two dealers. [All such parties other than Francis Ford settled with the FTC. The FTC ultimately held that Francis Ford's practices violated Sec. 5 of the FTC Act and ordered Francis Ford to cease and desist its credit repossession credit practices and adopt certain new ones.]

The narrow issue presented here is whether the F.T.C. should have proceeded by rulemaking in this case rather than by adjudication. The Supreme Court has said that an administrative agency, such as the F.T.C., "is not precluded from announcing new principles in the adjudicative proceeding and that the choice between rulemaking and adjudication lies in the first instance within the [agency's] discretion." *NLRB v. Bell Aerospace Co.*, 416 U.S. 267 (1974). *See also, Securities Comm'n v. Chenery Corp.*, 332 U.S. 194 (1947). But like all grants of discretion, "there may be situations where the [agency's] reliance on adjudication would amount to an abuse of discretion. . . ." *Bell Aerospace Co.*, 416 U.S. at 294, 94 S. Ct. at 1771. The problem is one of drawing the line. On that score the Supreme Court has avoided black-letter rules. ("[i]t is doubtful whether any generalized standard could be framed which would have more than marginal utility. . . .") Lower courts have been left, therefore, with the task of dealing with the problem on a case-by-case basis.

The Ninth Circuit recently made such an attempt in *Patel v. Immigration & Naturalization Serv.*, 638 F.2d 1199 (9th Cir. 1980). In *Patel*, the Immigration and Naturalization Service, by an administrative adjudication, added a requirement to a regulation governing permanent immigration to this country. The court disallowed the requirement because the requirement changed past practices through the "prospective pronouncement of a broad, generally applicable requirement, amount[ing] to 'an agency statement of general or particular applicability and future effect.'" In the court's view, the rule of law should have been established by rulemaking because, unlike *Bell Aerospace, supra,* the case before it called for a general standard, not a case-by-case determination. *Patel* cited Professor Davis for the view that courts should require agencies to use rulemaking procedures when the agency retroactively adopts new law or where the parties have relied on the precedents. 2 Davis, Administrative Law Treatise, §7:25 at 124 (1979). The thrust of the *Patel* holding, therefore, is that agencies can proceed by adjudication to enforce discrete violations of existing laws where the effective scope of the rule's impact will be relatively small; but an agency must proceed by rulemaking if it seeks to change the law and establish rules of widespread application.

In the present case, the F.T.C., by its order, has established a rule that would require a secured creditor to credit the debtor with the "best possible" value of the repossessed vehicle, and forbid the creditor from charging the debtor with overhead and lost profits. . . Framed according to *Patel,* the precise issue therefore is whether this adjudication changes existing law, and has widespread application. It does, and the matter should be addressed by rulemaking.

The F.T.C. admits that industry practice has been to do what Francis Ford does—credit the debtor with the wholesale value and charge the debtor for indirect expenses. But the F.T.C. contends that Francis Ford's particular practice violates state law; that the violation will not be reached by the proposed trade rule on credit practices; and that this adjudication will have only local application. The arguments are not persuasive. . . .

The F.T.C. could have formulated its position on . . . the credit practices of car dealerships in its proposed trade rule on credit practices. It did not do so. The pending rulemaking proceeding and this adjudication seek to remedy, more or less, the same credit practices. Although the former is directed against the practices, inter alia, of car dealers in their accounting of deficiencies, and the latter is directed against a car dealer by reason of his practices in failing to account for surpluses, both matters are covered by [a U.C.C. provision relied upon by the FTC]. If the rule for deficiencies is thought by the F.T.C. to be "appropriately addressed by rulemaking," it should also address the problem of accounting for surpluses by a rulemaking proceeding, and not by adjudication.

Ultimately, however, we are persuaded to set aside this order because the rule of the case made below will have general application. It will not apply just to Francis Ford. Credit practices similar to those of Francis Ford are widespread in the car dealership industry; and the U.C.C. section the F.T.C. wishes us to interpret exists in 49 states. The F.T.C. is aware of this. It has already appended a "Synopsis of Determination" to the order, apparently for the purpose of advising other automobile dealerships of the results of this adjudication. To allow the order to stand as presently written would do far more than remedy a discrete violation of a singular Oregon law as the F.T.C. contends; it would create a national interpretation of [the U.C.C. provision] and in effect enact the precise rule the F.T.C. has proposed, but not yet promulgated.

Under these circumstances, the F.T.C. has exceeded its authority by proceeding to create new law by adjudication rather than by rulemaking.

The order is vacated.

Notes

1. Why, as matter of policy, choose rulemaking over adjudication? Over the decades, numerous courts and commentators have observed that intertwined advantages of both effectiveness and fairness support agency use of rulemaking to make policy. Some notable effectiveness advantages include:

- Enabling better planning and allocation of constrained agency resources;
- Improving information gathering by allowing all interested persons to participate rather than just parties to a case;
- Avoiding the policy distortion that can occur in adjudications focused on determining adjudicative facts and individual rights based on them;
- Generating rules that are clearer and more accessible than those developed through case-by-case adjudication; and
- Generating legislative rules that carry the full force of law.

Overlapping fairness advantages include:

- Providing clearer and better notice to regulated parties of their obligations;
- Enhancing legitimacy by allowing all interested persons, rather than just parties to a case, to participate in the development of policies that affect them;
- Insofar as rules are generally prospective, avoiding the fairness problems associated with retroactive application of interpretations of law developed in adjudications;

- Avoiding the distorting effect that efforts to make general policy in an adjudication may have on individual rights;

- As rulemaking, unlike adjudication, produces rules that apply with equal legal force to everyone, avoiding the unfairness of selective application of the law.

See, e.g., David Shapiro, *The Choice of Rulemaking or Adjudication in the Development of Administrative Policy,* 78 Harv. L. Rev. 921 (1965).

2. Why, as a matter of policy, choose adjudication over rulemaking? Notwithstanding the long list you just read of nice things about rulemaking, *Chenery II* identified several factors that might lead an agency, such as the SEC, to choose adjudication to set policy. Justice Murphy explained:

> [P]roblems may arise in a case which the administrative agency could not reasonably foresee, problems which must be solved despite the absence of a relevant general rule. Or the agency may not have had sufficient experience with a particular problem to warrant rigidifying its tentative judgment into a hard and fast rule. Or the problem may be so specialized and varying in nature as to be impossible of capture within the boundaries of a general rule. In those situations, the agency must retain power to deal with the problems on a case-to-case basis if the administrative process is to be effective.

SEC v. Chenery Corp., 332 U.S. 194, 202–03 (1947).

3. The "mindsets" of rulemaking and adjudication. Rulemaking and adjudication generate different types of "records" for decision, and they also encourage decision-makers to react to these records in different ways. As Melvin Eisenberg explains, the adjudicative decisionmaker, particularly at common law, "is generally bound by the parties' proofs, . . . cannot rely either on his own prior knowledge or on independent inquiry," and is constrained by the adjudicative "norm of strong responsiveness" to decide the adjudication, including any policy issues, based upon the specific facts and narrow concerns of the particular parties. Where an adjudicator seeks to fashion a general policy, "the norm of strong responsiveness may conflict with the adjudicator's rulemaking function." Eisenberg, *Participation, Responsiveness, and the Consultative Process: An Essay for Lon Fuller,* 92 Harv. L. Rev. 410, 412–13 (1978). By contrast, the decisionmaker in a rulemaking, while still "obliged to attend to [the] arguments and proofs" of the participants, may gather additional information, and consider arguments and rules other than those asserted by the participants." *Id.* at 414. Unconstrained by the facts and circumstances of particular individuals, the rulemaker responds "to the more diffuse norm of serving the public's needs that is a general aspiration of democratic institutions." *Id.* at 431. Should this difference in "mindset" carry implications for the scope of agencies' discretion to choose between adjudication and rulemaking to fashion policy?

4. What legal constraints govern the choice between rulemaking and adjudication? At one point in *Chenery II,* the majority seems to signal a preference for rulemaking as opposed to adjudication. The Court observed:

> Since the Commission, unlike a court, does have the ability to make new law prospectively through the exercise of its rule-making powers, it has less reason to rely upon ad hoc adjudication to formulate new standards of conduct within the framework of the Holding Company Act. The function of filling in the interstices of the Act should be performed, as much as possible, through this quasi-legislative promulgation of rules to be applied in the future.

Chenery II, 332 U.S. at 202. The Court then proceeded, however, to rehearse various reasons why an agency might need to proceed via adjudication rather than rule-making. The Court explained:

> Not every principle essential to the effective administration of a statute can or should be cast immediately into the mold of a general rule. Some principles must await their own development, while others must be adjusted to meet particular, unforeseeable situations. In performing its important functions in these respects, therefore, an administrative agency must be equipped to act either by general rule or by individual order. To insist upon one form of action to the exclusion of the other is to exalt form over necessity.

Id. The Court therefore concluded, "the choice made between proceeding by general rule or by individual, ad hoc litigation is one that lies primarily in the informed discretion of the administrative agency." *Id.* at 203.

Later cases, such as *Bell Aerospace,* have emphasized the breadth of this agency discretion to choose between rulemaking and adjudication. As a result, in general, it is extremely difficult to persuade a reviewing court that an agency has abused its discretion by choosing adjudication when it should have instead used rulemaking. One important reason for this judicial hesitancy is that courts are understandably very reluctant to interfere with how agencies choose to deploy their constrained resources to carry out their statutory missions.

Still, as indicated by *Ford Motor Company v. FTC*, courts have resisted ceding absolute discretion to agencies to make this choice. Analyzing the relevant lower court decisions, William Araiza has identified:

> three basic themes that courts use to reject agency decisions to proceed by adjudication: a concern about the "functional" appropriateness of agency adjudication when functionally the matter seems better suited for treatment by rulemaking; a concern about the fairness of using an adjudication to establish a new agency policy when adjudicative results normally are applied retroactively; and a concern about the agency acting inconsistently with its own initial decision to use the rulemaking process.

William D. Araiza, *Agency Adjudication, the Importance of Facts, and the Limitations of Labels*, 57 Wash. & Lee L. Rev. 351, 355 (2000). More recently, Professor Araiza characterized *Ford Motor Company v. FTC* as "ultimately incorrect . . . a misfire," William D. Araiza, *Limits on Agency Discretion to Choose Between Rule-making and Adjudication: Reconsidering* Patel v. INS and Ford Motor Co. v. FTC, 58 ADMIN L. REV. 899, 901, 916 (2006), but he praised *Patel v. Immigration & Naturalization Services*, on which *Ford Motor Company* relied, as adopting a reasonable "anti-circumvention principle." *Id.* at 907.

5. Some states take greater control. Not all states courts are so willing to give agencies the freedom to choose between rulemaking and adjudication that *Chenery II* gave federal agencies. For instance, the Oregon Supreme Court concluded that, even though the particular enabling act at issue did not expressly require rulemaking, its broad and vague statutory standards indicated a legislative intent that the agency undertake its policymaking through rules rather than ad hoc orders. *Megdal v. Oregon State Bd. of Dental Exmrs.*, 605 P.2d 273 (1980).

6. Retroactive application of adjudications. We generally expect and accept that judicial pronouncements in cases of first impression have retroactive effect. But what about the "quasi-judicial" pronouncements that agencies produce via adjudication? Recall that the Chenery interests developed a scheme to preserve their control of a utility company and that the SEC rejected this scheme on the ground that it was not "fair and equitable" within the meaning of the Public Utility Holding Company Act of 1935. The *Chenery II* majority, over Justice Jackson's outraged dissent, explained that the propriety of applying the SEC's decision retroactively depended on a balancing test:

> That such action might have a retroactive effect was not necessarily fatal to its validity. Every case of first impression has a retroactive effect, whether the new principle is announced by a court or by an administrative agency. But such retroactivity must be balanced against the mischief of producing a result which is contrary to a statutory design or to legal and equitable principles. If that mischief is greater than the ill effect of the retroactive application of a new standard, it is not the type of retroactivity which is condemned by law. *See Addison v. Holly Hill Co.*, 322 U.S. 607, 620.

> And so in this case, the fact that the Commission's order might retroactively prevent Federal's management from securing the profits and control which were the objects of the preferred stock purchases may well be outweighed by the dangers inherent in such purchases from the statutory standpoint. If that is true, the argument of retroactivity becomes nothing more than a claim that the Commission lacks power to enforce the standards of the Act in this proceeding. Such a claim deserves rejection.

332 U.S. at 203-04.

Later case law has elaborated on the factors that courts should consider when applying *Chenery II*'s balancing test. The D.C. Circuit's decision in *Retail, Wholesale & Department Store Union v. NLRB*, 466 F.2d 380 (D.C. Cir. 1972), provides one of the most prominent discussions of these factors. That case held that a court determining whether to allow retroactive application of a "rule" announced in an administrative adjudication should consider:

> (1) whether the particular case is one of first impression, (2) whether the new rule represents an abrupt departure from well established practice or merely attempts to fill a void in an unsettled area of law, (3) the extent to which the party against whom the new rule is applied relied on the former rule, (4) the degree of the burden which a retroactive order imposes on a party, and (5) the statutory interest in applying a new rule despite the reliance of a party on the old standard.

Id. at 390. Later, in *Clark-Cowlitz Joint Operating Agency v. FERC*, 826 F.2d 1074 (D.C. Cir. 1987) (en banc), the D.C. Circuit both approved this non-exhaustive list but also added that it "boil[s] down . . . to a question of concerns grounded in notions of equity and fairness." *Id.* at 1082 n.6. Where an agency adjudication does not "substitut[e] . . . new law for old law that was reasonably clear" but instead merely contains "new applications of existing law, clarifications, and additions," the D.C. Circuit has instructed that agency adjudications are presumptively retroactive absent a showing of "manifest injustice." *Verizon Tel. Cos. v. FCC*, 269 F.3d 1098, 1109 (D.C. Cir. 2001).

Other principles may help a party avoid being sandbagged too brutally by retroactive application of new principles stated in administrative adjudications. Where deprivations of life, liberty, or property are in play, due process requires that a party have "fair notice of conduct that is forbidden or required." *FCC v. Fox Television Stations, Inc.*, 567 U.S. 239, 253 (2012) (*Fox II*). Also, as we will discuss further in Chapter 5, a reviewing court will reject an agency's policy change as arbitrary unless the agency offers a suitably reasonable explanation for the change. *FCC v. Fox Television Stations, Inc.*, 556 U.S. 502 (2009) (*Fox I*).

B. The Range of Procedural Forms

To this point, the materials in this chapter enable you to distinguish between rulemaking and adjudication. They illustrate what agencies can accomplish through each of those types of proceedings, and they address both the policy concerns and the legal constraints that bear on the choice of rulemaking or adjudication. We have yet to address procedures in detail, but you have seen the results of relatively formal, trial-like proceedings in *SEC v. Chenery Corp.* and *NLRB v. Bell Aerospace*, for example. You have also seen in *Storer Broadcasting* the results of what we generally call "informal rulemaking," a process involving public notice and submission of written comments. These trial-like and notice-and-comment procedures represent two points on a spectrum of procedural formality. At one end of that spectrum are trial-like procedures, which may be required (or chosen by the agency) for either adjudication or rulemaking. At the other end are very informal actions such as an agency head offering advice by telephone or an agency head writing a letter to communicate the agency's interpretation of a statute or regulation.

From Criminal Law and Civil Procedure, you are used to the proposition that decisionmakers must follow certain procedures. In the next two chapters, we will examine in detail the procedural requirements that govern rulemaking and adjudication. Here, we briefly consider how an agency should choose the form of process from the full range of the procedural spectrum.

———

Lesson 2B. Ralph received a memo from the Grants Division asking for advice as to procedures for making development grants under WTCA § 3. He asks Ben to prepare a draft of the procedures for development grants.

As part of the process, the agency will have to establish some sort of criteria to govern the grant award decisions and then review grant applications based upon those criteria to determine who gets the money and who does not. Most of the proposals will involve highly technical and specialized scientific research (e.g., the agency expects to receive many proposals to research genetic modification of grapes to enhance flavor, alcohol production, or disease resistance). Success in applying for grant money will depend, of course, on scientific merit, but some in the Division contend that the WTC should also consider other issues such as race, gender, and regional diversity, and support of less well-established research units. The process might also build in protection from political influence. The Division employs a number of scientists and, as is the custom in the sciences, they wish to constitute "juries" of outside scientists to evaluate the grant applications.

How would you advise Ben to design procedures for selecting the winning grantees? For instance, what materials would you have applicants submit? Who would judge the merit of the applications in the first instance? Should those decisionmakers have to explain their decisions to applicants — including the unsuccessful ones? Should applicants have a right to some sort of hearing? To an appeal? To counsel? How would you decide on the right amount and type of process?

Background to Two Excerpts

The following materials suggest the range, potential benefits, and drawbacks of possible procedural approaches, from very informal to a full-blown, trial-type hearing. William Andersen's essay introduces the use of informal communications, such as letters, staff manuals, and even oral responses to questions, none of which involves any sort of prior process or opportunity to be heard. Such informal guidance, which agencies issue in immense amounts, plays a vital role in guiding agency personnel and explaining agency policy and legal interpretations to the regulated community and regulatory beneficiaries. The excerpt from Judge Henry Friendly's article addresses the "due process explosion" that had been symbolized and in part triggered by the Supreme Court's decision in *Goldberg v. Kelly* five years earlier. With hearings now required in a wider range of situations, Judge Friendly urged "experimentation" in determining which procedures to choose, from the broad spectrum from a full trial to no process at all.

William R. Andersen, *Informal Agency Advice— Graphing the Critical Analysis**

54 ADMIN L. REV. 595, 609 (2002)

Informal advice and guidance is given by administrative agencies in quantities difficult to imagine. The magnitude of this material dwarfs statutes and agency legislative regulations. The forms of advice and guidance are numerous, but include memos, bulletins, staff manuals, letters, and oral responses to questions. This magnitude suggests the importance of informal advice and guidance in the day-to-day operation of the administrative process. In turn, it cautions that any legal principles we adopt to regulate the process must not make giving advice difficult, time-consuming, or expensive.

What explains the magnitude and ubiquity of informal advice and guidance? The benefits to the agency are real. Advice can encourage regulated parties to comply with agency preferences. Guidance to agency staff can enhance uniformity in enforcement. Informal advice can test reactions to new ideas before substantial time is invested in them. And informal advice can be very flexible—easy and quick to change in response to new conditions or new agency needs and free of cost/benefit and other regulatory requirements increasingly imposed on rulemaking.

Similarly, informal advice is of enormous value to the regulated parties. With good advice they know better how to plan their own affairs in light of regulatory requirements. The alternative—having "secret law" regularly applied but unknowable—has never been thought wise in a mature legal system. Moreover, leaving substantive rules in relatively general form and supplemented by more particular informal advice seems consistent with the general move from rules to standards. Finally, if the advice is formulated after consultation with regulated parties (as it often is), inputs are expanded, and opportunities for adjustment and negotiation may be increased.

Informal advice and guidance are also of value to the various groups that oversee the working of the administrative process, including the Congress, the President, the press, and the public. Oversight of these bodies will be more effective if greater knowledge of the details of agency practice is available.

However, informal agency advice comes at a price. Most importantly to our concerns here, informal agency action can result in the imposition of important new requirements on regulated parties without the benefit of the notice-and-comment procedure usually required by the Administrative Procedure Act (APA) for adoption of major policies. In addition, if agencies remain free to change their advice quickly, important investment-backed expectations may be disappointed.

Henry Friendly, *Some Kind of Hearing*

123 U. Pa. L. Rev. 1267, 1268–73, 1316 (1975)*

[W]e have witnessed a due process explosion in which the Court has carried the hearing requirement from one new area of government action to another, an explosion which gives rise to many questions of major importance to our society. Should the executive be placed in a position where it can take no action affecting a citizen without a hearing? When a hearing is required, what kind of hearing must it be? Specifically, how closely must it conform to the judicial model?

For a long time we have labored under the illusion that the two latter questions could be answered rather easily. We needed only to determine whether the issue was one of adjudicative or of legislative fact. If the former, a full trial-type hearing was demanded; if the latter, something substantially less would do. Although this approach is useful in many circumstances, it is only an approach. Moreover, it suffers from several significant defects. For one thing it does not indicate very accurately how to determine which issues are adjudicative and which are legislative. For another, with the vast increase in the number and types of hearings required in all areas in which the government and the individual interact, common sense dictates that we must do with less than full trial-type hearings even on what are clearly adjudicative issues. By contrast, more than mere notice and comment procedures may sometimes be desirable and even constitutionally necessary on subjects that conceptually would be regarded as rulemaking.

Although some may regret the loss of the old simplicity, its passing is all to the good. In an early opinion Mr. Justice Frankfurter, who had been a great administrative law teacher, explained that differences in the origin and function of administrative agencies "preclude wholesale transplantation of the rules of procedure, trial, and review which have evolved from the history and experience of courts." Despite this wise observation, the tendency to judicialize administrative procedures has grown apace in the United States. English judges and scholars consider that we have simply gone mad in this respect. Lord Diplock, who headed the English administrative law "team" in a 1969 exchange of views in which I participated, is reported to have said that the main value of the enterprise from the English standpoint had been to observe the horrible American examples of over-judicialization of administrative procedures and undue extension of judicial review, and to learn not to do likewise. The matter, however, is not that clear. Professor Davis was undoubtedly right when he observed in 1970, "The best answer to the overall question of whether we want more judicialization or less is probably that we need more in some contexts and less in other contexts."

A brief survey of the historical development of the hearing requirement, both statutory and constitutional, may be useful before engaging in analysis of that requirement's content.

The term "hearing," like "jurisdiction," is "a verbal coat of too many colors." Professor Davis has defined it as "any oral proceeding before a tribunal." Broad as that definition is, it may not be broad enough. Although the term "hearing" has an oral connotation, I see no reason why in some circumstances a "hearing" may not be had on written materials only. In addition the term "tribunal" is hardly apt to convey the notion that hearing requirements may be applied to bodies as diverse as an administrative law judge on the one hand or a city council on the other. The purpose of the hearing may range from the determination of a specific past event—did a government employee steal $50?—to an endeavor to ascertain community feeling about a proposed change in zoning or to determine the efficacy of a new drug.

The first great federal regulatory statute, the Interstate Commerce Act of 1887, made sparing use of the term "hearing." The general charter of the Commission, section 15, used the language, "if in any case in which an investigation shall be made by said Commission it shall be made to appear to the satisfaction of the Commission, either by the testimony of witnesses or other evidence." However, in proceedings in the circuit courts with respect to violations of the Act or refusals to obey an order of the Commission under section 15, the report of the Commission was regarded as merely prima facie evidence of the facts, which might be rebutted by the defendant. It was only in 1906, when the Hepburn Act greatly increased the powers of the Commission, that section 15 was altered to require a "full hearing," apparently in line with what had become Commission practice. Shortly thereafter, Mr. Justice Lamar, speaking for the Supreme Court in the well-known *Louisville & Nashville* case, said that this requirement, even in a proceeding relating to future rates,

> conferred the privilege of introducing testimony, and at the same time imposed the duty of deciding in accordance with the facts proved. . . . All parties must be fully apprised of the evidence submitted or to be considered, and must be given opportunity to cross-examine witnesses, to inspect documents and to offer evidence in explanation or rebuttal.

Scores of later federal statutes adopted the "hearing" language of the Hepburn Act, sometimes retaining the adjective "full," sometimes not. So far as action under such statutes was concerned, it was immaterial for many years whether Mr. Justice Lamar and his colleagues were simply construing a statute or were acting under the force of the Constitution as well.

Meanwhile, federal agencies became busily engaged in rulemaking, and until enactment of the Administrative Procedure Act (APA) in 1946, they generally were permitted to do this in whatever manner they chose. Even with the passage of the APA, only notice and comment procedures that fell far short of those described by Mr. Justice Lamar were prescribed for most agency rule-making. Furthermore, as the Supreme Court held in a subsequent case a rule made in compliance with these limited procedures could justify dismissal, without hearing of an application that would otherwise have required a "full hearing." . . .

On the other hand, the number of nonregulatory areas in which the Court has insisted on hearings has mushroomed; indeed, we have witnessed a greater expansion of procedural due process in the last five years than in the entire period since ratification of the Constitution.

. . . In the mass justice area the Supreme Court has yielded too readily to the notions that the adversary system is the only appropriate model and that there is only one acceptable solution to any problem, and consequently has been too prone to indulge in constitutional codification. There is need for experimentation, particularly for the use of the investigative model, for empirical studies, and for avoiding absolutes. . . .

Notes

1. What process should be used to establish grant criteria? Ben's project of designing a system for making grants will require establishing substantive standards for awards—i.e., the agency will need to decide what it is looking for in grant applications. We will learn more about the rulemaking procedures that an agency would actually need to use for this purpose in Chapter 3. But, for now, what procedures might you design? Whom should the agency consult? Should the agency rely on its own expertise and dispense with seeking outside input? If the agency decides to seek outside input, what would be a sensible means of doing so? Should it run some sort of "trial" to determine substantive standards for grants?

2. What procedures should the agency adopt to apply the grant criteria? In addition to determining substantive standards for grants, our friend Ben also needs to develop a proposal for procedural rules to govern awards of individual grants. In other words, we need some procedural rules to govern future adjudications. As we mentioned earlier, administrative law refers to trial-like processes as "formal," and refers to all other processes as "informal." So, we might say that the task, in administrative-law speak, is to determine just how "formal" or "informal" the adjudicative process for deciding individual grant applications should be.

For a menu, we might consider the following list of procedural elements associated with hearings identified by Judge Friendly:

(1) an unbiased tribunal;

(2) notice of the proposed action and the grounds asserted for it;

(3) an opportunity to give reasons challenging the proposed action;

(4) the right to call witnesses;

(5) the right to know any adverse evidence;

(6) the right to have the decision based only on the evidence presented;

(7) the right to be represented;

(8) a record;

(9) a statement of reasons for the final action; and

(10) hearing open to the public.

Which of these seem appropriate for determining who should get a grant? Should the procedures replicate a trial? What combination of elements might fairness or agency effectiveness require as a bare minimum? Should, for instance, a grant applicant have a right to a written statement of reasons for the agency's decision? Should an applicant have a right to appeal a denial? If so, should the applicant have a right to counsel for the purpose of appeal?

3. What about judicial review? In addition to the procedural elements listed above, Judge Friendly regarded judicial review as an integral part of the administrative process, but he recognized that it carries costs as well as benefits. Consider, in this regard, Judge Friendly's remarks on judicial review of agency action from the article excerpted above:

> Although I have not researched the state decisions, my impression is that, up to this time, judicial review in the area of mass justice has largely been limited to questions of fair procedure, and there has been little attempt to obtain review for lack of substantial evidence or even for arbitrariness or capriciousness. Would that it may remain so! The spectacle of a new source of litigation of this magnitude is frightening. Yet many state administrative procedure acts, not to speak of the supposed "common law" right of review, would seem to subject determinations of the sort here considered to substantive review. Surely this is an area where courts should exercise self-restraint; the agencies can promote this by fair procedures and adequate statements of reasons, remembering that one sufficiently outrageous example may burst the dike.

Friendly, *Some Kind of Hearing*, 123 U. PA. L. REV. at 1294–95. So, for Judge Friendly, at least some judicial review of agency action is more trouble than it is worth. Circling back to Lesson 2B, would judicial review of WTC denials of grant applications be more trouble than it would be worth? Can you think of any types of agency decisions that you think ought not be subject to judicial review because of expense or because courts would worsen the error rate?

4. The inquisitorial alternative to adversarial process. This reading is intended, in part, to try to undo whatever intuition you might be carrying around that a fair adjudicative process necessarily needs to follow the adversarial, trial-type model of our courts. Along these lines, it bears noting that not every legal culture has the same obsession for the adversarial model. An alternative model, used throughout continental Europe and in many countries that were never part of the British Empire, is called (perhaps unfortunately) the "inquisitorial model." The core distinction between the adversarial system and the inquisitorial system is that in the former the parties control the proceeding and the presentation of evidence, and in the latter the decisionmaker controls.

Social Security Disability hearings provide an important example of a system in American administrative law that veers away from an adversarial and toward an inquisitorial approach. SSD hearings are designed to be informal and non-adversarial. They are conducted by administrative law judges (ALJs) who, for those used to the relatively passive role of a district judge, exercise a surprising degree of control over the development of the record. As described in a study by three administrative law scholars,

> Before the hearing takes place, the ALJ decides whether the evidence in the file is adequate to resolve the issues or whether factual development of some type is necessary. The ALJ also decides what additional evidence is necessary, if any, and whether a vocational expert or medical expert should be called to appear at the hearing. As part of this process, the ALJ can order a consultative examination of the claimant through the DDS, and must do so if such an examination is necessary to complete the medical record.

Frank Bloch, Jeffrey Lubbers & Paul Verkuil, *Developing a Full and Fair Evidentiary Record in a Nonadversary Setting: Two Proposals for Improving Social Security Disability Adjudications*, 25 Cardozo L. Rev. 1, 26 (2003). The study's authors advised against proposals to make the hearing process more adversarial by adding a government attorney or representative to oppose claimants. Instead, they concluded, "[g]iven the potential downsides of experimenting with the adversary process in this setting and our judgment that such a step would fail to advance the crucial need to improve the record development process, we conclude that the best SSA 'representative' would be non-adversarial—a person who could help provide the ALJ with a timely and complete record for decision while not triggering a host of collateral issues." *Id.* at 58–59. Along similar lines, a federal district judge considered an experimental program in which an adversarial Social Security Representative was added to the hearing process to "sharpen factual issues." Here is the judge's reaction: "Has the quality of the hearing dispositions improved? The answer to this has to be a resounding no." *Salling v. Bowen*, 641 F. Supp. 1046, 1062 (W.D. Va. 1986).

5. Examples of varying levels of "formality" from across the procedural spectrum.
As we have developed in this chapter, administrative decisionmaking procedures encompass an almost infinite number of possibilities. In order to manage these alternatives, administrative law relies on two distinctions: that between adjudication and rulemaking, and that between formal (trial-like) and informal (anything that isn't trial-like). At this point, some examples arranged according to our models might be helpful.

We saw the Social Security adjudicatory process at the beginning of this chapter. It appears as #4 below along with several others. These individual procedural schemes have evolved from statutory mandates or due process requirements or both. As illustrated by the following graphic, they range along a spectrum from relatively formal procedures (#1—hearings before the NLRB) to very informal (#5—school disciplinary meetings) to no right to participation beyond requesting the agency's response (#6—IRS letter rulings).

ADJUDICATION

Trial-like procedures				Informal procedures		No Participation	
/	/	/	/	/	/		/
1	2	3	4	5		6	

(1) *National Labor Relations Board unfair labor practice proceeding.* These are very trial-like administration hearings. (Criminal trial would be in the far left hand corner if part of the administrative process.) The hearing resolves a labor controversy between two parties, although the agency nominally stands in place of the party it feels has been wronged.

(2) *Federal Trade Commission cease and desist order proceeding.* Also very trial-like hearing, but somewhat less so, perhaps because it does not involve two contending private parties. The government, represented by the FTC staff, brings an action before the agency's ALJ against an alleged violator of statutes enforced by the FTC.

(3) *Federal Energy Regulatory Commission.* Technically formal adjudication is required, but most of the proceedings involve little or no oral testimony. Facts are generally submitted in writing.

(4) *Social Security proceedings.* Formal adjudication is not technically required, but SSA hearings are relatively formal. Yet they are nonadversarial in most respects.

(5) *School discipline.* Some kind of hearing is required, but for minor disciplinary matters, after *Goss v. Lopez*, 419 U.S. 565 (1975), something like a conference might be sufficient.

(6) *IRS letter rulings.* These are very informal determinations of individuals' potential tax liability if they follow a particular course of action.

As with adjudications, rulemaking proceedings also range along a spectrum of formality. FDA proceedings (#1) use highly formal trial-like procedures. The SEC (#3) typically uses standard notice-and-comment procedures like those discussed in Chapter 3. And the IRS issues revenue rulings (#5) with no process at all. Note, however, that the rules identified in ##1–3 below, which require public participation, result in rules that are binding with the force of law. By contrast, ## 4–5, although formally considered to be "rules" under the Administrative Procedure Act, produce only informal guidance documents, not binding rules that can be enforced on their own terms.

RULEMAKING

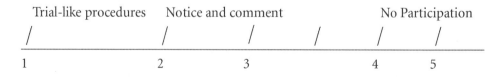

Trial-like procedures	Notice and comment			No Participation	
/	/	/	/	/	/
1	2	3		4	5

(1) *Food and Drug Administration rulemaking.* These rules must be made by the same trial-like procedures prescribed for formal adjudication under the APA. Some modifications of those procedures are permitted for rulemaking.

(2) *Federal Trade Commission Magnuson-Moss rulemaking.* Clearly informal rulemaking, but the procedures are more formal than required by §553 of the APA. For example, some opportunity to cross-examine might be provided.

(3) *Securities and Exchange Commission rulemaking.* Generally undertaken through the basic procedures of §553: notice, written comment, and statement of reasons. The rules have the force of law if properly promulgated.

(4) *Department of Health and Human Services guidelines or handbooks.* These announcements of general applicability are done with no formal public participation but the public may be consulted in informal ways, e.g., discussion with organizations representing the elderly. Such rules have no formal force, except as citizens are motivated to do what the agency wants.

(5) *Internal Revenue Service revenue rulings.* After a number of related letter rulings, the IRS might publish a revenue ruling which gives guidance to all taxpayers who might follow the same course. These are more rules than adjudications. No public procedures are followed.

Chapter 3

Rulemaking

James Landis, a renowned academic who also served successfully in several government positions, observed in his famous essay: "The ultimate test of the administrative [institution] is the policy that it formulates; not the fairness as between the parties of the disposition of a controversy on a record of their own making." JAMES LANDIS, THE ADMINISTRATIVE PROCESS 39 (1938). As we saw in Chapter 2, administrative agencies may develop policy through either adjudication or rulemaking. The strength of the administrative process, however, is its special mechanism for supporting and developing policy: rulemaking.

Fundamentally, rulemaking is a human enterprise, requiring communication among various interests within as well as outside an agency. Within an agency, different elements will have different sorts of expertise to contribute—for instance, at EPA, scientists, economists, and lawyers may all contribute to the development of a rule. An agency may also determine that it needs outside expertise to develop a rule. Frequently agencies hire consultants to provide the necessary expertise. Agencies develop internal procedures to help structure these various contributions to the decisionmaking process. Frankly, it is difficult to study this aspect of rulemaking in a general administrative law course because agencies' internal structures and procedures vary so widely. Still, you should always bear in mind that a great deal of the action in a rulemaking—sometimes all of the important action—occurs inside the agency, for the most part out of public view.

In this chapter, we will mostly focus on a more readily visible portion of the administrative law iceberg—the basic statutory templates for rulemaking procedure specified by the APA (or variations you might find in an enabling act, such as our WTCA). Topics include, among others:

- The APA template for formal (trial-type) rulemaking, and why courts very seldom require agencies to use this procedure.

- The default mode for rulemaking under the APA—the notice-and-comment process. On the face of the statute, this process looks extremely simple and straightforward. We shall learn how courts have, over the decades, complicated this process considerably.

- The APA's exceptions to the notice-and-comment process for certain types of rules—e.g., guidance documents, procedural rules, and rules exempted for good cause. We will explore the law, some of it rather hazy, delineating these exceptions.

The APA is not, however, the only source of procedural requirements for rule-making across agencies. Over the many decades since the APA's adoption, Congress has enacted various statutes, such as the Regulatory Flexibility Act, that add to the analytical requirements for rulemaking. In addition, presidents of both parties have issued executive orders that impose a centralized system of White House review on agency rulemaking. The upshot of these additional statutory and executive controls is that "real life" rulemaking for significant rules can be a far more difficult and time-consuming process than a person familiar only with the APA's skeletal requirements might think. Detailed coverage of these additional requirements is beyond the scope of this introductory casebook. We do, however, introduce you to some of them at the close of this chapter.

Before we begin tackling the basic statutory templates for rulemaking procedure, we will first examine a critical threshold issue: How does one determine the scope of agency rulemaking authority?

A. Determining the Existence and Scope of the Authority to Issue a Legislative Rule

Under the APA's extremely broad definition, the term "'rule' means the whole or a part of an agency statement of general or particular applicability and future effect designed to implement, interpret, or prescribe law or policy or describing the organization, procedure, or practice requirements of an agency . . . ." 5 U.S.C. § 551(4).

Administrative law distinguishes among various types of "rules" that fall within this definition. One important distinction is between "legislative" and "non-legislative" rules. Legislative rules establish legally binding requirements that the public, agencies, and the courts must follow and apply. We have seen several rules of this sort, including one setting air pollution standards (in *Whitman v. American Trucking* in Chapter 1) and one governing applications for broadcast licenses (in *United States v. Storer Broadcasting Co.* in Chapter 2). Non-legislative rules lack this binding force of law. The APA refers to two categories of non-legislative rules, "interpretative rules" and "general statements of policy," but it is now common to refer to them collectively as "guidance documents."

When an agency purports to issue a legislative rule, it is, of course, important to determine whether the rule falls within the agency's statutory authority. We can break this issue down into two legal questions. First, does the agency's enabling act authorize the agency to issue legislative rules at all? We discuss the courts' relatively straightforward and generous approach to this question in Notes 1–3 below.

Second, assuming the statute grants legislative rulemaking authority, does the rule fall within the scope of this authority? We introduce this topic with a prominent Supreme Court decision in which the majority and the dissenting opinions seem to clash over narrow and broad approaches to interpreting the scope of agency rulemaking authority. How would you articulate those approaches? Does either seem more persuasive at this point?

Lesson 3A. Brit served as Senator Bisby's chief of staff when the WTCA was enacted. She strongly encouraged the Senator to push through the Act, and is particularly skeptical of the wine industry's practices. Over time, however, she found life on the Hill to be less and less exciting, and she began to think that Senator Bisby's future was somewhat in doubt. She applied for a position at the WTC, where Carl, the agency's Chair, was happy to accommodate her. She has been assigned to the Rulemaking Division. Having been named Chief of the Rulemaking Division, Ben is extremely happy to have her because the Division is about to embark on the WTC's first really major rule. Ben assigns Brit to lead in this rulemaking.

Ben is primarily interested in developing a comprehensive labeling rule. He thinks the WTC should require disclosure of the grape varieties and any additives in all wines. He also has a personal interest in the health effects of wines because his sister is allergic to sulfites, which are in most wines. He would like to require disclosure of the health effects of all wine ingredients and of wine in general. He would also like to ban ingredients that cause significant health effects, particularly allergic reactions.

He and Brit discuss whether the disclosure requirements and ban that Ben proposes likely fall within the scope of the WTC's legislative rulemaking authority. In light of the following materials, do they?

Background of the *Brown & Williamson* Decision

As Justice O'Connor describes in the following decision, Congress and the Food and Drug Administration (FDA) struggled for decades over the health hazards created by tobacco. For most of that time, the FDA took the position that it did not have the authority to regulate tobacco products. Meanwhile, Congress over the years enacted various narrowly tailored provisions addressing cigarette package labeling, sales practices, and the like. In 1996, the FDA concluded, consistent with the plain language of the statute, that nicotine was a "drug" subject to regulation by the agency. The industry challenge to the FDA rule regulating tobacco products produced the following decision, in which the majority and dissent took distinctly different approaches to determining the scope of the agency's regulatory authority.

FDA v. Brown & Williamson Tobacco Corp.
529 U.S. 120 (2000)

JUSTICE O'CONNOR delivered the opinion of the Court.

This case involves one of the most troubling public health problems facing our Nation today: the thousands of premature deaths that occur each year because of tobacco use. In 1996, the Food and Drug Administration (FDA), after having expressly disavowed any such authority since its inception, asserted jurisdiction to regulate tobacco products. The FDA concluded that nicotine is a "drug" within the meaning of the Food, Drug, and Cosmetic Act (FDCA or Act), 21 U.S.C. § 301 *et seq.*, and that cigarettes and smokeless tobacco are "combination products" that deliver nicotine to the body. Pursuant to this authority, it promulgated regulations intended to reduce tobacco consumption among children and adolescents. The agency believed that, because most tobacco consumers begin their use before reaching the age of 18, curbing tobacco use by minors could substantially reduce the prevalence of addiction in future generations and thus the incidence of tobacco-related death and disease.

Regardless of how serious the problem an administrative agency seeks to address, however, it may not exercise its authority "in a manner that is inconsistent with the administrative structure that Congress enacted into law." *ETSI Pipeline Project v. Missouri*, 484 U.S. 495 (1988). And although agencies are generally entitled to deference in the interpretation of statutes that they administer, a reviewing "court, as well as the agency, must give effect to the unambiguously expressed intent of Congress." *Chevron U.S.A. Inc. v. Natural Resources Defense Council, Inc.*, 467 U.S. 837 (1984) [excerpted in subchapter 5G.3.b]. In this case, we believe that Congress has clearly precluded the FDA from asserting jurisdiction to regulate tobacco products. Such authority is inconsistent with the intent that Congress has expressed in the FDCA's overall regulatory scheme and in the tobacco-specific legislation that it has enacted subsequent to the FDCA. In light of this clear intent, the FDA's assertion of jurisdiction is impermissible.

I

The FDCA grants the FDA, as the designee of the Secretary of Health and Human Services (HHS), the authority to regulate, among other items, "drugs" and "devices." The Act defines "drug" to include "articles (other than food) intended to affect the structure or any function of the body." It defines "device," in part, as "an instrument, apparatus, implement, machine, contrivance, . . . or other similar or related article, including any component, part, or accessory, which is . . . intended to affect the structure or any function of the body." The Act also grants the FDA the authority to regulate so-called "combination products," which "constitute a combination of a drug, device, or biological product." The FDA has construed this provision as giving it the discretion to regulate combination products as drugs, as devices, or as both.

On August 11, 1995, the FDA published a proposed rule concerning the sale of cigarettes and smokeless tobacco to children and adolescents. The rule, which included several restrictions on the sale, distribution, and advertisement of tobacco products, was designed to reduce the availability and attractiveness of tobacco products to young people. A public comment period followed, during which the FDA received over 700,000 submissions, more than "at any other time in its history on any other subject."

On August 28, 1996, the FDA issued a final rule entitled "Regulations Restricting the Sale and Distribution of Cigarettes and Smokeless Tobacco to Protect Children and Adolescents." The FDA determined that nicotine is a "drug" and that cigarettes and smokeless tobacco are "drug delivery devices," and therefore it had jurisdiction under the FDCA to regulate tobacco products as customarily marketed . . . that is, without manufacturer claims of therapeutic benefit. First, the FDA found that tobacco products "affect the structure or any function of the body" because nicotine "has significant pharmacological effects." Specifically, nicotine "exerts psychoactive, or mood-altering, effects on the brain" that cause and sustain addiction, have both tranquilizing and stimulating effects, and control weight. Second, the FDA determined that these effects were "intended" under the FDCA because they "are so widely known and foreseeable that [they] may be deemed to have been intended by the manufacturers"; consumers use tobacco products "predominantly or nearly exclusively" to obtain these effects; and the statements, research, and actions of manufacturers revealed that they "have 'designed' cigarettes to provide pharmacologically active doses of nicotine to consumers." Finally, the agency concluded that cigarettes and smokeless tobacco are "combination products" because, in addition to containing nicotine, they include device components that deliver a controlled amount of nicotine to the body.

Having resolved the jurisdictional question, the FDA next explained the policy justifications for its regulations, detailing the deleterious health effects associated with tobacco use. It found that tobacco consumption was "the single leading cause of preventable death in the United States." According to the FDA, "[m]ore than 400,000 people die each year from tobacco-related illnesses, such as cancer, respiratory illnesses, and heart disease." The agency also determined that the only way to reduce the amount of tobacco-related illness and mortality was to reduce the level of addiction, a goal that could be accomplished only by preventing children and adolescents from starting to use tobacco. The FDA found that 82% of adult smokers had their first cigarette before the age of 18, and more than half had already become regular smokers by that age. It also found that children were beginning to smoke at a younger age, that the prevalence of youth smoking had recently increased, and that similar problems existed with respect to smokeless tobacco. The FDA accordingly concluded that if "the number of children and adolescents who begin tobacco use can be substantially diminished, tobacco-related illness can be correspondingly reduced because data suggest that anyone who does not begin smoking in childhood or adolescence is unlikely ever to begin."

Based on these findings, the FDA promulgated regulations concerning tobacco products' promotion, labeling, and accessibility to children and adolescents. The access regulations prohibit the sale of cigarettes or smokeless tobacco to persons younger than 18; require retailers to verify through photo identification the age of all purchasers younger than 27; prohibit the sale of cigarettes in quantities smaller than 20; prohibit the distribution of free samples; and prohibit sales through self-service displays and vending machines except in adult-only locations. The promotion regulations require that any print advertising appear in a black-and-white, text-only format unless the publication in which it appears is read almost exclusively by adults; prohibit outdoor advertising within 1,000 feet of any public playground or school;

prohibit the distribution of any promotional items, such as T-shirts or hats, bearing the manufacturer's brand name; and prohibit a manufacturer from sponsoring any athletic, musical, artistic, or other social or cultural event using its brand name. The labeling regulation requires that the statement, "A Nicotine-Delivery Device for Persons 18 or Older," appear on all tobacco product packages.

. . . .

We granted the federal parties' petition for certiorari, to determine whether the FDA has authority under the FDCA to regulate tobacco products as customarily marketed.

II

. . . .

A threshold issue is the appropriate framework for analyzing the FDA's assertion of authority to regulate tobacco products. Because this case involves an administrative agency's construction of a statute that it administers, our analysis is governed by *Chevron U.S.A. Inc. v. Natural Resources Defense Council, Inc.,* 467 U.S. 837 (1984). Under *Chevron,* a reviewing court must first ask "whether Congress has directly spoken to the precise question at issue." If Congress has done so, the inquiry is at an end; the court "must give effect to the unambiguously expressed intent of Congress." But if Congress has not specifically addressed the question, a reviewing court must respect the agency's construction of the statute so long as it is permissible. Such deference is justified because "[t]he responsibilities for assessing the wisdom of such policy choices and resolving the struggle between competing views of the public interest are not judicial ones," and because of the agency's greater familiarity with the ever-changing facts and circumstances surrounding the subjects regulated.

In determining whether Congress has specifically addressed the question at issue, a reviewing court should not confine itself to examining a particular statutory provision in isolation. It is a "fundamental canon of statutory construction that the words of a statute must be read in their context and with a view to their place in the overall statutory scheme." A court must therefore interpret the statute "as a symmetrical and coherent regulatory scheme," and "fit, if possible, all parts into an harmonious whole." Similarly, the meaning of one statute may be affected by other Acts, particularly where Congress has spoken subsequently and more specifically to the topic at hand. In addition, we must be guided to a degree by common sense as to the manner in which Congress is likely to delegate a policy decision of such economic and political magnitude to an administrative agency.

With these principles in mind, we find that Congress has directly spoken to the issue here and precluded the FDA's jurisdiction to regulate tobacco products.

A

Viewing the FDCA as a whole, it is evident that one of the Act's core objectives is to ensure that any product regulated by the FDA is "safe" and "effective" for its intended use. This essential purpose pervades the FDCA. For instance, [the Act] defines the FDA's "[m]ission" to include "protect[ing] the public health by ensuring that . . . drugs are safe and effective" and that "there is reasonable assurance of the safety and effectiveness of devices intended for human use." The FDCA requires premarket approval of any new drug . . . . If the FDA discovers after approval that a drug is unsafe or ineffective, it "shall . . . withdraw approval" of the drug. The Act also requires the FDA to classify all devices into one of three categories. . . . Even the "restricted device" provision pursuant to which the FDA promulgated the regulations at issue here authorizes the agency to place conditions on the sale or distribution of a device specifically when "there cannot otherwise be reasonable assurance of its safety and effectiveness." . . .

In its rulemaking proceeding, the FDA quite exhaustively documented that "tobacco products are unsafe," "dangerous," and "cause great pain and suffering from illness." It found that the consumption of tobacco products presents "extraordinary health risks," and that "tobacco use is the single leading cause of preventable death in the United States." It stated that "[m]ore than 400,000 people die each year from tobacco-related illnesses, such as cancer, respiratory illnesses, and heart disease, often suffering long and painful deaths," and that "[t]obacco alone kills more people each year in the United States than acquired immunodeficiency syndrome (AIDS), car accidents, alcohol, homicides, illegal drugs, suicides, and fires, combined." *Ibid.* Indeed, the FDA characterized smoking as "a pediatric disease," because "one out of every three young people who become regular smokers . . . will die prematurely as a result."

These findings logically imply that, if tobacco products were "devices" under the FDCA, the FDA would be required to remove them from the market. . . . Given the FDA's conclusions concerning the health consequences of tobacco use, there are no directions that could adequately protect consumers. . . .

. . . .

The FDCA's . . . provisions therefore make evident that were the FDA to regulate cigarettes and smokeless tobacco, the Act would require the agency to ban them. In fact, based on these provisions, the FDA itself has previously taken the position that if tobacco products were within its jurisdiction, "they would have to be removed from the market because it would be impossible to prove they were safe for their intended us[e]."

Congress, however, has foreclosed the removal of tobacco products from the market. . . . More importantly, Congress has directly addressed the problem of tobacco and health through legislation on six occasions since 1965. . . . Nonetheless, Congress stopped well short of ordering a ban. Instead, it has generally regulated the labeling and advertisement of tobacco products, expressly providing that it is the policy of Congress that "commerce and the national economy may be . . . protected to the maximum extent consistent with" consumers "be[ing] adequately informed about any adverse health effects." Congress' decisions to regulate labeling and advertising and to adopt the express policy of protecting "commerce and the national economy . . . to the maximum extent" reveal its intent that tobacco products remain on the market. Indeed, the collective premise of these statutes is that cigarettes and smokeless tobacco will continue to be sold in the United States. A ban of tobacco products by the FDA would therefore plainly contradict congressional policy.

The FDA apparently recognized this dilemma and concluded, somewhat ironically, that tobacco products are actually "safe" within the meaning of the FDCA. . . . [T]he FDA reasoned that, in determining whether a device is safe under the Act, it must consider "not only the risks presented by a product but also any of the countervailing effects of use of that product, including the consequences of not permitting the product to be marketed." Applying this standard, the FDA found that, because of the high level of addiction among tobacco users, a ban would likely be "dangerous." In particular, current tobacco users could suffer from extreme withdrawal, the health care system and available pharmaceuticals might not be able to meet the treatment demands of those suffering from withdrawal, and a black market offering cigarettes even more dangerous than those currently sold legally would likely develop. The FDA therefore concluded that, "while taking cigarettes and smokeless tobacco off the market could prevent some people from becoming addicted and reduce death and disease for others, the record does not establish that such a ban is the appropriate public health response under the act."

It may well be, as the FDA asserts, that "these factors must be considered when developing a regulatory scheme that achieves the best public health result for these products." But the FDA's judgment that leaving tobacco products on the market "is more effective in achieving public health goals than a ban," is no substitute for the specific safety determinations required by the FDCA's various operative provisions. Several provisions in the Act require the FDA to determine that the *product itself* is safe as used by consumers. That is, the product's probable therapeutic benefits must outweigh its risk of harm. In contrast, . . . although the FDA has concluded that a ban would be "dangerous," it has *not* concluded that tobacco products are "safe" as that term is used throughout the Act.

Consider 21 U.S.C. § 360c(a)(2), which specifies . . . [that] for all devices regulated by the FDA, there must at least be a "reasonable assurance of the safety and effectiveness of the device." . . . A straightforward reading of this provision dictates that the FDA must weigh the probable therapeutic benefits of the device to the consumer against the probable risk of injury. Applied to tobacco products, the inquiry is whether their purported benefits . . . satisfying addiction, stimulation and sedation, and weight control . . . outweigh the risks to health from their use. . . . In other words, the FDA is forced to contend that the very evil it seeks to combat is a "benefit to health." This is implausible.

. . . .

The dissent contends that our conclusion means that "the FDCA requires the FDA to ban outright 'dangerous' drugs or devices," and that this is a "perverse" reading of the statute. This misunderstands our holding. The FDA, consistent with the

FDCA, may clearly regulate many "dangerous" products without banning them. Indeed, virtually every drug or device poses dangers under certain conditions. What the FDA may not do is conclude that a drug or device cannot be used safely for any therapeutic purpose and yet, at the same time, allow that product to remain on the market. Such regulation is incompatible with the FDCA's core objective of ensuring that every drug or device is safe and effective.

. . . . The inescapable conclusion is that there is no room for tobacco products within the FDCA's regulatory scheme. If they cannot be used safely for any therapeutic purpose, and yet they cannot be banned, they simply do not fit.

B

In determining whether Congress has spoken directly to the FDA's authority to regulate tobacco, we must also consider in greater detail the tobacco-specific legislation that Congress has enacted over the past 35 years. At the time a statute is enacted, it may have a range of plausible meanings. Over time, however, subsequent acts can shape or focus those meanings. . . . As we recognized recently, . . . "a specific policy embodied in a later federal statute should control our construction of the [earlier] statute, even though it ha[s] not been expressly amended."

Congress has enacted six separate pieces of legislation since 1965 addressing the problem of tobacco use and human health. . . .

In adopting each statute, Congress has acted against the backdrop of the FDA's consistent and repeated statements that it lacked authority under the FDCA to regulate tobacco absent claims of therapeutic benefit by the manufacturer. In fact, on several occasions over this period, and after the health consequences of tobacco use and nicotine's pharmacological effects had become well known, Congress considered and rejected bills that would have granted the FDA such jurisdiction. Under these circumstances, it is evident that Congress' tobacco-specific statutes have effectively ratified the FDA's long-held position that it lacks jurisdiction under the FDCA to regulate tobacco products. Congress has created a distinct regulatory scheme to address the problem of tobacco and health, and that scheme, as presently constructed, precludes any role for the FDA.

. . . .

Taken together, these actions by Congress over the past 35 years preclude an interpretation of the FDCA that grants the FDA jurisdiction to regulate tobacco products. We do not rely on Congress' failure to act . . . in reaching this conclusion. Indeed, this is not a case of simple inaction by Congress that purportedly represents its acquiescence in an agency's position. To the contrary, Congress has enacted several statutes addressing the particular subject of tobacco and health, creating a distinct regulatory scheme for cigarettes and smokeless tobacco. In doing so, Congress has been aware of tobacco's health hazards and its pharmacological effects. It has also enacted this legislation against the background of the FDA repeatedly and consistently asserting that it lacks jurisdiction under the FDCA to regulate tobacco products as customarily marketed. Further, Congress has persistently acted to preclude a meaningful role for *any* administrative agency in making policy on the subject of tobacco and health. . . .

Under these circumstances, it is clear that Congress' tobacco-specific legislation has effectively ratified the FDA's previous position that it lacks jurisdiction to regulate tobacco. . . . Congress has affirmatively acted to address the issue of tobacco and health, relying on the representations of the FDA that it had no authority to regulate tobacco. It has created a distinct scheme to regulate the sale of tobacco products, focused on labeling and advertising, and premised on the belief that the FDA lacks such jurisdiction under the FDCA. As a result, Congress' tobacco-specific statutes preclude the FDA from regulating tobacco products as customarily marketed.

. . . .

C

Finally, our inquiry into whether Congress has directly spoken to the precise question at issue is shaped, at least in some measure, by the nature of the question presented. Deference under *Chevron* to an agency's construction of a statute that it administers is premised on the theory that a statute's ambiguity constitutes an implicit delegation from Congress to the agency to fill in the statutory gaps. In extraordinary cases, however, there may be reason to hesitate before concluding that Congress has intended such an implicit delegation.

This is hardly an ordinary case. Contrary to its representations to Congress since 1914, the FDA has now asserted jurisdiction to regulate an industry constituting a significant portion of the American economy. In fact, the FDA contends that, were it to determine that tobacco products provide no "reasonable assurance of safety," it would have the authority to ban cigarettes and smokeless tobacco entirely. Owing to its unique place in American history and society, tobacco has its own unique political history. Congress, for better or for worse, has created a distinct regulatory scheme for tobacco products, squarely rejected proposals to give the FDA jurisdiction over tobacco, and repeatedly acted to preclude any agency from exercising significant policymaking authority in the area. Given this history and the breadth of the authority that the FDA has asserted, we are obliged to defer not to the agency's expansive construction of the statute, but to Congress' consistent judgment to deny the FDA this power.

Our decision in *MCI Telecommunications Corp. v. American Telephone & Telegraph Co.*, 512 U.S. 218 (1994), is instructive. That case involved the proper construction of the term "modify" in § 203(b) of the Communications Act of 1934. The FCC contended that, because the Act gave it the discretion to "modify any requirement" imposed under the statute, it therefore possessed the authority to render voluntary the otherwise mandatory requirement that long distance carriers file their rates. We rejected the FCC's construction, finding "not the slightest doubt" that Congress had directly spoken to the question. In reasoning even more apt here, we concluded that "[i]t is highly unlikely that Congress would leave the determination of whether an industry will be entirely, or even substantially, rate-regulated to agency discretion . . . and even more unlikely that it would achieve that through such a subtle device as permission to 'modify' rate-filing requirements."

As in *MCI*, we are confident that Congress could not have intended to delegate a decision of such economic and political significance to an agency in so cryptic a fashion. To find that the FDA has the authority to regulate tobacco products, one must not only adopt an extremely strained understanding of "safety" as it is used throughout the Act . . . a concept central to the FDCA's regulatory scheme . . . but also ignore the plain implication of Congress' subsequent tobacco-specific legislation. It is therefore clear, based on the FDCA's overall regulatory scheme and the subsequent tobacco legislation, that Congress has directly spoken to the question at issue and precluded the FDA from regulating tobacco products.

. . . .

By no means do we question the seriousness of the problem that the FDA has sought to address. The agency has amply demonstrated that tobacco use, particularly among children and adolescents, poses perhaps the single most significant threat to public health in the United States. Nonetheless, no matter how "important, conspicuous, and controversial" the issue, and regardless of how likely the public is to hold the Executive Branch politically accountable, an administrative agency's power to regulate in the public interest must always be grounded in a valid grant of authority from Congress. And "'[i]n our anxiety to effectuate the congressional purpose of protecting the public, we must take care not to extend the scope of the statute beyond the point where Congress indicated it would stop.'" Reading the FDCA as a whole, as well as in conjunction with Congress' subsequent tobacco-specific legislation, it is plain that Congress has not given the FDA the authority that it seeks to exercise here. For these reasons, the judgment of the Court of Appeals for the Fourth Circuit is affirmed.

JUSTICE BREYER, with whom JUSTICE STEVENS, JUSTICE SOUTER, and JUSTICE GINSBURG join, dissenting.

The Food and Drug Administration (FDA) has the authority to regulate "articles (other than food) intended to affect the structure or any function of the body. . . ." Unlike the majority, I believe that tobacco products fit within this statutory language.

In its own interpretation, the majority nowhere denies the following two salient points. First, tobacco products (including cigarettes) fall within the scope of this statutory definition, read literally. . . . Cigarettes are "intended to affect" the body's "structure" and "function," in the literal sense of these words.

Second, the statute's basic purpose . . . the protection of public health . . . supports the inclusion of cigarettes within its scope. . . .

[T]he FDCA does not significantly limit the FDA's remedial alternatives. And the later statutes do not tell the FDA it cannot exercise jurisdiction, but simply leave FDA jurisdictional law where Congress found it.

The bulk of the opinion that follows will explain the basis for these latter conclusions. In short, I believe that the most important indicia of statutory meaning . . .

language and purpose . . . along with the FDCA's legislative history . . . are sufficient
to establish that the FDA has authority to regulate tobacco. The statute-specific
arguments against jurisdiction . . . are based on erroneous assumptions . . . . The
inferences that the majority draws from later legislative history are not persuasive, since . . . one can just as easily infer from the later laws that Congress did not
intend to affect the FDA's tobacco-related authority at all. And the fact that the FDA
changed its mind about the scope of its own jurisdiction is legally insignificant
because . . . the agency's reasons for changing course are fully justified. Finally, . . .
the degree of accountability that likely will attach to the FDA's action in this case
should alleviate any concern that Congress, rather than an administrative agency,
ought to make this important regulatory decision.

I

. . . .

After studying the FDCA's history, experts have written that the statute "is a
purposefully broad delegation of discretionary powers by Congress," and that, in
a sense, the FDCA "must be regarded as a *constitution*" that "establish[es] general
principles" and "permit[s] implementation within broad parameters" so that the
FDA can "implement these objectives through the most effective and efficient controls that can be devised." . . .

That Congress would grant the FDA such broad jurisdictional authority should
surprise no one. In 1938, the President and much of Congress believed that federal
administrative agencies needed broad authority and would exercise that authority
wisely . . . a view embodied in much Second New Deal legislation. . . .

Nor is it surprising that such a statutory delegation of power could lead after
many years to an assertion of jurisdiction that the 1938 legislators might not have
expected. . . .

After all, this Court has read more narrowly phrased statutes to grant what might
have seemed even more unlikely assertions of agency jurisdiction. *See, e.g., Permian
Basin Area Rate Cases*, 390 U.S. 747 (1968) (statutory authority to regulate interstate
"transportation" of natural gas includes authority to regulate "prices" charged by
field producers); *Phillips Petroleum Co. v. Wisconsin*, 347 U.S. 672 (1954) (independent gas producer subject to regulation despite Natural Gas Act's express exemption
of gathering and production facilities).

. . . .

II

. . . .

C

. . . .

The statute's language . . . permits the agency to choose remedies consistent with
its basic purpose . . . the overall protection of public health.

The second reason the FDCA does not require the FDA to select the more dangerous remedy [an outright ban] is that, despite the majority's assertions to the contrary, the statute does not distinguish among the kinds of health effects that the agency may take into account when assessing safety. . . .

Moreover, one cannot distinguish in this context between a "specific" health risk incurred by an individual and an "aggregate" risk to a group. . . . If unregulated smoking will kill 4 individuals out of a typical group of 1,000 people, if regulated smoking will kill 1 out of 1,000, and if a smoking ban (because of the black market) will kill 2 out of 1,000; then these three possibilities mean that in each group four, one, and two individuals, on average, will die respectively. And the risk to each individual consumer is 4/1,000, 1/1,000, and 2/1,000 respectively. A "specific" risk to an individual consumer and "aggregate" risks are two sides of the same coin; each calls attention to the same set of facts. . . . The FDA's history of regulating "replacement" drugs such as methadone shows that it has long taken likely actual alternative consumer behavior into account.

I concede that, as a matter of logic, one could consider the FDA's "safety" evaluation to be different from its choice of remedies. But to read the statute to forbid the agency from taking account of the realities of consumer behavior either in assessing safety or in choosing a remedy could increase the risks of harm . . . . Why would Congress insist that the FDA ignore such realities, even if the consequent harm would occur only unusually, say, where the FDA evaluates a product (a sleeping pill; a cigarette; a contact lens) that is already on the market, potentially habit forming, or popular? I can find no satisfactory answer to this question. . . .

[E]xperience counsels against an overly rigid interpretation of the FDCA that is divorced from the statute's overall health-protecting purposes.

. . . .

In my view, where linguistically permissible, we should interpret the FDCA in light of Congress' overall desire to protect health. That purpose requires a flexible interpretation that both permits the FDA to take into account the realities of human behavior and allows it, in appropriate cases, to choose from its arsenal of statutory remedies. A statute so interpreted easily "fit[s]" this, and other, drug- and device-related health problems.

. . . .

IV

I now turn to the final historical fact that the majority views as a factor in its interpretation of the subsequent legislative history: the FDA's former denials of its tobacco-related authority.

Until the early 1990's, the FDA expressly maintained that the 1938 statute did not give it the power that it now seeks to assert. It then changed its mind. The majority agrees with me that the FDA's change of positions does not make a significant legal difference.

. . . .

What changed? For one thing, the FDA obtained . . . evidence, which first became available in the early 1990's, . . . that the tobacco companies *knew* nicotine achieved appetite-suppressing, mood-stabilizing, and habituating effects through chemical (not psychological) means, even at a time when the companies were publicly denying such knowledge.

Moreover, scientific evidence of adverse health effects mounted, until, in the late 1980's, a consensus on the seriousness of the matter became firm. . . .

Finally, administration policy changed. Earlier administrations may have hesitated to assert jurisdiction for the reasons prior Commissioners expressed. Commissioners of the current administration simply took a different regulatory attitude.

Nothing in the law prevents the FDA from changing its policy for such reasons. . . . I agree with then-Justice Rehnquist's statement in a different case, where he wrote:

> "The agency's changed view . . . seems to be related to the election of a new President of a different political party. . . . A change in administration brought about by the people casting their votes is a perfectly reasonable basis for an executive agency's reappraisal of the costs and benefits of its programs and regulations. . . .

. . . .

V

. . . .

Insofar as the decision to regulate tobacco reflects the policy of an administration, it is a decision for which that administration, and those politically elected officials who support it, must (and will) take responsibility. And the very importance of the decision taken here, as well as its attendant publicity, means that the public is likely to be aware of it and to hold those officials politically accountable. . . .

. . . .

The majority finds that cigarettes are so dangerous that the FDCA would require them to be banned (a result the majority believes Congress would not have desired); thus, it concludes that the FDA has no tobacco-related authority. I disagree that the statute would require a cigarette ban. But even if I am wrong about the ban, the statute would restrict only the agency's choice of remedies, not its jurisdiction.

. . . .

The upshot is that the Court today holds that a regulatory statute aimed at unsafe drugs and devices does not authorize regulation of a drug (nicotine) and a device (a cigarette) that the Court itself finds unsafe. Far more than most, this particular drug and device risks the life-threatening harms that administrative regulation seeks to rectify. The majority's conclusion is counterintuitive. And, for the reasons set forth, I believe that the law does not require it.

Consequently, I dissent.

[Afterword: In 2009, President Obama signed into law the Family Smoking Prevention and Tobacco Control Act of 2009, Division A of Pub. L. 111-31, §§ 1 to 302, June 22, 2009, 123 Stat. 1776, which gave FDA express authority to regulate tobacco products. Does this fact have any bearing on your judgment with regard to whether Justice O'Connor or Justice Breyer had the better end of the argument in *Brown & Williamson*?]

Notes

1. Two questions about the WTC's authority to issue the rule Ben proposes. The FDA rule at issue in *Brown & Williamson* is considered to be a "legislative rule" because it would be binding on the public in much the same way as a statute. The same is true of the rule that Ben has asked Brit to develop.

Any agency attempt to adopt a legislative rule raises two questions. First, when does an agency have the authority to promulgate a legislative rule — a rule that will have the force of law? Second, if an agency has the authority to issue legislative rules, how should the courts go about determining the scope of the agency's rulemaking authority? Should they read the statute expansively in light of the statute's purpose, as in Justice Breyer's dissent, or restrictively as in Justice O'Connor's majority opinion? [Note: some use the term "substantive rule" in reference to legally binding rules. As noted above, and addressed at length in subchapter 3D.2, some rules that address substantive issues are not legally binding. We will use the term "legislative rule," which is nearly universally accepted in American administrative law to refer to rules that are legally binding.]

2. Statutory source of legislative rulemaking authority. All agency authority, including the authority to issue legislative rules, derives from statutes. Some statutes clearly grant specific authority to issue regulations with respect to particular issues. For example, the Clean Water Act provides that "the Administrator shall . . . publish . . . regulations providing guidelines for effluent limitations." 33 U.S.C. § 1314(b). Many statutes, however, include language such as Section 6(b) of the Federal Trade Commission Act, 15 U.S.C. § 46(g): "The Commission shall also have the power . . . (g) . . . to make rules and regulations for the purpose of carrying out the provisions of [the Act]."

The FTC relied upon this broad language to issue a legislative rule requiring the posting of octane ratings on service station gasoline pumps. In a landmark decision, the D.C. Circuit in *National Petroleum Refiners Ass'n v. FTC*, 482 F.2d 672 (D.C. Cir. 1973), *cert. denied*, 415 U.S. 951 (1974), upheld the rule as a valid implementation of the FTC's authority to prevent unfair trade practices. In so doing, the court said,

[T]here has been a . . . lack of hesitation in construing broad grants of rule-making power to permit promulgation of rules with the force of law as a means of agency regulation of otherwise private conduct. . . . Indeed, the general rule courts have adopted toward agencies' use of rule-making power . . . was stated succinctly and definitively for this court by Judge Fahy . . . :

"All authority of the Commission need not be found in explicit language. Section 16 [the general rule-making provision] demonstrates a realization by Congress that the Commission would be confronted with unforeseen problems of administration in regulating this huge industry and should have a basis for coping with such confrontation. While the action of the Commission must conform with the terms, policies and purposes of the Act, it may use means which are not in all respects spelled out in detail. . . ."

The need to interpret liberally broad grants of rule-making authority like the one we construe here has been emphasized time and again by the Supreme Court . . . :

In *American Trucking Association[s] v. United States*, 344 U.S. 298 (1953), we noted that it was not—

'a reasonable canon of interpretation that the draftsmen of acts delegating agency powers, as a practical and realistic matter, can or do include specific consideration of every evil sought to be corrected. . . . [O]ne of the reasons why regulatory agencies such as the Commission are created, . . . is the fond hope of their authors that they bring to their work the expert's familiarity with industry conditions which members of the delegating legislatures cannot be expected to possess '"

. . . .

In determining the legislative intent, our duty is to favor an interpretation which would render the statutory design effective in terms of the policies behind its enactment and to avoid an interpretation which would make such policies more difficult of fulfillment, particularly where, as here, that interpretation is consistent with the plain language of the statute. . . .

3. Should general rulemaking authority be interpreted to authorize legislative rules on substantive issues? Should courts be more restrictive than *Petroleum Refiners*, requiring instead specific legislative language authorizing legislative rules in particular areas? In the *Petroleum Refiners* opinion, the court was willing to infer the authority to make legislative rules from a general grant of rulemaking authority. Should a court be willing to infer legislative rulemaking authority based on a finding that such authority is necessary to carry out the intent of Congress, even though there is no express authority?

In *Chrysler v. Brown*, 441 U.S. 281 (1979), the Court rejected a rule where the agency had not been able to show that its regulation had been "reasonably within the contemplation of [the] grant of authority." The agency in *Chrysler* relied on an Executive Order as the authority for issuing regulations related to the disclosure of certain information. But regulatory authority must derive from a statute, and the Court held that the various statutes on which the Executive Order was based were not concerned with such public disclosure issues. Thus it is essential to establish that a general statutory grant of rulemaking authority is related to the substantive issues a regulation would address.

More recently, Thomas W. Merrill and Kathryn Tongue Watts have argued, based on extensive historical research, that:

> [T]hroughout most of the Progressive and New Deal eras, Congress followed a convention for signaling when an otherwise ambiguous rulemaking grant was intended to confer delegated authority to make rules with the force of law. Under this convention, rulemaking grants coupled with a statutory provision imposing sanctions on those who violate the rules were understood to authorize rules with the force of law; rulemaking grants not coupled with any provision for sanctions were understood to authorize only interpretive and procedural rules.

Thomas W. Merrill and Kathryn Tongue Watts, *Agency Rules with the Force of Law: The Original Convention*, 116 Harv. L. Rev. 467, 469 (2002). Merrill and Watts argue that the Supreme Court, which has never explicitly taken a position on the issue, should reject the approach of *Petroleum Refiners* and similar cases and return to the original convention. This would generally require specific statutory authority before an agency could issue a legislative rule with the force of law.

Which approach do you favor? How would adopting the "original convention" affect the arguments about the scope of the WTC's rulemaking authority?

4. Assuming a statute grants regulatory authority, how is the court to determine the scope of that authority? Whether a statute explicitly grants substantive regulatory authority, as in the Clean Air Act and Clean Water Act examples, or whether it uses general language of the sort addressed in *Petroleum Refiners*, courts must often determine the scope of that regulatory authority. *FDA v. Brown & Williamson* involved the scope of explicitly delegated regulatory authority. Lesson 3A involves the scope of the WTC's regulatory authority under general statutory language.

In the wake of *Brown & Williamson*, recent decisions suggest two principles as potential weapons for those challenging or supporting agency claims of regulatory authority. First, regulatory opponents will argue that courts should be reluctant to find implicit delegations of regulatory authority on issues of major significance. *Loving v. Internal Revenue Service*, 742 F.3d 1013 (D.C. Cir. 2014), involved a statute granting the IRS authority to "regulate the practice of representatives of persons before the Department of the Treasury." In rejecting the agency's claim of authority to regulate tax return preparers under this provision (essentially because tax return preparers do not "represent" taxpayers in the same way that lawyers represent their clients), the court noted that the "Supreme Court has stated that courts should not lightly presume congressional intent to implicitly delegate decisions of major economic or political significance to agencies." *Id.* at 1021. Emphasizing the widespread impact of the new rule, the D.C. Circuit concluded that, "as in *Brown & Williamson*, we are confident that the enacting Congress did not intend to grow such a large elephant in such a small mousehole." *Id.*

Second, arguments about the extent of the agency's authority to issue substantive rules should center on the substantive authority delegated to the agency. For example, the National Labor Relations Act authorizes the National Labor Relations Board to issue "such rules and regulations as may be necessary to carry out the provisions" of the Act. Despite statutory language very similar to *Petroleum Refiners*, the Fourth Circuit in *Chamber of Commerce of the United States v. NLRB*, 721 F.3d 152 (4th Cir. 2013), rejected a rule that would have required employers to post notices of employee rights under the National Labor Relations Act. Although the Board argued that the rule was "necessary" to inform employees of their rights under the Act, the court held that the Board's authority extended to resolving disputes—individualized adjudications—under the Act. Given that limited delegation, the Board had no authority to require that employees be informed of their rights so that they could file claims under the Act. This decision raises questions about the continued viability of the generous recognition of broad rulemaking authority in *Petroleum Refiners*.

Although attention to the specific substantive authority of the agency effectively limited the agency's authority in *Chamber of Commerce*, this emphasis favored the agency in *Monroe Energy, LLC v. EPA*, 750 F.3d 909 (D.C. Cir. 2014). In *Monroe Energy*, the D.C. Circuit held that the agency's failure to comply with a statutory deadline to issue a rule for a particular year did not eliminate the agency's authority to issue the rule. Although the agency violated a congressional instruction by missing the deadline, blocking the agency from issuing a late rule would have caused still greater disruption to the overall statutory scheme, which mandated a multi-year series of annual rules to achieve the desired results.

5. What is the best way to make the policy decision—a possible basis for interpreting rulemaking authority? One's answer to this question may depend in part on an assessment of the virtues of agency decisionmaking. Note that the net result of the *Brown & Williamson* decision was that tobacco policy was made by the courts in individual lawsuits, until Congress reentered the arena. Was that preferable to FDA policymaking?

When you look at the issue that way, you move away from the intricate details of statutory interpretation to the broader question of how best to develop government policy. Jim Rossi has identified three major models for agency decisionmaking that may be useful to this discussion. Jim Rossi, *Participation Run Amok: The Costs of Mass Participation for Deliberative Agency Decisionmaking*, 92 Nw. U. L. Rev. 173, 196–207 (1997). The first model, which he calls "Expertocratic Decisionmaking," emphasizes "specialized technical training, skill, and judgment," accompanied by rational explanation. Although this model has the obvious strength of scientific rationality, and presumably scientific accuracy, it cannot address value-laden judgments such as "the aesthetic impact of high-voltage power lines." Many agency decisions "involve competing values," so the ultimate decision is inherently political to a significant degree.

Rossi's second model is "Pluralism," which emphasizes interaction between decisionmakers and their various constituencies. In theory, "competition among interest groups . . . [is] the best means of approximating the public interest." Lobbying the agency and participating in the notice-and-comment rulemaking process are major aspects of this model with respect to legislative rulemaking. As with electoral politics itself, this model has limitations arising from the imbalance of power among competing interest groups and too much attention to those interests rather than to the relevant facts. Still, the model brings values into the picture in ways that Expertocratic Decisionmaking does not.

Rossi's third model, "Deliberative Democracy," essentially combines the best elements of the first two models. It insists upon dialogue based on reason, which inherently includes consideration of expertise and scientific rationality. And it emphasizes deliberation with the goal of achieving the public good, rather than the goal of satisfying competing interests. Rossi suggests that this approach "can justify bureaucracy as an element of 'sound governance,'" because the deliberative processes within the bureaucracy incorporate the most positive elements of these models.

Which of these theories seems like the most attractive approach to governance in general? To addressing the hazards of tobacco in particular? Rossi's models can transpose fairly neatly to Congress and the courts. In *Brown & Williamson*, the majority left regulatory power over tobacco with Congress, very much on the political, pluralistic side of the spectrum, as opposed to the scientific or rational side. In the likely event of congressional inaction, the majority also left policy development in the hands of the various state courts, where scientific proof may play a stronger role than politics, but where outcomes may vary wildly across the country. At the time, was the FDA likely to create better tobacco policies than either Congress or the courts? Which of these potential policymakers was in the best position to play the role of expert? To consider competing value choices? To deliberate? Lastly, to return to the question that started this note, should construction of the scope of an agency's statutory rulemaking authority depend on whom we think will make the best policies?

6. What if there were a rule but no legislative rulemaking authority? What is the status of an agency rule if the agency was not authorized to promulgate it as a legislative rule? As the Supreme Court recently confirmed, such a rule would be a mere "general statemen[t] of policy" or perhaps an "interpretive rule," both of which we discuss in subchapter 3D.2. It would not be binding and would not have the force of law. *Nat'l Park Hosp. Ass'n v. Dep't of the Interior*, 538 U.S. 803, 808–09, 820 (2003). We will use the term "non-legislative rule" to describe such statements.

7. How should the scope of the WTC's legislative rulemaking authority be interpreted? Assuming Ben establishes that the WTC has the authority to issue a legislative rule to implement § 5 of the WTCA, the next question is how to determine the scope of that authority. In *Brown & Williamson*, Justice O'Connor seems reluctant to recognize broad regulatory authority as she undertakes a rather tortuous journey through 35 years of legislative history and intervening events to conclude that "Congress has directly spoken" on the FDA's authority to regulate tobacco.

By contrast, Justice Breyer emphasizes that, "the statute's basic purpose—the protection of public health—supports the inclusion of cigarettes within its scope." Seemingly far more trusting of reliance upon regulation, he notes approvingly the assertion that, "in a sense, the FDCA 'must be regarded as a *constitution*' that 'establish[es] general principles' and 'permit[s] implementation within broad parameters' so that the FDA can 'implement these objectives through the most effective and efficient controls that can be devised.'" *Brown & Williamson*, 529 U.S. at 165 (citation and internal quotation marks omitted).

These distinctly different attitudes produce distinctly different results. Perhaps these different attitudes reflect different views of the best way to address this sort of policy issue. Consider Professor Rossi's three models of government decisionmaking, discussed in Note 5 above. Certainly Justice Breyer seems more comfortable with Expertocratic Decisionmaking, while Justice O'Connor seeks greater guidance from the political process, which is closer to Rossi's two other models.

Turning to Lesson 3A, what has Congress actually said about the WTC's authority to prescribe wine labels or to address health concerns? Section 5 of the WTCA is very broadly written to proscribe fraud and deceit in the wine industry. Section 8 grants the Commission authority to promulgate rules "for the purpose of carrying out the provisions of the Act." Could the contemplated labeling rules fairly be said to carry out § 5? What about a ban on ingredients that cause significant health effects?

Suppose that Ben, though he favors the policies behind the proposed rules, is concerned that they overreach agency authority. Brit counters that she was part of the promotion of the legislation on the Hill and she knows that the crucial members of Congress hoped that the WTC would be very aggressive, taking something like Justice Breyer's "constitutional approach." In the rulemaking, how much use can Brit make of what she knows about congressional opinion? Will it help if those views are reflected in a Committee Report?

8. May agencies create retroactive legislative rules? After thinking further about the potential for the labeling rule, Brit comes back to Ben with a suggestion that the rule include a provision that requires bottlers to supply retailers with revised labels and also requires the retailers to paste the new labels on the wine bottles in their possession. Ben is concerned that this rule might be impermissibly retroactive. Is it?

Under the APA, a "rule" is "an agency statement of general or particular applicability and future effect." 5 U.S.C. § 551(4). Most rules are specifically intended to govern future behaviors, as with the tobacco regulations at issue in *Brown & Williamson*. Sometimes, however, an agency may issue a rule that can be said to change the effects of past behavior. The Department of Health and Human Services (HHS) tried to do just that after a court struck down on procedural grounds a 1981 rule setting rates for hospital reimbursements under Medicare. The court's ruling resulted in higher reimbursement rates than would have been true under the 1981 rule. In 1984, HHS reissued the 1981 rule using the proper procedures and then sought to adjust all payments made after the 1981 rule had been struck down. In *Bowen v. Georgetown University Hospital*, 488 U.S. 204 (1988), the Court rejected what it considered to be a retroactive rule:

> It is axiomatic that an administrative agency's power to promulgate legislative regulations is limited to the authority delegated by Congress. In determining the validity of the Secretary's retroactive cost limit rule, the threshold question is whether the Medicare Act authorizes retroactive rulemaking.

> Retroactivity is not favored in the law. Thus, congressional enactments and administrative rules will not be construed to have retroactive effect unless their language requires this result. By the same principle, a statutory grant of legislative rulemaking authority will not, as a general matter, be understood to encompass the power to promulgate retroactive rules unless that power is conveyed by Congress in express terms. Even where some substantial justification for retroactive rulemaking is presented, courts should be reluctant to find such authority absent an express statutory grant. . . .

> The statutory provisions establishing the Secretary's general rulemaking power contain no express authorization of retroactive rulemaking. Any light that might be shed on this matter by suggestions of legislative intent also indicates that no such authority was contemplated.

In his concurring opinion, Justice Scalia took a slightly different approach, arguing that the APA definition of "rule," quoted above, does not permit any retroactive rules. Rules, he said, are agency statements of "future effect," having legal consequences only for the future. They contrast with adjudications, which decide the legal consequences of past acts. On this reading, no rule issued under the APA could be retroactive. He has yet to convince a majority of his position.

Despite *Bowen*'s reference to the absence of "express authorization of retroactive rulemaking," courts will recognize the authority to issue retroactive rules based upon indications in the statutory scheme or other indicators of congressional intent, despite the absence of express language authorizing retroactivity. For example, the D.C. Circuit in *Coalition for Common Sense in Government Procurement v. United States*, 707 F.3d 311 (D.C. Cir. 2013), upheld a rule retroactively imposing price caps on pharmaceuticals sold to military healthcare beneficiaries and requiring refunds for payments made above the price caps after the date of the statute authorizing the rule. In 2007, Congress had enacted the provision requiring price caps as of January 28, 2008, and had required the Secretary of Defense to "prescribe regulations to carry out this section." Although the Secretary did not issue the final rule until March 17, 2009, the court upheld the retroactive rule on the grounds that the statute itself had imposed the price caps as of January 28, 2008. Generally, where a court considers retroactivity necessary to achieve the goals of the statutory scheme, it is likely to find that Congress intended retroactivity.

9. When is a rule retroactive? *Bowen v. Georgetown University Hospital* provided a relatively clear test for determining whether an agency may issue a retroactive rule. The next question is when a rule should be considered retroactive. In his *Bowen* concurrence, Justice Scalia distinguished between "primary retroactivity," which is forbidden, and "secondary retroactivity," which is not. The former alters the "*past* legal consequences of past actions." Thus, the rule in *Bowen* had primary retroactive effect because it changed payments for the physicians' past actions. By contrast, an IRS rule "prescrib[ing] . . . that for the purposes of assessing future income tax liability, income from certain trusts that has previously been considered non-taxable will be taxable" in the *future* would have secondary retroactive effects. Such effects may substantially reduce the current value of a past investment—just as in Justice Scalia's trust example. This type of secondary retroactivity is nonetheless generally permissible so long as it is not the result of arbitrary action.

It is important to recognize that a rule is not retroactive if it imposes requirements or conditions previously adopted through adjudication or if it merely clarifies an existing statute or regulation. For example, in *Catholic Health Initiatives Iowa Corp. v. Sebelius*, 718 F.3d 914 (D.C. Cir. 2013), the D.C. Circuit upheld a 2004 rule governing behaviors prior to that date where the agency had adopted the same principle in an adjudicatory decision issued in 2000. Since the adjudicatory decision had effectively created the governing principle, the rule was not retroactive. Indeed, it is quite useful for an agency periodically to incorporate prior adjudicatory decisions into legislative rules, which are much more accessible to the general public.

Clay v. Johnson, 264 F.3d 744, 749 (7th Cir. 2001), illustrates the principle that a clarification of the existing law does not constitute a retroactive rule, even where the challenger thought it represented a change in the agency's position:

> However, a "rule simply clarifying an unsettled or confusing area of the law . . . does not change the law, but restates what the law according to the agency is and has always been." A clarifying rule, therefore, can be applied to the case at hand just as a judicial determination construing a statute can be applied to the case at hand.

Of course, the agency's new rule must truly be a clarification of an ambiguous provision, not a change of policy or position.

In light of these materials, is Ben correct that Brit's provision (described in note 8 above) would have illegal retroactive effect? Is it retroactive within Justice Scalia's definition of that term?

B. The Legislative Rulemaking Process— Formal, Informal, or a Mixture?

At the end of Chapter 2, we provided examples of the wide range of procedures that agencies might use to pursue either rulemaking or adjudication. In both cases, procedures may be highly formalized, to the point of appearing much like a judicial trial, or they may be very informal, sometimes involving no outside participation at all. When an agency seeks to issue a "legislative rule"—a rule that will be legally binding on the public—its procedural options are narrowed considerably. The materials in this subchapter address the procedural requirements that apply to the issuance of legislative rules.

1. When Is Formal, "Trial-Like" Process Required? Should It Be Used?

Lesson 3B.1. The Commission ultimately accepted Ben's recommendation that the WTC promulgate a legislative rule requiring disclosure of grape varieties, additives, and perhaps other information on wine labels. The WTC has not promulgated a rule of this dimension before, and Carl wants to assure that it follows the proper procedures. He asks Chris, the General Counsel, to have her staff review the statutory requirements and recommend procedures for this rulemaking. Ralph, the Assistant General Counsel for Litigation, is appalled at the informality of the rulemaking procedures established by WTCA § 8. He suggests that the Administrative Procedure Act must require greater formality (for Ralph, essentially trial-like process) for such an important decision.

How might the following materials help Ben determine whether Ralph is correct or whether a trial-like process is advisable? Does your analysis change if the WTC frames the rule as requiring proof that a winemaker makes all required disclosures as a condition of obtaining a wine merchant's license? (Hint: What does § 8 of the WTCA suggest?)

Background of the *Florida East Coast Railway* Decision

The Interstate Commerce Commission, established in 1887, is generally considered to be the first modern regulatory agency. Originally created to regulate railroad rates, the ICC eventually came to regulate the trucking industry, interstate bus lines, and even the telephone industry, before it was abolished in 1995. Generally, the purpose of rate regulation was to prevent unfair discrimination against certain shippers, to prevent monopolies (as railroads often are) from price gouging, and to assure a fair rate of return for railroads. In 1966, however, Congress specifically authorized the ICC to set daily rates for the use of railroad cars owned by other railroad companies in order to create incentives for those cars to be returned to their owners. The following case addressed the agency's attempt to implement that new authority using what we now call informal rulemaking, despite the fact that a 1917 amendment to the Interstate Commerce Act provided that the rate control decision could be made only "after hearing."

United States v. Florida East Coast Railway

410 U.S. 224 (1973)

MR. JUSTICE REHNQUIST delivered the opinion of the Court.

This case arises from the factual background of a chronic freight-car shortage on the Nation's railroads.... Congressional concern for the problem was manifested in the enactment in 1966 of an amendment to §1(14)(a) of the Interstate Commerce Act, [enlarging the [Interstate Commerce] Commission's authority to prescribe per diem charges for the use by one railroad of freight cars owned by another.]...

[Railroad cars owned by one company are often transferred to another company to get the goods to their final destination. The chronic freight-car shortage at issue arose because receiving companies were too slow in returning freight cars to their original companies. To alleviate the problem, the ICC proposed and ultimately adopted a rule requiring companies to pay "per diem" rates when they used freight cars owned by other companies. The purpose of the rule was to create an incentive to return the cars to their owners.]

. . . .

Before the enactment of the 1966 amendment to the Interstate Commerce Act, it was generally thought that the Commission's authority to fix per diem payments for freight car use was limited to setting an amount that reflected fair return on investment for the owning railroad, without any regard being had for the desirability of prompt return to the owning line or for the encouragement of additional purchases of freight cars by the railroads as a method of investing capital. The Commission concluded, however, that in view of the 1966 amendment it could impose additional "incentive" per diem charges to spur prompt return of existing cars and to make acquisition of new cars financially attractive to the railroads....

[The ICC imposed the charges by adopting a rule, which it promulgated using essentially the informal notice-and-comment process of §553 of the Administrative Procedure Act. The affected railroads challenged the rule on the ground that they were entitled to oral hearings and more extensive, trial-like procedures under §556 of the Administrative Procedure Act and §1(14)(a) of the Interstate Commerce Act.]

II. Applicability of Administrative Procedure Act

In *United States v. Allegheny-Ludlum Steel Corp.*, [406 U.S. 742 (1972)], we held that the language of §1(14)(a) of the Interstate Commerce Act authorizing the Commission to act "after hearing" was not the equivalent of a requirement that a rule be made "on the record after opportunity for an agency hearing" as the latter term is used in the Administrative Procedure Act. Since the 1966 amendment to §1(14)(a), under which the Commission was here proceeding, does not by its terms add to the hearing requirement contained in the earlier language, the same result should obtain here unless that amendment contains language that is tantamount to such a requirement. Appellees contend that such language is found in the provisions of that Act requiring that:

> '[T]he Commission shall give consideration to the national level of owner-ship of such type of freight car and to other factors affecting the adequacy of the national freight car supply, and shall, on the basis of such consider-ation, determine whether compensation should be computed. . . .'

While this language is undoubtedly a mandate to the Commission to consider the factors there set forth in reaching any conclusion as to imposition of per diem incentive charges, it adds to the hearing requirements of the section neither expressly nor by implication. We know of no reason to think that an administrative agency in reaching a decision cannot accord consideration to factors such as those set forth in the 1966 amendment by means other than a trial-type hearing or the presentation of oral argument by the affected parties. Congress by that amendment specified necessary components of the ultimate decision, but it did not specify the method by which the Commission should acquire information about those components.

Both of the district courts that reviewed this order of the Commission concluded that its proceedings were governed by the stricter requirements of §§ 556 and 557 of the Administrative Procedure Act, rather than by the provisions of § 553 alone. The conclusion of the District Court for the Middle District of Florida, which we here review, was based on the assumption that the language in § 1(14)(a) of the Interstate Commerce Act requiring rulemaking under that section to be done "after hearing" was the equivalent of a statutory requirement that the rule "be made on the record after opportunity for an agency hearing." Such an assumption is inconsistent with our decision in *Allegheny-Ludlum, supra.*

The District Court for the Eastern District of New York reached the same conclu-sion by a somewhat different line of reasoning. That court felt that because § 1(14)(a) of the Interstate Commerce Act had required a "hearing," and because that sec-tion was originally enacted in 1917, Congress was probably thinking in terms of a "hearing" such as that described in the opinion of this Court in the roughly con-temporaneous case of *ICC v. Louisville & Nashville R. Co.,* 227 U.S. 88, 93 (1913). The ingredients of the "hearing" were there said to be that "[a]ll parties must be fully apprised of the evidence submitted or to be considered, and must be given oppor-tunity to cross-examine witnesses, to inspect documents and to offer evidence in explanation or rebuttal." Combining this view of congressional understanding of the term "hearing" with comments by the Chairman of the Commission at the time of the adoption of the 1966 legislation regarding the necessity for "hearings," that court concluded that Congress had, in effect, required that these proceedings be "on the record after opportunity for an agency hearing" within the meaning of § 553(c) of the Administrative Procedure Act.

Insofar as this conclusion is grounded on the belief that the language "after hearing" of § 1(14)(a), without more, would trigger the applicability of §§ 556 and 557, it, too, is contrary to our decision in *Allegheny-Ludlum*. The District Court observed that it was "rather hard to believe that the last sentence of § 553(c) was directed only to the few legislative spots where the words 'on the record' or their equivalent had found their way into the statute book." This is, however, the language which Congress used, and since there are statutes on the books that do use these very words, adherence to that language cannot be said to render the provision nugatory or ineffectual. We recognized in *Allegheny-Ludlum* that the actual words "on the record" and "after . . . hearing" used in § 553 were not words of art, and that other statutory language having the same meaning could trigger the provisions of §§ 556 and 557 in rulemaking proceedings. But we adhere to our conclusion, expressed in that case, that the phrase "after hearing" in § 1(14)(a) of the Interstate Commerce Act does not have such an effect.

III. "Hearing" Requirement of § 1(14)(a) of the Interstate Commerce Act

Inextricably intertwined with the hearing requirement of the Administrative Procedure Act in this case is the meaning to be given to the language "after hearing" in § 1(14)(a) of the Interstate Commerce Act. Appellees, both here and in the court below, contend that the Commission procedure here fell short of that mandated by the "hearing" requirement of § 1(14)(a), even though it may have satisfied § 553 of the Administrative Procedure Act. The Administrative Procedure Act states that none of its provisions "limit or repeal additional requirements imposed by statute or otherwise recognized by law." 5 U.S.C. § 559. Thus, even though the Commission was not required to comply with §§ 556 and 557 of that Act, it was required to accord the "hearing" specified in § 1(14)(a) of the Interstate Commerce Act. Though the District Court did not pass on this contention, it is so closely related to the claim based on the Administrative Procedure Act that we proceed to decide it now.

. . . .

The term "hearing" in its legal context undoubtedly has a host of meanings. Its meaning undoubtedly will vary, depending on whether it is used in the context of a rulemaking-type proceeding or in the context of a proceeding devoted to the adjudication of particular disputed facts. It is by no means apparent what the drafters of the Esch Car Service Act of 1917, which became the first part of § 1(14)(a) of the Interstate Commerce Act, meant by the term. Such an intent would surely be an ephemeral one if, indeed, Congress in 1917 had in mind anything more specific than the language it actually used, for none of the parties refer to any legislative history that would shed light on the intended meaning of the words "after hearings." What is apparent, though, is that the term was used in granting authority to the Commission to make rules and regulations of a prospective nature.

. . . .

Under these circumstances, confronted with a grant of substantive authority made after the Administrative Procedure Act was enacted, we think that reference to that Act, in which Congress devoted itself exclusively to questions such as the nature and scope of hearings, is a satisfactory basis for determining what is meant by the term "hearing" used in another statute. Turning to that Act, we are convinced that the term "hearing" as used therein does not necessarily embrace either the right to present evidence orally and to cross-examine opposing witnesses, or the right to present oral argument to the agency's decisionmaker.

Section 553 excepts from its requirements rulemaking devoted to "interpretative rules, general statements of policy, or rules of agency organization, procedure, or practice," and rulemaking "when the agency for good cause finds . . . that notice and public procedure thereon are impracticable, unnecessary, or contrary to the public interest." This exception does not apply, however, "when notice or hearing is required by statute"; in those cases, even though interpretative rulemaking be involved, the requirements of § 553 apply. But since these requirements themselves do not mandate any oral presentation, it cannot be doubted that a statute that requires a "hearing" prior to rulemaking may in some circumstances be satisfied by procedures that meet only the standards of § 553. . . .

Similarly, even where the statute requires that the rulemaking procedure take place "on the record after opportunity for an agency hearing," thus triggering the applicability of § 556, subsection (d) provides that the agency may proceed by the submission of all or part of the evidence in written form if a party will not be "prejudiced thereby." Again, the Act makes it plain that a specific statutory mandate that the proceedings take place on the record after hearing may be satisfied in some circumstances by evidentiary submission in written form only.

We think this treatment of the term "hearing" in the Administrative Procedure Act affords sufficient basis for concluding that the requirement of a "hearing" contained in § 1(14)(a); in a situation where the Commission was acting under the 1966 statutory rulemaking authority that Congress had conferred upon it, did not by its own force require the Commission either to hear oral testimony, to permit cross-examination of Commission witnesses, or to hear oral argument. . . . Given the "open-ended" nature of the proceedings, and the Commission's announced willingness to consider proposals for modification after operating experience had been acquired, we think the hearing requirement of § 1(14)(a) of the Act was met.

Appellee railroads cite a number of our previous decisions dealing in some manner with the right to a hearing in an administrative proceeding. Although appellees have asserted no claim of constitutional deprivation in this proceeding, some of the cases they rely upon expressly speak in constitutional terms, while others are less than clear as to whether they depend upon the Due Process Clause of the Fifth and Fourteenth Amendments to the Constitution, or upon generalized principles of administrative law formulated prior to the adoption of the Administrative Procedure Act.

. . . .

ICC v. Louisville & Nashville R. Co., 227 U.S. 88 (1913), involved what the Court there described as a "quasi-judicial" proceeding of a quite different nature from the one we review here. The provisions of the Interstate Commerce Act . . . in effect at the time that case was decided, left to the railroad carriers the "primary right to make rates," but granted to the Commission the authority to set them aside, if after hearing, they were shown to be unreasonable. The proceeding before the Commission in that case had been instituted by the New Orleans Board of Trade complaint that certain class and commodity rates charged by the Louisville & Nashville Railroad from New Orleans to other points were unfair, unreasonable, and discriminatory. The type of proceeding there, in which the Commission adjudicated a complaint by a shipper that specified rates set by a carrier were unreasonable, was sufficiently different from the nationwide incentive payments ordered to be made by all railroads in this proceeding so as to make the *Louisville & Nashville* opinion inapplicable in the case presently before us.

The basic distinction between rulemaking and adjudication is illustrated by this Court's treatment of two related cases under the Due Process Clause of the Fourteenth Amendment. In *Londoner v. Denver*, 210 U.S. 373 (1908), cited in oral argument by appellees, the Court held that due process had not been accorded a landowner who objected to the amount assessed against his land as its share of the benefit resulting from the paving of a street. Local procedure had accorded him the right to file a written complaint and objection, but not to be heard orally. This Court held that due process of law required that he "have the right to support his allegations by argument, however brief; and, if need be, by proof, however informal." But in the later case of *Bi-Metallic Investment Co. v. State Board of Equalization*, 239 U.S. 441 (1915), the Court held that no hearing at all was constitutionally required prior to a decision by state tax officers in Colorado to increase the valuation of all taxable property in Denver by a substantial percentage. The Court distinguished Londoner by stating that there a small number of persons "were exceptionally affected, in each case upon individual grounds."

. . . While the line dividing them may not always be a bright one, these decisions represent a recognized distinction in administrative law between proceedings for the purpose of promulgating policy-type rules or standards, on the one hand, and proceedings designed to adjudicate disputed facts in particular cases on the other. Here, the incentive payments proposed by the Commission in its tentative order, and later adopted in its final order, were applicable across the board to all of the common carriers by railroad subject to the Interstate Commerce Act. No effort was made to single out any particular railroad for special consideration based on its own peculiar circumstances. . . . Though the Commission obviously relied on factual inferences as a basis for its order, the source of these factual inferences was apparent to anyone who read the order of December 1969. The factual inferences were used in the formulation of a basically legislative-type judgment, for prospective application only, rather than in adjudicating a particular set of disputed facts.

The Commission's procedure satisfied both the provisions of § 1(14)(a) of the Interstate Commerce Act and of the Administrative Procedure Act, and were not inconsistent with prior decisions of this Court. We, therefore, reverse the judgment of the District Court, and remand the case so that it may consider those contentions of the parties that are not disposed of by this opinion.

MR. JUSTICE DOUGLAS, with whom MR. JUSTICE STEWART concurs, dissenting.

The present decision makes a sharp break with traditional concepts of procedural due process. The Commission order under attack is tantamount to a rate order. Charges are fixed that nonowning railroads must pay owning railroads for boxcars of the latter that are on the tracks of the former. These charges are effective only during the months of September through February, the period of greatest boxcar use. For example, the charge for a boxcar that costs for $15,000 to $17,000 and that is five years of age or younger amounts to $5.19 a day. Box-cars costing between $39,000 and $41,000 and that are five years of age or younger cost the nonowning railroad $12.98 a day. The fees or rates charged decrease as the ages of the boxcars lengthen. This is the imposition on carriers by administrative fiat of a new financial liability. I do not believe it is within our traditional concepts of due process to allow an administrative agency to saddle anyone with a new rate, charge, or fee without a full hearing that includes the right to present oral testimony, cross-examine witnesses, and present oral argument. That is required by the Administrative Procedure Act, 5 U.S.C. § 556(d); § 556(a) states that § 556 applies to hearings required by § 553. Section 553(c) provides that § 556 applies "[w]hen rules are required by statute to be made on the record after opportunity for an agency hearing." A hearing under § 1(14)(a) of the Interstate Commerce Act fixing rates, charges, or fees is certainly adjudicatory, not legislative in the customary sense.

Notes

1. Let's review a little constitutional law. Justice Douglas in his dissent accuses the majority of breaking with "traditional concepts of procedural due process." Using the majority opinion and materials we have already discussed, make an argument as to why he was wrong on this point.

2. The APA—primary source of procedural requirements. Although the majority in *Florida East Coast* determined that the ICC's rulemaking did not implicate procedural due process, the agency did have to comply with statutory procedural requirements. The petitioner railroads contended that the ICC violated procedural requirements coming from two statutory sources—the Interstate Commerce Act (the agency's enabling act) and the Administrative Procedure Act (APA).

As we learned in Chapter 1, Congress adopted the APA in 1946 to provide an overarching set of procedures to govern actions by the growing administrative state. The APA's controls apply to "agencies," which the statute defines extremely broadly as including "each authority of the Government of the United States, whether or not it is within or subject to review by another agency." 5 U.S.C. § 551(1). Thus, for instance, although the Coast Guard is contained within the Department of Home-land Security, both are considered "agencies." The two most notable listed exceptions to the APA's broad, vague definition of "agency" are Congress and the federal courts. The most notable unlisted exception is the president, whom the courts, due to separation-of-powers concerns, have determined is not an "agency" subject to APA requirements.

Courts have often relied on three documents for special insights into the APA's meaning. The FINAL REPORT OF THE ATTORNEY GENERAL'S COMMITTEE ON ADMINISTRATIVE PROCEDURE (1941), which was prepared by leading scholars of the day, provided a detailed study of the operation of agencies and judicial review of their actions. World War II intervened before Congress could act on the FINAL REPORT, and the APA did not ultimately adopt the majority's recommendations. A compilation of legislative materials, ADMINISTRATIVE PROCEDURE ACT: LEGISLATIVE HISTORY (1946), provides valuable information about the drafters' intentions. After passage of the APA, the Attorney General developed a document to aid the agencies in bringing their procedures into compliance, ATTORNEY GENERAL'S MANUAL ON THE ADMINISTRATIVE PROCEDURE ACT (1947), which also provides useful interpretative guidance.

3. Section 553 and the notice-and-comment process for "informal" rulemaking. The primary source for rulemaking procedures in the APA is 5 U.S.C. § 553. Take a look at this provision in the appendix of the casebook—it won't take you long, it is astonishingly short. Ignoring certain complications that we will study later and boiling things down to the essentials, this provision creates a default template for rulemaking that requires an agency to: (1) issue a notice of proposed rulemaking; (2) accept comments on the proposal; (3) provide a "concise general statement of . . . basis and purpose" for its final rule; and (4) publish it thirty days before its effective date. We commonly refer to this notice-and-comment process as a type of "informal" rulemaking. The ICC used this procedure to create the rule that the railroads challenged in *Florida East Coast.*

4. Adding §§ 556 and 557 to get "formal" rulemaking. Now take a quicker look at 5 U.S.C. §§ 556 and 557. Don't worry about absorbing detail at this point—we are just trying to get the gist of things. Section 556 provides procedures for administrative hearings that can look quite a bit like a bench trial. Among other things, § 556 designates who can preside at such hearings, grants the presiding official powers needed to run them, specifies matters such as burden of proof, and defines the record. Section 557 specifies the types of decisions these hearings can produce, provides instructions regarding the contents of these decisions, provides for intra-agency review of decisions, and limits *ex parte* contacts.

5. Triggering formality. The railroads in *Florida East Coast* objected that the ICC should have used formal rulemaking procedures for the per diem rule they challenged. They needed two textual hooks to make this argument—one in the agency's enabling act and the other in § 553(c). Section 553(c) states that: "When rules are *required by statute* to be made *on the record after opportunity for an agency hearing,* sections 556 and 557 of this title apply *instead of this subsection*." (emphasis added). The "required by statute" language refers to the agency's enabling act. What was the textual hook in the ICC's enabling act, and how did it affect the railroads' argument for formality in *Florida East Coast*? What grounds did Justice Rehnquist give for rejecting this argument? It seems fair to say that Justice Rehnquist worked very hard to justify this rejection. Note 7 helps explain why he might have thought this strain worth the effort.

6. Comparing the triggers for formal rulemaking and formal adjudication. Once you have answered the questions in note 5, take a look at § 554(a), which begins the APA's initial provision governing adjudications. You will find language for triggering "formal" adjudication that parallels the language for triggering "formal" rulemaking in § 553(c). You might well think that, given this parallelism, the law for triggering formal proceedings would operate in the same way for both rulemaking and adjudication.

The courts, however, have been far quicker to interpret the APA as requiring formal, trial-like procedures for adjudication than for rulemaking. What is it about the nature of adjudication versus rulemaking that might have caused this differential treatment?

7. Are formal procedures well suited to rulemaking? In a now-classic 1972 study, Robert Hamilton critiqued the use of trial-like procedures for rulemaking. Examining formal rulemaking conducted by the Food and Drug Administration as required by the Federal Food, Drug and Cosmetic Act, Hamilton found that:

> The sixteen formal hearings that were held during the last decade vary from unnecessarily drawn out proceedings to virtual disasters. In not one instance did the agency complete a rulemaking proceeding involving a hearing in less than two years, and in two instances more than ten years elapsed between the first proposal and the final order. The *average* time lapse was roughly four years. The hearings themselves tended to be drawn out, repetitious and unproductive. The *Foods for Special Dietary Uses* hearing consumed over 200 days of testimony and amassed a transcript of more than 32,000 pages. Most of the hearing was devoted to cross-examination of expert government witnesses. Another proceeding involving the standard of identity for peanut butter developed a transcript of over 7,700 pages, largely directed to the question whether the product peanut butter should consist of 90 percent peanuts or 87½ percent peanuts. Both of these transcripts are largely monuments to free speech.

Robert Hamilton, *Procedures for the Adoption of Rules of General Applicability: The Need for Procedural Innovation in Administrative Rulemaking*, 60 CAL. L. REV. 1276, 1287–88 (1972). Hamilton identified several deficiencies in the process, including extensive cross-examination of government staff members that was "often intense, wide-ranging, and usually unproductive." Hamilton also found this type of process inappropriate because rulemaking typically hinges on issues of policy, for which trial-type process is not well-suited, and because the factual issues involved in rule-making "are often so broad as to be inappropriate for a trial-type hearing." More-over, Hamilton found that these burdens caused agencies to go to great lengths to avoid the process, even to the point of bargaining "with the affected industry in order to reach a consensus that avoids a hearing." Thus, the requirement of formal trial-type process in FDA rulemaking seems to have become more of a bargaining chip to produce agency concessions than an effective means of developing the record for a well-informed decision.

Interestingly, Hamilton also found that formal rulemaking processes worked reasonably well in the narrow, well-defined area of setting regional agricultural prices, so-called "marketing orders." In that arena, proceedings were typically completed within a few days. What purposes might trial-like hearings serve in the marketing order context? Why might formal rulemaking in this context be more successful than in FDA proceedings?

After a forty-year drought of scholarship on the subject of formal rulemaking, Aaron Nielson in 2014 argued that, "[i]f applied in appropriate circumstances, formal rulemaking—with its emphasis on accuracy and transparency—could improve the administrative process." Nielson maintained that many of the flaws Hamilton had identified could be corrected by careful legislation and tight control of the proceeding. For example, all parties sharing a certain interest could be required to conduct a single cross-examination. He suggests that formal rulemaking procedures offer "the potential to uproot an agency's faulty assumptions and increase the public's confidence in the regulatory process." He argues that we should at least experiment with formal rulemaking in some circumstances. Aaron L Nielson, *In Defense of Formal Rulemaking*, 75 Ohio St. L.J. 237, 241, 292 (2014).

Do you agree? When would you require formal rulemaking procedures? Does your answer depend upon the nature of the decision at issue—factual or policy? Specific factual question versus general factual question?

8. But just how formal does formal rulemaking need to be? We will study §§ 556 and 557 in more detail in the context of formal adjudications in Chapter 4. For the moment, though, note that the statutory procedures for formal rulemaking allow considerably more flexibility than may be widely understood. For example, the last sentence of § 556(d) provides that, "[i]n rule making . . . an agency may, when a party will not be prejudiced thereby, adopt procedures for the submission of all or part of the evidence in written form." In addition, there is nothing to prevent agencies from using the same summary judgment-style shortcut methods in formal rulemaking that they have developed for formal adjudication. The ICC long used a modified procedure whereby formal adjudication was conducted in writing unless a party could show an oral hearing was necessary. An agency faced with formal rulemaking requirements could establish a similar "modified" procedure for rule-making. Under such a procedure, a party to the rulemaking would have no right to an oral evidentiary hearing unless it could show a genuine issue of material fact that could only be resolved by an oral proceeding. If such a procedure is acceptable in the context of formal adjudication, it surely should be acceptable in rulemaking. In fact, the Supreme Court specifically approved the FDA's use of such a procedure in the rulemaking context in *Weinberger v. Hynson, Westcott & Dunning*, 412 U.S. 609 (1973). Given the kinds of facts that dominate most rulemaking proceedings—i.e., those facts for which testamentary proof is unnecessary—such an approach would eliminate almost all testimonial proceedings.

9. State APAs and rulemaking procedures. All states have administrative proce-dure acts or their equivalent, which have been studied extensively by Arthur Bon-field. BONFIELD, STATE ADMINISTRATIVE RULEMAKING 41 (1986). The development of state APAs has been heavily influenced by "model acts" issued by the National Conference of Commissioners of Uniform State Laws in 1946 (the year of the APA's adoption), 1961, 1981, and most recently, 2010. These model acts, and the state APAs that follow them, are all products of the same broad legal culture that produced the federal APA. It should therefore come as no surprise that they share many concepts and principles and give similar answers to similar questions (though sometimes using different language). For instance, like the federal APA, each of the model acts has incorporated the core distinction between adjudication and rulemaking and has specified procedures for these types of actions. These procedures include, among other things, analogues to formal adjudication (applicable to "contested cases") and to notice-and-comment rulemaking.

None of the model acts has included a provision for triggering trial-type rule-making proceedings akin to those specified in 5 U.S.C. §§ 556–57 of the federal APA. The 1981 MSAPA, § 3-104, does provide for "an oral proceeding" on request. The comments to this provision, however, made clear that an "oral proceeding" is not equivalent to a trial-type hearing. The 2010 MSAPA eliminates this right to an oral proceeding on request and instead provides that an agency need hold a "hear-ing" for rulemaking only where "required by law of this state" other than the model act itself. Unlike the federal APA, the 2010 MSAPA also does not include a "formal" template specifying procedures that a statutorily required hearing must follow.

10. What about procedures required by the Interstate Commerce Act? We aren't quite done with *Florida East Coast* yet. Remember that the railroads had two statu-tory arguments that the ICC had not provided enough procedure for its per diem rule. One, discussed in the notes above, involved triggering the formal, trial-type procedures of §§ 556 and 557. What was the railroads' other statutory argument? And how did the Court justify rejecting it?

2. Informal Rulemaking — Can the Courts Increase the Formality? Should Congress or the Agency Require More than the APA Minimum?

Lesson 3B.2. Recall that the Commission accepted the Rulemaking Division's recommendation for a major labeling rule requiring disclosure on wine labels of grape varieties, additives, and perhaps other information. The General Counsel's Office has advised Carl, the agency chair, that the WTC need not use formal trial-type process to issue this rule. Carl is delighted. He now asks Ben just what procedures will be required. He is concerned that a court might find very informal procedures inadequate, particularly on a hotly contested issue such as whether the information on wine labels is material to the consumer's purchasing decision. If consumers, for example, submit arguments that the information is material, a court may well want the WTC to consider industry responses to those comments, and vice versa. Carl wants to be sure that whatever procedures the agency adopts, they will satisfy a court.

Carl also wants to be sure, however, that the rulemaking process is productive. He notes that the Division's memorandum observed that the "public participation guidelines" as required by WTCA § 8(b)(5) are rather superficial, merely reiterating the requirements of APA § 553. He asks Ben to meet with him to discuss special guidelines for the labeling rule. He wants to assure broad participation and publicity for this rulemaking. He asks Chris, the General Counsel, to join them. Ben is surprised at how little Carl knows about the law and makes a respectful effort to inform him about it. The three of them then discuss additional steps they might take to give all interested persons an opportunity to participate. Carl, never forgetting his future, is particularly concerned that the industry perceive that the Commission has been sensitive to their interests. Ben is just as adamant about consumer interests.

Carl observes that rulemaking is essentially policymaking, and the process must facilitate inclusion of all points of view. He believes that rulemaking should follow the legislative hearing model he worked with in his years in the state assembly and Congress. Chris, who also has experience on the Hill, counters that one of her frustrations with the legislative process was the lack of factual support for much of the legislation. She hopes that the rulemaking will facilitate the development of a strong record containing a broad range of facts as well as comments.

In light of the following materials, what should Ben advise Carl as to rulemaking procedures that would both survive judicial review and produce a useful basis for the agency's ultimate decision?

Background of the *Vermont Yankee* Decision

The following decision occurred at a watershed moment in the development of modern administrative law. Although the federal government had been regulating industry to protect public health and safety since at least the steamboat explosions of the 1830s, the technical issues were relatively simple, and judicial review was quite limited. This changed with the advent of the nuclear age and the recognition of the health and safety threats of modern industrial activity. In this environment, two developments converged. First, Congress began enacting complex health and safety regulatory statutes, including the Atomic Energy Acts of 1946 and 1954, the Clean Air Act of 1970, and the Clean Water Act of 1972. These statutes, and many others, tasked federal agencies with examining scientifically and technically complex issues to determine how best to protect public health, safety, and the environment. Second, Congress and the courts expanded the availability of judicial review, placing law-trained judges in the position of reviewing complex agency decisions that could affect millions of lives but also cost millions of dollars.

The *Vermont Yankee* decision reflects the judicial struggle to determine how to review these agency decisions. With no technical expertise, some judges focused on improving process to improve decisions, while others insisted that the courts could not avoid the responsibility to review the substance of agency decisions.

The *Vermont Yankee* decision also serves as something of a review of principles governing rulemaking and adjudication. As explained in the decision, the saga began with an application for an operating license for the Vermont Yankee nuclear power plant—an adjudication. Various parties opposed to the plant intervened in the agency hearing, arguing that the license could not be issued without a showing that the plant's used nuclear fuel could be disposed of safely. Rather than have the hearing panel, known as the Atomic Safety and Licensing Board, decide that issue, the Nuclear Regulatory Commission initiated a rulemaking proceeding to determine the general question of the safety of the disposal of spent nuclear fuel. Once the rule was issued, it would be applied to every individual licensing proceeding. Nuclear opponents challenged the outcome of that rulemaking, arguing both that the agency's findings about safe disposal were invalid and that the NRC had not provided procedures necessary to develop an adequate record on the complex issues at hand. The D.C. Circuit ruled for the opponents on the procedural challenge, leading to this landmark decision.

Vermont Yankee Nuclear Power Corp. v. Natural Resources Defense Council
435 U.S. 519 (1978)

MR. JUSTICE REHNQUIST delivered the opinion of the Court.

In 1946, Congress enacted the Administrative Procedure Act, which as we have noted elsewhere was not only "a new, basic and comprehensive regulation of procedures in many agencies," but was also a legislative enactment which settled "long-continued and hard-fought contentions, and enacts a formula upon which opposing social and political forces have come to rest." Section 4 of the Act, dealing with rulemaking, requires in subsection (b) that "notice of proposed rule making shall be published in the Federal Register . . . ," describes the contents of that notice, and goes on to require in subsection (c) that after the notice the agency "shall give interested persons an opportunity to participate in the rule making through submission of written data, views, or arguments with or without opportunity for oral presentation. After consideration of the relevant matter presented, the agency shall incorporate in the rules adopted a concise general statement of their basis and purpose." Interpreting this provision of the Act in *United States v. Allegheny-Ludlum Steel Corp.*, 406 U.S. 742 (1972), and *United States v. Florida East Coast R. Co.*, 410 U.S. 224 (1973), we held that generally speaking this section of the Act established the maximum procedural requirements which Congress was willing to have the courts impose upon agencies in conducting rulemaking procedures. Agencies are free to grant additional procedural rights in the exercise of their discretion, but reviewing courts are generally not free to impose them if the agencies have not chosen to grant them. This is not to say necessarily that there are no circumstances which would ever justify a court in overturning agency action because of a failure to employ procedures beyond those required by the statute. But such circumstances, if they exist, are extremely rare.

Even apart from the Administrative Procedure Act this Court has for more than four decades emphasized that the formulation of procedures was basically to be left within the discretion of the agencies to which Congress had confided the responsibility for substantive judgments. In *FCC v. Schreiber*, 381 U.S. 279, 290 (1965), the Court explicated this principle, describing it as "an outgrowth of the congressional determination that administrative agencies and administrators will be familiar with the industries which they regulate and will be in a better position than federal courts or Congress itself to design procedural rules adapted to the peculiarities of the industry and the tasks of the agency involved." . . .

It is in the light of this background of statutory and decisional law that we granted certiorari to review two judgments of the Court of Appeals for the District of Columbia Circuit because of our concern that they had seriously misread or misapplied this statutory and decisional law cautioning reviewing courts against engrafting their own notions of proper procedures upon agencies entrusted with substantive functions by Congress. We conclude that the Court of Appeals has done just that in these cases, and we therefore remand them to it for further proceedings. . . .

A

Under the Atomic Energy Act of 1954, the Atomic Energy Commission was given broad regulatory authority over the development of nuclear energy. Under the terms of the Act, a utility seeking to construct and operate a nuclear power plant must obtain a separate permit or license at both the construction and the operation stage of the project. In order to obtain the construction permit, the utility must file a preliminary safety analysis report, an environmental report, and certain information regarding the antitrust implications of the proposed project.

[Ultimately, the utility must show that the facility will not threaten the public health and safety, and the Commission must carry out a thorough environmental review. At the time of this decision, the licensing decision was made only after a formal adjudicatory hearing before a three-person panel called the Atomic Safety and Licensing Board. That decision could be appealed to the Commission and then to the Court of Appeals. When Vermont Yankee applied for an operating license, the Natural Resources Defense Council (NRDC) intervened, arguing that the hazards of handling "spent fuel," the highly radioactive waste from the reactor's fuel, should prevent the grant of a license. As explained above, the NRC excluded this issue from the licensing proceeding, but it initiated a rulemaking proceeding to establish the effects of the nuclear fuel cycle.]

In November 1972, however, the Commission . . . instituted rulemaking proceedings "that would specifically deal with the question of consideration of environmental effects associated with the uranium fuel cycle in the individual cost-benefit analyses for light water cooled nuclear power reactors." The notice of proposed rulemaking offered two alternatives, both predicated on a report prepared by the Commission's staff entitled Environmental Survey of the Nuclear Fuel Cycle. The first would have required no quantitative evaluation of the environmental hazards of fuel reprocessing or disposal because the Environmental Survey had found them to be slight. The second would have specified numerical values for the environmental impact of this part of the fuel cycle, which values would then be incorporated into a table, along with the other relevant factors, to determine the overall cost-benefit balance for each operating license.

Much of the controversy in this case revolves around the procedures used in the rulemaking hearing which commenced in February 1973. In a supplemental notice of hearing the Commission indicated that while discovery or cross-examination would not be utilized, the Environmental Survey would be available to the public before the hearing along with the extensive background documents cited therein. All participants would be given a reasonable opportunity to present their position and could be represented by counsel if they so desired. Written and, time permitting, oral statements would be received and incorporated into the record. All persons giving oral statements would be subject to questioning by the Commission. At the conclusion of the hearing, a transcript would be made available to the public and the record would remain open for 30 days to allow the filing of supplemental written statements. . . .

After the hearing, the Commission's staff filed a supplemental document for the purpose of clarifying and revising the Environmental Survey. Then the Licensing Board forwarded its report to the Commission without rendering any decision. The Licensing Board identified as the principal procedural question the propriety of declining to use full formal adjudicatory procedures. The major substantive issue was the technical adequacy of the Environmental Survey.

In April 1974, the Commission issued a rule which adopted the second of the two proposed alternatives described above. The Commission also approved the procedures used at the hearing,[7] and indicated that the record, including the Environmental Survey, provided an "adequate data base for the regulation adopted." . . .

Respondents appealed from . . . the Commission's adoption of the rule. . . .

. . . .

After a thorough examination of the opinion itself, we conclude that while the matter is not entirely free from doubt, the majority of the Court of Appeals struck down the rule because of the perceived inadequacies of the procedures employed in the rulemaking proceedings. The court first determined the intervenors' primary argument to be "that the decision to preclude 'discovery or cross-examination' denied them a meaningful opportunity to participate in the proceedings as guaranteed by due process." The court then went on to frame the issue for decision thus:

> "Thus, we are called upon to decide whether the procedures provided by the agency were sufficient to ventilate the issues."

The court conceded that absent extraordinary circumstances it is improper for a reviewing court to prescribe the procedural format an agency must follow, but it likewise clearly thought it entirely appropriate to "scrutinize the record as a whole to insure that genuine opportunities to participate in a meaningful way were provided. . . ." The court also refrained from actually ordering the agency to follow any specific procedures, but there is little doubt in our minds that the ineluctable mandate of the court's decision is that the procedures afforded during the hearings were inadequate. . . .

In prior opinions we have intimated that even in a rulemaking proceeding when an agency is making a "'quasi-judicial'" determination by which a very small number of persons are "'exceptionally affected, in each case upon individual grounds,'" in some circumstances additional procedures may be required in order to afford the aggrieved individuals due process. It might also be true, although we do not think the issue is presented in this case and accordingly do not decide it, that a totally unjustified departure from well-settled agency procedures of long standing might require judicial correction.

---

7. The Commission stated:
"In our view, the procedures adopted provide a more than adequate basis for formulation of the rule we adopted. All parties were fully heard. Nothing offered was excluded. The record does not indicate that any evidentiary material would have been received under different procedures. Nor did the proponent of the strict 'adjudicatory' approach make an offer of proof—or even remotely suggest—what substantive matters it would develop under different procedures. In addition, we note that 11 documents including the Survey were available to the parties several weeks before the hearing, and the Regulatory staff, though not requested to do so, made available various drafts and handwritten notes. Under all of the circumstances, we conclude that adjudicatory type procedures were not warranted here."

But this much is absolutely clear. Absent constitutional constraints or extremely compelling circumstances the "administrative agencies 'should be free to fashion their own rules of procedure and to pursue methods of inquiry capable of permitting them to discharge their multitudinous duties.'" Indeed, our cases could hardly be more explicit in this regard. The Court has upheld this principle in a variety of applications. . . . And the basic reason for this decision was the Court of Appeals' serious departure from the very basic tenet of administrative law that agencies should be free to fashion their own rules of procedure.

We have continually repeated this theme through the years, most recently in *FPC v. Transcontinental Gas Pipe Line Corp.*, 423 U.S. 326 (1976), decided just two Terms ago. In that case, in determining the proper scope of judicial review of agency action under the Natural Gas Act, we held that while a court may have occasion to remand an agency decision because of the inadequacy of the record, the agency should normally be allowed to "exercise its administrative discretion in deciding how, in light of internal organization considerations, it may best proceed to develop the needed evidence and how its prior decision should be modified in light of such evidence as develops." We went on to emphasize:

> "At least in the absence of substantial justification for doing otherwise, a reviewing court may not, after determining that additional evidence is requisite for adequate review, proceed by dictating to the agency the methods, procedures, and time dimension of the needed inquiry and ordering the results to be reported to the court without opportunity for further consideration on the basis of the new evidence by the agency. Such a procedure clearly runs the risk of 'propel[ling] the court into the domain which Congress has set aside exclusively for the administrative agency.' *SEC v. Chenery Corp.*, 332 U.S. 194 (1947)."

Respondent NRDC argues that § [553] of the Administrative Procedure Act merely establishes lower procedural bounds and that a court may routinely require more than the minimum when an agency's proposed rule addresses complex or technical factual issues or "Issues of Great Public Import." We have, however, previously shown that our decisions reject this view. We also think the legislative history, even the part which it cites, does not bear out its contention. The Senate Report explains what eventually became § [553] thus:

> "This subsection states . . . the minimum requirements of public rule making procedure short of statutory hearing. Under it agencies might in addition confer with industry advisory committees, consult organizations, hold informal 'hearings,' and the like. Considerations of practicality, necessity, and public interest . . . will naturally govern the agency's determination of the extent to which public proceedings should go. Matters of great import, or those where the public submission of facts will be either useful to the agency or a protection to the public, should naturally be accorded more elaborate public procedures."

The House Report is in complete accord:

> "'[U]niformity has been found possible and desirable for all classes of both
> equity and law actions in the courts. . . . It would seem to require no argu-
> ment to demonstrate that the administrative agencies, exercising but a
> fraction of the judicial power may likewise operate under uniform rules
> of practice and procedure and that they may be required to remain within
> the terms of the law as to the exercise of both quasi-legislative and quasi-
> judicial power.'"

> . . . .

> "The bill is an outline of minimum essential rights and procedures. . . . It
> affords private parties a means of knowing what their rights are and how
> they may protect them. . . ."

> . . . .

> ". . . [The bill contains] the essentials of the different forms of administra-
> tive proceedings. . . ."

And the Attorney General's Manual on the Administrative Procedure Act 31, 35
(1947), a contemporaneous interpretation previously given some deference by this
Court because of the role played by the Department of Justice in drafting the legislation, further confirms that view. In short, all of this leaves little doubt that Congress
intended that the discretion of the *agencies* and not that of the courts be exercised in
determining when extra procedural devices should be employed.

There are compelling reasons for construing § [553] in this manner. In the first
place, if courts continually review agency proceedings to determine whether the
agency employed procedures which were, in the court's opinion, perfectly tailored to reach what the court perceives to be the "best" or "correct" result, judicial
review would be totally unpredictable. And the agencies, operating under this vague
injunction to employ the "best" procedures and facing the threat of reversal if they
did not, would undoubtedly adopt full adjudicatory procedures in every instance.
Not only would this totally disrupt the statutory scheme, through which Congress
enacted "a formula upon which opposing social and political forces have come to
rest," but all the inherent advantages of informal rulemaking would be totally lost.

Secondly, it is obvious that the court in these cases reviewed the agency's choice
of procedures on the basis of the record actually produced at the hearing, and not
on the basis of the information available to the agency when it made the decision to
structure the proceedings in a certain way. This sort of Monday morning quarter-
backing not only encourages but almost compels the agency to conduct all rulemaking proceedings with the full panoply of procedural devices normally associated
only with adjudicatory hearings.

Finally, and perhaps most importantly, this sort of review fundamentally mis-
conceives the nature of the standard for judicial review of an agency rule. The court
below uncritically assumed that additional procedures will automatically result in a

more adequate record because it will give interested parties more of an opportunity to participate in and contribute to the proceedings. But informal rulemaking need not be based solely on the transcript of a hearing held before an agency. Indeed, the agency need not even hold a formal hearing. Thus, the adequacy of the "record" in this type of proceeding is not correlated directly to the type of procedural devices employed, but rather turns on whether the agency has followed the statutory mandate of the Administrative Procedure Act or other relevant statutes. If the agency is compelled to support the rule which it ultimately adopts with the type of record produced only after a full adjudicatory hearing, it simply will have no choice but to conduct a full adjudicatory hearing prior to promulgating every rule. In sum, this sort of unwarranted judicial examination of perceived procedural shortcomings of a rulemaking proceeding can do nothing but seriously interfere with that process prescribed by Congress. . . .

In short, nothing in the APA, . . . , the circumstances of this case, the nature of the issues being considered, past agency practice, or the statutory mandate under which the Commission operates permitted the court to review and overturn the rulemaking proceeding on the basis of the procedural devices employed (or not employed) by the Commission so long as the Commission employed at least the statutory *minima*, a matter about which there is no doubt in this case.

There remains, of course, the question of whether the challenged rule finds sufficient justification in the administrative proceedings that it should be upheld by the reviewing court. Judge Tamm, concurring in the result reached by the majority of the Court of Appeals, thought that it did not. There are also intimations in the majority opinion which suggest that the judges who joined it likewise may have thought the administrative proceedings an insufficient basis upon which to predicate the rule in question. We accordingly remand so that the Court of Appeals may review the rule as the Administrative Procedure Act provides. We have made it abundantly clear before that when there is a contemporaneous explanation of the agency decision, the validity of that action must "stand or fall on the propriety of that finding, judged, of course, by the appropriate standard of review. If that finding is not sustainable on the administrative record made, then the Comptroller's decision must be vacated and the matter remanded to him for further consideration." The court should engage in this kind of review and not stray beyond the judicial province to explore the procedural format or to impose upon the agency its own notion of which procedures are "best" or most likely to further some vague, undefined public good.

[handwritten margin note: QUESTION #2 RE: JUSTIFIC. OF ADMIN. PROCEEDING]

. . . .

All this leads us to make one further observation of some relevance to this case. . . . Nuclear energy may some day be a cheap, safe source of power or it may not. But Congress has made a choice to at least try nuclear energy, establishing a reasonable review process in which courts are to play only a limited role. The fundamental policy questions appropriately resolved in Congress and in the state legislatures are *not* subject to reexamination in the federal courts under the guise of judicial review of agency action. Time may prove wrong the decision to develop nuclear energy, but it is Congress or the States within their appropriate agencies which must eventually make that judgment. In the meantime courts should perform their appointed function. . . . It is to insure a fully informed and well-considered decision, not necessarily a decision the judges of the Court of Appeals or of this Court would have reached had they been members of the decisionmaking unit of the agency. Administrative decisions should be set aside in this context, as in every other, only for substantial procedural or substantive reasons as mandated by statute, not simply because the court is unhappy with the result reached. . . .

Notes

1. APA § 553 requirements. The core concept for rulemaking procedures under the APA is "notice and comment." How would you describe the elements of "informal rulemaking" established by APA § 553? Who has authority to add more?

2. Should the WTC add procedures not required by statute? Under what circumstances should the WTC add additional procedures or at least modify the opportunities to participate in the notice-and-comment process? For example, they could provide for oral hearings. Participation is the dominant value in rulemaking. However, Jim Rossi has observed that participation is a mixed blessing. He notes that widespread participation is consistent with democratic norms, raises a wider number of issues, provides more potential solutions, and "may reveal the truth or falsity of factual claims about the state of the world or about the likely effects of policy proposals." Jim Rossi, *Participation Run Amok: The Costs of Mass Participation for Deliberative Agency Decisionmaking*, 92 Nw. U. L. Rev. 173, 213–14 (1997) (quoting Cass R. Sunstein, Democracy and the Problem of Free Speech 243 (1993)). However, he also points out that at some point excessive participation may hamper the agency's ability to consider the issue effectively and undermine effective deliberation. *See id.*

Do you agree that there can be too much participation? How would you limit participation to confront the problems presented by Professor Rossi? Are there other values to participation, in addition to its contribution to accurate decisionmaking, that might compel us to err on the side of more participation?

3. Competing visions of the judicial role over procedural control. One can think of *Vermont Yankee* as a 9-0 smackdown in which the Supreme Court told lower courts, in no uncertain terms, to quit adding procedural requirements to notice-and-comment rulemaking under the APA. This decision should also be understood as the Supreme Court's response to a long-standing debate among lower courts regarding how they should review agency rules, which had grown increasingly important to practical governance—procedurally and substantively—during the 1960s and 1970s. The following exchange from *Friends of the Earth v. AEC*, 485 F.2d 1031 (D.C. Cir. 1973), which features two lions of the D.C. Circuit, Judges

Bazelon and Leventhal, provides some flavor of the debate concerning control of procedure:

In Judge Bazelon's opinion:

> Where, as here, there is a possibility of imminent danger to life and health, emergency court review of administrative action must be more searching than in cases, such as ratemaking, involving purely economic interests. But it is not our duty, if for no other reason than that we lack the competence, to delve into complex scientific issues such as those involved here. . . . Our function is rather to insure that the agency provides "a framework for principled decision-making."

> This framework would ideally include the clash of opposing expert views in a setting involving some right of cross-examination, in the absence of unusual circumstances or emergency conditions. Under the circumstances of this case, and in light of continuing Commission proceedings, an adequate, if not ideal, framework has been provided.

> . . . .

> . . . In future proceedings it may be necessary for the Commission to seek out experts representing varied and opposing technical views to insure that issues such as these are resolved in the "crucible of debate through the clash of informed but opposing scientific and technological viewpoints." Only that sort of approach can "establish a decision-making process which assures a reasoned decision that can be held up to the scrutiny of the scientific community and the public."

Whereas Judge Leventhal observed:

> Chief Judge Bazelon has taken this occasion to discourse on his views, concerning issues not raised by the parties, as to how an agency should handle the proceedings involving safety and health, and to speculate as to what might be required in other circumstances or in the future. . . . Judge Bazelon's underlying approach . . . seems to be pointed toward distending the procedural requirements for rulemaking proceedings. He seems to be trying to chart a course whereby cross-examination will become routine in rule-making proceedings, subject to exceptions for unusual or emergency circumstances. The view developed in the majority opinion in *International Harvester* is that oral presentations in rule-making, however desirable, are not generally required, and that such requirements as may be evolving apply to crucial issues where alternative procedures are not adequate. Those alternatives may include focused written presentations, or oral submissions at legislative-type hearings, with questions submitted by parties through the hearing officer.

Judge Bazelon conceded that judges lack the substantive expertise "to delve into complex scientific issues," but seemed to think that they enjoy procedural expertise, as it were, necessary to improve agency rulemaking procedures. Judge Leventhal seemed less convinced on this point, limiting judicial intervention to "crucial" issues. Notwithstanding *Vermont Yankee,* might Judge Bazelon have been right? Should judges have discretion to insist that agencies provide cross-examination where rules implicate substantial danger to health and life—such as, just to give an example, a rule governing nuclear waste storage?

4. "Hybrid rulemaking," courtesy of Congress. Congress is free, of course, to override the APA in an agency's enabling act and require additional rulemaking procedures, producing a form of "hybrid rulemaking." As with the judicial efforts at formalizing notice-and-comment rulemaking, statutory efforts have had trouble finding the proper balance between judicialization and informality. The model for such provisions is the Magnuson-Moss/FTC Improvement Act rulemaking provision, 15 U.S.C. § 57a. Similar to Judge Leventhal's approach, the Magnuson-Moss Act provided that cross-examination should be permitted if found "to be required for a full and true disclosure with respect to [disputed issues of material fact]."

Judge Stephen Williams, now on the D.C. Circuit, studied the practical impact of the major hybrid rulemaking cases while he was still an administrative law professor. Stephen Williams, *"Hybrid Rulemaking" under the Administrative Procedure Act: A Legal and Empirical Analysis*, 42 U. Chi. L. Rev. 401 (1975). He found that when cross-examination was ordered, the challenging parties often did not even use it on remand. Rather, the right of cross-examination served the purpose of delay, and it served as a bargaining chip for challengers. Williams concluded for those and other reasons not only that cross-examination was inappropriate for rulemaking, but that it tended to frustrate the goal of elucidating the issues. *Id.* at 442–45. Williams found value, however, in procedures that tended to assure the public was fully aware of the basis for an agency's decisions, and in procedures allowing a give-and-take between the agency and affected parties. His analysis suggests that the more trial-like the procedures (such as written interrogatories), the less effective they are in achieving the goal of improving information and understanding. *Id.* at 448–55.

5. Can we negotiate the rule? Would we save time or effort or improve the product? Ben notes that WTCA § 8(b)(3) requires the Commission to consider whether the labeling rule should be negotiated. It refers to the Negotiated Rulemaking Act, 5 U.S.C. §§ 561 *et seq.*, which empowers agency heads to create a rulemaking committee to negotiate a rule if an agency head(s) determines that such a procedure would be "in the public interest," but does not require such a committee in order to engage in negotiated rulemaking. An agency head must consider the need for the rule, whether there are a limited number of identifiable interests who could be adequately represented on the committee, the risks of delay from using this process, and the chances that the committee will reach a consensus the agency can use as the basis for a proposed rule. If the agency decides to establish a negotiated rulemaking committee, it must publish notice and the proposed membership and duties of the committee in the *Federal Register*. The facilitator chairs the meetings and ensures that the committee complies with all record-keeping requirements of the Advisory Committee Act. 5 U.S.C. app. §5(b)(2). The committee may report on any consensus it reaches, or may explain in its report any failure to reach a consensus. The agency then may use the report as the basis for a proposed rule, following ordinary notice-and-comment procedures.

What should the Commission consider? Much of the early foundation for negotiated rulemaking was provided by Philip Harter. Philip Harter, *Negotiating Regulation: A Cure for Malaise*, 71 Geo. L.J. 1 (1982). Harter analyzed the conditions necessary for a successful negotiated rulemaking effort. He developed criteria raising these points:

a. Each party must have power to affect the decision;

b. Negotiation is difficult with large numbers of people and demands;

c. The issues must be readily apparent and the parties must be ready to decide them;

d. There must be pressure to resolve the matter;

e. Negotiation must have the potential to produce gain for all parties;

f. It cannot involve compromise of deeply held values;

g. The parties must be able to trade-off issues; and

h. Some kind of effective implementation process must be present.

Thomas McGarity noted several factors which may lead to failure to negotiate a particular rule. Thomas McGarity, *Some Thoughts on "Deossifying" the Rulemaking Process*, 41 Duke L.J. 1385 (1992). He found that negotiated rulemaking will be difficult: in an environment that is already conflict laden, with respect to "large generic rulemaking efforts with precedent-setting potential," where positions are already hardened, where a large number of parties have widely divergent interests, and when the power of each of the relevant interests is uneven. "[O]n the other hand, negotiated rulemaking might be entirely appropriate for new topics . . . where positions have not yet been formed and where large investments have not yet been made." *Id.* at 1439.

If the WTC decides that it should attempt to negotiate the labeling rule, how should it go about it? What procedures should Ben prescribe for negotiation? Who should be included in the negotiation? How can Ben assure that the interest of the public will be protected? Should the agency attempt to control or at least lead discussions, or should it more passively accommodate the views of interested parties? Is the agency a necessary participant? For some discussion of these questions, see Henry H. Perritt, Jr., *Negotiated Rulemaking Before Federal Agencies: Evaluation of Recommendations by the Administrative Conference of the United States*, 74 Geo. L.J. 1625 (1986).

6. The nature of factual issues in rulemaking. Chris is most interested in assuring factual support for a rule. What kind of factual questions will dominate the rulemaking? Consider the Seventh Circuit analysis in *United Air Lines v. CAB*, 766 F.2d 1107 (7th Cir. 1985), in which the now-defunct Civil Aeronautics Board (CAB) had issued a rule to constrain what the CAB considered to be anticompetitive practices in the airlines' implementation of their computer reservation systems (all of which shared certain similarities). Essentially arguing that the CAB had effectively made adjudicatory findings that airline practices (including its own) were anticompetitive, United Air Lines challenged the use of rulemaking to make this decision. The Seventh Circuit rejected the challenge as long as the CAB had issued "what is genuinely a rule":

> [T]he weight of authority, much of it in the Supreme Court and therefore beyond our power to reexamine, is overwhelming against forcing an administrative agency to hold an evidentiary hearing to resolve disputed questions of antitrust fact, though we can assume there would be an exception for a fact that could not rationally be found without providing an opportunity for cross-examination or some other trial-type procedural safeguard. Subject to this qualification, and provided that the agency issues what is genuinely a rule, which is to say a prospective regulation of general applicability, it is free to base the rule on the kind of findings normally made in an adjudicative proceeding, even if it conducts no evidentiary hearing. An important, perhaps controlling, precedent is *United States v. Florida East Coast Ry.*

Id. at 1118.

Why is it appropriate to treat this decision as rulemaking when the CAB essentially determined that the practices of the various airlines were anticompetitive? Were these adjudicatory facts or legislative facts? In the language of *Bi-Metallic*, construing *Londoner*, had the CAB "exceptionally affected [the airlines] . . . on individual grounds?"

How should the rulemakers at the WTC design the procedures to assure strong fact-gathering of the correct type? Does the Seventh Circuit suggest a category of facts that might require trial-like procedures? Will that category of facts likely be present in developing the labeling rule?

C. Implementing Notice-and-Comment Rulemaking

Although *Vermont Yankee* put a stop to courts explicitly imposing procedures such as cross-examination that go beyond the minimum requirements for notice-and-comment rulemaking, § 553 itself, as interpreted by the courts, imposes requirements that can trip up an agency seeking to promulgate an informal rule. These materials examine the requirements governing issuance of a proposed rule and a final rule after notice and comment.

1. How Does the Agency Initiate the Rulemaking Process?

Sections 553(b) and (c) of the APA govern agency initiation of the legislative rule-making process. Section 553(b) requires that an agency publish a notice of proposed rulemaking (NPRM) in the *Federal Register* (subject to some narrow exceptions), and lists the information that an agency must include in its NPRM. Section 553(c) requires the agency to give the public an opportunity to comment on its proposal. As described in the Notes below, the rulemaking process is also governed by various other requirements. The following materials are designed to help you grasp the specific statutory requirements for notice and comment and how those and other considerations guide agency implementation of the informal rulemaking process.

Lesson 3C.1. Brit, with lead responsibility for the labeling rulemaking, believes the WTC is ready to proceed. Under her direction, the WTC staff examined the literature concerning wine purchasing decisions and had a major public opinion firm conduct several surveys of consumers. Generally, the surveys show that the more expensive the wine, the more consumers pay attention to where the wine is from, what grapes were used, and any other information on the label. With respect to cheaper wines, particularly fruit wines (apple or strawberry wine, for example), consumers tend to be young and to pay little attention to information on the label beyond alcohol content. [Assume for this purpose that the WTCA reaches such fruit wines.]

Despite these differences, Brit has recommended, and the Commissioners have agreed, that any labeling rule should require grape quality and additive disclosures for all types of wines. Brit notes the survey results about cheap wines, but she considers it to be irrelevant because one of her goals is to promote the industry by increasing consumer appreciation of finer wines through clear labeling of ingredients.

Brit has decided to draft the NPRM herself. What information should she include in the NPRM? Can she leave out the information from the staff literature search since that information would be available to any member of the public conducting such a search? Can she leave out the information about cheap wines? Even if she can do either of these, should she? How should she publish the NPRM and otherwise seek public comment? The WTC has an e-mail list of all participants in the wine industry and of everyone else who has contacted the agency concerning wine regulation. Electronic communication would certainly be cheap and efficient. Would it be sufficient? Consider the following materials.

Background of *Nova Scotia Food Products*

The primary mechanism for challenging legislative rules is a petition for direct review of the rule in the Court of Appeals. *Vermont Yankee* is an example of such a challenge. In the following decision, by contrast, the company challenged the rule in question when the agency brought an enforcement action against the company. We will discuss these distinct approaches to judicial review in Chapter 5, but it is generally advisable to challenge a rule directly if possible, rather than wait for enforcement action.

In *Nova Scotia*, the company learned through pretrial discovery of "scientific data and the like upon which the Commissioner now says he relied but which were not made known to the interested parties." According to the district court, the factual record on review consisted of Tabs A-L of Exhibit D provided by the agency. Tab A, which the district court termed the "formal administrative record," consisted of the comments provided by industry and other interested parties in response to the proposed rule. Tabs B-L consisted of "everything that could be located in FDA files germane to the subject matter of the regulation and dated before its issuance." Although the opinion is not entirely clear on the point, it appears that most of the material in Tabs B-L was probably in the agency files at the time of the proposal, and much of the information would have been considered by the agency in preparing the proposal. The company argued, among other things, that the agency's failure to disclose the information in Tabs B-L during the rulemaking process rendered the rule invalid.

United States v. Nova Scotia Food Products Corp.

568 F.2d 240 (2d Cir. 1977)

GURFEIN, CIRCUIT JUDGE:

This appeal involving a regulation of the Food and Drug Administration is not here upon a direct review of agency action. It is an appeal from a judgment of the District Court for the Eastern District of New York (Hon. John J. Dooling, Judge) enjoining the appellants, after a hearing, from processing hot smoked whitefish except in accordance with time-temperature-salinity (T-T-S) regulations contained in 21 C.F.R. Part 122 (1977).

[Nova Scotia challenged the rule on several grounds, including an assertion that it is not feasible to prepare smoked whitefish under the conditions required by the FDA rule. After upholding the FDA's authority to issue the rule, the Second Circuit addressed procedural issues at interest to us here and below.]

II

Appellants contend that . . . the failure to disclose to interested persons the factual material upon which the agency was relying vitiates the element of fairness which is essential to any kind of administrative action. Moreover, they argue that the "concise general statement of . . . basis and purpose" by the Commissioner was inadequate. . . .

. . . .

2

The Scientific Data

Interested parties were not informed of the scientific data, or at least of a selection of such data deemed important by the agency, so that comments could be addressed to the data. Appellants argue that unless the scientific data relied upon by the agency are spread upon the public records, criticism of the methodology used or the meaning to be inferred from the data is rendered impossible.

We agree with appellants in this case, for although we recognize that an agency may resort to its own expertise outside the record in an informal rulemaking procedure, we do not believe that when the pertinent research material is readily available and the agency has no special expertise on the precise parameters involved, there is any reason to conceal the scientific data relied upon from the interested parties. As Judge Leventhal said in *Portland Cement Ass'n v. Ruckelshaus*, 486 F.2d 375, 393 (1973): "It is not consonant with the purpose of a rulemaking proceeding to promulgate rules on the basis of inadequate data, or on data that [in] critical degree, *is known only to the agency*." (Emphasis added.) This is not a case where the agency methodology was based on material supplied by the interested parties themselves. Here all the scientific research was collected by the agency, and none of it was disclosed to interested parties as the material upon which the proposed rule would be fashioned. Nor was an articulate effort made to connect the scientific requirements to available technology that would make commercial survival possible, though the burden of proof was on the agency. This required it to "bear a burden of adducing a reasoned presentation supporting the reliability of its methodology."

Though a reviewing court will not match submission against counter-submission to decide whether the agency was correct in its conclusion on scientific matters (unless that conclusion is arbitrary), it will consider whether the agency has taken account of all "relevant factors and whether there has been a clear error of judgment." In this circuit we have said that "it is 'arbitrary or capricious' for an agency not to take into account all relevant factors in making its determination."

If the failure to notify interested persons of the scientific research upon which the agency was relying actually prevented the presentation of relevant comment, the agency may be held not to have considered all "the relevant factors." We can think of no sound reasons for secrecy or reluctance to expose to public view (with an exception for trade secrets or national security) the ingredients of the deliberative process. . . .

We think that the scientific data should have been disclosed to focus on the proper interpretation of "insanitary conditions." When the basis for a proposed rule is a scientific decision, the scientific material which is believed to support the rule should be exposed to the view of interested parties for their comment. One cannot ask for comment on a scientific paper without allowing the participants to read the paper. Scientific research is sometimes rejected for diverse inadequacies of methodology; and statistical results are sometimes rebutted because of a lack of adequate gathering technique or of supportable extrapolation. Such is the stuff of scientific debate. To suppress meaningful comment by failure to disclose the basic data relied upon is akin to rejecting comment altogether. For unless there is common ground, the comments are unlikely to be of a quality that might impress a careful agency. The inadequacy of comment in turn leads in the direction of arbitrary decisionmaking. We do not speak of findings of fact, for such are not technically required in the informal rulemaking procedures. We speak rather of what the agency should make known so as to elicit comments that probe the fundamentals. Informal rule-making does not lend itself to a rigid pattern. Especially, in the circumstance of our broad reading of statutory authority in support of the agency, we conclude that the failure to disclose to interested persons the scientific data upon which the FDA relied was procedurally erroneous.

Notes

1. Notice of proposed rules. APA § 553(b) requires publication of the NPRM in the *Federal Register,* "unless persons subject thereto are named and either personally served or otherwise have actual notice. . . ." Particular statutes may have their own specific notice provisions. For example, § 8(b)(1) of the WTCA requires both that agencies publish in the *Federal Register* and that "they assure that all interested persons have actual notice of the proposed rulemaking."

Many states also require publication in state "registers" or otherwise. The 2010 MSAPA § 304(a) requires that a state agency publish a NPRM in the state "administrative bulletin." Section 304(b) also requires an agency to "mail the notice or send it electronically to each person that has made a timely request to the agency for a mailed or electronic copy of the notice."

If you were on an agency's rulemaking staff would you consider publication in the *Federal Register* to be adequate notice? Would you attempt to contact directly those who you know might wish to comment? Would this be fair to those interests who were not contacted?

2. What must be in the Notice of Proposed Rulemaking? At this point, Brit's attention is on what should be included in the NPRM. Section 553(b) requires that the notice include:

(1) a statement of the time, place, and nature of the public rulemaking proceedings;

(2) reference to the legal authority under which the rule is proposed; and

(3) either the terms or substance of the proposed rule or a description of the subjects and issues involved.

This seems quite simple, requiring little more than some basic introductory information and the text of the proposed rule itself. Indeed, the proposed rule in *Nova Scotia,* 34 Fed. Reg. 17176–17178 (October 23, 1969), easily meets that description at less than three pages of the *Federal Register.* These days, however, a glance at the proposed rules in *www.regulations.gov* reveals that agencies provide extensive discussion of the bases for their proposals. As you examine *Nova Scotia* and prepare to advise Brit about what to include in the NPRM, consider why this change has occurred.

3. Other requirements to be addressed. In addition to giving notice of the regulatory proposal, a NPRM must demonstrate that the agency has complied with several other statutes and Executive Orders, including the Regulatory Flexibility Act, the Paperwork Reduction Act, the Unfunded Mandates Act, and Executive Order

12,866, discussed later in subchapter 3F. Jeffrey S. Lubbers, A Guide to Federal Agency Rulemaking 149–97 (6th ed. 2018). We don't want to overwhelm you with detail as we explore the basic template for legislative rulemaking. Keep in the back of your mind, however, that these complexities await you out in the real world.

4. Pre-NPRM requirement in the WTCA. So, Ben and Brit must take special care in drafting the proposed rule. Ben notes that WTCA § 8(b)(2) requires an opportunity to comment before the rule is proposed. How should the WTC attempt to obtain those comments? Should the process for crafting the proposed rule be, say, open meetings and hearings generally focused on the issues?

5. The requirement of an opportunity to comment. Section 553(c) requires that the agency "give interested persons an opportunity to participate in the rulemaking through submission of written data, views, or arguments with or without opportunity for oral presentation." This is the core statutory requirement that *Vermont Yankee* held could not be embellished by the courts.

The APA does not establish a minimum length for the comment period. The standard minimum in practice is 30 days, although courts have upheld shorter periods that were reasonable under the circumstances. *See, e.g., Fla. Power & Light Co. v. United States*, 846 F.2d 765, 772 (D.C. Cir. 1988) (upholding a 15-day comment period). Executive Order 12,866 requires "a meaningful opportunity to comment . . . , which in most cases should include a comment period of not less than 60 days." Exec. Order 12,866, § 6(a), 58 Fed. Reg. 51735 (Sept. 30, 1993).

State practice is similar. Section 306 of the 2010 MSAPA, for example, requires a public comment period of at least 30 days.

6. *Nova Scotia*, the opportunity to comment, and the disclosure requirement. How does the *Nova Scotia* decision bear upon what Brit should include in the NPRM? Notice that the court did not rely upon § 553(b) and did not explicitly say that the information at issue had to be included in or disclosed by the NPRM. It held that "the failure to disclose to interested persons the scientific data upon which the FDA relied was procedurally erroneous."

Strictly speaking, neither the APA nor *Nova Scotia* specifically requires that the notice itself disclose the information underlying the proposed rule. The agency must disclose that information somehow, and the NPRM is the logical place to do that. Moreover, agencies are generally not required to disclose all of the information underlying a proposal, just the information necessary to allow effective comment. The failure to disclose relevant information known to the agency poses some risk of reversal on judicial review, but the agency may prevail if it can demonstrate that the public had been made aware of all the relevant issues and the key underlying information. These principles also apply to situations in which an agency learns new information material to its consideration of the rule, where that information is also available to the public. Exactly when an agency has complied with these requirements is a matter of judgment, not of simple line drawing. Jeffrey S. Lubbers, A Guide to Federal Agency Rulemaking 283–305 (6th ed. 2018).

Could the court in *Nova Scotia* have relied upon the statutory provision in § 553(b) to require notice through the NPRM? Could the court have relied upon §§ 553(b) and (c) in concert? What was the basis for the court's requirement that the agency disclose this information for consideration in the rulemaking process?

How committed will the agency be to its proposed rule and how likely is it to rework the proposed rule after public comment? If you were part of a rulemaking staff, how willingly would you modify your proposed rule? Many doubt that agency personnel have the flexibility to make major adjustments in a proposed rule once they are committed to it. It turns out that agencies often do make changes from the proposed rule to the final rule. In the next section we address the limitations on an agency's ability to make such changes.

7. Consider the APA—what about *Vermont Yankee*? Whatever a court may think about the procedures that an agency should use to pursue informal rulemaking, *Vermont Yankee* makes it quite clear that the court may not impose any procedural hurdles beyond the procedures required by the APA. What are the procedural requirements of § 553? *Nova Scotia* was decided before *Vermont Yankee*, as was *Portland Cement Ass'n v. Ruckelshaus*, 486 F.2d 375 (D.C. Cir. 1973), on which *Nova Scotia* was based. These cases are still considered to be good law and are frequently cited. Can you reconcile them with *Vermont Yankee*? If you have some difficulty, you are not the only one. Dissenting in *American Radio Relay League, Inc. v. FCC*, 524 F.3d 227, 246–47 (D.C. Cir. 2008), then-Judge Kavanaugh rejected the *Portland Cement* principle as contrary to the APA and the Supreme Court's decision in *Vermont Yankee*. Who was right, Judge Kavanaugh or the majority? As you will see in Note 6 following Lesson 3D.2 below, the Supreme Court recently re-emphasized the fundamental principles of *Vermont Yankee* in *Perez v. Mortgage Bankers Ass'n*, 135 S. Ct. 1199 (2015). How does this decision affect the debate about the requirements of *Portland Cement* and *Nova Scotia*?

8. The development of "E-Government." Brit is correct to think in terms of the use of electronic communication in rulemaking. In fact, the E-Government Act of 2002 established the Office of Electronic Government, which is responsible for encouraging effective use of electronic information and communication in all areas of government activity, including rulemaking. 44 U.S.C. § 3602. All agencies were, "to the extent practicable," to establish electronic dockets by March 2004. Moreover, there is now a central website, *www.regulations.gov*, through which the public can post comments on any proposed regulation. As Michael Herz reported:

> [A]t many agency websites, it is a relatively simple matter to learn the status of pending rulemakings and, in some cases, even to search the titles or even the text of materials that have been docketed. A dozen or more agencies also maintain subject or docket-specific listservs, so that subscribers receive e-mail notices of submissions, deadlines, or agency actions. While there is a ways to go in user-friendliness, the shift to e-rulemaking has undeniably made it far easier to learn about agency rule-makings, obtain relevant materials, and submit comments.

Michael Herz, *Rulemaking, in* Developments in Administrative Law and Regulatory Practice, 2002–2003 145–51 (Jeffrey S. Lubbers, ed. 2004). Both *regulations .gov* and individual agency websites have matured considerably since that report, making it much easier to identify rulemaking proceedings of interest and to file comments directly online.

Thus, it is clear that the WTC may use electronic communication both to make information available to the public and to receive comments. The WTC could certainly e-mail its NPRM to anyone on its relevant e-mail lists. But may the agency seek comment exclusively by using its own e-mail lists? *See* 5 U.S.C. § 553(b).

9. Optional oral hearings? The APA does not require an oral hearing but agencies often provide for some type of oral participation. Who should preside over these hearings? Should it be Ben as the leading staff person? Or should the WTC use an administrative law judge (ALJ) to assure independence?

10. Public petitions to initiate rulemaking. If the WTC decides not to promulgate a labeling rule, but to implement § 5 of the WTCA through a series of individual enforcement actions, Ben might well expect either the wine industry or consumer interests to ask the agency to issue a rule implementing § 5 in detail. Such petitions are specifically authorized by § 553(e) of the APA, which requires that "each agency give an interested person the right to petition for the issuance, amendment, or repeal of a rule."

Generally, agencies have broad discretion in responding to such petitions. At a minimum, however, § 555(e) requires that: "Prompt notice . . . be given of the denial in whole or in part of a written application, petition, or other request of an interested person made in connection with any agency proceeding. Except in affirming a prior denial or when the denial is self-explanatory, the notice shall be accompanied by a brief statement of the grounds for denial." Denials of rulemaking petitions are generally subject to judicial review under the "arbitrary and capricious" standard of review. As a general proposition, it is very difficult to persuade courts to order agencies to initiate rulemaking proceedings that they do not wish to pursue.

11. A peek inside the black box — what happens inside the agency during rulemaking? As we noted at the beginning of this chapter, a great deal of the policymaking work that goes into creating an agency rule occurs within the agency and is largely shielded from public view. Notably, much of this work occurs *before* the agency issues a statutorily required public notice. The issuance of an NPRM, particularly for an important rule, is an important bureaucratic event, and agencies invest significant resources into getting them right. Agencies, especially large, complex ones, must have internal systems for gathering and analyzing information and policy proposals. If you develop an area of practice that involves the rulemaking function of a particular agency, you will, of course, want to develop a clear understanding of its internal systems — with the idea, of course, of maximizing your ability to influence their operation.

Professor Thomas McGarity's study of the EPA provides us with an excellent example of one agency's internal systems for rulemaking. Thomas O. McGarity, *The Internal Structure of EPA Rulemaking*, 54 LAW & CONTEMP. PROBS. 57 (1991). Examining EPA twenty years after it was created by President Nixon, he describes an evolution of the agency's rulemaking into a highly refined and complex enterprise designed to identify all of the issues relevant to a proposal, obtain input from relevant offices within the agency and the government as a whole, and assure the accuracy and credibility of the agency's proposal. It is important to recognize that any agency will include several different types of actors. At the top are the political appointees. At EPA, for example, the Administrator is in charge. The Deputy Administrator helps run the entire agency, and the Assistant Administrators run each of the separate areas of the agency (e.g., Air, Water, Solid Wastes, depending upon how EPA is organized under any particular administration). These officials have primary and ultimate authority for policy decisions made within the agency. They are advised by the Office of General Counsel.

Below the political appointees are the various program offices, with expertise in particular technical areas. These may include scientists working on specific types of pollution, or they may include economists or other regulatory analysts who work with other branches of the agency.

As described by Professor McGarity, EPA relies upon a Steering Committee of responsible officials from relevant areas of the agency to coordinate all rulemaking efforts within the agency. This allows the agency to avoid duplication and to assure that everyone knows what is going on. If the Steering Committee gives the go-ahead, the agency forms a Workgroup "chaired by the project officer from the lead office," and including appropriate personnel from various offices within the agency, including the Office of General Counsel. The Workgroup advises upon and reviews the development of the rule. Once the Workgroup has prepared a draft of the proposed rule and supporting materials, the Steering Committee reviews the package and may resolve outstanding disputes. If the Steering Committee approves, the package is sent to "Red Border Review" by the agency's top management. The goal of this process is to produce a proposal that complies with any statutory requirements, achieves the current administration's policy goals, accurately reflects the available scientific or technical information, and will survive political and judicial review. Thus, an agency rulemaking decision is the result of a community of different contributors with a variety of experiences, expertise, personalities, and institutional and personal goals.

Justice, then Professor, Stephen Breyer made the following observation about the internal rulemaking process:

> The Environmental Protection Agency, for example, divided the problem of setting water pollution standards among several of its divisions; it staffed different divisions with people possessing different professional backgrounds (lawyers, business graduates, scientists); and it deliberately encouraged argument among them, in hope of giving top decision makers

a more objective view. NHTSA [National Highway Traffic Safety Administration] and the EPA also encouraged informal meetings between staff and industry scientists and engineers in the hope that direct contact among professionals would avoid the posturing that occurs when lawyers and top executives testify in formal meetings. . . .

STEPHEN BREYER, REGULATION AND ITS REFORM 112 (1982). You should always bear in mind that bureaucracies are not monolithic institutions but contain their own disparate communities. How might this affect your efforts to influence a rulemaking on behalf of a client?

2. What Must the Agency Do When It Issues the Final Rule?

Lesson 3C.2. Brit's staff sends Ben, the Director of the Rulemaking Division, a draft of a recommended labeling rule with a statement of basis and purpose. The document is lengthy and detailed, but the main provisions of the rule include:

- "All wine labels shall disclose all grape varieties and artificial ingredients or other additives used during the production of the labeled wine;" and

- "Wine may not be labeled 'special reserve' or by any similar designation unless it is distinguishable from the general run of wine sold by the manufacturer in terms of grapes, production process, or other indication of special quality."

The first of these provisions closely tracks the notice of proposed rulemaking. The staff reports that the primary dispute among commenters concerns the question of whether the information on wine labels matters to purchasers of wine. In terms of §5 of the WTCA, the question is whether the information is "material" to the purchase. Ben consults that part of the record referred to in the statement of basis and purpose as support for the staff recommendations. The Wine Merchants Association and other industry members submitted marketing studies showing that various different labeling practices over the years appeared to make no difference to wine sales, with one category of exceptions. Labels that prominently display celebrity endorsements or the names of very prominent wine makers appear to increase sales. The Wrath for Grapes and other consumer groups, on the other hand, submitted survey data showing that, when asked, consumers express a preference for full disclosure and say it would affect their purchasing decisions. These are consistent with previous studies considered by the Commission. The agency staff has recommended that the Commission conclude that labeling practices are material to consumer choice. Brit's draft of the Final Rule would respond to these various arguments as follows: "Considering the various comments, the Commission believes the disclosure requirement would best serve the public interest."

The second provision, concerning "special reserve" labels, did not appear in the notice of proposed rulemaking. The staff has nonetheless recommended that it be part of the final rule because several studies in the record demonstrate that consumers are particularly attracted to wines labeled with phrases such as "special reserve" or "estate bottled," which give the impression that the wine is of particularly high quality. Under this provision, a wine merchant may not use the term "special reserve" for its ordinary wines.

Ben is concerned that this first major WTC rulemaking effort must be able to withstand the seemingly inevitable attack in the courts. What guidance should he take from the following materials in preparing the final rule? Assuming he decides to go forward with the "special reserve" rule, how might it be challenged, and how could the WTC defend it?

There are two primary ways for opponents of a rule to challenge it at this stage. One is to argue that the agency failed to comply with § 553(c)'s requirement that the agency include a "concise general statement of [its] basis and purpose" when it issued its final rule. The other is to contend that the final rule is so different from the proposed rule that the agency deprived the public of a meaningful opportunity to comment on the final rule in violation of § 553(c). The following materials address each of these issues in turn.

Returning to *Nova Scotia*

Recall that *Nova Scotia* involved a challenge to an FDA rule governing the preparation of smoked whitefish. The excerpt above involved the question of whether, at the beginning of and during the rulemaking process, the agency had adequately disclosed information underlying the proposed and final rule. The following excerpt addresses the question of whether, at the end of the rulemaking process, the agency had complied with the § 553(c) requirement to include a "concise general statement of . . . basis and purpose" in the final rule. In its comments, the industry had argued at length about the temperature and salt concentration necessary to destroy toxic bacteria. It also argued that the proposed requirements would effectively destroy the product for certain types of fish.

United States v. Nova Scotia Food Products Corp.

568 F.2d 240 (2d Cir. 1977)

GURFEIN, CIRCUIT JUDGE:

. . . .

[The Commissioner acknowledged] in his "basis and purpose" statement required by the Administrative Procedure Act ("APA"), 5 U.S.C. § 553(c), that "adequate times, temperatures and salt concentrations have not been demonstrated for each individual species of fish presently smoked." The Commissioner concluded, nevertheless, that "the processing requirements of the proposed regulations are the safest now known to prevent the outgrowth and toxin formation of C. botulinum Type E." He determined that "the conditions of current good manufacturing practice for this industry should be established without further delay."

The Commissioner did not answer the suggestion by the Bureau of Fisheries that nitrite and salt as additives could safely lower the high temperature otherwise required, a solution which the FDA had accepted in the case of chub. Nor did the Commissioner respond to the claim of Nova Scotia through its trade association, the Association of Smoked Fish Processors, Inc., Technical Center that "(t)he proposed process requirements suggested by the FDA for hot processed smoked fish are neither commercially feasible nor based on sound scientific evidence obtained with the variety of smoked fish products to be included under this regulation." Nova Scotia, in its own comment, wrote to the Commissioner that "the heating of certain types of fish to high temperatures will completely destroy the product." It suggested, as an alternative, that "specific processing procedures could be established for each species after adequate work and experimention (sic) has been done but not before." We have noted above that the response given by the Commissioner was in general terms. He did not specifically aver that the T-T-S requirements as applied to whitefish were, in fact, commercially feasible . . . .

C

Appellants additionally attack the "concise general statement" required by APA, 5 U.S.C. § 553, as inadequate. We think that, in the circumstances, it was less than adequate. It is not in keeping with the rational process to leave vital questions, raised by comments which are of cogent materiality, completely unanswered. The agencies certainly have a good deal of discretion in expressing the basis of a rule, but the agencies do not have quite the prerogative of obscurantism reserved to legislatures. "Congress did not purport to transfer its legislative power to the unbounded discretion of the regulatory body." "We cannot discharge our role adequately unless we hold EPA to a high standard of articulation."

The test of adequacy of the "concise general statement" was expressed by Judge McGowan in the following terms:

> "We do not expect the agency to discuss every item of fact or opinion included in the submissions made to it in informal rulemaking. We do expect that, if the judicial review which Congress has thought it important to provide is to be meaningful, the 'concise general statement of . . . basis and purpose' mandated by Section 4 will enable us to see what major issues of policy were ventilated by the informal proceedings and why the agency reacted to them as it did."

And Judge Friendly has noted that "[i]n a case where a proposed standard under OSHA (Occupational Safety and Health Act) has been opposed on grounds as substantial as those presented here, the Department has the burden of offering some reasoned explanation."

The Secretary was squarely faced with the question whether it was necessary to formulate a rule with specific parameters that applied to all species of fish, and particularly whether lower temperatures with the addition of nitrite and salt would not be sufficient. Though this alternative was suggested by an agency of the federal government, its suggestion, though acknowledged, was never answered.

Moreover, the comment that to apply the proposed T-T-S requirements to white-fish would destroy the commercial product was neither discussed nor answered. We think that to sanction silence in the face of such vital questions would be to make the statutory requirement of a "concise general statement" less than an adequate safeguard against arbitrary decision-making.

We cannot improve on the statement of the District of Columbia Circuit in *Industrial Union Dep't, AFL-CIO v. Hodgson*, 499 F.2d 467, 475 (1974).

> "What we are entitled to at all events is a careful identification by the Secretary, when his proposed standards are challenged, of the reasons why he chooses to follow one course rather than another. Where that choice purports to be based on the existence of certain determinable facts, the Secretary must, in form as well as in substance, find those facts from evidence in the record. By the same token, when the Secretary is obliged to make policy judgments where no factual certainties exist or where facts alone do not provide the answer, he should so state and go on to identify the considerations he found to be persuasive."

One may recognize that even commercial infeasibility cannot stand in the way of an overwhelming public interest. Yet the administrative process should disclose, at least, whether the proposed regulation is considered to be commercially feasible, or whether other considerations prevail even if commercial infeasibility is acknowledged. This kind of forthright disclosure and basic statement was lacking in the formulation of the T-T-S standard made applicable to whitefish. It is easy enough for an administrator to ban everything. In the regulation of food processing, the worldwide need for food also must be taken into account in formulating measures taken for the protection of health. In the light of the history of smoked whitefish to which we have referred, we find no articulate balancing here sufficient to make the procedure followed less than arbitrary.

———

Now that we understand what must be included in an agency's statement of its basis and purpose for a final rule, we can turn to the other primary question regarding an agency's issuance of a final rule: whether the final rule departs so significantly from the proposed one that the public was deprived of its right to comment on the final rule in violation of § 553(c).

Background of *Natural Resources Defense Council v. EPA*

The following decision is a good example of the many complexities of environmental law. First, while it seems simple enough to set maximum pollution levels and expect compliance, the pollution control regime has to account for the many variations in industrial activity. Here, for example, the logging industry places cut timber into nearby rivers for transport to lumber mills. Water quality standards limit the amount of woody debris in the river, but the practical reality is that those standards will be exceeded in the area where the logs are first placed in the river.

The solution discussed here is to have a so-called zone of deposit where the standards can be exceeded, but to require compliance with the standards outside of that zone. This case involved a regulation governing the zone of deposit.

The second complexity illustrated here is the interaction between federal and state laws and agencies in setting and implementing environmental standards. Here, both EPA and the Alaska Department of Environmental Conservation play different roles in determining the appropriate zone of deposit. Consider how Alaska's role in determining the zone affected the outcome of this case, and whether, perhaps, the court should have given greater attention to the proceedings and decisions of the Alaska agency.

In addition to considering the particular issue addressed in this case, carefully examine the notes to determine the agency's various other responsibilities when it issues a final rule.

Natural Resources Defense Council v. U.S. EPA
279 F.3d 1180 (9th Cir. 2002)

THOMAS, CIRCUIT JUDGE:

Petitioners seek review of permits issued by the United States Environmental Protection Agency ("EPA") authorizing the operators of log transfer facilities in Alaska to release bark and woody debris into marine waters. We conclude that the EPA failed to provide adequate notice and opportunity for comment prior to issuing the final general permits, and we grant the petition for review in part.

I

[The Clean Water Act (CWA) prohibits all discharges of pollutants into the waters of the United States from a "point source" without a permit. Large polluting facilities typically must obtain individual permits, but EPA is authorized to issue "general permits," which] "are issued for an entire class of hypothetical dischargers in a given geographical region and are issued pursuant to administrative rulemaking procedures." . . . After a general permit has been issued, an entity that believes it is covered by the general permit submits a "notice of intent" to discharge pursuant to the general permit. A general permit can allow discharging to commence upon receipt of the notice of intent, after a waiting period, or after the permit issuer sends out a response agreeing that the discharger is covered by the general permit. . . .

Under the CWA, each state sets its own water quality standards, subject to review and approval by the EPA. Before approving a state's proposed standards, the EPA must be satisfied that the standards comply with the requirements of the CWA. Alaska has enacted water quality standards that have been approved by the EPA.

Before the EPA can issue either an individual or a general NPDES permit, the state in which the discharge will occur must certify, or waive its right to certify, that the discharge authorized by the permit will comply with the state's water quality standards.

II

Because of Alaska's unique and rugged terrain, most logs cut in Alaska are transported to market through marine waters. For transport, the logs are tied together into bundles that form log rafts. The bundles are placed into the water at log transfer facilities ("LTFs"). From these points, the bundles are towed to destinations such as sawmills and shipping ports.

During this process, particularly at the point where the logs are placed into the water, the logs rub against each other and sometimes against the bottom of the body of water. This friction, as well as the contact of the logs with the water itself, causes bark and woody debris to be rubbed or broken off and released into the water. Different methods of placing the logs into the water result in different amounts of bark and woody debris being released. Bark and woody debris remain in the water and do not decay for many years. In areas where the water lacks strong currents or where high amounts of bark and woody debris enter the water, the bark and woody debris can accumulate into significant concentrations. These accumulations of bark and woody debris create problems for marine life and worsen the quality of the water.

The EPA identified bark and woody debris as a pollutant in the early 1980s. Consequently, the EPA required new LTFs to obtain individual permits before discharging bark and woody debris.

. . . .

In the mid-1990s, the EPA came to the conclusion that the pre-1985 permits did not comply with the CWA.

. . . .

MODIFICATION BY EPA

Accordingly, the EPA proposed to modify all pre-1985 permits for LTFs in Alaska. The EPA issued for comment a draft general permit that would apply to nearly all LTFs in Alaska, including new LTFs and existing LTFs functioning under individual, post-1985 NPDES permits as well as LTFs functioning under pre-1985 permits. The proposed permit included changes in monitoring and reporting requirements, management practices, and effluent limitations. It also noted that Alaska proposed to allow a one-acre zone of deposit for bark and woody debris, defined by accumulations of 100 percent cover that exceed four inches' depth at any point, and to allow patchy distribution of bark beyond the one-acre zone of deposit.

A "zone of deposit," a creature of Alaska state law, is an area in which Alaska's water quality standards can be violated. Alaska's water quality standards consist of maximum levels for the amount of pollutants that can be in waters of different classifications. Bark and woody debris fall into the category "residues." The maximum amount of residue that can be in the highest class of water is defined as the amount that does not "make the water unfit or unsafe for use, . . . or cause a sludge, solid, or emulsion to be deposited beneath or upon the surface of the water, within the water column, on the bottom, or upon adjoining shorelines." The parties interpret this provision as meaning that, in general, any bark or woody debris released into the water would violate this standard. Because a zone of deposit is an area in which the standards can be violated, however, bark or woody debris can be released into an approved zone of deposit without violating Alaska's water quality standards.

The one-acre size for the zones had been prior practice for at least some pre-1985 permits and some post-1985 individual NPDES permits. As noted by the EPA in the draft general permit, the one-acre size for the zones stemmed from interim guidelines promulgated by the Alaska Timber Task Force ("ATTF") in 1985.

As it was required to do, the EPA sought certification from Alaska before it finalized the proposed general permit for LTFs in Alaska. The Alaska Department of Environmental Conservation ("ADEC") is the Alaska agency that provides such certification, and it follows its own public comment and review procedures before providing certification. The EPA noted this fact in the draft general permit, stating that "[p]ersons wishing to comment on State Certification of the proposed general NPDES permit should submit written comments within this public notice period to [ADEC]."

EPA SEEKS CERTIFICATION FROM AK.

In its first and second draft certifications, ADEC proposed that the zones of deposit be one acre of continuous bark coverage at least ten centimeters deep at any point. It also indicated that a zone of deposit could include patchy or discontinuous coverage outside the one acre of continuous coverage. It proposed that LTFs be required to submit remediation plans detailing "feasible" means of reducing bark and woody debris when an accumulation exceeded 1.5 acres of continuous coverage.

ADEC DRAFT CERTIFICATES

In its final draft certification, which apparently was not circulated to the public for comment, ADEC placed no specific size limit on zones of deposit. Instead, it authorized each LTF's zone to be its "project area," or the entire area of water covered by its operations. ADEC maintained the requirement that LTFs propose feasible remediation measures, but the requirement would be triggered by an accumulation of one acre of continuous coverage at least ten centimeters deep at any point, rather than 1.5 acres.

. . . .

The project-area definition for zones of deposit was incorporated into ADEC's final certification for the EPA's general LTF permit. The EPA accepted ADEC's certification.

EPA ACCEPTS AK CERT.

The EPA then issued final general permits. Instead of the one general permit originally proposed, the EPA issued two general permits: one for pre-1985 LTFs, AK-G70-0000, and one for post-1985 LTFs, AK-G70-1000. Both permits incorporated ADEC's project-area zone of deposit definition.

. . . .

III

A

Under the Administrative Procedure[] Act, the EPA must provide the public with notice and an opportunity to comment before it issues NPDES permits. Like other agencies, the EPA "must provide notice sufficient to fairly apprise interested persons of the subjects and issues before the Agency."

Of course, the final permit issued by the agency need not be identical to the draft permit. That would be antithetical to the whole concept of notice and comment. Indeed, it is "the expectation that the final rules will be somewhat different and improved from the rules originally proposed by the agency." Thus, "[t]he law does not require that every alteration in a proposed rule be reissued for notice and comment."

However, "a final rule which departs from a proposed rule must be a logical outgrowth of the proposed rule. . . . The essential inquiry focuses on whether interested parties reasonably could have anticipated the final rulemaking from the draft permit." In determining this, one of the salient questions is "whether a new round of notice and comment would provide the first opportunity for interested parties to offer comments that could persuade the agency to modify its rule." *Am. Water Works Ass'n v. EPA*, 40 F.3d 1266, 1274 (D.C. Cir. 1994); *see also Am. Med. Ass'n v. United States*, 887 F.2d 760, 768 (7th Cir. 1989) (stating that "the relevant inquiry is whether or not potential commentators would have known that an issue in which they were interested was 'on the table'").

On a petition for review from an agency decision, we determine in the first instance the adequacy of the agency's notice and comment procedure, without deferring to an agency's own opinion of the adequacy of the notice and comment opportunities it provided. A decision made without adequate notice and comment is arbitrary or an abuse of discretion.

B

In this instance, we conclude that the EPA's notice and comment procedure was inadequate because it did not afford interested parties the opportunity to comment on whether Alaska's proposed change in the zone of deposit definition conformed to the substantive requirements of Alaska law and, if not, whether the change required the issuance of a conditional permit or the denial of the permit altogether.

Under the CWA, the EPA has its own independent obligation to determine whether a permit will comply with the state's water quality standards.

In its draft permit, upon which public comment was solicited, the EPA noted:

> If issued, this general NPDES permit would authorize qualifying LTFs to discharge bark and woody debris into both near-shore and offshore marine waters in Alaska, except in areas excluded from coverage. The proposed general permit would not authorize new discharges into waters identified as critical or protected resources, waters which do not meet the ATTF siting

guidelines, and waters already exceeding State Water Quality Standards for parameters relating to bark and woody debris. ADEC proposes to grant a one-acre zone of deposit for those LTFs authorized under this general permit.

As noted earlier, the referenced one-acre zone of deposit area was consistent with then-existing Alaska regulatory practice. When it became apparent that Alaska's draft certification proposed a different practice, EPA's NPDES Unit Manager wrote the State [seeking an explanation of how Alaska's new practice complied with the Clean Water Act.] . . .

SEEKING EXPLANATION

Upon reviewing Alaska's response, the EPA issued a final permit approving Alaska's new zone of deposit definition. However, the public was never notified that Alaska was proposing to redefine the allowable zone of deposit, nor was the public afforded the opportunity to comment on the proposed change, either at the state or federal level.

NO PUB. COMMENT ON NEW DEFINITION

In determining the adequacy of EPA's notice and comment procedure as to this issue, the salient question is, as we have noted, "whether interested parties reasonably could have anticipated the final rulemaking from the draft permit." Given that the draft permit specifically referenced Alaska's proposed "one-acre zone of deposit" and conformance with the ATTF guidelines, interested parties could not have reasonably anticipated that the final permit would sanction the use of project-area zones of deposit that could exceed one acre. The fact that interested parties did not anticipate the paradigm shift from the draft to the final permit is underscored by the contents of the instant petition for review, which raises for the first time numerous issues about the proposed change in the conception of zones of deposit. These are precisely the type of comments that should have been directed in the first instance to the EPA, but which understandably were not because of the inadequate notice. Because the EPA's change of position from the draft permit was not "foreshadowed in proposals and comments advanced during the rulemaking," the "decision clearly caught petitioners . . . by surprise."

MAIN Q

Further, interested parties are entitled to be fairly apprised of the subjects and issues before the agency in a permitting process. . . . The public was not informed that EPA had raised the substantive issue about Alaska's proposed change in its definition of zones of deposit. Indeed, the proposed alteration was almost the only substantive issue left for resolution prior to issuance of the final permit. In short, the interested parties did not know that a fundamental change in the zone of deposit definition "was 'on the table.'"

The EPA argues that the draft permit's references to the role of state law and the state certification process and the fact that the proposed zones of deposit might allow "patchy or discontinuous" bark coverage outside the one-acre zone of continuous coverage were sufficient to put interested parties on notice. However, nuance and subtlety are not virtues in agency notice practice. If the EPA were contemplating approving entirely new constructs for allowable zones of deposit and departing from the ATTF guidelines, it should have said so explicitly. More importantly, there is no question that the change was substantive. The EPA acknowledged as much in its letter to the State, noting that "[t]he Department has changed its approach . . . from the approach contained in the ATTF Guidelines, which has been used for authorizing [zones of deposit] since the guidelines were developed." Given the draft permit's stated "heavy reliance" on the ATTF Guidelines, there is no doubt that there was a fundamental policy shift, rather than a natural drafting evolution, between the draft permit and the final permit. Given that the "final rule deviate[d] . . . sharply from the proposal," the EPA erred in not affording notice and soliciting further comments.

Notes

1. Making good use of the opportunity for public comment. Commenters have two basic goals in responding to an NPRM. The first is to make a persuasive case for their position. This includes appropriate legal arguments and citations, factual submissions (frequently including reports by substantive experts and extensive data), and logical arguments using all of the available materials.

The other basic goal is to create a record for judicial review. We will address judicial review at length in Chapter 5. It suffices at this point to understand that the arbitrary and capricious standard of review asks whether there is a "rational connection" among the law, the facts in the record, and the agency's ultimate conclusion. The commenter's task is to shape the record such that it would be very difficult or impossible for the agency to adopt a rule contrary to the commenter's interest without violating this principle.

The commenter faces several obstacles, which arise from the Balkanized nature of many agencies and the difficulty of making complex arguments to agency staff members who are already extremely busy. David Weinberg described this conundrum by explaining that:

> Commenting has always been a difficult art, because comments must serve several conflicting purposes. First and foremost, they must endeavor to persuade the target audience — typically agency staff or their consultants — to accept the commenter's suggestions or views. Typically, though, persuasive argument requires brevity and focus. Yet, second, comments must address all important issues raised by the proposal, not just the ones flagged for comment by the agency. Third, they must anticipate and be organized in a way consistent with the agency's analytical mechanisms. And, fourth, they must build the record for judicial review, should it prove necessary. . . .

> Several tensions run between these challenges. It is only human, after all, that some staff will be put off by a heavy-handed emphasis on legal standards. Telling a persuasive story may be hard when one understands that comment submissions are going to be sliced up, with different sections reviewed by different agency personnel (or contractors). And just how far

does one go in spotting, and addressing, secondary issues without eliminating one of the viable grounds for challenging an unacceptable rule . . . — that the agency did not give adequate notice of what it was considering?

David B. Weinberg, *D.C. Circuit Decision Highlights Need to Consider Comments on Proposed Rules*, 77 U.S.L.W. 2691 (2009). Judging by the descriptions in Lesson 3C.2, how well have the industry and consumer groups accomplished these goals?

2. What is the agency's task in issuing the final rule? The APA merely requires that an agency support a rule with a "concise general statement of . . . basis and purpose." 5 U.S.C. § 553(c). In a rulemaking involving long-distance telephone service, the FCC decided that $650 million was needed for a Universal Service Fund, which would subsidize poor and rural users of long-distance service. The Fifth Circuit described the agency's responsibility in colorful terms:

> The FCC does not explain how it actually derived that figure [$650 million], and instead seems to invoke the Goldilocks approach to rulemaking: noting that "[s]ome commentators argue that the size of the interstate access universal service mechanism is too large [while] [o]ther commentators argue that the size . . . is too small," the FCC apparently believes that its approach is just right because it falls reasonably within the range of estimates. The FCC also relies heavily on the fact that both the [long distance and local phone companies], which traditionally have had opposing interests, agree on the amount. An agency abdicates its role as a rational decision-maker if it does not exercise its own judgment, and instead cedes near-total deference to private parties' estimates—even if the parties agree unanimously as to the estimated amount.

Texas Office of Public Utility Counsel v. FCC, 265 F.3d 313, 328 (5th Cir. 2001). As this decision suggests, the agency's statement gets little if any credit for being "concise"; the focus is on whether the agency fully explained itself. We will examine the explanation requirement much more fully (perhaps to your dismay) when we address judicial review of agency action in Chapter 5.

3. Must the agency respond to the comments? What should affect the agency's judgment as to which comments must be answered? What factors should Ben and Brit use to evaluate the comments? How complete should answers to the comments be? The seminal decision on this issue, relied upon by the *Nova Scotia* court in the above excerpt, is *Portland Cement Ass'n v. Ruckelshaus*, 486 F.2d 375, 393–94 (D.C. Cir. 1973), which involved an engineer's comments on the validity of certain tests that were the basis for a proposed pollution control standard. EPA had added the comments to the record, but it had not directly addressed them. The court remanded on this (and several other issues) to get EPA's response:

> We are not establishing any broad principle that EPA must respond to every comment made by manufacturers on the validity of its standards or the methodology and scientific basis for their formulation. . . . This agency, particularly when its decisions can literally mean survival of persons

or property, has a continuing duty to take a "hard look" at the problems involved in its regulatory task, and that includes an obligation to comment on matters identified as potentially significant by the court order remanding for further presentation. Manufacturers' comments must be significant enough to step over a threshold requirement of materiality before any lack of agency response or consideration becomes of concern. The comment cannot merely state that a particular mistake was made in a sampling operation; it must show why the mistake was of possible significance in the results of the test. . . .

The D.C. Circuit later addressed this issue quite succinctly: "Although the FCA is not required 'to discuss every item of fact or opinion included in the submissions' it receives in response to a Notice of Proposed Rulemaking, it must respond to those 'comments which, if true, . . . would require a change in [the] proposed rule.'" *Louisiana Fed. Land Bank Ass'n, FCLA v. Farm Credit Admin.*, 336 F.3d 1075, 1080 (D.C. Cir. 2003).

[handwritten margin note: COMMENT TO BE ANSWERED]

The above decisions address comments of substantive significance. What about comments that arrive in large numbers, a phenomenon that has increased dramatically with interest groups' use of the internet? The pluralistic model of decisionmaking might suggest that an agency should be affected by the number of comments urging a certain position. Should there be any sense of majoritarianism? The D.C. Circuit, in *Natural Resources Defense Council v. EPA*, thought not. 822 F.2d 104, 122 n.17 (D.C. Cir. 1987) ("The number and length of comments, without more, is not germane to a court's substantial-evidence inquiry.") Do you agree?

4. To what extent may the agency change the rule without seeking additional comment? The staff's recommended "special reserve" provision of the labeling rule arguably represents a significant change from the rule that was proposed. Cautious as usual, Ben suggests that the WTC should publish a new NPRM to solicit comment on this aspect of the rule. Carl, who wants to demonstrate his aggressive leadership of the agency, wants the rule in place as quickly as possible. Brit argues this aspect of the rule will survive any challenge. Who is right?

In addition to *Natural Resources Defense Council v. EPA*, above, consider the following from *Louisiana Federal Land Bank Ass'n, FCLA v. Farm Credit Administration*, 336 F.3d 1075 (D.C. Cir. 2003). The Farm Credit Administration (FCA) proposed to eliminate certain geographic restrictions on lenders in the farm credit system. Such lenders make direct loans. They also participate in loans made by other lenders. The FCA proposed to eliminate geographic restrictions on both practices, but the final rule only eliminated them for one practice (loan participations) and not the other (direct loans). In response to an argument that the FCA was required to seek comment on this change, the court said,

> [T]he Final Rule . . . was a logical outgrowth — indeed a natural subset — of the proposal.

> . . . .

As the district court put the matter, "[n]owhere does the Proposed Rule indicate that removal of geographic restriction is an all-or-nothing proposal." Under these circumstances, we think the plaintiffs were clearly on notice that if they had anything to say specifically about the effect of removing geographic restrictions upon loan participations — either alone or in combination with the removal of restrictions upon other activities — then they should have said it during the period for comments on the Proposed Rule.

Just as *Louisiana Federal Land Bank Association* provided a "natural subset" test as a reasonable basis for judging an agency change from a proposed rule to a final rule, many decisions provide similar guidance. In *Long Island Care at Home, Ltd. v. Coke*, 551 U.S. 158, 175 (2007), for example, the Supreme Court upheld an agency decision to adopt a rule that was the opposite of the proposal. This might seem an obvious opportunity for a "logical outgrowth" challenge, but the agency had simply decided to stay with the status quo, rather than adopting the proposal. As the Court put it, "[s]ince the proposed rule was simply a proposal, its presence meant that the Department was considering the matter; after that consideration the Department might choose to adopt the proposal or to withdraw it . . . . We do not understand why such a possibility was not reasonably foreseeable." We might take from this a general principle that the pre-proposal status quo is always a possible outcome (except where a statute makes that impossible).

Two other decisions illustrate how particular circumstances can drive the outcome of a "logical outgrowth" dispute. In *Council Tree Communications, Inc. v. FCC*, 619 F.3d 235 (3d Cir. 2010), the Third Circuit addressed a final rule that would have changed a rule issued only three years before, but the agency had not mentioned the previous rule in the proposal. In that situation, the court thought it was unreasonable for commenters to expect that the agency might change such a recently adopted position without any mention of that prospect in the proposal. In *Allina Health Services v. Sebelius*, 746 F.3d 1102 (D.C. Cir. 2014), the D.C. Circuit found no logical outgrowth where the proposal said that the agency intended to "clarify" the issue at hand, and that "there should not be a major impact associated with this proposed change." When the final rule adopted a position that was the opposite of the proposal and that would have a "substantial financial effect," the court found that the proposal had not given adequate notice of such a substantial change. The fact that there were only two choices was not enough to give notice of the need to comment on the possibility of a significant change from the proposal.

Ultimately, these decisions represent common sense judgments about whether the proposal gave interested parties adequate notice of the issues ultimately addressed in the final rule. As the Supreme Court put it in *Long Island Care at Home*, "[t]he object, in short, is one of fair notice."

Unfortunately, common sense is often in the eye of the beholder. Professors Beerman and Lawson have argued that stringent application of the "logical outgrowth" test can render the rulemaking process highly unpredictable, forcing agencies to grapple with just how much change is allowed before a court will declare that the final rule is a material alteration and no longer a logical outgrowth of the proposal. This gives agencies a strong incentive to overproceduralize rulemaking by issuing, as we see today, highly detailed proposed rules with voluminous supporting material, and by conducting additional comment periods whenever a significant change is warranted by the comments. Raising the cost of making adjustments in response to comments gives agencies an incentive either to ignore the comments, which is contrary to the whole premise of legislative rulemaking, or to conduct a second round of notice and comment whenever it wants to make a change, which is contrary to Congress's intent in establishing the informal process embodied in § 553, as recognized by the Court in Vermont Yankee.

Jack M. Beerman and Gary Lawson, *Reprocessing Vermont Yankee*, 75 Geo. Wash. L. Rev. 856, 899 (2007).

Despite those concerns, the states may be even stricter. The 1981 MSAPA § 3-107 prohibited an agency from adopting a rule that is "substantially different from the proposed rule" and listed factors to be considered in making that determination. The Pennsylvania Supreme Court seemed to find that § 3-107 required more "expansive notice" than the logical outgrowth test. *Brocal Corp. v. Commonwealth Dep't of Transp.*, 528 A.2d 114 (Pa. 1987). But the 2010 MSAPA, § 308, specifically adopts the "logical outgrowth" test. The related comment describes the substance of the test as follows:

> Fair notice is met when changes between the adopted rule and the proposed rule are reasonably foreseeable from the proposed rule. Courts utilize several factors to apply the logical outgrowth test including: (1) any person affected by the adopted rule should have reasonably expected that the change from the published proposed rule would affect the person's interest; (2) the subject matter of the adopted rule or the issues determined by that rule are different from the subject matter or issues involved in the published rule proposed to be adopted; and (3) the effect of the adopted rule differs from the effect of the rule proposed to be adopted or amended.

How does this articulation of the test differ, if at all, from the federal version?

5. Achieving clarity in the final rule. Agencies try to write rules that are clear and understandable to the public, particularly to the industries they regulate. After all, agencies themselves benefit from clear, easily enforceable regulatory language. Despite that effort, some questions inevitably remain unanswered, and some provisions remain unclear. That is a primary reason that agencies (and those they regulate) rely heavily upon the nonlegislative rules discussed below in subchapter 3D.2.

6. The *Federal Register*—repository of final rules. The thousands and thousands of administrative rules and regulations that affect our lives, property, rights, and benefits should be systematically and periodically compiled, published, and made available to the public at large. To do otherwise would seem to constitute a violation of the most basic principles of fundamental due process under law. Yet, not until March 1936 were federal administrative rules of general applicability published with any semblance of order and regularity.

Before this date, publication of administrative rules was, at best, "a maximum of variety and confusion," with each agency, department, and subcomponent thereof printing and distributing its rules in whatever form or order it so desired. During this time, rules were usually printed in separate paper pamphlets, bulletins, or notices, which were easy to lose, difficult to retrieve, and infrequently propagated. Thus, citizens were bound by, and sometimes convicted of, violations of rules the existence and effectiveness of which were difficult, if not virtually impossible, to ascertain. In 1934, however, after *United States v. Smith*, 293 U.S. 633 (1934), which went all the way to the Supreme Court before it was discovered that the regulation upon which the charge was based had been revoked, the wave of public criticism over the chaotic state of publication of rules began to grow until it finally peaked in 1935 with the enactment of the Federal Register Act (FRA), 44 U.S.C. §§ 1501–1511. The FRA identified the nature of the documents to be published and the process by which publication occurs in the *Federal Register*. It also established the Administrative Committee of the Federal Register, which is charged with issuing its own rules.

In 1946, when Congress passed the Public Information Section of the APA (§ 3), the predecessor to the Freedom of Information Act, the Public Information Section not only reaffirmed a commitment to the publication of administrative rules of general effect, but also reinvigorated and enhanced the publication requirement. The Public Information Section was "not intended to repeal the Federal Register Act, but simply to require the publication of certain additional material." The amendment to § 3, known as the Freedom of Information Act (FOIA), in § 552(a)(1) retained the *Federal Register* requirements of the old section, most of which relate to publication of agency procedural action. Section 552(a)(1)(D) requires publication of substantive material that, coupled with the Federal Register Act, results in publication of massive amounts of information. Indeed, most criticism focuses on the fact that too much, not too little, is published.

Together, the FRA and FOIA create the *Federal Register* system. The *Federal Register* itself is a daily publication that contains the proposed rule and the initial publication of a final rule, along with lots of other government information. Permanent rules are compiled and published in the Code of Federal Regulations (CFR).

The *Federal Register* system is a major research source for "agency law." The *Federal Register* system attempts to provide several finding aids. The basic finding aids are organized according to individual agencies. This arrangement recognizes that practitioners usually specialize and hence each user is generally interested in the regulations of only one agency. (In further recognition of this fact, several agencies have agreed to publish on certain days of the week.) Each daily issue contains its own table of contents which is arranged alphabetically by agency. Each month, the system publishes an agency-by-agency cumulative index with broad topical headings.

7. Notice of the final rule — what is enough to allow enforcement? Section 552(a) (1) requires publication of final rules, and § 553(d) provides for a 30-day hiatus between publication and effective date. There are, however, some exceptions. Sometimes circumstances dictate that rules must be issued quickly (see discussion in subchapter 3D.1 of the exceptions to the requirement for notice and comment) and enforced immediately. Still, however, there must be some form of notice to those affected. The waving of arms and yelling of federal officials was sufficient notice to support a conviction for trespass on a temporary military security zone in *United States v. Ventura-Melendez*, 321 F.3d 230 (1st Cir. 2003). Even if a rule has not yet been published in the *Federal Register*, "actual and timely notice of the terms thereof" is enough to require compliance with the rule. *See* § 552(a)(1).

8. Rulemaking and new presidential administrations — the problem of "midnight regulations." As American politics have become increasingly polarized, the issue of "midnight regulations" has become a growing phenomenon. Any administration committed to its own policy goals will attempt to complete important rulemaking efforts before it is replaced, particularly if the replacement puts the other party in control.

It is clear that if a previous administration has completed the notice-and-comment process for a particular legislative rule, including having it signed by the appropriate official and published in the *Federal Register* before the end of the president's term, the subsequent administration would have to implement the entire rulemaking process again to withdraw or change the rule. The tricky questions arise when the rulemaking process has not quite been completed, as when the rule has been signed and transmitted to the *Federal Register*, but has not yet been published. Tricky questions also arise when, as occurred frequently under the second President Bush and also under President Obama, the new administration attempts to extend the effective date of new regulations so as to allow time to eliminate or change the regulation before it takes effect.

As to rules that have been transmitted to the *Federal Register* but have not yet been published, the D.C. Circuit held in *Kennecott Utah Copper Corp. v. Department of Interior*, 88 F.3d 1191, 1205 (D.C. Cir. 1996), that such rules could be withdrawn during the three-day "'confidential processing period' . . . *after* an agency transmits a document to the OFR [Office of Federal Register] and *before* the OFR makes the document available for public inspection." This left open, however, the question of whether rules could be withdrawn once they have been made available for public inspection but before they are published. *See* William M. Jack, Comment, *Taking Care That Presidential Oversight of the Regulatory Process Is Faithfully Executed: A Review of Rule Withdrawals and Rule Suspensions under the Bush Administration's Card Memorandum*, 54 ADMIN. L. REV. 1479, 1493–94 (2002). Under the language of the current rule, an agency may withdraw a filed document "with a timely letter signed by a duly authorized representative of the agency." 1 C.F.R. § 18.13 (2019).

Once a rule has been published, a new administration must pursue rulemaking to extend the effective date. Sometimes, as the second Bush administration discovered, provisions of the enabling act prevent changes after a rule has been issued by the agency. In *NRDC v. Abraham*, 355 F.3d 179 (2d Cir. 2004), the D.C. Circuit held that, since the rule had already been published in the *Federal Register*, an attempt to delay it was prevented by a provision of the enabling act stating that the agency "may not prescribe any amended standard" that is weaker than a standard already in place. For a thorough review of these transitional issues, see Jack M. Beerman, *Presidential Power in Transitions*, 83 B.U. L. Rev. 947 (2003).

9. The agency may not be done yet—political branch review of agency rules in Congress and the states. Political actors may, of course, attempt to alter or void a rule even after an agency has issued it in its final, official form. At the federal level, Congress may do so by passing a statute overturning an agency rule via normal legislative means, but this is a very difficult thing to do. Alternatively, Congress may, in theory, use the streamlined procedures of the Congressional Review Act (discussed at note 12 at the end of subchapter 1C.3 after the *Morrison* excerpt) to prevent a rule from taking effect. In general, congressional efforts to undo an agency rule are likely to take more of a "backdoor" form—e.g., an agency may find its funding under threat in the appropriations process. The president, too, has little formal control over agency rules once they have been formally promulgated and run the gauntlet of Executive Order 12,866 and other controls. (For more information on the White House's involvement in the rulemaking process, see subchapter 3F.) Of course, if the president is very interested in seeing a rule changed, his informal influence will be vast.

Formal political-branch review of agency rules at the state level presents a very different picture. *See generally* Arthur Bonfield, *State Law in the Teaching of Administrative Law: A Critical Analysis of the Status Quo*, 61 Tex. L. Rev. 95 (1982). In several states, the governor can veto or rescind agency rules. In California, the power to veto or rescind rules is committed to an Office of Administrative Law, subject to the governor's override power. Some states allow legislative vetoes; others follow the logic of *Chadha* and disallow them. A few states allow legislative rules review committees to challenge the legality of agency rules in court. A few states authorize legislative rules committees to object to agency rules, and, by doing so, shift the burden of persuasion to the agency to prove the lawfulness of its rule in subsequent litigation. (Bonfield calls this an objection with "bite.") Some states authorize a legislative rules review committee to suspend temporarily the operation of a rule— the legislature as a whole may extend this suspension or end it. The 2010 MSAPA provides for consideration of all final rules by a rules review committee, which is authorized to approve, disapprove and propose amendment, or disapprove of the final rule. If the committee disapproves of the final rule, the rule becomes effective upon the adjournment of the next session of the legislature unless the legislature acts to sustain the committee's disapproval.

How does political-branch review of agency rules work in your state?

D. Exceptions and Alternatives to Notice and Comment

Section 553, in addition to establishing notice and comment as the default mode for rulemaking, also provides that agencies need not use this process to issue several types of rules. Two of those exceptions, for procedural rules and rules issued with "good cause" for skipping notice and comment, have the same legal effect as rules that have completed the full notice-and-comment process. Another two exceptions, for what the APA calls "interpretive rules" and "general statements of policy," also do not require notice and comment, but these rules do not have the force of law. Modern administrative law vernacular often refers to these two types of "non-legislative" rules as "guidance documents" both because they are not technically binding and because they provide agency staff, regulated parties, and regulatory beneficiaries with valuable information concerning agency constructions of law and policy preferences.

Where an agency issues a rule without notice and comment that does not properly fall into one of these exceptions, the rule is subject to vacation by a reviewing court. Determining whether a rule falls within or outside of the exceptions is therefore critical. Regrettably, some of the relevant law—particularly the law that attempts to distinguish legislative rules from guidance documents—is vague and confusing. The materials below introduce you to it.

1. Exceptions to Notice and Comment—But Still Legally Binding

Lesson 3D.1. Recall from our last lesson the WTC's proposed special reserve rule stating, "[w]ine may not be labeled 'special reserve' or by any similar designation unless it is distinguishable from the general run of wine sold by the manufacturer in terms of grapes, production process, or other indication of special quality." The WTC had been contemplating jamming this provision into a legislative rule that the agency had been developing through notice and comment to address disclosures of information on labels. Suppose for the sake of argument that the agency concluded that this move would run an unacceptable risk of violating the "logical outgrowth" test on judicial review.

This conclusion presents the agency with a problem. Each year, wineries bottle their finest wines, the ones that might plausibly be labeled "special reserve," during the same two-month period. As that period approaches, and as pressure increases from wine consumer groups, Carl, the WTC's chair, wants to promulgate the special reserve rule as promptly as legally possible. He asks Ben to get the special reserve rule out quickly, one way or another.

Ben considers simply dispensing with notice and comment in light of the urgency of regulating the impending round of bottling by the wineries. Brit suggests a possible alternative approach. She argues that the agency might be able to avoid notice and comment by establishing a procedure under which wineries could file a "Notice of Special Reserve Labeling" with the Commission by a certain date. The Commission would commit itself to advise the wineries within two weeks of their filings whether the Commission considered the labels in compliance with §5 of the WTCA. If the Commission responded positively or failed to respond within the two week period, the winery would be assured that the Commission would not take enforcement action with respect to that year's batch of wines labeled "special reserve."

What do the following materials suggest as to the likely success of either of these approaches? (In forming your answer, be sure to consider WTCA §8(b) as well as the APA's §553.)

Background of *Public Citizen v. Department of State*

Section 553(b)(3)(A) of the APA provides an exception to the notice-and-comment requirement for "rules of agency organization, procedure, or practice." The term "agency organization" refers to such purely internal matters as who should report to whom within the agency, the organizational structure (as shown, for example, in an organization chart), and the like. The terms "procedure" and "practice" may well be synonymous. Disputes have focused on the term "procedure." But one person's procedure can be another person's substance. A strict procedural requirement, for example, can adversely affect someone who cannot comply or who must expend substantial resources to comply. In a widely quoted description of the procedural rule exception, the D.C. Circuit said that, "it covers agency actions that do not themselves alter the rights or interests of parties, although it may alter the manner in which the parties present themselves or their viewpoints to the agency." *American Hosp. Ass'n v. Bowen*, 834 F.2d 1037, 1047 (D.C. Cir. 1987).

In the following decision, the D.C. Circuit reviewed a challenge to an agency's reliance on the procedural rule exception where the challenger argued that the new rule had imposed substantial burdens on the challenger's operations.

Public Citizen v. Department of State
276 F.3d 634 (D.C. Cir. 2002)

Tatel, Circuit Judge:

When the State Department responds to Freedom of Information Act requests, it generally declines to search for documents produced after the date of the requester's letter. Challenging this "date-of-request cut-off" policy, appellant claims that the Department promulgated it without notice and opportunity to comment as required by the Administrative Procedure Act. . . . We reject [this] claim because the policy falls within the APA's exemption for "rules of agency organization, procedure or practice."

I.

The State Department processes FOIA requests in four stages. During the first stage, it mails a letter to the requester acknowledging receipt and assigning an identification number. This initial letter also informs the requester that the "cut-off date . . . is the date of the requester's letter" and that "no documents . . . originat[ing] after the date of [the] letter will be retrieved." During the second stage, the Department's Statutory Compliance & Research Division determines "which offices, overseas posts, or other records systems within the Department may reasonably be expected to contain the information requested." The Department then "task[s]" these various components to search for responsive documents. The speed at which the tasked component completes a search depends largely on available personnel, the nature of the request and the number of outstanding requests. "By far" the most frequently tasked component is the Department's Central Foreign Policy File, a centralized automated records system containing the "most comprehensive authoritative compilation of documents," including documents "that establish, discuss or define foreign policy," as well as "official record copies of incoming and outgoing Department communications." Consequently, the Central File has the "longest queue" of any Department component. During the third phase of FOIA request processing, the Department reviews the retrieved documents to determine whether it should withhold any, or portions thereof, pursuant to one of FOIA's nine exemptions. During the final phase, the Department copies the documents, redacts classified material and releases them to the requester.

In April 1998, appellant Public Citizen, a non-profit, public interest organization "dedicated to the study and promotion of public health and . . . consumer welfare," sent a FOIA request to the Department asking for records describing its "current system for managing word processing files . . . and electronic mail messages," as well as "disposition schedule[s] submitted to the National Archives concerning the transfer or disposal" of these materials. [Ultimately, the Department waived the "date-of-request cut-off" policy as to some of the requests, but it maintained it for others. Public Citizen pursued its APA rulemaking challenge as to the latter requests.] . . .

. . . Finding the policy a "rule[ ] of agency organization . . . or practice" exempt from notice and comment, the district court . . . granted summary judgment for the Department on Public Citizen's APA claim.

II.

We begin with Public Citizen's claim that the Department unlawfully promulgated the cut-off policy without the notice and opportunity to comment required by the APA. The Department responds that its cut-off policy is procedural and thus covered by the APA's exemption from notice and comment for "rules of agency organization, procedure, or practice," 5 U.S.C. §553(b)(3)(A). According to Public Citizen, the cut-off policy cannot be considered procedural because it "substantially . . . affects rights" by "needlessly multipl[ying] the number of FOIA requests that must be submitted to obtain access to records." We have, however, characterized agency rules as procedural even where their effects were far harsher than the Department's date-of-request cut-off policy. For example, in *Ranger v. FCC*, we found an agency rule establishing a cut-off date for the filing of radio license applications to be procedural even though the failure to observe the rule cost appellants a radio broadcast license.

As we recognized in *American Hospital Ass'n v. Bowen*, "[o]ver time, our circuit in applying the § 553 exemption for procedural rules has gradually shifted focus from asking whether a given procedure has a 'substantial impact' on parties to ... inquiring more broadly whether the agency action ... encodes a substantive value judgment." This "gradual move," we noted, "reflects a candid recognition that even unambiguously procedural measures affect parties to some degree." More recently, in *JEM Broadcasting Co. v. FCC*, we found that FCC "hard look rules," which required the dismissal of flawed license applications without leave to amend, were procedural despite their sometimes harsh effects. In doing so, we rejected the argument that the rules encoded substantive value judgments because they valued applications without errors over those with minor errors. Clarifying the *American Hospital* standard, we held that in referring to "value judgments" in that case, we had not intended to include "judgment[s] about what mechanics and processes are most efficient" because to do so would "threaten[ ] to swallow the procedural exception to notice and comment, for agency housekeeping rules often embody [such] judgment[s]."

Because the Department's cut-off policy applies to all FOIA requests, making no distinction between requests on the basis of subject matter, it clearly encodes no "substantive value judgment." To be sure, the policy does represent a "judgment" that a date-of-request cut-off promotes the efficient processing of FOIA requests, but a "judgment about procedural efficiency ... cannot convert a procedural rule into a substantive one." Consequently, we agree with the district court that the Department's cut-off policy represents a prototypical procedural rule properly promulgated without notice and comment.

Notes

1. **Determining whether an agency statement constitutes a "rule of procedure."** Would Brit's approach qualify as a procedural rule? It requires nothing more than certain filings with the Commission. Consider the following.

The *Public Citizen* court held that an agency statement of policy can be a procedural rule if it "encodes no 'substantive value judgment.'" Since the cut-off policy did not distinguish between FOIA requests based upon their content, the policy qualified as a procedural rule. As in the FCC cases discussed in *Public Citizen*, courts often find that agency statements qualify as procedural rules where they merely "alter the manner in which the parties present themselves or their viewpoints to the agency." Thus, a new requirement to use a certain type of form or to include certain types of information in an application would qualify as a procedural rule. Indeed, the *Public Citizen* court could well have relied upon this principle since the agency had merely required requesters to make additional requests for information obtained by the agency after the date of the initial request.

Exposing oneself to the Transportation Security Administration's full-body scanner during pre-flight security could be characterized as involving the manner in which people "present themselves . . . to the agency." But the D.C. Circuit in *Electronic Privacy Information Center v. U.S. Department of Homeland Security*, 653 F.3d 1 (D.C. Cir. 2011) (*EPIC*), held that the severity of the body scan intrusion on privacy was sufficient to preclude reliance on the procedural exception to replace magnetometers with body-scan machines without notice and comment. (We address the status of the full body scan as an administrative search in note 3 in subchapter 6C.) Two years later, a federal district court characterized the *EPIC* decision as meaning that an agency statement or policy that would otherwise qualify as a procedural rule "may still be subject to notice and comment if it intrudes upon other, important or fundamental rights or interests held by affected parties." *Nat'l Sec. Counselors v. Cent. Intelligence Agency*, 931 F. Supp. 2d 77 (D.D.C. 2013). This principle may well add a new weapon to the arsenal of those seeking to challenge agency reliance upon the procedural rule exception.

2. Sometimes there is a good reason — "good cause" — not to go through notice and comment. As Ben seeks a way to issue the "special reserve" rule quickly, he should consider a possibility suggested by *Utility Solid Waste Activities Group v. EPA*, 236 F.3d 749 (D.C. Cir. 2001), in which EPA relied upon the "good cause" exception to justify issuing a correction to a rule the agency had recently published. The EPA asserted that the need for the rule change (which would have changed the substance of the rule) arose from the fact that a word processing "search and replace" exercise had incorrectly changed the figure in question. The EPA also argued that it had the inherent power to correct its rule and that the nature of the change as a technical correction constituted "good cause." The court rejected both arguments and provided an instructive discussion of the "good cause" exception:

> EPA also thinks it qualified for the exception to notice and comment rulemaking contained in APA §553(b)[(3)](B). . . . The claim is that its statement in the Federal Register accompanying the amendment — the amendments contained only "minor, routine clarifications that will not have a significant effect on industry or the public" — amounted to a finding of good cause and a statement of reasons. There are three grounds in APA §553(b)[(3)](B) for finding good cause: notice and comment would be "impracticable, unnecessary, or contrary to the public interest." EPA does not tell us which of the three it meant to invoke, so we will discuss each. In doing so we are mindful of our precedents that the "good cause" exception is to be "narrowly construed and only reluctantly countenanced." The exception is not an "escape clause"; its use "should be limited to emergency situations."

With respect to the "impracticable" ground, the Attorney General's
Manual explains "that a situation is 'impracticable' when an agency finds
that due and timely execution of its functions would be impeded by the
notice otherwise required in [§ 553]," as when a safety investigation shows
that a new safety rule must be put in place immediately. United States
Department of Justice, Attorney General's Manual on the Administrative Procedure Act 30–31 (1947). This ground for finding good
cause cannot possibly apply here. There is no indication that 40 C.F.R.
§ 761.30(p), as it stood before the amendment, posed any threat to the environment or human health or that some sort of emergency had arisen. And
EPA made no finding to this effect.

With respect to the "unnecessary" prong of the exception, one court has
ruled that its use is "confined to those situations in which the administrative rule is a routine determination, insignificant in nature and impact,
and inconsequential to the industry and to the public." This formulation
comports with the explanation in the Attorney General's Manual that
"'[u]nnecessary' refers to the issuance of a minor rule in which the public
is not particularly interested." Attorney General's Manual at 31. EPA's
amendment of 40 C.F.R. § 761.30(p) does not fit that mold. As amended,
the rule greatly expanded the regulated community and increased the
regulatory burden. In the original rule, porous surfaces contaminated by
spills containing $>= 50$ ppm PCBs were not regulated by § 761.30(p) if the
resulting PCB surface contamination was less than 10 μg/100 cm^2. As we
understand the new regulations, these same surfaces now became subject
to § 761.30(p) because the 10 μg/100 cm^2 surface contamination trigger
has been repealed. While there may be other possible readings of this complex regulatory scheme, we need not reach them. EPA's amendment was,
without doubt, something about which these members of the public were
greatly interested.

As to the "public interest" ground for finding good cause, the Attorney
General's Manual states that this "connotes a situation in which the
interest of the public would be defeated by any requirement of advance
notice," as when announcement of a proposed rule would enable the sort
of financial manipulation the rule sought to prevent. Attorney General's
Manual at 31. Nothing of the sort is present here and nothing EPA said in
promulgating the amendment suggested that it needed to forego notice and
comment in order to prevent the amended rule from being evaded.

Section 553(b)(B) requires the agency to assert the good cause exception when
it issues the rule and to accompany a claim of good cause with findings and a
brief statement of reasons. However, courts have not taken a consistent approach
to this requirement. *Compare California v. Simon*, 504 F.2d 430 (TECA 1974), *cert.
denied*, 419 U.S. 1021 (1974) (justification could be inferred from the circumstances

surrounding the rule), *with Buschmann v. Schweiker*, 676 F.2d 352 (9th Cir. 1982) (rule's preamble did not satisfy the reasoning requirement).

3. Expedited rulemaking approaches that rely on the "good cause" exception. In recent years, agencies have taken to issuing so-called "interim-final rules," which agencies issue without notice and comment, relying on the "good cause" exception (typically the impracticability or public interest prong), but also inviting public comment and promising to consider public comment in finalizing the rule. The interesting question here is whether the use of this procedure improves the agency's chances of sustaining its "good cause" argument where the issue is a close one. Michael Asimow has identified several cases in which inviting and considering later comments strengthened the agency's position. He argues that interim-final rules have a useful "place as a well-accepted antidote to rulemaking ossification." Michael Asimow, *Interim-Final Rules: Making Haste Slowly*, 51 ADMIN. L. REV. 703, 723 n.78, 744 (1999).

A slightly different approach is the "direct final rule," which involves an agency publishing a rule it intends to adopt and inviting objections from the public. If there are no objections, the rule can simply become final at the appointed date. If there are objections, the rule is withdrawn and submitted to the usual notice-and-comment process. Ronald Levin has shown that this has been a useful and appropriate implementation of the "unnecessary" prong of the "good cause" exception and has defended it against charges that it undermines the procedural requirements of the APA. Ronald M. Levin, *More on Direct Final Rulemaking: Streamlining, Not Corner-Cutting*, 51 ADMIN. L. REV. 757, 766–67 (1999).

4. Good cause in the states. States often have some sort of good cause exemption, usually for emergencies or otherwise where there is a need for expedited action. The 2010 MSAPA replaces the "unnecessary, impracticable, or contrary to the public interest" formulation with two separate provisions. The first, § 309, authorizes dispensing with public process where "an agency finds that an imminent peril to the public health, safety, or welfare or the loss of federal funding for an agency program requires the immediate adoption of an emergency rule and publishes in a record its reasons for that finding." Section 310 then authorizes issuance of a direct final rule "with a statement by the agency that it does not expect the adoption of the rule to be controversial and that the proposed rule takes effect 30 days after publication if no objection is received." If the agency receives no objection, the rule becomes final.

5. Military, foreign affairs, and agency management exceptions. *Public Citizen v. Department of State* dealt with the exception for "agency organization, procedure, or practice." 5 U.S.C. § 553(b)(3)(A). The APA also creates exemptions for matters involving "a military or foreign affairs function," or "agency management or personnel or . . . public property, loans, grants, benefits, or contracts." 5 U.S.C. §§ 533(a)(1) and (2). It is perhaps self-evident that strictly internal matters should be exempt from notice and comment, but it is difficult to see a justification for avoiding public process with respect to public property, loans, grants, or benefits, which can affect millions. Should the agency be required to follow notice-and-comment procedures for internal instructions distributed only to its staff? For example, would an instruction from the Social Security Administration to its ALJs that they should not consider evidence of pain in disability cases be considered a procedural rule or a rule related to internal management?

6. Interagency agreements. What about interagency agreements? For example, the Equal Employment Opportunity Commission (EEOC), without notice-and-comment procedures, reached an understanding with the Department of Labor's Office of Federal Contract Compliance (OFCC) Programs, in which they agreed that complaints filed with EEOC and OFCC shall be promptly transmitted to the EEOC District Office. The Fourth Circuit said:

> [E]xamination of the practical implications of [the agreement] reveals that it has no substantive impact on Reynolds. It neither diminishes nor increases the company's rights and duties under the Executive Order and Title VII. It simply provides an expeditious means of transmitting to the commission complaints that should have been mailed to it in the first place. The commission could probably obtain the same result—prompt receipt of Title VII complaints—by stationing some of its own employees at the compliance office, but at far greater expense. By either method of operation the impact on Reynolds would be the same.

Reynolds Metals Co. v. Rumsfeld, 564 F.2d 663, 669 (4th Cir. 1977).

7. A "no harm-no foul" exception. Even if the WTC at some point fails to comply fully with the rulemaking provisions of the APA or the WTCA, the agency may nonetheless be able to prevail if it can show that a challenger was not prejudiced by the noncompliance. Section 706 of the APA, which establishes the standards governing judicial review, provides that in applying those standards, "due account shall be taken of the rule of prejudicial error." Courts generally take a dim view, however, of agencies arguing that it was all right that they skipped notice and comment because they would have adopted the same rule anyway. Allowing agencies to get away with this type of argument would eviscerate notice-and-comment requirements. Accordingly, the D.C. Circuit has explained, "an utter failure to comply with notice and comment cannot be considered harmless if there is any uncertainty at all as to the effect of that failure." *Sugar Cane Growers Coop. of Florida v. Veneman*, 289 F.3d 89, 96 (D.C. Cir. 2002).

But sometimes courts are a bit more forgiving of technical errors. In *Columbia Venture LLC v. South Carolina Wildlife Federation*, 562 F.3d 290 (4th Cir. 2009), the Fourth Circuit applied § 706 to uphold a FEMA determination despite the agency's failure to publish the required notice in the *Federal Register*. In 1999, FEMA had conducted the various studies needed to establish the "base flood elevation" for Richland County, South Carolina. The agency then sent the proposal to Richland County and published it in local newspapers, but it had not published it in the *Federal Register* as required by statute. Columbia Venture, a local developer whose land was not affected by the proposal, submitted supporting information and at one point wrote to FEMA that "your agency has provided more than adequate opportunities for all interested parties to submit pertinent information." Unfortunately for Columbia Venture, FEMA later issued revised maps and a new proposal that included some of Columbia Venture's land in the area that would be subject to floodplain restrictions. This time FEMA both notified everyone and published in the *Federal Register*. When FEMA ultimately adopted the new proposal, Columbia Venture challenged the agency's initial failure to provide the statutory notice. Despite Columbia Venture's involvement from the very beginning and its praise of the agency, the District Court found that the company had been prejudiced because it had been "deprived of the opportunity to elicit support from the public at-large." Wrong prejudice, according to the Fourth Circuit. The question is whether a party is prejudiced "with respect to its own arguments and claims" on the merits, not as to some effort to generate political support. The failure to comply with the letter of the APA did not matter where Columbia Venture had an adequate opportunity to comment on the proposal.

[handwritten margin note: PROPER Q RE: PREJUDICE]

2. Exceptions to Notice and Comment — Agency Statements That Are Not Legally Binding

In light of the burdens of the legislative rulemaking process, agencies rely increasingly on so-called interpretive rules or statements of policy. Both of these categories of "nonlegislative rule" are exempt from notice and comment. 5 U.S.C. § 553(b)(3)(A). Often issued by letter, internal memo, or manual, all permit prompt communication with internal agency personnel and with those affected by the agency's statute or regulations. The difficult question is whether a particular agency statement qualifies for these exceptions.

Lesson 3D.2. Now let's suppose that the WTC has managed to adopt the special reserve rule as a legislative rule and that it has withstood judicial review. Again, this provision states, "[w]ine may not be labeled 'special reserve' or by any similar designation unless it is distinguishable from the general run of wine sold by the manufacturer in terms of grapes, production process, or other indication of special quality."

Jordan, the General Counsel of the Wine Merchants Association, becomes concerned that the members of the Wine Merchants Association would have difficulty determining precisely when they could apply the "special reserve" label to their wines. He knows that the WTC could flesh out the meaning of the rule through a series of enforcement actions. He has in fact heard rumors that Ralph is considering such a charge in a complaint against Gallery. He thinks such an approach would be unfair and disruptive to his members. On behalf of the Association, therefore, Jordan asks the WTC to issue guidelines that would help his members understand when they would be in compliance with the "special reserve" rule and when they would not.

In response, Ben wants to issue guidelines that would create a "safe harbor," stating that the Commission will not challenge a special reserve claim if the wine contains: (a) at least 90% of the advertised grape variety, (b) 100% grapes grown at the vineyard, (c) 100% grapes harvested on the date on the label, and (d) no additives. The guidelines would also provide that, while any special reserve wine that stays within those limits will not be challenged, producers will be given the opportunity to justify other claims of special reserve status. Ben is concerned that he should use notice-and-comment procedures. Jordan, however, urges the Commission to provide guidance immediately because many of the Association's members are reluctant to continue offering such wines under a cloud of possible WTC action. On the other hand, Ben believes that the guidelines are so stringent that some wine producers will no doubt challenge them. Moreover, he is aware of wine consumer groups that are particularly concerned about the accuracy of "special reserve" designations. These groups are generally quite well-heeled and more than capable of paying for litigation should they so desire.

How do the following materials help Ben decide whether he should issue the guidelines immediately or set them down for notice-and-comment rulemaking? What, if anything, might Ben do to enhance the WTC's chances on judicial review if the agency issues the guidelines without notice and comment?

Background of *American Mining Congress*

The following decision is an example of a situation that often arises under both statutes and regulations. The statute or regulation states a requirement (or perhaps an exception to a requirement) that applies across an affected industry. But it is often unclear how the stated requirement applies in particular circumstances. Often at the request of the affected industry, the agency issues a statement explaining how the statutory or regulatory requirement applies. Although regulated industries want to know the agency's views, if they do not like what the agency says, they may challenge the agency's statement on procedural grounds. Remember that virtually any agency statement of future effect is by definition a "rule" under § 551(4) of the Administrative Procedure Act, and § 553 requires notice and comment unless the statement qualifies for an exception to that requirement. Here, the question is whether the agency statement qualifies as an "interpretative rule." The other similar exception is for "general statements of policy."

American Mining Congress v. Mine Safety & Health Administration

995 F.2d 1106 (D.C. Cir. 1993)

STEPHEN F. WILLIAMS, CIRCUIT JUDGE:

This case presents a single issue: whether Program Policy Letters of the Mine Safety and Health Administration, stating the agency's position that certain x-ray readings qualify as "diagnose[s]" of lung disease within the meaning of agency reporting regulations, are interpretive rules under the Administrative Procedure Act. We hold that they are.

. . . .

The [Federal Mine Safety and Health Act] extensively regulates health and safety conditions in the nation's mines and empowers the Secretary of Labor to enforce the statute and relevant regulations. In addition, the Act requires "every operator of a . . . mine . . . [to] establish and maintain such records, make such reports, and provide such information, as the Secretary . . . may reasonably require from time to time to enable him to perform his functions." The Act makes a general grant of authority to the Secretary to issue "such regulations as . . . [he] deems appropriate to carry out" any of its provisions.

Pursuant to its statutory authority, the Mine Safety and Health Administration (acting on behalf of the Secretary of Labor) maintains regulations known as "Part 50" regulations, which cover the "Notification, Investigation, Reports and Records of Accidents, Injuries, Illnesses, Employment, and Coal Production in Mines." Subpart C deals with the "Reporting of Accidents, Injuries, and Illnesses" and requires mine operators to report to the MSHA within ten days "each accident, occupational injury, or occupational illness" that occurs at a mine. Of central importance here, the regulation also says that whenever any of certain occupational illnesses are "*diagnosed*," the operator must similarly report the diagnosis within ten days. Among the occupational illnesses covered are "[s]ilicosis, asbestosis, coal worker's pneumoconiosis, and other pneumoconioses." An operator's failure to report may lead to citation and penalty.

As the statute and formal regulations contain ambiguities, the MSHA from time to time issues [Program Policy Letters] ("PPLs") intended to coordinate and convey agency policies, guidelines, and interpretations to agency employees and interested members of the public. One subject on which it has done so—apparently in response to inquiries from mine operators about whether certain x-ray results needed to be reported as "diagnos[es]"—has been the meaning of the term diagnosis for purposes of Part 50.

The first of the PPLs at issue here stated that any chest x-ray of a miner who had a history of exposure to pneumonoconiosis-causing dust that rated 1/0 or higher on the International Labor Office (ILO) classification system would be considered a "diagnosis that the x-rayed miner has silicosis or one of the other pneumonoconioses" for the purposes of the Part 50 reporting requirements. . . .

. . . .

The final PPL under dispute, PPL No. P92-III-2 (effective August 1, 1992), . . . restated the MSHA's basic view that a chest x-ray rating above 1/0 on the ILO scale constituted a "diagnosis" of silicosis or some other pneumoconiosis. The August 1992 PPL also modified the MSHA's position on additional readings. . . .

The MSHA did not follow the notice and comment requirements of 5 U.S.C. §553 in issuing any of the . . . PPLs. In defending its omission of notice and comment, the agency relies solely on the interpretive rule exemption of §553(b) (3)(A).

We note parenthetically that the agency also neglected to publish any of the PPLs in the Federal Register, but distributed them to all mine operators and independent contractors with MSHA identification numbers, as well as to interested operator associations and trade unions. *Compare* 5 U.S.C. § 552(a)(1)(D) (requiring publication in the Federal Register of all "interpretations of general applicability") *with id.* at § 552(a)(2)(B) (requiring agencies to make available for public inspection and copying "those statements of policy and interpretations which have been adopted by the agency and are not published in the Federal Register"). Petitioners here make no issue of the failure to publish in the Federal Register.

. . . .

The distinction between those agency pronouncements subject to APA notice and-comment requirements and those that are exempt has been aptly described as "enshrouded in considerable smog."

Given the confusion, it makes some sense to go back to the origins of the distinction in the legislative history of the Administrative Procedure Act. Here the key document is the *Attorney General's Manual on the Administrative Procedure Act* (1947), which offers "the following working definitions":

> *Substantive rules*—rules, other than organizational or procedural under section 3(a)(1) and (2) issued by an agency pursuant to statutory authority and which implement the statute, as, for example, the proxy rules issued by the Securities and Exchange Commission pursuant to section 14 of the Securities Exchange Act of 1934 (15 U.S.C. 78n). Such rules have the force and effect of law.
>
> *Interpretative rules*—rules or statements issued by an agency to advise the public of the agency's construction of the statutes and rules which it administers. . . .
>
> *General statements of policy*—statements issued by an agency to advise the public prospectively of the manner in which the agency proposes to exercise a discretionary power.

Our own decisions have often used similar language, inquiring whether the disputed rule has "the force of law." We have said that a rule has such force only if Congress has delegated legislative power to the agency and if the agency intended to exercise that power in promulgating the rule.

FORCE OF LAW

On its face, the "intent to exercise" language may seem to lead only to more smog, but in fact there are a substantial number of instances where such "intent" can be found with some confidence. The first and clearest case is where, in the absence of a legislative rule by the agency, the legislative basis for agency enforcement would be inadequate. The example used by the ATTORNEY GENERAL'S MANUAL fits exactly—the SEC's proxy authority under § 14 of the Securities Exchange Act of 1934, for example, forbids certain persons, "to give, or to refrain from giving a proxy" "in contravention of such rules and regulations as the Commission may prescribe." The statute itself forbids *nothing* except acts or omissions to be spelled out by the Commission in "rules or regulations." The present case is similar, as to Part 50 itself, in that §813(h) merely requires an operator to maintain "such records . . . as the Secretary . . . may reasonably require from time to time." Although the Secretary might conceivably create some "require[ments]" ad hoc, clearly some agency creation of a duty is a necessary predicate to any enforcement against an operator for failure to keep records. Analogous cases may exist in which an agency may offer a government benefit only after it formalizes the prerequisites.

Second, an agency seems likely to have intended a rule to be legislative if it has the rule published in the Code of Federal Regulations; 44 U.S.C. § 1510 limits publication in that code to rules "having general applicability and legal effect."

Third, "[i]f a second rule repudiates or is irreconcilable with [a prior legislative rule], the second rule must be an amendment of the first; and, of course, an amendment to a legislative rule must itself be legislative.'"

There are variations on these themes. For example, in *Chamber of Commerce v. OSHA* (D.C. Cir. 1980), the agency had on a prior occasion claimed that a certain statutory term, correctly understood, itself imposed a specific requirement on affected businesses. We found that interpretation substantively invalid, but noted the agency's power to promulgate such a requirement on the basis of more general authority. *Leone v. Mobil Oil Corp.* (D.C. Cir. 1975). The agency then issued a purported interpretive rule to fill the gap (without notice and comment), and we struck it down as an invalid exercise of the agency's legislative powers.

We reviewed a similar juxtaposition of different agency modes in *Fertilizer Institute v. EPA* (D.C. Cir. 1991). There a statute created a duty to report any "release" of a "reportable quantity" or "RQ" of certain hazardous materials, specifying the RQs but authorizing the EPA to change them by regulation. In the preamble to a legislative rule exercising its authority to amend the RQs, the EPA also expatiated on the meaning of the statutory term "release" — improperly broadening it, as petitioners claimed and as we ultimately found. But we rejected a claim that the agency's attempted exposition of the term "release" was not an interpretation and therefore required notice and comment.

In *United States v. Picciotto* (D.C. Cir. 1989), the Park Service had issued an indisputably legislative rule containing an "open-ended" provision stating that a "permit may contain additional reasonable conditions." Then, in a rule issued without notice and comment, it established some such conditions. We struck down the disputed condition, as it was not an interpretation of the prior regulation but an exercise of the legislative authority reserved by the prior legislative rule.

This focus on whether the agency *needs* to exercise legislative power (to provide a basis for enforcement actions or agency decisions conferring benefits) helps explain some distinctions that may, out of context, appear rather metaphysical. For example, in *Fertilizer Institute* we drew a distinction between instances where an agency merely "declare[s] its understanding of what a statute requires" (interpretive), and ones where an agency "go[es] beyond the text of a statute" (legislative). *See also Chamber of Commerce* (distinguishing between "constru[ing]" a statutory provision and "supplement[ing]" it). The difficulty with the distinction is that almost every rule may seem to do both. But if the dividing line is the necessity for agency legislative action, then a rule supplying that action will be legislative no matter how grounded in the agency's "understanding of what the statute requires," and an interpretation that spells out the scope of an agency's or regulated entity's pre-existing duty (such as EPA's interpretation of "release" in *Fertilizer Institute*), will be interpretive, even if, as in that case itself, it widens that duty even beyond the scope allowed to the agency under *Chevron U.S.A., Inc. v. NRDC* (1984).

Similarly, we have distinguished between cases where a rule is "based on specific statutory provisions" (interpretive), and where one is instead "based on an agency's power to exercise its judgment as to how best to implement a general statutory mandate" (legislative). A statute or legislative rule that actually establishes a duty or a right is likely to be relatively specific (and the agency's refinement will be interpretive), whereas an agency's authority to create rights and duties will typically be relatively broad (and the agency's actual establishment of rights and duties will be legislative). But the legislative or interpretive status of the agency rules turns not in some general sense on the narrowness or breadth of the statutory (or regulatory) term in question, but on the prior existence or non-existence of legal duties and rights.

Of course an agency may for reasons of its own choose explicitly to invoke its general legislating authority—perhaps, for example, out of concern that its proposed action might be invalid as an interpretation of some existing mandate, as was true in *Leone*, the case that set the legal landscape for *Chamber of Commerce*. In that event, even if a court believed that the agency had been unduly cautious about the legislative background, it would presumably treat the rule as an attempted exercise of legislative power.

In an occasional case we have appeared to stress whether the disputed rule is one with "binding effect"—"binding" in the sense that the rule does not "'genuinely leave[] the agency . . . free to exercise discretion.'" That inquiry arose in a quite different context, that of distinguishing *policy statements*, rather than interpretive rules, from legislative norms. The classic application is *Pacific Gas & Electric Co. v. FPC* (D.C. Cir. 1974). Indeed, the *agency's* theory in *Community Nutrition* [D.C. Cir. 1987] was that its pronouncement had been a policy statement.

But while a good rule of thumb is that a norm is less likely to be a general policy statement when it purports (or, even better, has proven) to restrict agency discretion, restricting discretion tells one little about whether a rule is interpretive. Nor is there much explanatory power in any distinction that looks to the use of mandatory as opposed to permissive language. While an agency's decision to use "will" instead of "may" may be of use when drawing a line between *policy statements* and legislative rules, the endeavor miscarries in the interpretive/legislative rule context.

PERMISSIVE
v.
~~AN~~ IMPERATIVE

Interpretation is a chameleon that takes its color from its context; therefore, an interpretation will use imperative language—or at least have imperative meaning—if the
interpreted term is part of a command; it will use permissive language—or at least
have a permissive meaning—if the interpreted term is in a permissive provision.

      . . . .

A non-legislative rule's capacity to have a binding effect is limited in practice
by the fact that agency personnel at every level act under the shadow of judicial
review. If they believe that courts may fault them for brushing aside the arguments
of persons who contest the rule or statement, they are obviously far more likely
to entertain those arguments . . . . Because the threat of judicial review provides a
spur to the agency to pay attention to facts and arguments submitted in derogation
of any rule not supported by notice and comment, even as late as the enforcement
stage, any agency statement not subjected to notice-and-comment rulemaking will
be more vulnerable to attack not only in court but also within the agency itself.

INCENTIVE
TO ENTERTAIN
OBJECTIONS

Not only does an agency have an incentive to entertain objections to an interpretive rule, but the ability to promulgate such rules, without notice and comment,
does not appear more hazardous to affected parties than the likely alternative.
Where a statute or legislative rule has created a legal basis for enforcement, an
agency can simply let its interpretation evolve ad hoc in the process of enforcement
or other applications (*e.g.*, grants). The protection that Congress sought to secure
by requiring notice and comment for legislative rules is not advanced by reading
the exemption for "interpretive rule" so narrowly as to drive agencies into pure ad
hocery—an ad hocery, moreover, that affords less notice, or less convenient notice,
to affected parties.

WHETHER
SOMETHING
IS INTERP.

Accordingly, insofar as our cases can be reconciled at all, we think it almost
exclusively on the basis of whether the purported interpretive rule has "legal effect,"
which in turn is best ascertained by asking (1) whether in the absence of the rule
there would not be an adequate legislative basis for enforcement action or other
agency action to confer benefits or ensure the performance of duties, (2) whether
the agency has published the rule in the Code of Federal Regulations, (3) whether
the agency has explicitly invoked its general legislative authority, or (4) whether the
rule effectively amends a prior legislative rule. If the answer to any of these questions is affirmative, we have a legislative, not an interpretive rule.

Here we conclude that the August 1992 PPL is an interpretive rule. The Part 50
regulations themselves require the reporting of diagnoses of the specified diseases,
so there is no legislative gap that required the PPL as a predicate to enforcement
action. Nor did the agency purport to act legislatively, either by including the letter
in the Code of Federal Regulations, or by invoking its general legislative authority. . . . The remaining possibility therefore is that the August 1992 PPL is a de facto
amendment of prior legislative rules, namely the Part 50 regulations.

A rule does not, in this inquiry, become an amendment merely because it supplies crisper and more detailed lines than the authority being interpreted. If that

were so, no rule could pass as an interpretation of a legislative rule unless it were confined to parroting the rule or replacing the original vagueness with another.

Although petitioners cite some definitions of "diagnosis" suggesting that with pneumoconiosis and silicosis, a diagnosis requires more than a chest x-ray — specifically, additional diagnostic tools as tissue examination or at least an occupational history. . . . A finding of a disease is surely equivalent, in normal terminology, to a diagnosis, and thus the PPLs certainly offer no interpretation that repudiates or is irreconcilable with an existing legislative rule.

We stress that deciding whether an interpretation is an amendment of a legislative rule is different from deciding the substantive validity of that interpretation. An interpretive rule may be sufficiently within the language of a legislative rule to be a genuine interpretation and not an amendment, while at the same time being an incorrect interpretation of the agency's statutory authority. Here, petitioners have made no attack on the PPLs' substantive validity. Nothing that we say upholding the agency's decision to act without notice and comment bars any such substantive claims.

Accordingly, the petitions for review are

Dismissed.

Notes

1. Interpretive rules and statements of policy as alternatives to legislative rules. The crucial characteristic of "legislative rules" is that they are legally binding. Assuming that the WTC has the authority to issue legislative rules and that it has followed the proper procedures for doing so, the WTC can enforce the terms of a legislative rule. It does not have to refer to the statute except to establish the authority to issue the rule.

In this subchapter's lesson, the "special reserve" rule is a legislative rule. It was issued through notice and comment. But what about the "guidelines" Ben is contemplating? Are they rules at all? Under the APA's definition? Under the WTCA's? If the guidelines are rules, do they have to go through notice and comment, or is there some basis for simply issuing them without any such process? Can the guidelines be considered to be an "interpretative rule" or a "general statement of policy" under §553(b)(3)(A)?

2. When should an informal issuance be considered an invalid legislative rule? Courts have struggled mightily with the issue addressed in *American Mining Congress*: how to determine whether an informally issued agency statement should be considered to be an invalid legislative rule because it was issued without notice and comment. William Funk has suggested a very simple approach, which he calls the "notice and comment test": "any rule not issued after notice and comment is an interpretive rule or statement of policy, unless it qualifies as a rule exempt from notice and comment on some other basis." William Funk, *When Is a "Rule" a Regulation? Marking a Clear Line Between Nonlegislative Rules and Legislative Rules*, 54 ADMIN. L. REV. 659, 663 (2002). If Professor Funk's approach were adopted, the answer to this issue would always be clear. Ben's task (and yours in trying to grasp these complexities) would be much easier.

As *American Mining Congress* demonstrates, the courts have not taken such a straightforward approach. Why not? The reason is that informal issuances can have an enormous practical impact on the public even if, strictly speaking, they are not legally binding. For example, a company that disagrees with an informal statement, such as the one in *American Mining Congress*, may feel compelled to comply with it in order to avoid enforcement action by the agency. Bill Funk would respond that such a company should challenge the merits of the agency's position, not the procedural validity of its statement. But the company would argue that it should not be effectively compelled to comply with an agency position that did not go through notice and comment.

Robert Anthony, who has strongly criticized agency misuse of informal issuances, also argues for a relatively simple rule. He emphasizes the distinction between "interpretative rules" and "general statements of policy." As to interpretative rules, an agency may state an interpretation without going through notice and comment and may state it in terms that appear to bind the public. After all, the agency would merely be stating its view of the meaning of a statute or regulation.

Anthony's concern with respect to interpretive rules is that agencies sometimes use that label when the informal statement does not truly qualify as an interpretation because it cannot be drawn from a statute or legislative rule through the interpretive method. What about *American Mining Congress*? Was the agency's statement an interpretation? What about Ben's proposed guidelines? Would they qualify as an interpretation?

As Anthony explains, the second category of non-legislative rules is "general statements of policy." These may not be stated in binding terms, and they may not be used to bind the public. If an agency statement that is not an interpretation were used, for practical purposes, to bind the public, Anthony would consider it to be an invalid legislative rule. If such a statement were not used to bind the public, Anthony would consider it to be a "general statement of policy" and exempt from the requirement for notice and comment.

In light of these considerations, Anthony suggests the following rule:

> There are two inquiries: First, does the rulemaking document interpret existing legislation? If so, it is exempt from notice-and-comment requirements, whether it is made binding or not. Second, if the document does not interpret, has the agency treated it as binding? If so, the document is an invalid spurious rule because it should have been promulgated through use of legislative procedures, ordinarily including full APA notice-and-comment formalities. If the agency has not made the document binding, it is excepted from notice-and-comment requirements as an exempt policy statement.

ROBERT
ANTHONY

Robert A. Anthony, *"Interpretive" Rules, "Legislative" Rules and "Spurious" Rules": Lifting the Smog*, 8 ADMIN. L.J. AM. U. 1, 11–12 (1994).

How would *American Mining Congress* come out under Anthony's test? What about Ben's guidelines? Which approach should the courts adopt — *American Mining Congress*, Funk, or Anthony?

Note that both *American Mining Congress* and Lesson 3D.2 involve statements in which the agency purports to derive specific numbers from the underlying language of the statute or regulation. Recent decisions have struggled with this prospect. In *Catholic Health Initiatives v. Sebelius*, 617 F.3d 490 (D.C. Cir. 2010), the court rejected an argument that a detailed investment code, including a "10% limit on equity investments" could be derived from the statutory term "reasonable costs." Noting *American Mining Congress*, the court wrote, "[w]e . . . have recognized that 'numerical limits cannot readily be derived by judicial reasoning,' although courts occasionally draw such limits." On the other hand, the Ninth Circuit in *Mora-Meraz v. Thomas*, 601 F.3d 933 (9th Cir. 2010), upheld as interpretive a Bureau of Prisons statement that an inmate may qualify for a drug rehabilitation program only if the inmate can show "substance dependence or abuse within his last twelve months 'on the street.'" Here, the Bureau's statement referred to the *Diagnostic and Statistical Manual of Mental Disorders*, which defines substance abuse in terms of symptoms occurring during a twelve-month period. In both cases, the courts applied the following principle, as recently and succinctly described in *Mendoza v. Perez*, 754 F.3d 1002 (D.C. Cir. 2014): "To be interpretative, a rule 'must derive a proposition from an existing document whose meaning compels or logically justifies the proposition.'" How could those courts have reached such different conclusions? And how does this principle apply to Ben's proposed approach in lesson 3D.2?

3. When is a policy statement not a "general statement of policy?" When it binds — whatever that means. Since the WTC would be issuing the guidelines at the request of the wine industry, Ben is more concerned about a challenge from consumer interests than from the WMA. After all, the guidelines are designed to make life easier for the industry. But high-end consumers are known to want strong assurances that "special reserve" labels are used for only the very elite wines. Ben is concerned about *Community Nutrition Institute v. Young*, 818 F.2d 943 (D.C. Cir. 1987), in which the D.C. Circuit struck down a similar safe harbor.

The FDA was authorized "to limit the amount of 'poisonous or deleterious substances' in food." In implementing that authority, the FDA informally identified so-called "action levels" for certain unavoidable contaminants, including aflatoxins in corn. The FDA said it would take enforcement action if contaminants were above these "action levels," but not if they were below them. The Community Nutrition Institute argued that this statement constituted an invalid legislative rule because it effectively bound the agency. The court agreed, citing the following criteria from *American Bus Ass'n v. United States*, 627 F.2d 525, 529 (D.C. Cir. 1980):

First, courts have said that, unless a pronouncement acts prospectively, it is a binding norm. Thus . . . a statement of policy may not have a present effect: "a 'general statement of policy' is one that does not impose any rights and obligations." . . .

The second criterion is whether a purported policy statement genuinely leaves the agency and its decisionmakers free to exercise discretion.

The *Community Nutrition Institute* court found that the FDA's action levels effectively bound the agency, limiting its ability to exercise its enforcement discretion. What does it mean, however, for an agency to be "bound" by a policy that it can change at any time? Dissenting, Judge Starr argued that the critical question was "whether the pronouncement has the force of law in subsequent proceedings." Since the action levels were not binding on any later proceedings, Judge Starr considered them to be a valid statement of enforcement policy.

Which view is better? The *Community Nutrition Institute* majority recognized the value of such informal statements:

Our holding today in no way indicates that agencies develop written guidelines to aid their exercise of discretion only at the peril of having a court transmogrify those guidelines into binding norms. We recognize that such guidelines have the not inconsiderable benefits of apprising the regulated community of the agency's intentions as well as informing the exercise of discretion by agents and officers in the field. It is beyond question that many such statements are non-binding in nature and would thus be characterized by a court as interpretative rules or policy statements. We are persuaded that courts will appropriately reach an opposite conclusion only where, as here, the *agency* itself has given its rules substantive effect.

If you were in Ben's shoes, would you recommend issuing the special reserve guidelines in light of *Community Nutrition Institute*? Is this situation distinguishable? Would the guidelines actually bind the WTC? Did the safe action level statements bind the FDA?

The Federal Circuit addressed the question of when an informal agency policy statement is considered to be binding on the agency:

The general consensus is that an agency statement, not issued as a formal regulation, binds the agency only if the agency intended the statement to be binding. . . . The primary consideration in determining the agency's intent is whether the text of the agency statement indicates that it was designed to be binding on the agency.

Farrell v. Dep't of Interior, 314 F.3d 584, 590–91 (Fed. Cir. 2002). Is agency intent the appropriate test? Could it allow the agency to state that its intent is not to be binding when it knows that regulated parties will feel they have to comply? Should that matter?

4. Trade-offs in issuing nonlegislative rules. Why has an exception from public procedures emerged for nonlegislative rules? Judge Williams suggests the dominant reason in *American Mining Congress*. Generally, we have chosen expedited disclosure of agency policy over participation. That is, we have decided to encourage agencies to disclose their policy judgments even at the cost of having pronouncements without public participation. Given the undeniable practical impact of nonlegislative rules on public conduct, would you continue to strike the same balance? Would you accept the danger of secret policies in order to obtain universal public participation in those cases where a policy is announced?

Notice that while the public trades participation rights for the opportunity to know agency policies, the agency also makes a trade-off. The agency trades legal enforceability for greater public knowledge of, and likelihood of compliance with, the agency's positions.

Of course, even if an agency statement qualified for an exception to notice-and-comment rulemaking, the agency could decide to undertake notice and comment anyway. Robert Anthony argued that agencies should "adhere to section 553's legislative notice-and-comment procedures for any substantive statement of general applicability (other than an interpretive rule) that (a) is intended to establish mandatory standards or to impose obligations upon private parties, or (b) is given that effect by the agency." Robert Anthony, *Interpretive Rules, Policy Statements, Guidances, Manuals, and the Like—Should Federal Agencies Use Them to Bind the Public?*, 41 DUKE L.J. 1311, 1373 (1992). He argues that this would reduce confusion about whether the agency expects full compliance with the position stated as informal guidance. He also argues that where informally stated positions are not fully final, "agencies should forthrightly declare in their nonlegislative policy documents that the stated policies are tentative, and that before they are applied finally to affected persons those persons will have a chance to challenge the policies." Consistent with that advice, he urged that agencies "assure that agency staff, counsel, administrative law judges, relevant state officials, and others who may apply policy statements or advise on the basis of such statements, are made aware that the policies set forth in such documents are tentative, and are subject to challenge . . . before they are applied."

Ben feels he has a good argument that the "safe harbor" does not require notice-and-comment procedures. However, considering both the advantages of avoiding notice-and-comment procedures in this case and Anthony's argument for voluntary use of such procedures, should Ben issue the guidelines immediately or recommend a rulemaking proceeding? Might he do both?

5. A key consideration—can the agency position be challenged within the agency? Notice that Anthony urges agencies to assure that internal agency decisionmakers, such as "agency staff, counsel, [and] administrative law judges" understand that nonlegislative rules are nonbinding and treat them accordingly. One helpful way to determine whether an informal agency statement qualifies as a valid nonlegislative rule is to ask whether it is possible to challenge the agency's stated position within the agency. If the agency considers the position taken in the informal statement to be binding on its own decisions, the statement is a legislative rule in disguise. On the other hand, if the agency is prepared to entertain challenges to the position and to justify it in a proceeding in which the position determines the outcome, the statement is probably a valid nonlegislative rule, and thus not required to go through notice-and-comment.

While the previous discussion may seem to provide a reasonably clear way of judging whether an agency statement is truly a nonlegislative rule, the distinction is often not so clear in practice. Consider, for example, *United States Telephone Ass'n v. FCC*, 28 F.3d 1232 (D.C. Cir. 1994), in which the FCC issued, without notice and comment, a statement identifying base penalty levels for various regulatory violations, as well as circumstances that would justify deviations from those base levels. The Commission, aware of the principles discussed in the previous paragraph, "labeled the standards as a policy statement and reiterated 12 times that it retained discretion to depart from the standards in specific applications." Despite the Commission's assertions, the court held that the agency had violated the APA by failing to go through notice and comment. In part, the court believed that the statement was so detailed and specific that it must have been intended "to cabin [the agency's] discretion. . . . It simply does not fit the paradigm of a policy statement, namely, an indication of an agency's current position on a particular regulatory issue." Moreover, the record demonstrated that the penalty schedule had been employed in over 300 cases, and only in 8 did the agency even purport to deviate from it. As analyzed by the court, 7 of those 8 applications did not truly qualify as deviations from the policy statement. Even the last case was ambiguous as to whether the FCC actually exercised judgment independent of the so-called policy statement or simply applied criteria within the statement to change a base amount. It seemed that the agency acted as if it were bound by the statement, rather than actually exercising independent judgment in each case. Thus, "the schedule of fines was intended to bind, no matter what 'policy statement' clothing it wore."

6. *Vermont Yankee* **prohibits requiring notice and comment when an agency changes a position taken in a previously issued informal interpretive statement.** Recall that the *Vermont Yankee* decision, discussed in subchapter 3B.2 above, struck down a D.C. Circuit attempt to impose on the informal rulemaking process procedures in addition to those required by the APA. As the Supreme Court said in *Vermont Yankee*, judicial imposition of additional procedures would "totally disrupt the statutory scheme, through which Congress enacted 'a formula upon which opposing social and political forces have come to rest.'"

Despite that admonition, the D.C. Circuit in a series of cases required notice and comment for an agency to change its position from a prior interpretive statement issued without notice and comment. The facts of *Alaska Professional Hunters Ass'n, Inc. v. FAA*, 177 F.3d 1030 (D.C. Cir. 1999), illustrate why the D.C. Circuit deemed notice and comment necessary in some situations. Beginning in the 1960s, the Federal Aviation Administration (FAA) Alaskan Region orally advised "guide pilots" that they were not covered by the regulations governing commercial pilots. Guide pilots fly their customers in small planes as part of their fishing or hunting guide service. This advice was based on the proposition that carrying passengers was merely incidental to the operation of the guide business. In 1998, without notice and comment, the FAA issued a "Notice to Operators" in which it interpreted its commercial pilot regulations to cover guide pilots. This shocked guide pilots, who built their businesses and invested in their equipment based upon the FAA's earlier position. In light of the pilots' decades long reliance on the previous advice and the likelihood that they would have had much to say about the new Notice, the D.C. Circuit required the FAA to go through notice and comment before implementing its new position.

In 2015, the Supreme Court firmly rejected the D.C. Circuit's decision in *Alaska Professional Hunters Association* in *Perez v. Mortgage Bankers Association*, 135 S. Ct. 1199 (2015). The Supreme Court in *Perez*, citing *Vermont Yankee*, held that the doctrine reflected in *Alaska Professional Hunters Association* "is contrary to the clear text of the APA's rulemaking provisions, and it improperly imposes on agencies an obligation beyond the 'maximum procedural requirements' specified in the APA." According to the Court, "the text of the APA answers the question" of whether a court may require notice and comment prior to the issuance of an interpretive rule. "[T]he APA provides that, unless another statute states otherwise, the notice-and-comment requirement 'does not apply' to 'interpretative rules, general statements of policy, or rules of agency organization, procedure, or practice.'" Thus, courts may not require notice and comment before the issuance of an interpretive rule unless the requirement derives from some statute other than the APA.

But what about the seemingly legitimate concerns that prompted the *Alaska Professional Hunters Association* decision and others like it? After all, private parties had made significant investments and otherwise relied upon agencies' interpretive statements. The more firmly and clearly agencies had made those earlier statements and the longer those statements had been in place, the more private parties legitimately considered them to be the rules governing their behaviors.

Much as it had in *Vermont Yankee*, the Court referred the challengers to the substantive review provisions of the APA. Noting that "[t]he APA contains a variety of constraints on agency decisionmaking—the arbitrary and capricious standard being among the most notable," the Court said it would be arbitrary and capricious to ignore serious reliance interests created by an agency's prior position. We will examine the arbitrary and capricious test and other standards of review in Chapter 5. For now, the lesson is that any challenge to an agency's rulemaking procedures must be based upon the requirements of the APA or some other statute.

In light of the Court's confirmation of *Vermont Yankee*'s prohibition on judicial interference with agency rulemaking procedures (and as something of a review), consider the continuing validity of the D.C. Circuit's decisions in *Nova Scotia* and *Portland Cement*, discussed in subchapter 3C.1 above. Does *Perez* strengthen then-Judge Kavanaugh's argument that these decisions violate *Vermont Yankee*?

7. Informal issuances are effective only with adequate notice. Although informally issued interpretations are not themselves binding, they can play an important role in notifying the public, particularly the regulated parties, of an agency's interpretation of a statute or regulation that is susceptible to more than one reasonable interpretation. As explained in subchapter 5G, a court may well defer to the agency's reasonable interpretation of a statute or regulation. However, where the agency seeks to enforce its interpretation against a particular company, the court may refuse to enforce the agency's interpretation if the company's interpretation was also reasonable, and the agency cannot prove that the company had notice of the agency's interpretation. This is particularly true where the agency is seeking a penalty for alleged past violations, much less so where the agency is simply seeking future compliance. *See Beaver Plant Operations, Inc. v. Herman*, 223 F.3d 25 (1st Cir. 2000) (refusing to impose a penalty for violation of an ambiguous OSHA regulation where there had been no proof that the company had actual notice of various informal issuances stating the agency's position).

8. Waivers or variances from legislative rules. Suppose that Ben is worried that no matter how he confines the special reserve rule it will prevent some bottlers, such as small, specialty brands, from marketing legitimately unique wines. How might a rule be individualized? Waiver or variance can be a valuable device for fine-tuning and assuring individual fairness in a generalized rulemaking process. Indeed, sixty years ago the Supreme Court suggested that the opportunity for waiver might be required in the interest of fundamental fairness. *Nat'l Broad. Co. v. U.S.*, 319 U.S. 190 (1943). Under what circumstances would you add a waiver provision in a rule? What procedures would you prescribe for the waiver process?

9. OMB weighs in on informal agency statements. Reflecting the various concerns about agency reliance upon informal statements, the Bush Office of Management and Budget (OMB) issued a Bulletin for Agency Good Guidance Practices. OMB, Final Bulletin for Agency Good Guidance Practices, 72 Fed. Reg. 3432 (Jan. 25, 2007). OMB's introductory discussion of the Bulletin provides a concise description of both the benefits and drawbacks of agency use of informal statements, which the Bulletin refers to as "guidance documents":

> In its 2002 Report to Congress, OMB recognized the enormous value of agency guidance documents in general. Well-designed guidance documents serve many important or even critical functions in regulatory programs. Agencies may provide helpful guidance to interpret existing law through an interpretive rule or to clarify how they tentatively will treat or enforce a governing legal norm through a policy statement. Guidance documents, used properly, can channel the discretion of agency employees, increase

efficiency, and enhance fairness by providing the public clear notice of the line between permissible and impermissible conduct while ensuring equal treatment of similarly situated parties.

Experience has shown, however, that guidance documents also may be poorly designed or improperly implemented. At the same time, guidance documents may not receive the benefit of careful consideration accorded under the procedures for regulatory development and review. These procedures include: (1) Internal agency review by a senior agency official; (2) public participation, including notice and comment under the Administrative Procedure Act (APA); (3) justification for the rule, including a statement of basis and purpose under the APA and various analyses under Executive Order 12866 (as further amended), the Regulatory Flexibility Act, and the Unfunded Mandates Reform Act; (4) interagency review through OMB; (5) Congressional oversight; and (6) judicial review. Because it is procedurally easier to issue guidance documents, there also may be an incentive for regulators to issue guidance documents in lieu of regulations.

[handwritten margin note: DOWNFALL OF GUIDANCE DOC]

Seeking to enhance the quality of guidance and to assure accountability, transparency, and consistency, OMB established various requirements for the handling of "significant guidance documents" by agencies other than independent agencies. Guidance documents qualify as "significant" if, for example, they would have an annual impact of $100 million or more on the national economy, would be inconsistent with actions or plans of other agencies, would materially alter budgetary impacts, or would raise novel issues of law or policy. Among other things, the Bulletin: (1) requires agencies to adopt procedures to assure significant guidance documents are "approved by appropriate senior agency officials," (2) prohibits agencies from departing from significant guidance documents without similar approvals, (3) mandates internet access to comprehensive lists of such guidance documents and a means of public response, and (4) prohibits the use of mandatory language ("must," "shall," "required") except to describe statutory or regulatory requirements. As to "economically significant guidance documents," (those with an annual economic impact of $100 million or a materially adverse effect on the economy or a sector of the economy), the Bulletin requires agencies to seek public comment and to respond to the comments, virtually imposing the requirements of § 553 of the APA on all economically significant guidance documents.

[handwritten margin note: OMB REQUIREMENTS]

How should Ben respond to the OMB Bulletin on guidance practices? What is the likely effect of the Bulletin on the agencies to which it applies and those affected by those agencies' programs?

On October 9, 2019, President Trump issued Exec. Order 13,981, *Promoting the Rule of Law Through Improved Agency Guidance Documents*, 84 Fed. Reg. 55,235 (Oct. 9, 2019) ("Guidance EO"). The Guidance EO overlaps with, and potentially expands on, the Bulletin. Like the Bulletin, the Guidance EO does not apply to independent agencies and requires certain guidance documents to be subjected to procedures akin to notice and comment, as well as to "review by the Office of Information and Regulatory Affairs (OIRA) under Executive Order 12866." Guidance EO at §§ 4(a)(iii)(A), (C). (EO 12,866 is discussed in greater detail in subchapter 3F.) Unlike the Bulletin, the Guidance EO requires that agencies "establish . . . a single, searchable, indexed database" of guidance documents. *Id.* at § 3(a). It applies to a wider range of guidance documents than the Bulletin, including those that "raise novel legal or policy issues," yet gives the OIRA Administrator seemingly broad discretion to determine which documents qualify as "significant" and to create exceptions for categories of documents. *Id.* at §§ 2(c)(iv); 4(a)(iii); 4(b). This (potentially) broader scope of the Guidance EO, balanced against the OIRA Administrator's contravening ability to limit its reach make it unclear how—if at all—the Guidance EO will impact agencies' use of guidance documents. For now, it is enough to know that the Guidance EO could further burden agencies' use of guidance documents, and to consider the possible consequences of that burden.

10. State exceptions to rulemaking procedural requirements. States have a variety of exceptions to participatory rulemaking procedures. Section 311 of the 2010 MSAPA, for example, would allow a state agency to issue a "guidance document" without notice and comment. Section 102(14) defines "guidance document" to include both interpretive statements and general statements of policy as we understand them under the APA. Consistent with the above discussion, § 311 would prohibit imposing a guidance document upon a private party without "an adequate opportunity to contest the legality or wisdom of a position taken in the guidance document," and it would require the agency to explain any deviation from the guidance document.

E. Issues of Integrity in the Rulemaking Process — Ex Parte Contacts and Bias

Control of the flow of information is critical in any decisionmaking process, and the optimal way to control this flow depends on the nature of the decision. In a judicial setting, we expect strict controls on *ex parte* contacts. It might be nice to take the judge out to dinner to explain what you really meant during oral argument without pesky opposing counsel around, but such conduct may get you disbarred. In a legislative setting, by contrast, we expect legislators to gather information from all quarters. (It is an unfortunate fact of life that many with whom those legislators do consult will tend to be among the well-heeled.)

It is also critical in any decisionmaking process to ensure that the decision maker is not unacceptably biased. Again, whether a given bias (or, less pejoratively, "attitude") is acceptable depends on the nature of the decision. Judges are not supposed to make their minds up about guilt before the trial. By contrast, we elect legislators precisely because they happen to have the attitudes that we prefer.

Translating these concerns to the administrative setting is complicated by the fact that agencies commonly wear both legislative and adjudicative hats. In this subchapter, we explore how due process, the APA, and related laws control *ex parte* contacts and bias in the legislative or rulemaking context.

The issue of *ex parte* contacts in rulemaking can be divided into three categories: *ex parte* contacts by the agency with (1) private parties; (2) members of the executive or legislative branch outside of the agency; and (3) agency employees. Lesson 3E and the three opinions included below address each of these categories in turn.

Lesson 3E. When Brit worked on Capitol Hill, she spent much of her time trying to convince federal agencies to adopt policies or take other actions that would benefit Senator Bisby's constituents. Now that she's on the other side, she is uncomfortable with those approaches by her former colleagues. Their phone calls and comments over drinks at the Hawk and Dove seem to violate the WTC's procedural integrity. She consults with Ben about the following situations. How should Ben advise Brit to handle them?

a. During the comment period on the rule, a lobbyist for a winery in Senator Bisby's state invited her to lunch. During lunch, he told her that a labeling rule would be a severe financial burden on his client. Moreover, he said, it would tend to hinder innovation in the wine industry and undermine the competitiveness of American wines on the world market. After the comment period had closed, he sent her two studies that he claimed supported his earlier assertions. Has the lobbyist or Brit violated any provisions of the APA or the WTCA? What should the WTC do about this?

b. Senator Bisby has demanded to see Carl about the proposed rule. He wants a meeting to discuss the costs that the proposal would impose on his state's wine industry. Brit knows that Senator Bisby would press Carl to exclude fruit wines from the rule because the country's largest producer of fruit wines is in Senator Bisby's state. Carl has also had a call from the president's Chief of Staff, who wants to discuss the rule's impact in major wine producing states. Those states also happen to be significant battlegrounds in the upcoming presidential election. Should Carl meet with Senator Bisby? With the Chief of Staff?

c. Brit has been intimately involved with the labeling rule from the very beginning, and appears intractably committed to it. She has been in almost constant contact with consumer groups and academic consultants. She has been particularly close to the Wrath for Grapes and has appeared on a number of its programs. While she was serving as staff chief to the Senate Beverage Committee (fictitious), Brit expressed strong anti-alcohol animus. In fact, Gallery and several other members of the industry denounced Brit in meetings with other members of the Committee. Indeed, it is rumored that Brit was "encouraged" to leave the Committee staff because of the efforts of the wine industry and other alcoholic beverage interests. However, during the rulemaking itself, Brit has appeared reasonable and objective. Nonetheless, Jordan, on behalf of the Association, asked the Commission to remove Brit from any further involvement in the labeling rule because of her obvious prejudgment of the industry and bias arising from previous acrimonious relationships. The Commission has referred the matter to Ben as Director of the Rulemaking Division. Must Ben remove Brit from her lead role in developing the rule? Should he?

Background of the "Integrity" Decisions

The three decisions below reflect the three types of contacts described above and in Lesson 3E. Remember that the three situations in Lesson 3E all involve what we frequently call the "legislative" rulemaking process. In each case, you should focus on why the decision comes out as it does and how the situation is distinct from the adjudicatory litigation process with which we are more familiar.

Home Box Office, Inc. v. F.C.C.

567 F.2d 9 (D.C. Cir. 1977) (per curiam)

Per Curiam

At the heart of these cases are the Commission's "pay cable" rules. . . . The effect of these rules is to restrict sharply the ability of cablecasters to present feature film and sports programs if a separate program or channel charge is made for this material. In addition, the rules prohibit cablecasters from devoting more than 90 percent of their cablecast hours to movie and sports programs and further bar cablecasters from showing commercial advertising on cable channels on which programs are presented for a direct charge to the viewer. Virtually identical restrictions apply to subscription broadcast television. . . .

During the pendency of this proceeding Mr. Henry Geller, a participant before the Commission and an amicus here, filed with the Commission a "Petition for Revision of Procedures or for Issuance of Notice of Inquiry or Proposed Rule Making." In this petition amicus Geller sought to call the Commission's attention to what were alleged to be violations in these proceedings of the *ex parte* communications doctrine set out by this court in *Sangamon Valley Television Corp. v. United States*, 269 F.2d 221 (D.C. Cir. 1959). The Commission took no action in response to the petition, and amicus now presses us to set aside the orders under review here because of procedural infirmity in their promulgation.

It is apparently uncontested that a number of participants before the Commission sought out individual commissioners or Commission employees for the purpose of discussing *ex parte* and in confidence the merits of the rules under review here. . . . In response to [an order of the court], the Commission filed a document over 60 pages long which revealed, albeit imprecisely, widespread *ex parte* communications involving virtually every party before this court, including amicus Geller.

. . . .

It is important to note that many contacts occurred in the crucial period between the close of oral argument on October 25, 1974 and the adoption of the First Report and Order on March 20, 1975, when the rulemaking record should have been closed while the Commission was deciding what rules to promulgate. The information submitted to this court by the Commission indicates that during this period broadcast interests met some 18 times with Commission personnel, cable interests some nine times, motion picture and sports interests five times each, and "public interest" intervenors not at all.

Although it is impossible to draw any firm conclusions about the effect of *ex parte* presentations upon the ultimate shape of the pay cable rules, the evidence is certainly consistent with often-voiced claims of undue industry influence over Commission proceedings, and we are particularly concerned that the final shaping of the rules we are reviewing here may have been by compromise among the contending industry forces, rather than by exercise of the independent discretion in the public interest the Communications Act vests in individual commissioners. Our concern is heightened by the submission of the Commission's Broadcast Bureau to this court which states that in December 1974 broadcast representatives "described the kind of pay cable regulation that, in their view, broadcasters 'could live with.'" If actual positions were not revealed in public comments, as this statement would suggest, and, further, if the Commission relied on these apparently more candid private discussions in framing the final pay cable rules, then the elaborate public discussion in these dockets has been reduced to a sham.

Even the possibility that there is here one administrative record for the public and this court and another for the Commission and those "in the know" is intolerable. Whatever the law may have been in the past, there can now be no doubt that implicit in the decision to treat the promulgation of rules as a "final" event in an ongoing process of administration is an assumption that an act of reasoned judgment has occurred, an assumption which further contemplates the existence of a body of material documents, comments, transcripts, and statements in various forms declaring agency expertise or policy with reference to which such judgment was exercised. Against this material, "the full administrative record that was before (an agency official) at the time he made his decision," *Citizens to Preserve Overton Park, Inc. v. Volpe* [excerpted in subchapter 5A], it is the obligation of this court to test the actions of the Commission for arbitrariness or inconsistency with delegated authority. Yet here agency secrecy stands between us and fulfillment of our obligation. As a practical matter, *Overton Park*'s mandate means that the public record must reflect what representations were made to an agency so that relevant

PUBLIC RECORD information supporting or refuting those representations may be brought to the attention of the reviewing courts by persons participating in agency proceedings. This course is obviously foreclosed if communications are made to the agency in secret and the agency itself does not disclose the information presented. Moreover, where, as here, an agency justifies its actions by reference only to information in the public file while failing to disclose the substance of other relevant information that has been presented to it, a reviewing court cannot presume that the agency has acted properly, but must treat the agency's justifications as a fictional account of the actual decisionmaking process and must perforce find its actions arbitrary.

JUDICIAL REVIEW

The failure of the public record in this proceeding to disclose all the information made available to the Commission is not the only inadequacy we find here. Even if the Commission had disclosed to this court the substance of what was said to it *ex parte*, it would still be difficult to judge the truth of what the Commission asserted it knew about the television industry because we would not have the benefit of an adversarial discussion among the parties. The importance of such discussion to the proper functioning of the agency decisionmaking and judicial review processes is evident in our cases. We have insisted, for example, that information in agency files or consultants' reports which the agency has identified as relevant to the proceeding be disclosed to the parties for adversarial comment. Similarly, we have required agencies to set out their thinking in notices of proposed rulemaking. This requirement not only allows adversarial critique of the agency but is perhaps one of the few ways that the public may be apprised of what the agency thinks it knows in its capacity as a repository of expert opinion. From a functional standpoint, we see no difference between assertions of fact and expert opinion tendered by the public, as here, and that generated internally in an agency: each may be biased, inaccurate, or incomplete failings which adversary comment may illuminate. Indeed, the potential for bias in private presentations in rulemakings which resolve "conflicting private claims to a valuable privilege," seems to us greater than in cases where we have reversed agencies for failure to disclose internal studies. We do not understand the rulemaking procedures adopted by the Commission to be inconsistent with these views since those procedures provide for a dialogue among interested parties through provisions for comment, reply-comment, and subsequent oral argument. What we do find baffling is why the Commission, which apparently recognizes that ready availability of private contacts saps the efficacy of the public proceedings, nonetheless continues the practice of allowing public and private comments to exist side by side....

LACK OF ADVERSARIAL DISCUSSION RE: EX PARTE

RULES

From what has been said above, it should be clear that information gathered *ex parte* from the public which becomes relevant to a rulemaking will have to be disclosed at some time. On the other hand, we recognize that informal contacts between agencies and the public are the "bread and butter" of the process of administration and are completely appropriate so long as they do not frustrate judicial review or raise serious questions of fairness. Reconciliation of these considerations in a manner which will reduce procedural uncertainty leads us to conclude that communications which are received prior to issuance of a formal notice of rulemaking do not, in general, have to be put in a public file. Of course, if the information contained in such a communication forms the basis for agency action, then, under well established principles, that information must be disclosed to the public in some form. Once a notice of proposed rulemaking has been issued, however, any agency official or employee who is or may reasonably be expected to be involved in the decisional process of the rulemaking proceeding, should "refus[e] to discuss matters relating to the disposition of a [rulemaking proceeding] with any interested private party, or an attorney or agent for any such party, prior to the [agency's] decision. . . ." If *ex parte* contacts nonetheless occur, we think that any written document or a summary of any oral communication must be placed in the public file established for each rulemaking docket immediately after the communication is received so that interested parties may comment thereon.

For the foregoing reasons, we must consider what steps should be taken to cure the procedural defect introduced by *ex parte* contacts. One option would be simply to vacate all of the rules under review and remand them to the Commission for consideration de novo. This approach has two defects, however. First, it is not possible for us to expunge from the Commission's collective memory what was said to it *ex parte*. Consequently, information untested by public scrutiny could influence the outcome of future proceedings if steps are not now taken to put this information on the public record. Second . . . we find it possible to uphold the Commission's rules relating to subscription broadcast television on the basis of the public record as it now stands. We further find no indication in the material already submitted to this court that the subscription broadcast rule amendments benefit persons who participated in *ex parte* contacts. We think the subscription broadcast rules ought, therefore, to remain in effect pending clarification of what was said to the Commission *ex parte*. Such clarification would, of course, require further proceedings to be held to determine what was said to the Commission. Since it does not seem possible for such an inquiry to be limited solely to contacts regarding subscription broadcast television given the overlap between issues and parties in these proceedings, and because it would be useful to remove any possible effect of the *ex parte* contacts in these proceedings, we think the best resolution of the procedural problem we face is to adopt the course taken in *Sangamon* itself. Therefore, we today remand the record to the Commission for supplementation with instructions "to hold, with the aid of a specially appointed hearing examiner, an evidential hearing to determine the nature and source of all *ex parte* pleas and other approaches that were made to" the Commission or its employees after the issuance of the first notice of proposed rulemaking in these dockets. "All parties to the former proceeding and to the present review may on request participate fully in the evidential hearing," and may further participate in any proceedings before the Commission which it may hold for the purpose of evaluating the report of the hearing examiner. The Commission is further instructed to file the supplemented record with this court within 120 days of the date of this opinion, together with its recommendations concerning our disposition of the subscription broadcast television segment of this review.

Sierra Club v. Costle

657 F.2d 298 (D.C. Cir. 1981)

Opinion for the Court filed by CIRCUIT JUDGE WALD.

[In a challenge to pollution control standards governing coal fired power plants, environmental groups charged that EPA had permitted extensive *ex parte* contacts after the close of the comment period. This portion of the opinion addresses complaints about two such contacts, one with the White House, the other with Senator Robert Byrd. The court began by describing the challenged contacts.]

. . . .

3. April 23, 1979 This was a 30–45 minute meeting held at then Senate Majority Leader Robert Byrd's request, in his office, attended by EPA Administrator Douglas Costle, Chief Presidential Assistant Stuart Eizenstat, and NCA officials. A summary of this meeting was put in the docket on May 1, 1979, and copies of the summary were sent to EDF and to other parties. In its denial of the petition for reconsideration, EPA was adamant that no new information was transmitted to EPA at this meeting.

. . . .

5. April 30, 1979 At 10:00 a.m., a one hour White House briefing was held for the President, the White House staff, and high ranking members of the Executive Branch "concerning the issues and options presented by the rulemaking." This meeting was noted on an EPA official's personal calendar which EDF obtained after promulgation in response to its FOIA request, but was never noted in the rulemaking docket.

. . . .

9. May 2, 1979 This was a brief meeting between Senator Byrd, EPA, DOE and NCA officials held ostensibly for Senator Byrd to hear EPA's comments on the NCA data. A 49 word, not very informative, memorandum describing the meeting was entered on the docket on June 1, 1979.

. . . .

At the outset, we decline to begin our task of reviewing EPA's procedures by labeling all post-comment communications with the agency as "ex parte." Such an approach essentially begs the question whether these particular communications in an informal rulemaking proceeding were unlawful. Instead of beginning with a conclusion that these communications were "ex parte," we must evaluate the various communications in terms of their timing, source, mode, content, and the extent of their disclosure on the docket, in order to discover whether any of them violated the procedural requirements of the Clean Air Act, or of due process.

. . . .

2. Meetings Held With Individuals Outside EPA

The statute does not explicitly treat the issue of post-comment period meetings with individuals outside EPA. Oral face-to-face discussions are not prohibited anywhere, anytime, in the Act. The absence of such prohibition may have arisen from the nature of the informal rulemaking procedures Congress had in mind. Where agency action resembles judicial action, where it involves formal rulemaking, adjudication, or quasi-adjudication among "conflicting private claims to a valuable privilege," the insulation of the decisionmaker from ex parte contacts is justified by basic notions of due process to the parties involved. But where agency action involves informal rulemaking of a policymaking sort, the concept of ex parte contacts is of more questionable utility.[501]

Under our system of government, the very legitimacy of general policymaking performed by unelected administrators depends in no small part upon the openness, accessibility, and amenability of these officials to the needs and ideas of the public from whom their ultimate authority derives, and upon whom their commands must fall. As judges we are insulated from these pressures because of the nature of the judicial process in which we participate; but we must refrain from the easy temptation to look askance at all face-to-face lobbying efforts, regardless of the forum in which they occur, merely because we see them as inappropriate in the judicial context.[503] Furthermore, the importance to effective regulation of continuing contact with a regulated industry, other affected groups, and the public cannot be underestimated. Informal contacts may enable the agency to win needed support for its program, reduce future enforcement requirements by helping those regulated to anticipate and shape their plans for the future, and spur the provision of information which the agency needs. The possibility of course exists that in permitting ex parte communications with rulemakers we create the danger of "one administrative record for the public and this court and another for the Commission." Under the Clean Air Act procedures, however, "[t]he promulgated rule may not be based

---

501.   ... *See generally* [Verkuil, *Jawboning Administrative Agencies: Ex Parte Contacts by the White House*, 80 Colum.L.Rev. 943, (1980)] at 975–76:

> It should not be forgotten that informal rulemaking involves "interested persons," rather than "parties" in the usual adjudicative sense of the term. The concept of "ex parte" implies a different decisional structure from that involving mere "interested persons." One can only have a contact without "parties" present in a proceeding where parties are involved, namely, adjudication or formal rulemaking.

503.   *See* Remarks of Carl McGowan (Chief Judge, U.S. Court of Appeals, D.C. Circuit), Ass'n of Amer. Law Schools, Section on Admin. Law (San Antonio, Texas, Jan. 4, 1981):

> I think it likely that ambivalence will continue to pervade the ex parte contact problem until we face up to the question of whether legislation by informal rulemaking under delegated authority is, in terms of process, to be assimilated to lawmaking by the Congress itself, or to the adversary trial carried on in the sanitized and insulated atmosphere of the courthouse. Anyone with experience of both knows that a courtroom differs markedly in style and tone from a legislative chamber. The customs, the traditions, the mores, if you please, of the processes of persuasion, are emphatically not the same. What is acceptable in the one is alien to the other.

(in part or whole) on any information or data which has not been placed in the docket. . . ." Thus EPA must justify its rulemaking solely on the basis of the record it compiles and makes public. . . .

(a) Intra-Executive Branch Meetings

We have already held that a blanket prohibition against meetings during the post-comment period with individuals outside EPA is unwarranted, and this perforce applies to meetings with White House officials. We have not yet addressed, however, the issue whether such oral communications with White House staff, or the President himself, must be docketed on the rulemaking record, and we now turn to that issue. The facts, as noted earlier, present us with a single undocketed meeting held on April 30, 1979, at 10:00 a. m., attended by the President, White House staff, other high ranking members of the Executive Branch, as well as EPA officials, and which concerned the issues and options presented by the rulemaking.

We note initially that section 307 [of the Clean Air Act] makes specific provision for including in the rulemaking docket the "written comments" of other executive agencies along with accompanying documents on any proposed draft rules circulated in advance of the rulemaking proceeding. Drafts of the final rule submitted to an executive review process prior to promulgation, as well as all "written comments," "documents," and "written responses" resulting from such interagency review process, are also to be put in the docket prior to promulgation. This specific requirement does not mention informal meetings or conversations concerning the rule which are not part of the initial or final review processes, nor does it refer to oral comments of any sort. Yet it is hard to believe Congress was unaware that intra-executive meetings and oral comments would occur throughout the rulemaking process. We assume, therefore, that unless expressly forbidden by Congress, such intra-executive contacts may take place, both during and after the public comment period; the only real issue is whether they must be noted and summarized in the docket.

The court recognizes the basic need of the President and his White House staff to monitor the consistency of executive agency regulations with Administration policy. He and his White House advisers surely must be briefed fully and frequently about rules in the making, and their contributions to policymaking considered. The executive power under our Constitution, after all, is not shared it rests exclusively with the President. The idea of a "plural executive," or a President with a council of state, was considered and rejected by the Constitutional Convention. Instead the Founders chose to risk the potential for tyranny inherent in placing power in one person, in order to gain the advantages of accountability fixed on a single source. To ensure the President's control and supervision over the Executive Branch, the Constitution and its judicial gloss vests him with the powers of appointment and removal, the power to demand written opinions from executive officers, and the right to invoke executive privilege to protect consultative privacy. In the particular case of EPA, Presidential authority is clear since it has never been considered an "independent agency," but always part of the Executive Branch.

The authority of the President to control and supervise executive policymaking is derived from the Constitution; the desirability of such control is demonstrable from the practical realities of administrative rulemaking. Regulations such as those involved here demand a careful weighing of cost, environmental, and energy considerations. They also have broad implications for national economic policy. Our form of government simply could not function effectively or rationally if key executive policymakers were isolated from each other and from the Chief Executive. Single mission agencies do not always have the answers to complex regulatory problems. An overworked administrator exposed on a 24-hour basis to a dedicated but zealous staff needs to know the arguments and ideas of policymakers in other agencies as well as in the White House.

We recognize, however, that there may be instances where the docketing of conversations between the President or his staff and other Executive Branch officers or rulemakers may be necessary to ensure due process. This may be true, for example, where such conversations directly concern the outcome of adjudications or quasi-adjudicatory proceedings; there is no inherent executive power to control the rights of individuals in such settings. Docketing may also be necessary in some circumstances where a statute like this one specifically requires that essential "information or data" upon which a rule is based be docketed. But in the absence of any further Congressional requirements, we hold that it was not unlawful in this case for EPA not to docket a face-to-face policy session involving the President and EPA officials during the post-comment period, since EPA makes no effort to base the rule on any "information or data" arising from that meeting. Where the President himself is directly involved in oral communications with Executive Branch officials, Article II considerations combined with the strictures of *Vermont Yankee* require that courts tread with extraordinary caution in mandating disclosure beyond that already required by statute.

The purposes of full-record review which underlie the need for disclosing ex parte conversations in some settings do not require that courts know the details of every White House contact, including a Presidential one, in this informal rulemaking setting. After all, any rule issued here with or without White House assistance must have the requisite factual support in the rulemaking record, and under this particular statute the Administrator may not base the rule in whole or in part on any "information or data" which is not in the record, no matter what the source. The courts will monitor all this, but they need not be omniscient to perform their role effectively. Of course, it is always possible that undisclosed Presidential prodding may direct an outcome that is factually based on the record, but different from the outcome that would have obtained in the absence of Presidential involvement. In such a case, it would be true that the political process did affect the outcome in a way the courts could not police. But we do not believe that Congress intended that the courts convert informal rulemaking into a rarified technocratic process, unaffected by political considerations or the presence of Presidential power. In sum, we find that the existence of intra-Executive Branch meetings during the post-comment period, and the failure to docket one such meeting involving the President, violated neither the procedures mandated by the Clean Air Act nor due process.

[(b) Meetings Involving Alleged Congressional Pressure]

Finally, EDF challenges the rulemaking on the basis of alleged Congressional pressure, citing principally two meetings with Senator Byrd. EDF asserts that under the controlling case law the political interference demonstrated in this case represents a separate and independent ground for invalidating this rulemaking. But among the cases EDF cites in support of its position, only *D.C. Federation of Civil Associations v. Volpe* [459 F.2d 1231 (D.C. Cir. 1971), *cert. denied*, 405 U.S. 1030 (1972), discussed below in subchapter 4C.3] seems relevant to the facts here.

In *D.C. Federation* the Secretary of Transportation, pursuant to applicable federal statutes, made certain safety and environmental findings in designating a proposed bridge as part of the interstate highway system. Civic associations sought to have these determinations set aside for their failure to meet certain statutory standards, and because of possible tainting by reason of improper Congressional influence. Such influence chiefly included public statements by the Chairman of the House Subcommittee on the District of Columbia, Representative Natcher, indicating in no uncertain terms that money earmarked for the construction of the District of Columbia's subway system would be withheld unless the Secretary approved the bridge. While a majority of this court could not decide whether Representative Natcher's extraneous pressure had in fact influenced the Secretary's decision, a majority did agree on the controlling principle of law: "that the decision [of the Secretary] would be invalid if based in whole or in part on the pressures emanating from Representative Natcher." In remanding to the Secretary for new determinations concerning the bridge, however, the court went out of its way to "emphasize that we have not found nor, for that matter, have we sought any suggestion of impropriety or illegality in the actions of Representative Natcher and others who strongly advocate the bridge." The court remanded simply so that the Secretary could make this decision strictly and solely on the basis of considerations made relevant by Congress in the applicable statute.

D.C. Federation thus requires that two conditions be met before an administrative rulemaking may be overturned simply on the grounds of Congressional pressure. First, the content of the pressure upon the Secretary is designed to force him to decide upon factors not made relevant by Congress in the applicable statute. Representative Natcher's threats were of precisely that character, since deciding to approve the bridge in order to free the "hostage" mass transit appropriation was not among the decisionmaking factors Congress had in mind when it enacted the highway approval provisions of Title 23 of the United States Code. Second, the Secretary's determination must be affected by those extraneous considerations.

In the case before us, there is no persuasive evidence that either criterion is satisfied. Senator Byrd requested a meeting in order to express "strongly" his already well-known views that the SO2 standards' impact on coal reserves was a matter of concern to him. EPA initiated a second responsive meeting to report its reaction to the reserve data submitted by the NCA. In neither meeting is there any allegation that EPA made any commitments to Senator Byrd. The meetings did underscore Senator Byrd's deep concerns for EPA, but there is no evidence he attempted actively to use "extraneous" pressures to further his position. Americans rightly expect their elected representatives to voice their grievances and preferences concerning the administration of our laws. We believe it entirely proper for Congressional representatives vigorously to represent the interests of their constituents before administrative agencies engaged in informal, general policy rulemaking, so long as individual Congressmen do not frustrate the intent of Congress as a whole as expressed in statute, nor undermine applicable rules of procedure. Where Congressmen keep their comments focused on the substance of the proposed rule and we have no substantial evidence to cause us to believe Senator Byrd did not do so here administrative agencies are expected to balance Congressional pressure with the pressures emanating from all other sources. To hold otherwise would deprive the agencies of legitimate sources of information and call into question the validity of nearly every controversial rulemaking.

United Steelworkers of America, AFL-CIO-CLC v. Marshall

647 F.2d 1189 (D.C. Cir. 1981)

Opinion for the court filed by CHIEF JUDGE J. SKELLY WRIGHT.

[Both unions and industry challenged a workplace lead exposure standard issued by the Occupational Safety and Health Administration, a unit of the Department of Labor. The Lead Industries Association (LIA) attacked the rule on the basis of the alleged prejudice of Richard Gross, the attorney who led the development of the rule.]

LIA aims its next procedural attack at OSHA staff attorneys who, LIA argues, acted essentially as advocates for a stringent lead standard by consulting with and persuading the Assistant Secretary as she drew her conclusions from the record. LIA would have us conclude that the agency decisionmaker engaged in ex parte, off-the-record contacts with one of the adverse sides in the rulemaking, thereby rendering the proceedings unfair. Grounding its contention somewhat equivocally on due process, the procedural principles inherent in hybrid rulemaking, and OSHA's own regulations providing for cross-examination, LIA asks us to invalidate the entire proceeding.

The key agency employee in question was Richard Gross, a lawyer in the Office of the Solicitor at OSHA, who served as a so-called "standard's attorney" throughout the rulemaking. His precise role is as ambiguous as it is important. LIA portrays him as a sort of guardian ad litem for a stringent lead standard who "horse-shed" expert witnesses to contrive a record that would support such a standard, and then impermissibly advocated before the Assistant Secretary to make certain she construed the record as he intended. OSHA portrays him rather as a neutral party with no particular cause other than developing the fullest and soundest scientific and economic record possible, and with no bias other than the general orientation toward worker health inevitable in any OSHA employee.

The standard's attorney was at the center of activity throughout the rulemaking. He worked with the regular OSHA staff in reviewing preliminary research and drafting the proposed standard, all the while offering informal legal advice. He helped organize the public hearings and, having immersed himself in the scientific literature and in the submitted public comments, he communicated regularly with the prospective expert witnesses. In these communications he briefed the witnesses on the issues they were to address in their testimony, explained the positions of the agency, the industry, and the unions on key questions, discussed the likely criticism of the experts' testimony, and asked the experts for any new information that supported or contradicted the OSHA proposal. During the hearing itself he conducted all initial questioning of OSHA witnesses and cross-examined all other witnesses. After the hearings he assisted the Assistant Secretary by reviewing the evidence in the record, preparing summaries, analyses, and recommendations, and helping draft the Preamble to the final standard.

In a proceeding to create a general rule it makes little sense to speak of an agency employee advocating for one "side" over another. . . . Therefore, although we have some doubt about calling the standard's attorney an "advocate" in the context of such rulemaking, we will assume he played that role so we can measure his conduct against the legal constraints on the agency.

We note at the outset that nothing in the Administrative Procedure Act bars a staff advocate from advising the decision maker in setting a final rule. The APA deals with ex parte contacts in two provisions. 5 U.S.C. § 554(d), which applies solely to adjudications, prohibits any off-the-record communication between an agency decision maker and any other person about a fact in issue, and in particular bars any prosecuting or investigating employee of the agency from participating in final decisions. Since an OSHA proceeding to set a safety and health standard is obviously rulemaking, and not adjudication, that provision cannot apply here. 5 U.S.C. § 557(d), which applies to formal rulemaking as well as adjudication, prohibits ex parte communications relevant to the merits of a proceeding between the agency and interested parties outside the agency. Even were we to ignore our own determination and Congress' that the OSH Act creates essentially informal rulemaking, this provision cannot apply to ex parte contacts wholly among agency employees.

Moreover, in establishing the special hybrid procedures in the OSH Act, Congress never intended to impose the separation-of-functions requirement it imposes in adjudications. The legislative history shows that Congress consistently turned back efforts to impose such formal procedures on OSHA standard-setting. Adding to informal rulemaking the special requirement of a substantial evidence test does not change the essential character of the rulemaking, especially under a statute like the OSH Act which does not even require a hearing before the agency sets a standard.

. . . .

Rulemaking is essentially an institutional, not an individual, process, and it is not vulnerable to communication within an agency in the same sense as it is to communication from without. In an enormously complex proceeding like an OSHA standard setting, it may simply be unrealistic to expect an official facing a massive, almost inchoate, record to isolate herself from the people with whom she worked in generating the record. In any event, we rest our decision not on our own theory of agency management, but on the state of the law.

Notes

1. Institutional integrity in the rulemaking process. The three scenarios in Lesson 3E involve arguments that the integrity of the rulemaking process has been compromised in three different ways. Ralph, as a litigator, is appalled at these apparent stains on the agency. He agrees with all three of the challenges. But is he right? This is rulemaking, not adjudication, and certainly not a formal trial. What are the differences between rulemaking and adjudication that bear on the resolution of these disputes?

2. *HBO*—A high-water mark, with lingering effects. The *HBO* opinion hinges on two previous decisions, *Citizens to Preserve Overton Park v. Volpe*, 401 U.S. 402 (1971), and *Sangamon Valley Television Corp. v. United States*, 269 F.2d 221 (D.C. Cir. 1959). As the *HBO* opinion reflects, *Overton Park*, which you will examine in subchapter 5A, was concerned about the adequacy of the record for judicial review in a dispute about a public park. *Sangamon Valley*, on the other hand, involved an FCC proceeding that, although labeled as rulemaking, effectively determined the private rights of broadcast license applicants.

Shortly after the *HBO* opinion was issued, another panel of the D.C. Circuit raised questions as to whether the strongest language of *HBO* would be the law even in the D.C. Circuit. In *Action for Children's Television v. FCC*, 564 F.2d 458, 474 (D.C. Cir. 1977), the Court offered a more temperate view of *ex parte* communications in a rulemaking about television for children:

> For the reasons set forth below, we agree with Judge MacKinnon [dissenting in *HBO*] that the [*HBO ex parte* pronouncement] should not apply—as the opinion clearly would have it—to every case of informal rulemaking. However, notwithstanding our views to the contrary, we hold only that *Home Box Office*'s broad proscription is not to be applied retroactively in the case *sub judice* inasmuch as it constitutes a clear departure from established law when applied to informal rulemaking proceedings. . . .

> In the absence of support for its position in the Administrative Procedure Act, the panel in *Home Box Office* justified its extension of an ex parte prohibition/disclosure rule throughout all manner of informal rulemaking by reasoning from our decision in *Sangamon Valley Television Corp.*,

where we held that ex parte contacts by interested parties with FCC members regarding the allocation of specific TV channels vitiated the ultimate allocation decision. . . . Although *Sangamon* did involve informal rulemaking, as opposed to licensing-by-adjudication, the court there agreed that "whatever the proceeding may be called it involved not only allocation of TV channels among communities *but also resolution of conflicting private claims to a valuable privilege* [i.e., a TV channel], and that basic fairness requires such a proceeding to be carried on in the open." Surely this is good law, especially in view of the fact that channel allocation via informal rulemaking is rather similar functionally to licensing via adjudication. The proceedings [here] however, present a different situation entirely, where the informal rulemaking undertaken did not involve such "conflicting private claims to a valuable privilege" but rather the possible formulation of programming policy revisions of general applicability. Nonetheless, *Home Box Office* would prohibit or require publication and opportunity for comment on all *ex parte* contacts, no matter how minor, during the notice and comment stage regardless of the nature of the inquiry. The novelty of this requirement should have been apparent to all.

. . . [In discussing a previous FCC rulemaking decision, *Sangamon Valley*] appears to say that because the Commission said it was not influenced by the ex parte contacts the reviewing court need not presume otherwise — a position not in harmony with the presumption of agency irregularity implicitly underwritten by the *Home Box Office* decision. We do not propose to argue that [the previous decision] stands for the proposition that ex parte contacts always are permissible in informal rulemaking proceedings — they are of course not — but we do think it can be read as supporting the proposition that ex parte contacts do not per se vitiate agency informal rulemaking action, but only do so if it appears from the administrative record under review that they may have materially influenced the action ultimately taken.

Do you agree that *ex parte* communication is less dangerous in rulemaking than in adjudication?

Despite the challenge to *HBO* in *Action for Children's Television*, the decision remains influential. Agencies typically keep a written docket of contacts from private interests related to their rulemaking proceedings. Reviewing an FCC rulemaking on long distance access charges, the Fifth Circuit said, "The APA permits *ex parte* contact between an agency and private parties as long as the agency adequately gives notice of such contact." *Texas Office of Pub. Util. Counsel v. FCC*, 265 F.3d 313, 327 (5th Cir. 2001). The court's statement appears to apply to all informal rulemaking, but the fact that this decision involved ratemaking may have placed it in the narrower realm of *Sangamon Valley* as a resolution of conflicts about private economic interests. Along those lines, the D.C. Circuit recently stated flatly (in a somewhat different context) that *"Home Box Office* was based on the due process clause. . . ." *Electric Power Supply Ass'n v. FERC*, 391 F.3d 1255, 1266 (D.C. Cir. 2004). Read that way, *HBO* is of no significance to most rulemakings. We examine the Due Process Clause in subchapter 4B.

3. Political contacts—a surprising legitimacy? As you consider Ben's concerns about discussions with Senator Brisby or the president's Chief of Staff, what guidance can you take from *Sierra Club v. Costle*? Is there any boundary to what a Senator's or president's aide can do? What constraints are there on what an agency may do in light of such contacts? What is the source of those constraints—the rights of the parties, as we would expect in an adjudication, or something else?

4. Brit's apparent anti-industry bias—a basis for removal? As lead attorney responsible for developing the labeling rule, Brit plays a crucial role in the rulemaking process. She guides the development of the record by agency personnel, and she probably controls the way information is transmitted to the ultimate decisionmakers, the Commissioners. In response to Jordan's petition, does the WTC have to remove her from her leadership role? Should it?

5. What if Commissioner Sarah had the same background as Brit? Commissioner Sarah has a history of strong-willed consumer advocacy. If she had cooperated closely with the Wrath for Grapes, as Brit did, and perhaps had made anti-alcohol pronouncements, should she be disqualified from the rulemaking? Unlike Brit, after all, she is an actual decisionmaker.

The D.C. Circuit addressed this issue in *United Steelworkers*, excerpted above. Dr. Eula Bingham, then head of the Occupational Safety and Health Administration (OSHA), had made several strong statements about the hazards of lead in the workplace and about the rights and needs of workers. Industry argued that she had prejudged the issues in the rulemaking. The court refused to vacate the lead exposure standard, however, due to the nature of rulemaking, as opposed to adjudication:

> Were it our task to assess the wisdom and propriety of an administrator's public conduct, we might well admonish Dr. Bingham for this speech. She served her agency poorly by making statements so susceptible to an inference of bias, especially statements to a group so passionately involved in the proceedings. But our task is rather to measure her conduct against the legal standards for determining whether an official is so biased as to be incapable of finding facts and setting policy on the basis of the objective record before her. . . .
>
> An administrative official is presumed to be objective and "capable of judging a particular controversy fairly on the basis of its own circumstances." Whether the official is engaged in adjudication or rulemaking, mere proof that she has taken a public position, or has expressed strong views, or holds an underlying philosophy with respect to an issue in dispute cannot overcome that presumption. . . .

When Congress creates an agency with an express mission in OSHA's case, to protect workers' health and safety the agency officials will almost inevitably form views on the best means of carrying out that mission. The subjective partiality of an official of such an agency does not invalidate a proceeding that the agency conducts in good faith.

This court has indeed required disqualification of an agency adjudicator when his public statements about pending cases revealed he "'has in some measure adjudged the facts as well as the law of a particular case in advance of hearing it.'" *Cinderella Career & Finishing Schools, Inc. v. FTC*, 425 F.2d 583, 591 (D.C. Cir. 1970). . . .

[This case] would lead us to vacate the lead standard only if Dr. Bingham had demonstrably made up her mind about important and specific factual questions and was impervious to contrary evidence. This test would be hard enough for petitioners to meet. But in *Ass'n of Nat'l Advertisers, Inc. v. FTC,* [627 F.2d 1151 (D.C. Cir. 1979), handed down after oral argument in the present case, we raised an even higher barrier to claims of bias in rulemaking proceedings. We stressed there the difference between the essentially "legislative" factfinding of a rulemaker and the trial-type factfinding of an adjudicator, and thus held that the *Cinderella* test was inappropriate. We concluded that an agency official must be disqualified from rulemaking "only when there has been a clear and convincing showing that [she] has an unalterably closed mind on matters critical to the disposition of the proceeding."

F. Rulemaking Beyond the APA: Additional Congressional and White House Controls

Suppose the WTC decides to move forward with a major legislative rule requiring fuller disclosures on wine labels. To comply with basic statutory requirements for rulemaking set forth in the APA and the agency's organic act, the WTC will, at some point, need to issue a "notice of proposed rulemaking" (NPRM) informing the public of the proposal. The agency will also need to comply with statutory requirements that allow the public to participate in the rulemaking process, typically by submitting comments on the proposed rule.

Administrative law courses tend to spend a lot of time exploring the basic, APA-style template for public participation in legislative rulemaking—as this casebook did earlier in this chapter. This focus is appropriate because this basic template applies broadly across many agencies, creating controls that are subject to judicial review. Still, this template represents only the proverbial tip of the iceberg of modern rulemaking. Now that you have learned the APA's rulemaking requirements, we can shift to introducing you to some of the other controls on the rulemaking process that Congress and presidents have created through statutes and executive orders.

Our chief focus will be on the requirements of Exec. Order 12,866, which has for several decades imposed centralized "White House" review of significant rules of executive agencies. This review is conducted by a relatively small but powerful agency, the Office of Information and Regulatory Affairs (OIRA), which is part of the Office of Management and Budget (OMB), which is in turn part of the Executive Office of the President. The dominant feature of Exec. Order 12,866 is that agencies must, before issuing notices of proposed significant rules or finally promulgating them, submit formal cost-benefit analyses to OIRA for review.

As you work through these materials, consider: What are the potential benefits of centralized White House review during the development of agency rules? And the drawbacks? Should it matter that Congress generally assigns rulemaking authority to agency heads rather than the president? Should it matter whether an agency enjoys "independent" status — such as the Federal Trade Commission or Securities and Exchange Commission? As you will see, Congress has developed the habit of passing statutes that require agencies to prepare various "impact statements" as part of rulemaking. Are they likely to improve the rulemaking process, or simply slow it?

This subchapter is designed to give you a big picture introduction to some of the issues and controversies that these extra-APA controls embed in the rulemaking process. If you find some of this material a bit daunting, do not be overly concerned — most people do.

———

Lesson 3F. When the WTC decided to move forward with a major legislative rule requiring fuller disclosure on wine labels, Brit recognized that the agency's internal procedures, which develop support for the rule, were the most important aspect of the rulemaking process. She suggested that her office (one of the WTC's several program offices) write the basic draft of the proposal with the technical assistance of the scientists in the Office of Technical Advice. That draft would then be circulated to the Policy Planning Office for its views and for the development of a cost-benefit analysis. The draft would also be reviewed by the enforcement staff, the Office of General Counsel (which will have to defend it in court), and the Office of the Director of Technical Advice.

After that review process, the draft would be circulated to interested agencies, such as the Department of Agriculture and the Food and Drug Administration. After receiving comments from these various offices inside government, Brit's office would write a proposed rule for issuance by the full Commission and publication for public comment.

After completing the agency's internal process for developing the proposed disclosure rule, Brit must ensure compliance with any additional procedural requirements imposed by executive order or statute before publishing an NPRM. Must the agency comply with Exec. Order 12,866? Why or why not? Assuming that the executive order does apply, what requirements does it impose before the WTC can publish its NPRM? What difficulties might the agency encounter in satisfying such requirements? Are there other statutory requirements, whether in the WTCA or other statutes, that the agency must address?

Materials on Executive Orders and Additional Statutory Controls

Congress has delegated to agencies an enormous amount of power to create legislative rules. On a moment's reflection, one might expect presidents, who are in charge of the executive branch, to take steps to coordinate and control the exercise of this power. Presidents of both parties have done so by imposing centralized review of rulemaking by executive order. Executive Order 12,866, which currently controls this process, appears below.

Congress, too, has played an important role in making the rulemaking process more complex than the framers of the APA contemplated in 1946. It has, in various statutes over the years, required agencies to prepare different types of "impact" statements in the course of rulemaking. People have been arguing for decades over whether these additional executive and legislative controls improve or distort the agency rulemaking process. Although it is surely too soon for you to form a definitive opinion, consider this issue as your work through the materials below.

Executive Order 12,866 (Sept. 30, 1993)
Regulatory Planning and Review

. . . .

The objectives of this Executive order are to enhance planning and coordination with respect to both new and existing regulations; to reaffirm the primacy of Federal agencies in the regulatory decision-making process; to restore the integrity and legitimacy of regulatory review and oversight; and to make the process more accessible and open to the public. . . .

Accordingly, by the authority vested in me as President by the Constitution and the laws of the United States of America, it is hereby ordered as follows:

. . .

Sec. 2. *Organization.* An efficient regulatory planning and review process is vital to ensure that the Federal Government's regulatory system best serves the American people.

. . .

(b) *The Office of Management and Budget.* Coordinated review of agency rulemaking is necessary to ensure that regulations are consistent with applicable law, the President's priorities, and the principles set forth in this Executive order, and that decisions made by one agency do not conflict with the policies or actions taken or planned by another agency. The Office of Management and Budget (OMB) shall carry out that review function. Within OMB, the Office of Information and Regulatory Affairs (OIRA) is the repository of expertise concerning regulatory issues, including methodologies and procedures that affect more than one agency, this Executive order, and the President's regulatory policies. To the extent permitted by law, OMB shall provide guidance to agencies . . . and shall be the entity that reviews individual regulations, as provided by this Executive order.

. . .

Sec. 3. *Definitions.* For purposes of this Executive order:

. . .

(b) "Agency," unless otherwise indicated, means any authority of the United States that is an "agency" under 44 U.S.C. 3502(1), other than those considered to be independent regulatory agencies, as defined in 44 U.S.C. 3502(10).

(c) "Director" means the Director of OMB.

(d) "Regulation" or "rule" means an agency statement of general applicability and future effect, which the agency intends to have the force and effect of law, that is designed to implement, interpret, or prescribe law or policy or to describe the procedure or practice requirements of an agency. It does not, however, include [rules issued through formal rulemaking, exempt from APA rulemaking requirements, or otherwise exempted by OIRA] . . . :

(e) "Regulatory action" means any substantive action by an agency (normally published in the **Federal Register**) that promulgates or is expected to lead to the promulgation of a final rule or regulation, including notices of inquiry, advance notices of proposed rulemaking, and notices of proposed rulemaking.

(f) "Significant regulatory action" means any regulatory action that is likely to result in a rule that may:

(1) Have an annual effect on the economy of $100 million or more or adversely affect in a material way the economy, a sector of the economy, productivity, competition, jobs, the environment, public health or safety, or State, local, or tribal governments or communities;

(2) Create a serious inconsistency or otherwise interfere with an action taken or planned by another agency;

(3) Materially alter the budgetary impact of entitlements, grants, user fees, or loan programs or the rights and obligations of recipients thereof; or

(4) Raise novel legal or policy issues arising out of legal mandates, the President's priorities, or the principles set forth in this Executive order.

Sec. 4. *Planning Mechanism.* [Requires agencies, including independent agencies, to prepare a regulatory agenda of rules under development and a regulatory plan, approved by the agency head, with OIRA to review and coordinate regulatory plans.]

. . .

Sec. 6. *Centralized Review of Regulations.* The guidelines set forth below shall apply to all regulatory actions, for both new and existing regulations, by agencies other than those agencies specifically exempted by the Administrator of OIRA:

(a) *Agency Responsibilities.* (1) Each agency shall (consistent with its own rules, regulations, or procedures) provide the public with meaningful participation in the regulatory process. In particular, before issuing a notice of proposed rulemaking, each agency should, where appropriate, seek the involvement of those who are intended to benefit from and those expected to be burdened by any regulation (including, specifically, State, local, and tribal officials). In addition, each agency should afford the public a meaningful opportunity to comment on any proposed regulation, which in most cases should include a comment period of not less than 60 days. Each agency also is directed to explore and, where appropriate, use consensual mechanisms for developing regulations, including negotiated rulemaking. . . . (3) [E]ach agency shall develop its regulatory actions in a timely fashion and adhere to the following procedures with respect to a regulatory action:

(A) Each agency shall provide OIRA, at such times and in the manner specified by the Administrator of OIRA, with a list of its planned regulatory actions, indicating those which the agency believes are significant regulatory actions within the meaning of this Executive order. . . .

(B) For each matter identified as, or determined by the Administrator of OIRA to be, a significant regulatory action, the issuing agency shall provide to OIRA:

(i) The text of the draft regulatory action, together with a reasonably detailed description of the need for the regulatory action and an explanation of how the regulatory action will meet that need; and (ii) An assessment of the potential costs and benefits of the regulatory action, including an explanation of the manner in which the regulatory action is consistent with a statutory mandate and, to the extent permitted by law, promotes the President's priorities and avoids undue interference with State, local, and tribal governments in the exercise of their governmental functions.

(C) For those matters identified as, or determined by the Administrator of OIRA to be, a significant regulatory action within the scope of section 3(f) (1), the agency shall also provide to OIRA the following additional information developed as part of the agency's decision-making process (unless prohibited by law):

(i) An assessment, including the underlying analysis, of benefits anticipated from the regulatory action (such as, but not limited to, the promotion of the efficient functioning of the economy and private markets, the enhancement of health and safety, the protection of the natural environment, and the elimination or reduction of discrimination or bias) together with, to the extent feasible, a quantification of those benefits;

(ii) An assessment, including the underlying analysis, of costs anticipated from the regulatory action (such as, but not limited to, the direct cost both to the government in administering the regulation and to businesses and others in complying with the regulation, and any adverse effects on the efficient functioning of the economy, private markets (including productivity, employment, and competitiveness), health, safety, and the natural environment), together with, to the extent feasible, a quantification of those costs; and

(iii) An assessment, including the underlying analysis, of costs and benefits of potentially effective and reasonably feasible alternatives to the planned regulation, identified by the agencies or the public (including improving the current regulation and reasonably viable nonregulatory actions), and an explanation why the planned regulatory action is preferable to the identified potential alternatives.

. . .

(E) After the regulatory action has been published in the Federal Register or otherwise issued to the public, the agency shall:

(i) Make available to the public the information set forth in subsections (a)(3)(B) and (C);

(ii) Identify for the public, in a complete, clear, and simple manner, the substantive changes between the draft submitted to OIRA for review and the action subsequently announced; and

(iii) Identify for the public those changes in the regulatory action that were made at the suggestion or recommendation of OIRA.

. . .

(b) *OIRA Responsibilities.* The Administrator of OIRA shall provide meaningful guidance and oversight so that each agency's regulatory actions are consistent with applicable law, the President's priorities, and the principles set forth in this Executive order and do not conflict with the policies or actions of another agency. . . .

(3) For each regulatory action that the Administrator of OIRA returns to an agency for further consideration of some or all of its provisions, the Administrator of OIRA shall provide the issuing agency a written explanation for such return, setting forth the pertinent provision of this Executive order on which OIRA is relying. If the agency head disagrees with some or all of the bases for the return, the agency head shall so inform the Administrator of OIRA in writing.

(4) [Provisions for openness and transparency in OIRA communications with those outside the executive branch.]

. . .

Sec. 7. *Resolution of Conflicts.* To the extent permitted by law, disagreements or conflicts between or among agency heads or between OMB and any agency that cannot be resolved by the Administrator of OIRA shall be resolved by the President, or by the Vice President acting at the request of the President, with the relevant agency head (and, as appropriate, other interested government officials). Vice Presidential and Presidential consideration of such disagreements may be initiated only by the Director, by the head of the issuing agency, or by the head of an agency that has a significant interest in the regulatory action at issue. Such review will not be undertaken at the request of other persons, entities, or their agents.

. . .

Sec. 9. *Agency Authority.* Nothing in this order shall be construed as displacing the agencies' authority or responsibilities, as authorized by law.

Sec. 10. *Judicial Review.* Nothing in this Executive order shall affect any otherwise available judicial review of agency action. This Executive order is intended only to improve the internal management of the Federal Government and does not create any right or benefit, substantive or procedural, enforceable at law or equity by a party against the United States, its agencies or instrumentalities, its officers or employees, or any other person.

. . .

THE WHITE HOUSE,

September 30, 1993.

Notes

1. Executive Order 12,866 and the development of centralized executive review. The federal APA has no provision for centralized formal executive review. Nonetheless, White House review of agency rules has become an entrenched part of the administrative state over the last forty years. The idea began with President Nixon, gained strength with Presidents Carter and Reagan, and has been embraced by every president since.

The basic provisions currently governing centralized review are set forth in Exec. Order 12,866, "Regulatory Planning and Review," which was issued by President Clinton in 1993. The Obama administration, in addition to revoking some modifications to the order made by President Bush, added some relatively minor supplements focusing, for instance, on retrospective review of existing rules.

As you have read, Exec. Order 12,866 requires agencies subject to its terms to submit "significant regulatory actions" for review by the Office of Information and Regulatory Affairs (OIRA), an agency within the Office of Management and Budget (OMB). Section 3(e)'s definition of "regulatory action" captures both proposed and final rules within its net. As part of this process, the agency submits a cost-benefit analysis of its action to OIRA. (Some details on carrying out cost-benefit analysis are discussed below in note 2.) Section 6(b) of the order charges OIRA's administrator with the tasks of "provid[ing] meaningful guidance and oversight so that each agency's regulatory actions are consistent with applicable law, the President's priorities, and the principles set forth [in the order itself] and do not conflict with the policies or actions of another agency."

Notably, OIRA has no express power to force agencies to rewrite their rules. Its formal power is limited to discussing the proposal with the agencies, delaying the issuance of regulations while changes are sought, and placing in the public file critical comments to which the agency must respond. OIRA's practical power resides largely in its ability to persuade and in its position as representative of the president. A 1987 study by the National Academy of Public Administration concluded, "OMB arguments are more than advisory but still less than mandatory." Agency officials on the receiving end of OIRA instructions have been known to disagree with this assessment. *See* Lisa Heinzerling, *Inside EPA: A Former Insider's Reflections on the Relationship between the Obama EPA and the Obama White House*, 31 PACE ENVTL. L. REV. 325 (2014) (explaining that when "OIRA calls an official at the agency and asks the agency to ask for an extension, . . . [i]t is clear, in such a phone call, that the agency is not to decline to ask for such an extension").

The results of OIRA review may take several forms. After negotiation, the agency may make the changes the OIRA staff believes are necessary to satisfy the requirements of the executive order. Under both Presidents Bush and Obama, OIRA review resulted in changes to some 80% of the rules subject to this process. Other possible results of OIRA review may be: clearance of the regulation without change, withdrawal of the rule by the agency, return of the rule for reconsideration by the agency, or suspension of review.

OIRA review is controversial. OIRA's relatively small staff is generally not as expert as the agency staff (except, perhaps, in the art of cost-benefit analysis). *See* Harold Bruff, *Presidential Management of Agency Rulemaking*, 57 GEO. WASH. L. REV. 533, 557 (1989) (criticizing desk officers, who conduct much of OIRA's actual review functions, as "typically young economists, lawyers, or policy analysts with little prior experience in government or with the programs they oversee"). Is it likely that OIRA, with its limited expertise, will be able to spur substantive improvements to, say, an EPA rule governing pollution emissions? Also, OIRA review can serve as a locus for gathering objections from across the White House, the broader executive branch, industry, and other interest groups, potentially clouding accountability. Does this aspect of OIRA review threaten to politicize the rulemaking process unduly? Or is this objection misplaced in a democracy rather than a pure technocracy? Another criticism is that OIRA's role in changing rules is largely hidden from public view despite language in the executive order that seems to demand transparency. It can be very hard, if not impossible, to determine just how OIRA review has affected the terms of an agency rule. Should we permit this degree of secrecy in the exercise of centralized control?

For critiques and defenses of OIRA review, see Cass R. Sunstein, *The Office of Information and Regulatory Affairs: Myths and Realities*, 126 HARV. L. REV. 1838 (2013) (contending, as a former administrator of OIRA, that its review function is essentially technical, not political); Lisa Heinzerling, *Inside EPA: A Former Insider's Reflections on the Relationship between the Obama EPA and the Obama White House*, 31 PACE ENVTL L. REV. 325 (2014) (contending, as a former high-ranking EPA official, that OIRA review distorts and delays agency rulemaking in an opaque manner that obscures accountability).

2. Performing formal cost-benefit analysis. Formal cost-benefit analysis requires considerable expertise and the development of complex data. A few aspects of cost-benefit analysis will be highlighted here, however.

Formal cost-benefit analysis is not a matter of simply listing benefits and drawbacks to a rule and then comparing them in a rough, intuitive way. Rather, formal cost-benefit analysis seeks to place a dollar value on all costs and benefits to the degree practicable. This can lead to uncomfortable results, such as an agency placing a dollar value on reductions in the risk of prison rape.

Any valuation must be discounted to present value. One dollar of benefit ten years from now is much less valuable than one dollar in the present. One of the most straightforward ways to determine present values incorporates interest rates. One million dollars invested at five percent for ten years would earn about $1.6 million; the same amount invested at 10% would earn about $2.7 million in 10 years. Thus, a present expenditure of $1 million must bring future benefits of one of those amounts, depending on the interest rate assumptions. An example of the effect of discounting to present value is offered in JACK HIRSHLEIFER, PRICE THEORY AND APPLICATIONS (3d ed. 1976):

> The Feather River Project is an enormous undertaking of the State of California conveying water from a dam and reservoir in the northern part of the state to numerous delivery points in the central and southern portions. The Table that follows shows the results of an independent assessment (made prior to construction) of the prospective costs and receipts of the project and of the net balance of the two, all calculated in terms of Present Values. Three alternative routes then under consideration were evaluated. The present-value calculation considered two alternative interest rates, 2.7% and 5%.
>
> While all the Present Values were negatives, the higher 5% interest rate was associated with relatively lower figures for both costs and receipts. Since the cost sequence is a series of positive payments at each date, and the receipts sequence also a series of positive elements, the larger the r [interest rate] the smaller the discounted sum for each. . . . But the Table shows that the impact of a higher r upon receipts is greater than upon costs. The reason is that costs

are typically incurred *earlier* in time than receipts are received, so that a rise in the discount factor $(1 + r)$ operates more powerfully to reduce the latter. *The higher the r, the less attractive the project* is a reliable general rule.

Present Values of the Feather River Project (millions of dollars)[1]

Interest Rate	Costs	Receipts	Net Present Value	Net Present Value Adjusted[2]
2.7%				
Route 1	$1241	$1079	$−162	$−97
Route 8A	1123	1012	−111	−46
Route 10A	1029	919	−110	−46
5%				
Route 1	1035	515	−520	−502
Route 8A	860	445	−415	−397
Route 10A	799	409	−391	−372

Constructing a cost-benefit analysis usually involves questions of both risk and uncertainty. Risk refers to situations in which information about the probability of an outcome's occurrence is available, whereas uncertainty refers to situations where there is no such information. Still, valuing a risk is difficult, and making a decision incorporating risk is tricky. For example, a manufacturer might know that one person in a million will have a fatal allergic reaction to a particular drug, but have no way of identifying such a person. Suppose the drug kills the HIV virus in 30 percent of the cases. If you were found to have the HIV virus, would you take the drug? If you were the Food and Drug Administration, would you approve the drug? Would you order the manufacturer to compensate the heirs of any person dying from the allergic reaction? Would you allow the manufacturer, if you could regulate pricing, to incorporate in its price the potential liability to those heirs?

Uncertainty and prediction raise similar but different problems. For one thing, since it is more difficult to quantify uncertainty, it is nearly impossible to offer concrete support for predictions about future cost or benefits under that condition. If you were part of a rulemaking staff, how would you deal with uncertainty? How would you attempt to support your predictions? If you were a reviewing court, how would you review an agency's efforts to deal with uncertainty?

One of the most compelling criticisms of formal cost-benefit analysis is that it is not possible (or at least not proper) to place a monetary value on life, so it is

---

1. Source: J.C. DeHaven and J. Hirshleifer, "Feather River Water for Southern California," *Land Economics*, v. 33 (Aug. 1957), p. 201. (Some technical footnotes omitted.)
2. Adjustment credits an allowance for flood-control benefits and salvage value.

not truly possible to compare the economic benefits of an activity to costs in terms of lives lost over time. Indeed, different agencies have used different amounts to reflect the value of a life. More broadly, critics argue that assigning dollar figures to non-market goods tends to overwhelm unquantifiable values such as the aesthetic beauty of a magnificent vista in the western National Parks or the calm quiet of a park from which traffic and other noises have been excluded.

Despite those criticisms, the use of cost-benefit analysis has become so pervasive that Cass Sunstein argues that the debate about whether to rely upon it in regulatory decisionmaking has ended "with a substantial victory" for its proponents. CASS R. SUNSTEIN, RISK AND REASON — SAFETY, LAW, AND THE ENVIRONMENT 5 (2002). Sunstein argues that we must use cost-benefit analysis if we are to make reasoned and reasonably accurate decisions that assure the greatest possible protection of life, health, and the environment. Intuitive and political judgments, too often driven by irrational assessments of risk, often cause us to misallocate resources to minimal risks and even to cause more harm than good. To Sunstein, cost-benefit analysis is inescapable. Recognizing its flaws, he argues for its careful use.

By contrast, Frank Ackerman and Lisa Heinzerling have challenged both the accuracy and the validity of reliance on cost-benefit analysis. Agreeing with Sunstein and others that "[t]here are hard questions to be answered about protection of human health and the environment," and that economics can provide "useful insights," they argue that:

> [F]ormal cost-benefit analysis often hurts more than it helps: it muddies rather than clarifies fundamental clashes about values. By proceeding as if its assumptions are scientific and by speaking a language all its own, economic analysis too easily conceals the basic human questions that lie at its heart and excludes the voices of people untrained in the field. Again and again, economic theory gives us opaque and technical reasons to do the obviously wrong thing.

FRANK ACKERMAN & LISA HEINZERLING, PRICELESS: ON KNOWING THE PRICE OF EVERYTHING AND THE VALUE OF NOTHING 5 (2004). In a subsequent article, they showed that a cost-benefit analysis requirement might well have prevented the elimination of lead from gasoline, which we now know was extraordinarily beneficial in terms of health and cost-benefit balance. They also showed that a cost-benefit analysis of damming the Grand Canyon for hydroelectric power favored protecting the Grand Canyon only because it used wildly optimistic figures about the cost of nuclear power. Reasonably accurate figures would have resulted in a conclusion supporting damming the Grand Canyon. They argue that cost-benefit analysis is not neutral but tends to favor industrial and economic interests, and for a variety of reasons it is not accurate. Frank Ackerman, Lisa Heinzerling & Rachel Massey, *Applying Cost-Benefit to Past Decisions: Was Environmental Protection Ever a Good Idea?*, 57 ADMIN. L. REV. 155 (2005).

How should the WTC approach this problem? Requiring detailed information on wine labels, for example, may improve purchasing decisions or even help a few asthmatics avoid harmful ingredients. But analyzing wines, identifying all the ingredients, and preparing and applying the correct labels all costs money. The increased cost may force up the price consumers pay for wines, and it may cause some wine industry workers to lose their jobs. How should the WTC determine and take into account the accuracy of such claims? Should it have to struggle with those difficult questions when the benefits of wine labels are fairly clear?

3. Sometimes it isn't legal for an agency to rely on cost-benefit analysis. Recall that all agency authority derives from statutes. The president may direct agencies in various ways, and he may order them to do cost-benefit analyses as part of his management functions. But he may not require an agency to use cost-benefit analysis as a rule of decision where doing so is inconsistent with the agency's statutory authority. Nor, of course, may the agency do so of its own accord.

Under what circumstances might an agency base its decision on cost-benefit analysis despite the fact that the statute does not specifically provide for it? In *Michigan v. EPA*, 135 S. Ct. 2699 (2015), although the Court split 5-4 on the result, all nine justices agreed that, absent contrary congressional instructions, reasonable agency rulemaking requires an agency somehow to consider the important costs of a regulation and ensure that they do not wildly outweigh benefits. The Court emphasized that it was not imposing a requirement of formal cost-benefit analysis on agencies, but *Michigan* seems to leave room for such analysis so long as Congress has not excluded it.

Congress does, however, sometimes exclude formal cost-benefit analysis as support for a rule. Section 6(b)(5) of the Occupational Health and Safety Act instructs OSHA to establish standards "which most adequately assure[ ], to the extent feasible, on the basis of the best available evidence, that no employee will suffer material impairment of health or functional capacity." This feasibility standard is quite common in environmental and safety statutes. Broadly speaking, it has been interpreted to require an agency to adopt rules that are as stringent as technically possible without causing significant harm to the regulated industry. In *American Textile Manufacturers Institute, Inc. v. Donovan*, 452 U.S. 490 (1981), the Court struck down an OSHA rule because the agency supported it with cost-benefit analysis rather than the more protective feasibility analysis that Congress intended the agency to use to better protect workers.

Executive Order 12,866 addresses the problem that some statutes forbid agencies from basing their rules on cost-benefit analysis by providing that the order's terms apply only to the extent permitted by law. It is quite common for executive orders to contain such limiting provisions to ensure that they do not violate other legal requirements.

4. Does the White House get to tell executive agencies how to exercise power that Congress delegated to them? The executive, consistent with our constitutional structure of government, has substantial authority to supervise the bureaucracy and its decisionmakers. Statutory delegations of rulemaking authority by their express terms, however, generally grant decisionmaking power to agency heads—not the president. Thus, by statute, it is the EPA's administrator, not the president, who is charged with promulgating a national ambient air quality standard. Is Exec. Order 12,866 consistent with this allocation of authority? According to the "unitary executive" school of thought, this point does not matter because the Constitution, by vesting the "executive power" in the president, necessarily overrides any statutory delegation of rulemaking discretion to agencies. To see how the order tries to finesse this issue, see its §§ 7 and 9. For discussion of the scope of presidential supervisory authority over agencies generally, see Peter L. Strauss, *Overseer, or "The Decider"? The President in Administrative Law*, 75 GEO. WASH. L. REV. 696, 732–38 (2007) (arguing, as the title suggests, that presidents lack legal authority to direct how agencies exercise their delegated discretion).

5. How does White House review affect the independent agencies? The distinction between "executive" and "independent" agencies clouds the issue of presidential control of agency rulemaking still further. Recall from the discussion in subchapter 1C that Congress has required that presidents have "cause" to remove the heads of various agencies. *See Humphrey's Ex'r v. United States*, 295 U.S. 602 (1935) (affirming for-cause limitation on removal of FTC commissioners). The point of this type of removal restriction is to provide some level of insulation for these "independent agencies" from presidential control. Proponents of the "unitary executive" theory of presidential power have never accepted the constitutionality of such restrictions, but they have been an entrenched part of American governance for more than one hundred years. Can presidents properly control rulemaking by independent agencies?

Presidents can avoid this issue by excluding independent agencies from the reach of their executive orders. *See* Exec. Order 12,866 § 3(b) (excluding independent agencies from the order's definition of "agency"). Sometimes, the White House urges independent agencies to comply with executive orders that, by their terms, do not bind them. The independent agencies sometimes respond by emphasizing that they cannot be required to comply and then complying substantially anyway.

The dynamic between the White House and independent agencies may, however, be changing with a remarkable power grab. In April 2019, OMB issued a memorandum explaining that all new rules, including those from independent agencies, should be submitted to OIRA before being made public. The purpose, according to the memo, is to allow OIRA to determine if a rule qualifies as a "major rule" under the Congressional Review Act (CRA). (The CRA is discussed at note 12 in subchapter 1C.3 after the *Morrison v. Olson* excerpt.) The memo is significant because it includes OIRA review of independent agency rules that would otherwise not be subject to the same level of White House scrutiny under Exec. Order 12,866. The ultimate impact of the memo remains to be seen, but it at least has the potential to increase White House interaction with independent agency rulemaking.

6. Executive Order 13,771—the new executive order on the block. Thanks to President Trump, after nearly three decades, Exec. Order 12,866 now has competition for the title of most significant executive order controlling agency rulemaking. On January 30, 2017, the president issued Exec. Order 13,771, "Reducing Regulation and Controlling Regulatory Costs." As is usual with such documents, it raises complexities that a quick summary will miss. At the core of the order, however, lie two requirements. First, the order imposes a type of "regulatory budget" on agencies that caps the "incremental costs" that an agency's regulations can impose on regulated parties. For fiscal year 2017, agency regulatory budgets were set at zero, precluding agencies from increasing aggregate compliance costs at all. Second, the order requires agencies to offset "any new incremental costs associated with new regulations . . . by the elimination of existing costs associated with at least two prior regulations." It remains somewhat unclear what effect this "one in, two out" order will have in practice, but it is certain to trigger difficult discussions within regulatory agencies and, eventually, judicial review. In response to some of the many questions raised by the order, the Office of Management and Budget has released a guidance memorandum, *Guidance Implementing Executive Order 13,771, Titled "Reducing Regulation and Controlling Regulatory Costs"* (Apr. 5, 2017).

Exec. Order 13,771 is presumably contributing to the very slow rate of adoption of regulations during the Trump administration. It is difficult to say how strong of an effect the order is actually having, however, given that the Trump administration is generally hostile to regulation in any event. It is extremely likely that any Democratic administration would make repealing Exec. Order 13,771 one of its first orders of business. It therefore seems unlikely to become a bipartisan fixture of the administrative state like Exec. Order 12,866.

7. Congressional and executive requirements for additional analysis. One can understand Exec. Order 12,866 as part of a broader legislative and executive movement to require agencies to produce various "impact" statements as part of legislative rulemaking. Other examples include:

- The Regulatory Flexibility Act, 5 U.S.C. §601 *et seq.* This act directs agencies to consider the impact of proposed regulations on small entities, including small businesses, nonprofits, and governmental jurisdictions. Among other requirements, unless an agency certifies that its rule will not have a "significant economic impact on a substantial number of small entities," it must include a regulatory flexibility analysis when it publishes its notice of proposed rulemaking.

- The Unfunded Mandates Reform Act, 2 U.S.C. §658 and §1501 *et seq.* This act requires agencies to include a regulatory impact analysis satisfying various statutory requirements for proposed or final rules that may "result in the expenditure by State, local, and tribal governments, in the aggregate, or by the private sector, of $100,000,000 or more (adjusted annually for inflation) in any 1 year."

- Exec. Order 12,630, *Governmental Actions and Interference with Constitutionally Protected Property Rights.* This order provides, "[s]ignificant takings implications should . . . be identified and discussed in notices of proposed rule-making and messages transmitting legislative proposals to the Congress, stating the departments' and agencies' conclusions on the takings issues."

- Exec. Order 13,132, *Federalism.* This order provides that rules that carry "federalism implications" and "impose[ ] substantial direct compliance costs on State and local governments" must include "a federalism summary impact statement."

Many observers wonder whether this habit of festooning the rulemaking process with impact statements and other procedural requirements could itself survive cost-benefit analysis. Put another way, it is fair to wonder: Is the government making it harder to regulate for no particularly good reason? Or, might making it harder to regulate *be* the reason?

8. The Information Quality Act—an obstacle to rulemaking? In 2001, Congress enacted the Information Quality Act (IQA). The purpose of the IQA is to assure the accuracy of information distributed by the federal government. One of the primary examples of such information is the Toxic Release Inventory, created by the 1986 Emergency Preparedness and Community Right to Know Act. The Toxic Release Inventory is a compilation of reports by private industry of their releases of toxic substances into the environment. The release of this information caused a significant public reaction and may have contributed to voluntary reductions by industry. This is an example of what might be called regulation by information.

The IQA directed OMB to issue guidelines "to Federal agencies for ensuring and maximizing the quality, objectivity, utility, and integrity of information (including statistical information) disseminated by Federal agencies." The IQA also requires federal agencies to adopt their own guidelines to achieve these goals. OMB has since issued the required guidelines, including a requirement for peer review of important scientific information disseminated by the federal government. 70 Fed. Reg. 2664 (Jan. 14, 2005). Although the OMB guidelines leave agencies with wide discretion to design their own system for employing peer review, the benefits of such a system could be significant for administrative government. *See* Louis J. Virelli III, *Scientific Peer Review and Administrative Legitimacy*, 61 ADMIN. L. REV. 723 (2009) (examining how scientific peer review can help contribute to the legitimacy of agency action).

In the rulemaking context, the OMB guidelines state that

> When an information product is a critical component of rule-making, it is important to obtain peer review before the agency announces its regulatory options so that any technical corrections can be made before the agency

becomes invested in a specific approach or the positions of interest groups have hardened. If review occurs too late, it is unlikely to contribute to the course of a rulemaking.

70 Fed. Reg. at 2668. Thus, it appears that rulemaking efforts may well be delayed while agencies implement the required peer review process. It is noteworthy, however, that the guidelines explicitly state that they do not create a right for relief at law or equity. Accordingly, while the new peer review procedures may delay rulemaking, private challenges to the implementation of those procedures should not cause delay.

In April 2019, the Executive Office of the President issued a Memorandum for the Heads of Executive Departments and Agencies titled *Improving Implementation of the Information Quality Act*. The memo offers twenty updates to the OMB Guidelines under the IQA. The updates cover a range of subjects, including how agencies characterize and verify data quality, disseminate and reuse data, help assure that the data they disseminate is reproducible, and handle public requests for correction of agency information. Proponents describe the memo as advancing the IQA's goals of promoting the integrity and reliability of government information, while critics contend that the memo's updates to the OMB Guidelines will, by design, inhibit agencies' ability to regulate by making their work more time-consuming and cumbersome, and by affirmatively empowering opponents to slow down the process through the aggressive use of requests for correction.

Chapter 4

The Process for Individual Decisions: Adjudication

As we discussed in Chapter 2, administrative adjudications focus on the resolution of matters involving individual circumstances. Although we tend to think of adjudications as the kinds of decisions that the judicial process makes through trial-like procedures, a bewildering array of agency decisions falls within the category of "adjudication." We easily recognize that a potential enforcement action against Gallery is an adjudication, probably with relatively formal procedures. But we have also seen that the WTC will be deciding about applications for grants to develop the wine industry. These, too, are adjudications, but the agency's procedures for those decisions would bear little relationship to formal trial-type process.

And there is a vast range of agency decisions between those two seeming extremes. The decisions to build a road through a park, to approve clean-up of a hazardous waste dump, to terminate benefits for someone who is no longer disabled, or to publicly identify someone as a shoplifter are all adjudications, with different types of procedures for each.

As we saw in studying the *Londoner* and *Bi-Metallic* decisions, one of the first tasks in analyzing any administrative decision is to determine whether it is legislative in nature (rulemaking), or whether it qualifies as an adjudication—an individualized decision. If the decision is an adjudication, the next question is what procedures, if any, are required by statute or by the Constitution.

Subpart A of this chapter examines procedures required by statute. We cannot emphasize enough that you must consider in detail the language of the relevant enabling act (the WTCA for our purposes) as well as the Administrative Procedure Act. This sometimes complex interaction determines the statutory requirements. Subchapter B addresses the constitutional requirement of procedural due process. Not all adjudications qualify for due process protections. We will consider how to determine whether due process applies and, if it does, what procedures it requires. Subchapter C deals with issues of integrity in agency adjudication, including problems associated with the combination of functions within an agency, judicial bias, *ex parte* contacts, and congressional pressure on agency adjudicators.

A. Adjudications — Procedures Required By Statute

As we saw with rulemaking, the universe of agency adjudication can be divided into two broad categories—formal and informal adjudication. We call an adjudication "formal" when it is subject to the statutory framework in §§ 554, 556, and 557 of the APA. We also sometimes refer to these proceedings as "trial-type" or "on-the-record."

Section 554 provides, in effect, that formal adjudication provisions apply "in every case of adjudication required by statute to be determined on the record after opportunity for agency hearing." 5 U.S.C. § 554(a). If this language looks familiar, it may be because you recollect from *Florida East Coast* back in Chapter 3 that parallel "trigger" language in § 553(c) governs applicability of formal rulemaking procedures. Notwithstanding the parallel language, courts have interpreted these two triggers quite differently. Section 554 also requires appropriate notice to proceed with a formal adjudication, establishes the rights of interested parties to participate in such adjudication, and imposes safeguards against judicial bias, including *ex parte* contacts.

Section 556 states that it applies "to hearings required by section . . . 554," thereby confirming the connection between the two provisions in triggering and imposing the requirements of formal adjudication. Section 556 also deals generally with how the initial hearing portion of the adjudication must be conducted and defines the exclusive record on which the agency may base its decision.

Section 557 applies to hearings "required to be conducted in accordance with section 556." It addresses the intra-agency review process, the parties' submissions to the agency employee presiding over the hearing, and additional prohibitions on *ex parte* contacts.

Unlike its thorough treatment of formal adjudication, the APA does not contain any express instructions for how to proceed with an informal adjudication—an adjudication that is not required by statute to be "determined on the record after opportunity for an agency hearing." As you will see later in this subchapter, although the courts initially treated informal adjudication as outside the bounds of the APA, the Supreme Court has since announced that § 555 is the governing provision for informal adjudication.

As you navigate through the materials on statutory procedure for adjudications, keep these sections in mind and try to ground what you learn about the courts' understanding of agency adjudication in the relevant provisions of the APA.

As General Counsel, Chris, with Ben's help, is responsible for developing the various procedures the WTC will follow in implementing the WTCA. For each of the various types of decisions the agency must make, they will have to determine whether the WTCA or the APA requires any particular form of process. To the extent that the agency has discretion, they will have to advise Carl and the other commissioners as to the appropriate procedures to achieve the agency's goals.

1. Formal or Informal Procedures?

Lesson 4A.1. Ralph has been pressing for an enforcement proceeding against Gallery or some other major company. But Carl is concerned that Ralph's preferred formal trial-like process would bog the agency down before it could get going. At Chris' direction, Ben has drafted regulations establishing the procedures to be followed when someone is charged under § 7(a)(1) of the WTCA with a violation of the Act. The new rules would provide that anyone entitled to a hearing under § 7(a)(1) would be given notice in writing of the charges, copies of or access to the evidence supporting the charge, and an opportunity to submit a written response. The § 7(a)(1) hearing would be presided over by the Commission itself (highly unlikely in most cases) or by a staff member hearing officer with appropriate expertise who has not otherwise been involved with the particular case. The draft rules provide that the Commission or hearing officer will entertain requests for oral appearances or cross-examination of witnesses, but it will grant such requests only if the requester demonstrates that the procedures will contribute materially to an accurate factual decision. The Commission or hearing officer will also provide a full written explanation of whatever decision it reaches on the charges. Ben believes that this approach will meet the need for accuracy and fairness while preserving efficiency.

Ben must first consider whether the WTC is required to comply with §§ 554, 556, and 557 of the APA, which are said to impose relatively formal requirements, including the appointment of an administrative law judge to hear the matter. In the course of his research, Ben has found the following passage in the Senate Report on the WTCA: "The Committee intends that any hearings held under § 7(a)(1) will assure that the due process rights of the parties are fully protected." Ben has also found the following colloquy from the brief House debate on the bill that became the WTCA:

Ms. Jones. I understand that if the Wine Trade Commission brings charges against a wine maker under Section 7 of the Act, any hearing would be before an administrative law judge and would have to comply with the formal hearing requirements of the Administrative Procedure Act. Can you confirm that understanding, Mr. Chairman?

Mr. Smith. Yes. That is my understanding as Chair of the Committee that reported the bill to the floor of the House.

In light of these references and the following materials, what should Ben expect Ralph (or the industry) to argue in addressing this question? How should Ben respond?

Background of *Dominion Energy Brayton Point*

In Chapter 3, we began the procedural discussion with the question of whether the APA or the WTCA required the agency to use formal trial-like process when issuing legislative rules. We begin this chapter with the same discussion as applied to agency adjudications. In both arenas (rulemaking and adjudication), the decisions reflect the continuing efforts of non-agency interests to impose procedural requirements upon agencies and the parallel efforts of agencies to minimize procedural requirements. In *Vermont Yankee*, the Supreme Court rejected efforts to impose additional procedures on the notice-and-comment rulemaking process in the absence of additional statutory requirements. The adjudicatory context is somewhat different in that the question of whether an agency must follow the formal adjudicatory procedures of §§ 556 and 557 of the APA depends upon the language of a statute other than the APA. As you will see in Note 1, the following decision is the fourth in a line of court of appeals decisions taking various approaches to answering this question. Since the Supreme Court has not yet addressed this issue, you will need to understand all of the arguments.

Dominion Energy Brayton Point, LLC v. Johnson

443 F.3d 12 (1st Cir. 2006)

SELYA, CIRCUIT JUDGE:

USGen New England, Inc., now Dominion Energy Brayton Point, LLC (Dominion), filed suit against the U.S. Environmental Protection Agency, its administrator, and its regional office (collectively, the EPA), alleging that the EPA failed to perform a non-discretionary duty when it refused to grant Dominion's request for a formal evidentiary hearing after issuing a proposed final National Pollution Discharge Elimination System (NPDES) permit. The district court dismissed the case for want of subject matter jurisdiction. On appeal, the central question presented concerns the effect of this court's decision in *Seacoast Anti-Pollution League v. Costle*, 572 F.2d 872 (1st Cir.1978), in light of the Supreme Court's subsequent decision in *Chevron U.S.A. Inc. v. Natural Resources Defense Council, Inc.*, 467 U.S. 837 (1984). Concluding, as we do, that *Seacoast* does not control, we affirm the judgment below.

I. Background

Dominion owns an electrical generating facility in Somerset, Massachusetts (the station). The station opened in the 1960s and, like most power plants of its era, utilizes an "open-cycle" cooling system. Specifically, the station withdraws water from the Lees and Taunton Rivers, circulates that water through the plant's generating equipment as a coolant, and then discharges the water (which, by then, has attained an elevated temperature) into Mount Hope Bay.

The withdrawals and discharges of water are regulated by the Clean Water Act (CWA). For the last three decades, these actions have been authorized by a series of NPDES permits issued by the EPA pursuant to section 402(a) of the CWA. The standards incorporated into those permits are determined under the thermal variance procedures laid out in section 316(a).

In 1998, the station applied for renewal of its NPDES permit and thermal variance authorization. The EPA issued a proposed final permit on October 6, 2003, in which it rejected the requested thermal variance. On November 4, Dominion sought review before the Environmental Appeals Board (the Board), and asked for an evidentiary hearing. The Board accepted the petition for review but declined to convene an evidentiary hearing.

LICENSE APPLICATION

On August 11, 2004, Dominion notified the EPA of its intent to file a citizen's suit under section 505(a)(2) of the CWA, 33 U.S.C. § 1365(a)(2), to compel the Board to hold an evidentiary hearing. Receiving no reply, Dominion proceeded to file its complaint in the United States District Court for the District of Massachusetts. The EPA moved to dismiss.

The district court granted the motion on jurisdictional grounds. . . .

II. The Legal Landscape

We set the stage for our substantive discussion by undertaking a brief review of the legal rules that frame the controversy at hand.

Before the EPA either issues an NPDES permit or authorizes a thermal variance, it must offer an "opportunity for public hearing." 33 U.S.C. §§ 1326(a), 1342(a). No definition of "public hearing" is contained within the four corners of the CWA.

CWA HEARING RULE

The Administrative Procedure Act (APA) is also part of the relevant legal landscape. Most pertinent here are those sections that combine to describe the procedures for formal administrative adjudications. *See* [5 U.S.C.]. §§ 554, 556, 557. These procedures apply "in every case of adjudication required by statute to be determined on the record after opportunity for an agency hearing." *Id.* § 554(a). The APA does not directly address whether these procedures apply when a statute simply calls for an "opportunity for public hearing" without any specific indication that the hearing should be "on the record."

APA RULES

In *Seacoast*, this court interpreted "public hearing" (as used in sections 402(a) and 316(a) of the CWA) to mean "evidentiary hearing"—in other words, a hearing that comports with the APA's requirements for a formal adjudication. Examining the legislative history of the APA, we adopted a presumption that "unless a statute otherwise specifies, an adjudicatory hearing subject to judicial review must be [an evidentiary hearing] on the record." Applying that presumption to the CWA, we concluded that "the statute certainly does not indicate that the determination need *not* be on the record." (emphasis in original).

SEACOAST

So viewed, *Seacoast* established a rebuttable presumption that, in the context of an adjudication, an organic statute that calls for a "public hearing" should be read to require an evidentiary hearing in compliance with the formal adjudication provisions of the APA. . . . Acquiescing in this construction, the EPA promulgated regulations that memorialized the use of formal evidentiary hearings in the NPDES permit process.

In 1984, a sea change occurred in administrative law and, specifically, in the interpretation of organic statutes such as the CWA. The Supreme Court held that "[w]hen a court reviews an agency's construction of the statute which it administers," the reviewing court first must ask "whether Congress has directly spoken to the precise question at issue." *Chevron*, 467 U.S. at 842. If Congress's intent is clear, that intent governs-both the court and the agency must give it full effect. If, however, Congress has not directly addressed the question and the agency has stepped into the vacuum by promulgating an interpretive regulation, a reviewing court may "not simply impose its own construction on the statute," but, rather, ought to ask "whether the agency's answer is based on a permissible construction of the statute."

This paradigm, sometimes called the *Chevron* two-step, increases the sphere of influence of agency action. If congressional intent is unclear and an agency's interpretation of a statute that it administers is reasonable, an inquiring court must defer to that interpretation. That is so even if the agency's interpretation is not the one that the court considers to be the best available interpretation.

Armed with the *Chevron* decision and a presidential directive to streamline regulatory programs, the EPA advanced a proposal to eliminate formal evidentiary hearings from the NPDES permitting process. In due course, the EPA adopted that proposal as a final rule. *See* Amendments to Streamline the NPDES Program Regulations: Round Two, 65 Fed.Reg. 30,886, 30,900 (May 15, 2000).

This revision depended heavily on a *Chevron* analysis. The agency began by "finding no evidence that Congress intended to require formal evidentiary hearings or that the text [of section 402(a)] precludes informal adjudication of permit review petitions." Then, it weighed the risks and benefits of employing informal hearing procedures for NPDES permit review, "determining that these procedures would not violate the Due Process Clause." Finally, it "concluded that informal hearing procedures satisfy the hearing requirement of section 402(a)."

It was under this new regulatory scheme that the EPA considered Dominion's request to renew its NPDES permit and to authorize a thermal variance. Thus, it was under this scheme that the EPA denied Dominion's request for an evidentiary hearing.

III. Analysis

. . . .

[T]he statute invoked by Dominion grants federal district courts jurisdiction over any citizen's suit brought "against the Administrator [of the EPA] where there is alleged a failure of the Administrator to perform any act or duty under [the CWA] which is not discretionary." . . . The crux of the case, therefore, is whether Dominion has pleaded the flouting of a non-discretionary duty.

One thing is crystal clear: on their face, the current EPA regulations do not establish a non-discretionary duty to provide the evidentiary hearing that Dominion seeks. Prior to the date of Dominion's request, the EPA vitiated the preexisting rule introducing evidentiary hearings into the NPDES permitting process. Dominion concedes this fact, but nonetheless relies on *Seacoast* as the source of a non-discretionary duty to convene an evidentiary hearing.

This reliance is misplaced. Even if *Seacoast* established a non-discretionary duty for section 505(a)(2) purposes when it was decided—a matter upon which we need not opine—Dominion's position ignores two important post-*Seacoast* changes in the legal landscape: the Supreme Court's decision in *Chevron* and the agency's subsequent promulgation of the current "no evidentiary hearing" rule.

. . . The *Chevron* two-step applies. At the first step, a court "must look primarily to the plain meaning of the statute, drawing its essence from the particular statutory language at issue, as well as the language and design of the statute as a whole." At this step, the court may "examine the legislative history, albeit skeptically, in search of an unmistakable expression of congressional intent." If the precedent at issue finds clarity at step one—that is, if the holding of the case rests on a perception of clear and unambiguous congressional intent—that precedent will govern. If, however, the precedent operates at *Chevron* step two—that is, if the case holds, in effect, that congressional intent is less than pellucid and proceeds to choose a "*best* reading" rather than "the *only permissible* reading," its stare decisis effect will, through *Chevron* deference, yield to a contrary but plausible agency interpretation.

Once this mode of analysis is understood and applied, Dominion's argument collapses. *Seacoast* simply does not hold that Congress clearly intended the term "public hearing" in sections 402(a) and 316(a) of the CWA to mean "evidentiary hearing." To the contrary, the *Seacoast* court based its interpretation of the CWA on a presumption derived from the legislative history of the APA—a presumption that would hold sway only in the absence of a showing of a contrary congressional intent. In other words, the court resorted to the presumption only because it could find no sign of a plainly discernible congressional intent. A statutory interpretation constructed on such a negative finding is antithetic to a conclusion that Congress's intent was clear and unambiguous.

WHY SEACOAST DOESN'T GOVERN

The short of it is that the *Seacoast* court, faced with an opaque statute, settled upon what it sensibly thought was the best construction of the CWA's "public hearing" language. Such a holding is appropriate at step two of the *Chevron* pavane, not at step one. Consequently, . . . *Seacoast* must yield to a reasonable agency interpretation of the CWA's "public hearing" requirement.

The only piece left to this puzzle is to confirm that the EPA's new regulations are, in fact, entitled to *Chevron* deference. This inquiry is a straightforward one. As our earlier discussion suggests (and as the *Seacoast* court correctly deduced), Congress has not spoken directly to the precise question at issue here. Accordingly, we must defer to the EPA's interpretation of the CWA as long as that interpretation is reasonable.

. . . The agency's conclusion that evidentiary hearings are unnecessary and that Congress, in using the phrase "opportunity for public hearing," did not mean to mandate evidentiary hearings seems reasonable—and Dominion, to its credit, has conceded the point.

. . . .

Dominion exhorts us to find that *Seacoast's* holding is actually an interpretation of the APA, not the CWA (and, therefore, the EPA's regulation is also an interpretation of the APA, not entitled to *Chevron* deference). Such a reading of *Seacoast* is plainly incorrect. While the *Seacoast* court relied on a presumption borrowed from the APA, the court's holding is an interpretation of the CWA and, specifically, of the term "public hearing" contained in sections 402(a) and 316(a). The EPA's regulations are also derived from the CWA. *See* 40 C.F.R. § 122.1(a) (explaining that 40 C.F.R. § 124 implements sections of the CWA). Because those changes implicate the statute that the EPA administers (i.e., the CWA), *Chevron* deference is appropriate. *See Chevron*, 467 U.S. at 842–43.

IV. Conclusion

We summarize succinctly. Although we in no way disparage the soundness of *Seacoast's* reasoning, . . . *Chevron* . . . and the interposition of a new and reasonable agency interpretation of the disputed statutory language have changed the picture. Because we, like the *Seacoast* court, cannot discern a clear and unambiguous congressional intent behind the words "public hearing" in the CWA and because the EPA's interpretation of that term constitutes a reasonable construction of the statute, deference is due. It follows inexorably that no non-discretionary duty to grant Dominion an evidentiary hearing on its permit application exists. Consequently, the jurisdictional requirements of section 505(a)(2) have not been satisfied.

We need go no further. For the reasons elucidated above, we conclude that the district court did not err in dismissing Dominion's action.

Affirmed.

Notes

1. Does the enabling act trigger § 554(a) of the APA? The threshold question is whether the language of § 7(a)(1) of the WTCA triggers § 554(a) of the Administrative Procedure Act. If it does, the proceedings are governed by §§ 556 and 557 of the APA, which we will examine in detail below.

In 1950, the Supreme Court held in *Wong Yang Sung v. McGrath*, 339 U.S. 33 (1950), that because the Constitution required an immigration statute to be interpreted as requiring a hearing prior to deportation, the statute had to be read to trigger § 554(a) of the APA. The Court said that the language of § 554(a) exempts "hearings of less than statutory authority, not those of more than statutory authority." Thus, it seemed that when a hearing was required by both statute and due process, the statute would be interpreted to require compliance with §§ 556 and 557 of the APA. Congress promptly amended the immigration statute so that it clearly did not impose the formal hearing requirements of the APA. And, as we will see in subchapter 4B.2, the Court sometimes recognizes very informal procedures as meeting the requirements of due process.

The circuit courts have followed three distinct approaches to resolving the issue of when a statutory "hearing" requirement triggers § 554(a) of the APA. The leading early case on the subject was *Seacoast Anti-Pollution League v. Castle*, 572 F.2d 872 (1st Cir. 1978). In *Seacoast*, the First Circuit emphasized the nature of the EPA decision at issue. The court noted that EPA's decision involved making "specific factual findings" affecting only "the rights of a specific applicant," that such factual questions "will frequently be sharply disputed," and that "[a]dversarial hearings will be helpful . . . in guaranteeing both reasoned decisionmaking and meaningful judicial review." The court also relied upon the legislative history of the APA, particularly the statement in the ATTORNEY GENERAL'S MANUAL that: "In fact, it is assumed that where a statute specifically provides for administrative adjudication (such as the suspension or revocation of a license) after opportunity for agency hearing, *such specific requirement for a hearing ordinarily implies the further requirement of a decision in accordance with evidence adduced at the hearing.*" (Emphasis supplied by the court.) On this basis, the court recognized a presumption "that, unless a statute otherwise specifies, an adjudicatory hearing subject to judicial review must be on the record."

Five years later, the Seventh Circuit, in *City of West Chicago, Illinois v. U.S. Nuclear Regulatory Commission*, 701 F.2d 632 (7th Cir. 1983), rather cryptically concluded that in the absence of the "three magic words" "on the record," "Congress must clearly indicate its intent to trigger the formal, on-the-record hearing provisions of the APA." The Seventh Circuit thus seemed to favor a presumption *against* formal adjudication—the very opposite to the *Seacoast* approach.

In 1989, the D.C. Circuit concluded, again quite cryptically, that the interpretive issue should be approached "within the framework that the Supreme Court decreed in *Chevron. Chemical Waste Mgmt., Inc. v. U.S. Envtl. Protection Agency*, 873 F.2d 1477 (D.C. Cir. 1989). In 2006, the First Circuit in *Dominion Energy* adopted the D.C. Circuit's approach, holding that, "*Seacoast* must yield to a reasonable agency interpretation of the CWA's 'public hearing' requirement."

Why did *Seacoast* have to yield? If you were the decisionmaker, which of the three interpretive approaches would you adopt in a challenge to the hearing provisions that Ben has proposed? The Supreme Court has not addressed this issue, and the Ninth Circuit continues to follow a *Seacoast*-like approach. *Marathon Oil Co. v. EPA*, 564 F.2d 1253 (9th Cir. 1977) (which is cited in *Seacoast*, by the way). Given the continued existence of a circuit split, there is an opportunity for Supreme Court resolution should the right case come along.

2. Sources of the dispute over the 554(a) trigger. The dispute over the triggering of § 554(a) and the application of §§ 556 and 557 plays out against the backdrop of two historical realities. First, as Gary Edles has explained: "The APA in 1946 focused on the requirements for formal hearings because they were the primary method of agency administration and formulation of policy regarding the significant economic regulatory programs of that era." Gary J. Edles, *An APA-Default Presumption for Administrative Hearings: Some Thoughts on "Ossifying" the Adjudication Process*, 55 ADMIN. L. REV. 787, 791 (2003). Thus, there was something of an assumption in the post-APA period that significant agency adjudicatory decisions would be made through a relatively formalized, largely trial-like hearing process. Even then, however, as recognized in *Seacoast Anti-Pollution League v. Costle*, the ATTORNEY GENERAL'S MANUAL explained that the formal hearing provisions of §§ 556 and 557 did not govern "the great mass of administrative routine as well as pensions, claims, and a variety of similar matters in which Congress has usually intentionally or traditionally refrained from requiring an administrative hearing." ATTORNEY GENERAL'S MANUAL ON THE ADMINISTRATIVE PROCEDURE ACT 41 (1947).

Edles argues that this history shows that formal hearing procedures were required for only a small percentage of agency adjudications, with agencies in most instances left to develop procedures appropriate to their particular programs. Cooley Howarth argues quite the opposite. He views the "great mass of administrative routine" referred to above as "non-adjudicative, non-rulemaking activities [that] usually call upon the agency to exercise a managerial or entrepreneurial discretion rather than engage in any truly adjudicative decisionmaking and hearing procedures [as] obviously inappropriate in most cases." Howarth asserts, consistent with *Seacoast*, "[i]f the decision of the agency was adjudicatory in nature and Congress had required a 'hearing,' §§ 554, 556 and 557 would apply." Cooley R. Howarth, Jr., *Restoring the Applicability of the APA's Adjudicatory Procedures*, 56 ADMIN. L. REV. 1043, 1048 n.28 (2004).

Whether Edles or Howarth is correct, the second historical reality is that regulation has expanded dramatically and become more intrusive, particularly after 1970. Agencies frequently exercise close oversight of private activities in ways that are arguably not suited to a judicial process model (e.g., requiring prompt clean-up of serious environmental hazards prior to determining liability, the issue at stake in *Chemical Waste Management*). This change in the nature of agency relationships with regulated parties, coupled with the sheer size of the regulatory effort, has created considerable pressure to streamline and simplify agency procedures. One approach agencies and courts have used to achieve that goal is to argue, as these materials demonstrate, that particular statutory hearing requirements do not trigger § 554(a) of the APA. Another approach, which we examine in subchapter 4A.3, is to seek flexibility within the provisions of §§ 556 and 557.

3. Should *Chevron* apply to this interpretive question? *Chevron v. NRDC*, on which the First Circuit relied in *Dominion Energy*, involved a challenge to EPA's interpretation of a substantive provision of the Clean Air Act. We will examine *Chevron* at greater length in Chapter 5. By contrast, the WTCA provision at issue in Lesson 4A.1(and the statutory provisions in all of the cases discussed here) involves procedures the agency must follow in reaching a decision. In *United States v. Mead*, 533 U.S. 218 (2001), which we will also see again later, the Supreme Court held that whether *Chevron* applies to a particular agency interpretation depends upon whether Congress intended courts to defer to that type of interpretation.

Should *Chevron* apply to the dispute over the hearing procedures that Ben has proposed? Professor Melissa Berry argues that Congress probably would not have intended such deference given the procedural (as opposed to substantive) nature of the decision and agencies' self-interest in the outcome. Melissa M. Berry, *Beyond Chevron's Domain: Agency Interpretations of Statutory Procedural Provisions*, 30 SEATTLE U.L. REV. 541 (2007). One of your editors argues that the legislative history of the Administrative Procedure Act demonstrates "that Congress would not have intended courts to defer to agencies with respect to this question." He concludes "that the APA should be seen as creating a presumption that courts are not to defer to agencies on this procedural question unless Congress clearly indicates the contrary." William S. Jordan, III, *Chevron and Hearing Rights: An Unintended Combination*, 61 ADMIN. L. REV. 249, 255 (2009).

On the other hand, the Supreme Court has held, in a separate but somewhat analogous case, that questions about an agency's statutory jurisdiction (i.e., the scope of an agency's substantive authority under its enabling act) are subject to *Chevron* deference. *See City of Arlington v. FCC*, 569 U.S. 290 (2013). (*City of Arlington* is discussed in greater detail in subchapter 5G.3.b.) So, if the Supreme Court is willing to defer to an agency's construction of the scope of its substantive power, does it follow that courts should defer to an agency's construction of procedural restrictions on that power?

Make the heroic assumption that you are Congress. Would you trust agencies to design their own procedures for adjudications that affect private interests? Would you trust the courts more?

4. Why didn't the *Dominion Energy* panel of the First Circuit have to follow *Seacoast*? Normally, judges on the U.S. Courts of Appeals must follow the precedents in their own circuits. In *Dominion Energy*, however, a 2006 First Circuit panel refused to apply the Circuit's *Seacoast* decision although the facts of the two cases were nearly identical. As we will see when we reach *Chevron*, the Supreme Court in *National Cable & Telecommunications Ass'n v. Brand X Internet Services*, 545 U.S. 967 (2005), held that where *Chevron* applies, a court is bound by its own prior interpretation of an agency's statute only if the prior decision indicated that the court had reached the only permissible interpretation. Noting that the *Seacoast* court had relied upon a "presumption only because it could find no sign of a plainly discernible congressional intent," the *Dominion Energy* panel was free under *Chevron* to uphold the agency's decision as long as it was reasonable.

5. How does a court decide that an agency interpretation is "reasonable" under *Chevron* Step 2? If *Chevron* applies, and if the statutory hearing requirement is ambiguous, the court must determine whether the agency's interpretation of that requirement is reasonable. We will return to this issue in Chapter 5, but the *Chemical Waste Management* decision provides a useful example in this context. *Chemical*

Waste Management involved the Resource Conservation and Recovery Act (RCRA), which required the EPA to "conduct a public hearing" before (1) suspending or revoking a permit for the operation of a hazardous waste disposal facility or assessing a civil penalty or (2) issuing a corrective action order requiring an investigation or environmental cleanup. As to the former (permit suspension or civil penalty), EPA regulations provided for a hearing meeting the "formal" requirements of §§ 554, 556, and 557 of the APA. As to the latter, however, the regulations challenged in *Chemical Waste Management* provided for informal proceedings in which the facility operator may "submit written information and argument for inclusion in the record, make an oral presentation at the hearing itself, and be assisted at hearing by legal and technical advisors." More important, the proceeding would not be before an independent ALJ, but before the Regional Judicial Officer or an agency attorney with no other connection to the case. These provisions do not comply with the requirements of §§ 554, 556, and 557.

The D.C. Circuit found the EPA's justification to be reasonable. It first explained that less formal adjudicative procedures are justified for corrective action orders because the factual questions surrounding those orders focus on whether and how best to cleanup hazards, rather than upon the existence of, or culpability for, any violations. Thus, the factual questions are fewer, more technical, and less dependent on witness credibility than those associated with a permit action. Next, faced with complaints that informal procedures would be less factually accurate or clear, the court held that the EPA could base its procedural decisions on the typical corrective action, which for the reasons stated above merits less formal treatment. The court concluded by stating "that the agency has provided a reasonable explanation for its choice of informal procedures [regarding corrective action orders] based on the number and nature of factual issues expected in a typical [corrective action] proceeding."

Why was it reasonable for the EPA to use formal procedures (including an independent ALJ and, usually, direct and cross-examination) for permit suspensions and civil penalties, but not for clean-up orders?

6. Section 554(a) triggered in an unusual context. Lesson 4A.1 and the cases discussed above all involve circumstances in which one might expect the decision to be made by an ALJ in a trial-like proceeding on a closed record. Each is an adjudication that would normally be decided initially by an ALJ or other low or mid-level agency official and subject to review by the agency head or other agency superiors. Each also seems part of the routine decisionmaking processes of the agency in question.

As always, however, it is important to recognize that legal principles may apply to contexts in which they may not immediately come to mind. An example is *Portland Audubon Society v. Endangered Species Committee*, 984 F.2d 1534 (9th Cir. 1993), which involved the long-running dispute over protection of the endangered northern spotted owl. The Endangered Species Act prohibits various actions that are likely to harm the habitat of an endangered species. The Act also provides, however, that an agency may obtain an exemption to the Act's prohibitions by applying to the statutorily created Endangered Species Committee. The Committee is also known as the "God Squad" because it may have ultimate power over the very existence of an endangered species.

The Committee "is composed of: the Secretary of Agriculture, the Secretary of the Army, the Chairman of the Council of Economic Advisors, the Administrator of the Environmental Protection Agency, the Secretary of the Interior, the Administrator of the National Oceanic and Atmospheric Administration, and 'one individual from each affected State' appointed by the President." When the Committee granted an exemption related to the spotted owl, environmental groups sued, claiming that members of the Committee had been subjected to improper *ex parte* contacts with, and pressure from, the White House. This claim depended upon the proposition that the Endangered Species Act triggered § 554(a), thereby imposing the requirements of § 557 on the Committee's decisionmaking process.

Although the application of the APA's formal adjudicatory procedures to this sort of high-level, multi-member committee is hardly intuitively obvious, the Ninth Circuit held that the Endangered Species Act did, indeed, trigger § 554(a). The court applied the following test: "The administrative proceeding must be 1) an adjudication; 2) determined on the record; and 3) after the opportunity for an agency hearing." Because the Committee decided "whether to grant or deny specific requests for exemptions based upon specific factual showings," the matter was an adjudication. And the statute specifically provided that the Committee's "determinations shall be 'on the record, based on the report of the Secretary, the record of the hearing held under subsection (g)(4) of this section and on such other testimony or evidence as it may receive.'"

The important lesson of this aspect of the decision is that you should never assume an agency decision or process fits (or does not fit) into any particular category. You must be able to identify the nature of the decision (an adjudication in this case), be aware of the types of procedural arguments that might be made about such decisions, and examine the specific statutory language to see whether there is an argument available even when it may not otherwise be apparent.

2. Informal Adjudicatory Procedures

Again, we refer to agency adjudications that are not subject to §§ 554, 556, and 557 of the APA as "informal." The vast majority of agency adjudications are, as it turns out, informal in this sense. The APA itself provides little guidance regarding how agencies should conduct informal adjudications. Do bear in mind, however, that informal adjudications that threaten deprivation of life, liberty, or property are subject to procedural due process limitations. In addition, an agency's enabling act (such as our WTCA) and agency procedural regulations are other sources of agency procedure. As a result, an adjudication that is "informal" in terms of the APA dichotomy can often require quite extensive procedures.

Lesson 4A.2. Ralph reviews Ben's efforts to design the process for making development grants under WTCA § 3 for the Grants Division. Most of the proposals involve scientific research. Ben's design deviates considerably from that of a trial. He provides that general notice of a "call for grants" shall be published in appropriate scientific journals. He recommends that the Grants Division draft an application form clearly stating the grant qualifications. Denial of a grant must be accompanied by the reasons for the denial. The denial may be challenged in writing to the Director of the Grants Division, but there is no right to an oral hearing, and the Director's decision will be final. Ralph asks whether such informal procedures will comply with the Constitution and, if they do, whether they comply with the WTCA and the APA.

How might the following opinion, combined with the materials in the previous subchapter, help Ben convince Ralph that his procedures satisfy statutory requirements? What if Ben's proposal complies with statutory and constitutional requirements? Should the WTC add more elements of the adversarial process as a matter of its own discretion?

Background of *Pension Benefit Guaranty Corp.*

In order to protect private pensions from company failures, Congress created the Pension Benefit Guarantee Corp. (PBGC) to take over company pension funds in certain circumstances. If a company terminates such a pension fund, the PBGC continues some of the payments, with the company liable for the reduced amounts paid by the PBGC. But if a company improperly terminates such a pension fund, the PBGC can reinstate the pension fund, which makes the company again liable for the full benefits of the pension program. In this case, the PBGC initially accepted a pension fund termination, but it later reinstated the fund, reimposing all costs on the company. As described below, the PBGC took this action without any particular procedures beyond informing the company of its decision.

Pension Benefit Guaranty Corp. v. LTV Corp.

496 U.S. 633 (1990)

Justice Blackmun delivered the opinion of the Court.

Petitioner PBGC [Pension Benefit Guaranty Corp.] is a wholly owned United States Government corporation, *see* 29 U.S.C. § 1302, modeled after the Federal Deposit Insurance Corporation. The Board of Directors of the PBGC consists of the Secretaries of the Treasury, Labor, and Commerce. The PBGC administers and enforces Title IV of ERISA. Title IV includes a mandatory Government insurance program that protects the pension benefits of over 30 million private sector American workers who participate in plans covered by the Title. In enacting Title IV, Congress sought to ensure that employees and their beneficiaries would not be completely "deprived of anticipated retirement benefits by the termination of pension plans before sufficient funds have been accumulated in the plans."

When a plan covered under Title IV terminates with insufficient assets to satisfy its pension obligations to the employees, the PBGC becomes trustee of the plan,

PBGC

BACK

taking over the plan's assets and liabilities. The PBGC then uses the plan's assets to cover what it can of the benefit obligations. The PBGC then must add its own funds to ensure payment of most of the remaining "nonforfeitable" benefits, i.e., those benefits to which participants have earned entitlement under the plan terms as of the date of termination. . . .

The cost of the PBGC insurance is borne primarily by employers that maintain ongoing pension plans. Sections 4006 and 4007 of ERISA require these employers to pay annual premiums. The insurance program is also financed by statutory liability imposed on employers who terminate under-funded pension plans. Upon termination, the employer becomes liable to the PBGC for the benefits that the PBGC will pay out. . . .

Termination can be undone by PBGC. . . . When a plan is restored, full benefits are reinstated, and the employer, rather than the PBGC, again is responsible for the plan's unfunded liabilities.

FACTS

This case arose after respondent The LTV Corporation (LTV Corp.) and many of its subsidiaries, . . . filed petitions for reorganization under Chapter 11 of the Bankruptcy Code. . . .

It is undisputed that one of LTV Corp.'s principal goals in filing the Chapter 11 petitions was the restructuring of LTV Steel's pension obligations, a goal which could be accomplished if the Plans were terminated and responsibility for the unfunded liabilities was placed on the PBGC. LTV Steel then could negotiate with its employees for new pension arrangements. LTV, however, could not voluntarily terminate the Plans because two of them had been negotiated in collective bargaining. LTV therefore sought to have the PBGC terminate the Plans.

[PBGC terminated the plan but then objected.]

. . . .

TERMINATION OF PLAN

The Director issued a notice of restoration on September 22, 1987, indicating the PBGC's intent to restore the terminated Plans. The PBGC notice explained that the restoration decision was based on (1) LTV's establishment of "a retirement program that results in an abuse of the pension plan termination insurance system established by Title IV of ERISA," and (2) LTV's "improved financial circumstances." Restoration meant that the Plans were ongoing, and that LTV again would be responsible for administering and funding them.

LTV refused to comply with the restoration decision. This prompted the PBGC to initiate an enforcement action in the District Court. The court vacated the PBGC's restoration decision, finding, among other things, that the PBGC had exceeded its authority under § 4047.

The Court of Appeals for the Second Circuit affirmed, holding that the PBGC's restoration decision was "arbitrary and capricious" or contrary to law under the APA, 5 U.S.C. § 706(2)(A), in various ways. [The Second Circuit based this determination on three substantive grounds.] Finally, the court concluded that the agency's restoration decision was arbitrary and capricious because the PBGC's decisionmaking process of informal adjudication lacked adequate procedural safeguards.

Because of the significant administrative law questions raised by this case, and the importance of the PBGC's insurance program, we granted certiorari.

. . . .

Finally, we consider the Court of Appeals' ruling that the agency procedures were inadequate in this particular case. Relying upon a passage in *Bowman Transportation, Inc. v. Arkansas-Best Freight System, Inc.* (1974), the court held that the PBGC's decision was arbitrary and capricious because the "PBGC neither apprised LTV of the material on which it was to base its decision, gave LTV an adequate opportunity to offer contrary evidence, proceeded in accordance with ascertainable standards . . . , nor provided [LTV] a statement showing its reasoning in applying those standards." The court suggested that on remand the agency was required to do each of these things.

The PBGC argues that this holding conflicts with *Vermont Yankee Nuclear Power Corp. v. Natural Resources Defense Council, Inc.* (1978) where, the PBGC contends, this Court made clear that when the Due Process Clause is not implicated and an agency's governing statute contains no specific procedural mandates, the APA establishes the maximum procedural requirements a reviewing court may impose on agencies. Although *Vermont Yankee* concerned additional procedures imposed by the Court of Appeals for the District of Columbia Circuit on the Atomic Energy Commission when the agency was engaging in informal rulemaking, the PBGC argues that the informal adjudication process by which the restoration decision was made should be governed by the same principles.

Respondents counter by arguing that courts, under some circumstances, do require agencies to undertake additional procedures. As support for this proposition, they rely on *Citizens to Preserve Overton Park, Inc. v. Volpe* (1971). In *Overton Park*, the Court concluded that the Secretary of Transportation's "post hoc rationalizations" regarding a decision to authorize the construction of a highway did not provide "an [a]dequate basis for [judicial] review" for purposes of the APA, 5 U.S.C. §706. Accordingly, the Court directed the District Court on remand to consider evidence that shed light on the Secretary's reasoning at the time he made the decision. Of particular relevance for present purposes, the Court in *Overton Park* intimated that one recourse for the District Court might be a remand to the agency for a fuller explanation of the agency's reasoning at the time of the agency action. Subsequent cases have made clear that remanding to the agency in fact is the preferred course. Respondents contend that the instant case is controlled by *Overton Park* rather than *Vermont Yankee*, and that the Court of Appeals' ruling was thus correct.

We believe that respondents' argument is wide of the mark. We begin by noting that although one initially might feel that there is some tension between *Vermont Yankee* and *Overton Park*, the two cases are not necessarily inconsistent. *Vermont Yankee* stands for the general proposition that courts are not free to impose upon agencies specific procedural requirements that have no basis in the APA. At most, *Overton Park* suggests that §706(2)(A), which directs a court to ensure that an agency action is not arbitrary and capricious or otherwise contrary to law, imposes a general "procedural" requirement of sorts by mandating that an agency take whatever steps it needs to provide an explanation that will enable the court to evaluate the agency's rationale at the time of decision.

Here, unlike in *Overton Park*, the Court of Appeals did not suggest that the administrative record was inadequate to enable the court to fulfill its duties under §706. Rather, to support its ruling, the court focused on "fundamental fairness" to LTV. With the possible exception of the absence of "ascertainable standards"—by which we are not exactly sure what the Court of Appeals meant—the procedural inadequacies cited by the court all relate to LTV's role in the PBGC's decisionmaking process. But the court did not point to any provision in ERISA or the APA which gives LTV the procedural rights the court identified. Thus, the court's holding runs afoul of *Vermont Yankee* and finds no support in *Overton Park*.

Nor is *Arkansas-Best*, the case on which the Court of Appeals relied, to the contrary. The statement relied upon (which was dictum) said: "A party is entitled, of course, to know the issues on which decision will turn and to be apprised of the factual material on which the agency relies for decision so that he may rebut it." That statement was entirely correct in the context of *Arkansas-Best*, which involved a formal adjudication by the Interstate Commerce Commission pursuant to the trial-type procedures set forth in §§5, 7 and 8 of the APA, 5 U.S.C. §§554, 556–557, which include requirements that parties be given notice of "the matters of fact and law asserted," §554(b)(3), an opportunity for "the submission and consideration of facts [and] arguments," §554(c)(1), and an opportunity to submit "proposed findings and conclusions" or "exceptions," §557(c)(1), (2). *See* 5 U.S.C. §554(a). The determination in this case, however, was lawfully made by informal adjudication, the minimal requirements for which are set forth in the APA, 5 U.S.C. §555, and do not include such elements. A failure to provide them where the Due Process Clause itself does not require them (which has not been asserted here) is therefore not unlawful.

We conclude that the PBGC's failure to consider all potentially relevant areas of law did not render its restoration decision arbitrary and capricious. We also conclude that the PBGC's anti-follow-on policy, an asserted basis for the restoration decision, is not contrary to clear congressional intent and is based on a permissible construction of §4047. Finally, we find the procedures employed by the PBGC to be consistent with the APA. Accordingly, the judgment of the Court of Appeals is reversed, and the case is remanded for further proceedings consistent with this opinion.

It is so ordered.

[JUSTICE WHITE, with whom JUSTICE O'CONNOR joined, concurred in part and dissented in part on the substantive rulings. JUSTICE STEVENS dissented on the substantive ruling.]

Notes

1. What are the statutory requirements if § 554(a) is not triggered? Ben can easily demonstrate that there is no statutory requirement for trial-like procedures for grant determinations. As we saw in Lesson 4A.1, § 7(a)(1) of the WTCA, which requires a "full hearing" for § 7 enforcement proceedings, might trigger formal adjudication. By contrast, § 3, which governs grants, makes no reference at all to hearings. The real questions for Ben are: (1) whether there are any other statutory requirements governing grant-making decisions, and (2) how best to design the WTC's grant consideration process given that the agency appears to have considerable flexibility in that regard.

2. Is the APA relevant at all? Consider § 555. For years, it was thought that the federal APA provided procedures for formal rulemaking, informal rulemaking, and formal adjudication but not informal adjudication. That is, the APA seemed to make no provision for adjudications for which an "on the record" hearing was not required. *Pension Benefit* changed that. Note that the Court said that the PBGC decision "was lawfully made by informal adjudication, the minimal requirements for which are set forth in the APA, 5 U.S.C. § 555." How does § 555 "set forth" those "minimal requirements," given that it makes no reference to informal adjudications? How would Ben describe those procedural requirements? Are they limited to informal adjudications? Do Ben's procedures comply with the APA requirements?

Note, in particular, that § 555(e) requires that an agency give prompt notice of any denial of any application or other request and that the agency accompany that notice with "a brief statement of the grounds for the denial." According to the D.C. Circuit, "the agency must explain why it decided to act as it did. The agency's statement must be one of 'reasoning'; it must not be just a 'conclusion'; it must 'articulate a satisfactory explanation' for its action." *Butte County v. Hogen*, 613 F.3d 190, 194 (D.C. Cir. 2010). The explanation must provide a "basis upon which [a court] could conclude that it was the product of reasoned decisionmaking." We will examine the adequacy of agency explanations in greater depth when we reach judicial review in Chapter 5.

3. Should *Vermont Yankee* apply to adjudications? Shortly after *Vermont Yankee* barred courts from "adding" procedures to informal rulemaking, the Supreme Court took the same narrow view of the judicial role with respect to adding procedures to formal adjudication. *Steadman v. SEC*, 450 U.S. 91 (1981). Should the judicial duty with respect to the adequacy of adjudicative procedures be treated the same as its duty with respect to the adequacy of rulemaking procedures? Does this hands-off procedural review make as much sense, theoretically or practically, in adjudication as it does in rulemaking?

4. Be sure to check the agency's enabling act. Suppose that, instead of procedures for grant awards, Ben designed procedures for the imposition of administrative penalties under WTCA § 11. Section 11(b) provides that hearings "shall not be subject to §§ 554 or 556 of Title 5, but shall provide a reasonable opportunity to be heard and to present evidence." Insofar as formal adjudicatory procedures do not apply, procedures for administrative penalties are necessarily "informal" in terms of the APA dichotomy. Congress has, however, imposed an independent procedural requirement in the enabling act itself, which the agency must obey. Suppose, for example, Ralph argues that § 11(b) requires some opportunity to cross-examine government witnesses. What argument might Ben make that the phrase should not be read to require such "formality"? Could a court impose this requirement consistent with *Pension Benefit* and *Vermont Yankee*?

The hearing provisions of § 11(b) of the WTCA are an example of the widespread phenomenon of Congress creating rights to administrative hearings, with decisions to be made on the basis of information presented at the hearings (i.e., "on the record"), but exempting the hearings from the formal adjudication requirements of the APA. Bill Funk argued in 1993 that this development was not justified by arguments that ALJ hearings are too costly and cumbersome and that it has eroded the basic protections of §§ 556 and 557. William Funk, *Close Enough for Government Work?—Using Informal Procedures for Imposing Administrative Penalties*, 24 SETON HALL L. REV. 1 (1993). Funk argued that the APA should be amended to achieve greater uniformity in such hearings and to assure greater fairness, particularly by requiring a neutral decisionmaker. Despite those concerns, many, if not most, record-based adjudicatory decisions are presided over by Administrative Judges (AJs), rather than ALJs, and are not governed by §§ 556 and 557 of the APA.

One lesson from this discussion is that you **must** examine the procedures contained in the enabling act as well as those in the APA and decisional law.

5. And never forget agency procedural rules. Agencies supplement and clarify statutory procedural requirements by adopting procedural rules that shape the adjudicatory process. For example, the Federal Trade Commission has set forth procedural rules for its formal adjudications at 16 C.F.R. 3.1–3.83 (Rules of Practice for Adjudicative Proceedings). Indeed, several of the lessons in this subchapter involve analyzing whether procedural rules designed by our good friend Ben (what, you have no imaginary friends?) satisfy statutory requirements of the APA and WTCA.

Review moment: Where the APA applies, must an agency use notice-and-comment procedures to promulgate procedural rules? Must the WTC use notice-and-comment rulemaking to promulgate procedural rules under the WTCA?

6. Should the WTC adopt adversarial procedures even if not required to do so? The foregoing material establishes that neither the WTCA nor the APA requires the WTC to adopt formal procedures for grant making. Stipulate for the moment that procedural due process, if applicable at all, will require very little at the grant application stage. As long as the WTC meets the minimal requirements of § 555, the agency has very broad discretion to choose between the very informal, essentially nonadversarial procedures that Ben has proposed, and additional elements of the adversary process (responsive pleadings or oral presentations, perhaps), up to a trial-type hearing.

Ralph, the inveterate litigator, would certainly argue for more adversarial process. Should Carl and the other commissioners go along with him?

We saw this issue in subchapter 2C, before we examined formal administrative hearings, and again in subchapter 3B.2, when we considered what, if any, procedures an agency should add to informal rulemaking beyond those imposed by the APA or the agency's substantive statute. Rather than worrying about the legal constraints, the WTC has the luxury of asking itself whether more adversarial elements are needed in order to achieve the accuracy, fairness, efficiency, and legitimacy that are always the goals of the administrative process.

In *Washington v. Harper*, 494 U.S. 210 (1990), the Supreme Court addressed arguments that more adversarial procedures should have been added to the medical review process that had resulted in a decision to force an inmate to take antipsychotic drugs:

> The primary point of disagreement between the parties is whether due process requires a judicial decisionmaker. . . . Respondent contends that only a court should make the decision to medicate an inmate against his will.

> [After applying the analysis of *Mathews v. Eldridge*, 424 U.S. 319, 335 (1976), excerpted in Subchapter 4B, the Court continued,] . . . we conclude that an inmate's interests are adequately protected, and perhaps better served, by allowing the decision to medicate to be made by medical professionals rather than a judge. The Due Process Clause "has never been thought to require that the neutral and detached trier of fact be law trained or a judicial or administrative officer." . . .

> Nor can we ignore the fact that requiring judicial hearings will divert scarce prison resources, both money and the staff's time, from the care and treatment of mentally ill inmates. . . .

> Respondent contends that the Policy is nonetheless deficient because it does not allow him to be represented by counsel. We disagree. "[I]t is less than crystal clear why lawyers must be available to identify possible errors in medical judgment." Given the nature of the decision to be made, we conclude that the provision of an independent lay adviser who understands the psychiatric issues involved is sufficient protection.

Although the Court's analysis appears in the due process framework of *Mathews v. Eldridge*, which we consider in subchapter 4B, its discussion bears on the WTC's choice of procedures here. Will Ben's proposed procedures achieve accurate results? Will they be fair? Would additional advocacy, by a lawyer or otherwise, improve the outcomes, particularly in light of inevitable resource constraints?

It may be that one or more particular elements of the adversarial process would be valuable, even if the overall process remains nonadversarial. In *Washington v. Harper*, for example, Justice Stevens dissented largely on the ground that the decisionmakers were not sufficiently neutral. He saw a danger that internal medical personnel might be unduly affected by the hospital's interest in maintaining order by medicating the inmate. Might there be a similar concern with respect to the WTC's grantmaking decisions? What if the Wrath of Grapes sought a grant to fund research into "the moral deterioration caused by wine drinking throughout the ages"?

7. Reliance upon expert decisionmakers. How do you think Justice Stevens, dissenting in *Harper*, would view the use of expert panels or "juries" in making the grants? Justice Kennedy observed: "Notwithstanding the risks that are involved, we conclude that an inmate's interests are adequately protected, and perhaps better served, by allowing the decision to medicate to be made by medical professionals rather than a judge." Since 1976, the FDA has offered those seeking approval of food additives and new drugs the opportunity to use a Public Board of Inquiry (PBOI) in lieu of formal adjudication. Sidney Shapiro studied this process:

> The FDA expected the PBOI to increase the effectiveness and the legitimacy of its decisions, but not all of its expectations were met. One anticipated benefit—a more expeditious process—did not materialize. The agency had underestimated the time and effort necessary to select PBOI members and to produce an initial decision.
>
> Despite these problems, the PBOI can be a useful method of resolving cases presenting difficult issues of scientific judgment, particularly when those issues generate significant public interest. In such cases, the potential benefits of increased accuracy and legitimacy are likely to outweigh the costs associated with the PBOI.

Sidney Shapiro, *Scientific Issues and the Function of Hearing Procedures: Evaluating the FDA's Public Board of Inquiry*, 1986 DUKE L.J. 288, 318. Why would science court decisions have more legitimacy? Why would they be perceived as increasing accuracy? Under what circumstances should the procedures parallel those used in the relevant discipline at the expense of procedures usually associated with legal proceedings? Justice Stevens, in footnote 20, stated: "The choice is not between medical experts on the one hand and judges on the other; the choice is between decisionmakers who are biased and those who are not." But will professionals always seem biased in our legal culture, which finds virtue in generalist, nonexperts?

8. Hearing procedures under the MSAPA. The states vary in their treatment of adjudicatory hearings, so you will need to check the particular statute where you practice. The Model State Administrative Procedure Act (MSAPA) has alternated between requiring a statutory trigger (as in the "on the record" language of § 554 of the APA) and imposing particular procedures unless a statute exempts a particular hearing from those procedures. The 2010 MSAPA is comparable to the federal APA. It requires particular adjudicatory procedures and protections for a "contested case," which is defined as "an adjudication in which an opportunity for an evidentiary hearing is required by the federal constitution, a federal statute, or the constitution or a statute of this state."

3. Formal Adjudicatory Procedures

Now that we have addressed what happens when a statutory hearing provision does not trigger § 554's requirement that an adjudication be "determined on the record after opportunity for an agency hearing" (i.e., when an informal adjudication occurs), the next step is to explore the requirements when a statutory hearing provision does trigger that requirement. The result, governed by §§ 554, 556, and 557, has come to be called formal adjudication.

Lesson 4A.3. Recall that in Lesson 4A.1, Ben drafted regulations establishing the procedures for conducting enforcement proceedings under § 7 of the WTCA. As described there, the proposed rules provide that anyone entitled to a hearing under § 7(a)(1) will be given notice in writing of the charges, copies of or access to the evidence supporting the charges, and an opportunity to submit a written response. Hearings will be conducted by the Commission itself (highly unlikely in most cases) or by a "hearing officer." The hearing officer will be a staff member with appropriate expertise who has not otherwise participated in the particular case. The Commission or hearing officer will entertain requests for oral appearances or cross-examination of witnesses, but will grant such requests only if the requester demonstrates that the procedures will contribute materially to an accurate factual decision. The Commission or hearing officer will also provide a full written explanation of whatever decision it reaches on the charges. Ben believes that this approach will meet the need for accuracy and fairness while preserving efficiency.

Assume the Commission's § 7(a)(1) hearings are governed by the formal adjudicatory requirements of the APA. Is Ben's draft, so far as it goes, consistent with those provisions? More specifically, does the APA allow the proposed limitations on oral appearances and cross-examination? Does the APA permit the Commission to conduct hearings? Hearing officers? Ben's sketch does not authorize discovery. Does it need to?

Background of *Citizens Awareness Network*

The following case continued the procedural battle reflected earlier in the *Dominion Energy Brayton Point* decision discussed in connection with Lesson 4A.1. Once again, the parties fought over whether a statutory hearing provision triggered the formal adjudication requirements of §§ 554, 556, and 557 of the APA. They apparently did not expect the analysis undertaken by the First Circuit.

Citizens Awareness Network v. United States
391 F.3d 338 (1st Cir. 2004)

SELYA, CIRCUIT JUDGE:

Disenchanted with its existing procedural framework for the conduct of adjudicatory hearings, the Nuclear Regulatory Commission (NRC or Commission) promulgated new rules designed to make its hearing processes more efficient. These new rules greatly reduce the level of formality in reactor licensing proceedings but, at the same time, place certain unaccustomed restrictions upon the parties. The petitioners and petitioner-intervenors are public interest groups. Supported by the Attorneys General of five states (who have filed a helpful amicus brief), they claim that the new rules violate a statutory requirement that all reactor licensing hearings be conducted in accordance with sections 554, 556, and 557 of the Administrative Procedure Act (APA), 5 U.S.C. §§ 554, 556 & 557.[1] In the alternative, they claim that the Commission has not put forth an adequate justification for so substantial a departure from prior practice and that, therefore, the new rules must be set aside as arbitrary and capricious. Fully cognizant of the gravity of our task, we have studied the complex statutory and regulatory framework and scrutinized the plenitudinous administrative record. After completing that perscrutation and grappling with an antecedent jurisdictional question, we find that the new procedures in fact comply with the relevant provisions of the APA and that the Commission has furnished an adequate explanation for the changes. Consequently, we deny the petitions for review.

I. Background

The NRC is the federal agency charged with regulating the use of nuclear energy, including the licensing of reactors used for power generation. The Atomic Energy Act requires the Commission to hold a hearing "upon the request of any person whose interest may be affected," before granting a new license, a license amendment, or a license renewal.

The NRC's predecessor agency, the Atomic Energy Commission (AEC), originally interpreted this provision as requiring on-the-record hearings in accordance with the APA. These hearings closely resembled federal court trials, complete with a full panoply of discovery devices and direct and cross-examination of witnesses by advocates for the parties. Such hearings proved to be very lengthy; some lasted as long as seven years.

In 1982, the NRC relaxed its approach for certain types of licensing proceedings. Although the results were heartening, the Commission nevertheless retained the full range of trial-like procedures for reactor licensing cases. The passage of time brought further changes: faced with the prospect of hearings on many license renewal applications in the near future—a large number of reactors were initially licensed in the decade from 1960 to 1970 and the standard term for such licenses was forty years—the Commission began to reassess its adjudicatory processes, focusing particularly on the procedures used in reactor licensing cases. The NRC's issuance, in 1998, of a policy on the conduct of adjudicatory proceedings marked the inception of this process. This policy statement reiterated the NRC's commitment

---

1. In the pages that follow, we use the modifiers "on the record" and "formal" interchangeably to refer to adjudications conducted in accordance with sections 554, 556, and 557 of the APA.

to expeditious adjudication and urged hearing officers to employ a variety of innovative case-management techniques in order to improve hearing efficiency.

While encouraging better utilization of existing procedures, the Commission also began pondering possible procedural revisions. In January of 1999, the NRC's general counsel drafted a legal memorandum concluding that the Atomic Energy Act did not require reactor licensing hearings to be on the record and, accordingly, that the Commission had the option of replacing the existing format with a truncated regime. Later that year, the Commission held a widely attended workshop on hearing procedures. Building on this foundation, the Commission published a notice of proposed rulemaking on April 16, 2001, suggesting a major revision of its hearing procedures. In an accompanying statement, the Commission took the position that section 189 of the Atomic Energy Act does not require reactor licensing proceedings to be on the record.

On January 14, 2004, the NRC published a final rule, along with a response to the comments that the proposed rule had generated. With minor exceptions, the final rule replicated the proposed rule. The statement of considerations for the final rule reiterated the Commission's view that reactor licensing hearings may be informal.

The new rules took effect on February 13, 2004. Although they apply to all adjudications conducted by the NRC, the petitioners only challenge their application to reactor licensing proceedings. We therefore confine our ensuing discussion to that aspect of the new rules.

Under the old protocol, all reactor licensing hearings were conducted according to the procedures outlined in 10 C.F.R. part 2, subpart G. The subpart G rules resemble those associated with judicial proceedings. They include a complete armamentarium of traditional discovery devices (*e.g.*, requests for document production, interrogatories, and depositions). The parties may make motions for summary disposition (although the hearing officer is not required to entertain them). There is an evidentiary hearing at which testimony is presented through direct and cross-examination of witnesses by the parties.

Under the new rules, reactor licensing hearings are, for the most part, to be conducted according to a less elaborate set of procedures described in 10 C.F.R. pt. 2, subpart L. The new subpart—which differs materially from the old subpart L—limns a streamlined hearing procedure. Unlike subpart G, subpart L does not provide for traditional discovery. Instead, parties in hearings governed by subpart L are required to make certain mandatory disclosures (akin to "open file" discovery) anent expert witnesses, expert witness reports, relevant documents, data compilations, and claims of privilege.

The hearings themselves also differ. Under subpart L, the presumption is that all interrogation of witnesses will be undertaken by the hearing officer, not the litigants. Parties are allowed to submit proposed questions in advance of the hearing, but the presiding officer is under no compulsion to pose them. Parties are not allowed to submit proposed questions during the hearing unless requested to do so by the presiding officer. Cross-examination is not available as of right, although a party may request permission to conduct cross-examination that it deems "necessary to ensure the development of an adequate record for decision." A party seeking leave to conduct cross-examination must submit a cross-examination plan, which will be included in the record of the proceeding regardless of whether the request is allowed.

The petitioners—we use that phrase broadly to include the petitioner-intervenors—took umbrage at these changes and brought these petitions for judicial review. Their primary claim is that the Commission erred in its determination that reactor licensing proceedings do not have to be fully formal adjudications. In their view, the new rules do not comply with the APA's requirements for on-the-record adjudication and, therefore, cannot stand. As a fallback, the petitioners assert that even if the new rules are not ultra vires, they must be set aside as arbitrary and capricious. . . .

III. The Merits

We divide our discussion of the merits into three segments, corresponding with the petitioners' most lively bruited points.

A. *Ultra Vires.*

The mainstay of the petitioners' challenge is the proposition that [the hearing provision of the Atomic Energy Act triggers the formal adjudication requirements of §§ 554, 556, and 557 of the APA]. . . .

. . . .

We . . . decline to resolve this issue. Because the new rules adopted by the Commission meet the requirements of the APA it does not matter what type of hearing the NRC is required to conduct in reactor licensing cases. . . .

We exercise plenary review over the Commission's compliance with the APA. The APA lays out only the most skeletal framework for conducting agency adjudications, leaving broad discretion to the affected agencies in formulating detailed procedural rules. In specific terms, the APA requires only that the agency provide a hearing before a neutral decisionmaker and allow each party an opportunity "to present his case or defense by oral or documentary evidence, to submit rebuttal evidence, and to conduct such cross-examination as may be required for a full and true disclosure of the facts." 5 U.S.C. § 556(d).[5]

The petitioners urge that the magnitude of the risks involved in reactor licensing proceedings warrant the imposition of a more elaborate set of safeguards. It is

---

5. The APA requires the presiding officer to be the agency, a member of the agency, or an administrative law judge. 5 U.S.C. § 556(b). In NRC hearings, 42 U.S.C. § 2241 explicitly authorizes the Commission to empanel safety and licensing boards consisting of one person "qualified in the conduct of administrative proceedings" and two persons with "such technical or other qualifications as the Commission deems appropriate" to preside at hearings under section 2239.

beyond cavil, however, that, short of constitutional constraints, a court may not impose procedural requirements in administrative cases above and beyond those mandated by statute (here, the APA). *Vt. Yankee Nuclear Power Corp. v. Natural Res. Def. Council, Inc.*, 435 U.S. 519, 543–44 (1978). Accordingly, we are not at liberty to impress on the Commission (or any other agency, for that matter) a procedural regime not mandated by Congress. The NRC's new rules will, therefore, succumb to the petitioners' first line of attack only if they fail to provide the minimal procedural safeguards actually demanded by the APA.

We turn now from the general to the particular. The rulemaking at issue here effected several changes in the Commission's procedures. The petitioners focus their challenge on two aspects of the newly minted process. First, they object to the Commission's decision to eliminate discovery. Second, they complain about the Commission's decision to circumscribe the availability of cross-examination. Because these are the only issues on which the petitioners have offered developed argumentation, we confine our analysis to those portions of the new rules.

We begin with the question of whether the new rules fall below the APA's minimum requirements by eliminating discovery. The Commission points out, and the petitioners do not seriously contest, that the APA does not explicitly require the provision of any discovery devices in formal adjudications. Thus, if the APA requires the Commission to provide any discovery to satisfy the standards for formal adjudications, that discovery must be necessary either to effectuate some other procedural right guaranteed by the APA or to ensure an adequate record for judicial review.

The petitioners suggest that discovery is necessary to realize the right of citizen-intervenors to present their case and submit an informed rebuttal. *See* 5 U.S.C. § 556. If discovery is unavailable, this thesis runs, citizen-intervenors will be unable to gather the evidence needed to support their contentions and, thus, will be shut out of meaningful participation in licensing hearings.

This thesis is composed of more cry than wool. The petitioners argue as if the new rules have eliminated all access to information from opposing parties—but that is a gross distortion. The new rules provide meaningful access to information from adverse parties in the form of a system of mandatory disclosure. Although there might well be less information available to citizen-intervenors under the new rules, the difference is one of degree. There is simply no principled way that we can say that the difference occasioned by replacing traditional discovery methods with mandatory disclosure is such that citizen-intervenors are left with no means of adequately presenting their case.

Nor do we think that full-dress discovery is essential to ensure a satisfactory record for judicial review. The Commission's final decision in any hearing must survive review based on the evidence adduced in the hearing. 5 U.S.C. § 556(e). The applicant bears the burden of proof in any licensing hearing, *id.* § 556(d), and it will have every incentive to proffer sufficient information to allow the agency to reach a reasoned decision. That same quantum of information should be adequate for a reviewing court to determine whether the agency's action is supportable.

To say more on this point would be to paint the lily. There is simply no discovery-linked conflict between the new rules and the APA's on-the-record adjudication requirement. The petitioners' first line of argument is, therefore, a dead end.

Turning to cross-examination, the petitioners' contentions fare no better: the new rules meet the APA's requirements. To explain this conclusion, we first must strip away the rhetorical flourishes in which the petitioners shroud their reasoning.

It is important to understand that, contrary to the petitioners' importunings, the new rules do not extirpate cross-examination. Rather, they restrict its use to situations in which it is "necessary to ensure an adequate record for decision." The legitimacy of this restriction must be weighed in light of the fact that the APA does not provide an absolute right of cross-examination in on-the-record hearings. The APA affords a right only to such cross-examination as may be necessary for a full and fair adjudication of the facts. Equally to the point, "[t]he party seeking to cross-examine bears the burden of showing that cross-examination is in fact necessary."

The Commission represents that, despite the difference in language, it interprets the standard for allowing cross-examination under the new rules to be equivalent to the APA standard. When an agency provides a plausible interpretation of its own procedural rules and there is no record or pattern of contrary conduct a court has no right either to slough off that interpretation or to deem it disingenuous. Given the Commission's stated interpretation, the new rules on cross-examination cannot be termed inconsistent with the dictates of the APA. Nor do we see how cross-examination that is not "necessary to ensure an adequate record for decision" could be necessary to ensure appropriate judicial review.

Because we find that the new rules meet the APA requirements for on-the-record adjudications, we hold that their promulgation does not exceed the Commission's authority. Consequently, the petitioners' ultra vires argument founders.

. . . .

IV. Conclusion

We need go no further. Procedural flexibility is one of the great hallmarks of the administrative process—and it is a feature that courts must be reluctant to curtail. Though the Commission's new rules may approach the outer bounds of what is permissible under the APA, we find the statute sufficiently broad to accommodate them. Similarly, the Commission's judgments as to when its procedures need fine-tuning and how they should be retooled are ones to which we accord great respect. We cannot say that the Commission's desire for more expeditious adjudications is unreasonable, nor can we say that the changes embodied in the new rules are an eccentric or a plainly inadequate means for achieving the Commission's goals. Accordingly, both of the instant petitions must be denied.

The petitions for judicial review are denied and dismissed.

Lipez, Circuit Judge.

Although I concur fully in Judge Selya's thoughtful and comprehensive opinion, I write separately to describe some oddities about this case which should not go unnoticed. The basic proposition of Judge Selya's decision is indisputably correct: the new rules promulgated by the Nuclear Regulatory Commission (NRC) to reduce the level of formality in reactor licensing proceedings comply with the "on-the-record" requirements of the Administrative Procedure Act (APA). Yet that legal proposition was largely an afterthought of the NRC in the effort to justify its new rules. Instead, the NRC principally argued in the long run-up to this case that 42 U.S.C. § 2239, which simply requires the Commission to hold a hearing "upon the request of any person whose interest may be affected" before granting a new license, did not invoke the requirements for formal adjudication (commonly referred to as "on-the-record" hearings) under the APA.

It is striking that so many smart people at the NRC could be so wrong for so long about the requirements of the APA. Although this history does not affect the outcome of this case, it should be noted as a cautionary tale about the power of analogy and the endurance of unexamined legal theories. This history also serves to explain some of the legitimate frustrations of the petitioners, who felt that they were dealing with a moving target as the NRC tried to justify its new regulations. With so much at stake in these nuclear reactor licensing proceedings, the rulemaking process should have followed a steadier course. For reasons I shall explain, this was not the rulemaking process at its best.

Terminology

The terminology for hearings under the APA can be imprecise and confusing. The everyday meaning of terms like "formal" and "informal" sometimes creeps into the discussion, although those terms have specific, functional definitions under the APA. As Judge Selya notes, the terms "formal" and "on-the-record" are generally used as shorthand for hearings that must be conducted pursuant to the requirements of 5 U.S.C. §§ 554, 556, and 557 of the APA. Other terms, too, are sometimes used to refer to such procedures — "trial-type" and "quasi-judicial." These vague and indefinite terms are particularly mischievous because they evoke images of courtroom trials, and they have contributed to the false impression that the APA's requirement of on-the-record hearings involves procedures more akin to civil trials than is actually the case.

To be specific, § 554 requires that, in cases of an "adjudication required by statute to be determined on the record after opportunity for an agency hearing," the agency must follow the procedures outlined in §§ 556 and 557. Although the statutory text at issue here is itself rather pithy, these procedures can be usefully condensed into the following ten points:

1. The agency must give notice of legal authority and matters of fact and law asserted. § 554(b).

2. The oral evidentiary hearing must be presided over by an officer who can be disqualified for bias. § 556(b).

3. Presiding officers cannot have ex parte communications. §§ 554(d), 557(d)(1).

4. Parties are entitled to be represented by attorneys. § 555(b).

5. The proponent of an order has the burden of proof. § 556(d).

6. A party is entitled to present oral or documentary evidence. § 556(d).

7. A party is entitled "to conduct such cross-examination as may be required for a full and true disclosure of the facts." § 556(d).

8. Orders can be issued only on consideration of the record of the hearing. § 556(d).

9. The transcript of testimony and exhibits is the exclusive record for decision and shall be made available to parties. § 556(e).

10. The decision must include "findings and conclusions, and the reasons or basis therefor, on all the material issues of fact, law, or discretion presented on the record." § 557(c)(3)(A).

See Richard J. Pierce, Jr., Administrative Law Treatise § 8.1 (4th ed. 2002). Strikingly, there is no reference to discovery in these statutory provisions of the APA, and cross-examination is assured only if necessary "for a full and true disclosure of the facts." 5 U.S.C. § 556(d). Most of these provisions relate to the conduct and responsibilities of the presiding officer or the basis for agency orders (on the record). Only a few relate to the conduct of the hearing itself. These APA requirements leave agencies with a great deal of flexibility in tailoring on-the-record hearing procedures to suit their perceived needs.

If hearings are not required to be "on the record," the procedures of §§ 556 and 557 are not triggered; the only section of the APA applicable to the proceedings is § 555, titled "Ancillary matters." Section 555(b) entitles a party to be represented by a lawyer, § 555(c) entitles people who have submitted data or evidence to retain copies of their submissions, and § 555(e) requires agencies to give prompt notice when they deny a petition made in connection with a proceeding, and to give a brief statement of the grounds for denial. Additionally, subsections (c) and (d) require that process, subpoenas, and other investigative demands must be made in accordance with law. Of course, these "informal" hearings must also comply with basic due process requirements.

From the beginning of its proposed rulemaking, the NRC repeatedly referred to the procedures outlined in the new regulations as "informal," as opposed to the outmoded formal procedures of the past. The clear implication was that the new informal procedures would not meet the APA's requirements for formal, on-the-record hearings. Thus, the NRC believed that it first had to establish that its authorizing statute, the Atomic Energy Act (AEA), did not require it to hold on-the-record hearings for reactor licensing.

Background to Rulemaking

Judge Selya outlines some of the important history of the rulemaking in this case. However, there is more to this curious history that is worth telling. From the 1998 Policy Statement to the Notice of Proposed Rulemaking, the NRC barely contemplated the possibility that it could reform its hearing procedures to its liking and still comply with the APA after all. . . .

. . . .

In the Notice of Proposed Rulemaking itself, which for the first time proposed specific changes to the NRC's hearing procedures, there was still no argument that the proposed procedures complied with the APA's requirements. Instead, the notice offered pages of legal analysis on the history of the AEA, all intended to justify the NRC's ability to promulgate new hearing procedures that are not subject to the APA's requirements for on-the-record hearings.

Other choices made by the NRC in its regulatory overhaul further emphasize the firmness of its conviction that the supposedly "informal" procedures it was proposing did not comply with the APA's requirements for on-the-record hearings. . . .

Strikingly, in the entire record of this rulemaking prior to the promulgation of the Final Rule, I can find only one footnote hinting that anyone at the NRC thought that it could reduce the formality of its procedures while at the same time complying with the strictures of the APA. In a footnote in its January 1999 memo, the OGC acknowledged the possibility of eliminating the "elements of Subpart G that go beyond the Administrative Procedure Act's requirements for 'on-the-record' hearings. One immediate effect would be to eliminate formal discovery in NRC adjudications." The memo contains no further discussion of how far beyond the APA's requirements the OGC understood Subpart G to go.

Not until publication of the Final Rule itself did the NRC assert for the first time that the new procedures comply with the APA's requirements for an on-the-record hearing—and even here, the NRC devotes only a few sentences to the issues of cross-examination, discovery, and the presiding officer. . . .

In considerable part, administrative agencies set the terms of the debate in the rulemaking process with the arguments they advance in support of their rulemaking initiatives. If certain arguments are unmistakably primary, those arguments will draw most of the attention during the administrative process, and during the judicial review that follows. Not surprisingly, opponents will believe that the primacy of the argument means that it is the most important argument to address. If, in the end, the dispositive issue on appeal is a different issue, addressed only glancingly in the administrative process, there has been enormous wasted effort, and the courts of appeal will be poorly served by appellate briefing that reflects the outdated emphases of the administrative process. That is precisely what happened here.

. . . .

Further History

The NRC's belated recognition that the new licensing procedures might in fact comply with the on-the-record requirements of the APA is all the more surprising because sources contemporaneous with the APA's passage suggest that flexibility has always been a hallmark of the APA, and that agencies have always had considerable discretion to structure on-the-record hearings to suit their particular needs. This flexibility is nowhere more evident than in determining the role of cross-examination in on-the-record hearings.

The Attorney General's Manual on the Administrative Procedure Act (1947) is a "key document" for interpreting the APA. We have described it as containing the "most authoritative" account of the history of the Act's passage. *See also Yankee Nuclear Power Corp. v. Natural Res. Def. Council, Inc.*, 435 U.S. 519, 546 (1978) (the Attorney General's Manual is "a contemporaneous interpretation previously given some deference by this Court because of the role played by the Department of Justice in drafting the legislation"). The Attorney General's Manual offers a vision of cross-examination entirely consistent with that advanced by the NRC in this rulemaking.

The Manual begins by stressing the general importance of cross-examination in on-the-record hearings, cautioning that "it is clear that the 'right to present his case or defense by oral or documentary evidence' does not extend to presenting evidence in affidavit or other written form so as to deprive the agency or opposing parties of opportunity for cross-examination." Technical evidence may be introduced in written form as long as its admission "would not prejudicially deprive other parties or the agency of opportunity for cross-examination. Thus, technical and statistical data may be introduced in convenient written form subject to adequate opportunity for cross-examination and rebuttal." *Id.*

The Attorney General's Manual goes on, however, to acknowledge that the general opportunity to cross-examine is subject to restrictions which become more salient as the complexity of the hearing's subject matter increases. On this point, the Manual quotes from the Report of the House Committee on the Judiciary on the APA. The Report cautions that the APA's provision for "such cross-examination as may be required for a full and true disclosure of the facts" does not

> confer a right of so-called "unlimited" cross-examination. Presiding officers will have to make the necessary initial determination whether the cross-examination is pressed to unreasonable lengths by a party or whether it is required for the "full and true disclosure of the facts" stated in the provision. Nor is it the intention to eliminate the authority of agencies to confer sound discretion upon presiding officers in the matter of its extent. The test is—as the section states—whether it is required "for a full and true disclosure of the facts." In many rule making proceedings where the subject matter and evidence are broadly economic or statistical in character and the parties or witnesses numerous, the direct or rebuttal evidence may

be of such a nature that cross-examination adds nothing substantial to the record and unnecessarily prolongs the hearings.

H.R.Rep. No.1980, 79th Cong., 2d Sess., 37.

The Attorney General's Manual and the House Report serve as good indicators that Congress, when it passed the APA, understood that agencies needed a considerable amount of flexibility in fashioning hearing procedures for on-the-record hearings. Despite the frequent use of terms like "trial-type" and "quasijudicial" over the years to refer to on-the-record hearings, agencies have always been able to adapt their procedures for on-the-record hearings under the APA. Today, this statute of general applicability governs the procedures for an enormous variety of hearings—everything from relatively simple claims for workers' compensation, to enforcement proceedings under the National Labor Relations Act or the Occupational Health and Safety Act, to complex rate-setting hearings before the Federal Energy Regulatory Commission.

. . . .

These sources, both contemporaneous with the APA's passage and modern, show that procedures in on-the-record hearings, despite sometimes being described as "trial-type" procedures, can in fact stray considerably from the procedures found in civil trials as the subjects of the administrative proceedings become more complex and more technical. This flexibility is inherent in the APA, and has been acknowledged by commentators and by courts. With these abundant sources pointing the way, the NRC's belated recognition that the APA could, in fact, accommodate its procedural reforms is all the more puzzling.

Conclusion

For most of the history of this rulemaking, the NRC argued that it did not have to comply with the APA's on-the-record requirements in refashioning its procedures for reactor licensing hearings. Belatedly, and then only sketchily, the NRC advanced the alternative argument that its proposed procedures complied with those on-the-record requirements. The staying power of old theories and flawed analogies (the repeated references to trial-type proceedings) may account for some of this delay. Whatever the reasons, the deleterious effect of this late insight on the rulemaking process and our review of it is undeniable. Countless hours were wasted during the administrative process fighting over the tired issue of whether 42 U.S.C. § 2239 requires reactor licensing hearings to be on the record. This tired issue dogged judicial review as well. Although we have done what *Chenery* requires—affirming on a basis advanced by the agency itself during the administrative process—we got there with too little help from the parties. There is a victory here for the NRC, but it should be a cause for self-examination rather than jubilation.

Notes

1. The NRC's procedural regulations. The NRC regulations at issue in *Citizens Awareness Network* are one of many examples of the regulations that agencies adopt to govern practice and hearings before the agency. The NRC's regulations, which appear at 10 C.F.R. Part 2, govern several subjects, including both adjudicatory hearings and rulemaking. 10 C.F.R. Subpart G governed reactor licensing hearings for many years until the NRC adopted Subpart L, the provision at issue in *Citizens Awareness Network*. Subpart G sets out very extensive procedures, including provisions for discovery. Agencies for many years assumed hearings should follow the judicial model. The NRC's Subpart G regulations are among the most formalized.

2. The potential informality of "formal" hearings. *Citizens Awareness* provides an object lesson in the importance of avoiding the tyranny of labels. As Judge Lipez explained in his concurrence:

> The terminology for hearings under the APA can be imprecise and confusing. The everyday meaning of terms like "formal" and "informal" sometimes creeps into the discussion, although those terms have specific, functional definitions under the APA. As JUDGE SELYA notes, the terms "formal" and "on-the-record" are generally used as shorthand for hearings that must be conducted pursuant to the requirements of 5 U.S.C. §§ 554, 556, and 557 of the APA. Other terms, too, are sometimes used to refer to such procedures—"trial-type" and "quasi-judicial." These vague and indefinite terms are particularly mischievous because they evoke images of courtroom trials, and they have contributed to the false impression that the APA's requirement of on-the-record hearings involves procedures more akin to civil trials than is actually the case.

The actual requirements of "formal" adjudication under the APA depend not on our intuitions of how judicial trials should work, but on the actual terms of the APA itself. We will be examining §§ 554, 556, and 557 in more detail as we march through this chapter. For a great introduction, however, find the spot in Judge Lipez's concurrence where he lists ten requirements for formal adjudication. For each of the ten, he provides a cite to the APA. Look up these cites, and do your best to make sense of them. (Really, you should do this. It will help.)

3. Administrative summary judgment. In civil litigation in federal court, litigants enjoy a Seventh Amendment right to jury trial for actions at common law. In the absence of a genuine issue of material fact, however, summary judgment can short-circuit this right to jury trial. In *Weinberger v. Hynson, Westcott & Dunning, Inc.*, 412 U.S. 609 (1973), the Supreme Court confirmed that agency procedural regulations can, in similar fashion, block the path to an oral hearing in administrative adjudication where a litigant fails to demonstrate that there is anything material for a hearing to resolve. Under 1962 amendments to the Federal Food, Drug, and Cosmetic Act of 1938, the FDA is required to deny approval of a "new drug application" in the absence of "substantial evidence" that the drug is effective for its intended purpose. The FDA promulgated regulations that established standards governing a statutory requirement that "substantial evidence" include "adequate and well-controlled investigations." The regulations also provided that, to obtain a hearing, an applicant would need to provide at least some evidence that its application satisfied these standards. The FDA withdrew a drug manufacturer's new drug application and denied its request for a hearing based on its failure to provide "substantial evidence" of efficacy. The Supreme Court held that, in light of the statutory and regulatory definition of "substantial evidence," the "FDA's so-called administrative summary judgment procedure" was "appropriate."

For support for its analysis, the Court turned to two precedents that you might recall from Chapter 2, *United States v. Storer Broadcasting Co.*, 351 U.S. 192 (1956), and *FPC v. Texaco*, 377 U.S. 33 (1964). The Court quoted *Texaco*:

> [T]he statutory requirement for a hearing under s 7 (of the Natural Gas Act) does not preclude the Commission from particularizing statutory standards through the rulemaking process and barring at the threshold those who neither measure up to them nor show reasons why in the public interest the rule should be waived.

412 U.S. at 620 (quoting *Texaco*, 377 U.S. at 39).

For an enthusiastic circuit court discussion of the validity of administrative summary judgment, see *Puerto Rico Aqueduct and Sewer Authority v. U.S. E.P.A.*, 35 F.3d 600, 606–09 (1st Cir. 1994) (noting, "it is unsurprising that most major agencies in the federal system have opted to make available procedures for the summary disposition of adjudicatory matters"). In *Puerto Rico Aqueduct*, the First Circuit observed that agency procedures are typically modeled on Fed. R. Civ. P. 56. Thus, an agency can deny a statutory hearing to a petitioner who fails to present a "genuine" issue of "material" fact. An issue is "genuine" where "a reasonable decisionmaker could decide in favor of either party under the applicable standard of proof." 35 F.3d at 605. A fact is "material" where it "may affect the outcome of the case." *Id. See also Crestview Parke Care Ctr. v. Thompson*, 373 F.3d 743, 750 (6th Cir. 2004) ("Given that federal district courts can decide cases as a matter of law without an oral hearing when it is clear there are no genuine material disputes to be resolved in a trial, it would be bizarre if administrative agencies, which are in many respects modeled after the federal courts and which indeed often have more informal proceedings than federal courts, could not follow a similar rule.").

Some Notes on Administrative Law Judges

1. Presiding officials for formal adjudications (are mostly ALJs). The First Circuit in *Citizens Awareness Network* explains in a footnote that the Atomic Energy Act authorizes the NRC to use special "safety and licensing boards" to preside at its hearings. Appropriately for a highly technical area, these boards consist of one member qualified to conduct hearings, typically a lawyer, and two members with technical expertise. This is an exception to the general requirement of § 556(a), which provides that "the taking of evidence" will be done by "the agency" (e.g., the five WTC commissioners), "one or more members of the body which comprises the agency" (e.g., one or more of the commissioners), or "one or more administrative law judges appointed under section 3105 of [the APA]." ALJs handle the vast majority of such hearings as agency heads are, not to put too fine a point on the matter, far too busy to do so.

2. Appointment of ALJs. Historically, ALJs were selected by designated agency officials from a list compiled by the Office of Personnel Management (OPM), an independent agency tasked with managing the federal workforce, of which ALJs are a part. The OPM list was based on candidates' scores on a civil service examination administered by OPM. Only the top three performers on the list at the time of selection were eligible for appointment by the agency as an ALJ. In general, individuals, including ALJs (hired based on their examination scores), were considered part of the "competitive service."

In 2018, President Trump issued Executive Order 13,843: *Executive Order Excepting Administrative Law Judges from the Competitive Service* (July 10, 2018) (EO). The EO was ostensibly issued in response to the Supreme Court's decision in *Lucia v. SEC*, 138 S. Ct. 2044 (2018) (discussed in connection with the president's appointment power in subchapter 1C.3), which held that SEC ALJs are "inferior officers" subject to the requirements of the Appointments Clause of Article II, rather than simply "employees" whose hiring is not directly controlled by the Constitution. The EO moved the position of ALJ from the competitive service to the excepted service, meaning the civil service exam is no longer required for appointment. Under the EO, ALJ appointments may be made directly by, and at the discretion of, agency heads. The only limiting feature of the EO is that ALJ candidates must either already be a judge or have a current license to practice law in the United States or one of its territories. EO at § 3(a)(ii). Proponents of the EO note that it will allow agencies to target subject matter experts in hiring, rather than non-experts who performed well on the civil service exam. Critics suggest that by removing OPM from the process, ALJ appointments will become more political, allowing an agency to staff its ranks of initial adjudicators with individuals who are sympathetic to the political views of the agency heads.

3. Removal and salary protections for ALJs. You remember from constitutional law that federal judges enjoy life tenure and salary protection to protect their decisional independence. ALJs have enjoyed a kind of substitute statutory protection for their decisional independence. By statute, salaries for ALJs are set at defined levels controlled by the Office of Personnel Management. 5 U.S.C. § 5372. To remove an ALJ, an agency must demonstrate good cause to the satisfaction of the Merit Systems Protection Board in formal proceedings. 5 U.S.C. § 7521.

This insulation from agency removal is coming under threat. As discussed in subchapter 1C.3, in *Free Enterprise Fund v. Public Co. Accounting Oversight Board*, 130 S. Ct. 3138 (2010), the Supreme Court took as a given that the president could remove SEC commissioners only for cause, and SEC commissioners could in turn remove PCAOB members only for cause. The Court held that this double insulation of Board members from presidential control was unconstitutional. To remove an ALJ, the MSPB must find good cause for removal, and the president needs good cause to remove MSPB members. In *Lucia v. SEC,* 138 S. Ct. 2044 (2018), the government contended that, to prevent ALJs from running afoul of *Free Enterprise Fund,* the Court should allow agencies to remove ALJs for inadequate performance or failure to follow instructions. The Court declined to reach this issue.

President Trump, as discussed in the preceding note, issued Executive Order 13,843 in the aftermath of *Lucia.* It states, "Civil Service Rules and Regulations shall [no longer] apply to removals" of ALJs, E.O. at § 3(b)(iii). The statutory requirements that ALJs may only be removed by the Merit Systems Protection Board, and only for cause, still apply. *See* 5 U.S.C. § 7521.

4. Types of ALJ decisions and their intra-agency review. Administrative adjudicative bureaucracies are usually structured somewhat like the judicial hierarchy, with two or more levels of decisionmakers. At a formal adjudication, the ALJ (or other authorized presiding official) compiles evidence, determines facts, and applies pertinent law and agency policy to reach a result. Under the APA, this result may be an "initial decision" or a "recommended decision." 5 U.S.C. § 557(b). An initial decision "becomes the decision of the agency without further proceedings unless there is an appeal to, or review on motion of, the agency within time provided by rule." *Id.* The recommended decision is, as the term suggests, only a recommendation from the presiding official; it becomes the decision of the agency only when adopted by the agency head.

In most administrative adjudicative systems, the agency head or administrative appellate authority has *de novo* control over all the issues and may substitute its judgment on appeal as to questions of fact as well as law and policy. Section 557(b) of the APA, for example, provides: "[O]n appeal from or review of the initial decision, the agency has all the powers which it would have in making the initial decision except as it may limit the issues on notice or by rule." Thus, although Congress has gone to considerable trouble (as discussed in notes 2 and 3) to protect the decisional independence of ALJs, it has expressly subjected ALJ decisions to plenary agency control. One rationale for this plenary control is that, as discussed in Chapter 2, agency adjudications are a vehicle for policymaking. Congress delegates policymaking power to agencies, not ALJs, and therefore, the theory goes, agencies must have plenary authority over the results of agency adjudications. Agency adjudicative orders are, however, subject to judicial review under terms discussed at considerable length in Chapter 5.

Not everyone, by the way, is totally convinced that plenary control over adjudication should be handed over to policymakers who owe their positions to political appointments. For Frederick Davis, this situation creates cause for concern:

> [One problem] involves the possible frustration or rejection of a judicial type decision on policy or political grounds by agency members who do not necessarily have the judicial competence of the ALJ. It may well be that the effective implementation of policy requires that final adjudicatory responsibility be vested in the agency itself or the appropriate cabinet member;

it may even be that this is technically a requirement of the Constitution. Nevertheless, the fact remains that under the present system the decision of an ALJ, reached after a trial-type hearing which includes many, if not most, of the procedures common to the judicial process, may nevertheless be rejected or modified by an "appellate" body which does not have a judicial composition.

Frederick Davis, *Judicialization of Administrative Law: The Trial-Type Hearing and the Changing Status of the Hearing Officer*, 1977 Duke L.J. 389, 406–07. Should administrative review authorities be staffed according to judicial-type standards rather than political or administrative motivations? Is there a difference?

Also, turning from policy to fact, how should agency heads approach their responsibility to review an ALJ's factual findings? Many fact determinations depend on assessments of witness credibility. Should an agency head exercise *de novo* review over credibility determinations made by ALJs who have heard testimony that the agency head has not? We will return to this issue in subchapter 5G.1, when we examine *Universal Camera Corp. v. NLRB*.

5. Before we go any further, here is an example to make things a bit more concrete. For a nice example of how the pieces of the puzzle we have been discussing fit together, consider the Federal Trade Commission's system of formal adjudication for enforcement hearings charging "unfair methods of competition" or "unfair or deceptive acts or practices." The FTC enforcement staff initiates the process with an investigation into alleged violations. If the staff finds evidence of a violation, they attempt to demonstrate to the Commission (the five commissioners that head the FTC) that there is "reason to believe" that the law has been violated. If the Commission agrees, it issues a "complaint" asserting that it has reason to believe the law has been violated. The private party named in the complaint may offer to settle the case and sign a "consent decree." If it does not, then the case goes to a formal administrative hearing. An ALJ is appointed and prehearing practice undertaken. The ALJ then conducts a hearing in which both sides present evidence in much the same manner as a judicial trial. After the hearing, the ALJ issues an "initial decision." If the ALJ finds a violation, the ALJ also issues a "cease and desist" order, compelling the party to stop the illegal practice. Either the respondent or the FTC enforcement staff may appeal the initial decision. If the decision is appealed, the Commission receives briefs and hears oral argument much like an appellate court. It then issues a final order and decision. This decision may be appealed to a federal circuit court of appeals and then, on certiorari, to the Supreme Court. When the order becomes final, the FTC staff monitors compliance with the order. Violation of the order may lead to "civil penalties."

6. Are ALJs "bound" by agency guidance? How should an ALJ handle questions of policy or statutory or regulatory interpretation? It is blackletter law that an agency must follow its own legislative rules. Legislative rules are binding on everyone, including the ALJ and the agency head, until they are changed through the legislative rulemaking process.

But what about nonlegislative rules or "guidance documents"—i.e., interpretive rules and policy statements? You will recall from subchapter 3B that, strictly speaking, guidance documents are not legally binding. Quite frequently, however, an agency will initiate an administrative enforcement action based upon a position that the agency has previously articulated in an interpretive rule or policy statement. When that happens, there is no doubt that the party against whom the enforcement action is brought may challenge the agency's position. It is also clear that the agency head (the Wine Trade Commission, for example), may agree with the party's challenge and reject its earlier guidance. The agency head will, however, need to explain its change of position.

A trickier question is whether an ALJ or other front-line adjudicator should regard herself as bound by agency guidance documents. On the one hand, as explained in note 4, it is clear that agencies, not ALJs, enjoy delegated authority to determine policy. On the other hand, if neither regulated parties nor the agency head are legally bound by such guidance, it might seem that ALJs should be free to reject them as well. Indeed, at some agencies, the ALJs do not consider themselves bound by the agency's guidance documents.

In the view of one of your editors, the effect of guidance documents on front-line adjudicators should be regarded, in a word, as "complicated." Charles H. Koch, Jr., *Policymaking by the Administrative Judiciary*, 56 Ala. L. Rev. 693 (2005). Professor Koch suggested that, since guidance documents do not technically bind the agency itself, front-line adjudicators, such as ALJs, should have at least some discretion to deviate from them where their literal application would be "unfair." One reason for allowing this discretion, in addition to fairness, is that it provides a path for policy change "to percolate up through the process," with each level playing "a role in sharpening the rule through interpretation." Still, the public expects agencies to act consistently with their pronouncements—regardless of whether, like interpretive rules and policy statements, they lack technical legal effect. Therefore, Professor Koch concluded that, in the usual case, a front-line adjudicator should give effect to agency guidance.

Of course, if an ALJ does take it upon herself to depart from an agency's guidance, the agency is free on review to exercise its plenary power to undo the deviation. Not all ALJ decisions, however, are appealed to agency heads. In those cases, if an ALJ were to deviate from an agency's informally stated position, the ALJ would become the policymaker despite the absence of any delegated authority to do so.

Some Quick Notes on Other Systems

1. **The split-enforcement model.** As we have seen, the archetypical modern agency can make rules, initiate enforcement actions for violations, and, ultimately, adjudicate these actions with binding orders. Although these orders are subject to judicial review, reasonable people may still be concerned by this type of combination of functions. In some administrative schemes, Congress has responded to such concerns (and potent lobbies) by adopting a split-enforcement model. Under this

model, one agency promulgates rules and initiates enforcement actions, but a separate agency adjudicates these actions.

This split-enforcement model leaves open the possibility that the rulemaking agency and the adjudicating agency might disagree on an issue of statutory or regulatory construction. The Supreme Court has determined that, when reviewing this type of disagreement, a court should extend any applicable deference to the rulemaking agency, not the adjudicating agency. The leading case on this point is *Martin v. Occupational Safety & Health Review Commission*, 499 U.S. 144 (1991). The Occupational Safety and Health Act (OSH Act) delegates authority to the Secretary of Labor to promulgate regulations and to initiate enforcement actions to protect workplace safety. Congress delegated to a different body, the Occupational Safety and Health Review Commission (OSHRC), the task of adjudicating enforcement actions. The two agencies disagreed regarding interpretation of a safety regulation governing the use of respirators. The Supreme Court held that deference should run to the Secretary "[b]ecause applying an agency's regulation to complex or changing circumstances calls upon the agency's unique expertise and policymaking prerogatives." The Secretary, who, after all, promulgated the regulation, was a better source than OSHRC regarding its meaning. Moreover, given that the Secretary is in charge of day-to-day enforcement, whereas OSHRC only hears contested citations, "the Secretary is more likely to develop the expertise relevant to assessing the effect of a particular regulatory interpretation."

2. Central panels of ALJs. In the federal system, ALJs, though insulated from the authority of agency heads, are considered part of the agencies for which they work. In many states, unlike the federal system, ALJs (or their equivalent) are housed in one agency, often referred to as a "panel." This central panel concept began in California in 1945. Now, about one-half of the states organize their presiding officials in this way. James G. Gilbert & Robert S. Cohen, *Administrative Adjudication in the United States*, 37 JNAALJ 222 n. 63 (2017) ("The 24 jurisdictions with confirmed central panels are Alaska, Arizona, California, Colorado, District of Columbia, Florida, Georgia, Iowa, Kansas, Louisiana, Maryland, Massachusetts, Michigan, Minnesota, New Jersey, North Carolina, North Dakota, Oregon, South Carolina, Tennessee, Texas, Washington, Wisconsin, and Wyoming."). The drafters of the 1981 MSAPA provided for the creation of a central panel, an "office of administrative hearings." MSAPA § 4-301 (1981).

According to John Hardwicke, Maryland's Chief ALJ, the central panel system has notable advantages: hearings are "more professional and conscientious," staff perform better before an independent judge than fellow staff, courts have more confidence in independent judges, disclosure of the real cost of litigation, and cost effectiveness. The panels also improve the performance of the ALJs themselves in several ways: facilitating training and professionalism, enabling impartial management, and eliminating "burnout" by adding variety to the ALJ's caseload. John Hardwicke, *The Central Hearing Agency: Theory and Implementation in Maryland*, 14 JNAALJ 5 (1994).

The relationship between the different levels of the adjudicatory bureaucracy is complicated by adoption of the independent ALJ panel in much the same way as in the split-function model at issue in *Martin*. How will the panel structure affect the allocation of roles, particularly policymaking, between the adjudicators and the agency? Does special independence of the ALJ improperly diminish the ultimate authority of the agency? Yet, isn't it inconsistent with the independent panel concept for the agency to have ultimate authority over the independent ALJ?

3. Alternative Dispute Resolution. By now, perhaps in your Civil Procedure class, you have learned something about alternative dispute resolution, or ADR. Perhaps it will come as little surprise that ADR has become part of administrative adjudication as well. Congress added to the APA, subchapter IV, "Alternative Means of Dispute Resolution in the Administrative Process," 5 U.S.C. §§ 571 *et seq.* Under this subchapter, subject to various exceptions, "[a]n agency may use a dispute resolution proceeding for the resolution of an issue in controversy that relates to an administrative program, if the parties agree to such proceeding." 5 U.S.C. § 572. Authorized methods of ADR include "any procedure that is used to resolve issues in controversy, including, but not limited to, conciliation, facilitation, mediation, fact-finding, minitrials, arbitration, and use of ombuds, or any combination thereof." 5 U.S.C. § 571(3).

4. Who May Participate in the Agency Hearing?

We have discussed some of the ways in which final adjudications under §§ 556 and 557 approximate trials, and we will continue to do so in the following subchapters on evidentiary standards and appeals within the agency. One way in which agency adjudication is notably different from a traditional trial is in the relatively wide range of potential participants in an adjudication. This subsection addresses the question of when an interested person or entity may participate in an agency hearing.

Lesson 4A.4. On Ralph's recommendation, the WTC found it had "reason to believe" that Gallery had violated WTCA § 5. In general, the major charges in the complaint were:

> Gallery had added cane sugar to its wines without disclosing that fact, and hence, failed "to state a material fact necessary in order to make the statements made, in light of the circumstances under which they were made, not misleading";

> Gallery claimed on its label and in advertising that certain of its wines were made from special high quality wine grapes, when in fact the wine is a mixture containing mostly high yield table grapes, and hence that Gallery engaged "in any act, practice, or course of business which operates or would operate as a fraud or deceit on any person"; and

> Gallery designated some of its wine as "special reserve" in violation of the special reserve rule and the guidelines interpreting it.

All efforts at settlement failed and Abby and Ralph are now locked in a hotly contested adjudicative hearing under WTCA §7 and the APA. Bud, the ALJ, has begun the prehearing stage of the adjudication. Ralph and Abby begin preparing their cases.

The Wrath for Grapes petitions to intervene. It is interested in demonstrating that alcohol is a dangerous drug, and hence the addition of sugar to increase the alcohol generated by fermentation should be prohibited. Both Ralph and Abby oppose Wrath's petition. Ralph believes that Wrath's involvement will only complicate the proceeding, and that in any case the WTC staff more than adequately represents the public interest. Abby is concerned that the Wrath will use the proceeding as a platform from which to disseminate its anti-alcohol propaganda.

Abby also notices that the Wrath's petition is signed by former Commissioner Fred as attorney for the Wrath. Although Fred left the WTC recently, he did not vote on the issuance of the complaint. Nonetheless, Abby considers claiming that his participation is a violation of the Ethics in Government Act and otherwise a conflict of interest in violation of the Code of Professional Responsibility. She asks the Commission to prohibit Fred from representing the Wrath in this hearing.

In light of the following materials, how should Bud assess the petition to intervene and Fred's participation?

Background of *Envirocare*

The following decision is unusual in upholding a denial of intervention despite the fact that the company seeking to intervene arguably would have constitutional standing by virtue of an alleged economic injury. Note carefully how administrative standing differs from judicial standing, why the Nuclear Regulatory Commission denied intervention in this case, and why it was upheld.

Envirocare of Utah, Inc. v. Nuclear Regulatory Commission
194 F.3d 72 (D.C. Cir. 1999)

RANDOLPH, CIRCUIT JUDGE:

Federal agencies may, and sometimes do, permit persons to intervene in administrative proceedings even though these persons would not have standing to challenge the agency's final action in federal court. Agencies, of course, are not constrained by Article III of the Constitution; nor are they governed by judicially-created standing doctrines restricting access to the federal courts. The criteria for establishing "administrative standing" therefore may permissibly be less demanding than the criteria for "judicial standing."

Is the converse true? May an agency refuse to grant a hearing to persons who would satisfy the criteria for judicial standing and refuse to allow them to intervene in administrative proceedings? This is the ultimate question posed in these consolidated petitions for judicial review of two orders of the Nuclear Regulatory

Commission refusing to grant Envirocare of Utah, Inc.'s requests for a hearing and for intervention in licensing proceedings.

I

Envirocare was the first commercial facility in the nation the Commission licensed to dispose of certain radioactive byproduct material from offsite sources. The Commission had licensed other companies to dispose of such radioactive waste, but only if the waste was produced onsite. In the late 1990s, the Commission granted the applications of two such companies for amended licenses to allow them to dispose of radioactive waste received from other sites. International Uranium (USA) Corporation's facility in Utah became licensed to receive and dispose of approximately 25,000 dry tons of waste still remaining from the Manhattan Project and currently stored in New York State. Quivira Mining Company's facility in New Mexico, some 500 miles from Envirocare's operation, also became licensed to dispose of specified amounts of such material from offsite sources.

In both licensing proceedings before the Atomic Safety and Licensing Board, Envirocare requested a hearing and sought leave to intervene to oppose the amendment. Envirocare's basic complaint was "that the license amendment permits [the company] to become a general commercial facility like Envirocare, but that the NRC did not require [the company] to meet the same regulatory standards the agency imposed upon Envirocare when Envirocare sought *its* license to become a commercial disposal facility for" radioactive waste. The Licensing Board rejected Envirocare's requests for a hearing and for leave to intervene in both cases, and in separate opinions several months apart, the Commission affirmed.

With respect to the proceedings to amend Quivira's license, the Commission ruled that Envirocare did not come within the following "standing" provision in the Atomic Energy Act: when the Commission institutes a proceeding for the granting or amending of a license, "the Commission shall grant a hearing upon the request of any person whose interest may be affected by the proceeding, and shall admit any such person as a party to such proceeding." In determining whether Envirocare possessed the requisite "interest" under this provision, the Commission looked to "current judicial concepts of standing." Envirocare alleged economic injury, claiming that the less stringent application of regulations to Quivira placed Envirocare at a competitive disadvantage. This allegation was sufficient, the Commission held, to meet the injury-in-fact requirements of constitutional standing. On the question of prudential standing, however, the Commission determined that "Envirocare's purely competitive interests, unrelated to any radiological harm to itself, do not bring it within the zone of interests of the AEA for the purpose of policing the license requirements of a competitor."

With respect to International Uranium's license, the Commission agreed with the Licensing Board that the case was "on all fours" with *Quivira*. As in that case, Envirocare's injury from International Uranium's competition was not within the Atomic Energy Act's zone of interests. In addition, the Commission made explicit its view that judicial standing doctrines were not controlling in the administrative context and that its duty was to interpret the "interest[s]" Congress intended to recognize in § 2239(a)(1)(A): "Our understanding of the AEA requires us to insist that a competitor's pecuniary aim of imposing additional regulatory restrictions or burdens on fellow market participants does not fall within those 'interests' that trigger a right to hearing and intervention under [§ 2239(a)(1)(A)]."

II

Envirocare spends all of its time arguing that in light of decisions of the Supreme Court and of this court, its status as a competitor satisfies the "zone of interests" test for standing. . . . We shall assume that Envirocare is correct. It does not follow that the Commission erred in refusing the company's motions for a hearing and for leave to intervene, at least in regard to International Uranium's license amendment. The Commission rightly pointed out, in *International Uranium* and in *Quivira*, that it is not an Article III court and thus is not bound to follow the law of standing derived from the "case or controversy" requirement. Judicially-devised prudential standing requirements, of which the "zone of interests" test is one, are also inapplicable to an administrative agency acting within the jurisdiction Congress assigned to it. The doctrine of prudential standing, like that derived from the Constitution, rests on considerations "about the proper—and properly limited—role of the courts in a democratic society."

Whether the Commission erred in excluding Envirocare from participating in International Uranium's licensing proceeding therefore turns not on judicial decisions dealing with standing to sue, but on familiar principles of administrative law regarding an agency's interpretation of the statutes it alone administers. *See Chevron U.S.A. Inc. v. Natural Resources Defense Council, Inc.*, 467 U.S. 837 (1984). The governing provision—42 U.S.C. § 2239(a)(1)(A)—requires the Commission to hold a hearing "on the request of any person whose interest may be affected by the proceeding" and to allow such a person to intervene.[3]

The term "interest" is not defined in the Act and it is scarcely self-defining. It could mean merely an academic or organizational interest in a problem or subject. . . . Or an interest in avoiding economic harm or in gaining an economic benefit from agency action directed at others. . . . Or an "interest" in "aesthetic, conservational

---

3. Although it appears that the Administrative Procedure Act applies to the Nuclear Regulatory Commission, Envirocare has not invoked the APA's administrative standing provision, which reads: "So far as the orderly conduct of public business permits, an interested person may appear before an agency or its responsible employees for the presentation, adjustment, or determination of an issue, request or controversy in a proceeding." 5 U.S.C. § 555(b). Commentators have noted that the role of § 555(b) is unclear and very few courts have attempted to delineate its scope. One scholar, relying on the prefatory language of the provision, argues that § 555(b) does not create "an absolute, or even a conditional, right to be a party." David L. Shapiro, *Some Thoughts on Intervention Before Courts, Agencies, and Arbitrators*, 81 HARV. L. REV. 721, 766 (1968). We express no view on whether § 555(b) would bring about a result different than the one reached by the Commission in its *International Uranium* opinion interpreting § 2239(a)(1)(A).

and recreational values." Or all of these. But whatever the judicial mind thinks of today as an "interest" affected by a proceeding is not necessarily what Congress meant when it enacted this provision in 1954. At the time, judicial notions of standing were considerably more restrictive than they are now. . . . It was not until the late 1950s that some decisions of this court began expanding the category of persons entitled to participate in agency proceedings on the theory that anyone who had standing to seek judicial review should have administrative standing. *See, e.g., Office of Communication of United Church of Christ v. FCC*, 359 F.2d 994, 1000–06 (D.C. Cir. 1966). (We will have more to say about these cases in a moment.)

Because we cannot be confident of what kinds of interests the 1954 Congress meant to recognize in §2239(a)(1)(A)—because, in other words, the statute is ambiguous—the Commission's interpretation of this provision must be sustained if it is reasonable. We think it is. For one thing, excluding competitors who allege only economic injury from the class of persons entitled to intervene in licensing proceedings is consistent with the Atomic Energy Act. The Act meant to increase private competition in the industry, not limit it. Before its passage in 1954, the federal government completely controlled nuclear energy. Through the Act, Congress sought to foster a private nuclear industry for peaceful purposes. In order to ensure that private industry would not undermine nuclear safety, the Act created an agency—what is today the Nuclear Regulatory Commission—to regulate the private sector. One of the Commission's statutory duties is authorizing the transfer and receipt of radioactive byproduct material. The statute describes the Commission's responsibility in this area as follows: "The Commission shall insure that the management of any byproduct material . . . is carried out in such a manner as the Commission deems appropriate to protect the public health and safety and the environment from radiological and nonradiological hazards associated with the processing and with the possession and transfer of such material. . . ."

Nothing in this provision, or in the rest of the Act, indicates that the license requirement was intended to protect market participants from new entrants. Envirocare points to the Act's policy statement which mentions "strengthen[ing] free competition in private enterprise." This statement refers to the Act's goal of creating a private nuclear energy industry. Allowing new competitors to enter the market strengthens competition. Permitting current license holders to initiate hearings for the purpose of imposing burdens on potential competitors does the opposite.

In rendering its interpretation of §2239(a)(1)(A), the Commission also properly took account of regulatory burdens on the agency. It wrote: "Competitors, though, whose only 'interest' is lost business opportunities, could readily burden our adjudicatory process with open-ended allegations designed not to advance public health and safety but as a dilatory tactic to interfere with and impose costs upon a competitor. Such an abuse of our hearing process would significantly divert limited agency resources, which ought to be squarely—genuinely—focused upon health and safety concerns." The Commission's concerns are not limited to byproduct disposal licenses. Those are only one of the many types of licenses the Commission grants. . . .

For these reasons, the view the Commission expressed in its *International Uranium* opinion—that competitors asserting economic injury do not demonstrate the type of interest necessary under § 2239(a)(1)(A)—is a permissible construction of the statute. And it appears to be a construction the Commission has adhered to for some time. The Commission stated that it has long been its practice to deny requests for a hearing under § 2239(a)(1)(A) when the petitioner alleged only economic injury. Envirocare has cited nothing to the contrary. In any event, even if the Commission's refusal to follow the developing law of judicial standing had been a departure from its usual practice, it gave adequate reasons for changing course.

We mentioned earlier several decisions of this court indicating that agencies should allow administrative standing to those who can meet judicial standing requirements: *Office of Communication of United Church of Christ v. FCC*, 359 F.2d 994, 1000–06 (D.C. Cir. 1966) [other decisions omitted]. None of these cases interpreted the administrative standing provision of the Atomic Energy Act. All were decided before *Chevron* and for that reason alone cannot control our decision today. Furthermore, despite some broad language in *Office of Communication* about administrative standing, the agency there equated standing to appear before it with standing to obtain judicial review and so the court had no occasion to examine whether the two concepts might be distinct. . . . In any event, as we have said, all of these cases were pre-*Chevron*. Judged by current law, none gave sufficient weight to the agency's interpretation of the statute governing intervention in its administrative proceedings.

Notes

1. Intervention in administrative adjudications. The concept of "intervention" is not unknown to private litigation. Anyone has a right to intervene as a party in federal court, for example, if they have an "interest relating to the property or transaction which is the subject of the action and the applicant is so situated that the disposition of the action may as a practical matter impair or impede the applicant's ability to protect that interest, unless the applicant's interest is adequately represented by existing parties." Fed. R. Civ. P. 24(a). Intervention is far from the norm, however, in private litigation because the "property or transaction" at issue is usually limited to the original participants. By contrast, intervention is quite common in administrative proceedings, which frequently involve issues affecting the broader public interest. On these issues, the party to the adjudication may not adequately represent all the potential effected interests.

> [S]ometimes adjudication should be made more like rule making. While an agency may well be justified in preferring to formulate its policies on a case-by-case basis rather than by rule making, safeguards may be necessary to ensure that non-parties to the adjudication who may be significantly affected by the new policy receive notice and have an opportunity to be heard. Such safeguards are desirable not only to protect individual rights but also to give the agency the benefit of pertinent facts, arguments, and

considerations which might not be before it but which interested persons could contribute. Nothing in the APA would prevent an agency engaged in a formal adjudication from giving public notice that the adjudication may result in the adoption of a new or significantly altered principle or policy which would have application beyond the parties to the proceeding. Neither would the Act prohibit an agency from making available an appropriate means for interested persons to participate. The notice should be given at that point in the proceeding when it first becomes clear that the adoption of such a new or significantly altered principle or policy becomes an issue or is proposed by the agency as a basis for its decision.

Brice Clagett, *Informal Action Adjudication—Rulemaking: Some Recent Developments in Federal Administrative Law*, 1971 Duke L.J. 51, 83–85.

The broad participation advocated in the above excerpt is central to what has become known as the public interest representation model of administrative law. Described in detail in Richard B. Stewart, *The Reformation of American Administrative Law*, 88 Harv. L. Rev. 1667 (1975), the public interest representation model envisioned the administrative process as, in large part, a resolution of conflicting private interests. This contrasts with an earlier vision of the administrative state as an expert, unbiased institution capable of fairly resolving public issues for all concerned. Increased intervention in administrative proceedings was one aspect of the growing influence of the public interest model. As with all pendulums, this one has swung to the point of generating criticism of the adverse effects of widespread interventions. The *Envirocare* decision may be seen as one example.

2. *Office of Communication*—a seminal decision on intervention. One of the earliest and most influential administrative intervention decisions was *Office of Communication of the United Church of Christ v. FCC*, 359 F.2d 994 (D.C. Cir. 1966), which involved a challenge to the renewal of a television station license in Mississippi. The petitioners argued that the license should be denied because the station had consistently presented biased coverage of racial issues and had otherwise failed to serve the public interest. The FCC denied intervention, limiting standing to those suffering economic injury or electrical interference. The court responded with an endorsement of liberal participation by those affected by agency decisions:

> It is important to remember that the cases allowing standing to those falling within either of the two established categories have emphasized that standing is accorded to persons not for the protection of their private interest but only to vindicate the public interest.

> . . . .

> The theory that the Commission can always effectively represent the listener interests in a renewal proceeding without the aid and participation of legitimate listener representatives fulfilling the role of private attorneys general is one of those assumptions we collectively try to work with so long as they are reasonably adequate. When it becomes clear, as it does to us

now, that it is no longer a valid assumption which stands up under the realities of actual experience, neither we nor the Commission can continue to rely on it. The gradual expansion and evolution of concepts of standing in administrative law attests that experience rather than logic or fixed rules has been accepted as the guide.

. . . .

Unless the Commission is to be given staff and resources to perform the enormously complex and prohibitively expensive task of maintaining constant surveillance over every licensee, some mechanism must be developed so that the legitimate interests of listeners can be made a part of the record which the Commission evaluates.

. . . .

The responsible and representative groups eligible to intervene cannot here be enumerated or categorized specifically; such community organizations as civic associations, professional societies, unions, churches, and educational institutions or associations might well be helpful to the Commission. These groups are found in every community; they usually concern themselves with a wide range of community problems and tend to be representatives of broad as distinguished from narrow interests, public as distinguished from private or commercial interests.

The Commission should be accorded broad discretion in establishing and applying rules for such public participation, including rules for determining which community representatives are to be allowed to participate and how many are reasonably required to give the Commission the assistance it needs in vindicating the public interest. The usefulness of any particular petitioner for intervention must be judged in relation to other petitioners and the nature of the claims it asserts as basis for standing. Moreover, it is no novelty in the administrative process to require consolidation of petitions and briefs to avoid multiplicity of parties and duplication of effort.

The fears of regulatory agencies that their processes will be inundated by expansion of standing criteria are rarely borne out. Always a restraining factor is the expense of participation in the administrative process, an economic reality which will operate to limit the number of those who will seek participation; legal and related expenses of administrative proceedings are such that even those with large economic interests find the costs burdensome. Moreover, the listening public seeking intervention in a license renewal proceeding cannot attract lawyers to represent their cause by the prospect of lucrative contingent fees, as can be done, for example, in rate cases.

We are aware that there may be efforts to exploit the enlargement of intervention, including spurious petitions from private interests not concerned with the quality of broadcast programming, since such private interests may sometimes cloak themselves with a semblance of public interest advocates. But this problem, as we have noted, can be dealt with by the Commission under its inherent powers and by rulemaking.

The court in *Office of Communication* spoke in very general terms about the benefits of broad public participation. Several points are worth noting. First, the court envisions intervention not only as a means of protecting private interests, but as a way to "vindicate the public interest." Second, the court is clearly skeptical of the agency's ability to achieve the public interest without broader input, due to both limited agency resources and the likelihood of an effective campaign by the license applicant. Third, the court suggests that broad agency discretion in both the recognition of particular intervenors and control of the proceedings themselves would avoid the alleged burdens of broad participation. The *Citizens Awareness Network* decision, excerpted in subchapter 4A.3 above, is an example of an agency's effective use of its discretion to manage administrative adjudications.

3. Statutes as the source of intervention rights. As discussed in a footnote to the *Envirocare* decision, § 555(b) of the APA provides that: "So far as the orderly conduct of public business permits, an interested person may appear before an agency or its responsible employees for the presentation, adjustment, or determination of an issue, request, or controversy in a proceeding. . . ." Some have suggested that this grants a right to intervene in agency proceedings. The *Envirocare* court declined to reach that argument. It seems likely that § 555(b) may authorize appearance before the agency, perhaps through written submissions or otherwise at the agency's discretion, but not full party status in administrative adjudications.

Note that the *Envirocare* decision itself hinges on the particular language and purposes of the Atomic Energy Act. Analysis of Wrath of Grapes's proposed intervention would similarly depend upon the language and purposes of the WTCA. How do the two differ?

One important difference between the two situations involves the nature of the agency decision. *Envirocare* involved a proposal to license a new facility, while the Wrath of Grapes has petitioned to intervene in an enforcement proceeding. Would you expect the Wrath of Grapes to have a stronger or weaker argument for intervention here than it would in a licensing proceeding? Consider *Bellotti v. United States Nuclear Regulatory Commission*, 725 F.2d 1380 (D.C. Cir. 1983), in which the NRC initiated an enforcement proceeding to amend a reactor license and require the utility in question to improve its performance. The Attorney General of Massachusetts petitioned to intervene to oppose continued operation of the reactor and to argue for more stringent measures. The court upheld the Commission's denial of intervention on the ground that the agency had the authority to determine the scope of the enforcement proceeding:

> We have no doubt that, as a general matter, such authority must reside in the Commission. To read the statute very broadly so that any proceeding necessarily implicates all issues that might be raised concerning the facility

in question would deluge the Commission with intervenors and expand many proceedings into virtually interminable, free-ranging investigations.

Id. at 1381. The court further explained that intervention would continue to be automatic for those who would be affected by changes to the license that reduce safety requirements. Such changes would not be in the nature of enforcement proceedings, but would be more akin to the original licensing decision. By contrast, where, as in an enforcement proceeding, the Commission acts to strengthen safety requirements, it has the discretion to deny intervention to those arguing that the requirements should be even more stringent. Parties like the Attorney General in *Bellotti*, or Wrath of Grapes here, would still have the right to petition the agency for changes they consider necessary to protect the public interest. *See* 5 U.S.C. § 555(e).

4. Managing intervention. If Bud allows the Wrath of Grapes to intervene, may he or should he limit the extent of its participation? If so, what limits should he prescribe? The APA limits intervention only "[s]o far as the orderly conduct of public business permits." The 2010 MSAPA requires a presiding officer to grant intervention if there is a statutory right to intervene or if the petitioner "has an interest that may be adversely affected by the outcome of the case and that interest is not adequately represented by existing parties." It also provides for permissive intervention in some circumstances. In either case, the 2010 MSAPA provides that, "[a] presiding officer may impose conditions at any time on an intervener's participation in the contested case." Basically, the presiding official has a great deal of discretion in both systems. What are the competing interests involved in the decision to permit intervention? What should the form of the intervention be? Consider the variety of possibilities. The possibilities vary from admitting the intervenor with the full rights of a party to some limited ability to submit written material on a narrow issue. What considerations should affect the decision to permit intervention and, if permitted, what should the form of the intervention be?

5. Is the Wrath of Grapes entitled to counsel? With respect to Abby's request to prevent Fred from representing the Wrath of Grapes, a threshold question would be whether there is a due process or statutory right to such representation. As we will see in subchapter 4B, it is unlikely that the Wrath of Grapes has a property or liberty interest that would trigger due process in this context. Even where due process applies, however, the Supreme Court has not been particularly committed to the proposition that due process includes the right to counsel in the administrative context. For example, in a prison discipline case, *Wolff v. McDonnell*, 418 U.S. 539, 561, 570 (1974), the Court said:

> The insertion of counsel into the disciplinary process would inevitably give the proceedings a more adversary cast and tend to reduce their utility as a means to further correctional goals. There would also be delay and very practical problems in providing counsel in sufficient numbers at the time and place where hearings are to be held. At this stage of the development of these procedures we are not prepared to hold that inmates have a right to either retained or appointed counsel in disciplinary proceedings.

Where an illiterate inmate is involved, however, or where the complexity of the issue makes it unlikely that the inmate will be able to collect and present the evidence necessary for an adequate comprehension of the case, he should be free to seek the aid of a fellow inmate, or if that is forbidden, to have adequate substitute aid in the form of help from the staff or from a sufficiently competent inmate designated by the staff.

What about the APA? Does it establish a right to be represented by counsel? Consider 5 U.S.C. § 555(b).

6. Can Fred represent the Wrath of Grapes? But in this case may the WTC bar Fred, the attorney for the Wrath of Grapes, from participating in this proceeding? The right to representation implies the right to representation of one's choice. *SEC v. Csapo*, 533 F.2d 7 (D.C. Cir. 1976). An agency's effort to disqualify an attorney necessarily limits that choice and hence these efforts are carefully reviewed. What behavior by counsel will warrant exclusion from the hearing? In *Ubiotica Corp. v. FDA*, 427 F.2d 376 (6th Cir. 1970), the exclusion of petitioner's counsel from oral participation in the hearing was found justified. Petitioner was not denied a fair hearing when his counsel was excluded due to dilatory, recalcitrant, obstructive, and contemptuous behavior, and the hearing was recessed to allow petitioner to obtain other counsel and to provide new counsel an opportunity to familiarize himself with the case.

In Fred's case, the problem isn't his personal behavior, but the fact that he has recently served on the Commission. The APA does not speak to this issue, but the Ethics in Government Act (key provisions at 18 U.S.C. § 207) limits the ability of government employees to appear before the agency in which they served. How does § 207 apply to Fred's representation of the Wrath of Grapes?

7. Should the government pay for representation? Are there circumstances in which the government should cover the cost of representation? Neither the Due Process Clause nor the APA requires counsel to be provided. The Equal Access to Justice Act (EAJA) provides fees to a party who prevails in some agency adjudications, as well as in court proceedings. But that may not be enough for a party with few resources. If you were an agency head, would there be circumstances in which you might fund the cost of participation in agency proceedings?

5. Managing the Hearing — Evidence and Standard of Proof

We now move to the hearing itself. Beware of your trial-based instincts as you consider what evidence should be admissible in administrative hearings. The following materials address both the question of admissibility and the question of adequacy to support a decision. We will see that question again when we reach judicial review.

Lesson 4A.5. Recall from Lesson 4A.4 that the WTC has charged Gallery with adding cane sugar to its wines without disclosing that fact, thus violating § 5(b) of the Act by "omit[ting] to state a material fact necessary in order to make the statements made, in light of the circumstances under which they were made, not misleading."

In preparing to support these charges, Ralph has discovered a body of work by the most eminent wine chemist in the world showing that adding cane sugar to promote fermentation significantly affects the quality of the wine. A paper written by the French chemist concludes that "adding sugar would destroy the purity and bouquet of the wine." Unfortunately, the chemist will not travel outside of France, and there is no way to compel him to do so. Therefore, Ralph wants to have an American wine chemist testify to explain the French chemist's detailed analysis of the substantial physical changes caused by the addition of cane sugar.

Abby, Gallery's counsel, wants to exclude that testimony as hearsay and because she will not be able to cross-examine the French chemist. She also hopes to make it as difficult as possible for Bud the ALJ to rule against Gallery. Accordingly, she would like to argue that, given the seriousness of the charges and their potential impact on Gallery's business, the WTC should have to prove them by clear and convincing evidence. She also contemplates arguing that the French chemist's analysis, at least viewed in isolation, cannot constitute "substantial evidence" sufficient to prove his findings.

Is Abby right about any of this?

Background of *Richardson v. Perales*

The following decision involved a dispute over a claim of disability. As is typical for such cases, much of the evidence takes the form of written reports from various physicians. At least some of those physicians have usually examined the claimant, but often physicians submit reports based upon information provided to them by other physicians. The question here is whether these various reports are admissible, and if they are, whether they are sufficient to support the agency's decision.

Richardson v. Perales
402 U.S. 389 (1971)

MR. JUSTICE BLACKMUN delivered the opinion of the Court.

In 1966 Pedro Perales, a San Antonio truck driver, then aged 34, height 5' 11", weight about 220 pounds, filed a claim for disability insurance benefits under the Social Security Act. [The Act provides that] the term "disability" means "inability to engage in any substantial gainful activity by reason of any medically determinable physical or mental impairment. . . ." [and] Section 205 (g) relating to judicial review, states, "The findings of the Secretary as to any fact, if supported by substantial evidence, shall be conclusive . . . ."

The issue here is whether physicians' written reports of medical examinations they have made of a disability claimant may constitute "substantial evidence" supportive of a finding of nondisability, within the § 205(g) standard, when the claimant objects to the admissibility of those reports and when the only live testimony is presented by his side and is contrary to the reports.

I

In his claim Perales asserted that on September 29, 1965, he became disabled as a result of an injury to his back sustained in lifting an object at work. He was seen by a neurosurgeon, Dr. Ralph A. Munslow, who first recommended conservative treatment. When this provided no relief, myelography was performed and surgery for a possible protruded intervertebral disc at L-5 was advised. The patient at first hesitated about surgery. . . . The patient was discharged from Dr. Munslow's care on January 25, 1966, with a final diagnosis of "Neuritis, lumbar, mild."

Mr. Perales continued to complain, but Dr. Munslow and Dr. Morris H. Lampert, a neurologist called in consultation, were still unable to find any objective neurological explanation for his complaints. Dr. Munslow advised that he return to work.

In April 1966 Perales consulted Dr. Max Morales, Jr., a general practitioner of San Antonio. Dr. Morales hospitalized the patient from April 15 to May 2. His final discharge diagnosis was: "Back sprain, lumbo-sacral spine."

Perales then filed his claim. As required by § 221 of the Act the claim was referred to the state agency for determination. The agency obtained the hospital records and a report from Dr. Morales. The report set forth no physical findings or laboratory studies, but the doctor again gave as his diagnosis: "Back sprain—lumbo-sacral spine," this time "moderately severe," with "Ruptured disk not ruled out." The agency arranged for a medical examination, at no cost to the patient, by Dr. John H. Langston, an orthopedic surgeon. This was done May 25.

Dr. Langston's ensuing report to the Division of Disability Determination was devastating from the claimant's standpoint. . . . Dr. Langston found no abnormalities of the lumbar spine. . . .

The agency again reviewed the file. The Bureau of Disability Insurance of the Social Security Administration made its independent review. The report and opinion of Dr. Morales, as the claimant's attending physician, were considered, as were those of the other examining physicians. The claim was again denied.

Perales requested a hearing before a hearing examiner. . . .

The requested hearing was set for January 12, 1967, in San Antonio. Written notice thereof was given the claimant with a copy to his attorney. The notice contained a definition of disability, advised the claimant that he should bring all medical and other evidence not already presented, afforded him an opportunity to examine all documentary evidence on file prior to the hearing, and told him that he might bring his own physician or other witnesses and be represented at the hearing by a lawyer.

. . . The attorney formally objected to the introduction of the several reports of Drs. Langston, Bailey, Mattson, and Lampert, and of the hospital records. Various grounds of objection were asserted, including hearsay [and] absence of an opportunity for cross-examination. . . .

At the two hearings oral testimony was submitted by claimant Perales, by Dr. Morales, by a former fellow employee of the claimant, by a vocational expert, and by Dr. Lewis A. Leavitt, a physician board-certified in physical medicine and rehabilitation, and chief of, and professor in, the Department of Physical Medicine at Baylor University College of Medicine. Dr. Leavitt was called by the hearing examiner as an independent "medical adviser," that is, as an expert who does not examine the claimant but who hears and reviews the medical evidence and who may offer an opinion. The adviser is paid a fee by the Government. The claimant, through his counsel, objected to any testimony by Dr. Leavitt not based upon examination or upon a hypothetical. Dr. Leavitt testified over this objection and was cross-examined by the claimant's attorney. He stated that the consensus of the various medical reports was that Perales had a mild low-back syndrome of musculo-ligamentous origin.

The hearing examiner, in reliance upon the several medical reports and the testimony of Dr. Leavitt, observed in his written decision, "There is objective medical evidence of impairment which the heavy preponderance of the evidence indicates to be of mild severity. . . . Taken altogether, the Hearing Examiner is of the conclusion that the claimant has not met the burden of proof." . . .

. . . .

II

We therefore are presented with the not uncommon situation of conflicting medical evidence. The trier of fact has the duty to resolve that conflict. We have, on the one hand, an absence of objective findings, an expressed suspicion of only functional complaints, of malingering, and of the patient's unwillingness to do anything about remedying an unprovable situation. We have, on the other hand, the claimant's and his personal physician's earnest pleas that significant and disabling residuals from the mishap of September 1965 are indeed present.

The issue revolves, however, around a system which produces a mass of medical evidence in report form. May material of that kind ever be "substantial evidence" when it stands alone and is opposed by live medical evidence and the client's own contrary personal testimony? The courts below have held that it may not.

III

The Social Security Act has been with us since 1935. It affects nearly all of us. The system's administrative structure and procedures, with essential determinations numbering into the millions, are of a size and extent difficult to comprehend. But, as the Government's brief here accurately pronounces, 'Such a system must be fair — and it must work.'

Congress has provided that the Secretary

'shall have full power and authority to make rules and regulations and to establish procedures . . . necessary or appropriate to carry out such provisions, and shall adopt reasonable and proper rules and regulations to regulate and provide for the nature and extent of the proofs and evidence and the method of taking and furnishing the same in order to establish the right to benefits hereunder.' s 205(a), 42 U.S.C. s 405(a).

Section 205(b) directs the Secretary to make findings and decisions; on request to give reasonable notice and opportunity for a hearing; and in the course of any hearing to receive evidence. It then provides:

> "Evidence may be received at any hearing before the Secretary even though inadmissible under rules of evidence applicable to court procedure."

In carrying out these statutory duties the Secretary has adopted regulations that state, among other things:

> 'The hearing examiner shall inquire fully into the matters at issue and shall receive in evidence the testimony of witnesses and any documents which are relevant and material to such matters. . . . The . . . procedure at the hearing generally . . . shall be in the discretion of the hearing examiner and of such nature as to afford the parties a reasonable opportunity for a fair hearing.' 20 C.F.R. s 404.927.

From this it is apparent that (a) the Congress granted the Secretary the power by regulation to establish hearing procedures; (b) strict rules of evidence, applicable in the courtroom, are not to operate at social security hearings so as to bar the admission of evidence otherwise pertinent; and (c) the conduct of the hearing rests generally in the examiner's discretion. There emerges an emphasis upon the informal rather than the formal. This, we think, is as it should be, for this administrative procedure, and these hearings, should be understandable to the layman claimant, should not necessarily be stiff and comfortable only for the trained attorney, and should be liberal and not strict in tone and operation. This is the obvious intent of Congress so long as the procedures are fundamentally fair.

IV

With this background and this atmosphere in mind, we turn to the statutory standard of 'substantial evidence' prescribed by s 205(g). The Court has considered this very concept in other, yet similar, contexts. The National Labor Relations Act, s 10(e), in its original form, provided that the NLRB's findings of fact 'if supported by evidence, shall be conclusive.' 49 Stat. 454. The Court said this meant 'supported by substantial evidence' and that this was

> 'more than a mere scintilla. It means such relevant evidence as a reasonable mind might accept as adequate to support a conclusion.' *Consolidated Edison Co. v. NLRB*, 305 U.S. 197, 229 (1938).

V

We may accept the propositions advanced by the claimant, some of them long established, that procedural due process is applicable to the adjudicative administrative proceeding involving "the differing rules of fair play, which through the years, have become associated with differing types of proceedings." . . .

The question, then, is as to what procedural due process requires with respect to examining physicians' reports in a social security disability claim hearing.

We conclude that a written report by a licensed physician who has examined the claimant and who sets forth in his report his medical findings in his area of competence may be received as evidence in a disability hearing and, despite its hearsay character and an absence of cross-examination, and despite the presence of opposing direct medical testimony and testimony by the claimant himself, may constitute substantial evidence supportive of a finding by the hearing examiner adverse to the claimant, when the claimant has not exercised his right to subpoena the reporting physician and thereby provide himself with the opportunity for cross-examination of the physician.

We are prompted to this conclusion by a number of factors that, we feel, assure underlying reliability and probative value:

1. The identity of the five reporting physicians is significant. Each report presented here was prepared by a practicing physician who had examined the claimant. A majority (Drs. Langston, Bailey, and Mattson) were called into the case by the state agency. Although each received a fee, that fee is recompense for his time and talent otherwise devoted to private practice or other professional assignment. We cannot, and do not, ascribe bias to the work of these independent physicians, or any interest on their part in the outcome of the administrative proceeding beyond the professional curiosity a dedicated medical man possesses.

2. The vast workings of the social security administrative system make for reliability and impartiality in the consultant reports. We bear in mind that the agency operates essentially, and is intended so to do, as an adjudicator and not as an advocate or adversary. This is the congressional plan. We do not presume on this record to say that it works unfairly.

3. One familiar with medical reports and the routine of the medical examination, general or specific, will recognize their elements of detail and of value. . . .

These are routine, standard, and unbiased medical reports by physician specialists concerning a subject whom they had seen. That the reports were adverse to Perales' claim is not in itself bias or an indication of nonprobative character.

4. The reports present the impressive range of examination to which Perales was subjected. . . .

5. So far as we can detect, there is no inconsistency whatsoever in the reports of the five specialists. Yet each result was reached by independent examination in the writer's field of specialized training.

6. Although the claimant complains of the lack of opportunity to cross-examine the reporting physicians, he did not take advantage of the opportunity afforded him . . . to request subpoenas for the physicians. . . .

7. Courts have recognized the reliability and probative worth of written medical reports even in formal trials and, while acknowledging their hearsay character, have admitted them as an exception to the hearsay rule. . . .

8. Past treatment by reviewing courts of written medical reports in social security disability cases is revealing. . . . The courts have reviewed administrative determinations, and upheld many adverse ones, where the only supporting evidence has been reports of this kind, buttressed sometimes, but often not, by testimony of a medical adviser such as Dr. Leavitt. In these cases admissibility was not contested, but the decisions do demonstrate traditional and ready acceptance of the written medical report in social security disability cases.

9. There is an additional and pragmatic factor which, although not controlling, deserves mention. This is what Chief Judge Brown has described as "[t]he sheer magnitude of that administrative burden," and the resulting necessity for written reports without "elaboration through the traditional facility of oral testimony." With over 20,000 disability claim hearings annually, the cost of providing live medical testimony at those hearings, where need has not been demonstrated by a request for a subpoena, over and above the cost of the examinations requested by hearing examiners, would be a substantial drain on the trust fund and on the energy of physicians already in short supply.

VI

1. Perales relies heavily on the Court's holding and statements in *Goldberg v. Kelly*, [397 U.S. 254 (1970)], particularly the comment that due process requires notice 'and an effective opportunity to defend by confronting any adverse witnesses . . . .' Kelly, however, had to do with termination of AFDC [welfare] benefits without prior notice. It also concerned a situation, the Court said, 'where credibility and veracity are at issue, as they must be in many termination proceedings.'

The Perales proceeding is not the same. We are not concerned with termination of disability benefits once granted. Neither are we concerned with a change of status without notice. Notice was given to claimant Perales. The physicians' reports were on file and available for inspection by the claimant and his counsel. And the authors of those reports were known and were subject to subpoena and to the very cross-examination that the claimant asserts he has not enjoyed. Further, the specter of questionable credibility and veracity is not present; there is professional disagreement with the medical conclusions, to be sure, but there is no attack here upon the doctors' credibility or veracity. Kelly affords little comfort to the claimant.

2. Perales also, as the Court of Appeals stated, would describe the medical reports in question as 'mere uncorroborated hearsay' and would relate this to Mr. Chief Justice Hughes' sentence in *Consolidated Edison Co. v. NLRB*: 'Mere uncorroborated hearsay or rumor does not constitute substantial evidence.'

Although the reports are hearsay in the technical sense, because their content is not produced live before the hearing examiner, we feel that the claimant and the Court of Appeals read too much into the single sentence from *Consolidated Edison*.

The contrast the Chief Justice was drawing, at the very page cited, was not with material that would be deemed formally inadmissible in judicial proceedings but with material "without a basis in evidence having rational probative force." This was not a blanket rejection by the Court of administrative reliance on hearsay irrespective of reliability and probative value. The opposite was the case.

3. The claimant, the District Court, and the Court of Appeals also criticize the use of Dr. Leavitt as a medical adviser. Inasmuch as medical advisers are used in approximately 13% of disability claim hearings, comment as to this practice is indicated. We see nothing "reprehensible" in the practice, as the claimant would describe it. The trial examiner is a layman; the medical adviser is a board-certified specialist. He is used primarily in complex cases for explanation of medical problems in terms understandable to the layman-examiner. He is a neutral adviser. This particular record discloses that Dr. Leavitt explained the technique and significance of electromyography. He did offer his own opinion on the claimant's condition. That opinion, however, did not differ from the medical reports. Dr. Leavitt did not vouch for the accuracy of the facts assumed in the reports. No one understood otherwise. We see nothing unconstitutional or improper in the medical adviser concept and in the presence of Dr. Leavitt in this administrative hearing.

4. Finally, the claimant complains of the system of processing disability claims. He suggests, and is joined in this by the briefs of amici, that the Administrative Procedure Act, rather than the Social Security Act, governs the processing of claims and specifically provides for cross-examination, 5 U.S.C. s 556(d). (1964 ed., Supp. V). . . .

We need not decide whether the APA has general application to social security disability claims, for the social security administrative procedure does not vary from that prescribed by the APA. Indeed, the latter is modeled upon the Social Security Act. The cited § 556(d) provides that any documentary evidence "may be received" subject to the exclusion of the irrelevant, the immaterial, and the unduly repetitious. It further provides that a "party is entitled to present his case or defense by oral or documentary evidence . . . and to conduct such cross-examination as may be required for a full and true disclosure of the facts" and in "determining claims for money or benefits . . . an agency may, when a party will not be prejudiced thereby, adopt procedures for the submission of all or part of the evidence in written form."

These provisions conform, and are consistent with, rather than differ from or supersede, the authority given the Secretary by the Social Security Act's §§ 205(a) and (b) "to establish procedures," and "to regulate and provide for the nature and extent of the proofs and evidence and the method of taking and furnishing the same in order to establish the right to benefits," and to receive evidence "even though inadmissible under rules of evidence applicable to court procedure." Hearsay, under either Act, is thus admissible up to the point of relevancy.

The matter comes down to the question of the procedure's integrity and fundamental fairness. We see nothing that works in derogation of that integrity and of that fairness in the admission of consultants' reports, subject as they are to being material and to the use of the subpoena and consequent cross-examination. This precisely fits the statutorily prescribed "cross-examination as may be required for a full and true disclosure of the facts." That is the standard. It is clear and workable and does not fall short of procedural due process.

. . . .

We therefore reverse and remanded for further proceedings. We intimate no view as to the merits. It is for the District Court now to determine whether the Secretary's findings, in the light of all material proffered and admissible, are supported by 'substantial evidence' within the command of s 205(g).

Notes

1. What evidence may be admitted? The *Perales* case actually treats two evidence issues: whether the written medical reports were admissible, and whether they could constitute substantial evidence sufficient to support the hearing examiner's (ALJ's) finding of nondisability on judicial review. The first issue turns on the applicable "rules" of evidence. You may have already studied the Federal Rules of Evidence that would apply to this type of question in federal court. If you have, we are sure you will agree that they are quite complex. Under Federal Rule of Evidence 803(18), Ralph's witness, the American chemist, could testify to explain the French chemist's work if it qualified as a "learned treatise."

Okay, are you ready for the APA's equivalent to the Federal Rules of Evidence? Brace yourself, here it is: Section § 556(d) of the APA provides that "[a]ny oral or documentary evidence may be received, but the agency as a matter of policy shall provide for the exclusion of irrelevant, immaterial, or unduly repetitious evidence." Given the complexities of administrative law, it seems only fair that it should sometimes be simple. But this does raise a question for you: Why is the APA's approach to the admissibility of evidence so radically different from that of the Federal Rules of Evidence?

As usual, the APA provides a default template. Congress has imposed stricter evidentiary rules on some agencies in their enabling acts, and agencies have discretion to adopt such rules on their own accord. *See, e.g.,* 29 C.F.R. § 2200.71 (providing that the Federal Rules of Evidence are applicable for adjudications before the Occupational Safety and Health Review Commission and its ALJs). Several decades ago, Richard Pierce found 280 different rules of evidence among federal agencies. Richard Pierce, *Use of the Federal Rules of Evidence in Federal Agency Adjudications,* 39 ADMIN. L. REV. 1 (1987). The overwhelming majority of them impose little if any restriction on the admission of hearsay, leaving it to the parties to argue over its weight.

2. What about cross-examination? Abby will not, of course, be able to cross-examine the French chemist. What is the extent of the right to cross-examine in the administrative process? In light of APA § 556(d), should Bud refuse to admit the French chemist's study, not because it is hearsay as presented, but because the author cannot be cross-examined?

3. What was the significance of Perales's failure to request subpoenas? In *Perales,* the Supreme Court qualified its holding that the written medical reports could constitute substantial evidence by noting, "the claimant has not exercised his right to subpoena the reporting physician and thereby provide himself with the opportunity for cross-examination of the physician." This qualification raises the question of whether Perales would have had an absolute right as a matter of due process to cross-examine the examining physicians who prepared the reports if he had bothered to subpoena them.

Courts have split on this issue. The Fifth Circuit has held that the better reading of *Perales* "is that by requesting a subpoena, a claimant has the right to cross-examine an examining physician" as a matter of due process. *Lidy v. Sullivan*, 911 F.2d 1075, 1077 (5th Cir. 1990). The Eighth Circuit, by contrast, has applied the balancing test of *Mathews v. Eldridge*, which we discuss in subchapter 4B.2, to conclude that a Social Security disability claimant has only a qualified right to use a subpoena to obtain cross-examination. *Passmore v. Astrue*, 533 F.3d 658, 663 (8th Cir. 2008). The court, using reasoning quite similar to *Perales*, concluded that the testifying physician's discussion of the examining physician's report, along with other medical evidence, was sufficiently reliable that Passmore had no absolute due process right to cross-examine the examining physician. The court went on to conclude that the ALJ in the case had not abused his discretion when he denied Passmore's request for a subpoena on the ground that Passmore had failed to explain "the important facts that the witness or document is expected to prove" that could not be obtained by other means. *See also Vladimirov v. Lynch*, 805 F.3d 955, 962 (10th Cir. 2015) (noting that, in removal proceedings, due process requires procedures that are "enough to insure a fair and reliable result," which does not include an absolute right to cross-examine); *Foxy Lady, Inc. v. City of Atlanta*, 347 F.3d 1332 (11th Cir. 2003) (rejecting claim that due process required that "gentlemen's clubs" have an absolute right to subpoena witnesses for administrative proceedings on revocation of liquor licenses). *But cf. Goldberg v. Kelly*, 397 U.S. 254, 270 (1970) (insisting, in seminal due process case, that, in administrative proceedings for termination of welfare benefits, "welfare recipients must . . . be given an opportunity to confront and cross-examine the witnesses relied upon by the department").

4. Can pure hearsay constitute "substantial evidence" on appeal? Near the opening of *Perales,* the Court characterizes the central issue as "whether physicians' written reports of medical examinations they have made of a disability claimant may constitute 'substantial evidence' supportive of a finding of nondisability, within the §205(g) standard, when the claimant objects to the admissibility of those reports and when the only live testimony is presented by his side and is contrary to the reports." The substantial evidence standard, which we discuss at length in subchapter 5G.1, applies generally to facts that agencies determine through formal adjudications. As *Perales* notes, the blackletter standard is that "substantial evidence" is "such relevant evidence as a reasonable mind might accept as adequate to support a conclusion." In essence, this standard checks whether there is reasonable support for a factual proposition in the record.

In holding that the Secretary's evidence of nondisability could, consistent with procedural due process, be regarded as "substantial," the Court rejected a classic concept of administrative law—the "residuum rule." The residuum rule holds that an agency decision may be based on inadmissible evidence, but some "residuum" of the evidence supporting the agency decision must be admissible in order to withstand judicial review under the substantial evidence test. Rather than rely on this sort of formalism, the Court instead performed a functional analysis, determining that the written medical reports constituted substantial evidence in light of a long list of factors that "assure[d] underlying reliability and probative value."

Of course, just because hearsay can constitute substantial evidence consistent with due process does not mean that all hearsay does. The Eleventh Circuit has declared, "hearsay may constitute substantial evidence in administrative proceedings as long as factors that assure the 'underlying reliability and probative value' of the evidence are present." *Basco v. Machin*, 514 F.3d 1177, 1182 (11th Cir. 2008). Factors bearing on this determination include "whether (1) the out-of-court declarant was not biased and had no interest in the result of the case; (2) the opposing party could have obtained the information contained in the hearsay before the hearing and could have subpoenaed the declarant; (3) the information was not inconsistent on its face; and (4) the information has been recognized by courts as inherently reliable." *Id. See also Hernandez-Guadarrama v. Ashcroft*, 394 F.3d 674, 682 (9th Cir. 2005) (explaining that due process imposes a fundamental fairness test on admission of hearsay; holding removal of alien violated due process where action was based solely on hearsay affidavit of self interested person whom the government had already deported).

5. Can an expert's testimony constitute substantial evidence without also including the underlying data? Suppose, for the sake of argument, that the French chemist did show up and testify at the WTC's enforcement action, but all he did was say, "but of course adding sugar destroys the purity and bouquet of the wine." He does not explain his underlying analysis that led to this conclusion. Can this testimony amount to substantial evidence?

In *Biestek v. Berryhill*, 139 S. Ct. 1148 (2019), the Court addressed a variation on this question that arose in another SSA disability determination. A vocational expert offered testimony concerning jobs that the claimant, Biestek, might be able to perform and the availability of such jobs in the national economy. In response to Biestek's attorney's questioning, the vocational expert explained that she based her numbers on her own individual labor market surveys. Biestek's attorney requested these surveys; the expert declined to supply them, citing confidentiality concerns; the ALJ announced he would not require their production, and the case continued. The ALJ partially denied Biestek's claim based on the vocational expert's testimony on the availability of jobs Biestek could perform.

On appeal, the Supreme Court characterized Biestek as arguing that the vocational expert's testimony "could not possibly constitute such [substantial] evidence because she had declined, upon request, to produce her supporting data." With this characterization in hand, the Court explained:

> Where Biestek goes wrong, at bottom, is in pressing for a categorical rule, applying to every case in which a vocational expert refuses a request for underlying data. Sometimes an expert's withholding of such data, when combined with other aspects of the record, will prevent her testimony from qualifying as substantial evidence. That would be so, for example, if the expert has no good reason to keep the data private and her testimony lacks other markers of reliability. But sometimes the reservation of data will have no such effect. Even though the applicant might wish for the data, the expert's testimony still will clear (even handily so) the more-than-a-mere-scintilla threshold. The inquiry, as is usually true in determining the substantiality of evidence, is case-by-case.

Biestek, 139 S. Ct. at 1157. The Court's holding was thus limited to rejecting a categorical rule requiring disclosure on request; it declined to "decide whether, in the absence of that rule, substantial evidence supported the ALJ in denying [claimant] benefits." *Id.*

6. Who bears the burden of proof? With respect to the burden of proof, § 556(d) of the APA provides that "the proponent of a rule or order has the burden of proof." In *Director, Office of Workers' Compensation Programs v. Greenwich Collieries*, 512 U.S. 267 (1994), the Supreme Court addressed the government's argument that § 556(d) referred only to the burden of going forward, not to the ultimate burden of persuasion. Rejecting that position, the Court held that "as of 1946 the ordinary meaning of burden of proof was burden of persuasion, and we understand the APA's unadorned reference to 'burden of proof' to refer to the burden of persuasion."

7. How great is the burden? The extent of the burden is also governed by § 556(d), which provides that:

> A sanction may not be imposed or rule or order issued except on consideration of the whole record or those parts thereof cited by a party and supported by and in accordance with the reliable, probative, and substantial evidence.

Recall that Abby seeks a heightened standard of proof in light of the seriousness of the charges against Gallery. She asserts that the common law required "clear and convincing evidence" to sustain what amount to charges of fraud. The Supreme Court rejected just this argument in *Steadman v. SEC*, 450 U.S. 91 (1981). Emphasizing *Vermont Yankee*'s admonition that the APA established the "maximum procedural requirements which Congress was willing to have the courts impose upon agencies in conducting rulemaking proceedings," the Court held that SEC proceedings, "subject to [§ 556(d)] of the APA, [are] governed by the preponderance-of-the-evidence standard."

8. The contents of the formal "record." We often refer to "formal" proceedings as "on the record" precisely because they are supposed to produce closed, well-defined records. The federal APA defines the record as "[t]he transcript of testimony and exhibits, together with all papers and requests filed in the proceeding." 5 U.S.C. § 556(e). The 1981 MSAPA § 4-221 lists eleven categories of information that might be included in a formal record. Both provide that this information should be the "exclusive" basis for decision.

The idea of an "exclusive" evidentiary record for decision is easy enough to state, but it becomes more puzzling on inspection. Every decisionmaker has to bring a wealth of background knowledge to the problem of fact finding in order to function. At a certain point, however, application of non-controversial background knowledge (e.g., rain falls from the sky) turns into unacceptable evidentiary assumptions. For instance, in *Razkane v. Holder*, 562 F.3d 1283 (10th Cir. 2009), Razkane requested a restriction on removal on the ground that it was more likely than not that he would be persecuted due to his homosexuality if he were returned to Morocco. The immigration judge (IJ) denied this request because he "found there was nothing in Razkane's appearance that would designate him as being gay because he did not 'dress in an effeminate manner or affect any effeminate mannerisms.'" The Tenth Circuit held that the IJ had improperly "elevated stereotypical assumptions to evidence upon which factual inferences were drawn and legal conclusions made." To support such a conclusion, there must be evidence about how Moroccans would treat Razkane, not about the IJ's impression of him.

9. Adding to the record through official notice. Bud the ALJ asserts at the prehearing conference that he will assume that wine drinkers choose wine on the basis of the quality of the grapes. Abby notes that this "finding" is pretty important and would like to prove otherwise. Ralph counters that proof is not necessary. How would this "evidence" get into the record? Besides being admitted through the process of "proof," information may enter the administrative adjudicative decision through "official notice" or "administrative notice." That is, the decisionmaker may rely on such information without having it introduced as "evidence." Ernest Gellhorn described operation of official notice:

> Official notice, like its judicial notice counterpart, involves reliance by the presiding officer [or examiner] on extra-record information. That is, the examiner in making a decision relies upon facts and opinions not supported by evidence "on the record." . . .
>
> . . . [I]n administrative adjudication, official notice is frequently confused with the process of decision-making. In reaching a conclusion, the examiner or agency may rely on its special skills, whether they include particular expertise in engineering, economics, medicine, or electricity, just as a judge may freely use his legal skills in reading statutes and applying decided cases in the preparation of his opinion. But such evaluations are not within the concept of official notice. Official notice is concerned with the *process of proof*, not with the *evaluation of evidence*. The difference between

an administrative tribunal's use of non-record information included in its expert knowledge, as a substitute for evidence or notice, and its application of its background in evaluating and drawing conclusions from the evidence that is in the record, is primarily a difference of degree rather than of kind. In principle, reliance upon the examiner's knowledge in the process of proof is permissible only within the confines of official notice, whereas the examiner's use of his experience in evaluating "proof" that has been offered is not only unavoidable but, indeed, desirable.

Ernest Gellhorn, *Rules of Evidence and Official Notice in Formal Administrative Hearings*, 1971 Duke L.J. 1.

Regarding the types of facts that are subject to official notice, the Attorney General's Manual on the Administrative Procedure Act (1947) explained:

> The recommendation of the Attorney General's Committee, which is thus apparently adopted was that "the permissible area of official notice be extended" so as to avoid "laborious proof of what is obvious and notorious," subject to rebuttal, as provided in section [556(e)].... [O]fficial notice should not be limited to the traditional matters of judicial notice but extends properly to all matters as to which the agency by reason of its functions is presumed to be expert, such as technical or scientific facts within its specialized knowledge.

Id. at 79–80.

A party that objects to a noticed fact "is entitled, on timely request, to an opportunity to show the contrary." 5 U.S.C. § 556(e). Note also that, independent of the APA, where deprivations of life, liberty, or property are at issue, due process may require a timely opportunity to respond to noticed facts. Regarding due process and official notice, the Ninth Circuit has explained:

> It is not necessary to warn that administrative notice will be taken of the fact that water runs downhill. Some propositions, however, may require that notice not be taken, or that warning be given, or that rebuttal evidence be allowed. The agency's discretion must be exercised in such a way as to be fair in the circumstances.

Castillo-Villagra v. INS, 972 F.2d 1017, 1028 (9th Cir. 1992).

10. How thoroughly must Bud explain his decision? What if the Commission ultimately decides the matter? Having examined the record and considered the various arguments, Bud is ready to prepare his decision. Section 557(c) of the APA provides that:

> All decisions, including initial, recommended, and tentative decisions, are a part of the record and shall include a statement of—
>
> (A) findings and conclusions, and the reasons or basis therefore, on all the material issues of fact, law, or discretion presented on the record....

There is no doubt that Bud must explain his decision, but how extensive should the reasons be? His judgment will be guided in part by the fact that the Commission itself will have ultimate responsibility for the decision. He must provide the detail that will allow the commissioners to understand all of the various issues and to reach their own conclusion. Equally important, if the Commission chooses not to review Bud's decision or otherwise allows it to stand as the decision of the agency, Bud's explanation will have to be sufficient to be sustained on judicial review. Referring to the above language of § 557(c), the Second Circuit wrote:

> The purposes of [§ 557(b)] "are to prevent arbitrary agency decisions, provide parties with a reasoned explanation for those decisions, settle the law for future cases, and furnish a basis for effective judicial review." *Armstrong v. CFTC*, 12 F.3d 401, 403 (3d Cir. 1993). Thus, so long as an agency has "articulate[d] a satisfactory explanation for its action including a 'rational connection between the facts found and the choice made,'" *Motor Vehicle Mfrs. Ass'n*, we will uphold its choice. . . .

Reddy v. Commodity Futures Trading Commission (CFTC), 191 F.3d 109 (2d Cir. 1999).

Since this will be one of the WTC's earliest and most significant decisions, it is highly likely that the Commission itself will take review. If it does, it must assure that a court can determine the basis for the Commission's ultimate conclusions. It can write its own opinion, of course (which can reach conclusions that differ from Bud's), or it can simply adopt Bud's decision as its own. Whatever the Commission does, a court must be able to determine how it resolved the issues. In *Armstrong v. CFTC*, 12 F.3d 401, 404 (3d Cir. 1993), the Third Circuit rejected an agency opinion stating only that "the ALJ reached a substantially correct result." The Third Circuit held "that a summary affirmance of all or part of an ALJ's opinion must leave no guesswork regarding what the agency has adopted. A decision by an ALJ that is only 'substantially correct' should be fully correct by the time an agency imprints its seal of approval."

If the WTC fails to meet the test articulated in *Reddy*, it is very unlikely to prevail on review. Justifications asserted sometime after the final decision are inherently suspect. Thus, courts generally discount "post hoc" rationales or reasons asserted for the first time in a challenge to the agency decision.

6. Appeal within the Agency and the Effect of Previous Judicial Decisions

As reflected in § 556(d) of the APA, an ALJ issues either an initial or recommended decision, with ultimate decisional authority in the head of the agency. Thus, either the agency staff or a private party may appeal some aspect of an ALJ's decision to the agency head. Appellants will naturally try to advance their causes by using any prior agency or judicial decisions that seem favorable. These materials examine the degree to which these past decisions, whether by the agency itself or a court, bind the agency.

Lesson 4A.6. Recall from Lesson 4A.4 that Ralph, as head of the Enforcement Division, charged Gallery with violating §5 of the WTCA by adding cane sugar without disclosure and by using table grapes, rather than the high quality wine grapes claimed on Gallery's label. Ralph also charged Gallery with violating the "special reserve" rule, which provides that wine shall not be labeled "special reserve . . . unless it is distinguishable from the general run of wine sold by that grower in terms of grapes, production process, or other indications of special quality." Ralph based the statutory misrepresentation charge on an enforcement decision the Commission had issued two years before, *Kajun Kabernet*. In this decision, the Commission had declared that misrepresentations or omissions violate §5(b) if they relate to practices that materially and deleteriously affect the quality of wine. Ralph introduced ample evidence to support a finding that Gallery had violated §5(b) as so interpreted by the Commission. Ralph took this position and offered this proof despite the fact that the Fifth Circuit had overruled *Kajun Kabernet*. Based on its reading of both the statutory text and legislative history, the court had concluded that Congress had plainly intended §5(b) to apply only where a misrepresentation or omission materially affects consumers' wine choices. Our favorite ALJ, Bud, followed the Fifth Circuit rather than the Commission. He found, correctly, that Ralph had failed to produce evidence of the effect of Gallery's disclosure practices on consumers. This omission was all the more glaring as Abby, representing Gallery, had produced several consumer preference studies showing that many consumers of the Gallery wine in question preferred its taste to that of wines made with nothing but wine grapes. Accordingly, Bud rejected the charge that Gallery had violated §5 through its misrepresentation and nondisclosure.

As for the special reserve charge, Gallery defended its "special reserve" label on the ground that the special reserve wines were made from grapes grown only in Oregon, while its other wines included grapes from California, Oregon, and Washington. Thus, Gallery argued, its special reserve wines were "distinguishable . . . in terms of grapes," as required by the special reserve rule. In response, Ralph relied on the *Interpretive Bulletin for Implementing the Special Reserve Rule*, which the Commission had issued soon after promulgating the special reserve rule. In the bulletin, the Commission had stated that the regulatory language "in terms of grapes" refers to the type of grape, rather than the geographic region where the grape is grown. Assume Gallery's special reserve wines were not distinguishable from its other wines on this basis.

In his initial decision, Bud correctly concluded that Gallery's special reserve wine did not meet the "type of grape" test set out in the Interpretive Bulletin, but he added that the rule itself, not the Interpretive Bulletin, provided the binding law. Finding that Gallery's marketing of its special reserve wines was consistent with a reasonable construction of the special reserve rule, Bud rejected this charge as well.

Ralph is preparing an appeal to the full Commission, and if he obtains a favorable decision, he naturally expects Gallery to petition for judicial review. In proceedings before the Commission on the statutory charge of misrepresentation and nondisclosure, what will be the significance of the Commission's previous decision in *Kajun Kabernet*? The Fifth Circuit's decision in *Kajun Kabernet*? Will Abby's consumer preference studies be of any help to her? Turning to the "special reserve" charge, how much force should the Interpretive Bulletin have on the agency? Was Bud right when he claimed that the bulletin did not "bind" him?

Suppose Gallery seeks judicial review after the Commission, following its own precedent in *Kajun Kabernet*, rules in favor of the Enforcement Division on the statutory charge. What will be the significance of the Fifth Circuit decision?

Background of *Nielsen Lithographing*

With some frequency, agencies may decide issues that have previously been addressed in the courts. Agencies are bound, of course, by Supreme Court decisions, but, as in the decision that follows, they sometimes reject decisions reached by the District or Circuit Courts. This refusal to follow judicial precedent, known as "non-acquiescence," reflects the distinctive role of agencies in a system of delegated authority.

Nielsen Lithographing Co. v. NLRB
854 F.2d 1063 (7th Cir. 1988)

POSNER, CIRCUIT JUDGE:

In labor negotiations, as in any negotiations, the party with more information has an edge. So when Nielsen Lithographing Company claimed during wage negotiations with its workers' union that it had to reduce wages and benefits in order to remain competitive with other printers, the union asked the company to let its accountants examine the books and other records — financial statements, tax returns, records of compensation paid managerial and supervisory personnel — that would substantiate (or refute) the company's claim of need. . . .

The company refused the demand for access to its books, and the union struck, and later filed charges with the Labor Board, which held that Nielsen's refusal to open its books to the union was an unfair labor practice and ordered Nielsen to cease the practice and rehire the workers who had struck and whom Nielsen had fired. . . .

In *NLRB v. Truitt Mfg. Co.* (1956), the Supreme Court held that it is an unfair labor practice for an employer who claims to be financially incapable of paying a wage increase requested by a union to refuse to let the union see the employer's books for purposes of verifying its claim. . . .

Nielsen, however, never claimed that it was *unable* to pay the existing scale of wages and benefits. It admitted to being profitable but said it wanted to bring its wage bill into line with the wages paid by competitors to whom it was losing sales. A company can survive, certainly in the short run and often in the long run, even though it is paying higher wages than its competitors. The company may have some other cost advantage; its competitors may price above their costs; the market may be expanding rapidly. The company will grow less rapidly than if its costs were lower and may stagnate or decline, but it need not die. There is thus no contradiction in a company's stating on the one hand that it is profitable and on the other hand that its costs are higher than its competitors' and it wants to reduce them. The Board concedes that if this is all Nielsen said, Nielsen had no duty to open its books to the union.

The Board found, however, that Nielsen had done more than express a desire for lower costs and higher profits; that it had said the wage cuts were necessary if the company was to remain competitive and reverse a trend of losing business to lower-cost competitors. The company's president had told the workers that "to survive we must be able to compete. Our business . . . and jobs are at stake if we can not. . . . If we don't [compete] the recent trend of losing even greater amounts of work to other companies will continue and the jobs of our employees will be lost." The Board held that this statement, and others like it, were sufficient under *Truitt* to create a duty of substantiation.

This is not an irrational extension of *Truitt*. A rational businessman is concerned with the long run as well as the short run. He wants to maximize the present value of his company's earnings; and if the company has a dismal future, its expected future earnings, and hence its present value, will be depressed as a result. An employer that in negotiations with its union claims that its wages are out of line with those of its competitors and as a result its future is bleak—however rosy the present may seem—makes a serious and factual claim, one that if true must cause the union to give serious consideration to making the concessions the employer is demanding, or at least making some concessions. Informed bargaining over the issue requires that the union have access to the data from which the company has projected its bleak future.

So at least the Board could reason within the analytical framework established in *Truitt*—so it did reason in this case. The problem is that right after it ruled in favor of the union we decided *NLRB v. Harvstone Mfg. Corp.* (7th Cir. 1986), a case similar to the present one, against the Board. Following earlier circuit precedent, we held that predictions that a business will falter—even that it will close—are "nothing more than truisms" and do not trigger the duty of disclosure under *Truitt*, a duty that we deemed limited to inability to pay during "the term [ordinarily three years] of the new collective bargaining agreement" being negotiated.

The Labor Board in its decision in this case had actually relied on the very decision that we reversed. Nielsen therefore asked for reconsideration but the Board refused, saying: "Respondent filed with the Board a motion for reconsideration contending . . . that the Board's order . . . directly conflicts with a certain decision of the United States [Court of] Appeals for the Seventh Circuit. The Board is of the opinion that the Respondent does not assert any matter not previously considered and that the Respondent's contentions are without merit." Period.

The decision alluded to so coyly was, of course, our *Harvstone* decision. How the Board could say that the motion for reconsideration did "not assert any matter not previously considered" by the Board perplexes us, since we did not think the Board gifted with prevision and therefore able to read and evaluate our decisions before they are rendered. In any event there is no reasoned discussion of our decision.

Yet if either in the present case or in *Harvstone* the Board had anticipated the substance of the analysis in our opinion in *Harvstone*, then perhaps its statement in the present case that the petition for reconsideration "did not assert any matter not previously considered" by the Board could be interpreted to mean that our opinion contained no argument that the Board had not considered. But a comparison of the Board's opinions in this case and in *Harvstone* with our opinion in *Harvstone* scotches any such contention—which anyway the Board does not make: at argument the Board's counsel speculated that the Board had not discussed our case only because it didn't think Nielsen would seek judicial review in this circuit. This, if so, was careless, given the wide venue (of which more shortly) for proceedings to review the Board's decisions. In any event counsel's speculation about the Board's motives is not especially plausible, since even if the Board had known that Nielsen was going to the Seventh Circuit it might have ignored our decision in *Harvstone* all the same; its "flagrant disregard of judicial precedent" is well known.

Granted, "flagrant disregard of judicial precedent" must not be confused with refusing to knuckle under to the first court of appeals (or the second, or even the twelfth) to rule adversely to the Board. The Supreme Court, not this circuit or even all twelve circuits that have jurisdiction to review orders of the Labor Board, is the supreme arbiter of the meaning of the laws enforced by the Board—a precept especially apt given the extraordinarily broad venue for proceedings to review Board orders, which virtually invites forum shopping of the kind exhibited in this case, and may in consequence cause a skewing of precedents at the circuit level. Although no circuit has rejected our decision in *Harvstone*, no circuit has followed it either (it is only two years old), and there are previous cases . . . that agree with the Board's position. This circuit is not authorized to interpret the labor laws with binding effect throughout the whole country, and the Board therefore is not obliged to accept our interpretation.

So the Board could have decided to stick by its guns and not bow to our decision in *Harvstone*—though it could also have defeated the company's effort at forum shopping simply by filing its petition to enforce its order in the Sixth Circuit (the natural venue for this case) and asking us to transfer the company's petition to review the order to that circuit, pursuant to 28 U.S.C. § 2112(a). We doubt whether, as some courts have suggested, we also have a nonstatutory "inherent" power to transfer a petition to review to another circuit, in order to defeat forum shopping. But that issue need not be decided here. The Board has not asked us to exercise such power; more to the point, it was content to file its petition for enforcement in this circuit, after the company had filed its petition for review here. . . .

If the Board wanted to stand pat on its *Harvstone* decision and try to take a decision by us adhering to our *Harvstone* decision to the Supreme Court, it could have done so merely by stating in response to Nielsen's petition for reconsideration that it had read our decision and disagreed with it. Instead it refused to acknowledge the pertinence of our decision to this case—and this despite the fact that the Board itself has been inconsistent with regard to the issue presented in this case.

The decisions we cited earlier that accuse the Board of "flagrant disregard of judicial precedent" were not accusing the Board of refusing to accept circuit precedent as binding, but of dealing with judicial precedent in a disingenuous, evasive, and in short dishonest manner. The Board's response to our *Harvstone* decision must be regarded in the same light. Faced with a conflict both in the circuits and its own decisions, the Board had the duty to take a stance, to explain which decisions it agreed with and why, and to explore the possibility of intermediate solutions. (For it is possible that the facts of this case place it halfway between *Truitt* and *Harvstone*. The company's ambiguous statements could be interpreted as a veiled threat of layoffs in the near if not the immediate future, thus upping the ante compared to *Harvstone* and perhaps bringing the case within the gravitational field of *Truitt*.) We do not follow stare decisis inflexibly; if the Board gives us a good reason to do so, we shall be happy to reexamine *Harvstone*. It has not done so. It has acted arbitrarily in its treatment of administrative as well as judicial precedent—and this is a pattern, too.

The petition for review is granted, the Board's order is set aside, and the matter is returned to the Board for such further proceedings as may be consistent with this opinion. We need not determine our course if the Board declines to follow *Harvstone*, its decision is again appealed to us and again reversed, and the Board on the third round decides to continue to stand fast; but presumably our present decision would stand as the law of the case in any subsequent proceeding in this court.

Notes

1. How should the Commission review the ALJ's decision? What standard of review must the Commission apply to Bud's findings and other judgments? Consider APA § 557(b): "On appeal from or review of the initial decision, the agency has all the powers which it would have in making the initial decision except as it may limit the issues on notice or by rule." What power does this sentence give the administrative review authority? Should agencies limit their review authority by rule?

2. Nonacquiescence, local courts, and national agencies. *Nielsen Lithographing* is just one of many "nonacquiescence" cases. Several agencies, including Treasury, National Labor Relations Board, and Social Security Administration, have policies of refusing to acquiesce in court decisions that conflict with the agency's national policy. If an agency nonacquiesces in a judicial decision, it obeys the judicial order in the particular case only and refuses to apply the rule of the decision in subsequent cases. Judge Posner recognized some legitimacy in nonacquiescence, but he also imposed some requirements on an agency that decides not to follow a lower court precedent on point. What arguments can there be for allowing an agency to nonacquiesce? If an agency chooses to nonacquiesce, how, if at all, should it respond to the judicial precedent?

Samuel Estreicher and Richard Revesz studied nonacquiescence on behalf of the Administrative Conference of the United States. Samuel Estreicher & Richard Revesz, *Nonacquiescence by Federal Administrative Agencies*, 98 YALE L.J. 679 (1989). They were not inclined to limit intercircuit nonacquiescence, an agency's refusal to follow one circuit's decision in matters in another circuit. The tough question for them was nonacquiescence as to cases in the same circuit, "intracircuit nonacquiescence." Agencies argue that the need to apply a national policy is just as compelling for intracircuit cases as for intercircuit cases. Estreicher and Revesz concluded that "such nonacquiescence can be justified only as an interim measure that allows the agency to maintain a uniform administration of its governing statute while it makes reasonable attempts to persuade the courts to validate its position." *Id.* at 743. Some believed, for example, that the Social Security Administration refused to follow court decisions but made no attempt to seek review by the Supreme Court. The Estreicher-Revesz proposal would force the agency to take steps towards ultimate judicial resolution of the question. At present, however, there is no explicit limit on an agency's authority to refuse to acquiesce in a circuit court precedent even within the circuit in which the decision was made.

It is important to understand that the doctrine of nonacquiescence permits an agency to reject a prior lower court decision that would otherwise be binding on the agency. This does not mean, however, that the agency will prevail on judicial review. We address the complexities of judicial review in the following note and in much detail in Chapter 5.

3. The legal force of judicial precedents on agencies. In addressing nonacquiescence questions, it is important to distinguish Supreme Court decisions from those of the lower federal courts. Agency freedom to "nonacquiesce" is rooted in the view that the lower courts are not, as Judge Posner noted, the "supreme arbiter[s]" of laws enforced by federal agencies with national jurisdiction. On this approach, the doctrine of judicial *stare decisis* does not bind an agency as it decides an issue previously addressed by a lower federal court. Given the Supreme Court's position atop the judicial hierarchy, its nationwide jurisdiction, and the natural impulse of the judiciary to keep some reins on the executive, it should come as little surprise that courts have not held, until *very* recently, that agencies can legitimately depart from Supreme Court precedent.

For an agency legal interpretation that disagrees with a judicial precedent to survive judicial review, the interpretation must survive two conceptually distinct hurdles. First, the interpretation must satisfy the agency's general obligation to give reasoned explanations for its significant decisions. Courts, as one might expect, take the view that it is profoundly irrational for agencies to ignore on-point judicial precedents. Thus, consistent with *Nielsen Lithographing*, an agency must at minimum give a reasoned explanation for its departure from relevant judicial precedents. The second hurdle the contrarian agency must overcome is that, even if a court's precedent does not bind the agency, it may bind the *court* itself. For instance, many circuit courts' rules provide that a panel decision has strictly binding force on later panels and can only be judicially reversed by an *en banc* or Supreme Court opinion. Until 2005, the most reasonable agency interpretation in the world could not overcome this buzz-saw of *stare decisis*.

Then came *National Cable & Telecommunications Ass'n v. Brand X*, 125 S. Ct. 2688 (2005), previously mentioned in Note 4 of subchapter 4A.1. To understand the impact of *Brand X*, one must first know that *Chevron, U.S.A., Inc. v. Natural Resources Defense Council*, 467 U.S. 837 (1984), explicitly recognized that certain agency statutory interpretations must be accepted by the courts as long as the interpretations are reasonable—even if they are not interpretations the courts would have chosen themselves. (This principle, called "*Chevron* deference," will be discussed in gory detail in Chapter 5.) In *Brand X*, the Supreme Court clarified that the *stare decisis* force of judicial precedent does not strip agencies of their entitlement to *Chevron* deference. Thus, an agency interpretation that is eligible for *Chevron* deference should survive the force of a contrary judicial precedent so long as the agency gives a reasonable explanation for its stance. The main caveat to this new doctrine is that, if the judicial precedent makes clear that the statutory language at issue has only one unambiguous interpretation, it follows that any contrary agency interpretation cannot be reasonable and must therefore fail.

4. Impact of the previous Commission decision? Is the Commission bound by its own prior adjudicatory interpretations of § 5? May it just change its mind? If it does, what must it do? How strongly should *stare decisis* apply to agency adjudicative decisionmaking? That is, under what circumstances may an agency decide not to follow *its own* prior decisions?

Administrative law has generally held that agencies are not bound by their own precedent if they give a reasoned explanation for the change. Judge Wald summarized the law regarding agency precedent: "Agency decisions that depart from established precedent without a reasoned explanation will be vacated as arbitrary and capricious." *Graphic Commun. Intern. Union v. Salem-Gravure*, 843 F.2d 1490, 1493 (D.C. Cir. 1988).

Should the law give agencies such freedom to deviate from past decisions? What factors might lead you to find some administrative precedent "binding" on an agency? For example, the Eighth Circuit found: "[The agency] is particularly entitled to a lesser degree of deference where, as here, it has reversed its long established precedent." *Brock v. Dun-Par Engineered Form Co.*, 843 F.2d 1135, 1137 (8th Cir. 1988). Should political shifts in Washington or the state capital be sufficient justification for a decision not to follow prior decisions? For further discussion (in the rulemaking context) of an agency's duty to explain its abandonment of old policies in favor of new ones, see *FCC v. Fox Television Stations, Inc.*, 129 S. Ct. 1800 (2009) (discussed in subchapter 5G.2 at note 7).

5. When should the agency use rulemaking rather than adjudication to announce binding policy?—A review. We return briefly to an issue we saw in Chapter 2. To what extent may the Commission decide to announce a policy, (e.g., regarding the percentage of the named grape a wine must contain before that variety can be claimed on the label) in an adjudication? Recall the Supreme Court in *NLRB v. Wyman-Gordon Co.* (excerpted in subchapter 2A.2) recognized that agencies, much like courts, can create "rules" via adjudication. Courts evolve rules through what we call the "common law" process. Indeed, learning to glean these rules has been the center of your legal education. Agencies, however, typically enjoy the additional authority to create legislative rules through a notice-and-comment process that allows for broad public participation.

Suppose the WTC decides to abandon an important interpretation of §5 that it had adopted in an earlier adjudication. May it do so via a later adjudication? Or must the agency use rulemaking? Which procedural device should the agency use? (You may want to take a look at the *Bell Aerospace* case excerpted in Chapter 2.)

6. Impact of the Interpretive Bulletin? Must Bud follow the Interpretive Bulletin, even though it is a not legislative rule? What is the effect of an informally issued agency rule on adjudication by ALJs? (You may wish to review note 6 of subchapter 4A.3.)

7. Administrative *res judicata*, or issue preclusion. Sometimes when two parties fully litigate a claim through the courts, the losing party tries to raise the same claim in another lawsuit. As you know from Civil Procedure, the doctrine of *res judicata* prohibits relitigation of a claim that has already been fully resolved between the parties through a final judgment. A similar doctrine, collateral estoppel, applies when one party seeks to relitigate an issue (as distinct from a claim) that had previously been fully litigated between the parties. These two doctrines are often referred to as "claim preclusion" and "issue preclusion," respectively.

As Justice Stewart succinctly explained, these doctrines serve to "relieve parties of the costs and vexation of multiple lawsuits, conserve judicial resources, and by preventing inconsistent decisions, encourage reliance on adjudication." *Allen v. McCurry*, 449 U.S. 90, 94 (1980).

The same sort of situation, and the same concerns, can arise in the context of administrative adjudication. For example, the California Supreme Court held that where a state administrative tribunal, acting in a "judicial capacity," determined that an individual had not committed welfare fraud, that decision precluded a later criminal prosecution on identical allegations. Since "the issues were identical in the two proceedings," and the burden of proof in the welfare proceeding was lower than the burden in the criminal case, the state could not proceed in the criminal prosecution given the finding in the administrative proceeding. *People v. Sims*, 651 P.2d 321 (Cal. 1982).

The United States Supreme Court recently confirmed that administrative adjudicatory decisions may preclude later relitigation of the same issues in court. In *B&B Hardware, Inc. v. Hargis Industries, Inc*, 135 S. Ct. 1293 (2015), B&B Hardware, owner of the trademark SEALTIGHT for its product (a type of fastener), successfully opposed Hargis' attempt to register a trademark for the name SEALTITE for its product (a very different type of fastener) at the U.S. Patent and Trademark Office. After losing before the agency, Hargis did not seek judicial review, which was clearly available.

Instead of appealing the agency decision to the courts, Hargis tried to make the same arguments in an ongoing district court action for trademark infringement involving the same parties and asserted trademarks. In holding that the administrative adjudicatory decision precluded judicial litigation of the same issues, Justice Alito usefully described the applicable principles and forcefully confirmed their application to administrative decisions:

> Sometimes two different tribunals are asked to decide the same issue. When that happens, the decision of the first tribunal usually must be followed by the second, at least if the issue is really the same. Allowing the same issue to be decided more than once wastes litigants' resources and adjudicators' time, and it encourages parties who lose before one tribunal to shop around for another. The doctrine of collateral estoppel or issue preclusion is designed to prevent this from occurring.
>
> . . . .
>
> This Court has long recognized that "the determination of a question directly involved in one action is conclusive as to that question in a second suit." The idea is straightforward: Once a court has decided an issue, it is "forever settled as between the parties," thereby "protect[ing]" against "the expense and vexation attending multiple lawsuits, conserv[ing] judicial resources, and foster[ing] reliance on judicial action by minimizing the possibility of inconsistent verdicts." In short, "a losing litigant deserves no rematch after a defeat fairly suffered."
>
> Although the idea of issue preclusion is straightforward, it can be challenging to implement. The Court, therefore, regularly turns to the Restatement (Second) of Judgments for a statement of the ordinary elements of issue preclusion. The Restatement explains that subject to certain well-known exceptions, the general rule is that "[w]hen an issue of fact or law is actually litigated and determined by a valid and final judgment, and the determination is essential to the judgment, the determination is conclusive in a subsequent action between the parties, whether on the same or a different claim." Restatement (Second) of Judgments § 27, p. 250 (1980); *see also id.,* § 28, at 273 (listing exceptions such as whether appellate review was available or whether there were "differences in the quality or extensiveness of the procedures followed").
>
> Both this Court's cases and the Restatement make clear that issue preclusion is not limited to those situations in which the same issue is before two *courts.* Rather, where a single issue is before a court and an administrative agency, preclusion also often applies. Indeed, this Court has explained that because the principle of issue preclusion was so "well established" at

common law, in those situations in which Congress has authorized agencies to resolve disputes, "courts may take it as given that Congress has legislated with the expectation that the principle [of issue preclusion] will apply except when a statutory purpose to the contrary is evident." This reflects the Court's longstanding view that "'[w]hen an administrative agency is acting in a judicial capacity and resolves disputed issues of fact properly before it which the parties have had an adequate opportunity to litigate, the courts have not hesitated to apply res judicata to enforce repose.'"

Id. at 1298–1303. The majority rejected Hargis' argument that the relevant statute should be read not to authorize issue preclusion as a result of this agency decision. Reflecting the proposition that the availability of administrative issue preclusion is a matter of congressional intent, the majority reiterated its earlier explanation "that absent a contrary indication, Congress presumptively intends that an agency's determination . . . has preclusive effect." In reaching its conclusion, the majority did not reach possible constitutional claims because they had not been adequately raised.

To what extent must a federal court give preclusive effect to state agency determinations? The Supreme Court in *University of Tennessee v. Elliott*, 478 U.S. 788, 798–99 (1986), concluded that ordinarily they must do so unless Congress intended otherwise. In a case asserting violations of Title VII of the Civil Rights Act of 1964 and of the Reconstruction civil rights statutes, the Court held that congressional intent dictated that an unreviewed state agency decision does not preclude a federal Title VII claim. As to the Reconstruction statutes, however, the Court found no such congressional intent to trump the usual operation of preclusion principles. The *Elliott* Court explained that federal courts should generally apply these principles to state agency determinations because:

> [G]iving preclusive effect to administrative factfinding serves the value underlying general principles of collateral estoppel: enforcing repose. This value, which encompasses both the parties' interest in avoiding the cost and vexation of repetitive litigation and the public's interest in conserving judicial resources, is equally implicated whether factfinding is done by a federal or state agency.

> Having federal courts give preclusive effect to the factfinding of state administrative tribunals also serves the value of federalism. . . . [T]he Full Faith and Credit Clause compels the States to give preclusive effect to the factfindings of an administrative tribunal in a sister State. The Full Faith and Credit Clause is of course not binding on federal courts, but we can certainly look to the policies underlying the Clause in fashioning federal common-law rules of preclusion. "Perhaps the major purpose of the Full Faith and Credit Clause is to act as a nationally unifying force," and this purpose is served by giving preclusive effect to state administrative factfinding rather than leaving the courts of a second forum, state or federal, free to reach conflicting results. Accordingly, we hold that when a state agency

"acting in a judicial capacity . . . resolves disputed issues of fact properly before it which the parties have had an adequate opportunity to litigate," federal courts must give the agency's factfinding the same preclusive effect to which it would be entitled in the State's courts.

In *University of Tennessee v. Elliott*, we see congressional intent overriding the application of traditional principles of collateral estoppel and preclusion to Title VII claims. Why would Congress override such concerns?

B. Constitutional Sources of Procedure in Adjudications

Many, if not most, procedural disputes about administrative adjudications involve the statutory issues addressed in subchapter 4A. It is important to recognize, however, that the Due Process Clauses of the Fifth and Fourteenth Amendments to the Constitution may impose procedural requirements where statutes do not, or perhaps beyond those imposed by statutes.

The "Great Clause" prevents government from affecting life, liberty, or property without adequate procedures. We saw the Due Process Clause at work in *Londoner v. City and County of Denver*. Once the Supreme Court determined that *Londoner* involved decisions about and based upon the particulars of certain individuals—in other words, adjudications—the Court required an individualized right to be heard. *Londoner* represents the first question in due process analysis. Does the dispute involve an adjudication? If it does, due process may attach. If it does not, and is legislative in nature (rulemaking), *Bi-Metallic* and *Vermont Yankee* establish that the applicable statutes alone will determine the procedural requirements.

Once we determine that a procedural dispute involves an adjudication, our inquiry must be divided into two overarching questions: What are the interests protected? And what procedures satisfy due process in a given context? These fundamental questions cause courts to employ a two-step approach. First, a court determines whether a due process interest (life, liberty, or property) has been affected by official conduct. Second, if the court finds a due process interest, it next determines whether the process used comported with due process in that particular context. As the Supreme Court said in *Morrissey v. Brewer*, 408 U.S. 471, 481 (1972): "Once it is determined that due process applies, the question remains what process is due." Put another way, the Due Process Clauses do not prohibit the government from depriving persons of life, liberty, or property. Rather, they require the government to do so through the appropriate procedures. The materials below seek to provide the foundation for determining whether a protected interest exists, and if so, how much process is required to adequately protect that interest. (Because of the scope of this course, we will confine ourselves to "procedural" due process issues, although some of the most controversial of current issues involve the extent of "substantive" due process.)

1. Interests Protected by Due Process

What does it mean to be deprived of liberty or property by the State? On the one hand, nearly every government action has some potentially negative consequence for individual liberty or property. On the other hand, too broad a reading of these terms could lead to endless procedural entanglements that would make it nearly impossible to govern. This subsection examines the Court's standards for establishing a protected property and liberty interest under the Due Process Clause.

a. Gateway to the Modern Due Process Era

Lesson 4B.1.a. Abby is assigned the case of one of the firm's clients, Mort, a small, local distributor. Mort owns a local liquor wholesale operation in which he distributes wine along with other alcoholic beverages. Mort is required by the WTCA to join the Wine Merchants' Association in order to continue carrying wine. Recently, the Association suspended Mort for violating the pricing disclosure provisions of its "Fair Marketing Practices" rules. The rules were promulgated under the language in § 6(b), authorizing the Association to "regulate the conduct of its members." The Association's adjudication board issued the suspension after an abbreviated hearing.

What do *Goldberg* and the notes that follow it suggest with regard to whether the Association's action against Mort implicates his due process rights?

Background of *Goldberg v. Kelly*

Often said to be the source of a "due process explosion," *Goldberg v. Kelly* involved individuals whom the state had initially determined met statutory requirements to receive certain welfare payments. This dispute arose when the state sought to terminate those payments. The attempted termination raised two distinct questions: (1) whether the welfare recipients had a property right to those payments under the Due Process Clause, and (2) if they had a property right in the payments, whether the welfare recipients had been given constitutionally sufficient process prior to termination of those payments.

Goldberg v. Kelly
397 U.S. 254 (1970)

MR. JUSTICE BRENNAN delivered the opinion of the Court.

The question for decision is whether a State that terminates public assistance payments to a particular recipient without affording him the opportunity for an evidentiary hearing prior to termination denies the recipient procedural due process in violation of the Due Process Clause of the Fourteenth Amendment.

PROCEDURAL HISTORY

This action was brought in the District Court for the Southern District of New York by residents of New York City receiving financial aid under the federally assisted program of Aid to Families with Dependent Children (AFDC) or under

New York State's general Home Relief program.[1] Their complaint alleged that the New York State and New York City officials administering these programs terminated, or were about to terminate, such aid without prior notice and hearing, thereby denying them due process of law. At the time the suits were filed there was no requirement of prior notice or hearing of any kind before termination of financial aid. However, the State and city adopted procedures for notice and hearing after the suits were brought, and the plaintiffs, appellees here, then challenged the constitutional adequacy of those procedures.

The State Commissioner of Social Services amended the State Department of Social Services' Official Regulations to require that local social services officials proposing to discontinue or suspend a recipient's financial aid do so according to a procedure that conforms to either subdivision (a) or subdivision (b) of § 351.26 of the regulations as amended. The City of New York elected to promulgate a local procedure according to subdivision (b). That subdivision, so far as here pertinent, provides that the local procedure must include the giving of notice to the recipient of the reasons for a proposed discontinuance or suspension at least seven days prior to its effective date, with notice also that upon request the recipient may have the proposal reviewed by a local welfare official holding a position superior to that of the supervisor who approved the proposed discontinuance or suspension, and, further, that the recipient may submit, for purposes of the review, a written statement to demonstrate why his grant should not be discontinued or suspended. The decision by the reviewing official whether to discontinue or suspend aid must be made expeditiously, with written notice of the decision to the recipient. The section further expressly provides that "[assistance] shall not be discontinued or suspended prior to the date such notice of decision is sent to the recipient and his representative, if any, or prior to the proposed effective date of discontinuance or suspension, whichever occurs later."

Pursuant to subdivision (b), the New York City Department of Social Services promulgated Procedure No. 68-18. A caseworker who has doubts about the recipient's continued eligibility must first discuss them with the recipient. If the caseworker concludes that the recipient is no longer eligible, he recommends termination of aid to a unit supervisor. If the latter concurs, he sends the recipient a letter stating the reasons for proposing to terminate aid and notifying him that within seven days he may request that a higher official review the record, and may support the request with a written statement prepared personally or with the aid of an attorney or other person. If the reviewing official affirms the determination of ineligibility, aid is stopped immediately and the recipient is informed by letter of the reasons

[handwritten margin note: PROCESS FOR TERMINATION]

---

1. AFDC was established by the Social Security Act of 1935. It is a categorical assistance program supported by federal grants-in-aid but administered by the States according to regulations of the Secretary of Health, Education, and Welfare. Home Relief is a general assistance program financed and administered solely by New York state and local governments. It assists any person unable to support himself or to secure support from other sources.

for the action. Appellees' challenge to this procedure emphasizes the absence of any provisions for the personal appearance of the recipient before the reviewing official, for oral presentation of evidence, and for confrontation and cross-examination of adverse witnesses. However, the letter does inform the recipient that he may request a post-termination "fair hearing." This is a proceeding before an independent state hearing officer at which the recipient may appear personally, offer oral evidence, confront and cross-examine the witnesses against him, and have a record made of the hearing. If the recipient prevails at the "fair hearing" he is paid all funds erroneously withheld. A recipient whose aid is not restored by a "fair hearing" decision may have judicial review. The recipient is so notified.

. . . .

Appellant does not contend that procedural due process is not applicable to the termination of welfare benefits. Such benefits are a matter of statutory entitlement for persons qualified to receive them. Their termination involves state action that adjudicates important rights. The constitutional challenge cannot be answered by an argument that public assistance benefits are "a 'privilege' and not a 'right.'" Relevant constitutional restraints apply as much to the withdrawal of public assistance benefits as to disqualification for unemployment compensation; or to denial of a tax exemption; or to discharge from public employment. The extent to which procedural due process must be afforded the recipient is influenced by the extent to which he may be "condemned to suffer grievous loss," *Joint Anti-Fascist Refugee Committee v. McGrath* (1951) (Frankfurter, J., concurring), and depends upon whether the recipient's interest in avoiding that loss outweighs the governmental interest in summary adjudication. Accordingly, as we said in *Cafeteria & Restaurant Workers Union v. McElroy* (1961), "consideration of what procedures due process may require under any given set of circumstances must begin with a determination of the precise nature of the government function involved as well as of the private interest that has been affected by governmental action." *See also Hannah v. Larche* (1960).

It is true, of course, that some governmental benefits may be administratively terminated without affording the recipient a pre-termination evidentiary hearing. But we agree with the District Court that when welfare is discontinued, only a pre-termination evidentiary hearing provides the recipient with procedural due process. For qualified recipients, welfare provides the means to obtain essential food, clothing, housing, and medical care. Thus the crucial factor in this context — a factor not present in the case of the blacklisted government contractor, the discharged government employee, the taxpayer denied a tax exemption, or virtually anyone else whose governmental entitlements are ended — is that termination of aid pending resolution of a controversy over eligibility may deprive an *eligible* recipient of the very means by which to live while he waits. Since he lacks independent resources, his situation becomes immediately desperate. His need to concentrate upon finding the means for daily subsistence, in turn, adversely affects his ability to seek redress from the welfare bureaucracy.

Moreover, important governmental interests are promoted by affording recipients a pre-termination evidentiary hearing. From its founding the Nation's basic commitment has been to foster the dignity and well-being of all persons within its borders. We have come to recognize that forces not within the control of the poor contribute to their poverty. This perception, against the background of our traditions, has significantly influenced the development of the contemporary public assistance system. Welfare, by meeting the basic demands of subsistence, can help bring within the reach of the poor the same opportunities that are available to others to participate meaningfully in the life of the community. At the same time, welfare guards against the societal malaise that may flow from a widespread sense of unjustified frustration and insecurity. Public assistance, then, is not mere charity, but a means to "promote the general Welfare, and secure the Blessings of Liberty to ourselves and our Posterity." The same governmental interests that counsel the provision of welfare, counsel as well its uninterrupted provision to those eligible to receive it; pre-termination evidentiary hearings are indispensable to that end.

Appellant does not challenge the force of these considerations but argues that they are outweighed by countervailing governmental interests in conserving fiscal and administrative resources. These interests, the argument goes, justify the delay of any evidentiary hearing until after discontinuance of the grants. Summary adjudication protects the public fisc by stopping payments promptly upon discovery of reason to believe that a recipient is no longer eligible. Since most terminations are accepted without challenge, summary adjudication also conserves both the fisc and administrative time and energy by reducing the number of evidentiary hearings actually held.

We agree with the District Court, however, that these governmental interests are not overriding in the welfare context. The requirement of a prior hearing doubtless involves some greater expense, and the benefits paid to ineligible recipients pending decision at the hearing probably cannot be recouped, since these recipients are likely to be judgment-proof. But the State is not without weapons to minimize these increased costs. Much of the drain on fiscal and administrative resources can be reduced by developing procedures for prompt pre-termination hearings and by skillful use of personnel and facilities. Indeed, the very provision for a post-termination evidentiary hearing in New York's Home Relief program is itself cogent evidence that the State recognizes the primacy of the public interest in correct eligibility determinations and therefore in the provision of procedural safeguards. Thus, the interest of the eligible recipient in uninterrupted receipt of public assistance, coupled with the State's interest that his payments not be erroneously terminated, clearly outweighs the State's competing concern to prevent any increase in its fiscal and administrative burdens. As the District Court correctly concluded, "[t]he stakes are simply too high for the welfare recipient, and the possibility for honest error or irritable misjudgment too great, to allow termination of aid without giving the recipient a chance, if he so desires, to be fully informed of the case against him so that he may contest its basis and produce evidence in rebuttal."

. . . .

Mr. Justice Black, dissenting.

In the last half century the United States, along with many, perhaps most, other nations of the world, has moved far toward becoming a welfare state, that is, a nation that for one reason or another taxes its most affluent people to help support, feed, clothe, and shelter its less fortunate citizens. The result is that today more than nine million men, women, and children in the United States receive some kind of state or federally financed public assistance in the form of allowances or gratuities, generally paid them periodically, usually by the week, month, or quarter. Since these gratuities are paid on the basis of need, the list of recipients is not static, and some people go off the lists and others are added from time to time. These ever-changing lists put a constant administrative burden on government and it certainly could not have reasonably anticipated that this burden would include the additional procedural expense imposed by the Court today.

. . . .

The more than a million names on the relief rolls in New York, and the more than nine million names on the rolls of all the 50 States were not put there at random. The names are there because state welfare officials believed that those people were eligible for assistance. Probably in the officials' haste to make out the lists many names were put there erroneously in order to alleviate immediate suffering, and undoubtedly some people are drawing relief who are not entitled under the law to do so. Doubtless some draw relief checks from time to time who know they are not eligible, either because they are not actually in need or for some other reason. Many of those who thus draw undeserved gratuities are without sufficient property to enable the government to collect back from them any money they wrongfully receive. But the Court today holds that it would violate the Due Process Clause of the Fourteenth Amendment to stop paying those people weekly or monthly allowances unless the government first affords them a full "evidentiary hearing" even though welfare officials are persuaded that the recipients are not rightfully entitled to receive a penny under the law. In other words, although some recipients might be on the lists for payment wholly because of deliberate fraud on their part, the Court holds that the government is helpless and must continue, until after an evidentiary hearing, to pay money that it does not owe, never has owed, and never could owe. I do not believe there is any provision in our Constitution that should thus paralyze the government's efforts to protect itself against making payments to people who are not entitled to them.

. . . .

This decision is thus only another variant of the view often expressed by some members of this Court that the Due Process Clause forbids any conduct that a majority of the Court believes "unfair," "indecent," or "shocking to their consciences." Neither these words nor any like them appear anywhere in the Due Process Clause. If they did, they would leave the majority of Justices free to hold any conduct unconstitutional that they should conclude on their own to be unfair or shocking to them.[6] Had the drafters of the Due Process Clause meant to leave judges such ambulatory power to declare laws unconstitutional, the chief value of a written constitution, as the Founders saw it, would have been lost. In fact, if that view of due process is correct, the Due Process Clause could easily swallow up all other parts of the Constitution. And truly the Constitution would always be "what the judges say it is" at a given moment, not what the Founders wrote into the document. A written constitution, designed to guarantee protection against governmental abuses, including those of judges, must have written standards that mean something definite and have an explicit content. I regret very much to be compelled to say that the Court today makes a drastic and dangerous departure from a Constitution written to control and limit the government and the judges and moves toward a constitution designed to be no more and no less than what the judges of a particular social and economic philosophy declare on the one hand to be fair or on the other hand to be shocking and unconscionable.

The procedure required today as a matter of constitutional law finds no precedent in our legal system. Reduced to its simplest terms, the problem in this case is similar to that frequently encountered when two parties have an ongoing legal relationship that requires one party to make periodic payments to the other. Often the situation arises where the party "owing" the money stops paying it and justifies his conduct by arguing that the recipient is not legally entitled to payment. The recipient can, of course, disagree and go to court to compel payment. But I know of no situation in our legal system in which the person alleged to owe money to another is required by law to continue making payments to a judgment-proof claimant without the benefit of any security or bond to insure that these payments can be recovered if he wins his legal argument. Yet today's decision in no way obligates the welfare recipient to pay back any benefits wrongfully received during the pre-termination evidentiary hearings or post any bond, and in all "fairness" it could not do so. These recipients are by definition too poor to post a bond or to repay the benefits that, as the majority assumes, must be spent as received to insure survival.

The Court apparently feels that this decision will benefit the poor and needy. In my judgment the eventual result will be just the opposite. While today's decision requires only an administrative, evidentiary hearing, the inevitable logic of the approach taken will lead to constitutionally imposed, time-consuming delays of a full adversary process of administrative and judicial review. . . . While this Court will perhaps have insured that no needy person will be taken off the rolls without a full "due process" proceeding, it will also have insured that many will never get on

---

6. I am aware that some feel that the process employed in reaching today's decision is not dependent on the individual views of the Justices involved, but is a mere objective search for the "collective conscience of mankind," but in my view that description is only a euphemism for an individual's judgment. Judges are as human as anyone and as likely as others to see the world through their own eyes and find the "collective conscience" remarkably similar to their own.

the rolls, or at least that they will remain destitute during the lengthy proceedings followed to determine initial eligibility.

For the foregoing reasons I dissent from the Court's holding. The operation of a welfare state is a new experiment for our Nation. For this reason, among others, I feel that new experiments in carrying out a welfare program should not be frozen into our constitutional structure. They should be left, as are other legislative determinations, to the Congress and the legislatures that the people elect to make our laws.

Notes

1. Two questions—when due process applies and what it requires. Checking her notes from law school, Abby recalls that she would have to establish both that due process applies to Mort's situation and that it requires more process than the WMA has already provided. Will *Goldberg v. Kelly* help with either of these issues? Mort is certainly not on welfare. In fact, he could probably continue to sell other alcoholic beverages and other items even if he could not sell wine.

2. The state action requirement: Does the Due Process Clause reach the WMA? A potentially serious obstacle for Abby might be that the Due Process Clause covers only government action, i.e., "state action." The Association, which has suspended Mort's license, is by definition a "private association," see §6(b) of the WTCA, which suggests that due process might not apply at all. Perhaps Mort's relationship with the WTCA is governed by the common law of contracts, instead.

Abby notes *Lugar v. Edmondson Oil Co.*, 457 U.S. 922 (1982), in which the Supreme Court carefully considered the scope of the state action requirement. It found that the state action requirement preserved a balance between protection of individuals against government conduct and avoiding government responsibility for actions for which it could not reasonably be blamed: "Our cases have accordingly insisted that the conduct allegedly causing the deprivation of a federal right be fairly attributable to the State." Fair attribution, it continued, required a two-part approach. "First, the deprivation must be caused by the exercise of some right or privilege created by the State or by a rule of conduct imposed by the state or by a person for whom the State is responsible." Second, the offending person must be a state actor, "because he is a state official, because he has acted together with or has obtained significant aid from state officials, or because his conduct is otherwise chargeable to the state." Resolution of these questions, the Court concluded, was fact-bound. In the prejudgment attachment case before it, the Court found state action "when the State has created a system whereby state officials will attach property on the *ex parte* application of one party to a private dispute."

In *Manhattan Community Access Corp. v. Halleck*, 139 S.Ct. 1921 (2019), the Supreme Court took up precisely the sort of fact-bound analysis described in *Lugar* when it decided whether a private nonprofit entity that was authorized by the City of New York to operate public access cable television stations was a state actor that, in turn, could be sued under the First Amendment for refusing to broadcast certain content. The Court, in a 5-4 decision, cited the standard in *Lugar*, but then went on to stress that the state action doctrine applies to traditional state functions—activities that have traditionally been the province of government. It concluded that neither the narrow version of what the nonprofit did (operating public access cable channels), nor the broader account (creating a public forum for speech) have traditionally been the exclusive function of government. As a result, the channel operator could not be considered a state actor and thus could not be held liable under the First Amendment. In dissent, Justice Sotomayor directly took issue with the majority's factual account of the case. She argued that the City had a property interest in the channels, thus making them a public forum whether the City chose to operate them itself or to authorize a private entity to do so.

The future impact of *Halleck* is unclear. The majority described its holding as "narrow," but its focus on whether the conduct in question is a traditional state function could be a basis for limiting the scope of state action in future cases.

3. Why did due process attach in *Goldberg*? Assuming there is state action, the next question is whether due process attaches to that action. The Fifth Amendment provides that "No person shall be . . . deprived of life, liberty, or property, without due process of law." Why did due process attach in *Goldberg*?

As discussed below, *Goldberg* is understood to have recognized a "new" form of property. But note that New York officials did "not contend that procedural due process is not applicable to the termination of welfare benefits." The Court addressed the issue only briefly in a paragraph that reflects the history of due process doctrine in very condensed form.

First, the Court said that "[t]he constitutional challenge cannot be answered by an argument that public assistance benefits are 'a privilege' and not a 'right.'" This statement reflected an earlier doctrine under which government benefits, such as employment or welfare payments, were considered to be "privileges." Since government could choose to create and fill jobs or fund and provide welfare benefits, it could also withdraw jobs or benefits at will. No one had a constitutional right to a government job or to welfare, so due process did not attach to their withdrawal. This distinction was rejected in *Cafeteria & Restaurant Workers Union v. McElroy*, 367 U.S. 886, 894 (1961), in which the court said, in words that have an unfortunate resonance today:

> The question remains whether Admiral Tyree's action in summarily denying Rachel Brawner access to the site of her former employment violated the requirements of the Due Process Clause of the Fifth Amendment. This question cannot be answered by easy assertion that, because she had no constitutional right to be there in the first place, she was not deprived of liberty or property by the Superintendent's action. "One may not have a constitutional right to go to Baghdad, but the Government may not prohibit one from going there unless by means consonant with due process."

Thus, the mere fact that there is no constitutional right to welfare, or in Mort's case to a wine merchant's license, does not mean there is no due process protection.

To this point, the Court said only that the privilege/right distinction did not prevent due process from attaching. The question remained how to determine whether due process attached to any particular interest affected by government action. As to this question, the *Goldberg* decision is somewhat ambiguous. *Goldberg* has come to be understood as recognizing the statutory entitlement to welfare benefits as a new form of property, which we discuss below. But at the time that narrow interpretation was not as clear as it is today. To the contrary, the Court's references to the extent of the benefit recipient's "grievous loss" and to the "precise nature of the government function involved as well as the private interest that has been affected" suggested that the availability and extent of due process protections were to be determined by a balancing of interests. As we will see, the balancing approach was quickly eclipsed with respect to the question of whether due process protection is available at all, but it emerged triumphant in governing the extent of procedural protections where due process does apply.

4. What is the "new" property interest? If *Goldberg* recognized a "new" property interest, what is it? In most cases, a property interest is simply something we have been given, purchased, or otherwise own under the common law of property. For example, another important procedural due process case, *Parratt v. Taylor*, 451 U.S. 527 (1981), involved deprivation of "certain hobby materials valued at $23.50," which a prisoner had ordered through the mail. As with most property, the prisoner had paid for it and could presumably sell it. One does not pay for and cannot sell the right to welfare benefits.

However, Justice Brennan in *Goldberg* defined a "new" concept of property as highlighted in *Goldberg*'s famous footnote 8:

> It may be realistic today to regard welfare entitlements as more like "property" than a "gratuity." Much of the existing wealth in this country takes the form of rights that do not fall within traditional common law concepts of property. It has been aptly noted that

> "[society] today is built around entitlement. The automobile dealer has his franchise, the doctor and lawyer their professional licenses, the worker his union membership, contract, and pension rights, the executive his contract and stock options; all are devices to aid security and independence. Many of the most important of these entitlements now flow from government: subsidies to farmers and businessmen, routes for airlines and channels for television stations; long term contracts for defense, space, and education; social security pensions for individuals. Such sources of security, whether private or public, are no longer regarded as luxuries or gratuities; to the recipients they are essentials, fully deserved, and in no sense a form of charity. It is only the poor whose entitlements, although recognized by public policy, have not been effectively enforced."

Charles Reich, *Individual Rights and Social Welfare: The Emerging Legal Issues*, 74 Yale L.J. 1245, 1255 (1965). *See also* Reich, *The New Property*, 73 Yale L.J. 733 (1964).

5. English and European due process concepts. The English equivalent of our due process jurisprudence is encompassed within the term "natural justice." Natural justice evolved in the English system over generations and no doubt crossed the Atlantic to shape our thinking about fair procedure. A prominent United Kingdom administrative law scholar noted the history of the concept:

> The rules requiring impartial adjudicators and fair hearings can be traced back to medieval precedent, and, indeed, they were not unknown in the ancient world. In their medieval guise they were regarded as part of the immutable order of things. . . .

William Wade & Christopher Forsyth, Administrative Law 467 (7th ed. 1994). By the 17th century, the force of this principle was so strong that Chief Justice Coke invoked it to void an act of parliament, a brazen act of judicial review in that system. *Dr. Bonham's Case*, 77 Eng. Rep. 638 (1610). The fundamental concept of a fair hearing had to evolve in this way because English jurists had no constitutional language such as the Due Process Clause from which to develop the law. In the nineteenth and first half of the twentieth centuries the doctrine lost force. But in 1963, the House of Lords rejuvenated the doctrine in *Ridge v. Baldwin*, [1964] AC 40, and it has been a pervasive part of UK administrative law since.

A similar concept has long been a fundamental part of French administrative law and that of most of continental Europe. In comparison with our due process jurisprudence, and in contrast to English natural justice, *droit administratif* has not been confined to procedural rules. L. Neville Brown & John Bell, French Administrative Law 205 (4th ed. 1993). *Droit administratif* has become part of the law of the European Union and the concept of natural justice has been incorporated into European procedural law. T.C. Hartley, The Foundations of European Community Law: An Introduction to the Constitutional and Administrative Law of the European Community 147 (2d ed. 1993).

b. The Property Interest as a Due Process Trigger

A few years after *Goldberg*, the Court refined and arguably simplified its approach to determining whether someone's interest constitutes a property right under the Due Process Clauses.

Lesson 4B.1.b. Abby understands that *Goldberg* recognized a "new" property. This modern concept of property was extended to any "entitlement." Abby, however, is still unclear as to how these constitutionally protected entitlements are to be defined.

What light do the next two cases and accompanying notes shed on this problem? And how might they affect analysis of the WMA's decision to suspend Mort's membership, as discussed in Lesson 4B.1.a?

Background of *Board of Regents v. Roth* and *Perry v. Sindermann*

The following decisions both involve the question of whether and when a faculty position at a state university could constitute a property right for due process purposes. Both draw upon the "entitlement" concept of *Goldberg v. Kelly*, but they reach opposite conclusions due to the factual differences between them.

Board of Regents v. Roth

408 U.S. 564 (1972)

MR. JUSTICE STEWART delivered the opinion of the Court.

In 1968 the respondent, David Roth, was hired for his first teaching job as assistant professor of political science at Wisconsin State University-Oshkosh. He was hired for a fixed term of one academic year. The notice of his faculty appointment specified that his employment would begin on September 1, 1968, and would end on June 30, 1969. The respondent completed that term. But he was informed that he would not be rehired for the next academic year.

The respondent had no tenure rights to continued employment. Under Wisconsin statutory law a state university teacher can acquire tenure as a "permanent" employee only after four years of year-to-year employment. Having acquired tenure, a teacher is entitled to continued employment "during efficiency and good behavior." A relatively new teacher without tenure, however, is under Wisconsin law entitled to nothing beyond his one-year appointment. There are no statutory or administrative standards defining eligibility for re-employment. State law thus clearly leaves the decision whether to rehire a nontenured teacher for another year to the unfettered discretion of university officials.

The procedural protection afforded a Wisconsin State University teacher before he is separated from the University corresponds to his job security. As a matter of statutory law, a tenured teacher cannot be "discharged except for cause upon written charges" and pursuant to certain procedures. A nontenured teacher similarly, is protected to some extent *during* his one-year term. Rules promulgated by the Board of Regents provide that a nontenured teacher "dismissed" before the end of the year may have some opportunity for review of the "dismissal." But the Rules provide no real protection for a nontenured teacher who simply is not re-employed for the next year. He must be informed by February 1 "concerning retention or non-retention for the ensuing year." But "no reason for non-retention need be given. No review or appeal is provided in such case."

In conformance with these Rules, the President of Wisconsin State University-Oshkosh informed the respondent before February 1, 1969, that he would not be rehired for the 1969–1970 academic year. He gave the respondent no reason for the decision and no opportunity to challenge it at any sort of hearing.

. . . .

The requirements of procedural due process apply only to the deprivation of interests encompassed by the Fourteenth Amendment's protection of liberty and property. When protected interests are implicated, the right to some kind of prior hearing is paramount. But the range of interests protected by procedural due process is not infinite.

[A] weighing process has long been a part of any determination of the *form* of hearing required in particular situations by procedural due process. But, to determine whether due process requirements apply in the first place, we must look not to the "weight" but to the *nature* of the interest at stake. We must look to see if the interest is within the Fourteenth Amendment's protection of liberty and property.

"Liberty" and "property" are broad and majestic terms. They are among the "[g]reat [constitutional] concepts . . . purposely left to gather meaning from experience. . . . [T]hey relate to the whole domain of social and economic fact, and the statesmen who founded this Nation knew too well that only a stagnant society remains unchanged." For that reason, the Court has fully and finally rejected the wooden distinction between "rights" and "privileges" that once seemed to govern the applicability of procedural due process rights. The Court has also made clear that the property interests protected by procedural due process extend well beyond actual ownership of real estate, chattels, or money. By the same token, the Court has required due process protection for deprivations of liberty beyond the sort of formal constraints imposed by the criminal process.

[handwritten margin note: EXPANSION OF "PROPERTY"]

Yet, while the Court has eschewed rigid or formalistic limitations on the protection of procedural due process, it has at the same time observed certain boundaries. For the words "liberty" and "property" in the Due Process Clause of the Fourteenth Amendment must be given some meaning.

[As discussed below, the Court found no liberty interest.]

. . . .

The Fourteenth Amendment's [procedural protection of property] is a safeguard of the security of interests that a person has already acquired in specific benefits. These interests — property interests — may take many forms.

. . . .

Certain attributes of "property" interests protected by procedural due process emerge from these decisions. To have a property interest in a benefit, a person clearly must have more than an abstract need or desire for it. He must have more than a unilateral expectation of it. He must, instead, have a legitimate claim of entitlement to it. It is a [purpose of the ancient institution of property to protect those claims upon which people rely in their daily lives, reliance that must not be arbitrarily undermined.] It is a purpose of the constitutional right to a hearing to provide an opportunity for a person to vindicate those claims.

[handwritten margin note: "MORE THAN DESIRE"]
[handwritten margin note: "RELIANCE"]

Property interests, of course, are not created by the Constitution. Rather, they are created and their dimensions are defined by existing rules or understandings that stem from an independent source such as state law—rules or understandings that secure certain benefits and that support claims of entitlement to those benefits. Thus, the welfare recipients in *Goldberg v. Kelly* (1970) had a claim of entitlement to welfare payments that was grounded in the statute defining eligibility for them. The recipients had not yet shown that they were, in fact, within the statutory terms of eligibility. But we held that they had a right to a hearing at which they might attempt to do so.

Just as the welfare recipients' "property" interest in welfare payments was created and defined by statutory terms, so the respondent's "property" interest in employment at Wisconsin State University-Oshkosh was created and defined by the terms of his appointment. Those terms secured his interest in employment up to June 30, 1969. But the important fact in this case is that they specifically provided that the respondent's employment was to terminate on June 30. They did not provide for contract renewal absent "sufficient cause." Indeed, they made no provision for renewal whatsoever.

Thus, the terms of the respondent's appointment secured absolutely no interest in re-employment for the next year. They supported absolutely no possible claim of entitlement to re-employment. Nor, significantly, was there any state statute or University rule or policy that secured his interest in re-employment or that created any legitimate claim to it. In these circumstances, the respondent surely had an abstract concern in being rehired, but he did not have a property interest sufficient to require the University authorities to give him a hearing when they declined to renew his contract of employment.

Our analysis of the respondent's constitutional rights in this case in no way indicates a view that an opportunity for a hearing or a statement of reasons for nonretention would, or would not, be appropriate or wise in public colleges and universities. For it is a written Constitution that we apply. Our role is confined to interpretation of that Constitution. . . .

Perry v. Sindermann

408 U.S. 593 (1972)

Mr. Justice Stewart delivered the opinion of the Court.

From 1959 to 1969 the respondent, Robert Sindermann, was a teacher in the state college system of the State of Texas. After teaching for two years at the University of Texas and for four years at San Antonio Junior College, he became a professor of Government and Social Science at Odessa Junior College in 1965. He was employed at the college for four successive years, under a series of one-year contracts. He was successful enough to be appointed, for a time, the cochairman of his department.

During the 1968–1969 academic year, however, controversy arose between the respondent and the college administration. The respondent was elected president of the Texas Junior College Teachers Association. In this capacity, he left his teaching duties on several occasions to testify before committees of the Texas Legislature, and he became involved in public disagreements with the policies of the college's Board of Regents. In particular, he aligned himself with a group advocating the elevation of the college to four-year status — a change opposed by the Regents. And, on one occasion, a newspaper advertisement appeared over his name that was highly critical of the Regents.

Finally, in May 1969, the respondent's one-year employment contract terminated and the Board of Regents voted not to offer him a new contract for the next academic year. The Regents issued a press release setting forth allegations of the respondent's insubordination.[1] But they provided him no official statement of the reasons for the nonrenewal of his contract. And they allowed him no opportunity for a hearing to challenge the basis of the nonrenewal. . . .

[The Court first discussed the denial of First Amendment rights.]

The respondent's lack of formal contractual or tenure security in continued employment at Odessa Junior College, though irrelevant to his free speech claim, is highly relevant to his procedural due process claim. But it may not be entirely dispositive.

We have held today in *Board of Regents v. Roth* that the Constitution does not require opportunity for a hearing before the nonrenewal of a nontenured teacher's contract, unless he can show that the decision not to rehire him somehow deprived him of an interest in "liberty" or that he had a "property" interest in continued employment, despite the lack of tenure or a formal contract. In *Roth* the teacher had not made a showing on either point to justify summary judgment in his favor.

Similarly, the respondent here has yet to show that he has been deprived of an interest that could invoke procedural due process protection. As in *Roth*, the mere showing that he was not rehired in one particular job, without more, did not amount to a showing of a loss of liberty.[5] Nor did it amount to a showing of a loss of property.

But the respondent's allegations — which we must construe most favorably to the respondent at this stage of the litigation — do raise a genuine issue as to his interest in continued employment at Odessa Junior College. He alleged that this interest, though not secured by a formal contractual tenure provision, was secured by a no less binding understanding fostered by the college administration. In particular, the respondent alleged that the college had a *de facto* tenure program, and that he had tenure under that program. He claimed that he and others legitimately relied upon

---

1. The press release stated, for example, that the respondent had defied his superiors by attending legislative committee meetings when college officials had specifically refused to permit him to leave his classes for that purpose.

5. The Court of Appeals suggested that the respondent might have a due process right to some kind of hearing simply if he *asserts* to college officials that their decision was based on his constitutionally protected conduct. We have rejected this approach in *Board of Regents v. Roth*.

an unusual provision that had been in the college's official Faculty Guide for many years:

> "*Teacher Tenure*: Odessa College has no tenure system. The Administration of the College wishes the faculty member to feel that he has permanent tenure as long as his teaching services are satisfactory and as long as he displays a cooperative attitude toward his co-workers and his superiors, and as long as he is happy in his work."

Moreover, the respondent claimed legitimate reliance upon guidelines promulgated by the Coordinating Board of the Texas College and University System that provided that a person, like himself, who had been employed as a teacher in the state college and university system for seven years or more has some form of job tenure.[6] Thus, the respondent offered to prove that a teacher with his long period of service at this particular State College had no less a "property" interest in continued employment than a formally tenured teacher at other colleges, and had no less a procedural due process right to a statement of reasons and a hearing before college officials upon their decision not to retain him.

We have made clear in *Roth*, that "property" interests subject to procedural due process protection are not limited by a few rigid, technical forms. Rather, "property" denotes a broad range of interests that are secured by "existing rules or understandings." A person's interest in a benefit is a "property" interest for due process purposes if there are such rules or mutually explicit understandings that support his claim of entitlement to the benefit and that he may invoke at a hearing.

A written contract with an explicit tenure provision clearly is evidence of a formal understanding that supports a teacher's claim of entitlement to continued employment unless sufficient "cause" is shown. Yet absence of such an explicit contractual provision may not always foreclose the possibility that a teacher has a "property" interest in re-employment. For example, the law of contracts in most, if not all, jurisdictions long has employed a process by which agreements, though not formalized in writing, may be "implied." Explicit contractual provisions may be supplemented by other agreements implied from "the promissor's words and conduct in the light of the surrounding circumstances." And, "[t]he meaning of [the promissor's] words and acts is found by relating them to the usage of the past."

A teacher, like the respondent, who has held his position for a number of years, might be able to show from the circumstances of this service—and from other relevant facts—that he has a legitimate claim of entitlement to job tenure. Just as this Court has found there to be a "common law of a particular industry or of a particular

---

6. The relevant portion of the guidelines, adopted as "Policy Paper 1" by the Coordinating Board on October 16, 1967, reads:
"A. Tenure
Tenure means assurance to an experienced faculty member that he may expect to continue in his academic position unless adequate cause for dismissal is demonstrated in a fair hearing, following established procedures of due process."

plant" that may supplement a collective-bargaining agreement, so there may be an unwritten "common law" in a particular university that certain employees shall have the equivalent of tenure. This is particularly likely in a college or university, like Odessa Junior College, that has no explicit tenure system even for senior members of its faculty, but that nonetheless may have created such a system in practice.

In this case, the respondent has alleged the existence of rules and understandings, promulgated and fostered by state officials, that may justify his legitimate claim of entitlement to continued employment absent "sufficient cause." We disagree with the Court of Appeals insofar as it held that a mere subjective "expectancy" is protected by procedural due process, but we agree that the respondent must be given an opportunity to prove the legitimacy of his claim of such entitlement in light of "the policies and practices of the institution." Proof of such a property interest would not, of course, entitle him to reinstatement. But such proof would obligate college officials to grant a hearing at his request, where he could be informed of the grounds for his nonretention and challenge their sufficiency.

Notes

1. **What do *Roth* and *Sindermann* add?** Can Abby demonstrate the elements necessary to establish a procedural due process interest in Association membership? What did *Roth* and *Sindermann* add to *Goldberg* and its predecessors? What are the keys to finding a property interest in Sindermann's teaching job and not in Roth's? What facts could you change in *Roth* to assure finding a property interest? How would you express the necessary element?

2. ***Castle Rock* — a more recent Supreme Court pronouncement.** In *Board of Regents v. Roth*, the Court wrote that, "[p]roperty interests, of course, are not created by the Constitution. Rather, they are created and their dimensions are defined by existing rules or understandings that stem from an independent source such as state law. . . ." In *Roth* itself, there was no basis for an entitlement claim, but in *Perry v. Sindermann* there was. Coupled with *Goldberg v. Kelly*, these decisions virtually invited a search for previously unrecognized "entitlements" that might trigger due process.

A more recent prominent example is *Town of Castle Rock v. Gonzales*, 125 S. Ct. 2796 (2005). Mrs. Gonzales had obtained a restraining order to protect herself and her children from her estranged husband. The order, reflecting statutory language to similar effect, included the following language directed to law enforcement:

> YOU SHALL USE EVERY REASONABLE MEANS TO ENFORCE THIS RESTRAINING ORDER. YOU SHALL ARREST, OR, IF AN ARREST WOULD BE IMPRACTICAL UNDER THE CIRCUMSTANCES, SEEK A WARRANT FOR THE ARREST OF THE RESTRAINED PERSON.

When her children disappeared around 5:30 p.m. while playing outside the family home, Mrs. Gonzales contacted the police and showed them the restraining order. The police advised her to wait until 10:00 p.m., and when she reappeared at that time they told her to wait until midnight. Her contact at 12:10 a.m. produced no further police effort, and the husband arrived at the police station at 3:20 a.m. He opened fire with an automatic weapon and was killed by police. The husband had already killed the three children, whose bodies were in his truck.

Mrs. Gonzales sued the town, arguing that the police had violated her constitutionally protected property right to enforcement of the restraining order. She asserted that the restraining order constituted an entitlement to a government benefit comparable to the welfare benefits in *Goldberg* or the *de facto* tenure promise in *Perry v. Sindermann.*

The Court rejected this argument for two reasons of interest to us here. First, the Court held that Colorado law did not establish a mandatory duty to enforce the restraining order. Language such as "USE EVERY REASONABLE MEANS," cited above, and the inherent need for the police to exercise discretion in enforcement meant that there was no property right to enforcement of the restraining order: "Respondent would have been assured nothing but the seeking of a warrant. This is not the sort of 'entitlement' out of which a property interest is created."

Second, the Court held that even if Mrs. Gonzales had been entitled to enforcement of the restraining order, that entitlement would not have constituted a property right triggering due process. To support this holding, the majority sought a way to distinguish entitlements that give rise to property interests from those that do not. It relied upon two propositions. First, "the right to have a restraining order enforced does not 'have some ascertainable monetary value,' as even our '*Roth*-type property-as-entitlement' cases have implicitly required." The internal quotations in the majority's assertion are not from prior decisions, but from a law review article. Thomas W. Merrill, *The Landscape of Constitutional Property*, 86 VA. L. REV. 885, 964 (2000). Second, "the alleged property interest here arises *incidentally*, not out of some new species of government benefit or service, but out of a function that government actors have always performed. . . ." Characterized this way, the indirect nature of the benefit was fatal to the claim, as it had been in *O'Bannon v. Town Court Nursing Center*, 447 U.S. 773 (1980). In *O'Bannon*, the Court had rejected an argument that nursing home residents on Medicaid had a due process right to a hearing before the nursing home could be excluded from the Medicaid program.

Justice Souter, in his concurring opinion in *Castle Rock*, may have provided an enduring means of distinguishing government entitlements that constitute property interests from those that do not:

> The Due Process Clause extends procedural protection to guard against unfair deprivation by state officials of substantive state-law property rights or entitlements; the federal process protects the property created by state law. But Gonzales claims a property interest in a state mandated process in and of itself.

Ms. Gonzales sought process (the making of an arrest), rather than substance (the retention of a job when certain standards are met).

[Justice Stevens, on the other hand, argued in dissent] that there was a mandatory duty to enforce the restraining order, and that "a citizen's property interest in such a commitment is just as concrete and worthy of protection as her interest in any other important service the government or a private firm has undertaken to provide." Comparing Mrs. Gonzales' right to enforcement of the restraining order to the right to government funded health care, Justice Stevens said: "Our cases have never required the object of an entitlement to be some mechanistic, unitary thing." Just as providing health care involves the exercise of judgment in making various decisions, so does enforcement of the restraining order. To him, they were the same.

Who has the better argument? Should Mrs. Gonzales have had a property right in enforcement of the restraining order that had been issued specifically for her benefit and the benefit of her children?

3. An alternative "rule of law" approach to whether due process attaches. Although *Goldberg* is said to have heralded a "due process revolution," and *Roth* has come to dominate the landscape in determining whether due process applies, Professors Sidney Shapiro and Richard Levy have argued that this analytical approach is seriously flawed. Sidney A. Shapiro & Richard E. Levy, *Government Benefits and the Rule of Law: Toward a Standards-Based Theory of Due Process*, 57 ADMIN. L. REV. 107 (2005).

Examining decisions dating back to the 18th Century, Shapiro and Levy show that there has long been a right to due process with respect to government benefits, including government employment, licenses, and social insurance. They argue that,

> *Goldberg v. Kelley* [sic], usually seen as the seminal new property decision, did not reflect an expansion of the scope of due process. The truly revolutionary decision was *Roth*, which replaced the open-ended and ambiguous due process analysis characterizing the Court's prior due process cases with a strict requirement of a protected interest in life, liberty, or property and incorporated the concept of legal entitlement to define property.

Id. at 119. Thus, the "due process revolution" actually narrowed the scope of due process protections by insisting upon recognition of discrete property or liberty interests.

Shapiro and Levy argue for a distinctly different approach to applying due process, one with roots in the nondelegation doctrine and the fundamental principle of adherence to the rule of law. They argue that the constitutional language "life, liberty, and property" was not meant to provide a list of discrete due process triggers. Rather, it was a "general phrase" intended to capture the principles of the Magna Carta, and the emphasis was on the concept of due process in dealing with government, not on any particular, narrowly understood trigger. *Id.* at 128–29.

In light of this history, Shapiro and Levy argue, in essence, that nondelegation theory requires that government actions be guided by standards, and rule of law principles require the application of due process to assure that standards are fol-lowed. They would even apply this principle to rulemaking, although they assert that it would make little difference in practice because the written notice-and-comment process meets the requirements of due process. *Id.* at 142–44. They conclude:

> If ours is to be a "government of laws and not of men," the rule of law, and hence due process, must apply to government benefits. The current entitlement-based approach leaves significant gaps in the application of due process to government benefits, provides at best a shaky foundation for the rule of law, and threatens to undermine the entire concept of property rights.
>
> The standards-based approach is a workable alternative that has its roots in due process cases dating back to the 1800s. This approach resonates with the idea of rule of law by emphasizing and preserving governmental regularity. Except in narrow areas where the Constitution itself permits standardless political discretion, governmental regularity requires legal standards that guide and control the execution of the law. Once legal standards are in place, it is the duty of all government officials to comply with them, regardless of the character of the right or interest at issue. Due process is a crucial con-stitutional mechanism for ensuring compliance with legal standards and therefore should apply whenever there are legal standards. The standards-based approach would therefore provide solid constitutional foundations for the rule of law, and it would do so without requiring wholesale changes in current practice or wholesale rejection of historical precedents.

Id. at 152–53.

What do you think of their argument? Who, in this context, are the activist judges, the ones who (as Shapiro and Levy would argue) narrowed due process rights in *Roth*, or the ones who would adopt the Shapiro and Levy "rule of law" theory of due process protections?

4. Does due process apply to an application for a government entitlement as well as to its termination? What if Mort did not yet have a wine merchant's license? Assuming such a license constitutes a property interest, would Mort have a due pro-cess right to be heard before his license application could be denied? How would you argue for Mort for the application of due process, or for the WTC against the application of due process?

The resolution of this question is at best uncertain. In *American Manufacturers Mutual Insurance Co. v. Sullivan*, 526 U.S. 40 (1999), the justices seem to have staked out opposing positions, although they did not have to resolve the issue. Work-ers' compensation claimants argued they were entitled to pre-deprivation hear-ings when insurers withheld payments pending "utilization review" to determine whether medical services were reasonable and necessary. For the majority, Chief Justice Rehnquist wrote that:

> [F]or an employee's property interest in the payment of medical benefits to attach under state law, the employee must clear two hurdles: First, he must

prove that an employer is liable for a work-related injury, and second, he must establish that the particular medical treatment at issue is reasonable and necessary. Only then does the employee's interest parallel that of the beneficiary of welfare assistance in *Goldberg* and the recipient of disability benefits in *Mathews*.

526 U.S. at 60–61. The claimants passed the first test but not the second, so they did not have a property interest that would trigger due process.

That would seem to resolve the issue against Mort, but Justice Ginsburg wrote in her concurring opinion that:

> I join Part III of the Court's opinion on the understanding that the Court rejects specifically, and only, respondents' demands for constant payment of each medical bill, within 30 days of receipt, pending determination of the necessity or reasonableness of the medical treatment. I do not doubt, however, that due process requires fair procedures for the adjudication of respondents' claims for workers' compensation benefits, including medical care.

526 U.S. at 61–62.

The courts of appeals have unanimously agreed "that a property interest in an application will arise if a statute narrows the decisionmaker's discretion to specific eligibility criteria and the statute creates a legitimate claim of entitlement to that benefit if the applicant meets the specific eligibility criteria." Virginia T. Vance, Note, *Applications for Benefits: Due Process, Equal Protection, and the Right to Be Free from Arbitrary Procedures*, 61 WASH. & LEE L. REV. 883, 890–91 (2004). In 2008, the Eleventh Circuit hinted otherwise, holding cryptically in an unpublished opinion that "applicants for benefits do not have a legitimate entitlement to those benefits that triggers due process protection." *Troup v. Fulton County*, 297 Fed. Appx. 934, 936 (11th Cir. 2008). In that case, however, the Eleventh Circuit noted that the claimant "did not meet the plan's disability retirement criteria, and could not establish [the] prima facie case of eligibility" necessary to create a legitimate claim of an entitlement in the context of an application for benefits. *Id.* at 936.

If Mort did not yet have a wine merchant's license, what would give rise to an argument that due process dictates certain minimum procedures when he applies for one? Consider two different sets of criteria that Mort might have to meet to obtain a wine merchant's license: (1) a showing that he has no criminal record and has completed training in the requirements governing wine merchant operations; or (2) a showing, to the satisfaction of the Director of the Bureau of Wine Merchant Licenses, that he understands the requirements governing wine merchant operations and is of good moral character. Which criteria are more likely to support an argument that due process attaches to Mort's application? Why? Should it matter?

5. Statutory procedures cannot substitute for constitutional protections when due process attaches—no "bitter with the sweet." In *Cleveland Board of Education v. Loudermill*, 470 U.S. 532 (1985), the Court rejected the argument that government-created entitlements can be defined to include the procedures provided for in the relevant statute. Under that argument, the statutory procedures themselves would always be sufficient, no matter how minimal or ineffective they might be. Termed the "bitter with the sweet," this concept had been accepted by a plurality of three justices in *Arnett v. Kennedy*, 416 U.S. 134 (1974).

Loudermill was dismissed from his position without a pre-termination hearing, but with a post-termination hearing in accordance with the applicable statute. The Court held that compliance with the statute was not enough to avoid constitutional scrutiny:

> [I]t is settled that the "bitter with the sweet" approach misconceives the constitutional guarantee. If a clearer holding is needed, we provide it today. The point is straightforward: the Due Process Clause provides that certain substantive rights—life, liberty, and property—cannot be deprived except pursuant to constitutionally adequate procedures. The categories of substance and procedure are distinct. Were the rule otherwise, the Clause would be reduced to a mere tautology. "Property" cannot be defined by the procedures provided for its deprivation any more than can life or liberty. The right to due process "is conferred, not by legislative grace, but by constitutional guarantee. While the legislature may elect not to confer a property interest in [public] employment, it may not constitutionally authorize the deprivation of such an interest, once conferred, without appropriate procedural safeguards."

> In short, once it is determined that the Due Process Clause applies, "the question remains what process is due." The answer to that question is not to be found in the Ohio statute.

But why should that be? If, following the logic of cases such as *Goldberg*, *Roth*, and *Sindermann*, a statute can create a property right, why can't a statute define the procedures that protect the right? Viewed one way, aren't those procedures a *part* of the property right created by the statute?

6. State due process analysis. State court analysis of due process questions under the U.S. Constitution or the applicable state constitution usually tracks very closely with federal due process law. For example, consider this Florida appellate court opinion, another involving academic employment. Dr. Spiegel had been employed as chairman of his department through seven successive one-year contracts. Two months into one such contract, the university sought to remove him as chairman without providing any reason for the action, and without providing any procedural protections. The court would have none of it:

> The question is whether Dr. Spiegel possessed a property interest in his 1988 contract as chairman of the department which could not be stripped from him without a showing of good cause and the affording of procedural due process. *See Board of Regents v. Roth.* It appears to us well settled that "[a] written contract with an explicit tenure provision clearly is evidence of a

formal understanding that supports a teacher's claim of entitlement to continued employment unless sufficient 'cause' is shown." *Perry v. Sindermann.*

We hold that Dr. Spiegel's contractual status and the potential right to compensation over and above that of a professor are protected property rights that cannot be withdrawn without notice and the opportunity to be heard. This is not, however, the sole concern we have with the manner in which Dr. Spiegel was removed. Removing him without charging misconduct or providing any other explanation for such action may well damage his standing with his associates and in the community generally. It may place upon him a stigma giving rise to suspicions as to the reason for his removal, damaging his reputation and impairing his ability to obtain employment elsewhere, factors which implicate his liberty interest protected by the Fourteenth Amendment. These reasons, standing alone, suggest the propriety of a hearing prior to the termination of his contract. Thus, we find that Dr. Spiegel possesses a constitutionally protected property interest in the benefits flowing from his chairmanship as well as his tenured position of professor entitling him to the procedural protections of Chapter 6C4-10, Florida Administrative Code.

Spiegel v. University of South Florida, 555 So. 2d 428, 429 (Fla. Dist. Ct. App. 1989). *See* 1 KOCH, ADMINISTRATIVE LAW AND PRACTICE, SECOND 119 (1997). Note that this decision was reached after *Paul v. Davis*, excerpted below, but it appears to give greater credence to the problem of reputational stigma than the U.S. Supreme Court did 13 years earlier.

c. The Liberty Interest as a Due Process Trigger

We tend to think of liberty as freedom from restraint. Thus, there is no doubt that due process requires a fair trial before the state can imprison someone. Administrative law rarely involves imprisonment (and when regulatory statutes provide for criminal penalties, they move to the realm of criminal law and process). But as the Court said in *Roth*, "'Liberty' and 'property' are broad and majestic terms." Just as property is not limited to traditional ownership interests, "the Court has required due process protection for deprivations of liberty beyond the sort of formal constraints imposed by the criminal process." 408 U.S. at 571–72. Indeed, as we will see below, *Roth* itself suggested that imposing a stigma that impugns an individual's "good name, reputation, honor, or integrity," 408 U.S. at 573, might constitute an infringement of liberty that would trigger due process.

Consider whether these principles can help Mort in the following scenario.

Lesson 4B.1.c. Many of Mort's customers have expressed concern about Mort's problems with the Association that led to his suspension for violating pricing disclosure rules. One customer, in fact, called Mort a "cheat" to his face when the customer found out that the Association questioned his pricing practices. Indeed, several customers have notified Mort that they are changing distributors. One of those customers was the local state university, to which Mort had supplied fine wines for various occasions. When a local reporter asked a university spokesman why it had changed distributors, the spokesman explained that: "It is university policy not to deal with businesses that cheat the public or otherwise engage in improper business practices."

Considering the following materials, can Abby raise a valid due process claim on Mort's behalf? Against whom would she raise it? What should she argue, and how should the government respond?

Background of *Paul v. Davis*

The following case involved what might well have been considered a "stigma" under *Roth*—the plaintiff's name was included on a list of known shoplifters. Examine carefully how the Court addressed this claim of stigma. Also, consider carefully how the Court distinguished this case from the seemingly comparable case of *Wisconsin v. Constantineau*.

Paul v. Davis
424 U.S. 693 (1976)

Mr. Justice Rehnquist delivered the opinion of the Court.

We granted certiorari in this case to consider whether respondent's charge that petitioners' defamation of him, standing alone and apart from any other governmental action with respect to him, stated a claim for relief under 42 U.S.C. § 1983 and the Fourteenth Amendment. For the reasons hereinafter stated, we conclude that it does not.

Petitioner Paul is the Chief of Police of the Louisville, Ky., Division of Police, while petitioner McDaniel occupies the same position in the Jefferson County, Ky., Division of Police. In late 1972 they agreed to combine their efforts for the purpose of alerting local area merchants to possible shoplifters who might be operating during the Christmas season. In early December petitioners distributed to approximately 800 merchants in the Louisville metropolitan area a "flyer," which began as follows:

"TO: BUSINESS MEN IN THE METROPOLITAN AREA

"The Chiefs of The Jefferson County and City of Louisville Police Departments, in an effort to keep their officers advised on shoplifting activity, have approved the attached alphabetically arranged flyer of subjects known to be active in this criminal field.

"This flyer is being distributed to you, the business man, so that you may inform your security personnel to watch for these subjects. These persons have been arrested during 1971 and 1972 or have been active in various criminal fields in high density shopping areas.

"Only the photograph and name of the subject is shown on this flyer, if additional information is desired, please forward a request in writing. . . ."

The flyer consisted of five pages of "mug shot" photos, arranged alphabetically. Each page was headed:

"November 1972 City of Louisville Jefferson County Police
Departments Active Shoplifters"

In approximately the center of page 2 there appeared photos and the name of the respondent, Edward Charles Davis III.

Respondent appeared on the flyer because on June 14, 1971, he had been arrested in Louisville on a charge of shoplifting. He had been arraigned on this charge in September 1971, and, upon his plea of not guilty, the charge had been "filed away with leave [to reinstate]," a disposition which left the charge outstanding. Thus, at the time petitioners caused the flyer to be prepared and circulated respondent had been charged with shoplifting but his guilt or innocence of that offense had never been resolved. Shortly after circulation of the flyer the charge against respondent was finally dismissed by a judge of the Louisville Police Court.

At the time the flyer was circulated respondent was employed as a photographer by the Louisville Courier-Journal and Times. The flyer, and respondent's inclusion therein, soon came to the attention of respondent's supervisor, the executive director of photography for the two newspapers. This individual called respondent in to hear his version of the events leading to his appearing in the flyer. Following this discussion, the supervisor informed respondent that although he would not be fired, he "had best not find himself in a similar situation" in the future.

Respondent thereupon brought this § 1983 action in the District Court for the Western District of Kentucky, seeking redress for the alleged violation of rights guaranteed to him by the Constitution of the United States. Claiming jurisdiction under 28 U.S.C. § 1343(3), respondent sought damages as well as declaratory and injunctive relief. Petitioners moved to dismiss this complaint. The District Court granted this motion, ruling that "[t]he facts alleged in this case do not establish that plaintiff has been deprived of any right secured to him by the Constitution of the United States."

> *PROCEDURAL HISTORY*

. . . .

Respondent's due process claim is grounded upon his assertion that the flyer, and in particular the phrase "Active Shoplifters" appearing at the head of the page upon which his name and photograph appear, impermissibly deprived him of some "liberty" protected by the Fourteenth Amendment. His complaint asserted that the "active shoplifter" designation would inhibit him from entering business establishments for fear of being suspected of shoplifting and possibly apprehended, and would seriously impair his future employment opportunities. Accepting that such consequences may flow from the flyer in question, respondent's complaint would appear to state a classical claim for defamation actionable in the courts of virtually every State. Imputing criminal behavior to an individual is generally considered defamatory *per se*, and actionable without proof of special damages.

Respondent brought his action, however, not in the state courts of Kentucky, but in a United States District Court for that State. He asserted not a claim for defamation under the laws of Kentucky, but a claim that he had been deprived of rights secured to him by the Fourteenth Amendment of the United States Constitution. Concededly if the same allegations had been made about respondent by a private individual, he would have nothing more than a claim for defamation under state law. But, he contends, since petitioners are respectively an official of city and of county government, his action is thereby transmuted into one for deprivation by the State of rights secured under the Fourteenth Amendment. . . .

The result reached by the Court of Appeals, which respondent seeks to sustain here, must be bottomed on one of two premises. The first is that the Due Process Clause of the Fourteenth Amendment and § 1983 make actionable many wrongs inflicted by government employees which had heretofore been thought to give rise only to state-law tort claims. The second premise is that the infliction by state officials of a "stigma" to one's reputation is somehow different in kind from the infliction by the same official of harm or injury to other interests protected by state law, so that an injury to reputation is actionable under § 1983 and the Fourteenth Amendment even if other such harms are not. We examine each of these premises in turn.

. . . .

The first premise would be contrary to pronouncements in our cases on more than one occasion with respect to the scope of § 1983 and of the Fourteenth Amendment. . . .

[S]uch a reading would make of the Fourteenth Amendment a font of tort law to be superimposed upon whatever systems may already be administered by the States. We have noted the "constitutional shoals" that confront any attempt to derive from congressional civil rights statutes a body of general federal tort law, *a fortiori*, the procedural guarantees of the Due Process Clause cannot be the source for such law.

The second premise upon which the result reached by the Court of Appeals could be rested—that the infliction by state officials of a "stigma" to one's reputation is somehow different in kind from infliction by a state official of harm to other interests protected by state law—is equally untenable. The words "liberty" and "property" as used in the Fourteenth Amendment do not in terms single out reputation as a candidate for special protection over and above other interests that may be protected by state law. While we have in a number of our prior cases pointed out the frequently drastic effect of the "stigma" which may result from defamation by the government in a variety of contexts, this line of cases does not establish the proposition that reputation alone, apart from some more tangible interests such as employment, is either "liberty" or "property" by itself sufficient to invoke the procedural protection of the Due Process Clause. As we have said, the Court of Appeals, in reaching a contrary conclusion, relied primarily upon *Wisconsin v. Constantineau* (1971). We think the correct import of that decision, however, must be derived from an examination of the precedents upon which it relied, as well as consideration of the other decisions by this Court, before and after *Constantineau*, which bear upon the relationship between governmental defamation and the guarantees of the Constitution. While not uniform in their treatment of the subject, we think that the weight of our decisions establishes no constitutional doctrine converting every defamation by a public official into a deprivation of liberty within the meaning of the Due Process Clause of the Fifth or Fourteenth Amendment.

In *United States v. Lovett* (1946), the Court held that an Act of Congress which specifically forbade payment of any salary or compensation to three named Government agency employees was an unconstitutional bill of attainder. The three employees had been proscribed because a House of Representatives subcommittee found them guilty of "subversive activity," and therefore unfit for Government service. The Court, while recognizing that the underlying charges upon which Congress' action was premised "stigmatized [the employees'] reputation and seriously impaired their chance to earn a living," also made it clear that "[w]hat is involved here is a Congressional proscription of [these employees], prohibiting their ever holding a government job."

Subsequently, in *Joint Anti-Fascist Refugee Comm. v. McGrath* (1951), the Court examined the validity of the Attorney General's designation of certain organizations as "Communist" on a list which he furnished to the Civil Service Commission. There was no majority opinion in the case; Mr. Justice Burton, who announced the judgment of the Court, wrote an opinion which did not reach the petitioners' constitutional claim. Mr. Justice Frankfurter, who agreed with Mr. Justice Burton that the petitioners had stated a claim upon which relief could be granted, noted that "publicly designating an organization as within the proscribed categories of the Loyalty Order does not directly deprive anyone of liberty or property." Mr. Justice Douglas, who likewise concluded that petitioners had stated a claim, observed in his separate opinion:

> "This is not an instance of name calling by public officials. This is a determination of status—a proceeding to ascertain whether the organization is or is not 'subversive.' This determination has consequences that are serious to the condemned organizations. Those consequences flow in part, of course, from public opinion. But they also flow from actions of regulatory agencies that are moving in the wake of the Attorney General's determination to penalize or police these organizations."

Mr. Justice Jackson, who likewise agreed that petitioners had stated a claim, commented:

> "I agree that mere designation as subversive deprives the organizations themselves of no legal right or immunity. By it they are not dissolved, subjected to any legal prosecution, punished, penalized, or prohibited from carrying on any of their activities. Their claim of injury is that they cannot attract audiences, enlist members, or obtain contributions as readily as before. These, however, are sanctions applied by public disapproval, not by law."

He went on to say:

> "[T]he real target of all this procedure is the government employee who is a member of, or sympathetic to, one or more accused organizations. He not only may be discharged, but disqualified from employment, upon no other ground than such membership or sympathetic affiliation. . . . To be deprived not only of present government employment but of future opportunity for it certainly is no small injury when government employment so dominates the field of opportunity."

Mr. Justice Reed, writing for himself, The Chief Justice, and Mr. Justice Minton, would have held that petitioners failed to state a claim for relief. In his dissenting opinion, after having stated petitioners' claim that their listing resulted in a deprivation of liberty or property contrary to the procedure required by the Fifth Amendment, he said:

> "The contention can be answered summarily by saying that there is no deprivation of any property or liberty of any listed organization by the Attorney General's designation. It may be assumed that the listing is hurtful to their prestige, reputation and earning power. It may be such an injury as would entitle organizations to damages in a tort action against persons not protected by privilege. . . . This designation, however, does not prohibit any business of the organizations, subject them to any punishment or deprive them of liberty of speech or other freedom."

Thus at least six of the eight Justices who participated in that case viewed any "stigma" imposed by official action of the Attorney General of the United States, divorced from its effect on the legal status of an organization or a person, such as loss of tax exemption or loss of government employment, as an insufficient basis for invoking the Due Process Clause of the Fifth Amendment.

In *Wieman v. Updegraff* (1952), the Court again recognized the potential "badge of infamy" which might arise from being branded disloyal by the government. But it did not hold this sufficient by itself to invoke the procedural due process guarantees of the Fourteenth Amendment; indeed, the Court expressly refused to pass upon the procedural due process claims of petitioners in that case. The Court noted that petitioners would, as a result of their failure to execute the state loyalty oath, lose their teaching positions at a state university. It held such state action to be arbitrary because of its failure to distinguish between innocent and knowing membership in the associations named in the list prepared by the Attorney General of the United States.

A decade after *Joint Anti-Fascist Refugee Comm. v. McGrath*, the Court returned to consider further the requirements of procedural due process in this area in the case of *Cafeteria Workers v. McElroy* (1961). Holding that the discharge of an employee of a Government contractor in the circumstances there presented comported with the due process required by the Fifth Amendment, the Court observed:

"Finally, it is to be noted that this is not a case where government action has operated to bestow a badge of disloyalty or infamy, *with an attendant foreclosure from other employment opportunity.*"

Two things appear from the line of cases beginning with *Lovett*. The Court has recognized the serious damage that could be inflicted by branding a government employee as "disloyal," and thereby stigmatizing his good name. But the Court has never held that the mere defamation of an individual, whether by branding him disloyal or otherwise, was sufficient to invoke the guarantees of procedural due process absent an accompanying loss of government employment.

It is noteworthy that in *Barr v. Matteo* (1959), and *Howard v. Lyons* (1959), this Court had before it two actions for defamation brought against federal officers. But in neither opinion is there any intimation that any of the parties to those cases, or any of the Members of this Court, had the remotest idea that the Due Process Clause of the Fifth Amendment might itself form the basis for a claim for defamation against federal officials.

It was against this backdrop that the Court in 1971 decided *Constantineau*. There the Court held that a Wisconsin statute authorizing the practice of "posting" was unconstitutional because it failed to provide procedural safeguards of notice and an opportunity to be heard, prior to an individual's being "posted." Under the statute "posting" consisted of forbidding in writing the sale or delivery of alcoholic beverages to certain persons who were determined to have become hazards to themselves, to their family, or to the community by reason of their "excessive drinking." The statute also made it a misdemeanor to sell or give liquor to any person so posted.

There is undoubtedly language in *Constantineau*, which is sufficiently ambiguous to justify the reliance upon it by the Court of Appeals:

"Yet certainly where the State attaches 'a badge of infamy' to the citizen due process comes into play. *Wieman v. Updegraff.* '[T]he right to be heard before being condemned to suffer grievous loss of any kind, even though it may not involve the stigma and hardships of a criminal conviction, is a principle basic to our society.' *Anti-Fascist Refugee Committee v. McGrath* (Frankfurter, J., concurring).

"Where a person's good name, reputation, honor, or integrity is at stake *because of what the government is doing to him*, notice and an opportunity to be heard are essential." (emphasis supplied).

The last paragraph of the quotation could be taken to mean that if a government official defames a person, without more, the procedural requirements of the Due Process Clause of the Fourteenth Amendment are brought into play. If read that way, it would represent a significant broadening of the holdings of *Wieman v. Updegraff*, and *Anti-Fascist Comm. v. McGrath*, relied upon by the *Constantineau* Court in its analysis in the immediately preceding paragraph. We should not read this language as significantly broadening those holdings without in any way adverting to the fact if there is any other possible interpretation of *Constantineau*'s language. We believe there is.

We think that the italicized language in the last sentence quoted, "because of what the government is doing to him," referred to the fact that the governmental action taken in that case deprived the individual of a right previously held under state law the right to purchase or obtain liquor in common with the rest of the citizenry. "Posting," therefore, significantly altered her status as a matter of state law, and it was that alteration of legal status which, combined with the injury resulting from the defamation, justified the invocation of procedural safeguards. The "stigma" resulting from the defamatory character of the posting was doubtless an important factor in evaluating the extent of harm worked by that act, but we do not think that such defamation, standing alone, deprived Constantineau of any "liberty" protected by the procedural guarantees of the Fourteenth Amendment.

This conclusion is reinforced by our discussion of the subject a little over a year later in *Board of Regents v. Roth* (1972). There we noted that "the range of interests protected by procedural due process is not infinite," and that with respect to property interests they are,

> "of course, ... not created by the Constitution. Rather, they are created and their dimensions are defined by existing rules or understandings that stem from an independent source such as state law rules or understandings that secure certain benefits and that support claims of entitlement to those benefits."

While *Roth* recognized that governmental action defaming an individual in the course of declining to rehire him could entitle the person to notice and an opportunity to be heard as to the defamation, its language is quite inconsistent with any notion that a defamation perpetrated by a government official but unconnected with any refusal to rehire would be actionable under the Fourteenth Amendment:

> "The State, *in declining to rehire the respondent*, did not make any charge against him that might seriously damage his standing and associations in his community. ...

> "Similarly, there is no suggestion that the State, *in declining to reemploy the respondent*, imposed on him a stigma or other disability that foreclosed his freedom to take advantage of other employment opportunities." (emphasis supplied).

Thus it was not thought sufficient to establish a claim under § 1983 and the Fourteenth Amendment that there simply be defamation by a state official; the defamation had to occur in the course of the termination of employment. Certainly there is no suggestion in *Roth* to indicate that a hearing would be required each time the State in its capacity as employer might be considered responsible for a statement defaming an employee who continues to be an employee.

This conclusion is quite consistent with our most recent holding in this area, *Goss v. Lopez*, 419 U.S. 565 (1975), that suspension from school based upon charges of misconduct could trigger the procedural guarantees of the Fourteenth Amendment. While the Court noted that charges of misconduct could seriously damage the student's reputation, it also took care to point out that Ohio law conferred a right upon all children to attend school, and that the act of the school officials suspending the student there involved resulted in a denial or deprivation of that right.

It is apparent from our decisions that there exists a variety of interests which are difficult of definition but are nevertheless comprehended within the meaning of either "liberty" or "property" as meant in the Due Process Clause. These interests attain this constitutional status by virtue of the fact that they have been initially recognized and protected by state law, and we have repeatedly ruled that the procedural guarantees of the Fourteenth Amendment apply whenever the State seeks to remove or significantly alter that protected status. In *Bell v. Burson* (1971), for example, the State by issuing drivers' licenses recognized in its citizens a right to operate a vehicle on the highways of the State. The Court held that the State could not withdraw this right without giving petitioner due process. In *Morrissey v. Brewer* (1972), the State afforded parolees the right to remain at liberty as long as the conditions of their parole were not violated. Before the State could alter the status of a parolee because of alleged violations of these conditions, we held that the Fourteenth Amendment's guarantee of due process of law required certain procedural safeguards.

In each of these cases, as a result of the state action complained of, a right or status previously recognized by state law was distinctly altered or extinguished. It was this alteration, officially removing the interest from the recognition and protection previously afforded by the State, which we found sufficient to invoke the procedural guarantees contained in the Due Process Clause of the Fourteenth Amendment. But the interest in reputation alone which respondent seeks to vindicate in this action in federal court is quite different from the "liberty" or "property" recognized in those decisions. Kentucky law does not extend to respondent any legal guarantee of present enjoyment of reputation which has been altered as a result of petitioners' actions. Rather his interest in reputation is simply one of a number which the State may protect against injury by virtue of its tort law, providing a forum for vindication of those interests by means of damages actions. And any harm or injury to that interest, even where as here inflicted by an officer of the State, does not result in a deprivation of any "liberty" or "property" recognized by state or federal law, nor has it worked any change of respondent's status as theretofore recognized under the State's laws. For these reasons we hold that the interest in reputation asserted in this case is neither "liberty" nor "property" guaranteed against state deprivation without due process of law.

Respondent in this case cannot assert denial of any right vouchsafed to him by the State and thereby protected under the Fourteenth Amendment. That being the case, petitioners' defamatory publications, however seriously they may have harmed respondent's reputation, did not deprive him of any "liberty" or "property" interests protected by the Due Process Clause. . . .

None of respondent's theories of recovery were based upon rights secured to him by the Fourteenth Amendment. Petitioners therefore were not liable to him under § 1983. The judgment of the Court of Appeals holding otherwise is

Reversed.

Mr. Justice Brennan, with whom Mr. Justice Marshall concurs and Mr. Justice White concurs in part, dissenting.

I dissent. The Court today holds that police officials, acting in their official capacities as law enforcers, may on their own initiative and without trial constitutionally condemn innocent individuals as criminals and thereby brand them with one of the most stigmatizing and debilitating labels in our society. If there are no constitutional restraints on such oppressive behavior, the safe-guards constitutionally accorded an accused in a criminal trial are rendered a sham, and no individual can feel secure that he will not be arbitrarily singled out for similar *ex parte* punishment by those primarily charged with fair enforcement of the law. The Court accomplishes this result by excluding a person's interest in his good name and reputation from all constitutional protection, regardless of the character of or necessity for the government's actions. The result, which is demonstrably inconsistent with our prior case law and unduly restrictive in its construction of our precious Bill of Rights, is one in which I cannot concur. . . .

The stark fact is that the police here have officially imposed on respondent the stigmatizing label "criminal" without the salutary and constitutionally mandated safeguards of a criminal trial. The Court concedes that this action will have deleterious consequences for respondent. For 15 years, the police had prepared and circulated similar lists, not with respect to shoplifting alone, but also for other offenses. Included in the five-page list in which respondent's name and "mug shot" appeared were numerous individuals who, like respondent, were never convicted of any criminal activity and whose only "offense" was having once been arrested. Indeed, respondent was arrested over 17 months before the flyer was distributed, not by state law enforcement authorities, but by a store's private security police, and nothing in the record appears to suggest the existence at that time of even constitutionally sufficient probable cause for that single arrest on a shoplifting charge. Nevertheless, petitioners had 1,000 flyers printed (800 were distributed widely throughout the Louisville business community) proclaiming that the individuals identified by name and picture were "subjects *known* to be *active* in this criminal field [shoplifting]," and trumpeting the "fact" that each page depicted *"Active Shoplifters"* (emphasis supplied).

Although accepting the truth of the allegation, as we must on the motion to dismiss, that dissemination of this flyer would "seriously impair [respondent's] future employment opportunities" and "inhibit him from entering business establishments for fear of being suspected of shoplifting and possibly apprehended," the Court characterizes the allegation as "mere defamation" involving no infringement of constitutionally protected interests. This is because, the Court holds neither a "liberty" nor a "property" interest was invaded by the injury done respondent's reputation and therefore no violation of § 1983 or the Fourteenth Amendment was alleged. I wholly disagree.

It is important, to paraphrase the Court, that "[w]e, too, [should] pause to consider the result should [the Court's] interpretation of § 1983 and of the Fourteenth Amendment be accepted." There is no attempt by the Court to analyze the question as one of reconciliation of constitutionally protected personal rights and the exigencies of law enforcement. No effort is made to distinguish the "defamation" that occurs when a grand jury indicts an accused from the "defamation" that occurs when executive officials arbitrarily and without trial declare a person an "active criminal." Rather, the Court by mere fiat and with no analysis wholly excludes personal interest in reputation from the ambit of "life, liberty, or property" under the Fifth and Fourteenth Amendments, thus rendering due process concerns *never* applicable to the official stigmatization, however arbitrary, of an individual. The logical and disturbing corollary of this holding is that no due process infirmities would inhere in a statute constituting a commission to conduct *ex parte* trials of individuals, so long as the only official judgment pronounced was limited to the public condemnation and branding of a person as a Communist, a traitor, an "active murderer," a homosexual, or any other mark that "merely" carries social opprobrium. The potential of today's decision is frightening for a free people. That decision surely finds no support in our relevant constitutional jurisprudence.

"In a Constitution for a free people, there can be no doubt that the meaning of 'liberty' must be broad indeed." "Without doubt it denotes not merely freedom from bodily restraint but also the right of the individual . . . generally to enjoy those privileges long recognized . . . as essential to the orderly pursuit of happiness by free men."[10] Certainly the enjoyment of one's good name and reputation has been recognized repeatedly in our cases as being among the most cherished of rights enjoyed by a free people, and therefore as falling within the concept of personal "liberty."

We have consistently held that

> "'[W]here a person's good name, reputation, honor, or integrity is at stake because of what the government is doing to him, notice and an opportunity to be heard are essential.'"

---

10. One of the more questionable assertions made by the Court suggests that "liberty" or "property" interests are protected only if they are recognized under state law or protected by one of the specific guarantees of the Bill of Rights. . . . We have never restricted "liberty" interests in the manner the Court today attempts to do. The Due Process Clause of the Fifth Amendment, like the Due Process Clause of the Fourteenth Amendment, protects "liberty" interests. But the content of "liberty" in those Clauses has never been thought to depend on recognition of an interest by the State or Federal Government, and has never been restricted to interests explicitly recognized by other provisions of the Bill of Rights. . . . It should thus be clear that much of the content of "liberty" has no tie whatsoever to particular provisions of the Bill of Rights, and the Court today gives no explanation for its narrowing of that content.

In the criminal justice system, this interest is given concrete protection through the presumption of innocence and the prohibition of state-imposed punishment unless the State can demonstrate beyond a reasonable doubt, at a public trial with the attendant constitutional safeguards, that a particular individual has engaged in proscribed criminal conduct. "[B]ecause of the certainty that [one found guilty of criminal behavior] would be stigmatized by the conviction . . . a society that values the good name and freedom of every individual should not condemn a man for commission of a crime when there is reasonable doubt about his guilt." . . .

Today's decision marks a clear retreat from *Jenkins v. McKeithen* (1969), a case closely akin to the factual pattern of the instant case, and yet essentially ignored by the Court. . . .

Thus, although the Court was divided on the particular procedural safeguards that would be necessary in particular circumstances, the common point of agreement, and the one that the Court today inexplicably rejects, was that the official characterization of an individual as a criminal affects a constitutional "liberty" interest.

Wisconsin v. Constantineau (1971), which was relied on by the Court of Appeals in this case, did not rely at all on the fact asserted by the Court today as controlling—namely, upon the fact that "posting" denied Ms. Constantineau the right to purchase alcohol for a year. Rather, *Constantineau* stated: "The *only* issue present here is whether the label or characterization given a person by 'posting,' though a mark of serious illness to some, is to others such a stigma or badge of disgrace that procedural due process requires notice and an opportunity to be heard." In addition to the statements quoted by the Court, the Court in *Constantineau* continued: "'Posting' under the Wisconsin Act may to some be merely the mark of illness, to others it is a stigma, an official branding of a person. The label is a degrading one. Under the Wisconsin Act, a resident of Hartford is given no process at all. This appellee was not afforded a chance to defend herself. She may have been the victim of an official's caprice. Only when the whole proceedings leading to the pinning of an unsavory label on a person are aired can oppressive results be prevented." "'[T]he right to be heard before being condemned to suffer grievous loss of any kind, *even though it may not involve the stigma and hardships of a criminal conviction*, is a principle basic to our society.'" quoting *Joint Anti-Fascist Refugee Comm. v. McGrath* (1951) (Frankfurter, J., concurring) (emphasis supplied). There again, the fact that government stigmatization of an individual implicates constitutionally protected interests was made plain.[15]

Thus *Jenkins* and *Constantineau*, and the decisions upon which they relied, are cogent authority that a person's interest in his good name and reputation falls

---

15. Even more recently, in *Goss v. Lopez* (1975), we recognized that students may not be suspended from school without being accorded due process safeguards. We explicitly referred to "the liberty interest in reputation" implicated by such suspensions, based upon the fact that suspension for certain actions would stigmatize the student. . . .

within the broad term "liberty" and clearly require that the government afford procedural protections before infringing that name and reputation by branding a person as a criminal. The Court is reduced to discrediting the clear thrust of *Constantineau* and *Jenkins* by excluding the interest in reputation from all constitutional protection "if there is any other possible interpretation" by which to deny their force as precedent according constitutional protection for the interest in reputation. The Court's approach oblivious both to Mr. Chief Justice Marshall's admonition that "we must never forget, that it is *a constitution* we are expounding," and to the teaching of cases such as *Roth* and *Meyer*, which were attentive to the necessary breadth of constitutional "liberty" and "property" interests, is to water down our prior precedents by reinterpreting them as confined to injury to reputation that affects an individual's employment prospects or, as "a right or status previously recognized by state law [that the State] distinctly altered or extinguished." The obvious answer is that such references in those cases (when there even were such references) concerned the particular fact situations presented, and in nowise implied any limitation upon the application of the principles announced. Discussions of impact upon future employment opportunities were nothing more than recognition of the logical and natural consequences flowing from the stigma condemned.

Moreover, the analysis has a hollow ring in light of the Court's acceptance of the truth of the allegation that the "active shoplifter" label would "seriously impair [respondent's] future employment opportunities." This is clear recognition that an official "badge of infamy" affects tangible interests of the defamed individual and not merely an abstract interest in how people view him; for the "badge of infamy" has serious consequences in its impact on no less than the opportunities open to him to enjoy life, liberty, and the pursuit of happiness. It is inexplicable how the Court can say that a person's status is "altered" when the State suspends him from school, revokes his driver's license, fires him from a job, or denies him the right to purchase a drink of alcohol, but is in no way "altered" when it officially pins upon him the brand of a criminal, particularly since the Court recognizes how deleterious will be the consequences that inevitably flow from its official act. Our precedents clearly mandate that a person's interest in his good name and reputation is cognizable as a "liberty" interest within the meaning of the Due Process Clause, and the Court has simply failed to distinguish those precedents in any rational manner in holding that no invasion of a "liberty" interest was effected in the official stigmatizing of respondent as a criminal without any "process" whatsoever.

I have always thought that one of this Court's most important roles is to provide a formidable bulwark against governmental violation of the constitutional safeguards securing in our free society the legitimate expectations of every person to innate human dignity and sense of worth. It is a regrettable abdication of that role and a saddening denigration of our majestic Bill of Rights when the Court tolerates arbitrary and capricious official conduct branding an individual as a criminal without compliance with constitutional procedures designed to ensure the fair and impartial ascertainment of criminal culpability. Today's decision must surely be a short-lived aberration.

Notes

1. Can Mort make a "liberty interest" argument? How might Abby assert a due process claim on Mort's behalf based upon the infringement of a "liberty interest"? *Paul v. Davis* seems to present a formidable obstacle. How can she make Mort's circumstances sound more like *Constantineau*? The Court in *Board of Regents v. Roth* (excerpted above) set the foundation for a "new liberty" interest to correspond with the "new property" interest created by *Goldberg*:

> [W]hile the Court has eschewed rigid or formalistic limitations on the protection of procedural due process, it has at the same time observed certain boundaries. For the words "liberty" and "property" in the Due Process Clause of the Fourteenth Amendment must be given some meaning.
>
> "While this Court has not attempted to define with exactness the liberty . guaranteed [by the Fourteenth Amendment], the term has received much consideration and some of the included things have been definitely stated. Without doubt, it denotes not merely freedom from bodily restraint but also the right of the individual to contract, to engage in any of the common occupations of life, to acquire useful knowledge, to marry, establish a home and bring up children, to worship God according to the dictates of his own conscience, and generally to enjoy those privileges long recognized . . . as essential to the orderly pursuit of happiness by free men." [*Meyers v. Nebraska*, 262 U.S. at 399 (1923).] In a Constitution for a free people, there can be no doubt that the meaning of "liberty" must be broad indeed.
>
> There might be cases in which a State refused to re-employ a person under such circumstances that interests in liberty would be implicated. But this is not such a case.
>
> The State, in declining to rehire the respondent, did not make any charge against him that might seriously damage his standing and associations in his community. It did not base the nonrenewal of his contract on a charge, for example, that he had been guilty of dishonesty, or immorality. Had it done so, this would be a different case. For "[w]here a person's good name, reputation, honor, or integrity is at stake because of what the government is doing to him, notice and an opportunity to be heard are essential." In such a case, due process would accord an opportunity to refute the charge before University officials. In the present case, however, there is no suggestion whatever that the respondent's "good name, reputation, honor, or integrity" is at stake.
>
> Similarly, there is no suggestion that the State, in declining to reemploy the respondent, imposed on him a stigma or other disability that foreclosed his freedom to take advantage of other employment opportunities. The State,

for example, did not invoke any regulations to bar the respondent from all other public employment in state universities. Had it done so, this, again, would be a different case. For "[t]o be deprived not only of present government employment but of future opportunity for it certainly is no small injury." The Court has held, for example, that a State, in regulating eligibility for a type of professional employment, cannot foreclose a range of opportunities "in a manner . . . that contravene[s] . . . Due Process," and, specifically, in a manner that denies the right to a full prior hearing. In the present case, however, this principle does not come into play.

. . . .

Hence, on the record before us, all that clearly appears is that the respondent was not rehired for one year at one university. It stretches the concept too far to suggest that a person is deprived of "liberty" when he simply is not rehired in one job but remains as free as before to seek another.

How did *Paul v. Davis* embellish on this statement regarding a new liberty interest? Did *Paul v. Davis* make raising a liberty interest more difficult? Will the effect on Mort's standing in the business community be sufficient to support a finding of a liberty interest? What might define "legal status," the significant altering of which must be present to find a liberty interest?

2. "Name-clearing" due process hearings. The Court noted the purpose of such a hearing in footnote 12 of *Roth*:

The purpose of such notice and hearing is to provide the person an opportunity to clear his name. Once a person has cleared his name at a hearing, his employer, of course, may remain free to deny him future employment for other reasons.

An after-the-fact hearing cannot retract official action that has unconstitutionally affected the reputation of an individual. Thus, the only practical remedy, other than a damage action, is the opportunity for a "name clearing" hearing.

For a post-*Paul v. Davis* example of facts giving rise to a "name clearing" hearing, consider *Hammer v. City of Osage Beach*, 318 F.3d 832 (8th Cir. 2003). Hammer was a City Manager who was terminated by the Mayor and City. Since he was an at-will employee, he had no property interest. But prior to his termination, the Mayor issued a press release accusing Hammer "of general improprieties and illegalities related to the City's health insurance, contract bids, and Hammer's termination of another City employee." In assessing whether these statements infringed Hammer's liberty interest so as to require a name-clearing hearing, the court applied a three-part test:

To establish the deprivation of a liberty interest, a public employee must make a three-part showing: (1) that the public employer's reasons for the discharge stigmatized the employee, seriously damaging his or her reputation or by foreclosing other employment opportunities; (2) that the employer made the reasons for the discharge public; and (3) that the employee denied the charges that led to the discharge.

Hammer, 318 F.3d at 839–40. Unlike the posting in *Paul v. Davis*, the facts of this case were enough to stigmatize the employee. Why? What about Mort's situation? *Board of Regents v. Roth* was initially interpreted as recognizing a liberty interest if government statements stigmatized someone. *Paul v. Davis* rejected the mere stigma of being listed as a shoplifter. It is said to establish a "stigma-plus" test for recognizing a liberty interest. What is the "plus"?

3. What if the WTC finds Mort has misled and defrauded customers? Assume that the WTC brings an administrative enforcement action against Mort and ultimately concludes, based on the record of an appropriate hearing, that Mort misled and defrauded customers in violation of § 5 of the WTCA. Assume also that any merchant who misleads or defrauds customers is prohibited from buying or selling alcoholic beverages in the state where Mort operates his business. When the state, having read a WTC press release about the case, orders Mort to stop buying or selling wine, does Mort have a due process right to be heard and to argue that he does not defraud customers?

Consider *Connecticut Department of Public Safety v. Doe*, 538 U.S. 1 (2003), in which a convicted sex offender argued that he had a due process right to prove that he was not dangerous before the state could make his name publicly available on a registry of convicted sex offenders. The Court rejected the argument on the principle that there is no need or use for a hearing if there are no facts in dispute. The statutory question was not whether the individual in question was still dangerous, but whether he was a convicted sex offender. How does that principle apply in Mort's case?

4. Due process rights for public school students (even if not for untenured professors). The *Paul v. Davis* majority distinguishes *Goss v. Lopez*, 419 U.S. 565 (1975), which held that students were entitled to due process before they could be suspended from school on charges of misconduct. In so doing, the Court noted that suspension might harm reputation, but it emphasized that Ohio had chosen to give all children a statutory right to an education—a property right. Thus, the public school student's entitlement to due process fell well within the entitlement concept recognized in *Goldberg*.

d. The Peculiar Case of Liberty Interests Within Prisons

Paul v. Davis raised the question of how to identify a "liberty interest." The Court noted that it would find a liberty interest if "a right or status previously recognized by state law was distinctly altered or extinguished" by state action. This suggested that liberty, like property, has its roots in state law, rather than in the Constitution or some other more fundamental source. That proposition became the basis for arguments made by prisoners in response to actions taken by prison authorities. With regret for what we have had to do to Mort's family, we offer the following scenario.

Lesson 4B.1.d. As if Mort weren't having enough problems of his own, his older son Brad is in prison, having been convicted of murder and sentenced to life without parole. Mort has learned that Brad is about to be moved to a Supermax prison due to his behavior in the maximum security prison in which he has been incarcerated. Conditions at the Supermax are more restrictive than any other form of incarceration in the state. In the Supermax almost every aspect of an inmate's life is controlled and monitored. Inmates must remain in their cells, which measure 7 by 14 feet, for 23 hours per day. A light remains on in the cell at all times, though it is sometimes dimmed, and an inmate who attempts to shield the light to sleep is subject to further discipline. During the one hour per day that an inmate may leave his cell, access is limited to one of two indoor recreation cells.

Incarceration at the Supermax is synonymous with extreme isolation. In contrast to any other prison in the state, including any segregation unit, Supermax cells have solid metal doors with metal strips along their sides and bottoms which prevent conversation or communication with other inmates. All meals are taken alone in the inmate's cell instead of in a common eating area. Opportunities for visitation are rare and in all events are conducted through glass walls. It is fair to say Supermax inmates are deprived of almost any environmental or sensory stimuli and of almost all human contact.

These conditions contrast with all other prison confinement. Even at maximum security prisons, inmates have an hour of outdoor exercise each day in good weather, can communicate from cell to cell in various ways, are allowed periodic visits by family (through glass panels), and otherwise have some degree of human interaction.

Abby has learned that the state prison system has adopted regulations under which an inmate will not be sent to the Supermax unless he represents an extremely serious threat to the security of prison employees or other inmates. Recalling *Paul v. Davis*, Abby thinks that when the state moved Brad it extinguished his pre-existing right not to be sent to the Supermax unless the state could show he met its very high standard of dangerousness. Brad was not given anything close to a trial-like hearing before the move. He was called to a meeting of prison officials, told what the charges were, and given a chance to respond orally. He was not permitted to call witnesses or to be represented by counsel.

Considering the following materials, what should Abby argue in an effort to raise a due process claim about Brad's move? How should the state respond?

Background of *Sandin v. Conner*

The following decision is the culmination of a series of cases in which the Supreme Court struggled with the question of whether prisoners can have any liberty interest at all and, if so, how to identify and protect those interests in the context of prison management. Consider the Court's brief flirtation (in *Hewitt v. Helms*, for example) with the *Roth*-like recognition of liberty interests based upon rules adopted by prison systems. Why did the court reject that approach, which it so strongly embraced in the context of identifying property interests?

Sandin v. Conner

515 U.S. 472 (1995)

CHIEF JUSTICE REHNQUIST delivered the opinion of the Court.

We granted certiorari to reexamine the circumstances under which state prison regulations afford inmates a liberty interest protected by the Due Process Clause.

DeMont Conner was convicted of numerous state crimes, including murder, kidnapping, robbery, and burglary, for which he is currently serving an indeterminate sentence of 30 years to life in a Hawaii prison. He was confined in the Halawa Correctional Facility, a maximum security prison in central Oahu. In August 1987, a prison officer escorted him from his cell to the module program area. The officer subjected Conner to a strip search, complete with an inspection of the rectal area. Conner retorted with angry and foul language directed at the officer. Eleven days later he received notice that he had been charged with disciplinary infractions. The notice charged Conner with "high misconduct" for using physical interference to impair a correctional function, and "low moderate misconduct" for using abusive or obscene language and for harassing employees.

Conner appeared before an adjustment committee on August 28, 1987. The committee refused Conner's request to present witnesses at the hearing, stating that "[w]itnesses were unavailable due to move [*sic*] to the medium facility and being short staffed on the modules." At the conclusion of proceedings, the committee determined that Conner was guilty of the alleged misconduct. It sentenced him to 30 days disciplinary segregation in the Special Holding Unit for the physical obstruction charge, and four hours segregation for each of the other two charges to be served concurrent with the 30 days. Conner's segregation began August 31, 1987, and ended September 29, 1987.

Conner sought administrative review within 14 days of receiving the committee's decision. Nine months later, the deputy administrator found the high misconduct charge unsupported and expunged Conner's disciplinary record with respect to that charge. But before the Deputy Administrator decided the appeal, Conner had brought this suit against the adjustment committee chair and other prison officials. . . . His amended complaint prayed for injunctive relief, declaratory relief and damages for, among other things, a deprivation of procedural due process in connection with the disciplinary hearing. . . .[3] . . .

---

3. The full text of the regulation reads as follows:

"Upon completion of the hearing, the committee may take the matter under advisement and render a decision based upon evidence presented at the hearing to which the individual had an opportunity to respond or any cumulative evidence which may subsequently

Our due process analysis begins with *Wolff* [*v. McDonnell*, 418 U.S. 539 (1974)]. There, Nebraska inmates challenged the decision of prison officials to revoke good time credits without adequate procedures. Inmates earned good time credits under a state statute that bestowed mandatory sentence reductions for good behavior, revocable only for "'flagrant or serious misconduct.'" We held that the Due Process Clause itself does not create a liberty interest in credit for good behavior, but that the statutory provision created a liberty interest in a "shortened prison sentence" which resulted from good time credits, credits which were revocable only if the prisoner was guilty of serious misconduct. The Court characterized this liberty interest as one of "real substance" and articulated minimum procedures necessary to reach a "mutual accommodation between institutional needs and objectives and the provisions of the Constitution." Much of *Wolff*'s contribution to the landscape of prisoners' due process derived not from its description of liberty interests, but rather from its intricate balancing of prison management concerns with prisoners' liberty in determining the amount of process due. Its short discussion of the definition of a liberty interest, led to a more thorough treatment of the issue in *Meachum v. Fano*, 427 U.S. 215 (1976).

Inmates in *Meachum* sought injunctive relief, declaratory relief and damages by reason of transfers from a Massachusetts medium security prison to a maximum security facility with substantially less favorable conditions. The transfers were ordered in the aftermath of arson incidents for which the transferred inmates were thought to be responsible, and did not entail a loss of good time credits or any period of disciplinary confinement. The Court began with the proposition that the Due Process Clause does not protect every change in the conditions of confinement having a substantial adverse impact on the prisoner. It then held that the Due Process Clause did not itself create a liberty interest in prisoners to be free from intrastate prison transfers. It reasoned that transfer to a maximum security facility, albeit one with more burdensome conditions, was "within the normal limits or range of custody which the conviction has authorized the State to impose." The Court distinguished *Wolff* by noting that there the protected liberty interest in good time credit had been created by state law; here no comparable Massachusetts law stripped officials of the discretion to transfer prisoners to alternate facilities "for whatever reason or for no reason at all."

Shortly after *Meachum*, the Court embarked on a different approach to defining state-created liberty interests. Because dictum in *Meachum* distinguished *Wolff* by focusing on whether state action was mandatory or discretionary, the Court in later cases laid ever greater emphasis on this somewhat mechanical dichotomy.

---

come to light may be used as a permissible inference of guilt, although disciplinary action shall be based upon more than mere silence. *A finding of guilt shall be made where:*
"(1) The inmate or ward admits the violation or pleads guilty.
"(2) *The charge is supported by substantial evidence.*" Haw.Admin.Rule § 17-201-18(b)(2) (1983) (emphasis added).

Greenholtz v. Inmates of Nebraska Penal and Correctional Complex, 442 U.S. 1 (1979), foreshadowed the methodology that would come to full fruition in *Hewitt v. Helms*, 459 U.S. 460 (1983). The *Greenholtz* inmates alleged that they had been unconstitutionally denied parole. Their claim centered on a state statute that set the date for discretionary parole at the time the minimum term of imprisonment less good time credits expired. The statute ordered release of a prisoner at that time, unless one of four specific conditions were shown. The Court apparently accepted the inmates' argument that the word "shall" in the statute created a legitimate expectation of release absent the requisite finding that one of the justifications for deferral existed, since the Court concluded that some measure of constitutional protection was due. Nevertheless, the State ultimately prevailed because the minimal process it had awarded the prisoners was deemed sufficient under the Fourteenth Amendment.

The Court made explicit in *Hewitt* what was implicit in *Greenholtz*. In evaluating the claims of inmates who had been confined to administrative segregation, it first rejected the inmates' claim of a right to remain in the general population as protected by the Due Process Clause on the authority of *Meachum, Montanye*, and *Vitek*. The Due Process Clause standing alone confers no liberty interest in freedom from state action taken "'within the sentence imposed.'" It then concluded that the transfer to less amenable quarters for nonpunitive reasons was "ordinarily contemplated by a prison sentence." Examination of the possibility that the State had created a liberty interest by virtue of its prison regulations followed. Instead of looking to whether the State created an interest of "real substance" comparable to the good time credit scheme of *Wolff*, the Court asked whether the State had gone beyond issuing mere procedural guidelines and had used "language of an unmistakably mandatory character" such that the incursion on liberty would not occur "absent specified substantive predicates." Finding such mandatory directives in the regulations before it, the Court decided that the State had created a protected liberty interest. It nevertheless, held, as it had in *Greenholtz*, that the full panoply of procedures conferred in *Wolff* were unnecessary to safeguard the inmates' interest and, if imposed, would undermine the prison's management objectives.

As this methodology took hold, no longer did inmates need to rely on a showing that they had suffered a "'grievous loss'" of liberty retained even after sentenced to terms of imprisonment. For the Court had ceased to examine the "nature" of the interest with respect to interests allegedly created by the State. In a series of cases since *Hewitt*, the Court has wrestled with the language of intricate, often rather routine prison guidelines to determine whether mandatory language and substantive predicates created an enforceable expectation that the state would produce a particular outcome with respect to the prisoner's conditions of confinement. . . .

By shifting the focus of the liberty interest inquiry to one based on the language of a particular regulation, and not the nature of the deprivation, the Court encouraged prisoners to comb regulations in search of mandatory language on which to base entitlements to various state-conferred privileges. Courts have, in response, and not altogether illogically, drawn negative inferences from mandatory language in the text of prison regulations. The Court of Appeals' approach in this case is typical: it inferred from the mandatory directive that a finding of guilt "shall" be imposed under certain conditions the conclusion that the absence of such conditions prevents a finding of guilt.

Such a conclusion may be entirely sensible in the ordinary task of construing a statute defining rights and remedies available to the general public. It is a good deal less sensible in the case of a prison regulation primarily designed to guide correctional officials in the administration of a prison. Not only are such regulations not designed to confer rights on inmates, but the result of the negative implication jurisprudence is not to require the prison officials to follow the negative implication drawn from the regulation, but is instead to attach procedural protections that may be of quite a different nature. Here, for example, the Court of Appeals did not hold that a finding of guilt could not be made in the absence of substantial evidence. Instead, it held that the "liberty interest" created by the regulation entitled the inmate to the procedural protections set forth in *Wolff*.

Hewitt has produced at least two undesirable effects. First, it creates disincentives for States to codify prison management procedures in the interest of uniform treatment. . . . The approach embraced by *Hewitt* discourages this desirable development: States may avoid creation of "liberty" interests by having scarcely any regulations, or by conferring standardless discretion on correctional personnel.

Second, the *Hewitt* approach has led to the involvement of federal courts in the day-to-day management of prisons, often squandering judicial resources with little offsetting benefit to anyone. . . .

In light of the above discussion, we believe that the search for a negative implication from mandatory language in prisoner regulations has strayed from the real concerns undergirding the liberty protected by the Due Process Clause. The time has come to return to the due process principles we believe were correctly established and applied in *Wolff* and *Meachum*. Following *Wolff*, we recognize that States may under certain circumstances create liberty interests which are protected by the Due Process Clause. But these interests will be generally limited to freedom from restraint which, while not exceeding the sentence in such an unexpected manner as to give rise to protection by the Due Process Clause of its own force, nonetheless imposes atypical and significant hardship on the inmate in relation to the ordinary incidents of prison life.

Conner asserts, incorrectly, that any state action taken for a punitive reason encroaches upon a liberty interest under the Due Process Clause even in the absence of any state regulation. Neither *Bell v. Wolfish*, 441 U.S. 520 (1979), nor *Ingraham v. Wright*, 430 U.S. 651 (1977), requires such a rule. *Bell* dealt with the interests of pretrial detainees and not convicted prisoners. The Court in *Bell* correctly noted that a detainee "may not be punished prior to an adjudication of guilt in accordance with due process of law." The Court expressed concern that a State would attempt to punish a detainee for the crime for which he was indicted via preconviction holding conditions. Such a course would improperly extend the legitimate reasons for which such persons are detained—to ensure their presence at trial.

The same distinction applies to *Ingraham*, which addressed the rights of school-children to remain free from arbitrary corporal punishment. The Court noted that the Due Process Clause historically encompassed the notion that the state could not "physically punish an individual except in accordance with due process of law" and so found schoolchildren sheltered. Although children sent to public school are lawfully confined to the classroom, arbitrary corporal punishment represents an invasion of personal security to which their parents do not consent when entrusting the educational mission to the State.

The punishment of incarcerated prisoners, on the other hand, serves different aims than those found invalid in *Bell* and *Ingraham*. The process does not impose retribution in lieu of a valid conviction, nor does it maintain physical control over free citizens forced by law to subject themselves to state control over the educational mission. It effectuates prison management and prisoner rehabilitative goals. Admittedly, prisoners do not shed all constitutional rights at the prison gate, but "'[l]awful incarceration brings about the necessary withdrawal or limitation of many privileges and rights, a retraction justified by the considerations underlying our penal system.'" Discipline by prison officials in response to a wide range of misconduct falls within the expected parameters of the sentence imposed by a court of law.

This case, though concededly punitive, does not present a dramatic departure from the basic conditions of Conner's indeterminate sentence. Although Conner points to dicta in cases implying that solitary confinement automatically triggers due process protection, this Court has not had the opportunity to address in an argued case the question whether disciplinary confinement of inmates itself implicates constitutional liberty interests. We hold that Conner's discipline in segregated confinement did not present the type of atypical, significant deprivation in which a state might conceivably create a liberty interest. The record shows that, at the time of Conner's punishment, disciplinary segregation, with insignificant exceptions, mirrored those conditions imposed upon inmates in administrative segregation and protective custody. We note also that the State expunged Conner's disciplinary record with respect to the "high misconduct" charge 9 months after Conner served time in segregation. Thus, Conner's confinement did not exceed similar, but totally discretionary confinement in either duration or degree of restriction. Indeed, the conditions at Halawa involve significant amounts of "lockdown time" even for inmates in the general population. Based on a comparison between inmates inside and outside disciplinary segregation, the State's actions in placing him there for 30 days did not work a major disruption in his environment.

Nor does Conner's situation present a case where the State's action will inevitably affect the duration of his sentence. Nothing in Hawaii's code requires the parole board to deny parole in the face of a misconduct record or to grant parole in its absence, even though misconduct is by regulation a relevant consideration. The decision to release a prisoner rests on a myriad of considerations. And, the prisoner is afforded procedural protection at his parole hearing in order to explain the circumstances behind his misconduct record. The chance that a finding of misconduct will alter the balance is simply too attenuated to invoke the procedural guarantees of the Due Process Clause. The Court rejected a similar claim in *Meachum*.

We hold, therefore, that neither the Hawaii prison regulation in question, nor the Due Process Clause itself, afforded Conner a protected liberty interest that would entitle him to the procedural protections set forth in *Wolff*. The regime to which he was subjected as a result of the misconduct hearing was within the range of confinement to be normally expected for one serving an indeterminate term of 30 years to life.

The judgment of the Court of Appeals is accordingly

Reversed.

JUSTICE GINSBURG, with whom JUSTICE STEVENS joins, dissenting.

Unlike the Court, I conclude that Conner had a liberty interest, protected by the Fourteenth Amendment's Due Process Clause, in avoiding the disciplinary confinement he endured. As JUSTICE BREYER details, Conner's prison punishment effected a severe alteration in the conditions of his incarceration. Disciplinary confinement as punishment for "high misconduct" not only deprives prisoners of privileges for protracted periods; unlike administrative segregation and protective custody, disciplinary confinement also stigmatizes them and diminishes parole prospects. Those immediate and lingering consequences should suffice to qualify such confinement as liberty depriving for purposes of Due Process Clause protection.

. . . .

I see the Due Process Clause itself, not Hawaii's prison code, as the wellspring of the protection due Conner. Deriving protected liberty interests from mandatory language in local prison codes would make of the fundamental right something more in certain States, something less in others. . . .

To fit the liberty recognized in our fundamental instrument of government, the process due by reason of the Constitution similarly should not depend on the particularities of the local prison's code. Rather, the basic, universal requirements are notice of the acts of misconduct prison officials say the inmate committed, and an opportunity to respond to the charges before a trustworthy decisionmaker.

JUSTICE BREYER, with whom JUSTICE SOUTER joins, dissenting.

The specific question in this case is whether a particular punishment that, among other things, segregates an inmate from the general prison population for violating a disciplinary rule deprives the inmate of "liberty" within the terms of the Fourteenth Amendment's Due Process Clause. The majority, asking whether that punishment "imposes atypical and significant hardship on the inmate in relation to the ordinary incidents of prison life," concludes that it does not do so. The majority's reasoning, however, particularly when read in light of this Court's precedents, seems to me to lead to the opposite conclusion. And, for that reason, I dissent. . . .

The Fourteenth Amendment says that a State shall not "deprive any person of life, liberty, or property, without due process of law." U.S. Const., Amdt. 14, § 1. In determining whether state officials have deprived an inmate, such as Conner, of a procedurally protected "liberty," this Court traditionally has looked either (1) to the nature of the deprivation (how severe, in degree or kind) or (2) to the State's rules governing the imposition of that deprivation (whether they, in effect, give the inmate a "right" to avoid it). Thus, this Court has said that certain changes in conditions may be so severe or so different from ordinary conditions of confinement that, whether or not state law gives state authorities broad discretionary power to impose them, the state authorities may not do so "without complying with minimum requirements of due process." The Court has also said that deprivations that are less severe or more closely related to the original terms of confinement nonetheless will amount to deprivations of procedurally protected liberty, provided that state law (including prison regulations) narrowly cabins the legal power of authorities to impose the deprivation (thereby giving the inmate a kind of right to avoid it).

If we apply these general pre-existing principles to the relevant facts before us, it seems fairly clear, as the Ninth Circuit found, that the prison punishment here at issue deprived Conner of constitutionally protected "liberty." For one thing, the punishment worked a fairly major change in Conner's conditions. In the absence of the punishment, Conner, like other inmates in Halawa's general prison population would have left his cell and worked, taken classes, or mingled with others for eight *hours* each day. As a result of disciplinary segregation, however, Conner, for 30 days, had to spend his entire time alone in his cell (with the exception of 50 *minutes* each day on average for brief exercise and shower periods, during which he nonetheless remained isolated from other inmates and was constrained by leg irons and waist chains).

Moreover, irrespective of whether this punishment amounts to a deprivation of liberty *independent* of state law, here the prison's own disciplinary rules severely cabin the authority of prison officials to impose this kind of punishment. They provide (among other things):

(a) that certain specified acts shall constitute *"high misconduct,"* Haw.Admin. Rule § 17-201-7a;

(b) that misconduct punishable by more than four hours in disciplinary segregation "shall be punished" through a prison "adjustment committee" (composed of three unbiased members), §§ 17-201-12, 13;

(c) that, when an inmate is charged with such misconduct, then (after notice and a hearing) "[a] finding of guilt shall be made" if the charged inmate admits guilt or the "charge is supported by substantial evidence," §§ 17-201-18(b), (b)(2); see §§ 17-201-16, 17; and

(d) that the "[s]anctions" for high misconduct that "may be imposed as punishment . . . shall include . . . [d]isciplinary segregation up to thirty days," § 17-201-7(b).

The prison rules thus: (1) impose a punishment that is substantial, (2) restrict its imposition as a punishment to instances in which an inmate has committed a defined offense, and (3) prescribe nondiscretionary standards for determining whether or not an inmate committed that offense. Accordingly, under this Court's liberty-defining standards, imposing the punishment would "deprive" Conner of "liberty" within the meaning of the Due Process Clause. Thus, under existing law, the Ninth Circuit correctly decided that the punishment deprived Conner of procedurally protected liberty and that the District Court should go on to decide whether or not the prison's procedures provided Conner with the "process" that is "due."

The majority, while not disagreeing with this summary of pre-existing law, seeks to change, or to clarify, that law's "liberty" defining standards in one important respect. The majority believes that the Court's present "cabining of discretion" standard reads the Constitution as providing procedural protection for trivial "rights," as, for example, where prison rules set forth specific standards for the content of prison meals. It adds that this approach involves courts too deeply in routine matters of prison administration, all without sufficient justification. It therefore imposes a minimum standard, namely that a deprivation falls within the Fourteenth Amendment's definition of "liberty" only if it "imposes atypical and significant hardship on the inmate in relation to the ordinary incidents of prison life."

I am not certain whether or not the Court means this standard to change prior law radically. If so, its generality threatens the law with uncertainty, for some lower courts may read the majority opinion as offering significantly less protection against deprivation of liberty, while others may find in it an extension of protection to certain "atypical" hardships that preexisting law would not have covered. There is no need, however, for a radical reading of this standard, nor any other significant change in present law, to achieve the majority's basic objective, namely to read the Constitution's Due Process Clause to protect inmates against deprivations of freedom that are important, not comparatively insignificant. Rather, in my view, this concern simply requires elaborating, and explaining, the Court's present standards (without radical revision) in order to make clear that courts must apply them in light of the purposes they were meant to serve. As so read, the standards will not create procedurally protected "liberty" interests where only minor matters are at stake.

Three sets of considerations, taken together, support my conclusion that the Court need not (and today's generally phrased minimum standard therefore does not) significantly revise current doctrine by deciding to remove minor prison matters from federal-court scrutiny. First, although this Court has said, and continues to say, that *some* deprivations of an inmate's freedom are so severe in kind or degree (or so far removed from the original terms of confinement) that they amount to deprivations of liberty, irrespective of whether state law (or prison rules) "cabin discretion," it is not easy to specify just *when*, or *how much* of, a loss triggers this protection. There is a broad middle category of imposed restraints or deprivations that, considered by themselves, are neither obviously so serious as to fall within, nor obviously so insignificant as to fall without, the Clause's protection.

Second, the difficult line-drawing task that this middle category implies helps to explain why this Court developed its additional liberty-defining standard, which looks to local law (examining whether that local law creates a "liberty" by significantly limiting the discretion of local authorities to impose a restraint). Despite its similarity to the way in which the Court determines the existence, or nonexistence, of "property" for Due Process Clause purposes, the justification for looking at local law is not the same in the prisoner liberty context. In protecting property, the Due Process Clause often aims to protect *reliance*, say, reliance upon an "entitlement" that local (*i.e.*, nonconstitutional) law itself has created or helped to define. In protecting liberty, however, the Due Process Clause protects, not this kind of reliance upon a government-conferred benefit, but rather an absence of government restraint, the very absence of restraint that we call freedom. . . .

Third, there is, therefore, no need to apply the "discretion-cabining" approach — the basic purpose of which is to provide a somewhat more objective method for identifying deprivations of protected "liberty" within a broad middle-range of prisoner restraints — where a deprivation is unimportant enough (or so similar in nature to ordinary imprisonment) that it rather clearly falls *outside* that middle category. . . . And, in my view, it should now simply specify that they do not.

. . . .

The upshot is the following: the problems that the majority identifies suggest that this Court should make explicit the lower definitional limit, in the prison context, of "liberty" under the Due Process Clause — a limit that is already implicit in this Court's precedent.

The Court today reaffirms that the "liberty" protected by the Fourteenth Amendment includes interests that state law may create. It excludes relatively minor matters from that protection. And, it does not question the vast body of case law, including cases from this Court and every Circuit, recognizing that segregation can deprive an inmate of constitutionally-protected "liberty."

. . . .

In sum, Conner suffered a deprivation that was significant, not insignificant. And, that deprivation took place under disciplinary rules that . . . do cabin official discretion sufficiently. I would therefore hold that Conner was deprived of "liberty" within the meaning of the Due Process Clause.

Other related legal principles, applicable here, should further alleviate the majority's fear that application of the Due Process Clause to significant prison disciplinary action, will lead federal courts to intervene improperly (as the majority sees it) "in the day-to-day management of prisons, often squandering judicial resources with little offsetting benefit to anyone." For one thing, the "process" that is "due" in the context of prison discipline is not the full blown procedure that accompanies criminal trials. Rather, "due process" itself is a flexible concept, which, in the context of a prison, must take account of the legitimate needs of prison administration when deciding what procedural elements basic considerations of fairness require.

More importantly for present purposes, whether or not a particular procedural element *normally* seems appropriate to a certain kind of proceeding, the Due Process Clause does not require process unless, in the *individual* case, there is a relevant factual dispute between the parties. . . .

Notes

1. How does *Sandin* affect the doctrine of *Paul v. Davis*? As noted in this lesson, Abby thinks she might be able to use *Paul v. Davis* to support her argument for Brad. What would she argue? How does *Sandin* affect that argument? Will she be able to base her argument in whole or in part on the state law under which an inmate is sent to the Supermax only if he represents an extremely serious threat to the security of prison employees or other inmates? If not, what can she argue?

2. Justice Ginsburg's dissent. Would Justice Ginsburg's approach make Abby's job easier? In basic concept, does this approach differ from Rehnquist's?

3. Justice Breyer's dissent. Would Abby be in a better position if she could convince a court to use Justice Breyer's approach? How does it differ from the other two? Abby certainly wants to avoid falling into Justice Breyer's third category "where a deprivation is unimportant enough . . . that it rather clearly falls *outside* that middle category." But how would she form an argument under either of the other two?

4. Are prison cases relevant outside prisons? To what extent are the prison "liberty interest" cases relevant outside of prisons? Mort suggests that the WMA is out to get him because he has been critical of them. He has challenged WMA standards as biased against small distributors like him. He thinks the WMA is trying to shut him up. Could Abby base a due process claim on the denial of a basic First Amendment liberty interest? What about basing it on a denial of Mort's liberty interest in operating his business?

The Court in *Roth* was unsympathetic to a First Amendment claim because the district court had stayed proceedings on that issue, and "the respondent has yet to prove that the decision not to rehire him was, in fact, based on his free speech activities." Justice Douglas dissented in *Roth*, saying:

> Respondent Roth, like Sindermann in the companion case, has no tenure under Wisconsin law and, unlike Sindermann, he had had only one year of teaching at Wisconsin State University-Oshkosh—where during 1968–1969 he had been Assistant Professor of Political Science and International Studies. Though Roth was rated by the faculty as an excellent teacher, he had publicly criticized the administration for suspending an entire group of 94 black students without determining individual guilt. He also criticized the university's regime as being authoritarian and autocratic. He used his classroom to discuss what was being done about the black episode; and one day, instead of meeting his class, he went to the meeting of the Board of Regents. [This potential First Amendment violation must be reviewed by the courts.]

In order to cast Mort's case according to Justice Ginsburg's approach in *Sandin*, how would Abby demonstrate a liberty interest derived from the Constitution itself?

5. What is the test for a liberty interest? How would you describe the current test for finding a liberty interest protected by procedural due process? Which liberty interest definition gives an official more discretion to act without regard to procedural due process? Is the test for finding a property interest clearer?

6. The life interest. Most due process cases involve either property or liberty interests. On occasion, the third interest, life, may be expanded through similar creative advocacy in order to raise a due process right. In the administrative context, these cases tend to relate to liberty type interests. In *Town Court Nursing Center v. Beal*, 586 F.2d 280 (3d Cir. 1978), *rev'd*, 447 U.S. 773 (1980), the major argument was that the decertification of a nursing home prevented the patients from staying in the facility of their choice. While allegations were made that transfers would endanger the life of the elderly patients, the dominant interest was liberty.

2. When Due Process Attaches, What Procedures Does It Require?

Once we have determined that a liberty or property interest has been affected by state action, the next question is whether the procedures provided for the deprived party to challenge that state action are adequate under the Due Process Clause. This question is necessarily relative—it depends on a determination by the court of whether the procedures available at the time of the deprivation gave the aggrieved party adequate notice of the contested action and a sufficient opportunity to be heard in opposition to that action. A complete lack of procedures will therefore tilt the analysis heavily in favor of the plaintiff/challenger, and a robust procedural regime will have the opposite effect. The relief granted for a due process violation is almost always procedural, such that a successful procedural due process claim will not likely lead to an invalidation of the contested state action, but rather to additional procedural mechanisms for the plaintiff to use in opposing that action.

Lesson 4B.2. Mort calls Abby quite upset: "My life is cursed." After the terrible difficulties with Brad, Mort's other son Nick thinks he was unfairly denied a position on the law review. Selection for law review is based on a "write-on" competition. Nick wrote his paper based upon criteria provided by the law review. The criteria said that the paper must demonstrate high quality writing, substantial research, incisive analysis, and original and creative thinking such that the paper would earn a grade of "A" if graded for a course. Nick submitted his paper on the assigned topic but was not one of the students selected. When he was not selected, he asked the editors for a written critique of his paper but they refused to provide any explanation for their decision. He then asked the faculty advisor to review his case. The advisor met with Nick and the review's editor-in-chief. After this conference, the advisor told Nick that he saw no reason to "second-guess" the editors. Nick then appealed to the law school dean. The dean refused to consider his request. Mort asks Abby to represent Nick and challenge the review's decision.

How might the following materials guide Abby?

Background of *Mathews v. Eldridge*

Recall that *Goldberg v. Kelly* involved welfare recipients whose benefits had been terminated by the state. In that context, the Court required many of the elements of a traditional evidentiary hearing (e.g., the right to present evidence orally, to cross-examine adverse witnesses, and to be given reasons for the determination—*see* Note 6 following *Mathews v. Eldridge*). Thus, the following decision came as something of a surprise in response to a seemingly similar claim about a termination of government benefits.

Mathews v. Eldridge

424 U.S. 319 (1976)

Mr. Justice Powell delivered the opinion of the Court.

The issue in this case is whether the Due Process Clause of the Fifth Amendment requires that prior to the termination of Social Security disability benefit payments the recipient be afforded an opportunity for an evidentiary hearing.

Cash benefits are provided to workers during periods in which they are completely disabled under the disability insurance benefits program created by the 1956 amendments to Title II of the Social Security Act. Respondent Eldridge was first awarded benefits in June 1968. In March 1972, he received a questionnaire from the state agency charged with monitoring his medical condition. Eldridge completed the questionnaire, indicating that his condition had not improved and identifying the medical sources, including physicians, from whom he had received treatment recently. The state agency then obtained reports from his physician and a psychiatric consultant. After considering these reports and other information in his file the agency informed Eldridge by letter that it had made a tentative determination that his disability had ceased in May 1972. The letter included a statement of reasons for the proposed termination of benefits, and advised Eldridge that he might request reasonable time in which to obtain and submit additional information pertaining to his condition.

In his written response, Eldridge disputed one characterization of his medical condition and indicated that the agency already had enough evidence to establish his disability. The state agency then made its final determination that he had ceased to be disabled in May 1972. This determination was accepted by the Social Security Administration (SSA), which notified Eldridge in July that his benefits would terminate after that month. The notification also advised him of his right to seek reconsideration by the state agency of this initial determination within six months.

Commence Action [handwritten annotation]

Instead of requesting reconsideration Eldridge commenced this action challenging the constitutional validity of the administrative procedures established by the Secretary of Health, Education, and Welfare for assessing whether there exists a continuing disability. . . .

Procedural due process imposes constraints on governmental decisions which deprive individuals of "liberty" or "property" interests within the meaning of the Due Process Clause of the Fifth or Fourteenth Amendment. The Secretary does not contend that procedural due process is inapplicable to terminations of Social Security disability benefits. . . .

In recent years this Court increasingly has had occasion to consider the extent to which due process requires an evidentiary hearing prior to the deprivation of some type of property interest even if such a hearing is provided thereafter. In only one case, *Goldberg v. Kelly*, 397 U.S. 254 (1970), has the Court held that a hearing closely approximating a judicial trial is necessary. In other cases requiring some type of pretermination hearing as a matter of constitutional right the Court has spoken sparingly about the requisite procedures. *Sniadach v. Family Finance Corp.*, 395 U.S. 337 (1969), involving garnishment of wages, was entirely silent on the matter. In *Fuentes v. Shevin*, 407 U.S. 67 (1972), the Court said only that in a replevin suit between two private parties the initial determination required something more than an *ex parte* proceeding before a court clerk. Similarly, *Bell v. Burson*, 402 U.S. 535 (1971), held, in the context of the revocation of a state-granted driver's license, that due process required only that the prerevocation hearing involve a probable-cause determination as to the fault of the licensee, noting that the hearing "need not take the form of a full adjudication of the question of liability." More recently, in *Arnett v. Kennedy*, 416 U.S. 134 (1974), we sustained the validity of procedures by which a federal employee could be dismissed for cause. They included notice of the action sought, a copy of the charge, reasonable time for filing a written response, and an opportunity for an oral appearance. Following dismissal, an evidentiary hearing was provided.

These decisions underscore the truism that "'[d]ue process,' unlike some legal rules, is not a technical conception with a fixed content unrelated to time, place and circumstances." "[D]ue process is flexible and calls for such procedural protections as the particular situation demands." Accordingly, resolution of the issue whether the administrative procedures provided here are constitutionally sufficient requires analysis of the governmental and private interests that are affected. More precisely, our prior decisions indicate that identification of the specific dictates of due process

Balancing Factors [handwritten annotation]

generally requires consideration of three distinct factors. First, the private interest that will be affected by the official action; second, the risk of an erroneous deprivation of such interest through the procedures used, and the probable value, if any, of additional or substitute procedural safeguards; and finally, the Government's interest, including the function involved and the fiscal and administrative burdens that the additional or substitute procedural requirement would entail.

We turn first to a description of the procedures for the termination of Social Security disability benefits, and thereafter consider the factors bearing upon the constitutional adequacy of these procedures. . . .

The continuing-eligibility investigation is made by a state agency acting through a "team" consisting of a physician and a nonmedical person trained in disability evaluation. The agency periodically communicates with the disabled worker, usually by mail—in which case he is sent a detailed questionnaire—or by telephone, and requests information concerning his present condition, including current medical restrictions and sources of treatment, and any additional information that he considers relevant to his continued entitlement to benefits.

(1)

Information regarding the recipient's current condition is also obtained from his sources of medical treatment. If there is a conflict between the information provided by the beneficiary and that obtained from medical sources such as his physician, or between two sources of treatment, the agency may arrange for an examination by an independent consulting physician. Whenever the agency's tentative assessment of the beneficiary's condition differs from his own assessment, the beneficiary is informed that benefits may be terminated, provided a summary of the evidence upon which the proposed determination to terminate is based, and afforded an opportunity to review the medical reports and other evidence in his case file. He also may respond in writing and submit additional evidence.

(2)

The state agency then makes its final determination, which is reviewed by an examiner in the SSA Bureau of Disability Insurance. If, as is usually the case, the SSA accepts the agency determination it notifies the recipient in writing, informing him of the reasons for the decision, and of his right to seek *de novo* reconsideration by the state agency. Upon acceptance by the SSA, benefits are terminated effective two months after the month in which medical recovery is found to have occurred.

(3)

If the recipient seeks reconsideration by the state agency and the determination is adverse, the SSA reviews the reconsideration determination and notifies the recipient of the decision. He then has a right to an evidentiary hearing before an SSA administrative law judge. The hearing is nonadversary, and the SSA is not represented by counsel. As at all prior and subsequent stages of the administrative process, however, the claimant may be represented by counsel or other spokesmen. If this hearing results in an adverse decision, the claimant is entitled to request discretionary review by the SSA Appeals Council, and finally may obtain judicial review. Should it be determined at any point after termination of benefits that the claimant's disability extended beyond the date of cessation initially established, the worker is entitled to retroactive payments. If, on the other hand, a beneficiary receives any payments to which he is later determined not to be entitled, the statute authorizes the Secretary to attempt to recoup these funds in specified circumstances. Despite the elaborate character of the administrative procedures provided by the Secretary, the courts below held them to be constitutionally inadequate, concluding that due

(4)

process requires an evidentiary hearing prior to termination. In light of the private and governmental interests at stake here and the nature of the existing procedures, we think this was error. . . .

Only in *Goldberg* has the Court held that due process requires an evidentiary hearing prior to a temporary deprivation. It was emphasized there that welfare assistance is given to persons on the very margin of subsistence:

> "The crucial factor in this context—a factor not present in the case of . . . virtually anyone else whose governmental entitlements are ended—is that termination of aid pending resolution of a controversy over eligibility may deprive an *eligible* recipient of the very means by which to live while he waits."

[PRIVATE INTEREST]

Eligibility for disability benefits, in contrast, is not based upon financial need. Indeed, it is wholly unrelated to the worker's income or support from many other sources, such as earnings of other family members, workmen's compensation awards, tort claims awards, savings, private insurance, public or private pensions, veterans' benefits, food stamps, public assistance, or the "many other important programs, both public and private, which contain provisions for disability payments affecting a substantial portion of the work force. . . ." As *Goldberg* illustrates, the degree of potential deprivation that may be created by a particular decision is a factor to be considered in assessing the validity of any administrative decision-making process. The potential deprivation here is generally likely to be less than in *Goldberg*, although the degree of difference can be overstated. As the District Court emphasized, to remain eligible for benefits a recipient must be "unable to engage in substantial gainful activity." Thus, in contrast to the discharged federal employee in *Arnett*, there is little possibility that the terminated recipient will be able to find even temporary employment to ameliorate the interim loss.

As we recognized last Term in *Fusari v. Steinberg*, 419 U.S. 379 (1975), "the possible length of wrongful deprivation of . . . benefits [also] is an important factor in assessing the impact of official action on the private interests." The Secretary concedes that the delay between a request for a hearing before an administrative law judge and a decision on the claim is currently between 10 and 11 months. Since a terminated recipient must first obtain a reconsideration decision as a prerequisite to invoking his right to an evidentiary hearing, the delay between the actual cutoff of benefits and final decision after a hearing exceeds one year.

[ERRONEOUS DEPRIVATION]

In view of the torpidity of this administrative review process, and the typically modest resources of the family unit of the physically disabled worker, the hardship imposed upon the erroneously terminated disability recipient may be significant. Still, the disabled worker's need is likely to be less than that of a welfare recipient. In addition to the possibility of access to private resources, other forms of government assistance will become available where the termination of disability benefits places a worker or his family below the subsistence level. In view of these potential sources of temporary income, there is less reason here than in *Goldberg* to depart from the ordinary principle, established by our decisions, that something less than an evidentiary hearing is sufficient prior to adverse administrative action.

An additional factor to be considered here is the fairness and reliability of the existing pretermination procedures, and the probable value, if any, of additional procedural safeguards. Central to the evaluation of any administrative process is the nature of the relevant inquiry. In order to remain eligible for benefits the disabled worker must demonstrate by means of "medically acceptable clinical and laboratory diagnostic techniques," that he is unable "to engage in any substantial gainful activity by reason of any *medically determinable* physical or mental impairment. . . ." (Emphasis supplied). In short, a medical assessment of the worker's physical or mental condition is required. This is a more sharply focused and easily documented decision than the typical determination of welfare entitlement. In the latter case, a wide variety of information may be deemed relevant, and issues of witness credibility and veracity often are critical to the decisionmaking process. *Goldberg* noted that in such circumstances "written submissions are a wholly unsatisfactory basis for decision." By contrast, the decision whether to discontinue disability benefits will turn, in most cases, upon "routine, standard, and unbiased medical reports by physician specialists" concerning a subject whom they have personally examined.[28] In *Richardson* [*v. Perales*, 402 U.S. 389 (1971),] the Court recognized the "reliability and probative worth of written medical report," emphasizing that while there may be "professional disagreement with the medical conclusions" the "specter of questionable credibility and veracity is not present." To be sure, credibility and veracity may be a factor in the ultimate disability assessment in some cases. But procedural due process rules are shaped by the risk of error inherent in the truthfinding process as applied to the generality of cases, not the rare exceptions. The potential value of an evidentiary hearing, or even oral presentation to the decisionmaker, is substantially less in this context than in *Goldberg*.

The decision in *Goldberg* also was based on the Court's conclusion that written submissions were an inadequate substitute for oral presentation because they did not provide an effective means for the recipient to communicate his case to the decisionmaker. Written submissions were viewed as an unrealistic option, for most recipients lacked the "educational attainment necessary to write effectively" and could not afford professional assistance. In addition, such submissions would not

---

28. The decision is not purely a question of the accuracy of a medical diagnosis since the ultimate issue which the state agency must resolve is whether in light of the particular worker's "age, education, and work experience" he cannot "engage in any . . . substantial gainful work which exists in the national economy. . . ." Yet information concerning each of these worker characteristics is amenable to effective written presentation. The value of an evidentiary hearing, or even a limited oral presentation, to an accurate presentation of those factors to the decisionmaker does not appear substantial. Similarly, resolution of the inquiry as to the types of employment opportunities that exist in the national economy for a physically impaired worker with a particular set of skills would not necessarily be advanced by an evidentiary hearing. The statistical information relevant to this judgment is more amenable to written than to oral presentation.

provide the "flexibility of oral presentations" or "permit the recipient to mold his argument to the issues the decision maker appears to regard as important." In the context of the disability-benefits-entitlement assessment the administrative procedures under review here fully answer these objections.

The detailed questionnaire which the state agency periodically sends the recipient identifies with particularity the information relevant to the entitlement decision, and the recipient is invited to obtain assistance from the local SSA office in completing the questionnaire. More important, the information critical to the entitlement decision usually is derived from medical sources, such as the treating physician. Such sources are likely to be able to communicate more effectively through written documents than are welfare recipients or the lay witnesses supporting their cause. The conclusions of physicians often are supported by X-rays and the results of clinical or laboratory tests, information typically more amenable to written than to oral presentation.

A further safeguard against mistake is the policy of allowing the disability recipient's representative full access to all information relied upon by the state agency. In addition, prior to the cutoff of benefits the agency informs the recipient of its tentative assessment, the reasons therefore, and provides a summary of the evidence that it considers most relevant. Opportunity is then afforded the recipient to submit additional evidence or arguments, enabling him to challenge directly the accuracy of information in his file as well as the correctness of the agency's tentative conclusions. These procedures, again as contrasted with those before the Court in *Goldberg*, enable the recipient to "mold" his argument to respond to the precise issues which the decisionmaker regards as crucial.

. . . .

In striking the appropriate due process balance the final factor to be assessed is the public interest. This includes the administrative burden and other social costs that would be associated with requiring, as a matter of constitutional right, an evidentiary hearing upon demand in all cases prior to the termination of disability benefits. The most visible burden would be the incremental costs resulting from the increased number of hearings and the expense of providing benefits to ineligible recipients pending decision. No one can predict the extent of the increase, but the fact that full benefits would continue until after such hearings would assure the exhaustion in most cases of this attractive option. Nor would the theoretical right of the Secretary to recover undeserved benefits result, as a practical matter, in any substantial offset to the added outlay of public funds. The parties submit widely varying estimates of the probable additional financial cost. We only need say that experience with the constitutionalizing of government procedures suggests that the ultimate additional cost in terms of money and administrative burden would not be insubstantial.

Financial cost alone is not a controlling weight in determining whether due process requires a particular procedural safeguard prior to some administrative decision. But the Government's interest, and hence that of the public, in conserving scarce fiscal and administrative resources is a factor that must be weighed. At some point the benefit of an additional safeguard to the individual affected by the administrative action and to society in terms of increased assurance that the action is just, may be outweighed by the cost. Significantly, the cost of protecting those whom the preliminary administrative process has identified as likely to be found undeserving may in the end come out of the pockets of the deserving since resources available for any particular program of social welfare are not unlimited.

But more is implicated in cases of this type than ad hoc weighing of fiscal and administrative burdens against the interests of a particular category of claimants. The ultimate balance involves a determination as to when, under our constitutional system, judicial-type procedures must be imposed upon administrative action to assure fairness. We reiterate the wise admonishment of Mr. Justice Frankfurter that differences in the origin and function of administrative agencies "preclude wholesale transplantation of the rules of procedure, trial and review which have evolved from the history and experience of courts." The judicial model of an evidentiary hearing is neither a required, nor even the most effective, method of decisionmaking in all circumstances. The essence of due process is the requirement that "a person in jeopardy of serious loss [be given] notice of the case against him and opportunity to meet it." All that is necessary is that the procedures be tailored, in light of the decision to be made, to "the capacities and circumstances of those who are to be heard," *Goldberg v. Kelly*, to insure that they are given a meaningful opportunity to present their case. In assessing what process is due in this case, substantial weight must be given to the good-faith judgments of the individuals charged by Congress with the administration of social welfare programs that the procedures they have provided assure fair consideration of the entitlement claims of individuals. This is especially so where, as here, the prescribed procedures not only provide the claimant with an effective process for asserting his claim prior to any administration action, but also assure a right to an evidentiary hearing, as well as to subsequent judicial review, before the denial of his claim becomes final.

We conclude that an evidentiary hearing is not required prior to the termination of disability benefits and that the present administrative procedures fully comport with due process.

Mr. Justice Brennan, with whom Mr. Justice Marshall concurs, dissenting.

For the reasons stated in my dissenting opinion in *Richardson v. Wright*, 405 U.S. 208 (1972), I agree with the District Court and the Court of Appeals that, prior to termination of benefits, Eldridge must be afforded an evidentiary hearing of the type required for welfare beneficiaries under Title IV of the Social Security Act. I would add that the Court's consideration that a discontinuance of disability benefits may cause the recipient to suffer only a limited deprivation is no argument. It is speculative. Moreover, the very legislative determination to provide disability benefits, without any prerequisite determination of need in fact, presumes a need by the recipient which is not this Court's function to denigrate. Indeed, in the present case, it is indicated that because disability benefits were terminated there was a foreclosure upon the Eldridge home and the family's furniture was repossessed, forcing Eldridge, his wife, and their children to sleep in one bed. Finally, it is also no argument that a worker, who has been placed in the untenable position of having been denied disability benefits, may still seek other forms of public assistance.

Notes

1. Does due process attach?—A brief review. The focus of these materials is on what due process requires when it attaches to a particular government decision. To get to that issue, however, there is always the threshold question of whether due process attaches. What should the parties argue in explaining whether due process attaches to the law review's decision about Nick's paper?

2. What does due process require? Assuming due process attaches, Abby must find the basis on which she can argue for additional or alternative procedures. Much of the law about procedural adequacy revolves around Justice Powell's three factors:

(1) the private interest that will be affected by the official action;

(2) the risk of an erroneous deprivation of such interest through the procedures used, and the probable value, if any, of additional or substitute procedural safeguards; and

(3) the Government's interest, including the function involved and the fiscal and administrative burdens that the additional or substitute procedural requirement would entail.

Do these factors make sense in Nick's case? Should these factors be given equal weight?

Despite identifying three factors, Justice Powell might be seen as compelling two balancing exercises: the balance of the individual's interest against the "government's interest" and the weighing of the cost of procedural moves against their benefits. Do you think such "cost-benefit" balancing is an appropriate method for evaluating procedural rights? Balancing tends to pit important interests against each other so that they are considered adverse but may not be in reality. Is there another method for guiding procedural design that does not require trading-off important community values? *See* Charles Koch, *A Community of Interest in the Due Process Calculus*, 37 Houston L. Rev. 635 (2000) (arguing that due process is a "community imperative" that should not involve trading the state's interest against the individual's).

3. Balancing at the attachment stage? As we saw in Note 3 after the *Goldberg* excerpt, the Court might well have taken a balancing approach to determining whether due process attached. In that connection, reconsider *Paul v. Davis*. Would you be more inclined to find that due process attached if the plaintiff could show that the distribution of shoplifter identification flyers was of little or no benefit to local businesses? That is, should the value to society of the governmental action affect the individual's right, i.e., the existence of either a property or liberty interest?

4. The balance of individual vs. government interest. In the wake of *Roth* and *Mathews v. Eldridge*, the courts balance the above factors to determine how much process is due. As Professor Koch suggests, there seem to be two balancing tests. The first is the interest of the individual against that of the government. How would Abby represent the balance of Nick's interest against the "government's interest"? Who is the "government," the law review, the law school, its students, its faculty, its alumni (both the law school's and the law review's), the state and its citizens? What is at stake in such a balance?

Which of Nick's individual interests should Abby assert? Jerry Mashaw criticized *Mathews* for taking too much of a "utilitarian" approach. Jerry Mashaw, *The Supreme Court's Due Process Calculus for Administrative Adjudication in* Mathews v. Eldridge: *Three Factors in Search of a Theory of Value*, 44 U. Chi. L. Rev. 28 (1976). He urged that due process theory should include individual dignity, equality, and tradition. An administrative process should satisfy the citizen involved. What procedural elements are most likely to add to the satisfaction of one who receives an adverse administrative decision?

5. The "cost/effectiveness" balancing test. The second type of balancing suggested by Justice Powell's three factors can be called "cost-effectiveness." That is, would the "probable value . . . of additional or substitute procedural safeguards" justify the cost of those procedural alternatives? Consider the procedures at issue in *Board of Curators of University of Missouri v. Horowitz*, 435 U.S. 78 (1978). There, the Supreme Court considered the procedures that should be available to students dismissed from medical school. The interest of society in adequate health care was great, but then that of a medical student is also great:

> Assuming the existence of a liberty or property interest, respondent has been awarded at least as much due process as the Fourteenth Amendment requires. The school fully informed respondent of the faculty's dissatisfaction with her clinical progress and the danger that this posed to timely graduation and continued enrollment. The ultimate decision to dismiss respondent was careful and deliberate. These procedures were sufficient under the Due Process Clause of the Fourteenth Amendment. . . .
>
> In *Goss v. Lopez* we held that due process requires . . . an "informal give-and-take" between the student and the administrative body dismissing him that would, at least, give the student "the opportunity to characterize his conduct and put it in what he deems the proper context." But we have frequently emphasized that "[t]he very nature of due process negates any concept of inflexible procedures universally applicable to every imaginable situation." The need for flexibility is well illustrated by the significant difference between the failure of a student to meet academic standards and the violation by a student of valid rules of conduct. This difference calls for far less stringent procedural requirements in the case of an academic dismissal.

. . . .

Academic evaluations of a student, in contrast to disciplinary determinations, bear little resemblance to the judicial and administrative fact-finding proceedings to which we have traditionally attached a full hearing requirement. In *Goss*, the school's decision to suspend the students rested on factual conclusions that the individual students had participated in demonstrations that had disrupted classes, attacked a police officer, or caused physical damage to school property. The requirement of a hearing, where the student could present his side of the factual issue, could under such circumstances "provide a meaningful hedge against erroneous action." The decision to dismiss respondent, by comparison, rested on the academic judgment of school officials that she did not have the necessary clinical ability to perform adequately as a medical doctor and was making insufficient progress toward that goal. Such a judgment is by its nature more subjective and evaluative than the typical factual questions presented in the average disciplinary decision. Like the decision of an individual professor as to the proper grade for a student in his course, the determination whether to dismiss a student for academic reasons requires an expert evaluation of cumulative information and is not readily adapted to the procedural tools of judicial or administrative decisionmaking.

. . . In *Goss*, this Court concluded that the value of some form of hearing in a disciplinary context outweighs any resulting harm to the academic environment. Influencing this conclusion was clearly the belief that disciplinary proceedings, in which the teacher must decide whether to punish a student for disruptive or insubordinate behavior, may automatically bring an adversary flavor to the normal student-teacher relationship. The same conclusion does not follow in the academic context. We decline to further enlarge the judicial presence in the academic community and thereby risk deterioration of many beneficial aspects of the faculty-student relationship.

6. Trial-like process? Can Abby argue that the Association must provide Mort with a trial-like hearing? Justice Brennan in *Goldberg* (excerpted above), after concluding the welfare benefits were "entitlements" protected by due process, explored the procedural adequacy of the state's method for terminating them:

We also agree with the District Court, however, that the pre-termination hearing need not take the form of a judicial or quasi-judicial trial. We bear in mind that the statutory "fair hearing" will provide the recipient with a full administrative review. Accordingly, the pre-termination hearing has one function only: to produce an initial determination of the validity of the welfare department's grounds for discontinuance of payments in order to protect a recipient against an erroneous termination of his benefits. Thus, a complete record and a comprehensive opinion, which would serve primarily to facilitate judicial review and to guide future decisions, need not be provided at the pre-termination stage. We recognize, too, that both welfare authorities and recipients have an interest in relatively speedy resolution of questions of eligibility, that they are used to dealing with one another informally, and that some welfare departments have very burdensome caseloads. These considerations justify the limitation of the pre-termination hearing to minimum procedural safeguards, adapted to the particular characteristics of welfare recipients, and to the limited nature of the controversies to be resolved. We wish to add that we, no less than the dissenters, recognize the importance of not imposing upon the States or the Federal Government in this developing field of law any procedural requirements beyond those demanded by rudimentary due process.

"The fundamental requisite of due process of law is the opportunity to be heard." The hearing must be "at a meaningful time and in a meaningful manner." In the present context these principles require that a recipient have timely and adequate notice detailing the reasons for a proposed termination, and an effective opportunity to defend by confronting any adverse witnesses and by presenting his own arguments and evidence orally. These rights are important in cases such as those before us, where recipients have challenged proposed terminations as resting on incorrect or misleading factual premises or on misapplication of rules or policies to the facts of particular cases. . . .

The city's procedures presently do not permit recipients to appear personally with or without counsel before the official who finally determines continued eligibility. Thus a recipient is not permitted to present evidence to that official orally, or to confront or cross-examine adverse witnesses. These omissions are fatal to the constitutional adequacy of the procedures.

The opportunity to be heard must be tailored to the capacities and circumstances of those who are to be heard. It is not enough that a welfare recipient may present his position to the decision maker in writing or secondhand through his caseworker. Written submissions are an unrealistic option for most recipients, who lack the educational attainment necessary to write effectively and who cannot obtain professional assistance. Moreover, written submissions do not afford the flexibility of oral presentations; they do not permit the recipient to mold his argument to the issues the decision maker appears to regard as important. Particularly where credibility and veracity are at issue, as they must be in many termination proceedings, written submissions are a wholly unsatisfactory basis for decision. The second-hand presentation to the decisionmaker by the caseworker has its own deficiencies; since the caseworker usually gathers the facts upon which the charge of ineligibility rests, the presentation of the recipient's side of the controversy cannot safely be left to him. Therefore a recipient must be allowed to state his position orally. Informal procedures will suffice; in this context due process does not require a particular order of proof or mode of offering evidence.

In almost every setting where important decisions turn on questions of fact, due process requires an opportunity to confront and cross-examine adverse witnesses. . . .

"The right to be heard would be, in many cases, of little avail if it did not comprehend the right to be heard by counsel." We do not say that counsel must be provided at the pre-termination hearing, but only that the recipient must be allowed to retain an attorney if he so desires. Counsel can help delineate the issues, present the factual contentions in an orderly manner, conduct cross-examination, and generally safeguard the interests of the recipient. We do not anticipate that this assistance will unduly prolong or otherwise encumber the hearing. Evidently HEW has reached the same conclusion.

Finally, the decisionmaker's conclusion as to a recipient's eligibility must rest solely on the legal rules and evidence adduced at the hearing. To demonstrate compliance with this elementary requirement, the decision maker should state the reasons for his determination and indicate the evidence he relied on, though his statement need not amount to a full opinion or even formal findings of fact and conclusions of law. And, of course, an impartial decision maker is essential. We agree with the District Court that prior involvement in some aspects of a case will not necessarily bar a welfare official from acting as a decision maker. He should not, however, have participated in making the determination under review.

Justice Brennan's opinion in *Goldberg* was the high-water mark of the Court's imposition of trial-like procedures under the Due Process Clause. What were the procedural elements required by *Goldberg*? Why did the Court require them on those facts? Would you conclude from Justice Brennan's opinion that the trial-like elements would be cost effective under the circumstances of *Goldberg*? What about in the case Abby must argue for Brad? Notice, by the way, that in *Horowitz*, we have an example of the Court emphatically ruling that due process did *not* require a trial-like process. Also consider: How far did *Mathews* cut back on *Goldberg*?

7. *Goss v. Lopez* — the due process minimum under a flexible standard. Several members of the *Goldberg* Court and several commentators criticized the resort to trial methods to vindicate due process rights. Might Justice Brennan be criticized for ignoring less direct and concrete costs? Or for ignoring the cost to the individuals? Should the costs be relevant to determining compliance with due process? Is there such a thing as too much procedure? Doctors are often criticized for ordering too many procedures (out of an abundance of caution or to increase their income), might the legal profession be criticized on similar grounds?

Goss v. Lopez, 419 U.S. 565 (1975), which was discussed in *Board of Curators v. Horowitz*, was something of a precursor to *Mathews v. Eldridge*. The decision is perhaps most notorious for the fact that the Court applied the profound principles of the Due Process Clause to something as seemingly trivial (but not to students or parents) and managerial in nature as public school discipline. Having recognized that the school discipline affected both property and liberty interests on the particular facts, the Court required only that an accused student be advised of the charges against him and be permitted to tell his side of the story to the school disciplinarian. The Court explained why, under these circumstances, the due process clause required that much, but no more:

> It also appears from our cases that the timing and content of the notice and the nature of the hearing will depend on appropriate accommodation of the competing interests involved. . . . Disciplinarians, although proceeding in utmost good faith, frequently act on the reports and advice of others; and the controlling facts and the nature of the conduct under challenge are often disputed. The risk of error is not at all trivial, and it should be guarded against if that may be done without prohibitive cost or interference with the educational process.

As the Court emphasized in *Horowitz*, *Goss v. Lopez* signaled a strong commitment to the proposition that due process is a flexible concept. Its requirements depend upon the circumstances. In the public school context, there must be at least "an informal give-and-take" in which the student has "the opportunity to characterize his conduct and put it in what he deems the proper context." This is the due process minimum, an opportunity to know the charges and to respond to them.

8. Determining the benefits of a procedure. What are the benefits of a particular procedure? Take the procedures discussed by Justice Brennan in the *Goldberg* quote above. Did he do a good job of measuring the benefit of each element in that context? On what information did he rely in evaluating the benefits of each procedural element?

How would Abby make an argument that an alternative or additional procedure would make the write-on process better? Would she argue that the procedure will make the decisions more accurate? What other types of benefits might she assert? What information could she rely on to show the established benefits of particular procedures? Now, go back to the list of procedural elements in note 3 after the Friendly excerpt in subchapter 2C. What procedures might Abby advocate using the *Mathews* analysis? What are her chances of having the law review's decision rejected on procedural due process grounds?

9. The problem of pre-deprivation process. Frequently, as in *Mathews v. Eldridge*, the question is whether a hearing is required before the government may terminate a benefit even if a substantial hearing is provided after the termination. Remember that the Court in *Goldberg* demanded a fairly extensive hearing before an entitlement determination. The Court felt that a prior hearing was necessary because the claimant might face a "grievous loss." *Mathews*, on the other hand, approved a process that made the adversarial hearing available after the preliminary determination to end the benefits. In *Gilbert v. Homar*, 520 U.S. 924, 930 (1997), Justice Rehnquist for the Court observed: "This Court has recognized, on many occasions, that where a State must act quickly, or where it would be impractical to provide pre-deprivation process, post-deprivation process satisfies the requirements of the Due Process Clause."

Perhaps the clearest case for dispensing with pre-determination process is when government responds to an emergency. Although more than a century old, *North American Cold Storage Co. v. Chicago*, 211 U.S. 306 (1908), remains the leading case on this point. Pursuant to a city ordinance, Chicago health officials ordered North American Cold Storage to turn over for destruction forty-seven barrels of allegedly putrid poultry. When the company refused, the City effectively shut down the business. Noting that putrid food "is in itself a nuisance, and a nuisance of the most dangerous kind, involving, as it does, the health, if not the lives, of persons who may eat it," the Court held that pre-destruction process was not required. Instead, the company's interests would be protected by a later "trial in an action brought for the destruction of his property. . . ."

On an issue that strikes close to home for many of us, consider whether a state should be able to suspend your driver's license without a pre-suspension hearing. Consider *City of Maumee v. Gabriel*, 518 N.E.2d 558, 562 (Ohio 1988), in which the court held that drivers were not constitutionally entitled to a pre-suspension hearing regarding their driver's license because of the state's powerful interest in keeping dangerous drivers off the road and the potential burdens of conducting pre-suspension hearings for all eligible drivers.

Under what circumstances would you approve of a process that provided the hearing after the initial determination? Would you take into account that the initial determination was the result of an extensive process including input from the private party, even though it did not involve a prior adversarial hearing? Remember that in *Goldberg* the Supreme Court suggested that an abbreviated pre-determination hearing might be adequate if followed by a more extensive hearing, and yet it required pre-determination procedures in the case before it.

10. Is there a violation of procedural due process when an agency employee harms a protected interest through negligence or through intentional but unauthorized conduct? The Supreme Court struggled with the question of how due process clause protections relate to property or other protected interests that might be harmed by the negligent or unauthorized acts of agency personnel.

In *Parratt v. Taylor*, 451 U.S. 527 (1981), the Supreme Court held that negligence was sufficient to constitute a deprivation. In that case, a prisoner lost a $23.50 hobby kit (a property interest even under the most traditional definition of property). The Court found that it was not necessary to prove that the deprivation was the result of authorized or even intentional official conduct. Justice Stevens, in a concurring opinion, however, urged that the word "deprived" itself suggests a protection only against affirmative abuses of power. In 1986, the Court changed course in *Daniels v. Williams*, 474 U.S. 327 (1986), when it held that negligence alone was not sufficient to create a deprivation in violation of due process. There a prisoner tripped over a pillow negligently left on a staircase. The court held that negligence was not enough because the Due Process Clause was "intended to secure the individual from the arbitrary exercise of the powers of government." A prior hearing cannot prevent negligent conduct because such conduct cannot by its nature be anticipated in order for a hearing to be held.

Similarly, intentional misconduct is not a deprivation triggering procedural due process. The Supreme Court established this doctrine in *Hudson v. Palmer*, 468 U.S. 517, 533 (1984). A prisoner alleged that, during a search of his prison cell, a guard deliberately and maliciously destroyed some of his property, including legal papers. As in the negligence cases, there was a tort remedy by which the prisoner could have been compensated. The guard was not acting pursuant to any established state procedure but, instead, was apparently pursuing a random, unauthorized personal vendetta against the prisoner. The Court denied due process coverage to such unauthorized misconduct because: "The state can no more anticipate and control in advance the random and unauthorized intentional conduct of its employees than it can anticipate similar negligent conduct." Again the key was that a pre-deprivation hearing was simply impossible. The state can no more instruct officials to hold a hearing before they commit intentional violations of rights than it can hold a hearing before an employee commits a negligent act.

11. The role of federalism. Federalism plays a substantial role in the above law of due process. For example, the Court refused in *Ingraham v. Wright*, 430 U.S. 651 (1977), to find that the due process clause required a hearing before the administration of corporal punishment in public schools. Much of the attitude of that opinion suggests that the Court wished to leave this issue with the states and allow state remedies to protect against abuse. It is important to note that the *Ingraham v. Wright* Court distinguished *Goss v. Lopez* by arguing that the purpose of corporal punishment was to correct the child's behavior so the child could stay in school. Thus, it did not involve a deprivation of a property interest, as in *Goss*.

12. Examples of *Mathews v. Eldridge* in action. Here are brief descriptions of several other prominent decisions in which the Court has applied (or declined to apply) *Mathews v. Eldridge* analysis in evaluating the adequacy of administrative decision-making procedures:

> *Wilkinson v. Austin*, 545 U.S. 209 (2005). This decision is the source of Lesson 4B.1.d, concerning Brad's transfer to the Supermax prison. With respect to the issue of whether due process attached, the Court held that the Supermax conditions imposed sufficiently "atypical and significant hardship" under the test of *Sandin v. Connor* to trigger due process protections. The process provided by the prison system included 48 hours' notice to the inmate of a hearing before a three member committee. The inmate was given notice of an extensive form used to evaluate his status and was given an opportunity to state his case in the hearing. He was not allowed to present witnesses. He had an opportunity to contest an adverse decision, the decision was subjected to multiple levels of review, and he was given

another review thirty days after being placed in the Supermax. In upholding these procedures, the Court balanced the harsh conditions (mitigated
somewhat by the fact of existing imprisonment) against the significant government interest in making a prompt decision while maintaining security.
The Court considered what it believed to be the low likelihood of error
given all the elements of the hearing process.

Hamdi v. Rumsfeld, 542 U.S. 507 (2004). In a highly publicized case concerning an American citizen captured in Afghanistan and designated an "enemy
combatant," the Court first found that due process applied despite the extensive powers of the president with respect to national security. Hamdi had
not been given any opportunity to contest his confinement. In a decision
that harkens back to *Goss v. Lopez*, the Court applied *Mathews v. Eldridge*
balancing to hold that Hamdi was entitled to "notice of the factual basis for
his classification, and a fair opportunity to rebut the Government's factual
assertions before a neutral decisionmaker." The Court did not require full
adversary process, and it acknowledged that the exigencies of the situation
might require reliance on hearsay and even a presumption that shifts the
burden to the detainee once the government has presented a credible case.

City of Los Angeles v. David, 538 U.S. 715 (2003). The City towed David's
car from a "no parking" space. After paying $134.50 to retrieve his car,
David sought a hearing to recover the money. Twenty-seven days after the
towing incident, the City held a hearing and denied David's request. David
claimed that the delay violated due process. Applying the *Mathews* factors,
the Court disagreed. With a mere private financial interest, a low likelihood
that delay would increase the likelihood of error, and a significant government interest in efficiency in light of the 4,000 vehicle impoundments each
year, the Court held that the City met the fundamental requirement of due
process: "the opportunity to be heard 'at a meaningful time and in a meaningful manner.'"

Cleveland Board of Education v. Loudermill, 470 U.S. 532 (1985). On a government employment application, Loudermill denied ever having been
convicted of a felony. He was dismissed without a hearing when authorities
discovered that the statement was false. On the merits, Loudermill argued
that he had been mistaken in believing the conviction to be a misdemeanor.
He received a post-termination hearing that recommended termination,
and the dismissal was upheld. Applying the *Mathews* factors, and particularly emphasizing that "the significance of the private interest in retaining
employment cannot be gainsaid," the Court found a due process violation.
The issue was not whether the statement was false, but whether Loudermill had lied. Given the discretionary nature of the employment decision,
the Court said that: "Even where the facts are clear, the appropriateness
or necessity of the discharge may not be; in such cases, the only meaningful opportunity to invoke the discretion of the decisionmaker is likely to

be before the termination takes effect." As to the government interest, the Court noted that a requirement to hear from the employee before dismissal would impose very little administrative burden, and that it was important to the government to avoid error because "[i]t is preferable to keep a qualified employee on than to train a new one."

13. What process is required in government contract disputes? You will recall from *Board of Regents v. Roth* that Roth lost because he did not have tenure. What is tenure? According to *Perry v. Sindermann*, it is: "A written contract . . . that supports a teacher's claim of entitlement to continued employment unless sufficient 'cause' is shown." Sindermann did not have tenure, but the Court held that he could trigger due process if he could show that there was "an unwritten 'common law' in a particular university that certain employees shall have the equivalent of tenure." In other words, he could prevail if he could show there was an unwritten contract that teachers would not be dismissed without a showing of cause.

Thus, it seems that government contracts automatically become property interests. Does this mean that contractual disputes with governments now require due process hearings? The answer is no, or at least not always. *Lujan v. G&G Fire Sprinklers, Inc.*, 532 U.S. 189 (2001), involved a California statute under which the state was authorized to withhold payment to a contractor if a subcontractor failed to comply with certain code requirements. The contractor argued that it was entitled to a due process hearing before any such payments could be withheld. Assuming that the contractual right to payment constituted a property right, the Court held that, "if California makes ordinary judicial process available to respondent for resolving its contractual dispute, that process is due process." The contractor could seek the disputed payment through a standard common law contract action.

14. Notice that it's not always *Mathews*. Although *Mathews v. Eldridge* dominates the landscape once it is determined that due process attached to a government decision, it does not always govern. In *Dusenbery v. United States*, 534 U.S. 161 (2002), Dusenbery was tried and convicted of various charges as a result of a search in which the government impounded several items of his property. While he was in prison, the government instituted statutorily authorized proceedings to take his property by forfeiture. The FBI sent certified mail notice to various appropriate addresses and published notice in the newspaper. Upon later learning of the forfeiture, Dusenbery claimed that inadequate notice violated his due process rights. The Court rejected an argument that *Mathews* balancing should apply and applied instead the "more straightforward test" (from *Mullane v. Central Hanover Bank & Trust*, 339 U.S. 306 (1950)) that notice must be "reasonably calculated under all the circumstances to apprise" the individual of the action. In so doing, the Court said it had "never viewed *Mathews* as announcing an all-embracing test for deciding due process claims."

Despite that disclaimer, a majority of the Court took an approach remarkably similar to *Mathews* balancing in *Jones v. Flowers*, 547 U.S. 220 (2006), which was factually close to *Dusenbery*. After Jones failed to pay taxes on his property in Little Rock, Arkansas, the state sold the property to Flowers at a tax sale after having sent

Jones a certified letter as notice of his tax delinquency. Although the post office returned that unopened packet and a later certified letter as "unclaimed," the state sold the property without any further specific effort to notify Jones. Quoting *Mullane*, the Court noted that assessing the adequacy of a particular form of notice requires balancing the "interest of the State" against "the individual interest sought to be protected by the Fourteenth Amendment." It then held that receipt of the returned letters was a "circumstance" that rendered the state's notice inadequate under the reasonableness test articulated in *Mullane*.

C. Issues of Integrity in Administrative Adjudications

In adjudications, as in rulemaking (*see* subchapter 3E), parties frequently challenge the integrity of the process or of the decisionmakers themselves. The following materials address four distinct areas in which such charges might be made: (1) problems arising from the combination of functions, in which the agency is in some sense both prosecutor and judge; (2) charges of bias; (3) *ex parte* contacts; and (4) congressional pressure.

1. May the Agency Both Prosecute and Decide? The Problem of "Combination of Functions"

One of the defining characteristics of modern administrative agencies is that they frequently decide adjudicatory disputes through a hearing structure remarkably similar to the judicial structure. In the federal courts, the contending parties appear before an independent Article III district judge who rules upon their dispute, subject to review in a court of appeals, and perhaps in the Supreme Court. We have seen several statutory schemes in which a hearing officer reaches an initial determination in a dispute, with the ultimate determination to be made by the head of the agency before review in the courts. For example, in the *Envirocare* decision, the parties initially appeared before the Atomic Safety and Licensing Board, and the company appealed the Board's ruling to the Nuclear Regulatory Commission.

In a significant departure from the judicial model, however, the agency itself, sometimes including the actual agency head, often initiates adjudicatory proceedings and participates as a party in the proceeding. For example, the adjudicatory process that gave rise to the Supreme Court's *Vermont Yankee* decision was initiated by the submission of a license application by the utility. The NRC staff reviewed the utility's application, decided that it met the various requirements, and appeared as a party in the licensing hearing in support of the application. Thus, one part of the agency participated as a party in a hearing before another part of the agency (the Atomic Safety and Licensing Board), with the decision ultimately made by another part of the agency—the agency head (the five members of the Nuclear Regulatory

Commission). Thus, the agency served as both prosecutor and ultimate decision-maker. That "combination of functions," quite common in administrative agencies, contrasts sharply with the judicial model and has prompted both constitutional challenges and statutory restrictions designed to protect the integrity of the agency adjudicatory process.

Lesson 4C.1. Abby now has a new client, Cuyahoga Canyon Vineyards (CCV), which is the target of one of Ralph's administrative enforcement actions. Some eighteen months after the original charge, CCV has lost before the ALJ and is now preparing arguments to the commissioners. Abby has learned that Ben recently left his position as Director of the Rulemaking Division to become the "attorney advisor" to Mick, a newly appointed commissioner. From her many conversations with Ben over the years, she knows he has worked very closely with Ralph since the very founding of the agency. He participated in discussions of virtually every important issue that came up, including what sort of industry behavior constituted a violation of § 5 of the WTCA. Indeed, he was consulted by Ralph with respect to every enforcement action the WTC filed before Ben took his new position. Abby is concerned that Ben's close involvement with the new commissioner would be adverse to her client's interest.

In light of the following materials, can Abby succeed in having Ben barred from advising Mick with respect to CCV's appeal?

Background of *Withrow v. Larkin*

The State of Wisconsin created a regulatory scheme governing the practice of medicine that raises the issues described in the introduction to this section. An Examining Board issues licenses to practice medicine and enforces the various rules governing those licenses. Here, the Board initiated an investigation into a physician's activities, including holding an "investigative hearing." The Board then would have held a "contested hearing," in which it would have determined whether the physician had violated the applicable rules, but a district court prohibited the Board from deciding the contested hearing on the ground that the combination of the investigative, prosecutorial, and decisional function in the same body violated due process.

Withrow v. Larkin

421 U.S. 35 (1975)

MR. JUSTICE WHITE delivered the opinion of the Court.

The statutes of the State of Wisconsin forbid the practice of medicine without a license from an Examining Board composed of practicing physicians. The statutes also define and forbid various acts of professional misconduct, proscribe fee splitting, and make illegal the practice of medicine under any name other than the name under which a license has issued if the public would be misled, such practice would constitute unfair competition with another physician, or other detriment to the profession would result. To enforce these provisions, the Examining Board is empowered . . . to warn and reprimand, temporarily to suspend the license, and "to institute criminal action or action to revoke license when it finds probable cause therefor under criminal or revocation statute. . . ." When an investigative proceeding before the Examining Board was commenced against him, appellee brought this suit against appellants, the individual members of the Board, seeking an injunction against the enforcement of the statutes.

. . . .

[Appellee's] practice in Wisconsin consisted of performing abortions at an office in Milwaukee. [The Board charged him with engaging in practices that are inimical to the public health and advised him of his hearing rights.] The hearing would be closed to the public, although appellee and his attorney could attend. They would not, however, be permitted to cross-examine witnesses. Based upon the evidence presented at the hearing, the Board would decide "whether to warn or reprimand if it finds such practice and whether to institute criminal action or action to revoke license if probable cause therefor exists under criminal or revocation statutes."

. . . .

The Board proceeded with its investigative hearing on July 12 and 13, 1973; numerous witnesses testified and appellee's counsel was present throughout the proceedings. Appellee's counsel was subsequently informed that appellee could, if he wished, appear before the Board to explain any of the evidence which had been presented.

On September 18, 1973, the Board sent to appellee a notice that a "contested hearing" would be held on October 4, 1973, to determine whether appellee had engaged in certain prohibited acts and that based upon the evidence adduced at the hearing the Board would determine whether his license would be suspended temporarily under [the relevant statute]. Appellee moved for a restraining order against the contested hearing. The District Court granted the motion on October 1, 1973. Because the Board had moved from purely investigative proceedings to a hearing aimed at deciding whether suspension of appellee's license was appropriate, the District Court concluded that a substantial federal question had arisen, namely, whether the authority given to appellants both "to investigate physicians and present charges [and] to rule on those charges and impose punishment, at least to the extent of reprimanding or temporarily suspending" violated appellee's due process rights. . . .

The Board complied and did not go forward with the contested hearing. Instead, it noticed and held a final investigative session on October 4, 1973, at which appellee's attorney, but not appellee, appeared. The Board thereupon issued "Findings of Fact," "Conclusions of Law," and a "Decision" in which the Board found that appellee had engaged in specified conduct proscribed by the statute.

. . . .

The District Court framed the constitutional issue, which it addressed as being whether "for the board temporarily to suspend Dr. Larkin's license at its own contested hearing on charges evolving from its own investigation would constitute a denial to him of his rights to procedural due process." The question was initially answered affirmatively, and in its amended judgment the court asserted that there was a high probability that appellee would prevail on the question. Its opinion stated that the "state medical examining board [did] not qualify as [an independent] decisionmaker [and could not] properly rule with regard to the merits of the same charges it investigated and, as in this case, presented to the district attorney." We disagree. On the present record, it is quite unlikely that appellee would ultimately prevail on the merits of the due process issue presented to the District Court, and it was an abuse of discretion to issue the preliminary injunction.

Concededly, a "fair trial in a fair tribunal is a basic requirement of due process." This applies to administrative agencies which adjudicate as well as to courts. Not only is a biased decisionmaker constitutionally unacceptable but "our system of law has always endeavored to prevent even the probability of unfairness." In pursuit of this end, various situations have been identified in which experience teaches that the probability of actual bias on the part of the judge or decisionmaker is too high to be constitutionally tolerable. Among these cases are those in which the adjudicator has a pecuniary interest in the outcome and in which he has been the target of personal abuse or criticism from the party before him.

The contention that the combination of investigative and adjudicative functions necessarily creates an unconstitutional risk of bias in administrative adjudication has a much more difficult burden of persuasion to carry. It must overcome a presumption of honesty and integrity in those serving as adjudicators; and it must convince that, under a realistic appraisal of psychological tendencies and human weakness, conferring investigative and adjudicative powers on the same individuals poses such a risk of actual bias or prejudgment that the practice must be forbidden if the guarantee of due process is to be adequately implemented.

[handwritten margin note: BURDEN OF UNCONSTIT. COMBINATION]

Very similar claims have been squarely rejected in prior decisions of this Court. In *FTC v. Cement Institute* (1948), the Federal Trade Commission had instituted proceedings concerning the respondents' multiple basing-point delivered-price system. It was demanded that the Commission members disqualify themselves because long before the Commission had filed its complaint it had investigated the parties and reported to Congress and to the president, and its members had testified before congressional committees concerning the legality of such a pricing system. At least some of the members had disclosed their opinion that the system was illegal. The issue of bias was brought here and confronted "on the assumption that such an opinion had been formed by the entire membership of the Commission as a result of its prior official investigations."

The Court rejected the claim, saying:

"[T]he fact that the Commission had entertained such views as the result of its prior ex parte investigations did not necessarily mean that the minds of its members were irrevocably closed on the subject of the respondents' basing point practices. Here, in contrast to the Commission's investigations, members of the cement industry were legally authorized participants in the hearings. They produced evidence—volumes of it. They were free to point out to the Commission by testimony, by cross-examination of witnesses, and by arguments, conditions of the trade practices under attack which they thought kept these practices within the range of legally permissible business activities."

In specific response to a due process argument, the Court asserted:

"No decision of this Court would require us to hold that it would be a violation of procedural due process for a judge to sit in a case after he had expressed an opinion as to whether certain types of conduct were prohibited by law. In fact, judges frequently try the same case more than once and decide identical issues each time, although these issues involve questions both of law and fact. Certainly, the Federal Trade Commission cannot possibly be under stronger constitutional compulsions in this respect than a court."

This Court has also ruled that a hearing examiner who has recommended findings of fact after rejecting certain evidence as not being probative was not disqualified to preside at further hearings that were required when reviewing courts held that the evidence had been erroneously excluded. The Court of Appeals had decided that the examiner should not again sit because it would be unfair to require the parties to try "issues of fact to those who may have prejudged them. . . ." But this Court unanimously reversed, saying:

"Certainly it is not the rule of judicial administration that, statutory requirements apart . . . a judge is disqualified from sitting in a retrial because he was reversed on earlier rulings. We find no warrant for imposing upon administrative agencies a stiffer rule, whereby examiners would be disentitled to sit because they ruled strongly against a party in the first hearing."

More recently we have sustained against due process objection a system in which a Social Security examiner has responsibility for developing the facts and making a decision as to disability claims, and observed that the challenge to this combination of functions "assumes too much and would bring down too many procedures designed, and working well, for a governmental structure of great and growing complexity."[16]

---

16. The decisions of the Courts of Appeals touching upon this question of bias arising from a combination of functions are also instructive. In *Pangburn v. CAB*, 311 F.2d 349 (1st Cir. 1962), the Civil Aeronautics Board had the responsibility of making an accident report and also reviewing the decision of a trial examiner that the pilot involved in the accident should have his airline transport pilot rating suspended. The pilot claimed that his right to procedural due process had been violated by the fact that the Board was not an impartial tribunal in deciding his appeal from the trial examiner's decision since it had previously issued its accident report finding pilot error

That is not to say that there is nothing to the argument that those who have investigated should not then adjudicate. The issue is substantial, it is not new, and legislators and others concerned with the operations of administrative agencies have given much attention to whether and to what extent distinctive administrative functions should be performed by the same persons. No single answer has been reached. Indeed, the growth, variety, and complexity of the administrative processes have made any one solution highly unlikely. Within the Federal Government itself, Congress has addressed the issue in several different ways, providing for varying degrees of separation from complete separation of functions to virtually none at all. For the generality of agencies, Congress has been content with § [554(d)] of the Administrative Procedure Act which provides that no employee engaged in investigating or prosecuting may also participate or advise in the adjudicating function, but which also expressly exempts from this prohibition "the agency or a member or members of the body comprising the agency."

[margin note: CONGRESS]

It is not surprising, therefore, to find that "[t]he case law, both federal and state, generally rejects the idea that the combination [of] judging [and] investigating functions is a denial of due process. . . ." Similarly, our cases, although they reflect the substance of the problem, offer no support for the bald proposition applied in this case by the District Court that agency members who participate in an investigation are disqualified from adjudicating. The incredible variety of administrative mechanisms in this country will not yield to any single organizing principle. . . .

Nor do we think the situation substantially different because the Board, when it was prevented from going forward with the contested hearing, proceeded to make and issue formal findings of fact and conclusions of law asserting that there was probable cause to believe that appellee had engaged in various acts prohibited by the Wisconsin statutes. These findings and conclusions were verified and filed with the district attorney for the purpose of initiating revocation and criminal proceedings. Although the District Court did not emphasize this aspect of the case before it, appellee stresses it in attempting to show prejudice and prejudgment. We are not persuaded.

Judges repeatedly issue arrest warrants on the basis that there is probable cause to believe that a crime has been committed and that the person named in the warrant has committed it. Judges also preside at preliminary hearings where they must decide whether the evidence is sufficient to hold a defendant for trial. Neither of these pretrial involvements has been thought to raise any constitutional barrier

[margin note: PROBABLE CAUSE]

---

to be the probable cause of the crash. The Court of Appeals found the Board's procedures to be constitutionally permissible:

> "[W]e cannot say that the mere fact that a tribunal has had contact with a particular factual complex in a prior hearing, or indeed has taken a public position on the facts, is enough to place that tribunal under a constitutional inhibition to pass upon the facts in a subsequent hearing. We believe that more is required. Particularly is this so in the instant case where the Board's prior contact with the case resulted from its following the Congressional mandate to investigate and report the probable cause of all civil air accidents."

against the judge's presiding over the criminal trial and, if the trial is without a jury, against making the necessary determination of guilt or innocence. Nor has it been thought that a judge is disqualified from presiding over injunction proceedings because he has initially assessed the facts in issuing or denying a temporary restraining order or a preliminary injunction. It is also very typical for the members of administrative agencies to receive the results of investigations, to approve the filing of charges or formal complaints instituting enforcement proceedings, and then to participate in the ensuing hearings. This mode of procedure does not violate the Administrative Procedure Act, and it does not violate due process of law. We should also remember that it is not contrary to due process to allow judges and administrators who have had their initial decisions reversed on appeal to confront and decide the same questions a second time around.

Here, the Board stayed within the accepted bounds of due process. Having investigated, it issued findings and conclusions asserting the commission of certain acts and ultimately concluding that there was probable cause to believe that appellee had violated the statutes.

The risk of bias or prejudgment in this sequence of functions has not been considered to be intolerably high or to raise a sufficiently great possibility that the adjudicators would be so psychologically wedded to their complaints that they would consciously or unconsciously avoid the appearance of having erred or changed position. . . .

That the combination of investigative and adjudicative functions does not, without more, constitute a due process violation, does not, of course, preclude a court from determining from the special facts and circumstances present in the case before it that the risk of unfairness is intolerably high. . . .

Notes

1. Assessing Ben's participation as a matter of due process. What guidance does *Withrow* provide with respect to Abby's challenge to Ben's participation? Why did the agency prevail in *Withrow*? Does the same logic apply to Ben?

Consider Justice White's footnote 16. Does it seem likely that the CAB could actually find pilot error in one proceeding and yet not find a basis for suspending the pilot's license in the other? In fact, the First Circuit noted that the CAB had done so in another case. Still, as Justice White expressed it, "under a realistic appraisal of psychological tendencies and human weakness" isn't this combination asking a good deal of an official's "honesty and integrity"? Is the argument for Ben's participation stronger or weaker than the CAB's argument in *Pangburn*?

Despite the freedom offered by *Withrow*, our administrative law continues to have a strong instinct for separation of functions. As you will see in the notes to 4C.2 below, the Supreme Court in *Williams v. Pennsylvania* recently held that due process requires the separation—at least in some instances—of prosecutorial and adjudicative functions. If you were creating, say, the disciplinary procedures for a state bar, would you separate those who make the decision to investigate from those who ultimately decide whether disciplinary action is appropriate? What factors might argue against such separation? *See, e.g., Kennedy v. L.D.,* 430 N.W.2d 833 (Minn. 1988).

2. Combination of functions under the APA. According to *Withrow,* procedural due process rarely prohibits the combination of functions. The APA, however, prohibits the combination of functions in adjudications. The Ninth Circuit in *Grolier Inc. v. FTC,* 615 F.2d 1215 (9th Cir. 1980), considered the scope of that prohibition:

> . . . In January 1976, four months before completion of the hearings, ALJ von Brand informed the parties that he had served as an attorney advisor to former FTC Commissioner A. Everett MacIntyre from 1963 through January 1971, during which period Grolier was intermittently investigated and charged by the FTC. Records available to Grolier indicated that Commissioner MacIntyre attended at least one meeting between it and representatives of the FTC.

> Upon learning of ALJ von Brand's advisory responsibilities during the eight-year period, Grolier requested that the judge disqualify himself from further participation in the proceedings. The judge denied the request, stating that he did not recall working on matters involving Grolier while serving as legal advisor to the Commissioner.

> . . . .

> Grolier argued before the FTC, and now argues before us, that failure to disqualify ALJ von Brand from the case violated both section 554(d) of the Administrative Procedure Act (APA) and the Due Process guarantee of the Fifth Amendment.

> . . . .

> In an effort to minimize any unfairness caused by this consolidation of responsibilities, the APA mandates an internal separation of the investigatory-prosecutorial functions from adjudicative responsibilities. . . . To violate section 554(d), then, an agency employee must, in the same or a factually related case, (1) engage in "investigative or prosecuting functions," and (2) "participate or advise in the decision." Neither Grolier nor the FTC contests the fact that ALJ von Brand's actions meet the latter of these two requirements. The point of their disagreement, and the issue which we must resolve, is whether ALJ von Brand meets the first requirement, *i.e.,* whether his employment as an attorney-advisor to Commissioner MacIntyre constituted "investigative or prosecuting functions" in this or a factually related case.

> . . . .

> It is evident that Congress intended to address these two concerns by separating investigative-prosecuting functions from adjudicative functions. Section 554(d)(1) expressly forbids ALJ acquisition of *ex parte* information.

This provision, along with 5 U.S.C. § 557(d)(1), illustrates Congress' concern over possible use in the decisional process of information received outside of the controlled adjudicative setting. Congress' second concern, precluding from adjudicative functions those who have developed a "will to win," is evident in the legislative history of the APA. . . .

Regarding the APA, the Supreme Court has stated that "it would be a disservice to our form of government and to the administrative process itself if the courts should fail, so far as the terms of the Act warrant, to give effect to its remedial purposes where the evils it was aimed at appear." We conclude that by forbidding adjudication by persons "engaged in the performance of investigative or prosecuting functions," Congress intended to preclude from decisionmaking in a particular case not only individuals with the title of "investigator" or "prosecutor," but all persons who had, in that or a factually related case, been involved with *ex parte* information, or who had developed, by prior involvement with the case, a "will to win." An attorney-advisor may, therefore, come within the prohibition of section 554(d) if he has had such involvement. The FTC decision to the contrary was error.

The FTC argues, however, that even if section 554(d) has the broad meaning that we conclude it does, ALJ von Brand and all other former attorney-advisors are exempted from the 554(d) prohibition by APA language immunizing "the agency or a member or members of the body comprising the agency." 5 U.S.C. § 554(d)(2)(C). It contends that the necessarily close relationship between attorney-advisors and agency members requires that an advisor be extended privileges coequal with his commission member's responsibilities so that he may freely advise the member on the full range of problems considered by the FTC. This argument would be compelling if made on behalf of an attorney-advisor or other FTC employee who must counsel the member at both the investigative and decisionmaking stages of a case. But ALJ von Brand is no longer an attorney-advisor; his ALJ position does not necessitate involvement in the adjudication of this particular case. The exemption from 554(d) was created only for those positions in which involvement in all phases of a case is dictated "by the very nature of administrative agencies, where the same authority is responsible for both the investigation-prosecution and the hearing and decision of cases." We reject the argument that ALJ von Brand is exempted from the 554(d) separation of functions.

Would this prohibition apply to Ben?

3. Separation of functions and agency management—FERC struggles with complexity. The concept of separating investigatory and prosecutorial functions on the one hand from decisionmaking functions on the other seems simple enough from the perspective of civil or criminal litigation. But agencies are far more complex than those relatively simple models. In addition to those functions, agencies conduct research, comply with environmental review requirements, audit their own and regulated industry performance, and perform many other tasks. Many agency staff responsibilities do not fit easily or obviously into the categories that must be separated, but they can be very important to assuring that the agency understands the issues before it in various contexts.

In 2002, the Federal Energy Regulatory Commission (FERC) issued a policy statement in which it sought to explain to the public and to guide its own staff with respect to the complex issues involved in separation of functions requirements. Separation of Functions, 101 FERC Para 61,340 (2002). FERC's statement reveals the complexity of managing an agency whose staff must act as investigator, prosecutor, and judge while also implementing many highly complex programs:

> The Commission believes generally that functions may be combined, that is, the same person may perform more than one function or perform a function that he typically does not otherwise perform, provided (1) such combination enhances the Commission's understanding of energy markets and related issues, and (2) parties in individual proceedings appear to and actually receive a fair and impartial adjudication of their claims. . . . In brief, this statement of administrative policy addresses those situations where a Commission staff member may perform multiple functions without running afoul of the Administrative Procedure Act (APA), 5 U.S.C. 554(d)(2) and 557(d). Simply put, it examines "who may talk to whom when." . . .
>
> . . . .
>
> 5. Generally, the Commission's advisory staff literally "advises" the Commission by preparing memoranda and draft orders, opinions, and rules for its consideration in specific docketed proceedings, and the Commission's trial staff literally "tries" cases in such proceedings before the Commission's ALJs. But the Commission has many staff members who are not trial staff but who also are not the traditional advisory staff. These include staff members who monitor the energy markets, investigate and enforce alleged violations of the law, audit companies' books, work with other Federal and state agencies on environmental matters, facilitate resolution of disputes, and communicate agency policy and action to the Congress, state officials, and the public.
>
> . . . .
>
> 6. Separating the Commission's functions has become more challenging recently because of fundamental changes in the industries regulated by the Commission, as well as the imperative for the Commission to oversee markets and reach out to members of the industry, state commissions, and citizen groups in pursuing its market-oriented goals. The Commission wants to be able to be open and responsive to those outside the Commission, and at the same time have access to advisors with the required expertise to aid the decision making process. Thus, as the Commission's

resources are limited, a combination of certain functions may be necessary to take advantage of that expertise while ensuring the integrity of the decision making process in pursuit of the important public interest objective of resolving critical matters correctly and on a timely basis. . . .

. . . .

13. . . . [T]he Commission's ALJs currently serve as true trial judges, generally not consulting advisory staff, and ensuring that the trials are a separate and distinct aspect of the decision making process. On the other hand, the Commission's advisory staff conduct technical conferences where they discuss issues with the parties, and subsequently advise the Commission on the appropriate course of action. The Commission has not separated these latter functions — nor does it intend to do so now — even though staff's participation in the technical conferences may have on occasion appeared to have been adversarial. Furthermore, under APA § 554, the Commission would not necessarily have to separate any functions in the licensing and ratemaking areas. Nevertheless, when the Commission has chosen to set certain cases, in particular rate cases, for hearing, it has separated, or not combined, the trial and advisory functions in factually-related proceedings regardless of the subject matter.

. . . .

14. In sum, especially with respect to regulatory agencies like the Commission, the APA does not require that there be a rigid line drawn between functions. Rather, the APA strikes a balance between "fairness and pragmatism." Thus, the protection of fair decisions can be balanced against the efficient use of staff resources so that the Commission may have access to the expertise that it needs to make sound decisions in highly technical, complex, or novel situations. At bottom, due process requires that there be an impartial decision maker to ensure that decisions are reasoned and unbiased and that all affected parties can play a meaningful role in the decision making process.

In that context, the policy statement provided specific advice to various different actors on the FERC staff. The following directive to the litigators illustrates the problem of trying to separate litigative functions when those involved in litigation also have many other responsibilities:

. . . [T]he litigator must separate his function from other functions once a matter is set for trial-type evidentiary hearing. Accordingly, until that time, a staff member who may ultimately be a litigator in a case may discuss the matter with anyone at the Commission, including the decision makers and their advisors. In effect, until that time, the "litigator" . . . would not be serving a litigation function. Accordingly, he may analyze tariff filings, review and help draft hearing orders, and participate in technical conferences. At this early stage in a proceeding, a would-be litigator would not have the "will to win" underlying the separation of functions rule so the protection of the process would be fairly balanced by the experience the litigator can contribute. He may also review and help draft other orders, including rehearing orders, provided the case was not set for hearing and did not involve a matter factually related to a case set for trial-type evidentiary hearing. Further, he may participate informally in the Commission's rulemakings (that is, he may review and help draft rules, and discuss the issues with the advisors and would not need to file formal comments), and otherwise contribute to generic policy discussions. In addition, he may perform other functions normally associated with staff who reach out and provide information to the public about Commission action.

20. Once a case is set for trial-type evidentiary hearing, a litigator may no longer serve an advisory function or give advice on the merits in that proceeding or in a factually-related proceeding, even after the record closes before the ALJ. . . .

4. Combination of functions issues in the MSAPA. The 2010 MSAPA, § 402, prohibits one "who has served as investigator, prosecutor or advocate at any stage in" a formal adjudicative proceeding (called a "contested case") from serving as a presiding officer or assisting or advising a presiding officer in that contested case. Similarly, one who is "subject to the authority, direction, or discretion of an individual who has served as investigator, prosecutor, or advocate at any stage in a contested case" may not serve as a presiding officer in that case.

This MSAPA provision also recognizes, as have the opinions excerpted here, that decisionmakers must make certain decisions at different stages of an adjudication and that this should not be grounds for disqualification. Thus, an "agency head that has participated in a determination of probable cause or other preliminary determination in an adjudication may serve as the presiding officer or final decision maker in the adjudication unless a party demonstrates" other grounds for disqualification.

5. A European perspective on combination of functions. Combination of functions is apparently not considered an offense to fundamental fairness in the French council of state model. Two English comparative administrative law commentators observed:

> The peculiar character of the Conseil d'Etat in handling administrative litigation lies in the dual functions of its members. At the same time they are judges of the administration and its central legal advisers. In the same afternoon, one person may act as a member of a judicial panel on tax cases and then come down in the lift to advise on the drafting of a new law on privatizing a television channel. Far from creating a conflict of interests, the dual function is seen as enriching administrative adjudication.

L. Neville Brown & John Bell, *Recent Reforms of French Administrative Justice*, 8 Civ. Just. Q. 71 (1989). Does our combination of functions law (generally requiring separation) also recognize some benefits in combining certain functions? What benefits might be gained? What combination could reap these benefits?

2. What's Enough to Taint a Decisionmaker? — Prior Statements and Other Possible Indications of Bias

The previous section addressed concerns about fairness or legitimacy that might arise from the structure of the agency adjudicatory process. The following materials address the prospect of actual personal bias, something about the circumstances of the particular decisionmaker that could render that person inappropriate to make the decision.

Lesson 4C.2. Abby has learned that Mick, the new Commissioner, has long been active in an anti-drunk driving organization. It turns out that his brother was killed by a drunk driver who had spent the day tasting wines at the various local wineries near their parents' home. In a fund raising letter for the organization several years earlier, Mick had written: "These wineries are concerned only with the bottom line. They have no concern for their customers or for the well-being of the public." Abby's client wants Mick barred from participation in the enforcement action.

What guidance can Abby take from the following materials?

Background of *Cinderella Career & Finishing Schools v. FTC*

The following decision involved Federal Trade Commission Chairman Paul Rand Dixon, who had been very outspoken about issues coming before the agency. Indeed, this court (the D.C. Circuit) and another had already criticized Chairman Dixon's actions in connection with his previous agency decisions. The court articulates a rule seemingly designed to assure fairness, but is it workable? Did the court overreact to the antics of one strong-minded agency head?

Cinderella Career & Finishing Schools v. FTC
425 F.2d 583 (D.C. Cir. 1970)

TAMM, CIRCUIT JUDGE:

. . . .

After the [Federal Trade] Commission filed its complaint under section 5 of the Federal Trade Commission Act which charged Cinderella with making representations and advertising in a manner which was false, misleading and deceptive, a hearing examiner held a lengthy series of hearings which consumed a total of sixteen days; these proceedings are reported in 1,810 pages of transcript. After the Commission had called twenty-nine witnesses and the petitioners twenty-three, and after the FTC had introduced 157 exhibits and petitioners 90, the hearing examiner ruled in a ninety-three page initial decision that the charges in the complaint should be dismissed.

Complainant's counsel appealed the hearing examiner's initial decision to the full Commission; oral argument was heard on the appeal on May 28, 1968, and the Commission's final order was issued on October 10, 1968. The full Commission reversed the hearing examiner as to six of the original thirteen charges and entered a cease and desist order against the petitioners, who then brought this appeal. For the reasons which follow we remand to the Commission for further proceedings.

. . . .

[A] ground which requires remand of these proceedings . . . is participation in the proceedings by the then Chairman of the Federal Trade Commission, Paul Rand Dixon.

Notice that the hearing examiner's dismissal of all charges would be appealed was filed by the Commission staff on February 1, 1968. On March 12, 1968, this court's decision was handed down in a prior appeal arising from this same complaint, in which we upheld the Commission's issuance of press releases which called attention to the pending proceedings. Then, on March 15, 1968, while the appeal from the examiner's decision was pending before him, Chairman Dixon made a speech before the Government Relations Workshop of the National Newspaper Association in which he stated:

> What kind of vigor can a reputable newspaper exhibit? The quick answer, of course, pertains to its editorial policy, its willingness to present the news without bias. However, that is only half the coin. How about ethics on the business side of running a paper? What standards are maintained on advertising acceptance? What would be the attitude toward accepting good money for advertising by a merchant who conducts a "going out of business" sale every five months? *What about carrying ads that offer college educations in five weeks*, fortunes by raising mushrooms in the basement, getting rid of pimples with a magic lotion, *or becoming an airline's hostess by attending a charm school*? Or, to raise the target a bit, how many newspapers would hesitate to accept an ad promising an unqualified guarantee for a product when the guarantee is subject to many limitations? Without belaboring the point, I'm sure you're aware that advertising acceptance standards could stand more tightening by many newspapers. *Granted that newspapers are not in the advertising policing business, their advertising managers are savvy enough to smell deception when the odor is strong enough.* And it is in the public interest, as well as their own, that their sensory organs become more discriminating. The Federal Trade Commission, even where it has jurisdiction, could not protect the public as quickly.

It requires no superior olfactory powers to recognize that the danger of unfairness through prejudgment is not diminished by a cloak of self-righteousness. We have no concern for or interest in the public statements of government officers, but we are charged with the responsibility of making certain that the image of the administrative process is not transformed from a Rubens to a Modigliani.

We indicated in our earlier opinion in this case that "there is in fact and law authority in the Commission, acting in the public interest, to alert the public to *suspected violations* of the law by *factual press releases* whenever the Commission shall have reason to believe that a respondent is engaged in activities made unlawful by the Act. . . ." This does not give individual commissioners license to prejudge cases or to make speeches which give the appearance that the case has been prejudged. [Conduct] such as this may have the effect of entrenching a Commissioner in a position which he has publicly stated, making it difficult, if not impossible, for him to reach a different conclusion in the event he deems it necessary to do so after consideration of the record. There is a marked difference between the issuance of a press release which states that the Commission has filed a complaint because it has "reason to believe" that there have been violations, and statements by a Commissioner after an appeal has been filed which give the appearance that he has already prejudged the case and that the ultimate determination of the merits will move in predestined grooves. While these two situations — Commission press releases and a Commissioner's pre-decision public statements — are similar in appearance, they are obviously of a different order of merit.

As we noted in our earlier opinion, Congress has specifically vested the administrative agencies both with the "power to act in an accusatory capacity" and with the "responsibility of ultimately determining the merits of the charges so presented."

Chairman Dixon, sensitive to theory but insensitive to reality, made the following statement in declining to recuse himself from this case after petitioners requested that he withdraw:

> As . . . I have stated . . . this principle "is not a rigid command of the law, compelling disqualification for trifling causes, but a consideration addressed to the discretion and sound judgment of the administrator himself in determining whether, irrespective of the law's requirements, he should disqualify himself."

To this tenet of self-appraisal we apply Lord Macaulay's evaluation more than 100 years ago of our American government: "It has one drawback — it is all sail and no anchor." We find it hard to believe that former Chairman Dixon is so indifferent to the dictates of the Courts of Appeals that he has chosen once again to put his personal determination of what the law requires ahead of what the courts have time and again told him the law requires. If this is a question of "discretion and judgment," Commissioner Dixon has exercised questionable discretion and very poor judgment indeed, in directing his shafts and squibs at a case awaiting his official action. We can use his own words in telling Commissioner Dixon that he has acted "irrespective of the law's requirements"; we will spell out for him once again, avoiding tired cliche and weary generalization, in no uncertain terms, exactly what those requirements are, in the fervent hope that this will be the last time we have to travel this wearisome road.

[The test for disqualification] has been succinctly stated as being whether "a disinterested observer may conclude that [the agency] has in some measure adjudged the facts as well as the law of a particular case in advance of hearing it." *Gilligan, Will & Co. v. SEC* (2d Cir. 1959). . . . In [*Texaco, Inc. v. FTC* (D.C. Cir. 1964)], Chairman Dixon made a speech before the National Congress of Petroleum Retailers, Inc. while a case against Texaco was pending before the examiner on remand. After restating the test for disqualification, this court said:

> [A] disinterested reader of Chairman Dixon's speech could hardly fail to conclude that he had in some measure decided in advance that Texaco had violated the Act.

We further stated that such an administrative hearing "must be attended, not only with every element of fairness but with the very appearance of complete fairness." We therefore concluded that Chairman Dixon's participation in the *Texaco* case amounted to a denial of due process.

After our decision in *Texaco* the United States Court of Appeals for the Sixth Circuit was required to reverse a decision of the FTC because Chairman Dixon refused to recuse himself from the case *even though he had served as Chief Counsel and Staff Director* to the Senate Subcommittee which made the initial investigation into the production and sale of the "wonder drug" tetracycline. Incredible though it may seem, the court was compelled to note in that case that:

> [The] Commission is a fact-finding body. As Chairman, Mr. Dixon sat with the other members as triers of the facts and *joined in making the factual determination* upon which the order of the Commission is based.
>
> *As counsel for the Senate Subcommittee, he had investigated and developed many of these same facts.*

It is appalling to witness such insensitivity to the requirements of due process; it is even more remarkable to find ourselves once again confronted with a situation in which Mr. Dixon, pouncing on the most convenient victim, has determined either to distort the holdings in the cited cases beyond all reasonable interpretation or to ignore them altogether. We are constrained to this harshness of language because of Mr. Dixon's flagrant disregard of prior decisions.

The rationale for remanding the case despite the fact that former Chairman Dixon's vote was not necessary for a majority is well established:

> Litigants are entitled to an impartial tribunal whether it consists of one man or twenty and there is no way which we know of whereby the influence of one upon the others can be quantitatively measured. . . .

For the reasons set forth above we vacate the order of the Commission and remand with instructions that the commissioners consider the record and evidence in reviewing the initial decision, without the participation of Commissioner Dixon.

Notes

1. How does the argument differ when it involves adjudication, not rulemaking? Abby recalls that there was a similar dispute about Brit's involvement in the labeling rulemaking (Lesson 3E). Jordan was unsuccessful in his effort to have Brit removed. Is Abby's case any stronger? Why?

2. How much evidence of bias is too much? A basic component of due process is the requirement for an impartial decisionmaker. This is also a fundamental principle of the ancient doctrine of "natural justice." Chief Justice Coke in his seminal *Dr. Bonham's* opinion, 77 Eng. Rep. 638 (1610) (noted in Note 5 after Lesson 4B.1.a), denied the College of Physicians the power to fine Dr. Bonham because half the fine would go to the College. Coke established the fundamental principle of "no man should be a judge in his own cause" (*nemo iudex in sua causa*) that prevailed even against acts of Parliament. The demands of modern government make the application of the demand for independent decisionmakers quite tricky. Factors such as large numbers, expertise, and consistency are at work as well.

How concrete does the evidence of bias have to be? For example, consider a case in which a patient challenged the panel constituted to conduct a medical malpractice arbitration because the panel was dominated by those in the health care business. The Michigan Supreme Court in *Morris v. Metriyakool*, 344 N.W.2d 736 (Mich. 1984), noted that an unacceptably high risk of bias as well as actual bias would not be tolerated. However, it concluded that the mere interest in insurance premiums on the part of the panelist would not create an unacceptably high risk of bias.

3. What about indirect pecuniary interest? Direct pecuniary interest seems a relatively easy instance of actual bias. As the pecuniary interest becomes less direct, the question becomes more difficult. Consider *Gibson v. Berryhill*, 411 U.S. 564 (1973), in which licensed independent optometrists filed charges of unprofessional conduct against licensed optometrists working for a corporation and sought to bar them from the practice of optometry. The challengers argued that working for a corporation constituted unprofessional conduct. The charges were heard by the Alabama Board of Optometry, whose members were required to be independent optometrists. The Court found an unacceptable conflict of interest where half of the state's optometrists worked for corporations.

How would *Gibson v. Berryhill* apply to Abby's case? What about a local planning board? Normally, every member of the community serving on a local planning board will have some indirect pecuniary interest in a matter coming before the board. Should all such boards be replaced? Define the pecuniary interest which should be considered as creating an unacceptable risk of bias.

4. "Appearance of complete fairness." The *Cinderella* court held that "an administrative hearing 'must be attended . . . with the very appearance of complete fairness.'" The principle may not be troubling as it was applied in *Cinderella*, but it is capable of very widespread application. In *Bunnell v. Barnhart*, 336 F.3d 1112 (9th Cir. 2003), for example, a Social Security claimant argued that essentially the same standard ("appearance of impropriety") was violated where the ALJ hearing her case was also the target (along with other ALJs) of a lawsuit by the claimant's lawyer. The Ninth Circuit joined two others in holding that the "appearance of impropriety" test does not apply to ALJs merely by virtue of their positions as ALJs within an agency:

> Administrative law judges are employed by the agency whose action they review. As the Second Circuit has specifically recognized, if the "appearance of impropriety" standard of 28 U.S.C. §455(a) [the federal judicial recusal statute] was applicable to administrative law judges, they would be forced to recuse themselves in every case.

To rule otherwise would create an incentive for litigants to manipulate the system in order to create an appearance of impropriety. Bunnell's counsel may have done just that in a case that later formed the basis of her claim discussed above. Lowry was a Social Security Disability litigator. In *Lowry v. Barnhart*, 329 F.3d 1019 (9th Cir. 2003), he sought a mandamus to prevent ALJ Hyatt and two other ALJs from hearing cases in which he was counsel. The court's description demonstrates the depth to which matters can sink if those involved let things get out of hand:

> Lowry says Hyatt uses "intimidation and anger as a tactic to shorten [his] hearings," refuses to hear evidence and denies him cross-examination. Hyatt also supposedly told two claimants that Lowry was a "poor attorney who does a poor job." Lowry began filing motions to recuse Hyatt from his cases, and Hyatt responded with letters to Lowry's clients defending his impartiality and encouraging them to ask Hyatt about their "rights to representation."
>
> Hyatt, for his part, doesn't think much of Lowry. He says Lowry uses too many leading questions, fails to submit necessary medical records and questionnaires, and acts in a generally "disrespectful and contemptuous" manner. He says that Lowry once called him a "baldfaced liar" on the record and then sat at counsel table laughing and smirking.
>
> In responding to Lowry's complaint, the agency itself had found that both sides of the dispute had acted unprofessionally, but that there were insufficient grounds for an investigation. The court denied relief on the ground that there was no private cause of action.

Normally, disputes of this sort, arising from behavior in the litigation itself, cannot be the basis for disqualifying an ALJ or other adjudicatory decisionmaker. Still, an ALJ must be careful, as indicated by *Bieber v. Department of the Army*, 287 F.3d 1358 (Fed. Cir. 2002). Bieber challenged his dismissal, which arose from persistent, widely disseminated, and obnoxiously stated complaints about his superiors' failure to control the workplace dress of his colleagues.

> In the course of the hearing, the administrative judge denigrated Bieber's concerns (for example, stating that "I really think what people wear to work is no concern of their fellow employees," and asking "[b]ut why . . . didn't

Mr. Bieber just shut up?" and repeatedly stated that he could not under-stand why Bieber "continued to be obsessed with [the dress code issue]." The administrative judge went so far as to state that Bieber's frequent berat-ing of his coworkers regarding their clothing "defies civility to me."[1] Bieber did not file a motion to recuse the administrative judge, and complains of bias for the first time on appeal to this court from the Board's decision.

Although the court found some of the ALJ's remarks to be "plainly inappro-priate," it denied relief, quoting the following instructive language from *Liteky v. United States*, 510 U.S. 540, 555 (1994):

> [O]pinions formed by the judge on the basis of facts introduced or events occurring in the course of the current proceedings, or of prior proceedings, do not constitute a basis for a bias or partiality motion *unless they display a deep-seated favoritism or antagonism that would make fair judgment impos-sible.* Thus, judicial remarks during the course of a trial that are critical or disapproving of, or even hostile to, counsel, the parties, or their cases, ordinarily do not support a bias or partiality challenge. They *may* do so if they reveal an opinion that derives from an extrajudicial source; and they *will* do so if they reveal such a high degree of favoritism or antagonism as to make fair judgment impossible.

As these materials indicate, courts rarely find undue bias based upon an ALJ's behavior during a hearing. In recent years, however, courts have severely criticized the behavior of Immigration Judges (who are not ALJs under the Administrative Procedure Act). In *Cham v. Attorney General of the U.S.*, 445 F.3d 683 (3d Cir. 2006), for example, the Third Circuit vacated a denial of asylum "when not a modicum of courtesy, of respect, or of any pretense of fairness is extended to a petitioner," and "under the 'bullying' nature of the immigration judge's questioning, a petitioner was ground to bits." Reviewing the transcript in detail, the court found that, "[t]he belligerence of the questioning and the tension in the courtroom fairly leap off the pages of the record," prejudicing the petitioner's ability to present his claims. At some point, the behavior of an ALJ or other administrative adjudicator may be suf-ficiently outrageous to constitute a violation of due process.

5. Mick's arguable personal animosity. To the extent that Mick has developed any animosity toward Cuyahoga Canyon Vineyards, it did not arise from the litigation itself, as discussed in the previous note, but from his family's experiences. Address-ing the problem of personal animosity arising from being the target of criticism, the New Jersey Supreme Court commented:

---

1. The administrative judge further stated: "I'm really groping to understand why you behaved as you did and I'm not hearing anything"; asked "[w]hat difference does it make to you what other people are wearing? What earthly difference, Mr. Bieber?"; and warned Bieber that "[y]ou're los-ing it."

> In this context [of a police superintendent conducting a hearing to discipline a police officer], actual bias becomes the touchstone of disqualification. The probability of actual bias is grounds for disqualification when the decisionmaker has a pecuniary interest in the outcome of the matter or has been the target of personal criticism from one seeking relief. Nothing here indicates that [the superintendent] had a pecuniary interest in the outcome of the proceeding or that he was engaged in a personal vendetta against [the police officer] because of criticism of him by [the officer] or anyone else.

Matter of Carberry, 556 A.2d 314 (N.J. 1989). The New Jersey court suggested that the risk that a reaction to criticism will skew a decision might lead to a finding of illegal bias. Under what circumstances would you find such a risk? Could the industry show some sort of "subliminal" bias?

6. Former government attorneys as ALJs. Recall that Bud, the WTC ALJ, had previously spent several years working as a government lawyer. Should Abby be concerned about Bud's background? Can she hope to challenge the decision because of the appearance of bias this suggests?

The Supreme Court has been very flexible regarding administrative judges' institutional associations. The leading case is *Schweiker v. McClure*, 456 U.S. 188 (1982). Under Medicare, the insurance carriers selected the presiding officials for appeals of their refusals to pay on a claim. As to this structure, the Court said:

> The hearing officers involved in this case serve in a quasi-judicial capacity, similar in many respects to that of administrative law judges. As this Court repeatedly has recognized, due process demands impartiality on the part of those who function in judicial or quasi-judicial capacities. We must start, however, from the presumption that the hearing officers who decide Part B claims are unbiased. This presumption can be rebutted by a showing of conflict of interest or some other specific reason for disqualification. But the burden of establishing a disqualifying interest rests on the party making the assertion.

> Fairly interpreted, the factual findings made in this case do not reveal any disqualifying interest under the standard of our cases. The District Court relied almost exclusively on generalized assumptions of possible interest, placing special weight on the various connections of the hearing officers with the private insurance carriers. The difficulty with this reasoning is that these connections would be relevant only if the carriers themselves are biased or interested. We find no basis in the record for reaching such a conclusion. As previously noted, the carriers pay all Part B claims from federal, and not their own, funds. Similarly, the salaries of the hearing officers are paid by the Federal Government. Further, the carriers operate under contracts that require compliance with standards prescribed by the statute and the Secretary. In the absence of proof of financial interest on the part of the carriers, there is no basis for assuming a derivative bias among their hearing officers.

Appellees further argued, and the District Court agreed, that due process requires an additional administrative or judicial review by a Government rather than a carrier-appointed hearing officer. Specifically, the District Court ruled that "[e]xisting Part B procedures might remain intact so long as aggrieved beneficiaries would be entitled to appeal carrier appointees' decisions to Part A administrative law judges." In reaching this conclusion, the District Court applied the familiar test prescribed in *Mathews v. Eldridge* (1976). We may assume that the District Court was correct in viewing the private interest in Part B payments as "considerable," though "not quite as precious as the right to receive welfare or social security benefits." We likewise may assume, in considering the third *Mathews* factor, that the additional cost and inconvenience of providing administrative law judges would not be unduly burdensome.

We focus narrowly on the second *Mathews* factor that considers the risk of erroneous decision and the probable value, if any, of the additional procedure. The District Court's reasoning on this point consisted only of this sentence:

"In light of [appellees'] undisputed showing that carrier-appointed hearing officers receive little or no formal training and are not required to satisfy any threshold criteria such as having a law degree, it must be assumed that additional safeguards would reduce the risk of erroneous deprivation of Part B benefits."

Again, the record does not support these conclusions. The Secretary has directed carriers to select as a hearing officer:

"'an attorney or other *qualified* individual with the ability to conduct formal hearings and with a general understanding of medical matters and terminology. The [hearing officer] must have a *thorough knowledge* of the Medicare program and the statutory authority and regulations upon which it is based, as well as rulings, policy statements, and general instructions pertinent to the Medicare Bureau.'"

The District Court did not identify any specific deficiencies in the Secretary's selection criteria. By definition, a "qualified" individual already possessing "ability" and "thorough knowledge" would not require further training. The court's further general concern that hearing officers "are not required to satisfy any threshold criteria" overlooks the Secretary's quoted regulation. Moreover, the District Court apparently gave no weight to the qualifications of hearing officers about whom there is information in the record. Their qualifications tend to undermine rather than to support the contention that accuracy of Part B decisionmaking may suffer by reason of carrier appointment of unqualified hearing officers.

"[D]ue Process is flexible and calls for such procedural protections as the particular situation demands." We have considered appellees' claims in light of the strong presumption in favor of the validity of congressional action and consistently with this Court's recognition of "congressional solicitude for fair procedure. . . ." Appellees simply have not shown that the procedures prescribed by Congress and the Secretary are not fair or that different or additional procedures would reduce the risk of erroneous deprivation of Part B benefits.

7. Recent Supreme Court discussions of "bias." The Supreme Court had four occasions in the last several years to discuss the problem of alleged judicial bias. Although none of these decisions involved an administrative agency adjudication, the principles apply to administrative adjudicators.

Bias arising from campaign contributions.

Ironically, among the most recent of these was a decision that drew upon the classic case with which we began these materials, *Withrow v. Larkin*, to rule that judicial campaign contributions can violate due process in a particularly egregious case. In *Caperton v. A.T. Massey Coal Co., Inc.*, 129 S. Ct. 2252 (2009), a jury imposed a $50 million verdict on Massey Coal Co. for fraudulent misrepresentation, concealment, and tortious interference. While the company's appeal was pending in the West Virginia Supreme Court, Dan Blankenship, Chair, President, and CEO of Massey Coal, made massive contributions to the campaign of Brent Benjamin for a seat on the court. Among other measures, Blankenship contributed more than two-thirds of the total funds raised to support Benjamin's campaign. Benjamin prevailed 53.3%-46.7% over an incumbent justice and then refused to recuse himself in response to the inevitable motion from plaintiff Caperton. The court ultimately ruled for the company by a vote of 3-2.

Noting that it had previously disqualified judges only from sitting in cases in which they had a "direct pecuniary interest" or in criminal contempt proceedings involving contempt for behavior in the judge's own courtroom, the U.S. Supreme Court, by a vote of 5-4, said:

> As new problems have emerged that were not discussed at common law, . . .
> the Court has identified additional instances which, as an objective matter,
> require recusal. These are circumstances "in which experience teaches that
> the probability of actual bias on the part of the judge or decisionmaker is
> too high to be constitutionally tolerable."

Withrow, 421 U.S. 35, 47. In *Withrow*, the Court applied this test to the structural question of bias that might arise from the combination of functions within an agency. In *Caperton*, the Court extended the test to personal bias that could arise from campaign contributions. The Court emphasized that the issue is not whether the judge is actually biased, which is difficult or impossible to determine, but rather:

> The inquiry is an objective one. The Court asks not whether the judge is
> actually, subjectively biased, but whether the average judge in his position
> is "likely" to be neutral, or whether there is an unconstitutional "potential
> for bias."

. . . .

> In defining these standards the Court has asked whether, "under a realistic appraisal of psychological tendencies and human weakness," the interest "poses such a risk of actual bias or prejudgment that the practice must be forbidden if the guarantee of due process is to be adequately implemented."

Withrow, 421 U.S. at 47. Other than massive campaign contributions, which are not relevant to the administrative context, what would be enough to require recusal of an ALJ or a commissioner of the WTC?

Bias from prior involvement with the case.

The Court's most recent foray into judicial bias, *Williams v. Pennsylvania*, 136 S. Ct. 1899 (2016), applied the objective "probability of actual bias" standard articulated by the Court in *Caperton* to address whether a state supreme court justice violated due process by declining to recuse himself from a case involving the revocation of a death sentence that the justice himself had personally approved while serving as the district attorney responsible for overseeing the prosecution.

Petitioner Williams was convicted of double murder and sentenced to death. Then-District Attorney of Philadelphia, Ronald Castille, approved the prosecutor's pursuit of the death penalty in Williams's case. Nearly thirty years later, Williams's execution was stayed and a new sentencing hearing was ordered based on a finding in a state post-conviction hearing that the prosecutor in Williams's murder trial improperly withheld exculpatory evidence in violation of *Brady v. Maryland*, 373 U.S. 83 (1963). The State asked the Pennsylvania Supreme Court to lift the stay, and Williams filed a recusal motion asking now-Chief Justice Ronald Castille to recuse himself from the case. Williams's recusal motion was based on the fact that Chief Justice Castille was the district attorney during Williams's murder trial and was leading the office at the time Williams alleged the *Brady* violation. The U.S. Supreme Court, applying the "probability of actual bias" test, held that the level of Chief Justice Castille's involvement in Williams's conviction and sentence created a significant enough risk of actual bias that due process required he recuse himself from the case. The Court explained:

> No attorney is more integral to the accusatory process than a prosecutor who participates in a major adversary decision. When a judge has served as an advocate for the State in the very case the court is now asked to adjudicate, a serious question arises as to whether the judge, even with the most diligent effort, could set aside any personal interest in the outcome. There is, furthermore, a risk that the judge "would be so psychologically wedded" to his or her previous position as a prosecutor that the judge "would consciously or unconsciously avoid the appearance of having erred or changed position."

. . . .

Even if decades intervene before the former prosecutor revisits the matter as a jurist, the case may implicate the effects and continuing force of his or her original decision. In these circumstances, there remains a serious risk that a judge would be influenced by an improper, if inadvertent, motive to validate and preserve the result obtained through the adversary process. The involvement of multiple actors and the passage of time do not relieve the former prosecutor of the duty to withdraw in order to ensure the neutrality of the judicial process in determining the consequences that his or her own earlier, critical decision may have set in motion.

Williams, 136 S. Ct. at 1906.

Bias arising from a personal relationship with a government official.

Justice Scalia dissented in *Caperton*, arguing that the majority created a "vast uncertainty" that will prompt extensive litigation that ultimately undermines public confidence in the judiciary. This dissent followed a previous decision in which he refused to recuse himself from a case in which Vice President Dick Cheney was a party. The case involved an effort to force the Vice President's office to divulge information concerning the National Energy Policy Study Group, which Mr. Cheney had chaired. While the litigation was pending, the Vice President, at Justice Scalia's invitation, joined an annual duck hunting expedition hosted by a friend of Justice Scalia. In a forceful opinion worthy of perusal in its entirety, *Cheney v. U.S. District Court for the District of Columbia*, 124 S. Ct. 1391 (2004), Justice Scalia attacked the proposition that he should recuse himself merely because his going hunting with his friend the Vice President may create an appearance of partiality:

> But while friendship is a ground for recusal of a Justice where the personal fortune or the personal freedom of the friend is at issue, it has traditionally *not* been a ground for recusal where *official action* is at issue, no matter how important the official action was to the ambitions or the reputation of the Government officer.

> A rule that required Members of this Court to remove themselves from cases in which the official actions of friends were at issue would be utterly disabling. Many Justices have reached this Court precisely because they were friends of the incumbent President or other senior officials—and from the earliest days down to modern times Justices have had close personal relationships with the President and other officers of the Executive.

He went on to describe various close personal and advisory relationships between presidents and Justices over the years. He issued something of a plaintive cry about the fishbowl in which public officials find themselves and the seemingly endless depths of cynicism about their behavior:

> The people must have confidence in the integrity of the Justices, and that cannot exist in a system that assumes them to be corruptible by the slightest friendship or favor, and in an atmosphere where the press will be eager to find foot-faults. . . .

The question, simply put, is whether someone who thought I could decide this case impartially despite my friendship with the Vice President would reasonably believe that I *cannot* decide it impartially because I went hunting with that friend and accepted an invitation to fly there with him on a Government plane. If it is reasonable to think that a Supreme Court Justice can be bought so cheap, the Nation is in deeper trouble than I had imagined.

Justice Scalia's discussion in *Cheney* highlights the potential differences between recusal at the Supreme Court and in the state and lower federal courts. One of your editors has argued that recusal at the Supreme Court is constitutionally different from recusal in other contexts, see Louis J. Virelli III, *The (Un)Constitutionality of Supreme Court Recusal Standards*, 2011 WIS. L. REV. 1181; Louis J. Virelli III, *Congress, the Constitution, and Supreme Court Recusal*, 69 WASH. & LEE L. REV. 1535 (2012), an idea that should be kept in mind when drawing parallels between the Court's recusal decisions and administrative law.

In general, however, the principles of fairness and impartiality inherent in judicial recusal are critical to all manner of legally sanctioned adjudication, including that performed in administrative agencies. The broader question of how recusal standards can and should be applied to administrative adjudicators was the topic of a recent recommendation adopted by the Administrative Conference of the United States. Admin. Conf. of the U.S., Recommendation 2018-4: *Recusal Rules for Administrative Adjudicators*, 84 Fed. Reg. 2139, 2139 (Feb. 6, 2019).

Bias and campaign statements—and a discussion of the nature of "impartiality."

In *Republican Party of Minnesota v. White*, 536 U.S. 765 (2002), the Court struck down as a violation of the First Amendment a state law that prohibited judicial candidate statements on disputed legal or political issues. Writing for the Court, Justice Scalia again discussed judicial bias, and in particular the problem of judicial "impartiality":

> One meaning of "impartiality" in the judicial context—and of course its root meaning—is the lack of bias for or against either *party* to the proceeding. Impartiality in this sense assures equal application of the law. That is, it guarantees a party that the judge who hears his case will apply the law to him in the same way he applies it to any other party. This is the traditional sense in which the term is used. *See* WEBSTER'S NEW INTERNATIONAL DICTIONARY 1247 (2d ed. 1950) (defining "impartial" as "[n]ot partial; esp., not favoring one more than another; treating all alike; unbiased; equitable; fair; just"). . . .

> B

> It is perhaps possible to use the term "impartiality" in the judicial context (though this is certainly not a common usage) to mean lack of preconception in favor of or against a particular *legal view*. This sort of impartiality would be concerned, not with guaranteeing litigants equal application of the law, but rather with guaranteeing them an equal chance to persuade

the court on the legal points in their case. . . . A judge's lack of predisposition regarding the relevant legal issues in a case has never been thought a necessary component of equal justice, and with good reason. For one thing, it is virtually impossible to find a judge who does not have preconceptions about the law. As then-JUSTICE REHNQUIST observed of our own Court:

"Since most Justices come to this bench no earlier than their middle years, it would be unusual if they had not by that time formulated at least some tentative notions that would influence them in their interpretation of the sweeping clauses of the Constitution and their interaction with one another. It would be not merely unusual, but extraordinary, if they had not at least given opinions as to constitutional issues in their previous legal careers. Indeed, even if it were possible to select judges who did not have preconceived views on legal issues, it would hardly be desirable to do so.

"Proof that a Justice's mind at the time he joined the Court was a complete *tabula rasa* in the area of constitutional adjudication would be evidence of lack of qualification, not lack of bias." . . .

C

A third possible meaning of "impartiality" (again not a common one) might be described as open-mindedness. This quality in a judge demands, not that he have no preconceptions on legal issues, but that he be willing to consider views that oppose his preconceptions, and remain open to persuasion, when the issues arise in a pending case. This sort of impartiality seeks to guarantee each litigant, not an *equal* chance to win the legal points in the case, but at least *some* chance of doing so. . . .

Respondents argue that the [statute at issue] serves the interest in open-mindedness, or at least in the appearance of open-mindedness, because it relieves a judge from pressure to rule a certain way in order to maintain consistency with statements the judge has previously made. The problem is, however, that statements in election campaigns are such an infinitesimal portion of the public commitments to legal positions that judges (or judges-to-be) undertake, that this object of the prohibition is implausible. Before they arrive on the bench (whether by election or otherwise) judges have often committed themselves on legal issues that they must later rule upon. More common still is a judge's confronting a legal issue on which he has expressed an opinion while on the bench. Most frequently, of course, that prior expression will have occurred in ruling on an earlier case. But judges often state their views on disputed legal issues outside the context of adjudication—in classes that they conduct, and in books and speeches. Like the ABA Codes of Judicial Conduct, the Minnesota Code not only permits but encourages this. *See* Minn. Code of Judicial Conduct, Canon 4(B) (2002) ("A judge may write, lecture, teach, speak and participate in other extra-judicial activities concerning the law . . . ."); Minn.Code of Judicial Conduct, Canon 4(B), Comment. (2002) ("To the extent that time permits, a judge is encouraged to do so . . . ."). That is quite incompatible with the notion that the need for open-mindedness (or for the appearance of open-mindedness) lies behind the prohibition at issue here.

Although the question of how the First Amendment relates to the speech of sitting judges has yet to be directly addressed by the Supreme Court, see, e.g., Louis J. Virelli III, *(A Bit More) On Judicial Speech and the First Amendment*, 79 OHIO ST. L.J. FURTHERMORE 83 (2018); Louis J. Virelli III, *What "Stop-and-Frisk" Can Teach Us about the First Amendment and Judicial Recusal*, 47 CONN. L. REV. ONLINE 13 (2014) (discussing the various First Amendment doctrines that could be brought to bear in connection with judicial recusal), much of what the Court said above about judges applies, perhaps even more strongly, to administrative law judges and to agency heads such as the commissioners of the WTC. The commissioners, in particular, are chosen largely as a result of their strongly held views and activism on behalf of their political parties.

3. With Whom May the Adjudicatory Decisionmaker Communicate — and About What?

It is common knowledge, at least among lawyers (and we hope among law students) that neither counsel for one of the parties to a lawsuit, nor one of the parties to the lawsuit, may speak to the judge about anything to do with the substance of the lawsuit without a representative of the other party or parties being present. This sort of *"ex parte"* communication would violate the canons of judicial ethics, basic principles of fairness, and probably due process. The prohibition on *ex parte* communications assures the independence and integrity of the judicial decision is based only on the facts and arguments in the record and known to the parties.

But the agency realm is very different from the judicial realm. Unlike judges, agency heads are part of the political world. They generally know many of the actors in that world, including those whose interests are affected by the decisions of their agency. These materials explore how concerns about *ex parte* communications apply to agency decisionmakers.

Lesson 4C.3. Abby learns that Commissioner Barney had served as "of counsel" in her firm while he was waiting for a change of administration and a government post. Barney and a senior partner of the firm were on law review together and remain friends. He and the partner regularly play golf. The partner informs Abby that he and Barney discussed the regulation of the wine industry and the firm's representation of Gallery. He cannot remember whether they discussed the current case since Barney joined the Commission, but he is sure they have discussed the labeling rule since his appointment.

How might the following opinion relate to the issues presented by this scenario?

Background of *PATCO v. FLRA*

The following decision involved one of the most ferocious political battles of the early Reagan administration. When the nation's air traffic controllers, represented by the Professional Air Traffic Controllers Organization (PATCO), went on strike, President Reagan fired thousands of strikers and the FAA sought to decertify PATCO as the union for the air traffic controllers. With thousands of flights canceled and passengers stranded around the country, it is hard to imagine a more high profile agency decision.

PATCO v. Federal Labor Relations Authority
685 F.2d 547 (D.C. Cir. 1982)

HARRY T. EDWARDS, CIRCUIT JUDGE:

. . . .

The Professional Air Traffic Controllers Organization (PATCO) has been the recognized exclusive bargaining representative for air traffic controllers employed by the Federal Aviation Administration since the early 1970s. Faced with the expiration of an existing collective bargaining agreement, PATCO and the FAA began negotiations for a new contract in early 1981. A tentative agreement was reached in June, but was overwhelmingly rejected by the PATCO rank and file. Following this rejection, negotiations began again in late July. PATCO announced a strike deadline of Monday, August 3, 1981.

Failing to reach a satisfactory accord, PATCO struck the FAA on the morning of August 3. Over seventy percent of the nation's federally employed air traffic controllers walked off the job, significantly reducing the number of private and commercial flights in the United States.

In prompt response to the PATCO job actions, the Government obtained restraining orders against the strike, and then civil and criminal contempt citations when the restraining orders were not heeded. The Government also fired some 11,000 striking air traffic controllers who did not return to work by 11:00 a.m. on August 5, 1981. In addition, on August 3, 1981, the FAA filed an unfair labor practice charge against PATCO with the Federal Labor Relations Authority. On that same day, an FLRA Regional Director issued a complaint on the unfair labor practice charge, alleging strike activity prohibited by 5 U.S.C. § 7116(b)(7) and seeking revocation of PATCO's certification under the Civil Service Reform Act. The complaint [gave notice of] a hearing for one week later, August 10, 1981.

John H. Fenton, Chief Administrative Law Judge of the FLRA, conducted hearings on the unfair labor practice charge. . . .

. . . Judge Fenton recommended that the FLRA revoke PATCO's exclusive recognition status and that PATCO "immediately cease to be legally entitled and obligated to represent employees in the unit." . . .

The FLRA General Counsel, the FAA and PATCO all filed exceptions to the A.L.J.'s recommended findings of fact and conclusions of law.

In seriatim opinions issued on October 22, 1981, the FLRA Members rejected the exceptions filed by the parties and affirmed the ALJ Decision.

Unfortunately, allegations of improprieties during the FLRA's consideration of this case forced us to delay our review on the merits. Only a day before oral argument, the Department of Justice, which represents the FAA in this review, informed the court that the Department of Justice Criminal Division and the FBI had investigated allegations of an improper contact between a "well-known labor leader" and FLRA Member Applewhaite during the pendency of the PATCO case.

. . . .

Following our remand on the *ex parte* communications issue, John M. Vittone, an Administrative Law Judge with the Civil Aeronautics Board, was appointed to preside over an evidentiary proceeding. . . .

[Three *ex parte* contacts were contested: (1) staff contacts with the members, (2) contacts with members of the executive branch and (3) social contacts by members. The ALJ found none of these contacts affected the outcome.]

. . . .

[1] On August 10, 1981 (one week after the unfair labor practice complaint against PATCO was filed), H. Stephan Gordon, the FLRA General Counsel, was in Member Applewhaite's office discussing administrative matters unrelated to the PATCO case. During Gordon's discussion with Member Applewhaite, Ms. Ellen Stern, an attorney with the FLRA Solicitor's office, entered Member Applewhaite's office to deliver a copy of a memorandum entitled "Decertification of Labor Organization Participating in the Conduct of a Strike in Violation of Section 7116(b)(7) of the Statute." Ms. Stern had prepared the memo at the request of Member Frazier. With General Counsel Gordon present, Ms. Stern proceeded to discuss her memorandum, which dealt with whether the Civil Service Reform Act makes revocation of a striking union's exclusive recognition status mandatory or discretionary and, assuming it is discretionary, what other disciplinary actions might be taken.

During Ms. Stern's discussion, both Member Applewhaite and General Counsel Gordon asked her general questions (*e.g.*, regarding the availability of other remedies and whether she had researched the relevant legislative history). General Counsel Gordon did not ask Member Applewhaite any questions or express any views on the issues discussed in the memorandum. Nor did Member Applewhaite express any opinion on the correct statutory interpretation. While the conversation at least implicitly focused on the PATCO case, the facts of the case and the appropriate disposition were not discussed. The discussion ended after ten or fifteen minutes.

[2] [Contact by the Secretary of Transportation. Presented separately below in the notes.]

. . . .

[3] Since 1974 Albert Shanker has been President of the American Federation of Teachers, a large public-sector labor union, and a member of the Executive Council of the AFL-CIO. Since 1964 Mr. Shanker has been President of the AFT's New York City Local, the United Federation of Teachers. Before joining the FLRA, Member Applewhaite had been associated with the New York Public Employment Relations Board. Through their contacts in New York, Mr. Shanker and Member Applewhaite had become professional and social friends.

During the week of September 20, 1981, Mr. Shanker was in Washington, D.C. on business. On September 21, Mr. Shanker made arrangements to have dinner with Member Applewhaite that evening. Although he did not inform Member Applewhaite of his intentions when he made the arrangements, Mr. Shanker candidly admitted that he wanted to have dinner with Member Applewhaite because he felt strongly about the PATCO case and wanted to communicate directly to Member Applewhaite his sentiments, previously expressed in public statements, that PATCO should not be severely punished for its strike. In particular, Mr. Shanker believed that revocation of PATCO's exclusive recognition status would be an excessive punishment. After accepting the invitation, Member Applewhaite informed Member Frazier and Chairman Haughton that he was having dinner with Mr. Shanker.

Member Applewhaite and Mr. Shanker talked for about an hour and a half during their dinner on September 21. Most of the discussion concerned the preceding Saturday's Solidarity Day Rally, an upcoming tuition tax credit referendum in the District of Columbia, and mutual friends from New York. Near the end of the dinner, however, the conversation turned to labor law matters relevant to the PATCO case. The two men discussed various approaches to public employee strikes in New York, Pennsylvania and the federal government. Mr. Shanker expressed his view that the punishment of a striking union should fit the crime and that revocation of certification as a punishment for an illegal strike was tantamount to "killing a union." The record is clear that Mr. Shanker made no threats or promises to Member Applewhaite; likewise, the evidence also indicates that Member Applewhaite never revealed his position regarding the PATCO case.

Near the end of their conversation, Member Applewhaite commented that because the PATCO case was hotly contested, he would be viewed with disfavor by whichever side he voted against. Member Applewhaite also observed that he was concerned about his prospects for reappointment to the FLRA in July 1982. Mr. Shanker, in turn, responded that Member Applewhaite had no commitments from anyone and urged him to vote without regard to personal considerations. The dinner concluded and the two men departed.

[Before the dinner, Member Applewhaite had favored a three-year revocation of the union's exclusive bargaining status, while Member Frazier had favored an indefinite revocation. The remaining Member had favored suspension rather than revocation. After the dinner and negotiations among the FLRA Members, Member Applewhaite ultimately joined Member Frazier supporting indefinite revocation.]

While these negotiations within the Authority were going on, Member Frazier became concerned that Mr. Shanker might have influenced Member Applewhaite's position in the case. On September 22, Member Frazier visited Member Applewhaite to inquire about his dinner with Mr. Shanker. Member Frazier understood Member Applewhaite to say that Shanker had said that if Member Applewhaite voted against PATCO, then Applewhaite would be unable to get work as an arbitrator when he left the FLRA. Member Frazier also understood Member Applewhaite to say that he was then leaning against voting for revocation. (A.L.J. Vittone found that Shanker had made no such threats during the dinner, and concluded that Member Frazier reached this conclusion based on some miscommunication or misunderstanding.)

. . . .

A.L.J. Vittone concluded: "The Shanker-Applewhaite dinner had no effect on the ultimate decision of Mr. Applewhaite in the PATCO case. Member Applewhaite's final decision in the PATCO case was substantially the same as the position he discussed at the September 21 meeting of the members." Later in his recommended findings, A.L.J. Vittone commented:

> It is clear that Mr. Shanker's message to Mr. Applewhaite was that revocation of certification was a drastic remedy out of proportion to the violation. However, as I stated in my findings, I do not believe tht (sic) the dinner had any effect on the final decision of the FLRA in the PATCO case. At the very most, the effect was transitory in nature, and occurred from September 21 to October 9.

. . . .

The Civil Service Reform Act requires that FLRA unfair labor practice hearings, to the extent practicable, be conducted in accordance with the provisions of the Administrative Procedure Act. Since FLRA unfair labor practice hearings are formal adjudications within the meaning of the APA, section 557(d) governs *ex parte* communications.

Section 557(d) was enacted by Congress as part of the Government in the Sunshine Act. The section prohibits *ex parte* communications "relevant to the merits of the proceeding" between an "interested person" and an agency decisionmaker, 5 U.S.C. § 557(d)(1)(A), (B) (1976), requires the agency decisionmaker to place any prohibited communications on the public record, *id.* § 557(d)(1)(C), grants the agency the authority to require an infringing party "to show cause why his claim or interest should not be dismissed, denied, disregarded, or otherwise adversely affected on account of [a] violation," *id.* § 557(d)(1)(D), and defines the time period during which the statutory prohibitions are applicable, *id.* § 557(d)(1)(E). The FLRA has adopted rules that, with minor variations, parallel the requirements of section 557(d).

Three features of the prohibition on *ex parte* communications in agency adjudications are particularly relevant to the contacts here at issue. First, by its terms, section 557(d) applies only to *ex parte* communications to or from an "interested person." Congress did not intend, however, that the prohibition on *ex parte* communications would therefore have only a limited application. A House Report explained:

> The term "interested person" is intended to be a wide, inclusive term covering any individual or other person with an interest in the agency proceeding that is greater than the general interest the public as a whole may have. The interest need not be monetary, nor need a person to [sic] be a party to, or intervenor in, the agency proceeding to come under this section. The term includes, but is not limited to, parties, competitors, public officials, and nonprofit or public interest organizations and associations with a special interest in the matter regulated. The term does not include a member of the public at large who makes a casual or general expression of opinion about a pending proceeding.

Second, the Government in the Sunshine Act defines an "*ex parte* communication" as "an oral or written communication not on the public record to which reasonable prior notice to all parties is not given, but . . . not includ[ing] requests for status reports on any matter or proceeding. . . ." 5 U.S.C. § 551(14) (1976). Requests for status reports are thus allowed under the statute, even when directed to an agency decisionmaker rather than to another agency employee. Nevertheless, the legislative history of the Act cautions:

> A request for a status report or a background discussion may in effect amount to an indirect or subtle effort to influence the substantive outcome of the proceedings. The judgment will have to be made whether a particular communication could affect the agency's decision on the merits. In doubtful cases the agency official should treat the communication as *ex parte* so as to protect the integrity of the decision making process.

Third, and in direct contrast to status reports, section 557(d) explicitly prohibits communications "relevant to the merits of the proceeding." The congressional reports state that the phrase should "be construed broadly and . . . include more than the phrase 'fact in issue' currently used in [section 554(d)(1) of] the Administrative Procedure Act." While the phrase must be interpreted to effectuate the dual purposes of the Government in the Sunshine Act, *i.e.*, of giving notice of improper contacts and of providing all interested parties an opportunity to respond to illegal communications, the scope of this provision is not unlimited. Congress explicitly noted that the statute does not prohibit procedural inquiries, or other communications "not relevant to the merits."

In sum, Congress sought to establish common-sense guidelines to govern *ex parte* contacts in administrative hearings, rather than rigidly defined and woodenly applied rules. The disclosure of *ex parte* communications serves two distinct interests. Disclosure is important in its own right to prevent the appearance of impropriety from secret communications in a proceeding that is required to be decided on the record. Disclosure is also important as an instrument of fair decisionmaking;

only if a party knows the arguments presented to a decisionmaker can the party respond effectively and ensure that its position is fairly considered. When these interests of openness and opportunity for response are threatened by an *ex parte* communication, the communication must be disclosed. It matters not whether the communication comes from someone other than a formal party or if the communication is clothed in the guise of a procedural inquiry. If, however, the communication is truly not relevant to the merits of an adjudication and, therefore, does not threaten the interests of openness and effective response, disclosure is unnecessary. Congress did not intend to erect meaningless procedural barriers to effective agency action. It is thus with these interests in mind that the statutory prohibition on *ex parte* communications must be applied.

Section 557(d) contains two possible administrative remedies for improper *ex parte* communications. The first is disclosure of the communication and its content. 5 U.S.C. § 557(d)(1)(C) (1976). The second requires the violating party to "show cause why his claim or interest in the proceeding should not be dismissed, denied, disregarded, or otherwise adversely affected on account of [the] violation." *Id.* § 557(d)(1)(D); *see also id.* § 556(d). Congress did not intend, however, that an agency would require a party to "show cause" after every violation or that an agency would dismiss a party's interest more than rarely. Indeed, the statutory language clearly states that a party's interest in the proceeding may be adversely affected only "to the extent consistent with the interests of justice and the policy of the underlying statutes." 5 U.S.C. § 557(d)(1)(D) (1976).

The Government in the Sunshine Act contains no specific provisions for judicial remedy of improper *ex parte* communications. However, we may infer from approving citations in the House and Senate Reports that Congress did not intend to alter the existing case law regarding *ex parte* communications and the legal effect of such contacts on agency decisions.

Under the case law in this Circuit, improper *ex parte* communications, even when undisclosed during agency proceedings, do not necessarily void an agency decision. Rather, agency proceedings that have been blemished by *ex parte* communications have been held to be *voidable*. In enforcing this standard, a court must consider whether, as a result of improper *ex parte* communications, the agency's decisionmaking process was irrevocably tainted so as to make the ultimate judgment of the agency unfair, either to an innocent party or to the public interest that the agency was obliged to protect.[32] In making this determination, a number of considerations may be

---

32. We have also considered the effect of *ex parte* communications on the availability of meaningful judicial review. Where facts and arguments "vital to the agency decision" are only communicated to the agency off the record, the court may at worst be kept in the dark about the agency's actual reasons for its decision. At best, the basis for the agency's action may be disclosed for the first time on review. If the off-the-record communications regard critical facts, the court will be particularly ill-equipped to resolve in the first instance any controversy between the parties. Thus, effective judicial review may be hampered if *ex parte* communications prevent adversarial decision of factual issues by the agency.

relevant: the gravity of the *ex parte* communications; whether the contacts may have influenced the agency's ultimate decision; whether the party making the improper contacts benefitted from the agency's ultimate decision; whether the contents of the communications were unknown to opposing parties, who therefore had no opportunity to respond; and whether vacation of the agency's decision and remand for new proceedings would serve a useful purpose. Since the principal concerns of the court are the integrity of the process and the fairness of the result, mechanical rules have little place in a judicial decision whether to vacate a voidable agency proceeding. Instead, any such decision must of necessity be an exercise of equitable discretion.

With the foregoing considerations in mind, we have analyzed A.L.J. Vittone's findings thoroughly and given careful thought to the positions urged by the parties. As we noted earlier, the vast majority of the reported contacts between FLRA Members and persons outside the Authority are not troubling. They relate to inquiries about the expected date of issuance of the FLRA's opinion, information from a third party regarding settlement efforts, statements regarding the running of PATCO's time to respond to Chairman Haughton's conditional dissent, and other communications unrelated to the merits of the case.

After extensive review of the three troubling incidents . . . we believe that they too provide insufficient reason to vacate the FLRA Decision or to remand this case for further proceedings before the Authority. The special evidentiary hearing before Judge Vittone was ordered by this court not because we assumed that the A.L.J. would find serious wrongs and improprieties, but because the allegations of misconduct were serious enough to require full exploration. Public officials are held to high standards of behavior, and only through a special inquiry could we clear the air of any doubt that the FLRA Decision in this case was not unfairly influenced.

After unavoidable time, effort and expense, both by the parties and by the individual FLRA Members, A.L.J. Vittone formulated his findings. Except as otherwise noted below, we accept them. We conclude that at least one and possibly two of the contacts documented by the A.L.J. probably infringed the statutory prohibitions on *ex parte* communications. The incidents reported by the A.L.J. also included some evident, albeit unintended, indiscretions in a highly charged and widely publicized case. Nevertheless, we agree with A.L.J. Vittone that the *ex parte* contacts here at issue had no effect on the ultimate decision of the FLRA. Moreover, we conclude that the statutory infringements and other indiscretions are not so serious as to require us to vacate the FLRA Decision or to remand the case to the Authority. On the facts of this case, we believe that to vacate and remand would be a gesture of futility.

. . . .

[As to each of the "three troubling incidents," the court concluded:]

. . . .

[1] When General Counsel Gordon met with Member Applewhaite on August 10, the General Counsel's office was prosecuting the unfair labor practice complaint

against PATCO before Chief A.L.J. Fenton. General Counsel Gordon was therefore a "person outside the agency" within the meaning of section 557(d) and the FLRA Rules. Still, the undisputed purpose of the meeting was to discuss budgetary and administrative matters. It was therefore entirely appropriate. The shared concerns of the Authority are not put on hold whenever the General Counsel prosecutes an unfair labor practice complaint.

. . . .

In hindsight, it may have been preferable if Member Applewhaite had postponed even this general conversation with Ms. Stern or if General Counsel Gordon had temporarily excused himself from Member Applewhaite's office. Nonetheless, we do not believe that this contact tainted the proceeding or unfairly advantaged the General Counsel in the prosecution of the case. Thus, we conclude that the conversation at issue here, even though possibly indiscreet and undesirable, does not void the FLRA Decision in this case.

[2] [The court found that the second contact by the Secretary of Transportation did not "taint the proceedings." Presented below in the notes.]

. . . .

[3] Of course, the most troublesome *ex parte* communication in this case occurred during the September 21 dinner meeting between Member Applewhaite and American Federation of Teachers President Albert Shanker — the "well-known labor leader" mentioned in Assistant Attorney General McGrath's affidavit. . . .

. . . .

We believe that Mr. Shanker falls within the intended scope of the term "interested person." Mr. Shanker was (and is) the President of a major public sector labor union. As such, he has a special and well-known interest in the union movement and the developing law of labor relations in the public sector. The PATCO strike, of course, was the subject of extensive media coverage and public comment. Some union leaders undoubtedly felt that the hard line taken against PATCO by the Administration might have an adverse effect on other unions, both in the federal and in state and local government sectors. Mr. Shanker apparently shared this concern. From August 3, 1981 to September 21, 1981, Mr. Shanker and his union made a series of widely publicized statements in support of PATCO. Mr. Shanker urged repeatedly in public statements that disproportionately severe punishment not be inflicted on PATCO. He spoke frequently on this subject, was interviewed about the PATCO strike on a nationally televised news program, and published a number of columns in the *New York Times* discussing the PATCO situation. Thus, Mr. Shanker's actions, as well as his union office, belie his implicit claim that he had no greater interest in the case than a member of the general public. Regardless of the amicus status of the AFL-CIO, and Mr. Shanker's lack of knowledge thereof, he was an "interested person" within the meaning of 5 U.S.C. § 557(d) (1976).

. . . .

We do not hold, however, that Member Applewhaite committed an impropriety when he accepted Mr. Shanker's dinner invitation. Member Applewhaite and Mr. Shanker were professional and social friends. We recognize, of course, that a judge "must have neighbors, friends and acquaintances, business and social relations, and be a part of his day and generation." Similarly, Member Applewhaite was not required to renounce his friendships, either personal or professional, when he was appointed to the FLRA. When Mr. Shanker called Member Applewhaite on September 21, Member Applewhaite was unaware of Mr. Shanker's purpose in arranging the dinner. He therefore had no reason to reject the invitation.

. . . .

We in no way condone Mr. Shanker's behavior in this case. Nor do we approve Member Applewhaite's failure to avoid discussion of a case pending before the Authority. Nevertheless, we do not believe that the Applewhaite/Shanker dinner, as detailed in A.L.J. Vittone's findings, irrevocably tainted the Authority's decision-making process or resulted in a decision unfair either to the parties or to the public interest.

As we have noted, the special evidentiary hearing ordered in this case has filled in much of the factual picture left incomplete by the McGrath affidavit and the FBI reports. One feature of the picture revealed by the inquiry is the contents of Member Applewhaite's and Mr. Shanker's dinner conversation. A.L.J. Vittone found that near the end of their conversation Member Applewhaite observed that "he was concerned about his prospects for reappointment in July 1982." He also commented that, "because the PATCO case was hotly contested, he would be viewed with disfavor by whichever side he voted against." In response, "Mr. Shanker urged Applewhaite to vote without regard to personal considerations."

Based essentially on this brief conversation, Member Frazier now proposes that Member Applewhaite had a personal interest in the outcome of the PATCO case. Member Frazier contends that the record shows that Member Applewhaite was concerned that if he voted in favor of PATCO, he would not be reappointed by the Administration, and that if he voted against PATCO (and was not reappointed), his career in labor law would suffer from organized labor's reaction to his vote. Because of these alleged personal interests in the outcome, Member Frazier argues that Member Applewhaite was disqualified from hearing the PATCO case.

We do not read as much into this conversation as does Member Frazier. It is not surprising that an agency member appointed by the President might be concerned about his prospects for reappointment. We are not so naive as to believe that such thoughts do not cross a member's mind. Nor would we assume that an Authority Member would believe that his decisions are irrelevant to the President's determination whether to reappoint him. Similarly, it is hardly surprising for Member Applewhaite to recognize that his decision in a hotly contested case would not receive universal approbation. The appropriate question here is not whether Member Applewhaite recognized that his decision might not be universally approved; rather, the correct inquiry is whether Member Applewhaite's concerns rendered him incapable of reaching a fair decision on the merits of the case before him.

. . . .

. . . Member Applewhaite did believe that he would be viewed with disfavor by whichever side he voted against. But Member Applewhaite explained that this was no different from any arbitration case in which he had ruled — one party wins and the other loses. . . . Thus, we believe that the evidentiary hearing has refuted "even the probability of unfairness." A remand on the basis of personal interest is therefore unnecessary.

Notes

1. What about Barney's conversations? Should the conversation between Barney and the senior partner alarm Abby? If she wished to be cautious, how might she proceed? Applewhaite's dinner with Shanker raises some tough questions. Administrative decisionmakers have numerous informal or social contacts with interested persons. These people express general and specific opinions. If a decisionmaker had to be disqualified every time this happened, no decisionmaker would be around long enough to make a decision. At what point should a decisionmaker be disqualified for informal contacts? If you were Applewhaite, would you have attended the Shanker dinner?

2. *Ex parte* communications and due process. The APA condemns *ex parte* communication in formal adjudications. Courts have also made some rather strong statements against such communications on due process grounds:

> Of course, one of the fundamental premises inherent in the concept of an adversary hearing, particularly if it is of the evidentiary type, is that neither adversary be permitted to engage in an *ex parte* communication concerning the merits of the case with those responsible for the decision. It is difficult to imagine a more serious incursion on fairness than to permit the representative of one of the parties to privately communicate his recommendations to the decision makers. To allow such activity would be to render the hearing virtually meaningless. We are of the opinion that due process forbids it.

Camero v. United States, 375 F.2d 777, 780–81 (Ct. Cl. 1967). Note that *Camero* preceded *Mathews v. Eldridge.* Would you apply *Mathews* to this issue, or is it like the problem of notice, which has its own distinct test? *See* Note 14 following Lesson 4B.2.

3. *Ex parte* contacts and separation of functions — the problem of non-expert decisionmakers who need expert advice. What is the relationship between the prohibition against *ex parte* communication and separation of functions? For example, suppose Ben, as head of the Rulemaking Division, met with Barney about the Gallery case to explain details of the applicable law. Would that violate the prohibition against separation of functions? Would it violate the prohibition against *ex parte* communication? What if he explained the significance of some of the facts in the record of the hearing?

One of the questionable scenarios in *PATCO* involved Member Applewhaite's inadvertent discussions with FLRA staff members. In *Seacoast Anti-Pollution League v. Costle*, 572 F.2d 872, 880 (1st Cir. 1978), petitioners objected to the Administrator's use of a panel of EPA scientists to assist him in reviewing the Regional Administrator's initial decision in a matter held to be governed by §§ 554, 556, and 557 of the APA. The objection was two-fold: first, that the Administrator should not have sought such help at all; and second, that the panel's report (the Report) to the Administrator included information not in the administrative record.

> Petitioners point out that by the EPA's own regulations "*[t]he Administrator shall decide* the matters under review on the basis of the record presented and any other consideration he deems relevant." It is true that when a decision is committed to a particular individual that individual must be the one who reviews the evidence on which the decision is to be based. *See Morgan v. United States* (1936). But it does not follow that all other individuals are shut out of the decision process. That conclusion runs counter to the purposes of the administrative agencies which exist, in part, to enable government to focus broad ranges of talent on particular multi-dimensional problems. The Administrator is charged with making highly technical decisions in fields far beyond his individual expertise. "The strength [of the administrative process] lies in staff work organized in such a way that the appropriate specialization is brought to bear upon each aspect of a single decision, the synthesis being provided by the men at the top." Therefore, "[e]vidence . . . may be sifted and analyzed by competent subordinates." The decision ultimately reached is no less the Administrators' simply because agency experts helped him to reach it.
>
> A different question is presented, however, if the agency experts do not merely sift and analyze but also add to the evidence properly before the Administrator. The regulation . . . cannot allow the Administrator to consider evidence barred from consideration by the APA. 5 U.S.C. § 556(e). "The transcript of testimony and exhibits, together with all papers and requests filed in the proceeding, constitutes the exclusive record for decision. . . ." To the extent the technical review panel's Report included information not in the record on which the Administrator relied, § 556(e) was violated. In effect the agency's staff would have made up for PSCO's failure to carry its burden of proof.
>
> Our review of the Report indicates that such violations did occur. . . . What is important is that the record did not support the conclusion until supplemented by the panel. The panel's work found its way directly into the Administrator's decision at page 27 where he discusses the Regional Administrator's concerns about insufficient data but then precipitously concludes: "On the recommendation of the panel, however, I find that . . .

local indigenous populations will not be significantly affected." This conclusion depends entirely on what the panel stated about the scientific literature.

Suppose the additional information comes from a recognized textbook, or from a prior staff report, or from the staff experts' general knowledge of the area. What sort of explanation or guidance would be acceptable, and what would not. Given the difficulty of determining whether experts inadvertently supplemented the record, should such consultation be banned entirely?

Should members of a collegial decisionmaking body be totally free to discuss matters among themselves? With their personal staff? With the personal staff of other members?

4. Contacts from other agencies. As with contacts within the agency, contacts from other agencies may be illegal *ex parte* communications. For example, in *PATCO*, the court found:

> During the morning of August 13, 1981, Secretary of Transportation Andrew L. Lewis, Jr. telephoned Member Frazier. Secretary Lewis stated that he was not calling about the substance of the PATCO case, but wanted Member Frazier to know that, contrary to some news reports, no meaningful efforts to settle the strike were underway. Secretary Lewis also stated that the Department of Transportation would appreciate expeditious handling of the case. Not wanting to discuss the PATCO case with Secretary Lewis, Member Frazier replied, "I understand your position perfectly, Mr. Secretary." Secretary Lewis then inquired whether Member Applewhaite was in Washington, D.C. at that time. Member Frazier replied that he was, but that Chairman Haughton was out of town. Although Member Frazier offered to convey the Secretary's message to Member Applewhaite, Secretary Lewis stated that he would call personally.

> . . . .

> Transportation Secretary Lewis was undoubtedly an "interested person" within the meaning of section 557(d) . . . Secretary Lewis' call clearly would have been an improper *ex parte* communication if he had sought to discuss the merits of the PATCO case. The Secretary explicitly avoided the merits, however, and mentioned only his view on the possibility of settlement and his desire for a speedy decision. On this basis, Solicitor Freehling and Member Frazier concluded the call was not improper.

> We are less certain that Secretary Lewis' call was permissible. Although Secretary Lewis did not in fact discuss the merits of the case, even a procedural inquiry may be a subtle effort to influence an agency decision. . . .

> We need not decide, however, whether Secretary Lewis' contacts were in fact improper. Even if they were, the contacts did not taint the proceedings or prejudice PATCO. Secretary Lewis' central concern in his conversations

with Member Frazier and Member Applewhaite was that the case be handled expeditiously. Member Applewhaite explicitly told Secretary Lewis that if he wanted the case handled more quickly than the normal course of FLRA business, then the FAA would have to file a written request. If, as A.L.J. Vittone found likely, Member Applewhaite's comments led to the FAA's Motion to Modify Time Limits, *that was exactly the desired result*. Once the FAA filed a motion, PATCO filed its own responsive motions, and the FLRA was able to decide the timing issue based on the pleadings before it.

Behind the prohibition against *ex parte* communication is the fear of improper advocacy or influence. In the above, we add the fear of political influence. Does that change the analysis? The court agreed that the Secretary's call did not influence the outcome but clearly considered such an attempt at influence to be improper. The FLRA is an independent agency and hence such an attempt at influence would clearly compromise its impartiality. Suppose the Secretary called about an adjudicative decision being considered by an executive agency? Suppose the call to an independent agency or an executive agency was from a high official in the executive office? Suppose he called about an adjudication being conducted by his agency? See *Portland Audubon Society v. Endangered Species Committee*, 984 F.2d 1534 (9th Cir. 1993), discussed in Note 6 after Lesson 4A.1, in which the Ninth Circuit remanded a "God Squad" decision based upon allegations of these sorts of political contacts.

5. The problem of congressional pressure. Congressional pressure can come through behind-the-scenes communications, which would clearly violate §557(d) of the APA. It can also come through actions or positions taken openly in the course of the legislative process. How far may Congress go in "advising" an agency of its views on specific matters before the agency? The Fifth Circuit in *Pillsbury Co. v. FTC*, 354 F.2d 952 (5th Cir. 1966), reviewed a circumstance in which agency adjudicators were forced to discuss their position on a pending administrative case:

> This is a petition by the Pillsbury Company to review and set aside an order of the Federal Trade Commission requiring Pillsbury to divest itself of the assets of Ballard & Ballard Company and of Duff's Baking Mix Division of American Home Products Corporation which the Federal Trade Commission found it had acquired in violation of §7 of the Clayton Act, as amended, and further requiring Pillsbury to restore the acquired companies to the status of "effective competitors." . . .

> When [FTC] Chairman Howrey appeared before the Senate subcommittee on June 1, 1955, he met a barrage of questioning by the members of the committee challenging his view of the requirements of §7 and the application of the per se doctrine announced by the Supreme Court in the Standard Stations case, in a Clayton Act §3 case, to §7 proceedings. A number of the members of the committee challenged the correctness of his and the Commission's position in holding that a mere showing of a substantial

increase in the share of the market after merger would not be sufficient to satisfy the requirement of §7 of a showing that "the effect of such acquisition may be substantially to lessen competition."

Much of the questioning criticized by the petitioner here is in the nature of questions and comments by members of the committee in which they forcefully expressed their own opinions that the per se doctrine should apply and that it was the intent of Congress that it should apply.

. . . .

[The following questions represent only a small sample of the questions reproduced by the court. eds.]

[Senator Kefauver]: "Then, Mr. Howrey, on the statement you made this morning, and as set forth in your opinion here, generally, insofar as dough mix or whatever it may be, in the southeastern part of the United States, Pillsbury had approximately 22 or 23 percent, and Duff and Ballard had 22 or 23 percent, and so somewhere they were winding up with between 45 and 48 percent of the dough-mix business in the southeastern part of the country. Those are rough figures, but that is substantially correct, is it not?"

[Mr. Howrey]: "Yes, that is substantially correct. I can give you the precise figures."

[Senator Kefauver]: "Well, they are in your opinion here. But that would be quite an obvious lessening of competition, particularly in view of the fact that there have been so many acquisitions prior to that time in the flour business. Wouldn't you have thought so?"

[Mr. Howrey]: "Yes, and I so said and so held."

[At this point, it should be noted that members of the Committee spoke as if the basic facts as to substantiality of shares in the market had already been determined. Actually, these facts were still being litigated before the Commission. The Commission order that Howrey was being questioned about held merely that a prima facie case as to substantiality had been made out by the Government. Pillsbury had not yet had its turn at bat.] . . .

[Senator Kefauver]: "I just want to say, as one who has been very much interested in this, Mr. Howrey—and we are just talking in the sense of being the best of friends here, because I think we all have, I hope we all have, the same interests—that I have been rather shocked and surprised with the turn that has been given to the amendment to the Clayton Act, having lived with it since the early 1940's. . . .

"Here, I cannot be sure, but it seems that you are applying no different treatment to section 7 of the Clayton Act than has always been applied to

Sherman Act cases. That was just not the intent of many of us who were interested in this legislation."

. . . .

At times similar statements of official position are elicited in Congressional hearings. In this context, the agencies are sometimes called to task for failing to adhere to the "intent of Congress" in supplying meaning to the often broad statutory standards from which the agencies derive their authority, *e.g.*, "substantially to lessen competition" or "to tend to create a monopoly." There are those who "take a rather dim view [of such] committee pronouncements as to what agency policy should be, save when this is incident to proposals for amendatory legislation." Although such investigatory methods raise serious policy questions as to the *de facto* "independence" of the federal regulatory agencies, it seems doubtful that they raise any constitutional issues. However, when such an investigation focuses directly and substantially upon the mental decisional processes of a Commission *in a case which is pending before it*, Congress is no longer intervening in the agency's *legislative* function, but rather, in its *judicial* function. At this latter point, we become concerned with the right of private litigants to a fair trial and, equally important, with their right to the appearance of impartiality, which cannot be maintained unless those who exercise the judicial function are free from powerful external influences. . . .

To subject an administrator to a searching examination as to how and why he reached his decision in a case still pending before him, and to criticize him for reaching the "wrong" decision, as the Senate subcommittee did in this case, sacrifices the appearance of impartiality—the *sine qua non* of American *judicial* justice—in favor of some short-run notions regarding the Congressional intent underlying an amendment to a statute, unfettered administration of which was committed by Congress to the Federal Trade Commission. It may be argued that such officials as members of the Federal Trade Commission are sufficiently aware of the realities of governmental, not to say "political," life as to be able to withstand such questioning as we have outlined here. However, this court is not so "sophisticated" that it can shrug off such a procedural due process claim merely because the officials involved should be able to discount what is said and to disregard the force of the intrusion into the adjudicatory process. We conclude that we can preserve the rights of the litigants in a case such as this without having any adverse effect upon the legitimate exercise of the investigative power of Congress. What we do is to preserve the integrity of the judicial aspect of the administrative process.

Was the Fifth Circuit too lenient on congressional efforts to "advise" an agency as to "congressional intent"? Would you restrain Congress more?

6. Congressional pressure on an informal adjudication. *Pillsbury* involved alleged congressional intrusion on a formal adjudication. The D.C. Circuit addressed informal adjudication in *D.C. Federation of Civic Ass'ns v. Volpe*, 459 F.2d 1231 (D.C. Cir. 1971):

> Briefly stated, the controversy concerns a projected bridge between the Georgetown waterfront in the District of Columbia and Spout Run in Virginia. . . . A source of continuous controversy since its conception, the proposed bridge was deleted from the Interstate Highway System in January, 1969, when the National Capital Planning Commission, the official planning body for the District, adopted "a comprehensive transportation plan which did not include the Three Sisters Bridge." The bridge was redesignated part of the Interstate System six months later after Representative Natcher, Chairman of the Subcommittee on the District of Columbia of the House Appropriations Committee, indicated unmistakably that money for construction of the District's subway system would be withheld if the bridge plan were not revived. To satisfy the Chairman, it was necessary, first, for the District of Columbia City Council to reverse its earlier position, and vote to approve the project. On August 9, 1969, the District government so voted, with the swing members loudly protesting that they would not have changed their votes but for the pressures exerted by Representative Natcher. The second prerequisite of redesignation was a decision by Transportation Secretary Volpe that the project should go ahead as part of the Interstate System. He announced that decision on August 12, 1969, and the project sprang full-blown back to life on the following day. . . .

> The author of this opinion is convinced that the impact of this pressure is sufficient, standing alone, to invalidate the Secretary's action. Even if the Secretary had taken every formal step required by every applicable statutory provision, reversal would be required, in my opinion, because extraneous pressure intruded into the calculus of considerations on which the Secretary's decision was based. Judge Fahy, on the other hand, has concluded that since critical determinations cannot stand irrespective of the allegations of pressure, he finds it unnecessary to decide the case on this independent ground.

> . . . .

> It is plainly not our function to establish the parameters of relevance. Congress has carried out that task in its delegation of authority to the Secretary of Transportation. Nor are we charged with the power to decide where or when bridges should be built. That responsibility has been entrusted by Congress to, among others, the Secretary, who has the expertise and information to make a decision pursuant to the statutory standards. So long as the Secretary applies his expertise to considerations Congress intended to make relevant, he acts within his discretion and our role as a reviewing court is constrained. We do not hold, in other words that the bridge can

never be built. Nor do we know or mean to suggest that the information now available to the Secretary is necessarily insufficient to justify construction of the bridge. We hold only that the Secretary must reach his decision strictly on the merits and in the manner prescribed by statute, without reference to irrelevant or extraneous considerations.

. . . .

To avoid any misconceptions about the nature of our holding, we emphasize that we have not found — nor, for that matter, have we sought — any suggestion of impropriety or illegality in the actions of Representative Natcher and others who strongly advocate the bridge. They are surely entitled to their own views on the need for the Three Sisters Bridge, and we indicate no opinion on their authority to exert pressure on Secretary Volpe. Nor do we mean to suggest that Secretary Volpe acted in bad faith or in deliberate disregard of his statutory responsibilities. He was placed, through the action of others, in an extremely treacherous position. Our holding is designed, if not to extricate him from that position, at least to enhance his ability to obey the statutory command notwithstanding the difficult position in which he was placed.

We conclude that the case should be remanded to the District Court with directions that it return the case to the Secretary for him to perform his statutory function in accordance with this opinion. . . .

To what extent should a legislator be permitted to attempt to influence an administrative decision? Here the Court held that had this been a formal adjudication, Natcher's conduct would have been clearly improper. *Volpe*, 459 F.2d at 1246 (discussing how in a formal adjudication, "plaintiffs could have forcefully argued that the [Secretary's] decision was invalid because . . . he had received *ex parte* communications."). Do you agree?

Chapter 5

Judicial Review of Agency Action

This chapter examines the web of doctrines that govern judicial review of agency action. These doctrines fall into two categories. One category governs whether a court will review the merits of an agency action at all. Doctrines in this category include, among others: jurisdiction, types of review, reviewability, sovereign immunity, standing (of various types), finality, ripeness, and exhaustion. The other category includes doctrines that govern the scope of review that a court should apply when reviewing agency action. The applicable standard of review may depend both on the type of procedure used to produce an action as well as on whether the issues in play revolve around fact, law, or policy determinations.

The first half of this long chapter focuses on doctrines that determine access to the courts. One major project is to explore the workings of the broadly applicable cause of action that the APA establishes for review of agency action. A brief tour of these provisions, 5 U.S.C. §§ 701–706, may therefore help orient you for further study. Here goes:

Section 701. Applications; definitions. This section addresses the issue of "reviewability." In most pertinent part, it provides:

(a) This chapter applies, according to the provisions thereof, except to the extent that—

(1) statutes preclude judicial review; or

(2) agency action is committed to agency discretion by law.

Translating and somewhat over-simplifying, there is a presumption that judicial review of final agency action is available under the APA unless some other law trumps it.

Section 702. Right of review. This section's first sentence specifies who can invoke the APA's cause of action to challenge agency action:

A person suffering *legal wrong* because of agency action, or *adversely affected or aggrieved by agency action* within the meaning of a relevant statute, is entitled to judicial review thereof.

Courts have construed this provision very broadly to authorize a plaintiff to challenge agency action for violating a statutory or constitutional provision so long as the plaintiff can demonstrate that her suit seeks to protect interests that "arguably" fall within the "zone of interests" protected by that provision. A person who has suffered the kind of harm necessary to sue under § 702 is sometimes said to have "statutory standing." Thanks to the doctrine of sovereign immunity, a plaintiff can sue the government only if the government permits the suit. Section 702's second sentence partially waives the government's sovereign immunity:

> An action in a court of the United States seeking relief other than money damages and stating a claim that an agency or an officer or employee thereof acted or failed to act in an official capacity or under color of legal authority *shall not be dismissed* nor relief therein be denied *on the ground that it is against the United States* or that the United States is an indispensable party.

Note that this waiver does not apply to suits for "money damages." The Supreme Court has construed this phrase to refer to compensatory damages rather than to all forms of monetary relief. A party seeking compensatory damages from the government must invoke an extra-APA waiver of sovereign immunity. The Federal Torts Claims Act (FTCA) provides one very important example of such a waiver and is discussed later in this chapter.

Section 703. Form and venue of proceeding. The central message of the first sentence of this section is that the APA's judicial review template cares about substance, not form:

> The form of proceeding for judicial review is the *special statutory review proceeding* relevant to the subject matter in a court specified by statute or, in the absence or inadequacy thereof, *any applicable form of legal action*, including actions for declaratory judgments or writs of prohibitory or mandatory injunction or habeas corpus, in a court of competent jurisdiction.

In other words, if an agency's enabling act includes adequate provisions governing how to seek judicial review of actions taken pursuant to that statute, then a litigant must follow those provisions. If the enabling act does not provide for an adequate "special statutory review proceeding," then the litigant may use whatever form of legal action seems apt. Litigants challenging agency action commonly seek injunctive or declaratory relief.

Section 704. Actions reviewable. This provision speaks to the timing of challenges to agency action. Its first sentence is relatively straightforward, providing:

> Agency action *made reviewable by statute* and *final agency action* for which there is no other adequate remedy in a court are subject to judicial review.

Just as in civil procedure, the default position, which sounds simple enough, is that a person must wait for an agency's action to become "final" before challenging it. We will explore the metaphysics of what "finality" means in this context later in the chapter.

The trickier part of § 704 controls application of the doctrine of "exhaustion." This doctrine, where it applies, requires a litigant to exhaust opportunities for review of an agency's action within the agency itself before challenging the action in court. The exhaustion doctrine thus respects agency autonomy, allows agencies to fix their own mistakes, and saves judicial time, among other virtues. The following sentence establishes preconditions for applying this doctrine to block suits brought by plaintiffs relying on the APA's cause of action:

> Except as otherwise expressly required by statute, *agency action otherwise final is final* for the purposes of this section whether or not there has been presented or determined an application for a declaratory order, for any form of reconsideration, or, *unless the agency otherwise requires by rule and provides that the action meanwhile is inoperative, for an appeal to superior agency authority.*

The upshot of this mouthful is that, for suits governed by the APA, an agency cannot invoke exhaustion doctrine to block judicial review of final agency actions unless: (a) the agency has adopted a rule requiring litigants to exhaust opportunities for review within the agency; and (b) the agency action at issue does not go into effect during the pendency of such internal review. A simple idea informing this rather complex sentence is that a person wishing to challenge an agency action in court should be able to easily determine whether she must first pursue administrative review.

Section 705. Relief pending review. This section authorizes both agencies and reviewing courts to stay the effective date of agency actions pending review to avoid irreparable injury to persons subject to them.

Section 706. Scope of review. This section is quoted in full and picked apart in the notes following the *Overton Park* excerpt in the next reading. It authorizes courts to "compel agency action unlawfully withheld or unreasonably delayed." It also instructs courts "to hold unlawful and set aside agency actions, findings, and conclusions" that are determined to be arbitrary, unlawful, or unsupported by substantial evidence. In other words, it establishes the standards of review governing various types of agency decisions and authorizes the courts to provide appropriate remedies.

Congratulations! You now have, at least on a surface level, worked through most of the APA's instructions on the who-what-when-how-and-why of challenging agency action in court. We will spend much of the following chapter figuring out how courts have amplified, clarified, and distorted these instructions over the decades. Along the way, we will also study various other constitutional, statutory, and prudential doctrines that shape judicial review of agency action.

A. An Overview (via *Overton Park*)

This section uses a foundational case of the modern administrative law canon, *Citizens to Preserve Overton Park v. Volpe*, to continue introducing you to the "big picture" of judicial review of agency action. Three fundamental concepts make especially important appearances. First, there is the issue of reviewability, which speaks to whether courts have authority to review a given agency action. Second, there is the question of scope of review (or standard of review), which asks how closely courts should review a given agency determination. Third, there is the problem of determining the "record" for the purpose of judicial review.

Lesson 5A. Gallery sells a brand of wine under the "Happy Hart" label. The logo on the label features a smiling deer (*i.e.*, a hart). The label also observes that consumption of red wine can "Make your heart happy, too!" The WTC brought a civil penalty action against Gallery under §11 of the Act on the ground that Gallery's health claim violated §5(b) because it both: (a) untruthfully suggested that red wine improves the heart health of all consumers who drink it; and (b) omits material facts concerning the damaging effects of wine consumption necessary to prevent the health claim from being misleading. In the §11 proceeding, the WTC concluded that the charged conduct did, in fact, violate the Act. In addition, the WTC ordered Gallery to pay a civil penalty equal to three times the profit it had earned on sales of Happy Hart. The WTC explained that it deemed this penalty appropriate in light of the gravity of Gallery's violation and as a means of deterring misconduct by either Gallery or other winemakers.

Gallery has asked its attorney, our friend Abby, to seek judicial review of the WTC's order. In this regard, consider:

a. Does the WTCA authorize judicial review of the amount of the penalty? If so, in what court?

b. Suppose, for the sake of argument, that the WTCA does not contain any language authorizing judicial review of administrative penalties ordered pursuant to §11. Would judicial review of the amount of the penalty nonetheless be available? How does *Overton Park*'s gloss on 5 U.S.C. §701 affect your answer?

c. Were Gallery to obtain judicial review of the amount of the administrative penalty, what standard of review should apply to the agency's conclusion that the Happy Hart label communicates a message that consumption of red wine is good for the hearts of all who drink it? (Consider the note discussing the scope of review provision of the APA, §706(2).)

d. In defending its treble-profit penalty in court, might the agency properly supplement its original explanation by arguing that this penalty was appropriate given that Gallery has a long history of regulatory violations relating to misleading health claims? (You will want to take a look at the discussion of *Chenery I* in the notes below.)

e. Suppose that the WTC had offered no explanation at all for its choice of civil penalty. Procedurally, on judicial review, what would be the proper way to obtain an explanation? (For this question, in addition to considering *Overton Park*, you will also want to take guidance from *Camp v. Pitts* in the notes below.)

f. To finish on a broad, normative note: Is it always a good idea for courts to review agency actions? Are there circumstances where we should trust agency judgment more than judicial judgment? Does Gallery's case fall into one of these circumstances? How about the Secretary's decision to fund a road through Overton Park?

Background of *Citizens To Preserve Overton Park, Inc. v. Volpe*

Most of us living in twenty-first century America do not devote a lot of thought to the interstate highway system. Most of its routes are older than most of us, and we take them for granted. Decisions made many decades ago regarding where to locate these routes, however, implicated a tremendous number of conflicting economic, social, and political interests — especially in cities, where freeways ripped the hearts out of many neighborhoods. The absence of people living in the green spaces of parks naturally made them tempting targets for the new highways. In response to this problem, Congress enacted statutory protections for parks. Most notably, §4(f) of the Department of Transportation Act instructed the Secretary of Transportation to refrain from approving projects using lands from public parks unless: "(1) there is no feasible or prudent alternative to the use of such land, and (2) such program includes all possible planning to minimize harm to such park."

Notwithstanding these protections, the Secretary of Transportation approved the expenditure of funds to run a section of Interstate 40 through Overton Park, a 342-acre park in the heart of Memphis, Tennessee. This decision was the culmination of decades of planning and discussion at city, state, and federal levels. The Citizens to Preserve Overton Park challenged the Secretary's decision in court both for failing to honor statutory restrictions on the use of parks and for failing to meet the procedural requirements of the APA. It would be difficult to overstate the importance of the resulting Supreme Court opinion for judicial control of agency action. As you read and reflect on the excerpt that follows, you will want to pay particular attention to (1) how the Court determined that the agency decision was subject to judicial review at all; (2) how the Court characterized the arbitrary-and-capricious standard of review; and (3) how the Court extended application of the concept of a "record" to informal proceedings.

Citizens to Preserve Overton Park, Inc. v. Volpe

401 U.S. 402 (1971)

Opinion of the Court by Mr. Justice Marshall, announced by Mr. Justice Stewart.

The growing public concern about the quality of our natural environment has prompted Congress in recent years to enact legislation designed to curb the accelerating destruction of our country's natural beauty. We are concerned in this case with §4(f) of the Department of Transportation Act of 1966, as amended, and §18(a) of the Federal-Aid Highway Act of 1968. These statutes prohibit the Secretary of Transportation from authorizing the use of federal funds to finance the construction of highways through public parks if a "feasible and prudent" alternative route exists. If no such route is available, the statutes allow him to approve construction through parks only if there has been "all possible planning to minimize harm" to the park.

Petitioners, private citizens as well as local and national conservation organizations, contend that the Secretary has violated these statutes by authorizing the expenditure of federal funds for the construction of a six-lane interstate highway through a public park in Memphis, Tennessee. Their claim was rejected by the District Court, which granted the Secretary's motion for summary judgment, and the Court of Appeals for the Sixth Circuit affirmed. After oral argument, this Court granted a stay that halted construction and, treating the application for the stay as a petition for certiorari, granted review. We now reverse the judgment below and remand for further proceedings in the District Court.

Overton Park is a 342-acre city park located near the center of Memphis. The park contains a zoo, a nine-hole municipal golf course, an outdoor theater, nature trails, a bridle path, an art academy, picnic areas, and 170 acres of forest. The proposed highway, which is to be a six-lane, high-speed, expressway, will sever the zoo from the rest of the park. Although the roadway will be depressed below ground level except where it crosses a small creek, 26 acres of the park will be destroyed. The highway is to be a segment of Interstate Highway I-40, part of the National System of Interstate and Defense Highways. I-40 will provide Memphis with a major east-west expressway which will allow easier access to downtown Memphis from the residential areas on the eastern edge of the city.

Although the route through the park was approved by the Bureau of Public Roads in 1956 and by the Federal Highway Administrator in 1966, the enactment of § 4(f) of the Department of Transportation Act prevented distribution of federal funds for the section of the highway designated to go through Overton Park until the Secretary of Transportation determined whether the requirements of § 4(f) had been met. Federal funding for the rest of the project was, however, available; and the state acquired a right-of-way on both sides of the park. In April 1968, the Secretary announced that he concurred in the judgment of local officials that I-40 should be built through the park. And in September 1969 the State acquired the right-of-way inside Overton Park from the city. Final approval for the project — the route as well as the design — was not announced until November 1969, after Congress had reiterated in § 138 of the Federal Aid Highway Act that highway construction through public parks was to be restricted. Neither announcement approving the route and design of I-40 was accompanied by a statement of the Secretary's factual findings. He did not indicate why he believed there were no feasible and prudent alternative routes or why design changes could not be made to reduce the harm to the park.

Petitioners contend that the Secretary's action is invalid without such formal findings and that the Secretary did not make an independent determination but merely relied on the judgment of the Memphis City Council. They also contend that it would be "feasible and prudent" to route I-40 around Overton Park either to the north or to the south. And they argue that if these alternative routes are not "feasible and prudent," the present plan does not include "all possible" methods for reducing harm to the park. Petitioners claim that I-40 could be built under the park by using either of two possible tunneling methods, and they claim that, at a minimum, by using advanced drainage techniques the expressway could be depressed below ground level along the entire route through the park including the section that crosses the small creek.

Respondents argue that it was unnecessary for the Secretary to make formal findings, and that he did, in fact, exercise his own independent judgment which was supported by the facts. In the District Court, respondents introduced affidavits, prepared specifically for this litigation, which indicated that the Secretary had made the decision and that the decision was supportable. These affidavits were contradicted by affidavits introduced by petitioners, who also sought to take the deposition of a former Federal Highway Administrator who had participated in the decision to route I-40 through Overton Park.

The District Court and the Court of Appeals found that formal findings by the Secretary were not necessary and refused to order the deposition of the former Federal Highway Administrator because those courts believed that probing of the mental processes of an administrative decisionmaker was prohibited. And, believing that the Secretary's authority was wide and reviewing courts' authority narrow in the approval of highway routes, the lower courts held that the affidavits contained no basis for a determination that the Secretary had exceeded his authority.

We agree that formal findings were not required. But we do not believe that in this case judicial review based solely on litigation affidavits was adequate.

A threshold question—whether petitioners are entitled to any judicial review—is easily answered. Section 701 of the Administrative Procedure Act, 5 U.S.C. § 701, provides that the action of 'each authority of the Government of the United States,' which includes the Department of Transportation, is subject to judicial review except where there is a statutory prohibition on review or where 'agency action is committed to agency discretion by law.' In this case, there is no indication that Congress sought to prohibit judicial review and there is most certainly no "showing of 'clear and convincing evidence' of a . . . legislative intent" to restrict access to judicial review.

Similarly, the Secretary's decision here does not fall within the exception for action "committed to agency discretion." This is a very narrow exception. Berger, *Administrative Arbitrariness and Judicial Review*, 65 Col. L. Rev. 55 (1965). The legislative history of the Administrative Procedure Act indicates that it is applicable in those rare instances where "statutes are drawn in such broad terms that in a given case there is no law to apply." S.Rep. No. 752, 79th Cong., 1st Sess., 26 (1945).

Section 4(f) of the Department of Transportation Act and § 138 of the Federal-Aid Highway Act are clear and specific directives. Both the Department of Transportation Act and the Federal-Aid to Highway Act provide that the Secretary "shall not approve any program or project" that requires the use of any public parkland "unless (1) there is no feasible and prudent alternative to the use of such land, and (2) such program includes all possible planning to minimize harm to such park. . . ." 23 U.S.C. § 138; 49 U.S.C. § 1653(f). This language is a plain and explicit bar to the use of federal funds for construction of highways through parks—only the most unusual situations are exempted.

Despite the clarity of the statutory language, respondents argue that the Secretary has wide discretion. They recognize that the requirement that there be no "feasible" alternative route admits of little administrative discretion. For this exemption to apply the Secretary must find that as a matter of sound engineering it would not be feasible to build the highway along any other route. Respondents argue, however, that the requirement that there be no other "prudent" route requires the Secretary to engage in a wide-ranging balancing of competing interests. They contend that the Secretary should weigh the detriment resulting from the destruction of parkland against the cost of other routes, safety considerations, and other factors, and determine on the basis of the importance that he attaches to these other factors whether, on balance, alternative feasible routes would be "prudent."

But no such wide-ranging endeavor was intended. It is obvious that in most cases considerations of cost, directness of route, and community disruption will indicate that parkland should be used for highway construction whenever possible. Although it may be necessary to transfer funds from one jurisdiction to another, there will always be a smaller outlay required from the public purse when parkland is used since the public already owns the land and there will be no need to pay for right-of-way. And since people do not live or work in parks, if a highway is built on parkland no one will have to leave his home or give up his business. Such factors are common to substantially all highway construction. Thus, if Congress intended these factors to be on an equal footing with preservation of parkland there would have been no need for the statutes.

Congress clearly did not intend that cost and disruption of the community were to be ignored by the Secretary. But the very existence of the statutes indicates that protection of parkland was to be given paramount importance. The few green havens that are public parks were not to be lost unless there were truly unusual factors present in a particular case or the cost or community disruption resulting from alternative routes reached extraordinary magnitudes. If the statutes are to have any meaning, the Secretary cannot approve the destruction of parkland unless he finds that alternative routes present unique problems.

Plainly, there is "law to apply" and thus the exemption for action "committed to agency discretion" is inapplicable. But the existence of judicial review is only the start: the standard for review must also be determined. For that we must look to § 706 of the Administrative Procedure Act, 5 U.S.C. § 706, which provides that a "reviewing court shall . . . hold unlawful and set aside agency action, findings, and conclusions found" not to meet six separate standards. In all cases agency action must be set aside if the action was "arbitrary, capricious, an abuse of discretion, or otherwise not in accordance with law" or if the action failed to meet statutory, procedural, or constitutional requirements. 5 U.S.C. §§ 706(2)(A), (B), (C), (D). In certain narrow, specifically limited situations, the agency action is to be set aside if the action was not supported by "substantial evidence." And in other equally narrow circumstances the reviewing court is to engage in a *de novo* review of the action and set it aside if it was "unwarranted by the facts." 5 U.S.C. §§ 706(2)(E), (F).

Petitioners argue that the Secretary's approval of the construction of I-40 through Overton Park is subject to one or the other of these latter two standards of limited applicability. First, they contend that the "substantial evidence" standard of § 706(2)(E) must be applied. In the alternative, they claim that § 706(2)(F) applies and that there must be a *de novo* review to determine if the Secretary's action was "unwarranted by the facts." Neither of these standards is, however, applicable.

Review under the substantial-evidence test is authorized only when the agency action is taken pursuant to a [formal] rulemaking provision of the Administrative Procedure Act itself, 5 U.S.C. § 553, or when the agency action is based on a public adjudicatory hearing. See 5 U.S.C. §§ 556, 557. The Secretary's decision to allow the expenditure of federal funds to build I-40 through Overton Park was plainly not an exercise of a rulemaking function. And the only hearing that is required by either the Administrative Procedure Act or the statutes regulating the distribution of federal funds for highway construction is a public hearing conducted by local officials for the purpose of informing the community about the proposed project and eliciting community views on the design and route. The hearing is nonadjudicatory, quasi-legislative in nature. It is not designed to produce a record that is to be the basis of agency action—the basic requirement for substantial-evidence review.

Petitioners' alternative argument also fails. *De novo* review of whether the Secretary's decision was "unwarranted by the facts" is authorized by § 706(2)(F) in only two circumstances. First, such *de novo* review is authorized when the action is adjudicatory in nature and the agency factfinding procedures are inadequate. And, there may be independent judicial factfinding when issues that were not before the agency are raised in a proceeding to enforce nonadjudicatory agency action. Neither situation exists here.

Even though there is no *de novo* review in this case and the Secretary's approval of the route of I-40 does not have ultimately to meet the substantial-evidence test, the generally applicable standards of § 706 require the reviewing court to engage in a substantial inquiry. Certainly, the Secretary's decision is entitled to a presumption of regularity. But that presumption is not to shield his action from a thorough, probing, in-depth review.

The court is first required to decide whether the Secretary acted within the scope of his authority. This determination naturally begins with a delineation of the scope of the Secretary's authority and discretion. As has been shown, Congress has specified only a small range of choices that the Secretary can make. Also involved in this initial inquiry is a determination of whether on the facts the Secretary's decision can reasonably be said to be within that range. The reviewing court must consider whether the Secretary properly construed his authority to approve the use of parkland as limited to situations where there are no feasible alternative routes or where feasible alternative routes involve uniquely difficult problems. And the reviewing court must be able to find that the Secretary could have reasonably believed that in this case there are no feasible alternatives or that alternatives do involve unique problems.

Scrutiny of the facts does not end, however, with the determination that the Secretary has acted within the scope of his statutory authority. Section 706(2)(A) requires a finding that the actual choice made was not "arbitrary, capricious, an abuse of discretion, or otherwise not in accordance with law." To make this finding the court must consider whether the decision was based on a consideration of the relevant factors and whether there has been a clear error of judgment. Although this inquiry into the facts is to be searching and careful, the ultimate standard of review is a narrow one. The court is not empowered to substitute its judgment for that of the agency.

The final inquiry is whether the Secretary's action followed the necessary procedural requirements. Here the only procedural error alleged is the failure of the Secretary to make formal findings and state his reason for allowing the highway to be built through the park.

Undoubtedly, review of the Secretary's action is hampered by his failure to make such findings, but the absence of formal findings does not necessarily require that the case be remanded to the Secretary. Neither the Department of Transportation Act nor the Federal-Aid Highway Act requires such formal findings. Moreover, the Administrative Procedure Act requirements that there be formal findings in certain rulemaking and adjudicatory proceedings do not apply to the Secretary's action here. And, although formal findings may be required in some cases in the absence of statutory directives when the nature of the agency action is ambiguous, those situations are rare. Plainly, there is no ambiguity here; the Secretary has approved the construction of I-40 through Overton Park and has approved a specific design for the project. . . . .

[T]here is an administrative record that allows the full, prompt review of the Secretary's action that is sought without additional delay which would result from having a remand to the Secretary.

That administrative record is not, however, before us. The lower courts based their review on the litigation affidavits that were presented. These affidavits were merely "*post hoc*" rationalizations, which have traditionally been found to be an inadequate basis for review. And they clearly do not constitute the "whole record" compiled by the agency: the basis for review required by § 706 of the Administrative Procedure Act.

Thus it is necessary to remand this case to the District Court for plenary review of the Secretary's decision. That review is to be based on the full administrative record that was before the Secretary at the time he made his decision. But since the bare record may not disclose the factors that were considered or the Secretary's construction of the evidence it may be necessary for the District Court to require some explanation in order to determine if the Secretary acted within the scope of his authority and if the Secretary's action was justifiable under the applicable standard.

The court may require the administrative officials who participated in the decision to give testimony explaining their action. Of course, such inquiry into the mental processes of administrative decisionmakers is usually to be avoided. *United States v. Morgan*, 313 U.S. 409, 422 (1941). And where there are administrative findings that were made at the same time as the decision, as was the case in *Morgan*, there must be a strong showing of bad faith or improper behavior before such inquiry may be made. But here there are no such formal findings and it may be that the only way there can be effective judicial review is by examining the decisionmakers themselves.

The District Court is not, however, required to make such an inquiry. It may be that the Secretary can prepare formal findings . . . that will provide an adequate explanation for his action. Such an explanation will, to some extent, be a "*post hoc rationalization*" and thus must be viewed critically. If the District Court decides that additional explanation is necessary, that court should consider which method will prove the most expeditious so that full review may be had as soon as possible.

[Separate opinion of Mr. Justice Black, with whom Mr. Justice Brennan joined, omitted.]

Mr. Justice Blackmun.

I fully join the Court in its opinion and in its judgment. I merely wish to state the obvious: (1) The case comes to this Court as the end product of more than a decade of endeavor to solve the interstate highway problem at Memphis. (2) The administrative decisions under attack here are not those of a single Secretary; some were made by the present Secretary's predecessor and, before him, by the Department of Commerce's Bureau of Public Roads. (3) The 1966 Act and the 1968 Act have cut across former methods and here have imposed new standards and conditions upon a situation that already was largely developed. This undoubtedly is why the record is sketchy and less than one would expect if the project were one which had been instituted after the passage of the 1966 Act.

Notes on Jurisdiction, Types of Review, and Reviewability

1. Jurisdiction. Although the excerpt from *Overton Park* that you just read does not discuss this issue, every case properly in federal court must satisfy the requirements for subject matter jurisdiction. The APA itself does not contain a jurisdictional grant, but this gap seldom presents a problem. Where no more specific statute applies, a litigant can rely on 28 U.S.C. § 1331, which grants jurisdiction to the district courts for civil actions "arising under" federal law. *See, e.g., Owner-Operators Indep. Drivers Ass'n v. Skinner*, 931 F.2d 582, 585 (9th Cir. 1991) ("[U]nless Congress specifically maps a judicial review path for an agency, review may be had in federal district court under its general federal question jurisdiction."). Often, however, an agency enabling act will include a provision allocating jurisdiction for review directly to the courts of appeals. This allocation of authority is workable because judicial review of agency action is generally conducted based on an administrative record created during agency proceedings, which eliminates the need for the fact-finding capabilities of the district courts. Congress frequently channels review to the D.C. Circuit, which accounts for its dominance in matters of administrative law.

2. "Types" of review. To challenge an agency action in court, a plaintiff will need to invoke some body of law granting a right to seek judicial review. In the parlance of administrative law, there are three different "types" of review—"general statutory review," "special statutory review," and "nonstatutory review." "General statutory review" refers to review conducted pursuant to the APA's cause of action, 5 U.S.C. §§ 701–706. *Overton Park* provides an example.

Congress is free, of course, to trump the APA's general templates when it wishes. In the context of judicial review, Congress often does so by including particular instructions in an agency's enabling act for seeking review of actions taken pursuant to that act. These instructions may determine such matters as who can seek judicial review, jurisdiction, limitations periods, finality requirements, and so on. Review conducted pursuant to this type of "special" scheme is called, naturally enough, "special statutory review." Section 9 of the WTCA is an example providing for special statutory review of orders, penalties, and rules issued by the WTC.

"Nonstatutory review" is rooted in a long history of the courts' common law and equitable authority that predates the relatively recent innovations of the APA's cause of action and enabling acts with special statutory review schemes. The name is misleading, as several forms that fall into this category have been codified. One codified form of nonstatutory review is mandamus, which you might recall Marbury used to try to get his commission from Madison. *See Marbury v. Madison*, 5 U.S. (1 Cranch) 137 (1803); 28 U.S.C. § 1361 (codifying district court jurisdiction for actions "in the nature of mandamus"). Another extremely important codified form of nonstatutory review is habeas corpus, which courts use to police the legality of detention. *See generally* 28 U.S.C. § 2241 *et seq.*

Nonstatutory review also includes suits brought by plaintiffs seeking declaratory or injunctive relief to block constitutional violations. *See Bell v. Hood*, 327 U.S. 678, 684 (1946) ("[I]t is established practice for this Court to sustain the jurisdiction of federal courts to issue injunctions to protect rights safeguarded by the Constitution.") Under very limited circumstances, federal courts will invoke equity to conduct nonstatutory review of statutory violations on the theory that the agency has acted *ultra vires. Leedom v. Kyne*, 358 U.S. 184 (1958) (allowing nonstatutory review of statutory claim where Board acted "in excess of its delegated powers and contrary to a specific prohibition in the Act"); *Griffith v. Federal Labor Relations Authority*, 842 F.2d 487, 493 (D.C. Cir. 1988) (characterizing this form of review as available only where the agency has "patently" misconstrued its authority and "disregarded a specific and unambiguous statutory directive"). *Bivens* actions, in which plaintiffs sue federal officials for damages for constitutional torts, are yet another form of nonstatutory review. *See Bivens v. Six Unknown Fed. Narcotics Agents*, 403 U.S. 388, 396 (1971).

3. *Overton Park* on reviewability. Recall from our earlier tour of the APA's cause of action that 5 U.S.C. § 701 creates a general presumption of reviewability of agency action subject to two exceptions:

> (a) This chapter applies, according to the provisions thereof, except to the extent that—
>
>> (1) statutes preclude judicial review; or
>>
>> (2) agency action is committed to agency discretion by law.

We will have much more to say on these two exceptions below. The first one— statutory preclusion—is relatively straightforward (although you may find certain judicial applications of it rather strained). The meaning of the second exception, which applies to agency actions "committed to agency discretion by law," is more opaque. What instructions did the Court give in *Overton Park* regarding how to apply these exceptions?

Notes on Scope of Review

4. Scope of review—moving beyond fact and law to policy. You no doubt remember from Civil Procedure the distinction drawn on appellate review between issues of law and issues of fact. Administrative law complicates this picture by adding doctrines for the review of agency discretionary decisions. The categories of "fact," "law," and "discretion" are, on their margins, fuzzy and easily manipulated. The balance of this note will nonetheless attempt to illustrate their basic natures.

With regard to "facts," note that approval of the route and design of I-40 required the Secretary to make various determinations of brute "fact" about the world—e.g., just where is Overton Park anyway, and how many acres of it would the proposed route destroy? The Secretary also needed to make more evaluative or predictive findings of "fact"—e.g., what would be the costs and benefits associated with building plausible alternative routes? In addition, to comply with the statute, the Secretary needed to determine whether any alternative routes outside the park were "feasible and prudent." To make this last determination, the Secretary required an understanding of just what this statutory phrase means. Issues such as these, which **require the application of law to fact for their resolution**, are sometimes called "mixed questions of law and fact." They may be said to stand on the border between the domains of "fact" and "law."

Without attempting an exhaustive definition, one can usefully think of the term "law" as capturing binding, generally applicable rules. For instance, in *Overton Park*, what it meant for an alternative route to be "prudent" presented an issue of law because Congress wrote this term into a statute that bound the Secretary. The Court concluded that an alternative route satisfies the "prudence" test so long as it does not present "uniquely difficult problems." Thus, the Secretary could not, as a matter of law, have properly concluded that an alternative route was "imprudent" simply because it was slightly more expensive than a route plunged through a park.

In addition to constraining agencies, statutes often grant them considerable decision-making freedom. For instance, recall from *Whitman v. American Trucking Ass'n* (excerpted in Chapter 1) that § 109(b)(1) of the Clean Air Act requires the EPA to set, for various pollutants, "ambient air quality standards the attainment and maintenance of which in the judgment of the Administrator . . . are requisite to protect the public health." This law does not specifically instruct the agency what emission levels to allow for any given pollutant. It thus leaves space for the agency to exercise *discretionary* judgment concerning these levels. Courts are not supposed to encroach upon the discretionary powers that Congress grants agencies—Congress wants the EPA, not the courts, to regulate air quality. As a general matter, courts are, however, supposed to ensure that agencies do not abuse their discretion. A good deal of administrative law is devoted to ironing out the tension between these two principles.

5. Scope of review—the APA's instructions. Here are the APA's instructions on scope of review:

> § 706. *Scope of review*
>
> To the extent necessary to decision and when presented, the reviewing court shall decide all relevant questions of law, interpret constitutional and statutory provisions, and determine the meaning or applicability of the terms of an agency action. The reviewing court shall—
>
> (1) compel agency action unlawfully withheld or unreasonably delayed; and
>
> (2) hold unlawful and set aside agency action, findings, and conclusions found to be—
>
>> (A) arbitrary, capricious, an abuse of discretion, or otherwise not in accordance with law;
>>
>> (B) contrary to constitutional right, power, privilege, or immunity;
>>
>> (C) in excess of statutory jurisdiction, authority, or limitations, or short of statutory right;
>>
>> (D) without observance of procedure required by law;
>>
>> (E) unsupported by substantial evidence in a case subject to sections 556 and 557 of this title or otherwise reviewed on the record of an agency hearing provided by statute; or
>>
>> (F) unwarranted by the facts to the extent that the facts are subject to trial de novo by the reviewing court.
>
> In making the foregoing determinations, the court shall review the whole record or those parts of it cited by a party, and due account shall be taken of the rule of prejudicial error.

Section 706 is not the final word on scope of judicial review—courts have interpreted (or ignored) it in ways you may find surprising. Still, it is important to be able to pick this statutory provision apart and determine which of its various subparts apply in various contexts.

Subpart (A) of §706(2) instructs courts to set aside agency action found to be "arbitrary, capricious, [or] an abuse of discretion." Administrative law regards these terms as synonymous and often uses the shorthand of referring to the "arbitrary" or "arbitrary and capricious" standard of review. This standard operates as a default, applying except where §706(2) specifies an alternative. As §706(2) does not specifically prescribe an alternative standard of review for policy determinations or facts found through informal procedures, arbitrariness review applies to such determinations.

Subparts (B)–(D) all instruct courts to review various types of issues of law. Notably, none of these provisions seems to hint at the possibility that courts should defer to agency determinations on any legal issues. On the face of the APA, it looks like courts, consistent with *Marbury*, are in charge of determining legal meaning. The problem of allocating power between courts and agencies to determine legal meaning will return with a vengeance, however, in the last part of this chapter, where we encounter, among other things, the *Chevron* doctrine.

Subparts (E) and (F) specifically address review of agency fact-finding. Subpart (E) provides that the "substantial evidence" standard governs review of facts found by an agency after formal, on-the-record proceedings. Subpart (F) calls for de novo review of agency fact-finding in limited, unclear circumstances and has largely fallen into disuse.

6. Scope of review—remember to check the enabling act. Congress can always trump the default provisions of the APA in an agency's enabling act, and it sometimes does so in provisions governing scope of judicial review. For instance, in some agency enabling acts, Congress has instructed courts to conduct "substantial evidence" review of facts that agencies find through informal proceedings. As explained in the previous note, such factual determinations would be subject to arbitrariness review under §706(2) of the APA. For an example of legislative departures from the APA's judicial review provisions, see §9 of the WTCA.

7. Scope of review—*Overton Park* on arbitrariness review for reasoned decisionmaking. Judicial review for rationality comes in two different types. One type reviews for rationality of outcomes. This approach does not check whether a decisionmaker actually had a reasonable explanation for its decision; rather, it just checks whether a reasonable decisionmaker *could* have made the decision. Courts apply this form of review to general verdicts as juries do not explain them. It is also the default standard that courts apply to constitutional challenges questioning the rationality of congressional legislation. A second type of more intrusive rationality review insists that a decisionmaker supply a reasonable explanation for its choice. Administrative law often refers to this approach as review for *reasoned decisionmaking*.

Overton Park is famous (well, in administrative law circles, anyway) for declaring that arbitrariness review of an agency's discretionary policy decisions entails review for reasoned decisionmaking. The Court explained:

> The court is first required to decide whether the Secretary acted within the scope of his authority. This determination naturally begins with a delineation of the scope of the Secretary's authority and discretion. As has been shown, Congress has specified only a small range of choices that the Secretary can make. Also involved in this initial inquiry is a determination of whether on the facts the Secretary's decision can reasonably be said to be within that range. The reviewing court must consider whether the Secretary properly construed his authority to approve the use of parkland as limited to situations where there are no feasible alternative routes or where feasible alternative routes involve uniquely difficult problems. And the reviewing court must be able to find that the Secretary could have reasonably believed that in this case there are no feasible alternatives or that alternatives do involve unique problems.

In other words, courts should: (a) determine the legal boundaries on permissible agency action, and (b) ensure that a reasonable decisionmaker *could* determine that the relevant facts offered rational support for the choice the Secretary made.

The next paragraph in *Overton Park* tightened the screws of judicial review by making clear that it takes more than a minimally rational *outcome* for an agency action to survive review for arbitrariness:

> Scrutiny of the facts does not end, however, with the determination that the Secretary has acted within the scope of his statutory authority. Section 706(2)(A) requires a finding that the actual choice made was not "arbitrary, capricious, an abuse of discretion, or otherwise not in accordance with law." To make this finding the court must consider whether the decision was based on a consideration of the relevant factors and whether there has been a clear error of judgment. Although this inquiry into the facts is to be searching and careful, the ultimate standard of review is a narrow one. The court is not empowered to substitute its judgment for that of the agency.

Thus, the agency's analytical path to its conclusion must make at least minimal sense to the reviewing court. There has been a great deal of controversy regarding whether this form of review for reasoned decisionmaking (called "hard look review" in some contexts) generates benefits worth its costs. We shall return to this problem below in our discussion of review of agency policymaking, which is the focus of the excerpt from *Motor Vehicle Mfgs. Ass'n v. State Farm Mut. Auto. Ins. Co.*, 463 U.S. 29 (1983), and the notes that follow it.

Notes Pertaining to Agency Explanations and Records

8. *Chenery* and the contemporaneous rationale rule. Hovering in the background of *Overton Park* and its explication of arbitrariness review is a venerable rule of administrative law that the validity of an agency's discretionary action depends on the validity of the rationale the agency had for that action at the time the agency took it. In other words, an agency cannot use a *post hoc* rationale to defend the reasonability of its action during judicial review. The seminal case on this point is *SEC v. Chenery Corp. [Chenery I]*, 318 U.S. 80 (1943), which reviewed the results of SEC efforts to enforce the Public Utility Holding Company Act of 1935, which was designed to force simplification of complex corporate structures in the public utilities industry. Section 11(e) of the Act permitted corporations to develop their own reorganization plans, but the SEC was to approve them only if they were "fair and equitable to the persons affected by the plan." In the *Chenery* matter, while a reorganization plan was under consideration, corporate insiders purchased preferred shares that would have allowed them to retain control of the reorganized entity. After a formal adjudication, the SEC issued an order conditioning approval of the reorganization on a requirement that the insiders divest themselves of these shares on the ground that their purchase had violated principles of equity expressed in judicial precedents. The Supreme Court disagreed with the agency's analysis of judicial precedent and remanded to the agency for further proceedings. Justice Frankfurter explained:

> . . . Since the Commission professed to decide the case before it according to settled judicial doctrines, its action must be judged by the standards which the Commission itself invoked. And judged by those standards, *i.e.,* those which would be enforced by a court of equity, we must conclude that the Commission was in error in deeming its action controlled by established judicial principles.

> But the Commission urges here that the order should nevertheless be sustained because "the effect of trading by management is not measured by the fairness of individual transactions between buyer and seller, but by its relation to the timing and dynamics of the reorganization which the management itself initiates and so largely controls." . . .

> But the difficulty remains that the considerations urged here in support of the Commission's order were not those upon which its action was based. The Commission did not rely upon "its special administrative competence"; it formulated no judgment upon the requirements of the "public interest or the interest of investors or consumers" in the situation before it. . . . [The Commission] purported merely to be applying an existing judge-made rule of equity. . . .

> . . . [T]he courts cannot exercise their duty of review unless they are advised of the considerations underlying the action under review. If the action rests upon an administrative determination—an exercise of judgment in an area which Congress has entrusted to the agency—of course it must not be set aside because the reviewing court might have made a different determination were it empowered to do so. But if the action is based upon a determination of law as to which the reviewing authority of the courts

does come into play, an order may not stand if the agency has misconceived the law. In either event the orderly functioning of the process of review requires that the grounds upon which the administrative agency acted be clearly disclosed and adequately sustained. . . . In finding that the Commission's order cannot be sustained, we are not imposing any trammels on its powers. . . . We merely hold that an administrative order cannot be upheld unless the grounds upon which the agency acted in exercising its powers were those upon which its action can be sustained.

The Court's opinion in *Chenery I* presupposed that the SEC might have legal authority to create a rule proscribing the kind of insider acquisitions at issue in the case. Note that an appellate court should affirm a lower court's decision that reaches a legally correct outcome "although the lower court relied upon the wrong [legal] ground or gave a wrong [legal] reason." *Helvering v. Gowran*, 302 U.S. 238 (1937). Why not take this approach to review of agency decisions? On such an approach, the Court in *Chenery I* might have affirmed the SEC's divesture order on the ground that, even though the agency used a mistaken understanding of equitable principles to justify its decision, it *could* have given a legally sufficient basis for its order at the time it issued it. Wouldn't such an approach streamline review and avoid useless remands?

On remand, the SEC once again ordered the *Chenery* insiders to divest, but this time the agency rested its decision on its view that the proposed reorganization transgressed the requirement of the Holding Company Act that reorganizations be "fair and equitable." This decision again made its way up to the Supreme Court, which ruled that the agency's creation of this new legal norm in a formal adjudication and its simultaneous application of it to Chenery was not impermissibly retroactive. *SEC v. Chenery Corp. [Chenery II]*, 332 U.S. 194 (1947) (excerpted in Chapter 2).

9. *Overton Park's* **stick for encouraging contemporaneous agency explanations.** Recall that one of the plaintiff's arguments in *Overton Park* was that the Secretary's action approving the route through the park was illegal due to his failure to issue formal findings supporting that action. On the surface, this argument failed because the Secretary's decision was an informal adjudication not subject to any statutory requirement of formal findings.

On another level, however, this argument was a great success. Although no statute required the Secretary to issue formal findings, under the *Chenery* principle, the validity of his action still depended on its contemporaneous rationale. One way to identify this contemporaneous rationale might be to ask the relevant agency officials, requiring them to give testimony or to submit affidavits. In *United States v. Morgan*, 313 U.S. 409 (1941), the Court recognized that this type of judicial scrutiny of the mental processes of administrators should generally be avoided. One very good reason to avoid such intrusions is the reality that high-ranking agency officials are very busy people charged with many responsibilities who must obviously rely on staff for a great deal of information. Taking discovery concerning their "real" motivations for an action, perhaps years after the fact, will generally be unproductive and a recipe for mischief. Such after-the-fact testimony will also naturally tend to have a flavor of *post hoc* rationalization. In light of such concerns, as *Overton Park* notes, the general rule is that, where "there are administrative findings that were made at the same time as the decision, as was the case in *Morgan*, there must be a strong showing of bad faith or improper behavior before such inquiry may be made." *Overton Park* ominously added, however, that, where an agency does not offer a contemporaneous explanation for an action and the "bare" administrative record does not adequately explain it, "it may be that the only way there can be effective judicial review is by examining the decisionmakers themselves." From a busy agency's point of view, this is a deeply alarming threat.

Not long after making this threat in *Overton Park,* the Court confirmed in *Camp v. Pitts*, 411 U.S. 138 (1973), that an agency could avoid it by offering a contemporaneous explanation for its actions. This case arose out of a challenge to an informal adjudication by the Comptroller of the Currency denying an application to organize a new national bank. The court of appeals held that the Comptroller's explanation for the denial had been inadequate, and remanded for a trial before the district court, which would determine for itself by a preponderance of the evidence whether the Comptroller's denial had been arbitrary and capricious. The Supreme Court reversed on the ground that the proper procedure in this case was to remand to the Comptroller for further proceedings rather than to hold a trial:

> In its present posture this case presents a narrow, but substantial, question with respect to the proper procedure to be followed when a reviewing court determines that an administrative agency's stated justification for informal action does not provide an adequate basis for judicial review. . . .
>
> The appropriate standard for review was . . . whether the Comptroller's adjudication was "arbitrary, capricious, an abuse of discretion, or otherwise not in accordance with law," as specified in 5 U.S.C. § 706(2)(A). In applying that standard, the focal point for judicial review should be the administrative record already in existence, not some new record made initially in the reviewing court. . . .
>
> If, as the Court of Appeals held and as the Comptroller does not now contest, there was such failure to explain administrative action as to frustrate effective judicial review, the remedy was not to hold a de novo hearing but, as contemplated by *Overton Park*, to obtain from the agency, either through affidavits or testimony, such additional explanation of the reasons for the agency decision as may prove necessary. We add a caveat, however. Unlike *Overton Park*, in the present case there was contemporaneous explanation of the agency decision. The explanation may have been curt, but it surely indicated the determinative reason for the final action taken: the finding that a new bank was an uneconomic venture in light of the banking needs and the banking services already available in the surrounding community. The validity of the Comptroller's action must, therefore, stand or fall on

the propriety of that finding, judged, of course, by the appropriate standard of review. If that finding is not sustainable on the administrative record made, then the Comptroller's decision must be vacated and the matter remanded to him for further consideration. It is in this context that the Court of Appeals should determine whether and to what extent, in the light of the administrative record, further explanation is necessary to a proper assessment of the agency's decision.

Thus, provided an agency gives a contemporaneous explanation for its action, a court generally should not conduct judicial proceedings (e.g., take affidavits or testimony from agency officials) to identify the agency's contemporaneous rationale. In effect, the court should accept the agency's "official story" as to why it took its action rather than use judicial proceedings to get at the "real story," as it were. Where a court determines that an agency's explanation for its action is inadequate, the court should generally vacate and remand to the agency for further consideration. The agency can then decide what action to take, generating a new record and explanation without judicial interference.

10. The agency record—definitional difficulties for informal actions. To conduct review of another entity's decision, a court must know what precisely it is supposed to examine. In other words, it needs to know what is in or out of the "record" for review. The term "record" has a connotation in law of a structured body of information created through trial procedures. In this vein, the APA itself defines the "record" for formal administrative proceedings as "[t]he transcript of testimony and exhibits, together with all papers and requests filed in the proceeding. . . ." 5 U.S.C. § 556(e).

This concept of the "record" does not apply neatly to informal agency actions that lack any formal process for determining a record's contents. In *Overton Park*, the Court nonetheless remanded to the district court "for plenary review of the Secretary's decision . . . based on the full administrative record that was before the Secretary at the time he made his decision." The Court was not specific about what this "full administrative record" might entail. In the absence of a formal definition, as in § 556(e), a functional approach must apply, defining the record as including information that the agency somehow considered in the course of making its decision. Aggressive application of this approach, however, might force inclusion into the record of every bit of information received by many different agency officials regarding a decision that may have taken the agency many years to make. *Overton Park* itself provides a good example of the difficulties of such an approach—the process of approving I-40's path through Memphis took years and involved any number of administrators. Taken to an extreme, this type of record-building exercise seems both needlessly time-consuming and difficult. The explosion of electronic records in the decades since *Overton Park* complicates this task still further. *Cf. Pinnacle Armor, Inc. v. U.S.,* 923 F. Supp. 2d 1226, 1237 (E.D. Cal. 2013) (observing that, to ensure manageability, courts narrowly construe the "record" for informal proceedings as including "only those documents directly or indirectly considered by the relevant decisionmakers").

The concept of the "record" transposes somewhat more easily to the context of notice-and-comment rulemaking. The APA, after all, requires the agency to produce a notice of proposed rulemaking, accept comments, and offer a public explanation for the rule it adopts. Building on these statutory requirements and judicial glosses on them, the Administrative Conference of the United States issued the following recommendation:

> "Rulemaking record" means the full record of materials before the agency in an informal rulemaking. The Conference contemplates that, in addition to materials required by law to be included in the rulemaking record, as well as all comments and materials submitted to the agency during comment periods, any material that the agency considered should be included as part of that record.
>
> "Considered" entails review by an individual with substantive responsibilities in connection with the rulemaking. To say that material was considered also entails some minimum degree of attention to the contents of a document. Thus, the rulemaking record need not encompass every document that rulemaking personnel encountered while rummaging through a file drawer, but it generally should include a document that an individual with substantive responsibilities reviewed in order to evaluate its possible significance for the rulemaking, unless the review disclosed that the document was not germane to the subject matter of the rulemaking. A document should not be excluded from the rulemaking record on the basis that the reviewer disagreed with the factual or other analysis in the document, or because the agency did not or will not rely on it. Although the concept resists precise definition, the term considered as used in this recommendation should be interpreted so as to fulfill its purpose of generating a body of materials by which the rule can be evaluated and to which the agency and others may refer in the future.

Administrative Record in Informal Rulemaking, ACUS Recommendation 2013-4 (June 14, 2013) (footnote omitted). It bears noting that ACUS perceived the need to make this recommendation because, over 40 years after *Overton Park*, courts and agencies have not developed a uniform, clear approach to this problem of defining the rulemaking record, creating "uncertainty" and "confusion." *Id.*

11. The agency record for informal proceedings is almost always what the agency says the record is. After reading the last note, you might be wondering how administrative law has for decades managed to avoid developing a clear means of defining records for informal proceedings. Part of the answer is that courts presume that the records that agencies submit for judicial review are proper, and courts are very reluctant to allow litigants to expand them. *Franks v. Salazar*, 751 F. Supp. 2d 62, 67 (D.D.C. 2010) ("A court that orders an administrative agency to supplement the record of its decision is a rare bird."); *See* Leland E. Beck, *Report to the Administrative Conference of the United States: Agency Practices and Judicial Review of Administrative Records in Informal Rulemaking* 66 (2013) (discussing case law governing supplementation of agency records; concluding that "cases in which a party rebuts the presumption and the certified administrative record is pierced are limited"). Accordingly, the Ninth Circuit has explained that it allows plaintiffs to supplement an agency's designated record only:

> (1) if necessary to determine whether the agency has considered all relevant factors and has explained its decision,
>
> (2) when the agency has relied on documents not in the record, [ ]
>
> (3) when supplementing the record is necessary to explain technical terms or complex subject matter, [or] . . .
>
> (4) when plaintiffs make a showing of agency bad faith.

Center for Biological Diversity v. U.S. Fish & Wildlife Serv., 450 F.3d 930, 943 (9th Cir. 2006).

12. An important counterexample—*Department of Commerce v. New York.* The Supreme Court's opinion in *Department of Commerce v. New York,* 139 S. Ct. 2551 (2019), illustrates the importance of controlling the record for review and provides a notable counterexample to the general rule that the record for informal proceedings is usually what the agency says it is. The state of New York, among many other plaintiffs, challenged the decision by Secretary of Commerce Ross to add a citizenship question to the census, notwithstanding analysis by Census Bureau staff concluding that this addition would lead to an undercount in minority communities. In a memo explaining this decision, Ross asserted that the Department of Justice had requested reinstatement of the citizen question to obtain more granular citizenship data that would be helpful for enforcing requirements of the Voting Rights Act. Shortly after the government submitted the administrative record purporting to include materials that Ross had considered, it submitted a memo explaining that Ross had been considering addition of a citizenship question since early 2017 and had *asked* DOJ to officially request that he do so. The plaintiffs argued that this memo demonstrated that the administrative record was incomplete, and they moved for completion of the record and extra-record discovery, including expert discovery and depositions of Secretary Ross and of the Acting Assistant Attorney General for the Civil Rights Division (AAG). After the district court granted these motions, the parties stipulated to the addition of 12,000 pages of material to the record. The government appealed the order authorizing depositions of the Secretary and the AAG; the Supreme Court stayed the Secretary's deposition but allowed other extra-record discovery, including the deposition of the AAG to proceed.

In an opinion by Chief Justice Roberts, five of the justices largely approved of the district court's moves to expand the record, albeit with reservations. The Chief Justice's discussion provides nice encapsulation of many of the principles we have explored in the last few notes:

> We now consider the District Court's determination that the Secretary's decision must be set aside because it rested on a pretextual basis, which the Government conceded below would warrant a remand to the agency.

We start with settled propositions. First, in order to permit meaningful judicial review, an agency must "disclose the basis" of its action. . . . *SEC v. Chenery Corp.*, 318 U.S. 80, 94 (1943) ("[T]he orderly functioning of the process of review requires that the grounds upon which the administrative agency acted be clearly disclosed and adequately sustained.").

Second, in reviewing agency action, a court is ordinarily limited to evaluating the agency's contemporaneous explanation in light of the existing administrative record. That principle reflects the recognition that further judicial inquiry into "executive motivation" represents "a substantial intrusion" into the workings of another branch of Government and should normally be avoided.

Third, a court may not reject an agency's stated reasons for acting simply because the agency might also have had other unstated reasons. Relatedly, a court may not set aside an agency's policymaking decision solely because it might have been influenced by political considerations or prompted by an Administration's priorities. Agency policymaking is not a "rarified technocratic process, unaffected by political considerations or the presence of Presidential power." . . .

Finally, we have recognized a narrow exception to the general rule against inquiring into "the mental processes of administrative decisionmakers." *Overton Park*, 401 U.S. at 420. On a "strong showing of bad faith or improper behavior," such an inquiry may be warranted and may justify extra-record discovery.

The District Court invoked that exception in ordering extra-record discovery here. Although that order was premature, we think it was ultimately justified in light of the expanded administrative record. Recall that shortly after this litigation began, the Secretary, prodded by DOJ, filed a supplemental memo that added new, pertinent information to the administrative record. The memo disclosed that the Secretary had been considering the citizenship question for some time and that Commerce had inquired whether DOJ would formally request reinstatement of the question. That supplemental memo prompted respondents to move for both completion of the administrative record and extra-record discovery. The District Court granted both requests at the same hearing, agreeing with respondents that the Government had submitted an incomplete administrative record and that the existing evidence supported a prima facie showing that the VRA rationale was pretextual. . . .

We agree with the Government that the District Court should not have ordered extra-record discovery when it did. At that time, the most that was warranted was the order to complete the administrative record. But the new material that the parties stipulated should have been part of the administrative record—which showed, among other things, that the VRA played an insignificant role in the decisionmaking process — largely justified such extra-record discovery as occurred (which did not include the deposition of the Secretary himself). We accordingly review the District Court's ruling on pretext in light of all the evidence in the record before the court, including the extra-record discovery.

Department of Commerce, 139 S. Ct. at 2574. Justice Thomas, joined by Justices Kavanaugh and Gorsuch, insisted that the evidence did not establish the "bad faith or improper behavior" required for extra-record discovery and "proves at most that the Secretary was predisposed to add a citizenship question to the census and took steps to achieve that end before settling on the VRA rationale he included in his memorandum." *Id.* at *25 (Thomas, J., concurring in part and dissenting in part).

A Note with a Big Picture Question

13. Is so much judicial review such a good idea? Law school tends to take a court-centered view of the world, and it is easy to develop the reflexive expectation that judicial review is a good thing. But is it always? Consider the nature of the decision at issue in *Overton Park*. After *years* of effort by local, state, and federal authorities, a location for I-40 through Memphis was selected. No matter where a new highway runs through a populated area, it must affect a huge number of distinct interests and make a huge number of people deeply unhappy. Was it the job of law or politics to resolve where the road should go? Put another way, which type of entity was better situated to make this decision: the various administrative authorities involved or the courts? Peter Strauss investigated the impact of the *Overton Park* decision and found that it completely disrupted a complex social policy and political balance that could not be regained so that the project was ultimately abandoned. Peter Strauss, *Revisiting Overton Park: Political and Judicial Controls over Administrative Actions Affecting the Community*, 39 UCLA L. Rev. 1251, 1328–1329 (1992). He concluded: "[C]onsideration of the different ways politics works at the agency and judicial levels ... suggests that in cases presenting issues engaging multiple interests and likely trade-offs, courts should be more assiduous to enforce full participation before the agency than correctness of outcome." How sensitive should a court be to its potential for distorting public policy?

B. Reviewability and "Agency Action" — § 551(13)

There is a threshold problem lurking in the APA's template for judicial review that we neglected to tell you about earlier. The APA's cause of action applies to review of "agency action," a phrase defined at § 551(13). It turns out that not everything an agency does counts as "agency action." If a plaintiff's suit does not implicate "agency action," then the APA's cause of action cannot apply. We now turn to the Supreme Court's construction of this phrase and how it limits the availability of judicial review. As you read the *Norton* excerpt below, consider: What policy concerns motivated the Court's decision to interpret "agency action" more narrowly than it might have?

Lesson 5B. Suppose the WTC has been up and running for some years. Throughout this time, Gallery has sent proposals to the WTC suggesting that it develop a national advertising campaign promoting wine in the way that the Department of Agriculture promotes beef via an organization the USDA created by rule for this purpose, the Cattlemen's Beef Promotion and Research Board (Beef Board). The Beef Board's promotional campaign is funded by an assessment imposed on the sale and importation of cattle. Its advertisements are generic, praising the virtues of beef and its consumption without singling out any particular kind of producer or type of beef. In like fashion, a generic ad campaign for wine might be focused on slogans such as: "Wine—It's What's With Dinner" or "Wine: It *Really* Does Cut Your Risk of Heart Attack!" In responses to Gallery's letters, the WTC has not rejected this proposal out of hand but has instead indicated that it requires additional study both to determine its potential benefits and to resolve important issues it raises concerning appropriate limitations on advertising alcoholic beverages. Tired of what it regards as bureaucratic torpor, Gallery asks Rock to determine whether the courts might be used to spur some action on the proposal. Rock assigns the task to Abby. What might *Norton v. SUWA* suggest to her on this point?

Background of *Norton v. Southern Utah Wilderness Alliance*

Different people have different ideas for how to enjoy the great outdoors. Some like to drive off-road vehicles (ORVs) over rough terrain. Others dislike ORVs for ripping up the ground and scaring off the wildlife. Members of the Southern Utah Wilderness Association (SUWA) fall into the latter category. They filed an action in court seeking to force the Bureau of Land Management (BLM) to exercise stricter controls over ORV use in "wilderness study areas," which the BLM has a statutory obligation to manage "so as not to impair the suitability of such areas for preservation as wilderness." 43 U.S.C. § 1782(c). SUWA's suit implicated the problem of judicial control of agency inaction, which is one of the great difficulties of administrative law. Agency actions, although great in number, are not infinite. They also provide a focal point for judicial review. By contrast, one might fairly say that agencies are, at any given moment, failing to take an infinite number of actions. Also, the power to force an agency to act carries with it the power to determine agency priorities for deployment of scarce resources. Administrative law generally accepts that, subject to statutory constraints, agencies, not courts, should determine agency priorities. On the other hand, immunizing agency inaction from judicial review raises a real concern that agencies could simply ignore statutory mandates with which they disagree. *Norton v. SUWA* is the Court's explication of how the APA steers a path between these concerns.

Norton v. Southern Utah Wilderness Alliance

542 U.S. 55 (2004)

Justice Scalia delivered the opinion of the Court.

In this case, we must decide whether the authority of a federal court under the Administrative Procedure Act (APA) to "compel agency action unlawfully withheld or unreasonably delayed," 5 U.S.C. § 706(1), extends to the review of the United States Bureau of Land Management's stewardship of public lands under certain statutory provisions and its own planning documents.

I

Almost half the State of Utah, about 23 million acres, is federal land administered by the Bureau of Land Management (BLM), an agency within the Department of Interior. For nearly 30 years, BLM's management of public lands has been governed by the Federal Land Policy and Management Act of 1976 (FLPMA), which "established a policy in favor of retaining public lands for multiple use management." *Lujan v. National Wildlife Federation*, 497 U.S. 871, 877 (1990). "Multiple use management" is a deceptively simple term that describes the enormously complicated task of striking a balance among the many competing uses to which land can be put, "including, but not limited to, recreation, range, timber, minerals, watershed, wildlife and fish, and [uses serving] natural scenic, scientific and historical values." 43 U.S.C. § 1702(c). A second management goal, "sustained yield," requires BLM to control depleting uses over time, so as to ensure a high level of valuable uses in the future. § 1702(h). To these ends, FLPMA establishes a dual regime of inventory and planning. Sections 1711 and 1712, respectively, provide for a comprehensive, ongoing inventory of federal lands, and for a land use planning process that "project[s]" "present and future use," § 1701(a)(2), given the lands' inventoried characteristics.

WILDERNESS AREAS

Of course not all uses are compatible. Congress made the judgment that some lands should be set aside as wilderness at the expense of commercial and recreational uses. A pre-FLPMA enactment, the Wilderness Act of 1964, provides that designated wilderness areas, subject to certain exceptions, "shall [have] no commercial enterprise and no permanent road," no motorized vehicles, and no man-made structures. 16 U.S.C. § 1133(c). The designation of a wilderness area can be made only by Act of Congress, see 43 U.S.C. § 1782(b).

Pursuant to § 1782, the Secretary of the Interior has identified so-called "wilderness study areas" (WSAs), roadless lands of 5,000 acres or more that possess "wilderness characteristics," as determined in the Secretary's land inventory. § 1782(a); see 16 U.S.C. § 1131(c). As the name suggests, WSAs (as well as certain wild lands identified prior to the passage of FLPMA) have been subjected to further examination and public comment in order to evaluate their suitability for designation as wilderness. In 1991, out of 3.3 million acres in Utah that had been identified for study, 2 million were recommended as suitable for wilderness designation. 1 U.S. Dept. of Interior, BLM, Utah Statewide Wilderness Study Report 3 (Oct. 1991). This recommendation was forwarded to Congress, which has not yet acted upon it. Until

Congress acts one way or the other, FLPMA provides that "the Secretary shall continue to manage such lands . . . in a manner so as not to impair the suitability of such areas for preservation as wilderness." 43 U.S.C. § 1782(c). This nonimpairment mandate applies to all WSAs identified under § 1782, including lands considered unsuitable by the Secretary. . . .

Protection of wilderness has come into increasing conflict with another element of multiple use, recreational use of so-called off-road vehicles (ORVs), which include vehicles primarily designed for off-road use, such as lightweight, four-wheel "all-terrain vehicles," and vehicles capable of such use, such as sport utility vehicles. . . . The use of ORVs on federal land has negative environmental consequences, including soil disruption and compaction, harassment of animals, and annoyance of wilderness lovers. Thus, BLM faces a classic land use dilemma of sharply inconsistent uses, in a context of scarce resources and congressional silence with respect to wilderness designation.

In 1999, respondents Southern Utah Wilderness Alliance and other organizations (collectively SUWA) filed this action in the United States District Court for Utah against petitioners BLM, its Director, and the Secretary. . . . SUWA [claimed] that BLM had violated its nonimpairment obligation under § 1782(a) by allowing degradation [due to ORV use] in certain WSAs. [Two other claims—that BLM violated statutory and regulatory obligations by failing to implement a land use plan and that it violated the National Environmental Policy Act of 1969 (NEPA) by failing properly to consider whether it should supplement its environmental analyses for areas subject to increased ORV use—are omitted.] SUWA contended that it could sue to remedy th[is] . . . failure[ ] to act pursuant to the APA's provision of a cause of action to "compel agency action unlawfully withheld or unreasonably delayed." 5 U.S.C. § 706(1).

The District Court entered a dismissal. . . . A divided panel of the Tenth Circuit reversed. The majority acknowledged that under § 706(1), "federal courts may order agencies to act only where the agency fails to carry out a mandatory, nondiscretionary duty." It concluded, however, that BLM's nonimpairment obligation was just such a duty, and therefore BLM could be compelled to comply. . . . We granted certiorari.

II

All . . . claims at issue here involve assertions that BLM failed to take action with respect to ORV use that it was required to take. Failures to act are sometimes remediable under the APA, but not always. We begin by considering what limits the APA places upon judicial review of agency inaction.

The APA authorizes suit by "[a] person suffering legal wrong because of agency action, or adversely affected or aggrieved by agency action within the meaning of a relevant statute." 5 U.S.C. § 702. Where no other statute provides a private right of action, the "agency action" complained of must be *final* agency action." § 704 (emphasis added). "Agency action" is defined in § 551(13) to include "the whole or a part of an agency rule, order, license, sanction, relief, or the equivalent or denial thereof, or *failure to act*." (Emphasis added.) The APA provides relief for a failure to act in § 706(1): "The reviewing court shall . . . compel agency action unlawfully withheld or unreasonably delayed."

Sections 702, 704, and 706(1) all insist upon an "agency action," either as the action complained of (in §§ 702 and 704) or as the action to be compelled (in § 706(1)). The definition of that term begins with a list of five categories of decisions made or outcomes implemented by an agency—"agency rule, order, license, sanction [or] relief." § 551(13). All of those categories involve circumscribed, discrete agency actions, as their definitions make clear: "an agency statement of . . . future effect designed to implement, interpret, or prescribe law or policy" (rule); "a final disposition . . . in a matter other than rule making" (order); a "permit . . . or other form of permission" (license); a "prohibition . . . or taking [of] other compulsory or restrictive action" (sanction); or a "grant of money, assistance, license, authority," etc., or "recognition of a claim, right, immunity," etc., or "taking of other action on the application or petition of, and beneficial to, a person" (relief). §§ 551(4), (6), (8), (10), (11).

The terms following those five categories of agency action are not defined in the APA: "or the equivalent or denial thereof, or failure to act." § 551(13). But an "equivalent . . . thereof" must also be discrete (or it would not be equivalent), and a "denial thereof" must be the denial of a discrete listed action (and perhaps denial of a discrete equivalent).

The final term in the definition, "failure to act," is in our view properly understood as a failure to take an *agency action*—that is, a failure to take one of the agency actions (including their equivalents) earlier defined in § 551(13). Moreover, even without this equation of "act" with "agency action" the interpretive canon of *ejusdem generis* would attribute to the last item ("failure to act") the same characteristic of discreteness shared by all the preceding items. See, e.g., *Washington State Dep't. of Social and Health Servs. v. Guardianship Estate of Keffeler*. A "failure to act" is not the same thing as a "denial." The latter is the agency's act of saying no to a request; the former is simply the omission of an action without formally rejecting a request—for example, the failure to promulgate a rule or take some decision by a statutory deadline. The important point is that a "failure to act" is properly understood to be limited, as are the other items in § 551(13), to a *discrete* action.

A second point central to the analysis of the present case is that the only agency action that can be compelled under the APA is action legally *required*. This limitation appears in § 706(1)'s authorization for courts to "compel agency action *unlawfully* withheld."[1] In this regard the APA carried forward the traditional practice prior to its passage, when judicial review was achieved through use of the so-called

---

1. Of course § 706(1) also authorizes courts to "compel agency action . . . unreasonably delayed"—but a delay cannot be unreasonable with respect to action that is not required.

prerogative writs—principally writs of mandamus under the All Writs Act, now codified at 28 U.S.C. § 1651(a). The mandamus remedy was normally limited to enforcement of "a specific, unequivocal command," *ICC v. New York, N.H. & H.R. Co.*, 287 U.S. 178, 204 (1932), the ordering of a "'precise, definite act . . . about which [an official] had no discretion whatever,'" *United States ex rel. Dunlap v. Black*, 128 U.S. 40, 46 (1888). . . . As described in the Attorney General's Manual on the APA, a document whose reasoning we have often found persuasive, § 706(1) empowers a court only to compel an agency "to perform a ministerial or non-discretionary act," or "to take action upon a matter, without directing *how* it shall act." Attorney General's Manual on the Administrative Procedure Act 108 (1947) (emphasis added). See also L. Jaffe, Judicial Control of Administrative Action 372 (1965); K. Davis, Administrative Law § 257, p. 925 (1951).

Thus, a claim under § 706(1) can proceed only where a plaintiff asserts that an agency failed to take a discrete agency action that it is required to take. These limitations rule out several kinds of challenges. The limitation to discrete agency action precludes the kind of broad programmatic attack we rejected in *Lujan v. National Wildlife Federation*, 497 U.S. 871 (1990). There we considered a challenge to BLM's land withdrawal review program, couched as unlawful agency "action" that the plaintiffs wished to have "set aside" under § 706(2).[2] *Id.*, at 879.

> "[R]espondent cannot seek *wholesale* improvement of this program by court decree, rather than in the offices of the Department or the halls of Congress, where programmatic improvements are normally made. Under the terms of the APA, respondent must direct its attack against some particular 'agency action' that causes it harm." *Id.*, at 891 (emphasis in original).

The plaintiffs in *National Wildlife Federation* would have fared no better if they had characterized the agency's alleged "failure to revise land use plans in proper fashion" and "failure to consider multiple use," in terms of "agency action unlawfully withheld" under § 706(1), rather than agency action "not in accordance with law" under § 706(2).

The limitation to *required* agency action rules out judicial direction of even discrete agency action that is not demanded by law (which includes, of course, agency regulations that have the force of law). Thus, when an agency is compelled by law to act within a certain time period, but the manner of its action is left to the agency's discretion, a court can compel the agency to act, but has no power to specify what the action must be. For example, 47 U.S.C. § 251(d)(1), which required the Federal Communications Commission "to establish regulations to implement" interconnection requirements "[w]ithin 6 months" of the date of enactment of the Telecommunications Act of 1996, would have supported a judicial decree under the APA

---

2. Title 5 U.S.C. § 706(2) provides, in relevant part: "The reviewing court shall— . . . (2) hold unlawful and set aside agency action . . . found to be—(A) arbitrary, capricious, an abuse of discretion, or otherwise not in accordance with law. . . ."

requiring the prompt issuance of regulations, but not a judicial decree setting forth the content of those regulations.

III

A

With these principles in mind, we turn to SUWA's first claim, that by permitting ORV use in certain WSAs, BLM violated its mandate to "continue to manage [WSAs] . . . in a manner so as not to impair the suitability of such areas for preservation as wilderness," 43 U.S.C. § 1782(c). SUWA relies not only upon § 1782(c) but also upon a provision of BLM's Interim Management Policy for Lands Under Wilderness Review, which interprets the nonimpairment mandate to require BLM to manage WSAs so as to prevent them from being "degraded so far, compared with the area's values for other purposes, as to significantly constrain the Congress's prerogative to either designate [it] as wilderness or release it for other uses."

Section 1782(c) is mandatory as to the object to be achieved, but it leaves BLM a great deal of discretion in deciding how to achieve it. It assuredly does not mandate, with the clarity necessary to support judicial action under § 706(1), the total exclusion of ORV use.

SUWA argues that § 1782 does contain a categorical imperative, namely the command to comply with the nonimpairment mandate. It contends that a federal court could simply enter a general order compelling compliance with that mandate, without suggesting any particular manner of compliance. It relies upon the language from the Attorney General's Manual quoted earlier, that a court can "take action upon a matter, without directing how [the agency] shall act," and upon language in a case cited by the Manual noting that "mandamus will lie . . . even though the act required involves the exercise of judgment and discretion." *Safeway Stores v. Brown*, 138 F.2d 278, 280 (Emerg. Ct. App. 1943). The action referred to in these excerpts, however, is discrete agency action, as we have discussed above. General deficiencies in compliance, unlike the failure to issue a ruling that was discussed in *Safeway Stores*, lack the specificity requisite for agency action.

The principal purpose of the APA limitations we have discussed—and of the traditional limitations upon mandamus from which they were derived—is to protect agencies from undue judicial interference with their lawful discretion, and to avoid judicial entanglement in abstract policy disagreements which courts lack both expertise and information to resolve. If courts were empowered to enter general orders compelling compliance with broad statutory mandates, they would necessarily be empowered, as well, to determine whether compliance was achieved—which would mean that it would ultimately become the task of the supervising court, rather than the agency, to work out compliance with the broad statutory mandate, injecting the judge into day-to-day agency management. To take just a few examples from federal resources management, a plaintiff might allege that the Secretary had failed to "manage wild free-roaming horses and burros in a manner that is designed to achieve and maintain a thriving natural ecological balance," or to "manage the

[New Orleans Jazz National] [H]istorical [P]ark in such a manner as will preserve and perpetuate knowledge and understanding of the history of jazz," or to "manage the [Steens Mountain] Cooperative Management and Protection Area for the benefit of present and future generations." 16 U.S.C. §§ 1333(a), 410bbb-2(a)(1), 460nnn-12(b). The prospect of pervasive oversight by federal courts over the manner and pace of agency compliance with such congressional directives is not contemplated by the APA. . . .

The judgment of the Court of Appeals is reversed, and the case is remanded for further proceedings consistent with this opinion.

It is so ordered.

Notes

1. **Is there any way out?** According to the Court, "a claim under § 706(1) can proceed only where a plaintiff asserts that an agency failed to take [a] a discrete agency action that it is [b] required to take." Could Abby style a claim for Gallery that would not violate one or the other of these requirements? Could SUWA have done so?

2. **"Agency action" is never indiscrete.** Where did the Court find the requirement of "discreteness" for "agency action"? Do you find Justice Scalia's analysis of this point persuasive?

3. **What drove this decision?** Stipulate, for the moment, that the APA's text is vague enough that, if the Court had wished to do so, it could have characterized BLM's alleged failure to implement its nonimpairment obligation as an "agency action" within the meaning of § 551(13). Given that it could have written a respectable opinion to this effect, what concerns seemed to block that path? Are these concerns consistent with those expressed in *Overton Park*?

4. **A word on mandamus and discretion.** The writ of mandamus, like habeas corpus and certiorari, is one of the "prerogative writs" developed at common law to control official action. Today, a mandamus-like power is codified (among other places) at 28 U.S.C. § 1361, which provides that "[t]he district courts shall have original jurisdiction of any action in the nature of mandamus to compel an officer or employee of the United States or any agency thereof to perform a duty owed to the plaintiff." Justice Scalia's opinion in *SUWA* stresses that mandamus may not be used to compel an official to exercise her discretion in any given manner; rather, mandamus only lies to compel "ministerial" acts. This position, for which there is a good deal of case-law support, would seem to block use of the writ to police abuses of discretion. It bears noting, however, that there is also support — some quite recent — for the proposition that mandamus may lie to correct egregious abuses of discretionary authority. *See, e.g., Cheney v. U.S. Dist. Ct. for the District of Columbia*, 542 U.S. 376 (2004) (noting that appellate courts may issue the writ against lower courts "in exceptional circumstances amounting to . . . a clear abuse of discretion"). We will briefly take up the topic of mandamus again in subchapter 5F below.

5. A pretty active example of an agency not acting. Sometimes when an agency does not do what someone wants it to do, the result is just disappointing inaction, not a reviewable "failure to act." For a good example, consider *Village of Bald Head Island v. U.S. Army Corps of Engineers*, 714 F.3d 186 (4th Cir. 2013). The Corps of Engineers had proposed dredging and maintenance activities that threatened beaches in nearby communities. After several studies and negotiations, the Corps developed a plan under which it would monitor the effects of its actions and would dispose of dredged beach-quality sand on the various beaches on a six-year cycle. It sent a letter describing these[proposed actions]and a second letter stating that its actions "shall be in accordance with" the earlier letter. The Corps then approved and undertook the project, with maintenance continuing as projected for several years, until the Corps informed the communities that it did "not have the funding for dredging the portion of the Channel nearest Bald Head Island or for disposing of beach-quality sand onto Bald Head Island beaches." Bald Head sued, arguing that the Corps' failure to fulfill its monitoring plan was a reviewable "failure to act." Despite the Corps' stated commitment to take the arguably "discrete" actions described in its monitoring plan, the court emphasized it could review an inaction only where it represented an agency's failure to take a *required* action. Neither the statutes, nor the regulations, nor the Corps' letter imposed any requirement to act. Ultimately, Bald Head was asking the court to involve itself in a "day-to-day managerial role over agency operations," which it could not do. According to the court, final agency action occurred when the Corps approved the plan. After that point, the agency was engaged in implementation of the program, with which the court could not interfere.

C. Preclusion of Review under § 701

In this subsection, we examine in more detail the problem of preclusion of review under § 701. Recall from *Overton Park* that the Supreme Court regards final agency action as presumptively reviewable. Section 701, however, identifies two ways to overcome this presumption. Section 701(a)(1) notes that Congress can preclude review by statute. The outer constitutional limits of this power are hazy and will likely never be definitively resolved. You may not be surprised to learn that courts often strongly resist construing statutes as precluding judicial review — at least for types of issues that courts tend to regard as systemically important.

Section 701(a)(2) blocks judicial review where agency actions are "committed to agency discretion by law." On its face, this provision is puzzling because, as we discussed earlier, many agency actions are subject to judicial review for arbitrariness or, equivalently, for "abuse of discretion." *See* 5 U.S.C. § 706(2)(A). So the mere fact that an agency action is discretionary cannot be enough to immunize it from judicial review — some sort of special discretion must be involved. *Overton Park* addressed this point by declaring that § 701(a)(2) blocks review where there is, in essence, "no law to apply" that confines agency discretion. But isn't there always some law to apply if we look hard enough for it?

Lesson 5C. The Wine Merchants Association, an industry self-regulatory body authorized by § 6(b) of the WTCA, suspended Abby's client Mort, a wholesale wine distributor, from its membership for one year for violating Association rules on pricing. The Wine Trade Commission later initiated an action under WTCA § 6(d) to suspend Mort's wine merchants license. Fortunately, Abby was able to negotiate a settlement with the Commission's compliance staff pursuant to which Mort would retain his license and could continue to sell wine even while suspended from the Association. As part of this settlement, Mort readily agreed to cease any offending practices.

The Association's governing board is very unhappy with the Commission's decision to let Mort off the hook. The Association has therefore asked its general counsel, Jordan, to seek judicial review of the Commission's settlement agreement with Mort.

Is this settlement agreement reviewable at the WMA's behest? What does § 9 of the WTCA suggest? The APA?

Background of *Webster v. Doe*

The work of a spy agency, such as the CIA, is by its nature secretive—thus, the "cloak" in "cloak and dagger." A republic committed to the rule of law, however, must exercise care to ensure that its secret intelligence services do not act arbitrarily and illegally. *Webster v. Doe* involved a clash between these two values. Doe, an exemplary employee of the CIA for nine years, was fired from his post as an undercover agent after he voluntarily revealed his homosexuality to the agency. He sued, claiming that this termination violated his constitutional rights, the APA's proscription of arbitrary agency action, and CIA regulations. The CIA contended that the courts could not review these claims. A plausible policy rationale supporting this contention is that courts should not be making sensitive decisions regarding whom the CIA employs as undercover agents. The legal basis for the CIA's argument lay in § 701(a) of the APA governing reviewability. As you read the excerpt below, consider closely the differing approaches that the majority, Justice O'Connor, and Justice Scalia took to applying this provision.

Webster v. Doe
486 U.S. 592 (1988)

Chief Justice Rehnquist delivered the opinion of the Court.

Section 102(c) of the National Security Act of 1947, 61 Stat. 498, as amended, provides that:

"[T]he Director of Central Intelligence may, in his discretion, terminate the employment of any officer or employee of the Agency whenever he shall deem such termination necessary or advisable in the interests of the United States. . . ." 50 U.S.C. § 403(c).

In this case we decide whether, and to what extent, the termination decisions of the Director under § 102(c) are judicially reviewable.

I

Respondent John Doe was first employed by the Central Intelligence Agency (CIA or Agency) in 1973 as a clerk-typist. He received periodic fitness reports that consistently rated him as an excellent or outstanding employee. By 1977, respondent had been promoted to a position as a covert electronics technician.

In January 1982, respondent voluntarily informed a CIA security officer that he was a homosexual. Almost immediately, the Agency placed respondent on paid administrative leave pending an investigation of his sexual orientation and conduct. On February 12 and again on February 17, respondent was extensively questioned by a polygraph officer concerning his homosexuality and possible security violations. Respondent denied having sexual relations with any foreign nationals and maintained that he had not disclosed classified information to any of his sexual partners. After these interviews, the officer told respondent that the polygraph tests indicated that he had truthfully answered all questions. The polygraph officer then prepared a five-page summary of his interviews with respondent, to which respondent was allowed to attach a two-page addendum.

On April 14, 1982, a CIA security agent informed respondent that the Agency's Office of Security had determined that respondent's homosexuality posed a threat to security, but declined to explain the nature of the danger. Respondent was then asked to resign. When he refused to do so, the Office of Security recommended to the CIA Director (petitioner's predecessor) that respondent be dismissed. After reviewing respondent's records and the evaluations of his subordinates, the Director "deemed it necessary and advisable in the interests of the United States to terminate [respondent's] employment with this Agency pursuant to section 102(c) of the National Security Act. . . ." . . .

Respondent then filed an action against petitioner in the United States District Court for the District of Columbia. Respondent's amended complaint asserted a variety of statutory and constitutional claims against the Director. Respondent alleged that the Director's decision to terminate his employment violated the Administrative Procedure Act (APA), 5 U.S.C. § 706, because it was arbitrary and capricious, represented an abuse of discretion, and was reached without observing the procedures required by law and CIA regulations. . . .

Petitioner moved to dismiss respondent's amended complaint on the ground that § 102(c) of the National Security Act (NSA) precludes judicial review of the Director's termination decisions under the provisions of the APA set forth in 5 U.S.C. §§ 701, 702, and 706. . . .

The District Court denied petitioner's motion to dismiss, and granted respondent's motion for partial summary judgment. The court determined that the APA

provided judicial review of petitioner's termination decisions made under § 102(c)   *DC FINDING*
of the NSA, and found that respondent had been unlawfully discharged because the
CIA had not followed the procedures described in its own regulations. . . .

A divided panel of the Court of Appeals for the District of Columbia Circuit . . .
decided that judicial review under the APA of the Agency's decision to terminate
respondent was not precluded by §§ 701(a)(1) or (a)(2). . . .

. . . We granted certiorari to decide the question whether the Director's decision to discharge a CIA employee under § 102(c) of the NSA is judicially reviewable
under the APA.

II

The APA's comprehensive provisions, set forth in 5 U.S.C. §§ 701–706, allow any
person "adversely affected or aggrieved" by agency action to obtain judicial review
thereof, so long as the decision challenged represents a "final agency action for which
there is no other adequate remedy in a court." Typically, a litigant will contest an
action (or failure to act) by an agency on the ground that the agency has neglected
to follow the statutory directives of Congress. Section 701(a), however, limits application of the entire APA to situations in which judicial review is not precluded by
statute, see § 701(a)(1), and the agency action is not committed to agency discretion
by law, see § 701(a)(2).

In *Citizens to Preserve Overton Park, Inc.* v. *Volpe,* 401 U.S. 402 (1971), this Court   *701(a)(1)*
explained the distinction between §§ 701(a)(1) and (a)(2). Subsection (a)(1) is con-   *v.*
cerned with whether Congress expressed an intent to prohibit judicial review; subsection (a)(2) applies "in those rare instances where 'statutes are drawn in such   *701(a)(2)*
broad terms that in a given case there is no law to apply.'" 401 U.S., at 410 (citing
S.Rep. No. 752, 79th Cong., 1st Sess., 26 (1945)).

We further explained what it means for an action to be "committed to agency
discretion by law" in *Heckler v. Chaney,* 470 U.S. 821 (1985). *Heckler* required the
Court to determine whether the Food and Drug Administration's decision not to
undertake an enforcement proceeding against the use of certain drugs in administering the death penalty was subject to judicial review. We noted that, under § 701(a)
(2), even when Congress has not affirmatively precluded judicial oversight, "review
is not to be had if the statute is drawn so that a court would have no meaningful
standard against which to judge the agency's exercise of discretion." 470 U.S., at 830.
Since the statute conferring power on the Food and Drug Administration to prohibit the unlawful misbranding or misuse of drugs provided no substantive standards on which a court could base its review, we found that enforcement actions
were committed to the complete discretion of the FDA to decide when and how they
should be pursued.

Both *Overton Park* and *Heckler* emphasized that § 701(a)(2) requires careful
examination of the statute on which the claim of agency illegality is based. . . . In the
present case, respondent's claims against the CIA arise from the Director's asserted
violation of § 102(c) of the NSA. As an initial matter, it should be noted that § 102(c)

allows termination of an Agency employee whenever the Director "shall *deem* such termination necessary or advisable in the interests of the United States" (emphasis added), not simply when the dismissal is necessary or advisable to those interests. This standard fairly exudes deference to the Director, and appears to us to foreclose the application of any meaningful judicial standard of review. Short of permitting cross-examination of the Director concerning his views of the Nation's security and whether the discharged employee was inimical to those interests, we see no basis on which a reviewing court could properly assess an Agency termination decision. The language of § 102(c) thus strongly suggests that its implementation was "committed to agency discretion by law."

So too does the overall structure of the NSA. Passed shortly after the close of the Second World War, the NSA created the CIA and gave its Director the responsibility "for protecting intelligence sources and methods from unauthorized disclosure." *See* 50 U.S.C. § 403(d)(3); S.Rep. No. 239, 80th Cong., 1st Sess., 2 (1947); H.R.Rep. No. 961, 80th Cong., 1st Sess., 3–4 (1947). Section 102(c) is an integral part of that statute, because the Agency's efficacy, and the Nation's security, depend in large measure on the reliability and trustworthiness of the Agency's employees. As we recognized in *Snepp v. United States*, 444 U.S. 507, 510 (1980), employment with the CIA entails a high degree of trust that is perhaps unmatched in Government service.

We thus find that the language and structure of § 102(c) indicate that Congress meant to commit individual employee discharges to the Director's discretion, and that § 701(a)(2) accordingly precludes judicial review of these decisions under the APA. We reverse the Court of Appeals to the extent that it found such terminations reviewable by the courts.

III

In addition to his claim that the Director failed to abide by the statutory dictates of § 102(c), respondent also alleged a number of constitutional violations in his amended complaint. Respondent charged that petitioner's termination of his employment deprived him of property and liberty interests under the Due Process Clause of the Fifth Amendment, denied him equal protection of the laws, and unjustifiably burdened his right to privacy. Respondent asserts that he is entitled, under the APA, to judicial consideration of these claimed violations. . . .

Petitioner maintains that, no matter what the nature of respondent's constitutional claims, judicial review is precluded by the language and intent of § 102(c). In petitioner's view, all Agency employment termination decisions, even those based on policies normally repugnant to the Constitution, are given over to the absolute discretion of the Director, and are hence unreviewable under the APA. We do not think § 102(c) may be read to exclude review of constitutional claims. We emphasized in *Johnson v. Robison*, 415 U.S. 361 (1974), that where Congress intends to preclude judicial review of constitutional claims its intent to do so must be clear. *Id.*, at 373–374. . . . We require this heightened showing in part to avoid the "serious constitutional question" that would arise if a federal statute were construed to deny any judicial forum for a colorable constitutional claim. *See Bowen v. Michigan Academy of Family Physicians*, 476 U.S. 667, 681, n. 12 (1986).

Our review of § 102(c) convinces us that it cannot bear the preclusive weight petitioner would have it support. As detailed above, the section does commit employment termination decisions to the Director's discretion, and precludes challenges to these decisions based upon the statutory language of § 102(c). A discharged employee thus cannot complain that his termination was not "necessary or advisable in the interests of the United States," since that assessment is the Director's alone. Subsections (a)(1) and (a)(2) of § 701, however, remove from judicial review only those determinations specifically identified by Congress or "committed to agency discretion by law." Nothing in § 102(c) persuades us that Congress meant to preclude consideration of colorable constitutional claims arising out of the actions of the Director pursuant to that section; we believe that a constitutional claim based on an individual discharge may be reviewed by the District Court. We agree with the Court of Appeals that there must be further proceedings in the District Court on this issue.

Petitioner complains that judicial review even of constitutional claims will entail extensive "rummaging around" in the Agency's affairs to the detriment of national security. But petitioner acknowledges that Title VII claims attacking the hiring and promotion policies of the Agency are routinely entertained in federal court, and the inquiry and discovery associated with those proceedings would seem to involve some of the same sort of rummaging. Furthermore, the District Court has the latitude to control any discovery process which may be instituted so as to balance respondent's need for access to proof which would support a colorable constitutional claim against the extraordinary needs of the CIA for confidentiality and the protection of its methods, sources, and mission.

Petitioner also contends that even if respondent has raised a colorable constitutional claim arising out of his discharge, Congress in the interest of national security may deny the courts the authority to decide the claim and to order respondent's reinstatement if the claim is upheld. For the reasons previously stated, we do not think Congress meant to impose such restrictions when it enacted § 102(c) of the NSA. Even without such prohibitory legislation from Congress, of course, traditional equitable principles requiring the balancing of public and private interests control the grant of declaratory or injunctive relief in the federal courts. On remand, the District Court should thus address respondent's constitutional claims and the propriety of the equitable remedies sought.

The judgment of the Court of Appeals is affirmed in part, reversed in part, and the case is remanded for further proceedings consistent with this opinion.

It is so ordered.

JUSTICE KENNEDY took no part in the consideration or decision of this case.

JUSTICE O'CONNOR, concurring in part and dissenting in part.

I agree that the Administrative Procedure Act (APA) does not authorize judicial review of the employment decisions referred to in § 102(c) of the National Security

Act of 1947. Because § 102(c) does not provide a meaningful standard for judicial review, such decisions are clearly "committed to agency discretion by law" within the meaning of the provision of the APA set forth in 5 U.S.C. § 701(a)(2). I do not understand the Court to say that the exception in § 701(a)(2) is necessarily or fully defined by reference to statutes "drawn in such broad terms that in a given case there is no law to apply." *See Citizens to Preserve Overton Park, Inc. v. Volpe*, 401 U.S. 402, 410 (1971). Accordingly, I join Parts I and II of the Court's opinion.

I disagree, however, with the Court's conclusion that a constitutional claim challenging the validity of an employment decision covered by § 102(c) may nonetheless be brought in a federal district court. Whatever may be the exact scope of Congress' power to close the lower federal courts to constitutional claims in other contexts, I have no doubt about its authority to do so here. The functions performed by the Central Intelligence Agency and the Director of Central Intelligence lie at the core of "the very delicate, plenary and exclusive power of the President as the sole organ of the federal government in the field of international relations." *United States v. Curtiss-Wright Export Corp.*, 299 U.S. 304, 320 (1936). The authority of the Director of Central Intelligence to control access to sensitive national security information by discharging employees deemed to be untrustworthy flows primarily from this constitutional power of the President, and Congress may surely provide that the inferior federal courts are not used to infringe on the President's constitutional authority. Section 102(c) plainly indicates that Congress has done exactly that, and the Court points to nothing in the structure, purpose, or legislative history of the National Security Act that would suggest a different conclusion. Accordingly, I respectfully dissent from the Court's decision to allow this lawsuit to go forward.

Justice Scalia, dissenting.

I agree with the Court's apparent holding in Part II of its opinion that the Director's decision to terminate a CIA employee is "committed to agency discretion by law" within the meaning of 5 U.S.C. § 701(a)(2). . . .

I

Before proceeding to address Part III of the Court's opinion, which I think to be in error, I must discuss one significant element of the analysis in Part II. Though I subscribe to most of that analysis, I disagree with the Court's description of what is required to come within subsection (a)(2) of § 701, which provides that judicial review is unavailable "to the extent that . . . agency action is committed to agency discretion by law." The Court's discussion suggests that the Court of Appeals below was correct in holding that this provision is triggered only when there is "no law to apply." Our precedents amply show that "commit [ment] to agency discretion by law" includes, but is not limited to, situations in which there is "no law to apply."

The Court relies for its "no law to apply" formulation upon our discussion in *Heckler v. Chaney*, 470 U.S. 821 (1985) — which, however, did not apply that as the sole criterion of § 701(a)(2)'s applicability, but to the contrary discussed the subject action's "general unsuitability" for review, and adverted to "tradition, case law, and sound reasoning." 470 U.S., at 831. Moreover, the only supporting authority for the "no law to apply" test cited in *Chaney* was our observation in *Citizens to Preserve Overton Park, Inc. v. Volpe*, 401 U.S. 402 (1971), that "[t]he legislative history of the Administrative Procedure Act indicates that [§ 701(a)(2)] is applicable in those rare instances where 'statutes are drawn in such broad terms that in a given case there is no law to apply.' S.Rep. No. 752, 79th Cong., 1st Sess., 26 (1945)," *id.*, at 410. Perhaps *Overton Park* discussed only the "no law to apply" factor because that was the only basis for nonreviewability that was even arguably applicable. It surely could not have believed that factor to be exclusive, for that would contradict the very legislative history, both cited and quoted in the opinion, from which it had been derived, which read in full: "The basic exception of matters committed to agency discretion would apply even if not stated at the outset [of the judicial review Chapter]. If, *for example*, statutes are drawn in such broad terms that in a given case there is no law to apply, courts of course have no statutory question to review." S.Rep. No. 752, 79th Cong., 1st Sess., 26 (1945) (emphasis added).

The "no law to apply" test can account for the nonreviewability of certain issues, but falls far short of explaining the full scope of the areas from which the courts are excluded. For the fact is that there is no governmental decision that is not subject to a fair number of legal constraints precise enough to be susceptible of judicial application—beginning with the fundamental constraint that the decision must be taken in order to further a public purpose rather than a purely private interest; yet there are many governmental decisions that are not at all subject to judicial review. A United States Attorney's decision to prosecute, for example, will not be reviewed on the claim that it was prompted by personal animosity. Thus, "no law to apply" provides much less than the full answer to whether § 701(a)(2) applies.

The key to understanding the "committed to agency discretion by law" provision of § 701(a)(2) lies in contrasting it with the "statutes preclude judicial review" provision of § 701(a)(1). Why "statutes" for preclusion, but the much more general term "law" for commission to agency discretion? The answer is, as we implied in *Chaney*, that the latter was intended to refer to "the 'common law' of judicial review of agency action," 470 U.S., at 832—a body of jurisprudence that had marked out, with more or less precision, certain issues and certain areas that were beyond the range of judicial review. That jurisprudence included principles ranging from the "political question" doctrine, to sovereign immunity (including doctrines determining when a suit against an officer would be deemed to be a suit against the sovereign), to official immunity, to prudential limitations upon the courts' equitable powers, to what can be described no more precisely than a traditional respect for the functions of the other branches reflected in the statement in *Marbury v. Madison*, 1 Cranch 137, 170–171 (1803), that "[w]here the head of a department acts in a case, in which executive discretion is to be exercised; in which he is the mere organ of executive will; it is again repeated, that any application to a court to control, in any respect, his conduct, would be rejected without hesitation." . . . Only if all that "common law" were embraced within § 701(a)(2) could it have been true that, as was generally understood, "[t]he intended result of [§ 701(a)] is to restate the existing law as to the area of reviewable agency action." Attorney General's Manual on the Administrative Procedure Act 94 (1947). Because that is the meaning of the provision, we have continued to take into account for purposes of determining reviewability, post-APA as before, not only the text and structure of the statute under which the agency acts, but such factors as whether the decision involves "a sensitive and inherently discretionary judgment call," *Department of Navy v. Egan*, 484 U.S. 518, 527 (1988), whether it is the sort of decision that has traditionally been nonreviewable, *ICC v. Locomotive Engineers*, 482 U.S. 270, 282 (1987); *Chaney, supra*, 470 U.S., at 832, and whether review would have "disruptive practical consequences," see *Southern R. Co. v. Seaboard Allied Milling Corp.*, 442 U.S. 444, 457 (1979). This explains the seeming contradiction between § 701(a)(2)'s disallowance of review to the extent that action is "committed to agency discretion," and § 706's injunction that a court shall set aside agency action that constitutes "an abuse of discretion." Since, in the former provision, "committed to agency discretion by law" means "of the sort that is traditionally unreviewable," it operates to keep certain categories of agency action out of the courts; but when agency action is appropriately in the courts, abuse of discretion is of course grounds for reversal.

All this law, shaped over the course of centuries and still developing in its application to new contexts, cannot possibly be contained within the phrase "no law to apply." It is not surprising, then, that although the Court recites the test it does not really apply it. Like other opinions relying upon it, this one essentially announces the test, declares victory and moves on. It is not really true "'that a court would have no meaningful standard against which to judge the agency's exercise of discretion,'" *ante*, quoting *Chaney*, 470 U.S., at 830. The standard set forth in § 102(c) of the National Security Act of 1947, 50 U.S.C. § 403(c), "necessary or advisable in the interests of the United States," at least excludes dismissal out of personal vindictiveness, or because the Director wants to give the job to his cousin. Why, on the Court's theory, is respondent not entitled to assert the presence of such excesses, under the "abuse of discretion" standard of § 706?

II

Before taking the reader through the terrain of the Court's holding that respondent may assert constitutional claims in this suit, I would like to try to clear some of the underbrush, consisting primarily of the Court's ominous warning that "[a] 'serious constitutional question' . . . would arise if a federal statute were construed to deny any judicial forum for a colorable constitutional claim."

The first response to the Court's grave doubt about the constitutionality of denying all judicial review to a "colorable constitutional claim" is that the denial of all judicial review is not at issue here, but merely the denial of review in United States district courts. As to that, the law is, and has long been, clear. Article III, § 2, of the Constitution extends the judicial power to "all Cases . . . arising under this Constitution." But Article III, § 1, provides that the judicial power shall be vested "in one supreme Court, and in such inferior Courts as the Congress may from time to time ordain and establish" (emphasis added). We long ago held that the power not to create any lower federal courts at all includes the power to invest them with less than all of the judicial power. . . .

Thus, if there is any truth to the proposition that judicial cognizance of constitutional claims cannot be eliminated, it is, at most, that they cannot be eliminated from state courts, and from this Court's appellate jurisdiction over cases from state courts (or cases from federal courts, should there be any) involving such claims. Narrowly viewed, therefore, there is no shadow of a constitutional doubt that we are free to hold that the present suit, whether based on constitutional grounds or not, will not lie.

It can fairly be argued, however, that our interpretation of § 701(a)(2) indirectly implicates the constitutional question whether state courts can be deprived of jurisdiction, because if they cannot, then interpreting § 701(a)(2) to exclude relief here would impute to Congress the peculiar intent to let state courts review Federal Government action that it is unwilling to let federal district courts review—or, alternatively, the peculiar intent to let federal district courts review, upon removal from state courts pursuant to 28 U.S.C. § 1442(a)(1), claims that it is unwilling to let federal district courts review in original actions. I turn, then, to the substance of the Court's warning that judicial review of all "colorable constitutional claims" arising out of the respondent's dismissal may well be constitutionally required. What could possibly be the basis for this fear? Surely not some general principle that all constitutional violations must be remediable in the courts. The very text of the Constitution refutes that principle, since it provides that "[e]ach House shall be the Judge of the Elections, Returns and Qualifications of its own Members," Art. I, § 5, and that "for any Speech or Debate in either House, [the Senators and Representatives] shall not be questioned in any other Place," Art. I, § 6. Claims concerning constitutional violations committed in these contexts—for example, the rather grave constitutional claim that an election has been stolen—cannot be addressed to the courts. Even apart from the strict text of the Constitution, we have found some constitutional claims to be beyond judicial review because they involve "political questions." The doctrine of sovereign immunity—not repealed by the Constitution, but to the contrary at least partly reaffirmed as to the States by the Eleventh Amendment—is a monument to the principle that some constitutional claims can go unheard. No one would suggest that, if Congress had not passed the Tucker Act, 28 U.S.C. § 1491(a)(1), the courts would be able to order disbursements from the Treasury to pay for property taken under lawful authority (and subsequently destroyed) without just compensation. And finally, the doctrine of equitable discretion, which permits a court to refuse relief, even where no relief at law is available, when that would unduly impair the public interest, does not stand aside simply because the basis for the relief is a constitutional claim. In sum, it is simply untenable that there must be a judicial remedy for every constitutional violation. Members of Congress and the supervising officers of the Executive Branch take the same oath to uphold the Constitution that we do, and sometimes they are left to perform that oath unreviewed, as we always are.

Perhaps, then, the Court means to appeal to a more limited principle, that although there may be areas where judicial review of a constitutional claim will be denied, the scope of those areas is fixed by the Constitution and judicial tradition, and cannot be affected by Congress, through the enactment of a statute such as § 102(c). That would be a rather counter-intuitive principle, especially since Congress has in reality been the principal determiner of the scope of review, for constitutional claims as well as all other claims, through its waiver of the pre-existing doctrine of sovereign immunity. On the merits of the point, however: It seems to me clear that courts would not entertain, for example, an action for backpay by a dismissed Secretary of State claiming that the reason he lost his Government job was that the President did not like his religious views — surely a colorable violation of the First Amendment. I am confident we would hold that the President's choice of his Secretary of State is a "political question." But what about a similar suit by the Deputy Secretary of State? Or one of the Under Secretaries? Or an Assistant Secretary? Or the head of the European Desk? Is there really a constitutional line that falls at some immutable point between one and another of these offices at which the principle of unreviewability cuts in, and which cannot be altered by congressional prescription? I think not. I think Congress can prescribe, at least within broad limits, that for certain jobs the dismissal decision will be unreviewable — that is, will be "committed to agency discretion by law."

Once it is acknowledged, as I think it must be, (1) that not all constitutional claims require a judicial remedy, and (2) that the identification of those that do not can, even if only within narrow limits, be determined by Congress, then it is clear that the "serious constitutional question" feared by the Court is an illusion. . . .

I think it entirely beyond doubt that if Congress intended, by the APA in 5 U.S.C. § 701(a)(2), to exclude judicial review of the President's decision (through the Director of Central Intelligence) to dismiss an officer of the Central Intelligence Agency, that disposition would be constitutionally permissible.

III

I turn, then, to whether that executive action is, within the meaning of § 701(a)(2), "committed to agency discretion by law." My discussion of this point can be brief, because the answer is compellingly obvious. . . . Given th[e] statutory text, and given (as discussed above) that the area to which the text pertains is one of predominant executive authority and of traditional judicial abstention, it is difficult to conceive of a statutory scheme that more clearly reflects that "commit[ment] to agency discretion by law" to which § 701(a)(2) refers.

It is baffling to observe that the Court seems to agree with the foregoing assessment, holding that "the language and structure of § 102(c) indicate that Congress meant to commit individual employee discharges to the Director's discretion."

Nevertheless, without explanation the Court reaches the conclusion that "a constitutional claim based on an individual discharge may be reviewed by the District Court." It seems to me the Court is attempting the impossible feat of having its cake and eating it too. . . .

Perhaps, then, a constitutional right is by its nature so much more important to the claimant than a statutory right that a statute which plainly excludes the latter should not be read to exclude the former unless it says so. That principle has never been announced—and with good reason, because its premise is not true. An individual's contention that the Government has reneged upon a $100,000 debt owing under a contract is much more important to him—both financially and, I suspect, in the sense of injustice that he feels—than the same individual's claim that a particular federal licensing provision requiring a $100 license denies him equal protection of the laws, or that a particular state tax violates the Commerce Clause. A citizen would much rather have his statutory entitlement correctly acknowledged after a constitutionally inadequate hearing, than have it incorrectly denied after a proceeding that fulfills all the requirements of the Due Process Clause. . . .

Today's result, however, will have ramifications far beyond creation of the world's only secret intelligence agency that must litigate the dismissal of its agents. If constitutional claims can be raised in this highly sensitive context, it is hard to imagine where they cannot. The assumption that there are any executive decisions that cannot be hauled into the courts may no longer be valid. Also obsolete may be the assumption that we are capable of preserving a sensible common law of judicial review.

I respectfully dissent.

Notes on Statutory Preclusion under § 701(a)(1)

1. Statutory preclusion can be harder than you might think. Recall that § 701(a)(1) states that Congress can preclude judicial review simply by enacting a statute to this effect. Be aware, however, that statutory language that looks on its surface like an attempt to preclude judicial review must be handled with care. The case law is littered with examples of courts straining to construe statutory language to allow judicial review. They are, after all, courts.

DeMore v. Hyung Joon Kim, 538 U.S. 510 (2003), provides a revealing example of this dynamic. 8 U.S.C. § 1226(c) states that, where an alien has been convicted of certain crimes, the Attorney General shall "take into custody" that alien pending removal proceedings. No bail is allowed. Kim, a lawful permanent resident alien, filed a habeas petition in which he claimed that INS's mandatory detention of him pending removal proceedings violated due process because INS "had made no determination that he posed either a danger to society or a flight risk." The possibility of express preclusion reared its head because § 1226(e) provides:

(e) Judicial Review

The Attorney General's discretionary judgment regarding the application of this section shall not be subject to review. No court may set aside any action or decision by the Attorney General under this section regarding the detention or release of any alien or the grant, revocation, or denial of bond or parole.

Six members of the Court agreed that this subsection did *not* preclude habeas review of Kim's constitutional claim, observing "respondent does not challenge a 'discretionary judgment' by the Attorney General or a 'decision' that the Attorney General has made regarding his detention or release. Rather, respondent challenges the statutory framework that permits his detention without bail." Recall from *Webster* that the Court will not interpret a statute to preclude judicial review absent a clear statement of congressional intent to this effect. The Court relied upon this clear statement rule, which the Court added applies with special force to preclusion of habeas review, to justify its conclusion that Kim's claim was reviewable.

Justice O'Connor (joined by Justices Scalia and Thomas) disagreed, and, in partial dissent, stated that "the signal sent by Congress in enacting § 1226(e) could not be clearer: '*No court* may set aside *any action or decision* . . . regarding the detention or release of any alien.' (Emphasis added [by Justice O'Connor]). There is simply no reasonable way to read this language other than as precluding all review, including habeas review, of the Attorney General's actions or decisions to detain criminal aliens pursuant to § 1226(c)."

The majority's efforts to avoid statutory preclusion in *DeMore* reflected the importance of protecting the role of courts in policing executive detention via habeas. This impulse reflects a broader theme that courts' determinations regarding statutory preclusion are sensitive to judicial perceptions of the importance of judicial review for a particular legal domain. In a leading law review article on statutory preclusion, Professor Ronald Levin offered the following summary of judicial tendencies regarding statutory preclusion:

> A critical reading of recent case law under section 701(a)(1) of the APA, which gives effect to statutory preclusion provisions, indicates that the Court tends to allow some issues to be precluded more readily than other issues. At the top of the scale, as *Doe* illustrates, the presumption against preclusion of constitutional grievances against an agency is practically irrebuttable. The Court also has proved less willing to find preclusion in cases involving administrative rules than in cases involving agency adjudication, and less willing to foreclose legal challenges than factual ones, especially where the legal issues are not within the administering agency's expertise. At the bottom of the hierarchy are issues of fact and application of law to fact, which the Court allows to be precluded more readily than any others.

Ronald M. Levin, *Understanding Unreviewability in Administrative Law*, 74 MINN. L. REV. 689, 739–40 (1990).

2. Implied statutory preclusion. Given that courts often strain to avoid interpreting express statutory language to preclude judicial review, you might think that courts

would never conclude that a statute precludes judicial review by implication—
but every now and then they do. For a leading example, consider *Block v. Community Nutrition Inst.*, 467 U.S. 340 (1984), which raised the question of "whether ultimate consumers of dairy products may obtain judicial review of milk market orders issued by the Secretary of Agriculture (Secretary) under the authority of the Agricultural Marketing Agreement Act of 1937 (Act)." Milk market orders are the product of a complex regulatory scheme designed to support milk prices payable to producers—*i.e.*, keep them higher than they would be if subject to the market's "destabilizing competition." Such orders therefore fly in the face of the consumer interest in obtaining milk on the cheap. Both milk producers and milk "handlers" (who process the milk into products sold to ultimate consumers) have the right to participate in the proceedings that produce milk market orders. A producer or handler who does not like how a milk market order turns out can seek review from the Secretary. The statute provides that a handler may not seek judicial review until it has exhausted its administrative remedies within the agency. By contrast, the regulatory scheme does not allow for consumer participation in the fashioning of milk market orders, nor does it expressly contemplate that consumers will seek administrative review of such orders.

The Community Nutrition Institute sued to challenge a milk market order anyway. The gist of its complaint was that the order made it uneconomic for milk handlers to process reconstituted milk—to the detriment of consumers. The Supreme Court held that this suit was blocked by statutory preclusion even though the statutory scheme contained no express language to this effect. The Court explained:

> The Act contemplates a cooperative venture among the Secretary, handlers, and producers the principal purposes of which are to raise the price of agricultural products and to establish an orderly system for marketing them. Handlers and producers—but not consumers—are entitled to participate in the adoption and retention of market orders. 7 U.S.C. §§ 608c(8), (9), (16)(B). The Act provides for agreements among the Secretary, producers, and handlers, 7 U.S.C. § 608(2), for hearings among them, §§ 608(5), 608c(3), and for votes by producers and handlers, §§ 608c(8)(A), (9)(B), (12), 608c(19). Nowhere in the Act, however, is there an express provision for participation by consumers in any proceeding. In a complex scheme of this type, the omission of such a provision is sufficient reason to believe that Congress intended to foreclose consumer participation in the regulatory process. . . .
>
> Allowing consumers to sue the Secretary would severely disrupt this complex and delicate administrative scheme. It would provide handlers with a convenient device for evading the statutory requirement that they first exhaust their administrative remedies. A handler may also be a consumer and, as such, could sue in that capacity. Alternatively, a handler would need only to find a consumer who is willing to join in or initiate an action in

the district court. The consumer or consumer-handler could then raise precisely the same exceptions that the handler must raise administratively. Consumers or consumer-handlers could seek injunctions against the operation of market orders that "impede, hinder, or delay" enforcement actions, even though such injunctions are expressly prohibited in proceedings properly instituted under 7 U.S.C. § 608c(15). Suits of this type would effectively nullify Congress' intent to establish an "equitable and expeditious procedure for testing the validity of orders, without hampering the Government's power to enforce compliance with their terms." S.Rep. No. 1011, 74th Cong., 1st Sess., 14 (1935). . . . For these reasons, we think it clear that Congress intended that judicial review of market orders issued under the Act ordinarily be confined to suits brought by handlers in accordance with 7 U.S.C. § 608c(15). . . .

The presumption favoring judicial review of administrative action is just that—a presumption. This presumption, like all presumptions used in interpreting statutes, may be overcome by specific language or specific legislative history that is a reliable indicator of congressional intent. . . . The congressional intent necessary to overcome the presumption may also be inferred from contemporaneous judicial construction barring review and the congressional acquiescence in it . . . or from the collective import of legislative and judicial history behind a particular statute. More important for purposes of this case, the presumption favoring judicial review of administrative action may be overcome by inferences of intent drawn from the statutory scheme as a whole. In particular, at least when a statute provides a detailed mechanism for judicial consideration of particular issues at the behest of particular persons, judicial review of those issues at the behest of other persons may be found to be impliedly precluded.

Id. at 346–49. *But cf. Sackett v. EPA*, 132 S. Ct. 1367, 1373 (2012) (rejecting argument that express authorization in Clean Water Act of judicial review of administrative penalties precluded judicial review of administrative compliance orders, noting that "if the express provision of judicial review in one section of a long and complicated statute were alone enough to overcome the APA's presumption of reviewability for all final agency action, it would not be much of a presumption at all").

3. Exclusivity of special statutory review proceedings. As we have seen, agency enabling acts often contain provisions creating special statutory review proceedings for judicial review of various agency actions. Section 9 of the WTCA provides a handy example of this practice. In addition to authorizing judicial review, a special statutory review provision may preclude other paths to review—e.g., if you can use a specific template for review created in an agency's enabling act, then you may not be able to use the APA's right of action or nonstatutory review.

In *Free Enterprise Fund v. Public Company Accounting Oversight Bd.*, 561 U.S. 477 (2010), the Court explained its framework for determining the exclusivity of special statutory review proceedings. The plaintiff in this case alleged that the Public Company Accounting Board (Board) was unconstitutional in part due to limitations on the power of the President to remove Board members. The Board's actions are subject to extensive control by the Securities and Exchange Commission (Commission), which has authority to review any Board rule or sanction. An aggrieved party may seek judicial review of the Commission's final orders or rules. 15 U.S.C. § 78y. A person disappointed by a Board action might thus appeal to the Commission and, if disappointed by the Commission's ruling, appeal again to the courts. The Court rejected the government's contention that this indirect statutory path to judicial review of Board actions was the exclusive route:

> Provisions for agency review do not restrict judicial review unless the "statutory scheme" displays a "fairly discernible" intent to limit jurisdiction, and the claims at issue "are of the type Congress intended to be reviewed within th[e] statutory structure." *Thunder Basin Coal Co. v. Reich*, 510 U.S. 200, 207, 212 (1994) (internal quotation marks omitted). Generally, when Congress creates procedures "designed to permit agency expertise to be brought to bear on particular problems," those procedures "are to be exclusive." *Whitney Nat. Bank in Jefferson Parish v. Bank of New Orleans & Trust Co.*, 379 U.S. 411, 420 (1965). But we presume that Congress does not intend to limit jurisdiction if "a finding of preclusion could foreclose all meaningful judicial review"; if the suit is "wholly collateral to a statute's review provisions"; and if the claims are "outside the agency's expertise." *Thunder Basin, supra*, at 212–213 (internal quotation marks omitted). These considerations point against any limitation on review here.

561 U.S. at 489–90.

To use the special statutory review scheme of § 78y to challenge the constitutionality of the Board, the plaintiffs could either: (1) choose a Board rule to challenge before the SEC, obtain a negative result, and then challenge that result in court; or (2) incur a Board sanction, appeal that sanction to the SEC, obtain a negative result, and then challenge that result in court. In the Supreme Court's view, neither of these circuitous paths was acceptable—in particular, the Court noted that it does not usually require plaintiffs to "'bet the farm . . . by taking the violative action' before testing the validity of the law." *Id.* at 490. The plaintiffs' claim, which was directed at the structure of the Board, was "collateral" to the review provisions of § 78y, which provide for review of Commission orders and rules. In addition, the plaintiffs' constitutional arguments did not implicate the agency's special expertise, but instead presented "standard questions of administrative law, which the courts are at no disadvantage in answering." *Id.* at 491. *Cf. Elgin v. Dept. of Treasury*, 567 U.S. 1 (2012) (applying *Free Enterprise* factors; holding that the Civil Service Reform Act, which creates an "elaborate" framework of "painstaking detail" for review by the Merit Systems Protection Board and the Federal Circuit of adverse employment actions, precluded jurisdiction in federal district court over constitutional claims).

Notes on "Committed to Agency Discretion" Preclusion under § 701(a)(2)

4. Is there ever "no law to apply"? You have now seen two instances where the Court has purported to apply its "no law to apply" standard to § 701(a)(2) analysis — *Overton Park* and *Webster.* Is there *ever* "no law to apply"? If the "no law to apply" principle is not driving the cases, what is?

5. Reconciling § 701(a)(2) and § 706(2)(A). Recall that § 706(2)(A) instructs courts to set aside agency actions for "abuse of discretion" yet § 701(a)(2) provides that agency actions "committed to agency discretion" by law are unreviewable. How are we to reconcile these two seemingly contradictory propositions? On this point, the Supreme Court recently advised:

> This Court has noted the "tension" between the prohibition of judicial review for actions "committed to agency discretion" and the command in § 706(2)(A) that courts set aside any agency action that is "arbitrary, capricious, an abuse of discretion, or otherwise not in accordance with law." *Heckler v. Chaney,* 470 U.S. 821, 829 (1985). A court could never determine that an agency abused its discretion if all matters committed to agency discretion were unreviewable. To give effect to § 706(2)(A) and to honor the presumption of review, we have read the exception in § 701(a)(2) quite narrowly, restricting it to "those rare circumstances where the relevant statute is drawn so that a court would have no meaningful standard against which to judge the agency's exercise of discretion." *Lincoln v. Vigil,* 508 U.S. 182, 191 (1993). The [Fish and Wildlife] Service contends that Section 4(b)(2) of the ESA is one of those rare statutory provisions.
>
> There is, at the outset, reason to be skeptical of the Service's position. The few cases in which we have applied the § 701(a)(2) exception involved agency decisions that courts have traditionally regarded as unreviewable, such as the allocation of funds from a lump-sum appropriation, *Lincoln,* 508 U.S., at 191, or a decision not to reconsider a final action, *ICC v. Locomotive Engineers,* 482 U.S. 270, 282 (1987). By contrast, this case involves the sort of routine dispute that federal courts regularly review: An agency issues an order affecting the rights of a private party, and the private party objects that the agency did not properly justify its determination under a standard set forth in the statute.

Weyerhauser Co. v. United States Fish and Wildlife Service, 139 S. Ct. 361, 370 (2018).

So, we have two types of discretion. There is what we might call "run of the mill" discretion, which is subject to review under § 706(2)(A), and there is exceptional discretion, which is protected from judicial review by § 701(a)(2). This exceptional discretion is "rare." To determine whether a particular agency action implicates it, the *Weyerhauser* Court instructs us to look to whether the relevant statute provides "no meaningful standard against which to judge the agency's discretion." In other words, we still look to whether there is "no law to apply." This instruction continues to be problematic insofar as there is always some law lying around for a willing court to apply (or, in effect, create). The "no law to apply" idea does, however, emphasize the narrowness of the protected category of unreviewable discretion. Consistent with Justice Scalia's opinion in *Webster*, the *Weyerhauser* Court also notes that past judicial practice plays a role in the analysis — *i.e.*, the Court has used § 701(a)(2) to knock out review of actions that "courts have traditionally regarded as unreviewable."

In *Weyerhauser* itself, the Court had little trouble determining that the agency action at issue implicated run-of-the-mill discretion unprotected by § 701(a)(2). Landowners had challenged a decision by the Fish and Wildlife Service (Service) refusing to exclude their property from "critical habitat" that the Service had designated for preservation of the dusky gopher frog. Section 4(b)(2) of the Endangered Species Act provides that the Secretary

> shall designate critical habitat . . . after taking into consideration the economic impact, the impact on national security, and any other relevant impact, of specifying any particular area as critical habitat. The Secretary may exclude any area from critical habitat if he determines that the benefits of such exclusion outweigh the benefits of specifying such area . . . unless he determines . . . that the failure to designate such area as critical habitat will result in the extinction of the species concerned.

16 U.S.C. § 1533(b)(2).

The Court conceded that the use of "may" in the second sentence of this provision "certainly confers discretion on the Secretary." 139 S. Ct. at 371. The dispositive point, however, was that the first sentence expressly "directs the Secretary to consider the economic and other impacts of designation when making his exclusion decisions." *Id.* Before exercising whatever discretion the "may" in the second sentence might impart, the Secretary had a legal obligation to follow the instructions of the first sentence. Weyerhauser claimed that the Service had ignored certain costs and overstated benefits in its analysis. The statute provided a "meaningful standard" for judging this claim, and § 701(a)(2) therefore did not block review.

6. Presumptive unreviewability of refusals to enforce. In the *Doe* excerpt above, there is a good deal of discussion of another critical case from the § 701(a)(2) canon — *Heckler v. Chaney*, 470 U.S. 821 (1985). In this case, prisoners sentenced to death petitioned the FDA to block the use of certain drugs for lethal injection. They contended, among other things, that although the FDA had approved these drugs for other uses, it had not approved them for use in human executions, and that the agency had an obligation to approve such use as "safe and effective." The FDA denied the petition, explaining that (a) its jurisdiction was unclear in this area; (b) its jurisdiction should not be exercised to interfere with state criminal justice systems; and (c) the agency would, even if its jurisdiction were clear, have declined to exercise it absent a "serious danger to public health or a blatant scheme to defraud." (Note that the FDA's affirmative denial of the petition distinguishes this case from the "failure to act" case we encountered earlier in this chapter, *Norton v. Southern Utah Wilderness Alliance*, in which the agency was accused of failing to implement its statutory and regulatory obligations.)

As the Court styled it, "this case turns on the important question of the extent to which determinations by the FDA *not to exercise* its enforcement authority over the use of drugs in interstate commerce may be judicially reviewed." The FDA contended that such decisions were not reviewable because they were "committed to agency discretion by law" under § 701(a)(2). The Court's analysis of this contention follows:

> . . . This Court has recognized on several occasions over many years that an agency's decision not to prosecute or enforce, whether through civil or criminal process, is a decision generally committed to an agency's absolute discretion. This recognition of the existence of discretion is attributable in no small part to the general unsuitability for judicial review of agency decisions to refuse enforcement.
>
> The reasons for this general unsuitability are many. First, an agency decision not to enforce often involves a complicated balancing of a number of factors which are peculiarly within its expertise. Thus, the agency must not only assess whether a violation has occurred, but whether agency resources are best spent on this violation or another, whether the agency is likely to succeed if it acts, whether the particular enforcement action requested best fits the agency's overall policies, and, indeed, whether the agency has enough resources to undertake the action at all. An agency generally cannot act against each technical violation of the statute it is charged with enforcing. The agency is far better equipped than the courts to deal with the many variables involved in the proper ordering of its priorities. . . .
>
> In addition to these administrative concerns, we note that when an agency refuses to act it generally does not exercise its coercive power over an individual's liberty or property rights, and thus does not infringe upon areas that courts often are called upon to protect. Similarly, when an agency does act to enforce, that action itself provides a focus for judicial review, inasmuch as the agency must have exercised its power in some manner. The action at least can be reviewed to determine whether the agency exceeded its statutory powers. Finally, we recognize that an agency's refusal to institute proceedings shares to some extent the characteristics of the decision of a prosecutor in the Executive Branch not to indict—a decision which has long been regarded as the special province of the Executive Branch, inasmuch as it is the Executive who is charged by the Constitution to "take Care that the Laws be faithfully executed."
>
> We of course only list the above concerns to facilitate understanding of our conclusion that an agency's decision not to take enforcement action should be presumed immune from judicial review under § 701(a)(2). For good

reasons, such a decision has traditionally been "committed to agency discretion," and we believe that the Congress enacting the APA did not intend to alter that tradition. In so stating, we emphasize that the decision is only presumptively unreviewable; the presumption may be rebutted where the substantive statute has provided guidelines for the agency to follow in exercising its enforcement powers. Thus, in establishing this presumption in the APA Congress did not set agencies free to disregard legislative direction in the statutory scheme that the agency administers. Congress may limit an agency's exercise of enforcement power if it wishes, either by setting substantive priorities, or by otherwise circumscribing an agency's power to discriminate among issues or cases it will pursue. How to determine when Congress has done so is the question left open by *Overton Park*.

After setting forth this analytical framework, the Court observed that the pertinent provision of the FDC Act relating to enforcement provided only that "[t]he Secretary is *authorized* to conduct examinations and investigations." This permissive language was insufficient to overcome the presumption of non-reviewability for decisions not to enforce.

Putting to one side the legal framework of *Chaney, should* agency decisions not to act be reviewable? Absent such review, what can force a recalcitrant agency to do its job?

7. (Not) committed to agency discretion by law—reviewability of refusals to initiate rulemaking. The Court was careful to note in *Chaney* that the case before it did not "involve the question of agency discretion not to invoke rulemaking proceedings." 470 U.S. at 825 n.2. A longtime leading case on this point is *American Horse Protection Ass'n, Inc. v. Lyng*, 812 F.2d 1 (D.C. Cir. 1987), which discussed the reviewability of the Secretary of Agriculture's refusal to initiate rulemaking to control "soring," the practice of deliberately injuring show horses to force them to use a desired gait. The D.C. Circuit explained why, notwithstanding *Chaney*, this refusal was reviewable—albeit under a highly deferential standard:

The *Chaney* Court relied on three features of nonenforcement decisions in arriving at its negative presumption. First, such decisions require a high level of agency expertise and coordination in setting priorities. Second, the agency in such situations will not ordinarily be exercising "its *coercive* power over an individual's liberty or property rights." Third, such nonenforcement decisions are akin to prosecutorial decisions not to indict, which traditionally involve executive control and judicial restraint. The first and second of these features are likely to be involved in an agency's refusal to institute a rulemaking, but the third is another matter.

Chaney says little about this third feature. To a degree, of course, it recapitulates and underscores the prior points about resource allocation and non-coercion. The analogy between prosecutorial discretion and agency nonenforcement is strengthened, however, by two other shared characteristics. First, both prosecutors and agencies constantly make decisions not to take enforcement steps; such decisions thus are numerous. Second, both types of nonenforcement are typically based mainly on close consideration of the facts of the case at hand, rather than on legal analysis. Refusals to institute rulemakings, by contrast, are likely to be relatively infrequent and more likely to turn upon issues of law. . . .

Furthermore, the Administrative Procedure Act ("APA") serves to distinguish between *Chaney* nonenforcement decisions and refusals to institute rulemakings. The *Chaney* Court noted that "when an agency *does* act to enforce, that action itself provides a focus for judicial review" since a court can "at least . . . determine whether the agency exceeded its statutory powers." APA provisions governing agency refusals to initiate rulemakings give a similar focal point. The APA requires agencies to allow interested persons to "petition for the issuance, amendment, or repeal of a rule," 5 U.S.C. § 553(e), and, when such petitions are denied, to give "a brief statement of the grounds for denial," *id.* § 555(e). These two provisions suggest that Congress expected that agencies denying rulemaking petitions must explain their actions.

Thus, refusals to institute rulemaking proceedings are distinguishable from other sorts of nonenforcement decisions insofar as they are less frequent, more apt to involve legal as opposed to factual analysis, and subject to special formalities, including a public explanation. *Chaney* therefore does not appear to overrule our prior decisions allowing review of agency refusals to institute rulemakings.

In the blockbuster global warming case, *Massachusetts v. EPA*, 549 U.S. 497, 527 (2007), the Supreme Court, citing *Lyng*, agreed that "[r]efusals to promulgate rules are . . . susceptible to judicial review, though such review is 'extremely limited' and 'highly deferential.'"

D. Who Gets to Sue — Standing

In this section, we examine three doctrines all of which go under the name "standing." Two of these doctrines — constitutional standing and prudential standing — limit who can sue in federal court. According to the Supreme Court, constitutional standing doctrine flows from Article III's limitation of the judicial power to resolution of cases and controversies. Therefore, a plaintiff who lacks constitutional standing cannot invoke the federal judicial power even if Congress seems to have granted that plaintiff a statutory right to review. By contrast, courts admit that prudential standing's limits on who can sue are judicial creations rather than constitutionally required. Congress, therefore, can trump prudential standing by statute. The line between constitutional and prudential standing has long been fuzzy. This difficulty may soon be a thing of the past, however, because the Supreme

Court has in recent years called into question the courts' authority to impose prudential limits on standing.

The third doctrine, which sometimes goes by the name "statutory standing," is quite different. Rather than speaking to the issue of whether a given plaintiff is blocked from suing by the Constitution or the courts, this doctrine speaks to whether the legislature has authorized a plaintiff to sue. Put another way, statutory standing speaks to whether the legislature has granted a plaintiff a cause of action. In the context of administrative law, the most important statutory grant of a cause of action lies in §702, which allows a plaintiff to challenge agency action provided she has been "adversely affected or aggrieved within the meaning of a relevant statute."

1. Constitutional Standing

The black letter of this doctrine is trivially easy to state. Simplifying somewhat, a plaintiff must have suffered an "injury in fact," this injury must be fairly traceable to the defendant's conduct, and it must be likely that a favorable court decision would provide redress for this injury.

Despite this surface simplicity, the doctrine of constitutional standing is notoriously slippery in theory and application. One root of this problem is that the justices of the Supreme Court are sharply divided over the purpose of constitutional standing doctrine. In part for this reason, they cannot agree on the meaning of "injury." Their judgments also vary regarding how strong a case a plaintiff must make on causation and redressability. As a result, many insist that the law of constitutional standing is an incoherent, politicized mess. Decide if you agree after reading the case and notes that follow.

Lesson 5D.1. The Wrath for Grapes, a citizens' group devoted to promoting temperance, petitioned the WTC for a rule requiring that each bottle of wine sold bear a label containing a clear warning that specifically identifies all major health and safety problems caused by alcohol consumption as well as the number of deaths each of these problems causes per year. The WTC denied the Wrath's petition. The Board of the Wrath is considering challenging this denial. Advise whether they likely would have *constitutional* standing to do so.

Background of *Lujan v. Defenders of Wildlife*

The Endangered Species Act (ESA) requires federal agencies to consult with the Secretary of the Interior to ensure that their actions do not "jeopardize the continued existence" of species that have been listed as threatened or endangered. On its merits, the *Lujan* case raised the question of how far this consultation requirement reaches around the world. During the Carter administration, a rule was promulgated extending this duty of consultation to agency actions in foreign countries. During the Reagan administration, a new rule restricted extra-territorial applicability of the consultation requirement to actions taken on the high seas. Environmental groups, including Defenders of Wildlife (Defenders), challenged the new regulation, which the Eighth Circuit threw out for contradicting the "plain language" of the ESA. The plaintiffs' victory did not last, however, as the Supreme Court reversed the Eighth Circuit on the threshold issue of constitutional standing without reaching the merits. The fundamental problem with the suit, according to the majority, was that the plaintiffs had not suffered the right type of "injury" necessary to create the "case or controversy" constitutionally required for federal courts to exercise judicial power. But wait: The plaintiff environmental groups were formed to protect wildlife, and no doubt many of their members found the new rule upsetting. Why not concede that anyone who finds illegal government action sufficiently upsetting to sue to fix it has been "injured" sufficiently to satisfy constitutional standing?

Lujan v. Defenders of Wildlife

504 U.S. 555 (1992)

Justice Scalia delivered the opinion of the Court with respect to Parts I, II, III-A, and IV, and an opinion with respect to Part III-B in which the Chief Justice, Justice White, and Justice Thomas join.

This case involves a challenge to a rule promulgated by the Secretary of the Interior interpreting § 7 of the Endangered Species Act of 1973 (ESA), in such fashion as to render it applicable only to actions within the United States or on the high seas. The preliminary issue, and the only one we reach, is whether the respondents here, plaintiffs below, have standing to seek judicial review of the rule.

I

The ESA seeks to protect species of animals against threats to their continuing existence caused by man. The ESA instructs the Secretary of the Interior to promulgate by regulation a list of those species which are either endangered or threatened under enumerated criteria, and to define the critical habitat of these species. Section 7(a)(2) of the Act then provides, in pertinent part:

> "Each Federal agency shall, in consultation with and with the assistance of the Secretary [of the Interior], insure that any action authorized, funded, or carried out by such agency . . . is not likely to jeopardize the continued existence of any endangered species or threatened species or result in the destruction or adverse modification of habitat of such species which is determined by the Secretary, after consultation as appropriate with affected States, to be critical." 16 U.S.C. § 1536(a)(2).

In 1978, the Fish and Wildlife Service (FWS) and the National Marine Fisheries Service (NMFS), on behalf of the Secretary of the Interior and the Secretary of Commerce respectively, promulgated a joint regulation stating that the obligations imposed by § 7(a)(2) extend to actions taken in foreign nations. The next year, however, the Interior Department began to reexamine its position. A revised joint regulation, reinterpreting § 7(a)(2) to require consultation only for actions taken in the United States or on the high seas, was proposed in 1983.

Shortly thereafter, respondents, organizations dedicated to wildlife conservation and other environmental causes, filed this action against the Secretary of the Interior, seeking a declaratory judgment that the new regulation is in error as to the geographic scope of § 7(a)(2), and an injunction requiring the Secretary to promulgate a new regulation restoring the initial interpretation. . . . The District Court denied the Secretary's motion [for summary judgment on the standing issue]. . . . The Eighth Circuit affirmed. . . .

II

While the Constitution of the United States divides all power conferred upon the Federal Government into "legislative Powers," Art. I, § 1, "[t]he executive Power," Art. II, § 1, and "[t]he judicial Power," Art. III, § 1, it does not attempt to define those terms. To be sure, it limits the jurisdiction of federal courts to "Cases" and "Controversies," but an executive inquiry can bear the name "case" (the Hoffa case) and a legislative dispute can bear the name "controversy" (the Smoot-Hawley controversy). Obviously, then, the Constitution's central mechanism of separation of powers depends largely upon common understanding of what activities are appropriate to legislatures, to executives, and to courts. . . . One of those landmarks, setting apart the "Cases" and "Controversies" that are of the justiciable sort referred to in Article III — "serv[ing] to identify those disputes which are appropriately resolved through the judicial process," *Whitmore v. Arkansas* (1990) — is the doctrine of standing. Though some of its elements express merely prudential considerations that are part of judicial self-government, the core component of standing is an essential and unchanging part of the case-or-controversy requirement of Article III.

Over the years, our cases have established that the irreducible constitutional minimum of standing contains three elements: First, the plaintiff must have suffered an "injury in fact" — an invasion of a legally-protected interest which is (a) concrete and particularized,[1] and (b) "actual or imminent, not 'conjectural' or 'hypothetical.'" Second, there must be a causal connection between the injury and the conduct complained of — the injury has to be "fairly . . . trace[able] to the challenged action of the defendant, and not . . . th[e] result [of] the independent action of some third party not before the court." Third, it must be "likely," as opposed to merely "speculative," that the injury will be "redressed by a favorable decision."

The party invoking federal jurisdiction bears the burden of establishing these elements. Since they are not mere pleading requirements but rather an indispensable part of the plaintiff's case, each element must be supported in the same way as any other matter on which the plaintiff bears the burden of proof, *i.e.*, with the manner and degree of evidence required at the successive stages of the litigation. At the pleading stage, general factual allegations of injury resulting from the defendant's

---

1. By particularized, we mean that the injury must affect the plaintiff in a personal and individual way.

conduct may suffice, for on a motion to dismiss we "presum[e] that general allegations embrace those specific facts that are necessary to support the claim." In response to a summary judgment motion, however, the plaintiff can no longer rest on such "mere allegations," but must "set forth" by affidavit or other evidence "specific facts," Fed.Rule Civ.Proc. 56(e), which for purposes of the summary judgment motion will be taken to be true. And at the final stage, those facts (if controverted) must be "supported adequately by the evidence adduced at trial."

SUIT RE: LEGALITY OF GOV'T ACTION When the suit is one challenging the legality of government action or inaction, the nature and extent of facts that must be averred (at the summary judgment stage) or proved (at the trial stage) in order to establish standing depends considerably upon whether the plaintiff is himself an object of the action (or forgone action) at issue. If he is, there is ordinarily little question that the action or inaction has caused him injury, and that a judgment preventing or requiring the action will redress it. *SUIT RE: UNLAW REG OF SOMEONE ELSE* When, however, as in this case, a plaintiff's asserted injury arises from the government's allegedly unlawful regulation (or lack of regulation) of *someone else,* much more is needed. In that circumstance, causation and redressability ordinarily hinge on the response of the regulated (or regulable) third party to the government action or inaction—and perhaps on the response of others as well. The existence of one or more of the essential elements of standing "depends on the unfettered choices made by independent actors not before the courts and whose exercise of broad and legitimate discretion the courts cannot presume either to control or to predict," and it becomes the burden of the plaintiff to adduce facts showing that those choices have been or will be made in such manner as to produce causation and permit redressability of injury. Thus, when the plaintiff is not himself the object of the government action or inaction he challenges, standing is not precluded, but it is ordinarily "substantially more difficult" to establish.

III

We think the Court of Appeals failed to apply the foregoing principles in denying the Secretary's motion for summary judgment. Respondents had not made the requisite demonstration of (at least) injury and redressability.

A [INJURY]

RESPONDENT'S "INJURY" [Respondents' claim to injury] is that the lack of consultation with respect to certain funded activities abroad "increas[es] the rate of extinction of endangered and threatened species." Of course, the desire to use or observe an animal species, even for purely aesthetic purposes, is undeniably a cognizable interest for purpose of standing. "But the 'injury in fact' test requires more than an injury to a cognizable interest. [It requires] that the party seeking review be himself among the injured." *WHAT HAD TO BE SHOWN TO WIN MSJ* [To survive the Secretary's summary judgment motion,] respondents had to submit affidavits or other evidence showing, through specific facts, not only that listed species were in fact being threatened by funded activities abroad, but also that one or more of respondents' members would thereby be "directly" affected apart from their "'special interest' in th[e] subject."

With respect to this aspect of the case, the Court of Appeals focused on the affidavits of two Defenders' members—Joyce Kelly and Amy Skilbred. Ms. Kelly stated that she traveled to Egypt in 1986 and "observed the traditional habitat of the endangered Nile crocodile there and intend[s] to do so again, and hope[s] to observe the crocodile directly, and that she "will suffer harm in fact as a result of [the] American . . . role . . . in overseeing the rehabilitation of the Aswan High Dam on the Nile . . . and [in] develop[ing] . . . Egypt's . . . Master Water Plan." Ms. Skilbred averred that she traveled to Sri Lanka in 1981 and "observed th[e] habitat" of "endangered species such as the Asian elephant and the leopard" at what is now the site of the Mahaweli Project funded by the Agency for International Development (AID), although she "was unable to see any of the endangered species;" "this development project," she continued, "will seriously reduce endangered, threatened, and endemic species habitat including areas that I visited . . . [, which] may severely shorten the future of these species;" that threat, she concluded, harmed her because she "intend[s] to return to Sri Lanka in the future and hope[s] to be more fortunate in spotting at least the endangered elephant and leopard." When Ms. Skilbred was asked at a subsequent deposition if and when she had any plans to return to Sri Lanka, she reiterated that "I intend to go back to Sri Lanka," but confessed that she had no current plans: "I don't know [when]. There is a civil war going on right now. I don't know. Not next year, I will say. In the future."

We shall assume for the sake of argument that these affidavits contain facts showing that certain agency-funded projects threaten listed species—though that is questionable. They plainly contain no facts, however, showing how damage to the species will produce "imminent" injury to Mss. Kelly and Skilbred. That the women "had visited" the areas of the projects before the projects commenced proves nothing. As we have said in a related context, "'[p]ast exposure to illegal conduct does not in itself show a present case or controversy regarding injunctive relief . . . if unaccompanied by any continuing, present adverse effects.'" And the affiants' profession of an "inten[t]" to return to the places they had visited before—where they will presumably, this time, be deprived of the opportunity to observe animals of the endangered species—is simply not enough. Such "some day" intentions—without any description of concrete plans, or indeed even any specification of *when* the some day will be—do not support a finding of the "actual or imminent" injury that our cases require.[2]

---

2. The dissent acknowledges the settled requirement that the injury complained of be, if not actual, then at least imminent, but it contends that respondents could get past summary judgment because "a reasonable finder of fact could conclude . . . that . . . Kelly or Skilbred will soon return to the project sites." This analysis suffers either from a factual or from a legal defect, depending on what the "soon" is supposed to mean. If "soon" refers to the standard mandated by our precedents-that the injury be "imminent," we are at a loss to see how, as a factual matter, the standard can be met by respondents' mere profession of an intent, some day, to return. But if, as we suspect, "soon" means nothing more than "in this lifetime," then the dissent has undertaken quite a departure from our precedents. Although "imminence" is concededly a somewhat elastic concept, it cannot be stretched beyond its purpose, which is to ensure that the alleged injury is not too speculative for

Besides relying upon the Kelly and Skilbred affidavits, respondents propose a series of novel standing theories. The first, inelegantly styled "ecosystem nexus," proposes that any person who uses *any part* of a "contiguous ecosystem" adversely affected by a funded activity has standing even if the activity is located a great distance away. This approach, as the Court of Appeals correctly observed, is inconsistent with our opinion in *National Wildlife Federation* [1990], which held that a plaintiff claiming injury from environmental damage must use the area affected by the challenged activity and not an area roughly "in the vicinity" of it. It makes no difference that the general-purpose section of the ESA states that the Act was intended in part "to provide a means whereby the ecosystems upon which endangered species and threatened species depend may be conserved." To say that the Act protects ecosystems is not to say that the Act creates (if it were possible) rights of action in persons who have not been injured in fact, that is, persons who use portions of an ecosystem not perceptibly affected by the unlawful action in question.

Respondents' other theories are called, alas, the "animal nexus" approach, whereby anyone who has an interest in studying or seeing the endangered animals anywhere on the globe has standing; and the "vocational nexus" approach, under which anyone with a professional interest in such animals can sue. Under these theories, anyone who goes to see Asian elephants in the Bronx Zoo, and anyone who is a keeper of Asian elephants in the Bronx Zoo, has standing to sue because the Director of AID did not consult with the Secretary regarding the AID-funded project in Sri Lanka. This is beyond all reason. Standing is not "an ingenious academic exercise in the conceivable," but as we have said requires, at the summary judgment stage, a factual showing of perceptible harm. It is clear that the person who observes or works with a particular animal threatened by a federal decision is facing perceptible harm, since the very subject of his interest will no longer exist. It is even plausible—though it goes to the outermost limit of plausibility—to think that a person who observes or works with animals of a particular species in the very area of the world where that species is threatened by a federal decision is facing such harm, since some animals that might have been the subject of his interest will no longer exist. It goes beyond the limit, however, and into pure speculation and fantasy, to say that anyone who observes or works with an endangered species, anywhere in the

Article III purposes—that the injury is """*certainly* impending,""". It has been stretched beyond the breaking point when, as here, the plaintiff alleges only an injury at some indefinite future time, and the acts necessary to make the injury happen are at least partly within the plaintiff's own control. In such circumstances we have insisted that the injury proceed with a high degree of immediacy, so as to reduce the possibility of deciding a case in which no injury would have occurred at all. . . . Our insistence upon these established requirements of standing does not mean that we would, as the dissent contends, "demand . . . detailed descriptions" of damages, such as a "nightly schedule of attempted activities" from plaintiffs alleging loss of consortium. That case and the others posited by the dissent all involve actual harm; the existence of standing is clear, though the precise extent of harm remains to be determined at trial. Where there is no actual harm, however, its imminence (though not its precise extent) must be established.

world, is appreciably harmed by a single project affecting some portion of that species with which he has no more specific connection.

B [REDRESSABILITY]

Besides failing to show injury, respondents failed to demonstrate redressability. Instead of attacking the separate decisions to fund particular projects allegedly causing them harm, the respondents chose to challenge a more generalized level of government action (rules regarding consultation), the invalidation of which would affect all overseas projects. This programmatic approach has obvious practical advantages, but also obvious difficulties insofar as proof of causation or redressability is concerned. As we have said in another context, "suits challenging, not specifically identifiable Government violations of law, but the particular programs agencies establish to carry out their legal obligations . . . [are], even when premised on allegations of several instances of violations of law, . . . rarely if ever appropriate for federal-court adjudication."

The most obvious problem in the present case is redressability. Since the agencies funding the projects were not parties to the case, the District Court could accord relief only against the Secretary: He could be ordered to revise his regulation to require consultation for foreign projects. But this would not remedy respondents' alleged injury unless the funding agencies were bound by the Secretary's regulation, which is very much an open question. . . . When the Secretary promulgated the regulation at issue here, he thought it was binding on the agencies. The Solicitor General, however, has repudiated that position here, and the agencies themselves apparently deny the Secretary's authority. (During the period when the Secretary took the view that §7(a)(2) did apply abroad, AID and FWS engaged in a running controversy over whether consultation was required with respect to the Mahaweli project, AID insisting that consultation applied only to domestic actions.)

Respondents assert that this legal uncertainty did not affect redressability (and hence standing) because the District Court itself could resolve the issue of the Secretary's authority as a necessary part of its standing inquiry. Assuming that it is appropriate to resolve an issue of law such as this in connection with a threshold standing inquiry, resolution by the District Court would not have remedied respondents' alleged injury anyway, because it would not have been binding upon the agencies. They were not parties to the suit, and there is no reason they should be obliged to honor an incidental legal determination the suit produced. . . .

A further impediment to redressability is the fact that the agencies generally supply only a fraction of the funding for a foreign project. AID, for example, has provided less than 10% of the funding for the Mahaweli project. Respondents have produced nothing to indicate that the projects they have named will either be suspended, or do less harm to listed species, if that fraction is eliminated. . . . [I]t is entirely conjectural whether the nonagency activity that affects respondents will be altered or affected by the agency activity they seek to achieve. There is no standing.

IV

The Court of Appeals found that respondents had standing for an additional reason: because they had suffered a "procedural injury." The so-called "citizen-suit" provision of the ESA provides, in pertinent part, that "any person may commence a civil suit on his own behalf (A) to enjoin any person, including the United States and any other governmental instrumentality or agency . . . who is alleged to be in violation of any provision of this chapter." The court held that, because § 7(a)(2) requires interagency consultation, the citizen-suit provision creates a "procedural righ[t]" to consultation in all "persons"—so that anyone can file suit in federal court to challenge the Secretary's (or presumably any other official's) failure to follow the assertedly correct consultative procedure, notwithstanding their inability to allege any discrete injury flowing from that failure. To understand the remarkable nature of this holding one must be clear about what it does *not* rest upon: This is not a case where plaintiffs are seeking to enforce a procedural requirement the disregard of which could impair a separate concrete interest of theirs (*e.g.*, the procedural requirement for a hearing prior to denial of their license application, or the procedural requirement for an environmental impact statement before a federal facility is constructed next door to them).[7] Nor is it simply a case where concrete injury has been suffered by many persons, as in mass fraud or mass tort situations. Nor, finally, is it the unusual case in which Congress has created a concrete private interest in the outcome of a suit against a private party for the government's benefit, by providing a cash bounty for the victorious plaintiff. Rather, the court held that the injury-in-fact requirement had been satisfied by congressional conferral upon all persons of an abstract, self-contained, noninstrumental "right" to have the Executive observe the procedures required by law. We reject this view.

We have consistently held that a plaintiff raising only a generally available grievance about government—claiming only harm to his and every citizen's interest in proper application of the Constitution and laws, and seeking relief that no more directly and tangibly benefits him than it does the public at large—does not state an Article III case or controversy. . . .

---

7. There is this much truth to the assertion that "procedural rights" are special: The person who has been accorded a procedural right to protect his concrete interests can assert that right without meeting all the normal standards for redressability and immediacy. Thus, under our case-law, one living adjacent to the site for proposed construction of a federally licensed dam has standing to challenge the licensing agency's failure to prepare an Environmental Impact Statement, even though he cannot establish with any certainty that the Statement will cause the license to be withheld or altered, and even though the dam will not be completed for many years. (That is why we do not rely, in the present case, upon the Government's argument that, *even if* the other agencies were obliged to consult with the Secretary, they might not have followed his advice.) What respondents' "procedural rights" argument seeks, however, is quite different from this: standing for persons who have no concrete interests affected-persons who live (and propose to live) at the other end of the country from the dam.

To be sure, our generalized-grievance cases have typically involved Government violation of procedures assertedly ordained by the Constitution rather than the Congress. But there is absolutely no basis for making the Article III inquiry turn on the source of the asserted right. Whether the courts were to act on their own, or at the invitation of Congress, in ignoring the concrete injury requirement described in our cases, they would be discarding a principle fundamental to the separate and distinct constitutional role of the Third Branch—one of the essential elements that identifies those "Cases" and "Controversies" that are the business of the courts rather than of the political branches. "The province of the court," as Chief Justice Marshall said in *Marbury v. Madison*, "is, solely, to decide on the rights of individuals." Vindicating the public interest (including the public interest in Government observance of the Constitution and laws) is the function of Congress and the Chief Executive. The question presented here is whether the public interest in proper administration of the laws (specifically, in agencies' observance of a particular, statutorily prescribed procedure) can be converted into an individual right by a statute that denominates it as such, and that permits all citizens (or, for that matter, a subclass of citizens who suffer no distinctive concrete harm) to sue. If the concrete injury requirement has the separation-of-powers significance we have always said, the answer must be obvious: To permit Congress to convert the undifferentiated public interest in executive officers' compliance with the law into an "individual right" vindicable in the courts is to permit Congress to transfer from the President to the courts the Chief Executive's most important constitutional duty, to "take Care that the Laws be faithfully executed," Art. II, §3. It would enable the courts, with the permission of Congress, "to assume a position of authority over the governmental acts of another and co-equal department," and to become "'virtually continuing monitors of the wisdom and soundness of Executive action.'" We have always rejected that vision of our role. ...

Nothing in this contradicts the principle that "[t]he ... injury required by Art. III may exist solely by virtue of 'statutes creating legal rights, the invasion of which creates standing.'" *Warth*, 422 U.S., at 500 (quoting *Linda R. S. v. Richard D.*, 410 U.S. 614, 617, n. 3 (1973)). Both of the cases used by *Linda R. S.* as an illustration of that principle involved Congress' elevating to the status of legally cognizable injuries concrete, de facto injuries that were previously inadequate in law (namely, injury to an individual's personal interest in living in a racially integrated community, and injury to a company's interest in marketing its product free from competition). As we said in *Sierra Club*, "[Statutory] broadening [of] the categories of injury that may be alleged in support of standing is a different matter from abandoning the requirement that the party seeking review must himself have suffered an injury." 405 U.S., at 738. Whether or not the principle set forth in *Warth* can be extended beyond that distinction, it is clear that in suits against the Government, at least, the concrete injury requirement must remain. ...

We hold that respondents lack standing to bring this action and that the Court of Appeals erred in denying the summary judgment motion filed by the United States.

The opinion of the Court of Appeals is hereby reversed, and the cause is remanded for proceedings consistent with this opinion.

It is so ordered.

Justice KENNEDY, with whom Justice SOUTER joins, concurring in part and concurring in the judgment. . . .

I agree with the Court's conclusion in Part III-A that, on the record before us, respondents have failed to demonstrate that they themselves are "among the injured." This component of the standing inquiry is not satisfied unless

> "[p]laintiffs . . . demonstrate a 'personal stake in the outcome.' . . . Abstract injury is not enough. The plaintiff must show that he 'has sustained or is immediately in danger of sustaining some direct injury' as the result of the challenged official conduct and the injury or threat of injury must be both 'real and immediate,' not 'conjectural' or 'hypothetical.'"

While it may seem trivial to require that Mses. Kelly and Skilbred acquire airline tickets to the project sites or announce a date certain upon which they will return, this is not a case where it is reasonable to assume that the affiants will be using the sites on a regular basis, see *Sierra Club v. Morton, supra,* nor do the affiants claim to have visited the sites since the projects commenced. With respect to the Court's discussion of respondents' "ecosystem nexus," "animal nexus," and "vocational nexus" theories, I agree that on this record respondents' showing is insufficient to establish standing on any of these bases. I am not willing to foreclose the possibility, however, that in different circumstances a nexus theory similar to those proffered here might support a claim to standing. See *Japan Whaling Assn. v. American Cetacean Society,* 478 U.S. 221, 231, n. 4 (1986) ("[R]espondents . . . undoubtedly have alleged a sufficient 'injury in fact' in that the whale watching and studying of their members will be adversely affected by continued whale harvesting").

In light of the conclusion that respondents have not demonstrated a concrete injury here sufficient to support standing under our precedents, I would not reach the issue of redressability that is discussed by the plurality in Part III-B.

I also join Part IV of the Court's opinion with the following observations. As Government programs and policies become more complex and far-reaching, we must be sensitive to the articulation of new rights of action that do not have clear analogs in our common-law tradition. Modern litigation has progressed far from the paradigm of Marbury suing Madison to get his commission, or Ogden seeking an injunction to halt Gibbons' steamboat operations. In my view, Congress has the power to define injuries and articulate chains of causation that will give rise to a case or controversy where none existed before, and I do not read the Court's opinion to suggest a contrary view. In exercising this power, however, Congress must at the very least identify the injury it seeks to vindicate and relate the injury to the class of persons entitled to bring suit. The citizen-suit provision of the Endangered Species Act does not meet these minimal requirements, because while the statute purports to confer a right on "any person . . . to enjoin . . . the United States and any other governmental instrumentality or agency . . . who is alleged to be in violation of any provision of this chapter," it does not of its own force establish that there is an injury in "any person" by virtue of any "violation." 16 U.S.C. § 1540(g) (1)(A).

The Court's holding that there is an outer limit to the power of Congress to confer rights of action is a direct and necessary consequence of the case and controversy limitations found in Article III. I agree that it would exceed those limitations if, at the behest of Congress and in the absence of any showing of concrete injury, we were to entertain citizen suits to vindicate the public's nonconcrete interest in the proper administration of the laws. While it does not matter how many persons have been injured by the challenged action, the party bringing suit must show that the action injures him in a concrete and personal way. This requirement is not just an empty formality. It preserves the vitality of the adversarial process by assuring both that the parties before the court have an actual, as opposed to professed, stake in the outcome, and that "the legal questions presented . . . will be resolved, not in the rarified atmosphere of a debating society, but in a concrete factual context conducive to a realistic appreciation of the consequences of judicial action." In addition, the requirement of concrete injury confines the Judicial Branch to its proper, limited role in the constitutional framework of Government. . . .

With these observations, I concur in Parts I, II, III-A, and IV of the Court's opinion and in the judgment of the Court.

JUSTICE STEVENS, concurring in the judgment.

Because I am not persuaded that Congress intended the consultation requirement in § 7(a)(2) of the Endangered Species Act of 1973 (ESA), 16 U.S.C. § 1536(a) (2), to apply to activities in foreign countries, I concur in the judgment of reversal. I do not, however, agree with the Court's conclusion that respondents lack standing because the threatened injury to their interest in protecting the environment and studying endangered species is not "imminent." Nor do I agree with the plurality's additional conclusion that respondents' injury is not "redressable" in this litigation.

I

In my opinion a person who has visited the critical habitat of an endangered species has a professional interest in preserving the species and its habitat, and intends to revisit them in the future has standing to challenge agency action that threatens their destruction. Congress has found that a wide variety of endangered species of fish, wildlife, and plants are of "aesthetic, ecological, educational, historical, recreational, and scientific value to the Nation and its people." 16 U.S.C. § 1531(a)(3). Given that finding, we have no license to demean the importance of the interest that particular individuals may have in observing any species or its habitat, whether those individuals are motivated by esthetic enjoyment, an interest in professional research, or an economic interest in preservation of the species. Indeed, this Court has often held that injuries to such interests are sufficient to confer standing, and the Court reiterates that holding today.

The Court nevertheless concludes that respondents have not suffered "injury in fact" because they have not shown that the harm to the endangered species will produce "imminent" injury to them. I disagree. An injury to an individual's interest in studying or enjoying a species and its natural habitat occurs when someone (whether it be the Government or a private party) takes action that harms that species and habitat. In my judgment, therefore, the "imminence" of such an injury should be measured by the timing and likelihood of the threatened environmental harm, rather than—as the Court seems to suggest—by the time that might elapse between the present and the time when the individuals would visit the area if no such injury should occur.

To understand why this approach is correct and consistent with our precedent, it is necessary to consider the purpose of the standing doctrine. Concerned about "the proper—and properly limited—role of the courts in a democratic society," we have long held that "Art. III judicial power exists only to redress or otherwise to protect against injury to the complaining party." The plaintiff must have a "personal stake in the outcome" sufficient to "assure that concrete adverseness which sharpens the presentation of issues upon which the court so largely depends for illumination of difficult . . . questions." For that reason, "[a]bstract injury is not enough. It must be alleged that the plaintiff 'has sustained or is immediately in danger of sustaining some direct injury' as the result of the challenged statute or official conduct. . . . The injury or threat of injury must be both 'real and immediate,' not 'conjectural,' or 'hypothetical.'"

Consequently, we have denied standing to plaintiffs whose likelihood of suffering any concrete adverse effect from the challenged action was speculative. In this case, however, the likelihood that respondents will be injured by the destruction of the endangered species is not speculative. If respondents are genuinely interested in the preservation of the endangered species and intend to study or observe these animals in the future, their injury will occur as soon as the animals are destroyed. Thus the only potential source of "speculation" in this case is whether respondents' intent to study or observe the animals is genuine. In my view, Joyce Kelly and Amy Skilbred have introduced sufficient evidence to negate petitioner's contention that their claims of injury are "speculative" or "conjectural." As Justice BLACKMUN explains, *post*, a reasonable finder of fact could conclude, from their past visits, their professional backgrounds, and their affidavits and deposition testimony, that Ms. Kelly and Ms. Skilbred will return to the project sites and, consequently, will be injured by the destruction of the endangered species and critical habitat.

[In the balance of his opinion, Justice Stevens explained why, in his view, the respondents had satisfied the redressability requirement of standing but that their claim failed on its merits.]

JUSTICE BLACKMUN, with whom JUSTICE O'CONNOR joins, dissenting. . . .

1

Were the Court to apply the proper standard for summary judgment, I believe it would conclude that the sworn affidavits and deposition testimony of Joyce Kelly and Amy Skilbred advance sufficient facts to create a genuine issue for trial concerning whether one or both would be imminently harmed by the Aswan and Mahaweli projects. In the first instance, as the Court itself concedes, the affidavits contained facts making it at least "questionable" (and therefore within the province of the factfinder) that certain agency-funded projects threaten listed species. The only remaining issue, then, is whether Kelly and Skilbred have shown that they personally would suffer imminent harm.

I think a reasonable finder of fact could conclude from the information in the affidavits and deposition testimony that either Kelly or Skilbred will soon return to the project sites, thereby satisfying the "actual or imminent" injury standard. The Court dismisses Kelly's and Skilbred's general statements that they intended to revisit the project sites as "simply not enough." But those statements did not stand alone. A reasonable finder of fact could conclude, based not only upon their statements of intent to return, but upon their past visits to the project sites, as well as their professional backgrounds, that it was likely that Kelly and Skilbred would make a return trip to the project areas. . . .

By requiring a "description of concrete plans" or "specification of when the some day [for a return visit] will be," the Court, in my view, demands what is likely an empty formality. . . .

2

The Court also concludes that injury is lacking, because respondents' allegations of "ecosystem nexus" failed to demonstrate sufficient proximity to the site of the environmental harm. To support that conclusion, the Court mischaracterizes our decision in *Lujan v. National Wildlife Federation*, 497 U.S. 871 (1990), as establishing a general rule that "a plaintiff claiming injury from environmental damage must use the area affected by the challenged activity." In *National Wildlife Federation*, the Court required specific geographical proximity because of the particular type of harm alleged in that case: harm to the plaintiff's visual enjoyment of nature from mining activities. One cannot suffer from the sight of a ruined landscape without being close enough to see the sites actually being mined. Many environmental injuries, however, cause harm distant from the area immediately affected by the challenged action. Environmental destruction may affect animals traveling over vast geographical ranges. It cannot seriously be contended that a litigant's failure to use the precise or exact site where animals are slaughtered or where toxic waste is dumped into a river means he or she cannot show injury.

The Court also rejects respondents' claim of vocational or professional injury. The Court says that it is "beyond all reason" that a zoo "keeper" of Asian elephants would have standing to contest his Government's participation in the eradication of all the Asian elephants in another part of the world. I am unable to see how the distant location of the destruction necessarily (for purposes of ruling at summary judgment) mitigates the harm to the elephant keeper. If there is no more access to a future supply of the animal that sustains a keeper's livelihood, surely there is harm.

[Justice Blackmun then gave a detailed analysis of why, contrary to the plurality's opinion, the respondents had satisfied the redressability requirement for standing.]

II

. . . .

The Court expresses concern that allowing judicial enforcement of "agencies' observance of a particular, statutorily prescribed procedure" would "transfer from the President to the courts the Chief Executive's most important constitutional duty, to 'take Care that the Laws be faithfully executed,' Art. II, §3." In fact, the principal effect of foreclosing judicial enforcement of such procedures is to transfer power into the hands of the Executive at the expense—not of the courts—but of Congress, from which that power originates and emanates.

Under the Court's anachronistically formal view of the separation of powers, Congress legislates pure, substantive mandates and has no business structuring the procedural manner in which the Executive implements these mandates. To be sure, in the ordinary course, Congress does legislate in black-and-white terms of affirmative commands or negative prohibitions on the conduct of officers of the Executive Branch. In complex regulatory areas, however, Congress often legislates, as it were, in procedural shades of gray. That is, it sets forth substantive policy goals and provides for their attainment by requiring Executive Branch officials to follow certain procedures, for example, in the form of reporting, consultation, and certification requirements. . . .

Congress legislates in procedural shades of gray not to aggrandize its own power but to allow maximum Executive discretion in the attainment of Congress' legislative goals. Congress could simply impose a substantive prohibition on Executive conduct; it could say that no agency action shall result in the loss of more than 5% of any listed species. Instead, Congress sets forth substantive guidelines and allows the Executive, within certain procedural constraints, to decide how best to effectuate the ultimate goal. The Court never has questioned Congress' authority to impose such procedural constraints on Executive power. Just as Congress does not violate separation of powers by structuring the procedural manner in which the Executive shall carry out the laws, surely the federal courts do not violate separation of powers when, at the very instruction and command of Congress, they enforce these procedures. . . .

I dissent.

Notes

1. Where is "standing" in the Constitution? Is it self-evident that the Constitution imposes "standing" limitations on the federal judicial power? What provisions of the Constitution did the justices in *Lujan* identify as bearing on standing? What, according to the various opinions above, is the purpose of constitutional standing doctrine? Do you find anyone's reasoning on this point persuasive?

2. If injury-in-fact seems clear to you, then maybe you should think about it some more. What types of "injuries" count as cognizable "injuries-in-fact"? They need not be economic—*Lujan* notes "the desire to use or observe an animal species, even for purely aesthetic purposes, is undeniably a cognizable interest for the purpose of standing." But it remains the case that "injury-in-fact" requires something more than merely being upset at illegal government action.

But does this limit make sense? Consider the facts of *Lujan*. Is there any reason to doubt that Ms. Skilbred and Ms. Kelly were worried about what might befall crocodiles, elephants, and leopards due to the agencies' change in consultation policy? If so, weren't they in some sense literally "injured" by the change? What more did they need to suffer to achieve "injury-in-fact"? Could timely purchase of tickets to Egypt and Sri Lanka have done the trick? Why should it matter whether the two plaintiffs had plans to be near crocodiles, elephants, and leopards?

Concurring, Justice Kennedy suggested that Congress has the power to "define injuries and articulate chains of causation" to create a constitutionally sufficient case or controversy. What did he mean by this claim? How might Congress have deployed this power to help out Skilbred and Kelly?

3. Associational standing—borrowing a member's injury. Perhaps you found it odd that in *Lujan v. Defenders of Wildlife* the standing battle focused on whether Skilbred and Kelly had firm plans to spend time near the habitats of crocodiles, elephants, and leopards. Surely, the Defenders of Wildlife—considered as an organization—suffers an injury whenever endangered species are threatened, and it makes little sense to require that an organization be "near" the animals in question.

Defenders of Wildlife could not base standing on this type of injury, however, in light of precedents such as *Sierra Club v. Morton*, 405 U.S. 727 (1972). In this case, Sierra Club sought declaratory and injunctive relief to block construction of a proposed ski resort in a national forest. It based its claim to standing on its long-standing organizational interest in protecting the environment. The Court rejected this basis for standing:

> The impact of the proposed changes in the environment of Mineral King will not fall indiscriminately upon every citizen. The alleged injury will be felt directly only by those who use Mineral King and Sequoia National Park, and for whom the aesthetic and recreational values of the area will be lessened by the highway and ski resort. The Sierra Club failed to allege that it or its members would be affected in any of their activities or pastimes by the Disney development. Nowhere in the pleadings or affidavits did the Club state that its members use Mineral King for any purpose, much less that they use it in any way that would be significantly affected by the proposed actions of the respondents. . . .

... It is clear that an organization whose members are injured may represent those members in a proceeding for judicial review. But a mere "interest in a problem," no matter how longstanding the interest and no matter how qualified the organization is in evaluating the problem, is not sufficient by itself to render the organization "adversely affected" or "aggrieved" within the meaning of the APA. The Sierra Club is a large and long-established organization, with a historic commitment to the cause of protecting our Nation's natural heritage from man's depredations. But if a "special interest" in this subject were enough to entitle the Sierra Club to commence this litigation, there would appear to be no objective basis upon which to disallow a suit by any other bona fide "special interest" organization however small or short-lived. And if any group with a bona fide "special interest" could initiate such litigation, it is difficult to perceive why any individual citizen with the same bona fide special interest would not also be entitled to do so.

Typically, organizations such as voluntary associations or trade groups get around the *Sierra Club* bar on ideological injury by invoking a derivative form of standing on behalf of their members. The Supreme Court stated the canonical test for this type of "associational standing" in *Hunt v. Washington Apple Advertising Comm'n*, 432 U.S. 333 (1977):

Thus we have recognized that an association has standing to bring suit on behalf of its members when: (a) its members would otherwise have standing to sue in their own right; (b) the interests it seeks to protect are germane to the organization's purpose; and (c) neither the claim asserted nor the relief requested requires the participation of individual members in the lawsuit.

The upshot of this derivative approach is that, to demonstrate standing, an organization such as Defenders of Wildlife typically submits affidavits from one or more members who explain why they have suffered the right type of injury for standing. This explains why *Defenders of Wildlife* turned, oddly enough, on the firmness of travel plans of Skilbred and Kelly.

In *Summers v. Earth Island Inst.*, 129 S. Ct. 1142 (2009), the Court insisted, by a 5-4 vote, that an organization invoking associational standing must identify particular injured members rather than rely on generalized claims that some member or other must have incurred the right kind of injury. Environmental organizations sued the Forest Service to challenge rules it had adopted exempting thousands of small salvage sales of timber from a notice-and-comment process that the plaintiffs claimed was statutorily required. The majority, in an opinion authored by Justice Scalia, rejected standing on the ground that the environmental groups had not identified any particular member who had specific enough plans to use any particular bit of forest that might be exempted at some point. Justice Breyer, writing for the four dissenting justices, contended: (a) all concede that the Forest Service has exempted small salvage sales many times in the past and that, unchecked, it will do so thousands of times in the future; (b) the environmental organizations are composed of hundreds of thousands of members—some of whom use the forests a lot; (c) some of these same forest lovers would, given the chance, avail themselves of notice-and-comment procedures to challenge exemptions; and, therefore, (d) the environmental organizations had shown that they (through their members) were threatened by a "realistic" threat of injury by the Forest Service's exemption policy, which should suffice for standing. 129 S. Ct. at 1155–58. Adopting Justice Breyer's approach might reduce the need for massive organizations such as Sierra Club to play the game of finding just the right member who can allege just the right assertions for standing. But does this leave much point to *Sierra Club v. Morton*?

4. Organizational standing. In addition to invoking associational standing, voluntary organizations, like other organizations recognized by law, can claim standing based on injuries that they suffer in their own right. For instance, Defenders of Wildlife would certainly have standing to sue someone who threw a rock through a window owned by the organization. The leading Supreme Court case on this form of "organizational standing" is *Havens Realty Corp. v. Coleman*, 455 U.S. 363 (1982), in which HOME, a nonprofit devoted to equal housing opportunity, sued Havens Realty Corp. for unlawful racial steering in violation of the Fair Housing Act. The Court held that HOME had adequately alleged injury by claiming that it had "devote[d] significant resources to identify and counteract the defendant's [sic] racially discriminatory steering practices." Put another way, Havens Realty had injured HOME by making its job harder and more expensive.

If *Sierra Club*'s bar on ideological injuries is to mean anything however, it cannot be the case that any expenditures that a voluntary organization makes in response to a defendant agency's action can count as an injury. For instance, if litigation expenses can count, then finding a non-ideological injury is just a matter of starting a lawsuit. This move, as you might expect, does not work. *See, e.g., Food & Water Watch, Inc. v. Vilsack*, 808 F.3d 905 (D.C. Cir. 2015) (explaining that litigation and advocacy expenses prompted by agency action do not give rise to organizational standing). Instead, an organization seeking to make use of *Havens Realty* must show that that defendant's action has "perceptibly impaired" the organization's ability to provide services.

5. Not very concrete guidance about what it means to be "concrete." Case law provides some fixed points for analysis of the "concreteness" of injuries. For instance, the justices have long agreed that an officious interest in insisting that the law be obeyed because it is, after all, the law, is too abstract to count as an injury. *Federal Election Commission v. Akins*, 524 U.S. 11 (1998). As we saw two notes ago, case law also insists that mere ideological injury does not suffice. *Sierra Club v. Morton*, 405 U.S. 727 (1972). On the other hand, an injury need not be physical or economic to qualify as concrete. For instance, damage to aesthetic or recreational interests can be concrete enough for standing. *Summers v. Earth Island Institute*, 555 U.S. 488 (2009).

The Court's most recent significant effort to distinguish the "concrete" from the "abstract" came in *Spokeo, Inc. v. Robins*, 136 S. Ct. 1540 (2016). The Fair Credit Reporting Act of 1970 (FCRA) imposes requirements governing the creation and use of "consumer reports" by "consumer reporting agencies." It also creates a cause of action authorizing an individual to sue for damages "[a]ny person who willfully fails to comply with any requirement [of the FCRA] with respect" to that individual. 15 U.S.C. § 1681(n)(a). Spokeo produced a consumer report about Robins that contained many inaccuracies; Robins invoked FCRA's private cause of action to sue Spokeo. The Ninth Circuit concluded that Robins had suffered an injury-in-fact that was both particularized and concrete given that "Spokeo violated his statutory rights, not just the statutory rights of other people," and that Robins's interest at stake was "individualized rather than collective." 742 F.3d at 413.

Justice Alito, writing for a six-justice majority, held that the Ninth Circuit had improperly conflated particularization and concreteness, which are separate requirements. He explained, not so helpfully, that to be "concrete" an injury must be "de facto," it must "exist," and it must be "real" rather than "abstract." It need not, however, be "tangible." He noted that many of the Court's precedents have confirmed "that intangible injuries can nevertheless be concrete." 136 S. Ct. at 1549 (citing examples of cases where intangible injuries to interests in free speech or free exercise of religion were sufficient for standing).

Determining whether an intangible injury is concrete enough for standing implicates both "history and the judgment of Congress." Regarding history, "it is instructive to consider whether an alleged intangible harm has a close relationship to a harm that has traditionally been regarded as providing a basis for a lawsuit in English or American courts." As for Congress, its judgment is "instructive and important" because it "is well positioned to identify intangible harms that meet minimum Article III requirements." This congressional power does not extend, however, to authorizing plaintiffs to sue for violation of any statutory right at all — a plaintiff still must suffer "a concrete injury even in the context of a statutory violation."

Turning to Robins's allegations, Justice Alito observed that it was easy to imagine some violations of FCRA that would not actually cause anyone any real harm — for example, a consumer report misidentifying someone's zip code. Robins therefore could not establish an injury-in-fact merely by "alleging a bare procedural violation" of the statute. The Ninth Circuit, because it "failed to appreciate the distinction between concreteness and particularization," had not properly addressed "whether the particular procedural violations alleged in this case entail a degree of risk [of harm to Robins] sufficient to meet the concreteness requirement." So the Court remanded to the Ninth Circuit to think it over.

Justice Ginsburg, joined by Justice Sotomayor, would have upheld standing for Robins given that he "complains of misinformation about his education, family situation, and economic status, inaccurate representations that could affect his fortune in the job market." Striking a broader note, she insisted that the "concreteness" requirement, properly understood, speaks merely to whether a litigant has a personal stake in the outcome of a case and whether that case involves genuinely adverse parties. *Id.* at 1555–56 (Ginsburg, J., dissenting) (collecting authority).

6. An injury can be "particularized" even though it is widely shared. The Supreme Court has in recent years clarified that its insistence on particularized injuries is a matter of constitutional rather than prudential standing. *Lexmark Intern., Inc. v. Static Control Components, Inc.*, 134 S. Ct. 1377, 1387 (2014). Thus, a plaintiff who raises "only a generally available grievance about government—claiming only harm to his and every citizen's interest in proper application of the Constitution and laws, and seeking relief that no more directly and tangibly benefits him than it does the public at large—does not state an Article III case or controversy." *Lujan v. Defenders of Wildlife*, 504 U.S. 555, 573–574 (1992). To be "particularized," an injury "must affect the plaintiff in a personal and individual way." *Spokeo, Inc. v. Robins*, 136 S. Ct. 1540, 1548 (2016).

But wait—hang on a second—suppose that a drug manufacturer sells a drug that harms millions of people by damaging their livers. Does it follow that none of the injured individuals can sue because they only have a generalized grievance? No—"[t]he fact that an injury may be suffered by a large number of people does not of itself make that injury a nonjusticiable generalized grievance. The victims' injuries from a mass tort, for example, are widely shared, to be sure, but each individual suffers a particularized harm." *Id.* at 1548 n.7. The drug in our hypothetical may have damaged millions of livers, but each individual plaintiff can claim injury to her particular liver.

7. The Supreme Court on "imminence" and probabilistic injury. If you found out that there is a 10% chance that a meteorite would hit you in the head one year from now and kill you, it would dampen your spirits *today*, wouldn't it? Put another way, one might reasonably say that a risk of future injury can cause injury in the present, no? If, however, one can always characterize future injury as present injury, then there may be little point to *Lujan's* requirement that an injury be "actual" or "imminent."

The Supreme Court's recent struggles with this issue have not been very illuminating. In *Clapper v. Amnesty Int'l USA*, 133 S. Ct. 1138 (2013), the Court issued a majority opinion that contradicted itself on the subject of probabilistic injury. The plaintiffs challenged a provision of the FISA Amendments of 2008, which authorized surveillance of individuals who are not "United States persons" and are reasonably believed to be outside the United States. The plaintiffs included attorneys and human rights organizations. They claimed injury-in-fact based on the "objectively reasonable likelihood" that authorized surveillance would compromise their communications with foreign contacts. They also claimed injury due to the costs they had incurred to try to preserve the confidentiality of their communications.

The Court rejected both theories by the 5-4 vote then usual in the Roberts Court for politically charged cases. Writing for the majority, Justice Alito stressed that the "objectively reasonable likelihood" standard espoused by the plaintiffs (and the Second Circuit) was inconsistent with the Court's requirement that "threatened injury must be *certainly impending* to constitute injury in fact and that allegations of possible future injury are not sufficient." 133 S. Ct. at 1147. The Court then spent several pages explaining that the plaintiffs' theory of injury depended on a long chain of speculative events (e.g., that the government would both target a plaintiff's particular contacts and use its new authorities to do so, etc.).

Given just this much, one might read *Clapper* as a clear instruction to lower courts to take a very tough line on probabilistic injury. This reading would fail to take account of note 5 of the majority opinion:

> Our cases do not uniformly require plaintiffs to demonstrate that it is literally certain that the harms they identify will come about. In some instances, we have found standing based on a "substantial risk" that the harm will occur, which may prompt plaintiffs to reasonably incur costs to mitigate or avoid that harm.

133 S. Ct. at 1150 n.5 (citations omitted). So, one of two standards should apply to a plaintiff's claim of injury that is based on a risk of future harm: Either (a) that a "substantial risk" of harm exists or else (b) that the harm is "certainly impending." The Court offered little express guidance in *Clapper* on choosing between the two.

In *Susan B. Anthony List v. Driehaus*, 134 S. Ct. 2334 (2014), the Court revisited the problem of risk-of-injury as injury and corrected the confusion in *Clapper* by sweeping it under the rug. The plaintiffs were advocacy organizations that challenged an Ohio statute that criminalized false statements about candidates in political campaigns. They based their claim to standing on the risk that the statute would be enforced against them. The Court noted that it had permitted pre-enforcement review where "the threatened enforcement is sufficiently imminent." This requirement is satisfied where a plaintiff alleges that it intends to violate the statute by taking actions that are "arguably affected by a constitutional interest" and demonstrates a "credible threat of prosecution." This approach is very hard to square with *Clapper*'s apparent preference, at least outside its footnotes, for a "certainly impending" injury. The Court neatly solved this problem by citing both of *Clapper*'s standards without acknowledging the tension between them, declaring that a "future injury may suffice if the threatened injury is 'certainly impending' or there is a '"substantial risk"' that the harm will occur.'"

Looking past the Court's doctrinal formulations in *Clapper* and *Susan B. Anthony*, it seems safe to say that these cases illustrate the practical point that the strictness of standing requirements can depend to a substantial degree on whether the majority deems judicial resolution of the merits a good idea. In *Clapper*, the Court was being asked to invalidate authority of the National Security Agency to collect intelligence on foreigners. The majority, it seems, was disinclined to do so. Along these very lines it observed, "we have often found a lack of standing in cases in which the Judiciary has been requested to review actions of the political branches in the fields of intelligence gathering and foreign affairs." By contrast, in *Susan B. Anthony*, the plaintiffs were asking the Court to invalidate a state statute that threatened to criminalize political speech. It comes as little surprise that the Court unanimously found that the plaintiffs had constitutional standing given this threat to core First Amendment values.

8. The D.C. Circuit on "imminence" and probabilistic injury. For an example of a lower court trying to make sense of the problem of probabilistic injury, consider the D.C. Circuit's efforts in *Public Citizen, Inc. v. Nat'l Highway Traffic Safety Admin.*, 489 F.3d 1279 (D.C. Cir. 2007). Public Citizen challenged a rule that NHTSA had adopted to implement a statutory requirement that new motor vehicles include a warning system for indicating when tires are underinflated. In essence, Public Citizen contended that NHTSA's rule did not go far enough in protecting public safety, thus increasing risk to the driving public. Commenting on the difficulties posed by such "increased risk" claims, the court explained:

> Opening the courthouse to these kinds of increased-risk claims would drain the "actual or imminent" requirement of meaning in cases involving consumer challenges to an agency's regulation (or lack of regulation). . . .
>
> To be sure, this Court has not closed the door to all increased-risk-of-harm cases. We have allowed standing when there was at least both (i) a substantially increased risk of harm and (ii) a substantial probability of harm with that increase taken into account. *See Mountain States Legal Found. v. Glickman*, 92 F.3d 1228, 1234–35 (D.C. Cir. 1996) . . .
>
> What increase in the risk of harm and what level of ultimate risk are high enough to be "substantial"—and thus to render the harm sufficiently "imminent"? *Mountain States* did not specify any hard-and-fast numerical rules; we have simply set forth a general principle: If the agency action causes an individual or individual members of an organization to face an increase in the risk of harm that is "substantial," and the ultimate risk of harm also is "substantial," then the individual or organization has demonstrated an injury in fact. . . .
>
> In applying the "substantial" standard, we are mindful, of course, that the constitutional requirement of imminence as articulated by the Supreme Court—even if this Court has said it does not completely bar increased-risk-of-harm claims—necessarily compels a very strict understanding of what increases in risk and overall risk levels can count as "substantial."

Id. at 1295–96 (some citations omitted). The Court gave Public Citizen the chance to submit supplemental briefing to demonstrate that its challenge to NHTSA's rule satisfied the *Mountain States* test for standing for increased risk claims. The panel subsequently ruled that Public Citizen's submission was riddled with statistical and analytical errors and therefore failed. 513 F.3d 234 (D.C. Cir. 2008).

9. Special solicitude for states. In *Massachusetts v. EPA*, 549 U.S. 497 (2007), a 5-4 majority of the Court ruled that the petitioner Massachusetts had constitutional standing to challenge EPA's rejection of a petition requesting that it use its rulemaking authority to regulate greenhouse gas emissions of motor vehicles. Writing for the majority, Justice Stevens explained that Massachusetts had satisfied the injury requirement by demonstrating that global warming threatened to cause rising sea levels, which in turn threatened coastal property owned by the state. Causation and redressability requirements were satisfied because, were EPA to initiate rulemaking, it might promulgate a rule limiting at least some greenhouse gas emissions and any move in that direction would reduce the risk of harm at least a little. To buttress its conclusion, the majority cited an obscure, one-hundred-year-old precedent, *Georgia v. Tennessee Copper Co.*, 206 U.S. 230 (1907), for the principle that states have a special claim to standing in the federal courts to protect their quasi-sovereign interests in "all the earth and air within [their] domain[s]." In light of the quasi-sovereign interests it sought to protect, Massachusetts was "entitled to special solicitude in . . . standing analysis." Chief Justice Roberts, writing for four justices, disputed the majority's reliance on *Tennessee Copper* and suggested its deployment amounted to a tacit admission that the majority's standing analysis needed all the help it could get. States are understandably quick to try to invoke "special solicitude" for their claims of standing, though it is not clear, in practice, how much real effect this "special solicitude" has.

10. Causation and redressability—how strong a connection is needed? Most discussion of constitutional standing revolves around determining whether a plaintiff can lay claim to a proper "injury." There are, however, two more prongs to constitutional standing analysis: causation and redressability. Regarding causation, *Lujan* declares, "there must be a causal connection between the injury and the conduct complained of—the injury has to be fairly traceable to the challenged action of the defendant, and not the result of the independent action of some third party not before the court." 504 U.S. at 560 (citation, brackets, ellipses, and quotation marks omitted). As for redressability, "it must be likely, as opposed to merely speculative, that the injury will be redressed by a favorable decision." *Id.* at 561 (citation and quotation marks omitted).

The bottom line with regard to both of these prongs is that sometimes courts take a strict approach to them, and sometimes they take a looser approach. For an example of a strict approach, consider *Simon v. Eastern Kentucky Welfare Rights Organization*, 426 U.S. 26 (1976). In this case, the petitioners challenged an IRS ruling that permitted hospitals to retain "charitable" status—and the tax advantages this status entailed—without offering non-emergency care to indigents such as the plaintiffs. The Court rejected standing for this claim on both causation and redressability grounds, and, along the way, toured some of its (then) recent precedent on the subject:

> The complaint here alleged only that petitioners, by the adoption of Revenue Ruling 69-545, had "encouraged" hospitals to deny services to indigents. The implicit corollary of this allegation is that a grant of respondents' requested relief, resulting in a requirement that all hospitals serve indigents as a condition to favorable tax treatment, would "discourage" hospitals from denying their services to respondents. But it does not follow from the

allegation and its corollary that the denial of access to hospital services in fact results from petitioners' new Ruling, or that a court-ordered return by petitioners to their previous policy would result in these respondents receiving the hospital services they desire. It is purely speculative whether the denials of service specified in the complaint fairly can be traced to petitioners' "encouragement" or instead result from decisions made by the hospitals without regard to the tax implications. . . .

It is equally speculative whether the desired exercise of the court's remedial powers in this suit would result in the availability to respondents of such services. So far as the complaint sheds light, it is just as plausible that the hospitals to which respondents may apply for service would elect to forgo favorable tax treatment to avoid the undetermined financial drain of an increase in the level of uncompensated services.

[I]ndirectness of injury, while not necessarily fatal to standing, "may make it substantially more difficult to meet the minimum requirement of Art. III: To establish that, in fact, the asserted injury was the consequence of the defendants' actions, or that prospective relief will remove the harm." Respondents have failed to carry this burden. Speculative inferences are necessary to connect their injury to the challenged actions of petitioners. Moreover, the complaint suggests no substantial likelihood that victory in this suit would result in respondents' receiving the hospital treatment they desire. A federal court, properly cognizant of the Art. III limitation upon its jurisdiction, must require more than respondents have shown before proceeding to the merits.

Do you agree that the impact of a court ruling forcing the IRS to condition charitable tax status on the provision of non-emergency services would be "purely speculative"? Surely such a ruling would increase the probability that a given non-profit hospital would offer care. Why shouldn't this link be strong enough to satisfy causation and redressability concerns?

Friends of the Earth, Inc. v. Laidlaw Environmental Services (TOC), Inc., 528 U.S. 167 (2000), by contrast, marks a looser approach. The plaintiff, FOE, filed a citizen suit against the defendant Laidlaw for discharging pollutants into a river in violation of the Clean Water Act. FOE sought injunctive relief as well as civil penalties. The district court imposed a civil penalty but denied injunctive relief because Laidlaw had achieved substantial compliance during the litigation. On appeal, Laidlaw contended that FOE lacked standing to pursue this civil penalty:

Laidlaw is right to insist that a plaintiff must demonstrate standing separately for each form of relief sought. But it is wrong to maintain that citizen plaintiffs facing ongoing violations never have standing to seek civil penalties.

We have recognized on numerous occasions that "all civil penalties have some deterrent effect." More specifically, Congress has found that civil penalties in Clean Water Act cases do more than promote immediate compliance by limiting the defendant's economic incentive to delay its attainment of permit limits; they also deter future violations. This congressional determination warrants judicial attention and respect. . . .

It can scarcely be doubted that, for a plaintiff who is injured or faces the threat of future injury due to illegal conduct ongoing at the time of suit, a sanction that effectively abates that conduct and prevents its recurrence provides a form of redress. Civil penalties can fit that description. To the extent that they encourage defendants to discontinue current violations and deter them from committing future ones, they afford redress to citizen plaintiffs who are injured or threatened with injury as a consequence of ongoing unlawful conduct. . . .

We recognize that there may be a point at which the deterrent effect of a claim for civil penalties becomes so insubstantial or so remote that it cannot support citizen standing. The fact that this vanishing point is not easy to ascertain does not detract from the deterrent power of such penalties in the ordinary case.

In *Laidlaw*, the Court conceded that it is reasonable to think that a party will respond to the financial incentives created by civil penalties. Can this stance be reconciled with the Court's approach in *Simon*? For another case taking a relaxed approach to redressability, see *Massachusetts v. EPA*, 549 U.S. 497 (2007) (holding that Massachusetts had standing to challenge EPA's rejection of a petition for rulemaking to limit greenhouse gas emissions from new motor vehicles; rejecting argument that Massachusetts could not satisfy redressability given that an EPA rule plainly could not solve the problem of global climate change; holding, in essence, that redressability was satisfied on an every-little-bit-helps theory).

11. A note that is more important than its brevity and placement might suggest — procedural violations and causation/redressability. An awful lot of administrative law, you have no doubt noticed, is procedural law, and plaintiffs frequently sue agencies for failure to follow procedural requirements. Forcing an agency to use a procedure does not, however, guarantee that the ultimate substantive result will be to the plaintiff's liking. For instance, as just mentioned in the preceding note, in *Massachusetts v. EPA*, the state challenged EPA's failure to initiate a rulemaking to limit greenhouse gas emissions from new motor vehicles. Massachusetts' claimed injury was that global climate change would cause seashore property it owned to be submerged. At the time of the litigation, one could not preclude the possibility that EPA, if forced to commence rulemaking, might promulgate a rule that did not limit greenhouse gas emissions and did nothing to redress Massachusetts' injury. Along these lines, one might think that plaintiffs could never (or at least seldom) be able to demonstrate standing to challenge procedural violations because plaintiffs will not be able to demonstrate a sufficient likelihood that forcing an agency to follow correct procedures will provide redress for their injuries. But that can't be right. To see how the Court has addressed this problem, take a look at note 7 in *Lujan*.

2. "Statutory" and Prudential Standing

This subchapter begins with the problem of determining whether a legislature has granted a plaintiff a cause of action to challenge agency action. This issue sometimes goes by the name of "statutory standing." It closes with some discussion of prudential standing, which courts use to block certain plaintiffs from bringing suit.

As you work through these materials, you will want to pay particular attention to how courts have interpreted the single most important statutory provision governing who can sue to challenge agency action, 5 U.S.C. § 702. This provision authorizes judicial review of agency action at the behest of "a person suffering legal wrong because of agency action, or adversely affected or aggrieved by agency action within the meaning of a relevant statute." As you will see, § 702 casts a very wide net.

Lesson 5D.2. The WTC has denied the Wrath for Grapes' petition for a rule that requires that each bottle of wine sold have a label containing a warning that specifically identifies all major health and safety problems caused by alcohol consumption as well as the number of deaths each of these problems causes per year. Assess whether the Wrath could satisfy *extra-constitutional* standing requirements for obtaining judicial review of this denial.

Background of *Cetacean Community v. Bush*

In the case that follows, the Ninth Circuit considered whether the Cetacean Community, composed of "all the world's whales, porpoises, and dolphins" and represented by a self-appointed attorney, had standing in federal court to contest the legality of the Navy's use of sonar. Before you discard the idea too quickly, consider that there are lots of plaintiffs who are not human beings, such as corporations and voluntary associations. Also, many plaintiffs who happen to be human beings are not legally competent due to factors such as disability or age. The Ninth Circuit's analysis contains a very clear and helpful review of both constitutional and statutory standing principles. Ultimately, the court's conclusion turned on its interpretation of a particular term that appears in both the Endangered Species Act and the APA. Consider whether you find this interpretation persuasive.

Cetacean Community v. Bush
386 F.3d 1169 (9th Cir. 2004)

WILLIAM A. FLETCHER, CIRCUIT JUDGE:

We are asked to decide whether the world's cetaceans have standing to bring suit in their own name under the Endangered Species Act ... and the Administrative Procedure Act. We hold that cetaceans do not have standing under these statutes.

I. Background

The sole plaintiff in this case is the Cetacean Community ("Cetaceans"). The Cetacean Community is the name chosen by the Cetaceans' self-appointed attorney for all of the world's whales, porpoises, and dolphins. The Cetaceans' challenge the

United States Navy's use of Surveillance Towed Array Sensor System Low Frequency Active Sonar ("SURTASS LFAS") during wartime or heightened threat conditions. The Cetaceans allege that the Navy has violated, or will violate, the Endangered Species Act ("ESA"), 16 U.S.C. §§ 1531–1544. . . .

The Navy has developed SURTASS LFAS to assist in detecting quiet submarines at long range. This sonar has both active and passive components. The active component consists of low frequency underwater transmitters. These transmitters emit loud sonar pulses, or "pings," that can travel hundreds of miles through the water. The passive listening component consists of hydrophones that detect pings returning as echoes. Through their attorney, the Cetaceans contend that SURTASS LFAS harms them by causing tissue damage and other serious injuries, and by disrupting biologically important behaviors including feeding and mating. . . .

The Cetaceans . . . seek to compel President Bush and Secretary of Defense Rumsfeld to undertake regulatory review of use of SURTASS LFAS during threat and wartime conditions. The Navy has specifically excepted such use of SURTASS LFAS from the current regulations. The Cetaceans seek an injunction ordering the President and the Secretary of Defense to consult with the National Marine Fisheries Service under the ESA, 16 U.S.C. § 1536(a). . . . They also seek an injunction banning use of SURTASS LFAS until the President and the Secretary of Defense comply with what the Cetaceans contend these statutes command.

Defendants moved to dismiss the Cetaceans' suit under Federal Rules of Civil Procedure 12(b)(1) for lack of subject matter jurisdiction and 12(b)(6) for failure to state a claim upon which relief can be granted. Without specifying which of these rules was the basis for its decision, the district court granted the motion to dismiss. The court held, *inter alia*, that the Cetaceans lacked standing under the ESA   and the Administrative Procedure Act ("APA").

The Cetaceans timely appeal. We review the district court's standing decision de novo. We agree with the district court that the Cetaceans have not been granted standing to sue by the ESA . . . or the APA. We therefore conclude that dismissal under Rule 12(b)(6) for failure to state a claim was correct, and we affirm the district court. . . .

III. Standing

Standing involves two distinct inquiries. First, an Article III federal court must ask whether a plaintiff has suffered sufficient injury to satisfy the "case or controversy" requirement of Article III. To satisfy Article III, a plaintiff "must show that (1) it has suffered an 'injury in fact' that is (a) concrete and particularized and (b) actual or imminent, not conjectural or hypothetical; (2) the injury is fairly traceable to the challenged action of the defendant; and (3) it is likely, as opposed to merely speculative, that the injury will be redressed by a favorable decision." If a plaintiff lacks Article III standing, Congress may not confer standing on that plaintiff by statute. *Lujan v. Defenders of Wildlife*, 504 U.S. 555, 576–77 (1992). A suit brought by a plaintiff without Article III standing is not a "case or controversy," and an Article III federal court therefore lacks subject matter jurisdiction over the suit. In that event, the suit should be dismissed under Rule 12(b)(1).

Second, if a plaintiff has suffered sufficient injury to satisfy Article III, a federal court must ask whether a statute has conferred "standing" on that plaintiff. Nonconstitutional standing exists when "a particular plaintiff has been granted a right to sue by the specific statute under which he or she brings suit." To ensure enforcement of statutorily created duties, Congress may confer standing as it sees fit on any plaintiff who satisfies Article III. Where it is arguable whether a plaintiff has suffered sufficient injury to satisfy Article III, the Supreme Court has sometimes insisted as a matter of "prudence" that Congress make its intention clear before it will construe a statute to confer standing on a particular plaintiff. If a plaintiff has suffered sufficient injury to satisfy the jurisdictional requirement of Article III but Congress has not granted statutory standing, that plaintiff cannot state a claim upon which relief can be granted. In that event, the suit should be dismissed under Rule 12(b)(6).

A. Article III Standing

Article III does not compel the conclusion that a statutorily authorized suit in the name of an animal is not a "case or controversy." As commentators have observed, nothing in the text of Article III explicitly limits the ability to bring a claim in federal court to humans. See U.S. Const. art. III; see also Cass R. Sunstein, *Standing for Animals (With Notes on Animal Rights)*, 47 UCLA L. Rev. 1333 (2000) (arguing that Congress could grant standing to animals, but has not); Katherine A. Burke, *Can We Stand For It? Amending the Endangered Species Act with an Animal-Suit Provision*, 75 U. Colo. L. Rev. 633 (2004) (same).

Animals have many legal rights, protected under both federal and state laws. In some instances, criminal statutes punish those who violate statutory duties that protect animals. In other instances, humans whose interests are affected by the existence or welfare of animals are granted standing to bring civil suits to enforce statutory duties that protect these animals. . . .

It is obvious that an animal cannot function as a plaintiff in the same manner as a juridically competent human being. But we see no reason why Article III prevents Congress from authorizing a suit in the name of an animal, any more than it prevents suits brought in the name of artificial persons such as corporations, partnerships or trusts, and even ships, or of juridically incompetent persons such as infants, juveniles, and mental incompetents.

If Article III does not prevent Congress from granting standing to an animal by statutorily authorizing a suit in its name, the question becomes whether Congress has passed a statute actually doing so. We therefore turn to whether Congress has granted standing to the Cetaceans under the ESA . . . or through the gloss of Section 10(a) of the APA.

B. Statutory Standing

1. The APA

Section 10(a) of the APA provides:

> A person suffering legal wrong because of agency action, or adversely affected or aggrieved by agency action within the meaning of a relevant statute, is entitled to judicial review thereof.

5 U.S.C. § 702. When a plaintiff seeks to challenge federal administrative action, Section 10(a) provides a mechanism to enforce the underlying substantive statute. Section 10(a) grants standing to any person "adversely affected or aggrieved by a relevant statute," making the relevant inquiry whether the plaintiff is hurt within the meaning of that underlying statute.

RULE

If a statute provides a plaintiff a right to sue, it is often said that the plaintiff has been granted a "private right of action." The phrase "private right of action" is sometimes used in the context of administrative law to refer to a right to challenge administrative action that is explicitly and directly provided by a particular statute, in contrast to a right to challenge administrative action granted only when the statute is read with the gloss of Section 10(a) of the APA. See, e.g., *Lujan v. National Wildlife Federation*, 497 U.S. 871, 882 (1990). This manner of speaking is somewhat misleading when a plaintiff seeks to challenge an administrative action, for the end result is the same whether the underlying statute grants standing directly or whether the APA provides the gloss that grants standing. In both cases, the plaintiff can bring suit to challenge the administrative action in question. In the first case, the substantive statute grants statutory standing directly to the plaintiff. In the second case, the substantive statute is enforced through Section 10(a) of the APA.

"ARGUABLY WITHIN"

In *Data Processing*, the Supreme Court construed Section 10(a) to grant standing to all those "arguably within the zone of interests" protected by the substantive statute whose duties the plaintiff was seeking to enforce. Under the reading of "arguably within" provided by *Data Processing*, courts grant standing fairly generously under the APA. As the Supreme Court wrote in *Clarke v. Securities Industry Association*, 479 U.S. 388, 399 (1987), the "zone of interests" test is "not meant to be especially demanding," and a court should deny standing only "if the plaintiff's interests are so marginally related to or inconsistent with the purposes implicit in the statute that it cannot reasonably be assumed that Congress intended to permit the suit."

2. The ESA

The ESA contains an explicit provision granting standing to enforce the duties created by the statute. The ESA's citizen-suit provision states that "any person" may "commence a civil suit on his own behalf ... to enjoin any person, including the United States and any other governmental instrumentality or agency ... who is alleged to be in violation of any provision of this chapter or regulation. ..." 16 U.S.C. § 1540(g)(1)(A). The ESA contains an explicit definition of the "person" who is authorized to enforce the statute:

> The term "person" means an individual, corporation, partnership, trust, association, or an other private entity; or any officer, employee, agent, department, or instrumentality of the Federal Government, or any State, municipality, or political subdivision of a State, or of any foreign government; any State, municipality, or political subdivision of a State; or any other entity subject to the jurisdiction of the United States.

Id. § 1532(13).

The ESA also contains separate definitions of "species," "endangered species," "threatened species," and "fish and wildlife." A "species" is defined as follows:

> The term "species" includes any subspecies of fish or wildlife or plants, and any distinct population segment of any species of vertebrate fish or wildlife which interbreeds when mature.

Id. § 1532(16). "Fish or wildlife" are defined as follows:

> The term "fish or wildlife" means any member of the animal kingdom, including without limitation any mammal, fish, bird . . . amphibian, reptile, mollusk, crustacean, arthropod or other invertebrate. . . .

Id. § 1532(8). An "endangered species" is defined as follows:

> The term "endangered species" means any species which is in danger of extinction throughout all or a significant portion of its range other than [certain dangerous species of insects].

Id. § 1532(6). Finally, a "threatened species" is defined as follows:

> The term "threatened species": means any species which is likely to become an endangered species within the foreseeable future throughout all or a significant portion of its range.

Id. § 1532(20).

It is obvious both from the scheme of the statute, as well as from the statute's explicit definitions of its terms, that animals are the protected rather than the protectors. The scheme of the ESA is that a "person," as defined in § 1532(13), may sue in federal district court to enforce the duties the statute prescribes. Those duties protect animals who are "endangered" or "threatened" under § 1532(6) and (20). The statute is set up to authorize "persons" to sue to protect animals whenever those animals are "endangered" or "threatened." Animals are not authorized to sue in their own names to protect themselves. There is no hint in the definition of "person" in § 1532(13) that the "person" authorized to bring suit to protect an endangered or threatened species can be an animal that is itself endangered or threatened.

We get the same answer if we read the ESA through Section 10(a) of the APA. The Supreme Court has specifically instructed us that standing under the ESA is broader than under the APA's "zone of interests" test. *Bennett v. Spear*, 520 U.S. 154, 163–64 (1997). Moreover, like the ESA, Section 10(a) of the APA grants standing to a "person." "Person" is explicitly defined to include "an individual, partnership, corporation, association, or public or private organization other than an agency." 5 U.S.C. §§ 551(2), 701(b)(2). Notably absent from that definition is "animal." *Data Processing* and *Clarke* instruct us that Section 10(a) means that we should read the underlying statute to grant standing generously, such that "persons" who are "adversely affected or aggrieved" are all persons "arguably within the zone of interests" protected by the underlying statute. But, as with the ESA, these cases do not instruct us to expand the basic definition of "person" beyond the definition provided in the APA....

Conclusion

We agree ... that "[i]f Congress and the President intended to take the extraordinary step of authorizing animals as well as people and legal entities to sue, they could, and should, have said so plainly." In the absence of any such statement in the ESA ... or the APA, we conclude that the Cetaceans do not have statutory standing to sue.

AFFIRMED.

Notes

1. "Statutory standing" as right of action. A complainant must do more than satisfy the requirements for constitutional standing to challenge an agency's alleged statutory violation. In addition, the complainant must, as *Cetacean Community* helpfully explains, be able to invoke a "private right of action." This requirement flows out of the general principle that not everyone has the right to seek judicial redress for any given violation of law. For instance, suppose a driver negligently runs into another car in a parking lot. Only a person who has suffered some legally cognizable harm from the negligence (e.g., the owner of the struck car) can properly sue the driver. A person who has no connection at all to the accident cannot properly sue no matter how outraged she is by the very thought of careless driving.

A statute might create a legal rule but not grant any person a right of action to contest its violation. In that case, persons wishing to contest a statutory violation would have to look elsewhere for a right of action. They might not find any. For instance, in *Alabama Power Co. v. Ickes*, 302 U.S. 464 (1938), a utility challenged federal loans extended to municipalities for the purpose of building electricity-distribution systems. The utility claimed that the statute authorizing the loan program was unconstitutional and that the agency issuing the loans had exceeded its statutory authority in any event. The Supreme Court ruled that the utility could not obtain judicial redress because it had no legal right to be free from lawful competition — even if that lawful competition had been made possible by a violation of law that the utility had no right to contest.

Many enabling acts solve this problem by including a specific statutory review scheme that creates a cause of action for contesting violations and designates which classes of plaintiffs may invoke it. For instance, as discussed in *Lujan* and *Cetacean Community*, the Endangered Species Act authorizes "any person" to obtain judicial review of violations of that Act. 16 U.S.C. § 1540(g). Also, as noted above, the APA's cause of action, 5 U.S.C. § 702, provides that "[a] person suffering legal wrong because of agency action, or adversely affected or aggrieved by agency action within the meaning of a relevant statute, is entitled to judicial review thereof." Our next note dives into the meaning of this important provision.

2. Section 702 and the "zone of interests." Section 702 is broadly understood as granting a cause of action to persons who have either suffered a "legal wrong" or have been "adversely affected or aggrieved by agency action within the meaning of a relevant statute." The "legal wrong" prong of § 702 requires a plaintiff to claim that the challenged action violated a "legal interest" or "legal right," which could be based on common law rights of property, contract, or tort, or a statute that confers a privilege. *Alabama Power*, discussed in note 1, provides a fine example of a plaintiff that lacked such a legal right—the plaintiff utility might suffer harm due to the government's extension of loans to competing municipal electrical systems, but the utility had no "legal right" to be free of such competition.

As a practical matter, a modern litigant need not worry about satisfying the "legal wrong" prong of § 702 because the Supreme Court has interpreted the "adversely affected or aggrieved" prong extremely broadly to open the doors wide to judicial review. The seminal case on this point is *Association of Data Processing Service Organizations v. Camp*, 397 U.S. 150 (1970). The petitioners, who were in the data processing service business, challenged a ruling by the Comptroller of the Currency that allowed national banks to provide data processing services to banks and bank customers. Thus, the petitioners were raising the kind of competitive injury claim rejected in *Alabama Power*.

The Court nonetheless ruled that petitioners had standing. As a threshold matter, the petitioners had plainly suffered an injury-in-fact sufficient for a constitutional "case" or "controversy." After noting this point, the Court explained:

> The question of standing . . . concerns, apart from the 'case' or 'controversy' test, the question whether the interest sought to be protected by the complainant is arguably within the zone of interests to be protected or regulated by the statute or constitutional guarantee in question. Thus the Administrative Procedure Act grants standing to a person 'aggrieved by agency action within the meaning of a relevant statute.' 5 U.S.C. s 702. . . .

> . . . [Section] 4 of the Bank Service Corporation Act of 1962, 12 U.S.C. s 1864, . . . provides:

> "No bank service corporation may engage in any activity other than the performance of bank services for banks."

> The Court of Appeals for the First Circuit held in *Arnold Tours, Inc. v. Camp*, 408 F.2d 1147, 1153, that by reason of s 4 a data processing company has standing to contest the legality of a national bank performing data processing services for other banks and bank customers:

"Section 4 had a broader purpose than regulating only the service corporations. It was also a response to the fears expressed by a few senators, that
without such a prohibition, the bill would have enabled 'banks to engage in
a nonbanking activity,' S.Rep.No.2105, and thus constitute 'a serious exception to the accepted public policy which strictly limits banks to banking.'
We think Congress has provided the sufficient statutory aid to standing
even though the competition may not be the precise kind Congress legislated against."

We do not put the issue in those words, for they implicate the merits. We
do think, however, that s 4 arguably brings a competitor within the zone of
interests protected by it.

In short, the "relevant statute" tried to make sure that banks stuck to banking. The
petitioners wanted banks to stick to banking, too — albeit for reasons that were
competitive rather than public-spirited. Given this congruence, the Court was willing to hold that the petitioners sought to protect an interest "arguably [notice the
weakness of this word] within the zone of interests to be protected or regulated by
the statute . . . in question."

Seventeen years later, in *Clarke v. Securities Industry Ass'n*, 479 U.S. 388 (1987),
the Court stressed the weakness of the "zone of interests" requirement still further:

The "zone of interest" test is a guide for deciding whether, in view of Congress' evident intent to make agency action presumptively reviewable, a particular plaintiff should be heard to complain of a particular agency decision.
In cases where the plaintiff is not itself the subject of the contested regulatory action, the test denies a right of review if the plaintiff's interests are *so
marginally related to or inconsistent with the purposes implicit in the statute
that it cannot reasonably be assumed that Congress intended to permit the suit.*
The test is not meant to be especially demanding; in particular, *there need be
no indication of congressional purpose to benefit the would-be plaintiff.*

(Emphasis added.) So, if *Clarke* is to be believed, § 702 may grant statutory standing
to would-be plaintiffs even if they are not members of a class Congress sought to
benefit.

If you find the preceding conclusion somewhat counter-intuitive, you might take
some comfort from the majority's analysis in *Air Courier Conference of America v.
American Postal Workers Union, AFL-CIO*, 498 U.S. 517 (1991). In this case, unions
representing postal workers challenged the Postal Service's decision to suspend its
statutory postal monopoly to permit private couriers to deliver letters to foreign
postal services, a practice called "international remailing." The unions were interested in protecting their members' jobs from competition. A narrow majority held
that this interest was not covered by § 702:

We must inquire then, as to Congress' intent in enacting the PES in order
to determine whether postal workers were meant to be within the zone of

interests protected by those statutes. The particular language of the statutes provides no support for respondents' assertion that Congress intended to protect jobs with the Postal Service. In fact, the provisions of 18 U.S.C. § 1696(c), allowing private conveyance of letters if done on a one-time basis or without compensation, and 39 U.S.C. § 601(a), allowing letters to be carried out of the mails if certain procedures are followed, indicate that the congressional concern was not with opportunities for postal workers but with the receipt of necessary revenues for the Postal Service.

Air Courier's seemingly tougher treatment of the scope of the "zone" did not last long. In *National Credit Union Administration v. First National Bank & Trust Co.*, 522 U.S. 479 (1998), a group of banks challenged the National Credit Union Administration's expansive interpretation of a statute limiting the scope of credit union membership. A five-justice majority held that the banks had satisfied § 702:

> Our prior cases, therefore, have consistently held that for a plaintiff's interests to be arguably within the "zone of interests" to be protected by a statute, there does not have to be an "indication of congressional purpose to benefit the would-be plaintiff." The proper inquiry is simply "whether the interest sought to be protected by the complainant is *arguably* within the zone of interests to be protected . . . by the statute." *Data Processing* (emphasis added). Hence in applying the "zone of interests" test, we do not ask whether, in enacting the statutory provision at issue, Congress specifically intended to benefit the plaintiff. Instead, we first discern the interests "arguably . . . to be protected" by the statutory provision at issue; we then inquire whether the plaintiff's interests affected by the agency action in question are among them.

> Section 109 provides that "[f]ederal credit union membership shall be limited to groups having a common bond of occupation or association, or to groups within a well-defined neighborhood, community, or rural district." 12 U.S.C. § 1759. By its express terms, § 109 limits membership in every federal credit union to members of definable "groups." Because federal credit unions may, as a general matter, offer banking services only to members, § 109 also restricts the markets that every federal credit union can serve. Although these markets need not be small, they unquestionably are limited. The link between § 109's regulation of federal credit union membership and its limitation on the markets that federal credit unions can serve is unmistakable. Thus, even if it cannot be said that Congress had the specific purpose of benefiting commercial banks, one of the interests "arguably . . . to be protected" by § 109 is an interest in limiting the markets that federal credit unions can serve. This interest is precisely the interest of respondents affected by the NCUA's interpretation of § 109. As competitors of federal credit unions, respondents certainly have an interest in limiting the markets that federal credit unions can serve, and the

NCUA's interpretation has affected that interest by allowing federal credit unions to increase their customer base.

The majority cited a series of cases, including *Data Processing* and *Clarke*, for support for the proposition that the "zone" test does not require that a plaintiff be a member of a class that Congress sought to benefit for the plaintiff to enjoy standing under § 702. *See Match-E-Be-Nash-She-Wish Band of Pottawatomi Indians v. Patchak*, 132 S. Ct. 2199, 2210 (2012) (confirming this point yet again).

To finish our tour of the "zone" with still more evidence of its breadth, consider *Bennett v. Spear*, 520 U.S. 154 (1997), which determined that ranchers satisfied the "zone of interests" test for the purpose of using the Endangered Species Act to sue the government to take water away from endangered fish:

> Whether a plaintiff's interest is "arguably . . . protected . . . by the statute" within the meaning of the zone-of-interests test is to be determined not by reference to the overall purpose of the Act in question (here, species preservation), but by reference to the particular provision of law upon which the plaintiff relies. As we said with the utmost clarity in *National Wildlife Federation*, "the plaintiff must establish that the injury he complains of . . . falls within the 'zone of interests' sought to be protected by the statutory provision whose violation forms the legal basis for his complaint."

> . . . [P]etitioners allege a violation of § 7 of the ESA, which requires . . . that each agency "use the best scientific and commercial data available," § 1536(a)(2). Petitioners contend that the available scientific and commercial data show that the continued operation of the Klamath Project will not have a detrimental impact on the endangered suckers, that the imposition of minimum lake levels is not necessary to protect the fish, and that by issuing a Biological Opinion which makes unsubstantiated findings to the contrary the defendants have acted arbitrarily and in violation of § 1536(a)(2). The obvious purpose of the requirement that each agency "use the best scientific and commercial data available" is to ensure that the ESA not be implemented haphazardly, on the basis of speculation or surmise. While this no doubt serves to advance the ESA's overall goal of species preservation, we think it readily apparent that another objective (if not indeed the primary one) is to avoid needless economic dislocation produced by agency officials zealously but unintelligently pursuing their environmental objectives. That economic consequences are an explicit concern of the ESA is evidenced by § 1536(h), which provides exemption from § 1536(a)(2)'s no-jeopardy mandate where there are no reasonable and prudent alternatives to the agency action and the benefits of the agency action clearly outweigh the benefits of any alternatives. We believe the "best scientific and commercial data" provision is similarly intended, at least in part, to prevent uneconomic (because erroneous) jeopardy determinations. Petitioners' claim that they are victims of such a mistake is plainly within the zone of interests that the provision protects.

Are you surprised by the conclusion that the ranchers' interest—maintaining their access to water that might otherwise keep endangered fish alive—fell into the zone of interests arguably protected by the ESA?

3. The zone-of-interests test spread beyond § 702. Although the Supreme Court developed the zone-of-interests test as a gloss on § 702, it later applied this test to determine whether plaintiffs could invoke more specific causes of action established by other statutes. Commenting on this practice in *Lexmark Intern., Inc. v. Static Control Components, Inc.*, 134 S. Ct. 1377 (2014), the Court explained:

> First, we presume that a statutory cause of action extends only to plaintiffs whose interests "fall within the zone of interests protected by the law invoked." *Allen*, 468 U.S., at 751. The modern "zone of interests" formulation originated in *Association of Data Processing Service Organizations, Inc. v. Camp*, 397 U.S. 150 (1970), as a limitation on the cause of action for judicial review conferred by the Administrative Procedure Act (APA). We have since made clear, however, that it applies to all statutorily created causes of action; that it is a "requirement of general application"; and that Congress is presumed to "legislat[e] against the background of" the zone-of-interests limitation, "which applies unless it is expressly negated." *Bennett v. Spear*, 520 U.S. 154, 163 (1997). It is "perhaps more accurat[e]," though not very different as a practical matter, to say that the limitation always applies and is never negated, but that our analysis of certain statutes will show that they protect a more-than-usually "expan[sive]" range of interests. *Bennett, supra*, at 164.

Complicating matters, alas, the Court has also advised that "the breadth of the zone of interests varies according to the provisions of law at issue, so that what comes within the zone of interests of a statute for purposes of obtaining judicial review of administrative action under the 'generous review provisions' of the APA may not do so for other purposes." *Id.* at 1389. Therefore, before applying an APA-style approach to a non-APA cause of action, you should check to make sure that the courts have not narrowed or expanded the reach of the zone in that context. *See, e.g., White Stallion Energy Center, LLC v. EPA*, 748 F.3d 1222 (D.C. Cir. 2014) (applying a tighter "zone" to a suit brought by an energy company relying on § 112 of the Clean Air Act to force EPA to impose stricter regulatory requirements on competitor energy companies) rev'd by *Michigan v. EPA*, 135 S. Ct. 2699 (2015).

4. The narrowing category of prudential standing. Rather than mooring prudential standing limitations in the text of the Constitution or some statute, courts admit that they make them up. On its face, this practice is hard to square with the Supreme Court's habit of intoning that the federal courts have a "virtually unflagging" obligation to resolve cases that fall within their jurisdiction. *See, e.g., Sprint Communications, Inc. v. Jacobs*, 134 S. Ct. 584, 591 (2013). In *Lexmark Intern., Inc. v. Static Control Components, Inc.*, 134 S. Ct. 1377 (2014), the Court partially resolved this tension by clarifying that certain doctrines that it has characterized as prudential in the past are, in fact, rooted in either constitutional or statutory concerns. Moreover, the Court suggested that it might, someday, eliminate the category of "prudential standing" altogether.

The *Lexmark* Court observed that prudential standing, though not "exhaustively" defined, has been generally associated with three principles: "the general prohibition on a litigant's raising another person's legal rights, the rule barring adjudication of generalized grievances more appropriately addressed in the representative branches, and the requirement that a plaintiff's complaint fall within the zone of interests protected by the law invoked."

Only the last of these three, the zone-of-interests test, was directly implicated in *Lexmark* itself. A party in this case sought to bring a somewhat unusual Lanham Act claim for unfair competition. Along the way to concluding that the party's claim satisfied the zone-of-interests test, the Court explained that it had, in the past, mischaracterized application of this test to non-APA causes of action as prudential. Properly understood, however, the zone-of-interests test is just a tool for determining how far Congress intended any given statutory cause of action to reach. It is therefore rooted in statutory meaning rather than in judicial notions of prudence.

Turning to "generalized grievances," the *Lexmark* Court emphasized that a string of recent cases had insisted that this limitation is constitutional, rather than, as some earlier cases had indicated, prudential. *See, e.g., Lance v. Coffman*, 549 U.S. 437 (2007) (*per curiam*) (collecting authority for the proposition that this bar is constitutional); *cf. FEC v. Akins*, 524 U.S. 11 (1998) (suggesting that this bar might be prudential).

As for third party standing, which generally blocks a litigant from suing to enforce somebody else's legal rights, the Court conceded that this limit was "harder to classify." Some cases, the Court admitted, characterize this doctrine as prudential in nature; other cases suggest that this doctrine speaks to whether a litigant can invoke a cause of action. Rather than indulge in still more dicta, the Court elected to leave this "doctrine's proper place in the standing firmament [for] another day."

Lexmark's unanimous opinion seems to signal that the Court thinks that the judiciary lacks a license to create additional limits on standing beyond those that it can moor in either the Constitution or statute. *Lexmark* is surely not the last word on this subject, however, and perhaps the Court will find itself unable to resist creating and imposing "prudential" limits on access to the courts from time to time. Along these lines, it bears noting that, just the year before in *United States v. Windsor*, a narrow majority, disregarding Justice Scalia's mockery, characterized the requirement that a case involve a genuinely adversarial clash between parties as merely "prudential." 133 S. Ct. 2675 (2013). *Windsor* was a highly-charged case that rejected the constitutionality of the Defense of Marriage Act's denial of statutory benefits to same-sex couples. Its approach to standing might therefore be a function of exceptional cases making for odd law.

5. Last prudential standing doctrine still standing? Third party standing. The Supreme Court offered its most recent significant discussion of third party standing doctrine in *Kowalski v. Tesmer*, 543 U.S. 125 (2004). In this case, the plaintiff-attorneys challenged the constitutionality of a Michigan statute and judicial practice that denies appellate counsel to indigent defendants who have been convicted after pleading guilty. The Court explained:

> We have adhered to the rule that a party "generally must assert his own legal rights and interests, and cannot rest his claim to relief on the legal rights or interests of third parties." This rule assumes that the party with the right has the appropriate incentive to challenge (or not challenge) governmental action and to do so with the necessary zeal and appropriate presentation. It represents a "healthy concern that if the claim is brought by someone other than one at whom the constitutional protection is aimed," the courts might be "called upon to decide abstract questions of wide public significance even though other governmental institutions may be more competent to address the questions and even though judicial intervention may be unnecessary to protect individual rights."
>
> We have not treated this rule as absolute, however, recognizing that there may be circumstances where it is necessary to grant a third party standing to assert the rights of another. But we have limited this exception by requiring that a party seeking third-party standing make two additional showings. First, we have asked whether the party asserting the right has a "close" relationship with the person who possesses the right. Second, we have considered whether there is a "hindrance" to the possessor's ability to protect his own interests.
>
> We have been quite forgiving with these criteria in certain circumstances. "Within the context of the First Amendment," for example, "the Court has enunciated other concerns that justify a lessening of prudential limitations on standing." And "[i]n several cases, this Court has allowed standing to litigate the rights of third parties when enforcement of the challenged restriction against the litigant would result indirectly in the violation of third parties' rights." Beyond these examples—none of which is implicated here—we have not looked favorably upon third-party standing.

After stating this standard, the majority determined that the plaintiff-attorneys lacked a "close" relationship with the group whose rights they sought to enforce—unidentified prisoners who would at some point be denied appellate counsel based on the operation of the allegedly unconstitutional statute. In addition, the Court ruled that these hypothetical, future "clients" did not face sufficient "hindrance" to justify granting third-party standing to the plaintiff-attorneys given that the prisoners, if denied appellate counsel, would have access to the Michigan state courts to appeal the constitutionality of such denial. That it would be harder for prisoners to press such an appeal *without* counsel did not impress the majority.

Why might the Court have been reluctant to let lawyers enjoy third-party standing? By way of review, why was it plausible to suppose that the lawyers in *Kowalski* had satisfied the requirements of constitutional standing? LIVELIHOOD → LIB OR PROP

E. Who Can Be Sued—Immunity Issues

When you sue the government, you are asking one part of the government—the courts—to discipline the actions of another part—typically some executive actor. This point suggests a basic question: Where do the courts get this power to tell other parts of the very same government what to do? The doctrine of sovereign immunity presupposes that courts get this power from the government itself as a matter of grace. In other words, you can sue the government only if the government lets you do so by waiving its sovereign immunity from suit in its own courts.

The U.S. Code is littered with waivers of the government's sovereign immunity. One of the most important lies in 5 U.S.C. § 702 of the APA, which provides that

> An action in a court of the United States seeking relief *other than money damages* and stating a claim that an agency or an officer or employee thereof acted or failed to act in an official capacity or under color of legal authority *shall not be dismissed* nor relief therein be denied *on the ground that it is against the United States* or that the United States is an indispensable party.

This waiver allows a party to seek injunctive or declaratory relief against the United States. (It can also be used to get money from the United States so long as that money does not fall within the technical meaning of "money damages." *Bowen v. Massachusetts*, 487 U.S. 879 (1988).)

Another extremely important, broadly applicable waiver can be found in the Federal Tort Claims Act (FTCA), 28 U.S.C. §§ 1346(b), 2671–80. In essence, the FTCA provides that, where a plaintiff sues a United States employee for a state law tort committed in the scope of that person's employment, the United States shall be substituted as the defendant. As detailed in the notes below, the FTCA's waiver of sovereign immunity is subject to a complex set of procedural and substantive restrictions.

Sovereign immunity protects the government itself from suit; official immunities, by contrast, protect the government's officials from suit. From the beginning of the Republic, plaintiffs have avoided restrictions on suing the government by suing the officers and employees through which the government necessarily acts. One might think that the courts would reject such suits as mere evasions of sovereign immunity. This is, indeed, how courts regard suits brought against government officials acting in their *official* capacities—*i.e.*, when you sue someone in her official capacity, you are really just suing the government.

Courts, nonetheless, have long policed government misconduct by permitting plaintiffs to sue government officials in their *individual* capacities. Courts have, for instance, permitted suits for injunctive relief against both federal and state officials to force them to obey the law. *American School of Magnetic Healing v. McAnnulty*, 187 U.S. 94 (1902) (injunctive relief available to block postmaster from halting mail service due to alleged fraud); *Ex parte Young*, 209 U.S. 123 (1908) (injunctive relief available against state attorney general to block enforcement of unconstitutional statute). Courts avoid the obvious problem that such suits are, functionally speaking, directed at the sovereign on the theory that an official cannot be acting on behalf of the sovereign while disobeying the law. In the federal system, this dodge lost much of its importance when in 1976 Congress amended § 702 of the APA to add a broad waiver of sovereign immunity for actions seeking equitable relief.

Alternatively, a plaintiff might sue an official for damages, which, in theory, would come out of the official's own pocket. Suppose a police officer breaks down your door and drags you into a waiting car. The traditional means of testing the legality of this action would be to sue the police officer on common law claims such as battery and false imprisonment; the police officer would counter with the defense of legal authority. You might also be inclined to sue the police officer for violating your Fourth Amendment rights. Section 1983 creates a cause of action that you can use for this purpose if the police officer works for a state or local government. If the police officer works for the federal government, then you might bring a *Bivens* action instead. *See Bivens v. Six Unknown Fed. Narcotics Agents*, 403 U.S. 388, 396 (1971) (holding that plaintiff had cause of action under the Constitution to seek damages from federal narcotics agents for alleged violation of the Fourth Amendment).

Of course, using damages suits against individuals to police against official misconduct poses obvious dangers. For one thing, it may be grossly unfair to government officials who must often make difficult and sometimes very fast decisions in contexts where the law is hazy. For another, the fear of being sued may make government officials too risk averse to perform their jobs well. The law has responded to such concerns by fashioning various immunities applicable to these damages actions. The FTCA, as noted above, provides a limited remedy against the United States for torts committed by its officials, but it also immunizes these officials from liability for common law torts that they commit in the scope of their employment. This FTCA-based immunity does not apply to constitutional torts committed by federal officials, and of course it does not apply to § 1983 claims against state or local officials for violations of constitutional or federal statutory rights. To cover these claims, courts have fashioned doctrines of "qualified immunity" for most officials and "absolute immunity" for others (such as judges).

The materials below provide more detail on this complex body of law. As you work through these materials, consider the following problem:

Lesson 5E. John is an enforcement officer with a regional WTC office. Last year, he inspected a large Gallery winemaking and storage facility. During this inspection, it seems that he forgot to set the parking brake on his vehicle. After he got out of the vehicle, it ran down a steep hill, through an open, garage-style door of a Gallery warehouse, and smashed into a large stack of cases of expensive wine. Gallery totaled up the damage in lost wine and smashed equipment at $30,000 and requested that the WTC pay that amount in compensation. The WTC found that figure too high and refused to pay.

Gallery has asked its attorney Abby to determine whether it could use the courts to obtain compensation for the damages it claims John caused. At this initial stage of her investigation, she is contemplating bringing a claim under state tort law and a constitutional claim on the theory that Gallery has been deprived of its property without due process. Who would be the proper defendant (or defendants) to such claims? How might the various immunity doctrines discussed below affect these claims? Also, indulging some review of due process, how should the constitutional claim fare if a court ever reaches the merits? (Note 4 below on the FTCA should be helpful for the state law tort claim.)

Background of *FDIC v. Meyer*

The introduction to this subchapter threw quite a bit of complex law at you. Much of this law reappears in the case excerpt that follows. The Federal Savings and Loan Insurance Corporation (FSLIC) was installed as receiver for a failing thrift institution, Fidelity Savings and Loan Association (Fidelity). In this capacity, FSLIC, acting through its "special representative" Robert Pattullo, fired Meyer from his job as a high-ranking official of Fidelity. Meyer sued both FSLIC and Pattullo for violating his due process rights by depriving him of a property interest in continued employment protected under California law. The jury awarded Meyer a verdict of $130,000 against FSLIC. The jury also, however, concluded that the official who actually carried out the firing, Pattullo, was not liable due to qualified immunity. FSLIC's statutory successor, the Federal Deposit Insurance Corporation (FDIC), appealed to the Ninth Circuit, which affirmed the jury's verdict. The Supreme Court reversed the judgment.

To keep track of the moving parts in this opinion, consider the following questions as you read it: (a) Why wasn't Meyer's constitutional tort claim "cognizable" under the FTCA? (b) Given the inapplicability of the FTCA, how did the Court justify concluding that sovereign immunity had been waived? (c) Given the waiver of sovereign immunity, why wasn't the jury's verdict in favor of Meyer upheld? and (d) What is wrong with extending *Bivens* claims to cover agencies as well as their officials?

Federal Deposit Insurance Corp. v. Meyer

510 U.S. 471 (1994)

Justice Thomas delivered the opinion of the Court.

In *Bivens v. Six Unknown Fed. Narcotics Agents*, 403 U.S. 388 (1971), we implied a cause of action for damages against federal agents who allegedly violated the Constitution. Today we are asked to imply a similar cause of action directly against an agency of the Federal Government. Because the logic of *Bivens* itself does not support such an extension, we decline to take this step.

I

On April 13, 1982, the California Savings and Loan Commissioner seized Fidelity Savings and Loan Association (Fidelity), a California-chartered thrift institution, and appointed the Federal Savings and Loan Insurance Corporation (FSLIC) to serve as Fidelity's receiver under state law. That same day, the Federal Home Loan Bank Board appointed FSLIC to serve as Fidelity's receiver under federal law. In its capacity as receiver, FSLIC had broad authority to "take such action as may be necessary to put [the thrift] in a sound solvent condition." 48 Stat. 1259, as amended, 12 U.S.C. § 1729(b)(1)(A)(ii) (repealed 1989). Pursuant to its general policy of terminating the employment of a failed thrift's senior management, FSLIC, through its special representative Robert L. Pattullo, terminated respondent John H. Meyer, a senior Fidelity officer.

Approximately one year later, Meyer filed this lawsuit against a number of defendants, including FSLIC and Pattullo, in the United States District Court for the Northern District of California. At the time of trial, Meyer's sole claim against FSLIC and Pattullo was that his summary discharge deprived him of a property right (his right to continued employment under California law) without due process of law in violation of the Fifth Amendment. In making this claim, Meyer relied upon *Bivens v. Six Unknown Fed. Narcotics Agents, supra*, which implied a cause of action for damages against federal agents who allegedly violated the Fourth Amendment. The jury returned a $130,000 verdict against FSLIC, but found in favor of Pattullo on qualified immunity grounds.

Petitioner Federal Deposit Insurance Corporation (FDIC), FSLIC's statutory successor, appealed to the Court of Appeals for the Ninth Circuit, which affirmed. First, the Court of Appeals determined that the Federal Tort Claims Act (FTCA or Act), 28 U.S.C. §§ 1346(b), 2671–2680, did not provide Meyer's exclusive remedy. Although the FTCA remedy is "exclusive" for all "claims which are cognizable under section 1346(b)," 28 U.S.C. § 2679(a), the Court of Appeals decided that Meyer's claim was not cognizable under § 1346(b). The court then concluded that the "sue-and-be-sued" clause contained in FSLIC's organic statute, 12 U.S.C. § 1725(c)(4) (repealed 1989), constituted a waiver of sovereign immunity for Meyer's claim and entitled him to maintain an action against the agency. Finally, on the merits, the court affirmed the jury's conclusion that Meyer had been deprived of due process when he was summarily discharged without notice and a hearing. We granted certiorari to consider the validity of the damages award against FSLIC. . . .

II

Absent a waiver, sovereign immunity shields the Federal Government and its agencies from suit. *Loeffler v. Frank*, 486 U.S. 549, 554 (1988); *Federal Housing Administration v. Burr*, 309 U.S. 242, 244 (1940). Sovereign immunity is jurisdictional in nature. Indeed, the "terms of [the United States'] consent to be sued in any court define that court's jurisdiction to entertain the suit." . . . Therefore, we must first decide whether FSLIC's immunity has been waived.

A

When Congress created FSLIC in 1934, it empowered the agency "[t]o sue and be sued, complain and defend, in any court of competent jurisdiction." 12 U.S.C. § 1725(c)(4) (repealed 1989). By permitting FSLIC to sue and be sued, Congress effected a "broad" waiver of FSLIC's immunity from suit. *United States v. Nordic Village, Inc.*, 503 U.S. 30, 34 (1992). In 1946, Congress passed the FTCA, which waived the sovereign immunity of the United States for certain torts committed by federal employees. 28 U.S.C. § 1346(b).[4] In order to "place torts of 'suable' agencies . . . upon precisely the same footing as torts of 'nonsuable' agencies," *Loeffler, supra*, 486 U.S., at 562 (internal quotation marks omitted), Congress, through the FTCA, limited the scope of sue-and-be-sued waivers such as that contained in FSLIC's organic statute. The FTCA limitation provides:

> "The authority of any federal agency to sue and be sued in its own name shall not be construed to authorize suits against such federal agency on claims which are cognizable under section 1346(b) of this title, and the remedies provided by this title in such cases shall be exclusive." 28 U.S.C. § 2679(a).

Thus, if a suit is "cognizable" under § 1346(b) of the FTCA, the FTCA remedy is "exclusive" and the federal agency cannot be sued "in its own name," despite the existence of a sue-and-be-sued clause.

The first question, then, is whether Meyer's claim is "cognizable" under § 1346(b). The term "cognizable" is not defined in the Act. In the absence of such a definition, we construe a statutory term in accordance with its ordinary or natural meaning. Cognizable ordinarily means "[c]apable of being tried or examined before a designated tribunal; within [the] jurisdiction of [a] court or power given to [a] court to adjudicate [a] controversy." BLACK'S LAW DICTIONARY 259 (6th ed. 1990). Under this definition, the inquiry focuses on the jurisdictional grant provided by § 1346(b).

Section 1346(b) grants the federal district courts jurisdiction over a certain category of claims for which the United States has waived its sovereign immunity and "render[ed]" itself liable. *Richards v. United States*, 369 U.S. 1, 6 (1962). This category includes claims that are:

> "[1] against the United States, [2] for money damages, . . . [3] for injury or loss of property, or personal injury or death [4] caused by the negligent or wrongful act or omission of any employee of the Government [5] while acting within the scope of his office or employment, [6] under circumstances

___

4. Section 1346(b) provides: "[T]he district courts . . . shall have exclusive jurisdiction of civil actions on claims against the United States, for money damages, . . . for injury or loss of property, or personal injury or death caused by the negligent or wrongful act or omission of any employee of the Government while acting within the scope of his office or employment, under circumstances where the United States, if a private person, would be liable to the claimant in accordance with the law of the place where the act or omission occurred."

where the United States, if a private person, would be liable to the claimant in accordance with the law of the place where the act or omission occurred." 28 U.S.C. § 1346(b).

A claim comes within this jurisdictional grant—and thus is "cognizable" under § 1346(b)—if it is actionable under § 1346(b). And a claim is actionable under § 1346(b) if it alleges the six elements outlined above. . . .

Applying these principles to this case, we conclude that Meyer's constitutional tort claim is not "cognizable" under § 1346(b) because it is not actionable under § 1346(b)—that is, § 1346(b) does not provide a cause of action for such a claim. As noted above, to be actionable under § 1346(b), a claim must allege, inter alia, that the United States "would be liable to the claimant" as "a private person" "in accordance with the law of the place where the act or omission occurred." A constitutional tort claim such as Meyer's could not contain such an allegation. Indeed, we have consistently held that § 1346(b)'s reference to the "law of the place" means law of the State—the source of substantive liability under the FTCA. [String cite omitted.] By definition, federal law, not state law, provides the source of liability for a claim alleging the deprivation of a federal constitutional right. To use the terminology of *Richards*, the United States simply has not rendered itself liable under § 1346(b) for constitutional tort claims. Thus, because Meyer's constitutional tort claim is not cognizable under § 1346(b), the FTCA does not constitute his "exclusive" remedy. His claim was therefore properly brought against FSLIC "in its own name." 28 U.S.C. § 2679(a).

FDIC argues that by exposing a sue-and-be-sued agency to constitutional tort claims, our interpretation of "cognizability" runs afoul of Congress' understanding that § 2679(a) would place the torts of "suable" and "nonsuable" agencies on the same footing. *See Loeffler*, 486 U.S., at 562. FDIC would deem all claims "sounding in tort"—including constitutional torts—"cognizable" under § 1346(b). Under FDIC's reading of the statute, only the portion of § 1346(b) that describes a "tort"— *i.e.*, "claims against the United States, for money damages, . . . for injury or loss of property, or personal injury or death caused by the negligent or wrongful act or omission of any employee of the Government"—would govern cognizability. The remaining portion of § 1346(b) would simply describe a "limitation" on the waiver of sovereign immunity.[6]

---

6. FDIC relies upon United States v. Smith, 499 U.S. 160 (1991), for its interpretation of the term "cognizable." In *Smith*, the "foreign country" exception, 28 U.S.C. § 2680(k), barred plaintiffs' recovery against the Federal Government for injuries allegedly caused by the negligence of a Government employee working abroad. We held that the FTCA provided plaintiffs' "exclusive remedy," even though the FTCA itself did not provide a means of recovery. *Smith* did not involve § 2679(a), the provision at issue in this case, but rather § 2679(b)(1), which provides that the FTCA remedy is "exclusive of any other civil action or proceeding for money damages . . . against the employee whose act or omission gave rise to the claim." The Court had no occasion in *Smith* to address the meaning of the term "cognizable" because § 2679(b)(1) does not contain the term. We therefore find *Smith* unhelpful in this regard.

We reject this reading of the statute. As we have already noted, § 1346(b) describes the scope of jurisdiction by reference to claims for which the United States has waived its immunity and rendered itself liable. FDIC seeks to uncouple the scope of jurisdiction under § 1346(b) from the scope of the waiver of sovereign immunity under § 1346(b). Under its interpretation, the jurisdictional grant would be broad (covering all claims sounding in tort), but the waiver of sovereign immunity would be narrow (covering only those claims for which a private person would be held liable under state law). There simply is no basis in the statutory language for the parsing FDIC suggests. Section 2679(a)'s reference to claims "cognizable" under § 1346(b) means cognizable under the whole of § 1346(b), not simply a portion of it.

B

Because Meyer's claim is not cognizable under § 1346(b), we must determine whether FSLIC's sue-and-be-sued clause waives sovereign immunity for the claim. FDIC argues that the scope of the sue-and-be-sued waiver should be limited to cases in which FSLIC would be subjected to liability as a private entity. A constitutional tort claim such as Meyer's, FDIC argues, would fall outside the sue-and-be-sued waiver because the Constitution generally does not restrict the conduct of private entities. In essence, FDIC asks us to engraft a portion of the sixth element of § 1346(b) — liability "under circumstances where the United States, if a private person, would be liable to the claimant" — onto the sue-and-be-sued clause.

On its face, the sue-and-be-sued clause contains no such limitation. To the contrary, its terms are simple and broad: FSLIC "shall have power . . . [t]o sue and be sued, complain and defend, in any court of competent jurisdiction in the United States." 12 U.S.C. § 1725(c)(4) (repealed 1989). In the past, we have recognized that such sue-and-be-sued waivers are to be "liberally construed," *Federal Housing Administration v. Burr*, 309 U.S., at 245, notwithstanding the general rule that waivers of sovereign immunity are to be read narrowly in favor of the sovereign. *See United States v. Nordic Village, Inc.*, 503 U.S., at 34. *Burr* makes it clear that sue-and-be-sued clauses cannot be limited by implication unless there has been a

> "clea[r] show[ing] that certain types of suits are not consistent with the statutory or constitutional scheme, that an implied restriction of the general authority is necessary to avoid grave interference with the performance of a governmental function, or that for other reasons it was plainly the purpose of Congress to use the 'sue and be sued' clause in a narrow sense." 309 U.S., at 245 (footnote omitted).

. . . Absent such a showing, agencies "authorized to 'sue and be sued' are presumed to have fully waived immunity." *International Primate Protection League v. Administrators of Tulane Ed. Fund*, 500 U.S. 72, 86, n. 8 (1991) (describing the holding in *Burr*).

FDIC does not attempt to make the "clear" showing of congressional purpose necessary to overcome the presumption that immunity has been waived. . . .

. . . Because "[n]o showing has been made to overcome [the] presumption" that the sue-and-be-sued clause "fully waived" FSLIC's immunity in this instance, we hold that FSLIC's sue-and-be-sued clause waives the agency's sovereign immunity for Meyer's constitutional tort claim.

III

Although we have determined that Meyer's claim falls within the sue-and-be-sued waiver, our inquiry does not end at this point. Here we part ways with the Ninth Circuit, which determined that Meyer had a cause of action for damages against FSLIC because there had been a waiver of sovereign immunity. The Ninth Circuit's reasoning conflates two "analytically distinct" inquiries. *United States v. Mitchell*, 463 U.S., at 218. The first inquiry is whether there has been a waiver of sovereign immunity. If there has been such a waiver, as in this case, the second inquiry comes into play—that is, whether the source of substantive law upon which the claimant relies provides an avenue for relief. It is to this second inquiry that we now turn.

Meyer bases his due process claim on our decision in *Bivens*, which held that an individual injured by a federal agent's alleged violation of the Fourth Amendment may bring an action for damages against the agent. In our most recent decisions, we have "responded cautiously to suggestions that *Bivens* remedies be extended into new contexts." *Schweiker v. Chilicky*, 487 U.S. 412, 421 (1988).[9] In this case, Meyer seeks a significant extension of *Bivens*: He asks us to expand the category of defendants against whom *Bivens*-type actions may be brought to include not only federal agents, but federal agencies as well.

We know of no Court of Appeals decision, other than the Ninth Circuit's below, that has implied a *Bivens*-type cause of action directly against a federal agency. Meyer recognizes the absence of authority supporting his position, but argues that the "logic" of *Bivens* would support such a remedy. We disagree. In *Bivens*, the petitioner sued the agents of the Federal Bureau of Narcotics who allegedly violated his rights, not the Bureau itself. Here, Meyer brought precisely the claim that the logic of *Bivens* supports—a *Bivens* claim for damages against Pattullo, the FSLIC employee who terminated him.

An additional problem with Meyer's "logic" argument is the fact that we implied a cause of action against federal officials in *Bivens* in part because a direct action against the Government was not available. In essence, Meyer asks us to imply a damages action based on a decision that presumed the absence of that very action.

---

9. For example, a *Bivens* action alleging a violation of the Due Process Clause of the Fifth Amendment may be appropriate in some contexts, but not in others. *Compare* Davis v. Passman, 442 U.S. 228, 248–249 (1979) (implying *Bivens* action under the equal protection component of the Due Process Clause in the context of alleged gender discrimination in employment), *with* Schweiker v. Chilicky, 487 U.S., at 429 (refusing to imply *Bivens* action for alleged due process violations in the denial of Social Security disability benefits on the ground that a damages remedy was not included in the elaborate remedial scheme devised by Congress).

Meyer's real complaint is that Pattullo, like many *Bivens* defendants, invoked the protection of qualified immunity. But *Bivens* clearly contemplated that official immunity would be raised. More importantly, Meyer's proposed "solution"—essentially the circumvention of qualified immunity—would mean the evisceration of the *Bivens* remedy, rather than its extension. It must be remembered that the purpose of *Bivens* is to deter the officer. *See Carlson v. Green*, 446 U.S. 14, 21 (1980) ("Because the *Bivens* remedy is recoverable against individuals, it is a more effective deterrent than the FTCA remedy against the United States"). If we were to imply a damages action directly against federal agencies, thereby permitting claimants to bypass qualified immunity, there would be no reason for aggrieved parties to bring damages actions against individual officers. Under Meyer's regime, the deterrent effects of the *Bivens* remedy would be lost.

Finally, a damages remedy against federal agencies would be inappropriate even if such a remedy were consistent with *Bivens*. Here, unlike in *Bivens*, there are "special factors counselling hesitation" in the creation of a damages remedy. *Bivens*, 403 U.S., at 396. If we were to recognize a direct action for damages against federal agencies, we would be creating a potentially enormous financial burden for the Federal Government. Meyer disputes this reasoning and argues that the Federal Government already expends significant resources indemnifying its employees who are sued under *Bivens*. Meyer's argument implicitly suggests that the funds used for indemnification could be shifted to cover the direct liability of federal agencies. That may or may not be true, but decisions involving "'federal fiscal policy'" are not ours to make. We leave it to Congress to weigh the implications of such a significant expansion of Government liability.

IV

An extension of *Bivens* to agencies of the Federal Government is not supported by the logic of *Bivens* itself. We therefore hold that Meyer had no *Bivens* cause of action for damages against FSLIC. Accordingly, the judgment below is reversed.

SO ORDERED.

Background of *U-Series Int'l Serv., Ltd. v. USA*

The plaintiff in this case sued both the United States and a DEA official, Snider, in connection with the civil forfeiture of property seized as part of an investigation into money laundering. As you read the case excerpt below (authored by a future United States Attorney General, by the way), keep in mind the following questions: (a) How did the court justify concluding that the United States had waived sovereign immunity for the due process claim against it? (b) How did the court justify concluding that the United States had not, by contrast, waived sovereign immunity for the conversion claim against it? (c) How did the court justify dismissing the *Bivens* claim that Snider, the DEA official, had violated the plaintiff's Fifth Amendment right to due process?

U-Series Int'l Serv., Ltd. v. U.S.A.

1995 U.S. Dist. LEXIS 16562 (S.D.N.Y. Nov. 6, 1995)

MUKASEY, DISTRICT JUDGE:

Plaintiff U-Series International Services, Inc. ("U-Series"), brings this action against the United States and Drug Enforcement Administration ("DEA") Forfeiture Counsel William J. Snider in his individual and official capacities, to challenge the civil forfeiture of its property—$200,000 worth of electronics equipment. The Amended Complaint alleges that the United States violated plaintiff's Fourth, Fifth and Fourteenth Amendment rights, and the law of nations, and that Snider is liable under both the Federal Tort Claims Act and a *Bivens* cause of action. Plaintiff also seeks to add as a defendant DEA Special Agent Dwayne M. Dodds in his individual and official capacities. . . .

. . . For the reasons set forth below, the United States' and William Snider's motions for summary judgment are granted; plaintiff's motion to add Dodds is denied for lack of personal jurisdiction; and the pendent state law claim against Tambor is dismissed for lack of subject matter jurisdiction.

I.

The following facts, viewed in the light most favorable to plaintiff, are based on affidavits, declarations and documentary exhibits. Plaintiff is a Nigerian corporation that imports electronics equipment from the United States for resale in Nigeria. (Comp. ¶¶ 4, 8) Zeev Tambor, doing business as Omega Import & Export, sells electronics equipment in New York. (*Id.* at ¶¶ 7, 9) In July 1992, plaintiff sent $30,000 to Omega for electronics equipment to be shipped to Nigeria. (*Id.* at ¶¶ 10–12) On July 22, 1992, pursuant to a search warrant issued by Magistrate Judge Ronald Hedges of the United States District Court for the District of New Jersey, DEA agents searched a cargo container docked at the Port of Newark, New Jersey and seized electronics goods worth $64,000, including items owned by plaintiff which were destined for Nigeria. (Dodds Decl. ¶ 4, Ex. B) The equipment was seized as a result of a DEA investigation which revealed that plaintiff and Tambor laundered money for Nigerian drug traffickers Gregory and Linus Odilibe. (Snider Decl., Ex. 22 at 2; Dodds Decl., Ex. B, ¶¶ 4, 7, 10, 21–23)

After seizing the property, the government commenced forfeiture proceedings by mailing a notice of seizure to plaintiff on September 21, 1992, via certified mail. (Snider Decl. ¶ 4(e), Ex. 5) The notice included the subject, date, and place of the forfeiture, as well as detailed instructions about how to contest the forfeiture in a U.S. District Court or to request remission or mitigation of the forfeiture by the DEA. (Snider Decl., Ex. 4) Plaintiff did not receive this notice until October 21, 1992. (Snider Decl. ¶ 4(d), Ex. 5; Okwuchukwu Aff. ¶ 22) Starting on September 30, 1992, the government also published notice of the seizure in USA Today for three weeks. (Snider Decl. ¶ 4(e), Exh. 6) Plaintiff, however, was not in the United

States during this period, and did not see the publication. (Okwuchukwu Aff. ¶ 22) Plaintiff did learn from Omega of the seizure notice in a telephone call on or about September 30, 1992; Omega then sent plaintiff a copy of the notice. (*Id.* at ¶ 20) Plaintiff then sought legal assistance at the U.S. Embassy in Nigeria, and retained K.C. Okoli, Esq., an attorney in New York. (*Id.* at ¶ 21)

Plaintiff did not file a claim and bond for judicial review within the specified period. On the last day of that period, October 20, 1992, plaintiff instead petitioned the DEA for remission or mitigation of forfeiture. (Snider Decl. ¶ 4(f)) As a result of plaintiff's failure to file a claim and bond, the DEA issued a Declaration of Forfeiture on January 8, 1993. (*Id.* at ¶ 4(g)) Thereafter, on April 21, 1993, the DEA denied plaintiff's petition (*Id.* at ¶ 4(h)), and its later request for reconsideration. (*Id.* at ¶ 4 (k)–(r)) On April 15, 1994, plaintiff filed this action, alleging Fourth and Fifth Amendment claims against the United States and individual DEA officers, and a breach of contract claim against Zeev Tambor. Plaintiff also seeks to add as a defendant Dwayne Dodds in his individual capacity. The United States and the individual agents have moved to dismiss or, in the alternative, for summary judgment.

II.

. . . .

The threshold issue is whether this court has subject matter jurisdiction to review the DEA's forfeiture decisions. Jurisdiction exists to review the constitutional adequacy of the procedures followed, but does not exist to review the merits of the forfeiture itself. . . .

Plaintiff asserts that this court has jurisdiction pursuant to 28 U.S.C. §§ 1331, 1332(a), 1343(a), 1346(b), 1350, 1355, 1356, and 5 U.S.C. § 702. For any claim to be maintained against the United States, there must be a clear and unequivocal waiver of sovereign immunity in the statute giving rise to the claim. *United States v. Testan*, 424 U.S. 392, 399 (1976). Although plaintiff improperly cites Section 702 of the Administrative Procedure Act (APA) as a basis for jurisdiction, that section does provide the necessary waiver of sovereign immunity for equitable suits challenging agency action. 5 U.S.C. § 702; *Califano v. Sanders*, 430 U.S. 99, 105 (1977). Thus, the combination of the federal question statute, 28 U.S.C. § 1331, which confers on federal courts jurisdiction to hear claims arising under federal law, and the APA, empowers this court to hear the case.

Contrary to the government's contention, this case does not fall within any of the exceptions to the APA's waiver of sovereign immunity. These exceptions are: (1) suits seeking money damages, (2) suits in which there is an adequate remedy at law, and (3) suits that are precluded from review by statute or raise issues committed to agency discretion. 5 U.S.C. §§ 704, 701(a)(1). This case does not fit within any of the exceptions to Section 702's waiver of sovereign immunity. Plaintiff does not seek money damages from the United States, but only the return of the seized electronics or the value thereof, which is a form of equitable relief. *See Marshall Leasing v. United States*, 893 F.2d 1096, 1099 (9th Cir. 1990). Moreover, this is not a case in which a remedy is available in another forum. No other forum adequately can address or redress a constitutional violation. *Id.* at 1100–01.

Finally, review of the adequacy of the notice to plaintiff is not a matter committed to agency discretion. By contrast, the decision to remit or mitigate the forfeiture is one committed to agency discretion, and is unreviewable in court. *See LaChance v. Drug Enforcement Admin.*, 672 F. Supp. 76, 79 (E.D.N.Y. 1987); *United States v. One 1987 Jeep Wrangler*, 972 F.2d 472, 479 (2d Cir. 1992). In this instance, however, plaintiff challenges not the merits of the denial of remission but the adequacy of the forfeiture notice, raising questions of due process which are not committed to agency discretion, and which are reviewable by this court. *Onwubiko v. United States*, 969 F.2d 1392, 1398 (2d Cir. 1992); *Montgomery v. Scott*, 802 F. Supp. 930, 934 (W.D.N.Y. 1992); *Sterling v. United States*, 749 F. Supp. 1202, 1208 (E.D.N.Y. 1990).

The next issue is whether the procedures used by the DEA afforded due process. [Judge Mukasey then explained that the plaintiff's due process claim failed because, inter alia, he had received actual notice.]

III.

Plaintiff contends also that the United States illegally converted its property and is subject to suit under the Federal Tort Claims Act (FTCA). The FTCA provides for a waiver of the sovereign immunity of the United States for claims

> for injury or loss of property, or personal injury or death caused by the negligent or wrongful act or omission of any employee of the Government while acting within the scope of his office or employment, under circumstances where the United States, if a private person, would be liable to the claimant in accordance with the law of the place where the act or omission occurred.

28 U.S.C. § 1346(b). Section 2680(c), however, provides an exception to that waiver, for "[a]ny claim arising in respect of the assessment or collection of any tax or customs duty, or the detention of any goods or merchandise by any officer of customs or excise or any other law-enforcement officer." 28 U.S.C. § 2680 (c).

The Supreme Court has given the § 2680(c) exception an expansive reading. *See Kosak v. United States*, 465 U.S. 848, 851–62 (1988). The Court reasoned that the language "any claim arising in respect of" encompassed claims resulting from negligent handling or storage of the detained property, and was not limited to damage caused by the detention itself. *Id.* at 853–55. Additionally, the Court reviewed the legislative history of the provision and found that Congress intended to ensure that certain government activities were not disrupted by fraudulent claims, or claims for which another remedy was available. The Court found this purpose validated its reading of the statute. *Id.* at 855–61. The *Kosak* Court declined to address the scope of the phrase "other law-enforcement officers." *Id.* at 852 n.6.

Applying the Supreme Court's broad interpretation, other courts have read the phrase "any other law-enforcement officer" to include various federal agents. *Schlaebitz v. United States Dept. of Justice*, 924 F.2d 193, 194 (11th Cir. 1991) (U.S.

marshals); *Ysasi v. Rivkind*, 856 F.2d 1520, 1525 (Fed. Cir. 1988) (INS agents). Those courts faced with the question of whether the phrase covers DEA agents engaged in the search and seizure of drug-related property, uniformly have answered in the affirmative.... Because the DEA agents in this case are covered by the § 2680(c) exception, defendant's motion for summary judgment is granted. [Editors' Note: In 2008, the Supreme Court held that § 2860(c) applies to all law enforcement officers, not just those operating in a customs or excise capacity. *Ali v. Federal Bureau of Prisons*, 552 U.S. 214 (2008).]

IV.

Plaintiff also brings a *Bivens* action against William J. Snider for violation of its Fifth amendment rights. To prevail on such a claim, plaintiff must demonstrate: (1) that Snider denied it a constitutional right, and (2) that Snider is not qualifiedly immune. *See Kinoy v. Mitchell*, 851 F.2d 591, 594 (2d Cir. 1988), *cert. denied*, 489 U.S. 1052 (1989). With respect to the first prong, plaintiff alleges that defendant deprived plaintiff of its property without due process in violation of the Fifth Amendment, through his failure to exercise "due care" as Forfeiture Counsel to the DEA. (Comp. ¶ 36(v.)) Plaintiff alleges no intentional or reckless behavior by Snider, nor does plaintiff allege bad faith. Essentially, plaintiff alleges that Snider violated its rights because he was negligent. The Supreme Court made it clear in *Daniels v. Williams*, 474 U.S. 327, 328 (1986) that mere lack of due care by a state official does not "deprive" an individual of life, liberty or property without due process of law in violation of the Fourteenth Amendment. *See also Stubbs v. Dudley*, 849 F.2d 83, 85 (2d Cir. 1988). Negligence cannot sustain a claim under the Fifth Amendment either. *See Shaner v. United States*, 976 F.2d 990, 995 n.7 (6th Cir. 1992); *Barbera v. Smith*, 836 F.2d 96, 99 (2d Cir. 1987).

Even if plaintiff's constitutional rights had been violated, this defendant would be protected by qualified immunity. That doctrine protects federal officials engaged in administrative or discretionary functions from personal liability in *Bivens* actions "insofar as their conduct does not violate clearly established statutory or constitutional rights of which a reasonable person would have known." *Harlow v. Fitzgerald*, 457 U.S. 800, 818 (1982). The critical question is whether defendant's actions were objectively reasonable. *See Barbera v. Smith*, 836 F.2d 96, 101 (2d Cir. 1987), *cert. denied*, 489 U.S. 1065 (1989). Plaintiff's own failure to assert a constitutional violation, as discussed above, makes it plain that Snider did not act contrary to well-established law. The agents seized plaintiff's property pursuant to a valid warrant, and followed all procedural requirements. Plaintiff does not allege that any such requirements were ignored, or that Agent Snider acted in bad faith during any part of the investigation or administrative review. Defendant's motion for summary judgment on the *Bivens* claim therefore is granted.

V.

Plaintiff's request to amend the complaint to add a *Bivens* claim against DEA agent Dwayne Dodds in his individual capacity must be denied based on improper service and, consequently, lack of personal jurisdiction. When suing a government official in his personal capacity in a *Bivens* action, a plaintiff must serve the officer himself; service on the government is not enough. *Armstrong v. Sears*, 33 F.3d 182, 186–187 (2d Cir. 1994); *Despain v. Salt Lake Area Metro Gang Unit*, 13 F.3d 1436, 1438 (10th Cir. 1994); *Micklus v. Carlson*, 632 F.2d 227, 240 (3d Cir. 1980). Plaintiff must serve the defendant as an "individual" in accordance with Fed. R. Civ. P. 4(e), rather than as an officer of the United States, as detailed by Fed. R. Civ. P. 4(i). *See* Armstrong, 33 F.3d at 186–187. Because a *Bivens* suit alleges personal wrongdoing by the federal agent and seeks relief from that agent's pocket, rather than from the government's, individual service, providing timely notice of the claims is essential. . . .

SO ORDERED.

Notes on Sovereign Immunity

1. Sovereign immunity—It's good to be king. Regarding sovereign immunity, the Supreme Court has explained:

> The immunity of a truly independent sovereign from suit in its own courts has been enjoyed as a matter of absolute right for centuries. Only the sovereign's own consent could qualify the absolute character of that immunity.

> The doctrine, as it developed at common law, had its origins in the feudal system. Describing those origins, Pollock and Maitland noted that no lord could be sued by a vassal in his own court, but each petty lord was subject to suit in the courts of a higher lord. Since the King was at the apex of the feudal pyramid, there was no higher court in which he could be sued. The King's immunity rested primarily on the structure of the feudal system and secondarily on a fiction that the King could do no wrong.

> We must, of course, reject the fiction. It was rejected by the colonists when they declared their independence from the Crown. . . . But the notion that immunity from suit is an attribute of sovereignty is reflected in our cases.

> Mr. Chief Justice Jay described sovereignty as the "right to govern"; that kind of right would necessarily encompass the right to determine what suits may be brought in the sovereign's own courts. Thus, Mr. Justice Holmes explained sovereign immunity as based "on the logical and practical ground that there can be no legal right as against the authority that makes the law on which the right depends."

Nevada v. Hall, 440 U.S. 410, 414–15 (1979) (footnotes and citations omitted), *overruled on other grounds by Franchise Tax Board v. Hyatt*, 139 S. Ct. 1485 (2019). Should a doctrine flowing out of such an archaic notion as "the king can do no wrong" play any role in modern jurisprudence?

2. Section 702's waiver of sovereign immunity sweeps beyond the APA. Recall that the second sentence of § 702 provides:

> An action in a court of the United States seeking relief other than money damages and stating a claim that an agency or an officer or employee thereof acted or failed to act in an official capacity or under color of legal authority shall not be dismissed nor relief therein be denied on the ground that it is against the United States or that the United States is an indispensable party.

Congress added this sentence to § 702 in 1976 as part of an effort to simplify challenges to government action seeking equitable relief. Given that Congress placed this sentence in the APA, one might think that it waives sovereign immunity only for claims brought pursuant to the APA itself under the authority of the first sentence of § 702 (which, you may recall, grants a cause of action to persons "adversely affected or aggrieved by final agency action within the meaning of the relevant statute").

Courts have nonetheless concluded that § 702 waives sovereign immunity to actions that seek equitable relief regardless of whether they rely on the APA's cause of action. The D.C. Circuit reiterated this point in *Trudeau v. FTC*, 456 F.3d 178 (D.C. Cir. 2006), in which the plaintiff Trudeau alleged that the FTC had issued a false press release about a settlement the agency had reached with him. In addition to invoking the APA's cause of action, Trudeau also brought an action directly under the First Amendment and a "nonstatutory action." The nonstatutory action relied on case law providing that, under very limited circumstances, a plaintiff can seek judicial review absent statutory authorization to press a claim that an agency has acted *ultra vires*. *Id.* at 190. The D.C. Circuit explained that the APA's waiver of sovereign immunity extended to these non-APA claims as well:

> We have previously, and repeatedly, rejected the FTC's first argument, expressly holding that the "APA's waiver of sovereign immunity applies to any suit whether under the APA or not." *Chamber of Commerce v. Reich*, 74 F.3d 1322, 1328 (D.C. Cir. 1996). There is nothing in the language of the second sentence of § 702 that restricts its waiver to suits brought under the APA. The sentence waives sovereign immunity for "[a]n action in a court of the United States seeking relief other than money damages," not for an action brought under the APA.

3. Section 702's waiver can apply to some claims seeking money — just not "money damages." The APA waives sovereign immunity only for claims not seeking "money damages." It bears noting, however, that "money damages" is a technical term referring to a type of substitutionary legal relief "intended to provide a victim with monetary compensation for an injury to his person, property, or reputation." *Bowen v. Massachusetts*, 487 U.S. 879, 893 (1988). A litigant can invoke the APA's waiver to obtain monetary relief so long as this relief is specific rather than compensatory in nature. *Dep't of the Army v. Blue Fox, Inc.*, 525 U.S. 255 (1999). Thus, in *Bowen*, the APA's waiver applied to a suit by the state of Massachusetts seeking to require the federal government to pay money allegedly owed under the Medicaid Act. The state was not seeking money as a substitutionary remedy to make up for some other loss; rather, it was seeking the specific relief of forcing the federal government to obey the statute, which happened to require the payment of money. 487 U.S. at 900.

4. More on the Federal Tort Claims Act. If you want money damages from the government, § 702 won't help, but the Federal Tort Claims Act (FTCA), 28 U.S.C. §§ 1346(b), 2671–80, might. Section 2674 provides broadly that "[t]he United States shall be liable, respecting the provisions of this title relating to tort claims, in the same manner and to the same extent as a private individual under like circumstances." Section 1346(b) elaborates that the district courts have:

> ... exclusive jurisdiction of civil action of claims against the United States, for money damages ..., for injury or loss of property, or personal injury or death caused by the negligent or wrongful act or omission of any employee of the Government while acting within the scope of his office or employment, under circumstances where the United States, if a private person, would be liable to the claimant in accordance with the law of the place where the act or omission occurred.

Note that the FTCA makes liability a function of the "law of the place where the act or omission occurred." Thus, the federal government's liability generally becomes, interestingly enough, a function of *state* law. An important corollary to this reliance on state law is that the FTCA does not waive sovereign immunity for constitutional torts of the sort that might be brought against a government official through a *Bivens* action. (*Bivens* actions are discussed in the *Meyer* excerpt above and in note 8 below.)

As discussed in the case excerpts above, a variety of procedural restrictions and substantive exceptions festoon the FTCA. For example, with regard to procedure, before a claimant may bring an FTCA claim in federal court, the claim must first be presented to and denied by the "appropriate" federal agency. 28 U.S.C. § 2675(a). Also, juries do not determine FTCA claims. *Id.* at § 2402.

Subparts (a) through (n) of § 2680 set forth a list of substantive exclusions from FTCA coverage—e.g., claims arising out of negligent transmission of the mail, detention of goods by law enforcement officers, quarantines, many intentional torts, and combatant activities of the military. Rather than work through them all, we will just take a moment to draw your attention to one of the most important and conceptually challenging of these exceptions, the discretionary function exception, which excludes:

> [a]ny claim based upon an act or omission of an employee of the Government ... based upon the exercise or performance or the failure to exercise or perform a *discretionary function* or duty on the part of a federal agency or an employee of the Government, whether or not the discretion involved be abused.

28 U.S.C. § 2680(a). Of course, by this point in an administrative law course, you have probably learned to view the term "discretion" with a wary eye, and you will not be surprised to learn that the courts have had trouble defining the scope of this discretionary-function exception. The Supreme Court has offered the following guidance:

The exception covers only acts that are discretionary in nature, acts that "involv[e] an element of judgment or choice," and "it is the nature of the conduct, rather than the status of the actor" that governs whether the exception applies. The requirement of judgment or choice is not satisfied if a "federal statute, regulation, or policy specifically prescribes a course of action for an employee to follow," because "the employee has no rightful option but to adhere to the directive."

Furthermore, even "assuming the challenged conduct involves an element of judgment," it remains to be decided "whether that judgment is of the kind that the discretionary function exception was designed to shield." Because the purpose of the exception is to "prevent judicial 'second-guessing' of legislative and administrative decisions grounded in social, economic, and political policy through the medium of an action in tort," when properly construed, the exception "protects only governmental actions and decisions based on considerations of public policy." . . .

When established governmental policy, as expressed or implied by statute, regulation, or agency guidelines, allows a Government agent to exercise discretion, it must be presumed that the agent's acts are grounded in policy when exercising that discretion. . . . The focus of the inquiry is not on the agent's subjective intent in exercising the discretion conferred by statute or regulation, but on the nature of the actions taken and on whether they are susceptible to policy analysis.[7]

United States v. Gaubert, 499 U.S. 315, 322–25 (1991) (citations omitted).

Finally, note well that the FTCA, in addition to contracting governmental immunity, also expands official immunity. In 1988, Congress amended the FTCA to provide that the remedy it authorizes against the United States is exclusive for claims arising out of a government employee's conduct "while acting within the scope of his office or employment." 28 U.S.C. § 2679(b)(1). This immunity does not extend to claims charging violation of the Constitution or federal statutes. § 2679(b)(2). It does, however, provide officials with broad immunity to common-law tort claims. The United States will be substituted as the party defendant in place of a defendant employee or officer upon the Attorney General's certification that the named defendant "was acting within the scope of his office or employment at the time of the incident out of which the claim arose." § 2679(d)(1).

---

7. There are obviously discretionary acts performed by a Government agent that are within the scope of his employment but not within the discretionary function exception because these acts cannot be said to be based on the purposes that the regulatory regime seeks to accomplish. If one of the officials involved in this case drove an automobile on a mission connected with his official duties and negligently collided with another car, the exception would not apply. Although driving requires the constant exercise of discretion, the official's decisions in exercising that discretion can hardly be said to be grounded in regulatory policy.

5. Congressional waivers of federal sovereign immunity—the Tucker Act. If you want to get money from the federal government without the aid of a tort claim, you might consider the Tucker Act, which provides that the U.S. Court of Federal Claims

> shall have jurisdiction to render judgment upon any claim against the United States founded either upon the Constitution, or any Act of Congress or any regulation of an executive department, or upon any express or implied contract with the United States, or for liquidated or unliquidated damages in cases not sounding in tort.

28 U.S.C. § 1491(a)(1). Notwithstanding its broad language, the Tucker Act does not create a substantive cause of action to recover money damages from the government. Instead, the Tucker Act's waiver of sovereign immunity allows courts to hear claims for money damages for violations of federal laws that create such a substantive right to compensation by their own force. *United States v. Mitchell*, 463 U.S. 206 (1983). The Tucker Act does, however, provide a relatively straightforward path for litigating contract and takings claims.

6. Congressional waivers of federal sovereign immunity—other possibilities. The preceding two notes have offered brief introductions to two broadly applicable statutory waivers of federal sovereign immunity—the FTCA and the Tucker Act. Bear in mind, however, that the U.S. Code contains many agency-specific waivers. *See, e.g., Thacker v. Tennessee Valley Authority*, 139 S. Ct. 1435 (2019) (noting that statutory provision stating that TVA could "sue and be sued in its corporate name" waived "at least some of the corporation's immunity"); *FDIC v. Meyer*, 510 U.S. 471, 475 (1994) (noting that statutory provision authorizing agency "[t]o sue and be sued, complain and defend, in any court of competent jurisdiction" waived agency immunity from suit)

Notes on Actions against Government Officials and Official Immunities

7. Suing officials in their *personal* capacities. It is common to distinguish between the "official" and "personal" (or "individual") capacities of government officials for the purpose of suing them. A suit against a government official acting in an "official" capacity is really just a suit against the government itself and therefore subject to the constraints of sovereign immunity. A suit for damages brought against a government official in his "personal" capacity seeks, in theory, to hold that official personally liable for his conduct even if it was performed in the course of the official's duties. For instance, one might sue a law enforcement official who broke down a door for trespass. Holding government officials personally liable for conduct performed in the course of their employment runs the obvious risk of deterring desirable regulatory or law-enforcement action. As a result, courts have developed the immunity doctrines discussed below to protect officials from litigation and liability.

8. *Bivens* actions for constitutional torts against federal officials. In *Bivens v. Six Unknown Fed. Narcotics Agents*, 403 U.S. 388, 396 (1971), the Supreme Court created the possibility for suits for damages against federal officials for violation of constitutional rights. *Bivens* held federal narcotics agents could be held liable for damages, absent official immunity, for violating the Fourth Amendment. The Court observed:

> Of course, the Fourth Amendment does not in so many words provide for its enforcement by an award of money damages for the consequences of its violation. But 'it is . . . well settled that where legal rights have been invaded, and a federal statute provides for a general right to sue for such invasion, federal courts may use any available remedy to make good the wrong done'. . . . The present case involves no special factors counseling hesitation in the absence of affirmative action by Congress. . . . [We] hold that petitioner is entitled to recover money damages for any injuries he has suffered as a result of the agents' violation of the Amendment.

Concurring, Justice Harlan stressed that constitutional rights were "federally protected interests" and that courts, as well Congress, had the power to fashion remedies to vindicate those interests.

In the decade following *Bivens*, the Court took an expansive approach to its reach. In *Carlson v. Green*, 446 U.S. 14 (1980), for instance, it held that federal prison officials could be sued for damages for violating a prisoner's Eighth Amendment rights by denying him proper medical care. Also, in *Davis v. Passman*, 442 U.S. 228 (1979), a narrow majority of the Court opined that a damages action would lie against a congressman for engaging in sex discrimination in violation of an employee's Fifth Amendment due process rights.

In later cases, however, the Court retrenched, explaining that it will not apply the *Bivens* remedy in a new context where it finds either that: (a) an "alternative, existing process for protecting the interest amounts to a convincing reason for the Judicial Branch to refrain from providing a new and freestanding remedy in damages" or (b) there are "special factors counseling hesitation before authorizing a new kind of federal litigation." *Wilkie v. Robbins*, 551 U.S. 537, 550 (2007). In *Ziglar v. Abbasi*, 137 S. Ct. 1843, 1857 (2017), the Court reiterated that "expanding" the reach of *Bivens* is a "disfavored" judicial activity and then rattled off a collection of precedents where it had declined to do so:

> For example, the Court declined to create an implied damages remedy in the following cases: a First Amendment suit against a federal employer, *Bush v. Lucas*, 462 U.S. 367, 390 (1983); a race-discrimination suit against military officers, *Chappell v. Wallace*, 462 U.S. 296, 297 (1983); a substantive due process suit against military officers, *United States v. Stanley*, 483 U.S. 669, 671–672 (1987); a procedural due process suit against Social Security officials, *Schweiker v. Chilicky*, 487 U.S. 412, 414 (1988); a procedural due process suit against a federal agency for wrongful termination, *FDIC v. Meyer*, 510 U.S. 471, 473–474 (1994); an Eighth Amendment suit against a private prison operator, [*Correctional Services Corp. v. Malesko*, 534 U.S. 61, 63 (2001)]; a due process suit against officials from the Bureau of Land

Management, *Wilkie v. Robbins*, 551 U.S. 537, 547–548, 562 (2007); and an Eighth Amendment suit against prison guards at a private prison, *Minneci v. Pollard*, 565 U.S. 118, 120 (2012).

The short of the matter is that, once a court characterizes your suit as trying to expand the reach of *Bivens* to a new context, you will, in all likelihood, lose.

9. Section 1983 actions against state officials. In the aftermath of the Civil War, the federal government adopted measures designed to protect the rights of the newly freed slaves from infringement by state authorities. Among the most prominent was a law now codified at 42 U.S.C. § 1983, which provides:

> Every person who, under color of any statute, ordinance, regulation, custom, or usage, of any State or Territory or the District of Columbia, subjects, or causes to be subjected, any citizen of the United States or other person within the jurisdiction thereof to the deprivation of any rights, privileges, or immunities secured by the Constitution and laws, shall be liable to the party injured in an action at law, suit in equity, or other proper proceeding for redress.

Teasing out what this statute means in practice is a proper topic for a treatise, but this note will offer a few observations. A plaintiff can use § 1983 to bring a damages action against a state official in her personal capacity for violations of rights established by the Constitution or certain federal statutes. The Court has not permitted plaintiffs to sue defendants in their official capacities as such actions are "really" against the state itself. Section 1983 actions do not lie against the states themselves because they are not "persons" within the statute's meaning. Local governments, however, do not enjoy this same immunity.

10. Absolute official immunity. Even if a cause of action for damages, such as might be brought via *Bivens* or § 1983, lies against an official, he or she might enjoy official immunity to that claim. In some contexts, this immunity is "absolute;" more often, it is "qualified." The Court explored the justifications and scope of absolute immunity in *Butz v. Economou*, 438 U.S. 478, 512 (1978):

> In *Bradley v. Fisher* (1872), the Court analyzed the need for absolute immunity to protect judges from lawsuits claiming that their decisions had been tainted by improper motives. . . . If a civil action could be maintained against a judge by virtue of an allegation of malice, judges would lose "that independence without which no judiciary can either be respectable or useful." Thus, judges were held to be immune from civil suit "for malice or corruption in their action whilst exercising their judicial functions within the general scope of their jurisdiction." . . .
>
> As the *Bradley* Court suggested, controversies sufficiently intense to erupt in litigation are not easily capped by a judicial decree. The loser in one forum will frequently seek another, charging the participants in the first with unconstitutional animus. Absolute immunity is thus necessary to

assure that judges, advocates, and witnesses can perform their respective functions without harassment or intimidation.

At the same time, the safeguards built into the judicial process tend to reduce the need for private damages actions as a means of controlling unconstitutional conduct. . . .

The absolute immunity from damages claims enjoyed by judges and prosecutors does not, of course, cover every action they might take in life; rather, it covers actions taken to further their respective judicial and prosecutorial functions. Noting the "functional" similarities between adjudication by the courts and adjudication by federal agencies, the *Butz* Court held that absolute immunity should also cover agency officials who perform adjudicative and prosecutorial-type functions in formal agency adjudications. *Id.* at 512–16.

Others who enjoy absolute immunity from damages claims include: witnesses, *Briscoe v. LaHue*, 460 U.S. 325 (1983); the president—for acts taken while in office, *Nixon v. Fitzgerald*, 457 U.S. 731 (1982); and legislators for their legislative acts, *Bogan v. Scott-Harris*, 523 U.S. 44 (1988).

11. Qualified official immunity. Government officials generally enjoy "qualified immunity" from claims for civil damages based on purported violations of federal statutory or constitutional rights. In *Harlow v. Fitzgerald*, 457 U.S. 800 (1982), the Court discussed the justification for and contours of this form of immunity:

The resolution of immunity questions inherently requires a balance between the evils inevitable in any available alternative. In situations of abuse of office, an action for damages may offer the only realistic avenue for vindication of constitutional guarantees. It is this recognition that has required the denial of absolute immunity to most public officers. At the same time, however, it cannot be disputed seriously that claims frequently run against the innocent as well as the guilty—at a cost not only to the defendant officials, but to society as a whole. These social costs include the expenses of litigation, the diversion of official energy from pressing public issues, and the deterrence of able citizens from acceptance of public office. Finally, there is the danger that fear of being sued will "dampen the ardor of all but the most resolute, or the most irresponsible [public officials], in the unflinching discharge of their duties." . . .

Consistently with the balance at which we aimed in *Butz*, we conclude today that bare allegations of malice should not suffice to subject government officials either to the costs of trial or to the burdens of broad-reaching discovery. We therefore hold that government officials performing discretionary functions generally are shielded from liability for civil damages insofar as their conduct does not violate clearly established statutory or constitutional rights of which a reasonable person would have known.

The Supreme Court has emphasized that the inquiry as to whether a law is clearly established must not be conducted at too abstract and general a level. The qualified immunity inquiry "must be undertaken in light of the specific context of the case, not as a broad general proposition. . . . The relevant, dispositive inquiry in determining whether a right is clearly established is whether it would be clear to a reasonable officer that his conduct was unlawful in the situation he confronted." *Brosseau v. Haugen*, 543 U.S. 194 (2004) (quotation marks omitted).

F. Timing the Challenge—Finality, Ripeness, and Exhaustion

A set of closely related doctrines governs when a litigant may obtain judicial review of agency action. The most prominent members of this set are finality, ripeness, and exhaustion. You may find it hard to tell them apart at times, but so do courts. These doctrines tend to overlap because they are all motivated to a degree by hostility to interlocutory review—much like the familiar final judgment rule that limits appellate review of district court decisions. In short, the core idea is that courts should try to avoid interfering with an agency's decision until the agency itself has finished with it. Application of this core idea, however, presents difficulties.

1. Finality and Ripeness

Under § 704, the default rule is that the APA's template for judicial review applies to "final agency action." Specific statutory review schemes in agency enabling acts typically impose this same precondition. The modern black-letter definition of finality is easy enough to state. For an agency action to be "final," it must both (a) "mark the 'consummation' of the agency's decisionmaking process"; and (b) determine "rights or obligations" or otherwise create "legal consequences." *Bennett v. Spear*, 520 U.S. 154, 178 (1997). Put another way, the agency must be finished with the action, and it must be legally meaningful. Often, application of these limits is trivially easy—e.g., a complaint initiating an administrative adjudication is not final. In other contexts, application is more difficult, especially because the line between practical effects and "legal consequences" is not always clear.

Ripeness, as the name suggests, relates to whether a final agency action is "ready" for review. This issue arises most often in connection with suits seeking review of a rule before an agency has enforced it in a particular adjudicative action. Ripeness depends on whether the agency action is "fit" for review as well as on the level of hardship that the plaintiff will suffer if review is postponed. *Abbott Laboratories v. Gardner*, 387 U.S. 136 (1967).

Lesson 5F.1. The WTC, acting pursuant to its legislative rulemaking authority, promulgated a "special reserve" rule providing that "[a]ny wine bottle label that includes a 'special reserve' or other designation of special quality must also include an objectively reasonable explanation for the label's claim of special quality." The statement of basis and purpose for the rule had relied on studies that purported to demonstrate that (a) claims of special quality (e.g., that a product is "new and improved") increase consumer purchases, and (b) roughly 20% of wines bearing "special reserve" (or similar) labels are objectively indistinguishable from their makers' "ordinary" wines. In the WTC's view, the disclosure rule was therefore an appropriate means to enforce §5(b) of the WTCA, which forbids the misleading omission of material facts in connection with the sale of wine.

One month after issuance of this rule, the WTC published in the *Federal Register* its Guidelines Interpreting the Special Reserve Rule. These guidelines state that "the agency's present view is that, to be 'objectively reasonable,' a claim of special quality must be based on superior production methods and/or quality of ingredients."

Promptly after issuance of the guidelines, Gallery's management asked its attorney Rock to challenge both the rule and the guidelines immediately. His first thought is to challenge both of them on the ground that they exceed the WTC's statutory authority. He is also considering challenging the guidelines on the additional ground that they should have been subjected to notice-and-comment.

What finality and ripeness issues might these challenges raise?

Background of *Abbott Laboratories v. Gardner*

Pharmaceutical companies brand their drugs with proprietary or trade names as part of their marketing efforts. Often, there are cheaper, generic substitutes available for a given branded drug. To address this issue, Congress enacted a law requiring pharmaceutical companies to print a drug's "established name" on labels or other printed materials that included the drug's "proprietary name." The FDA later adopted a rule requiring that the established name accompany each use of a proprietary name. Pharmaceutical companies, naturally, wanted judicial resolution of the legality of the labeling rule before deciding whether to obey it (and disrupt their marketing plans) or disobey it (and risk an enforcement action).

Before the *Abbott Laboratories* litigation, the general judicial practice had been to review rules in the context of review of agency adjudications. An agency would bring an enforcement action against a regulated party based on a rule, and the regulated party would later seek judicial review contesting the rule's validity. Taking this sort of wait-and-see approach to litigating rules has clear advantages. For instance, it ensures that judicial review, if it occurs, will be based on a concrete factual record that may illuminate the rule's legality. It also increases agencies' effective power to govern by enabling them to implement their rules without premature judicial interference. Some costs of this approach are also very clear, however. Most obviously, it increases the risk that regulated parties will be forced to obey illegal rules. In *Abbott Laboratories*, the Court concluded that the balance of interests favored allowing the pharmaceutical companies to obtain pre-enforcement review of FDA's labeling rule. Along the way to this result, the Court developed the canonical framework for determining whether an agency rule is "ripe" for review before its enforcement.

Abbott Laboratories v. Gardner
387 U.S. 136 (1967)

MR. JUSTICE HARLAN delivered the opinion of the Court.

In 1962, Congress amended the Federal Food, Drug, and Cosmetic Act to require manufacturers of prescription drugs to print the "established name" of the drug "prominently and in type at least half as large as that used thereon for any proprietary name or designation for such drug," on labels and other printed material. The "established name" is one designated by the Secretary of Health, Education, and Welfare; the "proprietary name" is usually a trade name under which a particular drug is marketed. The underlying purpose of the 1962 amendment was to bring to the attention of doctors and patients the fact that many of the drugs sold under familiar trade names are actually identical to drugs sold under their "established" or less familiar trade names at significantly lower prices. The Commissioner of Food and Drugs, exercising authority delegated to him by the Secretary, published proposed regulations designed to implement the statute. After inviting and considering comments submitted by interested parties the Commissioner promulgated the following regulation for the "efficient enforcement" of the Act:

> "If the label or labeling of a prescription drug bears a proprietary name or designation for the drug or any ingredient thereof, the established name, if such there be, corresponding to such proprietary name or designation, shall accompany each appearance of such proprietary name or designation."

A similar rule was made applicable to advertisements for prescription drugs.

The present action was brought by a group of 37 individual drug manufacturers and by the Pharmaceutical Manufacturers Association, of which all the petitioner companies are members, and which includes manufacturers of more than 90% of the Nation's supply of prescription drugs. They challenged the regulations on the ground that the Commissioner exceeded his authority under the statute by promulgating an order requiring labels, advertisements, and other printed matter relating to prescription drugs to designate the established name of the particular drug involved every time its trade name is used anywhere in such material. . . .

. . . The injunctive and declaratory judgment remedies are discretionary, and courts traditionally have been reluctant to apply them to administrative determinations unless these arise in the context of a controversy "ripe" for judicial resolution. Without undertaking to survey the intricacies of the ripeness doctrine it is fair to say that its basic rationale is to prevent the courts, through avoidance of premature adjudication, from entangling themselves in abstract disagreements over administrative policies, and also to protect the agencies from judicial interference until an administrative decision has been formalized and its effects felt in a concrete way by the challenging parties. The problem is best seen in a twofold aspect, requiring us to evaluate both the fitness of the issues for judicial decision and the hardship to the parties of withholding court consideration.

WHY THIS IS FIT FOR REVIEW

As to the former factor, we believe the issues presented are appropriate for judicial resolution at this time. First, all parties agree that the issue tendered is a purely legal one: whether the statute was properly construed by the Commissioner to require the established name of the drug to be used *every time* the proprietary name is employed. Both sides moved for summary judgment in the District Court, and no claim is made here that further administrative proceedings are contemplated. It is suggested that the justification for this rule might vary with different circumstances, and that the expertise of the Commissioner is relevant to passing upon the validity of the regulation. This of course is true, but the suggestion overlooks the fact that both sides have approached this case as one purely of congressional intent, and that the Government made no effort to justify the regulation in factual terms.

Second, the regulations in issue we find to be "final agency action" within the meaning of § [704] of the Administrative Procedure Act as construed in judicial decisions. An "agency action" includes any "rule," defined by the Act as "an agency statement of general or particular applicability and future effect designed to implement, interpret, or prescribe law or policy." The cases dealing with judicial review of administrative actions have interpreted the "finality" element in a pragmatic way. Thus in *Columbia Broadcasting System v. United States*, . . . this Court held reviewable a regulation of the Federal Communications Commission setting forth certain proscribed contractual arrangements between chain broadcasters and local stations. The FCC did not have direct authority to regulate these contracts, and its rule asserted only that it would not license stations which maintained such contracts with the networks. Although no license had in fact been denied or revoked, and the FCC regulation could properly be characterized as a statement only of its intentions, the Court held that 'Such regulations have the force of law before their sanctions are invoked as well as after. When as here they are promulgated by order of the Commission and the expected conformity to them causes injury cognizable by a court of equity, they are appropriately the subject of attack. . . .'

COLUMBIA COURT DEFINITION

WHY THIS IS FINAL

We find decision in the present case following *a fortiori* from these precedents. The regulation challenged here, promulgated in a formal manner after announcement in the Federal Register and consideration of comments by interested parties, is quite clearly definitive. There is no hint that this regulation is informal, or only the ruling of a subordinate official, or tentative. It was made effective upon publication, and the Assistant General Counsel for Food and Drugs stated in the District Court that compliance was expected.

The Government argues, however, that the present case can be distinguished from [prior] cases . . . on the ground that in those instances the agency involved could implement its policy directly, while here the Attorney General must authorize criminal and seizure actions for violations of the statute. In the context of this case, we do not find this argument persuasive. These regulations are not meant to advise the Attorney General, but purport to be directly authorized by the statute. Thus, if within the Commissioner's authority, they have the status of law and violations of them carry heavy criminal and civil sanctions. Also, there is no representation that the Attorney General and the Commissioner disagree in this area; the Justice Department is defending this very suit. It would be adherence to a mere technicality to give any credence to this contention. Moreover, the agency does have direct authority to enforce this regulation in the context of passing upon applications for clearance of new drugs or certification of certain antibiotics.

[IMPACT ON PETITIONER]

This is also a case in which the impact of the regulations upon the petitioners is sufficiently direct and immediate as to render the issue appropriate for judicial review at this stage. These regulations purport to give an authoritative interpretation of a statutory provision that has a direct effect on the day-to-day business of all prescription drug companies; its promulgation puts petitioners in a dilemma that it was the very purpose of the Declaratory Judgment Act to ameliorate. As the District Court found on the basis of uncontested allegations, "Either they must comply with the every time requirement and incur the costs of changing over their promotional material and labeling or they must follow their present course and risk prosecution." The regulations are clear-cut, and were made effective immediately upon publication; as noted earlier the agency's counsel represented to the District Court that immediate compliance with their terms was expected. If petitioners wish to comply they must change all their labels, advertisements, and promotional materials; they must destroy stocks of printed matter; and they must invest heavily in new printing type and new supplies. The alternative to compliance — continued use of material which they believe in good faith meets the statutory requirements, but which clearly does not meet the regulation of the Commissioner — may be even more costly. That course would risk serious criminal and civil penalties for the unlawful distribution of "misbranded" drugs.

It is relevant at this juncture to recognize that petitioners deal in a sensitive industry, in which public confidence in their drug products is especially important. To require them to challenge these regulations only as a defense to an action brought by the Government might harm them severely and unnecessarily. Where the legal issue presented is fit for judicial resolution, and where a regulation requires an immediate and significant change in the plaintiffs' conduct of their affairs with serious penalties attached to noncompliance, access to the courts under the Administrative Procedure Act and the Declaratory Judgment Act must be permitted, absent a statutory bar or some other unusual circumstance, neither of which appears here.

The Government does not dispute the very real dilemma in which petitioners are placed by the regulation, but contends that "mere financial expense" is not a justification for pre-enforcement judicial review. It is of course true that cases in this Court dealing with the standing of particular parties to bring an action have held that a possible financial loss is not by itself a sufficient interest to sustain a judicial challenge to governmental action. But there is no question in the present case that petitioners have sufficient standing as plaintiffs: the regulation is directed at them in particular; it requires them to make significant changes in their everyday business practices; if they fail to observe the Commissioner's rule they are quite clearly exposed to the imposition of strong sanctions.

RE: "MERE FINANCIAL EXPENSE"

RESPONSE

The Government further contends that the threat of criminal sanctions for non-compliance with a judicially untested regulation is unrealistic; the Solicitor General has represented that if court enforcement becomes necessary, "the Department of Justice will proceed only civilly for an injunction . . . or by condemnation." We cannot accept this argument as a sufficient answer to petitioners' petition. This action at its inception was properly brought and this subsequent representation of the Department of Justice should not suffice to defeat it.

Finally, the Government urges that to permit resort to the courts in this type of case may delay or impede effective enforcement of the Act. We fully recognize the important public interest served by assuring prompt and unimpeded administration of the Pure Food, Drug, and Cosmetic Act, but we do not find the Government's argument convincing. First, in this particular case, a pre-enforcement challenge by nearly all prescription drug manufacturers is calculated to speed enforcement. If the Government prevails, a large part of the industry is bound by the decree; if the Government loses, it can more quickly revise its regulation.

The Government contends, however, that if the Court allows this consolidated suit, then nothing will prevent a multiplicity of suits in various jurisdictions challenging other regulations. The short answer to this contention is that the courts are well equipped to deal with such eventualities. The venue transfer provision may be invoked by the Government to consolidate separate actions. Or, actions in all but one jurisdiction might be stayed pending the conclusion of one proceeding. A court may even in its discretion dismiss a declaratory judgment or injunctive suit if the same issue is pending in litigation elsewhere. In at least one suit for a declaratory judgment, relief was denied with the suggestion that the plaintiff intervene in a pending action elsewhere.

Further, the declaratory judgment and injunctive remedies are equitable in nature, and other equitable defenses may be interposed. If a multiplicity of suits are undertaken in order to harass the Government or to delay enforcement, relief can be denied on this ground alone. The defense of laches could be asserted if the Government is prejudiced by a delay. And courts may even refuse declaratory relief for the nonjoinder of interested parties who are not, technically speaking, indispensable.

In addition to all these safeguards against what the Government fears, it is important to note that the institution of this type of action does not by itself stay the effectiveness of the challenged regulation. There is nothing in the record to indicate that petitioners have sought to stay enforcement of the "every time" regulation pending judicial review. *See* 5 U.S.C. § 705. If the agency believes that a suit of this type will significantly impede enforcement or will harm the public interest, it need not postpone enforcement of the regulation and may oppose any motion for a judicial stay on the part of those challenging the regulation. It is scarcely to be doubted that a court would refuse to postpone the effective date of an agency action if the Government could show, as it made no effort to do here, that delay would be detrimental to the public health or safety. . . .

Notes on Ripeness

1. Unripe *Toilet Goods*. *Abbott* raises two distinct timing issues—finality and ripeness. The latter tends to arise where a petitioner brings a pre-enforcement, facial challenge to a rule rather than waiting until the agency seeks to apply the rule in an adjudicatory proceeding. *Abbott*'s application of the ripeness doctrine, with its fitness and hardship prongs, is commonly contrasted with the Court's application of this doctrine in a case decided the very same day, *Toilet Goods Ass'n v. Gardner*, 387 U.S. 158 (1967).

Toilet Goods addressed a pre-enforcement challenge to a rule that permitted FDA inspectors to suspend "certification service" if manufacturers of color additives denied inspectors access to their facilities. Uncertified color additives are considered "unsafe" and banned from interstate commerce. The petitioners contended that the rule exceeded the agency's statutory authority, but the Court ruled the challenge unripe:

> ... The Commissioner of Food and Drugs, exercising power delegated by the Secretary under statutory authority 'to promulgate regulations for the efficient enforcement' of the Act, issued the ... regulation after due public notice and consideration of comments submitted by interested parties ...

> ... [W]e agree with the Court of Appeals that the legal issue as presently framed is not appropriate for judicial resolution. This is not because the regulation is not the agency's considered and formalized determination, for we are in agreement with petitioners that ... there can be no question that this regulation—promulgated in a formal manner after notice and evaluation of submitted comments—is a 'final agency action' under § 10 of the Administrative Procedure Act, 5 U.S.C. § 704. Also, we recognize the force of petitioners' contention that the issue as they have framed it presents a purely legal question: whether the regulation is totally beyond the agency's power under the statute, the type of legal issue that courts have occasionally dealt with without requiring a specific attempt at enforcement.

> These points which support the appropriateness of judicial resolution are, however, outweighed by other considerations. The regulation serves notice only that the Commissioner may under certain circumstances order inspection of certain facilities and data, and that further certification of additives may be refused to those who decline to permit a duly authorized inspection until they have complied in that regard. At this juncture we have no idea whether or when such an inspection will be ordered and what reasons the Commissioner will give to justify his order. The statutory authority asserted for the regulation is the power to promulgate regulations 'for the efficient enforcement' of the Act, § 701(a). Whether the regulation is justified thus depends not only, as petitioners appear to suggest, on whether Congress refused to include a specific section of the Act authorizing such inspections, although this factor is to be sure a highly relevant one, but also

on whether the statutory scheme as a whole justified promulgation of the regulation. This will depend not merely on an inquiry into statutory purpose, but concurrently on an understanding of what types of enforcement problems are encountered by the FDA, the need for various sorts of supervision in order to effectuate the goals of the Act, and the safeguards devised to protect legitimate trade secrets. We believe that judicial appraisal of these factors is likely to stand on a much surer footing in the context of a specific application of this regulation than could be the case in the framework of the generalized challenge made here.

We are also led to this result by considerations of the effect on the petitioners of the regulation, for the test of ripeness, as we have noted, depends not only on how adequately a court can deal with the legal issue presented, but also on the degree and nature of the regulation's present effect on those seeking relief. The regulation challenged here is not analogous to those . . . where the impact of the administrative action could be said to be felt immediately by those subject to it in conducting their day-to-day affairs.

This is not a situation in which primary conduct is affected — when contracts must be negotiated, ingredients tested or substituted, or special records compiled. This regulation merely states that the Commissioner may authorize inspectors to examine certain processes or formulae; no advance action is required of cosmetics manufacturers. . . . Moreover, no irremediable adverse consequences flow from requiring a later challenge to this regulation by a manufacturer who refuses to allow this type of inspection. Unlike the other regulations challenged in this action, in which seizure of goods, heavy fines, adverse publicity for distributing 'adulterated' goods, and possible criminal liability might penalize failure to comply, a refusal to admit an inspector here would at most lead only to a suspension of certification services to the particular party, a determination that can then be promptly challenged through an administrative procedure, which in turn is reviewable by a court. Such review will provide an adequate forum for testing the regulation in a concrete situation.

Why was the challenge in *Abbott* fit for review but the challenge in *Toilet Goods* unfit? How did the cases differ with respect to the hardship prong of ripeness analysis?

2. Three looks at ripeness in one case from the national parks. *National Park Hospitality Ass'n v. Dept. of Interior*, 538 U.S. 803 (2003), offers a fairly recent and substantial discussion of ripeness doctrine from three justices. The National Park Service (NPS) enters concession contracts with firms that provide services at national parks. In 2000, NPS promulgated a final regulation declaring that "concession contracts" are not "contracts" within the meaning of the Contract Disputes Act (CDA), which provides for streamlined resolution of certain contract disputes with the government. The petitioner in *NPHA*, a trade association composed of national park concessioners, challenged the legality of NPS's rule. This challenge generated three different opinions on ripeness from the justices:

Justice THOMAS delivered the opinion of the Court. . . .

Ripeness is a justiciability doctrine designed "to prevent the courts, through avoidance of premature adjudication, from entangling themselves in abstract disagreements over administrative policies, and also to protect the agencies from judicial interference until an administrative decision has been formalized and its effects felt in a concrete way by the challenging parties." *Abbott Laboratories v. Gardner.* The ripeness doctrine is "drawn both from Article III limitations on judicial power and from prudential reasons for refusing to exercise jurisdiction," but, even in a case raising only prudential concerns, the question of ripeness may be considered on a court's own motion. . . .

We turn first to the hardship inquiry. The federal respondents concede that, because NPS has no delegated rulemaking authority under the CDA, the challenged portion of § 51.3 cannot be a legislative regulation with the force of law. They note, though, that "agencies may issue interpretive rules 'to advise the public of the agency's construction of the statutes and rules which it administers,'" and seek to characterize § 51.3 as such an interpretive rule.

We disagree. . . . NPS is not empowered to administer the CDA. Rather, the task of applying the CDA rests with agency contracting officers and boards of contract appeals, as well as the Federal Court of Claims, the Court of Appeals for the Federal Circuit, and, ultimately, this Court. Moreover, under the CDA, any authority regarding the proper arrangement of agency boards belongs to the Administrator for Federal Procurement Policy. . . . Consequently, we consider § 51.3 to be nothing more than a "general statemen[t] of policy" designed to inform the public of NPS' views on the proper application of the CDA.

Viewed in this light, § 51.3 does not create "adverse effects of a strictly legal kind," which we have previously required for a showing of hardship. . . . § 51.3 "do [es] not command anyone to do anything or to refrain from doing anything; [it] do[es] not grant, withhold, or modify any formal legal license, power, or authority; [it] do[es] not subject anyone to any civil or criminal liability; [and it] create[s] no legal rights or obligations."

Moreover, § 51.3 does not affect a concessioner's primary conduct. Unlike the regulation at issue in *Abbott Laboratories,* which required drug manufacturers to change the labels, advertisements, and promotional materials they used in marketing prescription drugs on pain of criminal and civil penalties, the regulation here leaves a concessioner free to conduct its business as it sees fit. . . .

Petitioner contends that delaying judicial resolution of this issue will result in real harm because the applicability *vel non* of the CDA is one of the factors a concessioner takes into account when preparing its bid for NPS concession contracts. Petitioner's argument appears to be that mere uncertainty as to the validity of a legal rule constitutes a hardship for purposes of the ripeness analysis. We are not persuaded. If we were to follow petitioner's logic, courts would soon be overwhelmed with requests for what essentially would be advisory opinions because most business transactions could be priced more accurately if even a small portion of existing legal uncertainties were resolved. In short, petitioner has failed to demonstrate that deferring judicial review will result in real hardship. . . .

No REAL HARDSHIP

We consider next whether the issue in this case is fit for review. Although the question presented here is "a purely legal one" and § 51.3 constitutes "final agency action" within the meaning of § 10 of the APA, 5 U.S.C. § 704, we nevertheless believe that further factual development would "significantly advance our ability to deal with the legal issues presented". While the federal respondents generally argue that NPS was correct to conclude that the CDA does not cover concession contracts, they acknowledge that certain types of concession contracts might come under the broad language of the CDA. Similarly, while petitioner and respondent Xanterra Parks & Resorts, LLC, present a facial challenge to § 51.3, both rely on specific characteristics of certain types of concession contracts to support their positions. In light of the foregoing, we conclude that judicial resolution of the question presented here should await a concrete dispute about a particular concession contract. . . .

Justice Stevens, concurring in the judgment. . . .

In our leading case discussing the "ripeness doctrine" we explained that the question whether a controversy is "ripe" for judicial resolution has a "twofold aspect, requiring us to evaluate both the fitness of the issues for judicial decision and the hardship to the parties of withholding court consideration." *Abbott Laboratories v. Gardner*, 387 U.S. 136, 148–149 (1967). Both aspects of the inquiry involve the exercise of judgment, rather than the application of a black-letter rule.

The first aspect is the more important and it is satisfied in this case. The CDA applies to any express or implied contract for the procurement of property, services, or construction. 41 U.S.C. § 602(a). In the view of the Park Service, a procurement contract is one that obligates the Government to pay for goods and services that it receives, whereas concession contracts authorize third parties to provide services to park area visitors. Petitioner, on the other hand, argues that the contracts provide for the performance of services that discharge a public duty even though the Government does not pay the concessionaires. Whichever view may better reflect the intent of the Congress that enacted the CDA, it is perfectly clear that this question of statutory interpretation is as "fit" for judicial decision today as it will ever be. . . .

The second aspect of the ripeness inquiry is less clear and less important. If there were reason to believe that further development of the facts would clarify the legal question, or that the agency's view was tentative or apt to be modified, only a strong showing of hardship to the parties would justify a prompt decision. In this case, it is probably correct that the hardship associated with a delayed decision is minimal. On the other hand, as the Park Service's decision to promulgate the regulation demonstrates, eliminating the present uncertainty about the applicable dispute resolution procedures will provide a benefit for all interested parties. If petitioner had alleged sufficient injury arising from the Park Service's position, I would favor the exercise of our discretion to consider the case ripe for decision. Because such an allegation of injury is absent, however, petitioner does not have standing to have this claim adjudicated. . . .

Justice BREYER, with whom Justice O'CONNOR joins, dissenting. . . .

[M]any of petitioner's members are parties to, as well as potential bidders for, park concession contracts. Those members will likely find that disputes arise under the contracts. And in resolving such disputes, the Park Service, following its regulation, will reject the concessioners' entitlement to the significant protections or financial advantages that the CDA provides. In the circumstances present here, that kind of injury, though a future one, is concrete and likely to occur.

For another thing, the challenged Park Service interpretation causes a present injury. If the CDA does not apply to concession contract disagreements, as the Park Service regulation declares, then some of petitioner's members must plan now for higher contract implementation costs. Given the agency's regulation, bidders will likely be forced to pay more to obtain, or to retain, a concession contract than they believe the contract is worth. . . .

Given this threat of immediate concrete harm (primarily in the form of increased bidding costs), this case is also ripe for judicial review. . . . [T]he case now presents a legal issue—the applicability of the CDA to concession contracts—that is fit for judicial determination. That issue is a purely legal one, demanding for its resolution only use of ordinary judicial interpretive techniques. The relevant administrative action, i.e., the agency's definition of "concession contract" . . . has been "formalized," *Abbott Laboratories v. Gardner*. It is embodied in an interpretive regulation issued after notice and public comment and pursuant to the Department of the Interior's formal delegation to the National Park Service of its own statutorily granted rulemaking authority. . . . The Park Service's interpretation is definite and conclusive, not tentative or likely to change; as the majority concedes, the Park Service's determination constitutes "final agency action" within the meaning of the Administrative Procedure Act.

The only open question concerns the nature of the harm that refusing judicial review at this time will cause petitioner's members. The fact that concessioners can raise the legal question at a later time, after a specific contractual dispute arises, militates against finding this case ripe. So too does a precedential concern: Will present review set a precedent that leads to premature challenges in other cases where agency interpretations may be less formal, less final, or less well suited to immediate judicial determination?

But the fact of immediate and particularized (and not totally reparable) injury during the bidding process offsets the first of these considerations. And the second is more than offset by a related congressional statute that specifies that prospective bidders for Government contracts can obtain immediate judicial relief from agency determinations that unlawfully threaten precisely this kind of harm. *See* 28 U.S.C. § 1491(b)(1) (allowing prospective bidder to object, for instance, to "solicitation by a Federal agency for bids . . . for a proposed contract" and permitting review of related allegation of "any . . . violation of statute or regulation in connection with a procurement or a proposed procurement"). This statute authorizes a potential bidder to complain of a proposed contractual term that, in the bidder's view, is unlawful, say, because it formally incorporates a regulation that embodies a specific, allegedly unlawful, remedial requirement. . . . That being so, *i.e.*, the present injury in such a case being identical to the present injury at issue here, I can find no convincing prudential reason to withhold Administrative Procedure Act review.

How did each opinion treat "fitness"? "Hardship"?

3. Ripeness and statutory provisions on pre-enforcement review. Many modern enabling acts expressly provide for pre-enforcement review of rules during some limited period of time following their promulgation. *See, e.g.*, 42 U.S.C. § 7607(b) (Clean Air Act provision allowing petitioners to challenge rules within 60 days of publication in the Federal Register); *cf.* WTCA § 9(c). Courts, however, sometimes dismiss claims brought within such statutorily prescribed periods for lack of ripeness. *Clean Air Implementation Project v. EPA*, 150 F.3d 1200 (D.C. Cir. 1998). This practice raises the problem that, by the time a rule is ripe for review, it may be too late to challenge it. To avoid this result, courts have held that time limits for review can run only against ripe claims. *Louisiana Environmental Action Network v. Browner*, 87 F.3d 1379 (D.C. Cir. 1996). A litigant, however, should take great care before relying on this principle to delay challenging a rule. *See Eagle-Picher Indus. v. EPA*, 759 F.2d 905 (D.C. Cir. 1985) (explaining that courts will use the ripeness doctrine to save a late-filed claim only where a timely claim would have been "indisputably not ripe"). Also, courts will generally allow a party to raise substantive (but not procedural) challenges to a rule after a statutory deadline where the party is defending itself against an agency enforcement action. *See, e.g.*, *JEM Broadcasting Co., Inc. v. FCC*, 22 F.3d 320, 324–25 (D.C. Cir. 1994).

Notes on Finality

4. Finality and fish— *Bennett*'s two-pronged test. In addition to ripeness, *Abbott* also discusses the timing doctrine of "finality," which, as the name suggests, blocks interlocutory review of agency action (much like the final judgment rule limits the availability of appeal from the district to the circuit courts). Section 704 of the APA generally limits review to "final agency action," and the judicial review provisions of agency enabling acts generally contain the same limitation. In *Abbott*, after characterizing its approach to finality as "pragmatic," the Court concluded that the FDA rule at issue satisfied this requirement given that it was "promulgated in a formal manner after announcement in the Federal Register and consideration of comments by interested parties," was "definitive," "effective upon publication" with compliance expected, and neither "informal" nor "only the ruling of a subordinate official, or tentative."

Thirty years later, the doctrine took a more formalistic turn in what was to become the Court's leading case on finality, *Bennett v. Spear*, 520 U.S. 154 (1997), which concerned a Biological Opinion issued by the Fish and Wildlife Service pursuant to the Endangered Species Act. This Biological Opinion informed the Bureau of Reclamation that operation of an irrigation project on the Klamath River threatened two varieties of sucker fish. It also identified "reasonable and prudent alternatives" for minimizing this impact, which included maintaining water levels in lakes that would reduce the amount of water available for irrigation.

The government argued against judicial review of this Biological Opinion on both standing and finality grounds based on its ostensibly "advisory" nature. The Court discounted this argument in light of the powerful legal forces that compel an "action agency," such as the Bureau of Reclamation, to take the Service's "advice." An action agency that rejects a Biological Opinion

> . . . runs a substantial risk if its (inexpert) reasons turn out to be wrong. A Biological Opinion of the sort rendered here alters the legal regime to which the action agency is subject. When it "offers reasonable and prudent alternatives" to the proposed action, a Biological Opinion must include a so-called "Incidental Take Statement"—a written statement specifying, among other things, those "measures that the [Service] considers necessary or appropriate to minimize [the action's impact on the affected species]". . . . 16 U.S.C. § 1536(b)(4). Any taking that is in compliance with these terms and conditions "shall not be considered to be a prohibited taking of the species concerned." § 1536(o)(2). Thus, the Biological Opinion's Incidental Take Statement constitutes a permit authorizing the action agency to "take" the endangered or threatened species so long as it respects the Service's "terms and conditions." The action agency is technically free to disregard the Biological Opinion and proceed with its proposed action, but it does so at its own peril (and that of its employees), for "any person" who knowingly "takes" an endangered or

threatened species is subject to substantial civil and criminal penalties, including imprisonment.

With the legal and practical force of Biological Opinions thus established, the Court turned to its finality analysis:

> The Government contends that petitioners may not obtain judicial review under the APA on the theory that the Biological Opinion does not constitute "final agency action," 5 U.S.C. §704, because it does not conclusively determine the manner in which Klamath Project water will be allocated:

GOV'T ARGUE

> "Whatever the practical likelihood that the [Bureau] would adopt the reasonable and prudent alternatives (including the higher lake levels) identified by the Service, the Bureau was not legally obligated to do so. Even if the Bureau decided to adopt the higher lake levels, moreover, nothing in the biological opinion would constrain the [Bureau's] discretion as to how the available water should be allocated among potential users."

MODERN TEST

> This confuses the question whether the Secretary's action is final with the separate question whether petitioners' harm is "fairly traceable" to the Secretary's action. . . . As a general matter, two conditions must be satisfied for agency action to be "final": First, the action must mark the "consummation" of the agency's decisionmaking process—it must not be of a merely tentative or interlocutory nature. And second, the action must be one by which "rights or obligations have been determined," or from which "legal consequences will flow." It is uncontested that the first requirement is met here; and the second is met because, as we have discussed above, the Biological Opinion and accompanying Incidental Take Statement alter the legal regime to which the action agency is subject, authorizing it to take the endangered species if (but only if) it complies with the prescribed conditions. In this crucial respect the present case is different from the cases upon which the Government relies, *Franklin v. Massachusetts*, 505 U.S. 788 (1992), and *Dalton v. Specter*, 511 U.S. 462 (1994). In the former case, the agency action in question was the Secretary of Commerce's presentation to the President of a report tabulating the results of the decennial census; our holding that this did not constitute "final agency action" was premised on the observation that the report carried "no direct consequences" and served "more like a tentative recommendation than a final and binding determination." And in the latter case, the agency action in question was submission to the President of base closure recommendations by the Secretary of Defense and the Defense Base Closure and Realignment Commission; our holding that this was not "final agency action" followed from the fact that the recommendations were in no way binding on the President, who had absolute discretion to accept or reject them. Unlike the reports in *Franklin* and *Dalton*, which were purely advisory and in no way affected the legal rights of the relevant actors, the Biological Opinion at issue here has direct and appreciable legal consequences.

Why the different results in *Franklin*, *Dalton*, and *Bennett*?

5. Finality—*Sackett* applies *Bennett* to an administrative compliance order. The Sacketts filled some property they owned near Priest Lake in northern Idaho with dirt and rock. *Sackett v. EPA*, 132 S. Ct. 1367 (2012). The EPA determined that the Sacketts had discharged pollutants into "navigable waters" without a permit, thus violating the Clean Water Act. The EPA could have brought a civil enforcement action in court to contest this alleged violation, with a maximum penalty of $37,500 per day per violation. 33 U.S.C. § 1319(a)(3), (d). Instead, the agency invoked its statutory authority to issue an administrative compliance order (ACO) ordering the Sacketts to restore the property immediately. The Sacketts sought a hearing before the EPA to make the case that they had not filled in "navigable waters" subject to the Act, but the agency denied this request. If a person subject to a compliance order does not comply and the agency later initiates a court action, then, according to the EPA, the maximum civil penalty doubles to $75,000 per day per violation. 132 S. Ct. at 1370. When the Sacketts sought relief from the ACO in federal court, the EPA objected that its action was not final and therefore not subject to review. The Supreme Court rejected this argument.

Consummation: The EPA argued that its action failed the consummation prong because its denial of the Sackett's request for a hearing had invited them to "engage in informal discussion [with EPA] of the [order's] terms and requirements" and to advise the agency of any inaccurate allegations. 132 S. Ct. at 1372. The Court rejected this effort, observing that EPA's invitation created no "entitlement to further agency review." More broadly, "[t]he mere possibility that an agency might reconsider in light of 'informal discussion' and invited contentions of inaccuracy does not suffice to make an otherwise final agency action nonfinal." *Id.* at 1372. Agencies, thus, cannot avoid finality by including a "why don't we have a nice chat maybe" provision in an order.

Rights/Obligations/Legal Consequences: The Court curtly observed that the ACO obligated the Sacketts to restore the land and to grant access to EPA for inspections. *Id.* at 1371. Taken at face value, the Court's brief analysis suggests that anytime an agency tells a person to do something, that agency has determined that person's legal obligations—at least if the agency is colorably acting within its authority. In addition, the government had taken the position that the ACO had doubled the civil penalties that would otherwise be available in a civil enforcement action from $37,500 per day per violation to $75,000 per day per violation. *Id.* at 1370. Unless the Sacketts complied with the EPA's order, these potential double penalties would continue to increase day by day until the matter was resolved by a district court in an action initiated by EPA at a time of its choosing. *See id.* at 1375 (Alito, J., concurring) (declaring "[i]n a nation that values due process, not to mention private property, such treatment is unthinkable"). In addition, the Sacketts faced the additional "legal consequence" that issuance of EPA's compliance order would make it more difficult to obtain a permit for the fill from the Corps of Engineers. *Id.* at 1372 (citing regulation providing that the Corps will process a permit for property subject to an EPA compliance order only where "clearly appropriate").

6. Finality—a return to pragmatism in *Hawkes*? In *U.S. Army Corps of Engineers v. Hawkes Co., Inc.*, 136 S. Ct. 1807 (2016), the Supreme Court signaled a retreat from a hard-edged, formalistic approach to *Bennett*'s requirement of legal consequences for finality. The plaintiffs in *Hawkes* challenged a jurisdictional determination (JD) in which the Corps determined that property included "waters of the United States" subject to permitting requirements of the Clean Water Act. The Corps argued that the JD did not constitute "final agency action" because it carried no legal consequences. The underlying idea here was that property either contains jurisdictional waters or it does not, and the fact that the Corps had expressed an opinion on this point did not actually change the underlying legal obligations imposed by the CWA.

The Supreme Court, in a majority opinion authored by Chief Justice Roberts disagreed, holding that the JD did constitute final agency action because it gave rise to "direct and appreciable legal consequences." *Id.* at 1814 (citing *Bennett*, 520 U.S. at 178). To find these legal consequences, the Chief Justice began by noting that, under a memorandum of agreement between the Corps and the EPA, a "negative JD" (*i.e.*, a finding that property does not contain jurisdictional waters) blocks these agencies from bringing civil enforcement actions under the CWA for five years. Although a negative JD does not block private parties from bringing citizen suits under the CWA, they cannot obtain civil liability for past violations. A negative JD thus "narrows the field of potential plaintiffs and limits the potential liability a landowner faces for discharging pollutants without a permit." *Id.* at 1814. A positive JD, like the one at issue in *Hawkes*, carries legal consequences insofar as it "represent[s] the denial of the safe harbor that negative JDs afford." *Id.*

After finding the formal legal consequences necessary to satisfy *Bennett*'s second prong, the Chief Justice characterized his conclusion as consistent with "the 'pragmatic' approach we have long taken to finality." *Hawkes*, 136 S. Ct. at 1815. As an example of this pragmatism, he cited *Frozen Food Express v. United States*, 351 U.S. 40, 76 (1956), which involved a challenge to an order of the Interstate Commerce Commission that identified commodities subject to a statutory exemption from regulation. Chief Justice Roberts observed that this "order 'had no authority except to give notice of how the Commission interpreted' the relevant statute, and 'would have effect only if and when a particular action was brought against a particular carrier.'" 136 S. Ct. at 1815 (quoting *Abbott Labs*, 387 U.S. at 150). The order thus carried no formal legal consequences. Nonetheless, the order "warns every carrier, who does not have authority from the Commission to transport those commodities, that it does so at the risk of incurring criminal penalties." *Id.* at 1815 (quoting *Frozen Food*, 351 U.S. at 44). This warning, even though it did not change the law, was final for the purpose of obtaining judicial review. Similarly, in *Hawkes*, "while no administrative or criminal proceeding can be brought for failure to conform to the approved JD itself, that final agency determination . . . warns [respondents] that if they discharge pollutants onto their property without obtaining a permit from the Corps, they do so at the risk of significant criminal and civil penalties." *Id.* This positive discussion of *Frozen Foods* in *Hawkes* seems to signal that an agency action that lacks formal legal consequences, such as a warning that conduct may incur significant potential liability, may be final in light of its practical impacts.

7. Finality — What if the agency says it hasn't bound anyone? Recall from Chapter 3 that "interpretative rules" and "general statements of policy" lack the kind of force of law enjoyed by "legislative rules." This characterization suggests that, unlike legislative rules, interpretative rules and policy statements cannot have the "legal consequences" that *Bennett*, at least, seems to require for finality — especially if the agency claims that it might change its position later. On the other hand, informal agency interpretations and policy statements can exert enormous practical pressure on regulated parties, which suggests that judicial review should be available.

As you might expect, courts do not allow agencies to avoid judicial review of rules simply by avoiding the use of legislative rulemaking procedures. In an early, influential analysis of this problem, the D.C. Circuit held that a letter from the Wage and Hour Administrator was sufficiently final for judicial review. The administrator sent the letter in response to an inquiry from an industry trade association about whether its members were covered by wage and hour legislation. After the Administrator said they were covered, the trade association sued. Emphasizing that the inquiry had not involved a "hypothetical set of facts" but the "actual and present operations" of the industry, the court found the requisite finality:

> When a published interpretation represents the initial views of an agency, approved by the Commission or person who heads the agency, when it is the product of the process provided by the agency for taking into account the position of agency staff as well as the outside presentation, when the interpretation is not labeled as tentative or otherwise qualified by arrangement for reconsideration, it has the feature of 'expected conformity' stressed in *Abbott Laboratories*. This embraces conformity not only by the businessman affected but by the agency personnel. And we see no basis for saying that this interpretative 'agency action' is not 'final' for purposes of the APA and judicial review.

> The matter of formality in the agency process helps show that the agency action involved is the product of the agency's process for assuring deliberation for this kind of action, but where that is not contested, informality in the communication does not negative the substance of what has been done and the reality that it is the 'final' such action of the agency.

> The opinion in this case was signed by the Administrator; it was rendered on a broad legal question affecting an entire industry group; we take it as satisfying the aspect of finality which requires an authoritative agency ruling.

National Automatic Laundry & Cleaning Council v. Schulz, 443 F.2d 689, 702 (D.C. Cir. 1971).

Nearly thirty years later, the D.C. Circuit took up the problem of the finality of informal actions again in another influential case, *Appalachian Power Co. v. Environmental Protection Agency*, 208 F.3d 1015 (D.C. Cir. 2000). Under Title V of the 1990 Amendments to the Clean Air Act, stationary sources of air pollution must obtain operating permits from state authorities. These state authorities administer permitting programs approved by EPA, which has promulgated rules specifying various requirements state permitting programs must meet. If EPA disapproves of a state's program, then the state loses its federal highway funds, and EPA takes over its permitting authority. In *Appalachian Power*, industrial concerns challenged the validity of an EPA "guidance" document that stated the agency's understanding of a rule it promulgated requiring state permitting programs to require monitoring of pollutant emissions:

> In a document entitled "Periodic Monitoring Guidance for Title V Operating Permits Programs," released in September 1998, EPA took a sharply different view of §70.6(a)(3) than do petitioners. The "Guidance" was issued over the signature of two EPA officials—the Director of the Office of Regulatory Enforcement, and the Director of the Office of Air Quality Planning and Standards. It is narrative in form, consists of 19 single-spaced, typewritten pages, and is available on EPA's internet web site (www.epa.gov)....

II.

> The phenomenon we see in this case is familiar. Congress passes a broadly worded statute. The agency follows with regulations containing broad language, open-ended phrases, ambiguous standards and the like. Then as years pass, the agency issues circulars or guidance or memoranda, explaining, interpreting, defining and often expanding the commands in the regulations. One guidance document may yield another and then another and so on. Several words in a regulation may spawn hundreds of pages of text as the agency offers more and more detail regarding what its regulations demand of regulated entities. Law is made, without notice and comment, without public participation, and without publication in the Federal Register or the Code of Federal Regulations. With the advent of the Internet, the agency does not need these official publications to ensure widespread circulation; it can inform those affected simply by posting its new guidance or memoranda or policy statement on its web site. An agency operating in this way gains a large advantage. "It can issue or amend its real rules, *i.e.*, its interpretative rules and policy statements, quickly and inexpensively without following any statutorily prescribed procedures." Richard J. Pierce, Jr., *Seven Ways to Deossify Agency Rulemaking*, 47 ADMIN. L. REV. 59, 85 (1995). The agency may also think there is another advantage—immunizing its lawmaking from judicial review.

> EPA tells us that its Periodic Monitoring Guidance is not subject to judicial review because it is not final, and it is not final because it is not "binding." *See* GUIDANCE at 19. It is worth pausing a minute to consider what is meant by "binding" in this context. Only "legislative rules" have the force

"BINDING"

and effect of law. A "legislative rule" is one the agency has duly promulgated in compliance with the procedures laid down in the statute or in the Administrative Procedure Act. If this were all that "binding" meant, EPA's Periodic Monitoring Guidance could not possibly qualify: it was not the product of notice and comment rulemaking in accordance with the Clean Air Act, 42 U.S.C. § 7607(d), and it has not been published in the Federal Register. But we have also recognized that an agency's other pronouncements can, as a practical matter, have a binding effect. If an agency acts as if a document issued at headquarters is controlling in the field, if it treats the document in the same manner as it treats a legislative rule, if it bases enforcement actions on the policies or interpretations formulated in the document, if it leads private parties or State permitting authorities to believe that it will declare permits invalid unless they comply with the terms of the document, then the agency's document is for all practical purposes "binding." See Robert A. Anthony, *Interpretative Rules, Policy Statements, Guidances, Manuals, and the Like—Should Federal Agencies Use Them to Bind the Public?*, 41 Duke L.J. 1311, 1328–29 (1992), and cases there cited . . . .

Of course, an agency's action is not necessarily final merely because it is binding. Judicial orders can be binding; a temporary restraining order, for instance, compels compliance but it does not finally decide the case. In the administrative setting, "two conditions must be satisfied for agency action to be 'final': First the action must mark the 'consummation' of the agency's decisionmaking process — it must not be of a merely tentative or interlocutory nature. And second, the action must be one by which 'rights or obligations have been determined,' or from which 'legal consequences will flow.'" *Bennett v. Spear*, 520 U.S. 154, 178 (1997). The first condition is satisfied here. The "Guidance," as issued in September 1998, followed a draft circulated four years earlier and another, more extensive draft circulated in May 1998. This latter document bore the title "EPA Draft Final Periodic Monitoring Guidance." On the question whether States must review their emission standards and the emission standards EPA has promulgated to determine if the standards provide enough monitoring, the Guidance is unequivocal—the State agencies must do so. *See* GUIDANCE at 6–8. . . .

On the issue whether the challenged portion of the Guidance has legal consequences, EPA points to the concluding paragraph of the document, which contains a disclaimer: "The policies set forth in this paper are intended solely as guidance, do not represent final Agency action, and cannot be relied upon to create any rights enforceable by any party." GUIDANCE at 19. This language is boilerplate; since 1991 EPA has been placing it at the end of all its guidance documents. See Robert A. Anthony, *supra*, 41 Duke L.J. at 1361; Peter L. Strauss, Comment, *The Rulemaking Continuum*, 41 Duke L.J. 1463, 1485 (1992) (referring to EPA's notice as "a charade, intended to keep the proceduralizing courts at bay"). Insofar as the "policies" mentioned in the disclaimer consist of requiring State permitting authorities to search for deficiencies in existing monitoring regulations and replace them through terms and conditions of a permit, "rights" may not be created but "obligations" certainly are—obligations on the part of the State regulators and those they regulate. At any rate, the entire Guidance, from beginning to end—except the last paragraph—reads like a ukase. It commands, it requires, it orders, it dictates. Through the Guidance, EPA has given the States their "marching orders" and EPA expects the States to fall in line, as all have done, save perhaps Florida and Texas. . . .

The short of the matter is that the Guidance, insofar as relevant here, is final agency action, reflecting a settled agency position which has legal consequences both for State agencies administering their permit programs and for companies like those represented by petitioners who must obtain Title V permits in order to continue operating.

It seems that the court is finding "legal consequences" based on the EPA's commitment to administer its "guidance" consistently. But don't we want agencies to act consistently? Consistency enables reliance, limits arbitrary discretion, and avoids favoritism. *See generally* Nicholas R. Parrillo, *Federal Agency Guidance and the Power to Bind: An Empirical Study of Agencies and Industries*, 36 YALE J. REG. 165 (2019) (finding, based on interviews of 135 agency officials and representatives of both industry and NGOs, that one important source of the "practically binding" effect of agency guidance is that regulated parties, regulatory beneficiaries, and Congress all demand consistency; concluding that pressures for consistency "spring from rule-of-law values that agencies would be remiss to ignore").

Note that, under *Appalachian Power*, an agency's action may be considered "final" even though the agency has not taken the procedural steps formally necessary to give a rule "legislative" force. But if a rule is "final" because it carries legal consequences, does it follow that the agency *should* have used legislative rulemaking procedures—which will usually entail notice-and-comment? The D.C. Circuit has, in recent years, answered this question in the affirmative, at least for purported policy statements. *See, e.g., Nat'l Mining Ass'n v. McCarthy*, 758 F.3d 243, 251 (D.C. Cir. 2014) (holding that proper policy statements lack the legal effects necessary for finality and are therefore categorically unreviewable; a rule that an agency has styled as a policy statement may, however, be a procedurally defective legislative rule subject to review). But see *California Communities against Toxics v. EPA*, 934 F.3d 627 (D.C. Cir. 2019) (acknowledging, in light of *Hawkes*, that a rule can be nonlegislative yet carry the direct legal consequences needed for finality).

It seems fair to suggest that the D.C. Circuit was trying pretty hard to characterize the EPA's guidance document in *Appalachian Power* as carrying formal legal consequences because they were needed for finality under *Bennett*'s two-pronged test that the Supreme Court had announced just a few years before. But, as discussed in note 6, the Supreme Court seemed to signal in *U.S. Army Corps of Engineers v. Hawkes Co., Inc.*, 136 S. Ct. 1807 (2016), that practical impacts can sometimes substitute for legal consequences. If this signal takes hold in the case law, then lower courts may be able to review guidance documents as final without bending over backwards, as in *Appalachian Power*, to characterize them as carrying formal legal consequences.

2. Exhaustion

The doctrine of exhaustion requires a litigant to invoke an agency's own internal remedies for correcting errors before seeking judicial review. It can be difficult to keep exhaustion straight from finality, but they are conceptually distinct. For instance, you will recall that under 5 U.S.C. § 557(b), an ALJ's initial decision becomes the decision of the agency if no one seeks review by the agency itself. The ALJ's decision thus will constitute "final" agency action even though the possibility of internal agency review has not been exhausted. Congress frequently imposes exhaustion requirements in agency enabling acts. Where Congress has not imposed a statutory exhaustion requirement, courts apply a "common law" version of the doctrine that they have fashioned over the years.

Lesson 5F.2. Suppose the following variation on health claims for red wine: Recently, Gallery began selling its "Great Hart" line of red wines. The labels for this line of wine note that scientific studies have shown that "moderate" consumption of red wine can decrease the chance of heart attack "substantially." They also include standard mandatory health and safety warnings advising pregnant women against consumption of alcohol and noting that alcohol impairs driving ability.

The WTC enforcement staff initiated a formal adjudication against Gallery on the ground that the Great Hart label violates WTCA § 5(b) by omitting material facts necessary to make its health benefit claims not misleading. In particular, the WTC staff objected that the label left the misleading impression that it is clear that the health benefits of red wine consumption outweigh its potential ill effects, and that therefore consumers should drink red wine to improve their health.

Our favorite ALJ, Bud, heard the case. The WTC staff's expert presented survey data showing that consumers understood the Great Hart labels as communicating a "wine is good for you" message. Gallery's expert presented survey data showing that consumers understood that the label communicated one discrete health benefit that wine might provide; they did not read the labels as making a claim that this health benefit outweighed any other potential effects. Gallery also observed that, as a commercial entity, it had a First Amendment right to convey truthful messages about its products. It therefore had a right to continue using its Great Hart labels as they were not misleading.

Bud issued an initial decision in favor of the staff. He determined that the WTC staff had demonstrated that the labels did convey a misleading impression that it is clear that red wine consumption is, on balance, healthy. Because the labels were misleading, the agency could forbid their use without infringing on Gallery's First Amendment right to commercial speech. Bud therefore ordered Gallery to cease-and-desist from using the Great Hart name and labels.

Just one week before, the WTC had published notice of a proposed rule forbidding inclusion of claims of health benefits on wine labels or other advertising.

A WTC rule provides that a party subject to an order issued via initial decision "may file an appeal of that order to the full Commission within thirty days of its issuance." Abby, Gallery's attorney, considers the WTC hostile to Gallery's cause and is wondering whether she could circumvent the agency and seek immediate judicial review of Bud's initial decision. What do the following materials suggest?

Background of *McCarthy v. Madigan*

This case assessed whether a federal prisoner pressing a *Bivens* claim arising out of alleged medical mistreatment needed to exhaust the prison's internal remedies before going to court. Justice Blackmun's opinion nicely lays out the doctrine of common law exhaustion. As you read, take note of the purposes served by this doctrine, the balancing test it requires, and the types of circumstances that may excuse exhaustion. Also, why do you think the plaintiff limited his claim for relief to monetary damages?

McCarthy v. Madigan
503 U.S. 140 (1992)

JUSTICE BLACKMUN delivered the opinion of the Court.

The issue in this case is whether a federal prisoner must resort to the internal grievance procedure promulgated by the Federal Bureau of Prisons before he may initiate a suit, pursuant to the authority of *Bivens v. Six Unknown Fed. Narcotics Agents*, 403 U.S. 388 (1971), solely for money damages.

While he was a prisoner in the federal penitentiary at Leavenworth, petitioner John J. McCarthy filed a pro se complaint in the United States District Court for the District of Kansas against four prison employees: the hospital administrator, the chief psychologist, another psychologist, and a physician. McCarthy alleged that respondents had violated his constitutional rights under the Eighth Amendment by their deliberate indifference to his needs and medical condition resulting from a back operation and a history of psychiatric problems. On the first page of his complaint, he wrote: "This Complaint seeks Money Damages Only."

The District Court dismissed the complaint on the ground that petitioner had failed to exhaust prison administrative remedies. Under 28 CFR pt. 542 (1991), setting forth the general "Administrative Remedy Procedure for Inmates" at federal correctional institutions, a prisoner may "seek formal review of a complaint which relates to any aspect of his imprisonment." § 542.10. . . .

To promote efficient dispute resolution, the procedure includes rapid filing and response timetables. An inmate first seeks informal resolution of his claim by consulting prison personnel. § 542.13(a). If this informal effort fails, the prisoner "may file a formal written complaint on the appropriate form, within fifteen (15) calendar days of the date on which the basis of the complaint occurred." § 542.13(b). Should the warden fail to respond to the inmate's satisfaction within 15 days, the inmate has 20 days to appeal to the Bureau's Regional Director, who has 30 days to respond. If the inmate still remains unsatisfied, he has 30 days to make a final appeal to the Bureau's general counsel, who has another 30 days to respond. §§ 542.14 and 542.15. If the inmate can demonstrate a "valid reason for delay," he "shall be allowed" an extension of any of these time periods for filing. § 542.13(b).

Petitioner McCarthy filed with the District Court a motion for reconsideration under Federal Rule of Civil Procedure 60(b), arguing that he was not required to exhaust his administrative remedies, because he sought only money damages which, he claimed, the Bureau could not provide. The court denied the motion.

The Court of Appeals [affirmed].

II

The doctrine of exhaustion of administrative remedies is one among related doctrines—including abstention, finality, and ripeness—that govern the timing of federal-court decisionmaking. Of "paramount importance" to any exhaustion inquiry is congressional intent. *Patsy v. Board of Regents of Florida*, 457 U.S. 496, 501 (1982). Where Congress specifically mandates, exhaustion is required. But where Congress has not clearly required exhaustion, sound judicial discretion governs. . . . Nevertheless, even in this field of judicial discretion, appropriate deference to Congress' power to prescribe the basic procedural scheme under which a claim may be heard in a federal court requires fashioning of exhaustion principles in a manner consistent with congressional intent and any applicable statutory scheme.

[handwritten margin note: CONGRESSIONAL INTENT]

A

This Court long has acknowledged the general rule that parties exhaust prescribed administrative remedies before seeking relief from the federal courts. See, e.g., *Myers v. Bethlehem Shipbuilding Corp.*, 303 U.S. 41, 50–51, and n. 9 (1938) (discussing cases as far back as 1898). Exhaustion is required because it serves the twin purposes of protecting administrative agency authority and promoting judicial efficiency.

[handwritten margin note: PURPOSE OF EXHAUSTION]

As to the first of these purposes, the exhaustion doctrine recognizes the notion, grounded in deference to Congress' delegation of authority to coordinate branches of Government, that agencies, not the courts, ought to have primary responsibility for the programs that Congress has charged them to administer. Exhaustion concerns apply with particular force when the action under review involves exercise of the agency's discretionary power or when the agency proceedings in question allow the agency to apply its special expertise. The exhaustion doctrine also acknowledges the commonsense notion of dispute resolution that an agency ought to have an opportunity to correct its own mistakes with respect to the programs it administers before it is haled into federal court. Correlatively, exhaustion principles apply with special force when "frequent and deliberate flouting of administrative processes" could weaken an agency's effectiveness by encouraging disregard of its procedures.

[handwritten margin note: CONGRESS (struck through)]

As to the second of the purposes, exhaustion promotes judicial efficiency in at least two ways. When an agency has the opportunity to correct its own errors, a judicial controversy may well be mooted, or at least piecemeal appeals may be avoided. And even where a controversy survives administrative review, exhaustion of the administrative procedure may produce a useful record for subsequent judicial consideration, especially in a complex or technical factual context.

B

Notwithstanding these substantial institutional interests, federal courts are vested with a "virtually unflagging obligation" to exercise the jurisdiction given them. "We have no more right to decline the exercise of jurisdiction which is given, than to usurp that which is not given." Accordingly, this Court has declined to require exhaustion in some circumstances even where administrative and judicial interests would counsel otherwise. In determining whether exhaustion is required, federal courts must balance the interest of the individual in retaining prompt access to a federal judicial forum against countervailing institutional interests favoring exhaustion. "[A]dministrative remedies need not be pursued if the litigant's interests in immediate judicial review outweigh the government's interests in the efficiency or administrative autonomy that the exhaustion doctrine is designed to further." Application of this balancing principle is "intensely practical," . . . because attention is directed to both the nature of the claim presented and the characteristics of the particular administrative procedure provided.

C

This Court's precedents have recognized at least three broad sets of circumstances in which the interests of the individual weigh heavily against requiring administrative exhaustion. First, requiring resort to the administrative remedy may occasion undue prejudice to subsequent assertion of a court action. Such prejudice may result, for example, from an unreasonable or indefinite timeframe for administrative action. See *Gibson v. Berryhill*, 411 U.S. 564, 575, n. 14 (1973) (administrative remedy deemed inadequate "[m]ost often . . . because of delay by the agency"). . . . Even where the administrative decisionmaking schedule is otherwise reasonable and definite, a particular plaintiff may suffer irreparable harm if unable to secure immediate judicial consideration of his claim. *Bowen v. City of New York*, 476 U.S., at 483 (disability-benefit claimants "would be irreparably injured were the exhaustion requirement now enforced against them"). . . . By the same token, exhaustion principles apply with less force when an individual's failure to exhaust may preclude a defense to criminal liability. . . .

Second, an administrative remedy may be inadequate "because of some doubt as to whether the agency was empowered to grant effective relief." For example, an agency, as a preliminary matter, may be unable to consider whether to grant relief because it lacks institutional competence to resolve the particular type of issue presented, such as the constitutionality of a statute. In a similar vein, exhaustion has not been required where the challenge is to the adequacy of the agency procedure itself, such that "'the question of the adequacy of the administrative remedy . . . [is] for all practical purposes identical with the merits of [the plaintiff's] lawsuit.'" Alternatively, an agency may be competent to adjudicate the issue presented, but still lack authority to grant the type of relief requested. *McNeese v. Board of Ed. for Community Unit School Dist. 187*, 373 U.S. 668, 675 (1963) (students seeking to integrate public school need not file complaint with school superintendent because the "Superintendent himself apparently has no power to order corrective action" except to request the Attorney General to bring suit). . . .

Third, an administrative remedy may be inadequate where the administrative body is shown to be biased or has otherwise predetermined the issue before it. . . . *Houghton v. Shafer*, 392 U.S. 639, 640 (1968) (in view of Attorney General's submission that the challenged rules of the prison were "validly and correctly applied to petitioner," requiring administrative review through a process culminating with the Attorney General "would be to demand a futile act"). . . .

III

In light of these general principles, we conclude that petitioner McCarthy need not have exhausted his constitutional claim for money damages. As a preliminary matter, we find that Congress has not meaningfully addressed the appropriateness of requiring exhaustion in this context. Although respondents' interests are significant, we are left with a firm conviction that, given the type of claim McCarthy raises and the particular characteristics of the Bureau's general grievance procedure, McCarthy's individual interests outweigh countervailing institutional interests favoring exhaustion. . . .

B

Because Congress has not required exhaustion of a federal prisoner's *Bivens* claim, we turn to an evaluation of the individual and institutional interests at stake in this case. The general grievance procedure heavily burdens the individual interests of the petitioning inmate in two ways. First, the procedure imposes short, successive filing deadlines that create a high risk of forfeiture of a claim for failure to comply. Second, the administrative "remedy" does not authorize an award of monetary damages—the only relief requested by McCarthy in this action. The combination of these features means that the prisoner seeking only money damages has everything to lose and nothing to gain from being required to exhaust his claim under the internal grievance procedure.

[handwritten margin note: BURDEN ON INDIVIDUAL]

The filing deadlines for the grievance procedure require an inmate, within 15 days of the precipitating incident, not only to attempt to resolve his grievance informally but also to file a formal written complaint with the prison warden. Then, he must successively hurdle 20-day and 30-day deadlines to advance to the end of the grievance process. Other than the Bureau's general and quite proper interest in having early notice of any claim, we have not been apprised of any urgency or exigency justifying this timetable. As a practical matter, the filing deadlines, of course, may pose little difficulty for the knowledgeable inmate accustomed to grievances and

[handwritten margin note: NO JUSTIFIC. FOR SHORT TIME-TABLE]

court actions. But they are a likely trap for the inexperienced and unwary inmate, ordinarily indigent and unrepresented by counsel, with a substantial claim. . . .

All in all, these deadlines require a good deal of an inmate at the peril of forfeiting his claim for money damages. The "first" of "the principles that necessarily frame our analysis of prisoners' constitutional claims" is that "federal courts must take cognizance of the valid constitutional claims of prison inmates." Because a prisoner ordinarily is divested of the privilege to vote, the right to file a court action might be said to be his remaining most "fundamental political right, because preservative of all rights." The rapid filing deadlines counsel strongly against exhaustion as a prerequisite to the filing of a federal-court action.

As we have noted, the grievance procedure does not include any mention of the award of monetary relief. Respondents argue that this should not matter, because "in most cases there are other things that the inmate wants." This may be true in some instances. But we cannot presume, as a general matter, that when a litigant has deliberately forgone any claim for injunctive relief and has singled out discrete past wrongs, specifically requesting monetary compensation only, that he is likely interested in "other things." The Bureau, in any case, is always free to offer an inmate administrative relief in return for withdrawal of his lawsuit. We conclude that the absence of any monetary remedy in the grievance procedure also weighs heavily against imposing an exhaustion requirement.

. . . The availability of a money damages remedy is, at best, uncertain, and the uncertainty of the administrative agency's authority to award relief counsels against requiring exhaustion.

We do not find the interests of the Bureau of Prisons to weigh heavily in favor of exhaustion in view of the remedial scheme and particular claim presented here. To be sure, the Bureau has a substantial interest in encouraging internal resolution of grievances and in preventing the undermining of its authority by unnecessary resort by prisoners to the federal courts. But other institutional concerns relevant to exhaustion analysis appear to weigh in hardly at all. The Bureau's alleged failure to render medical care implicates only tangentially its authority to carry out the control and management of the federal prisons. Furthermore, the Bureau does not bring to bear any special expertise on the type of issue presented for resolution here.

The interests of judicial economy do not stand to be advanced substantially by the general grievance procedure. No formal factfindings are made. The paperwork generated by the grievance process might assist a court somewhat in ascertaining the facts underlying a prisoner's claim more quickly than if it has only a prisoner's complaint to review. But the grievance procedure does not create a formal factual record of the type that can be relied on conclusively by a court for disposition of a prisoner's claim on the pleadings or at summary judgment without the aid of affidavits.

C

In conclusion, we are struck by the absence of supporting material in the regulations, the record, or the briefs that the general grievance procedure here was crafted with any thought toward the principles of exhaustion of claims for money damages. The Attorney General's professed concern for internal dispute resolution has not translated itself into a more effective grievance procedure that might encourage the filing of an administrative complaint as opposed to a court action. Congress, of course, is free to design or require an appropriate administrative procedure for a prisoner to exhaust his claim for money damages. Even without further action by Congress, we do not foreclose the possibility that the Bureau itself may adopt an appropriate administrative procedure consistent with congressional intent.

The judgment of the Court of Appeals is reversed.

It is so ordered.

CHIEF JUSTICE REHNQUIST, with whom JUSTICE SCALIA and JUSTICE THOMAS join, concurring in the judgment.

I agree with the Court's holding that a federal prisoner need not exhaust the procedures promulgated by the Federal Bureau of Prisons. My view, however, is based entirely on the fact that the grievance procedure at issue does not provide for any award of monetary damages. As a result, in cases such as this one where prisoners seek monetary relief, the Bureau's administrative remedy furnishes no effective remedy at all, and it is therefore improper to impose an exhaustion requirement. . . .

Background of *Darby v. Cisneros*

As the Court observed in *McCarthy*, courts follow Congress's instructions on exhaustion. In *Darby v. Cisneros*, the Court explained that a sentence in § 704 that had been largely ignored for over 45 years contained important limitations on agencies' authority to require litigants to exhaust administrative remedies before invoking the APA's cause of action to seek judicial review.

Darby v. Cisneros
509 U.S. 137 (1993)

JUSTICE BLACKMUN delivered the opinion of the Court.

This case presents the question whether federal courts have the authority to require that a plaintiff exhaust available administrative remedies before seeking judicial review under the Administrative Procedure Act (APA), 5 U.S.C. § 701 *et seq.*, where neither the statute nor agency rules specifically mandate exhaustion as a prerequisite to judicial review. At issue is the relationship between the judicially created doctrine of exhaustion of administrative remedies and the statutory requirements of § [704] of the APA.

Petitioner R. Gordon Darby is a self-employed South Carolina real estate developer who specializes in the development and management of multifamily rental projects. In the early 1980s, he began working with Lonnie Garvin, Jr., a mortgage banker, who had developed a plan to enable multifamily developers to obtain single-family mortgage insurance from respondent Department of Housing and Urban

Development (HUD). Respondent Secretary of HUD (Secretary) is authorized to provide single-family mortgage insurance under §203(b) of the National Housing Act. Although HUD also provides mortgage insurance for multifamily projects under §207 of the National Housing Act the greater degree of oversight and control over such projects makes it less attractive for investors than the single-family mortgage insurance option.

The principal advantage of Garvin's plan was that it promised to avoid HUD's "Rule of Seven." This rule prevented rental properties from receiving single-family mortgage insurance if the mortgagor already had financial interests in seven or more similar rental properties in the same project or subdivision. Under Garvin's plan, a person seeking financing would use straw purchasers as mortgage-insurance applicants. Once the loans were closed, the straw purchasers would transfer title back to the development company. Because no single purchaser at the time of purchase would own more than seven rental properties within the same project, the Rule of Seven appeared not to be violated. HUD employees in South Carolina apparently assured Garvin that his plan was lawful and that he thereby would avoid the limitation of the Rule of Seven.

Darby obtained financing for three separate multi-unit projects, and, through Garvin's plan, Darby obtained single-family mortgage insurance from HUD. Although Darby successfully rented the units, a combination of low rents, falling interest rates, and a generally depressed rental market forced him into default in 1988. HUD became responsible for the payment of over $6.6 million in insurance claims.

HUD had become suspicious of Garvin's financing plan as far back as 1983. In 1986, HUD initiated an audit but concluded that neither Darby nor Garvin had done anything wrong or misled HUD personnel. Nevertheless, in June 1989, HUD issued a limited denial of participation (LDP) that prohibited petitioners for one year from participating in any program in South Carolina administered by respondent Assistant Secretary of Housing. Two months later, the Assistant Secretary notified petitioners that HUD was also proposing to debar them from further participation in all HUD procurement contracts and in any nonprocurement transaction with any federal agency.

Petitioners' appeals of the LDP and of the proposed debarment were consolidated, and an Administrative Law Judge (ALJ) conducted a hearing on the consolidated appeals in December 1989. The judge issued an "Initial Decision and Order" in April 1990, finding that the financing method used by petitioners was "a sham which improperly circumvented the Rule of Seven." The ALJ concluded, however, that most of the relevant facts had been disclosed to local HUD employees, that petitioners lacked criminal intent, and that Darby himself "genuinely cooperated with HUD to try [to] work out his financial dilemma and avoid foreclosure." In light of these mitigating factors, the ALJ concluded that an indefinite debarment would be punitive and that it would serve no legitimate purpose; good cause existed, however, to debar petitioners for a period of 18 months.

Under HUD regulations,

> "[t]he hearing officer's determination shall be final unless, pursuant to 24 CFR part 26, the Secretary or the Secretary's designee, within 30 days of receipt of a request decides as a matter of discretion to review the finding of the hearing officer. The 30 day period for deciding whether to review a determination may be extended upon written notice of such extension by the Secretary or his designee. Any party may request such a review in writing within 15 days of receipt of the hearing officer's determination." 24 CFR § 24.314(c) (1992)."

Neither petitioners nor respondents sought further administrative review of the ALJ's "Initial Decision and Order."

On May 31, 1990, petitioners filed suit in the United States District Court for the District of South Carolina. They sought an injunction and a declaration that the administrative sanctions were imposed for purposes of punishment, in violation of HUD's own debarment regulations, and therefore were "not in accordance with law" within the meaning of § 10(e)(B)(1) of the APA, 5 U.S.C. § 706(2)(A).

Respondents moved to dismiss the complaint on the ground that petitioners, by forgoing the option to seek review by the Secretary, had failed to exhaust administrative remedies. . . .

The Court of Appeals for the Fourth Circuit reversed. It recognized that neither the National Housing Act nor HUD regulations expressly mandate exhaustion of administrative remedies prior to filing suit. The court concluded, however, that the District Court had erred in denying respondents' motion to dismiss, because there was no evidence to suggest that further review would have been futile or that the Secretary would have abused his discretion by indefinitely extending the time limitations for review. . . .

Section [704] of the APA bears the caption "Actions reviewable." It provides in its first two sentences that judicial review is available for "final agency action for which there is no other adequate remedy in a court," and that "preliminary, procedural, or intermediate agency action . . . is subject to review on the review of the final agency action." The last sentence of § [704] reads:

> "Except as otherwise expressly required by statute, agency action otherwise final is final for the purposes of this section whether or not there has been presented or determined an application for a declaratory order, for any form of reconsideration . . . , or, unless the agency otherwise requires by rule and provides that the action meanwhile is inoperative, for an appeal to superior agency authority." 5 U.S.C. § 704.

Petitioners argue that this provision means that a litigant seeking judicial review of a final agency action under the APA need not exhaust available administrative remedies unless such exhaustion is expressly required by statute or agency rule. According to petitioners, since § [704] contains an explicit exhaustion provision, federal courts are not free to require further exhaustion as a matter of judicial discretion.

Respondents contend that § [704] is concerned solely with timing, that is, when agency actions become "final," and that Congress had no intention to interfere with the courts' ability to impose conditions on the timing of their exercise of jurisdiction to review final agency actions. Respondents concede that petitioners' claim is "final" under § [704], for neither the National Housing Act nor applicable HUD regulations require that a litigant pursue further administrative appeals prior to seeking judicial review. However, even though nothing in § [704] precludes judicial review of petitioners' claim, respondents argue that federal courts remain free under the APA to impose appropriate exhaustion requirements.[9]

We have recognized that the judicial doctrine of exhaustion of administrative remedies is conceptually distinct from the doctrine of finality:

> "[T]he finality requirement is concerned with whether the initial decision-maker has arrived at a definitive position on the issue that inflicts an actual, concrete injury; the exhaustion requirement generally refers to administrative and judicial procedures by which an injured party may seek review of an adverse decision and obtain a remedy if the decision is found to be unlawful or otherwise inappropriate."

Whether courts are free to impose an exhaustion requirement as a matter of judicial discretion depends, at least in part, on whether Congress has provided otherwise, for "of 'paramount importance' to any exhaustion inquiry is congressional intent," We therefore must consider whether § [704], by providing the conditions under which agency action becomes "final for the purposes of" judicial review, limits the authority of courts to impose additional exhaustion requirements as a pre requisite to judicial review.

It perhaps is surprising that it has taken over 45 years since the passage of the APA for this Court definitively to address this question. . . .

While some dicta in these cases might be claimed to lend support to petitioners' interpretation of § [704], the text of the APA leaves little doubt that petitioners are correct. Under § [702] of the APA, "[a] person suffering legal wrong because of agency action, or adversely affected or aggrieved by agency action within the meaning of a relevant statute, *is entitled to judicial review thereof.*" Although § [702] provides the general right to judicial review of agency actions under the APA, § [704] establishes when such review is available. When an aggrieved party has exhausted all administrative remedies expressly prescribed by statute or agency rule, the agency

---

9. Respondents also have argued that under HUD regulations, petitioners' debarment remains "inoperative" pending review by the Secretary. But this fact alone is insufficient under § [704] to mandate exhaustion prior to judicial review, for the agency also must require such exhaustion by rule. Respondents concede that HUD imposes no such exhaustion requirement.

action is "final for the purposes of this section" and therefore "subject to judicial review" under the first sentence. While federal courts may be free to apply, where appropriate, other prudential doctrines of judicial administration to limit the scope and timing of judicial review, § [704], by its very terms, has limited the availability of the doctrine of exhaustion of administrative remedies to that which the statute or rule clearly mandates.

The last sentence of § [704] refers explicitly to "any form of reconsideration" and "an appeal to superior agency authority." Congress clearly was concerned with making the exhaustion requirement unambiguous so that aggrieved parties would know precisely what administrative steps were required before judicial review would be available. If courts were able to impose additional exhaustion requirements beyond those provided by Congress or the agency, the last sentence of § [704] would make no sense. To adopt respondents' reading would transform § [704] from a provision designed to "'remove obstacles to judicial review of agency action,'" into a trap for unwary litigants. Section [704] explicitly requires exhaustion of all intra-agency appeals mandated either by statute or by agency rule; it would be inconsistent with the plain language of § [704] for courts to require litigants to exhaust optional appeals as well.

Recourse to the legislative history of § [704] is unnecessary in light of the plain meaning of the statutory text. Nevertheless, we consider that history briefly because both sides have spent much of their time arguing about its implications. In its report on the APA, the Senate Judiciary Committee explained that the last sentence of § [704] was "designed to implement the provisions of section [557(b)]." Section [557(b)], provides, unless the agency requires otherwise, that an initial decision made by a hearing officer "becomes the decision of the agency without further proceedings unless there is an appeal to, or review on motion of, the agency within time provided by rule." The Judiciary Committee explained that

> "an agency may permit an examiner to make the initial decision in a case, which becomes the agency's decision in the absence of an appeal to or review by the agency. If there is such review or appeal, the examiner's initial decision becomes inoperative until the agency determines the matter. For that reason this subsection [§ 704] permits an agency also to require by rule that, if any party is not satisfied with the initial decision of a subordinate hearing officer, the party must first appeal to the agency (the decision meanwhile being inoperative) before resorting to the courts. In no case may appeal to 'superior agency authority' be required by rule unless the administrative decision meanwhile is inoperative, because otherwise the effect of such a requirement would be to subject the party to the agency action and to repetitious administrative process without recourse. There is a fundamental inconsistency in requiring a person to continue 'exhausting' administrative processes after administrative action has become, and while it remains, effective."

In a statement appended to a letter dated October 19, 1945, to the Judiciary Committee, Attorney General Tom C. Clark set forth his understanding of the effect of § [704]:

> "This subsection states (subject to the provisions of section [701]) the acts which are reviewable under section[s] [701 et seq.]. It is intended to state existing law. The last sentence makes it clear that the doctrine of exhaustion of administrative remedies with respect to finality of agency action is intended to be applied only (1) where expressly required by statute ... or (2) where the agency's rules require that decisions by subordinate officers must be appealed to superior agency authority before the decision may be regarded as final for purposes of judicial review."

Respondents place great weight on the Attorney General's statement that § [704] "is intended to state existing law." That law, according to respondents, "plainly permitted federal courts to require exhaustion of adequate administrative remedies." We cannot agree with this categorical pronouncement. With respect to the exhaustion of motions for administrative reconsideration or rehearing, the trend in pre-APA cases was in the opposite direction. . . .

Respondents in effect concede that the trend in the law prior to the enactment of the APA was to require exhaustion of motions for administrative reconsideration or rehearing only when explicitly mandated by statute. Respondents argue, however, that the law governing the exhaustion of administrative *appeals* prior to the APA was significantly different from § [704] as petitioners would have us interpret it. . . .

Nothing in this pre-APA history, however, supports respondents' argument that initial decisions that were "final" for purposes of judicial review were nonetheless unreviewable unless and until an administrative appeal was taken. The pre-APA cases concerning judicial review of federal agency action stand for the simple proposition that, until an administrative appeal was taken, the agency action was unreviewable because it was not yet "final." This is hardly surprising, given the fact that few, if any, administrative agencies authorized hearing officers to make final agency decisions prior to the enactment of the APA.

The purpose of § [704] was to permit agencies to require an appeal to "superior agency authority" before an examiner's initial decision became final. This was necessary because, under § [557(b)], initial decisions could become final agency decisions in the absence of an agency appeal. Agencies may avoid the finality of an initial decision, first, by adopting a rule that an agency appeal be taken before judicial review is available, and, second, by providing that the initial decision would be "inoperative" pending appeal. Otherwise, the initial decision becomes final and the aggrieved party is entitled to judicial review. . . .

We noted just last Term in a non-APA case that

> "appropriate deference to Congress' power to prescribe the basic procedural scheme under which a claim may be heard in a federal court requires

fashioning of exhaustion principles in a manner consistent with congressional intent and any applicable statutory scheme."

Appropriate deference in this case requires the recognition that, with respect to actions brought under the APA, Congress effectively codified the doctrine of exhaustion of administrative remedies in § [704]. Of course, the exhaustion doctrine continues to apply as a matter of judicial discretion in cases not governed by the APA. But where the APA applies, an appeal to "superior agency authority" is a prerequisite to judicial review *only* when expressly required by statute or when an agency rule requires appeal before review and the administrative action is made inoperative pending that review. Courts are not free to impose an exhaustion requirement as a rule of judicial administration where the agency action has already become "final" under § [704].

The judgment of the Court of Appeals is reversed, and the case is remanded for further proceedings consistent with this opinion.

It is so ordered.

Notes

1. Can Gallery circumvent the WTC? *McCarthy* provides a nice, concise statement of the "common law" of exhaustion. *Darby*, surprisingly enough, concludes that courts lack authority to impose common-law exhaustion requirements where judicial review is sought pursuant to the APA. If Gallery were to seek immediate judicial review of Bud's initial decision, would this effort be subject to *McCarthy*-type principles or to *Darby*'s?

McCarthy cites a variety of grounds for excusing exhaustion. Judicial application of these exceptions is not especially consistent. If *McCarthy* applies, would it make sense to excuse exhaustion on any of these grounds in Gallery's case?

2. Finality versus exhaustion. What light does *Darby* shed on the distinction between finality and exhaustion?

3. Issue exhaustion. One can distinguish between exhaustion of administrative remedies and issue exhaustion. The former may require a party to avail itself of available procedural steps for review within an agency (e.g., appeal to the agency itself). The latter may require that a party first present to the agency any issue that it later wishes to press on judicial review of the agency's decision. Of course, this rule is strongly analogous to the rule that appellate courts will not consider arguments not first presented to lower courts.

Issue exhaustion is sometimes required by an agency's organic statute and sometimes required by agency rule. Where neither statute nor rule requires issue exhaustion, courts have commonly done so pursuant to their own authority.

The Supreme Court took a soft approach to issue exhaustion in *Sims v. Apfel*, 530 U.S. 103 (2000). On judicial appeal of a denial of Social Security benefits, Sims pressed issues that she had not raised before the Social Security Appeals Council below. Writing for a narrow majority, Justice Thomas observed "the desirability of a court imposing a requirement of issue exhaustion depends on the degree to which the analogy to normal adversarial litigation applies in a particular administrative proceeding. . . . Where by contrast, an administrative proceeding is not adversarial, we think the reasons for a court to require issue exhaustion are much weaker." Writing for a four-justice plurality, Justice Thomas then stressed that the Social Security claims process is investigatory rather than adversarial, and that in this process ALJs and the Appeals Council have responsibility "to develop arguments both for and against granting benefits." Given this responsibility, it made little sense to demand issue exhaustion of claimants.

But one should not regard *Sims* as a free pass around issue exhaustion outside the non-adversarial, investigatory confines of the Social Security process. As Justice O'Connor observed in her concurrence, "[i]n most cases, an issue not presented to an administrative decisionmaker cannot be argued for the first time in federal court. On this underlying principle of administrative law, the Court is unanimous."

4. Exhaustion and rulemaking. Exhaustion doctrine seems most apt for application to adjudicatory proceedings, but a form of it is commonly applied to pre-enforcement challenges to rules as well. The D.C. Circuit has explained:

> Courts have long required a party seeking review of agency action to exhaust its administrative remedies before seeking judicial review. In this case, the administrative remedy was participation in the rulemaking proceedings during the comment period. Indeed, this court generally requires such participation as a prerequisite to a petition for direct review of the resulting regulations.

> The NRDC did not participate in the rulemaking proceedings in this case, but argues that we should not dismiss its petition for review because the agency in fact considered the statutory issue raised in the petition. The NRDC is correct. This court has excused the exhaustion requirements for a particular issue when the agency has in fact considered the issue. Thus, courts have waived exhaustion if the agency "has had an opportunity to consider the identical issues [presented to the court] . . . but which were raised by other parties," or if the agency's decision, or a dissenting opinion, indicates that the agency had "the opportunity to consider" "the very argument pressed" by the petitioner on judicial review.

Natural Res. Def. Council, Inc. v. U.S. E.P.A., 824 F.2d 1146 (D.C. Cir. 1987) (internal citations omitted). Requiring issue exhaustion may be perfectly "fair" to large, sophisticated entities that make it their business to keep careful track of agency rulemaking activity. But should this approach be applied to smaller entities without such resources at their disposal? *See Koretoff v. Vilsack*, 707 F.3d 394, 401 (D.C. Cir. 2013) (Williams, J., concurring) (suggesting that the court's approach to issue exhaustion in rulemaking should be revisited because its impact could be quite "severe" on smaller entities that are "unlikely to be adequately lawyered-up at the rulemaking stage").

5. Primary jurisdiction. At times, proceedings initiated before a court will raise issues over which an agency would have jurisdiction and could offer useful guidance. In such contexts, courts may invoke a cousin of exhaustion, the doctrine of "primary jurisdiction." Justice Breyer gave a concise description of this doctrine in *Pharmaceutical Research and Mfrs. of America v. Walsh*, 538 U.S. 644 (2003). The case arose out of a challenge brought by a pharmaceutical manufacturers' association to Maine Rx. The goal of the Maine Rx program was to obtain lower prices for prescription drugs for its participants by negotiating for rebates from manufacturers. Manufacturers that did not reach rebate agreements with Maine would find their Medicaid drug sales subject to "prior authorization" procedures. The pharmaceutical manufacturers' association sought a preliminary injunction to block operation of the program. A key issue was whether Maine Rx would impede operation of the Medicaid statute and was therefore preempted by it. The Supreme Court affirmed the First Circuit's vacation and reversal of the preliminary injunction issued by the District Court. In his concurring opinion, Justice Breyer advised:

> By vacating the injunction, we shall also help ensure that the District Court takes account of the Secretary's views in further proceedings that may involve a renewed motion for a preliminary injunction. It is important that the District Court do so. The Department of Health and Human Services (HHS) administers the Medicaid program. Institutionally speaking, that agency is better able than a court to assemble relevant facts (e.g., regarding harm caused to present Medicaid patients) and to make relevant predictions (e.g., regarding furtherance of Medicaid-related goals). And the law grants significant weight to any legal conclusion by the Secretary as to whether a program such as Maine's is consistent with Medicaid's objectives. See, e.g., *Chevron U.S.A. Inc. v. Natural Resources Defense Council, Inc.*, 467 U.S. 837 (1984); *Skidmore v. Swift & Co.*, 323 U.S. 134 (1944).

> The Medicaid statute sets forth a method through which Maine may obtain those views. A participating State must file a Medicaid plan with HHS and obtain HHS approval. A State must also promptly file a plan amendment to reflect any "[m]aterial changes in State law, organization, or policy, or in the State's operation of the Medicaid program." And the Secretary has said that a statute like Maine's is a "significant component of a state plan" with respect to which Maine is expected to file an amendment.

> In addition, the legal doctrine of "primary jurisdiction" permits a court itself to "refer" a question to the Secretary. That doctrine seeks to produce better informed and uniform legal rulings by allowing courts to take advantage of an agency's specialized knowledge, expertise, and central position within a regulatory regime. "No fixed formula exists" for the doctrine's application. Rather, the question in each instance is whether a case raises "issues of fact not within the conventional experience of judges," but within the purview of an agency's responsibilities; whether the "limited functions of review by the judiciary are more rationally exercised, by preliminary

resort" to an agency "better equipped than courts" to resolve an issue in the first instance; or, in a word, whether preliminary reference of issues to the agency will promote that proper working relationship between court and agency that the primary jurisdiction doctrine seeks to facilitate.

Where such conditions are satisfied—and I have little doubt that they are satisfied here—courts may raise the doctrine on their own motion. A court may then stay its proceedings—for a limited time, if appropriate—to allow a party to initiate agency review. Lower courts have sometimes accompanied a stay with an injunction designed to preserve the status quo. And, in my view, even if Maine should choose not to obtain the Secretary's views on its own, the desirability of the District Court's having those views to consider . . . is relevant to the "public interest" determination that often factors into whether a preliminary injunction should issue.

G. Scope of Review for Issues of Fact, Policy, and Law

This subchapter examines doctrines that speak to the problem of "scope of review," *i.e.*, how closely courts should review agency determinations of various types. The horns of the dilemma are these: On the one hand, it would make little sense for generalist courts to subject all reviewable agency decisions to de novo scrutiny. Such an approach would invite inefficiency, disrespect for administrative authority, and error. On the other hand, if courts were too passive, the risk of arbitrary agency action might rise to intolerable levels incompatible with the rule of law. The various doctrines of judicial deference to agency action that you will encounter in this subchapter derive from this dilemma.

Some of these doctrines are regrettably complex. Nonetheless, underlying them is (or should be) one simple inquiry: When does it make sense for a court to affirm an agency decision with which the court might not agree if it were exercising independent judgment? Suppose, for instance, that a court must review an EPA rule that permits a certain amount of pollutant X to be emitted into the air. This rule will depend on factual judgments regarding the effects of X in the atmosphere. Should a generalist court be quick to question such factual judgments by an expert agency? If your answer is, "probably not," then you will not be surprised to learn that judicial review of agency factual judgments is supposed to be, by and large, quite deferential. Suppose that EPA has an obligation under the Clean Air Act to set levels of X at a level "requisite to protect the public health with an adequate margin of safety." Even if EPA knew absolutely everything there is to know about X, these facts would not tell EPA *exactly* how high a level of X emissions to permit. The EPA would necessarily need to exercise policy judgment to draw this line. As with factual matters, administrative law, generally speaking, instructs courts to defer to reasonable agency policy judgments.

But should courts also extend such deference to agency determinations of law? On the one hand, in good *Marbury* fashion, we often think of courts as the masters of legal construction. But, on the other, policy expertise may come in quite handy when construing complex agency statutes such as the Clean Air Act. There are good reasons to leave courts in charge of statutory interpretation; there are also good reasons for courts to defer to an agency's construction of laws it is charged with administering. Given this much, perhaps it should not be too surprising that the doctrines governing judicial deference on issues of law are messy—as later discussion of the *Chevron* doctrine and its relatives will reveal.

1. Review of Agency Fact-Finding

Judicial review of agency fact-finding is generally supposed to be quite deferential. It is also, however, sensitive to the types of facts under review. For instance, courts often concede that they should be especially deferential to agency predictive judgments requiring technical expertise. In addition, the applicable standard of review may depend on the procedures an agency used to find its facts. Under § 706 of the APA, facts found through formal, on-the-record proceedings generally are subject to "substantial evidence" review; facts found informally are generally subject to "arbitrariness" review. The materials that follow explore the meanings of these standards. They also focus, to a considerable degree, on a problem created by the structure of formal adjudications. Sometimes, an ALJ and an agency will disagree on a finding of fact. Where this occurs, what weight, if any, should a reviewing court give to this disagreement?

Lesson 5G.1. Judge Byrd is to serve on a judicial panel assigned an appeal from a WTC cease-and-desist order issued pursuant to § 7 of the WTCA. The order resulted from an enforcement action that the WTC brought against Lubbockarillo Wines, Inc. (LW), a winemaker based in West Texas, relating to modestly-priced wines that LW markets under the "Purely Texas" (PT) name. The label for these wines bears a Texas flag and states, "Nothing But Lone Star Grapes!" It also indicates that the grapes for this wine were grown in Lubbock County, Texas. The WTC charged that use of this label violated § 5(a) as a "device, scheme, or artifice to defraud." Tracking the securities laws on which § 5's language was based, the WTC has determined that, to prove a § 5(a) violation, the agency must show that the charged party, in connection with the purchase or sale of wine in interstate commerce, acting with scienter (an intent to deceive, manipulate, or defraud), made a material misrepresentation or used a fraudulent device.

LW conceded that its sales satisfied the interstate commerce requirement. For its part, the WTC conceded that all of the fresh grapes used for the PT wines are, in fact, grown in Lubbock County, Texas, and that it is not misleading for LW, as is common in the trade, to use various additives as part of the winemaking process, such as sulfites and acid adjusters. The problem was that LW also adds Ultra-digo, a product that winemakers use to darken red wines and make their tastes more uniform. Ultra-digo is a grape concentrate sold by a California firm and made from California grapes. According to the WTC, the PT wine label's representations of "Purely Texas" and "Nothing But Lone Star Grapes!" were therefore false.

The proceedings before Bud, our favorite ALJ, focused on whether LW had used its label with an intent to deceive. LW's chief of marketing, William, explained that his firm had developed its "Purely Texas" line to tap into consumer demand for local products as well as state pride. He had been involved in every stage of the development of this line, and at no point had he or anyone else considered whether adding Ultra-digo might be inconsistent with the label's representations. William observed, without contradiction from the WTC, that adding undisclosed grape concentrates is a very common practice in the wine industry, especially for more modestly priced products. As he saw the matter, he and other employees at LW had regarded the Ultra-digo as just another additive necessary for the winemaking process rather than as a source of non-Texas grapes.

Bud dismissed the charge. He concluded that the labels were in fact true—the "grapes" used to make the wine were indeed all from Texas. Moreover, even if the labels were construed as misleading, the agency had failed to demonstrate that the presence of a small amount of grape concentrate in a product dominated by Texas grapes would be material to a reasonable consumer of PT wine. Also, Bud credited William's testimony as truthful, negating any inference of scienter.

The agency reversed. Its decisional memorandum explained that, although "Purely Texas" was too vague to be meaningful, the "Nothing But Texas Grapes!" portion of the label conveyed the false message that all the grape-based ingredients in the wine were from Texas. LW's own marketing plan demonstrated that this misrepresentation was material—the "homegrown" message of the label was designed to influence purchasers. William's testimony was self-serving and unpersuasive. The agency found it impossible to credit that the persons involved in planning the "Purely Texas" wine label were unaware that Ultra-digo is a grape concentrate from California. They therefore had to know that the "Nothing But Texas Grapes!" message was false, and they must have intended it to deceive.

How might the following materials help Judge Byrd understand how she should review the WTC's factfinding? As part of your answer, consider: What standard of review should apply? Does the type of procedure that the agency used affect your answer to this question? Would it under §706 of the APA? What role might the distinction between testimonial (a/k/a primary) and derivative (a/k/a secondary) inferences play in your analysis?

Background of *Universal Camera Corp. v. NLRB*

This case arose out of a dispute concerning why Universal Camera Corp. fired its employee, Chairman. The NLRB sought Chairman's reinstatement on the ground that he had been illegally terminated for giving testimony before the Board regarding union representation. An agency hearing examiner (whom we would now call an "administrative law judge" or "ALJ") who heard live testimony from witnesses in the case concluded that the agency had failed to prove that the firing had been a reprisal for the testimony. Instead, the examiner accepted the company's argument that it had fired Chairman for insubordination. On review of the record, the Board reversed this finding, and ordered Chairman's reinstatement. The Board then sought judicial enforcement of its order from the Second Circuit. Judge Hand's opinion focused on the problem of determining the significance of the Board's disagreement with its examiner on factual conclusions based on testimonial evidence.

A finding of fact by a trial court has a measure of "binding" force on appeal because the appellate court should reverse only if it determines that the finding was "clearly erroneous"—a standard which requires a "definite and firm conviction" that the trial court erred. This same familiar standard applies to district court review of the findings of a master in equity. By contrast, the APA provides that "on appeal from or review of" the decision of an "officer" who has presided at a hearing, "the agency shall . . . have all the powers which it would have in making the initial decision." 5 U.S.C. § 557(b). Judge Hand observed that this allocation of decision-making power precludes the possibility that an ALJ's initial decision can have binding effect on a reviewing agency in the way that a master's findings bind a district court. Thus, to justify reversing an ALJ's finding of fact, an agency need not first conclude that the ALJ has made a clear error.

This conclusion, however, still left the problem of determining whether, on *judicial* review of an *agency's* decision, the court should give any significance to the agency's disagreement with its ALJ concerning the facts of the case. Judge Hand concluded that such disagreement is significant, but he could see no principled way for a court to take it into account. He explained, "[w]e hold that, although the Board would be wrong in totally disregarding [the examiner's] findings, it is practically impossible for a court, upon review of those findings, to consider the Board's reversal as a factor in the court's own decision. This we say, because we cannot find any middle ground between doing that and treating such a reversal as error, whenever it would be such, if done by a judge to a master in equity." *NLRB v. Universal Camera*, 179 F.2d 749, 753 (2d Cir. 1950).

The Supreme Court, by contrast, did find a middle ground. As you read the following excerpt vacating Judge Hand's opinion, consider: What instructions did the Court give regarding how to conduct substantial evidence review of agency findings of fact? What weight should courts give to an ALJ's disagreement with the agency on a finding of fact? Why?

Universal Camera Corp. v. NLRB

340 U.S. 474 (1951)

Mr. Justice Frankfurter delivered the opinion of the Court.

The essential issue raised by this case is the effect of the Administrative Procedure Act and the legislation colloquially known as the Taft-Hartley Act on the duty of Courts of Appeals when called upon to review orders of the National Labor Relations Board.

The Court of Appeals for the Second Circuit granted enforcement of an order directing, in the main, that petitioner reinstate with back pay an employee found to have been discharged because he gave testimony under the Wagner Act and cease and desist from discriminating against any employee who files charges or gives testimony under that Act . . . .

I

Want of certainty in judicial review of Labor Board decisions partly reflects the intractability of any formula to furnish definiteness of content for all the impalpable factors involved in judicial review. But in part doubts as to the nature of the reviewing power and uncertainties in its application derive from history, and to that extent an elucidation of this history may clear them away.

The Wagner Act provided: "The findings of the Board as to the facts, if supported by evidence, shall be conclusive." This Court read "evidence" to mean "substantial evidence," and we said that "[substantial] evidence is more than a mere scintilla. It means such relevant evidence as a reasonable mind might accept as adequate to support a conclusion." *Consolidated Edison Co. v. National Labor Relations Board.* Accordingly, it "must do more than create a suspicion of the existence of the fact to be established, . . . it must be enough to justify, if the trial were to a jury, a refusal to direct a verdict when the conclusion sought to be drawn from it is one of fact for the jury."

"SUBSTANTIAL EVIDENCE"

The very smoothness of the "substantial evidence" formula as the standard for reviewing the evidentiary validity of the Board's findings established its currency. But the inevitably variant applications of the standard to conflicting evidence soon brought contrariety of views and in due course bred criticism. Even though the whole record may have been canvassed in order to determine whether the evidentiary foundation of a determination by the Board was "substantial," the phrasing of this Court's process of review readily lent itself to the notion that it was enough that the evidence supporting the Board's result was "substantial" when considered by itself. It is fair to say that by imperceptible steps regard for the fact-finding function of the Board led to the assumption that the requirements of the Wagner Act were met when the reviewing court could find in the record evidence which, when viewed in isolation, substantiated the Board's findings. This is not to say that every member of this Court was consciously guided by this view or that the Court ever explicitly avowed this practice as doctrine. What matters is that the belief justifiably arose that the Court had so construed the obligation to review.

Criticism of so contracted a reviewing power reinforced dissatisfaction felt in various quarters with the Board's administration of the Wagner Act in the years preceding the war. The scheme of the Act was attacked as an inherently unfair fusion of the functions of prosecutor and judge. Accusations of partisan bias were not wanting. The "irresponsible admission and weighing of hearsay, opinion, and emotional speculation in place of factual evidence" was said to be a "serious menace." No doubt some, perhaps even much, of the criticism was baseless and some surely was reckless. What is here relevant, however, is the climate of opinion thereby generated and its effect on Congress. Protests against "shocking injustices" and intimations of judicial "abdication" with which some courts granted enforcement of the Board's orders stimulated pressures for legislative relief from alleged administrative excesses . . . .

. . . [T]he legislative history of that [Administrative Procedure] Act hardly speaks with that clarity of purpose which Congress supposedly furnishes courts in order to enable them to enforce its true will. On the one hand, the sponsors of the legislation indicated that they were reaffirming the prevailing "substantial evidence" test. But with equal clarity they expressed disapproval of the manner in which the courts were applying their own standard. The committee reports of both houses refer to the practice of agencies to rely upon "suspicion, surmise, implications, or plainly incredible evidence," and indicate that courts are to exact higher standards "in the exercise of their independent judgment" and on consideration of "the whole record."

Similar dissatisfaction with too restricted application of the "substantial evidence" test is reflected in the legislative history of the Taft-Hartley Act. . . . [A]s the Senate Committee Report relates, "it was finally decided to conform the statute to the corresponding section of the Administrative Procedure Act where the substantial evidence test prevails. In order to clarify any ambiguity in that statute, however, the committee inserted the words "questions of fact, if supported by substantial evidence on the record considered as a whole. . . ." . . .

It is fair to say that in all this Congress expressed a mood. And it expressed its mood not merely by oratory but by legislation. As legislation that mood must be respected, even though it can only serve as a standard for judgment and not as a body of rigid rules assuring sameness of application. Enforcement of such broad standards implies subtlety of mind and solidity of judgment. But it is not for us to question that Congress may assume such qualities in the federal judiciary. . . .

It would be mischievous wordplaying to find that the scope of review under the Taft-Hartley Act is any different from that under the Administrative Procedure Act. The Senate Committee which reported the review clause of the Taft-Hartley Act expressly indicated that the two standards were to conform in this regard, and the wording of the two Acts is for purposes of judicial administration identical. And so we hold that the standard of proof specifically required of the Labor Board by the Taft-Hartley Act is the same as that to be exacted by courts reviewing every administrative action subject to the Administrative Procedure Act.

Whether or not it was ever permissible for courts to determine the substantiality of evidence supporting a Labor Board decision merely on the basis of evidence which in and of itself justified it, without taking into account contradictory evidence or evidence from which conflicting inferences could be drawn, the new legislation definitively precludes such a theory of review and bars its practice. The substantiality of evidence must take into account whatever in the record fairly detracts from its weight. This is clearly the significance of the requirement in both statutes that courts consider the whole record. Committee reports and the adoption in the Administrative Procedure Act of the minority views of the Attorney General's Committee demonstrate that to enjoin such a duty on the reviewing court was one of the important purposes of the movement which eventuated in that enactment.

To be sure, the requirement for canvassing "the whole record" in order to ascertain substantiality does not furnish a calculus of value by which a reviewing court can assess the evidence. Nor was it intended to negate the function of the Labor Board as one of those agencies presumably equipped or informed by experience to deal with a specialized field of knowledge, whose findings within that field carry the authority of an expertness which courts do not possess and, therefore, must respect. Nor does it mean that even as to matters not requiring expertise a court may displace the Board's choice between two fairly conflicting views, even though the court would justifiably have made a different choice had the matter been before it *de novo*. Congress has merely made it clear that a reviewing court is not barred from setting aside a Board decision when it cannot conscientiously find that the evidence supporting that decision is substantial, when viewed in the light that the record in its entirety furnishes, including the body of evidence opposed to the Board's view.

... A formula for judicial review of administrative action may afford grounds for certitude but cannot assure certainty of application. Some scope for judicial discretion in applying the formula can be avoided only by falsifying the actual process of judging or by using the formula as an instrument of futile casuistry. It cannot be too often repeated that judges are not automata. The ultimate reliance for the fair operation of any standard is a judiciary of high competence and character and the constant play of an informed professional critique upon its work. ...

But a standard leaving an unavoidable margin for individual judgment does not leave the judicial judgment at large even though the phrasing of the standard does not wholly fence it in. The legislative history of these Acts demonstrates a purpose to impose on courts a responsibility which has not always been recognized. ... The adoption in these statutes of the judicially-constructed "substantial evidence" test was a response to pressures for stricter and more uniform practice, not a reflection of approval of all existing practices. To find the change so elusive that it cannot be precisely defined does not mean it may be ignored. We should fail in our duty to effectuate the will of Congress if we denied recognition to expressed Congressional disapproval of the finality accorded to Labor Board findings by some decisions of this and lower courts, or even of the atmosphere which may have favored those decisions.

We conclude, therefore, that the Administrative Procedure Act and the Taft-Hartley Act direct that courts must now assume more responsibility for the reasonableness and fairness of Labor Board decisions than some courts have shown in the past. Reviewing courts must be influenced by a feeling that they are not to abdicate the conventional judicial function. Congress has imposed on them responsibility for assuring that the Board keeps within reasonable grounds. That responsibility is not less real because it is limited to enforcing the requirement that evidence appear substantial when viewed, on the record as a whole, by courts invested with the authority and enjoying the prestige of the Courts of Appeals. The Board's findings are entitled to respect; but they must nonetheless be set aside when the record before a Court of Appeals clearly precludes the Board's decision from being justified by a fair estimate of the worth of the testimony of witnesses or its informed judgment on matters within its special competence or both. . . .

Our power to review the correctness of application of the present standard ought seldom to be called into action. Whether on the record as a whole there is substantial evidence to support agency findings is a question which Congress has placed in the keeping of the Courts of Appeals. This Court will intervene only in what ought to be the rare instance when the standard appears to have been misapprehended or grossly misapplied. . . .

III

The Court of Appeals deemed itself bound by the Board's rejection of the examiner's findings because the court considered these findings not "as unassailable as a master's." They are not. Section 10(c) of the Labor Management Relations Act provides that "If upon the preponderance of the testimony taken the Board shall be of the opinion that any person named in the complaint has engaged in or is engaging in any such unfair labor practice, then the Board shall state its findings of fact. . . ." The responsibility for decision thus placed on the Board is wholly inconsistent with the notion that it has power to reverse an examiner's findings only when they are "clearly erroneous." Such a limitation would make so drastic a departure from prior administrative practice that explicitness would be required.

The Court of Appeals concluded from this premise "that, although the Board would be wrong in totally disregarding his findings, it is practically impossible for a court, upon review of those findings which the Board itself substitutes, to consider the Board's reversal as a factor in the court's own decision. This we say, because we cannot find any middle ground between doing that and treating such a reversal as error, whenever it would be such, if done by a judge to a master in equity." Much as we respect the logical acumen of the Chief Judge of the Court of Appeals, we do not find ourselves pinioned between the horns of his dilemma.

We are aware that to give the examiner's findings less finality than a master's and yet entitle them to consideration in striking the account, is to introduce another and an unruly factor into the judgmatical process of review. But we ought not to fashion an exclusionary rule merely to reduce the number of imponderables to be considered by reviewing courts. . . .

We do not require that the examiner's findings be given more weight than in reason and in the light of judicial experience they deserve. The "substantial evidence" standard is not modified in any way when the Board and its examiner disagree. We intend only to recognize that evidence supporting a conclusion may be less substantial when an impartial, experienced examiner who has observed the witnesses and lived with the case has drawn conclusions different from the Board's than when he has reached the same conclusion. The findings of the examiner are to be considered along with the consistency and inherent probability of testimony. The significance of his report, of course, depends largely on the importance of credibility in the particular case. To give it this significance does not seem to us materially more difficult than to heed the other factors which in sum determine whether evidence is "substantial." . . .

We therefore remand the cause to the Court of Appeals. On reconsideration of the record it should accord the findings of the trial examiner the relevance that they reasonably command in answering the comprehensive question whether the evidence supporting the Board's order is substantial. But the court need not limit its reexamination of the case to the effect of that report in its decision. We leave it free to grant or deny enforcement as it thinks the principles expressed in this opinion dictate.

Judgment vacated that cause remanded.

Background of *Penasquitos Village, Inc. v. NLRB*

Just as in *Universal Camera*, in *Penasquitos*, a reviewing court had to determine whether the NRLB's findings of fact were supported by "substantial evidence" notwithstanding its disagreements with the ALJ who heard live testimony. The NLRB had charged Penasquitos Village, Inc. (Penasquitos) with committing "unfair labor practices" in violation of the National Labor Relations Act by coercively interrogating and unlawfully discharging employees for union activity. The ALJ rejected the charges, in large part because he found the testimony of the discharged employees' supervisor, Zamora, credible. The NLRB rejected the ALJ's conclusions, finding Penasquitos liable on both claims. Penasquitos petitioned the Ninth Circuit to set aside the NLRBs' order; the NLRB cross-petitioned for enforcement.

Judge Wallace's lead opinion provides an illuminating discussion of the rationales for judicial deference to agency factfinding and the implications of those rationales for the problem of disagreement between ALJs and agencies. Pay particular attention to the distinction he draws between testimonial inferences (regarding witness credibility) and derivative inferences. Why treat them differently? Also, pay careful attention to how Judge Wallace applied these concepts as he reviewed the evidence supporting the charges. Judge Duniway, in his partial concurrence and dissent, expressed concerns regarding the dichotomy between testimonial and derivative inferences. What were these concerns? Did you find them persuasive? Would you have voted to uphold the agency's findings supporting either or both of the charges?

Penasquitos Village, Inc. v. National Labor Relations Board
565 F.2d 1074 (9th Cir. 1977)

Before DUNIWAY, CHOY and WALLACE, CIRCUIT JUDGES.

WALLACE, CIRCUIT JUDGE:

The National Labor Relations Board (the Board), reversing the decision of an administrative law judge, held that Penasquitos Village, Inc. and affiliated companies (Penasquitos) had engaged in coercive interrogation of employees in violation of section 8(a)(1) of the National Labor Relations Act (the Act), and had wrongfully discharged employees in violation of section 8(a)(3) of the Act. Penasquitos petitioned us to review and set aside the Board's order, alleging that it was not supported by substantial evidence. The Board cross-petitioned for enforcement. We refuse enforcement and set aside the order.

I.

. . . .

We treat as conclusive the factual determinations in a Board decision if they are "supported by substantial evidence on the record considered as a whole." 29 U.S.C. § 160(e)–(f). This statutorily mandated deference to findings of fact runs in favor of the Board, not in favor of the initial trier-of-facts, the administrative law judge. Nevertheless, the administrative law judge's findings of fact constitute a part of that whole record which we must review. We give those initial findings some weight, whether they support or contradict the Board's factual conclusions. See *Universal Camera Corp. v. NLRB* (1951).

The most difficult problem facing the reviewing court arises when, as in this case, the Board and the administrative law judge disagree on the facts. The Supreme Court has given the following general guidance to the courts of appeals faced with such a Board-administrative law judge conflict.

> We do not require that the examiner's findings be given more weight than in reason and in the light of judicial experience they deserve. The "substantial evidence" standard is not modified in any way when the Board and its examiner disagree. We intend only to recognize that evidence supporting a conclusion may be less substantial when an impartial, experienced examiner who has observed the witnesses and lived with the case has drawn conclusions different from the Board's than when he has reached the same conclusion. The findings of the examiner are to be considered along with the consistency and inherent probability of testimony. The significance of his report, of course, depends largely on the importance of credibility in the particular case.

Although this guidance is assertedly as precise as the nature of the problem permits, an analysis of both the cases, with emphasis on their facts, and basic policy considerations provides additional guidance to judicial review. Turning first to the cases, we have found no decision nor has one been cited to us, sustaining a finding of fact by the Board which rests solely on testimonial evidence discredited either expressly or by clear implication by the administrative law judge. A typical case demonstrating the need for independent, credited evidence is *Amco Electric v. NLRB* (9th Cir. 1966). There the legality of a discharge turned on a narrow question of fact: Did the discharged employee use the company's car radio to give orders to another employee or merely to contact the union steward? The trial examiner (now referred to as an administrative law judge) discredited the testimony of both the discharged employee and the employee receiving the call. The Board, however, disagreed and accepted the discharged employee's version. In refusing to enforce the Board's order against the company, we stated:

> Considering the record as a whole the only evidence which we believe supports the Board's findings is the (discredited) testimony of the (discharged employee). While the Board is not bound by the credibility determinations of the trial examiner, nevertheless the probative weight which may be properly given to testimony is severely reduced when an impartial experienced examiner who has observed the witnesses and lived with the case has drawn different conclusions.

> . . . .

The cases also demonstrate that, even when the record contains independent, credited evidence supportive of the Board's decision, a reviewing court will review more critically the Board's findings of fact if they are contrary to the administrative law judge's factual conclusions. This more rigorous review follows necessarily from the Supreme Court's statement in *Universal Camera Corp. v. NLRB* that the "substantiality of evidence (in support of the Board's decision) must take into account whatever in the record fairly detracts from its weight." . . .

We also conclude that basic policy considerations support the course these cases have taken and particularly the distinction often made in the cases between credibility determinations based on demeanor sometimes referred to as testimonial inferences, see *NLRB v. Universal Camera Corp.*, 190 F.2d 429, 432 (2d Cir. 1951) (Frank, J., concurring), on remand from 340 U.S. 474 (1951), and inferences drawn from the evidence itself sometimes referred to as derivative inferences. *Id.* These policy considerations can be illuminated by reference to the source of the deference accorded an administrative law judge's findings and the different source of the deference accorded the Board's findings.

Weight is given the administrative law judge's determinations of credibility for the obvious reason that he or she "sees the witnesses and hears them testify, while the Board and the reviewing court look only at cold records." *NLRB v. Walton Manufacturing Co.* (1962). All aspects of the witness's demeanor including the expression of his countenance, how he sits or stands, whether he is inordinately nervous, his coloration during critical examination, the modulation or pace of his speech and other non-verbal communication may convince the observing trial judge that the witness is testifying truthfully or falsely. These same very important factors, however, are entirely unavailable to a reader of the transcript, such as the Board or the Court of Appeals. But it should be noted that the administrative law judge's opportunity to observe the witnesses' demeanor does not, by itself, require deference with regard to his or her derivative inferences. Observation of demeanor makes weighty only the observer's testimonial inferences.

Deference is accorded the Board's factual conclusions for a different reason. Board members are presumed to have broad experience and expertise in labor-management relations. Further, it is the Board to which Congress has delegated administration of the Act. The Board, therefore, is viewed as particularly capable of drawing inferences from the facts of a labor dispute. Accordingly, it has been said that a Court of Appeals must abide by the Board's derivative inferences, if drawn from not discredited testimony, unless those inferences are "irrational," "tenuous" or "unwarranted." As already noted, however, the Board, as a reviewing body, has little or no basis for disputing an administrative law judge's testimonial inferences.

We emphasize that we do not hold that the administrative law judge's determinations of credibility based on demeanor are conclusive on the Board. Many circuits, including ours, have held that they are not. We simply observe that the special deference deservedly afforded the administrative law judge's factual determinations based on testimonial inferences will weigh heavily in our review of a contrary finding by the Board. In our view, this position is mandated by the Supreme Court's instruction that "(t)he significance of (the administrative law judge's) report, of course, depends largely on the importance of credibility in the particular case." *Universal Camera Corp. v. NLRB, supra. . . .*

II.

Applying these principles of judicial review to the present case, we conclude that the record considered as a whole does not contain substantial evidence of unfair labor practices.

A. Threats and Coercive Interrogation

The law regarding employer threats to and interrogations of employees is not in dispute here. Section 7 of the Act, 29 U.S.C. § 157, grants employees "the right to self-organization, to form, join or assist labor organizations, to bargain collectively through representatives of their own choosing, and to engage in other concerted activities for the purpose of collective bargaining." Section 8(a)(1) of the Act, 29 U.S.C. § 158(a)(1), implements this guarantee by making it an unfair labor practice to "interfere with, restrain, or coerce employees in the exercise of the rights guaranteed in section (7)." In light of this statutory language, the law regarding threats, at least of the type alleged in this case, needs no elaboration. Employer interrogation of employees regarding their concerted activities, however, requires some further comment. Such interrogation is not deemed per se unlawful. Some circumstances, such as, for example, an express reassurance by the employer of no retaliation or a history of free and open discussion of union activities, may preclude any possibility of coerciveness. Accordingly, the test is whether, under all the circumstances, the interrogation reasonably tends to restrain or interfere with the employees in the exercise of their protected rights.

In this case, the section 8(a)(1) charge is based on three separate incidents occurring over a six-month period coinciding with union efforts to organize some of Penasquitos' employees.

1. November 1973: The Rooftop Conversation

Employee Ruiz testified on direct examination that sometime in November 1973, supervisor Zamora, employee Hernandez and he were working on a roof when

> we saw Joe Alvarado (union field representative and organizer) drive up and so Jesus Zamora asked me who was that guy, you know. We thought he was a narc because of his car. And I told him he was from the Union. And he asked me who let the Union in, and I told him I didn't know. And then he said whoever did was probably going to get his (expletive deleted) laid off.

On cross-examination, Ruiz testified that when the car drove up, Zamora asked who the man was and he, Ruiz, responded that he did not know. In response to questions by the administrative law judge, Ruiz denied that he had told Zamora that the man was from the union because "I was too scared to tell him." According to Ruiz, Zamora, after getting down from the roof, learned the man's identity from another supervisor. Zamora testified that employees discussed the union with him openly and freely during work, that he thought at that time that the employees were already affiliated with the union, and that he had believed union representation was good because the employees were underpaid.

In light of this conflicting testimony, the administrative law judge was faced with a clear-cut question of credibility. He believed Zamora, whom he characterized "as an honest and forthright witness," and disbelieved Ruiz, whose testimony he characterized as "equivocal." The Board, on the basis of its own testimonial inferences, reversed this finding. There was no independent testimonial evidence or permissible derivative inferences to support the Board's conclusion that the threat was actually made. Accordingly, we overturn the Board's factual conclusion because it is not based on substantial evidence.

2. November 1973: The Hernandez Conversation

Employee Hernandez testified that in November 1973, while in the same room with Zamora, Zamora

> called me and asked me if I went into the Union and signed for them. I told him that this was the most convenient thing for everyone. For himself as well as us. And that is all. (Zamora) just smiled and left.

On cross-examination, Hernandez told essentially the same story, testifying that Zamora called to him, "Hey, Ricardo, if you can, if the Union comes in, are you going to sign with them? And I said, that is the most convenient thing for all of us."

The administrative law judge assumed that the conversation occurred, as testified to by Hernandez. Nevertheless, he refused to find an unfair labor practice because, under the circumstances, the conversation was not coercive. Particularly, in his view, General Counsel failed to establish, in conjunction with the interrogation, any employer anti-union animus that would supply the element of coercion.

. . . We conclude, therefore, that the Board's conclusion regarding the Hernandez conversation is not supported by substantial evidence.

3. April 1974: The Cuevas Conversation

Employee Cuevas testified that on April 4, 1974, following an injury and a trip to the doctor, he was sitting in the cafeteria when Zamora came in. Cuevas testified that during the conversation that ensued,

> I asked him if it was possible to go into the Union. And he answered me that it was possible because the (expletive referring to unions deleted), when they got a company, they didn't let go of it, until they got it in the Union. That it was not possible to go in right away, but later on he was going in. Then he asked me who was the one who started the (expletive deleted) with the Union. And I answered that it was Tony Rios and Ysidro Martinez, Ramon Valdez (and) Rodriguez.

Cuevas testified on cross-examination that Zamora did not ask him how he felt about the union, tell him not to join the union, express any feeling about whether the union was good or bad for the employees, or threaten to terminate anyone if they joined the union.

Zamora testified that he remembered talking to Cuevas following his injury and that while he could not relate the conversation, he thought that they discussed politics or the federal government. He conceded that the subject of the union may have come up because "like I said, the Union was discussed by everyone, you know. It was the thing." He testified that he felt all the employees "more or less" were for the union because all the employees discussed it openly during work and that he never attempted to find out which employees were doing the organizing because, through conversations with them, "I thought they were all in the Union."

In his opinion, the administrative law judge manifested some doubt that the limited query of Cuevas even occurred. Nevertheless, he based his ultimate conclusion of no violation on the absence of any coerciveness surrounding the conversation. He expressly credited Zamora's testimony, including the references to the practice of free and open discussion of the union by employees and supervisor, even during working hours. He also noted, as we do, the important fact that Cuevas, not Zamora, initiated the conversation about the union.

The Board, in reversing the administrative law judge's conclusions, relied on both discredited testimony and what can only be characterized as tenuous inferences. The discredited testimony concerned a purported conversation between Zamora and another supervisor at the timeclock. Former employee Rios testified that

> Zamora stated, while stamping his foot to the ground with anger (and referring to the employees in a obscene manner) . . . that we were going into the Union and therefore we were acting smart. But even so, he could fire us and he was going to do it.

On cross-examination, he testified that Zamora, stamping his foot, stated,

They think they are very smart because the Union is coming in. But whether it comes in or not, whether the Union comes in or not, I am going to try and I believe I am going to be able to fire them.

Employee Ruiz testified that he overheard Zamora use the same obscene expletive and then say "just because they think they are getting the Union in, they are going to do whatever they feel like doing. (Expletive deleted)!" Asked specifically by General Counsel if Zamora mentioned the word "fire" during the conversation, Ruiz responded that he had not.

The administrative law judge, as he did several other times in his decision, discredited Rios' testimony in the strongest terms. He noted further that "Rios' animosity toward Zamora was evident throughout his testimony" and that Rios "fabricated facts in an effort to make Zamora appear as a scoundrel." General Counsel, however, argues that the administrative law judge did not expressly discredit Ruiz' testimony. Ruiz did not, of course, testify that Zamora made references to firing employees, but the language he ascribed to Zamora, particularly the obscene expletives, could support a finding of anti-union animus. General Counsel, and the Board to the extent that it relies on this incident, fail, however, to give the administrative law judge's decision a fair reading. By clear implication, he did not accept Ruiz' recitation of the alleged conversation at the timeclock.

The Board's inferences from not discredited testimony are ... "tenuous" and "arbitrary".... The Board inferred that employee-supervisor relations were not friendly and open but rather hostile and tainted with anti-union animus, because Zamora testified that he was "a quiet dude," did not eat lunch with the employees, and once, more than two years prior to the incidents involved here, was run off the road by a disgruntled employee discharged for failure to work. Although such a derivative inference may have some weight standing alone, the contrary conclusions of the administrative law judge, based on testimonial inferences, make the substantiality of the Board's inference almost negligible.

B. The Discharges

It is axiomatic that an employer's discharge of an employee because of his union activities or sympathies violates section 8(a)(3) of the Act, 29 U.S.C. § 158(a)(3). We have stated that "the cases are legion that the existence of a justifiable ground for discharge will not prevent such discharge from being an unfair labor practice if partially motivated by the employee's protected activity; a business reason cannot be used as a pretext for a discriminatory firing." The determinative factual issue, therefore, is the employer's motive.

In this case, the administrative law judge and the Board disagreed on Penasquitos' motive. Whether, in light of this disagreement, the Board's conclusion is sustainable because it is based on substantial evidence is an extremely close question. We conclude, however, that the Board's finding of improper motive cannot be sustained, primarily because a significant number of the Board's derivative inferences were drawn from discredited testimony.

The keystone of the administrative law judge's finding of proper motive was his conviction that Zamora told the truth. Zamora testified that he observed Rios and Martinez working slowly and watching several women sunbathe in bikinis some distance from the employees' worksite. Upset with their performance, Zamora approached Rios and Martinez and stated that "if you want to see girls wearing bikinis there were some better ones at the beach." Zamora then left, verified with his superior that he had authority to fire, returned and discharged the two men. At the hearing before the administrative law judge, Martinez admitted that he was working at a slow pace on the day he was fired.

The administrative law judge relied on other evidence also. Several months prior to the discharge, Zamora and another supervisor watched for 5 or 10 minutes while Rios and two other employees stood under a tree, doing no work. When Zamora approached and demanded an explanation, the employees stated that they had no work to do and were waiting for quitting time. Zamora then suspended them a fact initially denied by the mendacious Rios during cross-examination but later clearly established.

In reaching a contrary conclusion regarding Zamora's motive, the Board relied on a variety of inferences. First, the Board transferred to Zamora's action in discharging Rios and Martinez the anti-union animus it found in his alleged threats and unlawful interrogations. But, as we concluded in part II,A, supra, that finding of anti-union animus was not supported by substantial evidence. The Board also ascribed an improper motive to Zamora for the discharge because of his alleged statements at the timeclock. Again, the witnesses testifying about that incident were not credited by the administrative law judge, see part II,A,3, supra, thus vitiating the inference the Board attempted to draw from it. . . .

The Board drew two inferences, however, from uncontroverted facts. First, the discharge was abrupt. Rios and Martinez received no warning prior to their discharge that a failure to speed up their work would result in termination. Second, the discharge came only two days after the Board's Regional Director issued a Decision and Direction of Election ordering an election among the Penasquitos employees under Zamora's supervision. These derivative inferences undoubtedly carry weight, which is not diminished by the fact that the administrative law judge drew a contrary inference from the timing of the discharge. As noted before, special deference is accorded the Board when, in the application of its expertise and experience, it derives such inferences from the facts of a labor dispute.

But in this case, credibility played a dominant role. The administrative law judge's testimonial inferences reduce significantly the substantiality of the Board's contrary derivative inferences. Particularly, removing the Board's finding of anti-union animus based upon alleged unlawful threats and interrogations, see part II,A, supra, leaves poorly substantiated the Board's other conclusion that the discharges were improperly motivated. Considering the record as a whole, we conclude that the Board's conclusion that Penasquitos committed unlawful labor practices is not supported by substantial evidence and must, therefore, be set aside.

ENFORCEMENT DENIED, ORDER SET ASIDE.

DUNIWAY, Circuit Judge (concurring in part and dissenting in part):

I concur in the result reached in part II A of Judge Wallace's opinion, but I have some reservations about the rationale by which that result is reached. I dissent from part II B of the opinion, and would enforce the part of the Board's order that is considered in part II B.

I.

My reservations relate to Judge Wallace's adoption of the dichotomy between "credibility determinations based on demeanor ... testimonial inferences" and those based on "inferences drawn from the evidence itself ... derivative inferences. ..." This distinction he finds in a concurring opinion of Judge Frank in *NLRB v. Universal Camera Corp.*, 2 Cir., 1951, on remand from *Universal Camera Corp. v. NLRB*, 1951. Judge Wallace is careful to emphasize that the administrative law judge's determinations of credibility are not conclusive, but I am concerned lest the dichotomy that he adopts may result in future decisions that are merely mechanical applications of labels, which hinder rather than help the intelligent and principled application or growth of the law. I fear that Judge Wallace's opinion may have just such an effect, one which, I am sure, he does not intend, and which he properly disavows.

The notion that special deference is owed to the determination of a trier of fact, whether judge, trial examiner, hearing officer (administrative law judge), or jury, because the trier "sees the witnesses and hears them testify, while the Board and the reviewing court look only at cold records," is deeply imbedded in the law. There must be thousands of appellate decisions that state and restate it in an infinite variety of ways. I could not disregard it if I would; indeed, I have no desire to do so. As a generalization, it is unassailable.

In his opinion, Judge Wallace fleshes it out:

> All aspects of the witnesses's demeanor including the expression of his countenance, how he sits or stands, whether he is inordinately nervous, his coloration during critical examination, the modulation or pace of his speech and other non-verbal communication may convince the observing trial judge that the witness is testifying truthfully or falsely. These same very important factors, however, are entirely unavailable to a reader of the transcript, such as the Board or the Court of Appeals.

Here is where I begin to have difficulty. I venture to suggest that, as to every one of the factors that Judge Wallace lists, one trier of fact may take it to indicate that the witness is truthful and another may think that it shows that the witness is lying.

I am convinced, both from experience as a trial lawyer and from experience as an appellate judge, that much that is thought and said about the trier of fact as a lie detector is myth or folklore. Every trial lawyer knows, and most trial judges will admit, that it is not unusual for an accomplished liar to fool a jury (or, even, heaven forbid, a trial judge) into believing him because his demeanor is so convincing. The expression of his countenance may be open and frank; he may sit squarely in the chair, with no squirming; he may show no nervousness; his answers to questions may be clear, concise and audible, and given without hesitation; his coloration may be normal neither pale nor flushed. In short, he may appear to be the trial lawyer's ideal witness. He may also be a consummate liar. In such a case, the fact finder may fit Iago's description of Othello:

> The Moor is of a free and open nature,
>
> That thinks men honest that but seem to be so;
>
> And will as tenderly be led by the nose as asses are.
>
> (*Othello*, Act 1, Sc. 3, 1. 405-8)

On the other hand, another fact finder seeing and hearing the same witness may conclude that he is just too good a testifier, that he is an expert actor, and that he is also a liar.

Conversely, many trial lawyers, and some trial judges, will admit that the demeanor of a perfectly honest but unsophisticated or timid witness may be or can be made by an astute cross-examiner to be such that he will be thought by the jury or the judge to be a liar. He may be unable to face the cross-examiner, the jury, or the judge; he may slouch and squirm in the chair; he may be obviously tense and nervous; his answers to questions may be indirect, rambling, and inaudible; he may hesitate before answering; he may alternately turn pale and blush. In short, he may, to the trier of fact, be a liar, but in fact be entirely truthful. Again, however, another fact finder, seeing and hearing the same witness, may attribute his demeanor to the natural timidity of the average not very well educated and non-public sort of person when dragged to court against his will and forced to testify and face a hostile cross-examiner, and conclude that the witness is telling the truth.

While there are innumerable cases that state and restate the importance of a witness's demeanor to the trier of fact, there are very few that deal with the proper effect of this or that aspect of demeanor. Those that I can find tend to confirm my view that myth and folklore are involved.

In *Quercia v. United States*, 1933, 289 U.S. 466, the Supreme Court reversed because the trial judge had commented to the jury:

> And now I am going to tell you what I think of the defendant's testimony. You may have noticed, Mr. Foreman and gentlemen, that he wiped his hands during his testimony. It is rather a curious thing, but that is almost always an indication of lying. Why it should be so we don't know, but that is the fact. I think that every single word that man said, except when he agreed with the Government's testimony, was a lie.

289 U.S. at 468.

[Judge Duniway then quoted a parade of horribles of outlandish judicial and administrative assessments of witness credibility.]

I write to suggest that Judge Wallace's dichotomy should not be taken to protect the myth and folklore behind an almost impenetrable wall. I do not want fact finders to believe that to make their findings almost totally unassailable they need only use the right incantation: "I don't (or I do) believe him because of his demeanor," or "on the basis of testimonial inferences."

I doubt if there are many cases in which the fact finder relies on demeanor alone. There may not be any; I hope that there are none. I think that in every case in which he thinks about what he is doing, the fact finder should and does consider both the demeanor of the witness and what he says the content of his testimony and weighs those factors in relation to the fact finder's knowledge of life's realities, the internal consistency of what the witness is saying, and its consistency, or lack of it, with the other evidence in the case, testimonial, documentary, and physical. The fact finding as to credibility of the witness should be, and is, based on all of these things. Judge Wallace's dichotomy seems to me to give to demeanor a more important effect than it ought to be given, considering the inherent ambiguities in demeanor itself. Anyone who really believes that he can infallibly determine credibility solely on the basis of observed demeanor is naive.

I do not at all mean to suggest that the demeanor of a witness is not, or ought not to be, an important factor in the process of fact finding. The law would not permit me to so hold if I wished to, and I do not wish to. . . .

II.

Having stated my doubts about Judge Wallace's dichotomy, I nevertheless agree with the result that he reaches in part II A of his opinion. The evidence as a whole, including the credibility rulings of the administrative law judge, seems to me too thin to be called substantial support for the Board's findings. I therefore concur in the result stated in part II A.

III.

I do not concur in part II B. As Judge Wallace observes, the question is "extremely close." In such a case, I give more weight to the experience and expertise of the Board than he does. I refer particularly to the two uncontradicted facts, the abruptness and the timing of the discharges. I cannot say that the inferences that the Board drew from these facts are "irrational" or "tenuous" or "unwarranted" . . . , or "arbitrary".

I would enforce that part of the Board's order that deals with the discharges of Rios and Martinez.

CHOY, Circuit Judge (concurring):

I concur in the results reached by Judge Wallace in both parts II A and II B.

However, I share the concern that Judge Duniway feels about Judge Wallace's treatment of demeanor evidence and testimonial inferences. I, therefore, concur in Judge Duniway's eloquent exposition of his reservations contained in part I of his concurring and dissenting opinion.

Notes

1. Substantial evidence as rationality test. In *Consolidated Edison Co. v. NLRB*, 305 U.S. 197, 229 (1938), the Supreme Court explained that an agency finding satisfies the substantial evidence test if it is supported by "such evidence as a reasonable mind might accept as adequate to support a conclusion." In *Universal Camera*, Justice Frankfurter added: "Nor does it mean that even as to matters not requiring expertise the court may displace the Board's choice between two fairly conflicting views, even though the court would justifiably have made a different choice had the matter been before it *de novo*." That is, applying this test, a court should affirm an agency's finding of fact so long as the court concludes the finding falls within the space where reasonable minds might disagree.

2. Substantial evidence, derivative and secondary inferences, and the significance of ALJ findings of fact. As we saw in both *Universal Camera* and in *Penasquitos*, administrative adjudication, like the judicial system, usually has a hearing level (where live testimony may be given) and then at least one level of review. As a result, a reviewing court will often confront a record with some findings or decisions by the presiding official (e.g., an ALJ) and an opinion based on review of that decision by the agency head.

On one level, an agency reversal of an ALJ's findings of fact should present no problem at all as the APA provides, "[o]n appeal from or review of the initial decision [by an ALJ], the agency has all the powers which it would have in making the initial decision except as it may limit the issues on notice or by rule." 5 U.S.C. § 557(b). The fly in this de novo-sounding ointment is that *Universal Camera* made clear that a contrary ALJ report is a part of the agency record available for judicial review, and that such a report may detract from the substantiality of the evidence for an agency's position.

As *Penasquitos* discussed at length, the weight that an ALJ's findings of fact will bear on judicial review is largely a function of whether these findings were rooted in the ALJ's credibility determinations. The basic theory behind this approach is that the ALJ, who hears and sees a witness, has access to demeanor evidence that an agency, reading a cold record, cannot see. Judge Frank, in his concurring opinion in *Universal Camera* on remand from the Supreme Court, gave a canonical (if rather dense) description of the review implications of this point:

> An examiner's finding binds the Board only to the extent that it is a 'testimonial inference,' or 'primary inference,' *i.e.*, an inference that a fact to which a witness orally testified is an actual fact because that witness so testified and because observation of the witness induces a belief in that testimony. The Board, however, is not bound by the examiner's 'secondary inferences,' or 'derivative inferences,' *i.e.*, facts to which no witness orally testified but which the examiner inferred from facts orally testified by witnesses whom the examiner believed. The Board may reach its own 'secondary inferences,' and we must abide by them unless they are irrational; in

that way, the Board differs from a trial judge (in a juryless case) who hears and sees the witnesses, for, although we are usually bound by his 'testimonial inferences,' we need not accept his 'secondary inferences' even if rational, but, where other rational 'secondary inferences' are possible, we may substitute our own. Since that is true, it is also true that we must not interfere when the Board adopts either (1) its examiner's 'testimonial inferences' and they are not absurd, or (2) his rational 'secondary inferences.'

190 F.2d 429, 432 (2d Cir. 1951).

Broadly speaking, "testimonial inferences" establish "brute" facts of the who-did-what-to-whom sort (e.g., What exactly did Zamora say to Ruiz?). A witness testifies as to some state of facts and the trier must "infer" whether or not the witness should be believed. "Secondary inferences" establish the legal significance of the brute facts and tend to depend to some degree on the decisionmaker's policy views. For example, suppose that it is clear from testimony that Universal Camera terminated Chairman for two reasons—he had in fact been insubordinate *and* his employer wanted to punish him for giving testimony before the Board. These testimonial inferences do not settle, by themselves, whether terminating Chairman amounted to an instance of an "unfair labor practice" within the meaning of the National Labor Relations Act. To reach this conclusion (one way or the other) requires a "secondary" inference, which determines whether the statutory phrase "unfair labor practice" captures termination due to a mix of permissible and impermissible motives. *Penasquitos* notes at least two reasons why courts should defer to an agency's secondary inferences. First, agencies are presumed to have greater expertise within their regulatory bailiwicks than generalist courts. Second, where Congress delegates power to an agency to administer an act, courts should be careful not to usurp this power with overly aggressive review.

The principle that ALJ testimonial inferences bear special weight has a procedural dimension insofar as courts have frequently stated that, in light of this principle, agencies must give detailed, specific explanations for their reversals of ALJ credibility determinations. *See, e.g., Tenneco Automotive, Inc. v. NLRB*, 716 F.3d 640, 651–52 (D.C. Cir. 2013) ("Because the Board never explained any basis for disagreement with the ALJ's findings, we have taken the findings into account in assessing whether there is substantial evidence to support the Board's judgment."); *Aylett v. Sec'y of Housing and Urban Dev.*, 54 F.3d 1560, 1566 (10th Cir. 1995) (where agency differs "with the ALJ's assessment of witness credibility," the agency "should fully articulate [its] reasons for so doing, and then, with heightened scrutiny, we must decide whether such reasons find support in the record") (collecting authority).

In addition to providing an excellent illustration of this characterization game, *Penasquitos* also provides a platform for questioning some of the premises commonly used to justify deference. Who, in your view, got the better of the great debate between Judges Wallace and Duniway over the significance of demeanor evidence for the weight of ALJ factual findings? As discussed above, one of the primary rationales for deference to agency secondary inferences is "expertise." Contrast the significance of agency expertise in the last two paragraphs of Judge Wallace's opinion with the significance it had in part III of Judge Duniway's opinion. Which judge got it right? More broadly, does the Board likely possess any "expertise" that gave it special insight into why Penasquitos discharged its employees? Under what circumstances should courts credit that agencies possess (and have exercised) relevant expertise?

3. Substantial evidence — sometimes you can take the expert's word for it. In *Biestek v. Berryhill*, 139 S. Ct. 1148 (2019), the Supreme Court examined the outer limits of when expert testimony may amount to "substantial evidence." Biestek applied for Social Security Disability benefits. His eligibility turned in part on whether there were a significant number of jobs in the national economy that he could still perform. As is common in such cases, the ALJ obtained testimony from a vocational expert on this issue. The vocational expert had five years of experience testifying during SSA hearings and ten years of experience counseling disabled persons regarding employment opportunities. The expert testified that Biestek could perform jobs such as "bench assembler" or "sorter" and that there were 360,000 such jobs in the national economy. Counsel for Biestek asked the expert for her foundation for these numbers; she responded that they were based on Bureau of Labor statistics and her own surveys; counsel requested the expert's surveys; she responded that she did not wish to produce them as they were part of confidential client files; counsel suggested redacting identifying names. The ALJ then put an end to this colloquy by declaring that he would not require production of the surveys. The ALJ later partially denied Biestek's claim on the ground that, for a four-year period, he could have obtained work in a sedentary occupation such as bench assembler or sorter. Biestek sought review on the theory that the expert's testimony "could not possibly constitute" substantial evidence "because she had declined, upon request, to produce her supporting data." 139 S. Ct. at 1153.

Justice Kagan, writing for a six-justice majority, rejected Biestek's argument for overreaching by seeking a categorical rule that "the testimony of a vocational expert who . . . refuses a request for supporting data about job availability can never clear the substantial-evidence bar." *Id.* at 1154. She summarized:

> Sometimes an expert's withholding of such data, when combined with other aspects of the record, will prevent her testimony from qualifying as substantial evidence. That would be so, for example, if the expert has no good reason to keep the data private and her testimony lacks other markers of reliability. But sometimes the reservation of data will have no such effect. Even though the applicant might wish for the data, the expert's testimony still will clear (even handily so) the more-than-a-mere-scintilla threshold. The inquiry, as is usually true in determining the substantiality of evidence, is case-by-case. *See, e.g., Richardson v. Perales*, 402 U.S. 389, 399, 410 (1971)] (rejecting a categorical rule pertaining to the substantiality of medical reports in a disability hearing). It takes into account all features of the vocational expert's testimony, as well as the rest of the administrative record. And in so doing, it defers to the presiding ALJ, who has seen the hearing up close.

That much is sufficient to decide this case. Biestek petitioned us only to adopt the categorical rule we have now rejected. He did not ask us to decide whether, in the absence of that rule, substantial evidence supported the ALJ in denying him benefits. Accordingly, we affirm the Court of Appeals' judgment.

Id. at 1157. *But see id.* at 1160 (Gorsuch, J., dissenting) ("The case hinges on an expert who (a) claims to possess evidence on the dispositive legal question that can be found nowhere else in the record, but (b) offers only a conclusion about its contents, and (c) refuses to supply the evidence when requested without showing that it can't readily be made available. What reasonable factfinder would rely on evidence like that?").

4. Substantial evidence and a duty to explain. In 2015's *T-Mobile South, LLC v. City of Roswell, Ga.,* 135 S. Ct. 808 (2015), the Supreme Court discussed the link between substantial evidence review and agencies' obligation under modern administrative law to explain their actions. T-Mobile South, LLC (T-Mobile) sought permission from the city of Roswell to build a cell tower. The City Council discussed the application at a two-hour meeting that T-Mobile arranged to have transcribed. During the meeting, T-Mobile made its case, and community residents declared their opposition. Members of the City Council commented on the proposal, discussing concerns that the tower did not fit the natural setting or residential zoning. They unanimously rejected the proposal. Two days later, the Planning and Zoning Division sent a letter to T-Mobile stating:

> Please be advised the City of Roswell Mayor and City Council denied the request from T-Mobile for a 108' mono-pine alternative tower structure during their April 12, 2010 hearing. The minutes from the aforementioned hearing may be obtained from the city clerk.

The City Council's minutes were approved and published the following month. Several days later, with these minutes in hand, T-Mobile filed suit in federal court, contending that the denial violated the Telecommunications Act of 1996 (the Act), which, to help ameliorate the problem that no one wants a cell tower in their backyard, provides, "[a]ny decision by a State or local government or instrumentality thereof to deny a request to place, construct, or modify personal wireless service facilities shall be in writing and supported by substantial evidence contained in a written record." 47 U.S.C. § 332(c)(7)(B)(iii).

The Supreme Court characterized the first question before it as "whether the statute requires localities to provide reasons when they deny applications to build cell phone towers." 135 S. Ct. at 814. The Court held that a statutory requirement of substantial evidence review justified an affirmative answer to this question because "[i]n order to determine whether a locality's denial was supported by substantial evidence as Congress directed, courts must be able to identify the reason or reasons why the locality denied the application." *Id.* One might object that such an agency explanation is not actually necessary as a court could, if it had a mind to do so, review the administrative record for itself to determine whether it contains substantial evidence for a given factual proposition. This approach, however, would be inconsistent with administrative law's *Chenery* principle (discussed at note 8 of Chapter 5A), which teaches that a court should review an agency's discretionary action based upon the agency's contemporaneous rationale for it. *Id.* By mandating application of the substantial evidence standard to siting decisions, Congress had "invoked . . . our recognition that 'the orderly functioning of the process of [substantial evidence] review requires that the grounds upon which the administrative agency acted be clearly disclosed.'" *Id.* at 815 (quoting *SEC v. Chenery Corp.*, 318 U.S. 80, 94 (1943)). To limit concerns that this duty of explanation might overload small administrative entities like city councils, the Court added that, "these reasons need not be elaborate or even sophisticated, but rather . . . simply clear enough to enable judicial review." *Id.*

5. The relation of substantial evidence review to arbitrariness review (of facts). As was noted earlier, according to the APA, the substantial evidence test applies to facts that agencies find via formal procedures (which, as a practical matter, means formal adjudication because formal rulemaking rarely happens). As the APA does not provide a specific standard applicable to facts found through informal proceedings, it follows that, where the APA applies, such facts should be subject to § 706's default arbitrariness standard of review. Thus, the arbitrariness standard applies to facts found through informal adjudication (such as we saw in *Overton Park*) and to the factual predicates underlying "informal" rules (e.g., those made through the APA's notice-and-comment procedures). Be aware, however, that Congress sometimes trumps the APA's default arbitrariness standard by including a provision in an agency's organic statute that subjects its rulemaking or informal adjudication efforts to substantial evidence review. *See, e.g.*, 29 U.S.C. § 655(f) (OSHA).

All of which raises the question: As applied to fact-finding, is there a lick of difference between substantial evidence and arbitrariness review? The judicial answer to this question is: It depends upon whom you ask. There is a good deal of authority for the proposition that the substantial evidence test is the somewhat stricter of the two. *See In re Gartside*, 203 F.3d 1305, 1312 (Fed. Cir. 2000) (noting that the substantial evidence standard "is considered to be a less deferential review standard than 'arbitrary, capricious.'"). *Cf. Nat'l Oilseed Processors Ass'n v. OSHA*, 769 F.3d 1173, 1178–79 (D.C. 2014) ("Although the 'substantial evidence' standard demands more stringent review . . . than would the APA's arbitrary and capricious standard, this court has cautioned, in view of an emerging consensus of the Courts of Appeals, that the difference between the two standards should not be exaggerated.") (citations and quotation marks omitted).

But hang on a moment: Substantial evidence review should toss out any unreasonable factual conclusion. If arbitrariness review is weaker, does it follow that this standard should permit some *unreasonable* factual conclusions to survive review? Such reasoning led Justice (then Judge) Scalia to write the following influential dicta:

> The "scope of review" provisions of the APA, 5 U.S.C. § 706(2), are cumulative. Thus, an agency action which is supported by the required substantial evidence may in another regard be "arbitrary, capricious, an abuse

of discretion, or otherwise not in accordance with law"—for example, because it is an abrupt and unexplained departure from agency precedent. Paragraph (A) of subsection 706(2)—the "arbitrary or capricious" provision—is a catchall, picking up administrative misconduct not covered by the other more specific paragraphs. Thus, in those situations where paragraph (E) has no application (informal rulemaking, for example, which is not governed by §§ 556 and 557 to which paragraph (E) refers), paragraph (A) takes up the slack, so to speak, enabling the courts to strike down, as arbitrary, agency action that is devoid of needed factual support. When the arbitrary or capricious standard is performing that function of assuring factual support, there is no substantive difference between what it requires and what would be required by the substantial evidence test, since it is impossible to conceive of a "nonarbitrary" factual judgment supported only by evidence that is not substantial in the APA sense—*i.e.*, not "'enough to justify, if the trial were to a jury, a refusal to direct a verdict when the conclusion sought to be drawn . . . is one of fact for the jury,'" . . .

Ass'n of Data Processing Serv. Orgs., Inc. v. Bd of Governors of the Fed. Reserve System, 745 F.2d 677, 683 (D.C. Cir. 1984).

Stipulate that the surface logic of Justice Scalia's analysis is hard to resist. *Universal Camera*, however, suggested that judicial review is sometimes a matter of "mood." Ought there be a difference between the "substantial evidence" and "arbitrary and capricious" moods?

6. Dealing with uncertainty. Agencies must "find" many "facts" that are impossible to determine with anything like certainty. For instance, EPA's conclusions regarding health impacts of limits on air pollutants are, necessarily, estimates. Uncertainty regarding facts leaves all the more space for interminable policy disagreement, of course. In light of such concerns, the Supreme Court instructs, "a reviewing court must be at its most deferential" when an agency is "making predictions, within its area of special expertise, at the frontiers of science." *Baltimore Gas & Elec. Co. v. Natural Resources Defense Council, Inc.*, 462 U.S. 87, 103 (1983) (affirming agency's assumption that permanent storage of certain nuclear wastes lacked significant environmental impacts for purposes of NEPA analysis and licensing of individual nuclear plants). Such deference should apply even where the predictions depend on facts that the agency cannot determine with certainty. *Id.*

2. Review of Agency Policymaking

Congress commonly charges agencies with broad, vague statutory missions. For instance, the Federal Trade Commission has the task of rooting out "unfair methods of competition." The EPA, as we have seen, is supposed to set air quality standards "requisite to protect the public health" with "an adequate margin of safety." Plainly, an agency must exercise discretionary judgment when implementing these types of tasks. One important project of administrative law has been to determine how courts should review the exercise of such policymaking discretion. If judicial review is too strict, then courts will find themselves infringing on discretion that Congress granted to "expert" agencies, not to the courts. On the reasonable assumption that agencies are generally better than courts at making substantive policy choices, excessive judicial interference may also lead to less effective and rational governance. On the other hand, if judicial review is too weak, the risk of lawless, arbitrary agency action will increase. In the materials that follow, you will see how courts have attempted to steer a middle course for judicial review of discretionary policymaking that avoids both abdication and overreaching.

Lesson 5G.2. Recall from Chapter 3 that the WTC promulgated a rule that a wine may not be labeled "special reserve" (or with any other similar description) "unless it is distinguishable from the general run of wine sold by that grower in terms of grapes, production process, or other indications of special quality." At one point, the WTC considered issuing "safe harbor" guidelines that clearly identified some wines as meriting "special reserve" labeling, but the agency ultimately decided against taking such action (partly out of concern that it would require additional notice-and-comment).

The agency's statement of basis and purpose for the special reserve rule had relied on a prominent, peer-reviewed study of market psychology for the proposition that claims of special quality can boost sales. In particular, the study had shown that prominent labels claiming that a detergent was "new and improved" caused sales to increase. The statement of basis and purpose also relied on a WTC-commissioned study that demonstrated that approximately 20% of wines bearing "special reserve" labels were objectively indistinguishable from "ordinary" wines. The WTC therefore concluded that a rule proscribing such improper use of "special reserve" labels was needed to prevent deception of consumers.

Assume for the purpose of this particular lesson that Carl tendered his resignation as WTC chair when a new administration rolled into town. He was replaced by Milton, a former congressman and longtime proponent of deregulation. Milton set about seeking WTC rules to repeal, and his eye fixed upon the special reserve rule.

A member of Milton's staff has sent a memo to the rulemaking division outlining reasons to repeal the rule. The memo contends that the rule was not properly supported by evidence that "special reserve" type labels are material to wine consumers (*i.e.*, wine is not detergent). Furthermore, many wine makers have complained to the agency that they have stopped using "special reserve" labels even for wines that in the makers' judgment deserve this designation. These wine makers say they fear that the WTC will disagree and impose sanctions. This chilling effect has caused wine consumers to lose access to truthful information regarding their potential purchases. In light of these concerns, the special reserve rule impedes rather than promotes the statutory goal of promoting wine sales and should be repealed.

Ben is disturbed by the new regime at the agency and, fortuitously, has been given a chance to act on this feeling. He has been asked to determine whether repeal of the special reserve rule (after another round of notice-and-comment) would likely survive judicial review given the rationales for this move stated in the memo. Would it?

Background of *Motor Vehicle Mfrs. Ass'n v. State Farm*

Here is another case that belongs in any "top three" list for modern American administrative law. Driving an automobile is one of the more dangerous things that most of us do from day to day; tens of thousands of people die per year on the roadways. To lessen this danger, any new car you purchase today will come equipped with passive safety restraints required by law (e.g., airbags). This legal requirement raises many interesting issues regarding the substance of policymaking. For instance, might a legislature achieve the same safety benefits without imposing costly regulatory requirements on manufacturers by imposing stiff fines on drivers and passengers who fail to buckle up? Alternatively, might regulators require installation of a simple device that prevents an automobile from starting if seat belts are not buckled? The National Highway and Traffic Safety Administration (NHTSA) actually tried this last move, requiring an "ignition interlock." Congress responded to resulting howls of protest from an angry public by overriding this requirement by statute.

From the viewpoint of general administrative law, the lasting significance of the *State Farm* case relates to judicial review of agency policy decisions. The procedural path to requiring passive restraints by regulation was long and tortured. As the majority opinion below observes, "[o]ver the course of approximately 60 rulemaking notices, the requirement [was] imposed, amended, rescinded, reimposed, and . . . rescinded again." In 1977, during the Carter administration, the Secretary of Transportation promulgated Motor Vehicle Safety Standard 208 (MS 208), which would have required auto manufacturers to install passive restraints in automobiles manufactured after 1982. These passive restraints could be automatic safety belts or airbags. In July 1980, NHTSA estimated that this requirement would, when fully implemented, save about 9,000 lives per year. Nonetheless, early in the Reagan administration during a sharp recession, a new Secretary of Transportation rescinded MS 208. Various interests, notably including the insurance industry, promptly challenged this rescission in court.

The resulting Supreme Court opinion includes canonical instructions for how courts should conduct arbitrariness review of agency policy decisions. As you read the excerpt below, you will naturally want to highlight the Court's abstract description of this standard of review. To understand its impact, you will also need to pay careful attention both to the agency's explanation for the rescission, as well as the specifics of the Court's response to it. Note that all nine justices agreed that the agency's treatment of airbags was arbitrary, but they split 5-4 on the agency's treatment of automatic safety belts. What does this split suggest regarding the nature of arbitrariness review? In a partial dissent, Justice Rehnquist suggested that, after an election, a new administration's regulatory "philosophy" might properly inform and justify policy changes. Do you agree?

Motor Vehicle Manufacturers Association v. State Farm Mutual Automobile Insurance Co.

463 U.S. 29 (1983)

JUSTICE WHITE delivered the opinion of the Court.

The development of the automobile gave Americans unprecedented freedom to travel, but exacted a high price for enhanced mobility. Since 1929, motor vehicles have been the leading cause of accidental deaths and injuries in the United States. In 1982, 46,300 Americans died in motor vehicle accidents and hundreds of thousands more were maimed and injured. While a consensus exists that the current loss of life on our highways is unacceptably high, improving safety does not admit to easy solution. In 1966, Congress decided that at least part of the answer lies in improving the design and safety features of the vehicle itself. But much of the technology for building safer cars was undeveloped or untested. Before changes in automobile design could be mandated, the effectiveness of these changes had to be studied, their costs examined, and public acceptance considered. This task called for considerable expertise and Congress responded by enacting the National Traffic and Motor Vehicle Safety Act of 1966, (Act), 15 U.S.C. §§ 1381 et seq. The Act, created for the purpose of "reduc[ing] traffic accidents and deaths and injuries to persons resulting from traffic accidents," 15 U.S.C. § 1381, directs the Secretary of Transportation or his delegate to issue motor vehicle safety standards that "shall be practicable, shall meet the need for motor vehicle safety, and shall be stated in objective terms." 15 U.S.C. § 1392(a). In issuing these standards, the Secretary is directed to consider "relevant available motor vehicle safety data," whether the proposed standard "is reasonable, practicable and appropriate" for the particular type of motor vehicle, and the "extent to which such standards will contribute to carrying out the purposes" of the Act. 15 U.S.C. § 1392(f)(1), (3), (4).

The Act also authorizes judicial review under the provisions of the Administrative Procedure Act (APA), 5 U.S.C. § 706, of all "orders establishing, amending, or revoking a Federal motor vehicle safety standard," 15 U.S.C. § 1392(b). Under this authority, we review today whether NHTSA acted arbitrarily and capriciously in revoking the requirement in Motor Vehicle Safety Standard 208 that new motor vehicles produced after September 1982 be equipped with passive restraints to protect the safety of the occupants of the vehicle in the event of a collision. Briefly summarized, we hold that the agency failed to present an adequate basis and explanation for rescinding the passive restraint requirement and that the agency must either consider the matter further or adhere to or amend Standard 208 along lines which its analysis supports.

I

The regulation whose rescission is at issue bears a complex and convoluted history. Over the course of approximately 60 rulemaking notices, the requirement has been imposed, amended, rescinded, reimposed, and now rescinded again.

As originally issued by the Department of Transportation in 1967, Standard 208 simply required the installation of seatbelts in all automobiles. It soon became apparent that the level of seatbelt use was too low to reduce traffic injuries to an acceptable level. The Department therefore began consideration of "passive occupant restraint systems"—devices that do not depend for their effectiveness upon any action taken by the occupant except that necessary to operate the vehicle. Two types of automatic crash protection emerged: automatic seatbelts and airbags. . . . The life-saving potential of these devices was immediately recognized, and in 1977, after substantial on-the-road experience with both devices, it was estimated by NHTSA that passive restraints could prevent approximately 12,000 deaths and over 100,000 serious injuries annually.

In 1969, the Department formally proposed a standard requiring the installation of passive restraints, thereby commencing a lengthy series of proceedings. In 1970, the agency revised Standard 208 to include passive protection requirements, and in 1972, the agency amended the standard to require full passive protection for all front seat occupants of vehicles manufactured after August 15, 1975. In the interim, vehicles built between August 1973 and August 1975 were to carry either passive restraints or lap and shoulder belts coupled with an "ignition interlock" that would prevent starting the vehicle if the belts were not connected. On review, the agency's decision to require passive restraints was found to be supported by "substantial evidence" and upheld.

In preparing for the upcoming model year, most car makers chose the "ignition interlock" option, a decision which was highly unpopular, and led Congress to amend the Act to prohibit a motor vehicle safety standard from requiring or permitting compliance by means of an ignition interlock or a continuous buzzer designed to indicate that safety belts were not in use. Motor Vehicle and Schoolbus Safety Amendments of 1974, 15 U.S.C. § 1410b(b).

The effective date for mandatory passive restraint systems was extended for a year until August 31, 1976. But in June 1976, Secretary of Transportation William Coleman initiated a new rulemaking on the issue. After hearing testimony and reviewing written comments, Coleman extended the optional alternatives indefinitely and suspended the passive restraint requirement. Although he found passive restraints technologically and economically feasible, the Secretary based his decision on the expectation that there would be widespread public resistance to the new systems. He instead proposed a demonstration project involving up to 500,000 cars installed with passive restraints, in order to smooth the way for public acceptance of mandatory passive restraints at a later date.

Coleman's successor as Secretary of Transportation disagreed. Within months of assuming office, Secretary Brock Adams decided that the demonstration project was unnecessary. He issued a new mandatory passive restraint regulation, known as [Modified Standard 208.] The Modified Standard mandated the phasing in of passive restraints beginning with large cars in model year 1982 and extending to all cars by model year 1984. The two principal systems that would satisfy the Standard were airbags and passive belts; the choice of which system to install was left to the manufacturers.

Over the next several years, the automobile industry geared up to comply with Modified Standard 208. As late as July, 1980, NHTSA reported:

> "On the road experience in thousands of vehicles equipped with airbags and automatic safety belts has confirmed agency estimates of the life-saving and injury-preventing benefits of such systems. When all cars are equipped with automatic crash protection systems, each year an estimated 9,000 more lives will be saved and tens of thousands of serious injuries will be prevented." NHTSA, Automobile Occupant Crash Protection, Progress Report No. 3, p. 4 (App. 1627).

In February 1981, however, Secretary of Transportation Andrew Lewis reopened the rulemaking due to changed economic circumstances and, in particular, the difficulties of the automobile industry. Two months later, the agency ordered a one-year delay in the application of the standard to large cars, extending the deadline to September 1982, and at the same time, proposed the possible rescission of the entire standard. After receiving written comments and holding public hearings, NHTSA issued a final rule (Notice 25) that rescinded the passive restraint requirement contained in Modified Standard 208.

II

In a statement explaining the rescission, NHTSA maintained that it was no longer able to find, as it had in 1977, that the automatic restraint requirement would produce significant safety benefits. This judgment reflected not a change of opinion on the effectiveness of the technology, but a change in plans by the automobile industry. In 1977, the agency had assumed that airbags would be installed in 60% of all new cars and automatic seatbelts in 40%. By 1981 it became apparent that automobile manufacturers planned to install the automatic seatbelts in approximately 99% of the new cars. For this reason, the life-saving potential of airbags would not be realized. Moreover, it now appeared that the overwhelming majority of passive belts planned to be installed by manufacturers could be detached easily and left that way permanently. Passive belts, once detached, then required "the same type of affirmative action that is the stumbling block to obtaining high usage levels of manual belts." For this reason, the agency concluded that there was no longer a basis for reliably predicting that the standard would lead to any significant increased usage of restraints at all.

In view of the possibly minimal safety benefits, the automatic restraint requirement no longer was reasonable or practicable in the agency's view. The requirement would require approximately $1 billion to implement and the agency did not believe it would be reasonable to impose such substantial costs on manufacturers and consumers without more adequate assurance that sufficient safety benefits would accrue. In addition, NHTSA concluded that automatic restraints might have an adverse effect on the public's attitude toward safety. Given the high expense and limited benefits of detachable belts, NHTSA feared that many consumers would regard the standard as an instance of ineffective regulation, adversely affecting the public's view of safety regulation and, in particular, "poisoning popular sentiment toward efforts to improve occupant restraint systems in the future."

State Farm Mutual Automobile Insurance Co. and the National Association of Independent Insurers filed petitions for review of NHTSA's rescission of the passive restraint standard. The United States Court of Appeals for the District of Columbia Circuit held that the agency's rescission of the passive restraint requirement was arbitrary and capricious. . . . [W]e granted certiorari, and . . . the Court of Appeals entered an order recalling its mandate.

III

Unlike the Court of Appeals, we do not find the appropriate scope of judicial review to be the "most troublesome question" in the case. Both the Motor Vehicle Safety Act and the 1974 Amendments concerning occupant crash protection standards indicate that motor vehicle safety standards are to be promulgated under the informal rulemaking procedures of § 553 of the Administrative Procedure Act. 5 U.S.C. § 553 (1976). The agency's action in promulgating such standards therefore may be set aside if found to be "arbitrary, capricious, an abuse of discretion, or otherwise not in accordance with law." 5 U.S.C. § 706(2)(A). *Citizens to Preserve Overton Park v. Volpe*, 401 U.S. 402, 414 (1971). We believe that the rescission or modification of an occupant protection standard is subject to the same test. Section 103(b) of the Motor Vehicle Safety Act, 15 U.S.C. § 1392(b), states that the procedural and judicial review provisions of the Administrative Procedure Act "shall apply to all orders establishing, amending, or revoking a Federal motor vehicle safety standard," and suggests no difference in the scope of judicial review depending upon the nature of the agency's action.

Petitioner Motor Vehicle Manufacturers Association (MVMA) disagrees, contending that the rescission of an agency rule should be judged by the same standard a court would use to judge an agency's refusal to promulgate a rule in the first place—a standard Petitioner believes considerably narrower than the traditional arbitrary and capricious test and "close to the borderline of nonreviewability." We reject this view. The Motor Vehicle Safety Act expressly equates orders "revoking" and "establishing" safety standards; neither that Act nor the APA suggests that revocations are to be treated as refusals to promulgate standards. Petitioner's view would render meaningless Congress' authorization for judicial review of orders revoking safety rules. Moreover, the revocation of an extant regulation is substantially different than a failure to act. Revocation constitutes a reversal of the agency's former views as to the proper course. A "settled course of behavior embodies the agency's informed judgment that, by pursuing that course, it will carry out the policies committed to it by Congress. There is, then, at least a presumption that those policies will be carried out best if the settled rule is adhered to." Atchison, T. & S.F.R. Co. v. Wichita Bd. of Trade, 412 U.S. 800, 807–808 (1973). Accordingly, an agency changing its course by rescinding a rule is obligated to supply a reasoned analysis for the change beyond that which may be required when an agency does not act in the first instance. . . .

The Department of Transportation accepts the applicability of the "arbitrary and capricious" standard. It argues that under this standard, a reviewing court may not set aside an agency rule that is rational, based on consideration of the relevant factors and within the scope of the authority delegated to the agency by the statute. We do not disagree with this formulation.[9] The scope of review under the "arbitrary and capricious" standard is narrow and a court is not to substitute its judgment for that of the agency. Nevertheless, the agency must examine the relevant data and articulate a satisfactory explanation for its action including a "rational connection between the facts found and the choice made." In reviewing that explanation, we must "consider whether the decision was based on a consideration of the relevant factors and whether there has been a clear error of judgment." *Citizens to Preserve Overton Park v. Volpe*, 401 U.S., at 416. Normally, an agency rule would be arbitrary and capricious if the agency has relied on factors which Congress has not intended it to consider, entirely failed to consider an important aspect of the problem, offered an explanation for its decision that runs counter to the evidence before the agency, or is so implausible that it could not be ascribed to a difference in view or the product of agency expertise. The reviewing court should not attempt itself to make up for such deficiencies: "We may not supply a reasoned basis for the agency's action that the agency itself has not given." *SEC v. Chenery Corp.*, 332 U.S. 194, 196 (1947). We will, however, "uphold a decision of less than ideal clarity if the agency's path may reasonably be discerned." For purposes of this case, it is also relevant that Congress required a record of the rulemaking proceedings to be compiled and submitted to a reviewing court, 15 U.S.C. § 1394, and intended that agency findings under the Motor Vehicle Safety Act would be supported by "substantial evidence on the record considered as a whole." S.Rep. No. 1301, 89th Cong., 2d Sess. p. 8 (1966); H.R.Rep. No. 1776, 89th Cong., 2d Sess. p. 21 (1966). . . .

V

The ultimate question before us is whether NHTSA's rescission of the passive restraint requirement of Standard 208 was arbitrary and capricious. We conclude, as did the Court of Appeals, that it was. We also conclude, but for somewhat different reasons, that further consideration of the issue by the agency is therefore required. We deal separately with the rescission as it applies to airbags and as it applies to seatbelts.

---

9. The Department of Transportation suggests that the arbitrary and capricious standard requires no more than the minimum rationality a statute must bear in order to withstand analysis under the Due Process Clause. We do not view as equivalent the presumption of constitutionality afforded legislation drafted by Congress and the presumption of regularity afforded an agency in fulfilling its statutory mandate.

A

FAILED TO CONSIDER REQ OF AIRBAG

The first and most obvious reason for finding the rescission arbitrary and capricious is that NHTSA apparently gave no consideration whatever to modifying the Standard to require that airbag technology be utilized. Standard 208 sought to achieve automatic crash protection by requiring automobile manufacturers to install either of two passive restraint devices: airbags or automatic seatbelts. There was no suggestion in the long rulemaking process that led to Standard 208 that if only one of these options were feasible, no passive restraint standard should be promulgated. Indeed, the agency's original proposed standard contemplated the installation of inflatable restraints in all cars. Automatic belts were added as a means of complying with the standard because they were believed to be as effective as airbags in achieving the goal of occupant crash protection. At that time, the passive belt approved by the agency could not be detached. Only later, at a manufacturer's behest, did the agency approve of the detachability feature—and only after assurances that the feature would not compromise the safety benefits of the restraint. Although it was then foreseen that 60% of the new cars would contain airbags and 40% would have automatic seatbelts, the ratio between the two was not significant as long as the passive belt would also assure greater passenger safety.

The agency has now determined that the detachable automatic belts will not attain anticipated safety benefits because so many individuals will detach the mechanism. Even if this conclusion were acceptable in its entirety, standing alone it would not justify any more than an amendment of Standard 208 to disallow compliance by means of the one technology which will not provide effective passenger protection. It does not cast doubt on the need for a passive restraint standard or upon the efficacy of airbag technology. In its most recent rule-making, the agency again acknowledged the life-saving potential of the airbag . . . .

Given the effectiveness ascribed to airbag technology by the agency, the mandate of the Safety Act to achieve traffic safety would suggest that the logical response to the faults of detachable seatbelts would be to require the installation of airbags. At the very least this alternative way of achieving the objectives of the Act should have been addressed and adequate reasons given for its abandonment. But the agency not only did not require compliance through airbags, it did not even consider the possibility in its 1981 rulemaking. Not one sentence of its rulemaking statement discusses the airbags-only option. Because, as the Court of Appeals stated, "NHTSA's . . . analysis of airbags was nonexistent," what we said in *Burlington Truck Lines v. United States*, 371 U.S., at 167, is apropos here:

> "There are no findings and no analysis here to justify the choice made, no indication of the basis on which the [agency] exercised its expert discretion. We are not prepared to and the Administrative Procedure Act will not permit us to accept such . . . practice. . . . Expert discretion is the life-blood of the administrative process, but 'unless we make the requirements for administrative action strict and demanding, expertise, the strength of

modern government, can become a monster which rules with no practical limits on its discretion.'"

We have frequently reiterated that an agency must cogently explain why it has exercised its discretion in a given manner; and we reaffirm this principle again today.

The automobile industry has opted for the passive belt over the airbag, but surely it is not enough that the regulated industry has eschewed a given safety device. For nearly a decade, the automobile industry waged the regulatory equivalent of war against the airbag and lost — the inflatable restraint was proven sufficiently effective. Now the automobile industry has decided to employ a seatbelt system which will not meet the safety objectives of Standard 208. This hardly constitutes cause to revoke the standard itself. Indeed, the Motor Vehicle Safety Act was necessary because the industry was not sufficiently responsive to safety concerns. The Act intended that safety standards not depend on current technology and could be "technology-forcing" in the sense of inducing the development of superior safety design. If, under the statute, the agency should not defer to the industry's failure to develop safer cars, which it surely should not do, *a fortiori* it may not revoke a safety standard which can be satisfied by current technology simply because the industry has opted for an ineffective seatbelt design.

Although the agency did not address the mandatory airbags option and the Court of Appeals noted that "airbags seem to have none of the problems that NHTSA identified in passive seatbelts," petitioners recite a number of difficulties that they believe would be posed by a mandatory airbag standard. These range from questions concerning the installation of airbags in small cars to that of adverse public reaction. But these are not the agency's reasons for rejecting a mandatory airbag standard. Not having discussed the possibility, the agency submitted no reasons at all. The short — and sufficient — answer to petitioners' submission is that the courts may not accept appellate counsel's post hoc rationalizations for agency action. *Burlington Truck Lines v. United States*, supra, 371 U.S., at 168. It is well-established that an agency's action must be upheld, if at all, on the basis articulated by the agency itself. *Ibid.*; *SEC v. Chenery Corp.*, 332 U.S. 194, 196 (1947).

Petitioners also invoke our decision in *Vermont Yankee Nuclear Power Corp. v. NRDC*, 435 U.S. 519 (1978), as though it were a talisman under which any agency decision is by definition unimpeachable. Specifically, it is submitted that to require an agency to consider an airbags-only alternative is, in essence, to dictate to the agency the procedures it is to follow. Petitioners both misread *Vermont Yankee* and misconstrue the nature of the remand that is in order. In *Vermont Yankee*, we held that a court may not impose additional procedural requirements upon an agency. We do not require today any specific procedures which NHTSA must follow. Nor do we broadly require an agency to consider all policy alternatives in reaching decision. It is true that a rulemaking "cannot be found wanting simply because the agency failed to include every alternative device and thought conceivable by the mind of man . . . regardless of how uncommon or unknown that alternative may have been. . . ." 435 U.S., at 551. But the airbag is more than a policy alternative to the passive restraint standard; it is a technological alternative within the ambit of the existing standard. We hold only that given the judgment made in 1977 that airbags are an effective and cost-beneficial life-saving technology, the mandatory passive-restraint rule may not be abandoned without any consideration whatsoever of an airbags-only requirement.

B

Although the issue is closer, we also find that the agency was too quick to dismiss the safety benefits of automatic seatbelts. NHTSA's critical finding was that, in light of the industry's plans to install readily detachable passive belts, it could not reliably predict "even a 5 percentage point increase as the minimum level of expected usage increase." 46 Fed.Reg., at 53,423. The Court of Appeals rejected this finding because there is "not one iota" of evidence that Modified Standard 208 will fail to increase nationwide seatbelt use by at least 13 percentage points, the level of increased usage necessary for the standard to justify its cost. Given the lack of probative evidence, the court held that "only a well-justified refusal to seek more evidence could render rescission non-arbitrary."

Petitioners object to this conclusion. In their view, "substantial uncertainty" that a regulation will accomplish its intended purpose is sufficient reason, without more, to rescind a regulation. We agree with petitioners that just as an agency reasonably may decline to issue a safety standard if it is uncertain about its efficacy, an agency may also revoke a standard on the basis of serious uncertainties if supported by the record and reasonably explained. Rescission of the passive restraint requirement would not be arbitrary and capricious simply because there was no evidence in direct support of the agency's conclusion. It is not infrequent that the available data does not settle a regulatory issue and the agency must then exercise its judgment in moving from the facts and probabilities on the record to a policy conclusion. Recognizing that policymaking in a complex society must account for uncertainty, however, does not imply that it is sufficient for an agency to merely recite the terms "substantial uncertainty" as a justification for its actions. The agency must explain the evidence which is available, and must offer a "rational connection between the facts found and the choice made." Generally, one aspect of that explanation would be a justification for rescinding the regulation before engaging in a search for further evidence.

In this case, the agency's explanation for rescission of the passive restraint requirement is not sufficient to enable us to conclude that the rescission was the product of reasoned decisionmaking. To reach this conclusion, we do not upset the agency's view of the facts, but we do appreciate the limitations of this record in supporting the agency's decision. We start with the accepted ground that if used, seatbelts unquestionably would save many thousands of lives and would prevent tens of thousands of crippling injuries. . . . We move next to the fact that there is no direct evidence in support of the agency's finding that detachable automatic belts cannot be predicted to yield a substantial increase in usage. The empirical evidence on the record, consisting of surveys of drivers of automobiles equipped with passive belts, reveals more than a doubling of the usage rate experienced with manual belts.[16] Much of the agency's rulemaking statement — and much of the controversy in this case — centers on the conclusions that should be drawn from these studies. The agency maintained that the doubling of seatbelt usage in these studies could not be extrapolated to an across-the-board mandatory standard because the passive seatbelts were guarded by ignition interlocks and purchasers of the tested cars are somewhat atypical.[17] Respondents insist these studies demonstrate that Modified Standard 208 will substantially increase seatbelt usage. We believe that it is within the agency's discretion to pass upon the generalizability of these field studies. This is precisely the type of issue which rests within the expertise of NHTSA, and upon which a reviewing court must be most hesitant to intrude.

But accepting the agency's view of the field tests on passive restraints indicates only that there is no reliable real-world experience that usage rates will substantially increase. To be sure, NHTSA opines that "it cannot reliably predict even a 5 percentage point increase as the minimum level of increased usage." But this and other statements that passive belts will not yield substantial increases in seatbelt usage apparently take no account of the critical difference between detachable automatic belts and current manual belts. A detached passive belt does require an affirmative act to reconnect it, but — unlike a manual seat belt — the passive belt, once reattached, will continue to function automatically unless again disconnected. Thus, inertia — a factor which the agency's own studies have found significant in explaining the current low usage rates for seatbelts — works in favor of, not against, use of the protective device. Since 20 to 50% of motorists currently wear seatbelts on some occasions, there would seem to be grounds to believe that seatbelt use by occasional users will be substantially increased by the detachable passive belts. Whether this is in fact the case is a matter for the agency to decide, but it must bring its expertise to bear on the question.

The agency is correct to look at the costs as well as the benefits of Standard 208. The agency's conclusion that the incremental costs of the requirements were no longer reasonable was predicated on its prediction that the safety benefits of the regulation might be minimal. Specifically, the agency's fears that the public may resent

---

16. Between 1975 and 1980, Volkswagen sold approximately 350,000 Rabbits equipped with detachable passive seatbelts that were guarded by an ignition interlock. General Motors sold 8,000 1978 and 1979 Chevettes with a similar system, but eliminated the ignition interlock on the 13,000 Chevettes sold in 1980. NHTSA found that belt usage in the Rabbits averaged 34% for manual belts and 84% for passive belts. Regulatory Impact Analysis (RIA) at IV-52, App. 108. For the 1978–1979 Chevettes, NHTSA calculated 34% usage for manual belts and 71% for passive belts. On 1980 Chevettes, the agency found these figures to be 31% for manual belts and 70% for passive belts. *Ibid.*

17. "NHTSA believes that the usage of automatic belts in Rabbits and Chevettes would have been substantially lower if the automatic belts in those cars were not equipped with a use-inducing device inhibiting detachment." Notice 25, 46 Fed.Reg., at 53,422.

paying more for the automatic belt systems is expressly dependent on the assumption that detachable automatic belts will not produce more than "negligible safety benefits." 46 Fed.Reg., at 53,424. When the agency reexamines its findings as to the likely increase in seatbelt usage, it must also reconsider its judgment of the reasonableness of the monetary and other costs associated with the Standard. In reaching its judgment, NHTSA should bear in mind that Congress intended safety to be the preeminent factor under the Motor Vehicle Safety Act:

"The Committee intends that safety shall be the overriding consideration in the issuance of standards under this bill. The Committee recognizes . . . that the Secretary will necessarily consider reasonableness of cost, feasibility and adequate leadtime." S.Rep. No. 1301, at 6.

"In establishing standards the Secretary must conform to the requirement that the standard be practicable. This would require consideration of all relevant factors, including technological ability to achieve the goal of a particular standard as well as consideration of economic factors. Motor vehicle safety is the paramount purpose of this bill and each standard must be related thereto." H.Rep. No. 1776, at 16.

The agency also failed to articulate a basis for not requiring nondetachable belts under Standard 208. It is argued that the concern of the agency with the easy detachability of the currently favored design would be readily solved by a continuous passive belt, which allows the occupant to "spool out" the belt and create the necessary slack for easy extrication from the vehicle. The agency did not separately consider the continuous belt option, but treated it together with the ignition interlock device in a category it titled "option of use-compelling features." 46 Fed.Reg., at 53,424. The agency was concerned that use-compelling devices would "complicate extrication of [a]n occupant from his or her car." *Ibid.* "To require that passive belts contain use-compelling features," the agency observed, "could be counterproductive [given] . . . widespread, latent and irrational fear in many members of the public that they could be trapped by the seat belt after a crash." *Ibid.* In addition, based on the experience with the ignition interlock, the agency feared that use-compelling features might trigger adverse public reaction.

By failing to analyze the continuous seatbelts in its own right, the agency has failed to offer the rational connection between facts and judgment required to pass muster under the arbitrary and capricious standard. We agree with the Court of Appeals that NHTSA did not suggest that the emergency release mechanisms used in nondetachable belts are any less effective for emergency egress than the buckle release system used in detachable belts. In 1978, when General Motors obtained the agency's approval to install a continuous passive belt, it assured the agency that nondetachable belts with spool releases were as safe as detachable belts with buckle releases. 43 Fed.Reg. 21,912, 21,913–14 (1978). NHTSA was satisfied that this belt design assured easy extricability: "the agency does not believe that the use of [such] release mechanisms will cause serious occupant egress problems . . ." 43 Fed. Reg. 52,493, 52,494 (1978). While the agency is entitled to change its view on the acceptability of continuous passive belts, it is obligated to explain its reasons for doing so.

The agency also failed to offer any explanation why a continuous passive belt would engender the same adverse public reaction as the ignition interlock, and, as the Court of Appeals concluded, "every indication in the record points the other way." We see no basis for equating the two devices: the continuous belt, unlike the ignition interlock, does not interfere with the operation of the vehicle. More importantly, it is the agency's responsibility, not this Court's, to explain its decision.

VI

"An agency's view of what is in the public interest may change, either with or without a change in circumstances. But an agency changing its course must supply a reasoned analysis . . ." *Greater Boston Television Corp. v. FCC*, 444 F.2d 841, 852 (CADC), *cert. denied*, 403 U.S. 923 (1971). We do not accept all of the reasoning of the Court of Appeals but we do conclude that the agency has failed to supply the requisite "reasoned analysis" in this case. Accordingly, we vacate the judgment of the Court of Appeals and remand the case to that court with directions to remand the matter to the NHTSA for further consideration consistent with this opinion.

So ordered.

JUSTICE REHNQUIST, with whom the CHIEF JUSTICE, JUSTICE POWELL, and JUSTICE O'CONNOR join, concurring in part and dissenting in part.

I join parts I, II, III, IV, and V-A of the Court's opinion. In particular, I agree that, since the airbag and continuous spool automatic seatbelt were explicitly approved in the standard the agency was rescinding, the agency should explain why it declined to leave those requirements intact. In this case, the agency gave no explanation at all. Of course, if the agency can provide a rational explanation, it may adhere to its decision to rescind the entire standard.

I do not believe, however, that NHTSA's view of detachable automatic seatbelts was arbitrary and capricious. The agency adequately explained its decision to rescind the standard insofar as it was satisfied by detachable belts.

The statute that requires the Secretary of Transportation to issue motor vehicle safety standards also requires that "[e]ach such . . . standard shall be practicable [and] shall meet the need for motor vehicle safety." 15 U.S.C. § 1392(a). The Court rejects the agency's explanation for its conclusion that there is substantial uncertainty whether requiring installation of detachable automatic belts would substantially increase seatbelt usage. The agency chose not to rely on a study showing a substantial increase in seatbelt usage in cars equipped with automatic seatbelts and an ignition interlock to prevent the car from being operated when the belts were not in place and which were voluntarily purchased with this equipment by consumers. It is reasonable for the agency to decide that this study does not support any conclusion concerning the effect of automatic seatbelts that are installed in all cars whether the consumer wants them or not and are not linked to an ignition interlock system.

The Court rejects this explanation because "there would seem to be grounds to believe that seatbelt use by occasional users will be substantially increased by the detachable passive belts," and the agency did not adequately explain its rejection of these grounds. It seems to me that the agency's explanation, while by no means a model, is adequate. The agency acknowledged that there would probably be some increase in belt usage, but concluded that the increase would be small and not worth the cost of mandatory detachable automatic belts. The agency's obligation is to articulate a "rational connection between the facts found and the choice made." I believe it has met this standard. . . .

The agency's changed view of the standard seems to be related to the election of a new President of a different political party. It is readily apparent that the responsible members of one administration may consider public resistance and uncertainties to be more important than do their counterparts in a previous administration. A change in administration brought about by the people casting their votes is a perfectly reasonable basis for an executive agency's reappraisal of the costs and benefits of its programs and regulations. As long as the agency remains within the bounds established by Congress, it is entitled to assess administrative records and evaluate priorities in light of the philosophy of the administration.

Notes

1. Identifying applicable standards of review. Regarding the lesson, what issues of fact or policy might repeal of the special reserve rule raise? Under the APA, what standards of review would apply to these issues? How about under the WTCA?

2. Precisely how did NHTSA blow it? All nine justices agreed that NHTSA's treatment of two kinds of passive restraint in Modified Standard 208 was arbitrary. What were these passive restraints, and where did NHTSA go wrong in its analysis of them? Only five justices condemned NHTSA's treatment of a third kind of passive restraint. What was it, and what prompted the justices' disagreement?

3. The basics of modern arbitrariness review of policymaking. How does a court determine whether an agency policy decision was "arbitrary" within the meaning of § 706(2)(A)? According to the Supreme Court in *Overton Park*, "To make this finding the court must consider whether the decision was based on a consideration of the relevant factors and whether there has been a clear error of judgment. Although this inquiry into the facts is to be searching and careful, the ultimate standard of review is a narrow one. The court is not empowered to substitute its judgment for that of the agency." In *State Farm*, Justice White added:

> Normally, an agency rule would be arbitrary and capricious if the agency has relied on factors which Congress has not intended it to consider, entirely failed to consider an important aspect of the problem, offered an explanation for its decision that runs counter to the evidence before the agency, or is so implausible that it could not be ascribed to a difference in view or the product of agency expertise.

Thus, judicial review of agency policymaking examines the rationality not just of an agency's policy choice, but also of the rationale the agency gave for it. Such review is supposed to be deferential. Generalizations about judicial review for agency arbitrariness should be handled with care, but, broadly speaking, such review divides into two kinds of inquiry: (a) Did the agency think about the stuff that Congress wanted the agency to think about as it makes policy (*i.e.*, did the agency base its policy choice on consideration of the "relevant factors")? and (b) Does the agency's explanation for its policy choice strike the reviewing court as at least minimally rational? For an argument that this approach to arbitrariness review is too ham-fisted and that courts should more carefully adjust review to fit the various constituent parts of policymaking, see Louis J. Virelli III, *Deconstructing Arbitrary and Capricious Review*, 92 N.C. L. Rev. (2014) (contending that arbitrariness review should discriminate among record building, reason giving, input scope and quality, and rationality).

Does Milton's memo's rationale for repealing the special reserve rule focus sufficiently on the "relevant factors" to be found within the WTCA? Assuming its factual claims are true, does the memo offer a sufficiently reasonable rationale for repeal?

4. Old fashioned arbitrariness review. Courts did not always review agency discretionary decisions so aggressively. *Pacific States Box & Basket Co. v. White*, 296 U.S. 176 (1935), provides a leading example of lax, old-fashioned arbitrariness review. In this case, the Court reviewed a due process challenge to an Oregon agency's rule that banned the use of certain types of containers for packing berries. In its decision, the Court held that the agency's action was entitled to the same presumption of regularity that generally applies to legislation:

> When such legislative action is called in question, if any state of facts *reasonably can be conceived* that would sustain it, there is a presumption of the existence of that state of facts, and one who assails the classification must carry the burden of showing . . . that the action is arbitrary.

296 U.S. at 185 (emphasis added). So, under the *Pacific States Box* regime, provided the agency, its counsel, or the court can dream up some sort of plausible rationale for an agency's action during subsequent litigation, it should be upheld. The Department of Transportation argued for a return to this standard in *State Farm*. For the Court's rejection of this invitation, see footnote 9 of *State Farm, supra*.

5. Modern arbitrariness review as "hard look." In an attempt to describe modern application of arbitrariness review to agency policymaking, courts coined the phrase "the hard look." Although *State Farm* never uses this phrase, many characterize it as the Supreme Court's adoption of this relatively strict approach to arbitrariness review.

Judge Leventhal sketched the outlines of the "hard look" doctrine in *Greater Boston Television Corp. v. FCC*, 444 F.2d 841, 850–51 (D.C. Cir. 1970). He suggested that a court should overturn agency policy decisions "if the court becomes aware, especially from a combination of danger signals, that the agency has not really taken a 'hard look' at the salient problems, and has not genuinely engaged in reasoned decisionmaking." 444 F.2d at 851. Notice the concept is that the court should assure that the agency took a hard look—not that the court should take a hard look. On this view, the "hard look" focuses on the validity and appropriateness of the administrative decisionmaking process, without intense scrutiny of the substantive merits of the decision itself. By focusing on agency process rather than outcome, judicial interference with agency policymaking authority is minimized—at least in theory.

Less than a decade later, Judge Wald offered a different take on who should do the "looking" required by "hard look review" in *National Lime Ass'n v. EPA*, 627 F.2d 416 (D.C. Cir. 1980):

> As originally articulated the words "hard look" described the agency's responsibility and not the court's. However, the phrase subsequently evolved to connote the rigorous standard of judicial review applied to increasingly utilized informal rulemaking proceedings or to other decisions made upon less than a full trial-type record. . . .

> As these newly-required records and rationales became more routinely available, the "hard look" taken began to appear more judicial than administrative, blurring the original meaning of that phrase.

416 F.2d at 451 n.126.

Regardless of which way one prefers to characterize the "hard look," one thing is plain: It can create *a lot* of work for agencies. To see one reason why, recall the *Chenery* teaching that discretionary agency actions stand and fall with the validity of the contemporaneous rationales that agencies offer for them. For a rule promulgated through notice-and-comment, this rationale should be stated in the "concise general statement of . . . basis and purpose" required by § 553(c). Mix this law together, and the result is that an agency that wishes its notice-and-comment rule to survive arbitrariness review will likely feel compelled to respond to any comment the agency fears a generalist court *might* deem significant. "Concise" statements therefore often run hundreds of pages in the Federal Register. Such effects of the "hard look" have led some to charge that it has made the rulemaking process too difficult and has thus, in law-review speak, "ossified" it.

Nor is the "hard look" necessarily easy for courts, as it can require them to immerse themselves in agency policymaking efforts that may be lengthy, technical, and difficult. The sheer length of the opinions in *Prometheus Radio Project v. FCC*, 373 F.3d 372 (3d Cir. 2004), which addressed challenges to a complex FCC order revising regulations on broadcast media ownership, illustrates this point. The bulk of Judge Ambro's majority opinion, which covered 56 pages of an F.3d reporter, was devoted to determining which parts of the order were or were not supported by "reasoned decisionmaking." After finding portions of the order wanting in this regard, the court remanded to the FCC for further proceedings. Chief Judge Scirica's partial dissent took a mere 55 pages to explain that the majority was wrong and that the FCC had adequately supported the entire order. "Reasoned decisionmaking," alas, is sometimes in the eye of the beholder.

But of course, just because "hard look" review may be hard and costly, it does not follow that it is a bad idea. A substantial law review literature explores this question. For examples of articles critical of the "hard look," see Thomas O. McGarity, *The Courts and the Ossification of Rulemaking: A Response to Professor Seidenfeld*, 75 Tex. L. Rev. 525, 530 (1997) (contending that hard-look review has played a "prominent role" in causing the demise of informal rulemaking and its benefits are dubious); Richard J. Pierce, Jr., *Seven Ways to Deossify Agency Rulemaking*, 47 Admin. L. Rev. 59 (1995) (placing much of the blame for the ossification of rulemaking on the courts' approach to judicial review). For a more favorable assessment of the hard look, see William S. Jordan, III, *Ossification Revisited: Does Arbitrary and Capricious Review Significantly Interfere with Agency Ability to Achieve Regulatory Goals through Informal Rulemaking*, 94 N.W. U. L. Rev. 393 (2000) (conducting a survey of D.C. Circuit opinions that administered a "hard look" and concluding that they did not significantly impede agency action). For a revisionist examination that contends that, at least at the Supreme Court level, the notion that *State Farm* "inaugurated an era of stringent judicial review of agency decisionmaking for rationality" is "flatly wrong," see Jacob Gersen & Adrian Vermeule, *Thin Rationality Review*, 114 Mich. L. Rev. 1355 (2016).

6. Discretion, relevant factors, and impermissible factors. Section 706(2)(A) requires courts to hold unlawful "agency action, findings, and conclusions found to be . . . arbitrary, capricious, [or] an abuse of discretion. . . ." The three descriptors at the end of the preceding quote are essentially synonymous. They each refer to a standard of review that preserves administrative discretion while assigning to the courts responsibility for preventing its abuse.

But just what is "discretion," anyway? Consider the following:

> . . . [P]erhaps the most characteristic instrument for making administrative decisions [is a rule that] . . . singles out a consideration as relevant, but provides no further rule for the application of the consideration. It therefore permits, indeed compels the administrator to resort to a whole complex of additional concepts and attitudes, official and personal, some of which he may explicitly formulate for the decision at hand, some of which he may not express, some of which he may be unaware of. . . . The mind focuses attention for a period of time on a group of authoritative decisional factors. But ultimately it reaches decision by an intuitive leap. It is this process which I would call the exercise of "discretion."

Louis Jaffe, Judicial Control of Administrative Action, 555–56 (1965).

Notice the key role played in Professor Jaffe's analysis by what the *State Farm* Court would later call the "relevant factors." Where administrative discretion is in play, a rule identifies various factors that an administrator has a *legal* obligation to consider as she exercises her discretion, but such a rule does not specify what policy judgments the administrator should make after considering them. For instance, § 109(b)(1) of the Clean Air Act instructs the EPA to develop primary ambient air quality standards "the attainment and maintenance of which in the judgment of the Administrator, ... allowing an adequate margin of safety, are requisite to protect the public health." 42 U.S.C. § 7409(b)(1). Thus, in developing such standards (or "NAAQSs"), the Administrator should, unsurprisingly, consider public health and safety. This statutory instruction obviously leaves the Administrator with a great deal of decisionmaking freedom as it does not provide remotely specific instructions concerning what levels of air pollutants are permissible.

Professor Jaffe also observed that some rules specify factors that an agency should *not* consider as it exercises policy discretion. For instance, judicial constructions of the Clean Air Act have settled that EPA should not consider implementation costs as it sets NAAQSs under its § 109(b)(1) authority. Therefore, any NAAQS based in part on such economic considerations would, in theory, be arbitrary and capricious due to the taint of an "impermissible factor" on the agency's decisionmaking process. *Cf. Whitman v. American Trucking Ass'ns, Inc.*, 531 U.S. 457, 471 n.4 (2001) (noting that a NAAQS based on "secret" consideration of implementation costs should be vacated as illegal).

Would it be arbitrary for NHTSA to consider economic costs in the course of setting a motor vehicle safety standard? Would it be arbitrary for NHTSA *not* to do so?

7. Politics, policy change, and arbitrariness review— *FCC v. Fox Television Stations, Inc.* Funny how the agency's regulatory approach discussed in *State Farm* had a way of changing every four years or so, no? Such changes in direction are, of course, to be expected in a system in which parties with different regulatory ideologies take turns exercising power based on mass elections. Accordingly, Justice Rehnquist in his partial dissent in *State Farm* noted that it is perfectly appropriate for an agency to change regulatory course to reflect a new administration's political outlook. More recently, in *Department of Commerce v. New York*, 2019 WL 2619437 (June 27, 2019), the Court realistically observed that "a court may not set aside an agency's policymaking decision solely because it might have been influenced by political considerations or prompted by an Administration's priorities. Agency policymaking is not a 'rarified technocratic process, unaffected by political considerations or the presence of Presidential power.'" *Id.* at *14 (quoting *Sierra Club v. Costle*, 657 F.2d 298, 408 (D.C. Cir. 1981)).

The Court's most revealing discussion of the relation of politics to arbitrariness review of policy changes appeared in a debate between Justices Scalia and Breyer in *FCC v. Fox Television Stations, Inc.*, 556 U.S. 502 (2009), which reviewed the FCC's decision to abandon its "fleeting expletives" policy. Congress has charged the FCC with the task of policing against "indecent" broadcasts. For many years, the agency followed a policy that it would not hold broadcasters liable for the broadcast of "fleeting expletives." Instead, "deliberate and repetitive use" was a prerequisite for a finding that a broadcast of nonliteral expletives was actionably indecent. But then Bono, Cher, and Nicole Ritchie all said variations of a word one really ought not say on television during various broadcasts on NBC and Fox. A congressional subcommittee responded by holding hearings in which it grilled FCC officials for failure to sanction indecent broadcasts. Following this treatment, the Commission determined that the Bono, Cher, and Ritchie broadcasts were actionably indecent, but it declined to sanction the broadcasting entities, NBC and Fox, because the broadcasts would have been permissible under the agency's earlier "fleeting expletives" precedents. To justify abandoning this policy, in the consolidated case involving Fox's broadcasts of Cher and Ritchie, the agency explained that its:

> ... prior "strict dichotomy between 'expletives' and 'descriptions or depictions of sexual or excretory functions' is artificial and does not make sense in light of the fact that an 'expletive's' power to offend derives from its sexual or excretory meaning." *Id.*, at 13308, ¶ 23. In the Commission's view, "granting an automatic exemption for 'isolated or fleeting' expletives unfairly forces viewers (including children)" to take "'the first blow'" and would allow broadcasters "to air expletives at all hours of a day so long as they did so one at a time." *Id.*, at 13309, ¶ 25.

Fox, 556 U.S. at 512–13 (Scalia, J.) (summarizing the FCC's explanation for its change in policy regarding the use of fleeting expletives). The FCC did not, however, advert to its grilling by the congressional subcommittee.

Justice Scalia, writing for a five-justice majority that included Justice Kennedy, held that the FCC's explanation survived review for arbitrariness. In the course of doing so, he explained that an agency, to provide a reasoned explanation for a policy change, must acknowledge awareness that it is making a change. It must also explain any rejection of factual findings that underlay its earlier policy and take into account "serious reliance interests" engendered by that policy. He stressed, however, that an agency's change in policy should not trigger a stricter standard of review:

> To be sure, the requirement that an agency provide reasoned explanation for its action would ordinarily demand that it display awareness that it is changing position. An agency may not, for example, depart from a prior policy *sub silentio* or simply disregard rules that are still on the books. And of course the agency must show that there are good reasons for the new policy. But it need not demonstrate to a court's satisfaction that the reasons for the new policy are *better* than the reasons for the old one; it suffices that the new policy is permissible under the statute, that there are good reasons for it, and that the agency *believes* it to be better, which the conscious change of course adequately indicates.

Fox, 556 U.S. at 515. In short, so long as the new policy is reasonable and legal, an agency can shift to it just because the agency *likes* the new policy better than the old one. This approach leaves space for an agency to choose among reasonable policy choices based on value judgments, which of course may change with electoral results.

By contrast, writing for a four-justice dissent, Justice Breyer, seeking to protect technocracy from politics, insisted that the law does not permit administrative agencies "to make policy choices for purely political reasons nor to rest them primarily upon unexplained policy preferences." *Fox*, 556 U.S. 547 (Breyer, J. dissenting). An explanation of a policy change therefore

> requires more than setting forth reasons why the new policy is a good one. It also requires the agency to answer the question, "Why did you change?" And a rational answer to this question typically requires a more complete explanation than would prove satisfactory were change itself not at issue. An (imaginary) administrator explaining why he chose a policy that requires driving on the right side, rather than the left side, of the road might say, "Well, one side seemed as good as the other, so I flipped a coin." But even assuming the rationality of that explanation for an initial choice, that explanation is not at all rational if offered to explain why the administrator changed driving practice, from right side to left side, 25 years later.

Id. at 549 (Breyer, J., dissenting) Muddying the waters, Justice Kennedy, who joined the relevant portion of Justice Scalia's opinion, also authored a solo concurrence in which he stated that he agreed with Justice Breyer that an agency seeking to justify a policy change "must explain why 'it now reject[s] the considerations that led it to adopt that initial policy.'" *Id.* at 535 (quoting Justice Breyer's dissent).

To see the potential impact of Justice Breyer's approach, consider his treatment of the Commission's "first blow" rationale. The Commission had explained that its abandoned policy "of granting an automatic exemption for isolated or fleeting expletives unfairly forces viewers (including children) to take the first blow." Justice Breyer responded that the "first blow" rationale could not explain a *"change"* in policy (his italics) because the Commission had long used this rationale to justify regulation of indecency even while at the same time maintaining its old fleeting expletives policy. *Id.* at 564 (Breyer, J., dissenting). Put another way, a problem that the FCC had known about for decades before its policy change could not, without further explanation, provide a sufficient basis for that policy change.

In sum, the *Fox* opinions present a choice between two approaches to the role that political preferences should play in judicial review of agency policy changes. Under one view (Scalia), a reviewing court should confine its inquiry to whether the new policy is supported by reasoned decisionmaking that takes into account the fact that the agency is changing its policy. This view leaves space for an agency to chop and change among "reasonable" policy options based on unstated political preferences. Under the other view (Breyer), the court should protect technocratic values by requiring agencies to answer the question, "Why change?" The members of the Court seemed to think that these two approaches are meaningfully different. By a 5-4 margin in *Fox*, they chose one approach or the other, but it wasn't immediately clear which one. Later case law has clarified that the Scalia approach controls. *See Encino Motorcars, LLC v. Navarro*, 136 S. Ct. 2117, 2126 (2016); *id.* at 2128 (Ginsburg,

J., concurring) (citing Justice Scalia's *Fox* analysis for the proposition that an agency need not demonstrate that a new policy is better than the old one it replaces).

8. Judicial ideology and arbitrariness review. Federal judges get their jobs in part because they know the right politicians. The arbitrariness standard of review is, by nature, open-ended; courts check whether an agency has been "reasonable"— whatever they may think that means—rather than whether an agency has violated some clear legal command. Does this combination of factors leave too much room for judges to impose their policy preferences on agencies under the guise of arbitrariness review?

Professors Sunstein and Miles investigated this question by analyzing every published appellate opinion issued between 1996 and 2006 that reviewed decisions by the EPA or NLRB under the arbitrariness or substantial evidence standards. Among their conclusions:

> Political commitments significantly influence the operation of hard look review in EPA and NLRB cases. When the agency decision is liberal, the Democratic validation rate is 72 percent and the Republican validation rate is 58 percent. When the agency decision is conservative, the Democratic validation rate drops to 55 percent and the Republican validation rate rises to 72 percent. For both Republican and Democratic appointees, then, the likelihood of a vote to validate is significantly affected by whether the agency's decision is liberal or conservative.

Thomas J. Miles & Cass R. Sunstein, *The Real World of Arbitrariness Review*, 75 U. Chic. L. Rev. 761, 767 (2008). Does this finding undermine the case for arbitrariness review of agency policy decisions? Or does it merely put numbers on an expected fact of life?

9. What should a court do when the agency's explanation for its action is arbitrary but looks curable? Remand without vacation. Suppose a court determines that an agency action fails review for arbitrariness because the agency's explanation for that action was defective. On its face, § 706(2) of the APA instructs the court to "set aside" that action. The court cannot fix the action by coming up with a better explanation without violating the *Chenery* principle (discussed at note 8 of subchapter 5A) and infringing on agency discretion. Subsequent to vacation of the agency action, the agency might exercise its discretion to take the action (or a similar one) again after developing a new rationale with sounder legal foundations. Or it might not.

Vacating a significant agency action, such as an important rule, can cause considerable disruption. This disruption might seem difficult to justify where it appears that the agency could fix the legal defect of its action with relative ease—e.g., by filling an analytical gap in its contemporaneous explanation. In response to such concerns, some courts, most notably the D.C. Circuit, have adopted a practice of *remand without vacation* where that outcome seems appropriate in light of (a) the level of disruption vacation would cause; and (b) the likelihood that the agency can rehabilitate its action. *See Allied-Signal, Inc. v. NRC*, 988 F.2d 146 (D.C. Cir. 1993). This remedy gives an agency the chance to address legal problems with its action without the disruption of vacation. The price for this benefit is that the agency action will remain in force after it has been found to be legally defective.

Not every judge thinks this practice is legal. *See Milk Train, Inc. v. Veneman*, 310 F.3d 747, 757 (D.C. Cir. 2002) (Sentelle, J., dissenting) (insisting that § 706 of the APA imposes a mandatory duty to set aside arbitrary action). For a leading scholar's alternative view that remand without vacation is well grounded in courts' equitable remedial powers, see Ronald M. Levin, *"Vacation" at Sea: Judicial Remedies and Equitable Discretion in Administrative Law*, 53 DUKE L.J. 291 (2003). *See also* Stephanie J. Tatham, *The Unusual Remedy of Remand Without Vacatur*, FINAL REPORT (ADMINISTRATIVE CONFERENCE OF THE UNITED STATES) (Jan. 3, 2014) (surveying courts' use of remand without vacation and academic commentary; concluding that this remedy should be regarded as valid under the APA).

3. Review of Law

Courts generally take the view that *they* are in charge of interpreting law. *Marbury v. Madison*, 5 U.S. 137, 177 (1803) (claiming for the courts the peculiar "province and duty . . . to say what the law is."). Their default position is that they interpret laws independently, without deferring to the views of nonjudicial actors. Thus, broadly speaking, the Supreme Court regards itself—not Congress or the President—as the arbiter of what the Constitution "means." Such judicial independence is commonly thought to play an integral role in maintaining the "rule of law" as it helps ensure that those charged with enforcing the law do not twist it to mean whatever they would like.

Administrative law, by way of the *Chevron* doctrine, among other devices, carves out substantial exceptions to the general principle of judicial interpretive control. The basic idea is that there are good reasons why courts should—either as a matter of policy or legal compulsion—give special weight to an agency's interpretations of laws it is charged with administering. Two core rationales for this stance are agency expertise and congressional delegation. In this vein, it is plausible to think that the EPA will often know better than the courts how best to make sense of a complicated statute such as the Clean Air Act (CAA); it is also plausible to think that Congress, by specifically charging EPA with the task of enforcing this statute, may have in some sense delegated power to the agency to determine what it means. Such reasoning leads to the conclusion that, although a court would not defer, for example, to the EPA's interpretation of the Due Process Clause, perhaps the court should defer to the EPA's interpretation of the CAA (or regulations that the agency has promulgated pursuant to it, for that matter).

Although the fundamental ideas underlying judicial deference to agency interpretations of law seem fairly straightforward, they have managed to flower into a complex body of law that attempts to specify: (a) what kinds of legal determinations by agencies warrant special deference; and (b) how much. The remainder of this chapter will work through some of the leading cases that speak to these matters.

a. Two Paradigms from Before the (R)evolution

We are not quite ready to rush off to systematic study of the *Chevron* doctrine. To make sense of both *Chevron* and the current state of the doctrine governing judicial review of agency statutory interpretations, it is helpful to understand some of the law that preceded *Chevron*. One reason is that it is almost always easier to understand a judicial opinion with some understanding of the legal backdrop informing it. Also, as you will see, the *Chevron* doctrine did not displace all of the pre-*Chevron* law on judicial review of agency statutory interpretations. Elements of the pre-*Chevron* law, notably including *Skidmore* deference, are still applied in some contexts today. Our last topic in this subchapter will address how courts are supposed to choose which of these deference doctrines to apply.

Lesson 5G.3.a. The WTC brought a § 7 enforcement action against Gallery, charging that it had violated § 5(b) of the WTCA in connection with its sale of hard apple cider under the "Apple Sue's" brand name. The labels for "Apple Sue's Cider" declare that it is "Nothing But Purest Apples!" The complaint against Gallery alleged that this label created a materially misleading impression that the cider is made entirely from freshly-pressed apples when in fact it is made in part from apple concentrate and contains preservatives. This enforcement action against Gallery marked the WTC's first assertion of regulatory authority over an alcoholic beverage made from a fruit other than grapes.

In the proceedings before the ALJ, Gallery, represented by its attorney, Abby, contested both the merits of the WTC's charge and, more to the present point, its regulatory authority to decide them. In Gallery's view, the WTC's statutory jurisdiction to regulate "wine" does not extend to apple cider, which is a different type of drink. As support for this argument, Gallery offered the testimony of an expert who explained that cider is a traditional drink made from apples that contain high levels of tannins and malic acid. By contrast, "apple wine" is generally made from dessert apples and has a much sweeter taste with less "bite." Apple cider typically has an alcohol content substantially less than 8%; higher percentages are commonly found in apple wine. To attain these higher alcohol levels, apple winemakers add additional sugar during the fermentation process. "Apple Sue's Cider" has an alcohol content of 8% and has levels of tannin and malic acid that are too high for the typical apple wine. The expert added that producers and consumers commonly regard apple wine and apple cider as different products. The WTC staff did not dispute any of this evidence.

Some potentially relevant legislative history appeared in a report on the WTCA issued by the Senate Committee on Beverage Regulation. This report states that "the statutory definition of 'wine' was intended to capture the common usage that alcoholic drinks made from raspberries, strawberries, and similar fruits are commonly considered 'fruit wines' by both producers and consumers." Gallery contended that this report demonstrated that Congress did not intend for the WTCA to regulate beverages understood by the public to be non-wines.

Bud the ALJ agreed that Apple Sue's Cider is not "wine" within the meaning of the WTCA and dismissed the complaint. On review, the WTC held otherwise, concluding both: (a) that Apple Sue's Cider fell within the agency's regulatory jurisdiction; and (b) that the "Nothing But Purest Apples" label was misleading. Assume that in the agency's decisional memorandum, it made the best available arguments in support of its claim of regulatory authority. Gallery has sought judicial review to overturn the agency's order, and Abby has made the best available arguments in response.

What, in your view, are the best arguments for and against the WTC's claim of authority to regulate Apple Sue's Cider? Feel free to look up dictionary definitions if they seem helpful. Which side should prevail on judicial review of this issue? (For the purposes of this lesson, don't read ahead to *Chevron* in the next subchapter.)

Background of *Skidmore v. Swift & Co.*

Employees of Swift & Co. agreed to spend several nights a week on company premises to respond to fire alarms. When not answering infrequent alarms, they stayed in a well-equipped "fire hall" with sleeping quarters, a pool table, a domino table, and a radio. The employees claimed that they were entitled to overtime under the Fair Labor Standards Act (FLSA) for this on-call time. The FLSA does not create a system for determining such disputes administratively. Instead, courts decide them. The FLSA does, however, create the post of Administrator with the power to initiate injunctive actions in court to require compliance with the Act. In the excerpt that follows, the Court discussed the level of deference that courts should give to the Administrator's views on construction and implementation of the Act. What is this level of deference (sometimes called "*Skidmore* respect")? What rationales support it? What role did the absence of administrative adjudication play in the Court's discussion? (You will want to remember this last query when you read note 2 discussing the *Hearst* doctrine.)

Skidmore v. Swift & Co.
323 U.S. 134 (1944)

Mr. Justice Jackson delivered the opinion of the Court.

Seven employees of the Swift and Company packing plant at Fort Worth, Texas, brought an action under the Fair Labor Standards Act, 29 U.S.C.A. § 201 et seq., to recover overtime, liquidated damages, and attorneys' fees, totaling approximately $77,000. The District Court rendered judgment denying this claim wholly, and the Circuit Court of Appeals for the Fifth Circuit affirmed.

It is not denied that the daytime employment of these persons was working time within the Act. Two were engaged in general fire hall duties and maintenance of fire-fighting equipment of the Swift plant. The others operated elevators or acted as relief men in fire duties. They worked from 7:00 a.m. to 3:30 p.m., with a half-hour lunch period, five days a week. They were paid weekly salaries.

Under their oral agreement of employment, however, petitioners undertook to stay in the fire hall on the Company premises, or within hailing distance, three and a half to four nights a week. This involved no task except to answer alarms, either because of fire or because the sprinkler was set off for some other reason. No fires occurred during the period in issue, the alarms were rare, and the time required for their answer rarely exceeded an hour. For each alarm answered the employees were paid in addition to their fixed compensation an agreed amount, fifty cents at first, and later sixty-four cents. The Company provided a brick fire hall equipped with steam heat and air-conditioned rooms. It provided sleeping quarters, a pool table, a domino table, and a radio. The men used their time in sleep or amusement as they saw fit, except that they were required to stay in or close by the fire hall and be ready to respond to alarms. It is stipulated that 'they agreed to remain in the fire hall and stay in it or within hailing distance, subject to call, in event of fire or other casualty, but were not required to perform any specific tasks during these periods of time, except in answering alarms.' The trial court found the evidentiary facts as stipulated; it made no findings of fact as such as to whether under the arrangement of the parties and the circumstances of this case . . . the fire hall duty or any part thereof constituted working time. It said, however, as a 'conclusion of law' that 'the time plaintiffs spent in the fire hall subject to call to answer fire alarms does not constitute hours worked, for which overtime compensation is due them under the Fair Labor Standards Act, as interpreted by the Administrator and the Courts,' and in its opinion observed, 'of course we know pursuing such pleasurable occupations or performing such personal chores does not constitute work.' The Circuit Court of Appeals affirmed.

. . . [W]e hold that no principle of law found either in the statute or in Court decisions precludes waiting time from also being working time. We have not attempted to, and we cannot, lay down a legal formula to resolve cases so varied in their facts as are the many situations in which employment involves waiting time. Whether in a concrete case such time falls within or without the Act is a question of fact to be resolved by appropriate findings of the trial court. This involves scrutiny and construction of the agreements between the particular parties, appraisal of their practical construction of the working agreement by conduct, consideration of the nature of the service, and its relation to the waiting time, and all of the surrounding circumstances. Facts may show that the employee was engaged to wait, or they way show that he waited to be engaged. His compensation may cover both waiting and task, or only performance of the task itself. Living quarters may in some situations be furnished as a facility of the task and in another as a part of its compensation. The law does not impose an arrangement upon the parties. It imposes upon the courts the task of finding what the arrangement was.

We do not minimize the difficulty of such an inquiry where the arrangements of the parties have not contemplated the problem posed by the statute. But it does not differ in nature or in the standards to guide judgment from that which frequently confronts courts where they must find retrospectively the effect of contracts as to matters which the parties failed to anticipate or explicitly to provide for.

Congress did not utilize the services of an administrative agency to find facts and to determine in the first instance whether particular cases fall within or without the Act. Instead, it put this responsibility on the courts. But it did create the office of Administrator, impose upon him a variety of duties, endow him with powers to inform himself of conditions in industries and employments subject to the Act, and put on him the duties of bringing injunction actions to restrain violations. Pursuit of his duties has accumulated a considerable experience in the problems of ascertaining working time in employments involving periods of inactivity and a knowledge of the customs prevailing in reference to their solution. From these he is obliged to reach conclusions as to conduct without the law, so that he should seek injunctions to stop it, and that within the law, so that he has no call to interfere. He has set forth his views of the application of the Act under different circumstances in an interpretative bulletin and in informal rulings. They provide a practical guide to employers and employees as to how the office representing the public interest in its enforcement will seek to apply it. *Wage and Hour Division, Interpretative Bulletin* No. 13.

The Administrator thinks the problems presented by inactive duty require a flexible solution, rather than the all-in or all-out rules respectively urged by the parties in this case, and his Bulletin endeavors to suggest standards and examples to guide in particular situations. In some occupations, it says, periods of inactivity are not properly counted as working time even though the employee is subject to call. Examples are an operator of a small telephone exchange where the switchboard is in her home and she ordinarily gets several hours of uninterrupted sleep each night; or a pumper of a stripper well or watchman of a lumber camp during the off season, who may be on duty twenty-four hours a day but ordinarily 'has a normal night's sleep, has ample time in which to eat his meals, and has a certain amount of time for relaxation and entirely private pursuits.' Exclusion of all such hours the Administrator thinks may be justified. In general, the answer depends 'upon the degree to which the employee is free to engage in personal activities during periods of idleness when he is subject to call and the number of consecutive hours that the employee is subject to call without being required to perform active work.' 'Hours worked are not limited to the time spent in active labor but include time given by the employee to the employer. . . .'

The facts of this case do not fall within any of the specific examples given, but the conclusion of the Administrator, as expressed in the brief amicus curiae, is that the general tests which he has suggested point to the exclusion of sleeping and eating time of these employees from the work-week and the inclusion of all other on-call time: although the employees were required to remain on the premises during the entire time, the evidence shows that they were very rarely interrupted in their normal sleeping and eating time, and these are pursuits of a purely private nature which would presumably occupy the employees' time whether they were on duty or not and which apparently could be pursued adequately and comfortably in the required circumstances; the rest of the time is different because there is nothing in the record to suggest that, even though pleasurably spent, it was spent in the ways the men would have chosen had they been free to do so.

There is no statutory provision as to what, if any, deference courts should pay to the Administrator's conclusions. And, while we have given them notice, we have had no occasion to try to prescribe their influence. The rulings of this Administrator are not reached as a result of hearing adversary proceedings in which he finds facts from evidence and reaches conclusions of law from findings of fact. They are not, of course, conclusive, even in the cases with which they directly deal, much less in those to which they apply only by analogy. They do not constitute an interpretation of the Act or a standard for judging factual situations which binds a district court's processes, as an authoritative pronouncement of a higher court might do. But the Administrator's policies are made in pursuance of official duty, based upon more specialized experience and broader investigations and information than is likely to come to a judge in a particular case. They do determine the policy which will guide applications for enforcement by injunction on behalf of the Government. Good administration of the Act and good judicial administration alike require that the standards of public enforcement and those for determining private rights shall be at variance only where justified by very good reasons. The fact that the Administrator's policies and standards are not reached by trial in adversary form does not mean that they are not entitled to respect. This Court has long given considerable and in some cases decisive weight to Treasury Decisions and to interpretative regulations of the Treasury and of other bodies that were not of adversary origin.

We consider that the rulings, interpretations and opinions of the Administrator under this Act, while not controlling upon the courts by reason of their authority, do constitute a body of experience and informed judgment to which courts and litigants may properly resort for guidance. The weight of such a judgment in a particular case will depend upon the thoroughness evident in its consideration, the validity of its reasoning, its consistency with earlier and later pronouncements, and all those factors which give it power to persuade, if lacking power to control.

. . . [I]n this case, although the District Court referred to the Administrator's Bulletin, its evaluation and inquiry were apparently restricted by its notion that waiting time may not be work, an understanding of the law which we hold to be erroneous. Accordingly, the judgment is reversed and the cause remanded for further proceedings consistent herewith.

Reversed.

Notes

1. *Skidmore* **deference.** What is the rationale for so-called *Skidmore* deference? What does its practice require of a reviewing court? What aspects of an agency's decision affect or should affect the "weight" of such deference?

2. *Hearst* and "mixed questions" of law and fact. In 1944 the Supreme Court issued not one but two opinions with lasting implications for judicial review of agency action. One of them was *Skidmore*. The other was *NLRB v. Hearst Publications, Inc.*, 322 U.S. 111 (1944), which stands for the ideas that the courts are in charge of determining pure questions of statutory interpretation but that they should defer to agency decisions regarding how to apply broad statutory terms to specific facts.

To tackle *Hearst*, start with the proposition that statements about "evidentiary facts" use language that avoids legal terms of art to characterize events that occur in the world. For instance, the proposition, "the defendant dropped a banana peel," is a matter of evidentiary fact. Determinations of "ultimate fact" (or "material fact") cloak evidentiary facts in language with legal significance. For instance, one might infer from the (evidentiary) fact that the defendant dropped a banana peel the (ultimate) fact that the defendant was "negligent." To use some of Judge Frank's language from the remand of *Universal Camera*, determinations of ultimate fact are the result of "derivative" or "secondary" inferences that decisionmakers draw from evidentiary facts. (See note 2 following *Universal Camera* and *Penasquitos* above.) Recall also from *Universal Camera* that judicial review of such factual determinations is supposed to be quite deferential.

Of course, any application of a legal term of art to a given set of facts about the world may raise problems concerning the legal term's meaning—one cannot decide who has been "negligent" without some notion of what this term means. Courts therefore sometimes speak of such determinations as presenting "mixed questions" of law and fact. The upshot of all this nomenclature is that several phrases—"ultimate fact," "material fact," "derivative inference," "secondary inference," and "mixed question"—all refer to the problem of characterizing facts in language with legal significance.

One can contrast "mixed questions" of law and fact with "pure" questions of law. By definition, it is impossible to determine a mixed question without knowing the facts of a particular case (e.g., did the defendant drop a banana peel?). By contrast, one can decide a pure question of law without knowing any particular facts about what particular person did what to whom. For instance, one does not need to know whether a given person ran a red light to determine whether running a red light is negligent per se.

In the *Hearst* case, the Court reviewed the NLRB's determination that newspaper-distributors called "newsboys" were "employees" within the meaning of the National Labor Relations Act. The NLRB's decision meant that the newsboys had a right to bargain collectively with their employers. This task required the Court to confront both a pure question of statutory interpretation and a mixed question of law and fact. The pure question was whether the term "employee" as used by the NLRA incorporates by reference common law standards for establishing an employment relationship, or whether its meaning is to be determined entirely by reference to the terms and purpose of the statute. Applying its own independent judgment, the Court held that statutory sources, not common law, determine the meaning of "employee." In essence, the Court said that the meaning of "employee" in any particular situation was to be determined in light of the statutory goal to "bring industrial peace," not by common-law concepts that may have no relationship to that goal.

This determination of "pure" law left open the mixed question of whether the newboys were "employees" as that term is used in the NLRA. To make this determination, one needs to know how the Hearst-newsboy relationship relates to the goal of achieving industrial peace. The Court explained that, at least where Congress has assigned the initial determination of the facts of a case to an agency, courts should defer to reasonable administrative determinations of such mixed questions:

> It is not necessary in this case to make a completely definitive limitation around the term 'employee.' That task has been assigned primarily to the agency created by Congress to administer the Act. Determination of 'where all the conditions of the relation require protection' involves inquiries for the Board charged with this duty. Everyday experience in the administration of the statute gives it familiarity with the circumstances and backgrounds of employment relationships in various industries, with the abilities and needs of the workers for self organization and collective action, and with the adaptability of collective bargaining for the peaceful settlement of their disputes with their employers. The experience thus acquired must be brought frequently to bear on the question who is an employee under the Act. Resolving that question, like determining whether unfair labor practices have been committed, 'belongs to the usual administrative routine' of the Board. *Gray v. Powell*, 314 U.S. 402, 411.

> In making that body's determinations as to the facts in these matters conclusive, if supported by evidence, Congress entrusted to it primarily the decision whether the evidence establishes the material facts. Hence in reviewing the Board's ultimate conclusions, it is not the court's function to substitute its own inferences of fact for the Board's, when the latter have support in the record. *Undoubtedly questions of statutory interpretation*, especially when arising in the first instance in judicial proceedings, *are for the courts to resolve, giving appropriate weight to the judgment of those whose special duty is to administer the questioned statute*. But where the question is one of *specific application of a broad statutory term* in a proceeding in which the agency administering the statute must determine it initially, *the reviewing court's function is limited*. Like the commissioner's determination under the Longshoremen's & Harbor Workers' Act, or that he was injured 'in the course of his employment', and the Federal Communications Commission's determination that one company is under the 'control' of another, *the Board's determination that specified persons are 'employees'*

under this Act is to be accepted if it has 'warrant in the record' and a reasonable basis in law.

In this case the Board found that the designated newsboys work continuously and regularly, rely upon their earnings for the support of themselves and their families, and have their total wages influenced in large measure by the publishers who dictate their buying and selling prices, fix their markets and control their supply of papers. Their hours of work and their efforts on the job are supervised and to some extent prescribed by the publishers or their agents. Much of their sales equipment and advertising materials is furnished by the publishers with the intention that it be used for the publisher's benefit. Stating that 'the primary consideration in the determination of the applicability of the statutory definition is whether effectuation of the declared policy and purposes of the Act comprehend securing to the individual the rights guaranteed and protection afforded by the Act,' the Board concluded that the newsboys are employees. The record sustains the Board's findings and there is ample basis in the law for its conclusion. [Emphasis added.]

In the preceding passage, what justifications does the Court offer for reviewing mixed questions regarding "specific application of a broad statutory term" deferentially? What approach does the Court prescribe for pure questions of statutory interpretation? Can you see the shadow of *Skidmore* anywhere?

3. Functional analysis. In a discussion of the scope of the deferential clear-error standard governing appellate review of district court fact-finding, Judge Posner has offered the following explanation for deferential review of mixed-questions:

The proper standard of review depends on the character of the ruling sought to be reviewed. If it is a ruling on a pure question of law, review is plenary because it is intolerable to have the law differ from district judge to district judge. If it is a pure question of fact — a "who did what where when and to whom" kind of question, "pure" in the sense that no legal knowledge or instruction is necessary to answer it — then the correct standard is clear error.

If it is a "mixed" question of law and fact or, the same thing under a different label, an "ultimate" question of fact — that is, if it is the application of a legal standard (such as negligence) to the pure facts (what the defendant did) to yield a legal conclusion (the defendant was or was not negligent) — then again, except in those few, mainly constitutional cases in which the Supreme Court has decreed plenary review of such determinations, the clear-error standard governs. The application of a legal rule or standard to the particular facts of particular cases will yield different outcomes from case to case depending on the facts of the individual case. So uniformity of outcome is unattainable; and as divergent applications of law to fact do not unsettle the law—doctrine is unaffected—a heavy appellate hand in these cases is unnecessary to assure the law's clarity and coherence.

Then too the court that finds the facts will know them better than the reviewing court will, and so its application of the law to the facts is likely to be more accurate.

Thomas v. General Motors Acceptance Corp., 288 F.3d 305, 307–308 (7th Cir. 2002) (internal citations omitted).

4. The continuing relevance of mixed questions in federal law. The mixed question concept is an important one to master in part because it can apply in a wide variety of contexts beyond administrative law—*cf.* Judge Posner's application of it to "negligence" above. In the particular context of federal administrative law, however, the *Hearst* approach has been eclipsed by the *Chevron* doctrine, which will appear in its full glory in our next case excerpt. Still, the *Hearst* approach certainly has not disappeared from the law, and, to understand the significance of *Chevron*, it is important to have a solid grasp of the doctrinal forms that preceded it. For a thoughtful, revisionist look at this topic that concludes that the Supreme Court still adheres to *Hearst* principles, see John H. Reese, *Bursting the* Chevron *Bubble: Clarifying Scope of Review in Troubled Times*, 73 FORD. L. REV. 1103 (2004).

b. The Chevron (R)evolution

The *Chevron* doctrine has come up any number of times in your reading of this casebook. Now, at last, you read an excerpt from *Chevron* itself. The *Chevron* doctrine has been characterized as the counter-*Marbury* of the administrative state—putting agencies rather than courts primarily in charge of determining statutory meaning. The author of the *Chevron* opinion, Justice Stevens, did not think so, however. He long maintained that the opinion simply applied well-established principles of deference. Regardless of whether *Chevron* changed everything or very little, you will need to be able to speak its language—if only to signal your literacy in administrative law to judges and other attorneys. To this end, you will want to identify precisely *Chevron*'s framework for deference as well as the Court's justifications for it. Do you find these justifications persuasive?

Lesson 5G.3.b. In 1984, the Supreme Court issued *Chevron, U.S.A., Inc. v. NRDC*, which is excerpted below. It has been cited and dissected in thousands of cases and law review articles over the last thirty-five years. Some regard it as the most important administrative law case of the modern era; others have concluded that *Chevron* created less substantive change than meets the eye. Be this debate as it may, no competent lawyer would address the problem of determining the meaning of a federal agency's organic statute without considering the potential implications of *Chevron*. In our preceding lesson, we confronted the problem of whether the WTC has jurisdiction over "Apple Sue's Cider." How does *Chevron* change judicial review of this point, if at all?

Background of *Chevron, U.S.A., Inc. v. NRDC*

The Clean Air Act Amendments of 1977 established an expensive permitting process applicable to "new or modified stationary sources" of air pollution in "non-attainment" states that had not yet managed to comply with standards created by EPA pursuant to the Clean Air Act. The new provisions naturally raised the problem of defining "stationary source." More specifically, suppose that a plant contains four smokestacks. Is each smokestack an individual "stationary source"? Or do they together constitute just one? This latter characterization implicates the "bubble concept," which encases an entire plant in a metaphorical bubble. Equipment in the plant may be added or altered, without triggering permitting requirements, so long as the total amount of emissions escaping the bubble does not increase.

To grasp the regulatory significance of these bubbles, now suppose that the four smokestacks in our example each emit 100 tons per year of air pollutants. The owner wishes to add new, super-efficient manufacturing equipment expected to double production. It will also, however, require a fifth smokestack that is also expected to emit 100 tons per year of air pollutants. If the bubble concept applies, the owner need not go through a difficult permitting process so long as it can shave 25 tons per year from the emissions of each of the four old smokestacks. This approach would keep total emissions escaping the bubble at 400 tons per year, but with greater production. If "stationary source" refers to individual smokestacks, however, then the new equipment will require permitting, including meeting some expensive pollution-reduction requirements. If the expense is too great, the owner will forgo building the fifth smokestack.

The Clean Air Act Amendments of 1977 do not contain any express provisions clearly governing whether "stationary source," as used by that statute, permits application of the "bubble concept." The EPA struggled for several years to determine its stance on this issue. In August 1980, the agency promulgated a rule that adopted a bifurcated approach that required application of the bubble concept for programs designed to *maintain* air quality but barred its application for programs designed to *improve* air quality in "nonattainment" states. The agency relied heavily on two recent D.C. Circuit court opinions to reach this result. In October 1981, after the Reagan administration had swept into power on a deregulatory agenda, the agency reversed course. Its new rule allowed "nonattainment" states implementing the permitting program to apply the bubble concept and adopt a plantwide definition of "stationary source." The Natural Resources Defense Council challenged this rule, and the D.C. Circuit, following its own earlier decisions, set the rule aside. The Supreme Court reversed, upholding the EPA's new definition as a "permissible construction of the statute which seeks to accommodate progress in reducing air pollution with economic growth."

Along the path to this conclusion, the Court accidentally revolutionized the law of judicial deference with the *Chevron* two-step, which you have already encountered repeatedly in this course. As you read the excerpt below, look for any available guidance concerning the nature of these steps and how to apply them. Examine carefully how the Court deployed the available statutory language, legislative history, and policy concerns. In particular, how does the Court's treatment of policy in *Chevron* compare to its treatment of policy in *State Farm*? On a broader note, what rationales justify *Chevron* deference? Are they persuasive?

Chevron, U.S.A., Inc. v. Natural Resources Defense Council
467 U.S. 837 (1984)

Justice Stevens delivered the opinion of the Court.

In the Clean Air Act Amendments of 1977, Congress enacted certain requirements applicable to States that had not achieved the national air quality standards established by the Environmental Protection Agency (EPA) pursuant to earlier legislation. The amended Clean Air Act required these "nonattainment" States to establish a permit program regulating "new or modified major stationary sources" of air pollution. Generally, a permit may not be issued for a new or modified major stationary source unless several stringent conditions are met. The EPA regulation promulgated to implement this permit requirement allows a State to adopt a plantwide definition of the term "stationary source."[2] Under this definition, an existing plant that contains several pollution-emitting devices may install or modify one piece of equipment without meeting the permit conditions if the alteration will not increase the total emissions from the plant. The question presented by these cases is whether EPA's decision to allow States to treat all of the pollution-emitting devices within the same industrial grouping as though they were encased within a single "bubble" is based on a reasonable construction of the statutory term "stationary source."

I

The EPA regulations containing the plantwide definition of the term stationary source were promulgated on October 14, 1981. Respondents filed a timely petition for review in the United States Court of Appeals for the District of Columbia Circuit pursuant to 42 U.S.C. § 7607(b)(1). The Court of Appeals set aside the regulations.

The court observed that the relevant part of the amended Clean Air Act "does not explicitly define what Congress envisioned as a 'stationary source, to which the permit program . . . should apply," and further stated that the precise issue was not "squarely addressed in the legislative history." In light of its conclusion that the legislative history bearing on the question was "at best contradictory," it reasoned

---

2. "(i) 'Stationary source' means any building, structure, facility, or installation which emits or may emit any air pollutant subject to regulation under the Act. "(ii) 'Building, structure, facility, or installation' means all of the pollutant-emitting activities which belong to the same industrial grouping, are located on one or more contiguous or adjacent properties, and are under the control of the same person (or persons under common control) except the activities of any vessel." 40 CFR §§ 51.18(j)(1)(i) and (ii) (1983).

that "the purposes of the nonattainment program should guide our decision here." Based on two of its precedents concerning the applicability of the bubble concept to certain Clean Air Act programs, the court stated that the bubble concept was "mandatory" in programs designed merely to maintain existing air quality, but held that it was "inappropriate" in programs enacted to improve air quality. Since the purpose of the permit program—its *"raison d'être,"* in the court's view—was to improve air quality, the court held that the bubble concept was inapplicable in these cases under its prior precedents. It therefore set aside the regulations embodying the bubble concept as contrary to law. We granted certiorari to review that judgment, and we now reverse.

The basic legal error of the Court of Appeals was to adopt a static judicial definition of the term "stationary source" when it had decided that Congress itself had not commanded that definition. Respondents do not defend the legal reasoning of the Court of Appeals. Nevertheless, since this Court reviews judgments, not opinions, we must determine whether the Court of Appeals' legal error resulted in an erroneous judgment on the validity of the regulations.

II

When a court reviews an agency's construction of the statute which it administers, it is confronted with two questions. First, always, is the question whether Congress has directly spoken to the precise question at issue. If the intent of Congress is clear, that is the end of the matter; for the court, as well as the agency, must give effect to the unambiguously expressed intent of Congress.[9] If, however, the court determines Congress has not directly addressed the precise question at issue, the court does not simply impose its own construction on the statute, as would be necessary in the absence of an administrative interpretation. Rather, if the statute is silent or ambiguous with respect to the specific issue, the question for the court is whether the agency's answer is based on a permissible construction of the statute.[11]

"The power of an administrative agency to administer a congressionally created . . . program necessarily requires the formulation of policy and the making of rules to fill any gap left, implicitly or explicitly, by Congress." *Morton v. Ruiz*, 415 U.S. 199, 231 (1974). If Congress has explicitly left a gap for the agency to fill, there is an express delegation of authority to the agency to elucidate a specific provision of the statute by regulation. Such legislative regulations are given controlling weight unless they are arbitrary, capricious, or manifestly contrary to the statute. Sometimes the legislative delegation to an agency on a particular question is implicit rather than

---

9. The judiciary is the final authority on issues of statutory construction and must reject administrative constructions which are contrary to clear congressional intent. [Massive string cite omitted.] If a court, employing traditional tools of statutory construction, ascertains that Congress had an intention on the precise question at issue, that intention is the law and must be given effect.

11. The court need not conclude that the agency construction was the only one it permissibly could have adopted to uphold the construction, or even the reading the court would have reached if the question initially had arisen in a judicial proceeding. [String cite omitted.]

explicit. In such a case, a court may not substitute its own construction of a statutory provision for a reasonable interpretation made by the administrator of an agency.

We have long recognized that considerable weight should be accorded to an executive department's construction of a statutory scheme it is entrusted to administer, and the principle of deference to administrative interpretations

"has been consistently followed by this Court whenever decision as to the meaning or reach of a statute has involved reconciling conflicting policies, and a full understanding of the force of the statutory policy in the given situation has depended upon more than ordinary knowledge respecting the matters subjected to agency regulations. See, *e.g., National Broadcasting Co. v. United States*, 319 U.S. 190; *Labor Board v. Hearst Publications, Inc.*, 322 U.S. 111; *Republic Aviation Corp. v. Labor Board*, 324 U.S. 793; *Securities & Exchange Comm'n v. Chenery Corp.*, 332 U.S. 194; *Labor Board v. Seven-Up Bottling Co.*, 344 U.S. 344.

". . . If this choice represents a reasonable accommodation of conflicting policies that were committed to the agency's care by the statute, we should not disturb it unless it appears from the statute or its legislative history that the accommodation is not one that Congress would have sanctioned."
United States v. Shimer, 367 U.S. 374, 382, 383 (1961).

Accord Capital Cities Cable, Inc. v. Crisp, 467 U.S. 691, 699–700 (1984).

In light of these well-settled principles it is clear that the Court of Appeals misconceived the nature of its role in reviewing the regulations at issue. Once it determined, after its own examination of the legislation, that Congress did not actually have an intent regarding the applicability of the bubble concept to the permit program, the question before it was not whether in its view the concept is "inappropriate" in the general context of a program designed to improve air quality, but whether the Administrator's view that it is appropriate in the context of this particular program is a reasonable one. Based on the examination of the legislation and its history which follows, we agree with the Court of Appeals that Congress did not have a specific intention on the applicability of the bubble concept in these cases, and conclude that the EPA's use of that concept here is a reasonable policy choice for the agency to make.

III

In the 1950's and the 1960's Congress enacted a series of statutes designed to encourage and to assist the States in curtailing air pollution. The Clean Air Amendments of 1970 "sharply increased federal authority and responsibility in the continuing effort to combat air pollution," but continued to assign "primary responsibility for assuring air quality" to the several States. Section 109 of the 1970 Amendments directed the EPA to promulgate National Ambient Air Quality Standards (NAAQS's) and § 110 directed the States to develop plans (SIP's) to implement the standards within specified deadlines. In addition, § 111 provided that major new sources of pollution would be required to conform to technology-based performance standards;

the EPA was directed to publish a list of categories of sources of pollution and to establish new source performance standards (NSPS) for each. Section 111(e) prohibited the operation of any new source in violation of a performance standard.

Section 111(a) defined the terms that are to be used in setting and enforcing standards of performance for new stationary sources. It provided:

"For purposes of this section: . . .

"(3) The term 'stationary source' means any building, structure, facility, or installation which emits or may emit any air pollutant."

In the 1970 Amendments that definition was not only applicable to the NSPS program required by § 111, but also was made applicable to a requirement of § 110 that each state implementation plan contain a procedure for reviewing the location of any proposed new source and preventing its construction if it would preclude the attainment or maintenance of national air quality standards.

In due course, the EPA promulgated NAAQS's, approved SIP's, and adopted detailed regulations governing NSPS's for various categories of equipment. In one of its programs, the EPA used a plantwide definition of the term "stationary source." In 1974, it issued NSPS's for the nonferrous smelting industry that provided that the standards would not apply to the modification of major smelting units if their increased emissions were offset by reductions in other portions of the same plant.[17] . . .

IV

The Clean Air Act Amendments of 1977 are a lengthy, detailed, technical, complex, and comprehensive response to a major social issue. A small portion of the statute expressly deals with nonattainment areas. The focal point of this controversy is one phrase in that portion of the Amendments.[22]

Basically, the statute required each State in a nonattainment area to prepare and obtain approval of a new SIP by July 1, 1979. . . . [T]he SIP's were required to contain a number of provisions designed to achieve the goals as expeditiously as possible.

Most significantly for our purposes, the statute provided that each plan shall

"(6) require permits for the construction and operation of new or modified major stationary sources in accordance with section 173. . . ."

Before issuing a permit, § 173 requires (1) the state agency to determine that there will be sufficient emissions reductions in the region to offset the emissions from the new source and also to allow for reasonable further progress toward attainment, or that the increased emissions will not exceed an allowance for growth established pursuant to § 172(b)(5); (2) the applicant to certify that his other sources in the

---

17. The Court of Appeals ultimately held that this plantwide approach was prohibited by the 1970 Act, see *ASARCO Inc.*, 578 F.2d, at 325–327. This decision was rendered after enactment of the 1977 Amendments, and hence the standard was in effect when Congress enacted the 1977 Amendments.

22. Specifically, the controversy in these cases involves the meaning of the term "major stationary sources" in § 172(b)(6) of the Act, 42 U.S.C. § 7502(b)(6).

State are in compliance with the SIP, (3) the agency to determine that the applicable SIP is otherwise being implemented, and (4) the proposed source to comply with the lowest achievable emission rate (LAER).

The 1977 Amendments contain no specific reference to the "bubble concept." Nor do they contain a specific definition of the term "stationary source," though they did not disturb the definition of "stationary source" contained in § 111(a)(3), applicable by the terms of the Act to the NSPS program. Section 302(j), however, defines the term "major stationary source" as follows:

> "(j) Except as otherwise expressly provided, the terms 'major stationary source' and 'major emitting facility' mean any stationary facility or source of air pollutants which directly emits, or has the potential to emit, one hundred tons per year or more of any air pollutant (including any major emitting facility or source of fugitive emissions of any such pollutant, as determined by rule by the Administrator)." . . .

VI

As previously noted, prior to the 1977 Amendments, the EPA had adhered to a plantwide definition of the term "source" under a NSPS program. After adoption of the 1977 Amendments, proposals for a plantwide definition were considered in at least three formal proceedings.

In January 1979, . . . [for] those areas that did not have a revised SIP in effect by July 1979, the EPA rejected the plantwide definition; on the other hand, it expressly concluded that the plantwide approach would be permissible in certain circumstances if authorized by an approved SIP. . . .

In April, and again in September 1979, the EPA published additional comments in which it indicated that revised SIP's could adopt the plantwide definition of source in nonattainment areas in certain circumstances. On the latter occasion, the EPA made a formal rulemaking proposal that would have permitted the use of the "bubble concept" for new installations within a plant as well as for modifications of existing units. . . .

Significantly, the EPA expressly noted that the word "source" might be given a plantwide definition for some purposes and a narrower definition for other purposes. It wrote:

> "Source means any building structure, facility, or installation which emits or may emit any regulated pollutant. 'Building, structure, facility or installation' means plant in PSD areas and in nonattainment areas except where the growth prohibitions would apply or where no adequate SIP exists or is being carried out."[28]

---

28. In its explanation of why the use of the "bubble concept" was especially appropriate in preventing significant deterioration (PSD) in clean air areas, the EPA stated: "In addition, application of the bubble on a plant-wide basis encourages voluntary upgrading of equipment, and growth in productive capacity."

The EPA's summary of its proposed Ruling discloses a flexible rather than rigid definition of the term "source" to implement various policies and programs. . . .

In August 1980, however, the EPA adopted a regulation that, in essence, applied the basic reasoning of the Court of Appeals in these cases. The EPA took particular note of the two then-recent Court of Appeals decisions, which had created the bright-line rule that the "bubble concept" should be employed in a program designed to maintain air quality but not in one designed to enhance air quality. Relying heavily on those cases, EPA adopted a dual definition of "source" for nonattainment areas that required a permit whenever a change in either the entire plant, or one of its components, would result in a significant increase in emissions even if the increase was completely offset by reductions elsewhere in the plant. The EPA expressed the opinion that this interpretation was "more consistent with congressional intent" than the plantwide definition because it "would bring in more sources or modifications for review," but its primary legal analysis was predicated on the two Court of Appeals decisions.

In 1981 a new administration took office and initiated a "Government-wide reexamination of regulatory burdens and complexities." 46 Fed.Reg. 16281. In the context of that review, the EPA reevaluated the various arguments that had been advanced in connection with the proper definition of the term "source" and concluded that the term should be given the same definition in both nonattainment areas and PSD areas.

In explaining its conclusion, the EPA first noted that the definitional issue was not squarely addressed in either the statute or its legislative history and therefore that the issue involved an agency "judgment as how to best carry out the Act." It then set forth several reasons for concluding that the plantwide definition was more appropriate. It pointed out that the dual definition "can act as a disincentive to new investment and modernization by discouraging modifications to existing facilities" and "can actually retard progress in air pollution control by discouraging replacement of older, dirtier processes or pieces of equipment with new, cleaner ones." Moreover, the new definition "would simplify EPA's rules by using the same definition of 'source' for PSD, nonattainment new source review and the construction moratorium. This reduces confusion and inconsistency." Finally, the agency explained that additional requirements that remained in place would accomplish the fundamental purposes of achieving attainment with NAAQS's as expeditiously as possible. These conclusions were expressed in a proposed rulemaking in August 1981 that was formally promulgated in October.

VII

In this Court respondents expressly reject the basic rationale of the Court of Appeals' decision. That court viewed the statutory definition of the term "source" as sufficiently flexible to cover either a plantwide definition, a narrower definition covering each unit within a plant, or a dual definition that could apply to both the entire "bubble" and its components. It interpreted the policies of the statute, however, to mandate the plantwide definition in programs designed to maintain clean air and to forbid it in programs designed to improve air quality. Respondents place a fundamentally different construction on the statute. They contend that the text of the Act requires the EPA to use a dual definition—if either a component of a plant, or the plant as a whole, emits over 100 tons of pollutant, it is a major stationary source. They thus contend that the EPA rules adopted in 1980, insofar as they apply to the maintenance of the quality of clean air, as well as the 1981 rules which apply to nonattainment areas, violate the statute.

Statutory Language

The definition of the term "stationary source" in § 111(a)(3) refers to "any building, structure, facility, or installation" which emits air pollution. This definition is applicable only to the NSPS program by the express terms of the statute; the text of the statute does not make this definition applicable to the permit program. Petitioners therefore maintain that there is no statutory language even relevant to ascertaining the meaning of stationary source in the permit program aside from § 302(j), which defines the term "major stationary source." We disagree with petitioners on this point.

The definition in § 302(j) tells us what the word "major" means—a source must emit at least 100 tons of pollution to qualify—but it sheds virtually no light on the meaning of the term "stationary source." It does equate a source with a facility—a "major emitting facility" and a "major stationary source" are synonymous under § 302(j). The ordinary meaning of the term "facility" is some collection of integrated elements which has been designed and constructed to achieve some purpose. Moreover, it is certainly no affront to common English usage to take a reference to a major facility or a major source to connote an entire plant as opposed to its constituent parts. Basically, however, the language of § 302(j) simply does not compel any given interpretation of the term "source."

Respondents recognize that, and hence point to § 111(a)(3). Although the definition in that section is not literally applicable to the permit program, it sheds as much light on the meaning of the word "source" as anything in the statute. As respondents point out, use of the words "building, structure, facility, or installation," as the definition of source, could be read to impose the permit conditions on an individual building that is a part of a plant. A "word may have a character of its own not to be submerged by its association." On the other hand, the meaning of a word must be ascertained in the context of achieving particular objectives, and the words associated with it may indicate that the true meaning of the series is to convey a common idea. The language may reasonably be interpreted to impose the requirement on any discrete, but integrated, operation which pollutes. This gives meaning to all of the terms—a single building, not part of a larger operation, would be covered if it emits more than 100 tons of pollution, as would any facility, structure, or installation. Indeed, the language itself implies a "bubble concept" of sorts: each enumerated item would seem to be treated as if it were encased in a bubble. While respondents insist that each of these terms must be given a discrete meaning, they also argue that § 111(a)(3) defines "source" as that term is used in § 302(j). The latter section, however, equates a source with a facility, whereas the former defines "source" as a facility, among other items.

We are not persuaded that parsing of general terms in the text of the statute will reveal an actual intent of Congress. We know full well that this language is not dispositive; the terms are overlapping and the language is not precisely directed to the question of the applicability of a given term in the context of a larger operation. To the extent any congressional "intent" can be discerned from this language, it would appear that the listing of overlapping, illustrative terms was intended to enlarge, rather than to confine, the scope of the agency's power to regulate particular sources in order to effectuate the policies of the Act.

Legislative History

In addition, respondents argue that the legislative history and policies of the Act foreclose the plantwide definition, and that the EPA's interpretation is not entitled to deference because it represents a sharp break with prior interpretations of the Act.

Based on our examination of the legislative history, we agree with the Court of Appeals that it is unilluminating. The general remarks pointed to by respondents "were obviously not made with this narrow issue in mind and they cannot be said to demonstrate a Congressional desire. . . ." . . . We find that the legislative history as a whole is silent on the precise issue before us. It is, however, consistent with the view that the EPA should have broad discretion in implementing the policies of the 1977 Amendments.

More importantly, that history plainly identifies the policy concerns that motivated the enactment; the plantwide definition is fully consistent with one of those concerns — the allowance of reasonable economic growth — and, whether or not we believe it most effectively implements the other, we must recognize that the EPA has advanced a reasonable explanation for its conclusion that the regulations serve the environmental objectives as well. Indeed, its reasoning is supported by the public record developed in the rulemaking process,[36] as well as by certain private studies.[37]

Our review of the EPA's varying interpretations of the word "source"—both before and after the 1977 Amendments—convinces us that the agency primarily responsible for administering this important legislation has consistently interpreted

---

36. See, for example, the statement of the New York State Department of Environmental Conservation, pointing out that denying a source owner flexibility in selecting options made it "simpler and cheaper to operate old, more polluting sources than to trade up. . . ." App. 128–129.

37. "Economists have proposed that economic incentives be substituted for the cumbersome administrative-legal framework. The objective is to make the profit and cost incentives that work so well in the marketplace work for pollution control. . . . [The 'bubble' or 'netting' concept] is a first attempt in this direction. By giving a plant manager flexibility to find the places and processes within a plant that control emissions most cheaply, pollution control can be achieved more quickly and cheaply." L. Lave & G. Omenn, Cleaning Air: Reforming the Clean Air Act 28 (1981) (footnote omitted).

it flexibly—not in a sterile textual vacuum, but in the context of implementing policy decisions in a technical and complex arena. The fact that the agency has from time to time changed its interpretation of the term "source" does not, as respondents argue, lead us to conclude that no deference should be accorded the agency's interpretation of the statute. An initial agency interpretation is not instantly carved in stone. On the contrary, the agency, to engage in informed rulemaking, must consider varying interpretations and the wisdom of its policy on a continuing basis. Moreover, the fact that the agency has adopted different definitions in different contexts adds force to the argument that the definition itself is flexible, particularly since Congress has never indicated any disapproval of a flexible reading of the statute.

Significantly, it was not the agency in 1980, but rather the Court of Appeals that read the statute inflexibly to command a plantwide definition for programs designed to maintain clean air and to forbid such a definition for programs designed to improve air quality. The distinction the court drew may well be a sensible one, but our labored review of the problem has surely disclosed that it is not a distinction that Congress ever articulated itself, or one that the EPA found in the statute before the courts began to review the legislative work product. We conclude that it was the Court of Appeals, rather than Congress or any of the decisionmakers who are authorized by Congress to administer this legislation, that was primarily responsible for the 1980 position taken by the agency.

Policy

The arguments over policy that are advanced in the parties' briefs create the impression that respondents are now waging in a judicial forum a specific policy battle which they ultimately lost in the agency and in the 32 jurisdictions opting for the "bubble concept," but one which was never waged in the Congress. Such policy arguments are more properly addressed to legislators or administrators, not to judges.

In these cases, the Administrator's interpretation represents a reasonable accommodation of manifestly competing interests and is entitled to deference: the regulatory scheme is technical and complex, the agency considered the matter in a detailed and reasoned fashion, and the decision involves reconciling conflicting policies. Congress intended to accommodate both interests, but did not do so itself on the level of specificity presented by these cases. Perhaps that body consciously desired the Administrator to strike the balance at this level, thinking that those with great expertise and charged with responsibility for administering the provision would be in a better position to do so; perhaps it simply did not consider the question at this level; and perhaps Congress was unable to forge a coalition on either side of the question, and those on each side decided to take their chances with the scheme devised by the agency. For judicial purposes, it matters not which of these things occurred.

Judges are not experts in the field, and are not part of either political branch of the Government. Courts must, in some cases, reconcile competing political interests, but not on the basis of the judges' personal policy preferences. In contrast, an agency to which Congress has delegated policy-making responsibilities may, within the limits of that delegation, properly rely upon the incumbent administration's views of wise policy to inform its judgments. While agencies are not directly accountable to the people, the Chief Executive is, and it is entirely appropriate for this political branch of the Government to make such policy choices — resolving the competing interests which Congress itself either inadvertently did not resolve, or intentionally left to be resolved by the agency charged with the administration of the statute in light of everyday realities.

When a challenge to an agency construction of a statutory provision, fairly conceptualized, really centers on the wisdom of the agency's policy, rather than whether it is a reasonable choice within a gap left open by Congress, the challenge must fail. In such a case, federal judges — who have no constituency — have a duty to respect legitimate policy choices made by those who do. The responsibilities for assessing the wisdom of such policy choices and resolving the struggle between competing views of the public interest are not judicial ones: "Our Constitution vests such responsibilities in the political branches."

We hold that the EPA's definition of the term "source" is a permissible construction of the statute which seeks to accommodate progress in reducing air pollution with economic growth. The judgment of the Court of Appeals is reversed.

It is so ordered.

Notes on Chevron *Deference*

1. What is a "stationary source"? How did the NRDC, the EPA, and the D.C. Circuit variously construe "stationary source"? What were their supporting arguments?

2. Deference round robin. How might *Skidmore* deference have applied to the facts presented in *Chevron*? How might *Hearst* principles have applied? And how might *Chevron* deference have applied to the facts of *Skidmore* and *Hearst*? By the way, Justice Stevens cited both of these cases in *Chevron*, which he declared was based on "well-settled principles." 467 U.S. at 845.

3. The *Chevron* "two-step" and its rationales. Justice Stevens' description of the judicial method for reviewing an agency's construction of a statute it administers calls for a two-step inquiry. At step one "is the question whether Congress has directly spoken to the precise question at issue. If the intent of Congress is clear, that is the end of the matter; for the court, as well as the agency, must give effect to the unambiguously expressed intent of Congress." 467 U.S. 842–43. As for step two: "If, however, the court determines Congress has not directly addressed the precise question at issue, the court does not simply impose its own construction on the statute, as would be necessary in the absence of an administrative interpretation" but should instead defer to an agency's "permissible" or "reasonable" construction. *Id.*

What rationales did the Court give for this deference framework? Do you find these rationales persuasive? Do they justify a blanket presumption that courts should defer to an agency's reasonable construction of its own enabling act?

Or did *Chevron* mark an unwise and improper cession of interpretive power by courts to agencies? *Cf Marbury v. Madison*, 5 U.S. 137, 177 (1803) ("It is emphatically the province and duty of the judicial department to say what the law is."). Notably, in the last several years, the view that *Chevron* is a dangerous violation of separation of powers has developed an audience on the Supreme Court. *Michigan v. EPA*, 135 S. Ct. 2699, 2712 (2015) (Thomas, J., concurring) (castigating *Chevron* for "wresting" from the courts "the ultimate authority to "say what the law is""); *Gutierrez-Brizuela v. Lynch*, 834 F.3d 1142, 1149 (10th Cir. 2016) (Gorsuch, J., concurring) (declaring that "*Chevron* and *Brand X* permit executive bureaucracies to swallow huge amounts of core judicial and legislative power").

4. Step one and the "traditional tools." How, at step one, should a reviewing judge determine whether Congress has declared its "unambiguously expressed intent"? Justice Stevens gave the following guidance, of sorts, in note 9 of *Chevron*:

> The judiciary is the final authority on issues of statutory construction and must reject administrative constructions which are contrary to clear congressional intent. If a court, employing *traditional tools of statutory construction*, ascertains that Congress had an intention on the precise question at issue, that intention is the law and must be given effect. [Emphasis added.]

Thus, in the course of determining "clear congressional intent," courts may use any interpretive method they have "traditionally" used. Given that debates over proper interpretive methods are interminable, Justice Stevens' instructions left a great deal of room for judicial maneuver. Judicial opinions applying step one have relied upon, *inter alia*: the "plain meaning" of statutory text, statutory structure, legislative purpose and policy, legislative history, dictionaries from various centuries, and the so-called "canons of construction." Which tools did the Court apply in *Chevron* itself? And how?

Ironically, the Supreme Court from time to time splits 5-4 on the issue of whether a statute clearly blocks or requires a given construction at step one. For a good example of such a 5-4 step-one split, reread *FDA v. Brown & Williamson Tobacco Corp.*, 529 U.S. 120 (2000), which is excerpted in Chapter 3.

5. Step one and canons of construction. Courts frequently invoke various "canons" of statutory construction as they construe ambiguous statutory language. For instance, under the canon of constitutional avoidance, "[w]here an otherwise acceptable construction of a statute would raise serious constitutional problems, the Court will construe the statute to avoid such problems unless such construction is plainly contrary to the intent of Congress." *Rust v. Sullivan*, 500 U.S. 173, 223 (1991) (O'Connor, J., concurring). Other notable "substantive" canons include: Courts should construe federal statutes where reasonably possible as applying "only within the territorial jurisdiction of the United States," *EEOC v. Arabian American Oil Co.*, 499 U.S. 244 (1991); courts should liberally construe federal statutes to favor the interests of Indian tribes, *Chickasaw Nation v. United States*, 534 U.S. 84 (2001); and courts should disfavor statutory retroactivity, *Bowen v. Georgetown Univ. Hospital*,

488 U.S. 204 (1988). There are many "linguistic" canons of construction as well; for instance, "under the established interpretative canons of *noscitur a sociis* and *ejusdem generis*, [w]here general words follow specific words in a statutory enumeration, the general words are construed to embrace only objects similar in nature to those objects enumerated by the preceding specific words." *Washington State Dept. of Social and Health Services v. Keffeler*, 537 U.S. 371, 384 (2003) (citation and quotation marks omitted). Which canons made appearances in *Chevron*, and how were they used?

Of course, as the Supreme Court has observed, the "[c]anons of construction need not be conclusive and are often countered . . . by some maxim pointing in a different direction." *Circuit Cities Stores, Inc. v. Adams*, 532 U.S. 105 (2001). This critique suggests that the canons may function less as meaningful guides to legislative meaning and more as after-the-fact justifications for constructions courts would favor anyway.

The bottom line to remember for immediate purposes is that courts at times use canons to resolve apparent statutory ambiguity, thus leaving no room for application of *Chevron* deference. *See INS v. St. Cyr*, 533 U.S. 289, 320 n.45 (2001) ("Because a statute that is ambiguous with respect to retroactive application is construed under our precedent to be unambiguously prospective, . . . there is, for *Chevron* purposes, no ambiguity in such a statute for an agency to resolve."); Kenneth A. Bamberger, *Normative Canons in the Review of Administrative Policymaking*, 118 YALE L. J. 64, 77–78 (2008) (explaining that the majority rule among courts, including the Supreme Court, is that courts should deploy normative canons of construction to eliminate statutory ambiguity that might otherwise leave room for the application of *Chevron* deference).

6. Step two and its relation to arbitrariness review. If a reviewing judge determines that an agency's statutory construction survives step one, how should she determine if it is sufficiently "permissible" or "reasonable" to survive step two? On a moment's reflection, step two presents a puzzle. To get by step one in the first place, an agency's construction must be reasonable in the sense that it does not violate the unambiguously expressed intent of Congress. How then, can a construction that survives step one *ever* be "unreasonable" at step two? On a practical note, one quasi-answer to the preceding question is that if an agency wins at step one, it is very likely to win at step two, which really does tend to be quite deferential.

Over the years, a number of scholars and judges have contended that *Chevron* step two should be regarded as a form of arbitrariness review applied to the policymaking function embedded in resolving statutory ambiguities. *See, e.g., Animal Legal Def. Fund, Inc. v. Glickman*, 204 F.3d 229, 234 (D.C. Cir. 2000) (noting "overlap" between step two and arbitrariness review under *State Farm*); Ronald M. Levin, *The Anatomy of* Chevron: *Step Two Reconsidered*, 72 CHI.-KENT L. REV. 1253, 1254 (1997) (arguing that step two and arbitrariness review should be regarded as "identical"). The metaphysics of the precise relation between step two and arbitrariness review under *State Farm* can, however, get tricky. According to the Second Circuit, for instance, although step two and *State Farm* both require forms of arbitrariness review, the former is less "exacting" than the latter. Still, under step two, "[a]n agency interpretation would surely be 'arbitrary' or 'capricious' if it were picked out of a hat, or arrived at with no explanation, even if it might otherwise be deemed reasonable on some unstated ground." *Catskill Mountains Chapter of Trout Unlimited, Inc. v. EPA*, 846 F.3d 492, 521–22 (2d Cir. 2017).

The Supreme Court has sent mixed signals on this issue. In *National Cable & Telecomm. Ass'n v. Brand X Internet Serv.*, 545 U.S. 967 (2005), the Court expressly stated that step two and arbitrariness review are different. This case addressed whether to sustain the FCC's conclusion that cable companies that sell broadband Internet service do not offer "telecommunications service" within the meaning of the Communications Act. Respondent MCI "vigorously argued" that the agency's construction was unreasonable under *Chevron* step two because it led the agency to regulate cable modem service differently than broadband DSL service. Justice Thomas, writing for the majority, responded that the arbitrariness standard rather than *Chevron* step two applied to this challenge because "[a]ny inconsistency bears on whether the Commission has given a reasoned explanation for its current position, not on whether its interpretation is consistent with the statute." *Id.* at 2710 n.4. But, again, if step two only checks for consistency with the statute, what does it add to step one?

In *Judulang v. Holder*, 132 S. Ct. 476 (20112), Justice Kagan, an administrative-law expert, added an interesting footnote to this debate. Under § 212(c) of the Immigration and Nationality Act, repealed in 1996, aliens subject to exclusion proceedings to bar them from entry into the country could seek discretionary relief. By its terms, § 212(c) did not authorize aliens subject to deportation proceedings to seek similar relief. Notwithstanding this gap, the courts and the Bureau of Immigration Appeals (BIA), motivated by equal protection concerns, adopted the position that potential deportees could also seek discretionary relief. Although § 212(c) was repealed in 1996, this avenue of discretionary relief remains available where the ground for removing a person from the country is a guilty plea entered prior to 1996. 132 S. Ct. at 481. In 2005, the BIA adopted a "comparable grounds" approach to determining whether a potential deportee could seek § 212(c)-style discretionary relief, which had the effect of narrowing its availability. The Government urged that the courts should review the BIA's decision under *Chevron* step two. Justice Kagan, writing for a unanimous court, disposed of this argument with the following footnote:

> The Government urges us instead to analyze this case under the second step of the test we announced in *Chevron U.S.A. Inc. v. Natural Resources Defense Council, Inc.*, 467 U.S. 837 (1984), to govern judicial review of an agency's statutory interpretations. Were we to do so, our analysis would be the same, because under *Chevron* step two, we ask whether an agency interpretation is "'arbitrary or capricious in substance.'" *Mayo Foundation for Medical Ed. and Research v. United States*, 131 S. Ct. 704, 711 (2011) (quoting

Household Credit Services, Inc. v. Pfennig, 541 U.S. 232, 242 (2004)). But we think the more apt analytic framework in this case is standard "arbitrary [or] capricious" review under the APA. The BIA's comparable-grounds policy . . . is not an interpretation of any statutory language—nor could it be, given that § 212(c) does not mention deportation cases.

Judulang, 132 S. Ct. at 483 n.7 (some citations omitted). Thus, according to Justice Kagan, *Chevron*'s step two asks the same basic question as arbitrariness review. *Chevron* was inapt for *Judulang*, however, because, in that case, the BIA's policy adjusting the availability of § 212(c)-style discretionary relief was not actually construing any statutory terms.

7. Flip-flops. The Supreme Court has frequently observed over the last two centuries that longstanding, uniform agency constructions are entitled to substantial judicial deference. *See, e.g., United States v. Vowell*, 9 U.S. 368 (1810). This canon of construction could have cut against the EPA in *Chevron* given the agency's changes in interpretive course with regard to the meaning of "stationary source." Rather than deploy this canon, however, the Court instead used *Chevron* as a chance to extol the virtues of agency interpretive flexibility, observing that an agency's initial interpretation of a statute that it is charged with administering is not "instantly carved in stone" and adding that agencies *should* "consider varying interpretations and the wisdom of [their] policies on a continuing basis." 467 U.S. at 863.

Does agency inconsistency matter after *Chevron*? It does in several ways. First, although *Chevron* leaves an agency free to change interpretive course, an agency must recognize that it is doing so and offer a reasoned justification for the change. *Cf. FCC v. Fox Television Stations, Inc.*, 556 U.S. 502 (2009). Second, regardless of what *Chevron* may have said about the virtues of interpretive flexibility, the Court has continued to cite agency consistency as a ground *for* deference—which in turn suggests that agency inconsistency tends to prompt closer judicial scrutiny. *See, e.g., Barnhart v. Walton*, 535 U.S. 212, 221–22 (2002); *Utah v. Evans*, 536 U.S. 452, 472 (2002). Third and on a closely related point, regardless of *Chevron*'s praise of flexibility, it seems that judges, in practice, may eye flip-flops with some suspicion. William N. Eskridge, Jr. & Lauren E. Baer, *The Continuum of Deference: Supreme Court Treatment of Agency Statutory Interpretations from* Chevron *to* Hamdan, 96 Geo. L.J. 1083, 1149 (2008) (demonstrating that affirmance rates indicate "that the Court has a preference for supporting interpretations that are stable, and ideally, ones that have been stable for some time").

8. A threshold limit on *Chevron*'s reach—what does it mean to "administer" a statute? Note that *Chevron* deference applies only where "a court reviews an agency's construction of a statute which it administers." The term "administer" requires that an agency bear some sort of particular responsibility for enforcing a statute. Thus, the EPA plainly can claim *Chevron* deference for some of its constructions of the Clean Air Act but not the Occupational Safety and Health Act. In addition to blocking application of *Chevron* to an agency's construction of another agency's statute, this principle also blocks application of *Chevron* to constructions of generally applicable statutes that many agencies play a role in administering. Thus, the EPA could not properly claim deference for its constructions of the APA itself, *Professional Reactor Operator Soc'y v. NRC*, 939 F.2d 1047 (D.C. Cir. 1991), nor of FOIA, *Al-Fayed v. CIA*, 254 F.3d 300 (D.C. Cir. 2001). And, of course, the agency could not claim deference for its interpretations of the Constitution (which is not a "statute" at least not in the relevant sense).

9. A threshold limit that dissolved—the "jurisdiction" problem. In our lesson, the WTC needed to figure out whether "apple cider" fell within the scope of its regulatory authority. The issue of whether *Chevron* should apply to an agency's interpretation of the scope of its "jurisdiction" (note the scare quotes) percolated through the case law and law reviews for some time. The key argument for refusing to apply *Chevron* is blocking agencies from power-grabs, seizing regulatory authority that Congress did not intend to delegate. The key counter-argument is that, in the administrative context, the distinction between jurisdictional and non-jurisdictional statutory constructions is illusory. In *City of Arlington v. FCC*, 133 S. Ct. 1863 (2013), the latter view, championed by Justice Scalia for many years, won a decisive victory, taking the "jurisdictional" issue off the *Chevron* table.

City of Arlington arose out of a tussle over the scope of FCC authority under the Telecommunications Act of 1996 to control siting decisions for cell phone towers by state and local authorities. Under the statute, state and local authorities must act on siting applications "within a reasonable period of time after a request is duly filed." 47 U.S.C. § 332(c)(7)(B)(ii). This vague language naturally raises the question: What is a "reasonable period of time"? The FCC has statutory authority to "prescribe such rules and regulations as may be necessary in the public interest to carry out" the provisions of the Communications Act. Responding to complaints of delay from wireless service providers, the FCC invoked this general rulemaking authority to issue a declaratory ruling setting time limits for determining siting applications. The cities of Arlington and San Antonio challenged this action on a variety of grounds, all rejected by the Fifth Circuit. The Supreme Court then granted certiorari solely on the issue of whether *Chevron* deference applies to agency assertions of "jurisdiction." During oral argument, the justices spent much of their time debating the meaning of "jurisdiction."

Justice Scalia's majority opinion attributed this confusion in part to reflexive transposition of the concept of jurisdiction from the judicial context, where it makes sense, to the agency context, where it is a "mirage." *Id.* at 1868. For courts, the issue of whether they have power (jurisdiction) is distinct from whether they use that power to determine the merits correctly. By contrast, for agencies,

> [b]oth their power to act and how they are to act is authoritatively prescribed by Congress, so that when they act improperly, no less than when they act beyond their jurisdiction, what they do is *ultra vires*. Because the question—whether framed as an incorrect application of agency authority or an assertion of authority not conferred—is always whether the agency has gone beyond what Congress has permitted it to do, there is no

principled basis for carving out some arbitrary subset of such claims as "jurisdictional."

Id. Returning to our lesson to make this discussion a little more concrete, Gallery might charge that the WTC has improperly exceeded its jurisdiction by claiming regulatory authority over apple cider. Or it might charge that the WTC misapplied its regulatory authority over "wine" to include apple cider. For Justice Scalia, these questions are functionally the same, and scholastic inquiries trying to separate them are worse than worthless. *Id.* at 1871 ("The federal judge as haruspex, sifting the entrails of vast statutory schemes to divine whether a particular agency interpretation qualifies as 'jurisdictional,' is not engaged in reasoned decisionmaking.").

Chief Justice Roberts authored a dissent for three justices. He explained that the "jurisdiction" question, properly understood, inquires whether Congress wished an agency to enjoy *Chevron* authority to imbue its construction of a particular statutory provision with the force of law. *Id.* at 1879–80. Courts should not defer to an agency on this threshold question of whether Congress wanted courts to defer to an agency. *Id.* at 1880. For a more recent case in which the Chief Justice had greater success deploying notions of congressional intent to restrict the applicability of *Chevron* deference, see note 7 of the next subchapter, discussing the extraordinary cases exception.

10. Previewing another threshold limit — does procedure matter? Notice that *Chevron* addressed a statutory definition that EPA had included in a rule promulgated through notice-and-comment. Did this fact have anything to do with the *Chevron* Court's willingness to defer? Should an agency's power to control interpretations of its enabling act depend on the procedures that it uses? This issue will return with a vengeance in the *Mead* excerpt in the next subchapter.

A Big Note on Auer *Deference to Regulatory Interpretations*

11. What about deference to an agency's interpretations of its *regulations*? The struggle over *Auer* deference. We have waited until the last note of this subchapter to throw yet another doctrine at you. *Auer* deference, formerly known as *Seminole Rock* deference, has required courts to defer to an agency's reasonable interpretation of its own *regulation* "unless it is plainly erroneous or inconsistent with the regulation." *Bowles v. Seminole Rock Co.*, 325 U.S. 410 (1945); *Auer v. Robbins*, 519 U.S. 452 (1997) (confirming this approach).

Auer deference has roots in the plausible proposition that the entity best placed to interpret a regulation is the agency that wrote it and applies it. Critics, however, have argued that *Auer* deference grants too much power to agencies to manipulate the meaning of regulations in enforcement actions. In the words of Justice Scalia, deferring to an agency's interpretation of its own regulation "contravenes one of the great rules of separation of powers: He who writes a law must not adjudge its violation." *Decker v. Nw. Envtl. Def. Ctr.*, 133 S. Ct. 1326, 1342 (2013) (Scalia, J., concurring and dissenting in part).

In response to such critiques, the Court took steps to limit agency manipulation of regulatory interpretations. In *Gonzales v. Oregon*, 546 U.S. 243 (2006), the Court ruled that *Auer* deference applies only to regulations that are genuine products of agency "expertise and experience." An agency therefore cannot reap the benefits of *Auer* deference by issuing a regulation that merely "parrots" statutory language. In *Christopher v. SmithKline Beecham Corp.*, 132 S. Ct. 2156 (2012), the Court imposed additional limits on the reach of *Auer* deference, blocking its application to interpretive flip-flops—especially where they take regulated parties by surprise.

But for opponents of *Auer* deference, including four members of the Court, these limitations were not enough. In 2019, the Court addressed the issue of whether to overrule *Auer* deference in *Kisor v. Wilkie*, 139 S. Ct. 2400 (2019). The Department of Veterans Affairs (VA) had denied benefits claims by James Kisor, a Vietnam War veteran suffering from post-traumatic stress disorder, for almost twenty-five years. The VA finally awarded benefits to him in 2006, when his claim was reopened. Based on an interpretation of its own regulation, however, the agency denied retroactive benefits to cover the period before this date. Kisor's challenge to this decision argued that *Auer* should be overruled. Although all nine justices voted to remand the case to give Kisor another chance to argue that he should be granted pre-2006 benefits, only four agreed that it was time to overrule *Auer*.

Justice Kagan wrote the lead opinion, which three other justices joined in full, and the Chief Justice joined in large part to add a fifth vote. Writing for this five-justice majority, Justice Kagan offered the following explanation for the reach and operation of *Auer* deference:

> First and foremost, a court should not afford *Auer* deference unless the regulation is genuinely ambiguous. . . . If uncertainty does not exist, there is no plausible reason for deference. The regulation then just means what it means—and the court must give it effect, as the court would any law. Otherwise said, the core theory of *Auer* deference is that sometimes the law runs out, and policy-laden choice is what is left over. . . .

> And before concluding that a rule is genuinely ambiguous, a court must exhaust all the "traditional tools" of construction. . . . To make that effort, a court must "carefully consider[ ]" the text, structure, history, and purpose of a regulation, in all the ways it would if it had no agency to fall back on. . . .

> If genuine ambiguity remains, moreover, the agency's reading must still be "reasonable." . . . In other words, it must come within the zone of ambiguity the court has identified after employing all its interpretive tools. . . .

> Still, we are not done—for not every reasonable agency reading of a genuinely ambiguous rule should receive *Auer* deference. We have recognized in applying *Auer* that a court must make an independent inquiry into whether the character and context of the agency interpretation entitles it to controlling weight. . . . The inquiry on this dimension does not reduce to any

exhaustive test. But we have laid out some especially important markers for identifying when *Auer* deference is and is not appropriate.

To begin with, the regulatory interpretation must be one actually made by the agency. In other words, it must be the agency's "authoritative" or "official position," rather than any more *ad hoc* statement not reflecting the agency's views. . . . The interpretation must at the least emanate from those actors, using those vehicles, understood to make authoritative policy in the relevant context. . . . If the interpretation does not do so, a court may not defer.

Next, the agency's interpretation must in some way implicate its substantive expertise. . . . So the basis for deference ebbs when "[t]he subject matter of the [dispute is] distan[t] from the agency's ordinary" duties or "fall[s] within the scope of another agency's authority." . . . When the agency has no comparative expertise in resolving a regulatory ambiguity, Congress presumably would not grant it that authority.[5]

Finally, an agency's reading of a rule must reflect "fair and considered judgment" to receive *Auer* deference. . . . That means, we have stated, that a court should decline to defer to a merely "convenient litigating position" or "*post hoc* rationalizatio[n] advanced" to "defend past agency action against attack."[6] And a court may not defer to a new interpretation, whether or not introduced in litigation, that creates "unfair surprise" to regulated parties. . . . That disruption of expectations may occur when an agency substitutes one view of a rule for another. Or the upending of reliance may happen without such an explicit interpretive change. This Court, for example, recently refused to defer to an interpretation that would have imposed retroactive liability on parties for longstanding conduct that the agency had never before addressed.

Id. at 2415–18 (numerous citations omitted). Your editors have identified at least five limiting factors on the reach of *Auer* deference articulated by the majority. Can you do the same? Are there underlying themes in Justice Kagan's description that can help us better understand the doctrine as a whole?

After describing the proper use of *Auer* deference going forward, Justice Kagan emphasized that *stare decisis* strongly weighed against overruling this doctrine,

---

5. For a similar reason, this Court has denied *Auer* deference when an agency interprets a rule that parrots the statutory text. See *Gonzales v. Oregon*, 546 U.S. 243, 257 (2006). An agency, we explained, gets no "special authority to interpret its own words when, instead of using its expertise and experience to formulate a regulation, it has elected merely to paraphrase the statutory language."

6. The general rule, then, is not to give deference to agency interpretations advanced for the first time in legal briefs. . . . . But we have not entirely foreclosed that practice. *Auer* itself deferred to a new regulatory interpretation presented in an *amicus curiae* brief in this Court. There, the agency was not a party to the litigation, and had expressed its views only in response to the Court's request. "[I]n the circumstances," the Court explained, "[t]here [was] simply no reason to suspect that the interpretation [did] not reflect the agency's fair and considered judgment on the matter in question." . . . .

given that it rested on a "long line of precedents" reaching back at least 75 years, its overruling would "cast doubt on many settled constructions of rules," and Congress has not acted, as it could, to overrule *Auer* by statute.

Justice Gorsuch's concurring opinion (writing for as many as four justices in some parts) strongly argued for jettisoning *Auer* deference. He argued that the APA, the Constitution, and policy considerations all counsel against judicial deference to agency interpretations of regulations. In addition to invoking the general *Marbury* principle that the judicial branch must have the final say on interpreting legal provisions, he contended that judicial deference to executive branch interpretations deprives individuals of the protection of independent courts and improperly expands executive power by providing agencies too much influence over the legal effect of their regulations. Instead of applying *Auer*'s strong form of deference, courts should instead exercise independent judgment to issues of regulatory interpretation and, following *Skidmore*, affirm only those interpretations that they find "persuasive."

Chief Justice Roberts and Justice Kavanaugh both wrote short concurring opinions. The Chief Justice emphasized that the practical difference between Justice Kagan's and Justice Gorsuch's approaches might not be that great as, given the limitations on *Auer* deference identified by Justice Kagan, "the cases in which *Auer* deference is warranted largely overlap with the cases in which it would be unreasonable for a court not to be persuaded by an agency's interpretation of its own regulation." *Id.* at 2424–25 (Roberts, C.J., concurring). Similarly, Justice Kavanaugh found a potentially powerful limit to *Auer* deference in the majority's instruction to courts to exhaust the "traditional tools" of construction before concluding that a regulation is sufficiently ambiguous to merit *Auer* deference. Justice Kavanaugh predicted that courts that assiduously apply these "traditional tools" will "almost always reach a conclusion about the best interpretation of the regulation at issue. After doing so, the court will then have no need to adopt or defer to an agency's contrary interpretation." *Id.* at 2448 (Kavanaugh, J., concurring).

Might this struggle over *Auer* portend anything for the fate of *Chevron* deference? Both the Chief Justice and Justice Kavanaugh were careful to note that *Kisor*'s treatment of *Auer* deference has no bearing on *Chevron* deference, which they contend raises different issues. Are they right about this?

c. Chevron's Reach — the Problem of Step Zero

Not all agency statutory constructions are created equal. For instance, in *Chevron* itself, the EPA's construction of "stationary source" was vetted through notice-and-comment rulemaking. At other times, an agency may issue a statutory construction in an opinion letter that involves little or no discernible process at all. Should *Chevron*'s supposedly strong form of deference apply whenever an agency construes a statute it administers? Or should *Chevron* deference be reserved for statutory constructions that somehow deserve it? The materials that follow address this problem of *Chevron*'s "step zero."

Lesson 5G.3.c. Suppose that the WTC promulgated, using proper procedures, the following disclosure-based variation of the special reserve rule: "Any wine bottle label that includes a 'special reserve' or other designation of special quality must also include an objectively reasonable explanation for the label's claim of special quality."

Later, without notice-and-comment, the WTC published in the *Federal Register* its Guidelines Interpreting the Special Reserve Rule. These guidelines provided that, to be "objectively reasonable, a claim of special quality must be based on superior production methods and/or quality of ingredients." They also warned "conduct in violation of the special reserve rule or these guidelines also constitutes an omission of material fact within the meaning of § 5(b) of the WTCA." The WTC explained in the guidelines themselves that they had not been subjected to notice-and-comment because they merely offered interpretations of terms in the Act and the special reserve rule.

After issuance of the guidelines, Abby's client Gallery distributed a run of its zinfandel bearing the label, "Our Favorite Zin in Years!" without any other explanation. Ralph of the WTC's enforcement bureau initiated an injunction action against Gallery pursuant to § 10(b), claiming that this label violates § 5(b) of the WTC as well as the special reserve rule as both have been interpreted in the guidelines.

How might *Mead* and the notes that follow it help Ben and Abby determine the guidelines' legal force?

Now suppose that the WTC had subjected these same guidelines—word for word—to notice and comment. Does their legal force change?

Background of *United States v. Mead Corp.*

The United States Customs Service classifies imports to determine tariffs owed under the Harmonized Tariff Schedule of the United States. To this end, 46 regional Customs offices across the United States issue 10,000 to 15,000 "ruling letters" per year. Customs Headquarters also issues ruling letters. At the pertinent time, Customs could modify or revoke a ruling letter without notice to anyone other than the addressee, and third parties were advised not to rely on them.

In 1993, Customs issued a Headquarters ruling letter classifying Mead Corporation's "day planners" as "bound" "diaries" subject to a 4% tariff. Mead sought administrative and judicial review. The Federal Circuit set aside the ruling letter, concluding that the day planners were neither "diaries" nor "bound." Along the way to this conclusion, the court held that Customs ruling letters were not entitled to *Chevron* deference because they were not preceded by notice-and-comment, did not carry the "force of law," and were not, unlike regulations, intended to reach "beyond the specific case subject to review."

The Supreme Court seized on the case to attempt to clarify the scope of *Chevron*'s applicability. It observed in the abstract that *Chevron* applies "when it appears that Congress delegated authority to the agency generally to make rules carrying the force of law, and that the agency interpretation claiming deference was promulgated in the exercise of that authority." Applying this new two-step, the Court agreed with the Federal Circuit that *Chevron* deference did not apply to the Customs ruling letter. *Skidmore* deference, however, did.

As you read the majority opinion, consider (a) How are we to tell whether Congress has delegated *Chevron*-style authority to an agency? (b) How did the Court justify its conclusion that Congress did not delegate such authority to Customs for its ruling letters? and (c) How did the Court justify its conclusion that Customs had no intent to imbue its ruling letters with the "force of law"? You will also want to pay careful attention to Justice Scalia's dissent, which touches on many of the administrative law concepts that you have encountered in this course. What, precisely, were Justice Scalia's objections?

United States v. Mead Corp.
533 U.S. 218 (2001)

JUSTICE SOUTER delivered the opinion of the Court.

The question is whether a tariff classification ruling by the United States Customs Service deserves judicial deference. The Federal Circuit rejected Customs's invocation of *Chevron U.S.A. Inc. v. Natural Resources Defense Council, Inc.*, 467 U.S. 837 (1984), in support of such a ruling, to which it gave no deference. We agree that a tariff classification has no claim to judicial deference under *Chevron*, there being no indication that Congress intended such a ruling to carry the force of law, but we hold that under *Skidmore v. Swift & Co.*, 323 U.S. 134 (1944), the ruling is eligible to claim respect according to its persuasiveness.

I

A

Imports are taxed under the Harmonized Tariff Schedule of the United States (HTSUS), 19 U.S.C. § 1202. Title 19 U.S.C. § 1500(b) provides that Customs "shall, under rules and regulations prescribed by the Secretary [of the Treasury,] . . . fix the final classification and rate of duty applicable to . . . merchandise" under the HTSUS. Section 1502(a) provides that

> "[t]he Secretary of the Treasury shall establish and promulgate such rules and regulations not inconsistent with the law (including regulations establishing procedures for the issuance of binding rulings prior to the entry of the merchandise concerned), and may disseminate such information as may be necessary to secure a just, impartial, and uniform appraisement of imported merchandise and the classification and assessment of duties thereon at the various ports of entry."[1]

---

1. The statutory term "ruling" is defined by regulation as "a written statement . . . that interprets and applies the provisions of the Customs and related laws to a specific set of facts." 19 CFR § 177.1(d)(1).

See also § 1624 (general delegation to Secretary to issue rules and regulations for the admission of goods).

The Secretary provides for tariff rulings before the entry of goods by regulations authorizing "ruling letters" setting tariff classifications for particular imports. 19 CFR § 177.8. A ruling letter

> "represents the official position of the Customs Service with respect to the particular transaction or issue described therein and is binding on all Customs Service personnel in accordance with the provisions of this section until modified or revoked. In the absence of a change of practice or other modification or revocation which affects the principle of the ruling set forth in the ruling letter, that principle may be cited as authority in the disposition of transactions involving the same circumstances." § 177.9(a).

After the transaction that gives it birth, a ruling letter is to "be applied only with respect to transactions involving articles identical to the sample submitted with the ruling request or to articles whose description is identical to the description set forth in the ruling letter." § 177.9(b)(2). As a general matter, such a letter is "subject to modification or revocation without notice to any person, except the person to whom the letter was addressed," § 177.9(c), and the regulations consequently provide that "no other person should rely on the ruling letter or assume that the principles of that ruling will be applied in connection with any transaction other than the one described in the letter," *ibid*. Since ruling letters respond to transactions of the moment, they are not subject to notice and comment before being issued, may be published but need only be made "available for public inspection," 19 U.S.C. § 1625(a), and, at the time this action arose, could be modified without notice and comment under most circumstances, 19 CFR § 177.10(c) (2000). A broader notice-and-comment requirement for modification of prior rulings was added by statute in 1993, Pub.L. 103-182, § 623, 107 Stat. 2186, codified at 19 U.S.C. § 1625(c), and took effect after this case arose.

Any of the 46 port-of-entry Customs offices may issue ruling letters, and so may the Customs Headquarters Office, in providing "[a]dvice or guidance as to the interpretation or proper application of the Customs and related laws with respect to a specific Customs transaction [which] may be requested by Customs Service field offices . . . at any time, whether the transaction is prospective, current, or completed," 19 CFR § 177.11(a). Most ruling letters contain little or no reasoning, but simply describe goods and state the appropriate category and tariff. A few letters, like the Headquarters ruling at issue here, set out a rationale in some detail.

B

Respondent, the Mead Corporation, imports "day planners," three-ring binders with pages having room for notes of daily schedules and phone numbers and addresses, together with a calendar and suchlike. The tariff schedule on point falls under the HTSUS heading for "[r]egisters, account books, notebooks, order books, receipt books, letter pads, memorandum pads, diaries and similar articles,"

HTSUS subheading 4820.10, which comprises two subcategories. Items in the first, "[d]iaries, notebooks and address books, bound; memorandum pads, letter pads and similar articles," were subject to a tariff of 4.0% at the time in controversy. Objects in the second, covering "[o]ther" items, were free of duty.

Between 1989 and 1993, Customs repeatedly treated day planners under the "other" HTSUS subheading. In January 1993, however, Customs changed its position, and issued a Headquarters ruling letter classifying Mead's day planners as "Diaries . . . , bound" subject to tariff under subheading 4820.10.20. That letter was short on explanation, but after Mead's protest, Customs Headquarters issued a new letter, carefully reasoned but never published, reaching the same conclusion. This letter considered two definitions of "diary" from the Oxford English Dictionary, the first covering a daily journal of the past day's events, the second a book including "'printed dates for daily memoranda and jottings; also . . . calendars. . . .'" Customs concluded that "diary" was not confined to the first, in part because the broader definition reflects commercial usage and hence the "commercial identity of these items in the marketplace." As for the definition of "bound," Customs concluded that HTSUS was not referring to "bookbinding," but to a less exact sort of fastening described in the Harmonized Commodity Description and Coding System Explanatory Notes to Heading 4820, which spoke of binding by "'reinforcements or fittings of metal, plastics, etc.'"

Customs rejected Mead's further protest of the second Headquarters ruling letter, and Mead filed suit in the Court of International Trade (CIT). The CIT granted the Government's motion for summary judgment, adopting Customs's reasoning without saying anything about deference. . . .

The Federal Circuit, however, reversed the CIT and held that Customs classification rulings should not get *Chevron* deference. . . . Rulings are not preceded by notice and comment as under the Administrative Procedure Act (APA), 5 U.S.C. § 553, they "do not carry the force of law and are not, like regulations, intended to clarify the rights and obligations of importers beyond the specific case under review." The appeals court thought classification rulings had a weaker *Chevron* claim even than Internal Revenue Service interpretive rulings, to which that court gives no deference; unlike rulings by the IRS, Customs rulings issue from many locations and need not be published.

The Court of Appeals accordingly gave no deference at all to the ruling classifying the Mead day planners and rejected the agency's reasoning as to both "diary" and "bound." It thought that planners were not diaries because they had no space for "relatively extensive notations about events, observations, feelings, or thoughts" in the past. And it concluded that diaries "bound" in subheading 4810.10.20 presupposed "unbound" diaries, such that treating ring-fastened diaries as "bound" would leave the "unbound diary" an empty category.

We granted certiorari, in order to consider the limits of *Chevron* deference owed to administrative practice in applying a statute. We hold that administrative implementation of a particular statutory provision qualifies for *Chevron* deference when it appears that Congress delegated authority to the agency generally to make rules carrying the force of law, and that the agency interpretation claiming deference was promulgated in the exercise of that authority. Delegation of such authority may be shown in a variety of ways, as by an agency's power to engage in adjudication or notice-and-comment rulemaking, or by some other indication of a comparable congressional intent. The Customs ruling at issue here fails to qualify, although the possibility that it deserves some deference under *Skidmore* leads us to vacate and remand.

II

A

When Congress has "explicitly left a gap for an agency to fill, there is an express delegation of authority to the agency to elucidate a specific provision of the statute by regulation," *Chevron*, 467 U.S., at 843–844, and any ensuing regulation is binding in the courts unless procedurally defective, arbitrary or capricious in substance, or manifestly contrary to the statute.[6] *See id.*, at 844; *United States v. Morton*, 467 U.S. 822, 834 (1984); APA, 5 U.S.C. §§ 706(2)(A), (D). But whether or not they enjoy any express delegation of authority on a particular question, agencies charged with applying a statute necessarily make all sorts of interpretive choices, and while not all of those choices bind judges to follow them, they certainly may influence courts facing questions the agencies have already answered. "[T]he well-reasoned views of the agencies implementing a statute 'constitute a body of experience and informed judgment to which courts and litigants may properly resort for guidance,'" *Bragdon v. Abbott*, 524 U.S. 624, 642, (1998) (quoting *Skidmore*, 323 U.S., at 139–140), and "[w]e have long recognized that considerable weight should be accorded to an executive department' construction of a statutory scheme it is entrusted to administer. . . ." *Chevron, supra*, at 844 (footnote omitted). The fair measure of deference to an agency administering its own statute has been understood to vary with circumstances, and courts have looked to the degree of the agency's care, its consistency, formality, and relative expertness, and to the persuasiveness of the agency's position, see *Skidmore, supra*, at 139–140. The approach has produced a spectrum of judicial responses, from great respect at one end, to near indifference at the other. Justice Jackson summed things up in *Skidmore v. Swift & Co*:

> "The weight [accorded to an administrative] judgment in a particular case will depend upon the thoroughness evident in its consideration, the validity of its reasoning, its consistency with earlier and later pronouncements, and all those factors which give it power to persuade, if lacking power to control." 323 U.S., at 140.

---

6. Assuming in each case, of course, that the agency's exercise of authority is constitutional, see 5 U.S.C. § 706(2)(B), and does not exceed its jurisdiction, see § 706(2)(C).

Since 1984, we have identified a category of interpretive choices distinguished by an additional reason for judicial deference. This Court in *Chevron* recognized that Congress not only engages in express delegation of specific interpretive authority, but that "[s]ometimes the legislative delegation to an agency on a particular question is implicit." 467 U.S., at 844. Congress, that is, may not have expressly delegated authority or responsibility to implement a particular provision or fill a particular gap. Yet it can still be apparent from the agency's generally conferred authority and other statutory circumstances that Congress would expect the agency to be able to speak with the force of law when it addresses ambiguity in the statute or fills a space in the enacted law, even one about which "Congress did not actually have an intent" as to a particular result. *Id.*, at 845. When circumstances implying such an expectation exist, a reviewing court has no business rejecting an agency's exercise of its generally conferred authority to resolve a particular statutory ambiguity simply because the agency's chosen resolution seems unwise, see *id.*, at 845–846, but is obliged to accept the agency's position if Congress has not previously spoken to the point at issue and the agency's interpretation is reasonable, see *id.*, at 842–845; cf. 5 U.S.C. §706(2) (a reviewing court shall set aside agency action, findings, and conclusions found to be "arbitrary, capricious, an abuse of discretion, or otherwise not in accordance with law").

We have recognized a very good indicator of delegation meriting *Chevron* treatment in express congressional authorizations to engage in the process of rulemaking or adjudication that produces regulations or rulings for which deference is claimed. *See, e.g., EEOC v. Arabian American Oil Co.,* 499 U.S. 244, 257 (1991) (no *Chevron* deference to agency guideline where congressional delegation did not include the power to "'promulgate rules or regulations'" (quoting *General Elec. Co. v. Gilbert,* 429 U.S. 125, 141 (1976)); *see also Christensen v. Harris County,* 529 U.S. 576, 596–597 (2000) (BREYER, J., dissenting) (where it is in doubt that Congress actually intended to delegate particular interpretive authority to an agency, *Chevron* is "inapplicable"). It is fair to assume generally that Congress contemplates administrative action with the effect of law when it provides for a relatively formal administrative procedure tending to foster the fairness and deliberation that should underlie a pronouncement of such force.[11] Thus, the overwhelming number of our cases applying *Chevron* deference have reviewed the fruits of notice- and-comment rulemaking or formal adjudication.[12] That said, and as significant as notice-and-

---

11. See Merrill & Hickman, Chevron's *Domain,* 89 Geo. L.J. 833, 872 (2001) ("[I]f *Chevron* rests on a presumption about congressional intent, then *Chevron* should apply only where Congress would want *Chevron* to apply. In delineating the types of delegations of agency authority that trigger *Chevron* deference, it is therefore important to determine whether a plausible case can be made that Congress would want such a delegation to mean that agencies enjoy primary interpretational authority").

12. [The Court cited 18 cases in which *Chevron* deference had been extended to interpretations promulgated via notice-and-comment rulemaking and cited 8 cases in which such deference had been extended to interpretations issued via adjudication. Eds.].

comment is in pointing to *Chevron* authority, the want of that procedure here does not decide the case, for we have sometimes found reasons for *Chevron* deference even when no such administrative formality was required and none was afforded, *see, e.g., NationsBank of N.C., N.A. v. Variable Annuity Life Ins. Co.*, 513 U.S. 251, 256–257 (1995).[13] The fact that the tariff classification here was not a product of such formal process does not alone, therefore, bar the application of *Chevron*.

There are, nonetheless, ample reasons to deny *Chevron* deference here. The authorization for classification rulings, and Customs's practice in making them, present a case far removed not only from notice-and-comment process, but from any other circumstances reasonably suggesting that Congress ever thought of classification rulings as deserving the deference claimed for them here.

B

No matter which angle we choose for viewing the Customs ruling letter in this case, it fails to qualify under *Chevron*. On the face of the statute, to begin with, the terms of the congressional delegation give no indication that Congress meant to delegate authority to Customs to issue classification rulings with the force of law. We are not, of course, here making any global statement about Customs's authority, for it is true that the general rulemaking power conferred on Customs, see 19 U.S.C. § 1624, authorizes some regulation with the force of law, or "legal norms,". . . . It is true as well that Congress had classification rulings in mind when it explicitly authorized, in a parenthetical, the issuance of "regulations establishing procedures for the issuance of binding rulings prior to the entry of the merchandise concerned," 19 U.S.C. § 1502(a).[15] The reference to binding classifications does not, however, bespeak the legislative type of activity that would naturally bind more than the parties to the ruling, once the goods classified are admitted into this country. And though the statute's direction to disseminate "information" necessary to "secure" uniformity, *ibid.*, seems to assume that a ruling may be precedent in later transactions, precedential value alone does not add up to *Chevron* entitlement; interpretive rules may sometimes function as precedents, see Strauss, *The Rulemaking Continuum*, 41 Duke L.J. 1463, 1472–1473 (1992), and they enjoy no *Chevron* status as a class. In any event, any precedential claim of a classification ruling is counterbalanced by the provision for independent review of Customs classifications by the CIT, see 28 U.S.C. §§ 2638–2640. . . .

It is difficult, in fact, to see in the agency practice itself any indication that Customs ever set out with a lawmaking pretense in mind when it undertook to make classifications like these. Customs does not generally engage in notice-and-comment

---

13. In *NationsBank*, we quoted longstanding precedent concluding that "[t]he Comptroller of the Currency is charged with the enforcement of banking laws to an extent that warrants the invocation of [the rule of deference] with respect to his deliberative conclusions as to the meaning of these laws." See also 1 M. Malloy, Banking Law and Regulation § 1.3.1, p. 1.41 (1996) (stating that the Comptroller is given "personal authority" under the National Bank Act).

15. The ruling in question here, however, does not fall within that category.

practice when issuing them, and their treatment by the agency makes it clear that a letter's binding character as a ruling stops short of third parties; Customs has regarded a classification as conclusive only as between itself and the importer to whom it was issued, 19 CFR § 177.9(c), and even then only until Customs has given advance notice of intended change, §§ 177.9(a), (c). Other importers are in fact warned against assuming any right of detrimental reliance. § 177.9(c).

Indeed, to claim that classifications have legal force is to ignore the reality that 46 different Customs offices issue 10,000 to 15,000 of them each year. Any suggestion that rulings intended to have the force of law are being churned out at a rate of 10,000 a year at an agency's 46 scattered offices is simply self-refuting. Although the circumstances are less startling here, with a Headquarters letter in issue, none of the relevant statutes recognizes this category of rulings as separate or different from others; there is thus no indication that a more potent delegation might have been understood as going to Headquarters even when Headquarters provides developed reasoning, as it did in this instance.

Nor do the amendments to the statute made effective after this case arose disturb our conclusion. The new law requires Customs to provide notice-and-comment procedures only when modifying or revoking a prior classification ruling or modifying the treatment accorded to substantially identical transactions, 19 U.S.C. § 1625(c); and under its regulations, Customs sees itself obliged to provide notice-and-comment procedures only when "changing a practice" so as to produce a tariff increase, or in the imposition of a restriction or prohibition, or when Customs Headquarters determines that "the matter is of sufficient importance to involve the interests of domestic industry," 19 CFR §§ 177.10(c)(1), (2). The statutory changes reveal no new congressional objective of treating classification decisions generally as rulemaking with force of law, nor do they suggest any intent to create a *Chevron* patchwork of classification rulings, some with force of law, some without.

In sum, classification rulings are best treated like "interpretations contained in policy statements, agency manuals, and enforcement guidelines." *Christensen*, 529 U.S., at 587. They are beyond the *Chevron* pale.

C

To agree with the Court of Appeals that Customs ruling letters do not fall within *Chevron* is not, however, to place them outside the pale of any deference whatever. *Chevron* did nothing to eliminate *Skidmore*'s holding that an agency's interpretation may merit some deference whatever its form, given the "specialized experience and broader investigations and information" available to the agency, 323 U.S., at 139, and given the value of uniformity in its administrative and judicial understandings of what a national law requires, *id.*, at 140. . . .

There is room at least to raise a *Skidmore* claim here, where the regulatory scheme is highly detailed, and Customs can bring the benefit of specialized experience to bear on the subtle questions in this case: whether the daily planner with room for brief daily entries falls under "diaries," when diaries are grouped with "notebooks and address books, bound; memorandum pads, letter pads and similar articles," HTSUS subheading 4820.10.20; and whether a planner with a ring binding should qualify as "bound," when a binding may be typified by a book, but also may have "reinforcements or fittings of metal, plastics, etc.," Harmonized Commodity Description and Coding System Explanatory Notes to Heading 4820, p. 687. A classification ruling in this situation may therefore at least seek a respect proportional to its "power to persuade," *Skidmore, supra,* at 140; see also *Christensen,* 529 U.S., at 587, *id.,* at 595 (STEVENS, J., dissenting); *id.,* at 596–597 (BREYER, J., dissenting). Such a ruling may surely claim the merit of its writer's thoroughness, logic, and expertness, its fit with prior interpretations, and any other sources of weight.

D

Underlying the position we take here, like the position expressed by Justice SCALIA in dissent, is a choice about the best way to deal with an inescapable feature of the body of congressional legislation authorizing administrative action. That feature is the great variety of ways in which the laws invest the Government's administrative arms with discretion, and with procedures for exercising it, in giving meaning to Acts of Congress. Implementation of a statute may occur in formal adjudication or the choice to defend against judicial challenge; it may occur in a central board or office or in dozens of enforcement agencies dotted across the country; its institutional lawmaking may be confined to the resolution of minute detail or extend to legislative rulemaking on matters intentionally left by Congress to be worked out at the agency level.

Although we all accept the position that the Judiciary should defer to at least some of this multifarious administrative action, we have to decide how to take account of the great range of its variety. If the primary objective is to simplify the judicial process of giving or withholding deference, then the diversity of statutes authorizing discretionary administrative action must be declared irrelevant or minimized. If, on the other hand, it is simply implausible that Congress intended such a broad range of statutory authority to produce only two varieties of administrative action, demanding either *Chevron* deference or none at all, then the breadth of the spectrum of possible agency action must be taken into account. Justice SCALIA's first priority over the years has been to limit and simplify. The Court's choice has been to tailor deference to variety. This acceptance of the range of statutory variation has led the Court to recognize more than one variety of judicial deference, just as the Court has recognized a variety of indicators that Congress would expect *Chevron* deference. . . .

We think, in sum, that Justice SCALIA's efforts to simplify ultimately run afoul of Congress's indications that different statutes present different reasons for considering respect for the exercise of administrative authority or deference to it. Without being at odds with congressional intent much of the time, we believe that judicial responses to administrative action must continue to differentiate between *Chevron* and *Skidmore,* and that continued recognition of *Skidmore* is necessary for just the reasons Justice Jackson gave when that case was decided. . . .

Since the *Skidmore* assessment called for here ought to be made in the first instance by the Court of Appeals for the Federal Circuit or the CIT, we go no further than to vacate the judgment and remand the case for further proceedings consistent with this opinion.

It is so ordered.

JUSTICE SCALIA, dissenting.

Today's opinion makes an avulsive change in judicial review of federal administrative action. Whereas previously a reasonable agency application of an ambiguous statutory provision had to be sustained so long as it represented the agency's authoritative interpretation, henceforth such an application can be set aside unless "it appears that Congress delegated authority to the agency generally to make rules carrying the force of law," as by giving an agency "power to engage in adjudication or notice-and-comment rulemaking, or . . . some other [procedure] indicati[ng] comparable congressional intent," and "the agency interpretation claiming deference was promulgated in the exercise of that authority."[1] What was previously a general presumption of authority in agencies to resolve ambiguity in the statutes they have been authorized to enforce has been changed to a presumption of no such authority, which must be overcome by affirmative legislative intent to the contrary. And whereas previously, when agency authority to resolve ambiguity did not exist the court was free to give the statute what it considered the best interpretation, henceforth the court must supposedly give the agency view some indeterminate amount of so-called *Skidmore* deference. We will be sorting out the consequences of the *Mead* doctrine, which has today replaced the *Chevron* doctrine, for years to come. I would adhere to our established jurisprudence, defer to the reasonable interpretation the Customs Service has given to the statute it is charged with enforcing, and reverse the judgment of the Court of Appeals.

I

Only five years ago, the Court described the *Chevron* doctrine as follows: "We accord deference to agencies under *Chevron* . . . because of a presumption that Congress, when it left ambiguity in a statute meant for implementation by an agency, understood that the ambiguity would be resolved, first and foremost, by the agency, and desired the agency (rather than the courts) to possess whatever degree of discretion the ambiguity allows," *Smiley v. Citibank (South Dakota), N. A.,* 517 U.S. 735, 740–741 (1996) (citing *Chevron, supra,* at 843–844). Today the Court collapses this doctrine, announcing instead a presumption that agency discretion does not exist unless the statute, expressly or impliedly, says so. While the Court disclaims any hard-and-fast rule for determining the existence of discretion-conferring intent, it asserts that "a very good indicator [is] express congressional authorizations to engage in the process of rulemaking or adjudication that produces regulations or rulings

---

1. It is not entirely clear whether the formulation newly minted by the Court today extends to both formal and informal adjudication, or simply the former.

for which deference is claimed." Only when agencies act through "adjudication[,] notice-and-comment rulemaking, or . . . some other [procedure] indicati[ng] comparable congressional intent [whatever that means]" is *Chevron* deference applicable—because these "relatively formal administrative procedure[s] [designed] to foster . . . fairness and deliberation" bespeak (according to the Court) congressional willingness to have the agency, rather than the courts, resolve statutory ambiguities. Once it is determined that *Chevron* deference is not in order, the uncertainty is not at an end—and indeed is just beginning. Litigants cannot then assume that the statutory question is one for the courts to determine, according to traditional interpretive principles and by their own judicial lights. No, the Court now resurrects, in full force, the pre-*Chevron* doctrine of *Skidmore* deference, whereby "[t]he fair measure of deference to an agency administering its own statute . . . var[ies] with circumstances," including "the degree of the agency's care, its consistency, formality, and relative expertness, and . . . the persuasiveness of the agency's position." The Court has largely replaced *Chevron*, in other words, with that test most beloved by a court unwilling to be held to rules (and most feared by litigants who want to know what to expect): th'ol' "totality of the circumstances" test.

The Court's new doctrine is neither sound in principle nor sustainable in practice.

A

As to principle: The doctrine of *Chevron*—that all authoritative agency interpretations of statutes they are charged with administering deserve deference—was rooted in a legal presumption of congressional intent, important to the division of powers between the Second and Third Branches. When, *Chevron* said, Congress leaves an ambiguity in a statute that is to be administered by an executive agency, it is presumed that Congress meant to give the agency discretion, within the limits of reasonable interpretation, as to how the ambiguity is to be resolved. By committing enforcement of the statute to an agency rather than the courts, Congress committed its initial and primary interpretation to that branch as well.

There is some question whether *Chevron* was faithful to the text of the Administrative Procedure Act (APA), which it did not even bother to cite.[2] But it was in

---

2. Title 5 U.S.C. §706 provides that, in reviewing agency action, the court shall "decide all relevant questions of law"—which would seem to mean that all statutory ambiguities are to be resolved judicially. See Anthony, *The Supreme Court and the APA: Sometimes They Just Don't Get It*, 10 Am. U. Admin. L.J. 1, 9–11 (1996). It could be argued, however, that the legal presumption identified by *Chevron* left as the only "questio[n] of law" whether the agency's interpretation had gone beyond the scope of discretion that the statutory ambiguity conferred. Today's opinion, of course, is no more observant of the APA's text than *Chevron* was—and indeed is even more difficult to reconcile with it. Since the opinion relies upon actual congressional intent to suspend §706, rather than upon a legal presumption against which §706 was presumably enacted, it runs head-on into the provision of the APA which specifies that the Act's requirements (including the requirement that judges shall "decide all relevant questions of law") cannot be amended except expressly. *See* §559.

accord with the origins of federal-court judicial review. Judicial control of federal executive officers was principally exercised through the prerogative writ of mandamus. *See* L. Jaffe, Judicial Control of Administrative Action 166, 176–177 (1965). That writ generally would not issue unless the executive officer was acting plainly beyond the scope of his authority. . . .

Statutory ambiguities, in other words, were left to reasonable resolution by the Executive.

The basis in principle for today's new doctrine can be described as follows: The background rule is that ambiguity in legislative instructions to agencies is to be resolved not by the agencies but by the judges. Specific congressional intent to depart from this rule must be found—and while there is no single touchstone for such intent it can generally be found when Congress has authorized the agency to act through (what the Court says is) relatively formal procedures such as informal rulemaking and formal (and informal?) adjudication, and when the agency in fact employs such procedures. The Court's background rule is contradicted by the origins of judicial review of administrative action. But in addition, the Court's principal criterion of congressional intent to supplant its background rule seems to me quite implausible. There is no necessary connection between the formality of procedure and the power of the entity administering the procedure to resolve authoritatively questions of law. The most formal of the procedures the Court refers to—formal adjudication—is modeled after the process used in trial courts, which of course are not generally accorded deference on questions of law. The purpose of such a procedure is to produce a closed record for determination and review of the facts—which implies nothing about the power of the agency subjected to the procedure to resolve authoritatively questions of law.

As for informal rulemaking: While formal adjudication procedures are prescribed (either by statute or by the Constitution), informal rulemaking is more typically authorized but not required. Agencies with such authority are free to give guidance through rulemaking, but they may proceed to administer their statute case-by-case, "making law" as they implement their program (not necessarily through formal adjudication). *See NLRB v. Bell Aerospace Co.*, 416 U.S. 267, 290–295 (1974); *SEC v. Chenery Corp.*, 332 U.S. 194, 202–203 (1947). Is it likely—or indeed even plausible—that Congress meant, when such an agency chooses rulemaking, to accord the administrators of that agency, and their successors, the flexibility of interpreting the ambiguous statute now one way, and later another; but, when such an agency chooses case-by-case administration, to eliminate all future agency discretion by having that same ambiguity resolved authoritatively (and forever) by the courts? Surely that makes no sense. It is also the case that certain significant categories of rules—those involving grant and benefit programs, for example, are exempt from the requirements of informal rulemaking. *See* 5 U.S.C. § 553(a)(2). Under the Court's novel theory, when an agency takes advantage of that exemption its rules will be deprived of *Chevron* deference, *i.e.*, authoritative effect. Was this either the plausible intent of the APA rulemaking exemption, or the plausible intent of the Congress that established the grant or benefit program? . . .

4

And finally, the majority's approach compounds the confusion it creates by breathing new life into the anachronism of *Skidmore*, which sets forth a sliding scale of deference owed an agency's interpretation of a statute that is dependent "upon the thoroughness evident in [the agency's] consideration, the validity of its reasoning, its consistency with earlier and later pronouncements, and all those factors which give it power to persuade, if lacking power to control"; in this way, the appropriate measure of deference will be accorded the "body of experience and informed judgment" that such interpretations often embody, 323 U.S., at 140. Justice Jackson's eloquence notwithstanding, the rule of *Skidmore* deference is an empty truism and a trifling statement of the obvious: A judge should take into account the well-considered views of expert observers.

It was possible to live with the indeterminacy of *Skidmore* deference in earlier times. But in an era when federal statutory law administered by federal agencies is pervasive, and when the ambiguities (intended or unintended) that those statutes contain are innumerable, totality-of-the-circumstances *Skidmore* deference is a recipe for uncertainty, unpredictability, and endless litigation. To condemn a vast body of agency action to that regime (all except rulemaking, formal (and informal?) adjudication, and whatever else might now and then be included within today's intentionally vague formulation of affirmative congressional intent to "delegate") is irresponsible.

II

The Court's pretense that today's opinion is nothing more than application of our prior case law does not withstand analysis. It is, to be sure, impossible to demonstrate that any of our cases contradicts the rule of decision that the Court prescribes, because the Court prescribes none. More precisely, it at one and the same time (1) renders meaningless its newly announced requirement that there be an affirmative congressional intent to have ambiguities resolved by the administering agency, and (2) ensures that no prior decision can possibly be cited which contradicts that requirement, by simply announcing that all prior decisions according *Chevron* deference exemplify the multifarious ways in which that congressional intent can be manifested: "[A]s significant as notice-and-comment is in pointing to *Chevron* authority, the want of that procedure here does not decide the case, for we have sometimes found reasons for *Chevron* deference even when no such administrative formality was required and none was afforded."

The principles central to today's opinion have no antecedent in our jurisprudence. *Chevron*, the case that the opinion purportedly explicates, made no mention of the "relatively formal administrative procedure[s]," that the Court today finds the best indication of an affirmative intent by Congress to have ambiguities resolved by the administering agency. Which is not so remarkable, since *Chevron* made no mention of any need to find such an affirmative intent; it said that in the event of statutory ambiguity agency authority to clarify was to be presumed. And our cases have followed that prescription.

[JUSTICE SCALIA then gave an extended analysis of various cases to buttress his point.]

. . . .

III

To decide the present case, I would adhere to the original formulation of *Chevron*. "'The power of an administrative agency to administer a congressionally created . . . program necessarily requires the formulation of policy and the making of rules to fill any gap left, implicitly or explicitly, by Congress,'" 467 U.S., at 843. We accordingly presume—and our precedents have made clear to Congress that we presume—that, absent some clear textual indication to the contrary, "Congress, when it left ambiguity in a statute meant for implementation by an agency, understood that the ambiguity would be resolved, first and foremost, by the agency, and desired the agency (rather than the courts) to possess whatever degree of discretion the ambiguity allows," *Smiley*, 517 U.S., at 740–741 (citing *Chevron*, [467 U.S.] at 843–844). *Chevron* sets forth an across-the-board presumption, which operates as a background rule of law against which Congress legislates: Ambiguity means Congress intended agency discretion. Any resolution of the ambiguity by the administering agency that is authoritative—that represents the official position of the agency—must be accepted by the courts if it is reasonable. . . .

Notes

1. Step zero: the problem of *Chevron's* reach. *Chevron* itself did not expressly indicate that the applicability of its strong form of deference depended on an agency's use of any given form of procedure. It was, nonetheless, amenable to this interpretation given that the EPA had promulgated its construction of "stationary source" through notice-and-comment rulemaking. Circuit courts split on this issue of procedural sensitivity, with some reserving *Chevron* deference to the interpretive products of notice-and-comment or formal adjudication. Around the turn of the millennium, the Supreme Court issued two especially important opinions addressing this problem, *Mead* itself and *Barnhart v. Walton*, 535 U.S. 212 (2002). As you will see, together, these opinions did not generate quite as much clarity as the Court might have wished.

2. *Mead* has its own two-step. *Mead* began its complex effort to delineate when *Chevron* applies by stating:

> We hold that administrative implementation of a particular statutory provision qualifies for *Chevron* deference when it appears [1] that Congress delegated authority to the agency generally to make rules carrying the force of law, and [2] that the agency interpretation claiming deference was promulgated in the exercise of that authority.

533 U.S. at 226–27. Thus, *Chevron* deference requires both a *delegation* of force-of-law power from Congress and *invocation* of that power by the agency.

How did the *Mead* majority justify its conclusion that the Customs ruling letter satisfied neither the delegation nor invocation requirements for *Chevron* deference? What role did the procedural provenance of the ruling letter play? Did the ruling letter purport to state a generally applicable rule? How did this matter to the Court?

3. Procedural authority as a signal of delegation of *Chevron* authority. The *Mead* Court observed generally that "[d]elegation of such [force-of-law] authority may be shown in a variety of ways, as by an agency's power to engage in adjudication or notice-and-comment rulemaking, or by some other indication of a comparable congressional intent." 533 U.S. at 227. What is it about agency powers to engage in notice-and-comment rulemaking or (formal?) adjudication that marks them as good signals that Congress has delegated *Chevron* authority to an agency?

4. *Barnhart* downplays procedure as a necessary signal. It is tempting to read *Mead* for the holding that the interpretive products of notice-and-comment rulemaking and formal adjudication should receive *Chevron* deference whereas interpretations produced with less procedure should not. Recall, however, that the Court was careful to stress in *Mead* that Congress can signal its delegation of *Chevron* power by means "other" than granting authority to engage in notice-and-comment rulemaking or formal adjudication. 533 U.S. at 227. Consistency with precedent demanded this loophole because the Court, just a few years before, had applied *Chevron* deference to a letter issued by the Comptroller of the Currency without such procedures. *See NationsBank of N.C., N.A. v. Variable Annuity Life Ins. Co.,* 513 U.S. 251 (1995) (discussed in footnote 13 of the majority opinion in *Mead*).

In *Barnhart v. Walton,* 535 U.S. 212 (2002), Justice Breyer seized on this loophole to downplay *Mead*'s focus on procedure in favor of a multi-factor approach to determining *Chevron*'s applicability. This case turned on interpretation of "disability" for the purpose of establishing eligibility for various Social Security benefits. The SSA had set forth its definition in an opinion letter as early as 1957. Decades later, and perhaps in response to the *Walton* litigation itself, the agency included this interpretation in a rule promulgated after notice-and-comment. All nine justices agreed that, in light of this rulemaking, the agency's interpretation was entitled to *Chevron* deference. But this was not enough for Justice Breyer, who, writing for an eight-justice majority over Justice Scalia's rather outraged dissent, added that, even absent this rulemaking, the Agency's interpretation would still have netted *Chevron*'s particular form of deference:

> [T]he Agency's interpretation is one of long standing. And the fact that the Agency reached its interpretation through means less formal than "notice and comment" rulemaking does not automatically deprive that interpretation of the judicial deference otherwise its due. If this Court's opinion in *Christensen* suggested an absolute rule to the contrary, our later opinion in *Mead* denied the suggestion. . . .

In this case, the interstitial nature of the legal question, the related expertise of the Agency, the importance of the question to administration of the
statute, the complexity of that administration, and the careful consideration the Agency has given the question over a long period of time all indicate that *Chevron* provides the appropriate legal lens through which to view
the legality of the Agency interpretation here at issue.

Id. at 221–22. *See also National Cable & Telecomm. Ass'n v. Brand X Internet Serv.*,
125 S. Ct. 2688, 2712–13 (2005) (Breyer, J., concurring) (emphasizing that *Mead*
does not require formal process as precondition for *Chevron* deference).

5. *Barnhart* applied. Combining *Mead* and *Barnhart*: Where an agency uses either
notice-and-comment rulemaking or relatively elaborate, "formal" adjudicative procedures to produce its statutory construction, the agency can safely expect *Chevron* deference to apply. Its statutory construction has sailed into one of *Mead*'s safe
harbors. Outside the safe harbors, an agency statutory construction might still win
Chevron deference based on a reviewing court's application of *Barnhart*'s multi-
factor test. This test is fact sensitive. Any given precedent applying *Barnhart* will
therefore likely have only limited significance for a later case with different facts. An
impressionistic reading of a few applications of *Barnhart* confirms that, where an
agency has relevant expertise and applies that expertise carefully to develop a statutory construction with general application, it has a decent chance to obtain *Chevron*
deference. Agency statutory constructions that seem slapdash do not.

Managed Pharmacy Care v. Sebelius, 716 F.3d 1235 (9th Cir. 2013), provides a
nice example of an agency statutory construction that deserved its *Chevron* deference under *Barnhart*. A state Medicaid plan must provide "methods and procedures" that are "sufficient to assure that payments are consistent with efficiency,
economy, and quality of care." 42 U.S.C. § 1396(a)(30)(A) ("Section 30(A)"). The
Secretary of Health and Human Services approved two State Plan Amendments
(SPAs) submitted by the state of California that reduced reimbursements for various medical services and equipment. Plaintiffs challenged this approval, arguing
that the SPAs violated § 30(A) because the state had failed to submit cost studies
in support of most of its proposed reductions. The agency does not read § 30(A)
as requiring such studies. The court observed that, although the Secretary had not
used notice-and-comment or formal adjudication, interested providers had, in fact,
"offered extensive input" on the decision to approve the SPAs. The court emphasized that implementing Medicaid is a "colossal undertaking" that is "nothing if
not complex." The executive branch had "been giving careful consideration to the
ins and outs of the program since its inception, and the agency is the expert in all
things Medicaid." The statutory terms subject to construction, such as "sufficiency"
and "efficiency," were "amorphous," and they required agency expertise to define.
Application of the *Barnhart* factors thus led to the conclusion that *Chevron* deference
should apply to the agency's construction of § 30(A). *See also Mylan Laboratories,
Inc. v Thompson*, 389 F.3d 1272, 1280 (D.C. Cir. 2004) (applying *Chevron* in light
of statutory complexity as well as the agency's expertise, "the careful craft of the

scheme it devised to reconcile various statutory provisions," and its reliance on its "previous determination of the same or similar issues and on its own regulations"); *Hospital Corp. of America v. Comm. of Internal Revenue*, 348 F.3d 136 (6th Cir. 2003) (holding that *Chevron* applied to Treasury regulation issued without notice-and-comment; stressing that the regulation had been promulgated "centrally by the Treasury Department, after careful consideration" (unlike *Mead*'s ruling letters)).

Fox v. Clinton, 684 F.3d 67 (D.C. Cir. 2012), provides a nice example of a court applying the *Barnhart* factors to conclude that a statutory construction did not deserve *Chevron* deference. The Bureau of Consular Affairs within the State Department issued a letter denying a request by Dr. Fox for a Certificate of Loss of Nationality. The court discussed several cases in which *Chevron* applied under *Barnhart* to agency statutory constructions that had been issued without notice-and-comment or formal procedures but that nonetheless were "clearly intended to have general applicability and the force of law." The agency letter to Dr. Fox did not merit this treatment, however, because "the Department offered little more than uncited, conclusory assertions of law in a short, informal document that does not purport to set policy for future CLN determinations." *Id.* at 78.

6. An additional threshold limitation — defective procedures. As we have seen, under *Mead* and *Barnhart*'s step-zero regime, an agency can, in essence, earn *Chevron* deference by using relatively open and formal procedures to develop a statutory interpretation. In *Encino Motorcars, LLC v. Navarro*, 136 S. Ct. 2117 (2016), the Court explained that an agency can lose the chance for *Chevron* deference by using defective procedures. The Court declared, "where a proper challenge is raised to the agency procedures, and those procedures are defective, a court should not accord *Chevron* deference to the agency interpretation." The Court characterized an agency's duty to "give adequate reasons for its decisions" as "[o]ne of the basic procedural requirements of administrative rulemaking." An explanation for a policy change must acknowledge the fact of change, show "good reasons for the new policy," and give due regard to reliance interests. *Id.* at 2126 (quoting *FCC v. Fox Televisions Stations, Inc.*, 556 U.S. 502, 515 (2009) (discussed at note 7 of Chapter 5G.2).

With these principles in hand, the Court denied *Chevron* deference to the Department of Labor's interpretation of a statutory exemption from the Fair Labor Standards Act's overtime protections. This new interpretation, which disavowed an earlier one, would have entitled "service advisors" working at automobile dealerships to overtime. The Court held that DOL had not provided "the reasoned explanation that was required in light of the Department's change in position and the significant reliance interests involved." As a result, the new rule was arbitrary, and arbitrary action "is itself unlawful and receives no *Chevron* deference." *Id.* (quoting *Mead*, 533 U.S. at 227).

As of this writing, it is unclear how much general significance *Encino*'s treatment of defective procedures will have on *Chevron*'s reach. As discussed in note 6 of Chapter 5G.3.b., a substantial body of case law and commentary, some of it from the Supreme Court, indicates that *Chevron* step two reviews agency statutory constructions for arbitrariness. This observation suggests that it would have been simpler for the Court to throw out DOL's interpretation at step two for a lack of reasoned decisionmaking rather than to add an additional wrinkle to the evolving *Chevron* step zero.

7. Yet another threshold limitation—a *Chevron* exception for extraordinary cases. Recall that the Supreme Court recently settled a debate over whether Chevron deference applies to determinations of agency "jurisdiction" in *City of Arlington v. FCC*, 133 S. Ct. 1863 (2013) (discussed at note 9 following the *Chevron* excerpt). Justice Scalia won the day with a majority opinion holding that, for the purpose of determining the scope of agency statutory authority, the distinction between jurisdictional and nonjurisdictional is both meaningless and confusing. Chief Justice Roberts's dissent countered that the majority was thinking about "jurisdiction" the wrong way—an easy thing to do, given the many meanings this term carries. *Id.* at 1879 (Roberts, C.J., dissenting). Properly understood, the "jurisdictional" question in this context boils down to determining whether Congress wished for *Chevron* to apply. *Id.* at 1879–80. The Chief Justice explained, "we do not defer to an agency's interpretation of an ambiguous provision unless Congress wants us to, and whether Congress wants us to is a question that courts, not agencies, must decide." *Id.* at 1883.

The Chief Justice found more success using congressional intent to restrict application of *Chevron* in *King v. Burwell*, 2015 U.S. Lexis 4248. This case raised the issue of whether the Affordable Care Act (ACA) authorizes subsidies for insurance purchased on federal (as opposed to state) exchanges. The implications of this case for the operation of the ACA would be hard to overstate. Without subsidies, millions of people would have dropped their insurance with profound implications for insurance markets. In short, the issue of statutory construction in King was a very, very big deal. And, therefore, according to the Chief Justice, Congress must not have intended *Chevron* to apply, and so it didn't:

> When analyzing an agency's interpretation of a statute, we often apply the two-step framework announced in Chevron. Under that framework, we ask whether the statute is ambiguous and, if so, whether the agency's interpretation is reasonable. This approach "is premised on the theory that a statute's ambiguity constitutes an implicit delegation from Congress to the agency to fill in the statutory gaps." *FDA v. Brown & Williamson Tobacco Corp.*, 529 U.S. 120, 159 (2000). "In extraordinary cases, however, there may be reason to hesitate before concluding that Congress has intended such an implicit delegation." *Ibid.*
>
> This is one of those cases. The tax credits are among the Act's key reforms, involving billions of dollars in spending each year and affecting the price of health insurance for millions of people. Whether those credits are available on Federal Exchanges is thus a question of deep "economic and political significance" that is central to this statutory scheme; had Congress wished to assign that question to an agency, it surely would have done so expressly. *Utility Air Regulatory Group v. EPA*, 134 S. Ct. 2427, 2444 (2014) (quoting

Brown & Williamson, 529 U.S., at 160). It is especially unlikely that Congress would have delegated this decision to the IRS, which has no expertise in crafting health insurance policy of this sort. *See Gonzales v. Oregon*, 546 U.S. 243, 266–267 (2006). This is not a case for the IRS. It is instead our task to determine the correct reading of Section 36B. *Id.* (some citations omitted).

So, if an issue of statutory construction raises extremely important policy questions, then *Chevron* should not apply because Congress would not want an agency to decide them. But hang on a second—the logic of *Chevron* is that agencies rather than courts are better positioned to fill the interpretive "gaps" that Congress inevitably leaves in agency enabling acts. Might it be all the more important for agencies rather than courts to resolve the really important statutory ambiguities?

8. *Chevron*, stare decisis, and resolution of Justice Scalia's ossification charge in *Brand X*. Note that a judicial opinion that affirms an agency interpretation as reasonable under *Chevron* leaves open the possibility that another, later agency interpretation might be reasonable, too. Judicial application of *Chevron* deference thus preserves a measure of agency interpretive freedom. Suppose, however, that a court determines that a particular agency interpretation does not qualify for *Chevron* deference. Applying *Skidmore*, the court decides that the agency's interpretation is not persuasive and adopts the construction it deems best. The question then arises: Can an agency later adopt a different, *Chevron*-eligible construction that trumps the "best" judicial construction, or will judicial stare decisis block this possibility? In *Mead*, Justice Scalia contended that the judicial construction must bind the agency. He also claimed that, because *Mead* expanded the range of circumstances in which courts would engage in non-deferential interpretation, it threatened to stifle agency interpretive freedom and freeze regulatory law into place.

The Court answered Justice Scalia's ossification charge in *National Cable & Telecomm. Ass'n v. Brand X Internet Serv.*, 125 S. Ct. 2688 (2005):

> A court's prior judicial construction of a statute trumps an agency construction otherwise entitled to *Chevron* deference only if the prior court decision holds that its construction follows from the unambiguous terms of the statute and thus leaves no room for agency discretion. This principle follows from *Chevron* itself. *Chevron* established a "presumption that Congress, when it left ambiguity in a statute meant for implementation by an agency, understood that the ambiguity would be resolved, first and foremost, by the agency, and desired the agency (rather than the courts) to possess whatever degree of discretion the ambiguity allows." *Smiley*, [517 U.S.] at 740–741. Yet allowing a judicial precedent to foreclose an agency from interpreting an ambiguous statute, as the Court of Appeals assumed it could, would allow a court's interpretation to override an agency's. *Chevron*'s premise is that it is for agencies, not courts, to fill statutory gaps. The better rule is to hold judicial interpretations contained in precedents to the same demanding *Chevron* step one standard that applies if the court is

reviewing the agency's construction on a blank slate: Only a judicial precedent holding that the statute unambiguously forecloses the agency's interpretation, and therefore contains no gap for the agency to fill, displaces a conflicting agency construction.

Justice Scalia retorted that, with this opinion, "[t]he Court today moves to solve this [ossification] problem of its own creation by inventing yet another breathtaking novelty: judicial decisions subject to reversal by Executive officers." *Id.* at 2719. He added that this result was both "bizarre" and "probably unconstitutional" because "Article III courts do not sit to render decisions that can be reversed or ignored by Executive officers." *Id.* at 2720. The majority responded:

> The dissent answers that allowing an agency to override what a court believes to be the best interpretation of a statute makes "judicial decisions subject to reversal by Executive officers." It does not. Since *Chevron* teaches that a court's opinion as to the best reading of an ambiguous statute an agency is charged with administering is not authoritative, the agency's decision to construe that statute differently from a court does not say that the court's holding was legally wrong. Instead, the agency may, consistent with the court's holding, choose a different construction, since the agency remains the authoritative interpreter (within the limits of reason) of such statutes. In all other respects, the court's prior ruling remains binding law (for example, as to agency interpretations to which *Chevron* is inapplicable). The precedent has not been "reversed" by the agency, any more than a federal court's interpretation of a State's law can be said to have been "reversed" by a state court that adopts a conflicting (yet authoritative) interpretation of state law.

125 S. Ct. at 2700–01.

9. Last but not least — does *Chevron* really matter? Standards of review instruct judges how to think as they review agency actions. Administrative law devotes considerable energy to developing and refining these standards. But do they affect outcomes very much? It is one thing for a judge to *think* that she is applying a standard of review. It is another thing for that standard of review to *affect* the judge's thinking in a way that changes outcomes. It could be that, regardless of the ostensible standard of review, case outcomes are driven by other factors — such as the persuasiveness of the agency's analysis, the complexity and technical difficulty of the agency's decision, the judge's respect for the particular agency, the agency's consistency over time, the judge's ideology, and so on.

A study by Eskridge and Baer that examined all 1,104 of the cases decided by the Supreme Court between the 1983 and 2005 terms in which the Court assessed an agency's statutory construction suggests that deference doctrines may have limited practical effects. Remarkably, the win rate for *Skidmore* cases was 73.5% and for *Chevron* cases was 76.2%. *See* William N. Eskridge Jr. & Lauren E. Baer, *The Continuum of Deference: Supreme Court Treatment of Agency Statutory Interpretations from* Chevron *to* Hamdan, 96 Geo. L.J. 1083, 1142 (2008). *See also* David Zaring, *Reasonable Agencies*, 96 Va. L. Rev. 135, 173–74 (2010) (surveying empirical studies on affirmance rates; observing that courts affirmed in *Chevron* cases about two-thirds of the time and that the rate for *Skidmore* cases, "though lower than *Chevron*, [was] not notably so"). The conclusion that deference doctrines do not actually matter much must now, however, take heed of Barnett and Walker's 2017 study, which examined 1,558 instances of judicial review of agency statutory constructions by the circuit courts. This study found that "agency interpretations were significantly more likely to prevail under *Chevron* deference (77.4%) than *Skidmore* deference (56%) or, especially, de novo review (38.5%)."

Empirical studies of agency "win rates" are informative, but one must be careful not to over-read them. It could be the case, for instance, that agencies push for more aggressive statutory constructions when they have *Chevron* on their side as opposed to *Skidmore*. If that is so, then *Chevron*'s effect on judges might be real enough but still not readily appear in agency win rates. On the other hand, courts do not choose randomly between applying *Chevron* and *Skidmore*, and we might reasonably expect *Skidmore* to be applied to interpretations that are, as a group, relatively weak. In that case, application of *Chevron* as opposed to *Skidmore* might not affect the real intensity of review, but we might still see higher *Chevron* win rates.

The upshot here is that, after decades of debate, we do not have a clear handle on how much deference doctrines matter to actual case outcomes. Still, even if the choice of standard of review might not matter much across the general run of cases, it might matter a lot in a particular case that you are litigating. Moreover, as an attorney, attention to form is an important part of your job. By deploying administrative law doctrines correctly, you communicate to judges, other attorneys, and sophisticated clients that you know what you are doing. That is a message you want to send.

Chapter 6

Agency Power to Gather Information

Information is at the heart of the regulatory process. The WTC, for example, must gather information about the content of wine, marketing practices, and consumer behaviors in order to develop rules implementing §5 of the WTCA. When the agency takes enforcement action against Gallery, it must do so on the basis of information about that particular company.

Much information is freely available in the public domain. The scientific literature will frequently include reports on the health effects of various substances or on the effect of product labeling on consumer purchasing decisions. The agency staff may research such information itself. Frequently, agencies contract with outside research firms or academic experts to gather publicly available information.

Inevitably, however, agencies need information that is closely held in private hands, particularly in the hands of regulated entities. This chapter examines agency power to require private parties to provide information, whether in the form of required filings or reports, responses to subpoenas and other demands for information, or being subjected to physical inspections.

A. Requiring Recordkeeping and Reports

Lesson 6A. When Carl appointed Ralph as head of the Enforcement Division, Carl pressed him to initiate a major enforcement action. Carl was confident he would be nominated to be the next undersecretary of commerce, except that Senator Bisby was not pleased with the WTC's performance under Carl. Senator Bisby sat on the relevant committee and his party controlled the Senate. Carl believed the Senator would "pull out all the stops" to block his nomination unless Carl could show effective leadership in implementing the WTCA. As he ushered Ralph out of his office, Carl slapped him on the shoulder and said, "I expect something showy and *soon*."

Ralph discovered that the staff had been exploring charges that Gallery had a practice of adding cane sugar to improve fermentation. The staff also asserted that Gallery added concentrated juice of high-yield table grapes to wines it labeled as made from the best wine grapes. Ralph thought that an extensive enforcement action against Gallery, the industry's largest producer, would be just what Carl had in mind. (As we saw in Lesson 4A.5, Ralph ultimately brought those charges against Gallery.)

Ralph reviewed the file the staff had already compiled. The file contained information taken from the reports required by WTCA §6(e). The staff planned to introduce those reports in the enforcement hearing. How would the following materials help Ralph determine whether he will be able to rely on these reports in the administrative hearing?

Background of *Marchetti v. United States*

The federal government is permitted to tax unlawful activities. It has done just that, in fact, with regard to wagering. The federal wagering tax statutes impose taxes on each wager placed, as well as on each individual accepting those wagers (the "occupational tax"), regardless of whether the wagers are legal under either state or federal law. The statutes also require each person who must pay the occupational tax to register with the Internal Revenue Service. In addition to providing personal information through their registration, those individuals must also preserve daily records indicating the total amount of wagers for which they are liable to be taxed that day. Petitioner Marchetti was in the business of accepting illegal wagers. He failed to register with the IRS or pay the occupational tax and was convicted. He argued post-conviction that the registration requirements and record keeping provisions of the wagering tax statutes violated his Fifth Amendment right against self-incrimination by forcing him to reveal his illegal gambling activities and therefore incriminate himself. The Court agreed to reexamine the question despite having ruled twice before that the registration and reporting requirements do not violate the Fifth Amendment.

Marchetti v. United States

390 U.S. 39 (1968)

Mr. Justice Harlan delivered the opinion of the Court.

Petitioner was convicted in the United States District Court for the District of Connecticut under two indictments which charged violations of the federal wagering tax statutes. The first indictment averred that petitioner and others conspired to evade payment of the annual occupational tax imposed by 26 U.S.C. §4411. The second indictment consisted of two counts: the first alleged a willful failure to pay the occupational tax, and the second a willful failure to register, as required by 26 U.S.C. §4412, before engaging in the business of accepting wagers.

After verdict, petitioner unsuccessfully sought to arrest judgment, in part on the basis that the statutory obligations to register and to pay the occupational tax violated his Fifth Amendment privilege against self-incrimination. The Court of Appeals for the Second Circuit affirmed. . . . For reasons which follow we have concluded that these provisions may not be employed to punish criminally those persons who have defended a failure to comply with their requirements with a proper assertion of the privilege against self-incrimination. The judgment below is accordingly reversed.

The provisions in issue here are part of an interrelated statutory system for taxing wagers. The system is broadly as follows. Section 4401 of Title 26 imposes upon those engaged in the business of accepting wagers an excise tax of 10% on the gross amount of all wagers they accept, including the value of chances purchased in lotteries conducted for profit. Parimutuel wagering enterprises, coin-operated devices, and state-conducted sweepstakes are expressly excluded from taxation. Section 4411 imposes in addition an occupational tax of $50 annually, both upon those subject to taxation under § 4401 and upon those who receive wagers on their behalf.

In addition, registrants . . . are required to preserve daily records indicating the gross amount of the wagers as to which they are liable for taxation, and to permit inspection of their books of account. Moreover, each principal internal revenue office is instructed to maintain for public inspection a listing of all who have paid the occupational tax, and to provide certified copies of the listing upon request to any state or local prosecuting officer. . . .

The issue before us is not whether the United States may tax activities which a State or Congress has declared unlawful. The Court has repeatedly indicated that the unlawfulness of an activity does not prevent its taxation, and nothing that follows is intended to limit or diminish the vitality of those cases. The issue is instead whether the methods employed by Congress in the federal wagering tax statutes are, in this situation, consistent with the limitations created by the privilege against self-incrimination guaranteed by the Fifth Amendment. We must for this purpose first examine the implications of these statutory provisions.

Wagering and its ancillary activities are very widely prohibited under both federal and state law. . . .

. . . .

Connecticut, in which petitioner allegedly conducted his activities, has adopted a variety of measures for the punishment of gambling and wagering. . . .

Information obtained as a consequence of the federal wagering tax laws is readily available to assist the efforts of state and federal authorities to enforce these penalties. Section 6107 of Title 26 requires the principal internal revenue offices to provide to prosecuting officers a listing of those who have paid the occupational tax. Section 6806(c) obliges taxpayers either to post the revenue stamp "conspicuously" in their principal places of business, or to keep it on their persons, and to produce it on the demand of Treasury officers. Evidence of the possession of a federal wagering tax stamp, or of payment of the wagering taxes, has often been admitted at trial in state and federal prosecutions for gambling offenses; such evidence has doubtless proved useful even more frequently to lead prosecuting authorities to other evidence upon which convictions have subsequently been obtained. Finally, we are obliged to notice that a former Commissioner of Internal Revenue has acknowledged that the Service 'makes available' to law enforcement agencies the names and addresses of those who have paid the wagering taxes, and that it is in "full cooperation" with the efforts of the Attorney General of the United States to suppress organized gambling.

In these circumstances, it can scarcely be denied that the obligations to register and to pay the occupational tax created for petitioner "real and appreciable," and not merely "imaginary and unsubstantial," hazards of self-incrimination. Petitioner was confronted by a comprehensive system of federal and state prohibitions against wagering activities; he was required, on pain of criminal prosecution, to provide information which he might reasonably suppose would be available to prosecuting authorities, and which would surely prove a significant "link in a chain" of evidence tending to establish his guilt. Unlike the income tax return . . . every portion of these requirements had the direct and unmistakable consequence of incriminating petitioner; the application of the constitutional privilege to the entire registration procedure was in this instance neither "extreme" nor "extravagant." It would appear to follow that petitioner's assertion of the privilege as a defense to this prosecution was entirely proper, and accordingly should have sufficed to prevent his conviction.

Nonetheless, this Court has twice concluded that the privilege against self-incrimination may not appropriately be asserted by those in petitioner's circumstances. We must therefore consider whether those cases have continuing force in light of our more recent decisions. Moreover, we must also consider the relevance of certain collateral lines of authority; in particular, we must determine whether either the "required records" doctrine, or restrictions placed upon the use by prosecuting authorities of information obtained as a consequence of the wagering taxes should be utilized to preclude assertion of the constitutional privilege in this situation. To these questions we turn.

The Court's opinion in *Kahriger* suggested that a defendant under indictment for willful failure to register under § 4412 cannot properly challenge the constitutionality under the Fifth Amendment of the registration requirement. For this point, the Court relied entirely upon Mr. Justice Holmes' opinion for the Court in *United States v. Sullivan*. The taxpayer in Sullivan was convicted of willful failure to file an income tax return, despite his contention that the return would have obliged him to admit violations of the National Prohibition Act. The Court affirmed the conviction, and rejected the taxpayer's claim of the privilege. It concluded that most of the return's questions would not have compelled the taxpayer to make incriminating disclosures, and that it would have been 'an extreme if not an extravagant application' of the privilege to permit him to draw within it the entire return.

The Court in Sullivan was evidently concerned, first, that the claim before it was an unwarranted extension of the scope of the privilege, and, second, that to accept a claim of privilege not asserted at the time the return was due would "make the taxpayer rather than a tribunal the final arbiter of the merits of the claim." . . .

The Court held in *Lewis* that the registration and occupational tax requirements do not infringe the constitutional privilege because they do not compel self-incrimination, but merely impose on the gambler the initial choice of whether he wishes at the cost of his constitutional privilege, to commence wagering activities. The Court reasoned that even if the required disclosures might prove incriminating, the gambler need not register or pay the occupational tax if only he elects to cease, or never to begin, gambling. There is, the Court said, "no constitutional right to gamble."

We find this reasoning no longer persuasive. The question is not whether petitioner holds a "right" to violate state law, but whether, having done so, he may be compelled to give evidence against himself. The constitutional privilege was intended to shield the guilty and imprudent as well as the innocent and foresighted; if such an inference of antecedent choice were alone enough to abrogate the privilege's protection, it would be excluded from the situations in which it has historically been guaranteed, and withheld from those who most require it.

Such inferences, bottomed on what must ordinarily be a fiction, have precisely the infirmities which the Court has found in other circumstances in which implied or uninformed waivers of the privilege have been said to have occurred. To give credence to such "waivers" without the most deliberate examination of the circumstances surrounding them would ultimately license widespread erosion of the privilege through "ingeniously drawn legislation." We cannot agree that the constitutional privilege is meaningfully waived merely because those "inherently suspect of criminal activities" have been commanded either to cease wagering or to provide information incriminating to themselves, and have ultimately elected to do neither.

The Court held in both *Kahriger* and *Lewis* that the registration and occupational tax requirements are entirely prospective in their application, and that the constitutional privilege, since it offers protection only as to past and present acts, is accordingly unavailable. This reasoning appears to us twice deficient: first, it overlooks the hazards here of incrimination as to past or present acts; and second, it is hinged upon an excessively narrow view of the scope of the constitutional privilege.

Substantial hazards of incrimination as to past or present acts plainly may stem from the requirements to register and to pay the occupational tax. In the first place, satisfaction of those requirements increases the likelihood that any past or present gambling offenses will be discovered and successfully prosecuted. It both centers attention upon the registrant as a gambler, and compels "injurious disclosure[s]" which may provide or assist in the collection of evidence admissible in a prosecution for past or present offenses. These offenses need not include actual gambling; they might involve only the custody or transportation of gambling paraphernalia, or other preparations for future gambling. Further, the acquisition of a federal gambling tax stamp, requiring as it does the declaration of a present intent to commence gambling activities, obliges even a prospective gambler to accuse himself of conspiracy to violate either state gambling prohibitions, or federal laws forbidding the use of interstate facilities for gambling purposes.

There is a second, and more fundamental, deficiency in the reasoning of *Kahriger* and *Lewis*. Its linchpin is plainly the premise that the privilege is entirely inapplicable to prospective acts; for this the Court in *Kahriger* could vouch as authority only a generalization. . . . We see no warrant for so rigorous a constraint upon the constitutional privilege. History, to be sure, offers no ready illustrations of the privilege's application to prospective acts, but the occasions on which such claims might appropriately have been made must necessarily have been very infrequent. We are, in any event, bid to view the constitutional commands as "organic living institutions" whose significance is "vital not formal."

The central standard for the privilege's application has been whether the claimant is confronted by substantial and "real," and not merely trifling or imaginary, hazards of incrimination. . . .

The hazards of incrimination created by §§ 4411 and 4412 as to future acts are not trifling or imaginary. Prospective registrants can reasonably expect that registration and payment of the occupational tax will significantly enhance the likelihood of their prosecution for future acts, and that it will readily provide evidence which will facilitate their convictions. Indeed, they can reasonably fear that registration, and acquisition of a wagering tax stamp, may serve as decisive evidence that they have in fact subsequently violated state gambling prohibitions. Insubstantial claims of the privilege as to entirely prospective acts may certainly be asserted, but such claims are not here, and they need only be considered when a litigant has the temerity to pursue them.

We must next consider the relevance in this situation of the "required records" doctrine, *Shapiro v. United States.* It is necessary first to summarize briefly the circumstances in *Shapiro.* Petitioner, a wholesaler of fruit and produce, was obliged by a regulation issued under the authority of the Emergency Price Control Act to keep and "preserve for examination" various records "of the same kind as he has customarily kept . . ." He was subsequently directed by an administrative subpoena to produce certain of these records before attorneys of the Office of Price Administration. Petitioner complied, but asserted his constitutional privilege. In a prosecution for violations of the Price Control Act, petitioner urged that the records had facilitated the collection of evidence against him, and claimed immunity from prosecution under § 202(g) of the Act. Petitioner was nonetheless convicted, and his conviction was affirmed.

On certiorari, this Court held both that § 202(g) did not confer immunity upon petitioner, and that he could not properly claim the protection of the privilege as to records which he was required by administrative regulation to preserve. On the second question, the Court relied upon the cases which have held that a custodian of public records may not assert the privilege as to those records, and reiterated dictum suggesting that the privilege which exists as to private papers cannot be maintained in relation to "records required by law to be kept in order that there may be suitable information of transactions which are the appropriate subjects of governmental regulation, and the enforcement of restrictions validly established." The Court considered that "it cannot be doubted" that the records in question had "public aspects," and thus held that petitioner, as their custodian, could not properly assert the privilege as to them.

We think that neither *Shapiro* nor the cases upon which it relied are applicable here.[14] Moreover, we find it unnecessary for present purposes to pursue in detail the question, left unanswered in *Shapiro*, of what "limits . . . the government cannot constitutionally exceed in requiring the keeping of records. . . ." It is enough that there are significant points of difference between the situations here and in *Shapiro* which in this instance preclude, under any formulation, an appropriate application of the "required records" doctrine.

Each of the three principal elements of the doctrine, as it is described in *Shapiro*, is absent from this situation. First, petitioner Marchetti was not, by the provisions now at issue, obliged to keep and preserve records "of the same kind as he has customarily kept"; he was required simply to provide information, unrelated to any records which he may have maintained, about his wagering activities. This requirement is not significantly different from a demand that he provide oral testimony. Second, whatever "public aspects" there were to the records at issue in *Shapiro*, there are none to the information demanded from Marchetti. The Government's anxiety to obtain information known to a private individual does not without more render that information public; if it did, no room would remain for the application of the constitutional privilege. Nor does it stamp information with a public character that the Government has formalized its demands in the attire of a statute; if this alone were sufficient, the constitutional privilege could be entirely abrogated by any Act of Congress. Third, the requirements at issue in *Shapiro* were imposed in "an essentially non-criminal and regulatory area of inquiry" while those here are directed at a "selective group inherently suspect of criminal activities." The United States' principal interest is evidently the collection of revenue and not the punishment of gamblers; but the characteristics of the activities about which information is sought, and the composition of the groups to which inquiries are made, readily distinguish this situation from that in *Shapiro*. There is no need to explore further the elements and limitations of *Shapiro* and the cases involving public papers; these points of difference in combination preclude any appropriate application of those cases to the present one.

---

14. The United States has urged that this case is not reached by *Shapiro* simply because petitioner was required to submit reports, and not to maintain records. Insofar as this is intended to suggest the crucial issue respecting the applicability of *Shapiro* is the method by which information reaches the Government, we are unable to accept the distinction. We perceive no meaningful difference between an obligation to maintain records for inspection, and such an obligation supplemented by a requirement that those records be filed periodically with officers of the United States. We believe, as the United States itself argued in *Shapiro*, that "[r]egulations permit records to be retained, rather than filed, largely for the convenience of the persons regulated." (Brief for the United States in No. 49, October Term 1947, at 21, n. 7).

Finally, we have been urged by the United States to permit continued enforcement of the registration and occupational tax provisions, despite the demands of the constitutional privilege, by shielding the privilege's claimants through the imposition of restrictions upon the use by federal and state authorities of information obtained as a consequence of compliance with the wagering tax requirements. . . .

The Constitution of course obliges this Court to give full recognition to the taxing powers and to measures reasonably incidental to their exercise. But we are equally obliged to give full effect to the constitutional restrictions which attend the exercise of those powers. We do not, as we have said, doubt Congress' power to tax activities which are, wholly or in part, unlawful. Nor can it be doubted that the privilege against self-incrimination may not properly be asserted if other protection is granted which "is so broad as to have the same extent in scope and effect" as the privilege itself. The Government's suggestion is thus in principle an attractive and apparently practical resolution of the difficult problem before us. Nonetheless, we think that it would be entirely inappropriate in the circumstances here for the Court to impose such restrictions.

The terms of the wagering tax system make quite plain that Congress intended information obtained as a consequence of registration and payment of the occupational tax to be provided to interested prosecuting authorities. This has evidently been the consistent practice of the Revenue Service. We must therefore assume that the imposition of use-restrictions would directly preclude effectuation of a significant element of Congress' purposes in adopting the wagering taxes. Moreover, the imposition of such restrictions would necessarily oblige state prosecuting authorities to establish in each case that their evidence was untainted by any connection with information obtained as a consequence of the wagering taxes; the federal requirements would thus be protected, only at the cost of hampering, perhaps seriously, enforcement of state prohibitions against gambling. We cannot know how Congress would assess the competing demands of the federal treasury and of state gambling prohibitions; we are, however, entirely certain that the Constitution has entrusted to Congress, and not to this Court, the task of striking an appropriate balance among such values. We therefore must decide that it would be improper for the Court to impose restrictions of the kind urged by the United States.

We are fully cognizant of the importance for the United States' various fiscal and regulatory functions of timely and accurate information; but other methods, entirely consistent with constitutional limitations, exist by which Congress may obtain such information. Accordingly, nothing we do today will prevent either the taxation or the regulation by Congress of activities otherwise made unlawful by state or federal statutes.

Nonetheless, we can only conclude, under the wagering tax system as presently written, that petitioner properly asserted the privilege against self-incrimination, and that his assertion should have provided a complete defense to this prosecution. This defense should have reached both the substantive counts for failure to register and to pay the occupational tax, and the count for conspiracy to evade payment of the tax. We emphasize that we do not hold that these wagering tax provisions are as such constitutionally impermissible; we hold only that those who properly assert the constitutional privilege as to these provisions may not be criminally punished for failure to comply with their requirements. If, in different circumstances, a taxpayer is not confronted by substantial hazards of self-incrimination, or if he is otherwise outside the privilege's protection, nothing we decide today would shield him from the various penalties prescribed by the wagering tax statutes.

The judgment of the Court of Appeals is

Reversed.

Mr. Justice Marshall took no part in the consideration or decision of this case. [For concurring and dissenting opinions, see *Grosso v. United States*, 390 U.S. 62 (1968).]

Notes

1. Statutory and regulatory reporting requirements. As always, an agency may act only pursuant to statutory authority. In this instance, §6(e) of the WTCA authorizes the Commission to "require . . . such reports as it deems necessary." Typically, an agency will promulgate legislative rules establishing the types of reports that regulated bodies must file with the agency. For example, the EPA requires the holders of water pollution permits both to monitor the contents of their discharges and to file periodic Discharge Monitoring Reports (DMRs). 40 C.F.R. §122.41(l)(4)(i). Reports such as DMRs or those required by the WTC are generally available to the public and frequently provide the basis for enforcement actions against the company submitting the report. In light of authority provided by §6(e) of the WTCA, the question here is not whether the WTC may require the information to be reported, but whether the WTC may rely upon the information in an enforcement action.

Note that §6(c) of the WTCA also authorizes the Commission to require the filing of "an application as prescribed by the Commission." An agency may require information to be provided in the application as well as in later reports.

2. Use of reports in enforcement actions. Under what circumstances may Ralph's staff introduce the reports required by WTCA §6(e) in the enforcement proceeding against Gallery? *Shapiro v. United States*, 335 U.S. 1 (1948), cited frequently in *Marchetti*, is the general rule and *Marchetti* is an exception. Will Gallery be able to claim the exception? One way Justice Harlan distinguished *Shapiro* was that, unlike the case before him, *Shapiro* involved an essentially non-criminal and regulatory area of inquiry. The WTC proceeding is a law enforcement proceeding. Indeed at the end, Gallery might face monetary penalties. Is this sufficiently criminal to raise the protections afforded to Marchetti? As it turns out, despite the similarity between "civil" penalties and criminal fines, administrative law enforcement proceedings, such as those under the WTCA, are not categorized as criminal. Still, Justice Harlan notes that one question left unanswered is what "limits . . . the government cannot constitutionally exceed in requiring the keeping of records." What do you think the answer to this question should be?

3. A contrary view from the states. Justice Kaufman, concurring and dissenting in *Craib v. Bulmash*, 777 P.2d 1120 (Cal. 1989), argued that the California Supreme Court should not follow *Shapiro* in interpreting the state constitution:

> While I recognize the state's need to verify compliance with valid police power regulations, I am troubled that, in many cases, the *Shapiro* rule gives regulatory agencies virtually the unchallengeable power to enforce its regulations by criminal prosecution based on compelled self-disclosure. It is wholly contrary to the state and federal guarantees against compelled self-incrimination to allow government the unbridled authority to compel an individual to provide self-incriminating testimonial evidence without at the same time preventing its use as evidence in the prosecution of that individual for any crimes disclosed therein. Accordingly, I would order defendant to produce the records the Division of Labor Standards Enforcement (Division) seeks to carry out its regulatory function, but require the government to forego their use in any subsequent criminal prosecution.
>
> . . . .
>
> The majority decision incorporates into California law the "required records doctrine" of *Shapiro*, a judicially created exception to the privilege against compelled self-incrimination, and by so doing denigrates the privilege and the principles upon which it is based. Such a decision, in my view, is unnecessary, unwarranted and ill-advised. As the Division averred at oral argument, criminal prosecution for failure to create and retain the wage and hour records or to pay prescribed wages is rarely pursued. Thus, criminal prosecution is apparently not essential to enforcement of the wage and hour laws. . . .
>
> . . . .
>
> I find the notion of balancing the governmental interest in obtaining compelled self-incriminating evidence against a claim for Fifth Amendment protection to be highly questionable. I have always thought the privilege to be absolute. Indeed, even in cases of the most compelling nature, the trial of an accused serial killer for example, it has never occurred to this court or the United States Supreme Court to allow the state to use evidence obtained in violation of the Fifth Amendment because the need is compelling.
>
> . . . .
>
> In sum, if *Shapiro*'s required-records doctrine mandates that we weigh the state's interest in compelling self-incriminating disclosures against the Fifth Amendment guaranty against such self-incrimination, then absent an affirmative showing by the regulatory agency that criminal prosecution is essential to enforce a valid regulatory scheme, the agency's obtaining such

records by compulsion must be conditioned on their unavailability for use in a criminal prosecution. In the absence of an applicable immunity provision, to avoid violation of the Constitution and to preserve the ability of the Division to perform its regulatory function, we should provide such immunity judicially.

If you were on the state supreme court, would you adopt Justice Kaufman's views?

4. The Paperwork Reduction Act. The burden of constantly increasing government reporting prompted the Paperwork Reduction Act of 1980, 44 U.S.C. §§ 3501–20. That act requires clearance by the Office of Management and Budget (OMB, the president's agency for supervising government) for all "information collection requests" that ask identical questions of ten or more sources outside the government, in an attempt to eliminate unnecessary or redundant reporting requirements. William Funk, *The Paperwork Reduction Act: Paperwork Reduction Meets Administrative Law*, 24 HARV. J. ON LEGIS. 1, 33 (1987). Congress made two major changes to that act in 1995. First, it made clear that an agency must obtain OMB clearance when it requires the collection of information for disclosure to others. Second, the amendment increased the agency's burden by requiring a certification of compliance with ten separate substantive requirements for new collections. These changes further strengthened the OMB's grip on agency information gathering operations. What are the pluses and minuses of giving the executive office such control over agency sources of information?

5. When can the agency release information to the public? Whenever private information comes into the hands of government, concerns arise about whether it can be released to the public. The WTCA addresses these concerns in § 6(g) by authorizing release of such information "if such release will further the Commission's law enforcement purposes." Moreover, it states that WTC employees who release such information without authority from the Commission or a court may be subjected to criminal punishment. More generally, government employees who release trade secrets or similar information "in any manner or to any extent not authorized by law" are subject to criminal fines and imprisonment, and they "shall be removed from office or employment." 18 U.S.C. § 1905. The question of when government-held information is available to the public is addressed at greater length in Chapter 7.

B. Agency Authority to Investigate — Subpoenas and the Like

Lesson 6B. Ralph has learned that Gallery has been boosting the sugar content of some of its wines, thereby enhancing their fermentation. But Gallery hasn't been adding sugar. Instead, it has contracted with a biotech firm, Magic Plants, to develop new strains of grapes by adding sugar cane genes to the DNA of traditional grape varieties. Gallery markets the resulting wines under names such as "Modern

Chardonnay." The label lists the name of the traditional grape variety, but it says nothing of the high-tech enhancement.

Ralph demands all records relevant to these grapes and wines from both Gallery and Magic Plants, both of whom have retained Abby to challenge the subpoenas. Both refuse to comply with the demands. Gallery argues that there is no basis for an argument that its practices violate § 5 of the WTCA, so the demands are not authorized. Magic Plants argues that it is not subject to the jurisdiction of the WTC.

In light of the following materials, what should Ralph and Abby argue for and against enforcement of the demands?

Background of *EEOC v. Karuk Tribe Housing Authority* and *EEOC v. Sidley Austin Brown & Wood*

The Equal Employment Opportunity Commission (EEOC) is responsible for, among other things, enforcing federal laws that make it illegal to discriminate against a job applicant or employee (who is at least forty years old) on the basis of age. As part of its enforcement responsibility, the EEOC has the power to obtain information via subpoenas. The following cases involve age discrimination claims by a member of the Karuk Tribe and by thirty-two recently demoted partners of a large law firm, respectively. In both cases, the EEOC subpoenaed information from the alleged violator and was refused. The EEOC asked a court to force the subpoenaed parties to comply and got two very different answers.

In *Karuk Tribe*, the Tribe resisted complying with the subpoena on the grounds that its sovereignty put it beyond the jurisdiction of the EEOC. The Ninth Circuit agreed, holding that the jurisdictional question of whether the statute applied to the Tribe should be answered by the courts before addressing the question of whether the subpoena is enforceable. Sidley tried to build on the holding in *Karuk Tribe* by arguing that it need only provide information under its subpoena sufficient to defeat EEOC jurisdiction over the former partners' claims. In a decision potentially in tension with the Ninth Circuit's ruling in *Karuk Tribe*, the Seventh Circuit in *Sidley Austin Brown* rejected Sidley's position, holding that Sidley must comply with at least those portions of the subpoena that go to the statute's applicability to the case at hand.

EEOC v. Karuk Tribe Housing Authority
260 F.3d 1071 (9th Cir. 2001)

McKeown, Circuit Judge:

This case raises issues at the intersection of administrative, Indian, and anti-discrimination law. We must decide whether the district court properly enforced an administrative subpoena issued to an Indian tribe in connection with an age-discrimination investigation. Robert Grant, a member of the Karuk Tribe ("the Tribe") and an employee of the Karuk Tribe Housing Authority (the "Housing

Authority"), filed an administrative complaint with the Equal Employment Opportunity Commission (the "EEOC"), alleging that he had been terminated because of his age. The EEOC opened an investigation and issued a subpoena to the Tribe, which refused to comply on the grounds that the Age Discrimination in Employment Act (the "ADEA") does not apply to Indian tribes, and that the Tribe enjoys sovereign immunity from the EEOC investigation.

The EEOC sought judicial enforcement of the subpoena. The district court issued an order enforcing the subpoena, from which the Tribe now appeals. We reverse.

The threshold question is whether the Tribe is immune from suit. We conclude that it is not. We next address whether the Tribe is subject to the ADEA in these circumstances. We conclude that it is not. Resolution of this issue is a pure question of law that is currently ripe for review and, therefore, is best resolved at the subpoena-enforcement stage, rather than in potential downstream litigation. To hold otherwise would frustrate the regulatory scheme, ignore the special status of the Tribe, and subject the Tribe to an unnecessary compliance burden. Thus, because the ADEA does not apply to the Tribe's employment relationship with Grant, we conclude that the Tribe need not comply with the subpoena.

Background

The Karuk Tribe Housing Authority owns 100 low-income housing units on tribal trust land in Northern California. . . . The Housing Authority, organized and authorized through a tribal ordinance, is a governmental arm of the Tribe. The Housing Authority, which provides safe and affordable housing to members of the Tribe, receives funding under the Native American Housing Assistance and Self-Determination Act. This legislation, passed in 1996, was particularly concerned with "the right of Indian self-determination and tribal self-governance." Although there is no formal requirement that only Tribe members may occupy the units, according to the Vice-Chairman of the Karuk Tribe and Acting Executive Director of the Karuk Tribe Housing Authority, ninety-nine of the units are occupied by Indian families. The record does not reveal how many of the Indians who occupy the units are members of the Tribe. According to the district court's order enforcing the subpoena, the Housing Authority employed twenty Indians and four non-Indians.

Grant, an enrolled member of the Tribe, worked as a maintenance supervisor for the Housing Authority for almost seven years, until he was terminated in November 1997. He was fifty-three years old at the time of his termination. Grant challenged his firing in internal tribal administrative proceedings, which are governed by written policies and procedures. After a hearing, the Board of Commissioners upheld the Housing Authority's actions. Grant further appealed to the Tribal Council, the highest governing body of the Tribe, which rejected his claim as well.

In February 1998, Grant filed a "Charge of Discrimination" with the EEOC on a standard form, alleging that he had been terminated because of his age. The EEOC subsequently opened an investigation based on its purported authority under 29 U.S.C. §626(a). Section 626(a) provides, "The Equal Employment Opportunity

Commission shall have the power to make investigations and require the keeping of records necessary or appropriate for the administration of this chapter in accordance with the powers and procedures provided in sections 209 and 211 of this title." Section 211(a), which is relevant here, provides,

> The Administrator or his designated representatives may investigate and gather data regarding the wages, hours, and other conditions and practices of employment in any industry subject to this chapter, and may enter and inspect such places and such records (and make such transcriptions thereof), question such employees, and investigate such facts, conditions, practices, or matters as he may deem necessary or appropriate to determine whether any person has violated any provision of this chapter, or which may aid in the enforcement of the provisions of this chapter.

The EEOC served on the Tribe a copy of the charge, along with a request for a written position statement and a list of questions. The Tribe responded that it would not provide the information, based on its position that the ADEA does not apply to Indian tribes. In March 1999, the EEOC served on the Housing Authority's custodian of records an administrative subpoena seeking various employment records. The Tribe responded with a letter explaining that it would not provide the requested information, again based on its view that the EEOC does not have jurisdiction over Indian tribes.

The EEOC filed an application to enforce the administrative subpoena in the United States District Court for the Northern District of California. The district court held that "the EEOC has jurisdiction over Indian tribes for the purpose of enforcing the ADEA," granted the EEOC's application, and issued an enforcement order. The Tribe timely appealed. We have jurisdiction . . . , and we reverse.

Discussion

[The court first held that the Tribe was not entitled to sovereign immunity in an action brought by the EEOC.]

II. Administrative Subpoena Enforcement

It bears repeating that we are not confronted here with an age-discrimination suit brought under the ADEA. Rather, the parties to this action have only reached the investigative stage, and this litigation is a suit to enforce an administrative subpoena. Before considering the applicability of the ADEA to the Tribe, therefore, we must first determine whether we should reach that question at this stage of the proceedings.

We begin with the Supreme Court's decision in *Endicott Johnson Corp. v. Perkins*, 317 U.S. 501 (1943). In *Endicott Johnson*, Secretary of Labor Frances Perkins issued an administrative subpoena to the petitioner, a government contractor, in the course of an investigation to determine whether the petitioner had violated the Walsh-Healey Act. Notably, the Walsh-Healey Act "applies only to contractors who voluntarily enter into competition to obtain government business on terms of which they are fairly forewarned by inclusion in the contract." The petitioner argued that he was not required to comply with the subpoena because the alleged violations of the Act occurred in plants that were not involved in government work and, therefore, were not covered by the Act. Stating that "[t]he evidence sought by the subpoena was not plainly incompetent or irrelevant to any lawful purpose of the Secretary in the discharge of her duties under the Act," the Supreme Court concluded that the subpoena should be enforced and that the question whether the Secretary had identified true violations of the Act could be resolved at a later stage of the proceedings.

The principle of *Endicott Johnson*—that courts should not refuse to enforce an administrative subpoena when confronted by a fact-based claim regarding coverage or compliance with the law—has been consistently reaffirmed by the Supreme Court. *Okla. Press Publ'g Co. v. Walling*, 327 U.S. 186, 216 (1946); *United States v. Morton Salt Co.*, 338 U.S. 632, 652–53 (1950); *United States v. Powell*, 379 U.S. 48, 57–58 (1964). It is also alive and well in this circuit, as illustrated by *EEOC v. Children's Hospital Medical Center*, 719 F.2d 1426 (9th Cir. 1983) (en banc), which sets forth current law governing the permissible grounds for challenging an administrative subpoena. In *Children's Hospital*, a private, class-action race discrimination suit ended with a consent decree. After entry of the consent decree, three employees filed claims with the EEOC against the hospital. The EEOC issued administrative subpoenas to the hospital, which refused to comply on the ground that any claims against the hospital were barred by the res judicata effect of the consent decree. The district court agreed with the hospital, reasoning that the EEOC lacked jurisdiction over the hospital because of the consent decree.

This court reversed, holding that it was premature to address the res judicata issue when the only action pending was litigation over enforcement of the administrative subpoenas. As we explained:

> The scope of the judicial inquiry in an EEOC or any other agency subpoena enforcement proceeding is quite narrow. The critical questions are: (1) whether Congress has granted the authority to investigate; (2) whether procedural requirements have been followed; and (3) whether the evidence is relevant and material to the investigation.

Put another way, courts must enforce administrative subpoenas unless "the evidence sought by the subpoena [is] 'plainly incompetent or irrelevant' to 'any lawful purpose' of the agency." Thus, in *Children's Hospital*, whether res judicata might bar a subsequent lawsuit was simply irrelevant to the inquiry whether the EEOC could issue administrative subpoenas that might uncover evidence for use in a later lawsuit: "[A] party may not defeat agency authority to investigate with a claim that could be a defense if the agency subsequently decides to bring an action against it."

The general rule of *Endicott Johnson* in favor of enforcement of administrative subpoenas thus stands. But it is not absolute. Although a party may not avoid an administrative subpoena on the ground that it has a valid defense to a potential subsequent lawsuit, such a challenge may, in limited circumstances, be mounted when the defense raised is "jurisdictional" in nature—i.e., when the agency lacks jurisdiction over the subject of the investigation. But even where this exception is concerned, the role of a court reviewing a subpoena attacked on jurisdictional grounds is "strictly limited." "As long as the evidence sought is relevant, material and there is some 'plausible' ground for jurisdiction, or to phrase it another way, unless jurisdiction is 'plainly lacking,' the court should enforce the subpoena."

Despite these seemingly straightforward ground rules, the inquiry into administrative subpoenas has been complicated by the fact that the words "coverage" and "jurisdiction" are sometimes used interchangeably, and often imprecisely. It is important to differentiate "coverage" from "jurisdiction," because these two different sorts of challenges lead to different results: factual challenges based on a lack of statutory "coverage" are clearly not permitted, while challenges based on "jurisdiction" may, in certain circumstances, result in a refusal to enforce a subpoena.

This distinction is not merely semantic. There is a difference, particularly in the case of an Indian tribe, between the determination whether an agency has regulatory jurisdiction to enforce a subpoena in the first instance, and the very different question whether a subpoena recipient has a defense to liability under the applicable statute.

Here, the Tribe's challenge to the EEOC subpoena—that the ADEA does not apply to Indian tribes, and that it enjoys sovereign immunity from the EEOC investigation—falls into a narrow category of cases that is ripe for determination at the enforcement stage. Our approach is consistent with *Burlington Northern*, where we held in the context of an Occupational Safety and Health Administration ("OSHA") inspection that

> [j]udicial intervention prior to an agency's initial determination of its jurisdiction is appropriate only where: (1) there is clear evidence that exhaustion of administrative remedies will result in irreparable injury; (2) the agency's jurisdiction is plainly lacking; and (3) the agency's special expertise will be of no help on the question of its jurisdiction.

Assuming that the Tribe is correct in its analysis with respect to jurisdiction, the prejudice of subjecting the Tribe to a subpoena for which the agency does not have jurisdiction results in irreparable injury vis-a-vis the Tribe's sovereignty. In addition, the EEOC does not have special expertise in interpretation of statutes with respect to Indians. By contrast, this special circumstance was not present in *Burlington Northern*.

For similar reasons, this case is also unlike *Endicott Johnson* and *Children's Hospital*. Both of those decisions involved parties that were clearly subject to the federal laws that authorized the administrative investigations. The questions that those courts declined to resolve concerned potential defenses to enforcement actions. In both cases, because the subpoenaed parties could, under some set of facts, be found in violation of federal law, it made sense for the court not to adjudicate the parties' fact-specific defenses at the administrative subpoena stage.

In juxtaposition, this case presents the question whether the Karuk Tribe Housing Authority, in its role as Grant's employer, is subject to the ADEA *at all*, whatever the facts of the actual discrimination charge may be. The Tribe asserts that it falls into a category of entity not subject to the ADEA, and thus not subject to investigation by the EEOC. Whether this is so is a pure question of law, the resolution of which does not depend on a factual inquiry, and which would not undermine the role of subpoena enforcement actions as "summary procedure[s]" designed to allow "speedy investigation of EEOC charges."

Here the jurisdictional question is particularly sensitive because it involves the Karuk Tribe, which, like other tribes, enjoys a unique legal status as a sovereign. In this context, the prejudice from compliance is real. *See Reich v. Great Lakes Indian Fish & Wildlife Comm'n*, 4 F.3d 490, 492 (7th Cir. 1993) ("The Commission should not be burdened with having to comply with a subpoena if, as the district court believed, the agency issuing it has no jurisdiction to regulate the wages that the Commission pays. Questions of regulatory jurisdiction are properly addressed at the subpoena-enforcement stage if, as here, they are ripe for determination at that stage. Compliance with a subpoena is a burden, and one that a person or institution that can show it is not subject to the regulatory regime in aid of which the subpoena was issued should not be required to bear." (citations omitted)). The Tribe's challenge to the EEOC's administrative subpoena is jurisdictional in nature and thus may be resolved here as a matter of law.

III. Applicability of the ADEA to Indian Tribes

[On the merits, the court held that the ADEA did not apply to the Tribe in this instance, essentially because the employment dispute was entirely "intramural," or within the Tribe and not involving others. Such disputes are to be resolved internally by the Tribe's sovereign government.] Because federal regulation of the employment relationship between the Karuk Tribe Housing Authority and Grant would "touch[ ] exclusive rights of self-governance in purely intramural matters," the ADEA does not apply in these circumstances. Thus, the EEOC is without regulatory jurisdiction over the Tribe with respect to the ADEA, and the district court should not have enforced the subpoena.

Reversed.

EEOC v. Sidley Austin Brown & Wood
315 F.3d 696 (7th Cir. 2002)

POSNER, CIRCUIT JUDGE:

In 1999, Sidley & Austin (as it then was) demoted 32 of its equity partners to "counsel" or "senior counsel." The significance of these terms is unclear, but Sidley does not deny that they signify demotion and constitute adverse personnel action within the meaning of the antidiscrimination laws. The EEOC began an investigation to determine whether the demotions might have violated the Age Discrimination in Employment Act. After failing to obtain all the information it wanted without recourse to process, the Commission issued a subpoena duces tecum to the firm, seeking a variety of documentation bearing on two distinct areas of inquiry: coverage and discrimination. The reason for the inquiry about coverage is that the ADEA protects employees but not employers. To be able to establish that the firm had violated the ADEA, therefore, the Commission would have to show that the 32 partners were employees before their demotion.

Sidley provided most of the information sought in the subpoena that related to coverage (but no information relating to discrimination, though Sidley claims that the demotions were due to shortcomings in performance rather than to age), but not all. It contended that it had given the Commission enough information to show that before their demotion the 32 had been "real" partners and so there was no basis for the Commission to continue its investigation. The Commission applied to the district court for an order enforcing the subpoena. The court ordered the firm to comply in full, and the firm appeals. . . .

. . . .

The law firm's argument proceeds in three steps: (1) the question whether the 32 demoted partners are within the ADEA's coverage is a jurisdictional question, which once answered against the Commission requires that the investigation cease; (2) the target of a subpoena need comply only up to the point at which it has produced evidence that establishes that there is no jurisdiction; (3) the Commission has no jurisdiction in this case because a partner is an employer within the meaning of the federal antidiscrimination laws if (a) his income included a share of the firm's profits, (b) he made a contribution to the capital of the firm, (c) he was liable for the firm's debts, and (d) he had some administrative or managerial responsibilities — and all these things, the firm argues, have been proved.

The facts as developed so far reveal the following:

> The firm is controlled by a self-perpetuating executive committee. Partners who are not members of the committee have some powers delegated to them by it with respect to the hiring, firing, promotion, and compensation of their subordinates, but so far as their own status is concerned they are at the committee's mercy. It can fire them, promote them, demote them (as it did to the 32), raise their pay, lower their pay, and so forth. The only firm-wide issue on which all partners have voted in the last quarter century was the merger with Brown & Wood and that vote took place after the EEOC began its investigation. Each of the 32 partners at the time of their demotion by the executive committee had a capital account with the firm, averaging about $400,000. Under the firm's rules, each was liable for the firm's

liabilities in proportion to his capital in the firm. Their income, however, was determined by the number of percentage points of the firm's overall profits that the executive committee assigned to each of them. Each served on one or more of the firm's committees, but all these committees are subject to control by the executive committee.

Sidley can obtain no mileage by characterizing the coverage issue as "jurisdictional." It is the law that the EEOC cannot protect employers; and it is also the law that like any agency with subpoena powers the EEOC is entitled to obtain the facts necessary to determine whether it can proceed to the enforcement stage. Among these are facts bearing on whether the 32 demoted partners were employees within the meaning of the age discrimination law. The Commission is entitled to the information that it thinks it needs in order to be able to formulate its theory of coverage before the court is asked to choose between the Commission's theory and that of the subpoenaed firm. Only if, as in *Reich v. Great Lakes Indian Fish & Wildlife Comm'n*, 4 F.3d 490 (7th Cir. 1993), the information that the subpoenaed firm resists furnishing is not even arguably relevant, because it is evident at the outset that whether the agency has any business conducting the investigation depends on a pure issue of statutory interpretation, can the court resolve the issue then and there without insisting on further compliance with the subpoena. . . .

. . . [C]haracterizing a threshold issue as "jurisdictional" [does not take] a case out of the general rule that enforcement of a subpoena cannot be resisted on the ground that the information the agency is seeking would not justify an enforcement action. The cases are legion that there is no *general* exception to the rule for issues going to the agency's jurisdiction. As explained in *United States v. Construction Products Research, Inc.*, "at the subpoena enforcement stage, courts need not determine whether the subpoenaed party is within the agency's jurisdiction or covered by the statute it administers; rather the coverage determination should wait until an enforcement action is brought against the subpoenaed party." Sidley gains nothing, therefore, from characterizing the coverage issue as jurisdictional, and so we need not decide whether the characterization is correct.

But the cases leave intact the principle that a subpoena may be challenged as unreasonable. And one basis on which it may be found unreasonable is that, as in *Great Lakes*, the agency clearly is ranging far beyond the boundaries of its statutory authority. As the Supreme Court explained in *United States v. Morton Salt Co.*, 338 U.S. 632, 652 (1950), "of course a governmental investigation into corporate matters may be of such a sweeping nature and so unrelated to the matter properly under inquiry as to exceed the investigatory power. But it is sufficient if the inquiry is within the authority of the agency, the demand is not too indefinite and the information sought is reasonably relevant." In *Endicott Johnson Corp. v. Perkins*, the Court noted that "the evidence sought by the subpoena was not plainly incompetent or irrelevant to any lawful purpose of the Secretary in the discharge of her duties under the Act, and it was the duty of the District Court to order its production for the Secretary's consideration"—implying therefore that had the evidence sought by the subpoena been "plainly incompetent or irrelevant to any lawful purpose," enforcement would have been denied.

Great Lakes was such a case; this one is not (not yet anyway, though it may become one, as we shall point out later). But the difference is not, as implied in *EEOC v. Karuk Tribe Housing Authority*, that *Great Lakes* involved an issue of jurisdiction and this case a "mere" issue of coverage and that there should be a special rule if not for jurisdictional defects then at least for "patent" jurisdictional defects. "Patent" is important to the issue of reasonableness, but not "jurisdictional." The Commission has the same right to obtain information bearing on its jurisdiction as to obtain any other information that it needs in order to decide whether there has been a violation of one of the laws that it enforces, while the recipient of the subpoena has the same right to challenge the subpoena as unreasonable because of lack of coverage as it does to complain that the subpoena is unreasonable because the recipient is outside the agency's jurisdiction. Suppose Sidley were conceded to have only eight employees, when an employer must have at least 20 employees in order to be subject to the ADEA. It would not follow that Sidley could not complain about the subpoena unless the issue were characterized as jurisdictional. The distinction for which *Karuk* contended would complicate litigation pointlessly by forcing judges to distinguish between jurisdictional and non-jurisdictional limitations on agencies' powers and to decide on which side of the line coverage issues belong. So, to repeat, whether the coverage issue in this case should be characterized as jurisdictional is irrelevant.

. . . .

[The court explained that the statutory question was not whether the 32 demoted partners were truly "partners" under state law or otherwise, but whether all partners are necessarily "employers" and thus unprotected by the ADEA. The court then examined in detail the complexities of the "partnership" arrangements at Sidley & Austin and the related caselaw.]

All that is clear amidst this welter of cases is that the coverage issue in the present case remains murky despite Sidley's partial compliance with the subpoena. The Commission is therefore entitled to full compliance, at least with regard to coverage, unless the additional documents the Commission is seeking are obviously irrelevant. What the Commission particularly wants to know is how unevenly the profits are spread across the entire firm. Are profits so concentrated in members of the executive committee, or in some smaller or larger set of partners, in relation to the profits that the executive committee allocated to the 32, that the latter occupied the same position they would have if they had been working at a comparable rank for one of the investment banks that once were partnerships but now are corporations? This might not be decisive but it would bear on the unavoidably multi-factored determination of whether this large law firm—which in recognition that conventional partnership is designed for much smaller and simpler firms has contractually altered the structure of the firm in the direction of the corporate form—should for purposes of antidiscrimination law be deemed the employer of some at least of the individuals whom it designates as partners.

But we think the district court acted prematurely in ordering order the subpoena complied with in its entirety. It is not only the law firm that has failed to argue the purpose of the exclusion of employers from the protection of the statute; it is also the EEOC. Without having proposed a standard or criterion to guide the determination, the Commission has not earned the right to force the law firm not merely to finish complying with the coverage portion of the subpoena but to go on and produce the voluminous and sensitive documentation sought relating to the question whether, if these 32 partners were employees, they were demoted on account of their age and therefore in violation of the age discrimination law. We are therefore vacating the district court's order and remanding the case with directions to order the law firm to comply fully with the part of the subpoena that requests documents relating to coverage, but upon completion of those submissions to make a determination whether the 32 demoted partners are arguably covered by the ADEA. If it is plain on the basis of uncontested facts that before their demotion the 32 were not employees and therefore were not protected by the Act, which would place the case under the principle of our *Great Lakes* decision, then, barring circumstances that we do not at present foresee, the court should excuse the firm from compliance with the part of the subpoena that requests documents relating to the merits.

We are not ruling that the 32 demoted partners were in fact employees within the meaning of the age discrimination law. Such a ruling would be premature. Sidley has respectable arguments on its side, not least that the functional test of employer status toward which the EEOC is leaning is too uncertain to enable law firms and other partnerships to determine in advance their exposure to discrimination suits   that it would be better if the courts and the Commission interpreted the employer exclusion to require treating all partners as employers, with perhaps a narrow sham exception. These issues will become ripe when Sidley finishes complying with the coverage part of the subpoena. We hold only that there is enough doubt about whether the 32 demoted partners are covered by the age discrimination law to entitle the EEOC to full compliance with that part, at least, of its subpoena.

VACATED AND REMANDED WITH DIRECTIONS.

[JUDGE EASTERBROOK concurred for reasons we need not consider.]

Notes

1. Statutory authority required. The threshold question is whether Ralph has the statutory authority to subpoena privately held information. Does he? See § 7(a)(2) of the WTCA.

2. The Court's tolerance of agency investigative power. The principal cases cited two venerable and still viable decisions, *Endicott Johnson Corp. v. Perkins*, 317 U.S. 501 (1943), and *Oklahoma Press Publishing Co. v. Walling*, 327 U.S. 186 (1946), in which the Supreme Court affirmed broad administrative discretion to conduct investigations. In *Oklahoma Press*, for example, the Court emphasized that the purpose of the subpoena was "to discover and procure evidence, not to prove a pending charge or complaint, but upon which to make one if, in the Administrator's judgment, the facts thus discovered should justify doing so." 327 U.S. at 201. In another leading case for administrative investigations, *United States v. Morton Salt*, the Court stated that "[e]ven if one were to regard the request for information in this case as caused by nothing more than official curiosity, nevertheless law-enforcing agencies have a legitimate right to satisfy themselves that corporate behavior is consistent with the law and the public interest." 338 U.S. 632, 652 (1950). Is such administrative freedom necessary or wise?

3. Agency jurisdiction to determine jurisdiction. Agencies have long been said to have jurisdiction to determine jurisdiction, and challenges to the coverage of the enforcement statute cannot be raised at the investigation stage. For example, the Federal Trade Commission (FTC) Act expressly denies the FTC jurisdiction over insurance companies regulated by a state insurance agency. Yet when the FTC opened an investigation against just such an insurance company, the Supreme Court, in a five-line *per curiam* opinion, reversed a Ninth Circuit decision questioning FTC jurisdiction to investigate the insurance company. *FTC v. Crafts*, 355 U.S. 9 (1957). Why would the Court be so lenient, particularly when it seems they should be especially vigilant in assuring that agencies act within their delegated authority?

Does *EEOC v. Karuk Tribe Housing Authority* threaten to change this principle? Is the genie about to escape, or would *EEOC v. Sidley Austin Wood & Brown*, if widely accepted, force the genie back into the bottle?

4. The "civil investigative demand." Ralph will rely upon § 7(a)(2) of the WTCA, which provides for a "civil investigative demand" (CID). Compare the limits on compulsory process in that section to the limits in APA § 555(d). In theory, a CID is limited by its authorizing statute, but courts often treat them the same as subpoenas. Both administrative review authorities and courts, however, are unwilling to hear interlocutory challenges to administrative discovery orders. So how would Abby challenge the CID? The only way to challenge an administrative discovery order in court is to refuse to comply and require the agency to seek judicial enforcement. However, agencies usually have procedural rules covering "motions to quash."

5. Can Abby use a CID or subpoena? Will Abby have some compulsory process available for her defense of Gallery in the enforcement action? Parties will want to obtain discovery from the government either in administrative or judicial challenges to government action. In a judicial proceeding, ordinary discovery rules apply with some special considerations for the government. What discovery rights does a party to an administrative adjudication have? The APA does not guarantee compulsory process, nor empower agencies to issue subpoenas. The APA provides only that a subpoena shall be issued to a party when an agency has subpoena authority. 5 U.S.C. § 555(d). This provision merely attempts to place the agency and private parties on an equal footing:

The purpose of this provision is to make agency subpoenas available to private parties to the same extent as to agency representatives. . . . It should be emphasized that [§ 555(d)] relates only to existing subpoena powers conferred upon agencies; it does not grant power to issue subpoenas to agencies which are not so empowered by other statutes.

ATTORNEY GENERAL'S MANUAL ON THE APA 67 (1946). Does WTCA § 7(a)(2), read in conjunction with APA § 555(d), limit compulsory process available to Abby? Should the APA be amended to grant a general right to compulsory process, at least in adjudications?

6. What about compulsory process for rulemaking? May Ben use this authority to obtain information for his rulemaking? Note that § 555 is denominated "ancillary matters," but § 7 of the WTCA covers proceedings to issue an order — adjudication. May Jordan use compulsory process to obtain information in order to participate in the rulemaking? If not, will he be totally dependent on the information compiled by the WTC and placed in the rulemaking record?

7. Use of the FOIA for "discovery." Abby, in the preliminary stages of the adjudication before a formal complaint has been issued, and Jordan, in rulemaking, may find the Freedom of Information Act (FOIA), 5 U.S.C. § 552 (discussed in Chapter 7), to be an alternative source of "discovery." The FOIA was intended to provide access to ordinary citizens, and hence no special form or particular language is necessary in making a request. Nonetheless, a request must "reasonably" describe the desired information. 5 U.S.C. § 552(a)(3). The agency must respond to the request within a short time, usually ten days after receipt. The agency may deny a request for information only if one of the exemptions discussed below covers the information. Documents containing some, but not all, exempt material must be edited; and the nonexempt, "reasonably segregable" material must be released. 5 U.S.C. § 552(b). A denial is expressly subject to judicial review under § 552(a)(4)(B). The burden always is on the agency to support its denial by showing that one of the exemptions applies. The scope of review is *de novo*.

C. Agency Authority to Investigate — Physical Inspections

Lesson 6C. As he digs for information about Gallery in the WTC's files, Ralph finds a collection of reports from agency inspectors. He learns that inspectors have been assigned to visit each wine merchant at least once a year to examine production practices and current labels and otherwise to assess compliance with the WTCA and the Commission's rules. From what he can tell, wine merchants generally consent to the inspections.

Sometimes, however, they do not cooperate. In examining the files on Gallery, Ralph has discovered a recent report showing that after the inspector was denied access to Gallery's plant, she climbed a nearby hill. From that vantage point, using strong binoculars, the inspector counted sacks of sugar as they were being unloaded.

Ralph wants to conduct a detailed investigation of Gallery's facilities, including assaying the wines in Gallery's vats. Will he need to get a warrant? If he does, will he be able to obtain one? If he does not need to get a warrant, can the information he obtains be used for a prosecution under § 10(c) of the WTCA? Can the WTC continue its usual monthly inspections? What if Gallery were to refuse to allow the monthly inspections?

How do the following materials help Ralph resolve these issues?

Background of *New York v. Burger*

Under the Fourth Amendment, government searches of private persons and property are generally prohibited without a warrant. Searches by administrative agencies, however, even if they end up resulting in criminal liability, are sometimes excepted from this warrant requirement. One such administrative exception to the warrant requirement is for "pervasively regulated industries," on the theory that pervasive regulation lowers a business owner's expectation of privacy in their business enough to justify a warrantless search. Prior to the Court's decision in *Burger*, the pervasive regulation exception depended on how long and how closely the industry had been regulated. In *Burger*, the Court revisited the pervasively regulated business exception in the context of a statutory provision authorizing warrantless searches of automotive junkyards and vehicle dismantlers. Despite the fact that the statute authorizing the searches was only enacted eight years earlier, the Court held that the automotive junkyard qualified as a pervasively regulated business, and therefore that the warrant exception applied.

New York v. Burger
482 U.S. 691 (1987)

JUSTICE BLACKMUN delivered the opinion of the Court.

This case presents the question whether the warrantless search of an automobile junkyard, conducted pursuant to a statute authorizing such a search, falls within the exception to the warrant requirement for administrative inspections of pervasively regulated industries. The case also presents the question whether an otherwise proper administrative inspection is unconstitutional because the ultimate purpose of the regulatory statute pursuant to which the search is done—the deterrence of criminal behavior—is the same as that of penal laws, with the result that the inspection may disclose violations not only of the regulatory statute but also of the penal statutes.

I

Respondent Joseph Burger is the owner of a junkyard in Brooklyn, N.Y. His business consists, in part, of the dismantling of automobiles and the selling of their parts. His junkyard is an open lot with no buildings. A high metal fence surrounds it, wherein are located, among other things, vehicles and parts of vehicles. At approximately noon on November 17, 1982, Officer Joseph Vega and four other plainclothes officers, all members of the Auto Crimes Division of the New York City Police Department, entered respondent's junkyard to conduct an inspection pursuant to N. Y. Veh. & Traf. Law § 415-a5 (McKinney 1986).[1] On any given day, the Division conducts from 5 to 10 inspections of vehicle dismantlers, automobile junkyards, and related businesses.

Upon entering the junkyard, the officers asked to see Burger's license and his "police book"—the record of the automobiles and vehicle parts in his possession. Burger replied that he had neither a license nor a police book. The officers then announced their intention to conduct a § 415-a5 inspection. Burger did not object. In accordance with their practice, the officers copied down the Vehicle Identification Numbers (VINs) of several vehicles and parts of vehicles that were in the junkyard. After checking these numbers against a police computer, the officers determined that respondent was in possession of stolen vehicles and parts. Accordingly, Burger was arrested and charged with five counts of possession of stolen property and one count of unregistered operation as a vehicle dismantler, in violation of § 415-a1.

In the Kings County Supreme Court, Burger moved to suppress the evidence obtained as a result of the inspection, primarily on the ground that § 415-a5 was unconstitutional. After a hearing, the court denied the motion. It reasoned that the junkyard business was a "pervasively regulated" industry in which warrantless administrative inspections were appropriate; that the statute was properly limited in "time, place and scope," and that, once the officers had reasonable cause to believe that certain vehicles and parts were stolen, they could arrest Burger and seize the property without a warrant. . . . For the same reasons, the Appellate Division affirmed.

The New York Court of Appeals, however, reversed. In its view, § 415-a5 violated the Fourth Amendment's prohibition of unreasonable searches and seizures. According to the Court of Appeals, "[t]he fundamental defect [of § 415-a5] . . . is that [it authorize[s] searches undertaken solely to uncover evidence of criminality and not to enforce a comprehensive regulatory scheme." . . .

---

1. This statute reads in pertinent part: [The statute requires all auto dismantlers to keep records of all vehicles and vehicle parts in their possession.]

. . . .

Upon request of an agent of the commissioner or of any police officer and during his regular and usual business hours, a vehicle dismantler shall produce such records and permit said agent or police officer to examine them and any vehicles or parts of vehicles which are subject to the record keeping requirements of this section and which are on the premises. . . . The failure to produce such records or to permit such inspection on the part of any person required to be registered pursuant to this section as required by this paragraph shall be a class A misdemeanor.

Because of the important state interest in administrative schemes designed to regulate the vehicle-dismantling or automobile junkyard industry, we granted certiorari.

II

A

The Court long has recognized that the Fourth Amendment's prohibition on unreasonable searches and seizures is applicable to commercial premises, as well as to private homes. *See v. City of Seattle*, 387 U.S. 541, 543, 546 (1967). An owner or operator of a business thus has an expectation of privacy in commercial property, which society is prepared to consider to be reasonable. This expectation exists not only with respect to traditional police searches conducted for the gathering of criminal evidence but also with respect to administrative inspections designed to enforce regulatory statutes. *See Marshall v. Barlow's, Inc.*, 436 U.S. 307, 312–313 (1978). An expectation of privacy in commercial premises, however, is different from, and indeed less than, a similar expectation in an individual's home. *See Donovan v. Dewey*, 452 U.S. 594, 598–599 (1981). This expectation is particularly attenuated in commercial property employed in "closely regulated" industries. The Court observed in *Marshall v. Barlow's, Inc.:* "Certain industries have such a history of government oversight that no reasonable expectation of privacy . . . could exist for a proprietor over the stock of such an enterprise."

The Court first examined the "unique" problem of inspections of "closely regulated" businesses in two enterprises that had "a long tradition of close government supervision." In *Colonnade Corp. v. United States*, 397 U.S. 72 (1970), it considered a warrantless search of a catering business pursuant to several federal revenue statutes authorizing the inspection of the premises of liquor dealers. Although the Court disapproved the search because the statute provided that a sanction be imposed when entry was refused, and because it did not authorize entry without a warrant as an alternative in this situation, it recognized that "the liquor industry [was] long subject to close supervision and inspection." We returned to this issue in *United States v. Biswell*, 406 U.S. 311 (1972), which involved a warrantless inspection of the premises of a pawnshop operator, who was federally licensed to sell sporting weapons pursuant to the Gun Control Act of 1968. While noting that "[f]ederal regulation of the interstate traffic in firearms is not as deeply rooted in history as is governmental control of the liquor industry," we nonetheless concluded that the warrantless inspections authorized by the Gun Control Act would "pose only limited threats to the dealer's justifiable expectations of privacy." We observed: "When a dealer chooses to engage in this pervasively regulated business and to accept a federal license, he does so with the knowledge that his business records, firearms, and ammunition will be subject to effective inspection."

The "*Colonnade-Biswell*" doctrine, stating the reduced expectation of privacy by an owner of commercial premises in a "closely regulated" industry, has received renewed emphasis in more recent decisions. In *Marshall v. Barlow's, Inc.*, we noted its continued vitality but declined to find that warrantless inspections, made pursuant to the Occupational Safety and Health Act of 1970 of *all* businesses engaged in inter-state commerce fell within the narrow focus of this doctrine. However, we found warrantless inspections made pursuant to the Federal Mine Safety and Health Act of 1977 proper because they were of a "closely regulated" industry. *Donovan v. Dewey, supra.*

Indeed, in *Donovan v. Dewey,* we declined to limit our consideration to the length of time during which the business in question—stone quarries—had been sub-ject to federal regulation. We pointed out that the doctrine is essentially defined by "the pervasiveness and regularity of the federal regulation" and the effect of such regulation upon an owner's expectation of privacy. We observed, however, that "the duration of a particular regulatory scheme" would remain an "important factor" in deciding whether a warrantless inspection pursuant to the scheme is permissible.

B

Because the owner or operator of commercial premises in a "closely regulated" industry has a reduced expectation of privacy, the warrant and probable-cause requirements, which fulfill the traditional Fourth Amendment standard of reason-ableness for a government search, have lessened application in this context. Rather, we conclude that, as in other situations of "special need," where the privacy interests of the owner are weakened and the government interests in regulating particular businesses are concomitantly heightened, a warrantless inspection of commercial premises may well be reasonable within the meaning of the Fourth Amendment.

This warrantless inspection, however, even in the context of a pervasively regu-lated business, will be deemed to be reasonable only so long as three criteria are met. First, there must be a "substantial" government interest that informs the regulatory scheme pursuant to which the inspection is made. *See Donovan v. Dewey* ("substan-tial federal interest in improving the health and safety conditions in the Nation's underground and surface mines"); *United States v. Biswell* (regulation of firearms is "of central importance to federal efforts to prevent violent crime and to assist the States in regulating the firearms traffic within their borders"); *Colonnade Corp. v. United States* (federal interest "in protecting the revenue against various types of fraud").

Second, the warrantless inspections must be "necessary to further [the] regula-tory scheme." For example, in *Dewey* we recognized that forcing mine inspectors to obtain a warrant before every inspection might alert mine owners or operators to the impending inspection, thereby frustrating the purposes of the Mine Safety and Health Act—to detect and thus to deter safety and health violations. *Id.,* at 603.

Finally, "the statute's inspection program, in terms of the certainty and regular-ity of its application, [must] provid[e] a constitutionally adequate substitute for a warrant." In other words, the regulatory statute must perform the two basic func-tions of a warrant: it must advise the owner of the commercial premises that the search is being made pursuant to the law and has a properly defined scope, and it must limit the discretion of the inspecting officers. To perform this first function, the statute must be "sufficiently comprehensive and defined that the owner of commercial property cannot help but be aware that his property will be subject to periodic inspections undertaken for specific purposes." In addition, in defining how a statute limits the discretion of the inspectors, we have observed that it must be "carefully limited in time, place, and scope."

III

A

Searches made pursuant to § 415-a5, in our view, clearly fall within this established exception to the warrant requirement for administrative inspections in "closely regulated" businesses. First, the nature of the regulatory statute reveals that the operation of a junkyard, part of which is devoted to vehicle dismantling, is a "closely regulated" business in the State of New York. The provisions regulating the activity of vehicle dismantling are extensive. An operator cannot engage in this industry without first obtaining a license, which means that he must meet the registration requirements and must pay a fee. Under § 415-a5(a), the operator must maintain a police book recording the acquisition and disposition of motor vehicles and vehicle parts, and make such records and inventory available for inspection by the police or any agent of the Department of Motor Vehicles. The operator also must display his registration number prominently at his place of business, on business documentation, and on vehicles and parts that pass through his business. § 415-a5(b). Moreover, the person engaged in this activity is subject to criminal penalties, as well as to loss of license or civil fines, for failure to comply with these provisions. That other States besides New York have imposed similarly extensive regulations on automobile junkyards further supports the "closely regulated" status of this industry.

In determining whether vehicle dismantlers constitute a "closely regulated" industry, the "duration of [this] particular regulatory scheme" has some relevancy. Section 415-a could be said to be of fairly recent vintage [1973], and the inspection provision of § 415-a5 was added only in 1979. But because the automobile is a relatively new phenomenon in our society and because its widespread use is even newer, automobile junkyards and vehicle dismantlers have not been in existence very long and thus do not have an ancient history of government oversight. Indeed, the industry did not attract government attention until the 1950's, when all used automobiles were no longer easily reabsorbed into the steel industry and attention then focused on the environmental and aesthetic problems associated with abandoned vehicles.

The automobile-junkyard business, however, is simply a new branch of an industry that has existed, and has been closely regulated, for many years. The automobile junkyard is closely akin to the secondhand shop or the general junkyard. Both share the purpose of recycling salvageable articles and components of items no longer usable in their original form. As such, vehicle dismantlers represent a modern, specialized version of a traditional activity. In New York, general junkyards and secondhand shops long have been subject to regulation. . . .

The history of government regulation of junk-related activities argues strongly in favor of the "closely regulated" status of the automobile junkyard.

Accordingly, in light of the regulatory framework governing his business and the history of regulation of related industries, an operator of a junkyard engaging in vehicle dismantling has a reduced expectation of privacy in this "closely regulated" business.

B

The New York regulatory scheme satisfies the three criteria necessary to make reasonable warrantless inspections pursuant to §415-a5. First, the State has a substantial interest in regulating the vehicle-dismantling and automobile-junkyard industry because motor vehicle theft has increased in the State and because the problem of theft is associated with this industry. In this day, automobile theft has become a significant social problem, placing enormous economic and personal burdens upon the citizens of different States. . . . Because contemporary automobiles are made from standardized parts, the nationwide extent of vehicle theft and concern about it are understandable.

Second, regulation of the vehicle-dismantling industry reasonably serves the State's substantial interest in eradicating automobile theft. It is well established that the theft problem can be addressed effectively by controlling the receiver of, or market in, stolen property. Automobile junkyards and vehicle dismantlers provide the major market for stolen vehicles and vehicle parts. Thus, the State rationally may believe that it will reduce car theft by regulations that prevent automobile junkyards from becoming markets for stolen vehicles and that help trace the origin and destination of vehicle parts.

Moreover, the warrantless administrative inspections pursuant to §415-a5 "are necessary to further [the] regulatory scheme." In this respect, we see no difference between these inspections and those approved by the Court in *United States v. Biswell* and *Donovan v. Dewey*. We explained in *Biswell*:

> "[I]f inspection is to be effective and serve as a credible deterrent, unannounced, even frequent, inspections are essential. In this context, the prerequisite of a warrant could easily frustrate inspection; and if the necessary flexibility as to time, scope, and frequency is to be preserved, the protections afforded by a warrant would be negligible."

Similarly, in the present case, a warrant requirement would interfere with the statute's purpose of deterring automobile theft accomplished by identifying vehicles and parts as stolen and shutting down the market in such items. Because stolen cars and parts often pass quickly through an automobile junkyard, "frequent" and "unannounced" inspections are necessary in order to detect them. In sum, surprise is crucial if the regulatory scheme aimed at remedying this major social problem is to function at all.

Third, §415-a5 provides a "constitutionally adequate substitute for a warrant." The statute informs the operator of a vehicle dismantling business that inspections will be made on a regular basis. Thus, the vehicle dismantler knows that the inspections to which he is subject do not constitute discretionary acts by a government official but are conducted pursuant to statute. Section 415-a5 also sets forth the scope of the inspection and, accordingly, places the operator on notice as to how to comply with the statute. In addition, it notifies the operator as to who is authorized to conduct an inspection.

Finally, the "time, place, and scope" of the inspection is limited to place appropriate restraints upon the discretion of the inspecting officers. The officers are allowed to conduct an inspection only "during [the] regular and usual business hours." §415-a5. The inspections can be made only of vehicle-dismantling and related industries. And the permissible scope of these searches is narrowly defined: the inspectors may examine the records, as well as "any vehicles or parts of vehicles which are subject to the record keeping requirements of this section and which are on the premises."

IV

A search conducted pursuant to §415-a5, therefore, clearly falls within the well-established exception to the warrant requirement for administrative inspections of "closely regulated" businesses. The Court of Appeals, nevertheless, struck down the statute as violative of the Fourth Amendment because, in its view, the statute had no truly administrative purpose but was "designed simply to give the police an expedient means of enforcing penal sanctions for possession of stolen property." ...

In arriving at this conclusion, the Court of Appeals failed to recognize that a State can address a major social problem *both* by way of an administrative scheme *and* through penal sanctions. Administrative statutes and penal laws may have the same *ultimate* purpose of remedying the social problem, but they have different subsidiary purposes and prescribe different methods of addressing the problem. An administrative statute establishes how a particular business in a "closely regulated" industry should be operated, setting forth rules to guide an operator's conduct of the business and allowing government officials to ensure that those rules are followed. Such a regulatory approach contrasts with that of the penal laws, a major emphasis of which is the punishment of individuals for specific acts of behavior. ...

If the administrative goals of §415-a5 are recognized, the difficulty the Court of Appeals perceives in allowing inspecting officers to examine vehicles and vehicle parts ... evaporates.

Nor do we think that this administrative scheme is unconstitutional simply because, in the course of enforcing it, an inspecting officer may discover evidence of crimes, besides violations of the scheme itself. ... The discovery of evidence of crimes in the course of an otherwise proper administrative inspection does not render that search illegal or the administrative scheme suspect.

Finally, we fail to see any constitutional significance in the fact that police officers, rather than "administrative" agents, are permitted to conduct the §415-a5 inspection. The significance respondent alleges lies in the role of police officers as enforcers of the penal laws and in the officers' power to arrest for offenses other than violations of the administrative scheme. It is, however, important to note that state police officers, like those in New York, have numerous duties in addition to those associated with traditional police work. As a practical matter, many States do not have the resources to assign the enforcement of a particular administrative scheme to a specialized agency. So long as a regulatory scheme is properly administrative, it is not rendered illegal by the fact that the inspecting officer has the power to arrest individuals for violations other than those created by the scheme itself. In sum, we decline to impose upon the States the burden of requiring the enforcement of their regulatory statutes to be carried out by specialized agents.

V

Accordingly, the judgment of the New York Court of Appeals is reversed, and the case is remanded to that court for further proceedings not inconsistent with this opinion.

It is so ordered.

Justice Brennan, with whom Justice Marshall joins, and with whom Justice O' Connor joins as to all but Part III, dissenting.

Warrantless inspections of pervasively regulated businesses are valid if necessary to further an urgent state interest, and if authorized by a statute that carefully limits their time, place, and scope. I have no objection to this general rule. Today, however, the Court finds pervasive regulation in the barest of administrative schemes. Burger's vehicle-dismantling business is not closely regulated (unless most New York City businesses are), and an administrative warrant therefore was required to search it. The Court also perceives careful guidance and control of police discretion in a statute that is patently insufficient to eliminate the need for a warrant. Finally, the Court characterizes as administrative a search for evidence of only criminal wrongdoing. As a result, the Court renders virtually meaningless the general rule that a warrant is required for administrative searches of commercial property. . . .

Notes

1. **When can an agency make a warrantless inspection?** Under what circumstances may Ralph obtain access to Gallery's plant without a warrant? There are well-established exceptions to the warrant requirement in the administrative context. These exceptions fall into four groups: emergency, consent, plain view, and licensing inspections.

(a) Emergency searches are permitted. Emergency searches have been upheld in numerous specific contexts: seizure of unwholesome food, compulsory smallpox vaccination, health quarantine, summary destruction of tubercular cattle, and fire inspections.

(b) Consent has been recognized as a valid exception to the warrant requirement. Consent here probably does not have to be as clear as that in a criminal context.

(c) Under the "plain view" doctrine, a warrant is not required to justify obtaining and using information that is available to government officers through the use of their senses as long as they are not otherwise engaged in an illegal search. Moreover, under the "open fields" doctrine, an official may generally conduct a warrantless search of outdoor property beyond the so-called "curtilage" of a private domicile, even if the property is privately owned, and even if the official is committing trespass.

(d) The Supreme Court has held, as in *New York v. Burger*, that by engaging in a pervasively regulated business one implies consent to warrantless searches. Implied consent has, therefore, been found to apply to pharmacies, coal mines, multi-family dwellings, nursing homes, and lobster fishing.

Ralph must struggle with the third and fourth of these exceptions to determine if the WTC can perform the inspection without a warrant.

2. How broad is the closely regulated business exception? In 2015, the Court set limits on the closely regulated business exception when it invalidated a statute permitting Los Angeles police officers to search hotel guest registries without a warrant. *Los Angeles v. Patel*, 135 S. Ct. 2443 (2015). The *Patel* Court noted that a "closely regulated industry . . . is an exception," and reminded us that since 1970, it had only treated four business as closely regulated for Fourth Amendment purposes: "liquor sales, firearms dealing, mining, [and] running an automobile junkyard." *Id.* at 2444 (citations omitted). Despite the fact that Los Angeles hotels are subject to numerous and often detailed regulations, the Court declined to apply the closely regulated business exception. It found that hotels do not present the same "clear and significant risk to the public welfare" as the four businesses that it had already determined to be closely regulated. *Id.* It instead held that hotel proprietors confronted with a warrantless search must be afforded an opportunity to challenge the justification for the search before complying. It is not entirely clear what effect *Patel* will have on the future of the closely regulated business exception. It at minimum shows that the Court was not willing to expand the exception beyond the boundaries set in *Burger*, but could be read more broadly as evidence of the Court's intent to limit the exception to the four industries it has already identified as closely regulated.

3. Searches at the border. With recent heightened public attention on federal immigration policy come questions about searches performed by agency actors at the border. On January 4, 2018, the Acting Director of U.S. Customs and Border Protection (CBP) issued a new directive regarding search of electronic devices, such as cell phones and tablets, at the border. U.S. Customs and Border Patrol, *CBP Directive No. 3340-049A: Border Search of Electronic Devices* ¶ 4 (Jan. 4, 2018) (CBP Directive).

Cell phone searches have been controversial in general under the Fourth Amendment. *See Riley v. California*, 573 U.S. 373 (2014) (holding that the sheer volume of information contained in a cell phone protects such devices from warrantless searches under the Fourth Amendment's "search incident to arrest" warrant exception).

The CBP Directive pointed out that courts have treated the environment at the border differently as a constitutional matter:

> Time and again, [the Supreme Court has] stated that "searches made at the border, pursuant to the longstanding right of the sovereign to protect itself by stopping and examining persons and property crossing into this country, are reasonable simply by virtue of the fact that they occur at the border." . . . Routine searches of the persons and effects of entrants [into the United States] are not subject to any requirement of reasonable suspicion, probable cause, or warrant. . . . As a constitutional matter, border search authority is premised in part on a reduced expectation of privacy associated with international travel. *See Flores-Montano*, 541 U.S. at 154 (noting that "the expectation of privacy is less at the border than it is in the interior").

CBP Directive at ¶ 4. It then went on to reconcile judicial concern over warrantless searches of electronic devices with the more permissive standards governing border searches in general. Although the CBP Directive did not acknowledge any constitutional protections for border searches of electronic devices, it did limit "advanced searches" (those involving the use of "external equipment" to give the investigator access to the device's contents) to "instances in which there is *reasonable suspicion* of activity in violation of the laws enforced or administered by CBP." *Id.* at ¶ 5 (emphasis added). By contrast, basic searches—those where the investigator accesses the device without the aid of additional hacking technology—do not require any degree of suspicion.

The CBP Directive has yet to be fully vetted by the courts, but courts that have considered its standards for warrantless searches of electronic devices are split as to whether some degree of reasonable suspicion is necessary before a warrantless search of a device is permissible. *Compare United States v. Vergara*, 884 F.3d 1309 (11th Cir. 2018) ("Border searches 'never' require probable cause or a warrant. And we require reasonable suspicion at the border only 'for highly intrusive searches of a person's body such as a strip search or an x-ray examination.'"), *with United States v. Wanjiku*, 919 F.3d 472, 489–90 (7th Cir. 2018) ("[T]he agents possessed reasonable suspicion to search [defendant's] electronic devices, including his cell phone . . . . We therefore need not reach the issue of what level of suspicion is required (if any) for searches of electronic devices at the border, and reserve that question for a case in which it matters to the outcome."). It remains to be seen whether courts will limit border authorities' access to electronic devices to instances where investigators have reasonable suspicion before conducting the search.

4. When can you just search everyone? The form of administrative search that the average citizen is most likely to encounter is a "checkpoint search." Examples of checkpoint searches are airport screenings and "patdowns" at public gatherings such as concerts and sporting events. Checkpoint searches do not require individualized suspicion under the Fourth Amendment because they "primarily ensure public safety instead of detect criminal wrongdoing." *Corbett v. Transp. Sec. Admin.*,

767 F.3d 1171, 1180 (11th Cir. 2014). As a result, administrative officials are permitted to search entire crowds of people based solely on their presence at a potentially dangerous location or event. But checkpoint searches are not given constitutional carte blanche. In *Corbett*, a recent challenge to the TSA's adoption of more invasive procedures for airport screenings, the Eleventh Circuit explained that the validity of suspicion-less checkpoint searches at airports "depends on 'the gravity of the public concerns served by the seizure, the degree to which the seizure advances the public interest, and the severity of the interference with individual liberty.'" *Id.* (quoting *Brown v. Texas*, 443 U.S. 47, 51 (1979)).

5. When do otherwise permissible warrantless searches go too far? As explained in the previous note, administrative searches that fall within one of the articulated exceptions generally do not require a warrant. In some cases, however, law enforcement officers engage in conduct that transforms what could have been a warrantless administrative search into one that requires a warrant under the Fourth Amendment. For example, "where an act authorizing administrative inspections 'fails to tailor the scope and frequency of such administrative inspections to the particular' governmental concern, and 'does not provide any standards to guide inspectors either in their selection of establishments to be searched or in the exercise of their authority to search,' a search warrant will be required." *Swint v. City of Wadley*, 51 F.3d 988, 998 (11th Cir. 1995) (quoting *Donovan v. Dewey*, 452 U.S. 594, 601 (1981)). In addition to a lack of standards to guide law enforcement, the use of excessive force in connection with administrative searches also raises a potential constitutional problem. Consider the following description of an administrative search on behalf of a state licensing agency in Florida:

> It was a scene right out of a Hollywood movie. On August 21, 2010, after more than a month of planning, teams from the Orange County Sheriff's Office descended on multiple target locations. They blocked the entrances and exits to the parking lots so no one could leave and no one could enter. With some team members dressed in ballistic vests and masks, and with guns drawn, the deputies rushed into their target destinations, handcuffed the stunned occupants—and demanded to see their barbers' licenses. The Orange County Sheriff's Office was providing muscle for the Florida Department of Business and Professional Regulation's administrative inspection of barbershops to discover licensing violations.

Berry v. Leslie, 767 F.3d 1144, 1146–47 (11th Cir. 2014), *vacated and rehearing en banc ordered by, Berry v. Orange Cty.*, 771 F.3d 1316 (11th Cir. 2014), *dismissed as moot by, Berry v. Orange Cty.*, 785 F.3d 553 (2015). Citing its earlier decision in *Swint*, the court went on to explain that "conducting a run-of-the-mill administrative inspection as though it is a criminal raid, when no indication exists that safety will be threatened by the inspection, violates clearly established Fourth Amendment rights." *Id.* at 1147. Although the case was dismissed as moot on appeal, the panel opinion makes clear that warrantless administrative searches will not be protected from the Fourth Amendment if they are seen as unnecessarily overzealous or criminal in nature.

6. What about the sacks of sugar? The staff asserts that the investigators counting the sacks of sugar from a public vantage point was not an "inspection." It quotes Chief Justice Burger's opinion in *Dow Chemical Co. v. United States*, 476 U.S. 227 (1986):

> In early 1978, enforcement officials of EPA, with Dow's consent, made an on-site inspection of two powerplants in this complex. A subsequent EPA request for a second inspection, however, was denied, and EPA did not thereafter seek an administrative search warrant. Instead, EPA employed a commercial aerial photographer, using a standard floor-mounted, precision aerial mapping camera, to take photographs of the facility from altitudes of 12,000, 3,000, and 1,200 feet. At all times the aircraft was lawfully within navigable airspace. . . .

> It may well be, as the Government concedes, that surveillance of private property by using highly sophisticated surveillance equipment not generally available to the public, such as satellite technology, might be constitutionally proscribed absent a warrant. But the photographs here are not so revealing of intimate details as to raise constitutional concerns. Although they undoubtedly give EPA more detailed information than naked-eye views, they remain limited to an outline of the facility's buildings and equipment. The mere fact that human vision is enhanced somewhat, at least to the degree here, does not give rise to constitutional problems. An electronic device to penetrate walls or windows so as to hear and record confidential discussions of chemical formulae or other trade secrets would raise very different and far more serious questions; other protections such as trade secret laws are available to protect commercial activities from private surveillance by competitors. We conclude that the open areas of an industrial plant complex with numerous plant structures spread over an area of 2,000 acres are not analogous to the "curtilage" of a dwelling for purposes of aerial surveillance; such an industrial complex is more comparable to an open field and as such it is open to the view and observation of persons in aircraft lawfully in the public airspace immediately above or sufficiently near the area for the reach of cameras.

> We hold that the taking of aerial photographs of an industrial plant complex from navigable airspace is not a search prohibited by the Fourth Amendment.

Suppose a staff member comes to Ralph claiming that he can "hack" into Gallery's files and find out how much cane sugar and table grape juice it uses. Would this be illegal? Consider the views of Justice Powell in *Dow Chemical*, concurring and dissenting in part:

Since physical trespass no longer functions as a reliable proxy for intrusion on privacy, it is necessary to determine if the surveillance, whatever its form, intruded on a reasonable expectation that a certain activity or area would remain private. An expectation of privacy is reasonable for Fourth Amendment purposes if it is rooted in a "source outside of the Fourth Amendment, either by reference to concepts of real or personal property law or to understandings that are recognized and permitted by society." Dow argues that, by enacting trade secret laws, society has recognized that it has a legitimate interest in preserving the privacy of the relevant portions of its open-air plants. As long as Dow takes reasonable steps to protect its secrets, the law should enforce its right against theft or disclosure of those secrets.

. . . .

I would reverse the decision of the Court of Appeals. EPA's aerial photography penetrated into a private commercial enclave, an area in which society has recognized that privacy interests legitimately may be claimed. The photographs captured highly confidential information that Dow had taken reasonable and objective steps to preserve as private. Since the Clean Air Act does not establish a defined and regular program of warrantless inspections, EPA should have sought a warrant from a neutral judicial officer. The Court's holding that the warrantless photography does not constitute an unreasonable search within the meaning of the Fourth Amendment is based on the absence of any physical trespass—a theory disapproved in a line of cases beginning with the decision in *Katz v. United States*. These cases have provided a sensitive and reasonable means of preserving interests in privacy cherished by our society. The Court's decision today cannot be reconciled with our precedents or with the purpose of the Fourth Amendment.

Try to visualize the internal discussions that led to the decision to hire a plane and fly over the Dow plant. What process should an agency undertake in deciding to conduct a search, either with a warrant or without? Should there have been some internal review before the WTC inspector climbed the hill near the Gallery facility? Assuming there is a sound argument that the "hacking" is not illegal, should Ralph nonetheless refuse to authorize this "search"?

7. What if a warrant is required? Several decisions discussed in *New York v. Burger* establish that even in compelling circumstances, a warrant might be required for administrative searches or inspections. *See Camara v. Mun. Court*, 387 U.S. 523 (1967); *See v. City of Seattle*, 387 U.S. 541 (1967). *Camara* involved a routine annual building code inspection designed to assure the safety of the building stock. The Court held that a warrant for such an administrative search could be based upon the reasonable needs of the administrative program, rather than particular information about the premises to be searched:

Finally, because the inspections are neither personal in nature nor aimed at the discovery of evidence of crime, they involve a relatively limited invasion of the urban citizen's privacy. . . .

Having concluded that the area inspection is a "reasonable" search of private property within the meaning of the Fourth Amendment, it is obvious that "probable cause" to issue a warrant to inspect must exist if reasonable legislative or administrative standards for conducting an area inspection are satisfied with respect to a particular dwelling. Such standards, which will vary with the municipal program being enforced, may be based upon the passage of time, the nature of the building (e.g., a multifamily apartment house), or the condition of the entire area, but they will not necessarily depend upon specific knowledge of the condition of the particular dwelling. . . . If a valid public interest justifies the intrusion contemplated, then there is probable cause to issue a suitably restricted search warrant. Such an approach neither endangers time-honored doctrines applicable to criminal investigations nor makes a nullity of the probable cause requirement in this area. It merely gives full recognition to the competing public and private interests here at stake and, in so doing, best fulfills the historic purpose behind the constitutional right to be free from unreasonable government invasions of privacy.

Thus, while the Court required some basis justifying the inspection, the justification could be based on "neutral criteria" in a legislative or administrative inspection plan, such as time or determination of a locality, rather than specific reason to believe a violation would be found.

The Supreme Court in *Marshall v. Barlow's, Inc.*, 436 U.S. 307 (1978), held that nonconsensual OSHA inspections may only be conducted pursuant to a warrant under the Occupational Safety and Health Act regulating workplace safety. The opinion illuminated the sort of showing that would meet the *Camara* test:

A warrant showing that a specific business has been chosen for an OSHA search on the basis of a general administrative plan for the enforcement of the Act derived from neutral sources such as, for example, dispersion of employees in various types of industries across a given area, and the desired frequency of searches in any of the lesser divisions of the area, would protect an employer's Fourth Amendment rights.[17] We doubt that the consumption of enforcement energies in the obtaining of such warrants will exceed manageable proportions.

---

17. The Secretary, Brief for Petitioner 9 n. 7, states that the Barlow inspection was not based on an employee complaint but was a "general schedule" investigation. "Such general inspections," he explains, "now called Regional Programmed Inspections, are carried out in accordance with criteria based upon accident experience and the number of employees exposed in particular industries." (citation omitted).

Does this standard mean that the WTC itself can establish its own warrant granting authority if it establishes "administrative standards"? Has it done so?

Since OSHA inspections involve health and safety, *Barlow's* raised questions about the lenient judicial approach to administrative searches that went before it. Many felt that the opinion placed an unnecessary obstacle in the way of workplace safety, in particular, and effective health and safety regulation in general. In his study of *Barlow's*, Mark Rothstein questioned both the negative and positive impacts of the decision:

> In his brief before the Supreme Court, the Secretary [of Labor] contended that "a warrant requirement would significantly impede the enforcement of the Occupational Safety and Health Act." Although a final judgment cannot be made at this time, it appears that the Court's decision will *not* have a significant adverse impact on OSHA enforcement. As was true with the decision in *Camara*, "both the burdens and the benefits of a search warrant requirement . . . seem to be overstated."

Mark Rothstein, *OSHA Inspections After* Marshall v. Barlow's, Inc., 1979 DUKE L.J. 63, 84.

8. Investigative hearings. An agency may institute an "investigative hearing" for any number of purposes. Such hearings are often challenged when they are or appear to be a prelude to taking enforcement action. The classic case on this issue is *Hannah v. Larche*, 363 U.S. 420 (1960). The Court drew a distinction between actual adjudications and investigations:

> "Due process" is an elusive concept. Its exact boundaries are undefinable, and its content varies according to specific factual context. Thus, when governmental agencies adjudicate or make binding determinations which directly affect the legal rights of individuals, it is imperative that those agencies use the procedures which have traditionally been associated with the judicial process. On the other hand, when government action does not partake of an adjudication, as for example, when a general fact-finding investigation is being conducted, it is not necessary that the full panoply of judicial procedures be used. Therefore, as a generalization, it can be said that due process embodies the differing rules of fair play, which through the years, have become associated with differing types of proceedings. Whether the Constitution requires that a particular right obtain in a specific proceeding depends upon a complexity of factors. The nature of the alleged right involved, the nature of the proceeding, are all considerations which must be taken into account. An analysis of these factors demonstrates why it is that the particular rights claimed by the respondents need not be conferred upon those appearing before purely investigative agencies. . . .

This case reached the Court before *Mathews v. Eldridge*, 424 U.S. 319 (1976), excerpted in subchapter 4B.2, but does it envision a similar type of balancing approach?

The Court held that the agency did not have to inform the investigation's target of the specific charges or the identity of the complainants, nor allow cross-examination of witnesses. Should investigative hearing requirements differ depending on whether the purpose of the hearing is to determine whether to bring an action or merely to gather information? Regardless, shouldn't some minimum procedural requirements apply in either case?

9. Interagency cooperation and parallel investigations. Ralph finds reference in the files to a Treasury Department investigation of Gallery. He calls a member of the Department's staff and finds that it had in fact investigated Gallery for possible tax violations but had decided to go no further. The WTC staff, however, believes that some information in that file might help Ralph. Can Ralph expect the Department to give him the file, and may he use information in that file? The D.C. Circuit's decision in *SEC v. Dresser Industries, Inc.*, 628 F.2d 1368 (D.C. Cir. 1980), seems to accept both parallel investigations by different agencies and cooperation between the two agencies. While the SEC was investigating questionable foreign payments for American companies, the Justice Department was developing information to be used in a criminal proceeding for illegal foreign payments. Refusing to prohibit the SEC from providing Justice with the fruits of its civil discovery, the court said:

> Effective enforcement of the securities laws requires that the SEC and Justice be able to investigate possible violations simultaneously. If the SEC suspects that a company has violated the securities laws, it must be able to respond quickly: it must be able to obtain relevant information concerning the alleged violation and to seek prompt judicial redress if necessary. Similarly, Justice must act quickly if it suspects that the laws have been broken. Grand jury investigations take time, as do criminal prosecutions. The SEC cannot always wait for Justice to complete the criminal proceedings if it is to obtain the necessary prompt civil remedy; neither can Justice always await the conclusion of the civil proceeding without endangering its criminal case. Thus we should not block parallel investigations by these agencies in the absence of "special circumstances" in which the nature of the proceedings demonstrably prejudices substantial rights of the investigated party or of the government.

> Dresser principally relies on an analogy to *United States v. LaSalle Nat'l Bank*, 437 U.S. 298 (1978), in which the Supreme Court said in dictum that the Internal Revenue Service (IRS) may not use its summons authority to investigate possible violations of the tax laws after it has referred those violations to Justice for criminal prosecution. Dresser argues that the SEC's transmittal of Dresser's file to Justice was equivalent to a "referral" under *LaSalle,* and thus that the SEC's power to enforce investigative subpoenas against Dresser in connection with that file lapsed at that time. Alternatively, Dresser suggests that, even if transmittal of the file was not analogous to a "referral" under *LaSalle,* initiation of the grand jury investigation

precluded subsequent enforcement of SEC investigative subpoenas into the same matters.

These two alternatives are vulnerable to the same objection: the *LaSalle* rule applies solely to the statutory scheme of the Internal Revenue Code, in which the IRS's civil authority ceases for all practical purposes upon referral of a taxpayer's case to Justice; it does not apply to the securities laws, in which the SEC's civil enforcement authority continues undiminished after Justice initiates a criminal investigation by the grand jury. . . .

Fulfillment of the SEC's civil enforcement responsibilities requires this conclusion. Unlike the IRS, which can postpone collection of taxes for the duration of parallel criminal proceedings without seriously injuring the public, the SEC must often act quickly, lest the false or incomplete statements of corporations mislead investors and infect the markets. Thus the Commission must be able to investigate possible securities infractions and undertake civil enforcement actions even after Justice has begun a criminal investigation. For the SEC to stay its hand might well defeat its purpose. . . .

[Relying heavily upon statutory provisions related to the SEC and DOJ, the court concluded as follows with respect to the agencies sharing information.] Where the agency has a legitimate noncriminal purpose for the investigation, it acts in good faith under the *LaSalle* conception even if it might use the information gained in the investigation for criminal enforcement purposes as well. In the present case the SEC plainly has a legitimate noncriminal purpose for its investigation of Dresser. It follows that the investigation is in good faith, in the absence of complicating factors. There is, therefore, no reason to impose a protective order [preventing the DOJ from using the information provided by the SEC].

10. Regulating through information. When Ralph discusses the staff reports with Carl, Carl urges that the WTC issue a press release immediately disclosing the results of their investigation. To what extent may the WTC use disclosure as a law enforcement device? Writing of the FTC, the D.C. Circuit has advised:

Since the Commission is charged by the broad delegation of power to it to eliminate unfair or deceptive business practices in the public interest, and since it is specifically authorized to make public information acquired by it, we conclude that there is, in fact and in law, authority in the Commission, acting in the public interest, to alert the public to suspected violations of the law by factual press releases whenever the Commission shall have reason to believe that a respondent is engaged in activities made unlawful by the Act which have resulted in the initiation of action by the Commission.

FTC v. Cinderella Career & Finishing Schs., 404 F.2d 1308, 1314 (D.C. Cir. 1968) (excerpted in subchapter 4C.2). How should Ralph react to Carl's suggestion that the Commission release information showing that Gallery mislabels its wine?

WTCA § 6(f) authorizes the release of required reports. Would it make a difference if the information were contained in the reports required by WTCA § 6(e)?

The WTC will need to be careful to assure that the information in its press release (and any other information that it disseminates) is accurate. This is obvious for several reasons, including the agency's need to maintain its own credibility. But it is also required by the Information Quality Act (IQA), an amendment to the Paperwork Reduction Act, 44 U.S.C. §§ 3501 *et seq.* The IQA, as implemented by OMB, requires all agencies to issue their own guidelines assuring the accuracy of their information, provide administrative processes through which affected persons may seek correction of agency information, and report periodically to OMB on their implementation of the Data Quality Act (DQA). According to the WASHINGTON POST:

> The Data Quality Act—written by an industry lobbyist and slipped into a giant appropriations bill in 2000 without congressional discussion or debate—is just two sentences directing the OMB to ensure that all information disseminated by the federal government is reliable. But the Bush administration's interpretation of those two sentences could tip the balance in regulatory disputes that weigh the interests of consumers and businesses.

Rick Weiss, *"Data Quality" Law Is Nemesis of Regulation*, WASH. POST, Aug. 16, 2004, at A1.

It would seem that agencies have a responsibility to assure the accuracy of information. Why would the WASHINGTON POST writer conclude that such a requirement is a "Nemesis of Regulation"? How should we balance the need to assure accuracy with the need to prevent overburdening agencies in their pursuit of the public interest?

Chapter 7

Open Government

Open government, or transparency, is often seen as the key to a successful democracy. Information about the federal government's doings can be obtained both in and out of the litigation process. As a litigant in judicial proceedings, the government is subject to discovery, although it can at times invoke special protections, such as executive privilege, to block access. In administrative adjudication, 5 U.S.C. § 555(d) requires an agency that has subpoena power to share that power with parties who appear before it. One need not, however, be tangled in adversary proceedings with the government to have a legal right to acquire information from it. Four broad, generally-applicable statutes provide (or constrain) such access.

The most important member of this group is the Freedom of Information Act (FOIA), 5 U.S.C. § 552. The original § 3 of the federal APA provided—on its face—for sweeping access to information. However, the section authorized agencies to withhold information if secrecy were required "in the public interest" or if the records related "solely to the internal management of an agency." Information could also be held confidential "for good cause found," and even if no good cause could be found for secrecy or confidentiality, the records were available only to persons "properly and directly concerned." Neither the statute nor its legislative history defined these broad phrases. There was no provision for review of an agency's wrongful denial of access to records. In sum, § 3 was a public information statute only to the extent agencies wished it to be, and they didn't! The failure of § 3 to provide access to government records, even to those directly affected by agency action, resulted in the congressional effort that culminated in 1966 with the FOIA. This new legislation substantially increased access by permitting "any person" to request government records, rather than only those persons "properly and directly concerned." The request need only "reasonably describe" the information sought. These changes indicated a shift of emphasis from providing access only to those citizens directly affected by an agency action to establishing a more informed electorate—an opening of the bureaucracy to any interested citizen.

The FOIA compels three different types of access. Subsection (a)(1) requires publication of select matters in the *Federal Register* (e.g., "substantive rules of general applicability"). Subsection (a)(2) requires that certain items be indexed and made available for public inspection and copying (e.g., "administrative staff manuals and instructions to staff that affect a member of the public"). Subsection (a)(3) mandates disclosure of other government records "upon [a] request" that "reasonably describes" the records sought and satisfies published agency rules governing "time, place, fees (if any), and procedures to be followed."

Subsection (b) lists nine exemptions to subsection (a)'s sweeping disclosure requirements. These exemptions protect sensitive information bearing on, among other things, national security, law enforcement, trade secrets, and embarrassing personal information. If an agency denies a FOIA request based on an exemption, the person seeking the information may challenge the denial in court. In such review proceedings, the judge ostensibly determines an exemption's applicability de novo, and the agency bears the burden of proof. A vast number of cases address the scope and applicability of the exemptions as they represent the tension between the FOIA's general mandate for disclosure and the strong policy reasons that exist in many contexts to preserve confidentiality. By and large, courts have adopted the strong disclosure bias intended by Congress, and hence these exemptions have been strictly construed.

Since enactment of the FOIA, Congress has passed several other major statutes governing control of government information, most notably: the Privacy Act (5 U.S.C. §552a), the Government in the Sunshine Act (5 U.S.C. §552b), and the Federal Advisory Committee Act (FACA) (5 U.S.C. Appx.). The Privacy Act limits the information that government may maintain or disclose concerning individuals and grants them a right to inspect and correct information recorded about them. Both the Sunshine Act and the FACA mandate public access to certain government proceedings. The Sunshine Act applies to agencies headed by multi-member collegial bodies—e.g., the Commissioners of the FTC. It requires that meetings among members to conduct agency business be held in public unless a statutory exception applies. The FACA applies to certain groups "established or utilized by one or more agencies" to obtain "advice or recommendations." A committee of scientists engaged by the EPA to advise it on the health effects of a pollutant might, for instance, fall within the purview of the FACA. If a committee is subject to this statute, it must conduct open meetings and make its documents available for public inspection—unless some exemption to these transparency requirements applies.

Every state now has some form of public access legislation. The particulars of these state acts vary, but they inevitably raise many of the same issues as the federal regime as all must balance conflicting policy interests favoring either openness or secrecy.

In the balance of this chapter, we will examine in more detail the operation of the FOIA and the FACA.

A. FOIA — The Scope of the Duty to Disclose under § 552(a)(3)(A)

As noted above, the FOIA's basic framework for addressing requests for government records is to establish an extremely broad duty of disclosure under § 552(a)(3)(A) and then to carve out limitations on this duty in § 552(b)'s list of exemptions. In this subchapter, we examine the initial scope of the government's duty to disclose under § 552(a)(3)(A). This provision declares:

> Except with respect to the records made available under paragraphs (1) and (2) of this subsection [which identify records that must be affirmatively disclosed or made available for inspection], and except as provided in subparagraph (E) [which blocks disclosures by intelligence agencies to foreign governmental entities], each agency, upon any request for records which
>
> > (i) reasonably describes such records and
> >
> > (ii) is made in accordance with published rules stating the time, place, fees (if any), and procedures to be followed, shall make the records promptly available to any person.

So, an "agency" must supply its "records" in response to "any request" that "reasonably describes" the requested records and complies with agency rules. But what is an "agency" within the meaning of the FOIA? And what are "records"? The following materials examine these and related questions.

Lesson 7A. Ben has been hired by the United States Trade Representative. He already knows his first assignment will be to defend certain wine standards at the World Trade Organization. Several Asian countries charge that these standards create a barrier to entry blocking their wines from the American market. He has two matters to clear up before he leaves on this mission.

The first is personal. Having started their D.C. careers together, he and Abby share a special bond. He calls to give her the news. To his delight, she too has momentous news to report. She has been offered a tenure-track position at a law school in Ohio. She will be moving west in a few months.

The second matter is professional. While he was director of the WTC's rulemaking division, he kept summaries of the record of each rulemaking in his own files. He passed these summaries on to Brit when she took over as director, and she kept them up-to-date. Fred, representing the Wrath for Grapes, learned of these summaries through his remaining WTC contacts. In its continuing effort to cause trouble and for no other noticeable purpose, the Wrath's leadership asked Fred to file a request for "summaries of any rulemaking records" under the Freedom of Information Act.

Do these summaries fall within the sweep of § 552(a)(3)(A)'s duty to disclose agency records? Does it matter why the Wrath wants them?

Background of *USDOJ v. Tax Analysts*

The respondent, Tax Analysts, as its name suggests, is in the business of providing information on developments in federal tax law to its readership. Today, with the prevalence of electronic databases, it is a relatively straightforward matter to keep track of developing case law for any given field, including tax. In 1979, this task was more difficult. Tax Analysts, however, found an extremely efficient way to collect information on civil litigation developments in federal tax law—just use the FOIA to ask the Department of Justice for copies of court decisions that it receives in tax cases as the representative of the federal government in litigation. The DOJ denied this request. A disappointed requester can seek judicial review "to enjoin the agency from withholding agency records and to order the production of any agency records improperly withheld." § 552(a)(4)(B). In the subsequent litigation, the DOJ denied that the documents in question were "agency records" or that they had been "improperly" "withheld." A decade after the request, the Court explained why the DOJ was wrong on these points.

United States Department of Justice v. Tax Analysts
492 U.S. 136 (1989)

Justice Marshall delivered the opinion of the Court.

The question presented is whether the Freedom of Information Act (FOIA or Act), requires the United States Department of Justice (Department) to make available copies of district court decisions that it receives in the course of litigating tax cases on behalf of the Federal Government. We hold that it does.

The Department's Tax Division represents the Federal Government in nearly all civil tax cases in the district courts, the courts of appeals, and the Claims Court. Because it represents a party in litigation, the Tax Division receives copies of all opinions and orders issued by these courts in such cases. Copies of these decisions are made for the Tax Division's staff attorneys. The original documents are sent to the official files kept by the Department.

. . . .

Respondent Tax Analysts publishes a weekly magazine, Tax Notes, which reports on legislative, judicial, and regulatory developments in the field of federal taxation to a readership largely composed of tax attorneys, accountants, and economists. As one of its regular features, Tax Notes provides summaries of recent federal court decisions on tax issues. To supplement the magazine, Tax Analysts provides full texts of these decisions in microfiche form. Tax Analysts also publishes Tax Notes Today, a daily electronic data base that includes summaries and full texts of recent federal court tax decisions.

In late July 1979, Tax Analysts filed a FOIA request in which it asked the Department to make available all district court tax opinions and final orders received by the Tax Division earlier that month. The Department denied the request on the ground that these decisions were not Tax Division records.

. . . .

In enacting the FOIA 23 years ago, Congress sought "'to open agency action to the light of public scrutiny.'" Congress did so by requiring agencies to adhere to "'a general philosophy of full agency disclosure.'" Congress believed that this philosophy, put into practice, would help "ensure an informed citizenry, vital to the functioning of a democratic society."

The FOIA confers jurisdiction on the district courts "to enjoin the agency from withholding agency records and to order the production of any agency records improperly withheld." §552(a)(4)(B). Under this provision, "federal jurisdiction is dependent on a showing that an agency has (1) 'improperly' (2) 'withheld' (3) 'agency records.'" Unless each of these criteria is met, a district court lacks jurisdiction to devise remedies to force an agency to comply with the FOIA's disclosure requirements.[3]

In this case, all three jurisdictional terms are at issue. Although these terms are defined neither in the Act nor in its legislative history, we do not write on a clean slate. Nine Terms ago we decided three cases that explicated the meanings of these partially overlapping terms. These decisions form the basis of our analysis of Tax Analysts' requests.

A

We consider first whether the district court decisions at issue are "agency records," a term elaborated upon both in *Kissinger* [1980] and in *Forsham* [1980]. *Kissinger* involved three separate FOIA requests for written summaries of telephone conversations in which Henry Kissinger had participated when he served as Assistant to the President for National Security Affairs from 1969 to 1975, and as Secretary of State from 1973 to 1977. Only one of these requests—for summaries of specific conversations that Kissinger had during his tenure as National Security Adviser—raised the "agency records" issue. At the time of this request, these summaries were stored in Kissinger's office at the State Department in his personal files. We first concluded that the summaries were not "agency records" at the time they were made because the FOIA does not include the Office of the President in its definition of "agency." We further held that these documents did not acquire the status of "agency records" when they were removed from the White House and transported to Kissinger's office at the State Department, a FOIA-covered agency:

> "We simply decline to hold that the physical location of the notes of telephone conversations renders them 'agency records.' The papers were not in the control of the State Department at any time. They were not generated in the State Department. They never entered the State Department's files, and they were not used by the Department for any purpose. If mere physical location of papers and materials could confer status as an 'agency record' Kissinger's personal books, speeches, and all other memorabilia stored in his office would have been agency records subject to disclosure under the FOIA."

Forsham, in turn, involved a request for raw data that formed the basis of a study conducted by a private medical research organization. Although the study had been

---

3. The burden is on the agency to demonstrate, not the requester to disprove, that the materials sought are not "agency records" or have not been "improperly withheld." ("Placing the burden of proof upon the agency puts the task of justifying the withholding on the only party able to explain it.")

funded through federal agency grants, the data never passed into the hands of the agencies that provided the funding, but instead was produced and possessed at all times by the private organization. We recognized that "[r]ecords of a nonagency certainly could become records of an agency as well," but the fact that the study was financially supported by a FOIA-covered agency did not transform the source material into "agency records." Nor did the agencies' right of access to the materials under federal regulations change this result. As we explained, "the FOIA applies to records which have been *in fact* obtained, and not to records which merely *could have been* obtained."

Two requirements emerge from *Kissinger* and *Forsham*, each of which must be satisfied for requested materials to qualify as "agency records." First, an agency must "either create or obtain" the requested materials "as a prerequisite to its becoming an 'agency record' within the meaning of the FOIA." In performing their official duties, agencies routinely avail themselves of studies, trade journal reports, and other materials produced outside the agencies both by private and governmental organizations. To restrict the term "agency records" to materials generated internally would frustrate Congress' desire to put within public reach the information available to an agency in its decisionmaking processes. As we noted in *Forsham*, "[t]he legislative history of the FOIA abounds with . . . references to records *acquired* by an agency."

Second, the agency must be in control of the requested materials at the time the FOIA request is made. By control we mean that the materials have come into the agency's possession in the legitimate conduct of its official duties. This requirement accords with *Kissinger's* teaching that the term "agency records" is not so broad as to include personal materials in an employee's possession, even though the materials may be physically located at the agency. This requirement is suggested by *Forsham* as well, where we looked to the definition of agency records in the Records Disposal Act. Under that definition, agency records include "all books, papers, maps, photographs, machine readable materials, or other documentary materials, regardless of physical form or characteristics, made or received by an agency of the United States Government *under Federal law or in connection with the transaction of public business. . . .*" (emphasis added).[5] Furthermore, the requirement that the materials be in

---

5. In *GTE Sylvania, Inc. v. Consumers Union of United States, Inc.* (1980), we noted that Congress intended the FOIA to prevent agencies from refusing to disclose, among other things, agency telephone directories and the names of agency employees. We are confident, however, that requests for documents of this type will be relatively infrequent. Common sense suggests that a person seeking such documents or materials housed in an agency library typically will find it easier to repair to the Library of Congress, or to the nearest public library, rather than to invoke the FOIA's disclosure mechanisms. To the extent such requests are made, the fact that the FOIA allows agencies to recoup the costs of processing requests from the requester may discourage recourse to the FOIA where materials are readily available elsewhere.

the agency's control at the time the request is made accords with our statement in *Forsham* that the FOIA does not cover "information in the abstract."[6]

Applying these requirements here, we conclude that the requested district court decisions constitute "agency records." First, it is undisputed that the Department has obtained these documents from the district courts. This is not a case like *Forsham*, where the materials never in fact had been received by the agency. The Department contends that a district court is not an "agency" under the FOIA, but this truism is beside the point. The relevant issue is whether an agency covered by the FOIA has "create[d] or obtaine[d]" the materials sought, not whether the organization from which the documents originated is itself covered by the FOIA.

Second, the Department clearly controls the district court decisions that Tax Analysts seeks. Each of the Tax Analysts' FOIA requests referred to district court decisions in the agency's possession at the time the requests were made. This is evident from the fact that Tax Analysts based its weekly requests on the Tax Division's logs, which compile information on decisions the Tax Division recently had received and placed in official case files. Furthermore, the court decisions at issue are obviously not personal papers of agency employees. The Department counters that it does not control these decisions because the district courts retain authority to modify the decisions even after they are released, but this argument, too, is beside the point. The control inquiry focuses on an agency's possession of the requested materials, not on its power to alter the content of the materials it receives. Agencies generally are not at liberty to alter the content of the materials that they receive from outside parties. An authorship-control requirement thus would sharply limit "agency records" essentially to documents generated by the agencies themselves. This result is incompatible with the FOIA's goal of giving the public access to all nonexempted information received by an agency as it carries out its mandate.

The Department also urges us to limit "agency records," at least where materials originating outside the agency are concerned, "to those documents 'prepared substantially to be relied upon in agency decisionmaking.'" This limitation disposes of Tax Analysts' requests, the Department argues, because district court judges do not write their decisions primarily with an eye toward agency decisionmaking. This argument, however, makes the determination of "agency records" turn on the intent of the creator of a document relied upon by an agency. Such a *mens rea* requirement is nowhere to be found in the Act. Moreover, discerning the intent of the drafters of a document may often prove an elusive endeavor, particularly if the document was

---

6. Because requested materials ordinarily will be in the agency's possession at the time the FOIA request is made, disputes over control should be infrequent. In some circumstances, however, requested materials might be on loan to another agency, "purposefully routed . . . out of agency possession in order to circumvent [an impending] FOIA request," or "wrongfully removed by an individual after a request is filed." We leave consideration of these issues to another day.

created years earlier or by a large number of people for whom it is difficult to divine a common intent.

B

We turn next to the term "withheld," which we discussed in *Kissinger*. Two of the requests in that case — for summaries of all the telephone conversations in which Kissinger had engaged while serving as National Security Adviser and as Secretary of State — implicated that term. These summaries were initially stored in Kissinger's personal files at the State Department. Near the end of his tenure as Secretary of State, Kissinger transferred the summaries first to a private residence and then to the Library of Congress. Significantly, the two requests for these summaries were made only after the summaries had been physically delivered to the Library. We found this fact dispositive, concluding that Congress did not believe that an agency "withholds a document which has been removed from the possession of the agency prior to the filing of the FOIA requests. In such a case, the agency has neither the custody nor control necessary to enable it to withhold." We accordingly refused to order the State Department to institute a retrieval action against the Library. As we explained, such a course "would have us read the 'hold' out of 'withhold. . . . A refusal to resort to legal remedies to obtain possession is simply not conduct subsumed by the verb withhold.'"[10]

The construction of "withholding" adopted in *Kissinger* readily encompasses Tax Analysts' requests. There is no claim here that Tax Analysts filed its requests for copies of recent district court tax decisions received by the Tax Division after these decisions had been transferred out of the Department. On the contrary, the decisions were on the Department's premises and otherwise in the Department's control when the requests were made. Thus, when the Department refused to comply with Tax Analysts' requests, it "withheld" the district court decisions for purposes of § 552(a)(4)(B).

The Department's counterargument is that, because the district court decisions sought by Tax Analysts are publicly available as soon as they are issued and thus may be inspected and copied by the public at any time, the Department cannot be said to have "withheld" them. The Department notes that the weekly logs it provides to Tax Analysts contain sufficient information to direct Tax Analysts to the "original source of the requested documents." It is not clear from the Department's

---

10. *Kissinger's* focus on the agency's present control of a requested document was based in part on the Act's purposes and structure. With respect to the former, we noted that because Congress had not intended to "obligate agencies to create or retain documents," an agency should not be "required to retrieve documents which have escaped its possession, but which it has not endeavored to recover." As for the Act's structure, we noted that, among other provisions, § 552(a)(6)(B) gives agencies a 10-day extension of the normal 10-day period for responding to FOIA requests if there is a need to search and collect the requested materials from facilities separate from the office processing the request. The brevity of this extension period indicates that Congress did not expect agencies to resort to lawsuits to retrieve documents within that period.

brief whether this argument is based on the term "withheld" or the term "improperly." But, to the extent the Department relies on the former term, its argument is without merit. Congress used the word "withheld" only "in its usual sense." When the Department refused to grant Tax Analysts' requests for the district court decisions in its files, it undoubtedly "withheld" these decisions in any reasonable sense of that term. Nothing in the history or purposes of the FOIA counsels contorting this word beyond its usual meaning. We therefore reject the Department's argument that an agency has not "withheld" a document under its control when, in denying an otherwise valid request, it directs the requester to a place outside of the agency where the document may be publicly available.

C

The Department is left to argue, finally, that the district court decisions were not "improperly" withheld because of their public availability. The term "improperly," like "agency records" and "withheld," is not defined by the Act. We explained in *GTE Sylvania*, however, that Congress' use of the word "improperly" reflected its dissatisfaction with § 3 of the Administrative Procedure Act, which "had failed to provide the desired access to information relied upon in Government decisionmaking, and in fact had become 'the major statutory excuse for withholding Government records from public view.'" Under § 3, we explained, agencies had "broad discretion . . . in deciding what information to disclose, and that discretion was often abused."

In enacting the FOIA, Congress intended "to curb this apparently unbridled discretion" by "clos[ing] the 'loopholes which allow agencies to deny legitimate information to the public.'" Toward this end, Congress formulated a system of clearly defined exemptions to the FOIA's otherwise mandatory disclosure requirements. An agency must disclose agency records to any person under § 552(a), "unless they may be withheld pursuant to one of the nine enumerated exemptions listed in § 552(b)." Consistent with the Act's goal of broad disclosure, these exemptions have been consistently given a narrow compass. More important for present purposes, the exemptions are "explicitly exclusive." As JUSTICE O'CONNOR has explained, Congress sought "to insulate its product from judicial tampering and to preserve the emphasis on disclosure by admonishing that the 'availability of records to the public' is not limited, 'except as *specifically* stated.'" It follows from the exclusive nature of the § 552(b) exemption scheme that agency records which do not fall within one of the exemptions are "improperly" withheld.[12]

The Department does not contend here that any exemption enumerated in § 552(b) protects the district court decisions sought by Tax Analysts. The

---

12. Even when an agency does not deny a FOIA request outright, the requesting party may still be able to claim "improper" withholding by alleging that the agency has responded in an inadequate manner. No such claim is made in this case. Indeed, Tax Analysts does not dispute the Court of Appeals' conclusion that the Department could satisfy its duty of disclosure simply by making the relevant district court opinions available for copying in the public reference facility that it maintains.

Department claims nonetheless that there is nothing "improper" in directing a requester "to the principal, public source of records." The Department advances three somewhat related arguments in support of this proposition. We consider them in turn.

First, the Department contends that the structure of the Act evinces Congress' desire to avoid redundant disclosures. An understanding of this argument requires a brief survey of the disclosure provisions of § 552(a). Under subsection (a)(1), an agency must "currently publish in the Federal Register" specific materials, such as descriptions of the agency, statements of its general functions, and the agency's rules of procedure. Under subsection (a)(2), an agency must "make available for public inspection and copying" its final opinions, policy statements, and administrative staff manuals, "unless the materials are promptly published and copies offered for sale." Under subsection (a)(3), the general provision covering the disclosure of agency records, an agency need not make available those materials that have already been disclosed under subsections (a)(1) and (a)(2). Taken together, the Department argues, these provisions demonstrate the inapplicability of the FOIA's disclosure requirements to previously disclosed, publicly available materials. "A *fortiori*, a judicial record that is a public document should not be subject to a FOIA request."

The Department's argument proves too much. The disclosure requirements set out in subsections (a)(1) and (a)(2) are carefully limited to situations in which the requested materials have been previously published or made available by the *agency itself*. It is one thing to say that an agency need not disclose materials that it has previously released; it is quite another to say that an agency need not disclose materials that some other person or group may have previously released. Congress undoubtedly was aware of the redundancies that might exist when requested materials have been previously made available. It chose to deal with that problem by crafting only narrow categories of materials which need not be, in effect, disclosed twice *by the agency*. If Congress had wished to codify an exemption for all publicly available materials, it knew perfectly well how to do so. It is not for us to add or detract from Congress' comprehensive scheme, which already "balances, and protects all interests" implicated by Executive Branch disclosure.[13]

It is not surprising, moreover, that Congress declined to exempt all publicly available materials from the FOIA's disclosure requirements. In the first place, such an exemption would engender intractable fights over precisely what constitutes public availability, unless the term were defined with precision. In some sense, nearly all of the information that comes within an agency's control can be characterized as publicly available. Although the form in which this material comes to an agency—*i.e.*, a report or testimony—may not be generally available, the information included in that report or testimony may very well be. Even if there

---

13. The obligations imposed under subsections (a)(1) and (a)(2) are not properly viewed as additions to the disclosure exemptions set out in subsection (b)....

were some agreement over what constitutes publicly available materials, Congress surely did not envision agencies satisfying their disclosure obligations under the FOIA simply by handing requesters a map and sending them on scavenger expeditions throughout the Nation. Without some express indication in the Act's text or legislative history that Congress intended such a result, we decline to adopt this reading of the statute.

The Department's next argument rests on the fact that the disclosure of district court decisions is partially governed by other statutes and by rules set by the Judicial Conference of the United States. The FOIA does not compel disclosure of district court decisions, the Department contends, because these other provisions are "more precisely drawn to govern the provision of court records to the general public." We disagree. As with the Department's first argument, this theory requires us to read into the FOIA a disclosure exemption that Congress did not itself provide. This we decline to do. That Congress knew that other statutes created overlapping disclosure requirements is evident from § 552(b)(3), which authorizes an agency to refuse a FOIA request when the materials sought are expressly exempted from disclosure by another statute. If Congress had intended to enact the converse proposition—that an agency may refuse to provide disclosure of materials whose disclosure is *mandated* by another statute—it was free to do so. Congress, however, did not take such a step.

The Department's last argument is derived from *GTE Sylvania*, where we held that agency records sought from the Consumer Products Safety Commission were not "improperly" withheld even though the records did not fall within one of subsection (b)'s enumerated exemptions. The Commission had not released the records in question because a district court, in the course of an unrelated lawsuit, had enjoined the Commission from doing so. In these circumstances, we held, "[t]he concerns underlying the Freedom of Information Act [were] inapplicable, for the agency . . . made no effort to avoid disclosure." We therefore approved the Commission's compliance with the injunction, noting that when Congress passed the FOIA, it had not "intended to require an agency to commit contempt of court in order to release documents. Indeed, Congress viewed the federal courts as the necessary protectors of the public's right to know."

Although the Department is correct in asserting that *GTE Sylvania* represents a departure from the FOIA's self-contained exemption scheme, this departure was a slight one at best, and was necessary in order to serve a critical goal independent of the FOIA—the enforcement of a court order. As we emphasized, *GTE Sylvania* arose in "a distinctly different context" than the typical FOIA case, where the agency decides for itself whether to comply with a request for agency records. In such a case, the agency cannot contend that it has "no discretion . . . to exercise."

The present dispute is clearly akin to those typical FOIA cases. No claim has been made that the Department was powerless to comply with Tax Analysts' requests. On the contrary, it was the Department's decision, and the Department's decision alone, not to make the court decisions available. We reject the Department's suggestion that *GTE Sylvania* invites courts in every case to engage in balancing, based on public availability and other factors, to determine whether there has been an unjustified denial of information. The FOIA invests courts neither with the authority nor the tools to make such determinations.

For the reasons stated, the Department improperly withheld agency records when it refused Tax Analysts' requests for copies of the district court tax decisions in its files.

JUSTICE BLACKMUN, dissenting.

The Court in this case has examined once again the Freedom of Information Act (FOIA). It now determines that under the Act the Department of Justice on request must make available copies of federal district court orders and opinions it receives in the course of its litigation of tax cases on behalf of the Federal Government. The majority holds that these qualify as agency records and that they were improperly withheld by the Department when respondent asked for their production. The Court's analysis, I suppose, could be regarded as a fairly routine one.

I do not join the Court's opinion, however, because it seems to me that the language of the statute is not that clear or conclusive on the issue and, more important, because the result the Court reaches cannot be one that was within the intent of Congress when the FOIA was enacted.

Respondent Tax Analysts, although apparently a nonprofit organization for federal income tax purposes, is in business and in that sense is a commercial enterprise. It sells summaries of these opinions and supplies full texts to major electronic databases. The result of its now-successful effort in this litigation is to impose the cost of obtaining the court orders and opinions upon the Government and thus upon taxpayers generally. There is no question that this material is available elsewhere. But it is quicker and more convenient, and less "frustrating," for respondent to have the Department do the work and search its files and produce the items than it is to apply to the respective court clerks.

This, I feel, is almost a gross misuse of the FOIA. What respondent demands, and what the Court permits, adds nothing whatsoever to public knowledge of government operations. That, I had thought, and the majority acknowledges, was the real purpose of the FOIA and the spirit in which the statute has been interpreted thus far. I also sense, I believe not unwarrantedly, a distinct lack of enthusiasm on the part of the majority for the result it reaches in this case.

If, as I surmise, the Court's decision today is outside the intent of Congress in enacting the statute, Congress perhaps will rectify the decision forthwith and will give everyone concerned needed guidelines for the administration and interpretation of this somewhat opaque statute.

Notes

1. What should happen to the summaries? Given Justice Marshall's view of "agency records" covered by the FOIA, does § 552(a)(3)(A) demand disclosure of the rulemaking summaries? Would it make any difference if Ben had taken his summaries home rather than passing them on to Brit?

2. What are "agencies"? For FOIA purposes, "'agency' as defined in § 551(1) of this title includes any executive department, military department, Government corporation, Government controlled corporation, or other establishment in the executive branch of the Government (including the Executive Office of the President), or any independent regulatory agency." 5 U.S.C. § 552(f)(1). Notably, this broad definition does not include, among others, the courts or Congress. Records in the possession of an agency may be "congressional records" and fall outside of the FOIA's reach if Congress has evidenced a clear intent to maintain control over them. For instance, records that Congress transfers to an agency with instructions to keep them confidential might remain "congressional records." *See, e.g., United We Stand America, Inc. v. IRS*, 359 F.3d 595, 599–600 (D.C. Cir. 2004).

Less obviously, FOIA's definition of "agency" does not capture offices within the Executive Office of the President that merely "advise and assist" the president rather than exercise substantial independent authority. *See Citizens for Responsibility and Ethics in Washington v. Office of Admin.*, 566 F.3d 219, 223 (D.C. Cir. 2009) (noting that courts have held that the Office of Science and Technology, Office of Management and Budget, and Council on Environmental Quality are agencies subject to the FOIA given that they wield "substantial authority independent of the President," whereas the Council of Economic Advisers and National Security Council are not). Advising the president is surely one of the most important functions a government official can have. Should the FOIA demand disclosure of purely "advisory" assistants to the president?

3. What are "agency records"? The original FOIA did not, oddly enough, define the term "record." In *Forsham v. Harris*, the Supreme Court looked to the definition of "record" in the Records Disposal Act, which provides:

> '[R]ecords' includes all books, papers, maps, photographs, machine readable materials, or other documentary materials, regardless of physical form or characteristics, *made or received* by an agency of the United States Government under Federal law or in connection with the transaction of public business ....

445 U.S. 169, 183 (1980) (quoting 44 U.S.C. § 3301) (italics added by Court). Parsing this passage, "record" grabs any material that might be construed as "documentary" in nature.

In a subsequent amendment to the FOIA, Congress confirmed that the term "record" is not format-sensitive but instead includes "any information that would be an agency record subject to the requirements of this section when maintained by an agency in any format, including an electronic format." 5 U.S.C. § 551(f)(2)(A). Congress has also clarified that the term "record" includes "any information described under subparagraph (A) that is maintained for an agency by an entity under Government contract, for the purposes of records management." 5 U.S.C. § 551(f)(2)

(B). Thus, an agency cannot avoid its FOIA obligations by the simple expedient of contracting with a third party to store materials.

For a "record" to be an "agency record," it must satisfy two conditions. First, the agency must "create or obtain" the material in question. Second, "the agency must be in control of the requested materials at the time the FOIA request is made." *United States Department of Justice v. Tax Analysts*, 492 U.S. 136, 144–45 (1989). Courts determine control in light of four factors:

> (1) the intent of the document's creator to retain or relinquish control over the records; (2) the ability of the agency to use and dispose of the record as it sees fit; (3) the extent to which agency personnel have read or relied upon the document; and (4) the degree to which the document was integrated into the agency's record system or files.

United We Stand Am., Inc. v. IRS, 359 F.3d 595, 599 (D.C. Cir. 2004).

An agency does not have an obligation to obtain records over which it has lost control. *Kissinger v. Reporters Committee for Freedom of the Press*, 445 U.S. 136, 158 (1980) (holding that Department of State did not "withhold" records in the form of Secretary's notes concerning official telephone conversations where request was made after notes had been "deeded" by Secretary to Library of Congress). Location is not dispositive. Records that are not in the physical custody of an agency may still be under its control and subject to the FOIA. *See Competitive Enterprise Inst. v. Office of Science and Technology Policy*, 827 F.3d 145, 150 (D.C. Cir. 2016) (observing that it would be senseless for the law to allow a department head to "deprive requestors of hard-copy documents by leaving them in a file at his daughter's house and then claiming that they are under her control"). On the other hand, records physically present in, say, an agency building may be personal possessions of agency officials or employees and not subject to the agency's control. *Tax Analysts*, 492 U.S. at 145.

4. A duty to disclose, not create. The FOIA "does not obligate agencies to create or retain documents; it only obligates them to provide access to those which it in fact has created and retained." *Kissinger*, 445 U.S. at 152. How far does this limit go? Suppose, for example, a requester asks the FTC to provide a breakdown of the industries involved in FTC deceptive practice complaints. The agency has not compiled this data, but it is contained in its investigative files. What is the agency's disclosure obligation? *Cf. Brown v. Perez*, 835 F.3d 1223 (10th Cir. 2016) (holding that agency was not obligated to produce "screenshot printouts" of menus for its scheduling software because doing so would require the agency to "open the software, input the relevant data, and recreate a screen image that could be captured and produced").

5. FOIA and grantees. Suppose the WTC issued a grant to a law professor to make recommendations about its rulemaking performance and that he made summaries for his own use that he kept in his own office. Would the professor's summaries be available under the FOIA? For a long time, one could have answered "no" on the basis of *Forsham v. Harris*, 445 U.S. 169 (1980), in which the Court held:

... We hold here that written data generated, owned, and possessed by a privately controlled organization receiving federal study grants [hereafter "grantee"] are not "agency records" within the meaning of the Act when copies of those data have not been obtained by a federal agency subject to the FOIA. Federal participation in the generation of the data by means of a grant from HEW does not make the private organization a federal "agency" within the terms of the Act. Nor does this federal funding in combination with a federal right of access render the data "agency records" of HEW, which *is* a federal "agency" under the terms of the Act.

Congress partially abrogated *Forsham* by including a two-sentence provision in the fiscal year 1999 appropriation for the Office of Management and Budget (OMB). Circular A-110 is the document that OMB uses to regulate grant-making by federal agencies to institutions of higher learning, hospitals, and other nonprofit institutions. The statutory provision instructed the agency to alter the circular "to require Federal awarding agencies to ensure that all data produced under an award will be made available to the public through the procedures established under the Freedom of Information Act." OMB interpreted this statutory command narrowly, instructing agencies to seek records in response to a "request for research data relating to published research findings produced under an award that were used by the Federal Government in developing an agency action that has the force and effect of law." *Circular A-110.36* (64 Fed. Reg. 54,926, Oct. 8, 1999). OMB's amendment to its circular also defines terms, such as "research data," in ways that sharply limit agencies' duty to request data from grantees.

6. "Reasonably describe." The FOIA was intended to provide access to ordinary citizens and hence no special form or particular language is necessary in making a request. Nonetheless, a request must "reasonably describe" the desired information. § 552(a)(3)(A). The FOIA's legislative history defines a reasonable description of records as one that enables "a professional employee of the agency who [is] familiar with the subject area of the request to locate the record with a reasonable amount of effort." H.R. Rep. No. 93-876, 93rd Cong., 2d Sess. 6 (1974), 1974 U.S.C.C.A.N. 6271. If you were writing a FOIA request, what would motivate you to be more vague than necessary? What impediments might stand in the way of your being as precise as you would like to be?

At what point does a FOIA request become unreasonably burdensome? The Second Circuit offered a little guidance on this point in *Ruotolo v. Department of Justice, Tax Div.*, 53 F.3d 4, 10 (2d Cir. 1995):

It is unreasonably burdensome to request information that would require "a page-by-page search through the 84,000 cubic feet of documents in the [CIA] Records Center"; a "search through every file in [the IRS's] possession to see if a reference to Scientology appeared"; a search of 3,500,000 files of patents as well as 1,000,000 other files. It is also unreasonably burdensome to require a search of the files of over 5,000 criminal cases upon a general request for data to be gleaned from documents which have not been created. In contrast, the Ruotolos specifically sought documents related to Vaughn indices, and it is clear that there were only 803 files to be searched. Certainly, the Tax Division should not be relieved from all duty to search under the circumstances.

7. Are some requesters better than others? "Any person" may make a FOIA request. 5 U.S.C. § 552(a)(3)(A). As used by FOIA, the term "person" casts a very broad net and is subject only to a few very limited exceptions. *See, e.g.*, § 552(a)(3)(E) (providing that foreign governments and their representatives cannot use FOIA to pry information out of agencies within the intelligence community). But should requests for commercial purposes be disfavored? Or at least subject to the true costs of disclosure? Do you agree with Justice Blackmun that the result in *Tax Analysts* "cannot be one that was within the intent of Congress"? For many agencies, the vast majority of FOIA requests come from commercial entities seeking to profit from agency records. Margaret B. Kwoka, *FOIA, Inc.*, 65 Duke L.J. 1361 (2016). Relatively few requests come from journalists. This disparity indicates that most of the effort involved in complying with FOIA requests serves private interests rather than a broader public interest in government transparency. Might a redesign of the FOIA be in order to address this problem?

8. Response times. Unless an agency decides to claim an applicable exemption, it is supposed to produce requested records "promptly." § 552(a)(3)(A). To move agencies along, § 552(a)(6) creates a complex set of short deadlines for determining whether to comply with requests and for resolving internal appeals. *See, e.g.*, § 552(a)(6)(A)(i) (giving agencies twenty days to "determine" whether to comply with a request). After an agency "determines" that it will comply, it generally should produce documents "within days or a few weeks." *Citizens for Responsibility and Ethics in Washington v. FEC*, 711 F.3d 180, 188 (D.C. Cir. 2013). Deadlines are subject to short extensions under "unusual circumstances." § 552(a)(6)(B)(i). An agency's failure to satisfy these deadlines eliminates a requester's obligation to pursue administrative remedies before seeking judicial review. § 552(a)(6)(C)(i).

According to statistics collected by the Office of Information Policy within the DOJ, federal agencies did a remarkable job speeding through the 818,271 FOIA requests they received in fiscal year 2017. *Summary of Annual FOIA Reports for Fiscal Year 2017.* The OIP reports that agencies took an average of 27.96 days to process "simple" requests, and they processed approximately 85% of "complex" requests in less than 140 days. Still, you may not want to hold your breath on your request. The government's glossy statistics are hard to square with a widespread acknowledgement that agencies' FOIA offices are notoriously under-resourced and that requesters often experience excessive delays. *Cf.* David E. McCraw, *The "Freedom from Information" Act: A Look Back at Nader, FOIA, and What Went Wrong*, 126 Yale L. J. Forum 232, 235–36 (2016) (characterizing the government statistic on "simple requests" as "misleading"; observing that a "different experience awaits those who make meaningful FOIA requests aimed at documents for use in investigative journalism or in-depth research"; adding, "responses stretching into the years remain a staple of FOIA").

9. Fees. Subject to statutory limits, an agency may charge fees for search, duplication, and review of documents where records are sought for a commercial purpose. The agency may charge for duplication fees where records are sought by educational or (non-commercial) scientific institutions for scholarly or scientific research or are sought by representatives of the news media. The agency may charge search and duplication fees for requests that fall into none of the preceding categories. § 552(a)(4)(A)(ii). Fees are to be waived or reduced where disclosure "is in the public interest because it is likely to contribute significantly to public understanding of the operations or activities of the government and is not primarily in the commercial interest of the requester." § 552(a)(4)(A)(iii).

10. Judicial review. An agency's denial of a FOIA request is subject to judicial review under § 552(a)(4)(B). The scope of review is ostensibly de novo, but as a practical matter, courts are highly deferential to agency refusals that implicate national security interests. If a court determines that agency records fall within § 552(a)(3)'s disclosure mandate, the court must order disclosure unless it determines that an exemption applies. The burden to justify application of an exemption lies with the agency. The court may award "reasonable attorney fees and other litigation costs reasonably incurred" by a plaintiff who has "substantially prevailed" in a FOIA action. § 552(a)(4)(E).

B. FOIA — A Tour of Exemptions

The preceding subchapter examined the scope of the disclosure requirement established by § 552(a)(3)(A). Now, attention turns to § 552(b)'s nine exemptions from this disclosure requirement. These exemptions cover a wide range of matters, including, as you might expect, national security (Exemption 1), trade secrets (Exemption 4), and certain private personal information (Exemptions 6 and 7(C)). The materials that follow will focus especially on Exemption 5, which "protects inter-agency or intra-agency memorandums or letters which would not be available by law to a party other than an agency in litigation with an agency." § 552(b)(5). The gist of this extremely important exemption is that, if a document would be shielded from discovery in civil litigation with the agency, then the document will be exempt from disclosure under the FOIA.

Lesson 7B. The Wrath has expanded its FOIA requests. In addition to Ben's and Brit's rulemaking summaries, it now asks for all intra-agency or inter-agency exchanges on the health or safety aspects of WTC wine regulation. Also, it seeks industry responses to the reporting requirements of WTCA § 6(e) and (f) as well as any staff compilation or analysis of information from those reports.

On another front, Carl left his post as WTC chair after being tapped by his party to run for governor. Usually his long absence from the state would be a problem, but, in this case, he was removed from some rancorous party in-fighting, making him the only candidate everyone in the party could support. His years of public service, including his "strong commitment to consumer protection" at the WTC, count heavily in his favor.

The Wrath is concerned about Carl's commitment to the wine industry during his years at the WTC. Therefore, the Wrath and its allies are "pulling out all the stops" to defeat him. To this end, the Wrath has requested access to his personnel files compiled by the U.S. government, including government investigations of his fitness to be WTC chair. They would also like to obtain the files compiled for the congressional confirmation hearings.

What, if any, of this information could the Wrath obtain through the FOIA?

Background of *NLRB v. Sears, Roebuck & Co.*

In the archetypical agency structure, an agency may both initiate an enforcement action and, later in the proceedings, adjudicate the merits. The National Labor Relations Board (NLRB) works a bit differently. This agency is charged by the National Labor Relations Act (NLRA) with adjudicating claims of unfair labor practices, but the job of determining whether to initiate such claims lies with the agency's Office of General Counsel. If the General Counsel decides not to bring a complaint, then the NLRB has nothing to adjudicate. As such, the General Counsel's policies and decisions regarding implementation of the NLRA are naturally a matter of intense interest to regulated parties. One of these regulated parties, Sears, Roebuck & Co. (Sears), filed a FOIA request seeking disclosure of "Appeals Memoranda" and "Advice Memoranda," which the Office of General Counsel generates in the course of determining whether to file complaints. The agency sought to shield these documents with Exemption 5, which covers "inter-agency or intra-agency memorandums or letters which would not be available by law to a party other than an agency in litigation with an agency."

The Supreme Court's opinion in the case remains one of the leading expositions on this exemption. Pay careful attention to how the Court steers a path between two important values. On the one hand, the law recognizes in many contexts a need for private, and therefore presumably more candid, discussion. Attorney-client privilege and the work product doctrine are obvious expressions of this value. On the other hand, in a society committed to due process, there should be no "secret law."

NLRB v. Sears, Roebuck & Co.
421 U.S. 132 (1975)

Mr. Justice White delivered the opinion of the Court.

The National Labor Relations Board (the Board) and its General Counsel seek to set aside an order of the United States District Court directing disclosure to respondent, Sears, Roebuck & Co. (Sears), pursuant to the Freedom of Information Act, of certain memoranda, known as "Advice Memoranda" and "Appeals Memoranda," and related documents generated by the Office of the General Counsel in the course of deciding whether or not to permit the filing with the Board of unfair labor practice complaints.

. . . .

Crucial to the decision of this case is an understanding of the function of the documents in issue in the context of the administrative process which generated them. We deal with this matter first. Under § 1 *et seq.* of the National Labor Relations Act, as amended by the Labor Management Relations Act, 1947, the process of adjudicating unfair labor practice cases begins with the filing by a private party of a "charge." Although Congress has designated the Board as the principal body which adjudicates the unfair labor practice case based on such charge the Board may adjudicate only upon the filing of a "complaint"; and Congress has delegated to the Office of General Counsel "on behalf of the Board" the unreviewable authority to determine whether a complaint shall be filed. In those cases in which he decides that a complaint shall issue, the General Counsel becomes an advocate before the Board in support of the complaint. In those cases in which he decides not to issue a complaint, no proceeding before the Board occurs at all. The practical effect of this administrative scheme is that a party believing himself the victim of an unfair labor practice can obtain neither adjudication nor remedy under the labor statute without first persuading the Office of General Counsel that his claim is sufficiently meritorious to warrant Board consideration.

In order to structure the considerable power which the administrative scheme gives him, the General Counsel has adopted certain procedures for processing unfair labor practice charges. Charges are filed in the first instance with one of the Board's 31 Regional Directors, to whom the General Counsel has delegated the initial power to decide whether or not to issue a complaint. A member of the staff of the Regional Office then conducts an investigation of the charge, which may include interviewing witnesses and reviewing documents. If, on the basis of the investigation, the Regional Director believes the charge has merit, a settlement will be attempted, or a complaint issued. If the charge has no merit in the Regional Director's judgment, the charging party will be so informed by letter with a brief explanation of the reasons. In such a case, the charging party will also be informed of his right to appeal within 10 days to the Office of the General Counsel in Washington, D.C.

If the charging party exercises this right, the entire file in the possession of the Regional Director will be sent to the Office of Appeals in the General Counsel's Office in Washington, D.C. The case will be assigned to a staff attorney in the Office of Appeals, who prepares a memorandum containing an analysis of the factual and legal issues in the case. This memorandum is called an "agenda minute" and serves as the basis for discussion at a meeting of the "Appeals Committee," which includes the Director and Associate Director of the Office of Appeals. At some point in this period, the charging party may make a written presentation of his case as of right and an oral presentation in the discretion of the General Counsel. If an oral presentation is allowed, the subject of the unfair labor practice charge is notified and allowed a similar but separate opportunity to make an oral presentation. In any event, a decision is reached by the Appeals Committee; and the decision and the reasons for it are set forth in a memorandum called the "General Counsel's Minute" or the "Appeals Memorandum." This document is then cleared through the General Counsel himself. If the case is unusually complex or important, the General Counsel will have been brought into the process at an earlier stage and will have had a hand in the decision and the expression of its basis in the Appeals Memorandum. In either event, the Appeals Memorandum is then sent to the Regional Director who follows its instructions. If the appeal is rejected and the Regional Director's decision not to issue a complaint is sustained, a separate document is prepared and sent by the General Counsel in letter form to the charging party, more briefly setting forth the reasons for the denial of his appeal. The Appeals Memoranda, whether sustaining or overruling the Regional Directors, constitute one class of documents at issue in this case.

The appeals process affords the General Counsel's Office in Washington some opportunity to formulate a coherent policy, and to achieve some measure of uniformity, in enforcing the labor laws. The appeals process alone, however, is not wholly adequate for this purpose: when the Regional Director initially decides to file a complaint, no appeal is available; and when the Regional Director decides not to file a complaint, the charging party may neglect to appeal. Accordingly, to further "fair and uniform administration of the Act," the General Counsel requires the Regional Directors, before reaching an initial decision in connection with charges raising certain issues specified by the General Counsel, to submit the matter to the General Counsel's "Advice Branch," also located in Washington, D.C. In yet other kinds of cases, the Regional Directors are permitted to seek the counsel of the Advice Branch.

When a Regional Director seeks "advice" from the Advice Branch, he does so through a memorandum which sets forth the facts of the case, a statement of the issues on which advice is sought, and a recommendation. The case is then assigned to a staff attorney in the Advice Branch who researches the legal issues presented by reading prior Board and court decisions and "prior advice determinations in similar or related cases," and reports, orally or in writing, to a Committee or "agenda" made up of various high-ranking members of the General Counsel's Office. The Committee recommendation is then arrived at and communicated to the General Counsel, together with the recommendation of the Regional Director and any dissenting views in the Committee. In special cases, the General Counsel may schedule special agendas and invite other staff members to submit their recommendations. In either event, the General Counsel will decide the issue submitted, and his "final determination" will be communicated to the Regional Director by way of an Advice Memorandum. The memorandum will briefly summarize the facts, against the background of which the legal or policy issue is to be decided, set forth the General Counsel's answer to the legal or policy issue submitted together with a "detailed legal rationale," and contain "instructions for the final processing of the case." Depending upon the conclusion reached in the memorandum, the Regional

Director will either file a complaint or send a letter to the complaining party advising him of the Regional Director's decision not to proceed and informing him of his right to appeal. It is these Advice Memoranda which constitute the other class of documents of which Sears seeks disclosure in this case.

This case arose in the following context. By letter dated July 14, 1971, Sears requested that the General Counsel disclose to it pursuant to the Act all Advice and Appeals Memoranda issued within the previous five years on [specified] subjects. . . . By letter dated July 23, 1971, the General Counsel declined Sears' disclosure request in full. The letter stated that Advice Memoranda are simply "guides for a Regional Director" and are not final; that they are exempt from disclosure under 5 U.S.C. § 552(b)(5) as "intra-agency memoranda" which reflect the thought processes of the General Counsel's staff. . . .

. . . .

The parties are in apparent agreement that Exemption 5 withholds from a member of the public documents which a private party could not discover in litigation with the agency. *EPA v. Mink* (1973). Since virtually any document not privileged may be discovered by the appropriate litigant, if it is relevant to his litigation, and since the Act clearly intended to give any member of the public as much right to disclosure as one with a special interest therein, it is reasonable to construe Exemption 5 to exempt those documents, and only those documents, normally privileged in the civil discovery context. The privileges claimed by petitioners to be relevant to this case are (i) the "generally . . . recognized" privilege for "confidential intra-agency advisory opinions. . . ."

That Congress had the Government's executive privilege specifically in mind in adopting Exemption 5 is clear. The precise contours of the privilege in the context of this case are less clear, but may be gleaned from expressions of legislative purpose and the prior case law. The cases uniformly rest the privilege on the policy of protecting the "decision making processes of government agencies"; and focus on documents "reflecting advisory opinions, recommendations and deliberations comprising part of a process by which governmental decisions and policies are formulated." The point, plainly made in the Senate Report, is that the "frank discussion of legal or policy matters" in writing might be inhibited if the discussion were made public; and that the "decisions" and "policies formulated" would be the poorer as a result. As a lower court has pointed out, "there are enough incentives as it is for playing it safe and listing with the wind," and as we have said in an analogous context, "[h]uman experience teaches that those who expect public dissemination of their remarks may well temper candor with a concern for appearances . . . to the *detriment of the decisionmaking process.*" *United States v. Nixon* (1974) (emphasis added).

Manifestly, the ultimate purpose of this long-recognized privilege is to prevent injury to the quality of agency decisions. The quality of a particular agency decision will clearly be affected by the communications received by the decision-maker on the subject of the decision prior to the time the decision is made. However, it is difficult to see how the quality of a decision will be affected by communications with respect to the decision occurring after the decision is finally reached; and therefore equally difficult to see how the quality of the decision will be affected by forced disclosure of such communications, as long as prior communications and the ingredients of the decisionmaking process are not disclosed. Accordingly, the lower courts have uniformly drawn a distinction between predecisional communications, which are privileged;[18] and communications made after the decision and designed to explain it, which are not. This distinction is supported not only by the lesser injury to the decisionmaking process flowing from disclosure of postdecisional communications, but also, in the case of those communications which explain the decision, by the increased public interest in knowing the basis for agency policy already adopted. The public is only marginally concerned with reasons supporting a policy which an agency has rejected, or with reasons which might have supplied, but did not supply, the basis for a policy which was actually adopted on a different ground. In contrast, the public is vitally concerned with the reasons which did supply the basis for an agency policy actually adopted. These reasons, if expressed within the agency, constitute the "working law" of the agency and have been held by the lower courts to be outside the protection of Exemption 5. Exemption 5, properly construed, calls for "disclosure of all 'opinions and interpretations' which embody the agency's effective law and policy, and the withholding of all papers which reflect the agency's group thinking in the process of working out its policy and determining what its law shall be."

This conclusion is powerfully supported by the other provisions of the Act. The affirmative portion of the Act, expressly requiring indexing of "final opinions," "statements of policy and interpretations which have been adopted by the agency," and "instructions to staff that affect a member of the public," 5 U.S.C. § 552(a)(2), represents a strong congressional aversion to "secret [agency] law," and represents an affirmative congressional purpose to require disclosure of documents which have "the force and effect of law." We should be reluctant, therefore, to construe Exemption 5 to apply to the documents described in 5 U.S.C. § 552(a)(2); and with respect at least to "final opinions," which not only invariably explain agency action already taken or an agency decision already made, but also constitute "final dispositions" of matters by an agency, we hold that Exemption 5 can never apply.

It is equally clear that Congress had the attorney's work-product privilege specifically in mind when it adopted Exemption 5 and that such a privilege had been recognized in the civil discovery context by the prior case law. The Senate Report

---

18. Our emphasis on the need to protect *pre-decisional* documents does not mean that the existence of the privilege turns on the ability of an agency to identify a specific decision in connection with which a memorandum is prepared. Agencies are, and properly should be, engaged in a continuing process of examining their policies; this process will generate memoranda containing recommendations which do not ripen into agency decisions; and the lower courts should be wary of interfering with this process.

states that Exemption 5 "would include the working papers of the agency attorney and documents which would come within the attorney-client privilege if applied to private parties," and the case law clearly makes the attorney's work-product rule of *Hickman v. Taylor* (1947), applicable to Government attorneys in litigation. Whatever the outer boundaries of the attorney's work-product rule are, the rule clearly applies to memoranda prepared by an attorney in contemplation of litigation which set forth the attorney's theory of the case and his litigation strategy.

Applying these principles to the memoranda sought by Sears, it becomes clear that Exemption 5 does not apply to those Appeals and Advice Memoranda which conclude that no complaint should be filed and which have the effect of finally denying relief to the charging party; but that Exemption 5 does protect from disclosure those Appeals and Advice Memoranda which direct the filing of a complaint and the commencement of litigation before the Board.

Under the procedures employed by the General Counsel, Advice and Appeals Memoranda are communicated to the Regional Director *after* the General Counsel, through his Advice and Appeals Branches, has decided whether or not to issue a complaint; and represent an explanation to the Regional Director of a legal or policy decision already adopted by the General Counsel. In the case of decisions *not* to file a complaint, the memoranda effect as "final" a "disposition," as an administrative decision can — representing, as it does, an unreviewable rejection of the charge filed by the private party. Disclosure of these memoranda would not intrude on predecisional processes, and protecting them would not improve the quality of agency decisions, since when the memoranda are communicated to the Regional Director, the General Counsel has already reached his decision and the Regional Director who receives them has no decision to make — he is bound to dismiss the charge. Moreover, the General Counsel's decisions not to file complaints together with the Advice and Appeals Memoranda explaining them, are precisely the kind of agency law in which the public is so vitally interested and which Congress sought to prevent the agency from keeping secret. . . .[22]

The General Counsel contends, however, that the Appeals Memoranda represent only the first step in litigation and are not final; and that Advice Memoranda are advisory only and not binding on the Regional Director, who has the discretion to file or not to file a complaint. The contentions are without merit. Plainly, an Appeals Memorandum is the first step in litigation only when the appeal is sustained and it directs the filing of a complaint; and the General Counsel's current characterization of an Advice Memorandum is at odds with his own description of the function of

---

22. The General Counsel argues that he makes no law, analogizing his authority to decide whether or not to file a complaint to a public prosecutor's authority to decide whether a criminal case should be brought, and claims that he does not adjudicate anything resembling a civil dispute. Without deciding whether a public prosecutor makes "law" when he decides not to prosecute or whether memoranda explaining such decisions are "final opinions," it is sufficient to note that the General Counsel's analogy is far from perfect. . . .

an Advice Memorandum in his statement to the House Committee. That statement says that the Advice Branch establishes "*uniform* policies" in those legal areas with respect to which Regional Directors are "required" to seek advice until a "definitive" policy is arrived at. This is so because if Regional Directors were "free" to interpret legal issues "the *law* could, as a practical matter and before Board decision of the issue, be one thing in one Region and conflicting in others." Therefore, the Advice Memorandum is created after consideration of "prior advice determinations in similar or related cases" and contains "instructions for the final processing of the case." In light of this description, we cannot fault the District Court for concluding that the Advice Memorandum achieves *a pro tanto* withdrawal from the Regional Director of his discretion to file or not to file a complaint. Nor can we avoid the conclusion that Advice Memoranda directing dismissal of a charge represent the "law" of the agency. Accordingly, Advice and Appeals Memoranda directing that a charge be dismissed fall outside of Exemption 5 and must be disclosed.

. . . .

Advice and Appeals Memoranda which direct the filing of a complaint, on the other hand, fall within the coverage of Exemption 5. The filing of a complaint does not finally dispose even of the General Counsel's responsibility with respect to the case. The case will be litigated before and decided by the Board; and the General Counsel will have the responsibility of advocating the position of the charging party before the Board. The Memoranda will inexorably contain the General Counsel's theory of the case and may communicate to the Regional Director some litigation strategy or settlement advice. Since the Memoranda will also have been prepared in contemplation of the upcoming litigation, they fall squarely within Exemption 5's protection of an attorney's work product. At the same time, the public's interest in disclosure is substantially reduced by the fact, as pointed out by the ABA Committee, that the basis for the General Counsel's legal decision will come out in the course of litigation before the Board; and that the "law" with respect to these cases will ultimately be made not by the General Counsel but by the Board or the courts.

We recognize that an Advice or Appeals Memorandum directing the filing of a complaint—although representing only a decision that a legal issue is sufficiently in doubt to warrant determination by another body—has many of the characteristics of the documents described in 5 U.S.C. § 552(a)(2). Although not a "final opinion" in the "adjudication" of a "case" because it does not effect a "final disposition," the memorandum does explain a decision already reached by the General Counsel which has real operative effect—it permits litigation before the Board; and we have indicated a reluctance to construe Exemption 5 to protect such documents. We do so in this case only because the decision-maker—the General Counsel—must become a litigating party to the case with respect to which he has made his decision. The attorney's work-product policies which Congress clearly incorporated into Exemption 5 thus come into play and lead us to hold that the Advice and Appeals Memoranda directing the filing of a complaint are exempt whether or not they are, as the District Court held, "instructions to staff that affect a member of the public."

Notes

1. Let's start with Exemption 5. Exemption 5 excuses from FOIA disclosure "inter-agency or intra-agency memorandums or letters that would not be available by law to a party other than an agency in litigation with the agency." Congress recently qualified the reach of this exemption, adding that it "shall not apply to records created 25 years or more before the date on which the records were requested." 5 U.S.C. § 552(b)(5). In *Sears*, Justice White advised, "it is reasonable to construe Exemption 5 to exempt those documents, and only those documents, normally privileged in the civil discovery context." What policy purposes support this approach?

2. Exemption 5 and the deliberative process privilege. The most commonly invoked grounds for blocking a FOIA request pursuant to Exemption 5 are the deliberative-process privilege, the work-product doctrine, and the attorney-client privilege. The following excerpt from *Mapother v. Dept. of Justice*, 3 F.3d 1533 (D.C. Cir. 1993), provides a concise discussion of the first of these grounds in the context of applying Exemption 5 to a DOJ report on the wartime activities of Kurt Waldheim, the former Secretary-General of the U.N. and former president of Austria:

> ... [W]e agree that the deliberative process privilege shields most of the Waldheim Report.
>
> Exemption 5 protects from disclosure "inter-agency or intra-agency memorandums or letters which would not be available by law to a party... in litigation with the agency." 5 U.S.C. § 552(b)(5). Included within this exemption is the deliberative process privilege, which "protect[s] the decisionmaking processes of government agencies" and "encourage[s] the frank discussion of legal and policy issues" by ensuring that agencies are not "forced to operate in a fishbowl." Nevertheless, this privilege, like all FOIA exemptions, must "be construed as narrowly as consistent with efficient Government operation."
>
> The deliberative process privilege protects materials that are both predecisional and deliberative. In this case, there is no dispute that the Report was delivered to the Attorney General before he made his decision to exclude Mr. Waldheim [thus barring him from entering the U.S.]. Hence, the Report is predecisional. Thus, it will be covered by the deliberative process privilege if, and only if, its contents are "deliberative" in character.
>
> The deliberative character of agency documents can often be determined through "the simple test that factual material must be disclosed but advice and recommendations may be withheld." Nevertheless, we have noted that the fact/opinion test, while offering "a quick, clear, and predictable rule of decision," is not infallible and must not be applied mechanically. This is so because the privilege serves to protect the deliberative process itself,

not merely documents containing deliberative material. Where an agency claims that disclosing factual material will reveal its deliberative processes, "we must examine the information requested in light of the policies and goals that underlie the deliberative process privilege."

On several occasions, we have permitted agencies to withhold factual material on the ground that its disclosure would expose an agency's policy deliberations to unwarranted scrutiny. . . .

In this case, the task assigned the OSI staff was . . . to cull the relevant documents, extract pertinent facts, organize them to suit a specific purpose, and to identify the significant issues they encountered along the way. It is in essence this task that the EPA Administrator's aides performed in *Montrose Chemical*, that the Air Force historians performed in *Russell* and *Dudman Communications*, and that our own judicial clerks perform in connection with many of the cases we decide. It is true that the products of such labors can loosely be characterized as factual, in the sense that the issues ultimately being addressed have a prominent factual component: What is the evidence indicating that DDT is dangerous? What actions did the Air Force undertake, and what results did it achieve in a certain set of operations? Was substantial evidence adduced on a particular point at trial? In cases such as this, however, the selection of the facts thought to be relevant clearly involves "the formulation or exercise of . . . policy-oriented judgment". . . . Such tasks are not "essentially technical" in nature; rather they are part of processes with which "[t]he deliberative process privilege . . . is centrally concerned." Given the need for deliberation to inform discretion and for confidentiality to protect deliberation, we have felt bound to shelter factual summaries that were written to assist the making of a discretionary decision. Given this principle, . . . the Waldheim Report would appear to have been properly withheld.

But see Trentadue v. Integrity Committee, 501 F.3d 1215, 1229 (10th Cir. 2007) (rejecting *Mapother* to the extent it "allows an agency to withhold factual material simply because it reflects a choice as to which facts to include in a document"; holding that factual content is protected only where it is "inextricably intertwined with deliberative materials" or where "disclosure of factual content would reveal deliberative information by allowing the public to easily infer the latter from the former").

3. Exemption 5 and work-product. Justice White in *Sears* recognized that Exemption 5 incorporates the attorney work-product doctrine, which protects documents prepared in anticipation of litigation. The Supreme Court offered further guidance on this point in *FTC v. Grolier, Inc.*, 462 U.S. 19, 26 (1983), in which it held that Exemption 5's work-product protection can cover a document even after the litigation for which it was prepared has ended:

By its own terms, Exemption 5 requires reference to whether discovery would normally be required during litigation *with the agency*. Under a literal reading of Rule 26(b)(3), the work-product of agency attorneys would not be subject to discovery in subsequent litigation unless there was a showing of need and would thus fall within the scope of Exemption 5. We need not rely exclusively on any particular construction of Rule 26(b)(3), however, because we find independently that the Court of Appeals erred in construing Exemption 5 to protect work-product materials only if related litigation exists or potentially exists. The test under Exemption 5 is whether the documents would be "routinely" or "normally" disclosed upon a showing of relevance. At the time this case came to the Court of Appeals, all of the Courts of Appeals that had decided the issue under Rule 26(b)(3) had determined that work-product materials retained their immunity from discovery after termination of the litigation for which the documents were prepared, without regard to whether other related litigation is pending or is contemplated. In addition, an overwhelming majority of the Federal District Courts reporting decisions on the issue under Rule 26(b)(3) were in accord with that view. "Exemption 5 incorporates the privileges which the Government enjoys under the relevant statutory and *case law* in the pre-trial discovery context." Under this state of the work-product rule it cannot fairly be said that work-product materials are "routinely" available in subsequent litigation.

Recall that Rule 26(b)(3) allows a litigant to obtain work-product containing factual information (but not attorney mental impressions or opinions) upon a showing that the litigant has a substantial need for it and will suffer undue hardship without it. Parsing *Grolier*, does this exception to work-product protection in civil litigation apply in the FOIA context?

4. Exemption 1—classified information. This exemption excuses from disclosure documents "properly classified" pursuant to executive order as secret "in the interest of national defense or foreign policy." Although review of a denial of a FOIA request ostensibly requires de novo review, courts have often adverted to the need to defer to agency judgment in this sensitive context.

5. Exemption 2—internal personnel rules. This exemption applies to matters "related solely to the internal personnel rules and practices of an agency." The Supreme Court in *Dept. of Air Force v. Rose*, 425 U.S. 352 (1976), found that the exemption covered information involving the daily routine of the bureaucracy "in which the public could not reasonably be expected to have an interest." Later lower-court cases applied this exemption to documents of broader significance where disclosure would "significantly risk[ ] circumvention of agency regulations or statutes." *See, e.g., Crooker v. BATF*, 670 F2d 1051, 1074 (D.C. Cir. 1981) (en banc) (upholding nondisclosure of portions of BATF manual discussing investigative techniques). Courts following this approach often distinguished between "High 2," which protected important substantive matters, and "Low 2," which protected relatively unimportant internal matters. The Supreme Court put an end to this distinction in *Milner v. Dep't of the Navy*, 562 U.S. 562 (2011). The Court explained that the exemption covers just "personnel rules and practices," which are "rules and practices dealing with employee relations or human resources." *Id.* at 570. Proper attention to the statutory language thus yielded the conclusion "that Low 2 is all of 2 (and that High 2 is not 2 at all)." *Id.*

6. Exemption 3 — other statutes. This exemption applies where another *non-disclosure* statute trumps the FOIA. To fall within Exemption 3, a statute must (a) eliminate agency discretion over disclosure; or (b) establish "particular criteria for withholding" or refer "to particular types of matters to be withheld." Also, a statute enacted after the OPEN FOIA Act of 2009 must specifically reference Exemption 3 to qualify for its coverage.

7. Exemption 4 — sensitive business information. Exemption 4 protects "[a] trade secrets and [b] commercial or financial information obtained from a person and privileged or confidential." The most litigated Exemption 4 issue has been whether information qualifies as "confidential." Until recently, the lead case on this point has been *Critical Mass Energy Project v. NRC*, 975 F.2d 871 (D.C. Cir. 1992) (en banc), which modified the approach of an earlier lead case, *Nat'l Parks and Conservation Ass'n v. Morton*, 498 F.2d 765 (D.C. Cir. 1974). *Critical Mass* drew a distinction between treatment of information that a person voluntarily submits to the government and information that a person submits under compulsion. The D.C. Circuit concluded that a voluntary submission should be treated as "confidential" for Exemption 4 so long "it is of a kind that would customarily not be released to the public by the person from whom it was obtained." This protective treatment helps ensure that people do not avoid submitting information to the government for fear of its disclosure. This concern does not apply with nearly so much force, however, where a person is required to submit information to the government. For this type of compelled information, *Critical Mass* followed *Nat'l Parks* in holding that the exemption applies only where disclosure would be likely "to cause substantial harm to the competitive position of the person from whom the information was obtained."

In *Food Marketing Inst. v. Argus Leader Media,* 139 S. Ct. 2356 (2019), the Supreme Court, in an opinion by Justice Gorsuch, swept away the *Critical Mass* framework, rejecting the "competitive harm" requirement as "inconsistent with the terms of the statute" and the result of a "selective tour through legislative history" marked by a "casual disregard of the rules of statutory interpretation." To determine the meaning of "confidential," the Court turned to the term's "ordinary, contemporary, common meaning" at the time of FOIA's enactment as explained by various dictionaries. This inquiry identified two conditions pertinent for determining if information communicated to another remains "confidential." First, to be confidential, information must be "customarily kept private, or at least closely held, by the person imparting it." Second, it is also possible that "information might be considered confidential only if the party receiving it provides some assurance that it will remain secret." The Court did not need to conclude whether this second condition is mandatory, however, because the government had promised to keep the information at issue in the case private.

The government's use of information obtained from others can create a line-drawing problem as Exemption 4 applies to information obtained from a "person," not to information produced by the government itself. *Board of Trade v. CFTC*, 627 F.2d 392 (D.C. Cir. 1980). Where an agency merely summarizes or reformulates information received from a "person," the information does not lose its protected character. Active government analysis of exempted data is not, however, exempted. *Philadelphia Newspapers, Inc. v. DHHS*, 69 F. Supp. 2d 63, 67 (D.D.C. 1999) (holding audit contained government analysis and therefore fell outside Exemption 4).

8. Exemptions 6 and 7(C) — personal privacy and the public interest in disclosure. Two FOIA exemptions, Exemption 6 and Exemption 7(C), protect personal privacy. Information need not be embarrassing or highly personal to implicate these protections, which can cover "[i]nformation such as place of birth, date of birth, date of marriage, employment history, and comparable data." *Department of State v. Washington Post Co.*, 456 U.S. 595, 600 (1982).

Exemption 6 protects "personnel and medical files and similar files the disclosure of which would constitute a clearly unwarranted invasion of privacy." Exemption 7(C) protects "records or information compiled for law enforcement purposes . . . to the extent that [their] production . . . could reasonably be expected to constitute an unwarranted invasion of personal privacy." Both of these exemptions require a balancing of privacy interests against the public interest to determine whether disclosure is unwarranted. Exemption 7(C) intentionally strikes a balance that favors privacy more than Exemption 6 in light of the sensitive nature of many law enforcement files. *Nat'l Archives and Records Admin. v. Favish*, 541 U.S. 157, 165–66 (2004).

A lead case governing application of both privacy exemptions is *Dept. of Justice v. Reporters Committee for Freedom of Press*, 489 U.S. 749 (1989), which applied Exemption 7(C) to a journalist's request to obtain "rap sheets" from the FBI regarding Medico. As the case made its way through the courts, the request was narrowed to cover only matters of public record regarding Medico's nonfinancial crimes.

The Court first determined that Medico had a cognizable privacy interest in maintaining the "practical obscurity" of information contained in any rap sheet the FBI might possess regarding him — even if the same information could, with sufficient labor, be culled from other public files. With a privacy interest established, it became necessary to determine whether any countervailing public interest "warrant[ed]" disclosure. The journalists claimed that disclosure was in the public interest because of Medico's ties to a congressman and dealings with the Department of Defense. The Court rejected this argument, explaining:

> Our previous decisions establish that whether an invasion of privacy is warranted cannot turn on the purposes for which the request for information

is made. . . . Thus, . . . the rights of the two press respondents in this case are no different from those that might be asserted by any other third party, such as a neighbor or prospective employer. As we have repeatedly stated, Congress "clearly intended" the FOIA "to give any member of the public as much right to disclosure as one with a special interest [in a particular document]." As Professor Davis explained: "The Act's sole concern is with what must be made public or not made public."

Thus whether disclosure of a private document under Exemption 7(C) is warranted must turn on the nature of the requested document and its relationship to "the basic purpose of the Freedom of Information Act 'to open agency action to the light of public scrutiny'" rather than on the particular purpose for which the document is being requested. In our leading case on the FOIA, we declared that the Act was designed to create a broad right of access to "official information." . . .

This basic policy of "'full agency disclosure unless information is exempted under clearly delineated statutory language,'" indeed focuses on the citizens' right to be informed about "what their government is up to." Official information that sheds light on an agency's performance of its statutory duties falls squarely within that statutory purpose. That purpose, however, is not fostered by disclosure of information about private citizens that is accumulated in various governmental files but that reveals little or nothing about an agency's own conduct. In this case—and presumably in the typical case in which one private citizen is seeking information about another—the requester does not intend to discover anything about the conduct of the agency that has possession of the requested records. Indeed, response to this request would not shed any light on the conduct of any Government agency or official. . . .

Respondents argue that there is a two-fold public interest in learning about Medico's past arrests or convictions: He allegedly had improper dealings with a corrupt Congressman, and he is an officer of a corporation with defense contracts. But if Medico has, in fact, been arrested or convicted of certain crimes, that information would neither aggravate nor mitigate his allegedly improper relationship with the Congressman; more specifically, it would tell us nothing directly about the character of the Congressman's behavior. Nor would it tell us anything about the conduct of the Department of Defense (DOD) in awarding one or more contracts to the Medico Company. Arguably a FOIA request to the DOD for records relating to those contracts, or for documents describing the agency's procedures, if any, for determining whether officers of a prospective contractor have criminal records, would constitute an appropriate request for "official information." Conceivably Medico's rap sheet would provide details to include in a news story, but, in itself, this is not the kind of public interest for which Congress enacted the FOIA. In other words, although there is undoubtedly some public interest in anyone's criminal history, especially if the history is in some way related to the subject's dealing with a public official or agency, the FOIA's central purpose is to ensure that the Government's activities be opened to the sharp eye of public scrutiny, not that information about private citizens that happens to be in the warehouse of the Government be so disclosed. Thus, it should come as no surprise that in none of our cases construing the FOIA have we found it appropriate to order a Government agency to honor a FOIA request for information about a particular private citizen.

What we have said should make clear that the public interest in the release of any rap sheet on Medico that may exist is not the type of interest protected by the FOIA. Medico may or may not be one of the 24 million persons for whom the FBI has a rap sheet. If respondents are entitled to have the FBI tell them what it knows about Medico's criminal history, any other member of the public is entitled to the same disclosure—whether for writing a news story, for deciding whether to employ Medico, to rent a house to him, to extend credit to him, or simply to confirm or deny a suspicion. There is, unquestionably, some public interest in providing interested citizens with answers to their questions about Medico. But that interest falls outside the ambit of the public interest that the FOIA was enacted to serve.

See also *Nat'l Archives and Records Administration v. Favish*, 541 U.S. 157 (2004) (holding that withholding of death-scene photographs of the suicide of Vince Foster, deputy counsel to President Clinton, was justified under Exemption 7(C)).

9. The Department of Justice on the Exemption 6 balance. The DOJ has summarized numerous efforts by courts to strike the Exemption 6 balance:

Although "the presumption in favor of disclosure is as strong [under Exemption 6] as can be found anywhere in the Act," courts have readily protected personal, intimate details of an individual's life. For example, as the Court of Appeals for the District of Columbia Circuit has noted, courts have traditionally upheld the nondisclosure of information concerning "marital status, legitimacy of children, identity of fathers of children, medical condition, welfare payments, alcoholic consumption, family fights, reputation" and similarly personal information. Furthermore, courts have consistently upheld protection for: (1) birth dates; (2) religious affiliations; (3) citizenship data; (4) social security numbers; (5) criminal history records; (6) incarceration of United States citizens in foreign prisons; (7) identities of crime victims; (8) financial information; (9) personal landline and cellular telephone numbers; (10) email addresses; and (11) medical information linked to individuals.

UNITED STATES DEPARTMENT OF JUSTICE GUIDE TO THE FREEDOM OF INFORMATION ACT, *Exemption 6*, 75–78 (Jan. 2014) (numerous footnotes omitted) (available at http://www.justice.gov/sites/default/files/oip/legacy/2014/07/23/exemption6.pdf).

10. Exemption 7 and law enforcement. The original version of Exemption 7 was quite simple. It covered "investigatory files compiled for law enforcement purposes except to the extent available by law to a party other than an agency." Exemption 7 has since become something of a mouthful and now covers:

> records or information compiled for law enforcement purposes, but only to the extent that the production of such law enforcement records or information
>
> > (A) could reasonably be expected to interfere with enforcement proceedings,
> >
> > (B) would deprive a person of a right to a fair trial or an impartial adjudication,
> >
> > (C) could reasonably be expected to constitute an unwarranted invasion of personal privacy,
> >
> > (D) could reasonably be expected to disclose the identity of a confidential source, . . . and, in the case of a record or information compiled by a criminal law enforcement authority in the course of a criminal investigation, or by an agency conducting a lawful national security intelligence investigation, information furnished by a confidential source,
> >
> > (E) would disclose techniques and procedures for law enforcement investigations or prosecutions, or would disclose guidelines for law enforcement investigations or prosecutions if such disclosure could reasonably be expected to risk circumvention of the law, or
> >
> > (F) could reasonably be expected to endanger the life or physical safety of any individual

The most sweeping provision in Exemption 7 may be subpart (A), which protects "law enforcement records or information" that "could reasonably be expected to interfere with enforcement proceedings." The D.C. Circuit has explained that "enforcement proceedings need not be currently ongoing; it suffices for them to be 'reasonably anticipated.'" *Sussman v. U.S. Marshals Service,* 494 F.3d 1106, 1113–14 (D.C. Cir. 2007). Mere speculation concerning the possibility of future enforcement actions does not suffice. Courts have permitted agencies to invoke this exemption on claims that disclosure might, among other things, enable their adversaries to determine the nature and scope of investigations directed against them; intimidate witnesses; or gain an improper advantage by learning the government's legal strategy prematurely.

11. Exclusions are different than exemptions. The 1986 amendments to the FOIA added a set of three "exclusions" that provide super protection from disclosure for three categories of especially sensitive information—criminal investigations or proceedings directed at persons who remain unaware of them; informant records held by criminal law enforcement agencies; and classified FBI records concerning foreign intelligence or international terrorism. Under specified circumstances, agencies may treat such "records as not subject to the requirements" of the FOIA. § 552(c)(1)–(3). As such, an agency that receives a request for such a record need not concede that it exists and then seek to justify nondisclosure under an exemption. It may instead respond that it has no record responsive to the FOIA request. *See generally* USDOJ GUIDE TO THE FREEDOM OF INFORMATION ACT, *Exclusions* (April 2019) (https://www.justice.gov/oip/foia-guide/exclusions/download).

12. Reverse FOIA. You may have a strong interest in blocking the government from releasing records that contain information about you that is arguably covered by a FOIA exemption. As Justice Rehnquist explained in *Chrysler v. Brown*, 441 U.S. 281 (1979), the FOIA itself will not help you block the release:

> That the FOIA is exclusively a disclosure statute is, perhaps, demonstrated most convincingly by examining its provision for judicial relief. Subsection (a)(4)(B) gives federal district courts "jurisdiction to enjoin the agency from withholding agency records and to order the production of any agency records improperly withheld from the complainant." That provision does not give the authority to bar disclosure, and thus fortifies our belief that Chrysler, and courts which have shared its view, have incorrectly interpreted the exemption provisions of the FOIA. The Act is an attempt to meet the demand for open government while preserving workable confidentiality in governmental decisionmaking. Congress appreciated that, with the expanding sphere of governmental regulation and enterprise, much of the information within Government files has been submitted by private entities seeking Government contracts or responding to unconditional reporting obligations imposed by law. There was sentiment that Government agencies should have the latitude, in certain circumstances, to afford the confidentiality desired by these submitters. But the congressional concern was with the *agency's* need or preference for confidentiality; the FOIA by itself protects the submitters' interest in confidentiality only to the extent that this interest is endorsed by the agency collecting the information.

> Enlarged access to governmental information undoubtedly cuts against the privacy concerns of nongovernmental entities, and as a matter of policy some balancing and accommodation may well be desirable. We simply hold here that Congress did not design the FOIA exemptions to be mandatory bars to disclosure.

But all hope is not lost for entities seeking to block disclosure via a "reverse FOIA" action. *Chrysler* explained that a party could use the APA's cause of action to challenge a disclosure on the ground that it would violate some law other than the FOIA and therefore be arbitrary or otherwise illegal. One common approach is to claim that a release of records would violate the Trade Secrets Act, which, absent an overriding regulation or statute, bars disclosure of confidential business information that would be protected by Exemption 4. *See CNA Fin. Corp. v. Donovan,* 830 F.2d 1132, 1151–52 (D.C. Cir. 1987).

C. The Federal Advisory Committee Act — and Government in the Sunshine

This last subchapter turns briefly to two additional, important statutes, which, like the FOIA, can be characterized as expressions of Justice Brandeis's observation that "[s]unlight is said to be the best of disinfectants." Agencies often seek advice from advisory committees of outside experts. To help ensure that such committees are not wasteful, duplicative, or dominated by special interests, Congress in 1972 enacted the Federal Advisory Committee Act, 5 U.S.C. § App., which imposes a variety of procedural, transparency, and balance requirements on such committees. In 1976, Congress passed the Government in the Sunshine Act, 5 U.S.C. § 552b. This Act opens to the public those meetings of multi-member agencies that conduct "official agency business." Like the FOIA, this transparency requirement is subject to many exceptions. As you read the materials below, you might reflect on whether these statutes shed too much light on things that might be better done in the dark.

Lesson 7C. Chris was very disappointed that she was not named Carl's successor as the WTC's chair. When she was asked to meet with the president's chief of staff, she had high hopes that a similar job would be offered. When she arrived at the White House, she was escorted to the Oval Office. The president asked her to become chair of the Administrative Conference of the United States (ACUS), which is a small agency that studies the administrative process and recommends improvements. ACUS is led by a single chairperson and has a small permanent staff. Membership of its "Conference" includes high-level agency officials, private practitioners, and academics. Researchers, working in tandem with committees of conference members, develop concrete, actionable recommendations for administrative reforms. The voting members of the Conference determine which recommendations to adopt formally.

Chris happily accepted the president's offer and is now frantically trying to figure out what her new responsibilities will entail and how she will discharge them. Once she is appointed, she would like to hold a series of meetings with the heads of agencies to discuss their ideas for reforms. Would these meetings trigger FACA obligations? Given the President's frequently stated desire to reduce the burden of federal regulation, Chris also contemplates meeting periodically with a select group of leaders from the business community to hear their advice on how to streamline administrative processes. Would these meetings trigger FACA obligations? More generally, is the Conference itself subject to FACA obligations?

Background of *Public Citizen v. Dep't of Justice*

The Federal Advisory Committee Act (FACA) defines the term "advisory committee" to include "any committee" or "similar group" that is "established or utilized" by the president or an agency to obtain "advice or recommendations." This definition posed a problem for the Department of Justice's practice of consulting the American Bar Association's Standing Committee on the Federal Judiciary (ABA

Committee) for assessment of potential appointees to the federal courts. On the face of the matter, the ABA Committee was quite obviously a committee "utilized" by the DOJ and president to obtain "advice or recommendations." Following this logic, the ABA Committee's work might seem subject to FACA requirements such as filing a charter, keeping detailed minutes, and opening meetings to the public. Even if that treatment of the ABA Committee sounds attractive to you, however, following this logic a little further suggests that the president triggers FACA every time she consults a non-governmental group with two or more people in it. In *Public Citizen v. Dep't of Justice,* the Supreme Court found a way around this result.

Public Citizen v. Department of Justice

491 U.S. 440 (1989)

JUSTICE BRENNAN delivered the opinion of the Court.

The Department of Justice regularly seeks advice from the American Bar Association's Standing Committee on Federal Judiciary regarding potential nominees for federal judgeships. The question before us is whether the Federal Advisory Committee Act (FACA), 5 U.S.C. App. § 1 *et seq.*, applies to these consultations and, if it does, whether its application interferes unconstitutionally with the President's prerogative under Article II to nominate and appoint officers of the United States; violates the doctrine of separation of powers; or unduly infringes the First Amendment right of members of the American Bar Association to freedom of association and expression. We hold that FACA does not apply to this special advisory relationship. We therefore do not reach the constitutional questions presented.

The Constitution provides that the President "shall nominate, and by and with the Advice and Consent of the Senate, shall appoint" Supreme Court Justices and, as established by Congress, other federal judges. Since 1952 the President, through the Department of Justice, has requested advice from the American Bar Association's Standing Committee on Federal Judiciary (ABA Committee) in making such nominations.

The American Bar Association is a private voluntary professional association of approximately 343,000 attorneys. It has several working committees, among them the advisory body whose work is at issue here. The ABA Committee consists of 14 persons belonging to and chosen by the American Bar Association. Each of the 12 federal judicial Circuits (not including the Federal Circuit) has one representative on the ABA Committee, except for the Ninth Circuit, which has two; in addition, one member is chosen at large. The ABA Committee receives no federal funds. It does not recommend persons for appointment to the federal bench of its own initiative.

Prior to announcing the names of nominees for judgeships on the courts of appeals, the district courts, or the Court of International Trade, the President, acting through the Department of Justice, routinely requests a potential nominee to complete a questionnaire drawn up by the ABA Committee and to submit it to the Assistant Attorney General for the Office of Legal Policy, to the Chair of the ABA

Committee, and to the committee member (usually the representative of the relevant judicial Circuit) charged with investigating the nominee.[9] The potential nominee's answers and the referral of his or her name to the ABA Committee are kept confidential. The committee member conducting the investigation then reviews the legal writings of the potential nominee, interviews judges, legal scholars, and other attorneys regarding the potential nominee's qualifications, and discusses the matter confidentially with representatives of various professional organizations and other groups. The committee member also interviews the potential nominee, sometimes with other committee members in attendance.

Following the initial investigation, the committee representative prepares for the Chair an informal written report describing the potential nominee's background, summarizing all interviews, assessing the candidate's qualifications, and recommending one of four possible ratings: "exceptionally well qualified," "well qualified," "qualified," or "not qualified." The Chair then makes a confidential informal report to the Attorney General's Office. The Chair's report discloses the substance of the committee representative's report to the Chair, without revealing the identity of persons who were interviewed, and indicates the evaluation the potential nominee is likely to receive if the Department of Justice requests a formal report.

If the Justice Department does request a formal report, the committee representative prepares a draft and sends copies to other members of the ABA Committee, together with relevant materials. A vote is then taken and a final report approved. The ABA Committee sends a copy of the final report in confidence to the Department of Justice, accompanied by a statement of whether its rating was supported by all committee members, or whether it only commanded a majority or substantial majority of the ABA Committee. After considering the report and other information the President and his advisors have assembled, including a report by the Federal Bureau of Investigation and additional interviews conducted by the President's judicial selection committee, the President then decides whether to nominate the candidate. If the candidate is in fact nominated, the ABA Committee's rating, though not its report, is made public at the request of the Senate Judiciary Committee.[10]

FACA was born of a desire to assess the need for the "numerous committees, boards, commissions, councils, and similar groups which have been established to advise officers and agencies in the executive branch of the Federal Government."

---

9. The Justice Department does not ordinarily furnish the names of potential Supreme Court nominees to the ABA Committee for evaluation prior to their nomination, although in some instances the President has done so.

10. The Senate regularly requests the ABA Committee to rate Supreme Court nominees if the Justice Department has not already sought the ABA Committee's opinion. As with nominees for other federal judgeships, the ABA Committee's rating is made public at confirmation hearings before the Senate Judiciary Committee.

§ 2(a).[11] Its purpose was to ensure that new advisory committees be established only when essential and that their number be minimized; that they be terminated when they have outlived their usefulness; that their creation, operation, and duration be subject to uniform standards and procedures; that Congress and the public remain apprised of their existence, activities, and cost; and that their work be exclusively advisory in nature. § 2(b).

To attain these objectives, FACA directs the Director of the Office of Management and Budget and agency heads to establish various administrative guidelines and management controls for advisory committees. It also imposes a number of requirements on advisory groups. For example, FACA requires that each advisory committee file a charter, § 9(c), and keep detailed minutes of its meetings. § 10(c). Those meetings must be chaired or attended by an officer or employee of the Federal Government who is authorized to adjourn any meeting when he or she deems its adjournment in the public interest. § 10(e). FACA also requires advisory committees to provide advance notice of their meetings and to open them to the public, § 10(a), unless the President or the agency head to which an advisory committee reports determines that it may be closed to the public in accordance with the Government in the Sunshine Act, 5 U.S.C. § 552b(c). § 10(d). In addition, FACA stipulates that advisory committee minutes, records, and reports be made available to the public, provided they do not fall within one of the Freedom of Information Act's exemptions and the Government does not choose to withhold them. § 10(b). Advisory committees established by legislation or created by the President or other federal officials must also be "fairly balanced in terms of the points of view represented and the functions" they perform. §§ 5(b), (c). Their existence is limited to two years, unless specifically exempted by the entity establishing them. § 14(a).

In October 1986, appellant Washington Legal Foundation (WLF) brought suit against the Department of Justice after the ABA Committee refused WLF's request for the names of potential judicial nominees it was considering and for the ABA Committee's reports and minutes of its meetings. [Public Citizen later intervened.] WLF asked the District Court for the District of Columbia to declare the ABA Committee an "advisory committee" as FACA defines that term. WLF further sought an injunction ordering the Justice Department to cease utilizing the ABA Committee as an advisory committee until it complied with FACA. In particular, WLF contended that the ABA Committee must file a charter, afford notice of its meetings, open those meetings to the public, and make its minutes, records, and reports available for public inspection and copying. The Justice Department moved to dismiss, arguing that the ABA Committee did not fall within FACA's definition of "advisory

---

11. Federal advisory committees are legion. During fiscal year 1988, 58 federal departments sponsored 1,020 advisory committees. Over 3,500 meetings were held, and close to 1000 reports were issued. Costs for fiscal year 1988 totaled over $92 million, roughly half of which was spent on federal staff support.

committee" and that, if it did, FACA would violate the constitutional doctrine of separation of powers. . . .

Section 3(2) of FACA defines "advisory committee" as follows:

"For the purpose of this Act—

"(2) The term 'advisory committee' means any committee, board, commission, council, conference, panel, task force, or other similar group, or any subcommittee or other subgroup thereof (hereafter in this paragraph referred to as 'committee'), which is—

"(A) established by statute or reorganization plan, or

"(B) established or utilized by the President, or

"(C) established or utilized by one or more agencies, in the interest of obtaining advice or recommendations for the President or one or more agencies or officers of the Federal Government, except that such term excludes (i) the Advisory Commission on Intergovernmental Relations, (ii) the Commission on Government Procurement, and (iii) any committee which is composed wholly of full-time officers or employees of the Federal Government."

Appellants agree that the ABA Committee was not "established" by the President or the Justice Department. Equally plainly, the ABA Committee is a committee that furnishes "advice or recommendations" to the President via the Justice Department. Whether the ABA Committee constitutes an "advisory committee" for purposes of FACA therefore depends upon whether it is "utilized" by the President or the Justice Department as Congress intended that term to be understood.

There is no doubt that the Executive makes use of the ABA Committee, and thus "utilizes" it in one common sense of the term. As the District Court recognized, however, "reliance on the plain language of FACA alone is not entirely satisfactory." "Utilize" is a woolly verb, its contours left undefined by the statute itself. Read unqualifiedly, it would extend FACA's requirements to any group of two or more persons, or at least any formal organization, from which the President or an Executive agency seeks advice. We are convinced that Congress did not intend that result. A nodding acquaintance with FACA's purposes, as manifested by its legislative history and as recited in § 2 of the Act, reveals that it cannot have been Congress' intention, for example, to require the filing of a charter, the presence of a controlling federal official, and detailed minutes any time the President seeks the views of the NAACP before nominating Commissioners to the Equal Employment Opportunity Commission, or asks the leaders of an American Legion Post he is visiting for the organization's opinion on some aspect of military policy.

Nor can Congress have meant—as a straightforward reading of "utilize" would appear to require—that all of FACA's restrictions apply if a President consults with his own political party before picking his Cabinet. It was unmistakably *not* Congress' intention to intrude on a political party's freedom to conduct its affairs as it chooses or its ability to advise elected officials who belong to that party by placing a federal employee in charge of each advisory group meeting and making its minutes public property. FACA was enacted to cure specific ills, above all the wasteful expenditure of public funds for worthless committee meetings and biased proposals; although its reach is extensive, we cannot believe that it was intended to cover every formal and informal consultation between the President or an Executive agency and a group rendering advice. As we said in *Church of the Holy Trinity v. United States* (1892), "frequently words of general meaning are used in a statute, words broad enough to include an act in question, and yet a consideration of the whole legislation, or of the circumstances surrounding its enactment, or of the absurd results which follow from giving such broad meaning to the words, makes it unreasonable to believe that the legislator intended to include the particular act." ...

Consideration of FACA's purposes and origins in determining whether the term "utilized" was meant to apply to the Justice Department's use of the ABA Committee is particularly appropriate here, given the importance we have consistently attached to interpreting statutes to avoid deciding difficult constitutional questions where the text fairly admits of a less problematic construction. It is therefore imperative that we consider indicators of congressional intent in addition to the statutory language before concluding that FACA was meant to cover the ABA Committee's provision of advice to the Justice Department in connection with judicial nominations.

Close attention to FACA's history is helpful, for FACA did not flare on the legislative scene with the suddenness of a meteor. Similar attempts to regulate the Federal Government's use of advisory committees were common during the 20 years preceding FACA's enactment. An understanding of those efforts is essential to ascertain the intended scope of the term "utilize."

. . . .

[Efforts to regulate advisory committees began in 1950 with Justice Department guidelines. In 1962, Congress failed to pass legislation regulating advisory committees but later that year the President issued Executive Order 11007 doing so. That Order formed the basis of the FACA.]

There is no indication, however, that Executive Order 11007 was intended to apply to the Justice Department's consultations with the ABA Committee. Neither President Kennedy, who issued the Order, nor President Johnson, nor President Nixon apparently deemed the ABA Committee to be "utilized" by the Department of Justice in the relevant sense of that term. Notwithstanding the ABA Committee's highly visible role in advising the Justice Department regarding potential judicial nominees, and notwithstanding the fact that the Order's requirements were established by the Executive itself rather than Congress, no President or Justice Department official applied them to the ABA Committee. As an entity formed privately, rather than at the Federal Government's prompting, to render confidential advice with respect to the President's constitutionally specified power to nominate federal judges—an entity in receipt of no federal funds and not amenable to the strict management by agency officials envisaged by Executive Order 11007—the ABA Committee cannot easily be said to have been "utilized by a department or agency in the same manner as a Government-formed advisory committee." That the Executive apparently did not consider the ABA Committee's activity within the terms of its own Executive Order is therefore unsurprising.

Although FACA's legislative history evinces an intent to widen the scope of Executive Order 11007's definition of "advisory committee" by including "Presidential advisory committees," which lay beyond the reach of Executive Order 11007, as well as to augment the restrictions applicable to advisory committees covered by the statute, there is scant reason to believe that Congress desired to bring the ABA Committee within FACA's net. FACA's principal purpose was to enhance the public accountability of advisory committees established by the Executive Branch and to reduce wasteful expenditures on them. That purpose could be accomplished, however, without expanding the coverage of Executive Order 11007 to include privately organized committees that received no federal funds. Indeed, there is considerable evidence that Congress sought nothing more than stricter compliance with reporting and other requirements—which *were* made more stringent—by advisory committees already covered by the Order and similar treatment of a small class of publicly funded groups created by the President. . . .

It is true that the final version of FACA approved by both Houses employed the phrase "established or utilized," and that this phrase is more capacious than the word "established" or the phrase "established or organized." But its genesis suggests that it was not intended to go much beyond those narrower formulations. The words "or utilized" were added by the Conference Committee to the definition included in the House bill. The Joint Explanatory Statement, however, said simply that the definition contained in the House bill was adopted "with modification." The Conference Report offered no indication that the modification was significant, let alone that it would substantially broaden FACA's application by sweeping within its terms a vast number of private groups, such as the Republican National Committee, not formed at the behest of the Executive or by quasi-public organizations whose opinions the Federal Government sometimes solicits. Indeed, it appears that the House bill's initial restricted focus on advisory committees established by the Federal Government, in an expanded sense of the word "established," was retained rather than enlarged by the Conference Committee. In the section dealing with FACA's range of application, the Conference Report stated: "The Act does not apply to persons or organizations which have contractual relationships with Federal agencies *nor to advisory committees not directly established by or for such agencies.*" (emphasis added). The phrase "or utilized" therefore appears to have been added simply to clarify that FACA applies to advisory committees established by the Federal Government in a generous sense of that term, encompassing groups formed indirectly by quasi-public organizations such as the National Academy of Sciences "for" public agencies as well as "by" such agencies themselves.

. . . .

In sum, a literalistic reading of § 3(2) would bring the Justice Department's advisory relationship with the ABA Committee within FACA's terms, particularly given FACA's objective of opening many advisory relationships to public scrutiny except in certain narrowly defined situations. A literalistic reading, however, would catch far more groups and consulting arrangements than Congress could conceivably have intended. And the careful review which this interpretive difficulty warrants of earlier efforts to regulate federal advisory committees and the circumstances surrounding FACA's adoption strongly suggests that FACA's definition of "advisory committee" was not meant to encompass the ABA Committee's relationship with the Justice Department. That relationship seems not to have been within the contemplation of Executive Order 11007. And FACA's legislative history does not display an intent to widen the Order's application to encircle it. Weighing the deliberately inclusive statutory language against other evidence of congressional intent, it seems to us a close question whether FACA should be construed to apply to the ABA Committee, although on the whole we are fairly confident it should not. There is, however, one additional consideration which, in our view, tips the balance decisively against FACA's application.

. . . .

[W]e are loath to conclude that Congress intended to press ahead into dangerous constitutional thickets in the absence of firm evidence that it courted those perils.

That construing FACA to apply to the Justice Department's consultations with the ABA Committee would present formidable constitutional difficulties is undeniable. The District Court declared FACA unconstitutional insofar as it applied to those consultations, because it concluded that FACA, so applied, infringed unduly on the President's Article II power to nominate federal judges and violated the doctrine of separation of powers. Whether or not the court's conclusion was correct, there is no gainsaying the seriousness of these constitutional challenges.

To be sure, "[w]e cannot press statutory construction 'to the point of disingenuous evasion' even to avoid a constitutional question." . . . [O]ur review of the regulatory scheme prior to FACA's enactment and the likely origin of the phrase "or utilized" in FACA's definition of "advisory committee" reveals that Congress probably did not intend to subject the ABA Committee to FACA's requirements when the ABA Committee offers confidential advice regarding presidential appointments to the federal bench. Where the competing arguments based on FACA's text and legislative history, though both plausible, tend to show that Congress did not desire FACA to apply to the Justice Department's confidential solicitation of the ABA Committee's views on prospective judicial nominees, sound sense counsels adherence to our rule of caution. Our unwillingness to resolve important constitutional questions unnecessarily thus solidifies our conviction that FACA is inapplicable.

JUSTICE KENNEDY, with whom THE CHIEF JUSTICE and JUSTICE O' CONNOR join, concurring in the judgment. . . .

Although one is perhaps more obvious than the other, this case presents two distinct issues of the separation of powers. The first concerns the rules this Court must follow in interpreting a statute passed by Congress and signed by the President. On this subject, I cannot join the Court's conclusion that the Federal Advisory Committee Act (FACA) does not cover the activities of the American Bar Association's Standing Committee on Federal Judiciary in advising the Department of Justice regarding potential nominees for federal judgeships. The result seems sensible in the abstract; but I cannot accept the method by which the Court arrives at its interpretation of FACA, which does not accord proper respect to the finality and binding effect of legislative enactments. The second question in the case is the extent to which Congress may interfere with the President's constitutional prerogative to nominate federal judges. On this issue, which the Court does not reach because of its conclusion on the statutory question, I think it quite plain that the application of FACA to the Government's use of the ABA Committee is unconstitutional.

Notes

1. The Constitution and FACA. The two excerpted opinions from *Public Citizen* reflect concern that FACA would have been unconstitutional if it had applied to the consultations with the ABA. What was the constitutional problem? How did the two opinions address it?

2. Should agency heads be able to consult in private with interest groups? How should the bureaucracy interact with the public, especially in the all-important area of policymaking? *Public Citizen* involved consultation by the president, but the question changes little for any high-level administrative decisionmaker. To what extent should a high official be permitted to consult (in private) with specially affected interest groups? Should an official in the Veterans' Affairs Department be permitted to consult with groups representing minority veterans? Should the Chair of the Consumer Product Safety Commission be permitted to meet with toy manufacturers, or the Administrator of the Food and Drug Administration with a group of doctors?

3. What does it mean to be a member of a committee subject to FACA? The FACA does not govern the activities of advisory committees "established or utilized by one or more agencies" that are "composed wholly of full-time officers or employees of the Federal Government." 5 U.S.C. App. § 3(2)(C). It therefore can be critical to determine whether a person who does not work for the federal government is functioning as a member of a committee. The D.C. Circuit addressed this problem in *In re Cheney*, 406 F.3d 723 (D.C. Cir. 2005) (en banc). This opinion was the culmination of a dispute over the National Energy Policy Development Group, which President Bush created in the Executive Office of the President for the purpose of developing a national energy policy. Chaired by Vice President Cheney, the NEPDG officially consisted only of federal agency officials. However, the Sierra Club alleged that "[e]nergy industry executives, including multiple representatives of single energy companies, and other non-federal employees, attended meetings and participated in activities of [the NEPDG] and Task Force Sub-Groups." Based upon that allegation, the Sierra Club and others argued that the NEPDG was subject to the requirements of the FACA. The D.C. Circuit disagreed:

> As to FACA, the critical question is whether plaintiffs have carried their burden of showing that the NEPDG or its so-called "Sub-Groups" were "advisory committees," that is, committees who were advising the President but were not "composed wholly of full-time, or permanent part-time, officers or employees of the Federal Government," 5 U.S.C.App. §3(2). While it is often easy to determine who is and who is not a federal employee, the question this lawsuit raises is different. Application of FACA depends on who is a member of a committee and who is not. On that subject, FACA is silent.
>
> In light of the severe separation-of-powers problems in applying FACA on the basis that private parties participated in, or influenced, or were otherwise involved with a committee in the Executive Office of the President, we must construe the statute strictly. We therefore hold that such a committee is composed wholly of federal officials if the President has given no one other than a federal official a vote in or, if the committee acts by consensus, a veto over the committee's decisions.
>
> Congress could not have meant that participation in committee meetings or activities, even influential participation, would be enough to make someone a member of the committee. When congressional committees hold hearings, it is commonplace for the Senate or House members of the committee to bring aides with them. The same is true when high-ranking Executive Branch officials serving on committees attend committee meetings. They, too, commonly bring aides with them. An aide might exert great influence, but no one would say that the aide was, therefore, a member of the committee. The situation is comparable if an individual, not employed by the federal government, attends meetings or participates in the activities of a Presidential committee whose official membership consists only of federal officials. The outsider might make an important presentation, he might be persuasive, the information he provides might affect the committee's judgment. But having neither a vote nor a veto over the advice the committee renders to the President, he is no more a member of the committee than the aides who accompany Congressmen or cabinet officers to committee meetings.

4. When must agency heads meet in public?—The government in the Sunshine Act. The Sunshine Act imposes an open-meetings requirement on agencies "headed by a collegial body composed of two or more individual members, a majority of whom are appointed to such position by the President with the advice and consent of the Senate." 5 U.S.C. §552b(a)(1). The Sunshine Act thus applies to multi-member agencies such as the Federal Communications Commission, the Federal Trade Commission, and the Securities and Exchange Commission. It does not apply to agencies headed by a single person, such as the Department of Justice or the Environmental Protection Agency.

Under the Sunshine Act, a "meeting" generally means "deliberations" by at least a quorum of agency members "where such deliberations determine or result in the joint conduct or disposition of official agency business." § 552b(a)(2). The Sunshine Act broadly declares "every portion of every meeting of an agency shall be open to public observation." § 552b(b). The next subsection, however, lists 10 exceptions to this transparency requirement. *See* § 552b(c). These exceptions mirror, imperfectly, the FOIA's exemptions from disclosure.

In *Common Cause v. Nuclear Regulatory Comm'n*, 674 F.2d 921 (D.C. Cir. 1982), the D.C. Circuit offered an overview of the purposes and operation of the Sunshine Act:

> The Government in the Sunshine Act establishes the policy that "the public is entitled to the fullest practicable information regarding the decisionmaking processes of the Federal Government." Every meeting of a multimember agency must be open to the public, except that specific portions of a meeting may be closed if the discussion is reasonably likely to fall within one or more of ten narrowly defined exemptions. 5 U.S.C. § 552b(c)(1)–(10) (1976). The Commission contends that these exemptions authorize closing of agency budget discussions. It places primary reliance on Exemption 9(B), which allows an agency to close a meeting or portion of a meeting which is likely to discuss matters whose "premature disclosure" would "be likely to significantly frustrate implementation of a proposed agency action." § 552b(c)(9)(B). The agency also contends that budget meetings may be closed because they encompass information protected under Exemption 2, matters related "solely to the internal personnel rules and practices of an agency," and Exemption 6, material of a personal nature whose disclosure would "constitute a clearly unwarranted invasion of personal privacy." §§ 552b(c)(2), 552b(c)(6). In light of the language, legislative history, and underlying purposes of the Sunshine Act, we reject the Commission's proposed interpretations of the Sunshine Act exemptions.
>
> Congress enacted the Sunshine Act to open the deliberations of multimember general agencies to public view. It believed that increased openness would enhance citizen confidence in government, encourage higher quality work by government officials, stimulate well-informed public debate about government programs and policies, and promote cooperation between citizens and government. In short, it sought to make government more fully accountable to the people. In keeping with the premise that "government should conduct the public's business in public," the Act established a general presumption that agency meetings should be held in the open. Once a person has challenged an agency's decision to close a meeting, the agency bears the burden of proof. Even if exempt subjects are discussed in one

portion of a meeting, the remainder of the meeting must be held in open session. . . .

Express language in the Sunshine Act also demonstrates that Congress did not intend to follow the FOIA pattern for predecisional discussions at agency meetings. The Sunshine Act applies to all "meetings," which are defined as deliberations which determine or result in "the joint conduct or disposition of official agency business[.]" 5 U.S.C. § 552b(a)(2) (1976). The legislative history demonstrates that "official agency business" means far more than reviewable final action. . . .

Exceptions to the Sunshine Act's general requirement of openness must be construed narrowly. Congress rejected the approach of establishing "functional categories" of agency business whose discussion could automatically be closed to the public. Instead the Sunshine Act provides for an examination of each item of business to ascertain whether it may be closed under the terms of one of ten specific exemptions. Exemptions must be interpreted in light of Congress' intention that agencies must "conduct their deliberations in public to the greatest extent possible." Nevertheless the Commission claims that Exemption 9(B) permits closing of agency budget meetings in their entirety.

Exemption 9(B) permits closing of meetings to prevent "premature disclosure" of information whose disclosure would be likely to "significantly frustrate implementation of a proposed agency action." For two reasons, the precept of narrow construction applies with particular force to this exemption, upon which the Commission principally relies. First, as we have seen, Congress decided not to provide any exemption for predecisional deliberations because it wished the process of decision as well as the results to be open to public view. . . .

Our *in camera* inspection of the transcripts of the July 27, 1981 and October 15, 1981 Commission meetings leads us to conclude that Exemption 9(B) does not support withholding of any portion of the transcripts.

5. Sunshine in surprising places. The Supreme Court of Texas confronted an inadvertent violation of its state open meetings act in *Acker v. Texas Water Commission*, 790 S.W.2d 299 (Tex. 1990):

DOGGETT, JUSTICE. The vital issue in this case is whether the decisionmaking of a state agency in a contested administrative case should be done openly or secretly. We believe the law requires openness.

Charles M. Acker received a favorable recommendation from the hearings examiner at the Texas Water Commission on a requested permit for a wastewater treatment plant. Thereafter, during a recess of a public hearing conducted by the three member Commission, Commissioners Hopkins and Roming were allegedly overheard conversing about this application in a restroom. This purported discussion concerned Acker's costs in complying with a city subdivision ordinance. When the public meeting reconvened, Commissioners Hopkins and Houchins voted to deny the application, and Commissioner Roming voted to grant it. Claiming a violation of the Texas Open Meetings Act had occurred, Acker brought suit seeking to set aside this order. The trial court granted Acker summary judgment based upon this asserted violation, but was reversed by the court of appeals on grounds that section 17 of the Texas Administrative Procedure and Texas Register Act [APTRA] allows private communications between agency members. We affirm the judgment, although not the reasoning, of the court of appeals and remand to the trial court for further proceedings.

The Open Meetings Act was enacted in 1967 for the purpose "of assuring that the public has the opportunity to be informed concerning the transactions of public business." It recognized the wisdom contained in the words of Justice Brandeis that: "Sunlight is said to be the best of disinfectants; electric light the most efficient policeman." L. BRANDEIS, OTHER PEOPLE'S MONEY 92 (1914 ed.). The executive and legislative decisions of our governmental officials as well as the underlying reasoning must be discussed openly before the public rather than secretly behind closed doors. In order to effect this policy, this statute requires that "every regular, special, or called meeting or session of every governmental body shall be open to the public." A "meeting" includes any deliberation involving a "quorum" or majority of the members of a governing body at which they act on or discuss any public business or policy over which they have control. Any verbal exchange between a majority of the members concerning any issue within their jurisdiction constitutes a "deliberation." When a majority of a public decisionmaking body is considering a pending issue, there can be no "informal" discussion. There is either formal consideration of a matter in compliance with the Open Meetings Act or an illegal meeting. We have previously noted that there is a broad scope to the coverage of the Open Meetings Act and a narrowness to its few exceptions. Its breadth is consistent with the recommendation of Woodrow Wilson that "Government ought to be all outside and no inside." Our citizens are entitled to more than a result. They are entitled not only to know what government decides but to observe how and why every decision is reached. The explicit command of the statute is for openness at every stage of the deliberations. Accordingly we have demanded exact and literal compliance with the terms of this statute.

Rather than applying it literally the court of appeals created a gaping hole in the Open Meetings Act through the meaning accorded to the subsequent enactment of section 17 of APTRA. That court held that APTRA authorizes a quorum of a state commission without any prior notice to meet and deliberate privately about any aspect of a pending contested proceeding.

This holding effectively eviscerates the Open Meetings Act for application to the executive branch of our government. In administrative review of contested issues from a to z—from alcoholic beverages to zoos, secrecy would suddenly be authorized. . . .

We hold that a meeting between a majority of the Commissioners to discuss among themselves contested issues outside a public hearing violates section 2 of the Open Meetings Act.

Should we prohibit two board members from informally discussing the board's business over dinner at a restaurant? Should two people who happen to be on the same board be prohibited from using the restroom at the same time and place? Absent some restrictions on decisionmakers meeting informally, an obvious danger exists that formal meetings will become mere shows. But is this a danger that can be practicably controlled at acceptable expense?

The Supreme Court partially addressed this problem for federal law by adopting a narrow construction of "meeting" in *FCC v. ITT World Communications, Inc.,* 466 U.S. 463 (1984). A telecommunications carrier claimed that three members of the Commission had violated the Sunshine Act by attending sessions of the "Consultative Process," which facilitates planning by European, American, and Canadian regulators. The Court rejected this claim on the ground that the Commissioners had not attended a "meeting" within the meaning of § 522(b)(a)(2), which defines this term as including "the deliberations of at least the number of individual agency members required to take action on behalf of the agency where such deliberations determine or result in the joint conduct or disposition of official agency business." This definition captures discussions that "effectively predetermine official actions." More broadly, to qualify as "meetings," discussions must be "sufficiently focused on discrete proposals or issues as to cause or be likely to cause the individual participating members to form reasonably firm positions regarding matters pending or likely to arise before the agency." 466 U.S. at 471 (quoting Berg & Klitzman, An Interpretive Guide to the Government in the Sunshine Act 9 (1978)). The Consultative Process gave regulators a chance to share background information and exchange views. As such, it did not qualify as a "meeting." Did Commissioners Hopkins and Roming have a "meeting" in the restroom?

6. Why don't appellate courts deliberate in public? In *Acker,* the Supreme Court of Texas applied its Open Meetings Act to a contested case determined by administrative adjudicators. But if so much sunshine is good for administrative adjudicators, how about for judges of the independent judiciary? Appellate courts, such as the Supreme Court of Texas itself as well as the Supreme Court of the United States, deliberate in secret—even though, in addition to determining legal rights and liabilities, they make critical policy decisions. Given the power, would you force the Supreme Court to deliberate in public? If not, would you extend the same privilege of secrecy to administrative decisionmakers? Should all discussions be open to the public and the press?

7. The effects of "openness" in congressional deliberations. Might too much "openness" damage the legislative policymaking process? After hearings, congressional committees meet for a "markup" session in which the members draft the final committee version of a bill. Discussing what he called the "real legislative activity of a [congressional] committee," Frank Cummings commented on the movement to open these meetings:

> In the name of "reform," "democracy," and other apple-pie objectives, the Congress in recent years has leaned toward holding its executive sessions open to the public.

> Do open markups really make a difference? Well, obviously, they make some, since they give the public and interested parties some insight into what is going on. Further, to a degree Congress will behave in a more responsible manner when conducting its business in public view subject to comment from the press. But the kind of give and take which has been characteristic of closed sessions is not likely to occur in open sessions. Thus, the principal consequences of opening executive sessions may turn out to be: (1) that the efficiency and speed of such sessions will be lessened; (2) that more time will be devoted to speech making and other plays to the grandstands; and (3) that the *real* business of legislative compromise may, to some extent, take place elsewhere—in private.

FRANK CUMMINGS, CAPITOL HILL MANUAL 46 (1976).

Appendix 1

Sample Enabling Act

Warning. The following **fictitious** enabling act is not law. It is intended as a tool to facilitate discussion. Its sections are derived from sections in actual legislation as described in the "Historical Notes."

WINE TRADE COMMISSION ACT
[fictitious]

Sec. 1. Enactment.

Be it enacted by the Senate and House of Representatives of the United States of America in Congress assembled, that an independent agency is hereby created and established to be known as the Wine Trade Commission (hereinafter referred to as the Commission) which shall be headed by a chair and four other commissioners who shall be appointed by the President with the advice and consent of the Senate. No more than three commissioners shall be of the same political party. The Commissioners shall serve for seven years but may be removed by the President for inefficiency, neglect of duty or malfeasance in office. The Commissioners shall have authority to employ and fix the compensation of such attorneys, special experts, clerks and other employees as they may find necessary for the proper performance of their duties and as appropriated by Congress. With the exception of the Commissioners, attorneys and special experts, all employees of the Commission shall be part of the classified civil service and shall enter the service under such rules and regulations as may be prescribed by the Commission and by the Office of Personnel

Management. The Federal Alcohol Administration Act, 27 U.S.C. §§ 201–212, is amended to remove all references to wine. The Secretary of Treasury shall hereafter have no jurisdiction over the wine industry.

Historical Note

This section was derived from the enactment clause of the Federal Trade Commission Act.

Sec. 2. Definitions.

(a) Association.

The Association is the Wine Merchants Association constituted under this Act.

(b) Commission.

The Commission is the Wine Trade Commission (WTC) created and established by this Act.

(c) Commissioners.

The Commissioners are the five members of the Commission who will administer the agency, issue rules and decide all cases. They shall be presided over by one of the members who shall chair the meetings.

(d) Order.

An order is the final disposition a specific dispute.

(e) Rule.

A rule is a statement of general applicability designed to implement, interpret, or prescribe law, policy or procedures.

(f) Wine.

Wine includes any alcoholic drink made primarily from fermented grapes or an equivalent fruit.

(g) Wine merchants.

Wine merchants are all growers, wholesalers and dealers in wine as defined by the Commission.

Sec. 3. A Plan for the Development of the American Wine Industry.

(a) Duty to promote.

The Commission shall promptly initiate and carry out a program for the promotion and development of the American wine industry.

(b) Development grants.

The Commission shall institute a program for development grants from such funds as Congress appropriates for that purpose. In order to assure compliance with the conditions of a grant, the Commission or its delegatee may enter the premise of the grant holder.

(c) Promotional plan.

The Commission is authorized and directed to prepare a comprehensive plan for the conduct of the development programs. The Commission shall transmit such comprehensive plan to the President and to each House of the Congress within 120 days of the establishment of the Administration.

Historical Note

This section was derived from the Solar Energy Research, Development and Demonstration Act of 1974, 42 U.S.C. §§ 5503 & 5564.

Sec. 4. Emergency Trust Fund.

(a) Creation of trust fund.

The Commission shall set and collect an annual fee from licensees under sec. 6. This fee will be allocated to a Trust Fund and the Trust Fund will be used to insure growers against crop failure or other natural disasters. The Trust Fund will be administered by the Commission in cooperation with each state.

(b) Disaster relief.

In the case of any person, the determination of whether or not he suffered a disaster covered by subsection (a) of this section, and of the day such disaster began, and the determination of the day on which such disaster ceased, shall be made by a State agency pursuant to an agreement entered into under subsection (c) of this section. Except as provided in subsections (d) and (e) of this section, any such determination shall be the determination of the Commission for purposes of this Act.

(c) Federal/state cooperation.

The Commission shall enter into an agreement with each State which is willing to make such an agreement under which any appropriate State agency or agencies will make the determinations referred to in subsection (a) of this section with respect to all persons in such State, or with respect to such class or classes of persons in the State as may be designated in the agreement at the State's request.

(d) Commission review of state determinations.

The Commission may on its own motion review a determination made by a State agency, pursuant to an agreement under this section, that a person is under a disaster and, as a result of such review, may determine that such person is not under a disaster, or that such disaster began on a day later than that determined by such agency, or that such disaster ceased on a day earlier than that determined by such agency.

(e) Hearing.

Any person dissatisfied with any determination under subsection (b) or (d) of this section shall be entitled to a hearing thereon by the Commission or its delegatee in accordance with the procedures set out in § 7(b).

(f) Payment to the states.

Each State which has an agreement with the Commission under this section shall be entitled to receive from the Trust Fund, in advance or by way of reimbursement, as may be mutually agreed upon, the cost to the State of carrying out the agreement under this section. The Commission shall from time to time certify such amount as is necessary for this purpose to the Managing Trustee of the Trust Fund, reduced or increased, as the case may be, by any sum (for which adjustment hereunder has not previously been made) by which the amount certified for any prior period was greater or less than the amount which should have been paid to the State under this subsection for such period; and the Managing Trustee, prior to audit or settlement by the General Accounting Office, shall make payment from the Trust Funds.

Historical Note

Subsection (a) of this section is new.

Subsections (b) to (f) of this section are derived from the Social Security programs disability provision, 42 U.S.C. § 421.

Sec. 5. Employment of Manipulative and Deceptive Devices.

It shall be unlawful for any person, directly or indirectly, by the use of any means or instrumentality of interstate commerce, or of the mail, in connection with the purchase or sale of wine:

(a) to employ any device, scheme, or artifice to defraud;

(b) to make any untrue statement of material fact or to omit to state a material fact necessary in order to make the statements made, in light of the circumstances under which they were made, not misleading; or

(c) to engage in any act, practice, or course of business which operates or would operate as a fraud or deceit upon any person.

Historical Note

This section was derived from § 17 of the Securities Act of 1933, 15 U.S.C. § 77q.

Sec. 6. Licensing Wine Merchants.

(a) License required.

It shall be unlawful for any person to act as a wine merchant in interstate commerce unless such person has first obtained a "wine merchants" license from the Commission.

(b) Wine Merchants Association.

The Commission shall cause a private association of wine merchants to be formed known as the "Wine Merchants Association" (the "Association"). The Association shall regulate the conduct of its members. The Association may make rules and these rules shall be binding on its members after review by the Commission. It shall be unlawful for any person to sell wine other than at retail unless that person is a member in good standing of the Association.

(c) License application.

A person may obtain a license as a wine merchant by filing with the Commission an application as prescribed by the Commission. A wine merchant license shall be granted to any member in good standing of the Association who is in compliance with all rules and regulations promulgated by the Commission in accordance with § 8(c) of this Act.

(d) Suspension and revocation of a license.

The Commission may by order, after the opportunity for a hearing as prescribed by the Commission, suspend or revoke a wine merchant's license of any who violates this Act, or the rules of the Commission promulgated in accordance with § 8 of this Act, or who ceases to be a member in good standing of the Association. A person whose license has been suspended may seek review of that order in accordance with § 9(a).

(e) Required reports.

The Commission may require any member of the Association to submit such reports as it deems necessary to carry out the purpose of this Act. Any person required to file a special report, who shall fail so to do within the time fixed by the Commission for filing the same and whose failure shall continue for thirty days after notice of such default, shall forfeit to the United States the sum of $1,000 for each and every day of the continuance of such failure, which forfeiture shall be payable into the Treasury of the United States, and shall be recoverable in a civil suit in the name of the United States brought in the district where the person resides or, if a corporation, where it has its principal office or in any district in which it does business. It shall be the duty of the various United States attorneys, under the direction of the Attorney General of the United States, to prosecute for the recovery of forfeitures. The costs and expenses of such prosecution shall be paid out of the appropriation for the expenses of the courts of the United States.

(f) Administrative Inspections.

Employees or agents of the Commission may enter during business hours the premises (including places of storage and production facilities) of any wine merchant for the purpose of inspecting or examining any records or other documents required to be kept by such wine merchant under this chapter or regulations issued pursuant thereto and any wines or potential raw ingredients of wines kept or stored by such wine merchant on such premises.

(g) Release of information.

In accordance with its rules and regulations, the Commission may release information obtained under this section if such release will further the Commission's law enforcement purpose. Any officer or employee of the Commission who shall make public any information obtained by the Commission without its authority unless directed by a court, shall be deemed guilty of a misdemeanor, and, upon conviction thereof, shall be punishable by a fine not exceeding $5,000, or by imprisonment not exceeding one year, or by fine and imprisonment, in the discretion of the court.

Historical Note

Subsections (a) to (d) of this section are derived from § 15 of the Securities and Exchange Act of 1934, 15 U.S.C. § 78o. Subsections (e) and (g) are derived from § 10 of the Federal Trade Commission Act, 15 U.S.C. § 50. Subsection (f) is derived from § 5146 of the Internal Revenue Code, 26 U.S.C. § 5146(b).

Sec. 7. Orders.

(a) Enforcement hearings and orders; civil investigative demands.

(1) Whenever the Commission has reason to believe that a person is violating this Act, or rules promulgated under § 8 of this Act, it shall issue and serve upon the person a complaint stating its charges in that respect. After a full hearing, the Commission may issue such orders as it finds necessary to cure the violation. The Commission shall provide for appeal of any initial decision of a violation of this Act.

(2) Whenever the Commission has reason to believe that any person may be in possession, custody, or control of any documentary material or information relevant to a violation of this Act, it may, before commencement of an enforcement action under this section, issue in writing and cause to be served on such person, a civil investigative demand requiring such person—

(A) to produce such documentary material for inspection and copying;

(B) to answer in writing written interrogatories with respect to such documentary materials or information;

(C) to give oral testimony concerning such documentary material or information; or

(D) to furnish any combination of such material, answers, or testimony.

(b) Appeals to the Commission.

A person denied disaster relief under § 4 may appeal that decision to the Commission. A person challenging a denial shall be afforded a conference with the Commission or its delegatee. The conference shall include rights of parties to have reasonable notice, to appear in person or by counsel or other qualified representative for the informal presentation of factual data, argument, or proof, to have notice of any contrary facts or information in the possession of the agency upon which it may rely in any way in making an adverse decision, to receive prompt decision and to be informed, briefly and generally in writing, of the factual or procedural basis for an adverse decision.

Historical Note

Subsection (a)(1) of this section is derived from subsection 5(b) of the Federal Trade Commission Act, 15 U.S.C. § 45.

Subsection (a)(2) is derived from the False Claims Act, 31 U.S.C. § 3733.

Subsection (b) of this section is suggested by the 1981 Model State Administrative Procedure Act, § 4-401.

Sec. 8. Rules.

(a) General Rulemaking Authority.

The Commission shall have the power to make rules and regulations for the purpose of carrying out the provisions of this Act.

(b) Procedures for rulemaking.

(1) The Commission shall initiate all such rulemaking with a Notice of Proposed Rulemaking. The notice shall be published in the *Federal Register.* In addition to publication, the Commission shall assure that all interested persons have actual notice of the proposed rulemaking.

(2) In addition to seeking information by other methods, the Commission before publication of the notice, shall solicit comments from interested members of the public on the subject matter of the possible rulemaking under consideration.

(3) Prior to publishing proposed rules in the *Federal Register,* the Commission shall consider whether the rule is appropriate for negotiated rulemaking under 5 U.S.C. § 561 et seq. The Commission may, within its discretion, determine to undertake negotiated rulemaking.

(4) The Commission shall issue a Regulatory Analysis with the proposed rule. The Regulatory Analysis shall estimate the costs and benefits of the

proposed rule and compare those costs and benefits with the costs and benefits of alternative courses of action.

(5) Except as provided in subsection (c), the Commission shall promulgate public participation guidelines for soliciting the input of interested parties in the formation and development of its rules. These guidelines shall set out any methods for identification and notification of interested persons and the method whereby interested persons may participate in the issuance of the rule. The guidelines shall set out the circumstances in which the Commission will establish and consult with an advisory panel.

(6) The Commission shall publish the final rule in the *Federal Register*. The final rule shall be accompanied by a Statement of Basis and Purpose, in compliance with 5 U.S.C. § 553(c), based on the rulemaking record.

(7) Any person may petition the Commission for an exemption from a final rule. After the opportunity for a hearing, the Commission shall determine whether to grant or deny an exemption.

(8) These procedures are inapplicable to a rule concerning only the internal management of an agency which does not directly and substantially affect the procedural or substantive rights or duties of any segment of the public.

(9) These procedures shall not apply in the case of any rule or circumstance referred to in subparagraphs (A) or (B) of subsection 553(b) of Title 5.

(c) Rules regarding wine merchant license.

After the opportunity for a full hearing, the Commission shall promulgate rules pertaining to eligibility for a wine merchant license. Such rules shall be based only on substantial evidence of record at such hearing and shall set forth, as part of the rule, detailed findings of fact on which the order is based.

Historical Note

Subsection (a)(1) of this section is derived from subsection 6(g) of the Federal Trade Commission Act, 15 U.S.C. 46(g). Subsection (b) combines §§ 3-101, 3-105 & 3-116 of the 1981 MSAPA and § 9-6.14:7.1 of the Virginia Administrative Process Act. Subsection (c) contains language from the Food, Drug, and Cosmetic Act, 21 U.S.C. § 371(e) (3). Subsection (b)(9) is derived from § 307(d) of the Clean Air Act, 42 U.S.C. § 7607(d) (1)(V).

Sec. 9. Judicial Review.

(a) Petition for review of an order.

(1) Any person who is subject to an order issued under this act may petition for review of the order in the court of appeals of the United States,

within any circuit where the act or practice in question was used or where such person resides or carries on business, by filing in the court, within 60 days from the date of the service of such order, a written petition praying that the order of the Commission be set aside.

(2) Upon such filing of the petition, the court shall have jurisdiction of the proceeding and of the question determined therein concurrently with the Commission until the filing of the record and shall have power to make and enter a decree affirming, modifying, or setting aside the order of the Commission, and enforcing the same to the extent that such order is affirmed, and to issue such writs as are ancillary to its jurisdiction or are necessary in its judgment to prevent injury to the public or to competitors *pendente lite.*

(3) The finding of the Commission as to the facts, if supported by evidence, shall be conclusive.

(4) To the extent that the order of the Commission is affirmed, the court shall thereupon issue its own order commanding obedience to the terms of such order of the Commission.

(5) The judgment and decree of the court shall be final, except that the same shall be subjected to review by the Supreme Court upon certiorari, as provided in section 240 of the Judicial Code.

(6) An order of the Commission shall become final—

(A) Upon the expiration of the time allowed for filing a petition for review, if no such petition has been duly filed within such time, but the Commission may thereafter modify or set aside its order;

(B) Upon the expiration of the time allowed for filing a petition for *certiorari*, if the order of the Commission has been affirmed, or the petition for review dismissed by the court of appeals, and no petition for certiorari has been duly filed; or

(C) Upon the denial of a petition for *certiorari*, if the order of the Commission has been affirmed or the petition for review dismissed by the court of appeals; or

(D) Upon the expiration of thirty days from the date of issuance of the mandate of the Supreme Court, if such Court directs that the order of the Commission be affirmed or the petition for review dismissed.

(b) Petition for review of an administrative penalty.

Any person against whom a civil penalty is assessed in accordance with § 11 or who commented on a proposed assessment may obtain review of a determination to assess or refuse to assess such civil penalties under that section. Any wine consumer shall be deemed to have had a nonspeculative injury from such determination.

(c) Petition for review of a rule.

(1) Not later than 60 days after a rule is promulgated under §8(b) or §8(c) by the Commission, any interested person may file a petition, in the United States Court of Appeals for the District of Columbia Circuit or for the circuit in which such person resides or has a principle place of business, for judicial review of the rule. Copies of the petition shall be forthwith transmitted by the clerk of the court to the Commission or other officer designated for that purpose. The provision of §2112 of Title 28 shall apply to the filing of the rulemaking record of proceedings on which the Commission based its rule and to the transfer of proceedings in the courts of appeals.

(2) For purpose of this section, the term "rulemaking record" means the rule, its statement of basis and purpose, the transcript of any oral hearing, if any, any written submissions, and any other information which the Commission considers relevant to such rule.

(3) Upon the filing of the petition under subsection (c)(1), the court shall have jurisdiction to review the rule in accordance with chapter 7 of Title 5 and to grant appropriate relief, including interim relief, as provided by such chapter. The court shall hold unlawful and set aside the rule on any ground specified in subparagraphs (A), (B), (C), or (D) of §706(2) of Title 5 (taking into account the rules of prejudicial error), or if the findings of fact upon which the rule is based are not supported by substantial evidence.

Historical Note

Section (a) follows closely the classic "petition for review" provision of §5 of the Federal Trade Commission Act, 15 U.S.C. §45. Section (b) contains language from the judicial review provision of the Federal Water Pollution Control Act, 33 U.S.C. §1319(g). Section (c) is derived from the judicial review provisions of the Magnuson-Moss Federal Trade Commission Improvement Act of 1975 amendments to the Federal Trade Commission Act, 15 U.S.C. §57a(e).

Sec. 10. Enforcement.

(a) Civil penalty for violation of an order.

Any person who violates an order of the Commission to cease and desist after it has become final, and while such order is in effect, shall forfeit and pay to the United States a civil penalty of not more than $10,000 for each violation, which shall accrue to the United States and may be recovered in a civil action brought by the United States. Each separate violation of such an order shall be a separate offense, except that in the case of a violation through continuing failure or neglect to obey a final order of the Commission, each day of continuance of such failure or neglect shall be deemed a separate offense.

(b) Injunction.

Whenever the Commission has reason to believe—

(1) that any person is engaged in a practice in violation of this act or a rule, promulgated under § 8 of this act, or

(2) that the enjoining thereof, pending the issuance of a complaint by the Commission under § 5 and until such complaint is dismissed by the Commission, or set aside by the court on review, or the order of the Commission to cease and desist made thereon has become final within the meaning of § 5, would be to the interest of the public, the Commission, by any of its attorneys designated by it for such purpose, may bring suit in a district court of the United States or in the United States court of any Territory, to enjoin the practice and upon proper showing a temporary injunction or restraining order shall be granted without bond. Any such suit shall be brought in the district in which such person, resides or transacts business.

(c) Criminal penalty.

Any person who willfully violates any provision of this Act, or rules promulgated under § 8 of this Act, shall, upon conviction, be fined not more than $100,000, or imprisoned not more than five years, or both.

Historical Note

Subsection (a) is derived from subsection (l) of § 5 of the Federal Trade Commission Act, 15 U.S.C. 45(l).

Subsection (b) is derived from an amendment to the Federal Trade Commission Act, 15 U.S.C. § 53(b).

Subsection (c) is derived from § 32 of the Securities Exchange Act of 1934, 15 U.S.C. § 78ff(a).

Sec. 11. Administrative Penalties.

(a) Violation.

(1) Whenever on the basis of any information available, the Commission finds that a wine merchant as defined by § 2 has violated this Act, or rules promulgated under § 8 of this Act, it may, after consultation with the State in which the violation occurs, assess a civil penalty.

(2) In determining the amount of any penalty, the Commission shall take into account the nature, circumstances, extent and gravity of the violation, or violations, and, with respect to the violator, ability to pay, any prior history of such violations, the degree of culpability, economic benefit or savings (if any) resulting from the violation, and such other matters as justice may require.

(b) Hearing.

Before issuing an order assessing a civil penalty, the Commission shall give to the person to be assessed such penalty written notice and the opportunity to request, within 30 days of the date the notice is received by such person, a hearing on the proposed order. Such hearing shall not be subject to §§ 554 or 556 of Title 5, but shall provide a reasonable opportunity to be heard and to present evidence.

(c) Rights of interested persons.

(1) Before issuing an order assessing a civil penalty, the Commission shall provide public notice of and reasonable opportunity to comment on the proposed issuance of such order.

(2) Any person who comments on a proposed assessment of a penalty shall be given notice of any hearing held under this section and of the order assessing such penalty. In any hearing held, such person shall have a reasonable opportunity to be heard and to present evidence.

(3) If no hearing is held before issuance of an order assessing a penalty any person who commented on the proposed assessment may petition, within 30 days after the issuance of such order, for such hearing, and the Commission shall immediately set aside such order and provide a hearing in accordance with sub-section (b). If the Commission denies a hearing, it shall provide to the petitioner and publish in the *Federal Register* notice of and the reasons for such denial.

(d) Finality of the order.

An order shall become final 30 days after its issuance unless a petition for judicial review is filed or a hearing is requested. If such a hearing is denied, such order shall become final 30 days after such denial.

(e) Collection.

If any person fails to pay an assessment of a civil penalty—

(1) after the order making the assessment has become final, or

(2) after a court in an action brought under § 9(b) has entered a final judgment in favor of the Commission or Association, the Commission shall request the Attorney General to bring a civil action in an appropriate district court to recover the amount assessed (plus interest at currently prevailing rates from the date of the final order). In such an action, the validity, amount, and appropriateness of such penalty shall not be subject to review.

Historical Notes

This section is derived from subsection 309(g) of the Federal Water Pollution Control Act, 33 U.S.C. § 1319(g).

Sec. 12. Citizen Suits.

(a) Authority to bring civil action; jurisdiction.

Except as provided in subsection (b) of this section, any person may commence a civil action on their own behalf—

(1) against any person (including (i) the United States, and (ii) any other governmental instrumentality or agency to the extent permitted by the Eleventh Amendment to the Constitution) who is alleged to be in violation of (A) a Commission rule or (B) an order issued by the Commission; or

(2) against the Commission where there is alleged a failure of the Commission to perform any act or duty under this Act which is not discretionary with the Commission. The district courts shall have jurisdiction, without regard to the amount in controversy or the citizenship of the parties, to enforce such rule or order, or to order the Commission to perform such act or duty, as the case may be.

(b) Notice.

No action may be commenced—

(1) under subsection (a)(1) of this section—

(A) prior to 60 days after the plaintiff has given notice of the violation (i) to the Commission, (ii) to the State in which the violation occurs, and (iii) to any alleged violator of the rule or order, or

(B) if the Commission or State has commenced and is diligently prosecuting a civil action in a court of the United States or a State to require compliance with the rule or order, but in any such action in a court of the United States or a State any person may intervene as a matter of right.

(2) under subsection (a)(2) of this section prior to 60 days after the plaintiff has given notice of such action to the Commission.

Notice under this subsection shall be given in such manner as the Commission shall prescribe by rule.

(c) Intervention by the Commission.

In such action under this section, the Commission, if not a party, may intervene as a matter of right.

(d) Award of costs.

The court, in issuing any final order in any action brought pursuant to subsection (a) of this section, may order any party, other than the government, to pay the costs of litigation (including reasonable attorney and expert witness fees), whenever the court determines that the award of such costs is appropriate. The court may order the government, when it is a party, to pay such costs to a prevailing party unless the court finds that the position of the government was substantially justified or that special circumstances make an award unjust.

(e) Nonrestriction of other rights.

Nothing in this section shall restrict any right which any person (or class of persons) may have under any statute or common law. Nothing in this section or in any other law of the United States shall be construed to prohibit, exclude, or restrict any State, local, or interstate authority from —

> (1) bringing any enforcement action or obtaining any judicial remedy or sanction in any State or local court, or

> (2) bringing any administrative enforcement action or obtaining any administrative remedy or sanction in any State or local administrative agency, department or instrumentality, against the United States, any department, agency, or instrumentality thereof, or any officer, agency, or employee thereof under State or local law.

Historical Note

This section is derived from §304 of the Clean Air Act, 42 U.S.C. §7604. Some of the language in the second sentence of subsection (d) comes from the Equal Access to Justice Act, 5 U.S.C. §504.

Sec. 13. Severability of Provisions.

If any provision of this Act, or the application thereof to any person or circumstance, is held invalid, the remainder of the Act and the application of such provision to any other person, or circumstance, shall not be affected thereby.

Appendix 2

Federal Administrative Procedure Act (5 U.S.C. §§ 551–559, 701–706, 3105, 1305, and 7521)

Sec.

551. Definitions

For the purpose of this subchapter—

(1) "agency" means each authority of the Government of the United States, whether or not it is within or subject to review by another agency, but does not include—

(A) the Congress;

(B) the courts of the United States;

(C) the governments of the territories or possessions of the United States;

(D) the government of the District of Columbia; or except as to the requirements of section 552 of this title —

(E) agencies composed of representatives of the parties or of representatives of organizations of the parties to the disputes determined by them;

(F) courts martial and military commissions;

(G) military authority exercised in the field in time of war or in occupied territory; or

(H) functions conferred by sections 1738, 1739, 1743, and 1744 of title 12; chapter 2 of title 41; subchapter II of chapter 471 of title 49; or sections 1884, 1891–1902, and former section 1641(b)(2), of title 50, appendix;

(2) "person" includes an individual, partnership, corporation, association, or public or private organization other than an agency;

(3) "party" includes a person or agency named or admitted as a party, or property seeking and entitled as of right to be admitted as a party, in an agency proceeding, and a person or agency admitted by an agency as a party for limited purposes;

(4) "rule" means the whole or a part of an agency statement of general or particular applicability and future effect designed to implement, interpret, or prescribe law or policy or describing the organization, procedure, or practice requirements of an agency and includes the approval or prescription for the future of rates, wages, corporate or financial structures or reorganization thereof, prices, facilities, appliances, services or allowances therefor or of valuations, costs, or accounting, or practices bearing on any of the foregoing;

(5) "rulemaking" means agency process for formulating, amending, or repealing a rule;

(6) "order" means the whole or a part of a final disposition, whether affirmative, negative, injunctive, or declaratory in form, of an agency in a matter other than rulemaking but including licensing;

(7) "adjudication" means agency process for the formulation of an order;

(8) "license" includes the whole or a part of an agency permit, certificate, approval, registration, charter, membership, statutory exemption or other form of permission;

(9) "licensing" includes agency process respecting the grant, renewal, denial, revocation, suspension, annulment, withdrawal, limitation, amendment, modification, or conditioning of a license;

(10) "sanction" includes the whole or a part of an agency —

(A) prohibition, requirement, limitation, or other condition affecting the freedom of a person;

(B) withholding of relief;

(C) imposition of penalty or fine;

(D) destruction, taking, seizure, or withholding of property;

(E) assessment of damages, reimbursement, restitution, compensation, costs, charges, or fees;

(F) requirement, revocation, or suspension of a license; or

(G) taking other compulsory or restrictive action;

(11) "relief" includes the whole or a part of an agency—

(A) grant of money, assistance, license, authority, exemption, exception, privilege, or remedy;

(B) recognition of a claim, right, immunity, privilege, exemption, or exception; or

(C) taking of other action on the application or petition of, and beneficial to, a person;

(12) "agency proceeding" means an agency process as defined by paragraphs (5), (7), and (9) of this section;

(13) "agency action" includes the whole or a part of an agency rule, order, license, sanction, relief, or the equivalent or denial thereof, or failure to act; and

(14) "ex parte communication" means an oral or written communication not on the public record with respect to which reasonable prior notice to all parties is not given, but it shall not include requests for status reports on any matter or proceeding covered by this subchapter.

553. Rule-making

(a) This section applies, according to the provisions thereof, except to the extent that there is involved—

(1) a military or foreign affairs function of the United States; or

(2) a matter relating to agency management or personnel or to public property, loans, grants, benefits, or contracts.

(b) General notice of proposed rulemaking shall be published in the Federal Register, unless persons subject thereto are named and either personally served or otherwise have actual notice thereof in accordance with law. The notice shall include—

(1) a statement of the time, place, and nature of public rulemaking proceedings;

(2) reference to the legal authority under which the rule is proposed; and

(3) either the terms or substance of the proposed rule or a description of the subjects and issues involved.

IF NOTICE OR HEARING IS REQUIRED, IN STATUTE THEN THIS APPLIES

Except when notice or hearing is required by statute, this subsection does not apply—

    (A) to interpretative rules, general statements of policy, or rules of agency organization, procedure, or practice; or

    (B) when the agency for good cause finds (and incorporates the finding and a brief statement of reasons therefor in the rules issued) that notice and public procedure thereon are impracticable, unnecessary, or contrary to the public interest.

(c) After notice required by this section, the agency shall give interested persons an opportunity to participate in the rulemaking through submission of written data, views, or arguments with or without opportunity for oral presentation. After consideration of the relevant matter presented, the agency shall incorporate in the rules adopted a concise general statement of their basis and purpose. When rules are required by statute to be made on the record after opportunity for an agency hearing, sections 556 and 557 of this title apply instead of this subsection.

(d) The required publication or service of a substantive rule shall be made not less than 30 days before its effective date, except—

    (1) a substantive rule which grants or recognizes an exemption or relieves a restriction;

    (2) interpretative rules and statements of policy; or

    (3) as otherwise provided by the agency for good cause found and published with the rule.

(e) Each agency shall give an interested person the right to petition for the issuance, amendment, or repeal of a rule.

554. Adjudications

(a) This section applies, according to the provisions thereof, in every case of adjudication required by statute to be determined on the record after opportunity for an agency hearing, except to the extent that there is involved—

    (1) a matter subject to a subsequent trial of the law and the facts de novo in a court;

    (2) the selection or tenure of an employee, except an administrative law judge appointed under section 3105 of this title;

    (3) proceedings in which decisions rest solely on inspections, tests, or elections;

    (4) the conduct of military or foreign affairs functions;

    (5) cases in which an agency is acting as an agent for a court; or

    (6) the certification of worker representatives.

(b) Persons entitled to notice of an agency hearing shall be timely informed of—

> **(1)** the time, place, and nature of the hearing;

> **(2)** the legal authority and jurisdiction under which the hearing is to be held; and

> **(3)** the matters of fact and law asserted.

When private persons are the moving parties, other parties to the proceeding shall give prompt notice of issues controverted in fact or law; and in other instances agencies may by rule require responsive pleading. In fixing the time and place for hearings, due regard shall be had for the convenience and necessity of the parties or their representatives.

(c) The agency shall give all interested parties opportunity for—

> **(1)** the submission and consideration of facts, arguments, offers of settlement, or proposals of adjustment when time, the nature of the proceeding, and the public interest permit; and

> **(2)** to the extent that the parties are unable so to determine a controversy by consent, hearing and decision on notice and in accordance with sections 556 and 557 of this title.

(d) The employee who presides at the reception of evidence pursuant to section 556 of this title shall make the recommended decision or initial decision required by section 557 of this title, unless he becomes unavailable to the agency. Except to the extent required for the disposition of ex parte matters as authorized by law, such an employee may not—

> **(1)** consult a person or party on a fact in issue, unless on notice and opportunity for all parties to participate; or

> **(2)** be responsible to or subject to the supervision or direction of an employee or agent engaged in the performance of investigative or prosecuting functions for an agency.

An employee or agent engaged in the performance of investigative or prosecuting functions for an agency in a case may not, in that or a factually related case, participate or advise in the decision, recommended decision, or agency review pursuant to section 557 of this title, except as witness or counsel in public proceedings. This subsection does not apply—

> **(A)** in determining applications for initial licenses;

> **(B)** to proceedings involving the validity or application of rates, facilities, or practices of public utilities or carriers; or

> **(C)** to the agency or a member or members of the body comprising the agency.

(e) The agency, with like effect as in the case of other orders, and in its sound discretion, may issue a declaratory order to terminate a controversy or remove uncertainty.

555. Ancillary matters

(a) This section applies, according to the provisions thereof, except as otherwise provided by this subchapter.

(b) A person compelled to appear in person before an agency or representative thereof is entitled to be accompanied, represented, and advised by counsel or, if permitted by the agency, by other qualified representative. A party is entitled to appear in person or by or with counsel or other duly qualified representative in an agency proceeding. So far as the orderly conduct of public business permits, an interested person may appear before an agency or its responsible employees for the presentation, adjustment, or determination of an issue, request, or controversy in a proceeding, whether interlocutory, summary, or otherwise, or in connection with an agency function. With due regard for the convenience and necessity of the parties or their representatives and within a reasonable time, each agency shall proceed to conclude a matter presented to it. This subsection does not grant or deny a person who is not a lawyer the right to appear for or represent others before an agency or in an agency proceeding.

(c) Process, requirement of a report, inspection, or other investigative act or demand may not be issued, made, or enforced except as authorized by law. A person compelled to submit data or evidence is entitled to retain or, on payment of lawfully prescribed costs, procure a copy or transcript thereof, except that in a nonpublic investigatory proceeding the witness may for good cause be limited to inspection of the official transcript of his testimony.

(d) Agency subpenas authorized by law shall be issued to a party on request and, when required by rules of procedure, on a statement or showing of general relevance and reasonable scope of the evidence sought. On contest, the court shall sustain the subpena or similar process or demand to the extent that it is found to be in accordance with law. In a proceeding for enforcement, the court shall issue an order requiring the appearance of the witness or the production of the evidence or data within a reasonable time under penalty of punishment for contempt in case of contumacious failure to comply.

(e) Prompt notice shall be given of the denial in whole or in part of a written application, petition, or other request of an interested person made in connection with any agency proceeding. Except in affirming a prior denial or when the denial is self-explanatory, the notice shall be accompanied by a brief statement of the grounds for denial.

556. Hearings; presiding employees; powers and duties; burden of proof; evidence; record as basis of decision

(a) This section applies, according to the provisions thereof, to hearings required by section 553 or 554 of this title to be conducted in accordance with this section.

(b) There shall preside at the taking of evidence—

    (1) the agency;

(2) one or more members of the body which comprises the agency; or

(3) one or more administrative law judges appointed under section 3105 of this title.

This subchapter does not supersede the conduct of specified classes of proceedings, in whole or in part, by or before boards or other employees specially provided for by or designated under statute. The functions of presiding employees and of employees participating in decisions in accordance with section 557 of this title shall be conducted in an impartial manner. A presiding or participating employee may at any time disqualify himself. On the filing in good faith of a timely and sufficient affidavit of personal bias or other disqualification of a presiding or participating employee, the agency shall determine the matters as a part of the record and decision in the case.

(c) Subject to published rules of the agency and within its powers, employees presiding at hearings may—

(1) administer oaths and affirmations;

(2) issue subpenas authorized by law;

(3) rule on offers of proof and receive relevant evidence;

(4) take depositions or have depositions taken when the ends of justice would be served;

(5) regulate the course of the hearing;

(6) hold conferences for the settlement or simplification of the issues by consent of the parties or by the use of alternative means of dispute resolution as provided in subchapter IV of this chapter;

(7) inform the parties as to the availability of one or more alternative means of dispute resolution, and encourage use of such methods;

(8) require the attendance at any conference held pursuant to paragraph (6) of at least one representative of each party who has authority to negotiate concerning resolution of issues in controversy;

(9) dispose of procedural requests or similar matters;

(10) make or recommend decisions in accordance with section 557 of this title; and

(11) take other action authorized by agency rule consistent with this subchapter.

(d) Except as otherwise provided by statute, the proponent of a rule or order has the burden of proof. Any oral or documentary evidence may be received, but the agency as a matter of policy shall provide for the exclusion of irrelevant, immaterial, or unduly repetitious evidence. A sanction may not be imposed or rule or order issued except on consideration of the whole record or those parts thereof cited by a party and supported by and in accordance with the reliable, probative, and substantial evidence. The agency may, to the extent consistent with the interests of justice and the policy of the underlying statutes administered by the agency, consider a violation of section 557(d) of this title sufficient grounds for a decision adverse to a party who has knowingly committed such violation or knowingly caused such violation to occur. A party is entitled to present his case or defense by oral or documentary evidence, to submit rebuttal evidence, and to conduct such cross-examination as may be required for a full and true disclosure of the facts. In rule making or determining claims for money or benefits or applications for initial licenses an agency may, when a party will not be prejudiced thereby, adopt procedures for the submission of all or part of the evidence in written form.

(e) The transcript of testimony and exhibits, together with all papers and requests filed in the proceeding, constitutes the exclusive record for decision in accordance with section 557 of this title and, on payment of lawfully prescribed costs, shall be made available to the parties. When an agency decision rests on official notice of a material fact not appearing in the evidence in the record, a party is entitled, on timely request, to an opportunity to show the contrary.

557. Initial decisions; conclusiveness; review by agency; submissions by parties; contents of decisions; record

(a) This section applies, according to the provisions thereof, when a hearing is required to be conducted in accordance with section 556 of this title.

(b) When the agency did not preside at the reception of the evidence, the presiding employee or, in cases not subject to section 554(d) of this title, an employee qualified to preside at hearings pursuant to section 556 of this title, shall initially decide the case unless the agency requires, either in specific cases or by general rule, the entire record to be certified to it for decision. When the presiding employee makes an initial decision, that decision then becomes the decision of the agency without further proceedings unless there is an appeal to, or review on motion of, the agency within time provided by rule. On appeal from or review of the initial decision, the agency has all the powers which it would have in making the initial decision except as it may limit the issues on notice or by rule. When the agency makes the decision without having presided at the reception of the evidence, the presiding employee or an employee qualified to preside at hearings pursuant to section 556 of this title shall first recommend a decision, except that in rulemaking or determining application for initial licenses—

(1) instead thereof the agency may issue a tentative decision or one of its responsible employees may recommend a decision; or

(2) this procedure may be omitted in a case in which the agency finds on the record that due and timely execution of its functions imperatively and unavoidably so requires.

(c) Before a recommended, initial, or tentative decision, or a decision on agency review of the decision of subordinate employees, the parties are entitled to a reasonable opportunity to submit for the consideration of the employees participating in the decisions—

(1) proposed findings and conclusions; or

(2) exceptions to the decisions or recommended decisions of subordinate employees or to tentative agency decisions; and

(3) supporting reasons for the exceptions or proposed findings or conclusions.

The record shall show the ruling on each finding, conclusion, or exception presented. All decisions, including initial, recommended, and tentative decisions, are a part of the record and shall include a statement of—

(A) findings and conclusions, and the reasons or basis therefor, on all the material issues of fact, law, or discretion presented on the record; and

(B) the appropriate rule, order, sanction, relief, or denial thereof.

(d) (1) In any agency proceeding which is subject to subsection (a) of this section, except to the extent required for the disposition of ex parte matters as authorized by law—

(A) no interested person outside the agency shall make or knowingly cause to be made to any member of the body comprising the agency, administrative law judge, or other employee who is or may reasonably be expected to be involved in the decisional process of the proceeding, an ex parte communication relevant to the merits of the proceeding;

(B) no member of the body comprising the agency, administrative law judge, or other employee who is or may reasonably be expected to be involved in the decisional process of the proceeding, shall make or knowingly cause to be made to any interested person outside the agency an ex parte communication relevant to the merits of the proceeding;

(C) a member of the body comprising the agency, administrative law judge, or other employee who is or may reasonably be expected to be involved in the decisional process of such proceeding who receives, or who makes or knowingly causes to be made, a communication prohibited by this subsection shall place on the public record of the proceeding:

(i) all such written communications;

(ii) memoranda stating the substance of all such oral communications; and

(iii) all written responses, and memoranda stating the substance of all oral responses, to the materials described in clauses (i) and (ii) of this subparagraph;

(D) upon receipt of a communication knowingly made or knowingly caused to be made by a party in violation of this subsection, the agency, administrative law judge, or other employee presiding at the hearing may, to the extent consistent with the interests of justice and the policy of the underlying statutes, require the party to show cause why his claim or interest in the proceeding should not be dismissed, denied, disregarded, or otherwise adversely affected on account of such violation; and

(E) the prohibitions of this subsection shall apply beginning at such time as the agency may designate, but in no case shall they begin to apply later than the time at which a proceeding is noticed for hearing unless the person responsible for the communication has knowledge that it will be noticed, in which case the prohibitions shall apply beginning at the time of his acquisition of such knowledge.

(2) This subsection does not constitute authority to withhold information from Congress.

558. Imposition of sanctions; determination of applications for licenses; suspension, revocation, and expiration of licenses

(a) This section applies, according to the provisions thereof, to the exercise of a power or authority.

(b) A sanction may not be imposed or a substantive rule or order issued except within jurisdiction delegated to the agency and as authorized by law.

(c) When application is made for a license required by law, the agency, with due regard for the rights and privileges of all the interested parties or adversely affected persons and within a reasonable time, shall set and complete proceedings required to be conducted in accordance with sections 556 and 557 of this title or other proceedings required by law and shall make its decision. Except in cases of willfulness or those in which public health, interest, or safety requires otherwise, the withdrawal, suspension, revocation, or annulment of a license is lawful only if, before the institution of agency proceedings therefor, the licensee has been given—

(1) notice by the agency in writing of the facts or conduct which may warrant the action; and

(2) opportunity to demonstrate or achieve compliance with all lawful requirements.

When the licensee has made timely and sufficient application for a renewal or a new license in accordance with agency rules, a license with reference to an activity of a continuing nature does not expire until the application has been finally determined by the agency.

559. Effect on other laws; effect of subsequent statute

This subchapter, chapter 7, and sections 1305, 3105, 3344, 4301(2) (E), 5372, and 7521 of this title, and the provisions of section 5335 (a) (B) of this title that relate to administrative law judges, do not limit or repeal additional requirements imposed by statute or otherwise recognized by law. Except as otherwise required by law, requirements or privileges relating to evidence or procedure apply equally to agencies and persons. Each agency is granted the authority necessary to comply with the requirements of this subchapter through the issuance of rules or otherwise. Subsequent statute may not be held to supersede or modify this subchapter, chapter 7, sections 1305, 3105, 3344, 4301(2) (E), 5372, or 7521 of this title, or the provisions of section 5335(a) (B) of this title that relate to administrative law judges, except to the extent that it does so expressly.

Judicial Review

701. Application; definitions

(a) This chapter applies, according to the provisions thereof, except to the extent that—

(1) statutes preclude judicial review; or

(2) agency action is committed to agency discretion by law.

(b) For the purpose of this chapter—

(1) "agency" means each authority of the Government of the United States, whether or not it is within or subject to review by another agency, but does not include—

(A) the Congress;

(B) the courts of the United States;

(C) the governments of the territories or possessions of the United States;

(D) the government of the District of Columbia;

(E) agencies composed of representatives of the parties or of representatives of organizations of the parties to the disputes determined by them;

(F) courts martial and military commissions;

(G) military authority exercised in the field in time of war or in occupied territory; or

(H) functions conferred by sections 1738, 1739, 1743, and 1744 of title 12; chapter 2 of title 41; subchapter II of chapter 471 of title 49; or sections 1884, 1891–1902, and former section 1641(b)(2), of title 50, appendix; and

(2) "person", "rule", "order", "license", "sanction", "relief", and "agency action", have the meanings given them by section 551 of this title.

702. Right of review

A person suffering legal wrong because of agency action, or adversely affected or aggrieved by agency action within the meaning of a relevant statute, is entitled to judicial review thereof. An action in a court of the United States seeking relief other than money damages and stating a claim that an agency or an officer or employee thereof acted or failed to act in an official capacity or under color of legal authority shall not be dismissed nor relief therein be denied on the ground that it is against the United States or that the United States is an indispensable party. The United States may be named as a defendant in any such action, and a judgment or decree may be entered against the United States: Provided, That any mandatory or injunctive decree shall specify the Federal officer or officers (by name or by title), and their successors in office, personally responsible for compliance. Nothing herein (1) affects other limitations on judicial review or the power or duty of the court to dismiss any action or deny relief on any other appropriate legal or equitable ground; or (2) confers authority to grant relief if any other statute that grants consent to suit expressly or impliedly forbids the relief which is sought.

703. Form and venue of proceeding

The form of proceeding for judicial review is the special statutory review proceeding relevant to the subject matter in a court specified by statute or, in the absence or inadequacy thereof, any applicable form of legal action, including actions for declaratory judgments or writs of prohibitory or mandatory injunction or habeas corpus, in a court of competent jurisdiction. If no special statutory review proceeding is applicable, the action for judicial review may be brought against the United States, the agency by its official title, or the appropriate officer. Except to the extent that prior, adequate, and exclusive opportunity for judicial review is provided by law, agency action is subject to judicial review in civil or criminal proceedings for judicial enforcement.

704. Actions reviewable

Agency action made reviewable by statute and final agency action for which there is no other adequate remedy in a court are subject to judicial review. A preliminary, procedural, or intermediate agency action or ruling not directly reviewable is subject to review on the review of the final agency action. Except as otherwise expressly required by statute, agency action otherwise final is final for the purposes of this section whether or not there has been presented or determined an application for a declaratory order, for any form of reconsideration, or, unless the agency otherwise requires by rule and provides that the action meanwhile is inoperative, for an appeal to superior agency authority.

705. Relief pending review

When an agency finds that justice so requires, it may postpone the effective date of action taken by it, pending judicial review. On such conditions as may be required and to the extent necessary to prevent irreparable injury, the reviewing court, including the court to which a case may be taken on appeal from or on application for certiorari or other writ to a reviewing court, may issue all necessary and appropriate process to postpone the effective date of an agency action or to preserve status or rights pending conclusion of the review proceedings.

706. Scope of review

To the extent necessary to decision and when presented, the reviewing court shall decide all relevant questions of law, interpret constitutional and statutory provisions, and determine the meaning or applicability of the terms of an agency action. The reviewing court shall—

(1) compel agency action unlawfully withheld or unreasonably delayed; and

(2) hold unlawful and set aside agency action, findings, and conclusions found to be—

(A) arbitrary, capricious, an abuse of discretion, or otherwise not in accordance with law;

(B) contrary to constitutional right, power, privilege, or immunity;

(C) in excess of statutory jurisdiction, authority, or limitations, or short of statutory right;

(D) without observance of procedure required by law;

(E) unsupported by substantial evidence in a case subject to section 556 and 557 of this title or otherwise reviewed on the record of an agency hearing provided by statute; or

(F) unwarranted by the facts to the extent that the facts are subject to trial de novo by the reviewing court.

In making the foregoing determinations, the court shall review the whole record or those parts of it cited by the party, and due account shall be taken of the rule of prejudicial error.

Administrative Law Judges

3105. Appointment of Administrative Law Judges

Each agency shall appoint as many administrative law judges as are necessary for proceedings required to be conducted in accordance with sections 556 and 557 of this title. Administrative law judges shall be assigned to cases in rotation so far as practicable, and may not perform duties inconsistent with their duties and responsibilities as administrative law judges.

1305. Administrative Law Judges

For the purposes of sections 3105 . . . of this title that relate to administrative law judges, the Office of Personnel Management may, and for the purpose of section 7521 of this title, the Merit Systems Protection Board may investigate, prescribe regulations, appoint advisory committees as necessary, recommend legislation, subpoena witnesses and records, and pay witness fees as established for the courts of the United States.

7521. Actions against Administrative Law Judges

(a) An action may be taken against an administrative law judge appointed under section 3105 of this title by the agency in which the administrative law judge is employed only for good cause established and determined by the Merit Systems Protection Board on the record after opportunity for hearing before the Board.

(b) The actions covered by this section are —

  (1) a removal;

  (2) a suspension;

  (3) a reduction in grade;

  (4) a reduction in pay; and

  (5) a furlough of 30 days or less;

  but do not include —

    (A) a suspension or removal [in the interest of a national security];

    (B) a reduction-in-force action . . . ; or

    (C) any action initiated [by the Special Counsel of the Board].

Index